Hasselback Guide to Economics Faculty, 2000-2001

I would like to review the following textbooks for adoption consideration.

Author/Title: ______________________________

Author/Title: ______________________________

Name: ______________________________

School: ______________________________

Address: ______________________________

Department: ______________________________

City/State: ____________________ Zip: __________

Telephone: ______________ E-mail: ______________

Office hours: ______________________________

Course(s) taught:

____

Enrollment(s): ______________________________

Offered: __________ Fall __________ Spring __________ Both

Text(s) used: ______________________________

Convention(s) or Meeting(s) you expect to attend in 2000:

____

Types of Multimedia technology (hardware) that are available in your classrooms and/or student labs:

____

Course(s) for which you are willing to review manuscripts:

____

Attn: Lori Braumberger, Marketing Manager,
Prentice Hall, One Lake Street, Upper Saddle River, NJ 07458
www.prenhall.com

THE PRENTICE HALL ECONOMICS FACULTY GUIDE

2000/2001

Compiled by

JAMES R. HASSELBACK

PRENTICE HALL, Upper Saddle River, NJ 07458

Editorial Director: *James C. Boyd*
Editorial Assistant: *Marie McHale*
Senior Marketing Manager: *Lori Braumberger*
Acquisitions editor: *Rod Banister*
Associate editor: *Gladys Soto*
Marketing Assistant: *Lauren Tarino*
Project editor: *Joseph F. Tomasso*
Manufacturer: *Victor Graphics Inc.*

Upper Saddle River, New Jersey 07458

Printed in the United States of America

10 9 8 7 6 5 4 3 2 1

ISBN 0-13-018027-0

Prentice-Hall International (UK) Limited, *London*
Prentice-Hall of Australia Pty. Limited, *Sydney*
Prentice-Hall Canada Inc., *Toronto*
Prentice-Hall Hispanoamericana, S.A., *Mexico*
Prentice-Hall of India Private Limited, *New Delhi*
Prentice-Hall of Japan, Inc., *Tokyo*
Prentice-Hall (Singapore) Pte Ltd
Editora Prentice-Hall do Brasil, Ltda., *Rio de Janeiro*

JAMES R. HASSELBACK

James R. Hasselback is a Professor of Taxation at Florida State University and has previously taught at Eastern Michigan University, the University of Florida, and Texas A&M University. A member of the American Accounting Association and the American Taxation Association, he has published over 145 papers in professional and academic journals, including *The Accounting Review*, *The Tax Adviser*, *Financial Management*, *Journal of Real Estate Taxation*, and the *American Business Law Journal*.

Dr. Hasselback has presented papers at numerous national and regional professional meetings, and served as chairman at tax sessions of professional conferences. He regularly presents continuing education seminars for Certified Public Accountants. He is co-author and technical editor on a two-volume introductory taxation series published by CCH Inc. for the past sixteen years. Jim has also served as technical editor on several publications by CCH Inc. and Harper-Collins Inc. He is a contributing author on *1999 U.S. Master Accounting Guide*, by CCH Incorporated. Jim is co-author with Irvin Gleim on the *Ninth Edition of Federal Tax Exam Questions and Explanations* and also on a recently published four volume *EA Review for the IRS Special Enrollment Exam*.

In addition to the *Guide to Economics Faculty*, Jim Hasselback compiles the *Accounting Faculty Directory* published by Prentice Hall. Published each year for 26 years, the *Accounting Faculty Directory* may be the most cited reference in the Accounting field. The other Directories in the business field include: a Directory of Management Faculty, a Directory of Finance Faculty, a Directory of Marketing Faculty, and a Directory of Business Law Faculty. An Engineering Faculty Directory was published in 1992 and 1995. A Computer Science Faculty Directory was published in 1994 and 1996. The Nursing Faculty Directory was published in January 1995.

Jim is the editor of *Accounting Perspectives*. The journal is published twice a year and focuses on faculty issues such as research productivity, promotion, movement, and gender issues related to those topics.

Dr. Hasselback teaches two courses, Income Tax Planning and Estate Planning, in Florida State University's Certificate in Financial Planning Program, both on campus and through the Internet. He taught for several years in the Florida State University's CPA Review Course.

Dear Economics Professor:

It is a great pleasure for us to present the **Prentice Hall Economics Faculty Directory, 2000-2001,** for your personal reference. Prentice Hall remains one of the leading publishers of undergraduate and graduate level publications designed for economics curricula world-wide, and this Directory, compiled by James R. Hasselback, is an expression of our gratitude to the many economics educators who have adopted our titles over the years. You can view the Economics Faculty Directory, as well as a complete catalog listing of Prentice Hall economics products, on the Prentice Hall web site located at **www.prenhall.com/phbusiness**

A catalog of our most current economics titles begins on page A-7. To order an examination copy of a Prentice Hall economics title, you may contact your local Prentice Hall representative, call our toll–free Faculty Service number (1-800-526-0485), or contact our Marketing manager,

Lori Braumberger
Prentice Hall Business Publishing
One Lake Street, Upper Saddle River, NJ 07458
Fax: 201-236-7172
e-mail: lori_braumberger@prenhall.com

It is our hope that this desk reference will prove to be a valuable resource for you.

Sincerely,

P.J. Boardman
Editor-in-Chief

Rod Banister
Senior Editor

Brian Kibby
Director of Marketing

Lori Braumberger
Senior Marketing Manager

Gladys Soto
Associate Editor

Lauren Tarino
Marketing Assistant

Marie McHale
Editorial Assistant

Should you wish to notify us of corrections or additions to **The Prentice Hall Guide to Economics Faculty**, please contact:

Dr. James R. Hasselback • College of Business, R-53A
Florida State University • Tallahassee, FL 32306-1042

Phone: (904) 644-7884 • Fax: (904) 894-2244

TABLE OF CONTENTS

PRINCIPLES OF ECONOMICS

TWO-SEMESTER PRINCIPLES OF ECONOMICS

NEW EDITION AVAILABLE SUMMER 2000!

ECONOMICS: Principles and Tools

Arthur O'Sullivan
Oregon State University

Steven M. Sheffrin
University of California, Davis

By emphasizing an active learning approach and focusing on the big picture – the framework of economics reasoning – this text emphasizes the key principles and ideas of economics and teaches students how to think like economists by showing them to use economics concepts in their every day lives and careers. By using key concepts repeatedly and using compelling real-world examples, the textbook presents material in a way that is understandable for average principles students.

FEATURES:

- Identifies, explains and uses **five key principles** to explain the key tools of economics:
  - *Opportunity Cost*
  - *The Marginal Principles*
  - *Diminishing Returns*
  - *The Spillover Principle*
  - *The Reality Principle*
- **Active learning involves students in "doing" economic analysis** throughout:
- ***Economic Detective*** exercises — invite students to use the tools of economics to explain puzzles or to answer questions.
- ***Using the Tools*** exercises that illustrate the key ideas of market equilibrium, government intervention, public goods, price fixing, imperfect information, market entry.
- ***Economics Experiments*** provide the opportunity for active learning in a group environment.
- Intersperses ***Test Your Understanding Questions and Problems*** throughout each chapter so students can check their understanding of the material.

CONTENTS:

15. Environmental Problems and Public Policy: Global Warming, Ozone Depletion, Acid Rain, and Urban Smog.
16. Imperfect Information and Disappearing Markets.
17. The Labor Market.
18. Interest Rates and Present Value.
19. Economic Challenges for the 21st Century.
20. The Big Ideas in Macroeconomics.
21. Behind the Economic Statistics.
22. Classical Economics: The Economy at Full Employment.
23. Why Do Economies Grow?
24. Coordinating Economic Activity: Aggregate Demand and Supply.
25. Keynesian Economics and Fiscal Policy.
26. Investment and Financial Intermediation.
27. Money, the Banking System, and the Federal Reserve.
28. Monetary Policy in the Short Run.
29. From the Short Run to the Long Run.
30. The Dynamics of Inflation and Unemployment.
31. Ten Questions (and Answers) about Government Debt and Deficits.
32. International Trade and Public Policy.
33. The World of International Finance.

©1998, 800 pp., Cloth (0-13-206368-9)

Macroeconomics: Principles and Tools

©1998, 500 pp., Paper (0-13-742842-1)

Microeconomics: Principles and Tools

©1998, 500 pp., Paper (0-13-742859-6)

SUPPLEMENTS:

- Instructor's Manual
- Study Guide
- Test Item File
- WIN CTB
- MAC CTB
- PHLIP/CW (prenhall.com/o'sullivan)
- PowerPoints (on the Web)
- Acetates
- Using Economic Experiments
- NY Times, Themes of the Times

PRINCIPLES OF ECONOMICS
Fifth Edition

Karl E. Case
Wellesley College

Ray C. Fair
Yale University

Written by an award-winning educator and a highly respected macroeconomist, the text is built on the pioneering "stories, graphs, and equations" pedagogy that has successfully made economics accessible and relevant to all types of students. This student-friendly text helps the student integrate the theory, issues, and policies into an "economic way of thinking." Known for its lively writing style, clear explanations, international perspective, well-crafted graphs, relevant examples, and unparalleled supplements package, the text supports both the instructor and student through this first, often difficult, course in Economics.

FEATURES:

- **"FAST FACTS"** integrated into every chapter illustrate the broad applica tions of theory and help explain the current events from around the world that are shaping our economic land scape.

- **WebCT Support**. Developed by educators, WebCt provides easy-to-use Internet tools to create on-line courses (no programming knowledge required). Case/Fair Web CT provides the rich content and enhanced features to help create full-length on-line courses, or simply produce on-line supplementary materials to enhance existing courses.

- **Uses a hands-on, student friendly approach that brings economics to life** - in terms students can understand and relate to.
  - Uses a variety of methods (stories, graphs, equations) to present and reinforce economic principles throughout - to accommodate the various learning styles of students.
  - Summarizes and highlights major economics principles - in yellow highlighting - to help students review key points.
  - Provides a point-by-point summary for each chapter.
  - Highlights key terms in the text and defines them in margins.

- Makes judicious use of examples to highlight special issues:
  - **Global Perspective** Boxes - illustrate that the global economy is inter-connected.
  - **"Applications"** Boxes - help students apply the principles they have learned to actual events.
  - **"Issues and Debates"** Boxes - gives students both sides of the story (e.g. debates over economic growth, desirability of government intervention, etc).
  - **An applied emphasis** - Numerous examples that make economics relevant to students.

CONTENTS:

(NOTE: Principles of Economics, 5/e includes Chapters 1-38; Principles of Microeconomics, 5/e includes Chapters 1-20, 35, 37, 38; Principles of Macroeconomics, 5/e includes Chapters 1-4, 5 (abridged), 21-38)

20. Current Topics in Applied Microeconomics: Health Care, Immigration, and Urban Problems.

MACROECONOMICS.

V. CONCEPTS AND PROBLEMS IN MACROECONOMICS.

21. Introduction to Macroeconomics.
22. Measuring National Output and National Income.
23. Macroeconomic Concerns: Unemployment, Inflation, and Growth.

VI. MACROECONOMIC PRINCIPLES AND POLICY.

24. Aggregate Expenditure and Equilibrium Output.
25. The Government and Fiscal Policy.
26. The Money Supply and the Federal Reserve System.
27. Money Demand, the Equilibrium Interest Rate, and Monetary Policy.

VII. MACROECONOMIC ANALYSIS AND ISSUES.

28. Money, the Interest Rate, and Output: Analysis and Policy.
29. Aggregate Demand, Aggregate Supply, and Inflation.
30. The Labor Market, Unemployment, and Inflation.
1. Deficit Reduction, Fed Behavior, Stabilization, Stock Market Effects, and Macro Issues Abroad.
32. Household and Firm Behavior in the Macroeconomy.

VIII. DEBATES IN MACROECONOMICS AND ECONOMIC GROWTH.

33. Debates in Macroeconomics: Monetarism New Classical Theory, and Supply-Side Economics.
34. Economic Growth and Productivity.

INTERNATIONAL ECONOMICS.

IX. THE GLOBAL ECONOMY.

35. International Trade, Comparative Advantage and Protectionism.
36. Open-Economy Macroeconomics: The Balance of Payments and Exchange Rates.
37. Economic Growth in Developing Nations.
38. Economies in Transition and Alternative Economic Systems.

©1999, 959 pp., Cloth (0-13-095710-0)

Principles of Macroeconomics Fifth Edition

©1999, 575 pp., Paper (0-13-095733-X)

Principles of Microeconomics Fifth Edition

©1999, 607 pp., Paper (0-13-095725-9)

SUPPLEMENTS:

- Instructor's Manual
- Study Guide
- Test Item File #1
- Test Item File #2
- Win PH Test Manager #1
- Win PH Test Manager #2
- MAC PH Test Manager #1
- MAC PH Test Manager #2
- PHLIP/CW (prenhall.com/case)
- PowerPoints (on the Web)
- Acetates
- Using Economics Experiments
- NY Times, Themes of the Times

ONE-SEMESTER PRINCIPLES OF ECONOMICS

ECONOMICS BY DESIGN: Principles and Issues

Second Edition

NEW EDITION

Robert A. Collinge

Ronald M. Ayers
both of University of Texas at San Antonio

This text is ideal for issues oriented courses that teach essential economic principles. Current issues and core principles of mainstream economics are presented in an intuitive manner that captures student interest. The text systematically combines this presentation with a wealth of relevant, up-to-date applications that engage today's students so that they'll retain essential concepts and be able to put these concepts to work in the real world.

FEATURES:

- **Fresh Examples, Current Applications**—Drawing from the abundance of economic issues, applications, and statistics found throughout modern life. As always, the goal is to provide applications to engage student interest so that they will retain economic concepts and be able to apply them long after their economics course is over.

- **Observation Points special-interest sections**—Features approximately 60 short applications of principles that illustrates for students how the abstract principles under discussion are put into practice in the real world, providing immediate reinforcement and relevance.

- **Quick Check Self-Tests**—Integrates brief, boxed self-assessment sections throughout the text that allow students to assess, reinforce, and challenge their understanding of recently covered topics.

NEW TO THIS EDITION:

- **Simplified Chapter Layout, Easier to Use**. The layout of the Second Edition adheres closely to the theme of a principles and issues textbook by concluding each chapter with an in depth discussion of selected issues.

- **Now Fourteen Chapters with More International Throughout**. Chapter 15, Global Economic Themes, has been eliminated in the Second Edition, with much of the material woven throughout the remaining fourteen chapters. The remaining international chapter has been revised to be more engaging and tied to current issues in international trade and finance.

- **More Accessible Macroeconomics Presentation**. The macro presentation has been made more accessible to entry-level student and the order of the presentation has been revised. Specifically, macro analysis is introduced in the context of a chapter on economic growth, followed by a chapter on money, and then by a chapter examining short-run instability.

- **Eight completely new Explorations have been added**. Other Explorations have been revised and updated where appropriate, some extensively. Each of the twenty-eight Explorations examines a different issue, including healthcare, crime and drugs, antitrust, discrimination, school vouchers, free trade, immigration, and much more!

- **Margin Notes**. Definitions of key terms are now provided in nearby margins as well as in the glossary. In addition, numerous Internet addresses are provided in the margins. These addresses refer students to web sites that relate to the discussion in the text.

- **Added Graphing and Internet Preparation**. The appendix material on graphing in Chapter One has been nearly doubled to meet the needs of more instructors. Approximately 100 web addresses and 28 web exercises make the book Internet-ready.

CONTENTS:

©2000, 624 pp., Paper (0-13-013298-5) (1329H-5)

SUPPLEMENTS

(Study Guide, Instructor's Manual, and Test Item File all have been prepared by the authors!)

- Study Guide
- Instructor's Manual
- Test Item File
- WIN PH Test Manager
- MAC PH Test Manager
- Companion Website - www.prenhall.com/collinge. All new to this edition, includes an on-line quiz with true/false, multiple-choice, and web-destination questions.
- PowerPoints—All new to this edition, approximately 50 slides per chapter provide detailed outlines with tables and graphs.
- Transparency Masters, downloadable from prenhall.com/collinge.

THE ECONOMIC WAY OF THINKING

Ninth Edition

NEW EDITION

Paul Heyne
University of Washington

Noted for its clear and informative style, this acclaimed text provides an in-depth discussion of a very specific and crucial set of economic principles and concepts, then applies these tools of analysis to a wide variety of familiar situations. The author presents conceptually demanding material in a lively, often witty fashion that is both accessible and pertinent for beginning students. The goal of this text is to help students think by developing the key insights into economic theory and applying these insights to numerous real-world examples.

This text gives students the opportunity to make sense out of the daily assertions of newspapers, political pundits, television, and the Internet.

FEATURES:

- **A focus on only the most crucial concepts**—and the real-world analytical power behind them. Develops key concepts with detailed explanations and a wealth of real-world, everyday applications.

- **Each concept is introduced with a real-life problem**. The examples contain high impact/high interest material and experiences that are familiar to students. Once the topic is introduced, the economic tool of analysis is carefully explained and then further developed.

- **Marginal notes reinforce the concept in accessible fashion**. The scripted notes, written as if they were in the author's handwriting, allow the students to feel as if the author is speaking directly to them.

- **Extended applications that challenge customary ways of thinking.** Challenges students to think critically about economic situations and to rethink their own assumptions about economics.

- **A market/property rights perspective**. Resents self-interest as a motive of government officials as well as of business decision-makers and other individuals. Shows that economics theory can explain social action that is not part of what we usually think of as "the economy".

CHANGES TO THIS EDITION:

- A reorganization of the first five chapters including expanded coverage of supply and demand.
- Marginal values now appear in Chapter 2 as part of the presentation of demand.
- Marginal costs and sunk costs, as well as opportunity costs, are covered in Chapter 3.
- Chapter 4 presents the interaction of demand and supply as a process of cooperation, facilitated by property rights and freedom to exchange. This is further discussed in Chapter 5.
- The chapters covering macroeconomics have been completely rewritten for this edition.
- The author's updated Responses to Discussion Questions are available for students to download from www.prenhall.com/heyne.
- The supplement package has been extensively expanded to enhance classroom lectures.

CONTENTS:

14. Markets and Government
15. The Overall Performance of Economic Systems
16. The Supply of Money
17. Monetary and Fiscal Policies
18. National Policies and International Exchange
19. Employment and Unemployment
20. Promoting Economic Growth
21. Economic Performance and Political Economy
22. The Limitations of Economics

©2000, 572 pp., Paper (0-13-013299-3)

SUPPLEMENTS:

- NEW—PHLIP/CW (Prentice Hall's Learning on the Internet Partnership/Companion Website). The online study guide, available free for students includes true/false, multiple-choice, and essay questions. Current Events articles offer an expanded look at the real world of economics.
- "Responses to Discussion Questions" written by author, offers detailed responses to all end-of-chapter questions.
- NEW—PowerPoint Lecture Presentation, with an average of 60 slides per chapter, are available to download from www.prenhall.com/heyne
- Test Bank, completely revised with 900 new questions added.
- Test Manager, Version 4.1 allows the instructor to manage a portfolio of tests and analyze student test results.
- Study Guide, prepared by the author, includes self-tests on the principle ideas of each chapter, as well as "Questions to Think About".

MODERN ECONOMICS

Jan S. Hogendorn
Colby College

This exciting textbook provides complete coverage of the principles in a concise presentation without sacrificing rigor. Students' understanding of the material is strengthened with gripping examples, many international.

CONTENTS:

I: INTRODUCTION.
1. What Is Economics?
2. The Market System.
3. Demand and Supply I: The Concept of Demand.
4. Demand and Supply II: The Concept of Supply, The Market Mechanism.
5. When Government Intervenes.
6. Revenues and Costs of the Firm and the Case of Perfect Competition.
7. Imperfect Markets I: Why They Exist and the Case ofMonopoly.
8. Imperfect Markets II: Monopolistic Competition and Oligopoly.
9. Controlling Market Power: Government Regulation and Antitrust Law.
10. Externalities: When Private and Social Costs and Benefits Diverge.
11. Factors of Production: Productivity and Incomes.
12. Wages, Rent, Interest, Profit.
13. Income Distribution and Poverty.

II: MACROECONOMICS.
14. An Introduction to Macroeconomics.
15. Measuring Economic Performance.
16. How Output and Income Are Determined: The Concept of Macroeconomic Equilibrium.
17. Pursuing the Fixed-Price Analysis.
18. A Contemporary Model of Aggregate Demand and Aggregate Supply.
19. Money and the Banking System.
20. The Tools of Monetary Policy.

21. The Conduct of Monetary Policy.
22. Fiscal Policy.
23. Deficits and Debt in a Modern Economy.
24. Stagflation.
25. Macroeconomic Innovation: "Heterodox" Ways to Fight Stagflation.
26. Economic Growth in Market Economies.

III: THE INTERNATIONAL ECONOMIC EXPERIENCE.

27. International Trade.
28. International Finance.
29. Reforming the Command Economies.
30. Economic Development of the LDCs.

© 1995, 832 pp., Cloth (0-13-103995-4)

SUPPLEMENTS:

- Study Guide
- Instructor's Manual with Test Bank

MACROECONOMICS

INTERMEDIATE MACROECONOMICS

MACROECONOMICS
Second Edition

NEW EDITION

Olivier Blanchard
Massachusetts Institute of Technology

This book conveys the excitement of macroeconomics, covering many of the main macroeconomic issues of the day—issues often missing from other texts. Its example-rich approach provides a strong emphasis on the role of expectations, the openness of modern economics, and the role of dynamics.

FEATURES:

- **The text is built on one underlying model** that provides an integrated view of macroeconomics. The model concentrates on the implications of equilibrium conditions in three sets of markets: goods, financial, and labor. Depending on the issue at hand, the parts of the model are developed in more detail while others are simplified or left in the background.

- **Theory and applications** are constantly used to explain what is happening around the world, from the introduction of a new currency in Western Europe, to the reduction of budget deficits in the United States. This approach conveys the fun of macroeconomics, and reinforces the lessons from the models making them more concrete and easier to grasp.

- **Boxes throughout each chapter** show how theoretical arguments can be used to understand events around the world.
  - **Focus boxes** use a macroeconomic episode or example to expand on a point made in the text.
  - **In Depth boxes** look at a particular macroeconomic episode in detail.
  - **Global Macro boxes** look at macroeconomic episodes from around the world and focus on real world applications

- **Detailed Application Boxes integrated throughout the text** shed light on the events happening around the world—events related to the new currency in Western Europe, the reduction of budget deficits in the United States, the transformation of Eastern Europe, the crisis in Asia, etc.

- **Digging deeper** - notes which expand on an argument in the text, often by indicating how an implicit assumption in the text could be relaxed, and what the implications might be.
- **Short appendixes** to some chapters show how a proposition in the text can be derived more rigorously or expanded.
- **Further reading section** at the end of each chapter indicate where to find more information, including Internet addresses.

NEW TO THIS EDITION:

- **NEW Organization**—The text is now organized around two main parts, a core of eleven chapters, followed by a set of three major extensions. The core looks at the short run, the medium run and the long run. The extensions look at expectations, openness and pathologies. The new organization allows flexibility to teach a quarter or a semester course, choice in the set and the organization of topics to be covered, and gives much more flexibility to teachers using the book.

- **NEW & UNIQUE Margin notes** create a dialogue with the reader, help reinforce more difficult passages, and allow for a deeper understanding of the concepts and the results derived along the way.

- **Appendix 3 on econometrics in macroeconomics** replaces Chapter 4 in the prior edition and can be found at the end of the text.

CONTENTS:

CHAPTER 19 – THE GOODS MARKET IN AN OPEN ECONOMY
CHAPTER 20 – OUTPUT, THE INTEREST RATE, AND THE EXCHANGE RATE

CHAPTER 21 – EXCHANGE RATE ADJUSTMENTS, EXCHANGE RATE CRISES, AND EXCHANGE RATE REGIMES

PATHOLOGIES

CHAPTER 22 – PATHOLOGIES I: HIGH UNEMPLOYMENT
CHAPTER 23 – PATHOLOGIES II: HIGH INFLATION
CHAPTER 24 - PATHOLOGIES III: TRANSITION IN EASTERN EUROPE, AND THE ASIAN CRISIS
CHAPTER 25 – SHOULD POLICY MAKERS BE RESTRAINED?

POLICY

CHAPTER 26 – MONETARY POLICY: A SUMMING UP
CHAPTER 27 – FISCAL POLICY: A SUMMING-UP
CHAPTER 28 – EPILOGUE: THE STORY OF MACROECONOMICS

©2000, 608 pp., Cloth, (0-13-013306-X)

SUPPLEMENTS
- Instructor's Manual
- Study Guide.
- Test Item File
- WIN PH Custom Test
- Active Graphs Software
- PHLIP/CW – (prenhall.com/blanchard) The Companion Website includes an online Study Guide free to students, with multiple choice and essay quizzes for each chapter
- Transparency Masters (on the Web)

AVAILABLE FALL 2000

MACROECONOMIC THEORY: An Integrated Approach

Steven Mathis
Shippensburg University

Janet Koscianski
Shippensburg University

This book develops microeconomic theory based on an approach which effectively integrates calculus, intuition, graphics, and applications. All topics are carefully and clearly presented, thus enabling students to readily comprehend the techniques by which individual topics can be examined and synthesized into the broader context of microeconomic analysis.

MACROECONOMICS: Theories and Policies
Sixth Edition

Richard T. Froyen
University of North Carolina, Chapel Hill

The author explains the difference among macroeconomists on issues of theory and policy while comparing and contrasting modern macroeconomic theory.

CONTENTS:
I. INTRODUCTION AND MEASUREMENT.
1. Introduction.
2. Measurement of Macroeconomic Variables.

II. MACROECONOMIC MODELS.
3. Classical Macroeconomics (I): Equilibrium Output and Employment.
4. The Classical System (II): Money, Prices, and Interest.
5. The Keynesian System (I): The Role of Aggregate Demand.

© 1999, 481 pp., Cloth, 0-13-099817-6

SUPPLEMENTS:

- Instructor's Manual with Test Bank
- Study Guide

THE MACROECONOMY: PRIVATE CHOICES, PUBLIC ACTIONS, AND AGGREGATE OUTCOMES
First Edition

Michael B. McElroy
North Carolina State University

By addressing the interests, needs, and abilities of students, this practical text prepares students for a lifetime of macroeconomic issues that will arise in their multiple roles of consumer, business decision-maker, voter, and opinion leader. The goal of the text is to help students reach a basic understanding of macroeconomics issues that will not evaporate soon after the final exam, but will become a part of an economic common sense to be drawn upon throughout their lives.

CONTENTS:

12. Consumption, Saving, and Investment.
13. Capital Markets.
14. Economic Growth.

V. MODELS, MEASUREMENT, AND PERFORMANCE.

15. Models and Measurement.
16. The Macroeconomy: Choices, Policies, and Outcomes.
    Appendix: National and International Macroeconomic Data.

Index.

© 1996, 487 pp., Cloth (0-02-378801-1)

SUPPLEMENTS:

- Instructor's Manual
- Test Item File
- Study Guide

MICROECONOMICS

INTERMEDIATE MICROECONOMICS

NEW EDITION AVAILABLE SUMMER 2000!

MICROECONOMICS

Fourth Edition

Robert S. Pindyck
Massachusetts Institute of Technology

Daniel L. Rubinfeld
University of California, Berkeley

Written by two of the most distinguished authors in the field, this fourth edition seeks to expose students to the **new topics** that play a central role in microeconomics over the past few years—game theory, competitive strategy, the roles of uncertainty and information, and the analysis of pricing by firms with market power. This highly acclaimed text demonstrates theory at work in real companies, industry and government. The emphasis on **relevance and application to both managerial and public-policy decision making** are focused goals of the book. It succeeds in showing how microeconomics can be used as **a tool for decision making.** This fresh treatment of the subject gives students an appreciation of its purpose and application outside the classroom walls.

CONTENTS:

I. INTRODUCTION: MARKETS AND PRICES.

1. Preliminaries.
2. The Basics of Supply and Demand.

II. PRODUCERS, CONSUMERS, AND COMPETITIVE MARKETS.

3. Consumer Behavior.
4. Individual and Market Demand.
5. Choice Under Uncertainty.
6. Production.
7. The Cost of Production.
8. Profit Maximization and Competitive Supply.
9. The Analysis of Competitive Markets.

III. MARKET STRUCTURE AND COMPETITIVE STRATEGY.

10. Market Power: Monopoly and Monopsony.
11. Pricing with Market Power.
12. Monopolistic Competition and Oligopoly.
13. Game Theory and Competitive Strategy.
14. Markets for Factor Inputs.
15. Investment, Time, and Capital Markets.

IV. INFORMATION, MARKET FAILURE, AND THE ROLE OF GOVERNMENT.

16. General Equilibrium and Economic Efficiency.

17. Markets with Asymmetric Information.
18. Externalities and Public Goods.

©1998, 699 pp., Cloth (0-13-272923-7) (27292-2)

SUPPLEMENTS:

- Study Guide
- Instructor's Manual
- Test Item File
- WIN PH Test Manager
- PowerPoints (on the Web)

PRICE THEORY AND APPLICATIONS

Sixth Edition

Jack Hirshleifer
University of California, Los Angeles

David Hirshleifer
University of Michigan

Rich with examples, this reality-based economics text continues its pioneering approach of integrating theory and applications, showing how microeconomic analysis sheds light on market behavior, guides personal and financial decisions, and explains behavior in such areas as politics, crime, and the family.

FEATURES:

- Helps students **cultivate the economic insight and intuition** necessary to tell what theories or propositions apply in any given context.

- Presents **'Examples'** which illustrate how economic models and principles help explain real-world phenomena; covering an enormous variety of topics.

- Intersperses **in-depth 'Applications'** throughout, extending basic theory to topics of special interest, such as the economics of charitable contributions, interdiction of narcotics supplies, the effects of import quotas, and minimum wage laws.

- Offers **unique coverage** on topics such as rationing and other non-price constraints; the voluntary provision of public goods, conflict and warfare, and more.

- Calculus used only in designated mathematical footnotes.

- Maintains **great breadth of vision**, including discussions and applications of economic analysis to historical phenomena; international examples and illustrations; and studies of topics and data from anthropology, law, biology, psychology, and other social sciences.

CONTENTS:

1. The Nature and Scope of Economics.
2. Working Tools.
3. Utility and Preference.
4. Consumption and Demand.
5. Applications and Extensions of Demand Theory.
6. The Business Firm.
7. Equilibrium in the Product Market—Competitive Industry.
8. Monopolies and Cartels.
9. The Product as a Variable.
10. Oligopoly and Strategic Behavior.
11. Demand for Factors of Production.
12. Resource Supply and Factor-Market Equilibrium.
13. Exchange, Transaction Costs, and Money.
14. The Economics of Time.
15. Welfare Economics: The Market and the State.
16. Government, Conflict, and Cooperation.

©1998, 608 pp., Cloth (0-13-190778-6) (19077-7)

SUPPLEMENTS:
- Instructor's Manual with Test Bank
- Study Guide

MICROECONOMICS
Fourth Edition

B. Curtis Eaton
Simon Fraser University

Diane F. Eaton

Douglas Alan
Simon Fraser University

This highly-regarded text teaches microeconomics as a way of looking at the world, using plenty of empirical data to focus the discussion. It is considered an upper mid-range text in its mathematical rigor while maintaining accessibility through examples and applications. Calculus is included in easy-to-refer-to footnotes.

CONTENTS:

©1999, 610 pp., Cloth (0-13-91108-5)

MANAGERIAL ECONOMICS

NEW EDITION AVAILABLE SUMMER 2000!

MICROECONOMICS
Fourth Edition

Robert S. Pindyck
Massachusetts Institute of Technology

Daniel L. Rubinfeld
University of California, Berkeley

See page A-19

MANAGERIAL ECONOMICS: ECONOMIC TOOLS FOR TODAYS DECISION MAKERS
Third Edition

Paul G. Keat
American Graduate School of International Management

Philip K.Y. Young
Pace University

NEW EDITION

One of the most distinctive features of this text is a running case study at the beginning and end of each chapter that explores the decision-making processes of managers within a hypothetical company. It creates a vivid, dynamic business setting for students highlighting microeconomic theory and the tools of quantitative analysis used in management decision-making. In addition, actual business examples from the popular press—including numerous international examples—are incorporated into the chapters to reinforce the connection between economic concepts and real business situations.

FEATURES:

- Each chapter starts and concludes with a **running case study** of a hypothetical company called "Global Foods", a hypothetical corporation competing in the soft drink industry. With this case situation as a backdrop, students are shown how mangers solve real business problems enabling them to apply economic principles to everyday business activity.

- **Current business examples** from the popular press (e.g., Business Week and the Wall Street Journal) are integrated throughout the text to highlight the relevance of economic concepts to current events.

- **UNIQUE** - International Application sections are interspersed throughout textbook. Nearly every chapter includes a special section called "International Application:" providing global application of the theory that shows the student how economic tools help businesses compete in the global economy.

NEW TO THIS EDITION:

- **NEW content has been included in chapter 15**—"The Role of the Government" has been completely rewritten and now includes topics in "doing business with the government" and "course theorem".

- Integrative chapter on economic concepts and tools—provides students with the analysis of the semiconductor industry and the competitive challenges of a company within that industry.

- Chapter 2 "The Firm and its Goals"—now includes new examples and a discussion on transactions costs and a discussion on Economic Value Added (EVA) and Market Value Added (MVA), which is a measure of wealth creation.

- Topics on isoquants, isocosts, and linear programming are **now treated in the appendix** in the back of the book.

- Complete explanation of linear programming and its uses—Includes references to Microsoft Excel spreadsheets to help solve LP problems.

- Industrial Economics material in chapter 10 has been completely rewritten and now shows the linkage of the structure-conduct –performance approach to Porter's strategy.

- Game Theory and its application to pricing and strategy is discussed in the chapter covering monopolistic competition and oligopoly.

CONTENTS:

©2000, 750 pp., Cloth (0-13-013538-0)

SUPPLEMENTS

- Excel Templates downloadable from www.prenhall.com/keat
- Instructors Manual with Test Item File
- Companion Website at www.prenhall.com/keat

MANAGERIAL ECONOMICS
Fourth Edition

H. Craig Petersen

W. Chris Lewis
both of Utah State University

This text offers a lively, applied presentation of analytical and empirical tools for managerial decision making. Students learn the connection between the theory and applications through devices such as case studies, real world data, and Windows-based software for students.

FEATURES:

- Concept/Example format introduces each basic economic concept and then applies it to a real-world problem—immediately relating economic principles to managerial decision making.

- Key Concepts sections throughout summarize material at frequent intervals.

- Integrated case studies and worked examples illustrate concepts and provide background for solving the end-of-chapter problems.

- Includes the highly successful **TOOLS software package** for a Windows environment for a more visual and student-friendly program. Self-contained, menu-driven, and easy to use with virtually no instruction, TOOLS allows instructors to assign more complicated, realistic problems. The software contains routines that enable students to solve problems involving time value of money, expected value and standard devia tion, trend projection and exponential smoothing, multiple regression, input-output analysis, and linear programming. Download from www.prenhall.com/petersen.

CONTENTS:

© 1999, 672 pp., Cloth, 0-13-976283-3

SUPPLEMENTS:

- Instructor's Manual with Test Bank
- TOOLS Software (on the Web)

MANAGERIAL ECONOMICS AND ORGANIZATION

First Edition

Zoltan J. Acs

Daniel A. Gerlowski
both of University of Baltimore

Managerial Economics and Organization is the *first* text to integrate the economics of organization into undergraduate managerial economics. The text begins with the economics of exchange and systematically develops the theory of economic organization. The approach is designed to accurately reflect the changing business environment through examination of organizational issues from a historical, technical and global perspective. Finally, *Managerial Economics and Organization* is more integrated with traditional business disciplines than other managerial economics texts.

CONTENTS:

© 1996, 464 pp., Cloth (0-02-300292-1)

SUPPLEMENTS:

- Instructor's Manual with Test Bank

FINANCIAL ECONOMICS

FINANCE

Zvi Bodie
Boston University

Robert C. Merton
Harvard University

This new text has a broader scope and greater emphasis on general principles than most introductory finance texts. The highly-acclaimed authors offer an approach which emphasizes the three "pillars" of finance—optimization over time, asset evaluation, and risk management. Their functional perspective on the financial system explains how financial institutions evolve over time and differ across national borders to fulfill a set of six basic economics functions which are the same everywhere and do not change.

FEATURES:

- Incorporates all sub-fields of finance—including **investments, institutions, and corporate finance**—within a single conceptual framework.

- Emphasis on general principles—the **three "pillars" of finance (opti mization over time, asset valuation, and risk management**) represent the basic "laws" and principles that apply across all the topical sub-fields of finance.

- Applies finance principles to personal decisions such as **life-cycle planning, saving and investing**, as well as to business financial decisions.

- Instructor's Resource CD Includes Spreadsheet Modeling Exercises. Shows students how to build their own Excel models.

- Provides complete integration of international material—Global examples are integrated directly into the text, rather than in separate boxed material.

- Contains **Quick Check Concept Questions**—At critical points in the text, helps students check their understanding of material previously pre sented.

- Special interest boxes throughout. Contains newspaper clippings and applications illustrating theories that encourages students to actively use the theory in dealing with their own affairs, and in interpreting the financial news.

- Includes End-of-chapter problems. Organizes problems by topic and level of difficulty. Offers complete step-by-step solutions for all problems in the Instructor's Manual, in a format that instructors can distribute to students.

- **UNIQUE Topics found in Bodie/Merton**. Life-cycle saving and resource allocation over time, Law of One Price and the Force of Arbitrage, Integrated risk management and Portfolio selection, Functions of the financial system and the dynamics of institutional change.

CONTENTS:

© 2000, 479 pp., Cloth, (0-13-310897-X)

SUPPLEMENTS:
- Instructor's Manual with Instructor's Resource CD (Excel, PowerPoints)
- Test Item File
- WIN Test Manager
- PHLIP/CW (Current Events articles, Online Study Guide, etc.)

ECONOMIC ISSUES

ECONOMICS BY DESIGN: Principles and Issues
Second Edition

Robert A. Collinge

Ronald M. Ayers
both of University of Texas at San Antonio

See Page A-11

THE ECONOMICS OF WOMEN, MEN AND WORK
Third Edition

Francine D. Blau
Cornell University

Marianne A. Ferber
University of Illinois, Urbana-Champaign

Anne E. Winkler
University of Missouri-St. Louis

This text introduces students to the findings of research on women, men, and work in the labor market and household.

FEATURES:

- Provides the most current research and data on women in the workplace and the home.

- Examines the **allocation of women's and men's time** spent in the market and the household, with special emphasis on analyzing recent participation trends.

- Reviews **gender differences** in occupations and earnings; and analyzes the role of gender differences in human capital and discrimination in explaining the differences.

- Considers relationships between recent changes in family structure and women's labor force participation and well-being, with particular attention to **dual-earner couples** and **female-headed households.**

- Focuses on policies intended to remedy employment discrimination, assist workers in meshing work and family responsibilities, and change the welfare system.

- Provides direct comparison of trends in labor force participation, gender gap, occupations, housework, marriage, divorce, single-parenthood and unwed births in U.S. with those in other economically-advanced nations.

CONTENTS:

© 1998, 396 pp., Paper, (0-13-565979-5)

THE MAKING OF ECONOMIC SOCIETY
Tenth Edition

Robert L. Heilbroner

William Milberg
both of the New School for Social Research

With its roots in history and eyes on the future, this solid book gives students a balanced perspective of why our economic society is the way it is and where it may be headed by tracing its development from the Middles Ages to the present. Showing that today's economic problems cannot be understood unless we have an understanding of how they first arose, it explores the catalytic role past economic trends and dynamics—particularly capitalism—have played in creating the present challenges we face, and offers suggestions on how we may deal with them most effectively.

CONTENTS:

©1998, 190 pp., Paper (0-13-874736-9) (87473-5)

NEW EDITION
AVAILABLE SUMMER 2000!

THE ECONOMICS OF POVERTY AND DISCRIMINATION
Seventh Edition

Bradley R. Schiller
American University

Emphasizing the complex economic, social, and political factors that create poverty and make its eradication so difficult, this book provides a broad overview of the dimensions of poverty and discrimination, the various explanations for these social ills, and the policy options for addressing them.

CONTENTS:

©1998, 320 pp., Paper (0-13-675083-4) (67508-2)

SUPPLEMENTS:

- Instructor's Manual with Test Bank (on the Web)

ECONOMIC HISTORY

THE MAKING OF ECONOMIC SOCIETY
Tenth Edition

Robert L. Heilbroner

William Milberg
both of the New School for Social Research

See page A-29

LABOR ECONOMICS

THE ECONOMICS OF WOMEN, MEN AND WORK
Third Edition

Francine D. Blau
Cornell University

Marianne A. Ferber
University of Illinois, Urbana-Champaign

Anne E. Winkler
University of Missouri-St. Louis

See page A-28

LABOR ECONOMICS AND LABOR RELATIONS
Eleventh Edition

Lloyd G. Reynolds
Yale University

Stanley H. Masters
SUNY at Binghamton

Colletta H. Moser
Michigan State University

A classic exploration of how labor markets are influenced by economic forces and the legal and institutional framework as well as an analysis of their interactions.

FEATURES:

- Combines the strengths of **early and more recent traditions of labor economics** that makes use of recent literature, both theoretical and empirical.

- Covers all topics from a **practical and theoretical** perspective.

- **Illustrates how collective bargaining works** and how it changes as the economic and legal environments also change.

©1998, 700 pp., Cloth (0-13-263310-8) (26331-9)

INTERNATIONAL ECONOMICS

NEW EDITION
AVAILABLE SUMMER 2000!

THE CHOICE: A Fable of Free Trade and Protectionism

Russel D. Roberts
Washington University

David Ricardo comes to life to discuss international trade theory and policy with Ed Johnson, a fictional American television manufacturer seeking protection from Japanese televisions. Their dialogue is a sophisticated, rigorous discussion of virtually every major issue in trade theory and policy. To illustrate the positive and normative effects of international trade and trade policy, Ricardo takes the reader and Ed Johnson into the future to see an America of free-trade and an America of complete self- sufficiency. The fictional element brings these topics to life so that students gain the intuition and understanding of how trade changes the lives of people and the industries they work in. The fundamental intuition of how international markets function including general equilibrium effects and policy analysis is provided.

FEATURES:

- Every major topic of trade policy is covered including comparative advantage, dumping, tariffs, optimal tariffs, quotas, trade agreements, and industrial policy.

- The fundamental intuition behind the standard graphical treatments of international trade and trade policy is provided. Students understanding of standard analyses of comparative advan tage, tariffs, quotas and short-run and long-run welfare effects of trade policies is enhanced.

- Students see how the theory works in the real world. The material comes to life in a unique way going beyond the standard boxed applications in books.

- Rich real-world issues are provided for students to discuss or research in depth, making economics fun without sacrificing rigor.

CONTENTS:

© 1994, 128 pp., paper, (0-13-083008-9)

WORLD ECONOMY: Resources, Location, Trade and Development
Third Edition

Anthony R. de Souza
Southwest Texas State University

Frederick P. Stutz
San Diego State University

Provides a sound theoretical and practical foundation for understanding the global economy in an era of shifting borders, restructuring economies, and regional realignments. Providing the most thorough treatment of the world economy and economic geography available, the text covers population, natural resources, and international trade and development. It combines economic theory with geography in addressing critical problems of growth, distribution, and development, and to explain their impact on international business.

CONTENTS:

© 1998, 596 pp., Cloth (0-13-727769-5)

INTERNATIONAL TRADE

NEW EDITION AVAILABLE SUMMER 2000!

THE CHOICE: A Fable of Free Trade and Protectionism

Russel D. Roberts
Washington University

See page A-31

COMPARATIVE ECONOMICS

COMPARATIVE ECONOMICS
Second Edition

James Angresano
Univesity of Texas, Austin

The text maintains a unique interdisciplinary approach that emphasizes the fluid, evolutionary nature of economics, while presenting additional aspects of economies not usually addressed in similar books. While integrating economic thought with economic history, it provides an alternative for students and teachers who wish to explore the variations of "mixed market economy" across countries.

CONTENTS:

©1996, 604 pp., Cloth (0-13-381633-8)

ECONOMICS OF DEVELOPMENT

THE ECONOMICS OF DEVELOPING COUNTRIES
Third Edition

Wayne E. Nafziger
Kansas State University

Written in exceptionally clear language, this comprehensive introduction to development economics features an abundance of real-world examples. It focuses on *real* problems of developing countries and their people.

CONTENTS:

©1997, 630 pp., cloth (0-13-339995-8)

SUPPLEMENTS:
- Instructor's Manual (on the Web)

ECONOMICS OF POVERTY AND DISCRIMINATION

NEW EDITION AVAILABLE SUMMER 2000!

THE ECONOMICS OF POVERTY AND DISCRIMINATION
Seventh Edition

Bradley R. Schiller
American University

See page A-30

U.S. ECONOMIC HISTORY

THE MAKING OF ECONOMIC SOCIETY
Tenth Edition

Robert L. Heilbroner

William Milberg
both of the New School for Social Research

See page A-29

HISTORY OF ECONMOMIC THOUGHT

COMPARATIVE ECONOMICS
Second Edition

James Angresano
Univesity of Texas, Austin

See page A-33

ECONOMIC HISTORY

THE MAKING OF ECONOMIC SOCIETY
Tenth Edition

Robert L. Heilbroner

William Milberg
both of the New School for Social Research

See page A-29

INDUSTRIAL ORGANIZATION

NEW EDITION
AVAILABLE SUMMER 2000!

THE STRUCTURE OF AMERICAN INDUSTRY
Ninth Edition

Walter Adams
Michigan State University

James W. Brock
Miami University, Ohio

The ninth edition of this widely-used reader continues to offer the leading real-world survey of contemporary American industries. Providing a sound new treatment of the role of public policy in a free-enterprise economy, this text illustrates the broadest possible range of American market structures through a series of carefully chosen and well-developed case studies of specific industries, all written by leading authorities in their field.

CONTENTS:

12. Public Policy, Walter Adams & James W. Brock.

©1995, 336 pp., Paper (0-02-300833-4)

AMERICAN INDUSTRY: STRUCTURE, CONDUCT, PERFORMANCE

Richard Caves
Harvard University

This popular volume provides a com pact account of the core concepts of the field of industrial organization and their application to American industry.

FEATURES:

- Focuses on the structures of markets, processes of competition among firms, levels of performance attained, and public policies regarding competition.
- Explains how the structures of markets shape competitive strategies and what competitive behavior implies for economic welfare.
- Includes recent scholarly evidence on the effects of deregulation and privati zation in the United States and public enterprises elsewhere.

CONTENTS:

1. The Business Sector and Its Organization.
2. Elements of Market Structure.
3. The Large Corporation.
4. Market Conduct.
5. Market Performance.
6. The Promotion of Competition and the Control of Monopoly.
7. Public Policy: Regulation and Public Enterprise. Selected Readings. Index.

© 1992, 144 pp., Paper, (0-13-029893-X)

BENEFIT—COST ANALYSIS

NEW EDITION AVAILABLE FALL 2000!

COST BENEFIT ANALYSIS: CONCEPTS AND PRACTICE

Anthony E. Boardman
University of British Columbia

David H. Greenberg
University of Maryland

Aidan R. Vining
Simon Fraser University

David L. Weimer
University of Rochester

Numerous **up-to-date illustrations and examples** show students how theories and techniques are applied to real-world situations. Provides a practical orientation and introduction to cost-benefit analysis through problem solving.

CONTENTS:

1. Introduction to Cost-Benefit Analysis.
2. Conceptual Foundations of Cost-Benefit Analysis
3. Valuing Benefits and Costs When Demand and Supply Curves Are Known.
4. Benefits and Costs in Different Time Periods: The Mechanics of Discounting.
5. The Social Discount Rate.
6. Dealing With Uncertainty: Expected Value and Sensitivity Analysis.
7. Option Price, Option Value, and Quasi-Option Value.
8. Existance Value.
9. Estimating Impacts From Demonstrations.
10. Estimating and Valuing Impacts from Observed Behavior.

11. Contingent Valuation: Using Surveys to Elicit Information About Costs and Benefits.
12. Shadow Prices from Secondary Sources.
13. Cost-Effectiveness Analysis and Cost-Utility Analysis.
14. Distributionally Weighted Cost-Benefit Analysis.
15. How Accurate is CBA?
A Selected Cost-Benefit Analysis Bibliography.
Author Index.
Subject Index.

©1996, 493 pp., Cloth (0-13-519968-9)

SUPPLEMENTS:

- Solutions Manual (on the Web)
- Extended Bibliography (on the Web)

GOVERNMENT AND BUSINESS

BUSINESS AND GOVERNMENT IN THE GLOBAL MARKETPLACE
Sixth Edition

Murray L. Weidenbaum
Washington University

Weidenbaum addresses the intricate relationship between the public sector and the private sector — why and how government intervenes in the economy and how business can respond. The Sixth Edition provides analyses from both perspectives, covering the ways in which government policy affects the activities of the modern corporation and the key responses on the part of business.

CONTENTS:

©1999, 397 pp., Paper (0-13-080625-0)

URBAN AND REGIONAL ECONOMICS

ECONOMICS OF CITIES AND SUBURBS
First Edition

William Thomas Bogart
Case Western Reserve University

Designed to convey the *excitement* of studying cities while developing a set of formal tools for analyzing their economies. Attempts to remove the division between "urban" economics and "regional" economics by demonstrating that the traditional intermetropolitan models of specialization and trade can also be extended to intrametropolitan analysis, thus unifying their treatment.

CONTENTS:

1. What Is a City?
2. Cities in History.
3. Market Areas and Central Place Theory.
4. Location of Economic Activity.
5. Intermetropolitan Trade.
6. Factor Abundance and Specialization.
7. Agglomeration and Metropolitan Growth.
8. Government Policy and Metropolitan Growth.
9. Clusters and Urban Form: Business Districts, Suburbs, and "Edge City."
10. Land Use Controls.
11. Intrametropolitan Competition and Economic Development Policy.
12. Urban Labor Markets and Poverty.
13. Housing Markets.
14. Housing Problems and Policies.
15. Transportation.

©1998, 500 pp., Cloth (0-13-569971-1) (56997-0)

FUNDAMENTALS OF URBAN ECONOMICS

John F. McDonald
University of Illinois, Chicago

This is the first modern text in urban economics that emphasizes urban economic growth. It approaches the various aspects of urban economics as part of *a coherent whole* rather than as separate isolated topics, and emphasizes the fundamental methods, models, and data used by economists to study cities.

CONTENTS:

I. ECONOMICS AND URBAN AREAS.
1. Introduction to Urban Economics.
2. Schools of Thought in Urban Economics.
3. Location Decisions, Agglomeration Economies, and the Origins of Cities.
4. Economic Functions of Cities.

II. LOCATION PATTERNS IN URBAN AREAS.
5. Introduction to Urban Location Patterns: Static Analysis.
6. Model of a Monocentric Urban Area.
7. Urban Employment Centers.
8. Urban Transportation.
9. Housing in Urban Areas.
10. The Public Sector in Urban Areas.

III. ECONOMIC GROWTH OF URBAN AREAS.
11. Models of Metropolitan Economic Growth.
12. Agglomeration Economies, Technical Change, and Urban Growth.
13. Labor, Capital, and Urban Growth.
14. Economic Development Policies for Urban Areas.

IV. THE CHANGING URBAN ECONOMY.
15. Urban Growth and Changing Location Patterns.
16. Urban Dimensions of Economic and Social Problems.

Appendix: Review of Some Mathematics and Microeconomic Theory.
Solutions to Selected Exercises.

©1997, 545 pp., Cloth (0-02-378852-6)

SUPPLEMENTS:

- Instructor's Manual with Solutions (on the Web)

URBAN ECONOMICS AND REAL ESTATE MARKETS

Denise DiPasquale
Harvard University

William C. Wheaton
Massachusetts Institute of Technology

This up-to-date, highly-accessible text presents a unique combination of *both* economic theory *and* real estate applications, providing students with the tools and techniques needed to understand the operation of urban real estate markets. It examines residential and non-residential real estate markets — from the perspectives of both macro- and micro-economics — as well as the role of government in real estate markets.

CONTENTS:

©1996, 378 pp., Cloth (0-13-225244-9)

REAL ESTATE

URBAN ECONOMICS AND REAL ESTATE MARKETS

Denise DiPasquale
Harvard University

William C. Wheaton
Massachusetts Institute of Technology

See description in left column

ECONOMETRICS

ECONOMIC STATISTICS AND ECONOMETRICS
Third Edition

Thad W. Mirer
State University New York, Albany

Designed for courses in economic statistics and introductory econometrics that aim to mix the development of technique with its application to real economic analysis. The text emphasizes formulating and interpreting regression models in economics, rather than on deriving and presenting technical material. It covers only those statistical topics that constitute a foundation for basic econometrics, and treats regression models in detail.

CONTENTS:

©1995, 464 pp., Cloth (0-02-381831-X); (U4845-6)

ECONOMETRIC ANALYSIS
Fourth Edition

NEW EDITION

William H. Greene
New York University

A standard text reference in courses that include basic techniques in regression analysis and extensions used when linear models prove inadequate or inappropriate. This text provides a broad survey of econometrics, with significant pedagogical work that will continue to serve as a modern, up–to–date reference for future practitioners. This book introduces students to the broad field of applied econometrics. An effective bridge to both on –the-job problems and to the professional literature, it features extensive applications and presents sufficient theoretical background to enable students to recognize new variants of the models that they learn about as merely natural extensions that fit within a common body of principles.

FEATURES:

- Surveys a wide range of topics in econometrics helping students to appreciate the important common foundation of all of the fields and use of the tools that they employ.

- Incorporates current topics in applied econometrics including GMM estimation methods, Lagrange multiplier tests, time series analysis, and the analysis of qualitative and limited dependent variable models.

- Provides a bridge to the professional literature by exposing students to material that will extend beyond many first courses.

- Includes extensive applications that makes the theory come to life and prepares students for problems they will likely encounter on the job.

NEW TO THIS EDITION:

- **FREE STUDENT VERSION OF LIMDEP** with the text! Packaged in the back of the text the student version of LIMDEP includes a large number of data sets, giving students realistic data sets and challenging empirical analyses as a routine part of their econometrics training.

- **NEW**—Increased number of examples using real data sets, with extensive examples worked out from current literature.

- **NEW**—Chapter 9 on large sample results and alternative estimators for the Classical Regression Model.

- **NEW**—Chapters 17 and 18 have been thoroughly revised to reflect current trends in time series analysis, including frequency domain and long–term memory models.

- **NEW**—Presents a greater emphasis on nonlinear models, including full chapters on nonlinear regression and nonlinear optimization.

CONTENTS:

Appendix A. Data Sets Used in Applications
Appendix B. Tables
Appendix C. Using EA-LIMDEP

© 2000, 1,100 pages, cloth, (0-13-013297-7)

SUPPLEMENTS:

- Solutions Manual
- LIMDEP Software

ECONOMETRIC MODELS, TECHNIQUES, AND APPRECIATIONS
Second Edition

Michael D. Intriligator
University of California, Los Angeles

Ronald G. Bodkin
University of Ottawa

Cheng Hsiao
University of California, Irvine

This text surveys the theories, techniques (model-building and data collection), and applications of econometrics. It focuses on those aspects of econometrics that are of major importance to students and researchers interested in performing, evaluating, or understanding econometric studies in a variety of areas.

CONTENTS:

©1996, 654 pp., Cloth (0-13-224775-5); (22477-4)

MATHEMATICAL ECONOMICS

MATHEMATICS FOR ECONOMIC ANALYSIS
First Edition

Knut Sydsaeter
University of Oslo

Peter I. Hammond
Stanford University

An introduction to those parts of mathematical analysis and linear algebra which are most important for economists.

CONTENTS:

©1995, 800 pp., Cloth (0-13-583600-X)

HEALTH ECONOMICS

NEW EDITION AVAILABLE SUMMER 2000!

ECONOMICS OF HEALTH AND HEALTH CARE
Second Edition

Sherman Folland
Oakland University

Allen C. Goodman
Wayne State University

Miron Stan
Oakland University

This comprehensive introduction to the economics of health and health care thoroughly develops and explains economic ideas and models and reflects the full spectrum of the most current health economics literature. It provides students with a solid working knowledge of the analytical tools of economics and econometrics ass applied to contemporary health care issues.

FEATURES:

- Organizes content around traditional and modern economic themes — such as supply and demand, technology, labor issues, and the economics of information.

- Provides a review of microeconomic concepts and tools and statistical tools for students who may need additional preparation or in those areas:

- Shows how economists analyze problems — using examples that are rele vant to health economics. Requires no calculus.

- Makes extensive use of ideas and models — with clear, thorough explanations of complex concepts.

CONTENTS:

© 1997, 666 pp.,cloth, (0-13-565987-6)

ALABAMA
- University of Alabama
- U of Alabama at Birmingham
- U of Alabama in Huntsville
- Alabama A&M University
- Alabama State University
- Athens State College
- Auburn University
- Auburn U at Montgomery
- Birmingham-Southern Coll
- Jacksonville State Univ
- University of Montevallo
- University of North Alabama
- Samford University
- University of South Alabama
- Troy State University
- Tuskegee University
- University of West Alabama

ALASKA
- Univ of Alaska Anchorage
- Univ of Alaska Southeast
- Univ of Alaska Fairbanks

ARIZONA
- University of Arizona
- Arizona State University
- Grand Canyon University
- Northern Arizona University

ARKANSAS
- Arkansas College
- University of Arkansas
- U of Arkansas at Little Rock
- U of Arkansas at Pine Bluff
- Arkansas State University
- Arkansas Tech University
- Univ of Central Arkansas
- Harding University
- Hendrix College
- Southern Arkansas Univ

CALIFORNIA
- Azusa Pacific University
- Biola University
- U of California-Berkeley
- Univ of California-Davis
- Univ of Calif-Irvine
- Univ of Calif, Los Angeles
- Univ of Calif, Riverside
- Univ of Calif, San Diego
- U of Calif, Santa Barbara
- U of Calif, Santa Cruz
- California Institute of Tech
- California Lutheran Univ
- Calif Polytechnic State U
- Calif State Poly U-Pomona
- Calif State U., Bakersfield
- Calif State Univ, Chico
- Calif St U-Dominguez Hills
- Calif State Univ-Fresno
- Calif State Univ, Fullerton
- Calif State Univ, Hayward
- Calif State Univ - Humboldt
- Calif State Univ, Long Beach
- Calif State U-Los Angeles
- Calif State Univ, Northridge
- Calif State Univ-Sacramento
- Calif St U San Bernardino
- Calif State U - San Marcos
- Calif State U, Stanislaus
- Chapman University
- Claremont McKenna College
- John F. Kennedy University
- La Sierra University
- University of LaVerne
- Loyola Marymount Univ
- Mount St. Mary's College
- Naval Postgraduate School
- Occidental College
- University of the Pacific
- Pacific Union College
- Pepperdine Univ-Malibu
- Point Loma Nazarene College
- University of Redlands
- Saint Mary's College
- University of San Diego
- San Diego State University
- University of San Francisco
- San Francisco State Univ
- San Jose State University
- Santa Clara University
- Sonoma State University
- Univ of Southern California
- Stanford University
- Woodbury University

COLORADO
- Adams State College
- Colorado College
- Univ of Colorado at Boulder
- U of Colorado at Co Springs
- Univ of Colorado at Denver
- Colorado State University
- University of Denver
- Fort Lewis College
- Mesa State College
- Metropolitan State College
- Univ of Northern Colorado
- Regis College of Regis Univ
- Univ of Southern Colorado
- U.S. Air Force Academy
- Western State College of CO

CONNECTICUT
- University of Bridgeport
- Central Connecticut St Univ
- Connecticut College
- University of Connecticut
- Eastern Conn State Univ
- Fairfield Universiy
- University of Hartford
- University of New Haven
- Quinnipiac College
- Sacred Heart University
- Southern Connecticut St Un
- Teikyo Post University
- Wesleyan University
- Western Conn State Univ
- Yale University

DELAWARE
- University of Delaware
- Delaware State College

FLORIDA
- Barry University
- Bethune-Cookman College
- Univ of Central Florida
- Embry-Riddle Aeronautical U
- University of Florida
- Florida A&M University
- Florida Atlantic Univ
- Florida Institute of Tech
- Florida International Univ
- Florida Southern College
- Florida State University
- Jacksonville University
- University of Miami
- University of North Florida
- Rollins College
- St. Thomas University
- University of South Florida
- Stetson University
- University of Tampa
- University of West Florida

GEORGIA
- Albany State College
- Augusta College
- Berry College
- Clark Atlanta University
- Clayton State College
- Columbus College
- Emory University
- Fort Valley State College
- Georgia College
- University of Georgia
- Georgia Institute Tech
- Georgia Southern University
- Georgia Southwestern Coll
- Georgia State University
- Kennesaw College
- Mercer Univ-Atlanta
- Mercer Univ-Macon
- Morehouse College
- Morris Brown College
- North Georgia College
- Oglethorpe University
- Piedmont College
- Valdosta State University
- West Georgia College

HAWAII
- Brigham Young Univ-Hawaii
- Chaminade University
- University of Hawaii at Hilo
- Univ of Hawaii at Manoa
- Hawaii Pacific University

IDAHO
- Boise State University
- University of Idaho
- Idaho State University

ILLINOIS
- Augustana College
- Bradley University
- University of Chicago
- Chicago State University
- DePaul University
- Eastern Illinois Univ
- Elmhurst College
- University of Illinois
- Univ of Illinois at Chicago
- Illinois Benedictine College
- Illinois Institute of Tech
- Illinois State University
- Illinois Wesleyan University
- Lewis University
- Loyola University of Chicago
- Millikin University
- North Central College
- Northeastern Illinois Univ
- Northern Illinois Univ
- Northwestern University
- Olivet Nazarene College
- Roosevelt University
- Sangamon State University
- Southern Illinois Univ
- So Illinois, Edwardsville
- Western Illinois University
- Wheaton College

INDIANA
- Anderson University
- Ball State University
- Butler University
- University of Evansville
- DePauw University
- Goshen College
- Indiana University
- Indiana Univ at Kokoma
- Indiana Univ Northwest
- Indiana Univ at South Bend
- Indiana Univ Southeast
- Indiana State University
- Indiana Wesleyan University
- University of Indianapolis
- Marian College
- University of Notre Dame
- Purdue University
- Purdue University at Calumet
- Saint Marys College
- Univ of Southern Indiana
- Taylor University
- Tri State University
- Valparaiso University

IOWA
- Buena Vista College
- Central University of Iowa
- Coe College
- Drake University
- Graceland College
- Grinnell College
- University of Iowa
- Iowa State University
- Loras College
- Luther College
- Morningside College
- University of Northern Iowa
- St. Ambrose University
- Simpson College
- Wartburg College

KANSAS
- Emporia State University
- Fort Hays State University
- University of Kansas
- Kansas State University
- Pittsburg State University
- Washburn Univ of Topeka
- Wichita State University

KENTUCKY
- Bellarmine College
- Berea College
- Brescia College
- Centre College
- Cumberland College
- Eastern Kentucky University
- University of Kentucky
- Kentucky State University
- University of Louisville
- Morehead State University
- Murray State University
- Northern Kentucky Univ
- Transylvania University
- Western Kentucky University

LOUISIANA
- Dillard University
- Grambling State University
- Louisiana State University
- Louisiana St in Shreveport
- Louisiana Tech University
- Loyola Univ-New Orleans
- Mc Neese State University
- University of New Orleans
- Nicholls State University
- Northeast Louisiana Univ
- Northwestern State U of LA
- Southeastern Louisiana Univ
- Southern University
- U of Southwestern Louisiana
- Tulane University

MAINE
- Bates College
- Bowdoin College
- Colby College
- Univ of Maine at Orono
- Univ of Southern Maine

MARYLAND
- University of Baltimore
- Frostburg State University
- Hood College
- Johns Hopkins University
- Loyola College in Maryland
- University of Maryland
- Univ Maryland-Baltimore Cnty
- Morgan State University
- Mount Saint Mary's College
- Salisbury State University
- Towson State University
- United States Naval Academy
- Western Maryland College

MASSACHUSETTS
- American International Coll
- Amherst College
- Assumption College
- Babson College
- Bentley College
- Boston College
- Boston University
- Brandeis University
- Clark University
- Fitchburg State College
- Framingham State College
- Harvard University
- College of the Holy Cross
- University of Massachusetts
- U Massachusetts at Boston
- U Massachusetts at Dartmouth
- U Massachusetts at Lowell
- Massachusetts Inst of Tech
- Merrimack College
- Mount Holyoke College
- Nichols College
- North Adams State College
- Northeastern University
- Regis College
- Salem State College
- Simmons College
- Smith College
- Stonehill College
- Suffolk University
- Tufts University
- Wellesley College
- Western New England College
- Westfield State College
- Wheaton College
- Williams College
- Worcester State College

MICHIGAN
- Adrian College
- Albion College
- Alma College
- Andrews University
- Aquinas College
- Calvin College
- Central Michigan University
- University of Detroit Mercy
- Eastern Michigan University
- Ferris State University
- GMI Engineering & Mgt Inst
- Grand Valley State Univ
- Hillsdale College
- Hope College
- Kalamazoo College
- Lake Superior State Univ
- Lawrence Technological Univ
- University of Michigan
- Univ of Michigan-Dearborn
- Univ of Michigan-Flint
- Michigan State University
- Michigan Technological Univ
- Northern Michigan Univ
- Northwood Institute
- Oakland University
- Olivet College
- Saginaw Valley State Univ
- Wayne State University
- Western Michigan University

MINNESOTA
- Gugsburg College
- Bemidji State University
- Bethel College
- Carleton College
- Concordia College MN
- Gustavus Adolphus College
- Hamline University
- Macalister College
- University of Minnesota
- U of Minnesota - Duluth
- Minnesota State U-Mankato
- Moorhead State University
- College of Saint Benedictine
- College of St. Catherine
- St. Cloud State University
- St. Olaf College
- College of St. Scholastica
- University of St. Thomas-MN
- Southwest State University
- Winona State University

MISSISSIPPI
- Alcorn State University
- Belhaven College
- Delta State University
- Jackson State University
- Millsaps College
- Mississippi College
- University of Mississippi
- Mississippi State Univ
- Mississippi Valley St Univ
- U of Southern Mississippi

MISSOURI
- Central Missouri State Univ
- Drury College
- Lincoln University
- Lindenwood College
- U of Missouri at Columbia
- U Missouri--Kansas City
- U Missouri at Rolla
- U Missouri--St. Louis
- Missouri Southern St Col
- Missouri Western St College
- Northeast Missouri State U
- Northwest Missouri St Univ
- Rockhurst College
- Saint Louis University
- Southeast Missouri St Univ
- Southwest Baptist Univ
- Southwest Missouri St Univ
- Washington University
- Webster University
- William Jewell College

MONTANA
- Eastern Montana College
- University of Montana
- Montana State University

NEBRASKA
- Chadron State College
- Creighton University
- University of Nebraska
- Univ of Nebraksa at Kearney
- Univ of Nebraska at Omaha
- Nebraska Wesleyan Univ
- Wayne State College

NEVADA
- Univ of Nevada, Las Vegas
- University of Nevada, Reno

NEW HAMPSHIRE
- Dartmouth College
- Keene State College
- New Hampshire College
- University of New Hampshire
- Plymouth State College
- Saint Anselm College

NEW JERSEY
Bloomfield College
Centenary College
Drew University
Fairleigh Dickinson-Madison
Fairleigh Dickinson-Teaneck
Kean College of New Jersey
Monmouth College
Montclair State College
New Jersey City University
New Jersey Inst Technology
Princeton University
Ramapo College of New Jersey
Rider College
Rowan College of New Jersey
Rutgers University-Camden
Rutgers University-Newark
Rutgers Univ-New Brunswick
Saint Peter's College
Seton Hall University
Stevens Institute of Tech
Stockton State College
Trenton State College
Upsala College
William Patterson College
NEW MEXICO
Eastern New Mexico Univ
University of New Mexico
New Mexico Highlands Univ
New Mexico State Univ
NEW YORK
Adelphi University
Alfred University
Barnard College
Canisius College
CUNY-Baruch College
CUNY-Brooklyn College
CUNY-Hunter College
CUNY-Lehman College
CUNY-Queens College
CUNY-Staten Island
Clarkson University
Colgate University
Columbia University
Cornell University
Dowling College
Elmira College
Fordham University
Hamilton College
Hartwick College
Hofstra University
Iona College
Ithaca College
LeMoyne College
Long Isl U, Brooklyn Campus
Long Island U-C.W. Post
Malloy College
Manhattan College
Marist College
Nazareth Col of Rochester
College of New Rochelle
New York University
New York Institute of Tech
Niagara University
Pace University
Rensselaer Poly Institute
University of Rochester
Rochester Inst of Technology
Russell Sage College
Saint Bonaventure Univ
St. Francis College
St. John Fisher College
St. John's University
St. Lawrence University
College of Saint Rose
Siena College
Skidmore College
SUNY College at Fredonia
State Un College at Geneseo
SUNY at Albany
SUNY at Binghamton
SUNY at Buffalo
SUNY at Cortland
SUNY - Empire State College
SUNY at New Paltz
SUNY at Old Westbury
SUNY College at Oneonta
SUNY at Oswego
SUNY at Plattsburgh
SUNY at Potsdam
SUNY College at Purchase
SUNY at Stony Brook
Syracuse University
Union College
United States Military Acad
Utica College
Vassar College
Yeshiva University
NORTH CAROLINA
Appalachian State Univ
Barton College
Campbell University
Catawba College
Davidson College
Duke University
East Carolina University
Elon College
Fayetteville State Univ
Gardner-Webb University
Greensboro College
Guilford College
Lenoir-Rhyn College
Meredith College
North Carolina at Ashville
University of North Carolina
North Carolina at Charlotte
North Carolina at Greensboro
North Carolina at Wilmington
North Carolina A&T State Un
North Carolina Central Univ
North Carolina State Univ
Pembroke State University
Pfeiffer College
Wake Forest University
Western Carolina University
Wingate College
Winston-Salem State Univ
NORTH DAKOTA
University of Mary
Minot State University
University of North Dakota
North Dakota State Univ
OHIO
University of Akron
Ashland University
Baldwin-Wallace College
Bowling Green State Univ
Capital University
Case Western Reserve Univ
Cedarville College
Central State Univ-Ohio
University of Cincinnati
Cleveland State University
University of Dayton
Dennison University
University of Findley
Franklin University
Heidelberg College
John Carroll University
Kent State University
Kenyon College
Marietta College
Miami University
Oberlin College
Ohio University
Ohio Northern University
Ohio State University
Ohio Wesleyan University
Otterbein College
University of Rio Grande
University of Toledo
Wittenberg University
The College of Wooster
Wright State University
Xavier University
Youngstown State University
OKLAHOMA
Cameron University
Univ of Central Oklahoma
East Central University
Northeastern State Univ
University of Oklahoma
Oklahoma Baptist University
Oklahoma Christian U Sci/Art
Oklahoma City University
Oklahoma State University
Southern Nazarene Univ
Southeastern Oklahoma State
Southwestern Oklahoma St Un
University of Tulsa
OREGON
Eastern Oregon State College
Lewis & Clark College
Linfield College
University of Oregon
Oregon State University
University of Portland
Portland State University
Reed College
Southern Oregon St College
Western Oregon State College
Willamette University
PENNSYLVANIA
Albright College
Allegheny College
Beaver College
Bloomsburg University
Bryn Mawr College
Bucknell University
California Univ of Penn
Carnegie Mellon University
Cheyney University
Clarion University
Dickinson College
Drexel University
Duquesne University
East Stroudsburg University
Edinboro University of PA
Elizabethtown College
Franklin and Marshall Coll
Gannon University
Geneva College
Gettysburg College
Grove City College
Holy Family College
Immaculata College
Indiana U of Pennsylvania
King's College
Kutztown University of PA
Lafayette College
LaSalle University
Lehigh University
Lincoln University
Lock Haven University
Lycoming College
Mansfield University of PA
Marywood College
Millersville Univ of PA
Moravian College
Mulhenberg College
University of Pennsylvania
Penn State University
Penn State Univ-Erie
Penn State Univ-Harrisburg
University of Pittsburgh
U of Pittsburgh at Johnstown
Robert Morris College
Saint Joseph's University
Saint Vincent College
University of Scranton
Shippensburg University
Slippery Rock University
Susquehanna University
Temple University
Villanova University
Washington & Jefferson Coll
West Chester University
Westminster College of PA
Widener University
Wilkes University
York College of Pennsylvania
RHODE ISLAND
Brown University
Bryant College
Providence College
Rhode Island College
University of Rhode Island
Salve Regina University
SOUTH CAROLINA
Benedict College
College of Charleston
The Citadel
Clemson University
Converse College
Francis Marion College
Furman University
Lander University
Presbyterian College
Univ of South Carolina
Univ So Carolina at Aiken
U South Carolina at Spartanb
South Carolina St College
Winthrop University
Wofford College
SOUTH DAKOTA
Augustana College SD
Northern State University
University of South Dakota
South Dakota State Univ
TENNESSEE
Austin Peay State University
Belmont College
Carson-Newman College
Christian Brothers College
East Tennessee State Univ
Fisk University
Freed Hardeman University
Memphis State University
Middle Tennessee State Univ
Rhodes College
University of the South
Southern Col of 7th Day Adv
University of Tennessee
Tennessee at Chattanooga
Univ of Tennessee at Martin
Tennessee State University
Tennessee Technological Un
Union University
Vanderbilt University
TEXAS
Amber University
Angelo State University
Baylor University
University of Dallas
Dallas Baptist University
East Texas State Univ
Hardin-Simmons University
University of Houston
Univ of Houston-Downtown
Univ of Houston-Clear Lake
Houston Baptist University
Howard Payne University
Lamar University
Univ of Mary Hardin-Baylor
McMurray University
Midwestern State University
University of North Texas
Prairie View A&M University
Rice University
St. Edward's University
St. Mary's University
University of St. Thomas-TX
Sam Houston State Univ
Southern Methodist Univ
Southwest Texas State Univ
Southwestern University
Stephen F. Austin St Univ
Tarleton State University
U of Texas at Arlington
Univ of Texas at Austin
Univ of Texas at Brownsville
Univ of Texas at Dallas
Univ of Texas at El Paso
Univ of Texas-Pan American
U of Texas of Permian Basin
Un of Texas at San Antonio
Univ of Texas at Tyler
Texas A&M University
Texas A&M - Corpus Christi
Texas A&M Univ-Kingsville
Texas A&M International Univ
Texas Christian University
Texas Lutheran College
Texas Southern University
Texas Tech University
Texas Wesleyan University
Texas Woman's University
Trinity University
West Texas A&M University
UTAH
Brigham Young University
Southern Utah University
University of Utah
Utah State University
Weber State University
Westminster U of Salt Lake C
VERMONT
Lyndon State College
Middlebury College
Norwich University
St. Michael's College
University of Vermont
VIRGINIA
Christopher Newport College
Emory and Henry College
George Mason University
Hampton University
James Madison University
Liberty University
Longwood College
Lynchburg College
Mary Baldwin College
Mary Washington College
Marymount University
Norfolk State University
Old Dominion University
Radford University
Regent University
University of Richmond
Roanoke College
Shenandoah University
University of Virginia
Virginia Commonwealth Univ
Virginia Military Institute
Virginia Poly Inst & St Un
Virginia State University
Washington and Lee Univ
College of William & Mary
WASHINGTON
Central Washington Univ
Eastern Washington Univ
Evergreen State College
Gonzaga University
Pacific Lutheran University
University of Puget Sound
Saint Martin's College
Seattle University
Seattle Pacific University
Walla Walla College
University of Washington
Washington State University
Western Washington Univ
Whitmore College
WASHINGTON DC
The American University
Catholic Univ of America
Univ of District of Columbia
Gallaudet University
George Washington Univ
Georgetown University
Howard University
WEST VIRGINIA
Fairmont State College
Shephard College
Marshall University
West Liberty State College
West Virginia University
West Virginia State College
WISCONSIN
Carroll College
Carthage College
Lakeland College
Marquette University
St. Norbert College
U of Wisconsin-Eau Claire
U of Wisconsin-Green Bay
U of Wisconsin-La Crosse
Univ of Wisconsin-Madison
Univ of Wisconsin-Milwaukee
Univ of Wisconsin-Oshkosh
Univ of Wisconsin-Parkside
U of Wisconsin-Platteville
U of Wisconsin-River Falls
U of Wisconsin-Stevens Point
Univ of Wisconsin-Superior
U of Wisconsin-Whitewater
WYOMING
University of Wyoming

THE 1999-2000 PRENTICE HALL
GUIDE TO ECONOMICS FACULTY

Compiled by
James R. Hasselback
Professor of Taxation
6753 Thomasville Rd, PMB 108-321
Tallahassee, Florida 32312
850-894-2244 Phone/Recorder/Fax
E-Mail: jhassel@cob.fsu.edu

Prentice Hall Inc. is publishing the fourth DIRECTORY OF ECONOMICS FACULTY. The Directory includes a listing of the Dean, Department Chairpersons, and full-time Economics faculty from almost 850 schools. It is compiled from information provided by the respective schools. The Directory is for the academic year 1999-2000. Only United States schools plus four foreign schools were included in the survey. The Directory is published every two years.

Updated information is provided on over 90 percent of the schools. Typically at least three requests went to any school listed as not responding. Only that information received by June 15, 1999 is included in the Directory. Information taken from college catalogs may be provided on nonresponding departments.

The department phone number follows the area code in the first line of each school. At the right side of the first line is the school's electronic-mail code. The fax number is shown in the second line. The department secretary/administration assistant is included at the end of the second line.

The columns are as follows:

Name Rank School-Phone Electronic-Mail Area Degr/Date/School Start
$ next to a Dean or Chairman indicates "Acting"

For the Chairperson, the title and rank are:

C	Chairman	D	Director	H	Head
Pr	Professor	Ac	Associate	As	Assistant

The electronic-mail column includes the individual's address. The individual address must be combined with the school electronic-mail address; for instance, jim@fsu. When an individual address includes an "@", that individual has a different school address from the school address listed in the first line of the school; the individual's complete electronic-mail address is included in the electronic-mail column. However, if an individual electronic-mail address ends with a "." then the school's address must be added to the individual address provided. Additional school addresses may be shown in a third line for the school. In some cases, an individual address was too long to fit in the column and was truncated with a "+" or was included in a line following the individual. Use the Super Computer to decipher this paragraph.

The degree column represents the highest earned degree or "all but dissertation," date received, and school.

The start column is for the year of beginning full-time employment at that school.

The teaching/research column is as follows:

A General Economics & Teaching
B Methodology & History of Econ Thought
C Mathematical & Quantitative Methods
D Microeconomics
E Macroeconomics & Monetary Economics
F International Economics
G Financial Economics
H Public Economics
I Health, Education, & Welfare
J Labor Economics
K Law & Economics
L Industrial Organization
M Business Adm & Business Economics
N Economic History
O Economic Development, Technological Change, & Growth
P Economic Systems
Q Agricultural & Natural Resource Economics
R Urban, Rural, & Regional Economics
T Demographic Economics
adapted from Journal of Economic Literature listing

In the second part of the Directory, individuals are listed in alphabetical order. The phone and electronic-mail columns are replaced with the individual's school.

Any mistakes in the Directory are my responsibility. However, some of the misinformation belongs to schools not providing complete information.

Any corrections, additional information, and new schools should be sent directly to me. If your school is not included, please send me a listing in a format similar to that provided in the Directory.

James R. Hasselback

1999-2000 GUIDE TO ECONOMICS FACULTY
ALPHABETICAL BY SCHOOL

NAME	RANK	PHONE	Electronic-Mail	RESR	DEGREE			START
Abilene Christian Univ	Abilene, TX		79699-0001 (915) 674-2565					coba.acu.edu
Dept of Management Sciences	College of Business Adm		Fax=674-2564					Darlene Mahaney
Lytle, Richard S.	Dean$	674-2503		Mktg	PHD	94	Ariz St	1991
Lynn, Monty L.	C-Ac	674-2593		Mgt	PHD	85	Brighm Yg	1985
Brister, Jozell	Assoc	674-2596			MS	73	North Tx	1980
Jackson, Don C.	Assoc	674-2634			DBA	65	Geo Wash	1987
Adams State College	Alamosa, CO		81102 (719) 587-7161					
Department of Economics	School of Business		Fax=587-7603					Ms. Dolly Maestas
Weston, Rafael R.	Dean	587-7161			PHD	72	Harvard	1988
Ellis, Theodore	Prof	587-7511			PHD	72	Colo St	1967
Larriviere, James	Asst	587-7303			PHD	95	Auburn	1997
Adelphi University	Garden City, NY		11530 (516) 877-4970					adelphi.edu
Department of Economics	Col of Arts & Sciences		Fax=877-4191					
Did Not Respond--1997-98 Listing								
Costello, Peter	Dean				PHD	66	Mich St	
Gleicher, David	C-Ac	877-4970		BJ	PHD	84	Columbia	1981
Machlis, David	Assoc			E	PHD	71	Rutgers	1968
Adrian College	Adrian, MI		49221-2575 (517) Ext 4432					adrian.adrian.edu
Economics Faculty	Department of Economics		Fax=264-3331					Pat Husband
phone: 265-5161								
Habib, Ahsan M.	Assoc	Ext 4330	ahabib		PHD	80	McMaster	1981
University of Akron	Akron, OH		44325-1908 (330) 972-7546					uakron.edu
Department of Economics	Buchtel Col Arts & Sci		Fax=972-5356					Sarah Thorley
Creel, Roger	Dean	972-7881	rcreel		PHD	69	Iowa St	1970
Byrne, Dennis	C-Pr	972-7939	dbyrne	AJL	PHD	75	Notre Dm	1975
Garofalo, Gasper A.	Prof	972-7548	ggarofalo	ADR	PHD	74	Pittsburgh	1979
Malhotra, Devinder	Prof	972-7937	dmalhotra	ADR	PHD	79	Kansas St	1979
McGuire, Robert A.	Prof	972-7521	rmcguire	AKN	PHD	78	U Wash	1990
Erickson, Elizabeth L.	Assoc	972-7973	eerickson	AOQ	PHD	72	Illinois	1969
King, Randall H.	Assoc	972-7975	king	ADJ	PHD	78	Ohio St	1978
Lin, Lung-Ho	Assoc	972-7974	llin	AE	PHD	71	Notre Dm	1970
Myers, Steven	Assoc	972-7421	smyers	ACJ	PHD	80	Ohio St	1979
Sellers, Gary	Assoc	972-7938	gsellers	AKL	PHD	77	Cincinnati	1976
Stratton, Richard	Assoc	972-7440	dickstratton	ADJ	PHD	77	Conn	1978
Ghosh, Sucharita	Asst	972-7549	sghosh	AEF	PHD	93	Kansas	1993
Su, Dongwei	Asst	972-7411	su	AC	PHD	97	Ohio St	1997
Yamarik, Steven	Asst	972-8491	yamarik	AE	PHD	96	N Carol	1997
University of Alabama	Tuscaloosa, AL		35487-0224 (205) 348-7842					cba.ua.edu
Dept Econ, Fnce & Legal Stds	Col Commerce & Bus Adm		Fax=348-0590					Sheila Smith, Prog Asst
Mason, J. Barry	Dean	348-7443	jbmason	Mktg	PHD	67	Alabama	1967
Russell Professor of Business Administration								
Helms, Billy P.	H-Pr	348-7842	bhelms	Fnce	PHD	73	Tennessee	1973
Fish, Mary	Prof	348-7842	mfish		PHD	63	Oklahoma	1965
Formby, John P.	Prof	348-8667	jformby		PHD	65	Colorado	1982
Hayes Professor of Economics								
Leathers, Charles G.	Prof	348-7842	cleather		PHD	68	Oklahoma	1968
Misiolek, Walter S.	Prof	348-8980	wmisiole		PHD	76	Cornell	1975
Senior Associate Dean & Director of Graduate Programs								
Schlesinger, Harris	Prof	348-7842	hsclesi		PHD	80	Illinois	1987
VanHoose, David D.	Prof	348-7842	dvanhoos		PHD	84	N Carol	1990
Cover, James P.	Assoc	348-8977	jcover		PHD	82	Virginia	1982
Elder, Harold W.	Assoc	348-7842	helder		PHD	82	Va Tech	1981
Hooks, Donald L.	Assoc	348-7842	dhooks		PHD	71	Tx A&M	1971
Pecorino, Paul	Assoc	348-0379	ppecorin		PHD	90	Duke	1994
Silver, J. Lew	Assoc	348-7842	jsilver		PHD	80	Duke	1990
Arce, Daniel G.	Asst	348-7842	darce		PHD	91	Illinois	1991
Heung, C. James	Asst	348-8971	chueng		PHD	97	Wisconsin	1997
Hoover, Gary A.	Asst	348-6033	ghoover		PHD	98	U Wash	1998
Temimi, Akram	Asst	348-8961	atemimi		PHD	96	Illinois	1996

U of Alabama at Birmingham	Birmingham, AL	35294-4460 (205) 934-8830						uab.edu
Department of Economics	School of Business	Fax=975-6234						Rose McCoy
email: @1=mail.business.uab.edu								
Lee, Seung-Dong	C-Ac	934-8830	sdlee	CDFQ	PHD	79	So Meth	1979
McCarl, Henry N.	Prof	934-8830	hmccarl	AR	PHD	69	Penn St	1969
Stanford, Robert	Prof	934-8830	stanford	C	PHD	71	Berkeley	1982
VanMatre, Joe G.	Prof	934-8830	jgv	C	PHD	70	Alabama	1971
Bos, Theodore	Assoc	934-8830	tedbos	CG	PHD	82	Illinois	1982
Dasgupta, Manabendra	Assoc	934-8830	dasgupta@1	CDHL	PHD	89	So Meth	1992
Ignatin, George	Assoc	934-8830	gig@1	AJK	PHD	69	Tx-Austin	1969
Culver, Sarah E.	Asst	934-8830	sculver	CEFG	PHD	93	Houston	1993
Wilson, Bradley	Asst	934-8830		CEF	PHD	97	Kansas	1997

U of Alabama in Huntsville	Huntsville, AL	35899 (256) 890-6590						uah.edu
Dept Economics & Finance	Col of Admin Science	Fax=890-6328						Ms. Liz Patillo
Billings, C. David	Dean	890-6735		H	PHD	69	Missouri	1981
Wilhite, Allen W.	C-Pr	890-6694		JK	PHD	81	Illinois	1988
Paul, Chris W.	Emer	890-6590		K	PHD	79	Tx A&M	1982
Schnell, John F.	Prof	890-6590		J	PHD	84	Illinois	1990
Schoening, Niles C.	Prof	890-6782		R	PHD	83	Tennessee	1983
Allen, W. David	Asst	890-6105		J	PHD	94	Arkansas	1994

Alabama A&M University	Normal, AL	35762 (205) 851-5085						asnaam.aamu.edu
Dept of Economics & Finance	School of Business	Fax=851-5874						Sibyl Moore
Jones, Barbara A. P.	Dean	851-5092		AP	PHD	73	Geo St	1997
Rahimian, Eric N.	C-Pr	851-5085		ADOF	PHD	75	Indiana	1975
Alexander, James	Prof	858-4794		EAOH	PHD	89	Tx-Austin	1983
Elike, Uchenna I.	Asst	858-8487		AOF	PHD	85	Alabama	1985
Mallick, Naresh	Asst	858-4792		CE	PHD	95	Illinois	2-99
Robbani, Mohammad G.	Asst	851-5095	aammgr01	GO	PHD	94	Fla Intl	9-94
Yousif, Salah A.	Asst	858-4788		AJ	MA		Howard	1976
Briggs, Charles	Inst	858-4787		A	MS	90	Alab A&M	1990
Gebremikael, Fesseha	Inst	858-4795		A	MS	97	Alab A&M	1996

Alabama State University	Montgomery, AL	36101-0271 (334) 229-4142						alasu.edu
Department of Business Adm	Col of Business Admin	Fax=265-9144						Ms. Jenette Williams
Vaughn, Percy J. Jr.	Dean	293-4124		Mktg	DBA	75	Tx Tech	1974
Yeh, Chiou-Nan	C-Pr	293-4130			PHD	74	Mass	1974
Bakir, Saad T.	Assoc	229-6805	sbakir	CM	PHD	77	Va Tech	1-93
Suwanakul, Sontachai	Assoc	293-6962			PHD	86	Arkansas	1989

Univ of Alaska Anchorage	Anchorage, AK	99508-8244 (907) 786-1770						uaa.alaska.edu
Department of Economics	Sch of Public Affairs	Fax=786-7739						Janet Burton
Huskey, Lee	C-Pr	786-1905	aflh	AJR	PHD	77	Wash U	1977
Goldsmith, O. Scott	Prof	786-7710		CH	PHD	76	Wisconsin	1975
Jackstadt, Stephen L.	Prof	786-1901		AEH	EDD	81	Indiana	1985
Knapp, Gunnar P.	Prof	786-7717	afgpk	QR	PHD	81	Yale	1981
Rohacek, Jerry K.	Prof	786-1662		DEN	MA	69	Ca-SnBarb	1973
Ross, Larry L.	Prof	786-1613		ADE	MS	71	Oregon	1971
Tuck, Bradford H.	Prof	786-1915		CDL	PHD	73	Boston U	1977
Vercella, Kit J.	Prof	786-1620		ADEO	MA	72	Ca-SnDgo	1974
Hill, Pershing J.	Assoc	786-1763		EFH	PHD	76	Wash St	1975

Univ of Alaska Fairbanks	Fairbanks, AK	99775-6080 (907) 474-7119						som.ucf.edu
Department of Economics	School of Management	Fax=474-5219						Francine Davis
Collins, James	D-As$	474-7119	ffjmc	Mgt	PHD	91	Tx-Austin	1991
Pippenger, Michael	H-As	474-6530	ffmkp		PHD	90	Purdue	1991
Goering, Gregory	Assoc	474-5572	ffgeg		PHD	90	Purdue	1990
Hermann, Mark	Assoc	474-7116	ffmlh		PHD	90	Wash St	1990
Logan, Robert	Assoc	474-6783	ffrrl		PHD	86	Iowa	1986
Read, Colin	Assoc	474-5975	ffclri		PHD	88	Queen's	1989
Giraud, Kelly	Asst	474-5199	ffklg		PHD	99	Colo St	
Reynolds, Douglas	Asst	474-6531	ffdmr		PHD			

Univ of Alaska Southeast	Juneau, AK	99801-8671 (907) 465-6405						alaska.edu
Economics Faculty	S of Edu, Lib Art & Sci	Fax=465-6406						Lisa Ward
Pugh, John R.	Dean	465-6417	jnjrp		MSSW		Tx-Austin	
Brown, William S.	Prof	465-6423	jfwsb		PHD	77	Colorado	1991

Albany State University	Albany, GA	31705 (912) 430-4772						asurams.edu
Economics Faculty	School of Business Adm	Fax=430-5119						Carol Crayton
Brown, Mollie B.	Dean	430-4788	mbbrown		PHD	76	Geo St	
Ojemakindel, Abiodun	Assoc	430-4772			PHD	89	LSU	1989
Shah, Umanglal	Asst	430-4772			MA	64	Houston	

Albion College — Albion, MI 49224-1899 (517) 629-0419 — albion.edu
Economics Faculty — Dept of Economics & Mgt Fax=629-0428 — Becky Ketchum

Name	Rank	Phone	E-mail	Fields	Degree	Yr	School	Since
McCarley, James F.	C-Pr	629-0294	jmccarley	J	PHD	70	Mich St	1965
Christiansen, Daniel S.	Prof	629-0425	christiansen	CD	PHD	75	Stanford	1981
Steinhauer, Larry	Prof	629-0423	lsteinauer		PHD	74	Chicago	1968
Bedient, John B.	Assoc	629-0343	jbedient		MBA	79	Indiana	1984
Saltzman, Gregory M.	Assoc	629-0422	gsaltzman		PHD	82	Wisconsin	1982
Hooks, Jon A.	Asst	629-0530	jhooks	G	PHD	89	Mich St	1989

Albright College — Reading, PA 19612-5234 (610) 921-7538 — joe.alb.edu
Economics Faculty — Dept of Econ & Business Fax=921-7530 — Mrs. Linda Reinhart

Name	Rank	Phone	E-mail	Fields	Degree	Yr	School	Since
Bell, Christine A.	C-As	921-7701			MBA	77	Temple	1989
Martin, David A.	Prof	921-7888			DA	80	Lehigh	1983
Moyer, James T.	Prof	921-7781			PHD	76	Lehigh	9-68
Schwartz, David Lamar	Prof	921-7782			MA	64	Mich St	1965
Lever, Jacqueline	Assoc	921-7704			PHD	82	Pittsburgh	1990
Saboori, Farhad	Assoc	921-7884			PHD	85	Indiana	1986

Alcorn State University — Alcorn State, MS 39096-9402 (601) 877-6411 — lorman.alcorn.edu
Dept of Social Sciences — Sch of Arts & Sciences Fax=877-6256 — Mrs. Regina Jones

Name	Rank	Phone	E-mail	Fields	Degree	Yr	School	Since
Edney, Norris	D-Pr	877-6120		Bio	PHD	69	Mich St	
Director, Division of Graduate Studies								
Morris, Alpha	C-Ac	877-6411		Soc	PHD	77	Miss St	
Gau, Carolina	Prof	877-6416			PHD		Missouri	
Gau, Paul K.	Prof	877-6417			PHD	71	Illinois	1972
Coordinator, Economics								

Alfred University — Alfred, NY 14802 (607) 871-2124 — ceramics
Dept of Business Adm — College of Business Fax=871-2114

Name	Rank	Phone	E-mail	Fields	Degree	Yr	School	Since
Szczerbacki, David	Dean	871-2124		Urba	PHD	84	SUNY-Buf	1981
Booker, James F.	Asst	871-2124			PHD	90	Colo St	1993
Mapalad, Claret	Asst	871-2124			PHD	94	Ca-Rivers	7-99

Allegheny College — Meadville, PA 16335-3902 (814) 332-3358 — alleg.edu
Economics Faculty — Department of Economics Fax=332-2789 — Ms. Kathy Uglow

Name	Rank	Phone	E-mail	Fields	Degree	Yr	School	Since
Adams, Earl W. Jr.	C-Pr	332-3331	eadams	AEGH	PHD	71	MIT	1972
Andrew Wells Robertson Professor of Economics								
Casler, Stephen D.	Prof	332-3337	scasler	ACEQ	PHD	83	Illinois	1988
Cupper, Robert Dean	Prof	332-2881	bcupper	ACD	PHD	74	Pittsburgh	1977
Afrasiabi, Ahmad	Assoc	332-3334	bafrasia	BCQR	PHD	85	W Virginia	1985
Baskan, Asuman	Assoc	332-3336	abaskan	CDFE	PHD	88	Lehigh	1987
Goldstein, Donald	Assoc	332-3340	dgoldste	ABG	PHD	91	Mass	1989
Moskwa, Antoni	Assoc	332-3339	amoskwa	AFCP	PHD	75	Warsaw	1982
Nonnenmacher, Tomas	Asst	332-3820	tnonnenm	DKLN	PHD	96	Illinois	1996

Alma College — Alma, MI 48801-1599 (517) 463-7183 — alma.edu
Economics Faculty — Department of Economics Fax=463-7277
Did Not Respond--1997-98 Listing

Name	Rank	Phone	E-mail	Fields	Degree	Yr	School	Since
Mueller, James V.	C-Ac	463-7183	mueller	ABEH	ABD		Ca-Irvine	1976
Choksy, George Dorian	Assoc	463-7390	choksy	DNRC	PHD	86	Tennessee	1989
Johnson, Denise H.	Asst	463-7015	johnson	CFJP	PHD	93	Mass	1994

American University — Washington, DC 20016-8029 (202) 885-3770 — american.edu
Department of Economics — Col of Arts & Sciences Fax=885-3790

Name	Rank	Phone	E-mail	Fields	Degree	Yr	School	Since
Mussell, Kay	Dean	885-2446	mussell		PHD	74	Iowa	1999
Feinberg, Robert M.	C-Pr	885-3788	feinberg		PHD	76	Virginia	1989
Blecker, Robert A.	Prof	885-3767	blecker		PHD	87	Stanford	1985
Bradford, Colin	Prof	885-3784	cbrad		PHD	70	Columbia	1998
Broder, Ivy E.	Prof	885-2125	ibroder		PHD	74	SUNY-SBr	1975
Hahnel, Robin E.	Prof	885-2712	rhahnel		PHD	79	American	1976
Lane, Julia I.	Prof	885-3781	jilane		PHD	82	Missouri	1990
Lerman, Robert I.	Prof	885-3770	rlerman		PHD	70	MIT	1989
Muller, Ronald E.	Prof	527-0990			PHD		American	1970
Sawers, Larry B.	Prof	885-3766	lsawers		PHD	69	Michigan	1969
Schydlowsky, Daniel M.	Prof	885-2521	dschyd		PHD	66	Harvard	1990
Thanh, Pham Chi	Prof	885-3777			PHD		NS Wales	1976
Wachtel, Howard M.	Prof	885-3784			PHD	69	Michigan	1969
Wisman, Jon D.	Prof	885-3158	jdwisma		PHD	74	American	1971
Ayittey, George B. N.	VAsoc	885-3779			PHD	81	Manitoba	1994
Floro, Maria Sagrario	Assoc	885-3139	mfloro	OGDQ	PHD	87	Stanford	1988
Golan, Amos	VAsoc	885-3784	agolan		PHD	88	Berkeley	1996
Graham, Fred C.	Assoc	885-3782	fgraham		PHD	85	Virginia	1988
Hazilla, Michael	Assoc	885-3148	hazilla		PHD	78	SUNY-Bin	1988
Husted, Thomas A.	Assoc	885-3773	husted		PHD	86	N Carol	1986

Name	Rank	Phone	Email	Fields	Degree	Yr	School	Hired
Isaac, Alan G.	Assoc	885-3785			PHD	86	Ca-Davis	1987
Meurs, Mieke E.	Assoc	885-3776	mmeurs		PHD	88	Mass	1989
Nickerson, David	Assoc	885-3762	dnick		PHD	82	Nrthwstrn	1992
Park, Walter G.	Assoc	885-3774	wgp		PHD	91	Yale	1991
Willoughby, John A.	Assoc	885-3759	jwillou		PHD	79	Berkeley	1979
Carey, Kevin	Asst	885-3747	kcarey	E	PHD	95	Princeton	1997

American International Coll Springfield, MA 01109-3189 (413) 737-6291 www.aic.edu
Department of Economics Sch Bus Adm/Sch Arts &S Fax=737-2803

Name	Rank	Phone	Email	Fields	Degree	Yr	School	Hired
Myers, Ed	Dean							
Peterson, Michael	Dean$	747-6230		Engr	PHD	98	Mass	
Orcutt, Bonnie	C-As	737-7000		ADJH	PHD	94	Clark	1992
Smolowitz, Ira E.	Prof	747-6369			PHD	84	Rensselaer	1988
Director, Center for Economic Education; Dean, Bureau of Business Research								

Amherst College Amherst, MA 01002-5000 (413) 542-2249 amherst.edu
Economics Faculty Department of Economics Fax=542-2090 Jeanne E. Reinle

Name	Rank	Phone	Email	Fields	Degree	Yr	School	Hired
Westhoff, Frank H.	C-Pr	542-2190	fwesthoff	ADHC	PHD	74	Yale	1973
Beals, Ralph E.	Prof	542-2570	rebeals	ACO	PHD	70	MIT	1966
Clarence Francis Professor of Economics								
Kohler, Heinz	Emer	542-2083	hkohler	APCD	PHD	61	Michigan	1961
Willard Long Thorp Professor of Economics								
Nicholson, Walter E.	Prof	542-2191	wenicholson	ACDK	PHD	70	MIT	1968
Ward H. Patton, Jr. Professor of Economics								
Woglom, Geoffrey R.	Prof	542-2433	grwoglom	AEG	PHD	74	Yale	1978
Yarbrough, Beth V.	Prof	542-2429	bvyarbrough	ADF	PHD	83	U Wash	1982
Barbezat, Daniel P.	Assoc	542-7948	dpbarbezat	ANO	PHD	88	Illinois	1988
Rivkin, Steven G.	Asst	542-2106	sgrivkin	AIJ	PHD	91	UCLA	1993
Takeyama, Lisa N.	Asst	542-2271	lntakeyama	ADLQ	PHD	92	Stanford	1994

Anderson University Anderson, IN 46012-3462 (765) 641-4358 anderson.edu
Department of Business School of Business Fax=641-4356 Chris Smith/Carol Whetsel

Name	Rank	Phone	Email	Fields	Degree	Yr	School	Hired
Armstrong, Ken D.	Dean		kenarm		PHD	85	Nrthwstrn	1990
Ritchey, Barry	Prof	641-4357		DHR	PHD	88	Syracuse	1991
Heberling, Gregory Dean	Assoc	641-4363			MBA		Ball St	1978
Truitt, Terry	Assoc	641-4354		G	PHD	96	Miss St	1995

Andrews University Berrien Spr, MI 49104-0024 (616) 471-3429 andrews.edu
Economics Department School of Business Fax=471-6158 Ruth Tidwell

Name	Rank	Phone	Email	Fields	Degree	Yr	School	Hired
Gibson, Ann	Dean	471-3102	gibson	Atg	PHD	92	Wash St	1992
Gashugi, Leonard K.	C-Pr	471-3581	gashugi	CF	PHD	92	Boston U	1979
Chuak, Sam	Prof	471-3453	chuahki	CD	PHD	92	Wash St	1998
Russell, Malcolm B.	Prof	471-3104	russell	EN	PHD	78	J Hopkins	1979
Shepard, Delynne	Asst	471-3429	shepard	EJ	PHD	95	Purdue	1995

Angelo State University San Angelo, TX 76909 (915) 942-2046 mailserv.angelo.edu
Dept Acct, Economics & Fnce C of Professional Stds Fax=942-2038 Marilyn Bumann
Did Not Respond--1997-98 Listing

Name	Rank	Phone	Email	Fields	Degree	Yr	School	Hired
Hegglund, Robert K.	Dean	942-2337		Mgt	PHD	72	Arkansas	1972
Sunderman, Norman A.	H-Pr	Ext 248	norman.sund+	Atg	DMA	69	Michigan	1986
Dane, Andrew J.	Prof	942-2046			PHD	75	Oklahoma	1973
Maddox, D. Pat	Assoc	942-2076			PHD	82	Tx Tech	1982

Appalachian State Univ Boone, NC 28608-2051 (828) 262-2148 appstate.edu
Department of Economics Walker College of Bus Fax=262-6105

Name	Rank	Phone	Email	Fields	Degree	Yr	School	Hired
Peacock, Kenneth E.	Dean	262-2058	peacockke	Atg	PHD	79	LSU	1983
Schieren, George A.	C-Ac	262-4033	schierenga	CDE	PHD	75	N Carol	1977
Combs, J. Paul	Prof	262-6161	compsjp	MR	PHD	73	N Car St	1971
Courbois, Jean-Pierre	Prof	262-2117	courboisjp	F	PHD	68	American	1968
Durden, Gary C.	Prof	262-6077	durdengc	EH	PHD	71	Fla St	1982
Elledge, Barry	Prof	262-6121	elledgebw	IM	PHD	70	N Car St	1969
Gaynor, Patricia E.	Prof	262-6129	gaynorpe	C	PHD	73	U Miami	1976
Millsaps, Steven	Prof	262-6080	millsapssw	CDQ	PHD	73	N Car St	1973
Perri, Timothy J.	Prof	262-2251	perritj	DJ	PHD	78	Ohio St	1980
Ellis, Larry V.	Assoc	262-6123	ellislv	E	PHD	78	Missouri	1978
Kirkpatrick, Rickey C.	Assoc	262-6127	kirkpatrickrc	FM	PHD	78	Tulane	1980
McRae, Larry T.	Assoc	262-6125	mcraelt	CDE	PHD	78	N Carol	1977
Wallace, Frederick H.	Assoc	262-6122	wallacefh	E	PHD	87	Rice	1986

Aquinas College Grand Rapids, MI 49506-1799 (616) 459-8281 aquinas.edu
Economics Faculty Economics Department Fax=732-4487
phone: 459-8281

Name	Rank	Phone	Email	Fields	Degree	Yr	School	Hired
Beversluis, Eric H.	C-Ac	Ext 3602	bevereri		PHD	70	Nrthwstrn	1988
Chaffee, Donald M. Jr.	Prof	Ext 4626	chaffdon		PHD	70	Ca-Davis	1992
Robertson, Gary L.	Assoc	Ext 4458	robergar		MA		Detroit	1969
Yamazaki, Masato	Asst	Ext 4466	yamaemas		PHD	84	Duke	1987

University of Arizona — Tucson, AZ 85721-0108 (520) 621-6224 bpavms.bpa.arizona.edu
Department of Economics — Col Business & Pub Adm Fax=621-7483 — Lanna Greffet, Adm Asst
email @1=ccit.arizona.edu

Name	Rank	Phone	Email	Field	Degree	Yr	School	Year
Zupan, Mark	Dean	621-2165			PHD	87	MIT	1996
Reynolds, Stanley	H-Pr	621-6251	sreynolds		PHD	83	Nrthwstrn	1982
Block, Michael K.	Prof	621-2854			PHD	72	Stanford	1981
Cox, James C.	Prof	621-2164	jcox		PHD	71	Harvard	1977
Fishback, Price V.	Prof	621-4421			PHD	83	U Wash	1990
Isaac, R. Mark	Prof	621-4831	misaac		PHD	80	Cal Tech	1980
Libecap, Gary D.	Prof	621-4821			PHD	76	Penn	1984
Director Karl Eller Center								
Marshall, Robert H.	Emer	621-5831			PHD	57	Ohio St	1957
Oaxaca, Ronald L.	Prof	621-4135	roaxaca		PHD	71	Princeton	1976
Rieber, Michael	Prof	621-4281			PHD	63	MIT	1978
Smith, Kenneth R.	Prof	621-6224	ksmith		PHD	68	Nrthwstrn	1980
Smith, Vernon L.	Prof	621-4747			PHD	55	Harvard	1975
Regents' Professor								
Taylor, Lester D.	Prof	621-6222	ltaylor		PHD	63	Harvard	1972
Tullock, Gordon	Prof	621-2640	gtullock		JD	47	Chicago	1987
Walker, Mark A.	Prof	621-6155	mwalker		PHD	70	Purdue	1990
Wells, Donald A.	Prof	621-6240	dwells		PHD	61	Oregon	1969
Zajac, Edward E.	Prof	621-2192	ezajac		PHD	54	Stanford	1983
Drabicki, John Z.	Assoc	621-4221	jdrabicki		PHD	73	Purdue	1970
Heckerman, Donald G.	Assoc	621-6065			PHD	67	MIT	1971
Kantor, Shawn E.	Assoc	621-6230			PHD	90	Cal Tech	1990
McBearty, James C.	Assoc	621-1639			PHD	68	Illinois	1968
McCabe, Kevin A.	Assoc	626-3165			PHD	85	Penn	1996
Sands, Barbara N.	Assoc	621-2166			PHD	85	U Wash	1985
Swanson, Gerald	Assoc	621-6220	gswanson		PHD	72	Illinois	1970
Broseta, Bruno	Asst	621-6238	bbroseta		PHD	94	Ca-SnDgo	1995
Horrace, William	Asst	62-6230	whorrace		PHD	96	Mich St	1996
Houser, Daniel	Asst	621-6224	dhouser		PHD	97	Minnesota	1997
Wooders, John C.	Asst	621-6231	jwooders		PHD	91	Cornell	1991
Billings, R. Bruce	Lect	621-4436	bbillings		PHD	69	Claremont	1965

Arizona State University — Tempe, AZ 85287-3806 (480) 965-3531 asu.edu
Department of Economics — College of Business Fax=965-0748

Name	Rank	Phone	Email	Field	Degree	Yr	School	Year
Penley, Larry E.	Dean	965-5516	larry.penley	Mgt	PHD	76	Georgia	1985
Blakemore, Arthur E.	C-Pr	965-3531	arthur.blakem+		PHD	77	S Illinois	1979
Boyes, William J.	Prof	965-3531	william.boyes		PHD	74	Claremont	1969
Brada, Josef C.	Prof	965-6524	josef.brada		PHD	71	Minnesota	1978
Burgess, Paul L.	Prof	965-8432	paul.burgess		PHD	69	Colorado	1969
DeSerpa, Allan C.	Prof	965-3531	allen.deserpa		PHD	70	Ca-SnBarb	1975
Faith, Roger L.	Prof	965-3531	roger.faith		PHD	73	UCLA	1981
Gooding, Elmer R.	Prof	965-5596	elmer.gooding		PHD	69	Kansas	1988
Happel, Stephen K.	Prof	965-5001	stephen.happel		PHD	76	Duke	1975
Hoffman, Dennis L.	Prof	965-3531	dennis.hoffman		PHD	78	Mich St	1979
Hogan, Timothy D.	Prof	965-3961	timothy.hogan		PHD	71	Va Tech	1970
Director of Center for Business Research								
Kingston, Jerry L.	Prof	965-7457	jerry.kingston		PHD	69	Penn St	1969
Low, Stuart A.	Prof	965-5498	stuart.low		PHD	79	Illinois	1979
McDowell, John M.	Prof	965-7109	john.mcdowell		PHD	79	UCLA	1978
McPheters, Lee R.	Prof	965-3961	lee.mcpheters		PHD	72	Va Tech	1976
Associate Dean, Graduate Program								
Melvin, Michael T.	Prof	965-6860	michael.melvin		PHD	80	UCLA	1980
Mendez, Jose A.	Prof	965-2723	jose.mendez		PHD	80	So Meth	1980
Ormiston, Michael B.	Prof	965-7350	michael.ormis+		PHD	77	J Hopkins	1984
Santos, Manuel	Prof		manuel.santos		PHD	84	Chicago	1999
Bank One Professor								
Ahn, Seung C.	Assoc	965-6574	seung.ahn		PHD	90	Mich St	1990
Cogley, Timothy	Assoc	965-3531	timothy.cogley		PHD	88	Berkeley	1999
Manelli, Alejandro	Assoc	965-3531	alejandro.man+		PHD	88	Berkeley	1997
Reffett, Kevin	Assoc	965-3531	kevin.reffett		PHD	90	Purdue	1995
Schlee, Edward E.	Assoc	965-5745	edward.schlee		PHD	88	Illinois	1990
Winkelman, Richard D.	Assoc	965-2128	richard.wink+		PHD	66	Illinois	1965
Chade, Hector	Asst	965-3531	hector.chade		PHD	96	Illinois	1997
Datta, Manjira	Asst	965-3531	manjira.datta		PHD	92	Cornell	1995
Hendricks, Lutz	Asst	965-1462	lutz.hendricks		PHD	96	Penn	1996

University of Arkansas — Fayetteville, AR 72701 (501) 575-ECON comp.uark.edu
Department of Economics — College of Business Adm Fax=575-7687

Name	Rank	Phone	Email	Field	Degree	Yr	School	Year
Williams, Doyle Z.	Dean	575-5949		Atg	PHD	65	LSU	1993
Ziegler, Joseph A.	H-Pr	575-3266		R	PHD	71	Notre Dm	1980
Britton, Charles R.	Prof			E	PHD	71	Iowa	1978
Curington, William P.	Prof			J	PHD	79	Syracuse	1989
Dixon, Bruce	Prof			TQ	PHD	76	Ca-Davis	1986
Gay, David E.	Prof			H	PHD	73	Tx A&M	1983
McKinnon, Thomas	Prof			NA	PHD	72	Miss	1981

Name	Rank	Phone	Email	Fields	Degree	Yr	School	Year
Murray, Tracy W.	Prof			F	PHD	69	Mich St	1978
Distinguished Professor & Chairholder, Phillips Petroleum Company Chair/IEB								
Farmer, Amy F.	Assoc			DK	PHD	91	Duke	1999
Ferrier, Gary D.	Assoc			DC	PHD	88	N Carol	1993
Horowitz, Andrew W.	Assoc			OFD	PHD	89	Wisconsin	1998
Schulman, Craig	Assoc			F	PHD	89	Tx A&M	1989
Sonstegaard, Miles H.	Assoc			H	PHD	58	Oregon	1969
Durham, Yvonne	Asst			LD	PHD	94	Arizona	1994
Kali, Raja	Asst			LOFD	PHD	96	Maryland	1999

U of Arkansas at Little Rock — Little Rock, AR 72204-1099 (501) 569-3354 — ualr.edu
Dept of Economics & Finance — College of Business Adm Fax=569-8898 — Karen Wisdom 569-3354

Name	Rank	Phone	Email	Fields	Degree	Yr	School	Year
Goolsby, William C.	Dean	569-3356	wcgoolsby	Fnce	PHD	74	Wisconsin	7-96
Terry, Andy	C-Ac	569-8872			PHD	89	Michigan	1989
Chisholm, Roger	Prof	569-8894	rkchisholm		PHD	67	Chicago	1985
Ford, Richard	Prof	569-8876	rkford		PHD	79	Arkansas	1981
Galchus, Kenneth	Prof	569-8893	kegalchus		PHD	70	Wash U	1976
Associate Dean								
Lindeman, Bruce	Prof	569-8870			PHD	68	Duke	1975
Pickett, John C.	Prof	569-3354			PHD	70	Missouri	1986
Shull, Ralph	Prof	569-8857			PHD	72	Arkansas	1971
Elder, Erick	Asst	569-8879	emelder		PHD	97	Pittsburgh	8-96
Hall, John	Asst	569-3355	jrhall		PHD	92	Indiana	
Holland, Larry C.	Asst	569-3042	lcholland		PHD	96	Okla St	1995
Keller, Anita	Inst	569-8873	apkeller		MBA	76	Ark St	1991

U of Arkansas at Pine Bluff — Pine Bluff, AR 71601 (870) 543-8575 — vx4500.uapb.edu
Economics Faculty — Sch of Business & Mgt Fax=543-8574 — Lula Smith

Name	Rank	Phone	Email	Fields	Degree	Yr	School	Year
Grayson, Barbara A.	Dean$	543-8577			EDD	83	Okla St	1987
Shahjahan, Mirza	Assoc	543-8575			PHD		Bonn	
Wu, Yeen-Kuen	Assoc	543-8575			MA		Atlanta	
Burkett, Evelyn	Asst	543-8575			MA		Houston	

Arkansas State University — State Univ, AR 72467-0239 (870) 972-3416 — cherokee.astate.edu
Dept of Economics & Dec Sys — College of Business Fax=972-3868 — Ms. Jeanette Gatlin

Name	Rank	Phone	Email	Fields	Degree	Yr	School	Year
Roderick, Roger D.	Dean	972-3035	roderick	Mgt	PHD	70	Illinois	1993
Brown, Christopher R.	C-Ac	972-3416	crbrown	AEKM	PHD	89	Tennessee	1990
Crawford, Jerry L.	Prof	972-3416	crawford	ADTM	PHD	69	Arkansas	1966
Dale, Lawrence Raymond	Prof	972-3810	dalex	ABPQ	PHD	79	Ohio U	1986
Kaminarides, John S.	Prof	972-3823	johnk	AFTO	PHD	68	Houston	1968
Director, Business Research								
Kesselring, Randall G.	Prof	972-3416	randyk	ACJF	PHD	80	Oklahoma	1984
Latanich, Gary A.	Assoc	972-3416	latanich	AREM	PHD	78	Nebraska	1981
Marburger, Daniel R.	Assoc	972-3416	marburge	AJMD	PHD	89	Ariz St	1989

Arkansas Tech University — Russellville, AR 72801-2222 (501) 968-0354 — atuvm.atu.edu
Dept of Business & Economics — School of Business Fax=968-0677

Name	Rank	Phone	Email	Fields	Degree	Yr	School	Year
Tyler, Thomas P.	Dean	968-0490			PHD	80	Arkansas	1967
Smith, Richard S.	H-Ac	968-0492			PHD	74	Tx-Austin	1991
Cole, Raymond E.	Prof	968-0491			PHD	76	Arkansas	1970
Moore, Joseph L.	Prof	968-0688			PHD	75	Arkansas	1988
Benefield, Michael E.	Asst	968-0264			PHD	89	Purdue	1995

Armstromg Atlantic St Univ — Savannah, GA 31419-1997 (912) 927-5286 — mailgate.armstrong.edu
Economics Faculty — Col of Arts & Sciences Fax=927-2398 — Sandy Ramey

Name	Rank	Phone	Email	Fields	Degree	Yr	School	Year
Townsend, Dabney	Dean				PHD	70	Emory	1997
Paul, Chris	C							
Saadatmand, Yassaman	Assoc	927-5548	yassaman_saad+	FO	PHD	88	NewHamp	1989
McGrath, Richard	Asst	927-5524	richard_mcgrath	DHG	PHD	97	Virginia	1997
Toma, Michael	Asst	927-5527	michael_toma	RE	PHD	96	GeoMason	1997

Ashland University — Ashland, OH 44805 (419) 289-5912 — ashland.edu
Department of Economics — College of Bus & Econ Fax=289-5949 — Linda Braun
Did Not Respond--1997-98 Listing

Name	Rank	Phone	Email	Fields	Degree	Yr	School	Year
Sears, Paul A.	Dean	289-5212	psears		PHD	90	Case Wes	8-97
Nadler, Mark A.	C-Ac	289-5912	mnadier		PHD	83	Iowa St	1989
A. L. Garber Family Chair of Economics								
Rafeld, Frederick J.	Prof	289-5746	rrafeld		PHD	68	Ohio St	9-70
Garcia, Javier	Assoc	289-5734	jgarcia		JD		Akron	1980
Rogers, Robert	Assoc	289-5739	rrogers1		PHD	83	Geo Wash	1993
Wasnich, Wendy	Asst	289-5735	wwasnich		MA		Ohio St	1985

Assumption College	Worcester, MA		01615-0005	(508) 767-7379			eve.assumption.edu	
Economic Faculty	Dept Econ & Global Stu		Fax=799-4502				Laurie Rochette	
Lynn, Stuart R.	C-Ac	767-7565	slynn	DBFO	PHD	71	N Carol	1987
Doyle, George A.	Prof	767-7579	gdoyle	FBOP	PHD	51	Fordham	1961
Hickey, Kevin L.	Assoc	767-7296	khickey		MLA	76	Harvard	1972
Kantarelis, Demetrius	Assoc	767-7557	dkantar	DCKL	PHD	83	Clark	1983
Fahy, Colleen A.	Asst	767-7558	cfahey	HLCD	PHD	89	SUNY-Bin	1994
White, Thomas J.	Asst	767-7556	twhite	EGQ	PHD	89	SUNY-Bin	1995
Asadoorian, Malcolm	Lect	767-7557		ACM	ABD		Clark	1997
Charlebois, Cecile M.	Lect	767-7004		AHJ	ABD		Clark	1980

Athens State University	Athens, AL		35611	(205) 233-8211			athens.edu	
Economics Faculty	School of Business		Fax=233-8164				Donna Thomas	
Haynes, James F.	Dean	233-8116	jfhaynes		PHD	80	Vanderbilt	1980
Newton, Dahlia	Asst	233-8175		A	MBA	80	W Carol	1987
Wilkes, William	Asst	233-8191	bwilkes	AF	DA	98	Mid Tenn	1996

Auburn University	Auburn, AL		36849-5242	(334) 844-4910			business.auburn.edu	
Department of Economics	College of Business		Fax=844-4615				Lola Burnett 844-2901	
Alderman, C. Wayne	Dean	844-4030	alderman	Atg	DBA	77	Tennessee	4-77
Laband, David N.	H-Pr	844-2903	labandn		PHD	81	Va Tech	1994
Barnett, Andy H.	Prof	844-4980	abarnett		PHD	78	Virginia	1982
Caudill, Steven B.	Prof	844-2907	scaudill		PHD	82	Florida	1981
Ekelund, Robert B. Jr.	Prof	844-2929	rekelund		PHD	67	LSU	1979
Lowder Eminent Scholar								
Garrison, Roger W.	Prof	844-2920	rgarrisn		PHD	81	Virginia	1983
Hebert, Robert F.	Prof	844-2927	rhebert		PHD	70	LSU	1974
Russell Professor								
Jackson, John D.	Prof	844-2906	jjackson		PHD	77	Claremont	1984
Kaserman, David L.	Prof	844-2905	kaserman		PHD	76	Florida	1986
Torchmark Professor								
Long, James E.	Prof	844-2911	jlong		PHD	74	Fla St	1974
Torchmark Professor								
Thompson, Henry L.	Prof	844-2910	hthompsn		PHD	81	Houston	1987
Whitten, David O.	Prof	844-2928	dwhitten		PHD	70	Tulane	1968
Ault, Richard W.	Assoc	844-2919	rault		PHD	83	Virginia	1983
Beard, Thomas Randolph	Assoc	844-2918	rbeard		PHD	88	Vanderbilt	1988
Beil, Richard O.	Assoc	844-2921	rbeil		PHD	88	Tx A&M	1988
Gropper, Daniel M.	Assoc	844-2908	dgropper		PHD	89	Fla St	1988
Saba, Richard P.	Assoc	844-2922	rsaba		PHD	74	Tx A&M	1974
Wells, John M.	Asst	844-2902	jwells		PHD	94	Tx A&M	1994

Auburn U at Montgomery	Montgomery, AL		36117-3596	(334) 244-3454			monk.aum.edu	
Department of Economics	School of Business		Fax=244-3792					
Lantz, Keith W.	Dean	224-3478	klantz	Atg	PHD	75	Iowa	1995
Gregorowicz, Phillip	H-Pr	244-3575	pgregorwic	EFGJ	PHD	82	N Illinois	1980
Deravi, M. Keivan	Prof	244-3555	dkeravi	DFGJ	PHD	85	Okla St	1985
on leave; Director of Center for Government & Public Affairs								
Hegji, Charles E.	Prof	244-3563	chegji	DFMJ	PHD	80	Wash U	1985
Lacy, Allen W.	Emer	244-3511	alacy	ETIH	PHD	71	Iowa St	1976
Chiles, Ted W.	Assoc	244-3512	tchiles	ADJM	PHD	90	Penn St	1990
Clark, Joy	Assoc	244-3561	jclark	APQB	PHD	88	Tx A&M	1988
Sollars, David L.	Assoc	244-3486	dsollars	KHAE	PHD	91	Fla St	1990
Assistant Dean								
Schneider, Lynn	Asst		lschneider		PHD	96	Houston	1998

Augsburg College	Minneapolis, MN		55454	(612) 330-1320			augsburg.edu	
Economics Faculty	Department of Economics		Fax=330-1149				Marta Kurck	
McNeff, Marie O.	Dean	330-1124			PHD	67	Nebraska	1968
Boeh, Jeanne	C-Ac	330-1760	boeh	I	PHD	89	Il-Chicago	1990
Gupta, Satya P.	Prof	330-1149	gupta		PHD	75	S Illinois	1976
Sabella, Edward M.	Prof	330-1152			PHD	71	Minnesota	1961

Augusta College	Augusta, GA		30904-2200	(706) 737-1560			admin.ac.edu	
Economics Faculty	School of Business Adm		Fax=667-4064		Ms. Nechelle N. Washington			
Widener, Jack K.	Dean	737-1418			MBA			
Brauer, Jurgen	Assoc	737-1560	jbrauer	AFIT	PHD	89	Notre Dm	1991
Leightner, Jonathan E.	Assoc	737-1560	jleightn	DTOP	PHD	89	N Carol	1989

Augustana College IL	Rock Island, IL		61201-2296	(309) 794-7457			augustana.edu	
Department of Economics	Div of Business & Educa		Fax=794-7605				Melody Reid	
Jurasek, Rick	Dean	794-7311	adcrj		PHD	75	Ohio St	1998
Ballman, Richard J. Jr.	C-Pr	794-7517	ecballman	ABDE	PHD	77	Iowa	1972
Lonergan, Janis	Prof	794-7472	balonergan	AFIC	PHD	79	S Illinois	1999
Marme, Christopher B.	Asst	794-7514	ecmarme	ACEO	PHD	94	Illinois	1988

Augustana College SD Sioux Falls, SD 57197 (605) 336-5226 inst.augie.edu
Department of Economics — Div of Social Sciences Fax=336-5229

Name	Rank	Phone	Email	Field	Degree	Yr	School	Since
Eggleston, Brian D.	C-Ac	336-5307	egglesto	ABQ	PHD	91	Wash St	1988
Nesiba, Reynold	Asst	336-5310	nesiba	EG	PHD	95	Notre Dm	1995
Sorenson, David	Asst			RG	PHD	97	W Virginia	1997

Austin Peay State University Clarksville, TN 37044 (931) 648-7788 apsu01.apsu.edu
Department of Economics — College of Business Fax=648-5985 — Ms. Penny Howard

Name	Rank	Phone	Email	Field	Degree	Yr	School	Since
Reagan, Carmen C.	Dean	648-7674	reaganc	Mktg	DBA	83	Miss St	1988
Meadows, Tommy C.	C-Pr	648-7747	meadowst	HJ	PHD	78	Clemson	1977
Kim, Kil-Joong	Prof	648-7788	kimk	FO	PHD	80	Cincinnati	1980
Ukpolo, Victor	Prof	648-6132	ukpolov	FO	PHD	85	American	1988
Langston, Vicky	Assoc	648-7851	langstonv	RM	PHD	83	Tx-Austin	1997
Redmon, Patrick	Assoc	648-7755	redmonp	IJ	PHD	93	Mich St	1998

Azusa Pacific University Azusa, CA 91702-7000 (626) 812-3085 apu.edu
Economics Faculty — School of Bus & Mgt Fax=815-3802 — Beverly Castle
Homepage: www.apu.edu:8080/sbm/

Name	Rank	Phone	Email	Field	Degree	Yr	School	Since
Bezjian, Ilene	Dean	812-3085		Mgt	DBA	86	US Intl	1-93
Conover, Roger	Asst	815-3823			MA	82	Ca-SnDgo	9-90
Verdugo, Paul	Asst	812-3091			MA	76	Ca Poly	9-80

Babson College Babson Park, MA 02457-0901 (781) 239-4580 babson.edu
Division of Economics — School of Management Fax=239-5239 — Linda Katz

Name	Rank	Phone	Email	Field	Degree	Yr	School	Since
Jones, Kent A.	C-Pr	239-4477	jones	F	PHD	81	Geneva	1982
Marthinsen, John E.	C-Pr	239-4324	martinsen	FD	PHD	74	Conn	1974
Bayer, Arthur A.	Prof	239-4321	bayer	AH	PHD	68	Mich St	1978
Casey, William L. Jr.	Prof	239-4244	casey	F	PHD	63	Boston C	1964
Moss, Laurence S.	Prof	239-5573	hoss	K	PHD	71	Columbia	1977
McAuliffe, Robert E. Jr.	Assoc	239-4515	mcaliffe	EL	PHD	82	Virginia	1982
Ricciardi, Joseph M.	Assoc	239-4530	ricciardi	EO	PHD	85	Tx-Austin	1985
Axarloglou, Kostas	Asst	239-5512	axarloglou	F	PHD	93	Michigan	1994
Gwin, Carl	Asst	239-4373	gwin	DLM	PHD	97	Indiana	1997
Han, Hsiang-Ling	Asst	239-5851	han	CE	PHD	92	Rochester	1997
Minniti, Maria	Asst	239-4296	minniti	E	PHD	97	NYU	1997
Polutnik, Lidija	Asst	239-4211	polutnik	HJ	PHD	94	Geo St	1991

Baldwin-Wallace College Berea, OH 44017-2088 (440) 826-2113 baldwinw.edu
Department of Economics — Div of Social Sciences Fax=826-3868 — Sandara Wojtolewicz

Name	Rank	Phone	Email	Field	Degree	Yr	School	Since
Rolleston, Barbara Sherman	C-Ac	826-2003	brollest	HR	PHD	83	Cornell	1983
Ebert, Robert R.	Prof	826-2033	rebert	DFP	PHD	74	Case Wes	1967
Heinicke, Craig W.	Assoc	826-2419	cheinicke	NOE	PHD	91	Toronto	1991
Miller, Dennis D.	Assoc	826-2002	dmiller	OQ	PHD	85	Colorado	1987
Peart, Sandra Joan	Assoc	826-2120	speart	BD	PHD	89	Toronto	1989
Ross, Thomas A.	Assoc	826-2118	tross	CG	MA		Bowl Gr	
Sage, Lewis C.	Assoc	826-2119	lsage	CIJ	PHD	85	Maryland	1985

Ball State University Muncie, IN 47306-0340 (765) 285-5360 bsuvc.bsu.edu
Department of Economics — College of Business Fax=285-8024 — Ms. Rita Disher

Name	Rank	Phone	Email	Field	Degree	Yr	School	Since
Palomba, Neil A.	Dean	285-8192			PHD	66	Minnesota	8-84
Flowers, Marilyn	C-Pr	285-5360		H	PHD	74	Va Tech	1990
Bohanon, Cecil E.	Prof	285-5363		H	PHD	81	Va Tech	1980
Cheng, Chu-Yuan	Prof	285-5366		OP	PHD	64	Geotown	1971
Coehlo, Philip R. P.	Prof	285-5376		NT	PHD	69	U Wash	1986
Deitsch, Clarence R.	Prof	285-5368		J	PHD	74	NewHamp	1974
Santoni, Gary J.	Prof	285-5365		E	PHD	72	New Mex	1988
Stone, Courtney C.	Prof	285-5378		EM	PHD	73	UCLA	1991
Van Cott, T. Norman	Prof	285-5370		FH	PHD	69	U Wash	1977
Green, Jeffery	Assoc	285-2056		C	PHD	72	Cornell	1972
Horowitz, John B.	Assoc	285-1436		HJ	PHD	88	Tx A&M	1989
Keil, Stanley R.	Assoc	285-5360		QR	PHD	73	Oregon	1973
Liu, Tung	Assoc	285-5360		C	PHD	90	Ca-SnDgo	1990
McClure, James Edward	Assoc	285-5375		J	PHD	83	Purdue	1982
Spector, Lee C.	Assoc	285-5360		E	PHD	85	Iowa	1985
Yoho, Devon L.	Assoc	285-8020		A	PHD	74	Missouri	1978
Director of Center for Economic Education								
Zegeye, Abera	Assoc	285-5379		A	PHD	77	Indiana	1974
Brandly, Mark	Asst			HL	PHD	98	Auburn	1998

University of Baltimore Baltimore, MD 21201-5779 (410) 837-4994 ubmail.ubalt.edu
Dept of Economics & Finance — Merrick Sch of Business Fax=837-5722 — Cindy Tannebaum
Did Not Respond--1997-98 Listing

Name	Rank	Phone	Email	Field	Degree	Yr	School	Since
Hatfield, John D.	Dean	837-4455	jhatfield	OrgC	PHD	76	Purdue	6-96
Gerlowski, Daniel A.	H-Ac	837-4987	dgerlowski	ALM	PHD	87	Pittsburgh	8-87

Acs, Zoltan J.	Prof	837-5012	zacs		PHD	80	New Sch	1989
Levy, David T.	Prof	837-5026	dlevy		PHD		N Carol	
Sawhney, Bansi L.	Prof	837-5049	bsawhney		PHD	75	Geo Wash	1971
Stevens, David W.	Prof	837-4727	dstevens		PHD	65	Colorado	
Executive Director of Jacob France Center								
Brownstein, Barry	Assoc	837-4960	bbrownstein		PHD	77	Rutgers	
Elkes, Lynne C.	Asst	837-4994						

Barnard College New York, NY 10027-6598 (212) 854-3454 barnard.columbia.edu
Economics Faculty Department of Economics Fax=854-8947
Homepage: www.econ.barnard.columbia.edu

Mehrling, Perry G.	C-Ac	854-4369	pmehrling	EGB	PHD	88	Harvard	1987
Burgstaller, Andre C.	Prof	854-3167	aburgstaller	EOB	PHD	79	Columbia	1977
Barrington, Linda	Asst	854-2082	lbarrington	NCI	PHD	91	Illinois	1991
Dye, Alan	Asst	854-3868	adye	N	PHD	91	Illinois	1995
Harrison, Sharon	Asst	854-3333	sharrison	E	PHD	97	Nrthwstrn	1997
Munasinghe, Lalith	Asst	854-5652	lmunasinghe	JC	PHD	95	Columbia	1997
Sethi, Rajiv	Asst	854-5140	rsethi	DQ	PHD	93	New Sch	1995

Barry University Miami Shores, FL 33161-6695 (305) 899-3500 barry.edu
Dept Economics & Finance Andreas Sch of Business Fax=892-6412

Scarborough, Jack W.	Dean	899-3500	jscarborough	Mgt	PHD	88	Maryland	8-89
Hervitz, Hugo M.	Prof	894-3514	hhervitz		PHD	83	Indiana	1982
Morrell, Stephen O.	Prof	899-3513	smorrell		PHD	77	Va Tech	1990
Cruz, Robert D.	Assoc	899-3522	rcryz		PHD	85	Penn	1993
Daghestani, Eddie	Assoc	899-3509	edaghestani		PHD	71	Colo St	1988
Payne, Bruce C.	Assoc	899-3519	bcp3090		PHD	77	LSU	8-98

Barton College Wilson, NC 27893 (252) 399-6418 e-mail.barton.edu
Economics Faculty School of Business Fax= Beth Jean Fitch

Eggers, Ronald E.	Dean	399-6417	reggers	Busi	MBA		E Carol	8-78
Jaggi, Anand P.	Prof	399-6423			PHD		Jabalpur	1971
Edmondson, Rob	Asst	399-6429	redmonds		MBA		Wake For	8-91

Bates College Lewiston, ME 04240 (207) 786-6099 abacus.bates.edu
Economics Faculty Department of Economics Fax=786-6123

Hughes, James W.	C-As	786-6193		J	PHD	87	Michigan	1987
Aschauer, David Alan	Prof	786-6099		E	PHD	84	Rochester	1990
Elmer W. Campbell Professor of Economics								
Murray, Michael P.	Prof	786-6085	mmurray	RH	PHD	74	Iowa St	1986
Phillips Professor of Economics								
Walther, Theodore	Prof	786-6008		FG	PHD	64	New Sch	1958
Williams, Anne D.	Prof	786-6091		O	PHD	76	Chicago	1981
Schwinn, Carl R.	Assoc	786-6090		IO	PHD	78	Cornell	1975
Maurer-Fazio, Margaret	Asst	786-6087		O	PHD	94	Pittsburgh	1985

Baylor University Waco, TX 76798-8003 (254) 710-2263 baylor.edu
Department of Economics Hankamer Sch Busines Fax=710-1092 Susan Armstrong

Maness, Terry S.	Dean	710-3411	terry_maness	Fnce	PHD	77	Indiana	1977
Truitt, W. James	C-Pr	710-2263	jim_truitt	D	PHD	68	Illinois	1968
Herman W. Lay Prof Private Enterprise, & Director Cntr/Priv Entrp								
Gardner, H. Stephen	Prof	710-6147	steve_gardner	FP	PHD	78	Berkeley	1978
Herman Brown Professor of Economics								
Gilbreath, L. Kent	Prof	710-3535	kent_gilbreath	GN	PHD	71	Florida	1973
Stevens Professor of Private Enterprise								
Green, Steven L.	Prof	710-4543	steve_green		PHD	84	Brown	1986
Henderson, James W.	Prof	710-4139	jim_henderson	IJ	PHD	81	So Meth	1981
Ben H. Williams Professor of Economics								
Kelly, Thomas M.	Prof	710-4146	tom_kelly	R	PHD	70	Okla St	1969
Director Center for Economic Analysis								
McKinney, Joseph A.	Prof	710-6141	joe_mckinney	F	PHD	70	Mich St	1976
Pisciotta, John L.	Assoc	710-6224	john_pisciotta		PHD	71	Tx-Austin	1980
Bawumia, Muhumudu	Asst	710-4141	mahumudu_ba+	F	PHD	95	Simon Fr	1996
North, Charles	Asst	710-6229	charles_north	K	PHD	99	Tx-Austin	1998
Taylor, Beck	Asst	710-4549	beck_taylor	D	PHD	97	Purdue	1997
Bowman, Judy C.	Lect	710-6174	judy_bowman		MS	74	Baylor	1974
Johnson, Karen R.	Lect	710-6149	karen_johnson		MIM		Baylor	1979
Newsome, Heather	Lect	710-6466	heather_news+		MS	96	Baylor	1996
Odegaard, Thomas A.	Lect	710-4892	tom_odegaard		MA	70	Rice	1985

Beaver College Glenside, PA 19038-3295 (215) beaver.edu
Economics Faculty Dept of Bus Adm & Econ Fax=

Biggs, William D.	C-Pr	572-2937		Mgt	PHD	74	Penn St	8-80
Morra, Wayne A.	Assoc	572-2125		ALR	PHD	84	Temple	8-81

Belhaven College Jackson, MS 39202-1789 (601) 968-5965 belhaven.edu
Economics Faculty Div of Business Adm Fax=968-9998

Name	Rank	Phone	E-mail	Fields	Degree	Yr	School	Year
Park, James W.	C-Pr	968-5965	jpark	AD	PHD	74	Alabama	1977
Penn, William M.	Prof	968-5966		AM	PHD	68	Duke	1981

Bellarmine College Louisville, KY 40205-0671 (502) 452-8240 bellarmine.edu
Department of Economics Rubel Sch of Business Fax=452-8004 Ms. Carol Huff

Name	Rank	Phone	E-mail	Fields	Degree	Yr	School	Year
Popper, Edward T.	Dean	452-8240			PHD	78	Harvard	1994
McCrickard, Myra J.	D-As	452-8240	mmcrick	CE	PHD	89	N Car St	1989
Slesnick, Frank L.	Prof	452-8240	slesnickf@a	AIKJ	PHD	72	Minnesota	1975
Dawson, John	Asst				PHD		N Car St	
Eller, Eric	Asst				PHD		Virginia	
Trawick, Michelle	Asst				PHD	96	N Car St	1999

Belmont University Nashville, TN 37212-3757 (615) 460-6175 mail.belmont.edu
Economics Faculty School of Business Fax=460-6455 Sue Kinzer

Name	Rank	Phone	E-mail	Fields	Degree	Yr	School	Year
Clapper, James M.	Dean	460-5511	clapperj	Mgt	PHD	74	Mass	1997
Cochran, Howard H. Jr.	Assoc	460-6477	cochran	AFM	DA	94	Mid Tenn	1989
Hodgin, Gary L.	Assoc	460-6333	hodging		PHD	85	Tennessee	1983
Thompson, Mary M.	Asst	460-6318	thompsonm		MA		Notre Dm	1983

Bemidji State University Bemidji, MN 56601-2699 (218) 755-2907 bemidji.mnus.edu
Department of Economics Col of Social & Nat Sci Fax=755-4100 Tammy Mayer

Name	Rank	Phone	E-mail	Fields	Degree	Yr	School	Year
Ley, Robert D.	C-Pr	755-2730			PHD	77	Wash St	1977
Johnson, Lowell E.	Prof	755-3709			PHD	75	Cornell	1976
Welle, Patrick G.	Prof	755-3873			PHD	86	Wisconsin	1982

Benedict College Columbia, SC 29204 (803) 253-5187
Business Adm & Econ Dept Sch Professional Prgms Fax=253-5225 Ms. Marlese Hodge

Name	Rank	Phone	E-mail	Fields	Degree	Yr	School	Year
Avery, Reginald S.	Dean	253-5212			PHD			8-96
Cole, John A.	C	253-5187						
Mahdi, Syed I.	Prof	253-5190			PHD	76	Mass	1975
Njoku, Anthanasius O.	Prof	253-5193			PHD	71	Illinois	1971

Benedictine University Lisle, IL 60532-0900 (630) Ext 6460 eagle.ibc.edu
Dept of Econ & Intl Bus Div of Social Science Fax=960-1126 Ms. Paticia Ariano
Did Not Respond--1997-98 Listing; phone: 960-1500

Name	Rank	Phone	E-mail	Fields	Degree	Yr	School	Year
Roth, Margarete P.	C-Pr	Ext 6465		FA	PHD	67	Cologne	1970
Lee, Soyon	Prof	Ext 6463		GO	PHD	77	N Illinois	1974

Bentley College Waltham, MA 02154-4705 (781) 891-3183 bentley.edu
Economics Faculty College of Business Fax=891-2896 Terry Lesanto

Name	Rank	Phone	E-mail	Fields	Degree	Yr	School	Year
Schlorff, H. Lee	Dean	891-2113	hschlorff	Atg	PHD	73	Missouri	1978
Clarke, William A.	C-Pr	891-2143	wclarke	AD	PHD	73	Rutgers	1972
Callan, Scott J.	Prof	891-2024	scallan	CDQ	PHD	85	Tx A&M	1987
Grubaugh, Stephen G.	Prof	891-2539	sgrubaugh	CF	PHD	82	Chicago	1981
Kuntz, Dale F.	Prof	891-2237	dkuntz	AEO	PHD	79	Conn	1975
Leeth, John D.	Prof	891-2029	jleeth	GCJ	PHD	83	N Carol	1987
Santerre, Rexford E.	Prof	891-2938	rsanterre	DHI	PHD	83	Conn	1983
Stollar, Andrew J.	Prof	891-2268	astollar	CFP	PHD	73	Boston C	1976
Sumner, Scott B.	Prof	891-2945	ssumner	EN	PHD	84	Chicago	1982
Thomas, Janet M.	Prof	891-2053	jthomas	DHQ	PHD	87	Boston C	1987
Zampieron, Alexander Alg	Prof	891-2126	azampieron	ABF	PHD	72	Fletcher	1965
Gulley, O. David	Assoc	891-2355	dgulley	EG	MA	89	Kentucky	1990
Mukerjee, Swati	Assoc	891-2956	smukerjee	DFI	PHD	86	Boston U	1989
Meyer, Christine	Asst		cmeyer	EFH	PHD	95	MIT	1995
Rhodus, W. Gregory	Asst	891-3483		ACG	MA	75	Conn	1992

Berea College Berea, KY 40404 (606) 986-9341 berea.edu
Economics Faculty Dept of Business & Econ Fax=986-4506 Becky Grandgeorge
phone: 986-9341

Name	Rank	Phone	E-mail	Fields	Degree	Yr	School	Year
Bolin, John	Dean	986-9341		Engl	PHD	70	Michigan	1970
Kazura, Martie	C-As	986-9341			MBA	90	Montana	1991
Sowell, Clifford	Prof	986-9341			PHD	78	Georgia	1981
Spears, Philip V.	Prof	986-9341			PHD	71	Kentucky	1968
Isaacs, Patricia	Assoc	986-9341			DBA	94	Kentucky	1989
Tolliver, R. Wayne	Assoc	986-9341			DBA	87	Kentucky	1975
Best, Michael	Asst	986-9341			PHD	94	Kentucky	1996
McCormack, Edward	Asst	986-9341			MBA	80	Estrn Ky	1985

Berry College Mt. Berry, GA 30149 (706) 236-2233 campbell.berry.edu
Economics Faculty Campbell Sch Business Fax=295-2921 Sandy Briggs
phone 232-5374

Name	Rank	Phone	Email	Field	Degree	Yr	School	Year
Lane, Michael R.	Dean	236-2233	mlane	Atg	PHD	80	Tx A&M	1998
Mixon, J. Wilson	Prof	Ext 2396			PHD	74	U Wash	1986
Shatto, Gloria M.	Prof	234-2707			PHD	66	Rice	1979
Sockwell, William D.	Assoc	Ext 2424			PHD	89	Vanderbilt	1988
Patrono, Michael Frank	Asst	Ext 2392			MS	88	Fla St	1989
Stephenson, E. Frank	Asst				PHD	97	N Carol	1997
Tohamy, Soumaya	Asst				PHD	94	Emory	1997
Waggle, J. Douglas	Asst	Ext 2585			PHD	94	Alabama	1994

Bethel College-MN St. Paul, MN 55112 (651) 638-6286 bethel.edu
Economics Faculty Business & Economics Fax=635-8712 Nikki Daniels

Name	Rank	Phone	Email	Field	Degree	Yr	School	Year
Essenburg, Timothy J.	C-Pr	638-6296	esstim	AI	PHD	91	Tennessee	1989
Abou-Zeid, Bassem	Assoc	638-6293	abobas	FG	PHD	90	Oklahoma	1990

Bethune-Cookman College Daytona Bch, FL 32015 (904) Ext 339 cookman.edu
Economics Faculty Division of Business Fax=255-3989
phone 255-1401

Name	Rank	Phone	Email	Field	Degree	Yr	School	Year
Long, Aubrey E.	C-Pr	Ext 355		Bus	PHD	80	Ohio St	1988
Nwefor, Ferdinand C.	Asst	Ext 527			PHD	97	Howard	1997
Ziegler, William	Asst	Ext 406			ABD		Nova SE	1991

Biola University LaMirada, CA 90639-0001 (562) 903-4770 biola.edu
Economics Faculty School of Business Fax=906-4545 Kathliene Pedrick, Ann Saxton

Name	Rank	Phone	Email	Field	Degree	Yr	School	Year
Strand, Larry D.	Dean	903-4770			MBA	69	S Calif	1986
Rundle, Steve	Asst	903-4770		DEFN	PHD	97	Claremont	1998

Birmingham-Southern Coll Birmingham AL 35254 (205) 226-4820 bsc.edu
Economics Faculty Div of Econ & Bus Admin Fax=226-3080 Dea Green

Name	Rank	Phone	Email	Field	Degree	Yr	School	Year
Blanshan, Sue A.	D	226-4820						
Schutte, David	Prof	226-4820	dschutte		PHD	81	Minnesota	1999
Cleveland, Paul	Assoc	226-4817	pclevela		PHD	85	Tx A&M	1995
Rossman, Kathleen	Asst	226-4820	krossman		PHD	99	Colorado	1999

Bloomfield College Bloomfield, NJ 07003 (973) Ext 339
Department of Economics Divison of Business Fax=743-3998 Monifa Mears Ext 339
Did Not Respond Again--1995-96 Listing

Name	Rank	Phone	Email	Field	Degree	Yr	School	Year
Powley, Ellen	C-Ac	Ext 414		Mktg	PHD		Pace	1991
Michailidis, Lazaros	Assoc	Ext 376			PHD	80	SUNY-Buf	1978
Gibson, Eleanor	Asst	Ext 378			MA		Columbia	1965

Bloomsburg Univ of Penn Bloomsburg, PA 17815-1301 (570) 389-4335 planetx.bloomu.edu
Department of Economics College of Arts & Sci Fax=389-2094

Name	Rank	Phone	Email	Field	Degree	Yr	School	Year
Liu, Hsien-Tung	Dean	389-4410						
Khan, Saleem M.	C-Pr	389-4681	skhan	AEOP	PHD	67	J Gutenb	1-78
Bohling, Peter H.	Prof	389-4343			PHD	77	Mass	1978
Haririan, Mehdi	Prof	389-4682			PHD	87	New Sch	1982
Lee, Woo Bong	Prof	389-4335			PHD	72	Rutgers	1977
Mohindru, Rajesh K.	Prof	389-4341			PHD	69	Penn	
Obutelewicz, Robert S.	Assoc	389-4342			PHD	71	Mass	
Patch, Elizabeth P.	Assoc	389-4737			PHD	90	Lehigh	
Ross, Robert P.	Assoc	389-4335			MA	58	Wash U	1967
Bagi, Sukhwinder	Asst	389-4839			PHD	87	Vanderbilt	

Boise State University Boise, ID 83725 (208) 426-3351 cobfac.boisestate.edu
Department of Economics Col of Bus & Economics Fax=426-3637 Elizabeth Ackerman

Name	Rank	Phone	Email	Field	Degree	Yr	School	Year
Lathen, William C.	Dean	426-1125	blathen	Atg	PHD	82	Ariz St	9-84
Skoro, Charles L.	C-Pr	385-1158	recskoro	JBI	PHD	77	Columbia	1982
Lichtenstein, Peter M.	Prof	385-1471	reclicht	PEF	PHD	74	Colorado	1975
Loucks, Christine	Prof	385-1468	reclouck	ELH	PHD	83	Wash St	1989
Payne, Richard D.	Prof	385-1477	recpayne	HEA	PHD	70	S Calif	1970
Reynolds, R. Larry	Prof	335-1469	recreyno	BID	PHD	77	Wash St	1979
Twight, Charlotte	Prof	385-1335	rectwigh	HKN	PHD	83	U Wash	1986
Draayer, Gerald F.	Assoc	385-1359	recdraay	HNA	PHD	70	Ohio U	1976
Raha, Arun	Asst	385-3465	recraha	EFO	PHD	91	Wash St	1990

Boston College — Chestnut Hl, MA 02467-3806 (617) 552-3670 — bc.edu
Department of Economics — College of Arts & Sci Fax=552-2308 — Kathleen Tubman

Name	Rank	Phone	Email	Fields	Degree	Yr	School	Since
Tresch, Richard W.	C-Ac	552-3670	tresch	H	PHD	73	MIT	1969
Anderson, James E.	Prof	552-3691		DF	PHD	69	Wisconsin	1969
Arnott, Richard J.	Prof	244-3674		DHR	PHD	75	Yale	1988
Bai, Jushan J.	Prof	552-3689		CE	PHD	92	Berkeley	1998
Belsley, David A.	Prof	552-3676		CD	PHD	65	MIT	1966
Cox, Donald C.	Prof	552-3677		DJ	PHD	80	Brown	1987
Gollop, Frank M.	Prof	552-3693		DO	PHD	74	Harvard	1979
Gottschalk, Peter	Prof	552-4517		CDIJ	PHD	73	Penn	1987
Kraus, Marvin C.	Prof	552-3692		DR	PHD	73	Minnesota	1972
Lewbel, Arthur	Prof	552-3678		CD	PHD	84	MIT	1998
Peek, Joe	Prof	552-3686		E	PHD	79	Nrthwstrn	1978
Quinn, Joseph F.	Prof	552-4623	quinnj	DJ	PHD	75	MIT	1975
Schiantarelli, Fabio	Prof	552-3687		CEF	PHD	81	LondonEc	1992
Baum, Christopher F.	Assoc	552-3673		CE	PHD	77	Michigan	1977
Ireland, Peter N.	Assoc	552-3687		E	PHD	91	Chicago	1998
Konishi, Hideo	Assoc			DHL	PHD	94	Rochester	1999
McLaughlin, Francis M.	Assoc	552-3675		JN	PHD	64	MIT	1961
Assistant Chairperson, Department of Economics								
Murphy, Robert G.	Assoc	552-3688		EF	PHD	84	MIT	1984
Ng, Serena	Assoc	552-2182		CE	PHD	93	Princeton	1996
Petersen, Harold A.	Assoc	552-4550		G	PHD	63	Brown	1960
Alger, I.	Asst			DL	PHD	97	Toulouse	1999
Butcher, Kristin F.	Asst	552-3696		DJ	PHD	93	Princeton	1995
Marcouiller, Douglas	Asst	552-3685		FO	PHD	94	Tx-Austin	1994
Monacelli, T.	Asst				PHD	99	NYU	1999

Boston University — Boston, MA 02215 (617) 353-4389 — bu.edu
Department of Economics — College of Arts & Sci Fax=353-4449 — Gloria Murray
Homepage: econ.bu.edu

Name	Rank	Phone	Email	Fields	Degree	Yr	School	Since
Berkey, Dennis	Dean			Math	PHD	74	Cincinnati	
Eaton, Jonathan	C-Pr	353-4142	eaton	FG	PHD	76	Yale	
Chamley, Christophe	Prof	353-4250	chamley	HEO	PHD	77	Harvard	
Cooper, Russell W.	Prof	353-7082	rcooper	CDE	PHD	79	Penn	
Associate Chair								
Doeringer, Peter B.	Prof	353-4438	doeringe	JL	PHD	66	Harvard	1974
Ellis, Randall P.	Prof	353-2741	ellisrp	CILQ	PHD	81	MIT	1981
Harris, John R.	Prof	353-8903	harrisjr	ER	PHD	67	Nrthwstrn	1975
Jones, Leroy P.	Prof	353-4123	jones	HLO	PHD	74	Harvard	1976
Director of Public Enterprise								
Kotlikoff, Laurence J.	Prof	353-4002	kotlikof	EH	PHD	77	Harvard	
Kyn, Oldrich	Prof	353-4539	okyn	CEP	PHD		Charles	1971
Lang, Kevin	Prof	353-5694	lang	JC	PHD	82	MIT	1987
Loury, Glenn C.	Prof	353-5662	gloury	DJ	PHD	76	MIT	1991
Lucas, Robert E. B.	Prof	353-4147	rlucas	CFJO	PHD	72	MIT	1976
Director, Undergrduate Studies								
Manove, Michael	Prof	353-3299	manove	D	PHD	70	MIT	1975
McGuire, Thomas G.	Prof	353-2995	tmcguire	HIL	PHD	76	Yale	1976
Miron, Jeffrey A.	Prof	353-4442	jmiron	EKN	PHD	84	MIT	1990
Mookherjee, Dilip M.	Prof	353-4392	dilipm	HLO	PHD	82	LondonEc	1995
Director, Institute for Economic Development								
Perron, Pierre	Prof			C	PHD	86	Yale	1997
Rosenthal, Robert W.	Prof	353-2742	rosentha	CD	PHD	71	Stanford	1987
Director of Graduate Studies								
Vogelsang, Ingo	Prof	353-2996	vogelsan	HL	PHD	69	Heidelbe	1981
Weiss, Andrew M.	Prof	353-3086	aweiss	DGJ	PHD	76	Stanford	1987
Donald, Stephen	Assoc	353-4824	ocker	CE	PHD	90	Brit Colum	1993
Leahy, John V.	Assoc			E	PHD	90	Princeton	1997
Ma, Ching-to Albert	Assoc	353-4010	ma	DIL	PHD	88	LondonEc	1987
Director, Industry Studies Program								
Tandon, Pankaj	Assoc	353-3089	ptandon	DO	PHD	79	Harvard	1978
Berman, Eli	Asst	353-6324	eli	CJ	PHD	93	Harvard	1993
Botticini, Maristella	Asst			N	ABD		Nrthwstrn	1997
Bui, Linda T.	Asst	353-4140	ltbui	HLQ	PHD	93	MIT	1993
Cati, Regina C.	Asst			C	PHD	95	Sao Paulo	1997
Gilchrist, Simon	Asst	353-6824	sgilchrist	C	PHD	90	Wisconsin	1995
Kortum, Sam	Asst	353-4822	kortum	ELO	PHD	92	Yale	1991
Minehart, Deborah	Asst	353-4436	minehart	CDL	PHD	94	Berkeley	1994
Neeman, Zvika	Asst	353-3184	zvika	CD	PHD	95	Nrthwstrn	1995

Bowdoin College — Brunswick, ME 04011 (207) 725-3340 — polar.bowdoin.edu
Economic Faculty — Department of Economics Fax=725-3691 — Ms. Irene Hilton

Name	Rank	Phone	Email	Fields	Degree	Yr	School	Since
DeCoster, Gregory Paul	C-Ac	725-3726	gdecoste	ER	PHD	85	Tx-Austin	1985
Fitzgerald, John M.	Prof	725-3593	jfitz	HC	PHD	83	Wisconsin	1983
Freeman, Albert Myrick III	Prof	725-3597	rfreeman	QD	PHD	65	U Wash	1965
William Shipman Professor of Economics								
Goldstein, Jonathan Paul	Prof	725-3595	jgoldste	EC	PHD	82	Mass	1979

Vail, David Jeremiah	Prof	725-3596	dvail	OQ	PHD	71	Yale	1970
Adams-Catlin Professor of Economics								
Connelly, Rachel E.	Assoc	725-3790	connelly	JT	PHD	85	Michigan	1985
Jones, Michael	Assoc	725-3598	mjones	F	PHD	79	Yale	1987
Austen, Andrew	Asst	725-3740	aausten	HC	PHD	91	Penn	1998
DeGraff, Deborah S.	Asst	725-3591	ddegraff	OT	PHD	89	Michigan	1991
Hornsten, James	Asst			L	ABD		Nrthwstrn	1999
Khan, B. Zorina	Asst	725-3841	bhkan	GN	PHD	91	UCLA	1996

Bowling Green State Univ	Bowling Gr, OH		43403-0268 (419) 372-2646				cba.bgsu.edu	
Department of Economics	College of Business		Fax=372-2875				Kelly M. Birr	
Sullivan, James A.	Dean	372-2747	jsulliv	Stat	PHD	71	Ohio St	1971
Hoag, John H.	C-Pr	372-8231	jhoag		PHD	72	Kansas	1972
Browne, M. Neil	Prof	372-8060	nbrown2		PHD	69	Tx-Austin	1968
Distinguished Teaching Professor								
Chittle, Charles R.	Emer	372-8180	chittle		PHD	69	Purdue	1965
Haas, Paul F.	Prof	372-2649	phaas		PHD	70	Boston C	1967
Kim, Kyoo H.	Prof	372-2735	kkim		PHD	78	Wisconsin	1978
Reed, J. David	Emer	372-2647	dreed		PHD	70	Kansas St	1968
Benedict, Mary Ellen	Assoc	372-8221	mbenedi@opie.		PHD	91	Car Mellon	1991
Douglas, Richard W. Jr.	Assoc	372-2648	rdougla		PHD	75	Iowa	1976
Fuerst, Timothy S.	Assoc	372-6868	tfuerst		PHD	90	Chicago	1993
Haight, Alan D.	Assoc	372-8111	ahaight		PHD	90	Wisconsin	1991
Quinn, J. Kevin	Assoc	372-8652	kquinn		PHD	89	American	1990
Vanderhart, Peter G.	Assoc	372-8070	pvander		PHD	91	Wisconsin	1991
Wilder, Lisa A.	Asst	372-8397	rosey		PHD	95	Va Tech	1995
Ziliak, Stephen T.	Asst	372-8055	ziliak		PHD	96	Iowa	1996

Bradley University	Peoria, IL		61625-0254 (309) 677-2296				bradley.bradley.edu	
Department of Economics	College of Business Adm		Fax=677-3374				Karen Olehy	
Lumpkin, James R.	Dean	677-2255	jrl	Mktg	PHD	80	Arkansas	7-96
Wojcikewych, Raymond	C-Ac	677-2296			PHD	80	Penn St	1977
Goldberg, Kalman	Prof	677-2301			PHD	54	Cornell	1952
Highfill, Jannett K.	Prof	677-2304			PHD	85	Kansas	1985
Sattler, Edward L.	Prof	677-2303			PHD	79	Illinois	1977
Scott, Robert C.	Prof	677-2297			PHD	75	Iowa	1975
Felder, Joseph	Assoc	677-2302			PHD	79	UCLA	1981
O'Brien, Kevin M.	Assoc	677-2299			PHD	88	Illinois	1992
Polley, William	Asst	677-2298			PHD	99	Iowa	1999

Brandeis University	Waltham, MA		02254-9110 (781) 736-2240				binah.cc.brandeis.edu	
Department of Economics	College of Arts & Sci		Fax=736-2263				Claire Cincotta	
Miller, Robin F.	Dean	736-3451						
Dolbear, F. Treanery Jr.	C-Pr	736-2244			PHD	63	Yale	1968
Clinton S. Darling Professor of Economics								
Carter, Anne P.	Prof	736-2242			PHD	49	Harvard	1971
Fred C. Hecht Professor of Economics								
McCulloch, Rachel	Prof	736-2245			PHD	73	Chicago	1987
Petri, Peter A.	Prof	736-2256			PHD	76	Harvard	1974
Jaffe, Adam B.	Assoc	736-2251			PHD	85	Harvard	
Jefferson, Gary H.	Assoc	736-2253			PHD	86	Yale	1984
Plummer, Michael G.	Assoc	736-2265			PHD	88	Mich St	1993
Chakraborty, Atreyea	Asst	736-2247			PHD	93	Boston C	

Brescia University	Owensboro, KY		42301-3023 (502) 686-4217				brescia.edu	
Economic Faculty	Wm Thompson Sch of Bus		Fax=686-4266				Nancy Rhodes	
Asefa, Sally Ann	C-Pr	686-4264	sallya		PHD	78	Iowa St	8-80

University of Bridgeport	Bridgeport, CT		06601-2449 (203) 576-4383				bridgeport.edu	
Dept of Business Economics	School of Business		Fax=576-4388					
Bassett, Glenn A.	Dean	576-4384		Mgt	PHD	78	Yale	1979
Kim, Gew-Rae	Asst	576-4372			PHD	92	CUNY	

Brigham Young University	Provo, UT		84602-2363 (801) 378-2859				byu.edu	
Department of Economics	Col Family,Home &SocSci		Fax=378-2844				Jearlene Leishman	
Pope, Clayne L.	Dean	378-2083			PHD	72	Chicago	1970
Jensen, Farrell	C-Pr	378-4057	fejensen		PHD	72	Kansas St	1982
Kearl, James R.	Prof	378-5812	jrkearl		PHD	75	MIT	1975
Lambson, Val E.	Prof	378-7765	lambson		PHD	83	Rochester	1989
McDonald, James B.	Prof	378-3463	jim_mcdonald		PHD	70	Purdue	1972
Pope, C. Arden III	Prof	378-2157	popea		PHD	81	Iowa St	1984
Pope, Rulon D.	Prof	378-3178	rpope		PHD	76	Berkeley	1982
Ransom, Michael R.	Prof	378-4736	ransom		PHD	83	Princeton	1988
Spencer, David E.	Prof	378-7277	david_spencer		PHD	74	Tx A&M	1986

Wimmer, Larry T.	Prof	378-3354	wimmer		PHD	68	Chicago	1963
GE and Honors								
Phillips, Kerk	Assoc	378-5928	kerk		PHD	91	Rochester	1992
Showalter, Mark	Assoc	378-4645	showalter		PHD	91	MIT	1991
Bradford, Scott	Asst	378-8358			PHD	98	Harvard	1998
Cardon, James H.	Asst	378-5735			PHD	96	Princeton	1996
Eide, Eric	Asst	378-5169	eide		PHD	93	Ca-SnBarb	1993
Snow, Karl N.	Asst	378-3182			PHD	91	Chicago	1995
Thurston, Norman	Asst	378-4883	norm_thurston	HIJ	PHD	95	Princeton	1995

Brigham Young Univ-Hawaii	Laie, HI		96762-1294 (808) 293-3580					byuh.edu
Economics Faculty	School of Business		Fax=293-3582					
Neal, William G.	Dean	293-3580		Sys	EDD	77	Va Tech	1984
Haynes, C. Beth	Prof	293-3587	haynesb	DG	PHD	81	Purdue	1994
Kimzey, Bruce W.	Prof	293-3585	kimzeyb		PHD	70	Wash St	1989
Woodbury, Denise	Assoc	293-3592	woodburd	AG	PHD	92	Utah	1996

Brown University	Providence, RI		02912 (401) 863-3836					brown.edu
Economic Faculty	Department of Economics		Fax=863-1970					
Lancaster, Anthony	C-Pr	863-2112	ec418000		PHD	64	St Cathe	
Borts, George H.	Prof	863-2458	george_borts		PHD	53	Chicago	1964
George S. and Nancy B. Parker Professor of Economics								
Buchinsky, Moshe	Prof	863-2951	buchins@pste3.	CJ	PHD	91	Harvard	
Galor, Oded	Prof	863-2117	oded_galor		PHD	84	Columbia	1986
Garber, Peter M.	Prof	863-2145	peter_garber		PHD	77	Chicago	1985
Grossman, Herschel I.	Prof	863-2606	herschel_gross+		PHD	65	J Hopkins	1973
Merton P. Stolz Professor in the Social Sciences								
Henderson, J. Vernon	Prof	863-2886	j_henderson		PHD	72	Chicago	1974
Eastman Professor of Political Economy								
Lumsdaine, Robin	Prof	863-3836			PHD	91	Harvard	
Page, Talbot	Prof	863-1988	talbot_page		PHD	72	Cornell	
Pitt, Mark M.	Prof	963-2970	mark_pitt		PHD	77	Berkeley	
Putterman, Louis G.	Prof	863-3837	ec424000		PHD	80	Yale	1980
Ryder, Harl E.	Prof	863-2179	ec415000		PHD	67	Stanford	1965
Schupack, Mark B.	Emer	863-3836	ec40500		PHD	60	Princeton	1970
Serrano, Roberto	Prof	863-2764	rserrano		PHD	92	Harvard	
Stein, Jerome L.	Emer	863-2143	jls		PHD	55	Yale	1956
Eastman Professor of Political Economy - Emeritus								
Vohra, Rajiv	Prof	863-3030	rajiv_vohra		PHD	83	J Hopkins	
Weil, David	Prof	863-1754	dnweil		PHD	90	Harvard	
Feldman, Allan M.	Assoc	863-2415	allan_feldman		PHD	72	J Hopkins	1977
Volij, Oscar	Assoc	863-2097	oscar-volij		PHD	94	Hebrew	
Driscoll, John	Asst	863-1584	john_driscoll		PHD	95	Harvard	1995
Elul, Ronel	Asst	863-2953	ronel-elul		PHD	95	Yale	
Friedberg, Rachel	Asst	863-7578	rachel_friedberg		PHD	93	MIT	
Ito, Harumi	Asst	863-2887	harumi_ito		PHD	97	Stanford	
Krebs, Tom	Asst	863-2097	tom_krebs		PHD	95	Columbia	1999
Krishna, Pravin	Asst	863-2170	pk@econ.pstc.		PHD	95	Columbia	1995
Nakajami, Tomoyuki	Asst	863-3836			PHD	99	Chicago	1999
Palacios-Huercta, Ignacid	Asst	863-2691	ipalacios		PHD	95	Chicago	
Spolaore, Enrico	Asst	863-2697	enrico_spolaore		PHD	93	Harvard	

Bryant College	Smithfield, RI		02917-1284 (401) 232-6338					bryant.edu
Department of Economics	College of Business		Fax=232-6319					
Briden, Earl	Dean	232-6440	ebriden		PHD	70	Brown	8-80
Mirmirani, Sam	C-Pr	232-6338	smirmira	IMO	PHD	85	Clark	1982
Ilacqua, Joseph A.	Prof	232-6098	jillacqua	AJ	EDD	93	Boston U	1968
Norton, R. D.	Prof	232-6307		FR	PHD	77	Princeton	1985
Sarkesian Professor of Business Economics								
Shaanan, Joseph	Prof	232-6340	jshaanan	FL	PHD	79	Cornell	
Sweeney, William B. Jr.	Prof	232-6097		AE	PHD	73	Sarasota	
Bates, Laurie	Assoc	232-6459	lbates	HD	PHD	89	Conn	
Mini, Peter S.	Assoc	232-6226		BN	PHD	65	Tulane	
Kim, Jong Sung	Asst	232-6129	jkim	AJ	PHD	98	J Hopkins	1998

Bryn Mawr College	Bryn Mawr, PA		19010-2899 (610) 526-5038					brynmawr.edu
Economics Faculty	Department of Economics		Fax=526-7475					
Ross, David R.	C-Ac	526-5180	dross		PHD	84	Nrthwstrn	1992
Farley, Noel J. J.	Prof	526-5179	nfarley		PHD	65	Yale	1971
Ceglowski, Janet E.	Assoc	526-5039	jceglows		PHD	86	Berkeley	1990
Newburger, Harriet B.	Assoc	526-5181	hnewburg		PHD	84	Wisconsin	1987

Bucknell University Lewisburg, PA 17837 (570) 577-1476 bucknell.edu
Department of Economics College of Arts & Sci Fax=577-3760 Alice VanBuskirk

Name	Rank	Phone	Email	Fields	Degree	Yr	School	Year
Gerdes, Eugenia Proctor	Dean	577-3292	egerdes		PHD	73	Duke	1974
Sackrey, Charles Melvin	C-Ac	577-1476	sackrey	A	PHD	65	Tx-Austin	1980
Griffith, Winston Harold	Prof	577-1476	wgrif	FOD	PHD	81	Howard	1987
Kresl, Peter K.	Prof	577-1478	kresl	FO	PHD	70	Tx-Austin	1969
Shackelford, Jean A.	Prof	577-1476	jshackel	ABE	PHD	74	Kentucky	1975
Amott, Teresa Louise	Assoc	577-1476	amott	JNAB	PHD	80	Boston C	1989
Knoedler, Janet T.	Assoc	577-1476	knoedler	LNO	PHD	91	Tennessee	9-92
Krohn, Gregory A.	Assoc	577-3448	krohn	EGA	PHD	85	Wisconsin	1983
Moohr, Michael	Assoc	577-1476	moohr	FNO	PHD	71	Cambridge	1975
White, Nancy E.	Assoc	577-1476	nwhite	RH	PHD	87	Colorado	1986
Ge, Wei	Asst	577-3452	weige	DFOR	PHD	93	Penn	9-95
Kinnaman, Thomas	Asst	577-1476	kinnaman	HQ	PHD	94	Virginia	9-94
O'Connor, Catherine	Asst	577-3442	cmoconnr	DJC	PHD	96	Virginia	9-96
Schneider, Geoffrey	Asst	577-1476	gschedr	NOBA	ABD	97	N Carol	9-96
Wolaver, Amy	Asst	577-1476	awolaver	IJH	PHD	98	Wisconsin	9-98

Buena Vista University Storm Lake, IA 50588-1798 (712) 749-2410 bvu.edu
Economics Faculty School of Business Fax=749-1462

Name	Rank	Phone	Email	Fields	Degree	Yr	School	Year
Parikh, Rajeev	Dean	749-2410	parikh	Fnce	PHD	82	SUNY-Buf	7-99
Russell, Paul	Prof	749-2422	russell		EDD	65	N Colo	9-67
Ullerich, Stan	Assoc	749-2419	ullerich	AQMA	PHD	95	Purdue	9-94

Butler University Indianapolis, IN 46208-3485 (317) 940-9221 butler.edu
Department of Economics College of Business Adm Fax=940-9455

Name	Rank	Phone	Email	Fields	Degree	Yr	School	Year
Fetter, Richard	Dean$	940-9221	rfetter		PHD	94	Indiana	1992
Main, Robert S.	C-Ac	940-9528	rmain	HQ	PHD	73	UCLA	1981
Rieber, William J.	Prof	940-9846	wrieber	F	PHD	79	Pittsburgh	1989
Grossman, Peter Z.	Assoc	940-9727	pgrossma	NL	PHD	92	Wash U	1994
Efroymson Chair in Economics								
Chin, Wiliam	VAsst	940-9652	wchin	H	ABD		Iowa St	1999
Gjerde, Kathy A. Paulson	Asst	940-8413	kpaulson	LJ	PHD	93	Purdue	1997
Meister, J. Patrick	VAsst	940-9761	pmeister	L	PHD	92	Michigan	1996

Calif Univ of Pennsylvania California, PA 15419-1394 (724) 938-4371 cup.edu
Dept of Business & Economics Eberly Col Sci & Tech Fax=938-5908 Shirley Elnikar

Name	Rank	Phone	Email	Fields	Degree	Yr	School	Year
Cignetti, Jess	Dean$	938-4169						
Brown, Burrell	C-Pr	938-4371		Mgt	JD	73	Pittsburgh	1989
Chawdhry, M. Arshad	Prof	938-5990			PHD	74	Illinois	1976
Cole, Ismail	Prof				PHD	86	Pittsburgh	1984
Omarzai, Mahmood	Prof				PHD	76	Indiana	1979
Park, Young J.	Prof	938-4371			PHD	74	Temple	1977
Tarullo, P. Ronald	Prof				PHD	76	Pittsburgh	1978
Mongell, Susan	Assoc				PHD		Pittsburgh	1990

U of California at Berkeley Berkeley, CA 94720-3880 (510) 642-3581 econ.berkeley.edu
Department of Economics Col of Letters & Sci Fax=642-6615 Casey Gardner
Homepage: http://elsa.berkeley.edu/econ/
email @1=uclink.berkeley.edu @2=haas.berkeley

Name	Rank	Phone	Email	Fields	Degree	Yr	School	Year
Adelman, Irma	Prof	642-6417			PHD	55	Berkeley	1979
Akerlof, George A.	Prof	642-5837	akerlof		PHD	66	MIT	1966
Anderson, Robert M.	Prof	642-5248			PHD	77	Yale	
Auerbach, Alan J.	Prof	643-0558	auerbach	GEH	PHD	78	Harvard	1994
Bardhan, Pranab K.	Prof	642-4527	bardhan		PHD		Cambridge	
Brown, R. Clair	Prof	643-7090	cbrown@1	J	PHD	73	Maryland	9-73
Card, David E.	Prof	643-2767	card		PHD	83	Princeton	
Craine, Roger	Prof	642-3021			PHD	72	Maryland	1977
Debreu, Gerard	Prof	642-7284	debreu		DSC	56	Paris	1962
DeVries, Jan	Prof	642-2813			PHD	70	Yale	
Eichengreen, Barry	Prof	642-2772	eichengr		PHD	79	Yale	1987
Farrell, Joseph V.	Prof	642-9854			PHD	81	Oxford	
Gilbert, Richard J.	Prof	642-1507	gilbert		PHD	76	Stanford	1976
Goldman, Steven M.	Prof	642-2787	goldman		PHD	66	Stanford	1979
Grossman, Gregory	Prof	642-4631	grossman		PHD	53	Harvard	1953
Katz, Michael	Prof	643-0661	katz@2		PHD		Oxford	
Keeler, Theodore E.	Prof	642-4411	keeler		PHD	71	MIT	1977
Lee, Ronald D.	Prof	642-4535			PHD	71	Harvard	1979
McFadden, Daniel L.	Prof	643-8428	mcfadden		PHD	62	Minnesota	1963
Obstfeld, Maurice	Prof	643-9646	obstfeld		PHD	79	MIT	
Pierce, James L.	Prof	642-4321	pierce		PHD	64	Berkeley	1976
Power, James	Prof	643-0709	powell		PHD	82	Stanford	1995
Quigley, John M.	Prof	643-7411	quigley		PHD	72	Harvard	1979
Rabin, Matthew J.	Prof	643-8622	rabin		PHD	89	MIT	
Reich, Michael	Prof	642-3647	mreich		PHD	74	Harvard	1974
Romer, Christina D.	Prof	642-1955	cromer		PHD	85	MIT	1988
Romer, David H.	Prof	642-1955	dromer		PHD	85	MIT	1988

Rothenburg, Thomas J.	Prof	642-5843	rothenbe		PHD	66	MIT	1966
Rubinfeld, Daniel L.	Prof	642-1959	rubinfld		PHD	72	MIT	1983
Ruud, Paul A.	Prof	642-6709	ruud		PHD	81	MIT	1981
Smale, Stephen	Prof	642-4367			PHD	57	Michigan	
Tyson, Laura D.	Prof	642-5222	tyson@2		PHD	74	MIT	1977
Williamson, Oliver E.	Prof	642-8697	owilliams@2		PHD	63	Car Mellon	1988
Yellen, Janet L.	Prof				PHD	71	Yale	
DeLong, J. Bradford	Assoc	643-4027	delong		PHD	87	Harvard	1995
Edlin, Aaron	Assoc	642-4719	edlin		PHD	93	Stanford	1995
Hall, Bronwyn H.	Assoc	642-3878	bhhall		PHD	88	Stanford	1987
Hermalin, Benjamin E.	Assoc	642-7575	hermalin@2		PHD	88	MIT	1988
Eissa, Nada	Asst	643-0708	eissa		PHD	95	Harvard	1995
Hoynes, Hilary	Asst	642-4639	hilary		PHD	95	Stanford	1995

Univ of California, Davis — Davis, CA 95616-8578 (530) 752-0741 — ucdavis.edu
Department of Economics — Col of Letters & Sci Fax=752-9382 — Gerri Refsland

Sheffrin, Steven M.	Dean	752-1576	smsheffrin	EH	PHD	76	MIT	1976
Quinzii, Martine	C-Pr	752-1567	mmquinzii	CDG	PHD	74	U Paris	1991
Bonanno, Giacomo F.	Prof	752-1574	gfbonanno	CD	PHD	75	LondonEc	1987
Brzeski, Andrzej	Emer	752-8491	abrzeski	AP	PHD	64	Berkeley	1963
Clark, Gregory	Prof	752-9242	gclark	NO	PHD	85	Harvard	1990
Feenstra, Robert	Prof	752-7022	rcfeenstra	F	PHD	81	MIT	1986
Hoover, Kevin D.	Prof	752-2129	kdhoover	BE	DPHI	85	Oxford	1985
Kaneda, Hiromitsu	Emer			AFOQ	PHD	64	Stanford	1973
Lindert, Peter H.	Prof	752-1983	phlindert	FN	PHD	67	Cornell	1978
Makowski, Louis	Prof	752-6142	lmakowski	DE	PHD	75	UCLA	1985
Mayer, Thomas	Emer	752-1550		BE	PHD	53	Columbia	1962
Olmstead, Alan L.	Prof	752-2043	alolmstead	HN	PHD	70	Wisconsin	1969
Roemer, John E.	Prof	752-3226	jeroemer	DP	PHD	74	Berkeley	1974
Shen, T. Y.	Emer			L	PHD	56	Yale	7-63
Silvestre, Joaquim	Prof	752-1570	jbsilvestre	D	PHD	73	Minnesota	1983
Tuma, Elias H.	Emer	752-1550	tuma@vfv.net	ANO	PHD	62	Berkeley	1967
Walton, Gary M.	Prof	757-4630	fte4efl@a	ADN	PHD	66	U Wash	1981
Wegge, Leon L.	Emer	752-1550	llwegge	F	PHD	63	MIT	1966
Woo, Wing T.	Prof	752-3035	wtwoo	EFOP	PHD	82	Harvard	1985
Baker, Michael	Assoc	752-2614	mbaker	H	PHD	90	Michigan	1-99
Helms, L. Jay	Assoc	752-2094	ljhelms	DHI	PHD	79	MIT	1985
Nehring, Klaus D.	Assoc	752-3379	kdnehring	DG	PHD	91	Harvard	1992
Salyer, Kevin D.	Assoc	752-8359	kdsalyer	EG	PHD	85	Ca-SnBarb	1990
Bergin, Paul	Asst	752-8398	prbergin	EF	PHD	96	Yale	1996
Branstetter, Lee	Asst	752-3033	branstet@polar.	FL	PH	96	Harvard	1996
Cameron, Colin	Asst	752-8376	accameron	CIJ	PHD	88	Stanford	1989
Jorda, Oscar	Asst	752-7021	ojorda	E	PHD	97	Ca-SnDgo	1997
Loeb, Susanna	Asst	752-8727	sloeb	JH	PHD	98	Michigan	7-98
Page, Marianne E.	Asst	752-1551	mepage	HJ	PHD	95	Michigan	1996
Swenson, Deborah	Asst	752-1569	deswenson	FH	PHD	91	MIT	1993
Gustafson, W. Eric	Emer		egustaf652@a	AO	PHD	59	Harvard	1978

Univ of Calif, Irvine — Irvine, CA 92697-5100 (949) 824-5788 — uci.edu
Department of Economics — Sch of Social Sciences Fax=824-2182 — Gay White/Iris Adam

Schonfeld, William R.	Dean	824-6801	wrschonf	PolS	PHD	70	Princeton	
Cohen, Linda	C-Pr	824-5189	lrcohen		PHD	79	Cal Tech	1988
Bell, Duran	Prof	824-7053	dbell		PHD	65	Berkeley	1965
Brownstone, David	Prof	824-6231	dbrownstone		PHD	80	Berkeley	1984
DeVany, Arthur S.	Prof	824-5269	asdevany		PHD	70	UCLA	1984
Fielding, Gordon J.	Emer	824-5448	gjfieldi		PHD	62	UCLA	1965
Glazer, Amihai	Prof	824-5974	aglazer		PHD	78	Yale	1978
Johnston, John	Emer	824-5581	jjohnsto		PHD	57	Wales	1978
Kassouf, Sheen T.	Emer	824-7161	rpellegr		PHD	65	Columbia	1965
Lave, Charles	Emer	824-6502	calave		PHD	68	Stanford	1964
Lilien, David M.	Prof	824-6232	dmlilien		PHD	77	MIT	1984
Luce, Ducan	Emer	824-6239	rdluce		PHD	50	MIT	1988
Margolis, Julius	Emer	824-7003	jmargoli		PHD	49	Harvard	1976
McGuire, Martin C.	Prof	824-6190	mcmcguir		PHD	64	Harvard	1992
Poirier, Dale	Prof				PHD	73	Wisconsin	1999
Small, Kenneth A.	Prof	824-5658	ksmall		PHD	76	Berkeley	1983
DiNardo, John	Assoc	824-3191	jdinardo		PHD	90	Princeton	1991
Garfinkel, Michelle	Assoc	824-3190	mgarfink		PHD	88	Brown	1991
Skaperdas, Stergios	Assoc	824-4167	sskapero		PHD	88	J Hopkins	1988
Black, Duncan	Asst				PHD	99	Brown	1999
Furuya, K.	Asst	824-1486	kfuruya		PHD	96	Berkeley	1996
Genicot, Garance	Asst				PHD	99	Cornell	1999
Lee, Jaewoo	Asst	824-8529	jwlee		PHD	92	MIT	1992
Moore, M.	Asst	824-4221	mpmoore		PHD	97	MIT	1997
Naito, Hisahiro	Asst				PHD	98	Michigan	1999
Ranjan, Priya	Asst	824-1926	pranjan		PHD	97	Columbia	1997
Richardson, Gary	Asst				PHD	99	Berkeley	1999
Tobias, Justin	Asst				PHD	99	Chicago	1999

Univ of Calif, Los Angeles Los Angeles, CA 90024-1447 (310) 825-1011 ucla.edu
Department of Economics Col of Letters & Sci Fax=206-2313
Did Not Respond--1997-98 Listing; email @1=econ.sscnet.ucla.edu

Name	Rank	Phone	Email	Fields	Degree	Yr	School	Since
Ellickson, Bryan C.	C-Pr	825-4556			PHD	70	MIT	1973
Aoki, Masanao	Emer	825-2360			PHD	65	Tokyo In	1983
Azariadis, Constantine C.	Prof	825-6682			PHD	75	Car Mellon	
Cameron, Trudy Ann	Prof	825-3925			PHD	82	Princeton	1984
Currie, Janet	Prof	206-8380			PHD	88	Princeton	1988
Demsetz, Harold	Emer	825-3651			PHD	59	Nrthwstrn	1971
Edwards, Sebastian	Prof	825-1011			PHD	81	Chicago	1985
Farmer, Roger E. A.	Prof	825-2523			PHD	82	W Ontario	1988
Hansen, Gary D.	Prof	825-3847			PHD	86	Minnesota	1987
Harberger, Arnold C.	Prof	825-7520			PHD	50	Chicago	
Intriligator, Michael D.	Emer	825-4144			PHD	63	MIT	1972
Klein, Benjamin	Prof	825-6547			PHD	70	Chicago	1978
Lal, Deepak	Prof	825-4521			PHD	65	Oxford	
Lamoreaux, Naomi	Prof	825-0225			PHD	79	J Hopkins	
Leamer, Edward E.	Prof	825-3557			PHD	70	Michigan	1975
Leijonhufvud, Axel S. B.	Emer	825-4126			PHD	87	Nrthwstrn	
Levine, David K.	Prof	825-3810			PHD	81	MIT	1981
McCall, John J.	Emer	825-1849			PHD	59	Chicago	
Ostroy, Joseph M.	Prof	825-4627			PHD	70	Nrthwstrn	
Riley, John G.	Prof	825-1541			PHD	72	MIT	1973
Rosenthal, Jean-Laurent	Prof	825-2490			PHD	88	Cal Tech	1988
Shapley, Lloyd S.	Prof	825-3723			PHD	53	Princeton	
Sokoloff, Kenneth L.	Prof	825-4249			PHD	82	Harvard	1980
Thomas, Duncan	Prof	825-5304			PHD	86	Princeton	
Thompson, Earl A.	Prof	825-4387			PHD	61	Harvard	1965
Zame, William	Prof	206-9463			PHD	70	Tulane	
Murphy, George G. S.	Emer	825-9397			PHD	57	U Wash	
Ozler, Sule	Assoc	825-2997			PHD	86	Stanford	1985
Vegh, Carlos	Assoc	825-7371			PHD	87	Chicago	
Asea, Patrick	Asst	206-6869			PHD	93	J Hopkins	
Hu, Wei-Yin	Asst	825-6838			PHD	94	Stanford	
Hubbard, Thomas	Asst	826-7652			PHD	96	Stanford	
Hyslop, Dean	Asst	826-9665			PHD	95	Princeton	
Lahiri, Amartya	Asst	825-8018			PHD	95	Maryland	
Lambertini, Luisa	Asst	206-1256			PHD	95	Berkeley	
McGarry, Kathleen	Asst	826-2833			PHD	92	SUNY-SBr	
Potter, Simon M.	Asst	206-6732			PHD	90	Wisconsin	1990
Sigman, Hilary	Asst	825-2443			PHD	93	MIT	
Williams, Darrell L.	Asst	206-2794	williams@1	GKL	PHD	91	Wash U	F-90
Yelowitz, Aaron	Asst	825-5665			PHD	94	MIT	

Univ of Calif, Riverside Riverside, CA 92521-0427 (909) Ext 1474 ucr.edu
Department of Economics Col Human, Arts & SocSc Fax=787-5685 Tala Martinez
Homepage: www.ucr.edu/chss/depts/econ/econhome.htm
phone 787-5037

Name	Rank	Phone	Email	Fields	Degree	Yr	School	Since
Velez-Iranez, Carlos	Dean	787-3594	carlos.velez		PHD	74	Ca-SnDgo	1994
Cullenberg, Stephen E.	C-Ac	Ext 1573	stephen.cullenbe	ABCP	PHD	87	Mass	1988
Bandyopadhayay, Taradas	Prof	Ext 1586	taradas.bandy+	AD	PHD	80	So Meth	1987
Carter, Susan B.	Prof	Ext 1589	susan.carter	AJNT	PHD	81	Stanford	1990
Chilcote, Ronald H.	Prof	Ext 1571	ronald.chilcote.	P	PHD	65	Stanford	1963
Gaffney, M. Mason	Prof	Ext 1574	mason.gaffney	AHR	PHD	56	Berkeley	1976
Griffin, Keith B.	Prof	787-4108	keith.griffin	AOP	DPHI	65	Oxford	1988
Khan, Azizur Rahman	Prof	Ext 1581	azizur.khan	FOPR	PHD	66	Cambridge	1988
Lippit, Victor D.	Prof	Ext 1582	victor.lippit	AOP	PHD	71	Yale	1971
Pattanaik, Prasanta	Prof	Ext 1592	prasanta.pattana	AO	PHD	68	Delhi	1991
Russell, R. Robert	Prof	Ext 1585	robert.russell	ADH	PHD	65	Harvard	1986
Sutch, Richard C.	Prof	Ext 1501	richard.sutch	AN	PHD	68	MIT	1998
Ullah, Aman	Prof	Ext 1591	aman.ullah	C	PHD	71	Delhi	1989
Dymski, Gary A.	Assoc	Ext 1570	gary.dymski	AEHP	PHD	87	Mass	1991
Fairris, David H.	Assoc	Ext 1578	david.fairris	AJP	PHD	84	Duke	1989
Gonzalez-Rivera, Gloria	Assoc	Ext 1590	gloria.gonzalez	CG	PHD	91	Ca-SnDgo	1991
Chauvet, Marcelle	Asst	Ext 1587	marcelle.chauvet	AE	PHD	95	Penn	1995
Cheng, Xu	Asst	Ext 1502	xu.cheng	CFO	PHD	99	Columbia	1998
Guo, Jang-Ting	Asst	Ext 1588	jangting.guo	AC	PHD	93	UCLA	1993
Helfand, Steven	Asst	Ext 1572	steven.helfand	AOQ	PHD	94	Berkeley	1995
Lee, Tae-Hwy	Asst	Ext 1509	tae.lee	ACG	PHD	90	Ca-SnDgo	1995

Univ of Calif, San Diego La Jolla, CA 92093-0508 (619) 534-3383 ucsd.edu
Department of Economics Thurgood Marshall Col Fax=534-7040 Beverly Applequist

Name	Rank	Phone	Email	Fields	Degree	Yr	School	Since
Hamilton, James D.	C-Pr	534-5986	jhamilto	D	PHD	83	Berkeley	1992
Attiyeh, Richard E.	Prof	534-6654		EI	PHD	66	Yale	1982
Vice Chancellor of Research and Dean, OGSR								
Bear, Donald V. T.	Emer	534-3383		AE	PHD	63	Stanford	1965
Carson, Richard T.	Prof	534-6319	rcarson	CQ	PHD	85	Berkeley	1985
Conlisk, John	Prof	534-3832	jconlisk	ET	PHD	65	Stanford	1968

Name	Rank	Phone	Email	Fields	Degree	Yr	School	Since
Crawford, Vincent	Prof	534-3952	vcrawfor	D	PHD	76	MIT	1976
Engle, Robert F.	Prof	534-4553	rengle	CGR	PHD	66	Cornell	1975
Chancellor's Associates Chair in Econometrics								
Granger, Clive W. J.	Prof	534-3856	cgranger	C	PHD	74	Nottinghm	1974
Chancellor's Associates Chair in Economics								
Groves, Theodore	Prof	534-2818	tgroves	DHM	PHD	70	Berkeley	1978
Heller, Walter P.	Prof	534-4692	wheller	DE	PHD	70	Stanford	1974
Machina, Mark J.	Prof	534-2391	mmachina	D	PHD	79	MIT	1979
Ramanathan, Ramu	Emer	534-6787	rramanat	CFO	PHD	67	Minnesota	1967
Ramey, Valerie	Prof	543-2388	vramey	E	PHD	87	Stanford	1987
Rauch, James E.	Prof	534-2405	jrauch	FO	PHD	85	Yale	1986
Sobel, Joel	Prof	534-4367	jsobel	D	PHD	78	Berkeley	1978
Starr, Ross	Prof	534-3879	rstarr	DE	PHD	72	Stanford	1980
White, Halbert L.	Prof	534-3502	hwhite	C	PHD	76	MIT	1979
Betts, Julian R.	Assoc	534-3369	jbetts	CJ	PHD	90	Queen's	1990
denHaan, Wouter	Assoc	543-0762	wdenhaan	AE	PHD	91	Car Mellon	1991
Flavin, Marjorie A.	Assoc	534-4649	mflavin	E	PHD	81	MIT	1992
Ramey, Garey	Assoc	534-5721	gramey	D	PHD	87	Stanford	1987
Timmermann, Allan	Assoc	534-3383	atimmerm	CG	PHD	92	Cambridge	1994
Watson, Joel	Assoc	534-3383	jwatson	CF	PHD	92	Stanford	1994
Elliott, Graham	Asst	534-3383	gelliott	CEF	PHD	94	Harvard	1994
Frieberg, Leora	Asst	534-2973	lfriedbe	HDJE	PHD	96	MIT	1996
Raphael, Steven	Asst	534-4828	sraphael	JF	PHD	96	Berkeley	1996
Riker, David	Asst	534-2958	driker	FEC	PHD	96	MIT	1996
Shachat, Jason	Asst	534-2988	jshachat	CD	PHD	96	Arizona	1996

U of Calif, Santa Barbara Santa Barbara CA 93106-9210 (805) 893-3670 econ.ucsb.edu
Department of Economics Col of Letters & Sci Fax=893-8830 Julie Sears, Manager

Name	Rank	Phone	Email	Fields	Degree	Yr	School	Since
Deacon, Robert T.	C-Pr	893-3569	deacon	QH	PHD	72	U Wash	1972
Bohn, Henning	Prof	893-4532	bohn	EF	PHD	86	Stanford	1992
Comanor, William S.	Prof	893-2287	eomanor	LD	PHD	64	Harvard	1975
Crouch, Robert L.	Prof	893-2152	rlcc	A	PHD	67	Essex	1973
DeCanio, Stephen J.	Prof	893-3130	decanio	NCD	PHD	72	MIT	1978
Frech, H. E. III	Prof	893-3569	frech	LAI	PHD	74	UCLA	1973
Kolstad, Charles	Prof	893-2108	kolstad	QLD	PHD	82	Stanford	1992
Krouse, Clement G.	Prof	893-3804	krouse	D	PHD	69	UCLA	1979
LeRoy, Stephen F.	Prof	893-2438	sleroy	GE	PHD	71	Penn	1997
Marshall, John M.	Prof	893-3670	marshall	A	PHD	69	MIT	1972
Mehra, Rajnish	Prof	893-3238	mehra	GF	PHD	78	Car Mellon	1988
Mercer, Lloyd J.	Prof	893-2895	mercer	ND	PHD	67	U Wash	1966
Morgan, W. Douglas	Prof	893-2653	dmorgan	HDE	PHD	69	Berkeley	1973
Phillips, Llad	Prof	893-2023	llad	JC	PHD	69	Harvard	1972
Sengupta, Jati K.	Prof	893-3797	sengupta	CO	PHD	62	Iowa St	1976
Shapiro, Perry	Prof	893-2253	pxshap	DH	PHD	67	Berkeley	1969
Sonstelie, Jon C.	Prof	893-2242	jon	HR	PHD	75	Nrthwstrn	1977
Stuart, Charles	Prof	893-3216	stuart	HKD	PHD	75	Lunds	1980
Qin, Cheng-Zhong	Assoc	893-2753	qin	D	PHD	89	Iowa	1989
Steigerwald, Douglas G.	Assoc	893-3151	doug	C	PHD	89	Berkeley	1988
Funkhouser, Ed	Asst	893-3490	funkhous	OJ	PHD	90	Harvard	1992
Garratt, Rodney J.	Asst	893-2849	garratt	AEH	PHD	91	Cornell	1991
Moon, Hyunsik Roger	Asst	893-5571	rmoon	C	PHD	98	Yale	1998
Proulx, Christopher	Asst	893-5572	rabbit	D	PHD	98	Michigan	1998
Nisbet, Mary J.	SLect	893-2284	nisbet	G	PHD	91	Glasgow	1991
Academic Coordinator								

Univ of Calif, Santa Cruz Santa Cruz, CA 95064 (408) 459-2743 cats.ucsc.edu
Department of Economics Social Sciences Fax=459-5077 Kim Tyler

Name	Rank	Phone	Email	Fields	Degree	Yr	School	Since
Friedman, Daniel	C-Pr	459-4981	dan	FG	PHD	77	Ca-SanCrz	1979
Dooley, Michael	Prof	459-3662	mpd	F	PHD	71	Penn	1992
Grieson, Ronald E.	Prof	459-2968	grieson	RHD	PHD	72	Rochester	1980
Hutchison, Michael M.	Prof	459-2600	hutch	EFG	PHD	83	Oregon	1985
Ibister, John W.	Prof	459-2246	isbister	O	PHD	69	Princeton	1968
Provost Merrill College								
Kaun, David E.	Prof	459-4745	nuclear	J	PHD	64	Stanford	1966
Kletzer, Kenneth M.	Prof	459-3407	kkletzer	FDOH	PHD	82	Berkeley	1992
Richards, Alan	Prof	459-4662	arr	ONQ	PHD	75	Wisconsin	1976
Singh, Nirvikar	Prof	459-4093	boxjenk	DLO	PHD	82	Berkeley	1982
Walsh, Carl E.	Prof	459-4082	walshc	E	PHD	76	Berkeley	1987
Wittman, Donald A.	Prof	459-4445	wittman	KD	PHD	70	Berkeley	1969
Cheung, Yin-Wong	Assoc	459-4247	cheung	C	PHD	90	Penn	1990
Elbaum, Bernard	Assoc	459-4248	elbaum	N	PHD	82	Harvard	1986
Fung, Kwok-Chiu	Assoc	459-3273	kcfung	F	PHD	70	Wisconsin	1989
Chinn, Menzie	Asst	459-2079	chinn	FCE	PHD	91	Berkeley	1991
Fairlie, Robert	Asst	459-3332	rfairlie	J	PHD	94	Nrthwstrn	1994
Kletzer, Lori Gladstein	Asst	459-3596	lketzer	J	PHD	86	Berkeley	1993
Shepherd, Robert J.	Lect	459-5080	shep		MSA	70	S Calif	

California Institute of Tech — Pasadena, CA 91125 (818) 395-4065 — caltech.edu
Economics Faculty — Div of Human & Soc Sci Fax=405-9841 — Susan G. Davis, Div Adm

Name	Rank	Phone	Field	Degree	Yr	School	Year
Ledyard, John O.	C-Pr	395-8482		PHD	67	Purdue	1985
Camerer, Colin	Prof	395-4054		PHD	81	Chicago	1994
Rea A. & Lela G. Axline Professor of Business Economics							
Davis, Lance E.	Prof	395-4092	N	PHD	56	J Hopkins	1968
Mary Stillman Harkness Professor of Social Science							
Grether, David M.	Prof	395-4068		PHD	69	Stanford	1970
Jackson, Matthew O.	Prof			PHD	88	Stanford	1997
Palfrey, Thomas R.	Prof	395-4088		PHD	81	Cal Tech	1986
Plott, Charles R.	Prof	395-4209		PHD	65	Virginia	1971
Edward S. Harkness Professor of Economics and Political Science							
Border, Kim Christian	Assoc	395-4218	C	PHD	79	Minnesota	1979
Bossaerts, Peter	Assoc	395-4028	G	PHD	86	UCLA	1990
Dubin, Jeffrey A.	Assoc	395-4059		PHD	82	MIT	1982
Fohlin, Caroline	Asst	395-4401	NFL	PHD	94	Berkeley	1994
Ghirardato, Paolo	Asst	395-4094	D	PHD	95	Berkeley	1995
Sherman, Robert P.	Asst	395-4337		PHD	91	Yale	1996
Wilkie, Simon	Asst	395-4216	L	PHD	90	Rochester	1995

California Lutheran Univ — Thousand OaksCA 91360-2787 (805) 493-3360 — clunet.edu
Economics Faculty — School of Business Fax=493-3719 — Joan Rensch

Name	Rank	Phone	Email	Field	Degree	Yr	School	Year
Maxey, Charles	Dean	493-3360	maxey	Soc	PHD	82	Illinois	1991
Akbari, Ali	Prof	493-3379	akbari		PHD	85	S Calif	1984
Damooei, Jamshid	Assoc	493-3357	damooei		PHD		Surrey	1987

Cal Polytechnic State U-SLO — S Luis Obispo CA 93407 (805) 756-2783 — cymbal.calpol
Economics Department — School of Business Fax=756-1473 — Eliane Yochum 756-2783
Did Not Respond--1997-98 Listing

Name	Rank	Phone	Field	Degree	Yr	School	Year
Boynton, William C.	Dean	756-2705	Atg	PHD	76	Mich St	9-85
Papakyriazis, Artemis	H-Pr	756-1765		PHD	82	Ca-Rivers	1982
Williamson, Daniel P.	H-Pr	756-1768		PHD	73	Ca-SnDgo	1970
Beardsley, George L.	Prof	756-2356		PHD	74	Penn	1975
Kersten, Timothy W.	Prof	756-2555		PHD	73	Oregon	1971
Marlow, Michael L.	Prof	756-1764		PHD	78	Va Tech	1988
Papakyriazis, Panagiotis A.	Prof	756-7176		PHD	74	Ca-SnDgo	1971
Rice, Walter E.	Prof	756-2285		PHD	73	Claremont	1964
Associate Dean							
Fanchon, Phillip F.	Assoc	756-1766		PHD	82	Ca-SnBarb	
Shiers, Alden F.	Assoc	756-2564		PHD	77	Ca-SnBarb	1975
Villegas, Daniel J.	Asst	756-1767		PHD	79	Stanford	1987

Calif State Poly U-Pomona — Pomona, CA 91768-4082 (909) 869-3842 — csupomona.edu
Economics Department — Cl Letters, Arts & SocS Fax=869-0987 — Rosie Pasos

Name	Rank	Phone	Email	Degree	Yr	School	Year
Burton, Maureen	C-Pr	869-3853	mburton	PHD	86	Ca-Rivers	1988
Al-Sabea, Taha H.	Prof	869-3855	thalsabea	PHD	68	S Calif	1968
Blumner, Sidney M.	Prof	869-3843	smblumner	PHD	68	Arizona	1967
Bray, Robert T.	Prof	869-3847	rtbray	PHD	72	UCLA	1965
Bresnock, Anne E.	Prof	869-4593	aebresnock	PHD	81	Colorado	1990
Ho, Franklin Y. H.	Prof	869-3854	fho	PHD	57	S Calif	1961
Jaques, David G.	Prof	869-3851	dgjaques	PHD	73	Claremont	1965
Rush, Lynda M.	Prof	869-3857	lmrush	PHD	84	Ca-Davis	1986
Safarzadeh, Mohammad R.	Prof	869-3852	mssafarzadeh	PHD	84	Claremont	1987
Shieh, John T.	Prof	869-3858	jtshieh	DBA	81	S Calif	1967
Shute, Laurence	Prof	869-3850	lshute	PHD	73	Columbia	1988
Sutton, James E.	Prof	869-3846	jesutton	BS	55	Wisconsin	1964
Ruiz, Nestor M.	Assoc	869-3972	nmruiz	PHD	89	Ca-Davis	1990

Calif State U., Bakersfield — Bakersfield, CA 93311-1099 (661) 664-2460 — csubak.edu
Economics Department — Sch of Arts & Sciences Fax=664-2049 — Sylvia O'Brien

Name	Rank	Phone	Email	Field	Degree	Yr	School	Year
Geigle, Ray	Dean	664-2221	rgeigle	PolS	PHD	71	U Wash	1970
Grammy, Abbas P.	C-Pr	664-2466	agrammy	ACOR	PHD	82	Colorado	1989
Evans, Mark O.	Prof	664-2460	mevans	AIQR	PHD	77	New Mex	1978
Falero, Frank Jr.	Prof	664-2462	ffalero	ADEG	PHD	67	Fla St	1972
Malixi, Margaret M.	Prof	664-2464	mmalixi	ACFP	PHD	88	Wisconsin	1988
Oswald, Donald J.	Assoc	664-2465	doswald	ABKN	PHD	74	Wash St	1961
Lynch, James G.	Lect	664-2470	jlynch	AFJ	PHD	98	Colorado	1999

Calif State Univ, Chico — Chico, CA 95929-0430 (530) 898-6141 — oavax.csuchico.edu
Department of Economics — Col of Behav & Soc Sci Fax=898-5901 — Annette Schmidt

Name	Rank	Phone	Field	Degree	Yr	School	Year
Hope, Barney F.	C-Pr	898-6141	RFO	PHD	79	Ca-Rivers	1977
Adams, Ronald G.	Prof	898-6141	ACKR	PHD	75	Kansas St	1971
Eckalbar, John C.	Prof	898-5808	CE	PHD	75	Colorado	1978
Fisher, Robert B.	Prof	895-5808	H	PHD		Oregon	1968
Francis, Gary E.	Prof	898-6141	ABGH	PHD	72	Colorado	1967

Gallo, David E.	Prof	898-5232		AEHQ	PHD	74	Oregon	1970
James, Robert G.	Prof	898-5997		EFG	PHD	78	Oregon	1981
Morlock, Mark J.	Prof	898-4784		J	PHD	78	Wash St	1980
O'Toole, James K.	Prof	898-5759		ADR	PHD	83	Va Tech	1984
Perelman, Michael A.	Prof	898-5321		N	PHD	71	Berkeley	1971
Shockley, Frederica	Prof	898-6141		HMOR	PHD	78	Geo St	1978
Coolidge, Cathleen J.	Assoc	898-6141		AHKL	PHD	83	Va Tech	1984

Calif St U-Dominguez Hills Carson, CA 90747 (310) 516-3446 csudh.edu
Economics Department Col of Arts & Sciences Fax=
Did Not Respond Again--1995-96 Listing

Palmer, Richard L.	Dean	516-3429		PolS	PHD	73	Claremont	1972
Billes, Frank V.	C-Pr	516-3446		AENP	PHD	74	UCLA	1972
Freed, Rodney Alan	Prof			ACR	PHD	77	Virginia	1979
Harris, James G.	Prof			AEDH	PHD	70	Oregon	1969
Kidane, Abraham Z.	Prof			AFOI	PHD	71	UCLA	1971
Moite, Leonard M.	Assoc			AEDJ	PHD	84	UCLA	1980

Calif State Univ-Fresno Fresno, CA 93740-0020 (559) 278-3916 csufresno.edu
Department of Economics Sch of Social Sciences Fax=278-7234 Sherry McCulloch

Gruenbaum, Ellen R.	Dean	278-3013	elleng	Anth	PHD	82	Conn	
Cypher, James M.	C-Pr	278-4935	james_cypher	OP	PHD	73	Ca-Rivers	1967
Allison, Robert J.	Prof		robert_allison	B	PHD	66	Colorado	1967
Bush, Paul D.	Prof	278-4933	paul_bush	AL	PHD	64	Claremont	1961
Leet, Don R.	Prof	278-4045	don_leet	TNA	PHD	72	Penn	1969
Shaffer, Linda J.	Prof	278-4936	linda_shaffer	CJ	PHD	78	Nrthwstrn	1984
Shaw, John A. Jr.	Prof	278-2673	john_shaw	DNF	PHD	69	Purdue	1965
Fayazmanesh, Sasan	Asst	278-2672		BCE	PHD	84	Ca-Rivers	1990
Houser, Scott	Asst	278-3045	scott_houser	HRI	PHD	96	Wisconsin	1996

Calif State Univ, Fullerton Fullerton, CA 92834-6848 (714) 278-2228 fullerton.edu
Department of Economics School of Bus Adm & Ec Fax=278-3097 Shelley Drath

Puri, Anil K.	C-Pr	278-3817	apuri	HR	PHD	77	Minnesota	1977
Chu, Kwang-Wen	Prof	278-3841	kchu	D	PHD	72	UCLA	1970
Dietz, James L.	Prof	278-3810	jdietz	O	PHD	74	Ca-Rivers	1973
Gill, Andrew M.	Prof	278-3076	agill	J	PHD	85	Wash St	1984
Hall, Jane V.	Prof	278-2236	jhall	Q	PHD	77	Berkeley	1981
Hettich, Walter	Prof	278-3756	whettich	H	PHD	67	Yale	1983
Long, Stewart L.	Prof	278-2243	slong	N	PHD	74	Illinois	1973
Michaels, Robert J.	Prof	278-2588	rmichaels	L	PHD	72	UCLA	1968
Naish, Howard F.	Prof	278-2241	hnaish	E	PHD	83	S Calif	1988
Rahmatian, Morteza	Prof	278-3859	mrahmatian	Q	PHD	82	Wyoming	1988
Solberg, Eric J.	Prof	278-2237	esolberg	J	PHD	74	Claremont	1973
Wolfson, Murray	Prof	278-3816	mwolfson	BC	PHD	63	Wisconsin	1986
Wong, David C.	Prof	278-3821	dwong	CO	PHD	84	Ca-SnBarb	1981
Brajer, Victor	Assoc	278-3818	vbrajer	DQ	PHD	83	New Mex	1987
Flessig, Adrian	Assoc	278-2228	aflessig	EF	PHD	93	N Car St	1999
Purkayastha, Dipankar	Assoc	278-3151	dpurkayastha	O	PHD	90	Wash St	1990
Battacharya, Radha S.	Asst	278-3652	rbattacharya	E	PHD	90	Penn St	1990
Dropsy, Vincent	Asst	278-3307	vdropsy	FE	PHD	90	S Calif	1989
Roy, Suddhasatwa	Asst	2778-381	9sroy	LF	PHD	96	Purdue	1998

Calif State Univ, Hayward Hayward, CA 94542-3068 (510) 885-3322 csuhayward.edu
Department of Economics Sch of Business & Econ Fax=885-2039

Tontz, Jay L.	Dean	885-3291	jtonz	EGM	PHD	66	N Carol	9-69
Ahiakpor, James C.	C-Pr	885-3330	jahiakop	BEO	PHD	81	Toronto	1991
Baird, Charles W.	Prof	885-3275	cbaird	BHJ	PHD	68	Berkeley	1972
Caassuto, Alexander E.	Prof	885-3922	acassuto	CEGM	PHD	73	UCLA	1971
Christiansen, Gregory B.	Prof	885-3301		BEHO	PHD	81	Wisconsin	1983
Kamath, Shyam J.	Prof	885-4275	skamath	BFMO	PHD	87	Simon Fr	1986
Leube, Kurt R.	Prof	885-3368	kleube	DBHK	DLE	71	Salzburg	1985
Lima, Anthony K.	Prof	885-3889	tlima	CEGM	PHD	80	Stanford	1979
Maxwell, Nan L.	Prof	885-3191	nmaxwell	ADJT	PHD	83	Fla St	1985
Ozaki, Robert S.	Prof	885-3137	rozaki	EFNO	PHD	60	Harvard	1960
Paringer, Lynn C.	Prof	885-3986		CDI	PHD	78	Wisconsin	1981
Shmanske, Steven	Prof	885-3334	sshmansk	CDHL	PHD	82	UCLA	1979
St. Clair, David J.	Prof	885-3327	dstclair	BENP	PHD	79	Utah	1979
Kahane, Leo H.	Assoc	885-3369	lkahane	CFL	PHD	91	Columbia	1991
Lopus, Jane S.	Assoc	885-3140	jlopus	AEH	PHD	90	Ca-Davis	1979

Humboldt State University Arcata, CA 95521-8299 (707) 826-3224 axe.humboldt.edu
Sch of Business & Economics Col of Professional Std Fax=826-6666 Patty Olson

Mullery, Colleen	C-Pr	826-6022	cbm1	Mgt	PHD	91	Port St	1990
Grobey, John H.	Prof	826-3347			PHD	75	U Wash	1967
Hackett, Steven C.	Assoc	826-3237			PHD	89	Tx A&M	1994
Eschker, Erik	Asst	826-3216	ee3		PHD	97	Ca-Davis	1998
Prince, Steven	Asst	826-5302	sjp12		PHD	93	Utah	1998

Calif State Univ, Long Beach Long Beach, CA 90840-4607 (562) 985-5061 csulb.edu
Department of Economics College of Liberal Arts Fax=985-5804 Karen Fawson

Name	Rank	Phone	Email	Field	Degree	Yr	School	Year
Abrahamse, Dorothy Z.	Dean	985-5381			PHD	67	Michigan	1967
Magaddino, Joseph P.	C-Pr	985-5061			PHD	72	Va Tech	1973
Anderson, Roy C.	Prof	985-5054			PHD	65	Tulane	1965
Beaumont, Marion S.	Prof	985-5076			PHD	67	Claremont	1967
Cole, Charles L.	Prof	985-5075			PHD	63	S Calif	1967
Crowther, Simeon J.	Prof	985-4634			PHD	70	Penn	1968
Edwards, Alejandra C.	Prof	985-5068			PHD	84	Chicago	1966
Farrell, Michael J.	Prof	985-5060			PHD	69	Stanford	1969
Glezakos, Constantine	Prof	985-5079			PHD	70	S Calif	1968
Grobar, Lisa M.	Prof	985-1652			PHD	89	Michigan	1989
Hall, Darwin C.	Prof	985-5045			PHD	77	Berkeley	1986
Hou, Jack W.	Prof	985-4710			PHD	89	Yale	1989
Ishimine, Tomotaka	Prof	985-5065			PHD	71	Wisconsin	1967
Medoff, Marshall H.	Prof	985-5077			PHD	73	Berkeley	1979
Muraoka, Dennis D.	Prof	985-5078			PHD	81	Ca-SnBarb	1982
Rooney, Robert F.	Prof	985-5086			PHD	65	Stanford	1970
Singh, Davinder	Prof	985-5071			PHD	78	S Carol	1983
Skov, Iva L.	Prof	985-5087			PHD	76	S Calif	1972
Stern, Andrew	Prof	985-5083			PHD	67	Columbia	1967
Radsich, Aleksander	Asst				PHD	99	Princeton	1999

Calif State U, Los Angeles Los Angeles, CA 90032-8124 (323) 343-2930 calstatela.edu
Dept of Economics & Stat School of Bus & Econ Fax=343-5462 Pat Tom

Name	Rank	Phone	Email	Field	Degree	Yr	School	Year
Haight, G. Timothy	Dean	343-2800	thaight	Fnce	DBA	80	Geo Wash	9-98
Lai, Kon Sun	C-Pr	343-2930	klai		PHD	87	Penn	1987
Canarella, Giorgio	Prof	343-2933	gcanare		PHD	73	Virginia	1973
Garston, Neil H.	Prof	343-2934	ngarsto		PHD	73	Brown	1975
Kim, Sun K.	Prof	343-2944			PHD	66	S Calif	1964
Larson, Tom Edward	Prof	343-2938	tlarson		PHD	86	Berkeley	1987
Sapra, Sunil	Prof	343-2941	ssapra		PHD	83	Columbia	1991
Tran, Dang	Prof	343-2949	dtran		PHD	77	Syracuse	1987
Wilson, Erika G.	Prof	343-2936	ewilson		PHD	79	S Calif	1968
Carrington, Samantha	Assoc	343-2946	scarrin		PHD	85	Ca-SnBarb	1986
Combs, Kathryn L.	Assoc	343-2946	kcombs		PHD	88	Minnesota	1986
Finney, Miles	Assoc	343-2937	mfinney		PHD	92	Houston	1991
Hsieh, Edward T.	Assoc	343-2939	ehsieh		PHD	88	Houston	1989
Mohanty, Madhu	Assoc	343-2935	mmahont		PHD	90	Wi-Milwa	1990
Pulchritudoff, Nikolai	Assoc	343-2943	npulchr		PHD	71	Ca-Davis	1972
Vaidya, Ashish K.	Assoc	343-2980	avaidya		PHD	90	Ca-Davis	1991
Yoon, Mann	Assoc	343-2936	myoon		PHD	91	Illinois	1991
Chen, Li Hseuh	Asst	343-2934			PHD	98	Michigan	1998

Calif State Univ, Northridge Northridge, CA 91330-8245 (818) 885-2462 csun.edu
Department of Economics Sch of Bus Adm & Econ Fax=885-4903 Lucy Larson

Name	Rank	Phone	Email	Field	Degree	Yr	School	Year
Hosek, William R.	Dean	677-2455	william.hosek		PHD	67	Ca-SnBarb	1988
Gifford, Adam Jr.	C-Pr	677-2462	adam.gifford		PHD	72	Ca-SnDgo	1975
Anderson, Gary M.	Prof	677-2462	gary.anderson	GLTR	PHD	87	GeoMason	1987
Blake, Daniel R.	Prof	677-2462	daniel.blake		PHD	71	Oregon	1971
Brown, William W.	Prof	677-2462	william.brown		MA	66	UCLA	1975
Johnson, Ivan C.	Prof	677-2462	ivan.johnson		PHD	71	W Ontario	1973
Krol, Robert	Prof	677-2462	robert.krol	FGT	PHD	82	S Illinois	1983
Lowenberg, Tony	Prof	677-2462	tony.lowenberg	GH	PHD	84	Simon Fr	1984
Roberts, William W.	Prof	677-2462	william.roberts		PHD	74	Ca-SnDgo	1973
Saft, Lester F.	Prof	677-2462	lester.saft		PHD	76	UCLA	1971
Chapman, Kenneth S.	Assoc	677-2462	kenneth.chapman	IG	PHD	86	Minnesota	1991
Evans, Keith D.	Assoc	677-2462	keith.evans		PHD	71	U Wash	1971
Ng, Kenneth	Assoc	677-2462	kenneth.ng	N	PHD	88	Rochester	1986
Svorny, Shirley V.	Assoc	677-2462	shirley.svorny	IG	PHD	79	UCLA	1978
Yu, Ben T.	Assoc	677-2462	ben.yu		PHD	78	U Wash	1984
Halcoussis, Dennis	Asst	677-2462	dennis.halcous+	C	PHD	92	Penn	1991
Marcal, Leah	Asst	677-4245	leah.marcal		PHD	96	Wisconsin	1996
Nadenichek, Jon	Asst	677-4571	jon.nadenichek		PHD	96	Rochester	1996
Tchakerian, Viken	Asst	677-2434	viken.tchakerian	N	PHD	91	UCLA	1991
Virts, Nancy L.	Asst	677-2434	nancy.virts	N	PHD	85	UCLA	1985

Calif State Univ, Sacramento Sacramento, CA 95819-6082 (916) 278-6223 csus.edu
Department of Economics Sch Social Sci & Int Ds Fax=278-5768 Nancy L. Carrillo

Name	Rank	Phone	Email	Field	Degree	Yr	School	Year
Sheley, Joseph	Dean	278-6504	sheleyj					
Lund, Peter D.	C-Pr	278-6223	pblund		PHD	67	Berkeley	1970
Calandri, Kevin	Prof	278-6131	calandrikv		PHD	85	Ca-Davis	1986
Gambles, Glenn C.	Prof	278-6731			PHD	70	Maryland	1969
Gutowsky, Albert R.	Prof	278-5588	arg		PHD	65	Oregon	1967
Henry, John F.	Prof	278-6193	henryjf		PHD	74	McGill	1970
Kerby, William C.	Prof	278-7112	kerbywc		PHD	71	Oregon	1967

Kerby, William C.: Director, Economic Education Center

McGowan, Susan Associate Dean	Prof	278-6504	susan.mcgowan	PHD	77	Ca-Davis	1974
Polkinghorn, Bette A.	Prof	278-7080	bapolkinghorn	PHD	72	Ca-Davis	1971
Scheel, Daniel Curtis	Prof	278-6919	dcs	PHD	70	Oregon	1969
Sexton, Terri A.	Prof	278-6484	sextont	PHD	81	Minnesota	1987
Yang, Yung Y.	Prof	278-6264	yangyy	PHD	74	Oregon	1974
Dube, Smile W.	Assoc	278-7519	dubes	PHD	89	Tx-Austin	1989
Quade, Ane M.	Assoc	278-7062		PHD	88	Illinois	1989

Calif St U, San Bernardino — S Bernardino, CA 92407-2397 (909) 880-5511 — csusb.edu
Department of Economics — Sch of Soc & Behave Sci Fax=880-7025 — Mary Schmidt

Conley, John	Dean	880-5500	jconley	SocS	PHD		Mich St	1977
Toruno, Mayo C.	C-Pr	880-5517	mtoruno	B	PHD	83	Ca-Rivers	1983
Asheghian, Par	Prof	880-5499	pasheghi	F	PHD	80	Geo St	1991
Charkins, Ralph James	Prof	880-5518	rcharkin	A	PHD	70	N Carol	1976
Moss, Richard L.	Prof	880-5513	moss	A	PHD	73	New Mex	1973
Pierce, Thomas J.	Prof	880-5515	tpierce	E	PHD	76	Notre Dm	1976
Rose, Nancy E.	Prof	880-5516	nrose	IN	PHD	85	MIT	1985
Konyar, Kazim	Assoc	880-5514	kkonyar	CQ	PHD	85	Ca-Rivers	1991
Nilsson, Eric A.	Assoc	880-5564	enilsson	FJ	PHD	89	Mass	1989
Rodriguez, Carolyn	Asst	880-7315	cbrod	E	PHD	95	Ca-Rivers	1995

Calif State U - San Marcos — San Marcos, CA 92069-1477 (760) 750-4152 — csusm.edu
Department of Economics — Col of Arts & Sciences Fax=750-4111 — Ksenija Jaksic

Rocha, Victor	Dean	750-4200	vrocha	BioS	PHD	70		
Rider, Robert L.	C-Ac	750-4140	rrider	CDHK	PHD	89	S Calif	1992
Arnold, Roger A.	Prof	750-4077	rarnold		PHD	79	Va Tech	
Brown, Robert W.	Asst	750-4176	rbrown	GIKH	PHD	91	Ca-SnBarb	1997
Ghiara, Ranjetta	Asst	750-4176	ghiara		PHD	94	Ca-Rivers	1994

Calif State U, Stanislaus — Turlock, CA 95382 (209) 667-3181 — stan.csustan.edu
Department of Economics — Col Arts, Letters & Sci Fax=667-3588 — Heidi Lofgren

Erickson, Edward C.	C-Pr	633-3338		PHD	70	S Calif	1970
Crist, William D.	Prof	667-3500	crist@toto.	PHD	72	Nebraska	1969
Lee, Albert Yin-Po	Emer	667-3339	aylee@koko.	PHD	70	S Illinois	1970
Renning, H. Dieter	Emer	667-3327		DR	61	Freiburg	1970
Jasek-Rysdahl, Kelvin	Asst	667-3182	kjasekry@toto.	PHD	96	Colo St	1996
Peterson, Elaine J.	Asst	667-3327	epeterso@toto.	PHD	96	Wisconsin	1996

Calvin College — Grand Rapids, MI 49546 (616) 957-7191 — calvin.edu
Dept of Economics & Business — Division of Social Sci Fax=957-6501 — Jen Candler

Roberts, Frank C.	Dean	957-6203	roberfr	PHD	73	Vanderbilt	1965
Hoksbergen, Roland G.	C-Pr	957-6188	hoksro	PHD	86	Notre Dm	1983
Monsma, George N. Jr.	Prof	957-6191	gmonsma	PHD	69	Princeton	1969
Tiemstra, John P.	Prof	957-6192	tmst	PHD	75	MIT	1975
Van Der Heide, Evert M.	Prof	957-6099	evheide	PHD	82	Wayne St	1982
Schaefer, Kurt C.	Assoc	957-6368	schk	PHD	84	Michigan	1987
DeVries, Rick	Asst	957-6247	redevrie	ABD	95	Notre Dm	1995
Vander Linde, Scott H.	Asst	957-6477	udls	PHD	89	Notre Dm	

Cameron University — Lawton, OK 73505-6377 (580) 581-2267 — cameron.edu
Economics Faculty — Department of Business Fax=581-2253

Amyx, Jack F.	AcDn	581-2267	Atg	EDD	72	Okla St	1964
Courington, John M.	Prof	581-2266		PHD	87	Okla St	1979
Horner, James	Prof	581-2269		PHD	85	Tx-Dallas	1976
Sukar, Abdul Hamid	Assoc	581-2845		PHD	89	Tx Tech	1987

Campbell University — Buies Creek, NC 27506 (910) 893-1390
Dept Bus Adm & Econ Box218 — Lundy-Fetterman Sch Bus Fax=893-1424 — Sandra McLeod
phone 893-1383

Folwell, Thomas H. Jr.	Dean	Ext 1380	MA		Duke	1963
Mostashari, Shahriar	C-Pr	Ext-1390	PHD	78	N Car St	1982
Cordato,	Prof		PHD		GeoMason	1993
Hsiao, Yu-Mong	Prof		PHD	85	N Car St	1984
Norwood, Dwight Lamar	Assoc		PHD	74	Arkansas	1973
Sikes, Ellen	Assoc		MS		N Carol	1966
Cwik,	Asst		ABD		Auburn	1998
Paleisek,	Inst		PHD		GeoMason	1993
Varma, Umesh C.	Inst		MS		Jackson	1988

Canisius College — Buffalo, NY 14208-1098 (716) 888-2670 — canisius.edu
Dept of Economics & Finance — Wehle Sch of Business Fax=888-2525 — Karen Akmenia

Name	Rank	Phone	Email	Field	Degree	Yr	School	Year
Shick, Richard A.	Dean	888-2160	shick	Fnce	PHD	73	SUNY-Buf	1978
Palumbo, George M.	C-Pr	888-2667	palumbo		PHD	77	Syracuse	1978
Hutton, Patricia A.	Prof	888-2673	hutton		PHD	80	Wisconsin	1981
Wilson, F. Scott	Prof	888-2674	wilson		PHD	76	Minnesota	1977
Lichtenstein, Larry	Assoc	888-2677	lichten		PHD	81	SUNY-Bin	1981
Zaporowski, Mark P.	Assoc	888-2679	zaporowsk		PHD	85	SUNY-Alb	1983
Eisenhauer, Joseph G.	Asst	888-2676	eisenhauer		PHD	91	SUNY-Buf	1986

Capital University — Columbus, OH 43209-2394 (614) 236-6595 — capital.edu
Dept of Business & Economics — College of Arts & Sci Fax=236-6596

Name	Rank	Phone	Email	Field	Degree	Yr	School	Year
McGary, Daina	Dean	236-6204			PHD		Union Gr	1979
Mittler, Dale	C-Pr	236-6595			MBA		Capital	1981
Baker, Stephen A.	Prof	236-6136			PHD	82	York UK	1987
Lawson, Robert	Asst	236-6138			PHD		Fla St	1996

Carleton College — Northfield, MN 55057 (507) 646-4109 — carleton.edu
Economics Faculty — Department of Economics Fax=646-4044 — Susan Quay

Name	Rank	Phone	Email	Field	Degree	Yr	School	Year
Hemesath, Michael	C-Ac	646-4105	mhemesat	AFP	PHD	88	Harvard	1989
Bierman, H. Scott	Prof	646-4108	sbierman	DHL	PHD	85	Virginia	1982
Lamson, George H.	Prof	646-4107	glamson	EF	PHD	71	Nrthwstrn	1969
Wadsworth W. Williams Professor of Economics								
Lewis, Stephen R. Jr.	Prof	646-4305		FO	PHD	63	Stanford	1987
President								
Paas, Martha W.	Prof	646-4103	mpaas	BNO	PHD	79	Bryn Mawr	1975
Strand, Stephen H.	Prof	646-4104	sstrand	DL	PHD	76	Vanderbilt	1981
Raymond Plank Professor of Economics								
Kanazawa, Mark T.	Assoc	646-4106	mkanazaw	DKNQ	PHD	87	Stanford	1985
Gibbons, Donna M.	Asst	646-5239	dgibbons	DOR	PHD	95	Brown	1993
Wahl, Jenny Bourne	Asst	646-4007	jwahl	JKN	PHD	86	Chicago	1998

Carnegie Mellon University — Pittsburgh, PA 15213-3890 (412) 268-2294 — andrew.cmu.edu
Department of Economics — Col of Human & Soc Sci Fax=268-7357 — Beverly M. Jones 268-3719
Homepage: http://bighurt.gsia.cmu.edu/economics/contents.htm

Name	Rank	Phone	Email	Field	Degree	Yr	School	Year
Stearns, Peter N.	Dean			Hst	PHD	63	Harvard	1991
Spear, Stephen E.	H-Pr	268-8831	ss1f		PHD	82	Penn	1982
Epple, Dennis N.	Prof	578-2289			PHD	74	Princeton	1974
Klepper, Steven I.	Prof	268-3235			PHD	75	Cornell	1980
Kydland, Finn	Prof				PHD	73	Car Mellon	1977
Lave, Lester B.	Prof	268-8837			PHD	63	Harvard	1963
James H. Higgins Professor of Economics								
McCallum, Bennett T.	Prof	268-2347			PHD	69	Rice	1981
H. J. Heinz Professor of Economics								
Meltzer, Allan H.	Prof	268-2283			PHD	58	UCLA	1957
John M. Olin University Professor of Political Economy and Public Policy								
Poole, Keith T.	Prof				PHD	78	Rochester	1982
Spatt, Chester S.	Prof	268-8834			PHD	79	Penn	1979
Srivastava, Sanjay	Prof				PHD	82	MIT	1982
Miller, Robert A.	Assoc	268-3701			PHD	82	Chicago	1982
Seppi, Duane J.	Assoc				PHD	88	Chicago	1986
Shaw, Kathryn L.	Assoc	268-7586			PHD	81	Harvard	1981
Sowell, Fallaw B.	Assoc	268-3697			PHD	86	Duke	1988
Zin, Stanley E.	Assoc				PHD	87	Toronto	1988
Citanna, Alessandro	Asst				PHD	95	Penn	1996
Parlour, Christine	Asst				PHD	95	Queen's	1995
Rajan, Uday	Asst				PHD	95	Stanford	1995
Routledge, Bryan	Asst				PHD	95	Brit Colum	1995
Smith, Anthony A.	Asst				PHD	91	Duke	1992
Tallarini, Thomas	Asst				PHD	95	Chicago	1995
Telmer, Chris I.	Asst				PHD	92	Queen's	1992
Thomas, Julia	Asst							
Wang, Cheng	Asst				PHD	94	W Ontario	1994
Yaron, Amir	Asst				PHD	94	Chicago	1994
Zhang, Harold H.	Asst				PHD	94	Duke	1994
Dalton, W. Robert	Adj				PHD	72	Missouri	1985
Quinlivan, Gary M.	Adj				PHD	83	SUNY-Alb	1989

Carroll College — Waukesha, WI 53186 (414) 547-1211 — carroll1.cc.edu
Dept of Business & Economics — Col of Arts & Sciences Fax=524-7139
Did Not Respond--1997-98 Listing

Name	Rank	Phone	Email	Field	Degree	Yr	School	Year
Moody, Merlene A.	C-Pr	514-7160	mmoody	Mgt	MBA	78	W Mich	1992
Kader, Ahmad A.	Prof	524-7173			PHD	74	W Virginia	1974
Debrecht, Dennis M.	Asst	524-7163			PHD	81	Iowa	1984

Carson-Newman College — Jefferson Cy, TN 37760 (423) 471-3316 — cncacc.cn.edu
Dept of Business & Economics — Division of Business Fax=471-3599 — Crystle Bacon

Name	Rank	Phone	E-mail	Fields	Degree	Yr	Institution	Since
Russell, C. W. Jr.	Dean	471-3441	russell	Mgt	JD	69	Tennessee	1991
Taylor, Millicent M.	C-Ac	471-3433	taylorm	DFCE	PHD	85	Tennessee	8-95
Ahlseen, Mark J.	Assoc	471-4803	ahlseen	DHJL	PHD	86	Tx A&M	1999

Carthage College — Kenosha, WI 53140-1994 (414) 551-5831 — cns.carthage.edu
Economics Faculty — Department of Economics Fax=551-6208 — Sandy Fredericks

Name	Rank	Phone	E-mail	Fields	Degree	Yr	Institution	Since
Schlack, Robert F.	C-Pr	551-5831	rfs	FPRC	PHD	77	Wayne St	1975
Maltsev, Yuri N.	Assoc	551-5880	yuri	DFJP	PHD	80	Inst Labor	1991
McClintock, Brent	Assoc	551-5852	btm	EFG	PHD	90	Colo St	1991

Case Western Reserve Univ — Cleveland, OH 44106-7206 (216) 368-2970 — po.cwru.edu
Economics Department — Weatherhead Sch of Mgt Fax=368-5039 — Lenora Mitchell

Name	Rank	Phone	E-mail	Fields	Degree	Yr	Institution	Since
Cameron, Kim S.	Dean	368-2046	ksc6	Mgt	PHD	78	Yale	1998
Peirce, William S.	C-Pr	368-4131	wsp	HOQ	PHD	66	Princeton	1966
Carlsson, Bo A.	Prof	368-4112	bxc4	DFMO	PHD	72	Stanford	1984
William E. Umstattd Professor of Industrial Economics; Assoc Dean								
Erdilek, Asim	Prof	368-4110	axe3	F	PHD	72	Harvard	1971
Fogarty, Michael S.	Prof	368-5535	msf3	RO	PHD	75	Pittsburgh	1986
Rosegger, Gerhard	Emer	368-4295	gxr2	OFND	DIUR	53	Austria	1965
Frank Tracy Carlton Professor Emeritus of Economics								
Shatten, Richard	Prof	368-5535	rxs90	HR	MBA	80	Harvard	1997
Professor for the Practice of Public Policy & Mgt; Director, Center Regional								
Baird, Robert N.	Assoc	368-4185	rnb	A	PHD	65	Kentucky	1965
University Marshal								
Bogart, William T.	Assoc	368-4296	wtb	HRDA	PHD	90	Princeton	1990
Dor, Avi	Assoc	368-0208	axd9	I	PHD	86	CUNY	1995
John R. Mannix Blue Cross & Blue Shield Professor of Health Care Economics								
Dubin, Robin A.	Assoc	368-3981	rad4	RCD	PHD	82	J Hopkins	1988
Helper, Susan	Assoc	368-5541	sxh23	ONM	PHD	87	Harvard	1990
Mudambi, Ram	Assoc	368-8845	rxm76	CLM	PHD	85	Cornell	1998
Rebitzer, James B.	Assoc	368-5537	jbr	J	PHD	85	Mass	1997
Cooper, David J.	Asst	368-1818		CD	PHD	92	Princeton	1999
Hanchate, Amresh	Asst	368-2184	adh2	OQDC	PHD	92	Wisconsin	1992
Leete, Laura	Asst	368-5870	lbl2	IJ	PHD	92	Harvard	1991
Slamim, Robert L.	Asst	368-5811	rls18	CD	PHD	95	Duke	1998

Catawba College — Salisbury, NC 28144-2488 (704) 637-4405 — catawba.edu
Economic Faculty — Ketner School of Bus Fax=637-4422 — Dorothy Earle
Did Not Respond--1997-98 Listing

Name	Rank	Phone	E-mail	Fields	Degree	Yr	Institution	Since
Carter, J. Alvin	C-Ac	637-4406		Mgt	MBA		Geo St	1968
Tseng, S. C.	Prof	637-4407			PHD	72	Oklahoma	

Catholic Univ of America — Washington, DC 20064 (202) 319-5236 — cua.edu
Dept of Economics & Business — Sch of Arts & Sciences Fax=319-4426 — Ms. Brenda Nichols
Did Not Respond--1997-98 Listing

Name	Rank	Phone	E-mail	Fields	Degree	Yr	Institution	Since
Suziedelis, Antanas	Dean	319-5115		Psy	PHD	57	Catholic	
Zampelli, Ernest M.	C-Ac	319-6683		DHQ	PHD	82	Maryland	9-85
Piedra, Alberto M.	Prof	319-5235		BNO	PHD			
Forbes, Kevin F.	Assoc	319-4794		DHLQ	PHD	82	Maryland	1983
Aguirre, Sophia	Asst	319-4957	aguirre	FG	PHD	92	Notre Dm	1993

Cedarville College — Cedarville, OH 45314-0601 (937) 766-7910 — cedarville.edu
Economic Faculty — Dept of Business Admin Fax=766-2760 — Susan Terkelsen

Name	Rank	Phone	E-mail	Fields	Degree	Yr	Institution	Since
Hazen, Marinus	C-Ac	766-7924	hazenm	Atg	PHD	97	Clev St	1983
Smith, Galen	Assoc	766-7923	smithg	ABFH	DMIN	98	Trinity	1981
Wheeler, Bert	Assoc	766-7714	wheelerb	AFOP	PHD	85	Tennessee	1992

Centenary College — Hackettstown, NJ 07840-9989 (908) Ext 2241 — centenarycollege.edu
Economics Faculty — Division of Business Fax=813-1984
phone 852-1400

Name	Rank	Phone	E-mail	Fields	Degree	Yr	Institution	Since
Quade, Robert	C-Ac	852-1400		Mktg	MBA	53	Iowa	8-86
Dunham, Heather	Prof		hdunham	ADEM	EDD	99	St Johns	8-82

Univ of Central Arkansas — Conway, AR 72035-0001 (501) 450-3109 — mail.uca.edu
Dept of Economics & Finance — College of Business Adm Fax=450-5302 — Barbara Hopp

Name	Rank	Phone	E-mail	Fields	Degree	Yr	Institution	Since
Horton, Joseph J.	Dean	450-3106			PHD	68	So Meth	7-96
Block, Walter	C-Pr				PHD	72	Columbia	9-97
Johnson, W. Clint	Prof				PHD	75	Tx Tech	1975
Cantrell, Pat	Assoc				PHD	83	So Meth	8-84
Kordsmeier, William F.	Assoc				PHD	86	Tx A&M	
Leonard, John	VAsst				PHD	81	Ca-SnBarb	9-98
McGarrity, Joseph	Asst				PHD	94	GeoMason	8-95
McLean, Roy	Asst				PHD	95	S Carol	9-97

Central Connecticut St Univ — New Britain, CT 06050-4010 (860) 832-2725 — ccsu.edu

Department of Economics — School of Arts & Sci Fax=832-2730

Name	Rank	Phone	E-mail	Field	Degree	Yr	School	Since
Higgins, June B.	Dean	832-2600	jhiggins	Psy	PHD	70	Rochester	1970
Pae, Ki-Tai	C-Pr	832-2725	pae		PHD	71	Conn	1971
Altieri, Paul L.	Prof	832-2735	altieri	E	PHD	76	Boston C	1975
Daigle, Ronald R.	Prof	832-2726	daigle	EG	PHD	75	Clark	1976
Kim, Ki Hoon	Prof	832-2727	kimk	FO	PHD	68	Conn	1967
Loughlin, James C.	Prof	832-2731	loughlin	DH	PHD	65	Clark	1968
Papathanasis, Anastasios	Prof	832-2733	papathanasis	LK	PHD	79	Ca-Davis	1984
Zottola, Armand J.	Prof	832-2732	zottola	JRT	PHD	70	Catholic	1970

Univ of Central Florida — Orlando, FL 32816-1400 (407) 823-3266 — bus.ucf.edu

Department of Economics — College of Business Adm Fax=823-3269 — Mrs. Frances Percival

Name	Rank	Phone	E-mail	Field	Degree	Yr	School	Since
Keon, Thomas L.	Dean	823-2181		Mgt	PHD	79	Mich St	8-97
Hofler, Richard A.	C-Pr	823-2606	richard.hofler	CIJ	PHD	82	N Carol	1989
McHone, W. Warren	Prof	823-2629	warren.mchone	R	PHD	80	Penn	1982
Rungeling, Brian S.	Prof	275-2592	brian.rungeling	J	PHD	69	Kentucky	1981
Braun, Bradley M.	Assoc	823-2343	brad.braun	D	PHD	86	Tulane	1986
Day, A. Edward	Assoc	823-2620	edward.day	D	PHD	76	Purdue	1983
Gibbs, W. Ernest	Assoc	823-5818	ernst.gibbs	D	PHD	87	Rutgers	1987
Hosni, Djehane	Assoc	823-2069	djehane.hosni	O	PHD	78	Arkansas	1977
Martin, Thomas L.	Assoc	823-5681	thomas.martin	B	PHD	81	Rice	1983
Pennington, Robert L.	Assoc	823-2886	robert.penning+	D	PHD	77	Tx A&M	1983
Soskin, Mark D.	Assoc	823-3266	mark.soskin	C	PHD	79	Penn St	1988
White, Kenneth R.	Assoc	823-5656	kenneth.white	C	PHD	71	Oklahoma	1968
Xander, James A.	Assoc	823-5657	james.xander	D	PHD	74	Georgia	1969
Agarwal, Rajshree	Asst	823-5570		L	PHD	94	SUNY-Buf	1995
Bisakha, Sen	Asst				PHD			
Co, Catherine	Asst	823-3763	catherine.co		PHD	95	Rutgers	1996
Elston, Julie Ann	Asst	823-2078			PHD			
Gallet, Craig	Asst	823-3720	craig.gallet	CDL	PHD	94	Iowa St	1996
Lee, Junsoo	Asst	823-2070		E	PHD	91	Mich St	
List, John	Asst	823-3719	john.list		PHD	96	Wyoming	1996
Strazicich, Mark	VAsst	823-5628			PHD			
Tomlin, KaSaundra	Asst	823-2601			PHD			
Euzent, Patricia	Inst	823-6075			MA		Clemson	1991
Moore, Barbara	Inst	823-5256			MAAE			
Zembrowski-Chanmala, Adriana	VInst				MAAE			

Central College of Iowa — Pella, IA 50219 (515) — central.edu

Economics Faculty — Dept Econ, Atg & Mgt Fax=

Name	Rank	Phone	E-mail	Field	Degree	Yr	School	Since
Iverson, Thomas	Prov	628-5175	iversont	Math	PHD	75	Claremont	1976
Vruwink, Carol J.	C-Ac	628-5258	vruwinkc		MS	82	Drake	1979
Glendening, Richard N.	Prof	628-5120	glendeningr	EFHO	PHD	93	Iowa St	1966
Wallace, Suzanne	Assoc	628-5318	wallaces	DJE	PHD	91	Georgia	1991

Central Michigan University — Mt. Pleasant, MI 48859-2372 (517) 774-3870 — cmich.edu

Department of Economics — College of Business Adm Fax=774-2040 — Debbie Clearwater

Name	Rank	Phone	E-mail	Field	Degree	Yr	School	Since
Arndt, Terry L.	Dean	774-7412	t.arndt	Atg	PHD	73	Arkansas	1993
Shields, Michael P.	C-Pr	774-6460	michael.p.shi+		PHD	75	Utah	1993
Basu, Bharati	Prof	774-3730	b.basu	FODJ	PHD	82	Rochester	1990
Cecen, A. Aydin	Prof	774-3677	a.cecen		PHD	86	Indiana	1987
Chakraborty, Debasish	Prof	774-3678	d.chakraborty		PHD	87	Pittsburgh	1988
Falls, Gregory A.	Prof	774-3655	g.falls		PHD	82	Purdue	1981
Natke, Paul A.	Prof	774-3653	p.natke		PHD	82	Notre Dm	1981
Zuberi, Habib A.	Prof	774-3372	h.zuberi		PHD	71	S Illinois	1971
Brunner, Lawrence P.	Assoc	774-3638	l.brunner		PHD	81	J Hopkins	1982
Clemmer, Richard B.	Assoc	774-3908	r.clemmer		PHD	81	Chicago	1982
Hill, James Richard	Assoc	774-3706	j.r.hill		PHD	80	Kentucky	1981
Barbour, G. Jeffrey	Asst	774-3380	j.barbour		PHD	73	Fla St	1971
Irwin, James R.	Asst	774-3697	j.irwin		PHD	86	Rochester	1989
McDevitt, Catherine L.	Asst	774-3648	c.mcdevitt		PHD	86	Rochester	1989
Zimmer, Basil G.	Asst	774-3600	b.zimmer		PHD	72	Rutgers	1969

Central Missouri State Univ — Warrensburg, MO 64093-5074 (660) 543-4246 — cmsu1.cmsu.edu

Dept of Economics & Finance — Harmon College Bus Adm Fax=543-8465 — Mrs. Nancy Dyer

Name	Rank	Phone	E-mail	Field	Degree	Yr	School	Since
Shaffer, Paul	Dean	543-4560	pshaffer	Mgt	PHD	74	Oklahoma	1986
Engelmann, Paul H.	C-Pr	543-4246	engelmann		PHD	76	Okla St	1972
Brock, Baird A.	Prof	543-8614	brock@macc.		PHD	77	Arkansas	1969
Karscig, Mark P.	Prof	543-4817	karscig		PHD	87	Pittsburgh	1981
Wilson, George W.	Prof	543-8597	gwilson		PHD	76	Okla St	1972
Andrews, Kim	Assoc	543-8623	andrews		PHD	94	Okla St	1990
Chambers, Catherine M.	Assoc	543-8605	chambers		PHD	90	Kentucky	1990
Chambers, Paul	Assoc	543-8610	pchambers		PHD	89	Kentucky	1990
Swanson, James A.	Assoc	543-8580	swanson		PHD	87	Wash St	1986
Kugler, Penny L.	Inst	543-8570	kugler		MA	88	Cen Mo St	1988

Univ of Central Oklahoma — Edmond, OK 73034-5209 (405) 974-5843 — ucok.edu
Department of Economics — College of Business Adm Fax=974-3853 — Ofelia Tovar
phone: 974-2000

Name	Rank	Phone	E-mail	Fields	Degree	Yr	School	Since
Harris, David J.	Dean	341-2980	dharris	Law	JD	86	Willamette	8-92
Metzger, Michael R.	C-Pr	341-2980	mmetzger	DIL	PHD	78	Stanford	1991
Caldwell, Jean	Prof	341-2980	jcaldwell	AN	EDD	82	N Illinois	1981
Maxwell, Don P.	Prof	341-2980	dmaxwell	ADEH	PHD	82	Okla St	1981
Shaaf, Mohammad	Prof	341-2980	mshaaf	BDEG	PHD	82	Tx Tech	1980
De los Santos, Tomas	Assoc	341-2980	tdelossantos	AEFO	PHD	88	Clark	1991
Smith, Paula	Assoc	Ext 2812	psmith	IJ	PHD	84	Okla St	1987
Johnson, Joseph T.	Asst	341-2980	jjohnson	AMR	PHD	80	Chicago	1992

Central State Univ-Ohio — Wilberforce, OH 45384 (937) 376-6421 — cesvax.ces.edu
Dept of Financial Systems — Col Business & Industry Fax=376-6206

Name	Rank	Phone	E-mail	Fields	Degree	Yr	School	Since
Showell, Charles H. Jr.	Dean	376-6441		BAdm	PHD	75	Ohio St	9-88
Vafaie, Massie S.	C-As	376-6421			PHD	79	Cincinnati	1991
Iwomi, Peter O.	Assoc	376-6446			EDD		Cincinnati	1981

Central Washington Univ — Ellensburg, WA 98926-7486 (509) 963-2664 — cwu.edu
Department of Economics — Sch of Business & Econ Fax=963-1992 — Barbara Cook

Name	Rank	Phone	E-mail	Fields	Degree	Yr	School	Since
Savoian, Roy T.	Dean	963-1955			PHD	79	Ca-SnBarb	1998
Saunders, Peter J.	C-Pr	963-1266		EHQ	PHD	81	Colorado	1988
Carbaugh, Robert John	Prof	963-3443		AFEK	PHD	74	Colo St	1985
Cocheba, Donald John	Prof	963-2411		QR	PHD	71	Wash St	1970
Distinguished Professor, Research (1992)								
Mack, Richard Stanley	Prof	963-2663		RQP	PHD	72	Colo St	1972
Distinguished Professor, Research (1988)								
Hedrick, David W.	Assoc	963-2664		AIO	PHD	84	Oregon	1987
Ghosh, Koushik	Asst	963-1014			PHD		Wash St	
Elkins, Ron	Inst	963-1043						1996

Centre College — Danville, KY 40422-1394 (606) 238-5231 — centre.edu
Department of Economics — Div of Social Studies Fax=236-7925 — Patsy McAfee

Name	Rank	Phone	E-mail	Fields	Degree	Yr	School	Since
Johnson, Bruce K.	C-Ac	238-5242	johnsonb	ADL	PHD	85	Virginia	1987
James Graham Brown Associate Professor of Economics								
Brownlee, Robert J.	Prof	238-5245	brownlee	AER	PHD	73	Syracuse	1978
Campbell, Charles W. III	Prof	238-5239	campbelc	AEHF	PHD	66	Virginia	1968
Blazer Professor of Economics								
Martin, Robert E.	Prof	238-5260	bmart	CD	PHD	79	So Meth	1996
Ewing T. Boles Professor of Economics								
Anderson, David A.	Assoc	238-5260	david	ACHK	PHD	92	Duke	1992
Winrich, J. Steven	Assoc	238-5237	winrich	APN	PHD	78	Kentucky	1981

Chadron State College — Chadron, NE 69337-2690 (308) 432-6290
Department Business & Econ — Sch Bus & Applied Sci Fax=432-6430 — Debby McDowell

Name	Rank	Phone	E-mail	Fields	Degree	Yr	School	Since
Crouse, Margaret	Dean	432-6365		HEc	PHD	84	Okla St	1979
Anderson, Tim	C-Pr	432-6290			EDD		Nebraska	1977
Afiat, Medhi	Prof	432-6290		MER	PHD	85	Kansas St	1985
Burke, Ronald L.	Prof	432-6290		MQE	PHD	70	Minnesota	1987

Chaminade University — Honolulu, HI 96816-1578 (808) 735-6744 — chaminade.edu
Department of Economics — College of Business Fax=735-4734 — James Moses

Name	Rank	Phone	E-mail	Fields	Degree	Yr	School	Since
Steelquist, John A.	Dean	739-4600	steelq	Mgt	PHD	82	Tx A&M	1-84
Klauser, Jack E.	Prof	735-4711			PHD	77	NYU	1970
Street, Barbara P.	Prof	377-5865		ACEI	PHD	86	Virginia	1981
Director, Master of Business Adminstration Program								

Chapman University — Orange, CA 92866 (714) 997-6684 — nexus.chapman.edu
Economics Faculty — Argyros Sch of Bus &Eco Fax=532-6081 — Iris Fallon, Office Mgr

Name	Rank	Phone	E-mail	Fields	Degree	Yr	School	Since
McDowell, Richard L.	Dean	997-6684	mcdowell	Adm	PHD	74	Tufts	1991
Adibi, Esmael	Prof	997-6693	adibi	AEFC	PHD	80	Claremont	1978
Director, A. Gary Anderson Center for Economic Research; Anderson Chair								
Booth, Donald R.	Prof	997-6804	booth	AD	PHD	70	UCLA	1959
Doti, James L.	Prof	997-6611	doti	AEC	PHD	76	Chicago	1974
President of the University								
Pierson, Lynne M.	Prof	997-6805	pierson	NE	PHD	78	Ca-Rivers	1972
Sfeir, Raymond	Assoc	997-6551	sfeir	AC	PHD	82	Ca-SnBarb	1985
Shabahang, Homa		997-6888	shabahan	F	PHD	83	Oklahoma	1991
Associate Dean								

College of Charleston	Charleston, SC	29424-0001 (843)						cofc.edu
Dept of Economics & Finance	Sch of Business & Econ	Fax=953-5697					Ms. Barbara Green	
Condon, Clarence M. III	Dean	953-5627	condonc		PHD	78	S Carol	1980
Morgan, J. Michael	C-Pr	953-8100	morganm		PHD	77	S Carol	1967
Clary, Betsy Jane	Prof	953-8107	claryb		PHD	81	Miss	1984
Jursa, Paul E.	Assoc	953-7836	jursap		PHD	72	Tx-Austin	1976
Flaherty, E. E.	VAsst	953-8100	flahertye		PHD	96	Fla St	1999
Hefner, Frank L.	Asst	953-8100	hefnerf		PHD	88	Kansas	1995
Snyder, Marcia	Inst	953-8100	snyderm		MA	95	London	1999

Cheyney U of Pennsylvania	Cheyney, PA	19319	(610) 399-2368					
Economics Faculty	Dept of Business Adm	Fax=399-2070					Idella Boone 399-2368	
Did Not Respond Again--1995-96 Listing								
Williams, Edward E.	C-Pr	399-2430		Mgt	PHD	75	Drexel	1972
Sawyer, Juliet	Assoc	399-2382						
Songha, W. A.	Assoc	399-2433						
Chowdhury, Ma Monayem	Asst	399-2022			PHD	78	Temple	

University of Chicago	Chicago, IL	60637-1561	(773) 702-9016					chicago.edu
Economics Faculty	Department of Economics	Fax=702-8490					Marda J. Gross; Julie Less	
Lucas, Robert E. Jr.	D-Pr	702-8179			PHD	64	Chicago	1974
John Dewey Distinguished Service Professor; 1995 Nobel Prize								
Scheinkman, Jose	C-Pr	702-8192			PHD	74	Rochester	1973
Alvin H. Baum Professor								
Becker, Gary S.	Prof	702-8168			PHD	55	Chicago	1970
Bowman, Mary Jean	Emer	702-8161			PHD	38	Harvard	1958
Chiappori, Pierre Andre	Prof				PHD	81	Paris	1997
Fogel, Robert W.	Prof	702-7709			PHD	63	J Hopkins	1981
Charles R. Walgreen Professor/Director, Center for Population Economics								
Friedman, Milton	Emer				PHD	46	Columbia	1946
Paul Snowden Russell Distinguished Service Professor Emeritus								
Galenson, David W.	Prof	702-8258			PHD	79	Harvard	1978
Hansen, Lars Peter	Prof	702-8170			PHD	78	Minnesota	1982
Homer J. Livingston Professor								
Harberger, Arnold C.	Emer				PHD	50	Chicago	1953
Gustavus F. and Ann M. Swift Distinguished Service Professor								
Heckman, James J.	Prof	702-0634			PHD	71	Princeton	1973
Henry Schultz Professor of Economics & Soc Sciences								
Johnson, D. Gale	Emer	702-8251			PHD	45	Iowa St	1944
Eliakim Hastings Moore Distinguished Service Professor								
Prescott, Edward C.	Prof				PHD	67	Car Mellon	1998
Rosen, Sherwin	Prof	702-8166			PHD	66	Chicago	1977
Edwin A. and Betty L. Bergman Professor of Economis & Social Sciences								
Sjaastad, Larry A.	Prof	702-8172			PHD	61	Chicago	1965
Sonnenschein, Hugo F.	Prof				PHD	64	Purdue	
President of University								
Stokey, Nancy	Prof	702-0915			PHD	78	Harvard	1990
Frederick Henry Prince Professor								
Telser, Lester G.	Emer	702-8193		1-98	PHD	56	Chicago	1958
Tolley, George S.	Prof	702-8199			PHD	55	Chicago	1966
Townsend, Robert M.	Prof	702-8178			PHD	75	Minnesota	1985
Charles E. Merriam Professor								
Philipson, Tomas J.	Assoc	702-9128			PHD	89	Penn	1996
Weir, David R.	VAsoc				PHD	83	Stanford	1995
Alvarez, Fernando	Asst				PHD	94	Minnesota	1996
Aquirregabiria, Victor	Asst				PHD	95	Compluten	1999
Campbell, Jeffrey	Asst				PHD	95	Nrthwstrn	1999
Ghatak, Maintreesh	Asst				PHD	96	Harvard	1996
Heller, Dana	Asst				PHD	98	Stanford	1998
Kyriazidou, Ekaterina	Asst				PHD	95	Nrthwstrn	1995
Levitt, Steven D.	Asst				PHD	94	MIT	1997
Mulligan, Casey	Asst	702-9017			PHD	93	Chicago	1993
Perktold, Josef	Asst				PHD	95	UCLA	1995
Vissing-Jorgensen,	Asst				PHD		MIT	1998
Yorukoglu, Mehmet	Asst				PHD	96	Rochester	1996
Sanderson, Allen	SLect	702-7815			MA	70	Chicago	
Tsiang, Grace	SLect	702-3410			PHD	91	Chicago	1990

Chicago State University	Chicago, IL	60628-1598	(773) 995-2186					csu.edu
Dept Geog, Econ & Anthrop	Col of Arts & Sciences	Fax=995-2030					Janie Davis	
Lindsey, Rachel I.	Dean	995-2105		Psyc	PHD	84	Chicago	1976
Bouman, Mark	C-Pr	995-2187	m-bouman		PHD	84	Minnesota	1984
Leach, Elroy M.	Prof	995-2173			PHD	85	Il-Chicago	1985
Pingkarawat, Nampeang	Prof	995-2340	man-ing		PHD	83	Il-Chicago	1982
Johnson, Mark	Assoc	995-2373	ma-johnson		PHD	85	Stanford	1995

Christian Brothers Univ — Memphis, TN 38104-5581 (901) 321-3489 — cbu.edu
Dept of Economics & Finance — School of Business Fax=321-3566 — Ms. Carolyn Denegri

Name	Rank	Phone	Email	Field	Degree	Yr	School	Year
House, Ray S.	Dean	321-3316	rhouse	Mktg	PHD	66	Miss	1985
Brittingham, Robert L.	C-Pr	321-3489	rbrittin	AD	PHD	73	St Louis	1989
Papachristou, Patricia T.	Prof	321-3301	ppapachr	TI	MBA	79	Memphis	1980
Bails, Dale G.	Assoc	321-3564	dbails		PHD	78	S Dakota	1995
Kamery, Rob H.	Assoc	321-3414	rkamery	ABJ	MS	81	Arkansas	1987
Poper, Frank J.	Assoc	321-3549	fpoper		PHD		NYU	1995

Christopher Newport Univ — Newport News VA 23606-2988 (757) 594-7176 — cnu.edu
Dept Econ & Fnce & Real Est — Col of Bus & Sci & Tech Fax=594-7808 — Ms. Iris Price

Name	Rank	Phone	Email	Field	Degree	Yr	School	Year
Webb, George R.	Dean	594-7184	gwebb		PHD	64	Va Tech	1973
Park, Sang O.	C-Pr	594-7265	spark	DFOR	PHD	63	N Carol	1982
Booker, H. Marshall	Prof	594-7174	mbooker	AFMO	PHD	65	Virginia	1971
Colonna, Carl M.	Assoc	594-7144	ccolona	AEIR	MA		Old Dom	1970
Sen, Swapan	Assoc	594-7148	swap		PHD	91	Nebraska	1998
Winder, Robert C.	Assoc	594-7176	rwinder		PHD	81	Rutgers	1991
Zestos, George K.	Assoc	594-7067	gzestos	CFHO	PHD	91	Indiana	1993
Rahim, Niazur	Asst	594-7727	nrahim		PHD	94	Va Comm	1998
Vachris, Michelle A.	Asst	594-7719	mvachris	DFHK	PHD	92	GeoMason	1994

University of Cincinnati — Cincinnati, OH 45221-0371 (513) 556-2600 — uc.edu
Department of Economics — McMicken Col Arts & Sci Fax=556-2669 — Geri Kirchner

Name	Rank	Phone	Email	Field	Degree	Yr	School	Year
Caruso, Joseph A.	Dean	556-5860	joseph.caruso	Chem	PHD	67	Mich St	
Gallo, Joseph C.	H-Pr	556-2605	joseph.gallo	L	PHD	69	Missouri	1967
Berry, Charles A.	Prof	556-2624	charles.berry	O	PHD	68	Cincinnati	1961
Herman, E. Edward	Prof	556-2611	edward.herman	J	PHD	65	McGill	1966
Leftwich, Howard M. — Coordinator of Labor & Employment Relations Program	Prof	556-2615	howard.leftw+	J	PHD	65	Illinois	1964
Mayer, Wolfgang — David Sinton Professor	Prof	556-2618	wolfgang.mayer	FD	PHD	71	SUNY-Buf	1970
Vredeveld, George	Prof	556-2948	george.vrede+		PHD	73	Indiana	1977
Wellington, Donald C.	Prof	556-2607		D	PHD	66	Chicago	
Whitmore, Harland W. Jr.	Prof	556-2622	harland.whit+	E	PHD	69	Mich St	1967
Escoe, Gisela Meyer	Assoc	556-3023	gisela.escoe	O	PHD	91	Ohio St	1991
Goddard, Haynes C.	Assoc	556-2621	haynes.goddard	H	PHD	70	Indiana	
Kelton, Christina — Director of Graduate Studies	Assoc	556-0525	chris.kelton		PHD	79	Wisconsin	1996
Mills, Jeffrey A.	Assoc	556-2619	jeffrey.mills	C	PHD	89	Wash U	1992
Pal, Debashis	Assoc	556-2630	debashis.pal	L	PHD	90	Florida	1994
Powers, John A.	Assoc	556-2616	john.powers	C	PHD	66	Purdue	1965
Way, Philip K.	Assoc	556-2613	philip.way	J	PHD	86	Warwick	1985
Williams, Nicolas	Assoc	556-2390	nicolas.will+	J	PHD	89	Nrthwstrn	1990
Zandvakili, Sourushe	Assoc	556-2629	sourushe.zand+	J	PHD	87	Indiana	1987

The Citadel — Charleston, SC 29409-0215 (843) 953-5056 — citadel.edu
Economics Faculty — Dept of Business Adm Fax=953-6764 — Ms. Georgeann Pringle

Name	Rank	Phone	Email	Degree	Yr	School	Date
Bebensee, Mark A.	H-Ac	953-5056	bebenseem	PHD	77	Duke	8-77
Sparks, Donald L.	Prof	953-5159	sparksd	PHD	85	London	8-86
Silver, Stephen J.	Assoc	953-5163	silvers	PHD	83	Maryland	8-90
Woolsey, W. William	Assoc	953-5161	woolseyw	PHD	86	GeoMason	8-86

CUNY-Baruch College — New York, NY 10010 (212) 802-6350 — cunyvm.cuny.edu
Dept of Economics & Finance — Zicklin School of Bus Fax=802-6353 — Sylvia Clark/Allison Davis

Name	Rank	Phone	Field	Degree	Yr	School	Year
Lirtzman, Sidney I.	Dean	802-6550	Mgt	PHD	55	Columbia	1973
Wolf, Avner	C-Pr	802-6350		PHD	83	Columbia	
Gutmann, Peter M.	Prof	802-6366	EF	PHD	57	Harvard	1963
Joyce, Theodore	Prof	802-6964		PHD	85	CUNY	1986
Lustgarten, Steven	Prof	802-6420		PHD	71	UCLA	
Marty, Alvin L.	Prof	802-5726		PHD	55	Berkeley	1960
O'Neill, June E. — Director, Center for the Study of Business and Government	Prof			PHD	70	Columbia	1987
Ross, Howard N.	Prof	802-6365		PHD	64	Columbia	1964
Stone, Irving	Prof	802-6369		PHD	62	Columbia	1962
Su, Vincent	Prof	802-6364		PHD	70	Rutgers	1971
Kleinberg, Norman L.	Assoc	802-6368		PHD	77	MIT	
Lee, Jae Won	Assoc	802-6360		PHD	69	CUNY	1972
Weiss, Jeffrey H.	Assoc	802-6357		PHD	81	Wisconsin	1981
Huckins, Larry E.	Asst	802-6381		PHD	83	Chicago	1980
Ma, Barry K.	Asst	802-6386		PHD	86	Stanford	1989
Pasupathy, Meenakshi	Asst	802-6378		PHD	96	Wash U	1996
Tansey, Francis B.	Lect	802-6356		MBA	65	CUNY	1967

CUNY-Brooklyn College — Brooklyn, NY 11210-2889 (718) 951-5317 — cunyvm.cuny.edu
Department of Economics — College of Liberal Arts Fax=951-4867 — Alycen Bray

Name	Rank	Phone	Area	Degree	Yr	Institution	Year
Bowers, Patricia F.	C-Pr	951-5317	G	PHD	65	NYU	1964
Bell, Robert	Prof	951-5686	M	PHD	72	Brunel	1986
Cherry, Robert D.	Prof	951-5264	AJ	PHD	69	Kansas	1977
Friedman, Hershey	Prof	951-5119	M	PHD	77	CUNY	1986
Laibman, David	Prof	951-5317	AP	PHD	73	New Sch	1967
Lazarcik, Gregor	Prof	951-5376	O	PHD	60	Columbia	1985
Sardy, Hyman	Prof	951-5326	C	PHD	63	New Sch	1957
Arenberg, Yuri	Assoc	951-5245	D	PHD	86	NYU	1985
Fox, Jerrald Mark	Assoc	951-5569	J	PHD	92	Union	1988
Goldberg, Paul A.	Assoc	951-5101	HP	PHD	84	Columbia	1978
Klein, Yehuda L.	Assoc	951-5275	CDQ	PHD	85	Berkeley	1985
Zelcer, Moishe	Assoc	951-5245	G	PHD	91	Baruch	1992
Thorne, Emanuel D.	Asst	951-5548	A	PHD	94	Yale	1994
Uctum, Merih	Asst	951-5097		PHD	89	Queens	1996

CUNY-Lehman College — Bronx, NY 10468-1589 (718) 960-8297 — cunyvm.cuny.edu
Economics Faculty — Dept of Economics & Atg Fax=960-1173 — Kim Pierce

Name	Rank	Phone	Degree	Yr	Institution	Year
Shreiber, Chanoch	C-Pr	960-8297	PHD	73	Columbia	
Cirace, John	Prof	960-8388	PHD	75	Columbia	
Sharav, Itzhak	Prof	960-8388	PHD	71	CUNY	9-67
Kayaalp, Orhan	Assoc	960-8598	PHD	84	CUNY	1979
Alexanderson, Peter	Asst	960-8598	JD			
Chatha, Jaspal	Asst	960-8461	PHD	85	New Sch	
DiLiberto, Maryann	Asst	960-8461	PHD	84	Columbia	
Fields, Judith M.	Asst	960-8384	PHD	84	NYU	1984
Honig, Susan	Asst	960-8389	MS		Pace	
Kamen, Michele	Asst	960-8384	MBA		St Johns	
Kraus, James A.	Asst	960-8159	JD		Columbia	
Ratowsky, Henry	Asst	960-8507	PHD	76	CUNY	1988
Rios, Roberto J.	Asst	960-8461	PHD	87	Columbia	1979
Tauber, Linda	Asst	960-8389	MBA			
Chung, Kuk-Soo	Lect	960-8386	MA		Yale	
Rodriguez, Ada	Lect	960-8389	MBA			

CUNY-Hunter College — New York, NY 10021 (212) — cunyvm.cuny.edu
Department of Economics — Sch of Arts & Sciences Fax= — Gigi Banks/B. Webb-Taylor

Name	Rank	Phone	Email	Degree	Yr	Institution	Year
Cohen, Ann H.	Dean	772-5121		PHD			8-98
Honig, Marjorie	C-Pr	772-5400	mahhc	PHD	71	Columbia	
Agbeyegbe, Terence	Prof	772-5405		PHD	83	Essex	1994
Chernick, Howard	Prof	772-5400		PHD	76	Penn	1982
Randall, Laura	Prof	772-5430		PHD	62	Columbia	
Reimers, Cordella W.	Prof	772-5400		PHD	77	Columbia	1982
Shull, Bernard Jr.	Prof	772-5437		PHD	57	Wisconsin	1970
Filer, Randall K.	Assoc	772-5399		PHD	79	Princeton	1986
Golbo, Devra L.	Assoc	772-5408		PHD	79	NYU	1987
Goodspeed, Timothy J.	Assoc	772-5434		PHD	86	Maryland	9-94
McLaughlin, Kenneth J.	Assoc	772-5439		PHD	87	Chicago	9-94
George, Nashwa E.	Asst	772-5404		PHD	88	Baruch	9-85
Jaeger, David	Asst	772-5435		PHD	95	Michigan	9-97
Liveson, Avi	Asst	772-5394		LLM	75	NYU	9-86
Osborne, Theresa	Asst	772-5400		PHD	97	Princeton	9-97
Bergman, Lila	Lect	772-5436		MBA	79	Fordham	9-85

CUNY-Queens College — Flushing, NY 11367-0904 (718) 997-5440 — qc1.qc.edu
Department of Economics — School of Gen Studies Fax=997-5466 — Ms. Barbara Crohn
email @1=qcvaxa.acc.qc.edu @2=cunyvm.cuny.edu @3=qc.edu

Name	Rank	Phone	Email	Area	Degree	Yr	Institution	Year
Hill, M. Anne	C-Pr	997-5455	mah$econ	JC	PHD	80	Duke	1989
Edelstein, Michael	Prof	997-5440		NOF	PHD	70	Penn	1974
Edwards, Linda N.	Prof	997-5464		JC	PHD	71	Columbia	1971
Franklin, Raymond S.	Prof	997-3070		JBP	PHD	66	Berkeley	1966
Gram, Harvey H.	Prof	997-5448	har$econ	FCE	PHD	73	Wisconsin	1974
Kaufmann, Hugo M.	Prof	997-5449	kaufmann@1	FE	PHD	68	Columbia	1967
Levenson, Albert M.	Prof	997-5444	albert_leve+@3	DFC	PHD	59	Columbia	1961
Lipsey, Robert E.	Emer	997-5443	relqc@2	FC	PHD	61	Columbia	1967
Riskin, Carl A.	Prof	997-5454	riskin@1	POQ	PHD	69	Berkeley	1974
Roistacher, Elizabeth A.	Prof	997-5453	elizabeth_ro+@3	RH	PHD	72	Penn	1974
Tabb, William K.	Prof	997-5451	wta$econ	RO	PHD	68	Wisconsin	1971
Thurston, Thom B.	Prof	997-5457	tbt$econ	EC	PHD	70	Berkeley	1971
Devereux, John J.	Assoc	997-5446	jdevereu	DFO	PHD	89	Chicago	1998
Dohan, Michael R.	Assoc	997-5464	dohan@1	PQ	PHD	69	MIT	1971
Field-Hendrey, Elizabeth	Assoc	997-5456	efh$econ	NJC	PHD	85	Duke	1989
Gabel, David J.	Assoc	997-5452	davidgabel@a	DNC	PHD	87	Wisconsin	1987
Nix, Joan	Assoc	997-5447	nix$econ	DG	PHD	89	NYU	1988
Solon, Babette S.	Emer	997-5445	sbo$econ	DJ	PHD	58	MIT	1961
Weiman, David F.	Assoc	997-5440	david_weiman@3	NOE	PHD	84	Stanford	1994
Bali, Turan	Asst	997-5443	tbali	GE	PHD	98	CUNY	1998
Feliciano, Zadia M.	Asst	997-5440	zadia_felic+@3	JFN	PHD	95	Harvard	1994
Chiremba, Daniel S.	Lect	997-3142		O	MA	69	New Sch	1969

CUNY-Col of Staten Island Staten Isl, NY 10314 (718) 982-2900 cunyvm.cuny.edu
Economics Faculty Dept Pol Sci,Econ &Phil Fax=982-2888

Name	Rank	Phone	Email	Fields	Degree	Yr	School	Year
Petratos, Vasilios	C-Ac	982-2903		BF	PHD	70	NYU	1974
Schwarz, Samuel	Prof	982-2897		KC	PHD	78	Columbia	1986
Meltzer, Yale L.	Asst	982-2896		EG	MBA	66	NYU	1983
Osakue, John U.	Asst	982-2898		FO	PHD	80	Nebraska	1991
White, Mark D.	Asst			C	PHD		Cincinnati	1997

Claremont McKenna College Claremont, CA 91711-6400 (909) 621-3394 mckenna.edu
Economics Faculty Department of Economics Fax=621-8249

Name	Rank	Phone	Email	Fields	Degree	Yr	School	Year
Fucaloro, Anthony	Dean	621-8117			PHD	69	Arizona	1974
Smith, Janet K.	C-Pr	607-3276			PHD	80	UCLA	1996
Arndt, Sven W.	Prof	621-8012			PHD	64	Berkeley	1990
Charles M. Stone Professor of Money, Credit & Trade								
Bjork, Gordon C.	Prof	607-3625			PHD	63	U Wash	1975
Jonathan B. Lovelace Professor								
Burdekin, Richard C. K.	Prof	607-2884			PHD	85	Houston	1989
Stubblebine, William Craig	Prof	621-8012			PHD	63	Virginia	1966
Teeples, Ronald K.	Prof	607-2964	rteeples		PHD	70	UCLA	1969
Boswell Professor of Economics								
Willett, Thomas D.	Prof	621-8012			PHD	67	Virginia	1977
Horton Professor of Economics								
Wright, Colin	Prof	607-3003			PHD	66	Chicago	1977
Norwood and Frances Berger Professor of Business & Soc								
Keil, Manfred W.	Assoc	607-3899	manfred_keil	ECJA	PHD	85	LondonEc	7-95
Bedard, Kelly	Asst	607-7140			PHD	96	Queen's	1998
Brown, William	Asst	607-3064			PHD	93	Clemson	1994
Harbaugh, Richard	Asst				PHD	97	Pittsburgh	1999
Helland, Eric	Asst	607-2654			PHD	95	U Wash	1998
Weidenmeir, Marc	Asst				PHD	99	Illinois	1999

Clarion Univ of Pennsylvania Clarion, PA 16214-1232 (814) 226-2627 vaxa.clarion.edu
Department of Economics College of Business Fax=226-1910 Sharon Bauer

Name	Rank	Phone	Email	Fields	Degree	Yr	School	Year
Grunenwald, Joseph P.	Dean	226-2600	gruney		DBA	81	Kent St	8-78
Balough, Robert S.	C-Pr	226-2627	balough		PHD	81	N Illinois	1981
Sanders, William V.	Prof	226-2623	sanders		PHD	81	Penn St	1981
Sohng, Soong Nark	Prof	226-2632	sohng		PHD	82	Wayne St	1981
Stine, William F.	Prof	226-2612	stine		PHD	83	Fordham	1981
Yang, Chin-Wei	Prof	226-2609	yang	DFHR	PHD	79	W Virginia	1981
Haggerty, Mark E.	Assoc	226-2614	haggerty		PHD	88	Wash St	1989
Smith, Lynn A.	Assoc	226-2633	lsmith		PHD	85	Pittsburgh	1989
Raehsler, Rod D.	Asst	226-2630	raehsler		PHD	93	Iowa	

Clark University Worcester, MA 01610-1477 (508) 793-7226 vax.clarku.edu
Economics Faculty Department of Economics Fax=793-8849 Ms. Peggy Moskowitz

Name	Rank	Phone	Email	Fields	Degree	Yr	School	Year
Gray, Wayne B.	C-Ac	793-7693	wgray		PHD	83	Harvard	1984
Hsu, Robert C.	Prof	793-7281	rhsu		PHD	70	Berkeley	1971
Ott, Attiat F.	Prof	793-7447	aott		PHD	62	Michigan	1969
Director, Institute for Economic Studies								
Puffer, Frank W.	Prof	793-7228	fpuffer		PHD	68	Brown	1968
Veendorp, Emiel C.	Prof	793-7101			PHD	63	Rice	1976
Weinrobe, Maurice D.	Prof	793-7248	mweinrobe		PHD	69	Cornell	1976
Brown, John C.	Assoc	793-7390	jbrown		PHD	86	Michigan	1986
Bernhofen, Daniel	Asst	793-7185	dbernhofen		PHD	94	Syracuse	1989
Geoghegan, Jacqueline	Asst	793-7709	jgeoghegan		PHD	95	Berkeley	1996
Liu, Zheng	Asst				PHD	97	Minnesota	1997

Clark Atlanta University Atlanta, GA 30314-4391 (404) 880-6770 sbus.cau.edu
Department of Economics School of Art & Science Fax=880-6276 Gwen Donaway

Name	Rank	Phone	Email	Fields	Degree	Yr	School	Year
Earvin, Larry	Dean	880-6770						
Bezuneh, Mesfin	C-Ac	880-6274			PHD	85	Va Tech	
Carter, Charlie	Assoc	880-6288			PHD	75	Illinois	
Nyomba, Ajamu	Asst	880-6286			PHD	91	Tx-Austin	
Yiheyis, Zelealm	Asst	880-6289			PHD			
Dadgie, Frank	Lect	880-6287			MA			

Clarkson University Potsdam, NY 13699-5785 (315) 268-2300 icarus.som.clarkson.edu
Faculty of Economics School of Business Fax=268-3810

Name	Rank	Phone	Email	Fields	Degree	Yr	School	Year
Menz, Fredric C.	Dean	268-6427		HQD	PHD	70	Virginia	1974
Atesoglu, H. Sonmez	Prof	268-7981		EFO	PHD	72	Pittsburgh	1977
Mullen, John K.	Prof	268-4283		GHR	PHD	78	SUNY-Bin	1977
Frascatore, Mark	Asst	268-3850		DHL	PHD	94	Va Tech	1994
MacDonald, John	Asst	268-3870		GM	PHD	87	Va Tech	1995
Mukherjee, Kankana	Asst	268-6604		EFG	PHD	97	Conn	1997

Clayton College & St Univ — Morrow, GA 30260-0285 (770) 961-3410 — mail.clayton.edu
Economics Faculty — School of Business Fax=961-0801 — Carol Leavell

Name	Rank	Phone	E-mail	Fields	Degree	Yr	School	Since
Miller, Ernest M. (Bud)	Dean	961-3410	ernestmiller		MBA	70	Harvard	1998
Arjomand, H. Lari	Prof	961-3417	lariarjomand		PHD	80	Oklahoma	1980
Haberland, Chris		961-3729	chrishaberland		MBA	76	Geo St	1987

Clemson University — Clemson, SC 29634-1309 (864) 656-3481 — clemson.edu
Department of Economics — Col Bus & Public Affrs Fax=656-4192 — Laura Cobb

Name	Rank	Phone	E-mail	Fields	Degree	Yr	School	Since
Trapnell, Jerry E.	Dean	656-3177	trapnel	Atg	PHD	77	Georgia	1986
Dougan, William R.	C-Pr	656-3497	douganw	HDEL	PHD	81	Chicago	1988
Benjamin, Daniel K.	Prof	656-3964	wahoo	DEGJ	PHD	75	UCLA	1985
Lindsay, Cotton M.	Prof	656-3955	lindsay	DHJK	PHD	68	Virginia	1984
J. Wilson Newman Professor								
Maloney, Michael T.	Prof	656-3430	maloney	DGKL	PHD	78	LSU	
McCormick, Robert E.	Prof	656-3441	sixmile	DGKH	PHD	78	Tx A&M	
Thompson, G. Richard	Prof	656-0946	tg	HLM	PHD	72	Virginia	
Wallace, Myles S.	Prof	656-3965	myles	EFC	PHD	76	Colorado	1980
Warner, John T.	Prof	656-3967	jtwarne	DJE	PHD	76	N Car St	1980
Yandle, T. Bruce Jr.	Prof	656-3970	yandle	QKH	PHD	70	Geo St	1969
Gordon, David B.	Assoc	656-3956	gd	DE	PHD	95	Chicago	1992
Placone, Dennis L.	Assoc	656-3951	dlplc	FPH	PHD	82	Pittsburgh	1976
Simon, Curtis J.	Assoc	656-3966	cjsmn	JOR	PHD	85	SUNY-Bin	1985
Tamura, Robert F.	Assoc	656-1242	rtamura	IJO	PHD	88	Chicago	1996
Hakes, John K.	Asst	656-3481	jhakes	HQC	PHD	96	Duke	1999
Thornberg, Christopher	Asst	656-3962	cthornb	FJL	PHD	97	UCLA	1997

Cleveland State University — Cleveland, OH 44115 (216) 687-4520 — csuohio.edu
Department of Economics — College of Arts & Sci Fax=687-9206 — Mrs. Karen Lee Scraga

Name	Rank	Phone	E-mail	Fields	Degree	Yr	School	Since
Steckol, Karen F.	Dean	687-3660	k.steckol		PHD	78	Memphis	1996
Harford, Jon D.	C-Ac	687-4524	j.harford	DHKQ	PHD	74	Stanford	1982
Mathur, Vijay K.	Prof	687-4526	v.mathur	DR	PHD	69	Wayne St	1968
Bell, Edward B.	Assoc	687-4519	e.bell	DHJ	PHD	73	Ohio St	1971
Chang, Myong-Hun	Assoc	687-4523	m.chang	LDMN	PHD	89	J Hopkins	1988
Song, Frank M.	Assoc	687-4525	f.song	EG	PHD	91	Ohio St	1991
Stein, Sheldon H.	Assoc	687-4537	s.stein	CER	PHD	78	J Hopkins	1976
Stewart, Douglas O.	Assoc	687-4515	d.o.stewart	DH	PHD	74	Michigan	1972
Taub, Allan J.	Assoc	687-4528	a.taub	CD	PHD	73	Nrthwstrn	1971

Coe College — Cedar Rapids, IA 52402 (319) 399-8619 — coe.edu
Economics Faculty — Dept of Bus Adm & Econ Fax=399-8830 — Ms. Malinda Svoboda

Name	Rank	Phone	E-mail	Fields	Degree	Yr	School	Since
Carstens, Pamela J.	C-Ac	399-8690	pcarsten		PHD	93	Iowa	1985
Sandberg, Michael L.	Prof	399-8713	msander	EJKM	PHD	76	Iowa	1976
Louie J. & Ella Pocho Bradsky Professor of Bus Adm; Assoc Dean of Faculty								
Wu, Mickey Tai Chuen	Prof	359-8727	mwu	ACEF	PHD	79	Kentucky	1979
George R. Baker Professor of Economics and Business Administration								
Hansen, Dwight W.	Assoc	399-8665	dhansen		MA	76	Nebraska	1978
Larew, Barbara	Assoc	399-8664	blarew		PHD	96	Iowa	1981
McDonald, Michael	Assoc	399-8551	mmcdonal		MA	81	Iowa	1981
Berri, David	Asst	399-8714			PHD	97	Colo St	1998
Ingram, David	Asst				PHD	97	Kansas St	1999

Colby College — Waterville, ME 04901-8852 (207) 872-3564 — colby.edu
Economics Faculty — Economic Department Fax=872-3263 — Dianne Labrec

Name	Rank	Phone	E-mail	Fields	Degree	Yr	School	Since
Findlay, David W.	C-Ac	872-3153	dwfindla	EGA	PHD	86	Purdue	1985
Dana Professor								
Gemery, Henry A.	Prof	878-3137	hagemery	NAB	PHD	67	Penn	1961
Pugh Family Professor of Economics								
Hogendorn, Jan S.	Prof	872-3142	jshogend	FOA	PHD	66	London	1966
Grossman Professor of Economics								
Meehan, James W.	Prof	872-3136	jwmeehan	DM	PHD	67	Boston C	1973
Herbert E. Wadsworth Professor of Economics								
Nelson, Randy A.	Prof	872-3567	ranelson	GM	PHD	79	Illinois	1987
Douglas Professor of Economics								
Reid, Clifford E.	Prof	872-3116	cereid	DCHR	PHD	73	Princeton	1987
Dana Professor								
Tietenberg, Thomas H.	Prof	872-3143	thtieten	QK	PHD	71	Wisconsin	1977
Mitchell Family Professor of Economics								
Barbezat, Debra A.	Assoc	872-3154	dabarbez	JIA	PHD	85	Michigan	1992
Donihue, Michael R.	Assoc	872-3115	mrdonihu	CEA	PHD	89	Michigan	1989
Franko, Patrice	Assoc	872-3347	pmfranko	FAO	PHD	88	Notre Dm	1986
Mansori, Kashif	Asst	872-3563	kmansori	EF	PHD	97	Princeton	1997

Colgate University Hamilton, NY 13346 (315) 228-7533 center.colgate.edu
Economics Faculty Economics Department Fax=228-7033 Ginger Irwin

Name	Rank	Phone	Email	Field	Degree	Yr	School	Since
Kato, Takao	C-Ac	228-7562	tkato	J	PHD	86	Queen's	1986
Haines, Michael R.	Prof	228-7536	mhaines	TN	PHD	71	Penn	1990
Banfi Vintners Professor of Economics								
Mandle, Jay R.	Prof	228-7540	jmandle	ON	PHD	69	Penn	
W. Bradford Wiley Professor of Economics								
Pinchin, Hugh M.	Prof	228-7539	hpinchin	F	PHD	70	Yale	1965
Waldman, Don E.	Prof	228-7535	dwaldman	L	PHD	76	Cornell	1981
Richard M. Kessler Professor of Economic Studies								
Baldani, Jeffrey P.	Assoc	228-7519	jbaldani	CD	PHD	83	Cornell	1982
Grapard, Ulla A.	Assoc	228-7538	ugrapard	AB	PHD	90	Cornell	1985
Khanna, Jyoti	Assoc	228-7527	jkhanna	H	PHD	90	Iowa	1992
Michl, Thomas R.	Assoc	228-7526	tmichl	EJ	PHD	84	New Sch	1983
Rask, Kevin N.	Assoc	228-7524	krask	QI	PHD	91	Duke	1991
Tiefenthaler, Jill M.	Assoc	228-7523	tiefenthaler	TO	PHD	91	Duke	1991
Turner, Robert W.	Assoc	228-7529	rturner	CH	PHD	84	MIT	1983
Sturges, David M.	Asst	228-8795	dsturges	EG	PHD	94	Yale	1995

The Colorado College Colorado Spr, CO 80903 (719) 389-6407 cc.colorado.edu
Economics Faculty Economics Department Fax=389-6927 C. Antonuccio/S. Fuller

Name	Rank	Phone	Email	Field	Degree	Yr	School	Since
Redmount, Esther R.	C-Ac	389-6412	eredmount		PHD	85	Virginia	1987
Becker, William S.	Prof	389-6416			PHD	70	LSU	1970
Bird, Michael C.	Prof	389-6445	mbird		PHD	68	Colorado	1968
Griffiths, L. Christopher	Prof	389-6417	cgriffiths		PHD	70	Colorado	1967
Hecox, Walter E.	Prof	389-6413	whecox		PHD	69	Syracuse	1970
Rittenberg, Libby T.	Prof	389-6410	lrittenberg		PHD	80	Rutgers	1989
Weida, William J.	Prof	389-6409			DBA	75	Colorado	1985
Kapuria-Foreman, Vibha	Assoc	389-6419	vkapuria		PHD	87	Pittsburgh	1989
Smith, Mark Griffin	Assoc	389-6411	msmith		PHD	87	Duke	1988

Univ of Colorado at Boulder Boulder, CO 80309-0256 (303) 735-5500 colorado.edu
Department of Economics College of Arts & Sci Fax=492-8960 Sue Stortz 492-5168

Name	Rank	Phone	Email	Field	Degree	Yr	School	Since
Spear, Petear	Dean	492-7294	peter.spear	Psy	PHD	70	Yale	1996
Carlos, Ann M.	C-Pr	492-8737	ann.carlos		PHD	80	W Ontario	1990
Glahe, Fred R.	Prof	492-5186	fred.glahe		PHD	64	Purdue	1965
Greenwood, Michael J.	Prof	492-7413	michael.greenw+		PHD	67	Nrthwstrn	1980
Howe, Charles W.	Prof	492-7245	charles.howe		PHD	59	Stanford	1970
Hsiao, Frank S. T.	Prof	492-7908	frank.hsiao		PHD	67	Rochester	1975
Kaempfer, William H.	Prof	492-4486	william.kaempfer		PHD	79	Duke	1981
Lillydahl, Jane H.	Prof	492-4599	jane.lillydahl		PHD	76	Duke	1976
Markusen, James R.	Prof	492-0748	james.markusen		PHD	73	Boston C	1990
Director, Carl McGuire Center for International Studies								
Maskus, Keith E.	Prof	492-7588	keith.maskus		PHD	81	Michigan	1981
McNown, Robert F.	Prof	492-8295	robert.mcnown		PHD	71	Ca-SnDgo	1971
Morey, Edward R.	Prof	492-6898	edward.morey		PHD	78	Brit Colum	1980
Poulson, Barry W.	Prof	492-7414	barry.poulson		PHD	65	Ohio St	1965
Roper, Don E.	Prof	492-7466	donald.roper		PHD	70	Chicago	1985
Singell, Larry D.	Prof	492-1809	larry.singell		PHD	65	Wayne St	1968
Waldman, Donald M.	Prof	492-6781	donald.waldman		PHD	79	Wisconsin	1984
Zax, Jeffrey S.	Prof	492-8268	jeffrey.zax		PHD	84	Harvard	1990
deBartolome, Charles	Assoc	492-4464	charles.debar+		PHD	85	Penn	1993
Rutherford, Thomas F.	Assoc	492-5169			PHD	87	Stanford	1995
Alberini, Anna	Asst	492-6653	anna.alberini		PHD	92	Ca-SnDgo	1995
Beauchemin, Kenneth	Asst	492-2651	kenneth.beauch+		PHD	95	Iowa	1995
Boileau, Martin	Asst	492-2108	martin.bioleau		PHD	94	Queen's	1998
Canals-Cerda, Jose	Asst	492-7869	jose.canals-c+		PHD	98	Virginia	
Chen, Yongmin	Asst	491-8736	yongmin.chen		PHD	92	Boston U	1996
Feeney, JoAnne	Asst	492-5923	jo.feeney		MA	91	Rochester	1990
Flores, Nicholas E.	Asst	492-8145	nicholas.flores		PHD	95	Ca-SnDgo	1995
Janeba, Eckhard	Asst	492-3021	edkhard.janeba		PHD	94	Bonn	
Robles, Jack	Asst	492-7407	jack.robles		PHD	96	Ca-SnDgo	1996

U of Colorado at Co Springs Colorado Spr, CO 80933-7150 (719) 262-4028 mail.uccs.edu
Department of Economics Letters, Arts, & Sci Fax=262-4558

Name	Rank	Phone	Email	Field	Degree	Yr	School	Since
Grobsmith, Elizabeth	Dean	262-4550		Antr	PHD			1986
Eubanks, Larry S.	C-Ac	262-4003		DHQ	PHD	80	Wyoming	1986
Ballantyne, A. Paul	Prof	262-4002		ABEO	PHD	65	Stanford	1967
Brock, John R. Jr.	VAsoc	262-4033		DHKL	PHD	88	Cornell	1998
Greenwood, Daphne T.	Assoc	262-4031		HJT	PHD	80	Oklahoma	1980
DeBoer, Dale	Asst	262-4032		DFO	PHD	93	Ca-Davis	1993

Univ of Colorado at Denver — Denver, CO 80217-3364 (303) 556-4413 — castle.cudenver.edu
Dept of Economics, CB 181 — Col Liberal Arts & Sci Fax=556-3547 — Lynn Ferguson, Adm Asst
email @1=carbon.cudenver.edu

Name	Rank	Phone	Email	Fields	Degree	Yr	School	Year
Smith, W. James	Dean	556-2557	jsmith		PHD	76	Colorado	
Medema, Steven G.	C-Pr	556-8511	smedema@1	BHDK	PHD	89	Mich St	1989
Helburn, Suzanne W.	Emer	556-8305	shelburn@1	BI	PHD	61	Indiana	1970
Johnson, Byron L.	Emer	556-2753			PHD	47	Wisconsin	1947
Mocan, Naci H.	Prof	556-8540	nmocan@1	CJI	PHD	89	CUNY	1990
Morris, John R. Jr.	Emer	556-2570	jrmorris@1	BI	PHD	66	Purdue	1970
Beckman, Steven R.	Assoc	556-3048	sbeckman	F	PHD	82	Ca-Davis	1988
Bramhall, David F.	Emer				PHD	61	Penn	
Hsiao, Mei-chu W.	Assoc	556-8322	mhsiao@1	OC	PHD	67	Rochester	1981
Zheng, Buhong	Assoc	556-8375	bzheng@1	O	PHD	93	W Virginia	1995
Argys, Laura M.	Asst	556-3949	largys	IOCD	PHD	93	Colorado	1990
Duncan, Brian	Asst	556-6763	bduncan@1	HC	PHD	98	Ca-SnBarb	1998
Polavarapu, Ramana V.	Asst	556-3950	rpolavar@1	IOCD	PHD	93	Ca-Davis	1993
Rees, Daniel I.	Asst	556-3348	drees@1	J	PHD	92	Cornell	1993

Colorado State University — Fort Collins, CO 80523-1771 (970) 491-6566 — colostate.edu
Department of Economics — Col of Liberal Arts Fax=491-2925 — Barbara Alldredge
Homepage: www.colostate.edu/depts/econ

Name	Rank	Phone	Email	Fields	Degree	Yr	School	Year
Huffert, Robert	Dean$	451-5421	rhoffert	PolS	PHD	74	Cornell	
Kling, Robert W.	C-Ac	491-6566	rkling	DQ	PHD	85	Kansas	1984
Cochrane, Harold	Prof	491-6653	hcochrane	EA	PHD	75	Colorado	1975
Fan, Chuen-mei	Prof	491-5438	cmfan	HD	PHD	72	Minnesota	1978
Fan, Liang-Shing	Prof	491-5336	lsfan	AOF	PHD	65	Minnesota	1968
Keller, Robert R.	Prof	491-5679	rkeller	EN	PHD	71	Wisconsin	1974
Driector, Honor's Program								
Ozawa, Terutomo	Prof	491-6076	tozawa	FO	PHD	66	Columbia	1974
Phillips, Ronnie J.	Prof	491-6079	rphillips	GB	PHD	80	Tx-Austin	1983
Shulman, Steven J.	Prof	491-6940	sshulman	JKEI	PHD	84	Mass	1984
Stanfield, James Ronald	Prof	491-6891	rstanfield	BA	PHD	72	Oklahoma	1976
Bernasek, Alexandra	Assoc	491-6856	abernasek	DA	PHD	92	Michigan	1992
Cutler, Harvey	Assoc	491-5704	hcutler	EC	PHD	85	U Wash	1980
Jianakoplos, Nancy A.	Assoc	491-6537	njianakoplos	CE	PHD	83	Ohio St	1990
Revier, Charles F.	Assoc	491-2929	crevier	EH	PHD	78	MIT	1974
Mushinski, David	Asst	491-3911	dmushinski	CHO	PHD	96	Wisconsin	1997
Weiler, Stephan	Asst	491-3883	sweiler	RO	PHD	94	Berkeley	1996

Columbia University — New York, NY 10027-6989 (212) 854-8057 — columbia.edu
Div of Finance & Economics — School of Business Fax=316-9355 — Shawn M. Patenaude
Homepage: www.columbia.edu/cu/economics
email @1=research.gsb.columbia.edu @2=claven.gsb.columbia.edu

Name	Rank	Phone	Email	Fields	Degree	Yr	School	Year
Feldberg, Meyer	Dean	854-6083			PHD	69	Capetown	1989
Edwards, Franklin R.	C-Pr	854-4202	fre1		PHD	64	Harvard	1980
Arthur F. Burns Professor of Free and Competitive Enterprise								
Adler, Michael	Prof	854-4682			DBA	68	Harvard	1968
Arzac, Enrique R.	Prof	854-4401	era1		PHD	68	Columbia	1971
Bartel, Ann	Prof	854-4419	apb2		PHD	74	Columbia	1976
Donaldson, John B.	Prof	854-4436	jd34		PHD	76	Car Mellon	1977
Greenwald, Bruce C. N.	Prof	854-3491			PHD	78	MIT	1991
Robert Heilbrunn Professo of Finance and Asset Management								
Heal, Geoffrey M.	Prof	854-6084	gmh1		PHD	68	Cambridge	1983
Paul Garett Professor of Public Policy and Business Responsibility								
Hubbard, R. Glenn	Prof	854-3493	rgh1		PHD	83	Harvard	1988
Russell L. Carson Professor of Finance and Economics								
Lichtenberg, Frank R.	Prof	854-4408	frl1		PHD	82	Penn	1983
Courtney C. Brown Professor of Business								
Mishkin, Frederic S.	Prof	854-8057	fsm3		PHD	76	MIT	1983
A. Barton Hepburn Professor of Economics								
Noam, Eli	Prof	854-4596	emn1		PHD	75	Harvard	1976
Patrick, Hugh T.	Prof	854-3497	hpatrick@2		PHD	60	Michigan	1984
R. D. Calkins Professor of International Business								
Sicherman, Nachum	Prof	854-4464	ns38		PHD	87	Columbia	1991
Siconolfi, Paolo	Prof	854-3474	ps17		PHD	87	Penn	1989
Wilkinson, Maurice	Prof	854-4481	mw16		PHD	65	Harvard	1965
Zeldes, Stephen P.	Prof	854-2492	spz1		PHD	84	Brown	1996
Harrison, Ann E.	Assoc	854-2760	aeh14		PHD	91	Princeton	1994
Himmelberg, Charles P.	Assoc	854-2622	cph15	DEL	PHD	90	Nrthwstrn	1995
Boivin, Jean	Asst				PHD	99	Princeton	1999
Fisman, Raymond	Asst				PHD	98	Harvard	1999
Willard, Kristen L.	Asst	854-4438	klw12	DFH	PHD	94	Princeton	9-94

Columbia University New York, NY 10027 (212) 854-3680 columbia.edu
Department of Economics College of Arts & Sci Fax=854-8059 Elizabeth Gold
Homepage: www.columbia.edu/cu/economics

Clarida, Richard	C-Pr	854-3652	rhc2	FE	PHD	83	Harvard	1988
Bagwell, Kyle W.	Prof	854-5890	kwb8	LF	PHD	86	Stanford	1996
Bhagwati, Jagdish	Prof	854-6297	jb38	F	PHD	67	MIT	1980
Casella, Alessandra	Prof	854-2459	ac186	EF	PHD	88	MIT	1993
Chichilnisky, Graciela	Prof	854-4092	gc9	FCQ	PHD	74	Berkeley	1979
Desai, Padma	Prof	854-2266	pd5	O	PHD	60	Harvard	1980
Dhrymes, Phoebus	Prof	854-4459	pjd1	B	PHD	61	MIT	1973
Dutta, Prajit	Prof	854-4742	pkd1	DLG	PHD	87	Cornell	1992
Ericson, Richard	Prof	854-5124	ree3	O	PHD	79	Berkeley	1985
Findlay, Ronald	Prof	854-5437	ref2	FB	PHD	60	MIT	1970
Goldberg, Pinelopi	Prof	854-3677		FLC	PHD	92	Stanford	1999
Lancaster, Kelvin	Prof	854-3679	kjl2	B	PHD	58	London	1966
McLaren, John	Prof	854-8267	jem18	OD	PHD	92	Princeton	1992
Mundell, Robert	Prof	854-3669	ram15	EF	PHD	56	MIT	1974
Phelps, Edmund	Prof	854-2060	esp2	EG	PHD	59	Yale	1971
Riordan, Michael H.	Prof	854-6984		LD	PHD	81	Berkeley	1999
Sala-i-Martin, Xavier	Prof	854-7055	xs23	OE	PHD	90	Harvard	1996
Weinstein, David E.	Prof	854-6880		FL	PHD	91	Michigan	1999
Wellisz, Stanislaw	Prof	854-8033	sw11	O	PHD	54	Harvard	1964
Idson, Todd	Assoc	854-4067	ti18	JC	PHD	86	Columbia	1990
Kahn, Matthew	Assoc	854-5489	mk214	JQR	PHD	93	Chicago	1993
Newman, Andrew F.	Assoc	854-8277	an61	DLO	PHD	89	Harvard	1993
O'Flaherty, Brendan	Assoc	854-2449	bo2	RA	PHD	80	Harvard	1987
Perotti, Roberto	Assoc	854-5712	rp41	E	PHD	91	MIT	1991
Rivera-Batiz, Francisco L.	Assoc	854-4478	flr9	FOJ	PHD	79	MIT	1991
Amarante, Massimiliano	Asst	854-5488		DC	PHD	99	MIT	1999
Cameron, Stephen	Asst	854-4818	sc337	JC	PHD	93	Chicago	1994
Chaudhuri, Shubham	Asst	854-4661	sc301	HOD	PHD	93	Princeton	1994
Das, Mitali	Asst	854-4641	md448	IDC	PHD	98	MIT	1998
Dehijia, Rajeev	Asst	854-4659	rd247	DJC	PHD	97	Harvard	1998
Edlund, Lena	Asst	854-5489		J	PHD	96	SSE	1999
Henry, Marc	Asst	854-3690	mh530	CG	PHD	98	LondonSE	1998
Kockesen, Levent	Asst	854-2512		DL	PHD	99	NYU	1999
Madajewicz, Margaret	Asst			DLO	PHD	98	Harvard	1999
Miller, Ronald	Asst	854-5713	rm170	EO	PHD	94	Princeton	1994
Miyagawa, Eiichi	Asst	854-3926	em347	DH	PHD	98	Rochester	1998
Pande, Rohini	Asst	854-5712		OD	PHD		London	1999
Pfaff, Alexander	Asst	854-4190	ap196	DQ	PHD	95	MIT	1995
Tay, Abigail	Asst	854-3685		LHI	PHD	99	Stanford	1999

Columbus State University Columbus, GA 31907-5645 (706) 568-2280 colstate.edu
Dept of Business Adm Turner College of Bus Fax=568-2184

Johnson, Robert S.	Dean	568-2044	johnson_robert		PHD	64	Virginia	1993
Bill Heard Chair of Business Administration								
Daniels, Michael J.	Prof		daniels_michael	JKR	PHD	79	Geo St	1980
Associate Dean								

Concordia College MN Moorhead, MN 56562 (218) 299-4411 gloria.cord.edu
Economics Faculty Dept of Econ & Bus Adm Fax=299-3947 Leslie Hartford

Petree, Daniel L.	C-Ac	299-3115		JT	PHD	93	Kansas	1995
Moewes, David S.	Prof	299-3488		EH	PHD	82	Utah	1968
Hiestand, Thomas W.	Assoc	299-3483		CD	PHD	74	Kansas St	1972
Kabir, MD Mahbabul	Asst	299-3199		FO	PHD	98	Nebraska	1997
Alshawa, Alaa	Inst	299-3070		EG	MA	94	Ohio	1997

Connecticut College New London, CT 06320-4196 (203) 439-2248 conncoll.edu
Economics Faculty Department of Economics Fax=439-5332 Gina Foster

Cruz-Saco, Maria A.	C-Ac	447-1911	macru	O	PHD	83	Pittsburgh	1990
Pack, Spencer J.	Prof	447-1911	sjpac	B	PHD	83	NewHamp	1981
Peppard, Donald M. Jr.	Prof	447-1911	dmpep	R	PHD	75	Mich St	
Visgilio, Gerald R.	Prof	447-1911	grvis	K	PHD	73	Rhode Isl	
Howes, Candance	Assoc	447-1911	chow	DF	PHD	91	Berkeley	1995
Jensen, Rolf W.	Assoc	447-1911	rwjen	O	PHD	81	Mass	
McKenna, Edward J.	Assoc	774-1911	ejmck	E	PHD	81	SUNY-SBr	

University of Connecticut Storrs, CT 06269-1063 (860) 486-3022 uconnvm.uconn.edu
Department of Economics Col of Lib Arts & Scien Fax=486-4463 Sharon Syrene

Mackinnon, Ross D.	Dean	486-4447	mackinn	Geog	PHD	68	Nrthwstrn	1996
Miller, Stephen M.	H-Pr	486-3853	smiller	EF	PHD	72	SUNY-Buf	1970
Allen, Polly R.	Prof	486-3955	pallen	FE	PHD	70	Brown	1976
Barth, Peter S.	Prof	486-3023	barth	J	PHD	65	Michigan	1973
Carstensen, Fred V.	Prof	486-0614	carsten	N	PHD	76	Yale	1982
Hallwood, C. Paul	Prof	445-3478	hallwood	F	PHD	88	Aberdeen	1986

Heffley, Dennis R.	Prof	486-4669	dheffley	RI	PHD	75	Ca-SnBarb	193
Langlois, Richard N.	Prof	486-3472	langlois	B	PHD	81	Stanford	1983
McEachern, William A.	Prof	486-3272	mceacher	H	PHD	75	Virginia	1978
Miceli, Thomas J.	Prof	486-5810	miceli	KR	PHD	88	Brown	1987
Ray, Subhash C.	Prof	486-3967	ray	CD	PHD	81	Ca-SnBarb	1982
Sacks, Stephen R.	Prof	486-4859	sacks	H	PHD	71	Berkeley	1971
Segerson, Kathleen	Prof	486-4567	segerson	QD	PHD	84	Cornell	1986
Wright, Arthur W.	Prof	486-3773	wright	KD	PHD	69	MIT	1979
Ahking, Francis W.	Assoc	486-3026	anking	EF	PHD	81	Va Tech	1980
Alpert, William T.	Assoc	322-3466	alpert	J	PHD	79	Columbia	1983
Cosgel, Metin M.	Assoc	486-4662	cosgel	N	PHD	89	Iowa	1989
Cunningham, Steven R.	Assoc	486-3550	cunning	EB	PHD	89	Fla St	1989
Harmon, Oskar R.	Assoc	322-3466	harmon	H	PHD	80	Rutgers	1982
Kimenyi, Samson M.	Assoc	486-3027	kimenyi	HI	PHD	86	GeoMason	1991
Landau, Daniel L.	Assoc	596-4080	lanau	O	PHD	74	Chicago	1981
Lott, William F.	Assoc	486-3885	wlott	C	PHD	69	N Car St	1969
Minkler, Alanson P.	Assoc	486-4070	minkler	DK	PHD	88	Ca-Davis	1989
Randolph, Susan M.	Assoc	486-4171	randolph	O	PHD	83	Cornell	1984
Sazama, Gerald W.	Assoc	486-3366	shazam	H	PHD	67	Wisconsin	1966
Chisik, Richard	Asst	486-4762	chisik	FL	PHD	97	Nrthwstrn	1997
Couch, Kenneth A.	Asst	486-4570	couchch	J	PHD	92	Wisconsin	1995
Lin, Emily	Asst	486-4752	lin	HJ	PHD	98	Michigan	1998
Morand, Oliver	Asst	486-6546	morand	DO	PHD	97	Ariz St	1997
Ross, Stephen	Asst	486-3533	ross	R	PHD	94	Syracuse	1994

Converse College Spartanburg, SC 29302-0006 (803) 596-9603 converse.edu
Dept of Economics & Business Col of Arts & Sciences Fax=583-9158 Mrs. Kathy Flowe

Lever, Joe Ann	Dean	596-9091		Biol	MA			1962
Hughes, Woodrow W. Jr.	C-As	596-9089	woodyhughes		PHD	89	S Carol	1986
Young, Madelyn V.	Asst	596-909			PHD	91	Geo St	1991

Cornell University Ithaca, NY 14853-7601 (607) 255-4254 cornell.edu
Department of Economics Col of Arts & Sciences Fax=255-2818

Mitra, Tapan	C-Pr	255-4062	tm19		PHD	75	Rochester	
Basu, Kaushik	Prof	255-2525	kb40	DHLO	PHD	76	LondonEc	
Blume, Lawrence E.	Prof	255-9530	lb19		PHD	77	Berkeley	
Coate, Stephen	Prof	255-1912	sc163		PHD	88	Nrthwstrn	
Davis, Tom E.	Prof	255-5007			PHD	56	J Hopkins	
Easley, David A.	Prof	255-6283	dae3	DGC	PHD	79	Nrthwstrn	9-79
Henry Scarborough Professor of Social Sciences								
Ehrenberg, Ronald G.	Prof	225-3026	rg2		PHD	70	Nrthwstrn	1985
Irving M. Ives Professor of Industrial & Labor Relations and Economics								
Frank, Robert H.	Prof	256-4254	rhf3		PHD	72	Berkeley	1972
Goldwin Smith Professor of Economics, Ethics, and Public Policy								
Hay, George A.	Prof	256-3378	ghay@law.mail.		PHD	69	Nrthwstrn	1979
Edward Cornell Professor Law and Professor of Economics								
Kanbur, Sanjiv	Prof	255-6209	sk145		PHD	81	Oxford	
Lee Teng-hui Professor of World Arts								
Kiefer, Nicholas M.	Prof	255-6315	nmk		PHD	76	Princeton	1980
Ta-Chung Liu Professor of Economics								
Majumdar, Mukul K.	Prof	255-3640	mkm5		PHD	70	Berkeley	
H.T. & R.I. Warshow Professor of Economics								
Masson, Robert T.	Prof	255-6288	rtm2		PHD	69	Berkeley	1976
McClelland, Peter D.	Prof	256-6285			PHD	67	Harvard	1968
Possen, Uri M.	Prof	255-6387	ump1		PHD	71	Yale	1971
Schuler, Richard E.	Prof	255-7579	res1	Engr	PHD	72	Brown	1972
Shell, Karl	Prof	255-5277	ks22		PHD	65	Stanford	1986
Robert Julius Thorne Professor of Economics								
Staller, George J.	Prof	255-4955	gjs3		PHD	59	Cornell	1960
Thorbecke, Erik	Prof	255-2066	et17		PHD	57	Berkeley	1974
H. Edward Babcock Professor of Economics and Food Economics								
Wan, Henry Y. Jr.	Prof	255-6211	hyw1		PHD	61	MIT	
Hong, Youngmaio	Assoc	255-5130	yh20		PHD	93	Ca-SnDgo	7-93
Lyons, Thomas P.	Assoc	255-9534	tp14		PHD	83	Cornell	1988
Conlin, Michael	Asst	255-6284	mec20	LJ	PHD	95	Wisconsin	8-95
Cozzi, Guido	Asst	255-6337	gc49		PHD	98	NYU	
O'Donoghue, Ted	Asst	255-6287	edo1		PHD	96	Berkeley	
Subramanian, Shankar	Asst	255-2355	ss55	OQ	PHD	88	Berkeley	8-93

Creighton University Omaha, NE 68178-0130 (402) 280-2612 creighton.edu
Dept of Economics & Finance College of Business Adm Fax=280-2172 Ms. Shirley Gust

Pitts, Robert E.	Dean	280-2852	rpitts		PHD	77	S Carol	1997
Wingender, John R.	C-Pr	280-2612		Fnce	PHD	85	Nebraska	
Allen, Robert F.	Prof	280-2442	rallen	DKL	PHD	69	Mich St	1986
Goss, Ernest P.	Prof	280-4757	egoss	RC	PHD	83	Tennessee	1992
MacAllister Chair in Regional Economics								
Murthy, N. R. Vasudeva	Prof	280-2128	vmurthy	CDH	PHD	75	SUNY-Bin	1979

Nitsch, Thomas O.	Emer	280-2887	tnitsch	ENP	PHD	63	Ohio St	1969
Phillips, Joseph M. Jr. Associate Dean	Prof	280-2342	jphillips	EO	PHD	82	Notre Dm	1988
Fitzsimmons, Edward L.	Assoc	280-2170	efitzsimmons	AD	PHD	84	Nebraska	1984
Funk, Herbert J.	Emer			AC	PHD	64	Iowa St	1967
Stockhausers, Gerard L. S.J. Associate Dean	Assoc	280-2614	gstock	AEFN	PHD	85	Michigan	1985
Cahill, Neil S.J.	Asst	280-2686	ncahill	AN	MA	47	St Louis	1962
Knudsen, James J.	Asst	280-2281	jimknu	CHJ	PHD	89	Iowa St	1989

Cumberland College — Williamsburg, KY 40769-7984 (606) — cc.cumber.edu
Economics Faculty — Dept of Business Admin Fax=
phone 549-2200

Hubbard, Harold F.	C-Pr	539-4254	hhubbard	BAdm	MBA	60	Kentucky	7-60
Carter, Jane	Assoc	539-4274	jcarter		MBA	85	Kentucky	1985
Tan, Chin	Assoc	539 4457			MBA	88	Tenn Tech	1988
Briley, James	Asst	539-4305	jbriley		PHD	98	Tx Tech	1985

University of Dallas — Irving, TX 75062-4799 (972) 721-5308 — acad.udallas.edu
Department of Economics — Constantin C of Lib Art Fax=721-4034 — Kate Hohlt

Thurow, Glenn E.	Dean	721-5242	gthurow	PolS	PHD	68	Harvard	1974
Bostaph, Samuel H.	C-Ac	721-5308	bostaph	BNP	PHD	76	S Illinois	1981
Doyle, William	Asst	721-5054	bdoyle	GN	PHD	91	Tennessee	1991
Weston, Samuel C.	Asst	721-5238	sweston	B	PHD	87	Pittsburgh	1987

Dallas Baptist University — Dallas, TX 75211-9299 (214) 333-5244 — dbu.edu
Department of Economics — College of Business Fax=333-5293 — Shirtly Mitchell

Smiles, Ronald	C-Pr	333-5253	rons	R	PHD	87	Tx-Arlin	1987
Ellis, Charles M.	Prof				PHD	73	Alabama	
Kakoli, Philip	Asst	333-5218	philip	F	MBA	88	DallasBpt	1988

Dartmouth College — Hanover, NH 03755-3514 (603) 646-2617 — dartmouth.edu
Department of Economics — Col of Arts & Sciences Fax=646-2122 — Julie Guillette/Karen Pelletie
Homepage: http://www.dartmough.edu/artsci/economics/

Berger, Edward M.	Dean							
Blanchflower, David Graham	C-Pr	646-2536			PHD	85	London	1989
Aizenman, Joshua Champion Internation Professor	Prof	646-2531			PHD	81	Chicago	1990
Fischel, William Alan	Prof	646-2940			PHD	73	Princeton	1973
Gustman, Alan Leslie Loren M. Berry Professor	Prof	646-2641			PHD	69	Michigan	1969
Irwin, Douglas A.	Prof	646-2942			PHD	88	Columbia	1997
Kohn, Meir G.	Prof	646-2648			PHD	73	MIT	1978
Marion, Nancy P.	Prof	646-2511			PHD	77	Princeton	1976
Menge, John A.	Prof	646-2529			PHD	59	MIT	1956
Scott, John T.	Prof	646-2941			PHD	76	Harvard	1977
Skinner, Jonathan John French Professor	Prof	646-2535			PHD	83	UCLA	1995
Venti, Steven F.	Prof	646-2526			PHD	82	Harvard	1982
Staiger, Douglas O.	Assoc	646-2979			PHD	90	MIT	1998
Anderson, Patricia Mary	Asst	646-2532			PHD	91	Princeton	1991
Baicker, Katherine	Asst	646-2943			PHD	98	Harvard	1998
Durell, Alan	Asst	646-2202			PHD	99	Harvard	1999
Edmonds, Eric V.	Asst	646-2944			PHD	99	Princeton	1999
Lusardi, Annamaria	Asst	646-2099			PHD	92	Princeton	1993
Pavcnik, Nina	Asst	646-2537			PHD	99	Princeton	1999
Sacerdote, Bruce I.	Asst	646-2121			PHD	98	Harvard	1998
Samwick, Andrew A.	Asst	646-2893			PHD	93	MIT	1994
Slaughter, Matthew J.	Asst	646-2939			PHD	94	MIT	1994

Davidson College — Davidson, NC 28036-1719 (704) 892-2398 — davidson.edu
Economics Faculty — Department of Economics Fax=892-2874 — Barbara M. Carmack

Hess, Peter N. Gail M. and Ernst G. Doe Professor of Economics	C-Pr	892-2249	pehess	OT	PHD	82	N Carol	1980
Appleyard, Dennis R. James B. Duke Professor of International Studies	Prof	892-2456	deappleyard	F	PHD	66	Michigan	1990
Martin, David W.	Prof	892-2253	damartin	GQ	PHD	84	Illinois	1984
Ross, Clark G. Frontis Johnston Professor of Economics	Prof	892-2204	clross	P	PHD	76	Boston C	1979
Baker, Ben	Assoc	892-2397	bebaker	G	MA	83	S Carol	1997
Kumar, Vikram	Assoc	892-2265	vikumar	E	PHD	87	Vanderbilt	1986
Chaston, Kelly	Asst	892-2574	kechaston	DL	PHD	97	Boston C	1997
Simpson, Murray S.	Asst	892-2454	musimpson	O	PHD	94	Illinois	1993

University of Dayton — Dayton, OH 45469-2251 (937) 229-2416 udayton.edu
Dept of Economics & Finance — School of Business Adm Fax=229-2477 Ms. Sandy L. Murphy

Name	Rank	Phone	E-mail	Field	Degree	Yr	School	Since
Gould, Sam B.	Dean	229-3731	gould	Mgt	PHD	75	Mich St	1985
Gustafson, Elizabeth F.	C-Ac	229-2406	gustafso	C	PHD	74	N Carol	1983
Beladi, Hamid	Prof	229-2407	beladi	F	PHD	83	Utah St	1988
Frasca, Ralph R.	Prof	229-2405	frasca	A	PHD	75	Indiana	1972
Weiler, John E.	Prof	229-2453	weiler	H	PHD	73	Cincinnati	1967
Hadley, Lawrence H.	Assoc	229-2403	hadleyla	J	PHD	75	Conn	1977
Ruggiero, John	Assoc	229-2550	ruggiero	R	PHD	95	Syracuse	1995
Poitras, Marc	Asst	229-2419	poitras	A	PHD	95	GeoMason	1998

University of Delaware — Newark, DE 19716-2720 (302) 831-2563 be.udel.edu
Department of Economics — Col of Business & Econ Fax=831-6968 Gail E. Walford, Off Coor

Name	Rank	Phone	E-mail	Field	Degree	Yr	School	Since
Biederman, Kenneth R.	Dean$	831-2551	biederk	G	PHD	71	Purdue	1991
Butkiewicz, James L.	C-Pr	831-1891	butkiewj	E	PHD	77	Virginia	1976
Associate Dean								
Abrams, Burton A.	Prof	831-1900	abramsb	EH	PHD	74	Ohio St	1974
Anderson, Lee G.	Prof	831-2650		Q	PHD	70	U Wash	1974
Professor, College of Marine Studies								
Grubb, Farley	Prof	831-1905	grubbf	N	PHD	84	Chicago	1983
Hoffman, Saul D.	Prof	831-1907	hoffmans	TJ	PHD	77	Michigan	1977
Koford, Kenneth	Prof	831-1909	kofordk	H	PHD	77	UCLA	1979
Lewis, Kenneth A.	Prof	831-1912	lewisk	CE	PHD	69	Princeton	1973
Associate Chair, Economics								
Link, Charles R.	Prof	831-1921	linkc	J	PHD	71	Wisconsin	1701
Miller, Jeffrey B.	Prof	831-1911	millerj	EP	PHD	76	Penn	1976
Mulligan, James G.	Prof	831-1918	mulligaj	L	PHD	80	Minnesota	1980
O'Neill, James B.	Prof	831-2559	oneillj	A	PHD	71	Purdue	1971
Director, Center for Economic Education								
Seidman, Laurence S.	Prof	831-1917	seidmanl	H	PHD	74	Berkeley	1982
Settle, Russell F.	Prof	831-1914	settler	H	PHD	74	Wisconsin	1974
Agnello, Richard J.	Assoc	831-1901	agnellor	C	PHD	70	J Hopkins	1968
Beck, Stacie E.	Assoc	831-1915	becks	GEF	PHD	87	Penn	1986
Black, David E.	Assoc	831-1902	blackd	HO	PHD	69	MIT	1975
Craig, Eleanor D.	Assoc	831-1904	craige	H	MA	61	Penn	1962
Associate Chair								
Donnelley, Lawrence P.	Assoc	831-2652		O	PHD	70	Brown	1968
Associate Provost, International Programs and Special Sessions								
Falaris, Evangelos M.	Assoc	831-1768	falarise	O	PHD	79	Minnesota	1986
Latham, William R. III	Assoc	831-6846	lathamw	RC	PHD	73	Illinois	1971
Thornton, James R.	Assoc	831-1919	thorntoj	P	PHD	74	Cornell	1973
Whited, Toni	Assoc	831-2563	whitedt	GE	PHD	90	Princeton	1994
Ying, John S.	Assoc	831-1903	yingj	L	PHD	87	Berkeley	1987
Arnold, Michael	Asst	831-1916	arnoldm	LD	PHD	92	UCLA	1992
Parsons, George R.	Asst	831-6792		Q	PHD	85	Wisconsin	1985
College of Marine Studies								
Stockman, David	Asst	831-1903	stockmad	CE	PHD	97	Chicago	1998

Delaware State University — Dover, DE 19901-2277 (302) 739-2705 dsc.edu
Dept of Accounting & Finance — School of Management Fax=739-3517 Ms. Claudia L. Daniels

Name	Rank	Phone	E-mail	Field	Degree	Yr	School	Since
Williamson, Joan W.	C-Ac	739-2705		Atg	PHD	97	Delaware	
Bieker, Richard F.	Prof	739-3526			PHD	70	Kentucky	
Ikein, Augustine	Assoc	739-3587		Soc	PHD	88	Atlanta	
Kwak, Young-sik	Assoc	739-3524			PHD	94	Miss	1993
Christopher, Jan E.	Asst	739-7644		CDMR	PHD	93	Howard	1994

Delta State University — Cleveland, MS 38733 (601) 846-4185 dsu.deltast.edu
Division of Econ & Finance — School of Business Fax=846-4215 Cathy Conico

Name	Rank	Phone	E-mail	Field	Degree	Yr	School	Since
Stewart, William S.	Dean	846-4200		Mgt	PHD	77	Miss	8-97
Moore, B. C.	C-Pr	846-4185	bmoore	AG	PHD	95	Miss	8-86
Hinton, William Valentine	Prof	846-4196			PHD	82	Arkansas	8-87
Wood, Clinton F.	Prof	846-4209			JD	80	Miss	8-84
Sridharan, K. P.	Assoc	846-4196		ACFG	PHD	92	Miss	8-92
Denson, Chad	Asst				PHD	87	La Tech	8-97
Wagoner, Charles	Asst	846-4188		ACFG	PHD	93	Tulane	8-95
Walker, Craig	Asst	846-4189		ACFG	PHD	96	So Meth	8-96

Denison University — Granville, OH 43023 (614) 587-6245 cc.denison.edu
Economics Faculty — Department of Economics Fax=587-6348 Judy Thompson

Name	Rank	Phone	E-mail	Field	Degree	Yr	School	Since
LaRoe, Ross M.	C-Ac	587-6473	laroe	AHQ	PHD	82	American	1985
Bartlett, Robin L.	Prof	587-6574	barlett	AJ	PHD	74	Mich St	1973
Laura C. Harris Chair								
Behdad, Sohrab	Prof	587-6404	behdad	BF	PHD	70	Mich St	1985
King, Paul G.	Prof	587-6314	king	OAQ	PHD	71	Illinois	1967
John Harris Chair								
Lucier, Richard L.	Prof	587-6462	lucier	ADF	PHD	72	Claremont	1971
Miller, Timothy I.	Prof	587-6403	millert	CE	PHD	79	S Illinois	1978
Boyd, David W.	Assoc	587-6317	boyd	KLD	PHD	91	Ohio St	1991
Boyd, Laura A.	Assoc	587-6316	boydl	JI	PHD	91	Ohio St	1991
Ziegert, Andrea	Asst	587-6575	ziegert		PHD	85	N Carol	1997

University of Denver Denver, CO 80208-2685 (303) 871-2685 du.edu
Department of Economics Arts, Humanities & SocS Fax=871-2605 Mary Ann Hones-Chavis

Name	Rank	Phone	Email	Fields	Degree	Yr	School	Since
Mott, Tracy L.	C-Ac	871-2569	tmott	BE	PHD	82	Stanford	1991
Burford, William E.	Assoc	871-2256	wburford	AJM	PHD	70	Ohio St	1969
retiring December 1999								
Freeman, Katherine	Assoc	871-2151		AD	PHD	78	Fla St	1983
Ho, Peter S. W.	Assoc	871-2259	pho	FO	PHD	89	Stanford	1987
Director, Asian Studies Program								
Urquhart, Robert	Assoc	871-2258	rurquhar	BN	PHD	88	New Sch	1988
Directory, Cultural & Critical Studies Program								
Wray, L. Randall	Assoc	871-2245	lwray	E	PHD	88	Wash U	1987
Mazzucato, Mariana	Asst	871-2146	mmazz;uca	CL	PHD	98	New Sch	1997

DePaul University Chicago, IL 60604-2287 (312) 362-8781 wppost.depaul.edu
Department of Economics Col Arts & Sci/Cl Comm Fax=362-5452 Sue Schoeben

Name	Rank	Phone	Email	Fields	Degree	Yr	School	Since
Patten, Ronald J.	Dean	362-6783		Atg	PHD	63	Alabama	7-89
Oppenheimer, Margaret M.	C-Pr	362-8651		JDK	PHD	74	Nrthwstrn	9-76
Batavia, Bala	Prof	362-8781		CD	PHD	74	N Car St	1976
Ciecka, James E.	Prof	362-8781		CD	PHD	70	Purdue	1970
Diamond, James J.	Emer			EC	PHD	62	Nrthwstrn	9-55
Ghoshal, Animesh	Prof	362-8008		DE	PHD	74	Michigan	1981
Krautmann, Anthony C.	Prof	362-6176		DL	PHD	85	Iowa	1985
Mark, Adolph E.	Emer			A	PHD	63	Illinois	9-61
Sander, William III	Prof	362-5240		RD	PHD	78	Cornell	1989
Wiltgen, Richard J.	Prof	362-8016		B	PHD	74	Illinois	1973
Berdell, John	Assoc	362-8781		NE	PHD	91	Cambridge	1991
Bucci, Gabriella A.	Assoc	362-6787		DH	PHD	88	J Hopkins	1989
Choi, Jin	Assoc	362-8842		GMC	PHD	82	Iowa St	8-88
Donley, Thomas D.	Assoc	362-8887		C	PHD	93	Wisconsin	8-90
Miller, Michael S.	Assoc	362-8477		E	PHD	80	Pittsburgh	1980
Mondschean, Thomas H.	Assoc	362-5210		EG	PHD	89	Wisconsin	1987
Owen, Laura J.	Assoc	362-8771		NJ	PHD	91	Yale	1990
Dill, Floyd R.	Asst	362-8309		N	PHD	73	Cornell	1975
Epstein, Seth	Asst	362-8112		D	PHD	88	Arizona	1992

DePauw University Greencastle, IN 46135-0037 (765) 658-4878 depauw.edu
Dept of Economics & Mgt College of Liberal Arts Fax=658-4177 Dot Grundlock
Did Not Respond--1997-98 Listing

Name	Rank	Phone	Email	Fields	Degree	Yr	School	Since
Wachter, Daniel R.	C-Ac	658-4879	dwachter		PHD	82	Purdue	1979
Catanese, Anthony V.	Prof	658-4884	mcatanes		PHD	72	S Illinois	1979
Field, William Joseph	Prof	658-4886			PHD	80	Michigan	1979
English, Mary P.	Assoc	658-4355			PHD	89	So Meth	1988
Associate Dean of Academic Affairs								

University of Detroit Mercy Detroit, MI 48219-0900 (313) 993-1238 udmercy.edu
Department of Economics Col of Liberal Arts Fax=993-1166

Name	Rank	Phone	Email	Fields	Degree	Yr	School	Since
Byrne, Donald R.	Prof	993-3391			PHD	71	Notre Dm	1966
Pemberton, Donald K.	Prof	993-1097			PHD	70	Kansas	1969
Shen, Raphael	Prof	993-1148			PHD	75	Mich St	1977
Song, Yoon K.	Prof	993-1095			PHD	69	Illinois	1969
Brorby, Bruce M.	Asst	993-1600			MA	67	Detroit	1971
Assistant Dean								
Mosby, James B.	Asst	993-1096			MA	70	Detroit	1972
Schad, Tom	Asst							

Dickinson College Carlisle, PA 17013-2896 (717) 245-1381 dickinson.edu
Economics Faculty Department of Economics Fax=245-1854 Isabel L. Houston
Did Not Respond--1997-98 Listing

Name	Rank	Phone	Email	Fields	Degree	Yr	School	Since
Koont, Sinan	C-As	245-1381	koont	CFE	PHD	87	Mass	1986
Barone, Charles A.	Assoc		barnone	AO	PHD	78	American	1975
Bergsten, Gordon S.	Assoc	245-1529	bergsten	BNDE	PHD	77	Berkeley	1984
Bellinger, William K.	Asst	245-1358	bellinger_w	JE	PHD	85	Nrthwstrn	1981
Burczak, Ted A.	Asst	245-1264	burczak	ELF	PHD	94	Mass	
Skrabis, Kristin	Asst	245-1596	skrabis	QD				

Dillard University New Orleans, LA 70122 (504) 286-4699 dillard.edu
Economics Faculty Division of Business Fax=286-4851 Helen Bougere 286-4698
Homepage: http://www.dillard.edu

Name	Rank	Phone	Email	Fields	Degree	Yr	School	Since
Chase, Edgar L. III	C-Pr	286-4697		Atg	JD		Loyola	
Mengistu, Tadessa	Assoc	286-4698			PHD	86	Indiana	
Fugar, Christian	Asst	286-4699			PHD	89	Howard	
Sheriff, Mohamed A.	Asst	286-4698			PHD	91	Howard	

Univ of District of Columbia — Washington, DC 20008 (202) 282-3723 — udcvax.bitnet
Dept Atg, Fnce, & Economics — C of Professional Stds Fax=274-7022 — Carolyn Lynch
Did Not Respond--1997-98 Listing

Name	Rank	Phone	E-mail	Field	Degree	Yr	School	Since
Taylor, Alfred O.	Dean	282-3701		Edu	EDD	91	Va Tech	1969
Quigley, Herbert G.	C-Pr	282-3726			DBA	77	Geo Wash	1969
Ezeani, Eboh	Prof	282-3723		O	PHD	76	American	1976
Whitman, Raymond D.	Prof	282-3750		JHA	PHD	71	Columbia	1985
Boland, Dennis	Assoc	282-3723		BA	PHD	70	Illinois	1976
Omar, Hanai	Assoc	282-3750		AH	MS		Maryland	1976

Dowling College — Oakdale, NY 11769-1999 (516) 244-3155
Department of Economics — Sch of Arts & Sciences Fax=589-6644 — Lynn Ellen Lotz

Name	Rank	Phone	E-mail	Field	Degree	Yr	School	Since
Caraway, James E.	Dean	244-3232			EDD		Tennessee	
Raji, Seyed	Prof	244-3118			PHD	72	NYU	
Gullason, Edward T.	Assoc	244-3167			PHD	86	Penn	
Sonny, Jacob	Assoc	244-3117			PHD	71	New Sch	
Greer, Mark	Asst	244-3239			PHD	90	Michigan	1994

Drake University — Des Moines, IA 50311-4505 (515) 271-3122 — drake.edu
Department of Economics — College of Arts & Sci Fax=271-2055 — Nancy A. Smith

Name	Rank	Phone	E-mail	Field	Degree	Yr	School	Since
Troyer, Ron	Dean			Soc	PHD	80	W Mich	1980
University Professor								
Boal, William M.	C-Ac	271-3129	william.boal		PHD	85	Stanford	1995
Berry, Dale A.	Prof	271-2895	dale.berry		PHD	66	Indiana	1962
Hewett, Roger S.	Assoc	271-3834	roger.hewett		PHD	84	Illinois	1981
Hosseinzadeh, Esmail	Assoc	271-4026	ismael.zadeh		PHD	87	New Sch	1988
Weaver, Janice E.	Assoc	271-2898	janice.weaver		PHD	76	Illinois	1983

Drew University — Madison, NJ 07940-4037 (201) 408-3434 — drew.drew.edu
Department of Economics — College of Liberal Arts Fax=408-3143 — Lydia Feldman
Did Not Respond--1997-98 Listing

Name	Rank	Phone	E-mail	Field	Degree	Yr	School	Since
Cucchi, Paolo M.	Dean				PHD	72	Princeton	1984
Smith, Bernard	C-Ac	408-3595		HOP	PHD	89	Yale	1986
Cole, Donald P.	Prof	408-3429		AH	PHD	68	Ohio St	1966
Curtis, Fred	Prof	408-3432		BJO	PHD	83	Mass	1978
Seneca, Rosalind S.	Prof	408-3433		DL	PHD	71	Penn	1981
Isenberg, Dorene L.	Assoc	408-3435		E	PHD	86	Ca-Rivers	
Colton, Nora Ann	Asst	408-3665		FPT	DPHL	92	Oxford	1994
Dickens, Edwin T.	Asst	408-3024		EG	PHD	90	New Sch	1996

Drexel University — Philadelphia, PA 19104-2875 (215) 895-2123 — duvm.ocs.drexel.edu
Economics & Intl Business — College of Business Adm Fax=895-6975

Name	Rank	Phone	E-mail	Field	Degree	Yr	School	Since
Lewis, Pamela S.	Dean	895-2111	lewisps	Mgt	PHD	88	Tennessee	1997
Madan, Vibhas	C-Ac	895-2124	madanv		PHD	89	Mich St	1989
Koziara, Edward C.	Prof	895-6994	koziarec		PHD	65	Wisconsin	1966
McCain, Roger A. III	Prof	895-2176	mccainra		PHD	71	LSU	1988
Yan, Chiou-shuang	Prof	895-6972	yancsj		PHD	66	Purdue	1967
Hammoudeh, Shawka M.	Assoc	895-6673	hammousm		PHD	80	Kansas	1990
Jeon, Bang Nam	Assoc	895-2125	jeonbana		PHD	87	Indiana	1988
Lester, Bijou	Assoc	895-6973	lesterby		PHD	81	Penn	1988
Jensen, Paul	Asst	895-2123			PHD	97	Penn St	1997
Soller, Elizabeth	Asst	895-2123			PHD	97	Indiana	1997
Tang, Linghui	Asst	895-1034			PHD	98	Syracuse	1998

Drury College — Springfield, MO 65802 (417) 873-7509 — lib.drury.edu
Economics Faculty — Breech S Bus Adm & Econ Fax=873-7537 — Judy Gibson

Name	Rank	Phone	E-mail	Field	Degree	Yr	School	Since
Zimmerer, Thomas W.	D-Pr	873-7509		Mgt	PHD	71	Arkansas	
Rohlf, William D. Jr.	Prof	865-8731			PHD	72	Kansas St	1972
Mullins, Steven	Assoc				PHD	83	Okla St	1982

Duke University — Durham, NC 27708-0097 (919) 660-1800 — econ.duke.edu
Economics Department — College of Arts & Sci Fax=684-8974 — Betty Henderson 660-1852

Name	Rank	Phone	E-mail	Field	Degree	Yr	School	Since
McElroy, Marjorie B.	C-Pr	660-1815	mcelroy		PHD	69	Nrthwstrn	1976
Bollerslev, Tim	Prof			CG	PHD	86	Ca-SnDgo	1999
DeMarchi, Neil B.	Prof	660-1834	demarchi		PHD	70	Austr Natl	1983
Goodwin, Craufurd	Prof	684-3936	goodwin	ABFN	PHD	58	Duke	9-62
James D. Duke Professor								
Grabowski, Henry G.	Prof	660-1839	grabow		PHD	67	Princeton	1972
Graham, D. A	Prof	660-1802	dag		PHD	69	Duke	1969
Kelley, Allen C.	Prof	660-1825	kelley		PHD	64	Stanford	1972
James D. Duke Professor								
Sloan, Frank A.	Prof	660-1820	fsloan		PHD	69	Harvard	1993
Alexander McMahon Professor								
Smith, V. Kerry	Prof	660-1805	kerrys	QDC	PHD	70	Rutgers	1994

Tauchen, George	Prof	660-1812	get		PHD	78	Minnesota	1977
Tower, Edward	Prof	660-1818	tower		PHD	71	Harvard	1974
Director, Undergraduate Studies								
Treml, Vladimir G.	Emer	660-1841	treml		PHD	63	N Carol	1967
Vernon, John M.	Prof	660-1829	vernon		PHD	66	MIT	1969
Wallace, T. Dudley	Emer	660-1855	wallace					
James D. Duke Professor								
Weintraub, E. Roy	Prof	660-1838	erw		PHD	69	Penn	1970
Yohe, William P.	Emer	660-1835	yohe		PHD	59	Michigan	1958
Kimbrough, Kent P.	Assoc	660-1811	kent		PHD	80	Chicago	1980
Mendoza, Enrique	Assoc	660-1814	mendozae		PHD	89	W Ontario	1997
Zhou, Lin	Assoc	660-1801	linzhou	CF	PHD	89	Princeton	1996
An, Mark	Asst	660-1808	man		PHD	93	Cornell	1993
Connolly, Michelle	Asst	660-1819	connolly		PHD	96	Yale	1997
Coppejans, Mark	Asst	660-1804	mtc		PHD	96	Nrthwstrn	1996
Crawford, Gregory	Asst	660-1828	gsc		PHD	96	Stanford	1996
Peretto, Pietro	Asst	660-1807	peretto	EFLM	PHD	94	Yale	9-94
Quadrini, Vincenzo	Asst	660-1817	quadrini		PHD	96	Penn	1998
Sieg, Holger	Asst	660-1856	hs25		PHD	96	Car Mellon	1996
Yang, Dennis	Asst	660-1821	yang		PHD	93	Chicago	1992
Burmeister, Edwin	Resr		eb	GC	PHD	65	MIT	
Toniolo, Gianni	Resr	660-1885	giannit		LAUR	66	Venice	

Duquesne University Pittsburgh, PA 15282-0104 (412) 396-5831 duq.edu
Economic Sciences Division School of Bus & Admin Fax=396-4764 Cathy Hramika

Murrin, Thomas J.	Dean	396-5157			DMS		Duquesne	1991
Bober, Stanley	Prof	396-6263			PHD	62	NYU	1964
Rethwisch, Kurt	Prof	396-6258			PHD	69	Maryland	1967
Bond, Richard E.	Assoc	396-6262			PHD	69	Maryland	1969
Marlin, Matthew R.	Assoc	396-6250			PHD	81	Fla St	1987
Davies, Anthony	Asst	396-5831			PHD	94	SUNY-Alb	1999
Hettler, Paul	Asst	396-6246			PHD	98	Pittsburgh	1999

Earlham College Richmond, IN 47374-4095 (765) 983-1525 earlham.edu
Economics Faculty Department of Economics Fax=983-1207 Cheri Gaddis

Diskin, Jonathan	C-Ac	983-1427	jond		PHD	89	Mass	1988
Klose, Gilbert	Prof	983-1206	gilk		MA		Nrthwstrn	1960

East Carolina University Greenville, NC 27858-4353 (252) 328-6006 mail.ecu.edu
Department of Economics College of Arts & Sci Fax=328-6743 Mrs. Kimberly Moore

Sparrow, Keats	Dean	328-6249	sparrowk		PHD		Kentucky	
Bays, Carson W.	C-Pr	328-6006	baysc	IKL	PHD	74	Michigan	1982
Bishop, John A.	Prof	328-6756	bishopj	DHI	PHD	87	Alabama	1988
Baldwin, Marjorie L.	Assoc	328-6383	baldwinm	DIJ	PHD	88	Syracuse	1989
Parker, Randall E.	Assoc	328-6755	parkerr	EN	PHD	86	Kentucky	1986
Rothman, Philip	Assoc	328-6151	rothmanp	CE	PHD	90	NYU	1992
Whitehead, John C.	Assoc	328-6821	whiteheadj	DQ	PHD	89	Kentucky	1989
Zeager, Lester A.	Assoc	328-6408	zeagerl	DIJ	PHD	87	Pittsburgh	1986
DeSimone, Jeffrey	Asst	328-6742	desimonej	DIJ	PHD	98	Yale	1999
Ghent, Linda	VAsst	328-6751	ghentl	DJ	PHD	92	N Car St	1993
Haab, Timothy C.	Asst	328-6006	haabt	CDQ	PHD	95	Maryland	1995
Holmes, George M.	Asst	328-4165	holmesg	CIJ	PHD	99	N Carol	1999
Schumacher, Edward	Asst	328-1083	schumachere	DIJ	PHD	94	Fla St	1994

East Central University Ada, OK 74820-6899 (405) Ext 274 ecok.edu
Dept of Business Admin School of Business Fax=
Did Not Respond Again--1995-96 Listing; phone: 332-8000

Mitchusson, Linda C.	Dean	Ext 649		Atg	PHD	75	Arkansas	1996
Gaster, Walter D.	C-Pr	Ext 525		Mktg	DBA	82	La Tech	1970
Steger, Eric K.	Prof	Ext 267			PHD	80	La Tech	1970

East Stroudsburg University E Stroudsburg PA 18301 (570) 422-3251 esu.edu
Department of Economics Sch of Arts & Sciences Fax=422-3777 Melanie Deuerlein

Liberman, Michael	Dean$	422-3494			PHD	71	Nebraska	1971
Hartman, Harrison G.	C-Pr	422-3251		J	PHD	76	NYU	1964
Bunjun, Seewoonundun	Prof	422-3240		D	PHD	79	Penn St	1979
Christofides, Constantinos A	Prof	422-3329		CRT	PHD	77	Lehigh	1971
Kidman, Peter N.	Prof	422-3830		K	PHD	71	W Virginia	1977
DeCosmo, Michael C.	Assoc	422-3108			MBA	84	Lehigh	1984
Kane, Mamadou	Assoc	422-3279		EFN	MA	72	NYU	1973
Kercsmar, John	Assoc	422-3829		M	PHD	85	Houston	
Nyamwange, Richard	Assoc	422-3404		D	MBA	82	Long Isl	1987
Behr, Todd	Asst	422-3831		EH	MBA	78	Lehigh	1989
Neelakantan, P.	Asst	422-3823		D	PHD	92	SUNY-Buf	1992

East Tennessee State Univ — Johnson City, TN 37614-0686 (423) 439-4202 — etsu.edu
Dept of Economics & Finance — College of Business Fax=439-5274 — Ms. Mimi Mick

Name	Rank	Phone	Email	Field	Degree	Yr	School	Year
Spritzer, Allan D.	Dean	439-5489	i64sprit	Mgt	PHD	71	Cornell	1981
Followill, Richard A.	C-Pr	439-4202	followil	Fnce	PHD	87	Alabama	1996
Bartell, H. Robert	Prof	439-4402			PHD	63	Columbia	1989
Director, Center of Banking								
Hippie, F. Steb	Prof	439-4202			PHD	72	So Meth	1982
Alavi, Jafar	Assoc	439-4202			PHD	86	Tennessee	1985
Dotterweich, Douglas P.	Assoc	439-4202			PHD	78	Delaware	1984
Everett, Michael David	Assoc	439-4202			PHD	67	Wash U	1977
Mackara, W. Frederick	Assoc	439-4202			PHD	76	Tx A&M	1975
Mason, W. Joe Jr.	Assoc	439-4202			PHD	87	S Carol	1984
Smith, Jon L.	Assoc	439-4202			PHD	82	S Carol	1980
Warren, J. Harold	Assoc	439-4202			PHD	69	Okla St	1969
Baryla, Edward	Asst	439-4202			PHD	95	Alabama	1995
Jennings, Donna	Asst	439-4202			PHD	95	Vanderbilt	1994
Pillutla, Padmaja	Asst	439-4202			ABD		Wash St	1998
Trogen, Paul	Asst	439-4202			PHD	95	Fla St	1995

Eastern Conn State Univ — Willimantic, CT 06226-2295 (203) 465-5239 — ecsu.ctstateu.edu
Economics Faculty — Department of Economics Fax=456-2231 — Ms. Jean Stencil

Name	Rank	Phone	Email	Field	Degree	Yr	School	Year
Horrocks, Robert	Dean	456-5293						
Parzych, Kenneth M.	C-Pr	456-5239	parzych		PHD	70	Conn	
Lombard, John	Prof				PHD	78	Conn	
Free, Rhona C.	Assoc	456-2231			PHD	83	Notre Dm	1983
Mann, Prem S.	Assoc	456-5216			PHD	88	UCLA	1986
Pachis, Dimitrios S.	Assoc				PHD	82	Mass	
Associate Vice President for Academic Affairs								
Roy, Tapan K.	Assoc	456-5502			PHD	80	Temple	1977

Eastern Illinois Univ — Charleston, IL 61920-3099 (217) 581-2719 — eiu.edu
Department of Economics — College of Sciences Fax=581-5997 — Lois Luallen

Name	Rank	Phone	Email	Field	Degree	Yr	School	Year
Wall, Lida	Dean	581-3328		Comm	PHD		Ohio St	1995
Karbassioon, Ebrahim	C-Pr	581-5429	cfexk		PHD	81	Nebraska	1980
Corley, Edward M.	Prof	581-2378	efemc		PHD	64	Okla St	1967
Dao, Minh Quang	Prof	581-6329	cfmqd		PHD	87	Illinois	1987
Lenihan, Patrick M.	Prof	581-6330	cfpml		PHD	68	Wisconsin	1967
Nordin, Harold D.	Prof	581-6331	cfhdn		PHD	76	Illinois	1967
Sidwell, Richard J.	Prof	581-3812	cfrjs		PHD	72	Utah	1970
Thompson, William F.	Prof	581-2927			PHD	79	Arkansas	1981
Bates, Lawrence W.	Assoc	581-2710	cflwb		PHD	75	Tx-Austin	1970
Brodsky, Noel	Assoc	581-6334	cfnb		PHD	88	Illinois	1988
Bruehler, James	Assoc	581-2719	cfjrb		PHD	93	Illinois	1993
Champlin, Dell	Assoc	581-2719	cfdpc		PHD	90	Utah	1995
Fahy, Paul R	Assoc	581-6332	cfprf		PHD	76	Conn	1976
Mason, Timothy I.	Assoc	581-6966	cftim		PHD	87	Indiana	1909
Moshtagh, Ali R.	Assoc	581-6967	cfam1		PHD	88	Arkansas	1987
Grant, Alan	Asst	581-7794	cfapq		PHD	96	Kansas St	1997

Eastern Kentucky University — Richmond, KY 40475-3176 (606) 622-1769 — eku.edu
Department of Economics — Col of Arts & Sciences Fax=622-2359 — Mrs. Laura A. Weitkamp

Name	Rank	Phone	Email	Field	Degree	Yr	School	Year
Hart, Dominick J.	Dean$	622-1405			PHD	70	S Carol	1970
Ruppel, Fred J.	C-Ac	622-1769	econruppe		PHD	84	Maryland	1997
O'Connor, J. Francis	Prof	622-1769	ecooconnor		PHD	74	Minnesota	1989
Watkins, Thomas G.	Prof	622-4980	ecowatkins		PHD	79	Iowa St	1984
Wright, Virginia B.	Prof	622-1390	ecowrigh		PHD	71	Geo Wash	1982
Dickey, Steven W.	Assoc	622-4987	ecodicke		PHD	85	S Illinois	1983
Payne, James E.	Assoc	622-1771	ecopayne		PHD	89	Fla St	1992
Harter, John F. R.	Asst	622-1773	ecoharte		PHD	92	Purdue	1999
Houston, Robert G.	Asst	622-2160	ecohoust		ABD	99	Kentucky	1998
Wuilleumier, Rudolph B.	Asst	622-2411	ecowuill		BS	67	Estrn Ky	1971

Eastern Michigan University — Ypsilanti, MI 48197 (734) 487-3395 — online.emich.edu
Department of Economics — Col of Arts & Science Fax=481-3240 — Ms. Deborah Wright
Homepage: http://www.emich.edu
email @1=emich.edu

Name	Rank	Phone	Email	Field	Degree	Yr	School	Year
Fish, Barry A.	Dean	487-4345	barry.fish@1		PHD	71	Wayne St	1970
Hanna, Raouf S.	H-Pr	487-3395	raouf.hanna@1		PHD	73	Indiana	1977
Chung, Young-Iob	Prof	487-6833	eco_chung		PHD	65	Columbia	1966
Edgren, John A.	Prof	487-3068	eco_edgren		PHD	79	Michigan	1979
Moreland, Kemper W.	Prof	487-0279	eco_moreland		PHD	80	Wisconsin	1980
Pearson, Donald W.	Prof	487-0008	eco_pearson		PHD	70	Tx-Austin	1969
Vogt, Michael G.	Prof	487-0006	eco_vogt		PHD	76	Wisconsin	1978
Woodland, Bill M.	Prof	487-0269	eco_woodland		PHD	81	Purdue	1981
Abdullah, Dewan A.	Assoc	487-0072	eco_abdullah		PHD	84	Kentucky	1988
Erenburg, Sharon J.	Assoc	487-0385	eco_erenburg		PHD	86	Illinois	1987
Esposto, Alfredo G.	Assoc	487-0004	eco_esposto		PHD	83	Temple	1990
Hayworth, Steve	Assoc	487-0009	eco_hayworth		PHD	87	MIT	1977
Thornton, James	Assoc	487-0080	eco_thornton		PHD	91	Oregon	1991
Crary, David B.	Asst	487-0001	eco_crary		PHD	82	Maryland	1980

Eastern New Mexico Univ — Portales, NM 88130 (505) — emnu.edu
Department of Economics — College of Business Fax=562-2252

Name	Rank	Phone	Email	Field	Degree	Yr	School	Year
Huybregts, Gerry	Dean	562-2343	gerry.huybregts	Mgt	PHD	88	UCLA	1988
Brunsen, William	C-Pr	562-2744	brunsenb	GHMA	PHD	76	Virginia	1987
Bice, Douglas	Asst	562-2342			PHD	96	Kentucky	1997
McFerrin, Randy	Asst	562-2369			PHD	95	Tx A&M	1995

Eastern Oregon University — LaGrande, OR 97850-2899 (541) 962-3508 — eou.edu
Department of Economics — School of Arts & Sci Fax=962-3893 — Dawna Flanagan

Name	Rank	Phone	Email	Field	Degree	Yr	School	Year
Ellston, Sandra	Dean	962-3629	ellston		PHD	80	Oregon	9-96
Johnson, Jeffery	C	962-3578	jjohnson		PHD	78	Ca-Rivers	9-82
Johnson, Colleen	Assoc	962-3340	johnsonc	AEJM	PHD	88	Wash St	9-86
Steenstra, Alex	Asst	962-3371	steensa	ABDQ	PHD	97	Utah	9-97

College of Eastern Utah — Price, UT 84501 (435) 613-2120 — ceu.edu
Economics Faculty — Dept of Social Science Fax=613-4102 — Linda Jensen

Name	Rank	Phone	Email	Field	Degree	Yr	School	Year
Hekmat, Ali	C-Pr	637-2120	ahekmat	E	PHD	93	Wi-Milwa	1994

Eastern Washington Univ — Cheney, WA 99004-2431 (509) 359-2281 — ewu.edu
Department of Economics — Ltrs, Art & Soc Science Fax=359-6732 — Nancy Millard

Name	Rank	Phone	Email	Field	Degree	Yr	School	Year
Chertox, Jeffers	Dean	359-2287		Soc	PHD	73	Oregon	
Trulove, William T.	C-Pr	359-2212			PHD	73	Oregon	1969
Bonsor, Thomas W.	Prof	359-2428			MA	55	Tufts	1958
Bunting, David C.	Prof	359-7947			PHD	72	Oregon	1971
Karier, Thomas M.	Prof	359-6517			PHD	85	Berkeley	1981
Kiser, Larry L.	Prof	359-2422			PHD	73	Rutgers	1971
Liu, Tsung-Hua	Prof	359-2430			PHD	69	Toronto	1970
Brown, Lisa Jo	Assoc	359-2838			PHD	86	Colorado	1981
Orr, Douglas V.	Assoc	359-2424			PHD	82	Colorado	1991

Edinboro University of PA — Edinboro, PA 16444 (814) 732-2407 — vax.edinboro.edu
Dept of Business Adm & Econ — Sch of Sci, Mgt & Tech Fax=732-2422 — Ms. Kathleen Schruers

Name	Rank	Phone	Email	Field	Degree	Yr	School	Year
Randall, Eric	Dean	732-2400	erandall		PHD			1977
Hannan, Michael J.	C-Pr	732-2407	hannan		PHD	88	W Virginia	1988
Dunn, James R.	Prof	732-2907	dunn		PHD	81	SUNY-Bin	1974
Adams, Robert J.	Assoc	732-2895	adamsr		PHD	71	Penn St	1977
Hannes, Lance E.	Assoc	732-2707	hannes		MBA	87	SUNY-Buf	1978

Elizabethtown College — Elizabethtown PA 17022-2298 (717) 361-1270 — etown.edu
Economics Faculty — Department of Business Fax=361-1487 — Ms. Eunice Ginder
phone: 361-1270

Name	Rank	Phone	Email	Field	Degree	Yr	School	Year
Evans, Hugh G. Jr.	C-Ac	Ext 1276	evanshg		MA	66	Penn St	1968
Hoppie, Maurice R.	Assoc	Ext 1277	hoppiemr		PHD	85	Tennessee	1980
Stone, Richard G.	Assoc	Ext 1284	stonerg		PHD	80	Temple	1987

Elmhurst College — Elmhurst, IL 60126-3296 (630) 617-3122 — elmhcx9.elmhurst.edu
Center for Bus & Economics — Div of Social Sciences Fax=617-6497 — Gail Herff

Name	Rank	Phone	Email	Field	Degree	Yr	School	Year
Heiney, Joseph N.	D-Pr	279-4100	josephh		PHD	83	Chicago	1977
Coleman Foundation Distinguished Chair in Business								
Thoma, George A. Jr.	Prof	617-3098	georget		PHD	73	N Illinois	1970
Schmitz, Suzanne	Asst	617-3115	susans		PHD	89	Kentucky	1990
Wan, Siaw-Peng	Asst	617-3112	siawpeng		PHD	94	Illinois	1995

Elmira College — Elmire, NY 14901 (607) 735-1942 — elmira.edu
Economics Faculty — Department of Economics Fax=735-1701 — Dawn Haupt

Name	Rank	Phone	Email	Field	Degree	Yr	School	Year
Hoffman, Naphtali	C-Ac	735-1942			PHD	80	Case Wes	1976
Kahwar, Mariam	Asst	735-4930			PHD	97	J Hopkins	1997

Elon College — Elon College, NC 27244-2020 (336) 584-2566 — numen.elon.edu
Department of Economics — Love School of Business Fax=538-2643 — Mrs. Jane Gilliam

Name	Rank	Phone	Email	Field	Degree	Yr	School	Year
Burbridge, John J.	Dean	584-2566	burbridg	Mgt	PHD	70	Lehigh	1996
Lilly, Gregory A.	C-As	584-2700	lillyg	CDA	PHD	88	Duke	1990
Tiemann, Thomas K.	Prof	584-2558	tiemann	RC	PHD	75	Vanderbilt	1984
Barbour, James L.	Assoc	584-2106	barbour	AB	PHD	87	Kentucky	1990
Das, Jayoti	Asst	584-2570	dastina	FL	PHD	93	Cincinnati	1996
DeLoach, Stephen B.	Asst	584-2560	deloach	EF	PHD	93	Mich St	1996
Redington, Douglas B.	Asst	584-2105	redingto	Q	PHD	89	Wyoming	1995

Embry-Riddle Aeronautical U	Daytona Bch, FL		32114-3900 (904) 226-6694				bart.db.erau.edu	
Economics Faculty	Business Administration		Fax=226-6696					
Harraf, Abe	C-Pr	226-6694			PHD	84	Utah St	
Vasigh, Bijan	Prof	226-6722			PHD	84	SUNY-Bin	
Tacker, Thomas L.	Assoc	226-6701			PHD	87	N Carol	
Kornecki, Lucyna	Asst	226-4963			PHD	80	Krakow	
Marett, Pamela	Asst	226-6721			PHD	82	Tennessee	

Emory University	Atlanta, GA		30322-2240 (404) 727-6364				emory.edu	
Economics Faculty	Department of Economics		Fax=727-4639	Susan Lee/L. Bassel/L. McNutt				
Sanderson, Steve	Dean	727-6062						
Chirinko, Robert	C-Ac$	727-6645	rchirin	EGH	PHD	82	Nrthwstrn	1994
Aranson, Peter H.	Prof	727-6648	paranso	HKL	PHD	72	Rochester	1981
Benston, George J.	Prof	727-7831		GKLM	PHD	63	Chicago	9-87
John H. Harland Professor of Finance, Economics, and Accounting								
Muth, Richard F.	Prof	727-0328	rmuth	N	PHD	58	Chicago	1983
Fuller E. Callaway Professor of Economics								
Rubin, Paul	Prof	727-6365	prubin	K	PHD	70	Purdue	1991
Schaffer, Beverly K.	Prof	727-6361	bschaff	D	PHD	67	Duke	1965
Carlson, Leonard	Assoc	727-6375	econlac	DJN	PHD	77	Stanford	1975
Chakravorty, Ujjayant	Assoc	727-1381	unc	QRH	PHD	89	Hawaii	1999
Curran, Christopher	Assoc	727-6355	econcc	CDK	PHD	72	Purdue	1970
Dezhbakhsh, Hashem	Assoc	727-4679	econhd	CG	PHD	89	Ohio St	1992
Levy, Daniel	Assoc	727-2941	econdl	EC	PHD	90	Ca-Irvine	1992
Arbatskaya, Maria	Asst			DL	ABD		Indiana	9-99
Beelders, Owen	Asst	727-6650	obeelde	CG	PHD	98	Rochester	1997
Carpenter, Robert	Asst	727-2770	econrc	EL	PHD	92	Wash U	1992
Islam, Nazrul	Asst	727-8643	nislam	ECO	PHD	93	Harvard	1997
Mazumdar, Joy	Asst	727-7833	jmazumd	FEO	PHD	96	Michigan	1996
Ozden, Caglar	Asst	727-0355	cozden	FL	PHD	98	Stanford	1998
Schrag, Joel	Asst	727-6363	jschrag	DKL	PHD	93	Berkeley	1993

Emory and Henry College	Emory, VA		24327-0947 (540) 944-4121				ehc.edu	
Economics Faculty	Dept of Econ & Business		Fax=944-6223					
Love, Barry A.	C-Ac	944-4121			PHD	78	Virginia	1984
Holbert L. Harris Professorship in Free Enterprise								
Dobkins, Linda H.	Asst	944-6194	lhdobkin	ROF	PHD	95	Va Tech	1996

Emporia State University	Emporia, KS		66801-5087 (316) 341-5347				esumail.emporia.edu	
Div Mgmt, Mktg, Fin & Econ	School of Business		Fax=341-5418				Ginger Tabares	
Hashmi, Sajjad A.	Dean	341-5274			PHD	66	Penn	8-83
Jones Distinguished Professor								
Titus, Varkey K.	C-Ac	341-5347			PHD	80	Wash St	8-79
Ghosh, Dipak	VProf	341-5891			PHD	94	Tulane	1997
Catlett, Robert B.	Asst	341-5678			MA	75	Nebraska	1976
Janssen, Arthur J.	Asst	341-5401			MA		Missouri	1976

University of Evansville	Evansville, IN		47722 (812) 479-2851				evansville.edu	
Dept of Atg, Econ & Finance	School of Business Adm		Fax=479-2872				Sherry Hawkins	
phone 1-800-423-8633 ext 2851								
Reeder, David B.	Dean	479-2866	dr4	Atg	MBA	80	Kentucky	1968
Blalock, M. Gale	C-Ac	479-2868	gb3		PHD	80	Okla St	1977
Zimmer, Michael A.	Prof	479-2864	m23		PHD	77	Tennessee	1976

Evergreen State College	Olympia, WA		98505 (360) Ext 6513					
Economics Faculty	Pol Economy & Soc Chg		Fax=					
Hahn, Jeanne	C	866-6000		PolS	ABD	68	Chicago	1972
Bohmer, Peter G.		866-6000			PHD	85	Mass	1987
Bowerman, Priscilla V.		866-6000			MPHI	71	Yale	1973
Academic Dean								
Bruner, Bill		866-6000			BA	67	W Wash	1981
Lidman, Russell M.		866-6000			PHD	72	Wisconsin	1974
Nasser, Alan		866-6000			PHD	71	Indiana	1975
Nisbet, Charles T.		866-6000			PHD	67	Oregon	1971
Weeks, Gregory C.		866-6000			PHD	78	Wash St	1981
Womeldorf, Thomas		866-8600			PHD	89	American	1991

Fairfield University	Fairfield, CT		06430-5195 (203) Ext 2866				fairi.fairfield.edu	
Department of Economics	Col of Arts & Sciences		Fax=254-4119				Sally Williams	
phone: 254-4000								
Grossman, Orin L.	Dean	254-4000	olgrossman	Musi	PHD	75	Yale	1993
Deak, Edward J.	C-Pr	254-4000	deak	LRK	PHD	74	Conn	1970
Buss, James A.	Assoc	254-4000	jabuss	EOP	PHD	72	Conn	1975
Lane, Philip J.	Assoc	254-4000	lane	EGR	PHD	83	Tufts	1981

LeClair, Mark S. | Assoc 254-4000 mleclair | FGC PHD 87 Rutgers 1988
Miners, Laurence A. | Assoc 254-4000 miners | CIJA PHD 79 N Carol 1981
Nantz, Kathryn A. | Assoc 254-4000 nantz | JDPA PHD 87 Purdue 1986
Kelly, Robert A. | Asst 254-4000 rakelly | HKC PHD 71 Geotown 1978
Miners, Cathy | VAsst 254-4000 cminers | EG PHD 81 N Carol 1998
Parsons, Christina | Asst 254-4000 ccuuha | HR PHD 97 Ohio St 1997

Fairleigh Dickinson Univ | Madison, NJ 07940 (973) 443-8721 | alpha.fdu.edu
Dept of Social Sci & Econ | Becton C of Arts & Sci Fax=443-8799 | Doris Owen
Greer, Martin | Dean$ 443-8750 greer | Eng PHD Illinois 1970
Woolley, Peter J. | C 443-8721 woolley | PHD 89 Pittsburgh 1987
Englander, Frederick | Prof 443-8832 englander | DE PHD 75 Rutgers
Greenfield, Robert L. | Prof 443-8846 | GP PHD 79 Rutgers 8-79
Jonnard, Claude | Prof 443-8810 jonnard | A PHD
Lee, Eric Y. | Prof | F PHD 73 Columbia
Koppl, Roger | Assoc 443-8800 koppl | BEG PHD 88 Auburn 1988

Fairleigh Dickinson Univ | Teaneck, NJ 07666-1914 (201) 692-7215 | alpha.fdu.edu
Atg, Ec, Fn, Tx Lw, Intl Bus | Silbermann Col of Bus Fax=692-7219 | Mrs. Eileen Kerrigan
Lerman, Paul | Dean 692-7200 | Quan PHD 74 NYU 9-72
Angkatavanich, Virote | C-Pr 692-7215 | AEFG PHD 67 New Sch 1963
Djimopoulos, Evangelos | Prof 692-7292 | ADEF PHD 69 Columbia
Anastasopoulos, Petros | Assoc 692-7268 | ADE PHD 84 New Sch 1986
Kessler, Adam | Assoc 692-7214 | ACDE PHD 78 NYU
Kjetsaa, Richard W. | Assoc 692-7295 | AEG PHD 85 Fordham
Oseghale, Braimoh | Assoc 692-7267 | F PHD 89 Temple 1994
Kiernan, Joseph J. | Asst 692-7298 | AEG PHD 80 Fordham

Fairmont State College | Fairmont, WV 26554-2470 (304) 367-4261 | mail.fscwv.edu
Department of Economics | Sch of Business & Econ Fax=366-4870 | Sherrie Strowderman
Schaupp, Rebecca | C-Pr 367-4261 ras | EDD W Virginia 1984
Khalil, Mohamad | C-Pr 367-4727 mak | C PHD 88 W Virginia 1988
Alshallah, Mohamed | Assoc 367-4750 mha | AF MBA Bridgepr 1988
Laughlin, William | Assoc 367-4726 wml | AE MA Cincinnati 1966
Potter, William | Assoc 367-4724 potter | AN MA Memphis 1970

Fayetteville State Univ | Fayetteville, NC 28301-4298 (910) 486-1617 | sbel.uncfsu.edu
Dept of Economics & Finance | Sch of Business & Econ Fax=486-1033 | Ms. Vera Watkins
Davis, Charles | Dean 486-1267 cdavis | Mktg PHD 81 Tennessee 1993
Nijhawan, Inder P. | C-Pr 486-1618 nijhawan | PHD 71 N Carol
Jonsson, Petur | Assoc 486-1984 jonsson | PHD 86 Penn St
Okpala, Amon O. | Assoc 486-1594 okpala | PHD 84 LSU 1984
Roayaei, A. Jean | Assoc 486-1592 roayaei | PHD 84 Fla St

Ferris State University | Big Rapids, MI 49307-2284 (616) 592-2431 | ferris.edu
Econ & Applied Stat Dept | College of Business Fax=592-3521 | Kay Anderson
Rallo, Joseph C. | Dean 592-2422 | Mgt PHD 80 Syracuse 1992
Teferra, Daniel | C-Pr 592-2767 dteferra | PHD 79 Wisconsin 1980
Afifi, Ashraf S. | Prof 592-2766 aafifi | ADH PHD 83 Kansas 1980
Ferdowsi, Abdollah | Prof 592-2738 ferdowsa | PHD 82 Mich St 1984
Olson, Dennis D. | Asst 592-2766 dolson | ABD Minnesota 1972

University of Findlay | Findlay, OH 45840-3695 (419) 424-4539 | lucy.findlay.edu
Economics Faculty | College of Business Fax=424-6781 | Ms. Kathy Bradford
Mathern, Dennis C. | D-Ac 424-4546 mathern | Mktg PHD 98 Bowl Gr
Gupta, Shiv K. | Prof 424-4548 | AJ DBA 83 London 1983
Gamba, Maria V. | Asst 424-4718 | AD MS Wright St 1988

Fisk University | Nashville, TN 37208-3051 (615) 329-8570
Economics Faculty | Div of Business Admin Fax=329-8758 | Mrs. Eula Black
Cambronero, Alfredo | C-As 329-8698 | DOE PHD 92 Vanderbilt 1992

Fitchburg State College | Fitchburg, MA 01420-2697 (978) 665-3397 | fsc.edu
Economics Faculty | Social Sciences Dept Fax=665-4530
Micciche, Pasquale E. | C-Pr 665-3429 | Hst PHD 76 Boston U 1969
Wiegersma, Nancy A. | Prof 665-3088 | PHD 76 Maryland 1979
Lwamugira, Pirudas L. | Assoc 665-3281 | PHD 90 Temple 1991
Turk, Michael | Assoc 665-3731 | PHD 76 Harvard 1982

University of Florida	Gainesville, FL		32611-7140 (352) 392-0151					dale.cba.ufl.edu
Department of Economics	College of Business Adm Fax=392-7860							Dian Studstill
Kraft, John L.	Dean	392-2397	kraftj		PHD	71	Pittsburgh	1990
Kenny, Lawrence W.	C-Pr	392-0151	kenny	DHJ	PHD	77	Chicago	1975
Adams, James D.	Prof	392-0124	adams	OJ	PHD	76	Chicago	1979
Berg, Sanford V.	Prof	392-0132	berg	T	PHD	70	Yale	1971
Exec Dir Public Utility Research Ctr;Public Utilities & Distinguished Serv Pr								
Blair, Roger Duncan	Prof	392-0179	rblair	KT	PHD	68	Mich St	1970
Huber Hurst Professor of Business and Legal Studies								
Denslow, David A. Jr.	Prof	392-0171	denslow	EH	PHD	74	Yale	1970
Distinguished Service Professor								
Dinopoulos, Elias	Prof	392-8150	dinopoe	FO	PHD	85	Columbia	1988
Lanzillotti, Robert F.	Prof	392-2397	lanz	T	PHD	53	Berkeley	1969
Dir Public Pol Resr Center; American Econ Int Free Enterprise Eminent Scholar								
Lewis, Tracy R.	Prof	392-7489		TDQ	PHD	75	Ca-SnDgo	1991
James Walter Eminent Scholar in Economics								
Romano, Richard E.	Prof	392-4812	romano	THOD	PHD	82	Pittsburgh	1982
Rush, Mark	Prof	392-0318	rush	EF	PHD	82	Rochester	1982
Sappington, David A.	Prof	392-3904	sapping	TD	PHD	80	Princeton	1989
Lanzillotti-McKethan Eminent Scholar								
Slutsky, Steven M.	Prof	392-8106	slutsky	DH	PHD	75	Yale	1984
Smith, Stanley K.	Prof	392-0171	stans	J	PHD	76	Michigan	1976
Director, Bureau of Economic and Business Research								
Vernon, Jack R.	Prof	392-6612	vernon	E	PHD	61	Nrthwstrn	1967
West, Carol Taylor	Prof	392-0171	carolw	RQC	PHD	74	Michigan	1909
Director, Forcasting Program Bureau of Economics and Business Research								
Bomberger, William A.	Assoc	392-0135	billb		PHD	73	Brown	1977
Goddard, Frederick O.	Assoc	392-0972	fgoddard		PHD	67	Duke	1966
Hamilton, Johnathan H.	Assoc	392-2999	hamilton	HRD	PHD	82	MIT	1984
Horowitz, Ann R.	Assoc	392-0198	horowitz		PHD	66	Indiana	1972
Toda, Yasushi	Assoc	392-0112	toda	RP	PHD	69	Harvard	1974
Waldo, Douglas G.	Assoc	392-1370	waldo	EFO	PHD	80	N Carol	1981
Ai, Chunrong	Asst	392-7859	aic	CT	PHD	90	MIT	1994
Werner, Megan	Asst	392-0475	wernermj	CHQ	PHD	94	Ca-SnDgo	1994
Xu, Bin	Asst	392-0122	xub	FO	PHD	95	Columbia	1995

Florida A&M University	Tallahassee, FL		32307-4800 (850) 599-3138					famu.edu
Department of Economics	Coll of Arts & Sciences Fax=561-2290							Mrs. Pamela H. Leonard
Perry, Aubrey	Dean	599-3430		Psyc				
Burggraf, Shirley	Prof	599-3126		CE	PHD	68	Case Wes	1968
Daniels, Rudolph	Prof	561-2052		DJQ	PHD	80	Fla St	1977
Oguledo, Victor I.	Assoc	561-2053		FL	PHD	89	Nebraska	1990
Taylor, Addis C.	Assoc	599-3138		JM	PHD	83	Fla St	1976
Bierhanzal, Elwood	Asst							
Thomas, Michael	Asst							
Auzenne, George R.	Lect	561-2057		LM	MS	63	Boston	1976

Florida Atlantic Univ	Boca Raton, FL		33431-0991 (561) 297-3220					fau.edu
Department of Economics	Col of Social Sciences Fax=297-2542							Patricial Spitale
Register, Charles A.	C-Pr	297-3222	cregister	JL	PHD	84	Okla St	1997
Hung, Chao-shun	Prof	297-3223	hung	D	PHD	82	Tx A&M	1982
Stronge, William B.	Prof	297-2833	strongew		PHD	71	Iowa St	1971
Bosshardt, William D.	Assoc		bwbosshar	F	PHD	91	Purdue	1995
Director of Center for Economic Education								
Manage, Neela D.	Assoc	297-3226	manage	FE	PHD	81	Geo Wash	1981
Yuhn, Ky-hyang	Assoc	297-3224	yuhn	ECG	PHD	85	N Illinois	8-93
Benchekroun, Hassan	Asst	726-3222		DL	PHD	98	Laval	1999
Gupta, Srabana	Asst	726-5251		DL	PHD	95	Florida	1995
McCown, James	Asst	296-8502	jmccown	FE	PHD	97	Ohio St	1997
Vishwasrao, Sharmila	Asst	297-3229	svishwas	F	PHD	94	Purdue	1995

Florida Institute of Tech	Melbourne, FL		32901-6975 (407) 674-7167					fit.edu
Dept of Economics	School of Business Fax=674-8896							S. Farinella
Hollingsworth, A. Thomas	Dean	674-7327	aholling	Mgt	PHD	69	Mich St	1990
Hott, David D.	C-Ac	674-7167	dhott		PHD	77	Lehigh	1995
Slotkin, M.	Asst	674-7267	mslotkin		PHD	95	N Carol	1996

Florida International Univ	Miami, FL		33199 (305) 348-2316					fiu.edu
Department of Economics	College of Arts & Sci Fax=348-1524							Deuixieme Maison #314/316
Herriott, Arthur	Dean	348-2866	herriott	Chem	PHD	67	Florida	1993
Liossatos, Panagis S.	C-Pr	348-3288	liossato	CODR	PHD	68	Penn	1981
Alonso, Irma T. de	Prof	348-2318	alonsoi	OCFI	PHD	69	York-Eng	1981
Carvajal, Manuel J.	Prof	348-3290	carvajal	JITQ	PHD	74	Florida	1981
Jorge, Antonio	Prof	348-2072		BPO	PHD		Villanova	
Salazar-Carrillo, Jorge	Prof	348-3283	salazar	OFA	PHD	67	Berkeley	
Director, Center of Economic Research & Education								

Name	Rank	Phone	Email	Field	Degree	Yr	School	Hired
Wilkins, Mira	Prof	348-3352	wilkinsm	NF	PHD	57	Cambridge	1974
Witte, Ann D.	Prof	348-3286	wittea	DHK	PHD	71	N Car St	1996
Anbarci, Nejat M.	Assoc	348-2735	anbarcin	DC	PHD	88	Iowa	1995
Boyd, John H. III	Assoc	348-3287	boydj	DC	PHD	86	Indiana	1998
Karayaicin, Ali Cem	Assoc	348-3285	karayalc	EF	PHD	89	Columbia	1989
Lipner, Kenneth	Assoc	919-5859	lipnerk	RJA	PHD	77	Rutgers	1981
Roy, Santanu	Assoc	348-6362	roys	DLQF	PHD	91	Cornell	1998
Syropoulos, Constantinos	Assoc	348-2592	syropoul	FLO	PHD	89	Yale	1996
Willumsen, Maria Jose	Assoc	348-3400	willumse	RO	PHD	84	Cornell	1984
Bhat, Mahadev G.	Asst	348-1210	bhatm	Q	PHD	91	Tennessee	1994
Lemke, Robert J.	Asst	348-6031	lemker	DJ	PHD	97	Wisconsin	1997
Mitra, Devashish	Asst	348-3893	mitrad	FLO	PHD	96	Columbia	1996
Thomakos, Dimitrios	Asst	348-6639	thomakos	CEO	PHD	98	Columbia	1998
Gummerson, A.	Lect	348-2381	gummerso	AEF	PHD	71	Wisconsin	1989

Florida Southern College — Lakeland, FL 33801-5698 (941) — flsouthern.edu
Dept of Bus & Economics — Division of Bus Adm — Fax=680-4126

Name	Rank	Phone	Email	Field	Degree	Yr	School	Hired
Hopkins, Duane L.	C-As	680-4285		Mktg	MBA		Harvard	1982
Brown, Carl C.	Prof	680-4290		EFHL	PHD	79	Okla St	1980
William F. Chatlos Professorship in Business & Economics								
Buccino, Joan G.	Prof	680-4277		A	PHD	90	S Fla	1980
Dorotha Tanner Chair in Ethics in Business & Economics								
Lebrenz, Eugene R.	Prof	680-4274		J	EDD		N Illinois	1987
Bias, Peter V.	Assoc	680-4282		ER	PHD	89	Cincinnati	1988

Florida State University — Tallahassee, FL 32306-2180 (850) 644-5001 — garnet.acns.fsu.edu
Department of Economics — College of Soc Sciences Fax=644-4535 — Fran Loeb 644-7089

Name	Rank	Phone	Email	Field	Degree	Yr	School	Hired
Cnudde, Charles F.	Dean	644-5488	ccnudde	PolS	PHD	67	N Carol	1987
Cobbe, James H.	C-Pr	644-7091	jcobbe	O	PHD	77	Yale	1976
Adamovich, Ljubisa S.	Prof	644-7097	ladamovi	E	PHD	61	Belgrade	1967
Benson, Bruce L.	Prof	644-7094	bbenson	K	PHD	78	Tx A&M	1987
VeDoe Moore Distinguished Research Professor								
Canterbery, E. Ray	Prof	644-7209	rcanterb	F	PHD	66	Wash U	1970
Downing, Paul B.	Prof	644-7648			PHD	67	Wisconsin	1980
on leave								
Fournier, Gary M.	Prof	644-7080	gfournie	L	PHD	81	Virginia	1980
Gapinski, James H.	Prof	644-7081	jgapinsk	O	PHD	71	SUNY-Buf	1979
Gwartney, James D.	Prof	644-7645	ljgwartney	A	PHD	69	U Wash	1968
on leave								
Hirsch, Barry T.	Prof	644-2833	bhirsch	J	PHD	77	Virginia	1990
Research Associate, Pepper Institute on Aging & Public Policy								
Holcombe, Randall G.	Prof	644-7095	holcombe	H	PHD	76	Va Tech	1988
DeVoe Moore Professor								
Koo, Anthony Y.	VProf	644-7086	ykoo	F	PHD	46	Harvard	
Macesich, George	Prof	644-7079		E	PHD	58	Chicago	1959
Macpherson, David A.	Prof	644-3586	dmacpher	J	PHD	87	Penn St	1992
Research Director, Pepper Institute on Aging & Public Policy								
Marquis, Milton H.	Prof	644-7204	mmarquis	E	PHD	85	Indiana	1986
Norrbin, Stefan C.	Prof	644-7206	snorrbin	F	PHD	86	Ariz St	1990
Director of Graduate Studies								
Rasmussen, David W.	Prof	644-7659	drasmuss	K	PHD	69	Wash U	1968
Director, DeVoe Moore Center								
Rockwood, Charles E.	Emer	644-7088	crockwoo	O	PHD	63	Indiana	1960
Schlagenhauf, Don E.	Prof	644-3817	dschlage	E	PHD	77	Illinois	1998
Brim Eminent Scholar Chair								
Serow, William J.	Prof	644-1762	wserow	T	PHD	72	Duke	1981
Director, Center for Study of Population								
Sliger, Bernard F.	Prof	644-4772		A	PHD	55	Mich St	1972
Sorensen, Phillip E.	Prof	644-7093		Q	PHD	66	Berkeley	1971
Beaumont, Paul M.	Assoc	644-7085	beaumont	C	PHD	84	Penn	1988
Mason, Patrick L.	Assoc			J	PHD	91	New Sch	1999
McCaleb, Thomas S.	Assoc	644-1816	mccaleb		PHD	75	N Carol	1980
Prasad, Kislaya	Assoc	644-7083	kprasad	D	PHD	88	Syracuse	1988
Sass, Tim R.	Assoc	644-7087	tsass	L	PHD	84	U Wash	1990
Schmertmann, Carl P.	Assoc	644-7100	schmertmann	C	PHD	88	Berkeley	1990
Zuehlke, Thomas W.	Assoc	644-7208	tzuehlke	C	PHD	83	Florida	1983
Burke, Mary A.	Asst	644-5003	mburke	D	PHD	98	J Hopkins	1997

Fordham University — New York, NY 10458 (718) 817-4048 — murray.fordham.edu
Department of Economics — Col of Arts & Sciences Fax=817-3518 — Angela Bates

Name	Rank	Phone	Email	Field	Degree	Yr	School	Hired
Himmelberg, Robert	Dean			Hist	PHD	63	Penn St	
Salvatore, Dominick	C-Pr	817-4048			PHD	71	CUNY	1970
Cammarosano, Joseph R.	Prof	817-4057			PHD	56	Fordham	1955
Dowling, Edward T.	Prof	817-4062			PHD	73	Cornell	1973
Vinod, Hrishinesh D.	Prof	817-4065			PHD	65	Harvard	1982
Basu, Parantap	Assoc	817-4061			PHD	85	Ca-SnBarb	1988
Brent, Robert J.	Assoc	817-4058			PHD	76	Manchest	1980

Name	Rank	Phone	Email	Fields	Degree	Yr	School	Joined
Diulio, Eugene A.	Assoc	817-4055			PHD	66	Columbia	1963
Assistant Chair, Undergraduate Education								
Leighton, Linda S.	Assoc	817-4054			PHD	78	Columbia	1979
Champ, Bruce	Asst	817-4056			PHD	90	Minnesota	1994
Geddes, Raymond R.	Asst	817-4049			PHD	91	Chicago	1991
James, Duncan	Asst	817-4066			PHD	98	Arizona	1999
McLeod, Darryl L.	Asst	817-4063			PHD	82	Berkeley	1984
Reagle, Derrick	Asst	817-3866			PHD	98	Vanderbilt	1998
Rowland, Patrick	Asst	817-4051			PHD	98	Ca-SnBarb	1996
Schwalbenberg, Henry M.	Asst	817-4059			PHD	88	Columbia	1988
Assistant Chair, Graduate Education								
Winczewski, Greg A.	Asst	817-4050			PHD	92	Fordham	1995

Fort Hays State University — Hays, KS 67601-4099 (785) 628-5805 — fhsu.edu
Dept of Economics & Finance — College of Business Fax=628-4418 — Linda Kepka

Name	Rank	Phone	Email	Fields	Degree	Yr	School	Joined
Gamble, Ralph C. Jr.	C-Pr	628-5805	rgamble	AEG	PHD	89	Okla St	1984
Parker, Carl D.	Prof	628-5805	cparker	DIJM	PHD	71	Okla St	1976
Director, Employee Relations								
Rickman, Bill D.	Prof	628-5318	brickman	DEJ	PHD	82	Okla St	1972
Lee, Jimmy	Assoc	628-5868	jlee	EKL	PHD	91	Penn St	1989
Gilson, Preston	Asst	628-4107	pgilson	F	PHD	93	St Louis	1988
Johansen, Thomas C.	Asst	628-5867	tjohanse	GE	PHD	90	Okla St	1989
Terry, Rory	Asst	628-5337	rterry	GE	PHD	92	Utah	1997

Fort Lewis College — Durango, CO 81301-3999 (970) 247-7294 — fortlewis.edu
Department of Economics — School of Business Adm Fax=247-7623 — Iris Mobley
Homepage: http://ww.fortlewis.edu/soba/soba.html

Name	Rank	Phone	Email	Fields	Degree	Yr	School	Joined
Cave, John E. Jr.	Dean	247-7294	cave_s	BusA	PHD	75	Minnesota	1990
Atencio, Leonard D.	Prof	247-7589	anencio_l		PHD	69	Kansas St	1968
Clay, James P.	Prof	247-7591	clay_j		PHD	74	Kansas St	1982
Lynch, Vernon E. Jr.	Prof	247-7404	lynch_v		PHD	76	Arizona	1972
Lehman, Dale E.	Assoc	247-7494	lehman_d		PHD	81	Rochester	1983
Hai, Wen	Asst	247-7494	wai_w		PHD	91	Ca-Davis	1992

Fort Valley State College — Fort Valley, GA 31030-3298 (912) 825-6270 — fvs3.fvsc.peachnet.edu
Dept of Business Adm & Econ — Sch of Arts & Sciences Fax=825-6394 — Shuri Rand
Did Not Respond--1997-98 Listing

Name	Rank	Phone	Email	Fields	Degree	Yr	School	Joined
Crumbley, Isaac	Dean	825-6454		Biol	PHD			
Bhuiyan, Mohammad	H	825-6270			PHD	93	Florida	9-96
Yasin, Jehad	Assoc	825-6270	jyasin	ETAC	PHD	87	Fla St	9-88

Framingham State College — Framingham, MA 01701-9101 (508) 626-4850 — compsvc.frc.mass.edu
Economics Faculty — Dept of Econ & Bus Adm Fax=626-4040 — Marie Dinallo
Did Not Respond--1997-98 Listing

Name	Rank	Phone	Email	Fields	Degree	Yr	School	Joined
Wallace, Robert	C-Pr	626-4888			PHD	72	Nrthwstrn	
Barr, Joseph E.	Prof	626-4852			PHD	76	Boston C	
Dunne, Maureen E.	Prof	626-4861			MBA		Detroit	
Krier, Donald F.	Prof	626-4884			PHD	69	Boston C	1973
McKinney, Marie M.	Prof	626-4853			PHD	83	SUNY-Bin	1985
White, Charles	Prof	626-4892	cwhite	EC	PHD	81	Chicago	9-85
Doyle-Burke, Christine	Assoc	626-4886			MA		Boston C	
MacRitchie, Donald R.	Assoc	626-4881			MA	85	Boston C	1987
Meaney, Martha M.	Assoc	626-4880			MA		Boston C	
Rogers, Mary T.	Assoc	626-4858			PHD	89	Mass	
Anderson, Thomas	Asst	626-4857			PHD	87	Iowa	
Devine, Robert	Asst	626-4882			MA		Northeas	
Ding, John	Asst	626-4016			PHD	91	Mass	
Farina, Louis	Asst	626-4885			MBA		Babson	
Ryan, Peter C.	Asst	626-4844			PHD	77	Mass	
Soriano, Beverly	Asst	626-4856			MS		Bentley	

Francis Marion University — Florence, SC 29501-0547 (843) 661-1432 — fmarion.edu
Economics Faculty — School of Business Fax=661-1165 — Carol Austin

Name	Rank	Phone	Email	Fields	Degree	Yr	School	Joined
Goebel, E. L. (Jack)	Dean	661-1430		Mgt	PHD	68	Georgia	8-95
Rinehart, James R.	C-Pr	661-1426			PHD	62	Virginia	
Phillip N. Truluck Professor of Economics and Public Policy								
Kyer, Ben L.	Prof	661-1436			PHD	84	W Virginia	
Marcis, John G.	Assoc	661-1412			PHD		Missouri	
O'Brien, M. Barry	Assoc	661-1407			PHD	86	S Carol	
Pompe, Jeffrey	Assoc	661-1438			PHD	90	Fla St	

Franklin University — Columbus, OH 43215-5399 (614) 341-6330 — franklin.edu
Div Atg, Fnce & Intl Bus — Col of Business & Tech Fax=228-8478

Name	Rank	Phone	Email	Fields	Degree	Yr	School	Joined
Newton, James E.	C-Pr	341-6330	newtonj		PHD	97	Ohio St	
Assistant Dean								

Franklin and Marshall Coll Lancaster, PA 17604-3003 (717) 291-3916 acad.fandm.edu
Economics Faculty Department of Economics Fax=291-4369 Maryfrances Mason

Whitesell, William E.	C-Pr	291-3938	w_whitesell		PHD	63	Tx-Austin	1965
Henry P. & Mary B. Stager Professor of Economics								
Callari, Antonino	Prof	291-3947	a_callari		PHD	81	Mass	1979
Caniglia, Alan S.	Prof	291-3945	a_caniglia		PHD	83	Virginia	1982
Flaherty, Sean	Prof	291-3940	s_flaherty	J	PHD	81	Berkeley	1980
A'Hearn, Brian	Asst	291-3990	b_ahearn		PHD	94	Berkeley	1999
Ortiz, L.	Asst	291-3920	l_ortiz		PHD	98	Berkeley	1996
Shabbir, Tayyeb	Asst	291-3936	t_shabbir		PHD	87	Penn	1998
Zein-Elabdin, Eiman	Asst	291-4045	e_zein-elabdin		PHD	93	Tennessee	1995

Freed Hardeman University Henderson, TN 38340-2399 (901) 989-6091 fhu.edu
Economics Faculty School of Business Fax=989-6065 Mrs. Estelle Maxwell

Wilson, Dwayne H.	Dean	989-6091	dwilson	CDEQ	PHD	91	Miss	8-75
Director of the Free Enterprise Center								
Perkins, Garey B.	Assoc	989-6983	gperkins	DEQ	PHD	71	Tennessee	8-98
Brooks, Rickey A.	Asst	989-6054	rbrooks	DEF	MBA	91	Miss	8-92

Frostburg State University Frostburg, MD 21532-1099 (301) 687-4386 fre.fsu.umd.edu
Department of Economics School of Business Fax=687-4760 Ms. Yvonne R. Beal

Wilkinson, Steven P.	Dean	687-4089			PHD	77	S Illinois	8-87
Stair, Anthony G.	C-Ac	687-4788			PHD	93	W Virginia	1984
Dalton, Margaret M.	Prof	687-4386			PHD	86	W Virginia	1981
Mizak, Daniel A.	Prof	687-4096			PHD	84	Pittsburgh	1977
McLellan, Jacquelynne W.	Assoc	687-4394			PHD	93	Wayne St	1994
Neral, John A.	Assoc	687-4265			PHD	89	Pittsburgh	1986
Rossi, Armond A.	Asst	687-4407			PHD	93	W Virginia	1988
Kiriazis, David M.	Lect	687-4390			PHD	97	Wayne St	

Furman University Greenville, SC 29613 (864) 294-2132 furman.edu
Economics Faculty Dept of Econ & Bus Adm Fax=294-2990 Brenda Chandler

Roe, R. David	C-Pr	294-3320			PHD	78	Duke	1977
Horney, Mary Jean	Prof	294-3315			PHD	77	Duke	1979
Frederick W. Symmes Professor of Economics								
Stanford, Richard A.	Prof	294-3322			PHD	71	Georgia	1968
David C Garrett Jr. Professor of Economics								
Khandke, Kailash	Asst				PHD	93	Ca-Davis	1995
Peterson, Kenneth D.	Asst	294-3043			PHD	91	SUNY-SBr	1990

Gallaudet University Washington DC 20002-3695 (202) 651-5040 gallaudet.gallua.edu
Dept of Economics & Finance School of Management Fax=651-5516
Did Not Respond--1997-98 Listing

Sutcliffe, Ronald E.	Dean	651-5312		Bus	PHD	80	Maryland	1980
Chaikind, Stephen B.	C-Pr	651-5040			PHD	78	CUNY	1989
Rashid, Khadijat	Asst	651-5040			MBA	93	Maryland	

Gannon University Erie, PA 16541-0001 (814) 871-7585 gannon.edu
Dept of Econ, Fnce & Bus Adm Dahlkemper Sch of Bus Fax=871-7210

Prokop, Duane R.	C	871-7576	prokopool	Mktg	MBA	78	Youngstwn	1-81
Aburachis, Abdelrahman E.	Prof	871-7584	aburachidol	G	PHD	72	Pittsburgh	
Brooker, Robert F.	Assoc	871-7586	brookercol	C	PHD	85	N Car St	1982
Mahan, Gary P.	Assoc	871-7588	mahancon		PHD	78	N Car St	1977
Bennett, Charles A.	Asst	871-7585	bennett	A	MA	68	Fordham	1968

Gardner-Webb University Boiling Spr, NC 28017 (704) 434-4375 gardner-webb.edu
Economics Faculty Broyhill Sch of Mgt Fax=434-4738 Sharon Webb

Honts, Arlen K.	Dean	434-2361	ahonts	Mgt	PHD	97	Vanderbilt	1993
Bottoms, I. Glenn	Prof	434-4377	gbottoms		PHD	81	Geo St	1983
Negbenebor, Anthony I.	Prof	434-3820	anegbenebor		PHD	88	Miss St	1989

Geneva College Beaver Falls, PA 15010-3599 (724) 847-6615 geneva.edu
Economics Faculty Dept of Bus, Atg & Mgt Fax=847-6696 B. Dawson

Nutter, J. Randall	C-Pr	847-6613	jrn	Mgt	DBA	91	Nova SE	1992
Fong, Tat P.	Asst	847-6615	tfong	F	PHD	91	Pittsburgh	1996

George Fox University Newberg, OR 97132-2697 (503) Ext 2810 georgefox.edu
Economics Faculty Dept of Business & Econ Fax=554-2829 Konay Ford Ext 2810
phone 544-2810

Head, Tom	C-Ac	Ext 2811	thead		MA	80	Berkeley	
Dykema, Eugene R.	Prof	Ext 2812	edykema		PHD	83	Notre Dm	
Worden, Debra	Asst	Ext 2816	dworden		PHD	84	Purdue	

George Mason University	Fairfax, VA	22030-4444 (703) 993-1130					sba01.gmu.edu	
Department of Economics	College of Arts & Sci	Fax=993-1133					Carol J. Hlavinka	
Williams, Walter E.	C-Pr	993-1148			PHD	72	UCLA	1981
John M. Olin Distinguished Professor of Economics								
Bennett, James T.	Prof	993-1155			PHD	70	Case Wes	1975
William P. Snavely Professor of Economics								
Bloch, Howard Ruben	Prof	993-1157			PHD	64	Princeton	
Buchanan, James M.	Prof	993-2327			PHD	48	Chicago	1983
University Professor of Economics								
Congleton, Roger D.	Prof	993-2328			PHD	78	Va Tech	1988
Cowen, Tyler	Prof	993-1136			PHD	87	Harvard	
Crain, W. Mark	Prof	993-2325			PHD	76	Tx A&M	
Heiner, Ronald A.	Prof	993-2322			PHD	75	UCLA	1989
Rowley, Charles K.	Prof	993-4026			PHD	64	Nottinghm	1984
Vaughn, Karen I.	Prof	993-1146			PHD	71	Duke	1978
Wagner, Richard E.	Prof	993-2324			PHD	66	Virginia	1988
Holbert I. Harris Professor of Economics								
Levy, David M.	Assoc	993-2319			PHD	79	Chicago	1983
Meyer, Carrie A.	Assoc	993-1143			PHD	88	Illinois	1988
Reid, Joseph D.	Assoc	993-1159			PHD	74	Chicago	1983
Thorbecke, Willem	Assoc	993-1150			PHD	88	Berkeley	
Wiest, Philip Ray	Assoc	993-1131			PHD	76	Pittsburgh	
Caplan, Bryan	Asst	993-1124			PHD	97	Princeton	1997
Hanson, Robin	Asst				PHD	99	Cal Tech	1999
Menes, Rebecca	Asst				PHD	97	Harvard	1999
Ramirez, Carlos D.	Asst	993-1145			PHD	93	Harvard	
Sellgrew, Andrew	Asst				PHD	98	Chicago	1999

George Washington Univ	Washington, DC	20052	(202) 994-6150				gwu.edu	
Department of Economics	Columbian C Arts & Sci	Fax=994-6147					Peter Van Ripen	
Lefton, Lester A.	Dean	994-6210			PHD			
Watson, Harry S.	C-Pr	994-6685	hsw	H	PHD	81	Indiana	1980
Aschheim, Joseph	Prof	994-6153		E	PHD	54	Harvard	1964
Boulier, Bryan L.	Prof	994-8088	mortile	JT	PHD	74	Princeton	1981
Bradley, Michael D.	Prof	994-8089	mbrad	E	PHD	82	N Carol	1987
Brock, Gerald W.	Prof	994-3989	gbrock	L	PHD	73	Harvard	1990
Cordes, Joseph J.	Prof	994-6151	cordes	H	PHD	77	Wisconsin	1975
Dunn, Robert M. Jr.	Prof	994-7379	rmdunn	F	PHD	67	Stanford	1978
Goldfarb, Robert S.	Prof	994-7581	gldfrb	BJ	PHD	68	Yale	1980
Holman, Mary A.	Prof	994-6156		L	PHD	63	Geo Wash	1963
Kaminsky, Graciela	Prof	994-6686	graciela	F	PHD	83	MIT	1998
Kwoka, John E. Jr.	Prof	994-6922	kwoka	L	PHD	72	Penn	1981
Labadie, Pamela A.	Prof	994-7068	labadie	E	PHD	84	Chicago	1996
Millar, James R.	Prof	994-6342	millar	P	PHD	65	Cornell	1989
Parsons, Donald O.	Prof	994-3984	dopars	J	PHD	70	Chicago	1997
Pelzman, Joseph	Prof	994-7108	jpelz	F	PHD	76	Boston C	1980
Trost, Robert P.	Prof	994-9011	trost	C	PHD	77	Florida	1981
Yezer, Anthony M.	Prof	994-6755	yezer	R	PHD	74	MIT	1972
Joshi, Sumit	Assoc	994-6154	sumjos	CD	PHD	91	Indiana	1992
Joutz, Frederick L.	Assoc	994-4899	bmark	EC	PHD	87	U Wash	1988
Malik, Arun	Assoc	994-5471	amalik	Q	PHD	84	J Hopkins	1992
Moore, Michael Owen	Assoc	994-6157	mom	F	PHD	88	Wisconsin	1988
Phillips, Robert F.	Assoc	994-8619	rphil	C	PHD	85	Columbia	1985
Smith, Stephen C.	Assoc	994-8086	scsmith	O	PHD	83	Cornell	1983
Suranovic, Steven M.	Assoc	994-7579	smsuan	F	PHD	87	Cornell	1988
Vonortas, Nicholas S.	Assoc	994-6458	vonortas	OL	PHD	89	NYU	
Fon, Vincy	Asst	994-7580	vfon	CD	PHD	81	Kansas	1979
Jain, Sanjay	Asst	994-8087	sjain	ODL	PHD	95	Princeton	1994
Snyder, Christopher	Asst	994-6581	csnyder	L	PHD	94	MIT	1994
Soares, Jorge	Asst	994-0192	jsoares	E	PHD	96	Rochester	1998
Bailey, Mary Ann	Adj	994-5838	mabaily	I	PHD	74	MIT	1983
Solomon, Elinor H.	Adj	994-6581	esolomon	E	PHD	48	Harvard	1982

Georgetown University	Washington, DC	20057-1045	(202) 687-5830				georgetown.edu	
Department of Economics	College of Arts & Sci	Fax=687-6102						
Lawton, Robert B.	Dean	687-4043	lawtonr	Hist	PHD	77	Harvard	
Cuddington, John T.	C-Pr	687-6103	duddingj		PHD	78	Wisconsin	1986
Albrecht, James W.	Prof	687-6105	albrecht		PHD	76	Berkeley	1992
Canzoneri, Matthew B.	Prof	687-5911	canzonem		PHD	75	Minnesota	1985
Evans, Martin D. D.	Prof	687-1570	evansm12	EFG	PHD	87	Princeton	1996
McNelis, Paul D.	Prof	687-5573	mcnelisp		PHD	74	J Hopkins	1977
Schwartz, Marius	Prof	687-6112	schwarm2		PHD	82	UCLA	1982
Viksnins, George J.	Prof	687-5890	viksning		PHD	64	Geotown	1968
Vroman, Susan	Prof	687-6024	vromans		PHD	77	J Hopkins	1978
Brown, Douglas M.	Assoc	687-5772	browndm		PHD	69	W Virginia	1972
Collins, Susan M.	Assoc	687-5781	collins1		PHD	84	MIT	1992
Diba, Behzad T.	Assoc	687-5682	dibab		PHD	84	Brown	1988
Gale, Ian L.	Assoc	687-5732	galei		PHD	86	Princeton	1995

Name	Rank	Phone	Email	Fields	Degree	Yr	School	Year
Oweiss, Ibrahim M.	Assoc	687-5582	bweissi		PHD	69	Minnesota	1967
Rogers, Carol Ann	Assoc	687-5816	rogersc		PHD	83	Princeton	1984
Kahn, Daniel S.	Asst	687-6244	kahnd		PHD	95	Columbia	1994
Lagunoff, Roger D.	Asst	687-1510	lagunoffr		PHD	89	Minnesota	1996
Mehrez, Gil	Asst	687-6172	mehrezg		PHD	95	Berkeley	1995
Olley, G. Steven	Asst	687-7144	olleys	L	PHD	92	Wisconsin	1997
Westbrook, M. Daniel	Asst	687-5880	westbrom		PHD	78	Ohio St	1978
Kazmer, Daniel R.	Lect				PHD	73	MIT	

University of Georgia	Athens, GA	30602-6252	(706) 542-1311				rigel.econ.uga.edu	
Department of Economics	Terry College of Bus		Fax=542-3376				Judy A. Griffin	
Benson, P. George	Dean	542-8100		Stat	PHD	77	Florida	1998
DeLorme, Charles D. Jr.	H-Pr	542-3682	delorme	EH	PHD	66	LSU	1968
Atkinson, Scott E.	Prof	542-3691	atknsn	CQK	PHD	72	Colorado	1985
Bateman, Fred	Prof	542-3692	bateman	N	PHD	65	Tulane	1991
Nicholas A. Beadles Professor								
Danielsen, Albert L.	Prof	542-3807	daniel	MH	PHD	66	Duke	1963
Kamerschen, David R.	Prof	542-3681	davidk	DK	PHD	64	Mich St	1974
Jasper N. Dorsey Professor								
Keenan, Donald C.	Prof	542-3668	keenan	CHR	DSC	78	Wash U	1978
Lee, Dwight R.	Prof	542-3970	lee	DHM	PHD	72	Ca-SnDgo	1985
Bernard B. & Eugenia A. Ramsey Professor								
Lovell, Knox	Prof	542-3689	knox	D	PHD	66	Duke	1994
Herman & Mary Virginia Terry Professor								
Cornwell, Christopher M.	Assoc	542-3670	cornwl	CHJ	PHD	85	Mich St	1988
Lastrapes, William D.	Assoc	542-3569	last	CEF	PHD	86	N Carol	1990
Selgin, George A.	Assoc	542-2734	selgin	EN	PHD	86	NYU	1989
Snow, Arthur	Assoc	542-3752	snow	DH	PHD	79	Wisconsin	1989
Trandel, Gregory A.	Assoc	542-3673	trandel	GK	PHD	92	Princeton	1989
Warren, Ronald S.	Assoc	542-3693	warren	JC	PHD	76	N Carol	1985
White, Lawrence H.	Assoc	542-3696	lwhite	ENB	PHD	82	UCLA	1988
Aarstol, Michael P.	Asst	542-3698	aarstol	EO	PHD	96	Stanford	1996
Holman, Jill Ann	Asst	542-1311	holman	EF	PHD	97	Colorado	1997
Klein, Peter G.	Asst	542-3697	klein	GKL	PHD	95	Berkeley	1995
Mustard, David B.	Asst	542-1311	mustard	DJK	PHD	97	Chicago	1997

Georgia College	Milledgeville GA	31061-4090	(912) 453-4210				gac.peachnet.edu	
Dept of Economics & Finance	School of Business		Fax=445-5249				Janis Zarkowsky	
Did Not Respond--1997-98 Listing								
Jones, Jo Ann	Dean	453-5497			PHD	77	La Tech	1976
Wolfenbarger, J. Larry	C-Pr	453-4210		ABPE	PHD	74	Tennessee	1987
Jones, Kenneth D.	Prof	471-2063			PHD	77	La Tech	1987
Dean, Graduate School								
Samprone, Joseph C. Jr.	Prof	454-2596		AD	PHD	75	Ca-SnBarb	1983
Speir, Edwin G.	Prof	453-4444			PHD	65	Denver	1981
President of the College								
Farr, William Kendrick	Assoc	454-2593		ADQ	PHD	85	Georgia	1985

Georgia Institute Tech	Atlanta, GA	30318-6015	(404) 894-4919				econ.gatech.edu	
School of Economics	Allen Col Mgt, Plcy & I		Fax=894-1890				Carolyn Stephens/M. Johnson	
Hawkins, Robert G.	Dean	894-2601			PHD	66	NYU	1993
email: robert.hawkins@iac.gatech.edu								
Ries, Christine P.	C-Pr	894-4919	christine.ries		PHD	77	Chicago	1997
Biven, W. Carl	Prof	894-1885	carl.biven	EB	PHD	56	St Louis	1958
Boston, Thomas D.	Prof	894-5020	thomas.boston	JN	PHD	76	Cornell	1985
Cebula, Richard J.	Prof	894-4914	richard.cebula	EDR	PHD	71	Geo St	1992
Chu, Kong	Prof	894-1886	kong.chu	OC	PHD	64	Tulane	1968
Schaffer, William A.	Prof	894-4915	william.schaffer	R	PHD	63	Duke	1963
Tarpley, Fred A. Jr.	Prof		fred.tarpley	D	PHD	67	Tulane	1962
Belton, Willie J. Jr.	Assoc	894-4388	willie.belton	E	PHD	86	Penn St	1987
McCarty, Marilu H.	Assoc	894-2621	marilu.mccarty	EH	PHD	72	Geo St	1972
Shaban, Radwan Ali	Assoc	894-4909	radwan.shaban	DO	PHD	85	Stanford	1991
Li, Haizheng C.	Asst	894-3542	clifford.li	C	PHD	97	Colorado	1997
McCabe, Mark J.	Asst	385-0512	mccabe.mark	L	PHD	91	MIT	1998
Mrozek, Janusz R.	Asst	894-0353	janusz.mrozek	QD	PHD	95	Stanford	1993
Nair, Usha C.	Asst	894-4903	usha.nair	F	PHD	95	Purdue	1996

Georgia Southern University	Statesboro, GA	30460-8151	(912) 681-5161				gsvms2.cc.gasou.edu	
Dept of Finance & Economics	College of Business Adm		Fax=871-1835				Barbara Focht, Kaye Brammen	
Gooding, Carl W.	Dean	681-5106	cgooding	Mgt	PHD	76	Georgia	1986
Whitaker, William M.	C-Pr	681-5161	wmw		PHD	68	Kentucky	1989
on leave								
White, John B.	C-Pr$	681-5161	jwhite	Fnce	PHD	85	Virginia	1989
Coston, Robert D.	Prof	681-5162	rcoston		PHD	73	Arkansas	1970
Davis, Elynor G.	Prof	681-5020	edavis		PHD	78	Tx A&M	1979
Jones, Marcia Noreen	Prof	681-0404	mjones		PHD	86	Illinois	1986

Name	Rank	Phone	Email	Fields	Degree	Yr	School	Since
Levernier, William B.	Assoc	681-5227	sdfinbl		PHD	88	W Virginia	1989
Brock, Greg J.	Asst	681-5161	gbrock	PO	PHD	89	Ohio St	1999
Brown, John H.	Asst	681-0896	jbrown		PHD	89	Mich St	1994
Grant, Darren P.	Asst	681-5036	dgrant		PHD	95	Fla St	1996
Koch, S.	Asst	681-5161	skoch		PHD	97	Penn St	1998
McPherson, S.	Asst	681-5161	sjhanson		PHD	97	Indiana	1997

Georgia Southwestern Coll Americus, GA 31709-4693 (912) 931-2079 business.gsw.edu
Economic Faculty Div of History & Pol Sc Fax=
Did Not Respond--1997-98 Listing

Name	Rank	Phone	Email	Fields	Degree	Yr	School	Since
Baringer, Richard L.	C-Pr	931-2079		Hst	PHD	69	G Peabdy	
Huddleston, Kenneth M.	Asst	931-2079			MBA		Geo St	

Georgia State University Atlanta, GA 30303-3083 (404) 651-2626 gsuvm1.gsu.edu
Department of Economics Sch of Policy Studies Fax=651-4985 Caroline Patton Griffin

Name	Rank	Phone	Email	Fields	Degree	Yr	School	Since
Bahl, Roy W. Jr.	Dean	651-3993	prcrwb	HR	PHD	65	Kentucky	1988
Skogstad, Samuel L.	C-Pr	651-4967	prcsls	EFO	PHD	65	Wash U	1994
Cheng, Juei Ming	Prof	651-2769		CO	PHD	68	Purdue	1968
Cummings, Ronald G.	Prof	651-1888	prcrgc	Q	PHD	68	Kansas	1993
Noah Langdale Jr. Eminent Scholar Chair of Environmental Policy								
Ihlanfeldt, Keith R.	Prof	651-3968	prckri	HR	PHD	78	Wash U	1981
Kaufman, Bruce E.	Prof	651-2922	ecobek	JN	PHD	78	Wisconsin	1977
Martinez, Jorge L.	Prof	651-3989	prcjlm	DF	PHD	78	Wash U	1977
Ratajczak, Donald	Prof	651-3282	ecfdon	MN	PHD	72	MIT	1973
Director of the Economic Forecasting Center								
Rushing, Francis W.	Prof	651-3782	prcfwr	ANP	PHD	67	N Carol	1974
Holder of the Eugenia A. and Bernard B. Ramsey Chair of Private Enterprise								
Saposnik, Rubin	Emer	651-2626		D	PHD	59	Minnesota	1970
Sjoquist, David L.	Prof	651-3995	prcdls	DR	PHD	71	Minnesota	1970
Stephan, Paula E.	Prof	651-3988	prcpes	JO	PHD	71	Michigan	1971
Associate Dean								
Farnham, Paul G.	Assoc	651-2624	ecopgf	DHI	PHD	78	Berkeley	1977
Gurmu, Shiferaw	Assoc	651-1907	prcsg	CI	PHD	92	Indiana	1998
Hotchkiss, Julie L.	Assoc	651-3986	prcjlh	CJ	PHD	89	Cornell	1989
Long, C. Richard	Emer	651-2626		BE	PHD	68	Vanderbilt	1968
Moore, Robert E.	Assoc	651-3756	prcrem	FO	PHD	88	Cornell	1989
Seaman, Bruce A.	Assoc	651-2775	ecobas	DL	PHD	78	Chicago	1978
Walker, Mary Beth	Assoc	651-3751	prcmbw	DC	PHD	86	Rice	1991
Wallace, Sally	Assoc	651-3959	prcskw	GH	PHD	88	Syracuse	1991
on leave in Moscow, USAID/GSU Tax Reform Policy project								
Xu, Yongsheng	Assoc	651-2626		DHC	PHD	92	Tulane	1999
Edmiston, Kelly D.	Asst	651-3519	prckde	EGHR	PHD	98	Tennessee	1998
Lavry, Susan K.	Asst	651-2626		HC	PHD	96	Indiana	1999
Mansfield, Jon	VAsst	651-2626	ecojxm	AM	PHD	92	Geo St	1996
Pitts, M. Melinda	Asst	651-4979	prcmmp	IJ	PHD	97	N Car St	1998
Rioja, Felix K.	Asst	651-0417	profkr	EFG	PHD	97	Ariz St	1997
Scafidi, Benjamin P.	Asst	651-2977	prcbps	HIR	PHD	97	Virginia	1998
Taylor, Laura L.	Asst	651-2873	prclot	C	PHD	94	N Car St	1994
Terrebonne, Peter	Asst	651-4379	ecorpt	A	PHD	92	Emory	1992
Valev, Neven T.	Asst	651-0418	prcntv	EF	PHD	97	Purdue	1998

Gettysburg College Gettysburg, PA 17325-1486 (717) 337-6670 cc.gettysburg.edu
Economics Faculty Department of Economics Fax=337-6638 Ms. Betty Smith

Name	Rank	Phone	Email	Fields	Degree	Yr	School	Since
Gondwe, Derrick K.	C-Pr	337-6673	dgondwe	ABEO	PHD	78	Manitoba	1977
Fender, Ann Harper	Prof	337-6671	fondera	ADNL	PHD	76	J Hopkins	1978
Railing, William F.	Prof	337-6678	wrailing	AHP	PHD	58	Cornell	1964
Fletcher, Jean W.	Assoc	337-6674	fletcher	AJD	PHD	83	Wash U	1986
Nirro, Katsuyuki	Assoc	337-6676	niirok	AC	PHD	75	Pittsburgh	1972
Stillwaggon, Eileen	Asst	337-6675	estillwa	AFQO	PHD	79	American	1995

Gonzaga University Spokane, WA 99258-0009 (509) 323-3403 jepson.gonzaga.edu
Department of Economics Sch of Business Adm Fax=323-5811 Brenda Lobdell
phone: 323-4220

Name	Rank	Phone	Email	Fields	Degree	Yr	School	Since
Barnes, Clarence H.	Dean	323-3402	barnes		PHD	73	Tennessee	9-73
Beck, John H.	D-Ac	323-3429	beck	BH	PHD	76	Mich St	1988
Bennett, Randall W.	Prof	323-3411	bennett	HL	PHD	84	Mich St	1988
Wiseman, A. Clark	Prof	323-3432	wiseman	AFQ	PHD	68	U Wash	1981

Goshen College Goshen, IN 46526 (219) goshen.edu
Economics Faculty Dept of Atg, Bus & Econ Fax=535-7660

Name	Rank	Phone	Email	Fields	Degree	Yr	School	Since
Kein, Paul	Dean	535-7503	dean		PHD		Harvard	7-97
Good, Delmar	C-Pr	535-7452	delgg	AH	PHD	70	Illinois	2-67
Gunden, Randal G.	Assoc	535-7454	randygg	EIO	ABD		Notre Dm	1984

```
Graceland College              Lamoni, IA        50140-1699  (515) 784-5170           graceland.edu
Economics Faculty              Division of Soc Sc-Econ  Fax=784-5410
Peterson, Rebecca              C      784-5170
Anders, Steven L.              Prof   784-5175  anders      ARD    PHD   88 Kansas St  1978
  Associate Dean of Faculty
Beck, Paul                     Assoc  784-5176  beck        AFJE   PHD   94 Missouri   1992
Davis, Victor                  Inst   784-5173  vdavis      ACHD   ABD      Wisconsin  1998
```

```
Grambling State University     Grambling, LA     71245       (318) 274-6290           alpha0.gram.edu
Economics Department           College of Business      Fax=274-2191              Ms. Ollie Pruitt
Dhanani, Karim                 Dean   274-2275              Atg    DBA   86 La Tech    9-77
Bashir, Abdel H.               H-As   274-6289  bashirah           PHD   90 Wisconsin  1990
Cadet, Marc                    Assoc  274-2794                     PHD   91 Kansas St  9-68
Ghebreyohannes, Keleta         Assoc  274-2795                     PHD      Colo St    9-81
Ghebreyesus, Ghirmay           Asst   274-2779  ghebreg     EFJO   PHD   88 Strathcl   1990
Melancon, Melissa              Asst   274-3825                     ABD      La Tech
```

```
Grand Canyon University        Phoenix, AZ       85017-1097  (520) 589-2867        grand-canyon.edu
Department of Economics        College of Business      Fax=589-2532                  Sue Sharkey
Smith, Anne                    Dean   589-2825  asmith
Houlihan, Colleen              Asst   589-2418  houlihan    L      PHD   98 Illinois   1998
```

```
Grand Valley State Univ        Allendale, MI     49401       (616) 895-2535                gvsu.edu
Department of Economics        Seidman Sch Bus & Adm    Fax=895-3286                Thelma Cathey
Homepage: gvsu.edu/~econ.index.htm
Mielke, David E.               Dean   895-2163  mielked     Atg    PHD   81 Wisconsin  1999
Singh, Harinder                C-Pr   895-2545  singhh             PHD   85 Il-Chicago 1995
Gonce, Richard A.              Prof   895-2540              ABDK   PHD   66 Wisconsin  1972
Reifel, John W.                Prof   895-2541  reifelj     AHOR   PHD   72 Mich St    1971
Dalmia, Sonia                  Asst   895-2535  dalmias            PHD   99 Iowa       1999
Isely, Paul N.                 Asst   895-2499  iselyp             PHD   95 Purdue     1997
Sicilian, Paul                 Asst   895-2542  siciliap    ACDJ   PHD   91 Illinois   1987
Simons, Gerald P.              Asst   895-2538  simonsg            PHD   95 Kansas     1995
Thorsnes, Paul E.              Asst   895-2539  thorsnep           PHD   94 Oregon     1995
```

```
Greensboro College             Greensboro, NC    27401-1875  (910) 272-7102         gborocollege.edu
Economics Faculty              Div of Business Adm      Fax=271-6634
Jones, Thomas O. Jr.           C-Pr   272-7102              BAdm   DBA   72 Geo Wash   1986
  Fred L. Proctor Sr. Professor of Business Administration
Kondeas, Alexander G.          Asst   272-7102              EG     PHD   98 Auburn     1999
Oerther, Frederick J.          Asst   272-7102                     PHD   89 GeoMason   1990
```

```
Grinnell College               Grinnell, IA      50112-0806  (515)                    grinnell.edu
Department of Economics        Div of Social Studies    Fax=269-3408
Seiz, Janet A.                 C-Ac   269-4868  seiz        BO     PHD   85 Duke       1989
Bateman, Bradley W.            Prof   269-3145  bateman     B      PHD   84 Kentucky   1987
Mutti, John                    Prof   269-3143  mutti       FHQ    PHD   74 Wisconsin  1987
  Sydney Meyer Professor of International Economics
Ferguson, William D.           Assoc  269-3132  ferguso1    JE     PHD   89 Mass       1989
Montgomery, Mark               Assoc  269-3146  montgome    JQH    PHD   82 Wisconsin  1989
Munyon, Paul G.                Assoc  269-3142  munyon      L      PHD   75 Harvard    1982
Powell, Irene                  Assoc  269-3125  powelli     IL     PHD   85 Wisconsin  1989
```

```
Grove City College             Grove City, PA    16127-2104  (724) 458-2056            moses.gcc.edu
Economics Faculty              Department of Economics  Fax=458-3852
  email @1=gcc.edu
Sparks, John A.                C-Pr   458-2056              BLaw   JD    69 Michigan   1976
Herbener, Jeffrey M.           Prof   458-2204  jmherbener@1       PHD   82 Okla St    1997
Mateer, G. Dirk                Assoc  458-2056  mateeargd          PHD   91 Fla St     1993
Miller, Tracy C.               Assoc  458-2013  millertc           PHD   86 Chicago    1995
```

```
Guilford College               Greensboro, NC    27410       (336) 316-2282             guilford.edu
Economics Faculty              Department of Economics  Fax=316-2950
Williams, Robert G.            C-Pr   316-2282              POFE   PHD   78 Stanford   1978
Williams, Robert B.            Assoc  316-2218              HQRL   PHD   84 N Carol    1987
```

```
Gustavus Adolphus College      Saint Peter, MN   56082-1498  (507) 933-7414                  gac.edu
Economics Faculty              Dept of Economics & Mgt  Fax=933-6032                 Connie Baum
Johnson, Bruce H.              C-Ac   933-7011                     PHD   79 Houston    1986
Bungum, John L.                Assoc  933-7406                     PHD   77 Nebraska   1979
Reese, David A.                Assoc  933-7405                     PHD   80 Va Tech    1979
Abraham, Elizabeth             Asst   933-6273                     ABD      Arizona    1997
Estenson, Paul                 Asst   933-7408                     PHD   86 Nebraska   1986
Misdzar, Sujetlana             Asst   933-7409                     PHD   96 Minnesota  1994
Rauch, James                   Asst   933-7420                     PHD   94 Nebraska   1998
```

Hamilton College	Clinton, NY		13323	(315) 859-4450			hamilton.edu	
Economics Faculty	Department of Economics		Fax=859-4477				Dawn Woodward	
Balkan, Erol M.	C-Ac	859-4180	ebalkan	OF	PHD	88	SUNY-Bin	1987
Bradfield, James	Prof	859-4190	jbradfie	GD	PHD	73	Rochester	1976
Jensen, Elizabeth J.	Prof	859-4437	ejensen	LN	PHD	84	MIT	1983
Jones, Derek C.	Prof	859-4381	djones	PJ	PHD	74	Cornell	1972
Georges, Christophre	Assoc	859-4472	cgeorges	EJB	PHD	89	Michigan	1989
Hagstrom, Paul Alan	Assoc	859-4146	phagstro	JHI	PHD	91	Wisconsin	1991
Pliskin, Jeffrey L.	Assoc	859-4143	jpliskin	CF	PHD	85	Michigan	1982
Kayser, Hilke A.	Asst	859-4234	hkayser	HIQ	PHD	94	Wisconsin	1993
Owen, Ann	Asst	859-4419	aowen	EO	PHD	95	Brown	1997
Lutzker, Adam	Inst		alutzker	EB	ABD		Michigan	1995

Hamline University	St. Paul, MN		55104-1284	(651) 523-2295			piper.hamline.edu	
Economics Faculty	Dept of Mgmt and Econ		Fax=523-2956				Katina Krull 523-2295	
email @1=gw.hamline.edu								
Aziz, Fahima	C-As	523-2262	fazia@1	DJ	PHD	95	Minnesota	1994
Jessup, Paul F.	Prof	523-2261	pjessup	G	PHD	66	Nrthwstrn	1988
William Kahlert Professor								
Akhavi-Pour, Hossein	Assoc	523-2223	hakhavi	FO	PHD	79	Kansas	1988
Bochnak, Mary	Assoc	523-2377	mbochnak	M	PHD	82	Minnesota	1990
Gunderson, Elizabeth W.	Assoc	523-2263	egunders	C	PHD	91	Union In	1980

Hampton University	Hampton, VA		23668	(757) 727-5205			unixvax.hampton.edu	
Dept of Banking & Finance	School of Business		Fax=727-5048				Alvita Shirinzadeh	
Adeyigh, Janet	Dean	727-5361		Atg	PHD	80	Missouri	
Pyatt, Edward J.	C-Pr	727-5762		Fnce	PHD	85	Temple	1984
Byniyan, Mohammad	Assoc	727-5886			PHD		Geo St	
Sarki, Ayuba J.	Assoc	727-5860			PHD	84	Georgia	1982

Hardin-Simmons University	Abilene, TX		79698-6220	(915) 670-1357			hsutx.edu	
Department of Economics	School of Business		Fax=670-1573				Clara Stovall	
Monhollon, Jimmie R.	Dean	670-1508			PHD	61	Vanderbilt	1995
Distinguished Professor								
Hill, John A.	Asst	670-5871			PHD	95	Tennessee	1998
Monhollon, Michael	VAsst	670-5870			JD	84	Virginia	1998

Harding University	Searcy, AR		72149-0001	(501) 279-4470			harding.edu	
Economics Faculty	School of Business		Fax=279-4195				Debi Adcock	
McLeod, Randall J.	Dean	279-4201	rmmcleod	Mktg	JD	74	Memphis	8-88
Diffine, Donald P.	Prof	279-4470	d.diffine		PHD	75	Miss	1971
Robertson, Marvin	Prof	279-4307	robertson	FDK	JD	73	Arkansas	8-79

University of Hartford	W Hartford, CT		06117-1599	(800) 768-4581			mail.hartford.edu	
Dept of Econ, Fnce, Ins & AS	Barney Sch Bus & P Adm		Fax=768-4911				Marcia Osbourne	
Norgaard, Corine T.	Dean	768-4243	norgaard	Atg	PHD	65	Tx-Austin	1996
Kolluri, Bharat R.	C-Pr	768-4581	kollur	CEGH	PHD	77	SUNY-Buf	1976
Giannoros, Demetrios	Prof	768-4835	giannaros	AEMP	PHD	81	Boston U	
Panik, Michael J.	Prof	768-4836	panik	CDHO	PHD	70	Boston C	1968
Rassekh, Farhad	Assoc	768-5007	rassekh	ADFO	PHD	83	Houston	1989
Singamsetti, Nageswara Rao	Assoc	768-4779	singamset	CDLM	PHD	73	SUNY-Buf	1974
James, Harvey Jr.	Asst	768-4864	hjames	ADKL	PHD	95	Wash U	1995

Hartwick College	Oneonta, NY		13820	(607) 431-4940			hartwick.edu	
Department of Economics	Div Social & Behav Sci		Fax=431-4954					
Gotsch, Susan	Dean		gotschs					
Malone, Laurence J.	C-Ac	431-4943	malonel	ABFN	PHD	91	New Sch	1986
Alexander, Peter	Assoc		alexanderp	ACDL	PHD	90	Mass	1997
Cochi Ficano, Carlena	Asst		cochificanoc	ACDJ	PHD	97	Cornell	1997

Harvard University	Cambridge, MA		02138	(617) 495-2144			harvard.edu	
Department of Economics	Faculty of Arts & Sci		Fax=495-7730				Patricia Shanahan 495-2185	
Homepage: http://www.economics.harvard.edu								
Knowles, Jeremy R.	Dean							
Williamson, Jeffrey G.	C-Pr	495-2438	jwilliam		PHD	61	Stanford	1983
Laird Bell Professor of Economics								
Alesina, Alberto F.	Prof	495-8388	aalesina		PHD	86	Harvard	1988
Paul Sack Associate Professor of Political Economy								
Barro, Robert J.	Prof	495-3203	vbarro		PHD	70	Harvard	1987
Campbell, John	Prof	496-6448	john_campbell	GE	PHD	84	Yale	7-94
Otto Eckstein Professor of Applied Economics								
Caves, Richard E.	Prof	495-2127	rcaves		PHD	58	Harvard	1962
Nathaniel Ropes Professor of Political Economy								
Chamberlain, Gary	Prof	495-1869	gchamberlain		PHD	75	Harvard	1987
Director of Graduate Studies								

Name	Rank	Phone	Email	Field	Degree	Yr	School	Year
Cooper, Richard N.	Prof	495-5076	rcooper		PHD	62	Harvard	1981
Maurits C. Boas Professor ofInternational Economics								
Cutler, David M.	Prof	496-5216	dcutler		PHD	91	MIT	
Feldstein, Martin S.	Prof	495-2167	mfeldstein		DPHL	67	Oxford	1969
George F. Baker Professor of Economics								
Friedman, Benjamin M.	Prof	495-4246	bfriedman		PHD	71	Harvard	1972
William Joseph Maier Professor of Political Economy								
Fudenberg, Drew D.	Prof	496-5895	dfudenberg		PHD	81	MIT	1987
Goldin, Claudia D.	Prof	495-3934	cgoldin		PHD	72	Chicago	1990
Green, Jerry R.	Prof	495-3950	jgreen@hbs.edu		PHD	70	Rochester	1973
David A. Wells Professor of Political Economy								
Griliches, Zvi	Prof	495-2181	zgriliches		PHD	57	Chicago	1969
Paul M. Warburg Professor of Economics								
Hart, Oliver D'Arcy	Prof	496-3461	ohart		PHD	74	Princeton	1993
Andrew Turner Professor of Economics								
Helpman, Eihanen	Prof	495-4690	ehelpman		PHD		Harvard	1974
Houthakker, Hendrick S.	Emer	495-2442			ECD	49	Amsterdm	
Henry Lee Professor of Economics								
Jorgenson, Dale W.	Prof	495-4661	djorgenson		PHD	59	Harvard	1969
Frederick E. Abbe Professor of Economics								
Katz, Lawrence F.	Prof	495-5148	lkatz		PHD	85	MIT	1986
Kornai, Janos	Prof	495-1236	jkornai		DSC	66	Hungaria	1986
Mankiw, N. Gregory	Prof	495-4301	ngmankiw		PHD	84	MIT	1985
Marglin, Stephen A.	Prof	495-3759	smarglin		PHD	65	Harvard	
Walter S. Barker Professor of Economics								
Maskin, Eric S.	Prof	495-4167	emaskin		PHD	76	Harvard	
Medoff, James L.	Prof	495-4209	jmedoff		PHD	75	Harvard	
Meyer Kestnbaum Professor of Labor & Industry								
Perkins, Dwight H.	Prof	495-2164	dwight_perkins		PHD	64	Harvard	1963
Harold Hitchings Burbank Professor of Political Economy								
Rosovsky, Henry	Emer	495-4151			PHD	59	Harvard	1965
Lewis P. and Linda L. Geyser University Professor, Emeritus								
Roth, Alvin E.	Prof	495-6009	al-roth		PHD	74	Stanford	
Sachs, Jeffrey D.	Prof	495-4112	jsachs		PHD	80	Harvard	1983
Galen L. Stone Professor of International Trade								
Shleifer, Andrei	Prof	495-5046	ashleifer		PHD	86	MIT	1991
Weitzman, Martin L.	Prof	495-5133	mweitzman		PHD	67	MIT	1989
Ernest E. Monrad Professor of Economics								
Davis, Donald R.	Assoc	496-6416	donald_davis		PHD	92	Columbia	1992
Glaeser, Edward L.	Assoc	495-0575			PHD	92	Chicago	
Hall, Brian J.	Assoc	495-3961	bhall		PHD	83	Harvard	1993
Hoxby, Caroline Minter	Assoc	496-3588	choxby	JH	PHD	94	MIT	7-94
Mandler, Michael A.	Assoc	495-0586	mmandler		PHD	87	Yale	
Tornell, Aaron	Assoc	496-6284	atornell		PHD	87	MIT	
Foote, Chris	Asst	495-0968	clfoote		PHD	96	Michigan	
Laibson, David	Asst	496-3402	dlaibson	DE	PHD	94	MIT	7-94
LaPorta, Rafael	Asst	495-2144	rlaporta		PHD	94	Harvard	
McHale, John	Asst	496-4310	jmchale		PHD	96	Harvard	
Metrick, Andrew P.	Asst	496-7081	ametrick		PHD	94	Harvard	
Porter, Jack	Asst	495-2896	jporter		PHD	96	MIT	
Wolfram, Catherine	Asst	495-9293	cworlfram		PHD	96	MIT	
Wolcowitz, Jeffrey	SLect	495-2109	j_wolcowitz	HDRJ	PHD	82	Harvard	7-78
Jenkins, Glenn P.	Lect				PHD	72	Chicago	1972

University of Hawaii-Hilo	Hilo, HI		96720-4091 (808) 974-7400				hawaii.edu	
Bus Adm & Economics Div	School of Business		Fax=974-7685				Mitzi Hennessey	
email @1=sob.uhh.hawaii.edu								
Hammes, David L.	C-Pr	974-7523	hammes		PHD	85	Simon Fr	1988
Cauley, Jon	Prof	974-7384	jcaualey@1		PHD	71	Colorado	
Hahn, Youngki	Prof	974-7767	yhahn		PHD	71	Ca-Rivers	
Im, Eric I.	Prof	974-7462	eim		PHD	82	Hi-Manoa	
Sakai, Marcia	Assoc	974-7457	msakai@1		PHD	85	Hi-Manoa	1991

Univ of Hawaii at Manoa	Honolulu, HI		96822-2223 (808) 956-8496				hawaii.edu	
Department of Economics	Col of Social Sciences		Fax=956-4347		Irene Uemoto/Carolyn Paet			
Dubanoski, Richard A.	Dean	956-6570	dickd	Psyc	PHD	66	Minnesota	
Mason, Andrew	C-Pr	956-8730	amason		PHD	75	Michigan	1975
La Croix, Sumner J.	Prof	956-7061	lacroix		PHD	81	U Wash	1981
Lee, Chung H.	Prof	956-8427	lchung		PHD	66	Berkeley	1980
Mak, James	Prof	956-8280	jmak		PHD	70	Purdue	1970
Moncur, James E. T.	Prof	956-7143	jmoncur		PHD	71	Wash St	1969
Naya, Seiji	Prof	586-2355	naya		PHD	66	Wisconsin	1961
Rose, Louis	Prof	956-8118	lrose		PHD	70	UCLA	1969
Roumasset, James A.	Prof	956-7496	jimr		PHD	73	Wisconsin	1976
Yeh, Yeong-Her	Prof	956-7749	yeongher		PHD	66	Minnesota	1965
Bonham, Carl S.	Assoc	956-7605	bonham		PHD	89	Tx-Austin	1989
Gangnes, Byron S.	Assoc	956-7285	gangnes		PHD	90	Penn	1990
Russo, Gerard G.	Assoc	956-7065	russo		PHD	89	Nrthwstrn	1987
Cheong, Kwang-Soo	Asst	956-7653	kscheong		PHD	94	Stanford	1994
Konan, Denise	Asst	956-6310	konan		PHD	93	Colorado	1993

Hawaii Pacific University
Economics Faculty
Honolulu, HI 96813 (808) 544-0283 hpu.edu
Department of Economics Fax=566-2403 Jennifer Loo

Name	Rank	Phone	Email	Areas	Degree	Yr	School	Since
Romig, Rodney	Dean	544-0283	rromig		PHD	75	Nebraska	8-87
Drabkin, Eric	C-As	544-9393	edrabkin	MCEF	PHD	93	UCLA	1994
Mardfin, Ward	Assoc	233-3213			PHD	79	Hi-Manoa	1992
Scholland, Ken	Assoc	544-1177		MLFB	MSFB		Geotown	1991
Abrams, Eric	Asst	544-0816	eabrams		PHD	97	Iowa	1997
Espiritu, Antonina	Asst	544-0892	aesprit		PHD	98	Nebraska	1998
Lucas, Eruesto	Asst	544-0842	elucas		PHD	69	Hi-Manoa	1993
Sarauiti, Brett	Asst	544-0826	basarauit		PHD	97	Nrthwstrn	1997

Heidelberg College
Economics Faculty
Tiffin, OH 44883 (419) heidelberg.edu
Dept of Bus Adm & Econ Fax=448-2124

Name	Rank	Phone	Email	Areas	Degree	Yr	School	Since
Wickham, William T.	C-Pr	448-2280		Mgt	PHD	56	Case Wes	1977
Rennie, Henry	Prof	448-2221		CFG	PHD	73	Ohio St	1993
Chudzinski, James	Assoc	448-2109		AJH	PHD	88	Tx Tech	1988
Kirklin, Wayne	Assoc	448-2036		G	MBA		NYU	1978
Cook, John	Asst	448-2280		AG	PHD	94	Kentucky	1995
Keener, Gary	Asst	448-2280		AHKR	PHD	93	Kentucky	1991

Hendrix College
Economics Faculty
Conway, AR 72032-3080 (501) 329-6811 mercury.hendrix.edu
Dept of Econ & Business Fax=450-1200

Name	Rank	Phone	Email	Areas	Degree	Yr	School	Since
Rupert, Lyle M.	C-Ac	450-1237	rupert	Atg	MBA	85	Chicago	1987
Scott, Ralph D.	Prof	450-1306			PHD	83	Tulane	1979
Berry, Stanley Keith	Assoc	450-1233			PHD	79	Vanderbilt	1989
Stanley, Tom D.	Assoc	450-1276			PHD	82	Purdue	1986

Hillsdale College
Economics Faculty
phone: 437-7341
Hillsdale, MI 49242-1298 (517) 437-7341
Dept Econ, Bus Adm, Atg Fax=437-3923

Name	Rank	Phone	Email	Areas	Degree	Yr	School	Since
Ebeling, Richard M. (Ludwig von Mises Chair)	C-Ac				MA	80	Rutgers	1988
Wolfram, Gary	Assoc				PHD	76	Berkeley	1989
Coppock, Lee	Asst				PHD	94	GeoMason	1994

Hofstra University
Dept Economics & Geography
Hempstead, NY 11550-1090 (516) 463-5592 hofstra.edu
Col Liberal Arts & Sci Fax=463-6519 Stephanie Colace

Name	Rank	Phone	Email	Areas	Degree	Yr	School	Since
Firestone, Bernie	Dean	463-5441						
Moghadam, Fatemeh	C-Pr	463-5598	ecofzm	NOQ	PHD	79	Oxford	
Guttmann, Robert P.	Prof	463-5602	ecorpg	F	PHD	79	London	
Christensen, Paul P.	Assoc	463-6024	ecoppc	B	PHD	76	Wisconsin	
DeFreitas, Gregory E.	Assoc	463-5040	ecoged	J	PHD	79	Columbia	
Kozlov, Nicholas N.	Assoc	463-6954	econnk	P	PHD	88	NewHamp	
Duffy, Niev	Asst	463-5599	econjd	ITJ	PHD	96	NYU	

College of the Holy Cross
Economics Faculty
Worcester, MA 01610-2395 (508) 793-3362 holycross.edu
Department of Economics Fax=793-3708 Mrs. Beverly Bylund

Name	Rank	Phone	Email	Areas	Degree	Yr	School	Since
Gottschang, Thomas R.	C-Ac	793-2678	tgottsch	AOP	PHD	82	Michigan	1979
Carter, John R.	Prof	793-2676	jcarter	CDL	PHD	76	Cornell	1976
O'Connell, John F.	Prof	793-2680	joconnel	CDIJ	PHD	70	Wisconsin	1974
Schap, David J.	Prof	793-2688	dschap	CDK	PHD	82	Wash U	1981
Anderton, Charles H.	Assoc	793-3441	canderto	ACDF	PHD	86	Cornell	1986
Kosicki, George	Assoc	793-2689	gkosicki	ADJL	PHD	85	Cornell	9-85
Rask, Kolleen J.	Assoc	793-2768	krask	EFOP	PHD	89	Yale	1989
Sanchez, Nicolas	Assoc	793-3362	nsanchez	DENO	PHD	72	S Calif	1977
Cahill, Miles B.	Asst	793-2682	mcahill	AEJ	PHD	95	Purdue	1995
Dupree, Jill L.	Asst	793-2334	jvanston	FNT	PHD	96	Colorado	1996
Kiel, Katherine A.	Asst	793-2743	kkiel	CDQR	PHD	89	Ca-SnDgo	1998

Holy Family College
Economics Faculty
phone: 637-7700
Philadelphia, PA 19114-2094 (215) Ext 3274 hfc.edu
Business Adm Division Fax=637-5037

Name	Rank	Phone	Email	Areas	Degree	Yr	School	Since
DiPrimio, Anthony	H	Ext 3415			PHD			7-98
Tokar, Bette L.	Prof	Ext 3274	btokar	AFED	EDD	93	Temple	9-75
Mazzarella, James	Asst	Ext 3404			PHD	87	Columbia	

Hood College
Economics Faculty
Frederick, MD 21701-8575 (301) 696-3685 hood.edu
Dept of Economics & Mgt Fax=696-3771 Colette Cooney

Name	Rank	Phone	Email	Areas	Degree	Yr	School	Since
Dahms, Joseph E.	C-Ac	696-3687	dahms	NOP	PHD	83	American	1978
Obar, Ruth I.	Asst	696-3689	robar	CEF	PHD	96	Alabama	1994
Banks, Nina	Lect	696-3685		AJ	ABD		Mass	1993

Hope College	Holland, MI 49422-9000 (616)						hope.cit.hope.edu	
Economics Faculty	Dept of Econ & Bus Adm Fax=395-7922						Joy Forgwe	
Heisler, James B.	C-Pr	395-7915		PD	PHD	75	Nebraska	1981
Lunn, John E.	Prof	395-7931		LD	PHD	80	UCLA	1992
Gentenaar, Robert	Assoc	395-7579		EC	PHD	77	Mich St	1977
Klay, Robin	Assoc	395-7581		BO	PHD	73	Princeton	1979
Steen, Todd P.	Assoc	395-7582		JT	PHD	93	Harvard	1988

University of Houston	Houston, TX 77204-5882 (713) 743-3800						uh.edu	
Department of Economics	Col of Social Science Fax=743-3798							
Rozelle, Richard	Dean	743-4000						
Antel, John J.	C-Pr	743-3808	jantel	J	PHD	82	UCLA	1981
Bhargava, Alok	Prof	743-3837		C	PHD	82	London	1989
Craig, Steven C.	Prof	743-3812	econ30	HR	PHD	81	Penn	1989
Dechert, W. Davis	Prof	743-3800		C	PHD	77	Cornell	
DeGregori, Thomas R.	Prof	743-3838	econ1m	O	PHD	65	Tx-Austin	1967
Gregory, Paul R.	Prof	743-3828		P	PHD	69	Harvard	1972
Mayor, Thomas H.	Prof	743-3801		AK	PHD	65	Maryland	1969
Papell, David H.	Prof	743-3807	econh	E	PHD	81	Columbia	1984
Ruffin, Roy J.	Prof	743-3827		F	PHD	67	Nrthwstrn	1976
Smith, Barton A.	Prof	743-3834		ADR	PHD	74	Chicago	1973
Steele, Henry B.	Prof	743-3835		A	PHD	57	MIT	
Bean, Richard N.	Assoc	743-3831		N	PHD	71	U Wash	1970
Juhn, Chinhui	Assoc	743-3823		J	PHD	91	Chicago	1992
Kohlhase, Janet E.	Assoc	743-3799		RHD	PHD	80	Penn	1983
Wilcox, Nathaniel	Assoc	743-3840		D	PHD	92	Chicago	1991
Ben-Gad, Michael	Asst	743-3800		E	PHD	95	Chicago	1995
Murray, Chris	Asst	743-3835		E	PHD	98	U Wash	1998
Palumbo, Michael G.	Asst	743-3824		H	PHD	92	Virginia	1992
Thompson, Peter	Asst	743-3841			PHD	94	Florida	1996

Univ of Houston-Clear Lake	Houston, TX 77058-1098 (281) 283-3185						cl.uh.edu	
Economics Faculty	Sch of Bus & Public Adm Fax=283-3951						Noel Turner	
Cummings, W. Theodore	Dean	283-3100	ted	Mktg	PHD	78	Ariz St	1980
Perdue, D. Grady	C-Pr	283-3213		Fnce	PHD	85	Alabama	9-84
Cloninger, Dale O.	Prof	283-3210			DBA	73	Fla St	9-74
Hodgin, Robert F.	Assoc	283-3211			DA	80	Illin St	9-81
Halil, Kiymaz	Asst	283-3208						1-97

Univ of Houston-Downtown	Houston, TX 77002-1001 (713) 221-8017						dt.uh.edu	
Finance, Atg, & Comp Inf Sys	College of Business Fax=226-5238						Ms. Marie Cepeda	
Bizzell, Bobby G.	Dean	221-8179		Mgt	PHD	71	Tx-Austin	1989
Nazemzadah, Asghar	C-Pr				PHD	83	Fla St	1989
Islam, Anisul	Assoc				PHD	84	Alberta	1990
Marvasti, Akbar B.	Assoc				PHD	85	LSU	1990

Houston Baptist University	Houston, TX 77074-3298 (281) 649-3325						hbu.edu	
Economics Area	Col of Business & Econ Fax=649-3436							
Homepage: www.hbu.edu								
Gillette, Lynn G.	Dean	649-3325			PHD	81	Tx A&M	1998
Matthews, Warren T.	Assoc	649-3207	warren		PHD	72	Tx A&M	1995

Howard University	Washington, DC 20059 (202) 806-1595						howard.edu	
Dept Law, Economics & Comm	College of Business Fax=797-6393							
Harvey, Barron H.	Dean	806-1507		Atg	PHD	77	Nebraska	1982
Lindsey, Debra A.	Assoc	806-1638			PHD	83	Howard	
Paschall, Samuel S.	Assoc	806-1575			JD	80	Howard	1980
Aiyegoro, Ademois	Asst	806-1658			PHD	90	GeoMason	
Ekanem, Frank	Asst	806-1639		EGHR	PHD	74	Geo Wash	1987
Hull, Everson W.	Asst	806-1542			PHD	77	Howard	
Straight, Ronald L.	Asst	806-1531			DBA	79	Geo Wash	1988

Howard University	Washington, DC 20059 (202) 806-6717						fac.howard.edu	
Department of Economics	College of Arts & Sci Fax=806-5262						Santina Merchant Huff	
Lee, Clarence	Dean				PHD			
Palmer, Ransford W.	C-Pr	806-6717	palmer	HO	PHD	66	Clark	1973
Betsey, Charles L.	Prof	806-6717	cbetsey	J	PHD	76	Michigan	1990
Chandler, Clevelend	Prof	806-6717	cchandler	R	PHD	69	Maryland	1976
Green, Rodney D.	Prof	806-6717	alaec06@a	R	PHD	80	American	1977
Huang, Lien-fu	Prof	806-6717	lhuang	I	PHD	71	Rochester	
Hung, Gregory	Prof	806-6717	ghung	O	PHD	65	Virginia	
Kwack, Sung Y.	Prof	806-6717	skwack	E	PHD	68	Berkeley	
McDonald, Vincent R.	Prof	806-6717	vmcdonald		PHD	68	Maryland	
Wadhawan, Satish C.	Prof	806-6717	swadhawan	FO	PHD		Nehru	

Name	Rank	Phone	Email	Fields	Degree	Yr	School	Since
Blank, Emily	Assoc	806-6717	eblank	J	PHD	85	Boston C	1985
Dompere, Kofi	Assoc	806-6717	kdompere	HEC	PHD	80	Temple	1977
Lee, Byung	Assoc	806-6717	blee	CDH	PHD	73	Catholic	8-73
Perkins, Mary	Assoc	806-6717		D	PHD	82	American	
email=jcolvin@erols.com								
Dorsainvil, Kathleen	Asst	806-6717	kdorsainvil	CEO	PHD	97	Penn St	1995
Hunte, C. Kenrick	Asst	806-6717		OF	PHD		Ohio St	
email=kenjacks@errols.com								
Meepagaia, Gaminie	Asst	806-6717	gmeepagala	C	PHD	86	SUNY-Alb	1988
Staab, Martin	Lect	806-6177	mstaab	EQ	PHD		Indiana	

Howard Payne University — Brownwood, TX 76801-2794 (915) 649-8704 — hputx.edu
Dept of Business Adm — School of Business Adm Fax=649-8928 — Mary Hill

Name	Rank	Phone	Email	Fields	Degree	Yr	School	Since
Plagens, Les	Dean	649-8705	lplagens		PHD	84	Tx A&M	1997
Spraberry, Hubert O.	Prof	649-8704	hspraber		PHD	85	Tx Tech	1986

University of Idaho — Moscow, ID 83844-3240 (208) 885-6294 — uidaho.edu
Department of Economics — Col of Business & Econ Fax=885-8939 — Karen L. Gillespie
Homepage: http://www.uidaho.edu/~econ

Name	Rank	Phone	Email	Fields	Degree	Yr	School	Since
Dangerfield, Byron J.	Dean	885-6478	bdange	Mgt	PHD	85	U Wash	1987
Ghazanfar, Shaikh M.	H-Pr	885-7144	ghazi	HOB	PHD	69	Wash St	1968
DiNoto, Michael J.	Prof	885-7148	dnt@crow.csrv.	JR	PHD	73	SUNY-Buf	1970
Miller, Jon R.	Prof	885-7506	jrmecon	BQ	PHD	74	Wash U	1989
Coffman, Richard B.	Assoc	885-7155	richardc	DL	PHD	72	U Wash	1978
Lyman, R. Ashley	Assoc	885-7145	alyman	DC	PHD	72	Nrthwstrn	1976

Idaho State University — Pocatello, ID 83209-8053 (208) 236-2346 — isu.edu
Department of Economics — Col of Arts & Sciences Fax=236-3186 — Sue Ann Bowman

Name	Rank	Phone	Email	Fields	Degree	Yr	School	Since
Hjelm, Victor S.	Dean	236-3053	hjelvict	PolS	PHD	66	Colorado	1968
Stegner, Tesa	C-Ac	236-2346	stegtesa	AHQ	PHD	89	Wash St	1992
Norman, Lee	Prof	236-2385	normlee	ALN	PHD	80	Utah	1981
Benson, C. Scott	Assoc	236-2860	bensscot	ABEF	PHD	88	Ca-Davis	1990
Green, Gregory G.	Asst	236-2943	greegreg	ACEF	PHD	97	Temple	1997
Hill, Cynthia D.	Asst	236-4945	hillcynt	AIJQ	PHD	97	Wash St	1998
Tokle, Robert J.	Asst	236-3835	toklrobe	AGL	PHD	86	Iowa St	1986

University of Illinois — Champaign, IL 61820 (217) 333-0120 — uiuc.edu
Department of Economics — Col of Comm & Bus Admin Fax=244-6678 — Marsha DAvis-Hubert
email: @1=igpa.uiuc.edu @2=srwilliams.econ.uiuc.edu

Name	Rank	Phone	Email	Fields	Degree	Yr	School	Since
Arnould, Richard J.	H-Pr	333-0120	rarnould	DIKL	PHD	68	Iowa St	1967
Alston, Lee	Prof	333-7664	l-alston	NQ	PHD	78	U Wash	1988
Baer, Werner	Prof	333-8388	w-baer	EFO	PHD	58	Harvard	1974
Bera, Anil K.	Prof	333-4596	a-bera	C	PHD	83	Austr Natl	1983
Brueckner, Jan K.	Prof	333-4557	jbrueckn	DHR	PHD	76	Stanford	1976
Cho, In-Koo	Prof	333-4579	inkoocho	CDE	PHD	86	Princeton	1998
DeBrock, Lawrence	Prof	333-4553	ldebrock	DIL	PHD	80	Cornell	1979
Gahvari, Firouz	Prof	333-7651	fgahvari	DH	PHD	81	UCLA	1994
Giertz, J. Fred	Prof	244-4822	fredg@1	HO	PHD	70	Nrthwstrn	1980
Gottheil, Fred	Prof	333-4591	fgotthei	AB	PHD	59	Duke	1959
Grinols, Earl L.	Prof	333-4595	grinols	DFO	PHD	77	MIT	1984
Hendricks, Wallace E.	Prof	333-6028	wally-h	J	PHD	73	Berkeley	1973
Koenker, Roger	Prof	333-4558	rkoenker	CL	PHD	74	Michigan	1983
Leuthold, Jane H.	Prof	333-4517	leuthold	HO	PHD	68	Wisconsin	1967
Neal, Larry	Prof	333-4678	l-neal	EGN	PHD	68	Berkeley	1967
Rashid, Salim	Prof	333-7388	s-rashid	BGO	PHD	76	Yale	1981
Resek, Robert W.	Prof	244-4827	r-resek	CR	PHD	61	Harvard	1961
Shafer, Wayne	Prof	333-0645		CD	PHD	72	Ca-SnBarb	1990
Taub, Bart	Prof	333-3467	b-taub	E	PHD	81	Chicago	1989
Yannelis, Nicholas C.	Prof	333-4584	nyannelis	D	PHD	83	Rochester	1988
Arvan, Lanny D.	Assoc	333-4587	l-arvan	CD	PHD	81	Nrthwstrn	1980
Conley, John	Assoc	333-4590	jpconley	DGH	PHD	90	Rochester	1989
Esfahani, Hadi S.	Assoc	333-2681	esfahani	EFLO	PHD	84	Berkeley	1984
Husby, Ralph D.	Assoc	333-6865	r-husby	EJ	PHD	69	Cornell	1967
Krasa, Stefan	Assoc	333-7698	skrasa	DG	PHD	87	Vienna	1990
Villamil, Anne P.	Assoc	244-6330	avillami	EG	PHD	88	Minnesota	1988
Williams, Steven R.	Assoc	333-4516	srw@2	CD	PHD	82	Nrthwstrn	1992
Williamson, H. F. Jr.	Assoc	333-4511	billw	AR	PHD	69	Yale	1964
Bernhardt, Dan	Asst	244-5708	danber	DGJL	PHD	86	Car Mellon	1998
Capps, Cory	Asst	333-1260	cocapps	IL	ABD		Nrthwstrn	1998
Deltas, George M.	Asst	333-4586	deltas	CDKL	PHD	96	Yale	1995
Hallock, Kevin F.	Asst	333-4842	hallock	HJ	PHD	95	Princeton	1995
Kim, Soyoung	Asst	265-0682	kim11	EF	PHD	96	Yale	1997
Powers, Elizabeth	Asst	244-4818	epowers	IJR	PHD	94	Penn	1996
Xiao, Zhijie	Asst	333-4520	zxiao	CL	PHD	97	Yale	1997

Univ of Illinois at Chicago	Chicago, IL		60607-7121 (312) 996-2684					uic.edu
Department of Economics	Col of Business Admin		Fax=996-3344				Ms. Lynn Lacey	
Rucci, Anthony	Dean	996-2671	ajrucci		PHD	78	Bowl Gr	1998
Chiswick, Barry R.	H-Pr	996-2683	brchris	J	PHD	67	Columbia	1978
Ayal, Eliezer B.	Emer	355-0506	eayal	O	PHD	61	Cornell	1970
Bassett, Gilbert W.	Prof	996-5777	gib	C	PHD	73	Michigan	1973
Camacho, Antonio	Prof	996-8651	acamacho	D	PHD	65	Minnesota	1973
Chaloupka, Frank J. IV	Prof	413-2367	fjc	I	PHD	88	CUNY	1988
Chiswick, Carmel U.	Prof	996-8721	cchis4	T	PHD	72	Columbia	1978
Hoffman, Elizabeth	Prof	413-3450	ehoffman	N	PHD	79	Cal Tech	1997
Provost								
Kosobud, Richard F.	Prof	996-2266	kosobud	D	PHD	63	Penn	1966
Lehrer, Evelyn L.	Prof	996-2363	elechrer	T	PHD	78	Nrthwstrn	1980
Director, Undergraduate Studies								
McDonald, John F.	Prof	996-2362	mcdonald	R	PHD	71	Yale	1971
Miller, Oscar	Prof	996-5247	omiller	A	MA	46	Chicago	1948
Officer, Lawrence H.	Prof	996-2671	lofficer	F	PHD	65	Harvard	1987
Persky, Joseph J.	Prof	996-2687	jpersky	R	PHD	71	Harvard	1974
Stokes, Houston H.	Prof	996-0971	hhstokes	D	PHD	69	Chicago	1967
Tam, Mo-Yin S.	Prof	413-2360	moyintam	P	PHD	74	SUNY-SBr	1974
Karras, Georgios	Assoc	996-2321	gkarras	E	PHD	90	Ohio St	1990
Peck, Richard M.	Assoc	996-2365	rmpeck	D	PHD	83	Princeton	1981
Pieper, Paul J.	Assoc	996-5214	pieper	E	PHD	84	Nrthwstrn	1982
Director of Graduate Studies								
Stanford, William G.	Assoc	996-0970	wgstan	C	PHD	84	Nrthwstrn	1983
Ierulli, Kathryn	Asst	996-3913	kierulli	D	PHD	94	Chicago	1993
Moses, Ronald P.	Asst	996-2599	rpmoses	F	PHD	69	Chicago	1964
Akarca, Ali	Lect	996-1416	akarca	E	MS	72	Nrthwstrn	1985
Roberts, Helen	Lect	995-0378	hroberts	E	PHD	95	Chicago	1995

Univ Illinois at Springfield	Springfield, IL		62794-9243 (217) 206-7174					uis.edu
Department of Economics	Col of Business & Mgt		Fax=206-7543				Ruth Mullenix	
Munkirs, John R.	Dean	206-6533	jmunk1	BN	PHD	73	Oklahoma	1972
Siddiquee, Baker A.	H-Ac	206-7174	bsidd1	EFO	PHD	88	Manitoba	1987
Ayers, Michael	Assoc	206-7174	mayer1	HR	PHD	73	Oklahoma	1971
Mouhammed, Adil	Assoc	786-6299	amouh1	FP	PHD	85	Nebraska	1988
Scannell, Nancy	Asst	206-7174	nscan1	AG	PHD	92	Il-Chicago	1996

Illinois Institute of Tech	Chicago, IL		60661-3691 (312) 906-6500					stuart.iit.edu
Department of Business Adm	Stuart Sch of Business		Fax=906-6549					
Hassan, M. Zia	Dean	906-6515		Mgt	PHD	65	Ill Tech	1960
Hall, W. Clayton	Assoc				PHD	64	Illinois	
Tourk, Khairy A.	Assoc				PHD	71	Berkeley	

Illinois State University	Normal, IL		61790-4200 (309) 438-8625					ilstu.edu
Dept of Economics Box 4200	Col of Arts & Sciences		Fax=438-5228				Janice Pritchett	
Ramsey, David D.	C-Ac	438-8625	ddramsey	DEH	PHD	67	Minnesota	1973
Chizmar, John F.	Prof	438-7301	jfchizmar	CM	PHD	71	Boston C	1971
Cohn, Raymond L.	Prof	438-7892	rlcohn	DN	PHD	77	Oregon	1983
Hiebert, L. Dean	Prof	438-7509	dhieber	ADE	PHD	72	Wisconsin	1973
Nelson, Michael A.	Prof	438-8720	manelson	G	PHD	80	Purdue	1981
Ostrosky, Anthony L. Jr.	Prof	438-7071	alostros	ADEC	PHD	73	Pittsburgh	1973
Ram, Rati	Prof	438-7101	rram		PHD	76	Chicago	1982
Distinguished Professor								
Singh, Ram Das	Prof	438-3005	rdsingh	TIO	PHD	70	N Delhi	1981
Skaggs, Neil T.	Prof	438-7204	ntskaggs	BDE	PHD	80	Duke	1979
Goel, Rajeev Kumar	Assoc	438-2360	rkgoel	CO	PHD	87	Houston	1989
Mohammadi, Hassan	Assoc	438-7777	hmohamma	E	PHD	88	Wash St	1988
Rich, Daniel P.	Assoc	438-7647	dprich	DJ	PHD	87	Houston	1987
Walbert, Mark S.	Assoc	438-3935	mswalber	CDE	PHD	84	New Mex	1984
Antecol, Heather	Asst	438-2996		JIG	PHD	98	McMaster	8-99
Carlson, J. Lon	Asst	438-8625	lcarlson	PQ	PHD	84	Illinois	1986
Hasan, Nazmul	Asst	438-3747		G	PHD	93	Illinois	1993
Zhang, Kevin	Asst	438-8928	khzhang	F	PHD	96	Colorado	8-97

Illinois Wesleyan University	Bloomington, IL		61702-2900 (309) 556-3266					titan.iwu.edu
Department of Economics	Business & Econ Div		Fax=556-3719				Sue Olson	
Leekley, Robert M.	C-Ac	556-3266	bleekley	H	PHD	74	Mich St	1974
Chapman, Margaret L.	Prof	556-3191	mchapman	L	PHD	77	Illinois	1977
Seeborg, Michael C.	Prof	556-3184	mseeborg	J	PHD	76	Utah	1989
Robert S. Eckley Distinguished Professor of Economics								
Ossella, Ilaria	Asst	556-3906	iossella	O	PHD	99	Cornell	1999
Stumph, Carolyn F.	Asst	556-3826	cstumph	E	PHD	99	Lehigh	1998

Immaculata College — Immaculata, PA 19345-0901 (610) Ext 3472 — immaculata.edu
Economics Faculty — Dept of Econ, Atg & Bus Fax=251-1668
phone: 647-4400

Name	Rank	Phone	Email	Field	Degree	Yr	School	Year
Coyle, Sister Ann	Assoc	Ext 3470			MA		Temple	1978
Sumpta, Sister Virginia A.	Assoc	Ext 3147			MA		Catholic	1968
Henry, Jacqueline	Asst	Ext 3031			MA		Cen Mich	1998
Ryan, Julie	Asst	Ext 3463			MA		St MryCA	1999

Indiana University — Bloomington, IN 47405-5301 (812) 855-1021 — indiana.edu
Department of Economics — Col of Arts & Sciences Fax=855-3736 — Amy Ruff

Name	Rank	Phone	Email	Field	Degree	Yr	School	Year
Lowengrub, Morton	Dean	855-2392	lowengru	Math	PHD	61	Duke	
Becker, Robert	C-Pr	855-3014	becker		PHD	78	Rochester	1978
Alexeev, Michael	Prof	855-7103	malexeev		PHD	84	Duke	1992
Becker, William	Prof	855-3577	beckerw		PHD	73	Pittsburgh	1979
Buffie, Edward F.	Prof	855-9566	ebuffie		PHD	82	Yale	1992
Gardner, Roy J.	Prof	855-6383	gardner		PHD	75	Cornell	1983
Chancellor								
Kniesner, Thomas J.	Prof	855-7256	kniesne		PHD	76	Ohio St	1988
Trivedi, Pravin K.	Prof	855-3567	trivedi		PHD	70	LondonEc	1987
von Furstenberg, George	Prof	855-4764	vonfurst		PHD	66	Princeton	1970
Rudy Professor of Economics								
Walker, James M.	Prof	855-2760	walkerj		PHD	78	Tx A&M	1984
Williams, Arlington W.	Prof	855-4564	williama		PHD	78	Arizona	1979
Chang, Fwu-Ranq	Assoc	855-6070	changf		PHD	85	Chicago	1983
Kaganovich, M.	Assoc	855-6967	mkaganov		PHD	85	USSR	1991
Leeper, Eric M.	Assoc	855-9157	eleeper		PHD	89	Minnesota	1995
Rotella, Elyce J.	Assoc	885-7858	rotella		PHD	77	Penn	1981
Witte, Willard E.	Assoc	855-2080	witte		PHD	75	Wisconsin	1981
Ming, Xing	Asst	855-1021	xming		PHD	95	Rice	1995
Pedroni, Peter	Asst	855-7925	ppedroni		PHD	93	Columbia	1993
Raff, Horst	Asst	855-7928	hraff		PHD	91	W Ontario	1993
Schmidt, David R.	Asst	855-2543	drschmid		PHD	94	CIT	1993

Indiana University — Bloomington, IN 47405-5301 (812) 855-9219 — indiana.edu
Dept Bus Econ & Pub & Policy — Kelley Sch of Business Fax=855-3354 — Amy Ruff

Name	Rank	Phone	Email	Field	Degree	Yr	School	Year
Dalton, Dan R.	Dean	855-8489	dalton	Mgt	PHD	79	Ca-Irvine	1979
Fratianni, Michele	C-Pr	855-9219	fratiann		PHD	71	Ohio St	1971
Baye, Michael R.	Prof	855-9219	mbaye	DIO	PHD	83	Purdue	1997
Davidson, Larry	Prof	855-9219	davidso		PHD	77	N Carol	1990
Green, Jeffery	Prof	855-8924	green		PHD	67	Illinois	1985
Jaffee, Bruce	Prof	855-8796	jaffee		PHD	71	J Hopkins	1971
Kang, Keejoon	Prof	855-9219	kang		PHD	80	U Wash	1980
Rasmusen, Eric	Prof	855-9219	erasmuse		PHD	84	MIT	1992
VonHagen, Jurgen	Prof	855-9219	vonhagen		PHD	86	Bonn	1987
Lyon, Tom	Assoc	855-9219	tlyon		PHD	89	Stanford	1989
Maxwell, John	Asst	855-9219	jwmax		PHD	93	Queen's	1992
Marcus, Morton	Lect	855-5507	marcus		MA	63	Wash U	1973

Indiana U-Purdue U/Indy — Indianapolis IN 46202-5140 (317) 274-4756 — iupui.edu
Department of Economics — School of Liberal Arts Fax=274-0097 — Jeannette Rowe

Name	Rank	Phone	Email	Field	Degree	Yr	School	Year
Sandy, Robert	C-Ac	274-2176	icjz100	J	PHD	77	Mich St	1974
Kirk, Robert	Prof	274-3995	rkirk	HR	PHD	69	Iowa St	1972
Spechler, Martin	Prof	274-7379	mspechle	BFNP	PHD	71	Harvard	1986
Steinberg, Richard	Prof	274-8671	rsteinbe	HL	PHD	84	Penn	1991
Bilodeau, Marc	Assoc	274-5684	mbilodea	HL	PHD	90	W Ontario	1996
Bivin, David	Assoc	274-7207	1qty100	E	PHD	80	Purdue	1985
Carlin, Paul S.	Assoc	274-0990	pcarlin	J	PHD	85	Pittsburgh	1985
Chakrabarti, Subir	Assoc	274-2412	imxl100	C	PHD	85	Iowa	1985
Harris, Robert	Assoc	274-0095	rharris	A	PHD	79	Ohio St	1981
Director, Center for Economic Education								
Rangazas, Peter	Assoc	274-8641	prangaza	EH	PHD	83	Indiana	1989
Rooney, Patrick	Assoc	348-7203	rooney	JH	PHD	87	Notre Dm	1987
Wilhelm, Mark	Assoc		mowilhel	CH	PHD	90	NYU	1998
Burke, Jonathan L.	Asst		jolburke	C	PHD	85	MIT	1998
Chu, Tianshu	VAsst			O			Minnesota	1999
Deb, Partha	Asst	274-5216	pdeb	C	PHD	91	Rutgers	1991
Kaviani, Mohammad	Asst	274-0096	mkaviani		MA	85	Indiana	1986
Olili, Una O.	Asst			O	PHD	97	Nrthwstrn	1999
Royalty, Anne B.	Asst			J	PHD	93	Yale	1999
Russell, Steven	Asst	274-0420	shrusse		PHD	89	Minnesota	1993
Warner, Geoffrey	Asst		gwarnear	I	PHD	94	CUNY	1998
Askari, Ammar	Lect	348-7290	aaskari		PHD	95	Indiana	1989

Indiana Univ at Kokomo — Kokomo, IN 46904-9003 (317) — iuk.indiana.edu
Economics Faculty — Div of Business & Econ Fax=

Name	Rank	Phone	Email	Field	Degree	Yr	School	Year
Von der Embse, Thomas J.	Dean	455-9446		Mgt	PHD	68	Ohio St	1990
Pendse, Dilip C.	Assoc	455-9279			PHD	71	Oregon St	
Pulikonda, Naga	Assoc	455-9282			PHD	77	Illinois	
Parkison, Kathy	Asst	455-9462			PHD	83	Purdue	1993

Indiana Univ South Bend	South Bend, IN		46634-7111 (219) 237-4346					iusb.edu
Economics Faculty	Div of Business & Econ		Fax=237-4866				Dorothea Solymosi	
Swanda, John R.	Dean	237-4346	jswanda	L	PHD	68	Illinois	1968
Agbetsiafa, Douglas K.	Prof	237-4208	dagbetsiafa	AGO	PHD	80	Notre Dm	1980
Bartholomew, A. Wayne	Prof	237-4397	wbarthol	AET	PHD	72	Cornell	1972
Herschede, Alfred J.	Prof	237-4303	aherschede	ADP	PHD	76	Illinois	1976
Joray, Paul A.	Prof	237-4227	pjoray	ADJ	PHD	71	Illinois	1971
Kochanowski, Paul S.	Prof	237-4243	pkochanowski	CDR	DBA	72	Indiana	1972
Konzelmann, Suzanne	Assoc	237-4142	skonzelmann	ADJ	PHD	91	Notre Dm	1989

Indiana Univ Northwest	Gary, IN		46408-1197 (219) 980-6633					iunbus1.iun.indiana.edu
Economics Faculty	Div of Business & Econ		Fax=980-6579				Karen Peterson	
Coffin, Donald A.	Dean	980-6636	don	JNR	PHD	79	W Virginia	1987
Lynch, Gary	Prof	980-6907	gary	RTE	PHD	70	Wash St	1981
Bhatia, Shyam L.	Assoc	980-6634	bhatia	FDEL	PHD	76	Indiana	1976
Olmsted, George M.	Assoc	980-6909	george	HI	PHD	84	Nrthwstrn	1987

Indiana Univ Southeast	New Albany, IN		47150-6405 (812) 941-2362					iusmail.ius.indiana.edu
Department of Economics	Div of Business & Econ		Fax=941-2672				Mrs. Lydia Garza	
Dufrene, Uric	Dean	941-2325	udufrene	Fnce	PHD	92	Miss	1992
Altmann, James L.	Prof	941-2307	jaltmann	DM	PHD	78	Wisconsin	1978
Alse, Janardhanan	Asst	941-2520	jalse	FE	PHD	93	Wisconsin	1992
Faulk, Dagney	Asst	941-2362	dfaulk	R	PHD	99	Geo St	1999
Schansberg, D. Eric	Asst	941-2527	dshansb	HJC	PHD	91	Tx A&M	1992

Indiana U of Pennsylvania	Indiana, PA		15705-1087 (724) 357-2640					grove.iup.edu
Economics Faculty	Humanities & Social Sci		Fax=357-6485				Mrs. Mary Anne Lupinetti	
Carter, Brenda	Dean	357-2280	brenda_carter		PHD			
Karatjas, Nicholas	C-Pr	357-4855	karatjas	ADI	PHD	76	SUNY-SBr	1978
Asamoah, Yaw	Prof	357-2641	osebo	FO	PHD	85	Wash U	1984
Dyal, James A.	Prof	357-4856	jimdyal	JR	PHD	75	Illinois	1977
Martel, Arthur H.	Prof	357-4775	amartel	JK	PHD	74	Mass	1970
Radell, Willard W.	Prof	357-4776	willard_radell	NP	PHD	80	Illinois	1981
Stonebraker, Robert J.	Prof	357-4770	bobstone	EK	PHD	73	Princeton	1971
Cross, John W.	Assoc	357-4781	jwcross	EG	MA	68	Mass	1969
Radakovic, George	Assoc	357-4826	georad	JR	PHD	79	Pittsburgh	1986
Brewer, Stephanie M.	Asst	357-2640		DHF	PHD	99	Indiana	1999
Jezefowicz, James J.	Asst	357-2640		CEL	PHD	99	SUNY-Alb	1999

Indiana State University	Terre Haute, IN		47809 (812) 237-2160					scifac.indstate.edu
Department of Economics	College of Arts & Sci		Fax=237-4349				Martha Bridges	
Weixlmann, Joseph	Dean	237-2788	asceix@amber.	Engl	PHD	73	Kansas	1976
Conant, John L.	C-Pr	237-2163	econjlc	DJB	PHD	84	Tennessee	1981
Burkett, Paul G.	Prof	237-2164	ecburke	EO	PHD	84	Syracuse	1991
Fischbaum, Marvin N.	Prof	237-2171	ecfisch	DP	PHD	65	Columbia	1965
Parks, Terrance C.	Prof	237-2173	ecparks	OED	PHD	74	Illinois	1966
Richards, Donald G.	Prof	237-2179	ecparmi	FO	PHD	83	Conn	1985
Chen, Aimin	Assoc	237-2175	ecchen	PD	PHD	90	Penn St	1991
Guell, Robert	Assoc	237-2169	ecguell	HC	PHD	91	Syracuse	1991
Kyle, James T.	Assoc	237-2159	eckyle	J	ABD	63	Indiana	1963
Lotspeich, Richard	Assoc	237-2176	eclotsp	PQ	PHD	86	New Mex	1990

Indiana Wesleyan	Marion, IN		46953-4999 (765) 677-2303					indwes.edu
Dept of Atg, Business & Econ	Division of Social Sci		Fax=677-2380				Linda MacKay	677-2289
Martin, Glenn R.	C-Pr	677-2300	gmartin	Hist	PHD	73	Ball St	1967
Showalter, Jerry	C-Ac	677-2289	jshowalt	Atg	MACC	67	Ball St	1967
Pongracic, Ivan	Asst	677-2145	ipongrac	AEFP	MA	68	Zagreb	1987

University of Indianapolis	Indianapolis, IN		46227-3697 (317) 788-3378					gandlf.uindy.edu
Department of Economics	School of Business		Fax=788-3300					
Livesay, Robin R.	Dean	788-3370		Mgt	PHD	74	Ohio St	1979
O. T. Fitzwater Professor of Business								
Gurtunca, Esen Z.	Prof	788-3287			PHD	73	Purdue	1974
Donald W. Tanselle Professor of Economics								
Conrad, James M.	Assoc	788-3232			PHD	70	Kentucky	1979

Iona College	New Rochelle, NY		10801-1890 (914) 633-2216					iona.edu
Dept of Economics	Col of Arts & Science		Fax=633-2608					
Did Not Respond--1997-98 Listing								
Rosenberg, Warren	Dean			Bio	PHD	82	NYU	1981
Pescatrice, Donn R.	C-Pr	637-2729		CDE	PHD	75	Purdue	1983
Acker, Mary H.	Assoc	633-2215	mhal	FG	PHD	82	Fordham	1982
Jantzen, Robert H.	Assoc	637-2731	rhj1	CIJ	PHD	82	Northeas	1982
Spagnolo, John A.	Assoc	637-2730		R	PHD	82	Fordham	1978

University of Iowa	Iowa City, IA		52242-1000 (319) 335-0829					uiowa.edu
Department of Economics	Henry B. Tippie Col Bus		Fax=335-1956					Shari Tolander
Fethke, Gary C.	Dean	335-0868	gary-fethke		PHD	68	Iowa	1974
Whiteman, Charles H.	C-Pr	335-0834	whiteman		PHD	81	Minnesota	1980
Albrecht, William P.	Prof	335-3125	william-albrecht		PHD	65	Yale	1965
Fethke, Carol	Prof	335-0504	carol-fethke		PHD	71	Iowa	1975
Forsythe, Robert	Prof	335-0865	robert-forsythe		PHD	75	Car Mellon	1981
Associate Dean								
Fuller, John W.	Prof	335-0038	john-w-fuller		PHD	68	Wash St	1979
Horowtiz, Joel	Prof	335-0844	joel-horowitz		PHD	67	Cornell	1982
Joseph, Hyman	Prof	335-0837	hyman-joseph		PHD	69	Nrthwstrn	1966
McCloskey, Deirdre N.	Prof	335-2290	deirdre-mcclos+		PHD	70	Harvard	1980
Nelson, Forrest D.	Prof	335-0854	forrest-nelson		PHD	75	Rochester	1980
Neumann, George R.	Prof	335-0850	george-neumann		PHD	74	Nrthwstrn	1984
Nordquist, Gerald L.	Emer	335-0833	gerald-nordquist		PHD	60	Iowa	1968
Pogue, Thomas F.	Prof	335-0843	thomas-pogue		PHD	68	Yale	1965
Riezman, Raymond G.	Prof	335-0829	raymond-riezman		PHD	77	Minnesota	
Savin, Nathan E.	Prof	335-0855	gene-savin		PHD	69	Berkeley	1986
Sgontz, Larry G.	Emer	r35-0852	larry-sgontz		PHD	64	Illinois	1964
Siebert, Calvin D.	Prof	335-0851	calvin-siebert		PHD	66	Berkeley	1965
Wu, Shih-Yen	Emer	335-0846	shih-yen-wu		PHD	60	Nrthwstrn	1964
Balch, Michael S.	Assoc	335-0847	michael-balch		PHD	65	NYU	1971
Blume, Andreas	Assoc	335-0931	andreas-blume		PHD	89	Ca-SnDgo	1989
Ingram, Marlynne B. F.	Assoc	335-0897	beth-ingram		PHD	86	Iowa	1988
Paarsch, Harry	Assoc	335-0936	harry-paarsch		PHD	87	Stanford	1996
Page, Scott	Assoc	335-1015	scott-page	H	PHD	93	Nrthwstrn	1997
Ravikumar, B.	Assoc	335-0841	ravikumar		PHD	89	Iowa	1996
Solow, John L.	Assoc	335-0845	john-solow		PHD	83	Stanford	1981

Iowa State University	Ames, IA		50011-1070 (515) 294-6740					iastate.edu
Department of Economics	Col Liberal Arts & Sci		Fax=294-0221					Diana McLaughlin
Allen, Benjamin	Dean	294-2422	ballen	Tran	PHD	74	Illinois	1979
Miranowski, John A.	C-Pr	294-6741	jmirski	Q	PHD	75	Harvard	1995
Adams, Jean W.	Prof	294-5886	jwadams	L	PHD	73	Illinois	1972
Adams, Roy Dean	Prof	294-5886	radams	HE	PHD	72	Illinois	1972
Choi, Eun Kwan	Prof	294-5999	kchoi		PHD	78	Iowa	1985
on leave to Chinese Univ of Hong Kong								
Enders, Walter	Prof	294-6314	enders	EF	PHD	75	Columbia	1974
Fletcher, Lehman B.	Prof	294-5820	lbf	O	PHD	69	Berkeley	1960
Harl, Neil E.	Prof	294-6354	harl	QK	PHD	65	Iowa St	1964
Huffman, Wallace E.	Prof	294-6359	whuffman	J	PHD	72	Chicago	1974
Lapan, Harvey E.	Prof	294-5917	hlapan	DF	PHD	71	MIT	1972
Mattila, John Peter	Prof	294-5813	jpm	J	PHD	69	Wisconsin	1973
Merrill, William C.	Prof	294-6846	wmerrill	O	PHD	64	Berkeley	1964
Orazem, Peter F.	Prof	294-5827	pfo	J	PHD	83	Yale	1982
Sandler, Todd M.	Prof	294-5783	tsandler	HD	PHD	71	SUNY-Bin	1980
Tesfatsion, Leigh S.	Prof	294-0138	tesfatsi	E	PHD	75	Minnesota	1990
Vandewetering, Hylke	Prof	294-5888	hivdw	O	PHD	64	Iowa St	1964
Falk, Barry L.	Assoc	294-5875	bfalk	E	PHD	82	Minnesota	1980
Hallam, Arne	Assoc	294-5861	ahallam	D	PHD	83	Berkeley	1983
Quirmbach, Herman C.	Assoc	294-6221	hcqbach	L	PHD	83	Princeton	1990
Schroeter, John R.	Assoc	294-5876	johns	L	PHD	81	Minnesota	1983
Bilias, Yannis G.	Asst	294-3664	billas	C	PHD	95	Illinois	1995
Bose, Subir	Asst	294-5860	bose	D	PHD	96	Yale	1996
Morelli, Massimo	Asst	294-4720	morelli	D	PHD	96	Harvard	1996
Reed, Robert	Asst	294-5245	robreed	EF,I	PHD	98	Penn St	1990
Vesterlund, Lise	Asst	294-7396		H	PHD	97	Wisconsin	1997

Ithaca College	Ithaca, NY		14850 (607) 274-3200					ithaca.edu
Department of Economics	Sch of Humanities & Sci		Fax=274-3474					Tina Bennett
Erlich, Howard	Dean	274-3102		Comm	PHD	75	Mass	
Musgrave, Frank W.	C-Pr$	274-3613		IJ	PHD	68	Rutgers	1968
Mieczkowski, Bogdan	Prof	274-3607		AF	PHD	54	Illinois	1954
Hinderliter, Roger H.	Assoc	274-3582		BE	PHD	70	Wash U	1970
Kacapyr, Elia W.	Assoc	274-3200		AG	PHD	85	Geo St	1985
Kolberg, William	Assoc	274-3609		AQ	PHD	84	Rhode Isl	1984

Jackson State University	Jackson, MS		39217-0560 (601) 968-2531					ccaix.jsums.edu
Dept Econ, Finance & Gen Bus	Sch Business Box 17760		Fax=968-2690					Ella King
Glover, Glenda	Dean	968-2411		Atg	PHD	90	Geo Wash	1994
Hurley, John F.	C-Ac	968-2531	jhurley		PHD	71	Illinois	1972
Freeman, Patricia A.	Assoc	968-2610	pfreeman		PHD	88	LSU	1998
Grass, R. Gail	Assoc	968-2028	ggrass		PHD	89	Harvard	1989
Anyamolo, Dennis	Asst	968-2608	danyame		PHD	92	Howard	
Assad, Jean-Claud	Asst	968-2604	jassad		PHD	87	Howard	1991
Didia, Dal	Asst	968-2606	jdidia		PHD	93	LSU	1997
Jeffries, Christopher N.	Asst	968-2607	cjeffrie		PHD	88	Fla St	1992
McGill-Tillman, Patricia	Inst	968-2605			MA	65	Atlanta	1968
Opara-Nadi, Gregory	Inst	968-2679	goparana		MBA	77	Rust	

Jacksonville University Jacksonville, FL 32211-3394 (904) 745-7432 mail.ju.edu
Economics Faculty College of Business Fax=745-7467 Kim MacLean

Name	Rank	Phone	Email	Field	Degree	Yr	School	Since
Mullins, Terry W.	Dean	Ext 7431	tmullin	Mgt	PHD	78	Houston	1998
Brady, James J.	Prof	Ext 7442	jbrady		PHD	69	Notre Dm	
Jessie Ball duPont Professor of Economics								
Pordeli, Hassan	Prof	Ext 7450	hpordel		PHD	83	Nebraska	1983
Hugh F. Culverhouse Professor of Economics								
Buck, John	Asst	745-7431	jbuck		PHD	89	Wisconsin	1994

Jacksonville State Univ Jacksonville, AL 36265-1602 (205) 782-5776 succ.jsu.edu
Finance, Econ & Accounting Col Commerce & Bus Adm Fax=782-5312 Ms. Pat Upton

Name	Rank	Phone	Email	Field	Degree	Yr	School	Since
Fielding, William T.	Dean	782-5505	fielding		PHD	76	S Carol	1968
Scrogins, William A.	H-Pr	782-5388	scroggin	Fnce	DBA	85	Miss St	8-79
Bennett, Doris S.	Assoc	782-5514	dbennett		PHD	79	Alabama	1986
Calcagno, Peter	Asst	782-5392	calcagno		PHD	97	Auburn	1997
Carter, Shawn	Asst	792-5199	scarter		PHD	97	Tx A&M	1998
McCarty, Cynthia S.	Asst	782-5777	cmccarty		PHD	94	N Carol	1990

James Madison University Harrisonburg, VA 22807 (540) 568-3216 jmu.edu
Economics Program Col of Business MSC0204 Fax=568-3010 Mrs. Loretta Grunewald

Name	Rank	Phone	Email	Field	Degree	Yr	School	Since
Reid, Robert D.	Dean	568-3252	reidrd	Mkgt	EDD	85	Va Tech	9-86
Ahmed, Ehsan	D-Pr	586-3214	ahmedex	EC	PHD	83	Mich St	1984
Director Office of Economic Services								
Carrier, Ronald E.	Prof	568-6241		A	PHD	60	Illinois	1971
President								
Fields, T. Windsor	Prof	568-3097	fieldstw	EC	PHD	78	Virginia	1990
Horn, Robert N.	Prof	568-3219	hornrn	JD	PHD	78	NewHamp	1978
Kohen, Andrew I.	Prof	568-3220	kohenai	JD	PHD	73	Ohio St	1976
Rosser, J. Barkley Jr.	Prof	568-3212	rosserjb	R	PHD	76	Wisconsin	1977
Varghese, K. Thomas	Prof	568-3206	varghekt	E	PHD	71	Wayne St	1970
Wood, William C.	Prof	568-3243	woodwc	DA	PHD	80	Virginia	1989
Director, Center for Economic Education								
Jerome, Robert T. Jr.	Assoc	568-3029	jeromert	DF	PHD	82	Virginia	1981
Kreutzer, David W.	Assoc	568-3218	kreutzdw	FH	PHD	84	GeoMason	1984
Milliman, Scott R.	Assoc	568-3213	millimsr	DQ	PHD	85	Wisconsin	1986
Rosser, Marina V.	Assoc	568-3094	rossermv	FP	PHD	79	MoscowSt	1987
Smith, Vardaman Russell	Assoc	568-3221	smithvr	B	PHD	80	Penn St	1979
Brunton, Bruce G.	Asst	581-3211	bruntobg	FNO	PHD	89	Utah	1984
Doyle, Joanne M.	Asst	568-3030	doylejm	DC	PHD	93	Boston C	1993
Elwood, S. Kirk	Asst	568-3098	elwoodsk	EFC	PHD	93	Ca-Davis	1992

John Carroll University Cleveland, OH 44118 (216) 397-4508 jcvaxa.jcu.edu
Dept of Economics & Finance School of Business Fax=397-1728 Barbara Lovequist

Name	Rank	Phone	Email	Field	Degree	Yr	School	Since
Navratil, Frank J.	Dean	397-4521	navratil	G	PHD	74	Notre Dm	1973
Zlatoper, Thomas J.	C-Pr	397-4583	zlatoper	ACD	PHD	80	Nrthwstrn	1984
Soper, John C.	Prof	397-3027	jsoper	ENA	PHD	70	Mass	1982
Calkins, Lindsay Noble	Assoc	397-4467	calkins	ADH	PHD	86	Michigan	1986
Cima, Lawrence R.	Assoc	397-4534	lrcima	ADEF	PHD	82	W Virginia	1971
Jacques, Kevin T.	Asst	397-4508	kjacques	EG	PHD	90	Mich St	1999
Simmons, Walter O.	Asst	397-4659	wsimmons	JKNO	PHD	94	Wayne St	1995
Welki, Andrew M.	Asst	397-4550	welki	HR	PHD	83	Penn St	1982

John F. Kennedy University Walnut Creek CA 94596 (925) 295-0600 jfku.edu
1250 Arroyo Way Econ Faculty School of Management Fax=295-0604

Name	Rank	Phone	Email	Field	Degree	Yr	School	Since
Baltodano, Josefina	Dean	295-0600	jeb		JD			7-98

Johns Hopkins University Baltimore, MD 21218-2585 (410) 516-7601 jhu.edu
Department of Economics Sch of Arts & Sciences Fax=516-7600 Donna Althoff 516-7677
email @1=jhunix.hcf.jhu.edu @2=zauq.econ.jhu.edu

Name	Rank	Phone	Email	Field	Degree	Yr	School	Since
Kessler, Herbert L.	Dean	516-8212	hlk		PHD			
Maccini, Louis J.	C-Pr	516-7607	maccini		PHD	70	Nrthwstrn	1969
Ball, Laurence M.	Prof	516-7605	ball		PHD	86	MIT	1994
Gersovitz, Mark	Prof	516-7612			PHD	75	Yale	1994
Hamilton, Bruce W.	Prof	516-7613	hamilba		PHD	72	Princeton	1973
Harrington, Joseph E.	Prof	516-7615	harringt@1		PHD	84	Duke	1983
Karni, Edi	Prof	516-7608	karni@1		PHD	71	Chicago	1981
Khan, M. Ali	Prof	516-8545	zmak@2		PHD	73	Yale	1988
Moffitt, Robert A.	Prof	516-7611	moffitt		PHD	75	Brown	1995
Ridder, Geert	Prof	516-7614	gridder		PHD	87	Amsterdm	1998
Young, H. Peyton	Prof	516-6118	pyoung		PHD	70	Michigan	1994
Carroll, Christopher D.	Assoc	516-7602	carroll		PHD	90	MIT	1995
de Lima, Pedro F.	Assoc	516-7606	delima		PHD	92	Wisconsin	1993
Chan, Jimmy	Asst	516-7610	chan@1		PHD	98	Berkeley	1998

Kalamazoo College Kalamazoo, MI 49006-3295 (616) 337-7028 kzoo.edu
Dept of Economics & Business Liberal Arts Education Fax=337-5733 Sandy Rook 337-7053

Name	Rank	Phone	Email	Fields	Degree	Yr	School	Hired
Hussen, Ahmed M.	C-Pr	337-7025	hussen	DQ	PHD	78	Oregon St	1985
McKinney, Hannah J.	Asst	337-7024	mckinney	HJR	PHD	84	Penn	1988
Moffit, Tim	Asst	337-7031	moffit	M	MBA	84	Dartmouth	1994
Reinert, Kenneth	Asst	337-7027	reinert	FDE	PHD	88	Maryland	1993
Rochon, Louis-Phillip	Asst	337-7023	lprochon		PHD	98	New Sch	1999
Stull, Charles	Inst	337-7053	cstull		ABD		Wisconsin	

University of Kansas Lawrence, KS 66045-2113 (785) 864-3501 ukans.edu
Department of Economics Col Liberal Arts & Sci Fax=864-5270 Leanea Wales
email @1=bschool.wpo.ukans.edu @2=eagle.cc.unkans.edu

Name	Rank	Phone	Email	Fields	Degree	Yr	School	Hired
Sicilian, Joseph M.	C-Ac	864-3501	jsic@2	D	PHD	77	Purdue	1977
El-Hodiri, Mohamed A.	Prof	864-2838			PHD	66	Minnesota	1966
Lien, Da-Hsiang D.	Prof	864-2848	dlien@2	O	PHD	86	Cal Tech	1986
Weiss, Thomas J.	Prof	864-2840	t-weiss	NF	PHD	67	N Carol	1967
Wu, De-Min	Prof	864-2849			PHD	63	Wisconsin	1964
Bhattacharya, Gautam	Assoc	864-2869	gbhattacharya@1	LDO	PHD	80	Rochester	1980
Comolli, Paul M.	Assoc	864-2863	pcomolli@1	QF	PHD	75	Purdue	1975
Faurot, David J.	Assoc	864-2865	dfaurot@1	J	PHD	75	Nrthwstrn	1975
Frevert, Peter	Assoc	864-2860	pfrevert@1	DF	PHD	64	Purdue	1964
Iwata, Shigeru	Assoc	864-2867	shigeru	EJ	PHD	88	UCLA	1988
Rosenbloom, Joshua L.	Assoc	864-2839	jrosenbloom	NJ	PHD	88	Stanford	1988
Zhang, Jianbo	Assoc	864-2861		D	PHD	90	Penn St	1990
Asiedu, Elizabeth	Asst	864-2843	asiedu	F	PHD	98	Illinois	1998
Earnhart, Dietrich	Asst	864-2866	earnhart	QK	PHD	95	Wisconsin	8-97
Keating, John W.	Asst	864-3501	keating@1	E	PHD	89	Nrthwstrn	8-97
Larudee, Mehrene	Asst	864-2837	mehrene	F	ABD		Mass	1984
Popp, David	Asst	864-2868	dpopp	O	PHD	97	Yale	8-97
Shin, Kwanho	Asst	864-3501		E	ABD		UCLA	1984

Kansas State University Manhattan, KS 66506-4001 (785) 532-7357 ksu.edu
Department of Economics Col of Arts & Sciences Fax=532-6919 Velda Deutsch

Name	Rank	Phone	Email	Fields	Degree	Yr	School	Hired
Nicholls, Peter	Dean	532-6900	nicholls	Math	PHD		Cambridge	1991
Ragan, James F. Jr.	H-Pr	532-7357	jfrjr	JA	PHD	75	Wash U	1977
Babcock, Michael W.	Prof	532-4571	mwb	RQ	PHD	73	Illinois	1972
Nafziger, E. Wayne	Prof	532-4579	nafwayne	OPF	PHD	67	Illinois	1966
Thomas, Lloyd B. Jr.	Prof	532-4584	lbt	EA	PHD	70	Nrthwstrn	1968
Akkina, Krishna Rao	Assoc	532-4570	krishna	ECO	PHD	72	Minnesota	1972
Bratsberg, Bernt	Assoc	532-4572	bernt	JD	PHD	91	Ca-SnBarb	1991
Cassou, Steven P.	Assoc	532-6342	scassou	EC	PHD	89	Minnesota	1996
Chang, Yang-Ming	Assoc	532-4573	ymchang	DCF	PHD	84	SUNY-Buf	1984
Gormely, Patrick J.	Assoc	532-4576	gormely	OF	PHD	67	Duke	1967
Oldfather, Michael	Assoc	532-4580	mon812	EJ	PHD	80	Ohio	1983
Weisman, Dennis	Assoc	532-4588	weisman	LKD	PHD	93	Florida	1993
Bidarkota, Prasad V.	Asst	532-7357	pbidarko	CEG	PHD	96	Ohio St	1999
Lu, Xiaohua	Asst	532-4575	xlu	LDC	PHD	95	Tx-Austin	1997
Sadler, Michael A.	Asst	532-4574	msadler	EO	PHD	97	Tx-Austin	1996
Stock, Wendy A.	Asst	532-4583	stockwn	JCQ	PHD	96	Mich St	1996
Trenary, Roger C.	Inst	532-4585	trenary	A	MA	72	Wayne St	1977

Kean University Union, NJ 07083 (908) 527-2238 kean.edu
Dept Econ, Fnce & Geography Sch Bus, Govt & Tech Fax=353-8656 Elaine Mahon

Name	Rank	Phone	Email	Fields	Degree	Yr	School	Hired
Anderson, Charles E.	Dean	527-2531			PHD	75	Stanford	7-88
Kempey, William M.	O-Pr	527-2390			PHD	70	NYU	9-78
Kim, Youn Suk	Prof	527-2489			PHD	73	New Sch	9-74
Carreno, Eufronio	Assoc	527-2374		DEFO	PHD	80	Rutgers	9-88
Jackson, Peter	Assoc	527-2429			PHD		Harvard	
Saffer, Henry	Assoc	527-2400			PHD	77	CUNY	9-85
Yamoah, David A. Associate Dean	Assoc	527-2794			PHD	90	Rutgers	9-87
Condon, Carol M.	Asst	527-2391			PHD	78	Columbia	9-85
Griffith, Jacqueline	Asst	527-3210			MBA			
Skoorka, Bruce	Asst	527-2429			PHD	92	NYU	
Tully, Cathyann	Asst	527-2428						

Keene State College Keene, NH 03431-4183 (603) 358-2544 keene.edu
Department of Economics Sciences & Soc Sciences Fax=358-2257 Mary Ann Williams

Name	Rank	Phone	Email	Fields	Degree	Yr	School	Hired
Leversee, Gordon J.	Dean	358-2544	gleverse		PHD	73	Duke	1981
Duston, Thomas E.	Assoc	358-2625	tduston		PHD	72	Brown	1984
Sherry, Robert L.	Assoc	358-2626			PHD	79	Yale	1984

Kennesaw State University — Kennesaw, GA 30144-5591 (770) 423-6091 ksumail.kennesaw.edu
Dept of Economics & Finance — Coles College of Bus Fax=499-3209 Julee Childre/Iona Pearson

Name	Rank	Phone	E-mail	Fields	Degree	Yr	School	Year
Mescon, Timothy S.	Dean	423-6342	tmescon		PHD	79	Georgia	1990
Tutterow, Roger C.	C-Ac	423-6091	rtuttero	CDGM	PHD	90	Geo St	1991
Brotman, Billie Ann	Prof	423-6496	bbrotman	AGIM	PHD	78	Notre Dm	1989
Bumgarner, Mary	Prof	423-6341	mbumgarn	AERH	PHD	84	Geo St	1985
Curley, Michael D.	Prof	423-6091	mcurley	ADMG	PHD	74	Kentucky	1984
Gilliam, Kenneth P.	Prof	423-6319	kgilliam	ACD	PHD	76	Lehigh	1984
Park, Jong-Heum	Prof	423-6429	jpark	ADFO	PHD	74	Okla St	1988
Prime, Penelope B.	Prof	423-6579	pprime	ADFO	PHD	87	Michigan	1991
Anderson, Thomas C.	Assoc	423-6111	tanderso	ADM	PHD	72	Berkeley	1985
Goodwin, Randall B.	Assoc	423-6101	rgoodwin	ADM	PHD	82	Georgia	1982
Sabbarese, Donald M.	Assoc	423-6094	dsabbare	AEM	PHD	84	Geo St	1978
Tiwari, Kashi N.	Assoc	423-6086	ktiwari	CEG	PHD	81	So Meth	1988

Kent State University — Kent, OH 44242-0001 (330) 672-2366 bsa3.kent.edu
Department of Economics — College of Business Adm Fax=672-2448 Diane Williams Ext 221
phone 672-2366

Name	Rank	Phone	E-mail	Fields	Degree	Yr	School	Year
Stevens, George E.	Dean	672-2772	gstevens	ADMS	DBA	79	Kent St	1995
Kent, Richard J.	C-Ac	Ext 216	rkent	E	PHD	76	Berkeley	1983
Casper, Cheryl A.	Prof	Ext 259	ccasper	D	PHD	75	Case Wes	1973
McKee, David L.	Prof	Ext 214	dmckee	OR	PHD	66	Notre Dm	1967
Mount, Randall I.	Prof	Ext 327	rmount	CD	PHD	69	Purdue	1966
Upton, Charles W.	Prof	Ext 311	cupton	EQ	PHD	69	Car Mellon	8-09
Williams, Donald R.	Prof	Ext 399	dwilliams	J	PHD	84	Nrthwstrn	1983
Butler, Alison	Asst		abutler	FEO	PHD	89	Oregon	1999
Ellis, Michael A.	Asst	Ext 211	mellis	EF	PHD	91	Tx A&M	1990
Qi, Min	Asst	Ext 261	mqi	CDFG	PHD	96	Ohio St	1996
Wilson, Kathryn S.	Asst	Ext 253	kwilson	DHIJ	PHD	96	Wisconsin	1996

University of Kentucky — Lexington, KY 40506-0034 (606) 257-3626 pop.uky.edu
Department of Economics — Gatton Col Bus & Econ Fax=323-1920

Name	Rank	Phone	E-mail	Fields	Degree	Yr	School	Year
Furst, Richard W.	Dean	257-8939		Fnce	DBA	68	Wash U	1981
Blomquist, Glenn C.	C-Pr	257-3924	gcblom	IHQ	PHD	77	Chicago	1980
Ali, Mukhtar M.	Prof	257-7636	mmali	C	PHD	69	Wisconsin	1969
Berger, Mark C.	Prof	257-1282	mberger	J	PHD	81	Ohio St	1981
Fackler, James S.	Prof	257-7649	eco134@1	E	PHD	77	Indiana	1982
Garen, John E.	Prof	257-3581	jgaren	J	PHD	82	Ohio St	1982
Gift, Richard E.	Prof	257-7640	regift01	FB	PHD	65	Duke	1965
Harvey, Curtis E.	Prof	257-4634	charv1	P	PHD	63	S Calif	1963
Jensen, Richard A.	Prof	257-1266	rjensen	D	PHD	80	Nrthwstrn	1980
Krislov, Joseph	Prof	257-3057	eco192	JN	PHD	54	Wisconsin	1954
Scott, Frank A. Jr.	Prof	257-7643	fscott	GH	PHD	79	Virginia	1979
Toma, Eugenia F.	Prof	257-1156	pub702	H	PHD	77	Va Tech	1977
Gillette, Robert	Assoc	257-1411	jrgill01	A	PHD	86	Tx A&M	1994
Hoyt, William H.	Assoc	257-2518	whoyt	RHG	PHD	86	Iowa	1969
Kim, Yoonbai	Assoc	257-2838	ykim01	EFG	PHD	87	Stanford	1991
Toma, Mark	Assoc	268-4966	mtoma	E	PHD	51	Va Tech	1989
Waller, Christopher J.	Assoc	257-0226	cjwall	E	PHD	86	Wash St	1998
Bollinger, Christopher R.	Asst	257-9524	crboll	CDJ	PHD	93	Wisconsin	1998
Hoyt, Gail Mitchell	Asst	257-2517	ghoyt	A	PHD	92	Kentucky	1994
Murray, Sheila	Asst	257-5581	semurr01	I	PHD	95	Maryland	1995
Thompson, Eric	Asst	257-1386	ecthom1	R	PHD	92	Wisconsin	1995
Trask, Kathleen	Asst	257-9681	katrask	FO	PHD	98	Penn St	1998

Kentucky State University — Frankfort, KY 40601 (502) 227-6708 gwmail.kysu.edu
Dept of Bus Adm-Economics — School of Business Fax=227-6404 Carmon Harrod

Name	Rank	Phone	E-mail	Fields	Degree	Yr	School	Year
Lee, Dae Sung	Dean	227-6714	dslee	ADEC	PHD	69	Mass	1969
Amadi, Confidence	Asst	227-6921		G	DBA	94	La Tech	1998
Assibey-Mensah, Albert	Asst	227-6284		AG	PHD	94	Cincinnati	1994
Sokoloff, Joel J.	Asst	227-6914		ACE	MA	67	Mass	1974

Kenyon College — Gambier, OH 43022-9623 (740) 427-5657 kenyon.edu
Economics Faculty — Department of Economics Fax=427-5276 April Farmer

Name	Rank	Phone	E-mail	Fields	Degree	Yr	School	Year
Gensemer, Bruce L.	C-Pr	427-5283	gensemer	HPDI	PHD	66	Michigan	1966
Harrington, David E.	Assoc	427-5393	harrington	QRHC	PHD	84	Wisconsin	1986
Himmelright Associate Professor in Economics								
Keeler, James	Assoc	427-5285	keeler	CEB	PHD	81	Indiana	1984
Kynski, Kathy	Assoc	427-5328	krynski	CDIJ	PHD	86	Wisconsin	7-86
Himmelright Associate Professor of Economics								
Melick, William R.	Assoc	427-5291	melickw	EGCF	PHD	87	Ohio St	7-98
Trethewey, Richard L.	Assoc	427-5270	trethewe	NFKB	PHD	71	U Wash	1969
Cooke, Priscilla	Asst	427-5281	cookep	OQCD	PHD	95	U Wash	7-97
Sayre, Edward A.	VAsst	427-5000	sayree	JROA	PHD	99	Texas	7-99

Kettering University — Flint, MI 48504-4898 (810) 762-7952 — kettering.edu
Economics Faculty — Management Department Fax=762-9944

Name	Rank	Phone	Email	Field	Degree	Year	School	Since
Pouck, David W.	C	762-7959						
Ioannatos, Petros	Asst	762-1955			PHD	89	Wayne St	
Wing, Martin M.	Asst	762-7986			PHD	89	Wayne St	

King's College — Wilkes-Barre, PA 18711 (570) Ext 5972 — kings.edu
Dept of Economics & Finance — McGowan Sch of Business Fax=826-5989 — Janet Meade
phone 208-5900

Name	Rank	Phone	Email	Field	Degree	Year	School	Since
Schoen, Edward J.	Dean	208-5932	ejschoen	Law	JD	68	Geotown	9-72
John S. Davis Distinguished Service Professor in Business								
Hosseini, Hamid S.	C-Ac	208-5900			PHD	77	Oregon	9-86
Singer, Russell	C-As	208-5900	rjsinger		BS	58	Wilkes	9-67
Arnold, Thomas R.	Prof	208-5900	trarnold		PHD	70	Syracuse	6-60
Herve A. LeBlanc Distinguished Service Professor in Liberal Arts								
Rose, Margarita M.	Asst	208-5900	mmrose		PHD	89	Notre Dm	9-90

Kutztown University of PA — Kutztown, PA 19530-0730 (610) 683-4584 — kutztown.edu
Department of Economics — College of Business Fax=683-4573 — Mrs. Donna DeLong

Name	Rank	Phone	Email	Field	Degree	Year	School	Since
Hartz, Theodore A.	Dean	683-4575	jartz	Fnce	MBA		Lehigh	1977
Hvidding, James M.	C-Pr	683-4593	hvidding	EB	PHD	76	Maryland	1986
Daneshyar, Arifeen M.	Prof	683-4592	daneshya	AE	PHD	76	S Illinois	1984
Margolis, H. Albert	Prof	683-1372	margolis	NC	PHD	69	Purdue	1976
Luizer, James C.	Assoc	683-4595		JC	PHD	84	Lehigh	1984
Sraiheen, Abdulwahab	Assoc	683-4597	sraiheen	CM	PHD	86	Penn St	1990
Zelleke, Girma	Assoc	683-4598	zelleke	FO	PHD	84	Colorado	1986

Lafayette College — Easton, PA 18042-1776 (610) 330-5298 — lafayette.edu
Economics Faculty — Dept of Econ & Business Fax=330-5715 — Mrs. Carol Riffert/Carolyn Lee

Name	Rank	Phone	Email	Field	Degree	Year	School	Since
Heavey, Jerome F.	C-Ac	330-5300	heaveyj	DHP	PHD	76	Penn St	1973
Chambers, Donald	Prof	330-5303	chambers	MG	PHD	81	N Carol	1992
Walter E. Hanson/KPMG Professor of Business & Finance								
Hochman, Harold M.	Prof	330-5315	hochmanh	HIK	PHD	65	Yale	1992
Wm. E. Simon Professor of Political Economics								
Seifried, Edmond J.	Prof			JM	PHD	71	W Virginia	1978
Ahene, Rexford A.	Assoc	330-5305	ahener	OR	PHD	83	Wisconsin	1982
Averett, Susan	Assoc	330-5307	averetts	CJI	PHD	91	Colorado	1991
Beckman, Mary P.	Assoc	330-5301	beckmanm	OP	PHD	86	Notre Dm	1985
Bodenhorn, Howard	Assoc	330-5308	bodenhoh	AN	PHD	90	Rutgers	1993
Bruggink, Thomas H.	Assoc	330-5307	bruggint	CQ	PHD	79	Illinois	1978
DeVault, James M.	Assoc	330-5312	devaultj	EFQ	PHD	90	Wisconsin	1989
on leave Fall 1999								
Gamber, Edward N.	Assoc	330-5310	gambere	EC	PHD	86	Va Tech	1992
Hutchinson, Gladstone	Asst	330-5304	hutchins	AO	PHD	90	Clark	1992
on leave Fall 1999								
Shively, Phillip	Asst	330-5313	shivelp	CG	PHD	97	Michigan	1997

Lake Superior State Univ — Sault S Marie MI 49783-1626 (906) 635-2426 — lakers.lssu.edu
Economics Faculty — Sch of Business & Econ Fax=635-2821 — Ms. Laurine Kelly

Name	Rank	Phone	Email	Field	Degree	Year	School	Since
Mugavero, Daniel C.	C-Ac	635-2662	dmugavero	Atg	MBA	67	Mich St	9-76
Erikkila, John	Prof	635-2108		ADEF	PHD	87	W Ontario	9-90
Harger, Bruce T.	Prof	635-2421		A	PHD	91	Mich St	9-67
Gaertner, Robert C.	Assoc	635-2177		DM	MBA	65	Notre Dm	1-70

Lakeland College — Sheboygan, WI 53082-0359 (414) 565-1543 — lakeland.edu
Economics Faculty — Dept of Business Admin Fax=565-1206

Name	Rank	Phone	Email	Field	Degree	Year	School	Since
Schilcutt, J. Garland	C-Pr	565-1271		M	LLD		Marian	1958
Kudek, James F.	Assoc	565-1273		ABCD	MBA		Wi-Milwa	1982
Qastin, Abdul Masesh	Assoc	565-1269		DGNP	PHD		Kennedy W	1985
Schwartz, Adina Tzur	Assoc	565-1296		AEFG	MA		Wi-Milwa	1986
Botana, Joseph D.	Asst	565-1336		AFND	MBA		Roosevelt	1990

Lamar University — Beaumont, TX 77710 (409) 880-8647 — lamar.edu
Dept of Economics & Finance — College of Business Fax=880-1752 — Mrs. Cloris Moser

Name	Rank	Phone	Email	Field	Degree	Year	School	Since
Moore, Gary A.	Dean$	880-8603	moore	J	PHD	74	Nebraska	1998
Hawkins, Charles F.	C-Pr	880-8647		RK	PHD	80	LSU	1966
Regents' Professor of Economics								
Allen, Charles L.	Prof	880-8656		RC	PHD	78	Arkansas	1979
Choi, Jai-Young	Prof	880-8062		DF	PHD	82	Oklahoma	1982
Montano, Carl B.	Prof	880-8651		OQ	PHD	82	Mich St	1981
Parigi, Sam F.	Prof	880-8652		J	PHD	64	Tx-Austin	1961
Regents' Professor of Economics								
Price, Donald I.	Prof	880-8655		MO	PHD	80	Arkansas	1981
Allen, Joel L.	Asst	880-8657		B	MS	60	Baylor	1960

Lander University — Greenwood, SC 29649 (864) 388-8232 — lander.edu
Economic Faculty — School of Business Adm Fax=388-8890 — Joyce Shelton
Did Not Respond--1997-98 Listing

Name	Rank	Phone	Email	Fields	Degree	Yr	School	Since
Molander, J. Dale	Dean	388-8232		Mktg	PHD	66	U Wash	1989
Dumont, David A.	Prof	388-8354		ADJR	PHD	77	SUNY-Alb	1972
Caines, W. Royce	Assoc	388-8355		ALPQ	PHD	88	Clemson	1988
Barnhart, Cora M.	Asst	388-8355		AMO	PHD	95	Clemson	1996

LaSalle University — Philadelphia, PA 19141-1199 (215) — lasalle.edu
Department of Economics — College of Arts & Sci Fax=

Name	Rank	Phone	Email	Fields	Degree	Yr	School	Since
Ratkus, Mark J.	C-As	951-1178	ratkus	O	PHD	76	Notre Dm	1973
George, David L.	Assoc	951-1185	george	ABN	PHD	84	Temple	1979
Grady, John	Assoc	951-1360	grady	BE	MA		Temple	1960
Paulin, Elizabeth	Assoc	951-1181	paulin	J	PHD	87	Tx-Austin	1988
Robison, H. David	Assoc	951-1184	robison	LQC	PHD	83	Maryland	1988
Cairo, Joseph P.	Asst	951-1177	caiaro	BE	MA		Penn	1963
Mshomba, Richard	Asst	951-1116	mshomba	FO	PHD	92	Illinois	1991

La Sierra University — Riverside, CA 92515-8247 (909) 785-2064 — lasierra.edu
Economics Faculty — Sch of Business & Mgt Fax=785-2700 — Vernell Kaufholtz

Name	Rank	Phone	Email	Fields	Degree	Yr	School	Since
Felder, Henry E.	Dean	785-2064	hfelder	Mtg	PHD	75	Stanford	7-95
Sellvanoff, George A.	C-Pr	785-2313	gselivan	AF	PHD	64	American	1984
Ogum, George	Assoc		gogum		DBA	90	Memphis	1997
Thomas, Johnny	Asst	785-2085	jthomas	C	MBA	88	LomaLinda	1989

University of LaVerne — LaVerne, CA 91750 (909) 593-3511 — ulvacs.ulaverne.edu
School of Bus & Global Study — College of Grad & Prof Fax=392-2704 — Barbara Buchanan

Name	Rank	Phone	Email	Fields	Degree	Yr	School	Since
Relf, William	Dean	593-3511			PHD		Claremont	1995
Ispahani, Ahmed S.	Prof	593-3511	ispahani		PHD	66	S Calif	1964
Park, Gon Yung	Prof	593-3511			PHD	93	Brown	1995
Thakur, Rita	Prof	593-4206			MBA		NW Mo St	1978

Lawrence Technological Univ — Southfield, MI 48075-1058 (248) 204-3520 — ltu.edu
Dept of Humanities — Col of Arts & Sciences Fax=204-3518 — Joyce McKissen

Name	Rank	Phone	Email	Fields	Degree	Yr	School	Since
Rodgers, James	Dean	204-3500	rodgers	Engl	PHD	79	E Anglia	1968
Hotelling, Harold	C-Ac	204-3520	hotelling	KL	PHD	82	Duke	9-89
Stevens, Flumo	Prof	204-3508	stevens	G	PHD	74	Nebraska	1987

Lehigh University — Bethlehem, PA 18015-3117 (610) 758-3420 — lehigh.edu
Department of Economics — College of Bus & Econ Fax=758-4677 — Diane Oechsle

Name	Rank	Phone	Email	Fields	Degree	Yr	School	Since
Hyclak, Thomas J.	C-Pr	758-3425	tjh7	JR	PHD	76	Notre Dm	1979
Aronson, J. Richard	Prof	758-3411	jra1	HG	PHD	64	Clark	1965
William L. Clayton Professor of Business and Economics								
Innes, Jon T.	Prof	758-3417	jti1	EB	PHD	67	Oregon	1987
King, Arthur E.	Prof	758-4451	aek0	FP	PHD	76	Ohio St	1976
McNamara, John R.	Prof	758-3415	njm1	MO	PHD	71	Rensselaer	1973
Lee Iacocca Professor of Business & Economics								
Munley, Vincent G.	Prof	758-3428	vgm0	HI	PHD	79	SUNY-Bin	1980
Thornton, Robert J.	Prof	758-3460	rjt1	JI	PHD	70	Illinois	1970
Charles W. MacFarlane Professor of Economics								
Dearden, James A.	Assoc	758-5129	jad8	DH	PHD	87	Penn St	1989
Deily, Mary E.	Assoc	758-4951	med4	LQ	PHD	85	Harvard	1991
Gunter, Frank R.	Assoc	758-4540	frg2	FK	PHD	85	J Hopkins	1984
McDonald, Judith Ann	Assoc	758-5345	djm0	FE	PHD	86	Princeton	1990
O'Brien, Anthony P.	Assoc	758-3442	ao01	NE	PHD	86	Berkeley	1987
Taylor, Larry W.	Assoc	758-3416	lwt0	CE	PHD	84	N Carol	1984
Chisholm, Darlene C.	Asst	758-3422	dcc0	LD	PHD	91	U Wash	1991
Watkins, Todd A.	Asst	758-4954	taw4	LO	PHD	95	Harvard	1992
Thomas, John R.	Inst	758-4775	jrt3		PHD	96	SanDiego	1995

LeMoyne College — Syracuse, NY 13214-1399 (315) 445-4465 — maple.lemoyne
Economics Faculty — Department of Economics Fax=445-4540

Name	Rank	Phone	Email	Fields	Degree	Yr	School	Since
Ruwe, Marcia	Dean	445-4310	ruweml		DBA	82	Kentucky	1995
Shepard, Edward M.	C-Ac	445-4465	shepard	HJL	PHD	87	Boston C	1990
Arora, Harjit K.	Prof	445-4436	arora	EFH	PHD	84	Wi-Milwa	1987
Blackley, Dixie M.	Prof	445-4437	black_d	DRC	PHD	84	Syracuse	1982
Blackley, Paul R.	Prof	445-4465	black_p	HR	PHD	82	Syracuse	1982
Saunders, Kent T.	Asst	445-4488	sanuders	ADG	PHD	95	Clemson	1998

Lenoir-Rhyne College — Hickory, NC 28603 (704) 328-7225 — lrc.edu
Dept of Economics & Pol Sci — Div of Social & Beh Sci Fax=328-7338 — Dottie Crafton

Name	Rank	Phone	Email	Fields	Degree	Yr	School	Since
Ashman, H. Lowell	C-Pr	328-7213	l_ashman		PHD	73	Utah	1975
Mauney, William M.	Prof	328-7218	mauneyw	AE	MA	76	Appalach	1967
Centennial Professor of Economics - Director Broyhill Institute								
Wright, Jeffrey J.	Prof	328-7217	wright_jj	AFK	PHD	87	Conn	1989

Lewis University Romeoville, IL 60441 (815) Ext 531
Department of Economics College of Business Fax=Ext 3330
Did Not Respond Again--1995-96 Listing; phone 838-0500
Perrone, James Dean Ext 360 Ecol
Hill, Lawrence G. C-Pr Ext 377 PHD 76 N Illinois 1968
Marker, William Inst Ext 260 MA 85 N Illinois 1988

Lewis & Clark College Portland, OR 97219-7899 (503) 768-7606 lclark.edu
Department of Economics Col of Arts & Sciences Fax=768-7611 Kim Spir
Schleef, Harold C-Pr 768-7603 Fnce PHD 77 Chicago
Hart-Landsberg, Martin Prof 768-7624 marty POFA PHD 74 Wisconsin 1978
Goodstein, Eban Assoc 768-7626 eban QDGL PHD 89 Michigan 1995
Bekar, Clifford T. Asst 768-7612 bekar HPIL ABD Simon Fr
Grant, James H. Asst 768-7623 grant CDJA PHD 79 Mich St 1987
Zahrt Geib, Elizabeth Asst 768-7605 zahrt GEBJ PHD 97 Calif 1997

Liberty University Lynchburg, VA 24502-2269 (804) 582-2480 liberty.edu
Dept Econ & Finance & MIS School of Bus & Govt Fax=582-2366 Sharon Woods
Adkins, Robert T. Dean 582-2480 Mktg PHD 77 Arkansas 1991
Mateer, Robert N. C-Pr 582-2338 MBA 64 Tulane 1984
Lai, T. H. Assoc 582-2910 AEFG PHD 84 Ohio St 9-85
Rencher, Robert Assoc 582-7743 MBA 81 Fairl Dick 1991
Torrell, Timothy Asst 582-2338 ACPQ PHD 98 Auburn 1998

Lincoln University-MO Jefferson Cty MO 65101-0029 (573) 681-5489 luag.lu.edu
Dept of Bus & Economics Col Bus & Prof Studies Fax=681-6074
Linhardt, Wayne C. Dean 681-5489 ABD Nova SE 1965
LePage, James Assoc 681-6081 PHD Kansas 1984
Arabian, Ghodratollah Asst 681-6077 PHD 85 Indiana 1984

Lincoln University-PA Lincoln Univ, PA 19352 (610) Ext 3394
Dept of Economics & Bus Adm Div of Social Sciences Fax= Melanie Murray Ext 3394
Did Not Respond Again--1995-96 Listing; phone 932-8300
Dadson, William K. C-Pr Ext 6191 PHD 83 Denver
Ramdas, Ganga P. Asst Ext 3376 PHD 87 Temple

Lindenwood University St. Charles, MO 63301-1695 (636) 949-2000 lc.lindenwood.edu
Economics Faculty Div Management & LCIE Fax=949-4910
Hagan, Oliver Dean 916-1920 hagan DMGT Webster 9-90
Hafer, Gail Assoc 949-4930 hafer PHD 87 S Illinois 9-93
Kamm, Judy Asst 949-4832 kamm MS Mo-StLou 8-96

Linfield College McMinnville, OR 97128-6894 (503) 434-2405 linfield.edu
Economics Faculty Dept of Economics & Bus Fax=434-2566 Jean Claus
Kiehl, Sandra C-Ac 434-2252 skiehl Mgt PHD 89 Port St 1988
Hansen, David Prof 434-2253 dhansen MS Portland 1969
Chambers, Scott Assoc 434-2401 schamb PHD 88 Ca-Davis 1990
Grant, Randy R. Assoc 434-2402 rgrant PHD 96 Nebraska 1993
Summers, Jeffrey A. Assoc 434-2297 jsummer PHD 87 Purdue 1992

Lock Haven University Lock Haven, PA 17745 (570) 893-2163 eagle.lhup.edu
Dept Hist, Pol S, Econ & Mgt College of Arts & Sci Fax=893-2830 Gale Spangler
Johnson, Roger Dean 893-2136 PHD
DeLavan, Nelson C 893-2646 Hst BA Tx Tech 1968
Carroll, Richard R. Prof 893-2447 PHD 73 Kentucky 1977
Chatterton, R. Edward Prof 893-2222 PHD 80 Wash St 1982
Wion, Douglas A. Assoc 893-2217 PHD 80 Penn St 1980

Long Isl U, Brooklyn Campus Brooklyn, NY 11201-5372 (718) 488-1025 liunet.edu
Department of Economics Conolly C Liberal A & S Fax=780-4106 Ms. Mina Pacheco
Cohen, David B. Dean Biol PHD 73 NYU
Varma, Ranbir C-Pr 834-1025 AFOP PHD 57 New Sch 1959
Lombardi, Waldo J. Prof ACD PHD 70 Columbia
Zewail, Amin A. Assoc AEHR PHD 75 Fordham

Long Island U.-C.W. Post Brookville, NY 11548-0570 (516) 299-2321 eagle.liunet.edu
Department of Economics College of Liberal Arts Fax=299-4169 Rhonda Pereira
Sherwin, Paul Dean 299-2236 PHD Yale
Gafar, John S. C-Pr 299-2371 PHD 79 W Indies 1980
Mourdoukoutas, Panos Prof 299-2322 PHD 83 SUNY-SBr 1984
Solar, Donald Prof 299-2321 PHD 63 Columbia 1965
Roy, Udayan Assoc 299-2405 PHD 91 SUNY-SBr
Zeineldin, Aly Assoc 299-2370 PHD 79 NYU
Lu, Laura Asst 299-2369 PHD 89 SUNY-SBr

Longwood College Farmville, VA 23909 (804) 395-2042 lwcnet.lwc.edu
Dept of Economics & Finance School of Bus & Econ Fax=395-2203 Ms. Janet Evans

Farmer, Berkwood M.	Dean	395-2045	bfarmer	Q	PHD	70	N Car St	1991
Flanigan, Mary A.	C-Ac	395-2042	mflaniga	Atg	PHD	95	Va Comm	1989
Shaw, Sue O.	Prof	395-2371	sshaw		PHD	67	Harvard	1986
Adusei, Edward O.	Assoc	395-2459	eadusei		PHD	88	Va Tech	1992
Brastow, Raymond T.	Assoc	395-2370	rbrastow	J	PHD	87	U Wash	1987
Marks, Melanie B.	Assoc	395-2372	mmerrell		PHD	93	Tx A&M	1993

Loras College Dubuque, IA 52004-0178 (319) loras.edu
Department of Economics Div Soc Sci & Beh Stds Fax=

Simon, Peter J.	C-Ac	588-7915	psimon		PHD	89	N Illinois	1989
Giannakouros, George	Prof	588-7646	ggiannak		PHD	74	Iowa	1966
O'Connor, Dennis A.	Prof	588-7519	doconnor		PHD	84	Notre Dm	1983
Sula, Laddie J.	Prof	588-7507	lsula		PHD	76	Geo St	1983

Louisiana State University Baton Rouge, LA 70803-6306 (225) 388-5211 lsu.edu
Department of Economics College of Business Adm Fax=388-3807 Mary Jo Neathery

Clark, Thomas D. Jr.	Dean	388-3211			DBA	77	Fla St	8-95
Rice, G. Randolph	C-Pr	388-3799	rrice	C	PHD	70	Kentucky	1969
Thomas J. Singletary Business Partnership Professor								
Beard, Thomas R.	Emer	388-3787	trbreard	E	PHD	63	Duke	1961
LSU Alumni Professor Emeritus								
Culbertson, W. Patton Jr.	Prof	388-3783	wculber	F	PHD	72	Tx-Austin	
Hill, R. Carter	Prof	388-1490	eohill	C	PHD	75	Missouri	
Marjory B. Ourso Excellence in Teaching Professor								
Johnson, David B.	Prof	388-3796		H	PHD	68	Virginia	
Jones, Lamar B.	Prof	388-3803	bajone	J	PHD	65	Tx-Austin	1967
Associate Director of EMBA								
Koray, Faik A.	Prof	388-3801	eokora	EF	PHD	84	Duke	1984
Director Graduate Studies								
McMillin, W. Douglas	Prof	388-3798	eodoug	E	PHD	79	LSU	1985
South Central Bell Business Partnership Professor								
Moore, William J.	Prof	388-3792	eomoore	IJ	PHD	70	Tx-Austin	
Gulf Coast Coca Cola Business Partnership Professor								
Newman, Robert J.	Prof	388-3794	eonewm	IJ	PHD	80	UCLA	1983
South Central Bell Business Partnership Professor								
Richardson, James A.	Prof	388-6743	parich	H	PHD	71	Michigan	1970
Alumni Professor of Economics; Director Public Administration Institute								
Scott, Loren C.	Emer	388-3779	lscott	J	PHD	69	Okla St	1969
Turnbull, Geoffrey K.	Prof	388-3795	eoturn	DH	PHD	83	Wi-Milwa	1984
CJ Brown Distinguished Professor of Real Estate; Gulfcoast Bottling Dist Prof								
Miyagiwa, Kaz	Assoc	388-3793	kmiyagi	FO	PHD	85	Tx-Austin	8-95
Palivos, Theodore	Assoc	388-3791	eopali	F	PHD	92	Penn St	1992
Mack Hornbeak Business Partnership Professor								
Terrell, Dek	Assoc	388-3785	mdterre	C	PHD	91	Duke	8-96
Mack H. Hornbeak Business Professorship Professor								
McCracken, Michael	Asst	388-3782	mmccrac	C	PHD	98	Wisconsin	8-98
Okten, Cagla	Asst	388-5211		L	PHD	99	Nrthwstrn	8-99
Papageorgio, Chris	Asst	388-3790	cpapa	E	PHD	96	Pittsburgh	8-97
Ringel, Jeanne	Asst	388-3780	jringel	D	PHD	97	Maryland	8-97

Louisiana St in Shreveport Shreveport, LA 71115-2399 (318) 797-5241 lsuvm.sncc.lsu.edu
Dept of Economics & Finance College of Business Adm Fax=797-5208 Donna Carney

Harju, Melvin W.	Dean	797-5027			PHD	72	Florida	8-77
Vines, Timothy	C-Ac	797-5241			PHD	92	Tennessee	1989
Austin, John A.	Prof	797-5022			PHD	72	Ariz St	1983
Brendler, Michael D.	Prof	797-5019			PHD	77	Tx A&M	1977
Jones, Charlotte	Prof	797-5383			DBA	85	La Tech	1984
Hsieh, Eric	Assoc	797-5145			PHD		LSU	1989

Louisiana Tech University Ruston, LA 71272-0001 (318) 257-4149 cab.latech.edu
Dept of Economics & Finance College of Admin & Bus Fax=257-4253 Brenda Sanderson

Emery, John T.	Dean	257-4526	emery	Fnce	PHD	69	U Wash	1994
Anderson, Dwight C.	H-Pr	257-4149	anderson	Fnce	PHD	74	Alabama	1979
Darrat, Ali F.	Prof	257-3874	darrat	EG	PHD	81	Indiana	1987
Gilley, Otis W.	Prof	257-3768	gilley	D	PHD	79	Purdue	1988
Smith, Lawrence C.	Prof	257-2112			PHD	68	Miss	1970
Chopin, Marc	Assoc	257-4464	chopin@cab.	DL	PHD	92	Tx A&M	1992
O'Boyle, Edward John	Assoc	257-3701			PHD	72	St Louis	1977
Barkoulas, John	Asst	257-4149		EGF	PHD		Boston C	1997

University of Louisville — Louisville, KY 40292-0001 (502) 852-7836 — ulkyvm.louisville.edu
Department of Economics — Col Business & Pub Adm Fax=852-7672 — Charlotte Ford

Name	Rank	Phone	E-mail	Field	Degree	Yr	School	Since
Taylor, Robert L.	Dean	852-7684	rltaylo1	Mgt	DBA	72	Indiana	8-84
Coomes, Paul A.	D-Ac	852-4841	pacoom01	R	PHD	85	Tx-Austin	1985
Gohmann, Stephan F.	Prof	852-4844	sfgohm01	J	PHD	84	N Car St	1988
Nahata, Babu L.	Prof	852-4864	b0naha01	D	PHD	77	N Illinois	8-78
Nelson, John P.	Prof	852-7901	jpnelso01	H	PHD	68	Kentucky	
Chou, Nan-Ting	Assoc	852-4840	ntchou01	E	PHD	86	Ohio St	1991
Vahaly, John	Assoc	852-4863	j0vaha01	R	PHD	75	Vanderbilt	1975
Davidson, Audrey	Asst	852-4839	abdavi01	L	PHD	93	Auburn	1993
Haworth, Barry	Asst	852-4845	bmhawo01	L	PHD	94	Ca-Davis	1995
Hilmer, Michael	Asst	852-4858	mjhilm01	H	PHD	96	Ca-SnBarb	8-97
Izyumov, Alexei	Asst	852-4842	a0izyu01	F	PHD	85	USSR	8-97

Loyola College in Maryland — Baltimore, MD 21210-2699 (410) 617-2357 — loyola.edu
Department of Economics — Sellinger Sch Bus & Mgt Fax=617-2118 — Bonnie Nauman

Name	Rank	Phone	E-mail	Field	Degree	Yr	School	Since
Lorenzi, Peter	Dean	617-2301	plorenzi	Mgt	PHD	78	Penn St	1995
Larson, John C.	C-Pr	617-2476	jlarson	E	PHD	77	Minnesota	1974
Derrick, Frederick W.	Prof	617-2712	fderrick	CI	PHD	76	N Car St	1982
DiLorenzo, Thomas J.	Prof	617-2755		KLH	PHD	80	Va Tech	1992
Scott, Charles E.	Prof	617-2618	cscott	MJH	PHD	79	Vanderbilt	1985
Walters, Stephen J. K.	Prof	617-2313	swalters	KL	PHD	82	UCLA	1981
Williams, Nancy A.	Assoc	617-2825	nwilliams	QH	PHD	84	Berkeley	1987
Burger, John	Asst	617-2357	jburger	FE	PHD	99	N Carol	1999
Hilton S.J., F. G.	Asst	617-2544	fhilton	QF	PHD	96	Wisconsin	1996

Loyola University - Chicago — Chicago, IL 60611-2196 (312) 915-6062 — luc.edu
Department of Economics — School of Business Adm Fax=915-8508 — Sylvia Bravo

Name	Rank	Phone	E-mail	Field	Degree	Yr	School	Since
Bryan, William R.	Dean	915-6113	wbryan	Fnce	PHD	61	Wisconsin	9-95
Cain, Louis P.	C-Pr	915-6075	lcain	ADNR	PHD	69	Nrthwstrn	1968
Cinar, E. Mine	Prof	915-6066	mcinar	ACDO	PHD	76	Tx A&M	1983
Malliaris, Tassos	Prof	915-6063	tmallia	ACG	PHD	72	Oklahoma	1972
Gabriel, Paul E.	Assoc	915-6070	pgabrie	ADJ	PHD	87	Kentucky	1990
Gobin, Roy T.	Assoc	915-6074	tgobin	AEHO	PHD	78	Illinois	1978
Hayford, Marc D.	Assoc	915-6073	mhayfor	AE	PHD	87	Brown	1986
Merriman, David F.	Assoc	915-6071	dmerrim	ADHO	PHD	83	Wisconsin	1987
Mirza, David B.	Assoc	915-6062	dmirza	AF	PHD	73	Nrthwstrn	1969
Vanderporten, Bruce S.	Assoc	915-6076	bvander	ACD	PHD	73	Wayne St	1978
Surdam, David	Asst	915-6067	dsurdam	AILN	PHD	94	Chicago	1994

Loyola Univ-New Orleans — New Orleans, LA 70118 (504) 865-3544 — beta.loyno.edu
Department of Economics — College of Business Adm Fax=865-3496

Name	Rank	Phone	E-mail	Field	Degree	Yr	School	Since
O'Brien, J. Patrick	Dean	865-3547		AEHR	PHD	77	Okla St	1995
Walker, Deborah L.	C-Ac	865-3924		ABDJ	PHD	87	GeoMason	1987
Barnett, William	Assoc	865-2165		DEFK	PHD	74	Mich St	1974
Dauterive, Jerry W.	Assoc	865-3545		ADH	PHD	76	Tx Tech	1979
Associate Dean								
Mundell, Cyril Lee	Assoc	865-2549		AC	PHD	76	N Carol	1981
Saliba, Michael T.	Assoc	865-2681		ADM	PHD	72	Oklahoma	1973
Wood, J. Stuart	Assoc	865-2171		GM	PHD	80	NYU	1984

Loyola Marymount Univ — Los Angeles, CA 90045-8410 (310) 338-7373 — lmumail.lmu.edu
Department of Economics — College of Liberal Arts Fax=338-1950 — M. Edwards/B. Bernard

Name	Rank	Phone	E-mail	Field	Degree	Yr	School	Since
Chan, Kenyon	Dean	338-2716	kchan		PHD	74	UCLA	1998
Singleton, Robert	C-As	338-7373	rsinglet	AJR	PHD	83	UCLA	1982
Devine, James N.	Prof	338-2948	jdevine	AEJN	PHD	81	Berkeley	1985
Earley, Joseph E.	Assoc	338-4572	jearley	AC	PHD	74	Fordham	1974
Konow, James D.	Assoc	338-2956	jkonow	ACD	PHD	93	UCLA	1989
Shoukry, Kamal	Assoc	338-8215	kshoukry	ABCE	PHD	72	S Calif	1980
Thimester, Renate	Assoc	338-2817	rthimest	ABKM	PHD	67	Alabama	1971
Zekavat, Seid M.	Assoc	338-7372	szekavat	ACG	PHD	64	S Calif	1964
Eusufzai, Zaki	Asst	338-2822	zeusufza	ACFD	PHD	94	UCLA	1989
Fuentes, Gabriel	Asst	338-5956	gfuentes	DLO	PHD	94	Berkeley	1994

Luther College — Decorah, IA 52101-1045 (319) 387-1340 — luther.edu
Dept of Economics & Business — Div of Social Sciences Fax=387-1088 — Jeri Laursen

Name	Rank	Phone	E-mail	Field	Degree	Yr	School	Since
Kaschins, Edward A.	H-Pr	387-1130			PHD	73	Iowa	1961
Lund, Mark	Prof				PHD	75	Iowa St	1978
Leake, Richard S.	Assoc				MBA		Wisconsin	1975
Gomoroall, C. Nicholas	Asst				PHD	91	Cornell	1991

Lycoming College — Williamsport, PA 17701-5192 (570) 321-4100 — lycoming.edu
Economics Faculty — Dept of Economics Fax=321-4161 — Carolyn Vander Weide

Name	Rank	Phone	E-mail	Field	Degree	Yr	School	Since
Madresehee, Mehrdad	C-Ac	321-4179	madreseh	FKLR	PHD	85	Wash St	1986
Sprunger, Philip W.	Asst	321-4178	sprunger	AJQH	PHD	93	Indiana	1993
Yerger, David B.	Asst	321-4154	yerger	JFTN	PHD	94	Penn St	1996

Lynchburg College — Lynchburg, VA 24501-3199 (804) 544-8256 — lynchburg.edu
Dept of Economics — Sch of Business & Econ Fax=544-8639 — Virginia Kern

Name	Rank	Phone	E-mail	Fields	Degree	Yr	School	Since
Husted, Stewart W.	Dean	522-8621		Mgt	PHD	77	Mich St	9-89
Messerschmidt, Daniel C.	C-Pr	522-8458			PHD	84	Iowa St	1985
Prinzinger, Joseph M.	Prof	522-8329			PHD	74	Geo St	1987
Turek, Joseph H.	Assoc	522-8542			PHD	87	SUNY-Alb	1986

Lyndon State College — Lyndonville, VT 05851 (802) 626-6200 — queen.lsc.vsc.edu
Economics Faculty — Business Adm Department Fax=626-9770

Name	Rank	Phone	E-mail	Fields	Degree	Yr	School	Since
Tero, Paul F.	Dean	626-6406		Psy	PHD	85	Rochester	6-97
Bradley, David B.	C-Pr	626-6482	bradleyd	Atg	MBA	82	Plymouth	9-81
Siegel, Rachel S.	Assoc	626-9371	siegelr	CGQN	MBA	89	Yale	9-90

Lyon College — Batesville, AR 72501-2317 (870) 698-4258 — lyon.edu
Department of Economics — Business & Econ Div Fax=698-4622 — Peggy Weaver

Name	Rank	Phone	E-mail	Fields	Degree	Yr	School	Since
Cooper, Thomas E.	C-Ac	698-4364	tcooper	DGHL	PHD	84	Princeton	1987
Anne J. Stewart Professor of Economics								
Cohen, Richard H.	Asst	793-1740	rcohen	EG	PHD	92	Indiana	1998

Macalester College — St. Paul, MN 55105-1899 (612) 696-6227 — mac.cc.macalstr.edu
Economics Faculty — Economics Department Fax= — Nancy H. Jones

Name	Rank	Phone	E-mail	Fields	Degree	Yr	School	Since
Sukhatme, Vasant A.	C-Pr	696-6744	sukhatme	ADO	PHD	77	Chicago	1978
Edward J. Noble Professor of Economics								
Egge, Karl A.	Prof	696-6227	egge	AGM	PHD	73	Ohio St	1970
F. R. Bigelow Professor of Economics								
Ferderer, J. Peter	Assoc	696-6093	ferderer	EFN	PHD	89	Wash U	1996
Krueger, Gary J.	Assoc	696-6222	krueger	ACP	PHD	89	Wisconsin	1989
Bunn, Julie A.	Asst	696-6776	bunn	AFQ	PHD	93	Stanford	1992
Moe, Karine S.	Asst	696-6227	moe	AJ	PHD	95	Minnesota	1995
Robertson, Raymond	Asst			AEF	PHD	97	Texas	1999

Univ of Maine — Orono, ME 04469-5774 (207) 581-1850 — umit.maine.edu
Department of Economics — Col Liberal Arts & Sci Fax=581-1851 — Ms. Debra A. Perro

Name	Rank	Phone	E-mail	Fields	Degree	Yr	School	Since
Wihry, David F.	C-Ac	581-1850	david.wihry	HIA	PHD	72	Syracuse	1969
Burke, Melvin	Prof	581-1853	melvin.burke	O	PHD	67	Pittsburgh	1966
Duchesneau, Thomas D.	Prof	581-1858	rec360	AO	PHD	69	Boston C	1967
Hunt, Gary	Prof	581-1861	gary.hunt	AR	PHD	84	Colorado	1993
Lutz, Mark A.	Prof	581-1859		AB	PHD	72	Berkeley	1970
Townsend, Ralph E.	Prof	581-1852	ralph.townsend	CHQA	PHD	83	Wisconsin	1980
Breece, James H.	Assoc	581-1863	james.breece	AEF	PHD	82	Boston C	1983
Montgomery, Michael	Assoc	581-1857		AE	PHD	88	Florida	1991
Kearney, Adrienne	Asst	581-1854	adrienne.kearney	AF	PHD	92	Penn St	1997
Mueller, Richard	Asst	581-1864	richard.mueller	JA	PHD	97	Tx-Austin	1996
McCallie, John	Lect	581-1856	john.mccallie	EA	PHD	90	Auburn	1992

Manhattan College — Riverdale, NY 10471 (718) 862-7462 — manhattan.edu
Dept of Economics & Finance — School of Business Fax=862-8032

Name	Rank	Phone	E-mail	Fields	Degree	Yr	School	Since
Suarez, James M.	Dean	862-7440			PHD	72	Columbia	1984
Tomer, John F.	C-Pr	862-7462	jtomer@juno.com		PHD	73	Rutgers	1983
Geisst, Charles R.	Prof	862-7242	cgeisst@a	N	PHD	72	LondonEC	1985
Abdulahad, Faraj	Assoc	862-7220	fabdulah	F	PHD	68	Boston C	1970
Robbins, Edward	Assoc	862-7110			PHD	86	Stanford	1997
Shojai, Siamack	Assoc	862-7239			PHD	84	Fordham	1989
Topyan, Kudret	Assoc	862-7887			PHD	92	CUNY	1991
Maclachlan, Fiona C.	Asst	862-7466			PHD	91	NYU	1992

Mansfield University of PA — Mansfield, PA 16933 (717) 662-4510 — mnsfld.edu
Economics Faculty — Business & Economics Fax=662-4111

Name	Rank	Phone	E-mail	Fields	Degree	Yr	School	Since
Welch, Paula	C-Ac	662-4512	pwelch		MBA	80	Syracuse	1976
Yacovissi, William A.	Prof	662-4764	wyacoviss		PHD	89	SUNY-Bin	1976
Carpenter, Bruce E.	Assoc	662-4761	bcarrpent		PHD	90	Conn	1987

Marian College — Indianapolis, IN 46222-1997 (317) 929-0269 — marian.edu
Economics Faculty — Business Fax=955-6434
Did Not Respond Again--1995-96 Listing

Name	Rank	Phone	E-mail	Fields	Degree	Yr	School	Since
Merle, Jill A.	C-As	929-0269			MBA	89	Indiana	1989
Schuttler, Robert D.	Inst	929-0269			MBA	80	Evansville	1985

Marietta College — Marietta, OH 45750-4029 (740) 376-4633 — marietta.edu
Brachman Dp Econ, Mgt & Atg — College of Business Fax=376-7501 — Paula Lewis

Name	Rank	Phone	E-mail	Fields	Degree	Yr	School	Since
Potash, Sidney	C-Pr	376-4633	potashs	Mgt	PHD	79	SUNY-Buf	1974
Delemeester, Gregory	Assoc	376-4630	delemeeg	DJK	PHD	89	Tx A&M	1986
Milton Friedman Chair in Economics								
Khorassani, Jacqueline	Asst	376-4621	khorassj	AEFH	PHD	97	W Virginia	1994

Marist College	Poughkeepsie, NY 12601-1387 (914) 575-3225						marist.edu	
Economic Faculty	School of Management Fax=575-3640						Jean Talbot	
Badovick, Gordon J.	Dean	575-3225	jZGB	Mktg	PHD	88	Oregon	1990
Kobos, Chester	C-As	575-3000	JZII	Fnce	PHD	72	Fordham	1982
Black, Geoffrey	Asst	Ext 2911	geoff.black	QHN	PHD	95	U Wash	1995
Davis, Ann E.	Asst	575-3000	JZFL	RT	PHD	83	Boston C	1981
Morley, John	Asst	575-3000	JZ78	N	PHD	87	Yale	1995

Marquette University	Milwaukee, WI 53201-1881 (414) 288-7377						biz.mu.edu	
Department of Economics	College of Business Adm Fax=288-5757						April Fleischmann	
Brush, Brian C.	C-Pr	288-3367	brush	DL	PHD	73	N Carol	1968
Davis, John B.	Prof	288-5438	davis	BI	PHD	85	Mich St	
Smiley, William G.	Prof	288-5664	smiley	DN	PHD	73	Iowa	1973
Booth, Douglas E.	Assoc	288-7310	booth	DQ	PHD	72	U Wash	
Breeden, Charles H.	Assoc	288-3370	breedenc	DHK	PHD	77	Va Tech	1979
Chowdhury, Abdur R.	Assoc	288-3417	chowdhur	EFO	PHD	83	Kentucky	1989
Clark, David E.	Assoc	288-3339	clarkde	DR	PHD	86	SUNY-Bin	1985
Crane, Steven E.	Assoc	288-1450	crane	DHLR	PHD	81	Colorado	1980
Daniels, Joseph P.	Assoc	288-3368	danielsj	EFG	PHD	92	Indiana	1989
Hunter, William J.	Assoc	288-1449	hunter	DH	PHD	79	Va Tech	1982
Associate Dean								
McGibany, James M.	Assoc	288-7187	mcgibanyj	CER	PHD	83	Mich St	1983
Nourzad, Farrokh	Assoc	288-3570	nourzad	CEO	PHD	82	Kansas	1981
Toumanoff, Peter	Assoc	288-7523	toumanof	DOPC	PHD	77	U Wash	1995

Marshall University	Huntington, WV 25755-2320 (304) 696-6492						marshall.edu	
Div of Finance & Economics	College of Business Fax=696-4344							
Kent, Calvin A.	Dean	696-2614	kent		PHD	67	Missouri	1993
Adkins, Roger L.	C-Pr	696-2609	adkinsr		PHD	81	Kansas St	1981
Akkihal, Ramchandra G.	Prof	696-2613	akkihal		PHD	69	Tennessee	1970
Kontos, Nicholas C.	Assoc	696-2606	kontos		MA	58	Indiana	1961
Shuklian, Steve	Assoc	696-2605	shuklian		PHD	88	Utah	1988
Smith, Harlan II	Assoc	696-3233	smithh		PHD	89	Yale	1991
Wilkins, Allen J.	Assoc	696-3351	wilkins		PHD	84	Wisconsin	1985
Zapalska, Alina	Assoc	696-3234	zapalska		PHD	91	Kentucky	1991
Burton, Mark L.	Asst	696-2382	burtonm		PHD	91	Tennessee	1999
Newsome, Mike	Asst	696-2709	newsome		PHD	97	Kentucky	1999

University of Mary	Bismarck, ND 58504-9652 (701) 255-7500						umary.edu	
Economics Faculty	Division of Business Fax=255-7687							
phone 255-7500								
Borgelt, Marvin	C-Ac	Ext 439	mborgelt	Mgt	MBA	82	Maryland	9-82
Door, Randy	Assoc	Ext 438			MS		N Dak St	

Mary Baldwin College	Staunton, VA 24401 (540) 887-7053						cit.mbc.edu	
Economics Faculty	Department of Economics Fax=887-7137							
Did Not Respond--1997-98 Listing								
Klein, Judy L.	C-Ac	887-7053	jklein	BC	PHD	86	London	1982
Diduch, Amy	Asst	887-7114	adiduch	J	PHD	95	Harvard	1995

Univ of Mary Hardin-Baylor	Belton, TX 76513 (254) 295-4644						umbh.edu	
Dept Atg, Economics & Fnce	School of Business Fax=295-4535							
Did Not Respond--1997-98 Listing								
Baldwin, Lee E.	Dean	295-4644	lbaldwin	Mgt	PHD	80	North Tx	1992
Fabritius, Michael	Prof	295-4655	mfabriti	ABDE	PHD	87	Tx-Austin	1987
Claude McBryde Professor of Finance-Economics								

Mary Washington College	FredericksburgVA 22401-5358 (540) 654-1483						mwu.edu	
Economics Faculty	Department of Economics Fax=654-1074						Jane Clark 654-1066	
Greenlaw, Steven A.	C-Ac	654-1483	greenla	EFA	PHD	87	SUNY-Bin	1982
Rycroft, Robert S.	Prof	654-1500	rrycroft	CHJG	PHD	78	Maryland	1977
Ray, Margaret A.	Assoc	654-1485	mray	LQRA	PHD	88	Tennessee	
Stageberg, Stephen P.	Assoc	654-1486	sstagebe	CFN	PHD	84	Geotown	1982
Hansen, Bradley	Asst	654-1484	bhansen	N	PHD	95	Wash U	1995

Univ Maryland-Baltimore Co	Baltimore, MD 21228-5398 (410) 455-2137						umbc2.umbc.edu	
Department of Economics	Col of Arts & Sciences Fax=						Iris Bachelor	
Did Not Respond Again--1995-96 Listing								
Burchard, Robert	Dean$	455-2386		Biol	PHD	65	Minnesota	
Sorkin, Alan L.	C-Pr	455-2173			PHD	66	J Hopkins	1974
Bradley, Michael E.	Prof	455-2170			PHD	67	Cornell	
Goldfarb, Marsha G.	Prof	455-2171			PHD	68	Nrthwstrn	1973
Gindling, Thomas H.	Assoc	455-3629	gindling	O	PHD	87	Cornell	

Name	Rank	Phone	Degree	Yr	School	Year
Lord, William A.	Assoc	455-2498	PHD	84	Indiana	1987
McConnell, Virginia D.	Assoc	455-2068	PHD	78	Maryland	
Mitch, David F.	Assoc	455-2157	PHD	82	Chicago	1983
Peake, Charles F.	Assoc	455-2168	PHD	68	Maryland	1967
Takacs, Wendy E.	Assoc	455-2174	PHD	76	J Hopkins	1981
Wu, Roland Y.	Assoc	455-2176	PHD	71	Stanford	
Carroll, Kathleen A.	Asst	455-2169	PHD	76	J Hopkins	1980
Knapp, Kimberly A.	Asst	455-3243	PHD	88	Brown	
Lamdin, Douglas J.	Asst	455-2672	PHD	91	Maryland	1989
Humphreys, Brad	Inst	455-2177	MA	91	J Hopkins	
Davis, Mary	Lect	455-3177	MBA	78	Maryland	

University of Maryland College Park, MD 20742-7211 (301) 405-3266 umd.edu
Department of Economics Col Behav & Social Sci Fax=405-3542 Martha Best 405-3506

Name	Rank	Phone	Degree	Yr	School	Year
Goldstein, Irwin	Dean	405-1679	PHD	64	Maryland	1991
Straszheim, Mahlon R.	C-Pr	405-3266	PHD	66	Harvard	
Almon, Clopper Jr.	Prof	405-4604	PHD	62	Harvard	1966
Ausubel, Lawrence M.	Prof	405-3495	PHD	84	Stanford	1992
Betancourt, Roger R.	Prof	405-3479	PHD	69	Wisconsin	1980
Calvo, Guillermo	Prof	405-3553	PHD	74	Yale	1994
Cramton, Peter C.	Prof	405-6987	PHD	84	Stanford	1993
Cropper, Maureen L.	Prof	405-3266	PHD	73	Cornell	1980
Dorsey, John W.	Prof	405-3501	PHD	65	Harvard	1989
Drazen, Allen	Prof	405-3477	PHD	76	MIT	1990
Evans, William N.	Prof	405-3486	PHD	87	Duke	1987
Haltiwanger, John C.	Prof	405-3490	PHD	81	J Hopkins	1987
Hulten, Charles R.	Prof	405-3549	PHD	73	Berkeley	1985
Kelejian, Harry	Prof	405-3492	PHD	68	Wisconsin	1968
Montgomery, Edward B. on leave	Prof	405-3498	PHD	82	Harvard	1990
Murrell, Peter	Prof	405-3476	PHD	77	Penn	1977
Oates, Wallace	Prof	405-3496	PHD	65	Stanford	1979
Panagariya, Arvind	Prof	405-3546	PHD	78	Princeton	1978
Prucha, Ingmar R.	Prof	405-3499	PHD	77	Vienna	1981
Qian, Yingyi	Prof		PHD	90	Harvard	1999
Schelling, Thomas	Prof	405-3494	PHD	51	Harvard	1991
Schwab, Robert M.	Prof	405-3478	PHD	80	J Hopkins	1980
Wallis, John J.	Prof	405-3552	PHD	81	U Wash	1983
Coughlin, Peter J.	Assoc	405-3482	PHD	76	SUNY-Alb	1982
Lyon, Andrew B.	Assoc	405-3493	PHD	86	Princeton	1987
Sakellaris, Plutarchos	Assoc	405-3509	PHD	92	Harvard	1992
Sanders, Seth	Assoc		PHD	93	Chicago	1999
Shea, John	Assoc	405-3491	PHD	90	MIT	1996
Vincent, Daniel	Assoc	405-3485	PHD	87	Princeton	1998
Binder, Michael	Asst	405-3466	PHD	95	Penn	1995
Chao, John	Asst	405-4366	PHD	95	Yale	1995
Gelbach, Jonah	Asst	405-3512	PHD	98	MIT	1998
Hellerstein, Judith	Asst	405-3545	PHD	94	Harvard	1996
Kranton, Rachel E.	Asst	405-3487	PHD	93	Berkeley	1993
Pries, Michael	Asst		PHD	99	Stanford	1999
Rodriguez, Francisco	Asst	405-3480	PHD	98	Harvard	1998

Marymount University Arlington, VA 22207-4299 (703) 284-5910 marymount.edu
Economics Faculty School of Business Adm Fax=527-3830 Sara Caltrider/Danielle Laky

Name	Rank	Phone	Email	Field	Degree	Yr	School	Year
Sigethy, Robert	Dean	284-5910	rsigethy	Mgt	PHD	80	American	1983
Long, Teresa M.	C-Pr	284-5918	tlong		PHD	80	Iowa St	1981
Hassanein, Saad A.	Prof	234-5938	shassanein		PHD	88	Catholic	1988
Marshall, Louise	Prof	284-5932	lmarshall		PHD	89	Maryland	1976

Marywood University Scranton, PA 18509-1598 (717) ac.marywood.edu
Economics Faculty Social Science Dept Fax=
Did Not Respond--1997-98 Listing

Name	Rank	Degree	Yr	School	Year
Barrett, Jack	C	PHD			
Fagal, Frederick F. Jr.	Assoc	PHD	81	Syracuse	1987

University of Massachusetts Amherst, MA 01003-7510 (413) 545-2590 econs.umass.edu
Department of Economics Col of Arts & Science Fax=545-2921 Judy Dietel

Name	Rank	Phone	Email	Degree	Yr	School	Year
Boyce, James K.	C-Pr	545-3815	boyce	PHD	85	Oxford	1985
Bausor, Randall S.	Prof	545-0595	bausor	PHD	78	Duke	1979
Bowles, Samuel S.	Prof	545-1373	bowles	PHD	65	Harvard	1973
Brimmer, Andrew F.	VProf			PHD	57	Harvard	
Costrell, Robert M.	Prof	545-1374	costrell	PHD	78	Harvard	1978
Crotty, James R.	Prof	545-2768	crotty	PHD	73	Car Mellon	1974
Deere, Carmen D.	Prof	545-0455	deere	PHD	78	Berkeley	1977
Epstein, Gerald A.	Prof	545-6355	gepstein	PHD	81	Princeton	1987
Flaherty, Diane P.	Prof	545-4703	gibson	PHD	78	NYU	

Folbre, Nancy	Prof	545-3283	folbre		PHD	79	Mass	1985
Gintis, Herbert M.	Prof	545-6363	gintis		PHD	69	Harvard	1975
Katzner, Donald W.	Prof	545-6350			PHD	65	Minnesota	1975
Kotz, David M.	Prof	545-4536	dmkotz		PHD	75	Berkeley	
Pollin, Robert N.	Prof	577-0126	pollin		PHD	82	New Sch	1998
Rao, J. Mohan	Prof	545-4808	rao@mit.edu		PHD	82	Harvard	1989
Resnick, Stephen A.	Prof	545-0947			PHD	64	MIT	
Shepherd, William G.	Prof	545-0443			PHD	63	Yale	1986
Wolff, Richard D.	Prof	545-6351		ABNP	PHD	69	Yale	9-73
Ballou, Dale	Assoc	545-6358	rdballou		PHD	89	Yale	
Friedman, Gerald	Assoc	545-6357	gfriedma		PHD	86	Harvard	1984
Heim, Carol E.	Assoc	545-0854	cheim	NRE	PHD	82	Yale	1-81
Badgett, Lee	Asst	545-0159	lbadgett		PHD	90	Berkeley	1997
Ndikumana, Leonce	Asst	545-6359	ndiku		PHD	96	Wash U	1996
Saunders, Lisa F.	Asst	545-0546	saunders		PHD	87	Berkeley	1987

U Massachusetts at Boston Boston, MA 02125-3393 (617) 287-6950 umb.edu
Department of Economics Col of Arts & Sciences Fax=287-6976 Ms. Yvonne Ceurvels

Terkla, David G.	C-Pr	287-6952	david.terkla	QRH	PHD	79	Berkeley	1987
Albelda, Randy P.	Prof	287-6963	albelda	JI	PHD	83	Mass	1988
Chiong, Winston R.	Prof	287-6957	chiong	E	PHD	74	Boston C	1982
Ferleger, Louis	Prof	287-6964	ferleger	NOQ	PHD	78	Temple	1978
Gershenberg, Irving	Prof	287-6954	gershenberg	FOL	PHD	67	Berkeley	1982
MacEwan, Arthur	Prof	287-6956	macewan	FOI	PHD	69	Harvard	1975
Wolozin, Harold	Prof	287-6961	wolozin	B	PHD	55	Columbia	1966
Campen, James T.	Assoc	287-6962	campen	EG	PHD	76	Harvard	1976
Cotton, Jeremiah	Assoc	287-6965	cotton	IJ	PHD	83	Michigan	1985
Lynde, Catherine	Assoc	287-5600	catherine.lynde	EF	PHD	85	Ca-Davis	1983
Stevenson, Mary H.	Assoc	287-6958	stevenson	JIR	PHD	74	Michigan	1972
Kapler, Janis	Asst	287-6955	kapler	FL	PHD	93	American	1993
Trost, Alice	Asst	287-6960	trost	RH	PHD	95	SUNY-Bin	1992

U Massachusetts-Dartmouth No Dartmouth MA 02747-2300 (508) 999-8257 umassd.edu
Department of Economics Col of Arts & Sciences Fax=999-9125

Schaaf, Judy	Dean	999-8268						
Hogan, William V.	C-Pr	999-8257	whogan		PHD	76	Cornell	1976
Berger, David E.	Prof	999-8256	dberger	IJOR	PHD	72	Wash U	1972
Esposito, Frances F.	Prof	999-8280	fesposito		PHD	67	Boston C	1967
Georgianna, Daniel L.	Prof	999-8414	dgeorgianna		PHD	77	Mass	1977
Ohly, John H.	Assoc	999-8518		A	PHD	76	Boston U	1977
Shadbegian, Ronald	Asst	999-8337	rshadbegian	HKQ	PHD	91	Clark	1993
Walgreen, Sonia	VLect	999-8337			MA	63	Boston C	1984

U of Massachusetts at Lowell Lowell, MA 01854-2881 (978) 934-2780 uml.edu
Department of Economics Col of Arts & Sciences Fax=934-3071 Judy 934-2820

Kleniewski, Nancy	Dean	934-3847		Soc	PHD			
Sanz, Ernesto	C-Pr	934-2780	ernesto.sanz	FNP	PHD	75	Boston C	
Cederlund, Albert M.	Prof	934-2783		HL	PHD	75	Clark	
MacBeth, Thomas G.	Prof	934-2790		AC	PHD	62	S Calif	
McDonough, Carol C.	Prof	934-2784		DN	PHD	69	Boston C	1970
Sihag, Balbir S.	Prof	934-2786		CI	PHD	78	MIT	1980
Carter, Michael J.	Assoc	934-2794		CEQ	PHD	81	Stanford	
Dery, George C.	Assoc	934-2788		CD	MA		Boston C	
Goodwin, Susan A.	Assoc	934-3450		G	PHD	75	Tufts	
Vice Chancellor of Administration & Finance								
Lahiri, Supriya	Assoc	934-2789	lahiris	CQ	PHD	75	Delhi	
Snoonian, Paul E.	Assoc	934-2793		EQ	PHD	71	Mich St	

Mass College of Liberal Arts North Adams, MA 01247-4100 (413) 662-5311 mecn.mass.edu
Economics Faculty Business Adm & Econ Pgm Fax=662-5306 Barbara P. Sunskis

Foss, Deborah	C							
Hajizadeh, Avaz	Assoc	Ext 5329			PHD	85	Rensselaer	
Kahn, Abraham	Assoc	Ext 5306			MA	79	SUNY-Alb	
Ovitsky, Nancy L.	Asst	Ext 5307			PHD	82	Illinois	
Zomorrodian, Reza	Asst	Ext 5303			EDD	90	Mass	

Massachusetts Inst of Tech Cambridge, MA 02142 (617) 253-3361 mit.edu
Department of Economics Sch Humanities &Soc Sci Fax=253-1330 John Arditi

Khoury, Phillip S.	Dean	253-3450	khoury@mitvma	Hist	PHD	80	Harvard	
Schmalensee, Richard L.	Dean	253-2957	rschmal	O	PHD	70	MIT	1977
Gordon Y. Billard Professor Economics & Management								
Blanchard, Olivier J.	H-Pr	253-8891	blanchar	G	PHD	77	MIT	1985
Class of 1941 Professor of Economics								
Angrist, Joshua D.	Prof	253-8909	angrist	J	PHD	89	Princeton	1996
Banerjee, Abhijit V.	Prof	253-8855	banerjee	G	PHD	88	Harvard	1993

Name	Rank	Phone	Email	Field	Degree	Yr	School	Since
Caballero, Ricardo	Prof	253-0489	caball	E	PHD	88	MIT	1992
Diamond, Peter A.	Prof	253-3363	pdiamond	E	PHD	63	MIT	1966
Institute Professor								
Dornbusch, Rudiger	Prof	253-3648	rudi	F	PHD	71	Chicago	1975
on leave; Ford International Professor of Economics								
Ellison, Glenn D.	Prof	253-8702	gellison	L	PHD	92	MIT	1994
on leave								
Fisher, Franklin M.	Prof	253-3373	ffisher	P	PHD	60	Harvard	1960
Giavazzi, Francesco	VProf				PHD			1999
Gruber, Jonathan H.	Prof	253-8892	gruberj	G	PHD	92	Harvard	1992
Harris, Jeffrey E.	Prof	253-2677	jeffrey	I	PHD	75	Penn	1976
Hausman, Jerry A.	Prof	253-3644	jhausman	C	DPHI	73	Oxford	1973
John and Jennie S. MacDonald Professor of Economics								
Holmstrom, Bengt	Prof	253-0506	bengt	L	PHD	78	Stanford	1995
Paul A. Samuelson Professor of Economics								
Joskow, Paul L.	Prof	253-6664	pjoskow	O	PHD	72	Yale	1972
on leave; Mitsui Professor of Economics and Management								
Krugman, Paul R.	Prof	253-1551	krugman	F	PHD	77	MIT	1979
on leave; Ford International Professor of Economics								
Maskin, Eric S.	Prof				PHD	76	Harvard	1999
visiting from Harvard								
Newey, Whitney K.	Prof	253-6420	wnewey	CDH	PHD	83	MIT	6-90
Piore, Michael J.	Prof	253-3377	mpiore	J	PHD	66	Harvard	1966
David W. Skinner Professor of Political Economy								
Porter, Robert H.	Prof				PHD	81	Princeton	1999
visiting from Northwestern University								
Poterba, James M.	Prof	253-6673	poterba	H	DPHI	83	Oxford	1983
Mitsui Professor of Economics								
Rose, Nancy E.	Prof	253-8956	nrose@sloan	L	PHD	85	MIT	1985
Ross, Stephen A.	Prof	258-8371	sross	G	PHD	69	Harvard	1998
Franco Modiglani Professor of Finance and Economics								
Snyder, James M. Jr.	Prof	253-2669	millett		PHD	85	Cal Tech	
Temin, Peter	Prof	253-3126	ptemin	N	PHD	64	MIT	1965
Elish Gray II Professor								
Thurow, Lester C.	Prof	253-2932	lthurow	F	PHD	64	Harvard	1968
Jerome and Dorothy Lemelson Professor of Economics and Management								
Tirole, Jean	VProf	253-8884	tirolecict.fr	O	PHD	81	MIT	1984
Weil, Philippe	VProf				PHD	85	Harvard	1999
Wheaton, William C.	Prof	253-1723	wheaton	R	PHD	72	Penn	1972
Acemoglu, Daron	Assoc	253-1927	daron	J	PHD	92	LondonEc	1993
Athey, Susan	Assoc	253-6407	athey	L	PHD	95	Stanford	1995
Castle Krob Career Development Associate Professor of Economics								
Costa, Dora L.	Assoc	253-2989	costa	N	PHD	93	Chicago	1993
on leave; Ford Career Development Associate Professor of Economics								
Pischke, Jorn-Steffen	Assoc	253-1942	jsp	J	PHD	92	Princeton	1993
on leave								
Ventura, Jaume	Assoc	253-6878	jaume	E	PHD	95	Harvard	1995
on leave								
Autor, David	Asst			J	PHD	99	Harvard	1999
Duflo, Ester	Asst		eduflo	O	PHD	99	MIT	1999
Feiedberg, Leora	VAsst				PHD			1999
Gabaix, Xavier	Asst		xgabaiz	G	PHD	99	Harvard	1999
on leave								
Irwin, Douglas	VAsst				PHD		Columbia	1999
Kuersteiner, Guido	Asst	253-2118	gkuerste	E	PHD	92	Princeton	1997
Mullainathan, Sendhlil	Asst	258-8047	mullain		PHD	98	Harvard	1998
Spector, David	Asst	258-9268	spector	E	PHD	96	LondonEc	1996
Wells, Robin	Asst	258-9491	rewells	L	PHD	89	Berkeley	1996
on leave								
Ellison, Sara	Lect	253-3821	sellison	L	PHD	93	MIT	1997
on leave								

McMurry University	Abilene, TX 79697 (915) 691-6396						
Economic Faculty	School of Business Fax=691-6268						
Valentine, John	Dean	793-3850		MBA		Abilene	1980
Williams, Eugene	Prof	793-3860		PHD	71	Arkansas	1988

McNeese State University	Lake Charles, LA 70609-1415 (318) 475-5522					ucsvm.mcneese.edu	
Dept Atg, Fnce & Econ 91415	College of Business Fax=475-5010					Bridgett Friend	
Bailey, Eldon R.	Dean	475-5514		Atg	PHD	70 LSU	1964
Burckel, Daryl V.	H-Pr	475-5522		Atg	DBA	86 Miss St	1992
Foshee, Andrew W.	Prof	475-5562			PHD	80 LSU	1978
Kurth, Michael M.	Prof	475-5558			PHD	82 Va Tech	1984
McNiel, Douglas W.	Prof	475-5560	dmcniel		PHD	77 Okla St	1984

University of Memphis	Memphis, TN		38152-6460 (901) 678-2432					memphis.edu
Department of Economics	Fogelman Col Bus & Econ Fax=678-2685							
Wetherbe, James	Dean$	678-2432			PHD	80	Tx Tech	1999
Reid, John Joseph	C-Ac	678-4627	jjreid	EF	PHD	62	Virginia	1966
Chang, Cyril F.	Prof	678-3565	cchang	IM	PHD	79	Virginia	1981
Ciscel, David H.	Prof	678-2281	dhciscel	LM	PHD	71	Houston	1973
Daniel, Coldwell III	Prof	678-2473	cdaniel1	IL	PHD	68	Virginia	1970
Depperschmidt, Thomas O.	Prof	678-4628	tdpprsch	KH	PHD	65	Tx-Austin	1966
Evans, Richard D.	Prof	678-3632	revans1	CM	PHD	70	Harvard	1978
Fung, Kwok-Kwan	Prof	678-4626	kkfung	OP	PHD	70	Harvard	1975
Gnuschke, John E.	Prof	678-2281	jgnuschk	MR	PHD	75	Missouri	1976
Director, Ctr for Manpower Studies and Bureau of Business & Economic Research								
Gootzeit, Michael J.	Prof	678-4625	mgoot	BE	PHD	66	Purdue	1975
Heath, Julia A.	Prof	678-2785	jheath	JI	PHD	86	S Carol	1986
Kemme, David M.	Prof	678-5408	dmkemme	FCP	PHD	80	Ohio St	1994
Morris Chair of Excellence in International Econ								
Okunade, Albert A.	Prof	678-2672	aokunade	JI	PHD	86	Arkansas	1987
Rubin, Rose M.	Prof	678-4622	rmrubin	JI	PHD	68	Kansas St	1994
White-Means, Shelley L.	Prof	678-2456	swhitmns	DJI	PHD	83	Nrthwstrn	1988
Smith, William	Assoc	678-3675	wtsmith	EF	PHD	87	Virginia	1993
Bose, Pinaki	Asst	678-5528	psbose	LD	PHD	90	NYU	9-95

Mercer University-Atlanta	Atlanta, GA		30341-4415 (770) 986-3199					mercer.edu
Economics Faculty	Stetson Sch Bus & Econ Fax=986-3337							
Joiner, W. Carl	Dean	986-3169	joiner_wc		PHD	78	Alabama	1974
Biegeleisen, J. Alan	Assoc	986-3338	biegeleis_ja		PHD	83	Geo St	1982
Jalili, Reza	Assoc	986-3325	jalili_ar		PHD	94	NewHamp	1993
Yu, Tie-Liu	Assoc	986-3368	yu_tl		PHD	90	Miss St	1990
Connell, James A.	Asst	986-3195	connell_ja		DBA	92	La Tech	1996

Mercer University-Macon	Macon, GA		31207-0001 (912)					mercer.edu
Economic Faculty	Stetson Sch Bus & Econ Fax=752-2635							
Joiner, William Carl	Dean	752-2832		Mgt	PHD	78	Alabama	1974
Andrews, Charles Haynes	Prof	752-2832			PHD	67	Vanderbilt	1973
Stetson Professor of Economics								
Mounts, William S. Jr.	Prof	752-2832			PHD	77	Georgia	1978
Barber, G. Russell Jr.	Assoc	752-2162			PHD	90	Miss	1973
Shippen, Benjamin S.	Asst	752-4055			PHD	95	Fla St	1995

Meredith College	Raleigh, NC		27607-5298 (919) 760-8475					meredith.edu
Economic Faculty	Dept Business & Econ Fax=760-8470							
Wessels, Susan B.	H-As	760-8475		Atg	MBA	72	DePaul	1978
Ammann, Alan	Assoc	760-8472			DBA	78	Miss St	1990
Chappell, Glenn	Assoc	760-8473			PHD		Tennessee	1991
Wakeman, Douglas	Assoc	760-8482			PHD	86	N Carol	1987
York, Anne	Asst	760-8483			PHD		N Car St	1999

Merrimack College	North Andover MA 01845		(978) Ext 4245					merrimack.edu
Dept of Economics	Div of Liberal Arts Fax=837-5078							Linda Trimble
phone 837-5000								
Ledoux, Arthur	Dean	837-5244		Phil	PHD		Notre Dm	
Laramie, Anthony J	C-Pr	837-5216			PHD	88	Clark	
Amariglio, Jack	Prof	Ext 4313			PHD	84	Mass	
Charos, Evangelos N.	Prof	Ext 4247			PHD	84	NewHamp	1983
Donovan, Elaine M.	Assoc	837-5447			PHD	81	Houston	
Looney, Lawrence J.	Assoc	Ext 4245			MA		Boston C	
Tontar, Charles F.	Assoc	Ext 4165			MA		New Sch	

Mesa State College	Grand JunctionCO 81502		(970) 248-1656					mesas.mesa.colorado.edu
Business Administration	Professional Studies Fax=248-1930							Joy Donofrio, Ellin ALstatt
Did Not Respond--1997-98 Listing								
Phillips, William	Dean	248-1656			PHD	70	Nebraska	1997
Polson, Houston	C	248-1656		Law	JD	80	Creighton	1994
Rees, David M.	Assoc				PHD	73	Oregon	1983

Metropolitan St Coll Denver	Denver, CO		80217-3362 (303) 556-3217					mscd.edu
Department of Economics	School of Business Fax=556-3966							
Robertson, James W.	Dean	556-3245	robertsoj	Atg	PHD	63	U Wash	9-98
Cochran, John	C-Pr	556-3218	cochran		PHD	85	Colorado	1984
Akacemn, Mohammed	Prof	556-4649	akacem		PHD	84	Colorado	1991
Call, Stephen T.	Prof	556-3916	calls		PHD	77	Indiana	1979
Erickson, Erick Lee	Prof	556-3038	erickson		PHD		New Mex	1984
Kulkarni, Kishore G.	Prof	556-2675	kulkarnk		PHD	82	Pittsburgh	1989
Pasternak, Richard E.	Prof	556-4935	pastern		PHD	62	Alabama	1968
Fleisher, Arthur A. III	Assoc	556-4079	fleishet		PHD	87	GeoMason	1990
Gilliam, Lynde O.	Assoc	556-3037	gilliaml		PHD	80	Colo St	1986

University of Miami Coral Gables, FL 33124-6550 (305) 284-5540 exchange.sba.miami.edu
Department of Economics Sch of Business Admin Fax=284-2985 Ms. Denise Eutsey

Sugrue, Paul K.	Dean	284-4643	psugrue	Mas	PHD	77	Mass	1977
Robins, Philip K.	C-Pr	284-5664	pkrobins	IJ	PHD	72	Wisconsin	1982
Connolly, Michael B.	Prof	284-4898	mconnolly	F	PHD	69	Chicago	1987
Fishe, Raymond P. H.	Prof	284-4397	rfishe	CD	PHD	79	Florida	1981
Holtmann, Alphonse G.	Prof	284-1721	hholtmann	DI	PHD	63	Wash U	1981
Foley, James W.	Assoc	284-4641	jfoley	O	PHD	69	Mich St	1968
Locay, Luis	Assoc	284-1502	llocay	DJOT	PHD	83	Chicago	1989
Streeter, Lanny E.	Assoc	284-1627	lstreeter	C	PHD	70	Illinois	1967
Austin, Adrian	Asst	284-3338	aaustin	CG	PHD	98	Duke	1998
Ederington, William	Asst	284-1626	wedering	F	PHD	98	Wisconsin	1998
Katzman, Brett E.	Asst	284-1654	bkatzman	DL	PHD	96	Duke	1996
Kelly, David	Asst	284-3725	dkelly	E	PHD	95	Car Mellon	1998
Minier, Jenny	Asst	284-1628	jminier	EO	PHD	98	Wisconsin	1998
Solnick, Sara J.	Asst	284-3736	ssolnick	DIJ	PHD	96	Penn	1996

Miami University Oxford, OH 45056-1675 (513) 529-2836 muohio.edu
Department of Economics R.T. Farmer Sch Bus Adm Fax=529-6992 Sandra Richardson

Short, Daniel G.	Dean	529-3631	dshort	Atg	PHD	77	Michigan	7-95
Ferguson, J. David	C-Pr	529-2836	fergusjd	EF	PHD	74	Brown	1970
Brock, James W.	Prof	529-2846	brockj	AK	PHD	81	Mich St	1979
Bill R. Moeckel Professor of Business								
Davis, George K.	Prof	529-2842	davisgk	EO	PHD	84	So Meth	1985
Dunlevy, James A.	Prof	529-5333	dunlevja	JF	PHD	74	Nrthwstrn	1980
Erekson, O. Homer	Prof	529-2836	ereksooh	HR	PHD	80	N Carol	1978
Associate Dean								
Even, William E.	Prof	529-2865	evenwe	JC	PHD	84	Iowa	1983
Hall, Thomas E.	Prof	529-2862	hallte	EC	PHD	82	Ca-SnBarb	1982
Hart, William R.	Prof	529-4352	hartwr	EA	PHD	76	Wash U	1974
Hutchinson, William K.	Prof	529-2856	hutchiwk	EF	PHD	75	Iowa	1972
McBride, Mark E.	Prof	529-2864	mcbridme		PHD	79	Wash U	1983
Miller, Norman C.	Prof	529-2854	millergm	EF	PHD	66	Pittsburgh	1985
Julian G. Lange Professor of Economics & American Enterprise								
Noble, Nicholas R.	Prof	529-6288	noblenr	EC	PHD	78	Cincinnati	1976
Seiver, Daniel A.	Prof	529-2863	seiverda	TG	PHD	74	Yale	1978
Sullivan, Dennis H.	Prof	529-2867	sullivdh	HI	PHD	75	Princeton	1973
Williamson, Samuel H.	Prof	529-2851	williash	NI	PHD	68	Purdue	1983
Curme, Michael A.	Assoc	529-6215	curmema	JD	PHD	89	Illinois	1988
Ghosal, Vivek	Assoc	529-6668	ghosalv	DE	PHD	88	Florida	1990
Granderson, Gerald	Assoc	529-2841	grandegd	DG	PHD	93	N Carol	1993
Gupta, Barnali	Assoc	529-4116	guptab	DR	PHD	90	Florida	1993
Lage, Maureen J.	Assoc	529-2840	lagemj	AE	PHD	91	Penn St	1990
Mehdizadeh, Mostafa	Assoc	727-3311	mehdizm	A	PHD	80	Oklahoma	1982
Middleton Campus								
Platt, Glenn	Assoc	529-2869	plattgj	CR	PHD	93	Car Mellon	1993
Raynold, Prosper	Assoc	529-4348	raynolp	EG	PHD	89	LSU	1989
Lyons, John S.	Asst	529-2853	lyonsjs	NO	PHD	77	Berkeley	1985
Miller, Gerald M.	SInst	529-2838	millergm	DC	MA	73	Brown	1971
Assistant Chairperson								

University of Michigan Ann Arbor, MI 48109-1220 (734) 764-2355 umich.edu
Department of Economics Col Lit,Science, & Arts Fax=764-2769 Carolyn Dymond
email @1=econ.lsa.umich.edu

Goldenberg, Edie	Dean	764-0322		PolS	PHD	74	Stanford	
Slemrod, Joel B.	C-Pr	936-3914	joel.slemrod		PHD	80	Harvard	1987
Solon, Gary R.	C-Pr	763-1306	gsolon		PHD	83	Princeton	1983
Adams, William James	Prof	764-5273	jimadams		PHD	73	Harvard	1973
Bound, John	Prof	747-2319	jbound@psc.lsa.		PHD	87	Harvard	
Brown, Charles C.	Prof	763-6867	charlieb		PHD	74	Harvard	1985
Courant, Paul N.	Prof	763-2499	pnc		PHD	74	Princeton	1973
Cross, John D.	Prof	763-3479	jcross		PHD	65	Princeton	1965
Deardorff, Alan V.	Prof	764-6817	alandear		PHD	71	Cornell	1970
Gramlich, Edward M.	Prof	764-3490			PHD	65	Yale	1976
Holbrook, Robert S.	Prof	763-1282	rsh		PHD	65	Berkeley	1965
Howrey, E. Philip	Prof	763-1087	eph	CE	PHD	64	N Carol	9-73
Hymans, Saul H.	Prof	764-3299	shymans		PHD	64	Berkeley	1964
Johnson, George	Prof	764-2374	gjohnson		PHD	66	Berkeley	
Juster, F. Thomas	Prof	764-4207			PHD	56	Columbia	1973
Laitner, John	Prof	763-9620	jlaitner@1		PHD	76	Harvard	1975
Lam, David A.	Prof	764-2355	davidl@1		PHD	83	Berkeley	1983
Lillard, Lee	Prof	647-5609	lillard@isr.		PHD	72	N Car St	
Porter, Richard C.	Prof	769-9419	rporter		PHD	57	Yale	1964
Salant, Stephen W.	Prof	764-2370	ssalant		PHD	73	Penn	1981
Saxonhouse, Gary R.	Prof	764-3296	grsaxon		PHD	71	Yale	1970
Shapiro, Matthew D.	Prof	764-5419	shapiro		PHD	84	MIT	1989
Simon, Carl P.	Prof	763-3074	cpsimon	CDT	PHD	70	Nrthwstrn	7-72
Stachetti, Ennio	Prof	764-8022	ennio		PHD	83	Wisconsin	1992

Stafford, Frank P.	Prof	936-0323	fstaffor		PHD	68	Chicago	1974
Stern, Robert M.	Prof	764-2373	rmstern		PHD	58	Columbia	1961
Weisskopf, Thomas E.	Prof	763-3037	tomw		PHD	66	MIT	1972
Whatley, Warren	Prof	764-5256	wwhatley	NJOR	PHD	82	Stanford	1981
White, Michelle J.	Prof	763-3096	micwhite		PHD	73	Princeton	1984
Barsky, Robert	Assoc	764-9476	barsky@1		PHD	86	MIT	
Basu, Susanto	Assoc	764-5359	sbasu		PHD	92	Harvard	1992
Hanson, Gordon H.	Assoc		gohanson	FO	PHD	92	MIT	
Kimball, Miles S.	Assoc	764-2375	mkimball		PHD	87	Harvard	1987
Kuhn, Kai-uwe	Assoc	763-5317	kukuhn@1					
Levinsohn, James A.	Assoc	763-2319	jamesl		PHD	88	Princeton	1987
Mackie-Mason, Jeffrey K.	Assoc	764-7438	jmm		PHD	86	MIT	1986
Smith, Lones A.	Assoc	764-2357	lones	D	PHD	91	Chicago	
Tesar, Linda L.	Assoc	763-2254	ltesar	FGE	PHD	90	Rochester	
Charles, Kerwin	Asst	764-8075	kcharles		PHD	95	Cornell	1995
Chen, Yan	Asst	763-9619	yanchen@1		PHD	94	Cal Tech	1994
Cullie, Julie	Asst	764-2367	jbcullie					
Kilian, Lutz	Asst	764-2320	lkilian					
Kossoudji, Sherrie A.	Asst	764-2381	kossoudj		PHD	84	Michigan	1987
Li, David	Asst	763-9561	davidli		PHD	92	Harvard	1992
Sakata, Shinichi	Asst	764-2368	ssakata@1					
Sonanathan, Rohini	Asst	647-5611	rohinis@1					
Sonmez, Tayfun O.	Asst	763-9238	tsonmez@1	CDH	PHD	95	Rochester	1995
Van't Veld, Klaas	Asst	763-5319	kvtveld					
Gerson, Janet	Lect	764-2355	jgerson	AD	PHD	81	Michigan	
Thompson, Frank W.	Lect	763-2392	fthom		PHD	73	Harvard	1990
Wolfe, Janet C.	Lect	763-2515	janwolfe		MPP	80	Michigan	1987

Univ of Michigan-Dearborn	Dearborn, MI		48128-1491	(313) 593-5096			umd.umich.edu	
Dept of Social Science	Col of Arts, Sci & Ltrs		Fax=593-5645				Deborah Przybylo	
Bord, Donald	Dean$	593-5490	dbord@sb-fl		PHD	76	Dartmouth	1984
Hull, Brooks B.	C-Pr	593-5332	bhull@ca.f1.	LQ	PHD	82	U Wash	1981
Roehl, Richard Associate Dean	Prof	593-5490	rroehl@um-fl	BJNR	PHD	68	Berkeley	1976
Twomey, Michael J.	Prof	593-5176	mwomey@ca-fl	FNO	PHD	73	Cornell	1977
Crowell, Elizabeth	Assoc	436-9183	ecrowell@ca-fl	DHIJ	PHD	71	Indiana	1978
Smith, Patricia	Assoc	593-5205	psmith@ca-fl	IJK	PHD	86	Va Tech	1988
Bergeron, Suzanne	VAsst	593-5155	sbergo@ca-fl	BENO	PHD	98	Notre Dm	1998
Ellis, Steffany G.	Asst	436-9180	sellis@ca-fl	CEFG	PHD	93	NC-Charl	1992
Pietrykowski, Bruce Assistant Dean	Asst	593-5490	bpietryk@ca-fl	BJNR	PHD	90	New Sch	1988
Shah, Parth	Asst	593-5147	pshah@ca-fl	EFO	PHD	90	Auburn	1991

Univ of Michigan-Flint	Flint, MI		48502-2186	(810) 762-3280			crob.flint.umich.edu	
Department of Economics	Col of Arts & Sciences		Fax=762-3687				Judy J. Bedore	
Zeff, Jacqueline L.	Dean	762-3234	zeff_j	Engl	PHD	73	Pittsburgh	1991
Reddy, Nallapu N.	C-Pr	762-3280	reddy_n		PHD	67	Penn St	1974
Kowal, Lubomyr M.	Prof	762-3280	kowal_l		PHD	65	Illinois	1966
Nas, Tevfik F.	Prof	762-3280	nas_t		PHD	77	Fla St	1982
Weber, Charles T.	Assoc	762-3280	weber_c		PHD	77	Wayne St	1977
Johnston, Charles W.	Asst	762-3280	johnston_c		PHD	88	Tx-Austin	1988
Olmstead, Jennifer C.	Asst	762-3280	olmstead_j		PHD	94	Ca-Davis	1993
Perry, Mark J.	Asst	762-3280	perry_m		PHD	93	GeoMason	1996

Michigan State University	East Lansing, MI		48824-1038	(517) 355-7583			pilot.msu.edu	
Department of Economics	College of Business		Fax=432-1068				Terie Snyder	355-5238
Henry, James B.	Dean	355-8378	jhenry	Fnce	PHD	70	Syracuse	7-94
Goddeeris, John H.	C-Pr	355-5238	goddeeri		PHD	80	Wisconsin	1980
Allen, Bruce T.	Prof	355-7739	allenb		PHD	65	Cornell	1965
Baillie, Richard Pasant Chair of Economics & Finance	Prof	355-1864	baillie	CFG	PHD	78	LondonEc	8-86
Ballard, Charles L.	Prof	353-2961	ballard		PHD	83	Stanford	1983
Biddle, Jeff E.	Prof	353-7862	biddle		PHD	85	Duke	1985
Boyer, Kenneth D.	Prof	353-9088	boyerkd		PHD	75	Michigan	1984
Brown, Byron W.	Prof	355-2364	brownb		PHD	66	J Hopkins	1978
Davidson, Carl	Prof	355-7756	davidso4		PHD	87	Wisconsin	1982
Fisher, Ronald C.	Prof	353-4582	fisherr1		PHD	77	Brown	1976
Holzer, Harry J.	Prof	355-8320	holzer		PHD	83	Harvard	1983
Kreinin, Mordechai E. University Distinguished Professor	Prof	355-6579	kreinin		PHD	54	Michigan	1959
Liedholm, Carl E.	Prof	355-1812	liedhol1		PHD	65	Michigan	1967
Linz, Susan	Prof	355-7280	linz		PHD	80	Illinois	1988
Mackey, M. Cecil	Prof	355-8306	mackey		PHD	55	Illinois	1980
Martin, Lawrence W.	Prof	353-3528	martinl3		PHD	81	Maryland	1982
Matusz, Steven J.	Prof	353-8719	matusz		PHD	83	Penn	1983
Menchik, Paul L.	Prof	355-4553	menchik		PHD	76	Penn	1979
Meyer, Jack	Prof	355-7749	jmeyer		PHD	74	Stanford	1983

Name	Rank	Phone	E-mail	Field	Degree	Yr	School	Hired
Neumark, David B.	Prof	353-7275	nuemarkd		PHD	87	Harvard	1995
Obst, Norman P.	Prof	353-5252	obst		PHD	70	Purdue	1973
Pecchenino, Rowena A.	Prof	353-6621	rowenap		PHD	85	Wisconsin	1985
Schmidt, Peter J.	Prof	355-8381	schmidtp		PHD	70	Mich St	1977
University Distinguished Professor								
Segerstrom, Paul S.	Prof	355-9647	segerst1		PHD	84	Rochester	1984
Strauss, John	Prof	355-1863	jstrauss		PHD	81	Mich St	1992
Wilson, John D.	Prof	432-3116	wilsonjd		PHD	79	MIT	1998
Woodbury, Stephen A.	Prof	355-4587	woodbur2		PHD	81	Wisconsin	1982
Wooldridge, Jeffrey	Prof	353-5972	wooldri1	C	PHD	86	Ca-SnDgo	9-91
Amsler, Christine E.	Assoc	355-3774	amsler		PHD	80	Penn	1980
Cookingham, Mary E.	Assoc	355-0293	cookingh		PHD	80	Berkeley	1979
Creane, Anthony J.	Assoc	355-4667	creane		PHD	91	Virginia	1990
Glomm, Gerhard	Assoc	355-7349	glomm		PHD	88	Minnesota	1995
Irvine, F. Owen	Assoc	353-9008	irvinef		PHD	76	MIT	1982
Papke, Leslie E.	Assoc	355-3773	papke		PHD	87	MIT	1990
Asdrubali, Pierfederuo	Asst	353-7281	asdrubal		PHD	96	Brown	1997
deJong, Robert	Asst	353-9933	dejongr		PHD	93	Free	1997
Giles, John	Asst				PHD	99	Berkeley	1999
Mullin, Wallace P.	Asst	353-9934	wpmullin		PHD	92	MIT	1992

Michigan Technological Univ Houghton, MI 49931-1295 (906) 487-2669 mtu.edu
Economics Faculty School of Bus & Eng Adm Fax=487-1863 Nancy G. Johnson

Name	Rank	Phone	E-mail	Field	Degree	Yr	School	Hired
Klippel, R. Eugene	Dean	487-2669	reklippe	Mktg	PHD	91	Penn St	1994
Campbell, Gary A.	Prof	487-2803	gcampbe	Q	PHD	82	Penn St	1982
Gale, James R.	Prof	487-2674	jrgale	E	PHD	72	Iowa	1971
Joyce, B. Patrick	Prof	487-2677	pjoyce	D	PHD	74	Missouri	1972
Monson, Terry D.	Prof	487-3124	tmonson	F	PHD	72	Minnesota	1977
Associate Dean								
Merz, Thomas E.	Assoc	487-2805	temerz		PHD	80	Pittsburgh	1980
Nelson, Paul A.	Assoc	487-2809	pnelson	M	PHD	74	Wisconsin	1972
Roberts, Mark C.	Assoc	487-2771	mroberts		PHD	85	Arizona	1985

Middle Tennessee State Univ Murfreesboro, TN 37132 (615) 898-2520 frank.mtsu.edu
Dept of Economics & Finance College of Business Fax=898-5596 Thenartis Ellis

Name	Rank	Phone	E-mail	Field	Degree	Yr	School	Hired
Elam, Rick	Dean	898-2764	relam	Atg	PHD	73	Missouri	1996
Lee, John T.	C-Pr	898-2520	jtlee		PHD	77	Georgia	1984
DePrince, Albert E. Jr.	Prof	898-5995	adeprince	GM	PHD	78	NYU	1991
Fayissa, Bichaka	Prof	898-2385	bfayissa	D	PHD	82	Tennessee	1980
Ford, William F.	Prof	898-2889	wfford	GHM	PHD	66	Michigan	1991
Weatherford Chair								
Graddy, Duane B.	Prof	898-2525	dgraddy	GHA	PHD	74	Lehigh	1972
Hannah, Richard	Prof	898-2228	rhannah	J	PHD	81	Utah	1992
Kawahito, Kiyoshi	Prof	898-5751	kkawah;ito	FE	PHD	71	Maryland	1971
Kyle, Reuben	Prof	898-5617	rkyle	L	PHD	72	Tennessee	1972
Director, Bureau of Business & Economic Research								
Zietz, Joachim	Prof	898-5619	jzietz	EC	PHD	81	Gottingen	1989
Eff, E. Anthon	Assoc	898-2387	aeff	RB	PHD	89	Tx-Austin	1990
Evans, Boyd	Assoc	898-5473		A	MA	64	Auburn	1965
Nguyen, Nghiep H.	Assoc	898-5117	nnguyen	L	PHD	81	Tennessee	1981
Norman-Zietz, Emily	Assoc	898-5497		M	PHD	94	Fla St	1993
Sarver, Lee	Assoc	898-5919	lsarver	M	PHD	87	Tennessee	1991
Deme, Mamit	Asst	898-5750	mdeme	FE	PHD	90	Tx-Austin	1990

Middlebury College Middlebury, VT 05753-6125 (802) 443-5327 middlebury.edu
Economics Faculty Department of Economics Fax=443-2084 Amy Holbrook
phone: 443-5000

Name	Rank	Phone	E-mail	Field	Degree	Yr	School	Hired
Ramaswamy, Sunder	C-As	Ext 5322	ramaswam	DFO	PHD	90	Purdue	1990
Claudon, Michael Paul	Prof	Ext 5324	claudon	FLMP	PHD	71	J Hopkins	1970
Colander, David C.	Prof	Ext 5302	colandaer	ABE	PHD	76	Columbia	1982
Christian A. Johnson Distinguished Professor of Economics								
Sommers, Paul M.	Prof	Ext 5325	psommers	CDT	PHD	76	Ca-SnDgo	1976
Wonnacott, Paul	Prof	Ext 5590	gwonnaco	EF	PHD	59	Princeton	1994
Alan R. Holmes Visiting Professor in Monetary Economics								
Wunnava, Phanindra V.	Prof	Ext 5024	wunava	ACIJ	PHD	86	SUNY-Bin	1985
Barlow, Tammy	VAsst	tbarlow		HQ	PHD	99	Mass	1999
Carpenter, Jeffrey	Asst		jcarpent	DL	PHD	99	Mass	1999
Crowley, Patrick	Asst	Ext 2536	pcrowley	BEF	PHD	95	McGill	1998
Elder, John	Asst	Ext 2546	jelder	CEG	PHD	95	Virginia	1998
Isham, Jonathan T. Jr.	Asst		jisham	OQ	PHD	94	Ca-Rivers	1997
Kelly, Thomas	Asst	Ext 2432	tkelly	OQ	PHD	97	Ca-Rivers	1997
Matthews, Peter H.	Asst	Ext 5591	pmatthew	BCEJ	PHD	95	Yale	1995
Pyle, William	Asst		wpyle	EP	PHD	97	Duke	1999

Midwestern State University Wichita Falls TX 76308-2099 (940) 397-4248 nexus.mwsu.edu
Department of Economics Div of Business Admin Fax=397-4280 Ms. Karin Patterson

Fukasawa, Yoshikazu	Dean	397-4360		EF	PHD	79	Kansas St	1978
Welch, Robert G.	H-Pr	397-4290		ADP	PHD	62	Oregon St	1966
Krienke, Albert B.	Prof	397-4722		DP	PHD	67	Tx A&M	1965
Martinez, John	Prof	397-4662		ABCO	PHD	84	Oklahoma	1997
Rodriguez, Louis J.	Prof	397-4211		EF	PHD	63	LSU	1981
President								
Harmel, Robert	Assoc	397-4365		DL	PHD	74	Iowa St	1989

Millersville Univ of PA Millersville, PA 17551-0302 (717) 872-3679 millersv.edu
Dept of Economics Sch of Human & Soc Sci Fax=871-2326 Ms. Beth A. Crumling

Montgomery, Barbara	Dean	872-3553						
Suliman, Osman	C-Pr	872-3679			PHD	84	Indiana	1993
Hamid, M. Khalil	Prof	872-3560			PHD	66	Iowa	1968
Margolis, Marvin S.	Prof	872-3561			PHD	69	Purdue	1981
Gumpper, Michael R.	Asst	872-3944			PHD	97	Kentucky	1995
Madden, Kirsten K.	Asst	872-3576			PHD	95	N Carol	1996

Millikin University Decatur, IL 62522-2084 (217) 424-6284 mail.millikin.edu
Dept of Economics & Finance Tabor Sch of Business Fax=424-6286 Pamela J. Goodman
Homepage: http://www.millikin.edu/academics/tabor/

Zemke, Douglas	Dean	424-6284						
Liberatore, Anthony F.	Assoc	546-6446	aliberat		PHD	78	Conn	1984
Watson, James O.	Assoc	424-6380	jwatson		PHD	76	Purdue	1979
Cohn, Cheryl L.	Asst	827-8478	ccohn		DA	85	Illin St	1984
area code (309)								

Millsaps College Jackson, MS 39210-0001 (601) 974-1274 millsaps.edu
Economic Faculty Esle Sch of Management Fax=974-1260 Ms. Carol Heatherly

Boxx, Randy	Dean	974-1270	boxxwr	Mgt	PHD	71	Arkansas	1999
Taylor, Patrick A.	C-Ac	974-1274	taylorpa	AD	PHD	85	Alabama	1984
Director of BBA Program								
Brooking, Carl G.	Prof	974-1261	brookcg	CDK	PHD	74	Penn	1981
The McRae Chair of Business Administration								
Taylor, Susan W.	Assoc	974-1278	taylorsw	AFH	PHD	89	LSU	1992
The J. A. Brown Chair of Business Administration								

University of Minnesota Minneapolis, MN 55455-0413 (612) 625-6353 atlas.socsci.umn.edu
Department of Economics College of Liberal Arts Fax=624-0209 Sara Shuford
email @1=maroon.tc.umn.edu @2=plato.econ.umn.edu @3=mailbox.mail.umn.edu

Rosenstone, Steven	Dean				PHD	79	Berkeley	1996
Chari, V. V.	C-Pr	626-7151	chari		PHD	81	Car Mellon	1994
Allen, Beth Elaine	Prof	625-8213			PHD	78	Berkeley	1992
Chipman, John S.	Prof	625-2816	jchipman		PHD	51	J Hopkins	1955
Regents' Professor								
Coen, Edward	Emer				PHD	53	London	
Feldman, Roger D.	Prof	624-5669	feldm002@1		PHD	76	Rochester	1985
Foster, Edward M.	Prof	624-6567	foster		PHD	61	MIT	1983
Director Graduate Studies								
Geweke, John F.	Prof	625-7563	geweke		PHD	75	Minnesota	1990
Hurwicz, Leo	Prof	625-5808	hurwicz		LLM	38	Warsaw	1951
Kehoe, Timothy J.	Prof	625-1589	tkehoe		PHD	79	Yale	1987
Mohring, Herbert D.	Emer	625-6520	mohring		PHD	59	MIT	1961
Prescott, Edward C.	Prof	625-3810	prescott		PHD	67	Car Mellon	1980
Regent's Professor								
Richter, Marcel K.	Prof	625-7832			PHD	59	MIT	1959
Ruttan, Vernon W.	Emer	625-4707	vruttan@1		PHD	52	Chicago	1976
Regents' Professor								
Schuh, G. Edward	Prof	625-0669	schuh@3		PHD	61	Chicago	1979
Smith, Harlan	Emer	625-8035			PHD	49	Chicago	
Swan, Craig E.	Prof	625-6353	cswan		PHD	70	Yale	1969
Holmes, Thomas J.	Assoc	625-4512	holmes		PHD	85	Nrthwstrn	1995
McLennan, Andrew M.	Assoc	625-7504	mclennan		PHD	82	Princeton	1987
Ohanian, Lee E.	Assoc	624-4060	ohanian		PHD	93	Rochester	1995
Werner, Jan	Assoc	625-0708	jwerner		PHD		Bonn	1987
Gownsaukaran, Gautam	Asst	625-8310	gautam		PHD	95	Yale	1995

U of Minnesota - Duluth Duluth, MN 55812-2496 (218) 726-7284 ub.d.umn.edu
Department of Economics Sch of Business & Econ Fax=726-6509 Becky Skurla

Knudsen, Kjell R.	Dean	726-7288	kknudsen	Mgt	PHD	73	Minnesota	1974
Jesswein, Wayne A.	H-Pr	726-7297	wjesswei	FA	PHD	69	Illinois	1968
Anderson, Curtis L.	Prof	726-7568	canderso	QA	PHD	81	Wyoming	1980
Lichty, Richard W.	Prof	726-7219	rlichty	R	PHD	71	Kansas St	1971
Peterson, Jerrold M.	Prof	726-7256	jpeterson	HE	PHD	70	Illinois	1969
Raab, Raymond L.	Prof	726-8508	rraab1	L	PHD	71	Colo St	1970
Steinnes, Donald N.	Prof	726-8243	dsteinne	C	PHD	72	Nrthwstrn	1975
O'Brien, A. Maureen	Assoc	726-7981	mobrien	J	PHD	83	W Virginia	1982
Vose, David	Assoc	726-8756	dvose	QA	PHD	66	Wisconsin	1966

Minnesota State U, Mankato — Mankato, MN 56002-8400 (507) 389-2969 — mankato.msus.edu
Dept Economics & Intl Bus — Col of Social & Beh Sci Fax=389-6377 — Barbara Lutz

Name	Rank	Phone	E-mail	Fields	Degree	Yr	School	Since
Coultrap-McQuin, Susan	Dean	389-5717	susan.coutrap-+		PHD		Iowa	1995
Sharma, Ved P.	C-Pr	389-2711	ved.sharma	CDT	PHD	77	Wash U	1976
Askalani, Mohamed H.	Prof	389-5328	mohamed.askal+	AC	PHD	70	Iowa St	1969
Chowdhury, Ashok K.	Prof	389-6014	ashok.chowd+	AC	PHD	80	Iowa St	1980
Hickerson, Steven	Prof	389-5330	steven.hicker+	ABK	PHD	80	Nebraska	1980
Renner, Donald E.	Prof	389-5249	donald.renner	ACHR	PHD	78	Cincinnati	1979
Schiming, Richard C.	Prof	389-5323	richard.schim+	AE	PHD	74	Ohio St	1981
Simonson, Robert D.	Prof	389-5324	robert.simonson	AJ	PHD	79	Nebraska	1981
Skorr, Arlen J.	Prof	389-2712	arlen.skorr	AE	PHD	70	Nebraska	1965
Smith, Gerald A.	Prof	389-5325	gerald.smith	AOQ	PHD	79	LSU	1979
Wells, Arnold R.	Prof	389-5248	arnold.wells	ADM	PHD	66	Minnesota	1966
Abel, David R.	Asst	389-2969	david.abel	AE	ABD		Minnesota	1969
Tix, Paul	Asst	389-2711	paul.tix	AC	MS		N Dak St	1984

Minot State University — Minot, ND 58702-5002 (701) 858-3130 — warp6.cs.misu.nodak.edu
Div Social Sci-Dept of Econ — Col of Arts & Sciences Fax=839-6933 — Mrs. Robyn Miller

Name	Rank	Phone	E-mail	Fields	Degree	Yr	School	Since
Elhardt, Dale G.	Dean	858-3159		Soci	PHD	88	Colo St	1970
Lomire, Patricia M.	C-Pr	858-3130						
Huenneke, Steve	Assoc	858-3135		AR	PHD	92	Kansas St	1991
Yang, Bill	Asst	858-3151		LG	PHD	93	Iowa	1997

Mississippi College — Clinton, MS 39058 (601) 925-3214 — mc.edu
Dept Business Adm-Economics — School of Business Fax=925-3954 — Shea Elkins

Name	Rank	Phone	E-mail	Fields	Degree	Yr	School	Since
Roberts, Lloyd	Dean	925-3419			PHD	74	Miss	1982
Hood, Frank	Prof	925-3413			PHD	72	Miss	1972
Lee, Gerald R.	Prof	925-3220			PHD	73	Miss	1970

University of Mississippi — University, MS 38677 (601) 232-7730 — bus.olemiss.edu
Dept of Economics & Finance — School of Business Adm Fax=232-5087 — Ms. Cynthia Jeffries

Name	Rank	Phone	E-mail	Fields	Degree	Yr	School	Since
Womer, N. Keith Associate Dean	Prof	232-7076			PHD	70	Penn St	1986
Belongia, Michael T.	Prof	232-7785		E	PHD	82	N Car St	1993
Shughart, William F. II	Prof	232-7076			PHD	78	Tx A&M	1988
Smith, Lewis	Prof	232-5924		E	PHD	71	Tennessee	1971
Chappell, William	Assoc	232-5708			PHD	83	S Carol	1987
Conlon, John	Assoc	232-5708			PHD	78	Chicago	1987
Dorsey, Robert	Assoc	232-7575		ED	PHD	89	Arizona	1989
Mayer, Walt	Assoc	232-5980		E	PHD	86	Florida	1987
Moen, Jon R.	Assoc	232-5467			PHD	87	Chicago	1990
Tosh, Dennis S.	Assoc	232-5101			PHD	80	Geo St	1980
Van Boening, Mark V.	Assoc	232-5841	vanboen	BDL	PHD	91	Arizona	1990
Wolcott, Susan	Assoc				PHD	88	Stanford	1999
Razzolini, Laura	Asst	232-7530		D	PHD	94	So Meth	1994

Mississippi State Univ — Miss St, MS 39762-9580 (601) 325-2341 — cobilan.msstate.edu
Dept Finance & Economics — Col of Business & Indus Fax=325-1977 — Kate Carrithers

Name	Rank	Phone	E-mail	Fields	Degree	Yr	School	Since
Freedman, Sara M.	Dean	325-2580		Mgt	PHD	76	N Carol	1998
Verrall, George	C-Ac	325-1978			DBA	72	Miss St	1965
Grimes, Paul W.	Prof	325-1987			PHD	84	Okla St	1987
Campbell, Charles A.	Assoc	325-7477	ccampell		PHD	85	Tennessee	1985
Sanderson, Patricia L.	Assoc	325-1970			PHD	77	Oklahoma	1979
Millea, Meghan	Asst	325-7476			PHD	98	Nebraska	1998
Phelps, Janie	Asst	325-2561			PHD	98	Kansas	1998
Rogers, Kevin	Asst	325-1982			PHD	96	Georgia	1996

Mississippi Valley St Univ — Itta Bena, MS 38941-1400 (601) 254-3601 — cypress.mcsr.olemiss.edu
Economics Faculty — Department of Business Fax=254-3600 — Mrs. Mary Carter

Name	Rank	Phone	E-mail	Fields	Degree	Yr	School	Since
Chowdhury, A. A. Farhad	C-Pr$	254-3606	achowdhu		PHD	93	Miss St	1993
Kim, Juho	Prof	254-3604			PHD	73	Oklahoma	1973
Rajanikauth, N.	Inst	254-3609			MBA		Miss St	1987

Univ of Missouri-Columbia — Columbia, MO 65211 (573) 882-4574 — missouri.edu
Department of Economics — Col of Arts & Sciences Fax=882-2697 — Sheila Akers Adm Asst

Name	Rank	Phone	E-mail	Fields	Degree	Yr	School	Since
Podgursky, Michael J.	C-Pr	882-4574	podgurskym	IJ	PHD	80	Wisconsin	1995
Hicks, W. Whitney	Prof	882-3483	hicksw	O	PHD	65	Stanford	1965
Menezes, Carmen F.	Prof	882-6094	menezesc	DF	PHD	66	Nrthwstrn	1965
Ratti, Ronald A.	Prof	882-6474	rattir	EFG	PHD	75	So Meth	1975
Wallace, Richard L. Vice President for Academic Affairs	Prof	882-1154	wallacer		PHD	65	Vanderbilt	1967
Geiss, Charles G.	Assoc	882-6073	geissc	C	PHD	74	N Carol	1972
Johnson, Walter L.	Assoc	882-3871	johnsonw	AEGH	PHD	63	Duke	1965
Mandy, David M.	Assoc	882-1763	mandyd	CD	PHD	87	Illinois	1994

Name	Rank	Phone	E-mail	Fields	Degree	Yr	Institution	Year
Mueser, Peter R.	Assoc	882-6427	mueserp	DJT	PHD	83	Chicago	1985
Raymon, Neil A.	Assoc	882-3072	raymonn	CDEF	PHD	77	Colorado	1983
Gao, Ting	Asst	884-8005	gaot	FJ	PHD	98	Michigan	1998
Jensen, Mark	Asst	882-9125	jensenm	EC	PHD	94	Wash U	1997
Ni, Xiagoguang	Asst	882-6878	nix	EH	PHD	91	Minnesota	1990
Pham, Van	Asst	882-3161	phamv	FL	PHD	98	Cornell	1998
Troske, Kenneth	Asst	882-4229	troskek	J	PHD	92	Chicago	1997
Wang, Xinghe	Asst	882-4954	wangx	CDO	PHD	90	Iowa	1990

U Missouri--Kansas City Kansas City, MO 64110-2499 (816) 235-1314 cctr.umkc.edu
Department of Economics Col of Arts & Sciences Fax=235-5263 Ms. Sheila Steverson

Name	Rank	Phone	E-mail	Fields	Degree	Yr	Institution	Year
Durig, James	Dean	235-2538		Chem	PHD	62	MIT	1993
Ward, John O.	C-Pr	235-1309	wardj	KIO	PHD	70	Oklahoma	1969
Brazelton, W. Robert	Prof	235-2831		EP	PHD	61	Oklahoma	1963
Hubbell, L. Kenneth	Prof	235-2835		GHM	PHD	70	Nebraska	1968
Olson, Gerald W.	Prof	235-1317		CGH	PHD	73	Rutgers	1971
Shepherd, A. Ross	Prof	235-2836		DF	PHD	63	Syracuse	1967
Sturgeon, James I.	Prof	235-3837		BO	PHD	74	Oklahoma	1977
Vorst, Karen S.	Prof	235-2838		EC	PHD	80	Indiana	1980
Wagner, F. Eugene	Prof	235-2840		AJO	PHD	67	Syracuse	1967
Wray, Randall	Prof	235-5687			PHD	88	U Wash	1999
Eaton, Peter J.	Assoc	235-2832		CI	PHD	76	Florida	1979
Forstater, Mathew B.	Asst	235-5687		ABF	PHD	96	New Sch	1999
Jepsen, Lisa	Lect	235-5687			PHD	98	Vanderbilt	1998
Kelsy, Michael	Lect	235-5105		CQ	PHD	91	Tennessee	1996
Young, Ben	Lect	235-1314		A	PHD	73	Oklahoma	1993

University Missouri - Rolla Rolla, MO 65409-1250 (573) 341-4800 umr.edu
Department of Economics Col of Arts & Sciences Fax=341-4866 Leatta Nichols
Homepage: http://www.umr.edu/~econ

Name	Rank	Phone	E-mail	Fields	Degree	Yr	Institution	Year
Johnson, Walter D.	C-Pr	341-4809	wjohnson	Ecol	PHD	71	Oklahoma	1988
Gelles, Gregory	C-Ac	341-4825	gelles		PHD	89	W Virginia	1989
Hentzel, David	Prof	341-4827	hentzel		PHD	67	S Illinois	1969
Bryant, Richard R.	Assoc	341-4823	rrbryant		PHD	84	Ca-Davis	1977
Manning, Linda M.	Assoc	341-4828	lindam		PHD	90	Il-Chicago	1989
Sen, Amit	Asst	341-6688	samit		PHD	97	N Carol	1997
Thompson, Philip B.	Asst	341-4893	philthom		PHD	88	Arizona	1994

U Missouri--St. Louis St. Louis, MO 63121-4499 (314) umslvma.umsl.edu
Department of Economics Col of Arts & Sciences Fax= Gloria Axe

Name	Rank	Phone	E-mail	Fields	Degree	Yr	Institution	Year
Young, David	Dean	516-5501						
Phares, Donald	C-Pr	516-5551	c1706	HR	PHD	70	Syracuse	1969
Feigenbaum, Susan K.	Prof	516-5554		DHKP	PHD	80	Wisconsin	1988
Ireland, Thomas R.	Prof	516-5558	strirel		PHD	68	Virginia	1972
Levin, Sharon G.	Prof	516-5560	c4878	DJ	PHD	73	Michigan	1974
Sorensen, Robert L.	Prof	516-5562	c1752	KMAO	PHD	71	Va Tech	1970
Graduate Coordinator								
McBride, Timothy	Assoc	516-5530	stdmcbr	IH	PHD	87	Wisconsin	1991
Rose, David C.	Assoc	516-5307	srose	CDIJ	PHD	87	Virginia	1985
Winkler, Anne E.	Assoc	516-5563	c4934	JT	PHD	89	Illinois	1989
Greene, Clinton	Asst	516-5565		CE	PHD	92	Ca-Davis	1994
Kridel, Donald	Asst	516-5553		CD	PHD	87	Arizona	1993
McCorkle, Sarapage	Asst	516-5248	ssmccor	A	EDD	87	Mo-StLou	1970
Director, Center for Economic Education								
Allison, Michael	Lect	516-5306	smallis	CE	ABD		Virginia	1993
Phares, Kathleen	Lect	516-5570	skphare	A	MA	76	Mo-StLou	1977
Sulter, Mary	Lect	516-5248	smsuite	A	MIEE		Delaware	
Associate Director, Center for Economic Education								

Missouri Southern St Col Joplin, MO 64801-1595 (417) 625-9319 vm.mssc.edu
Economics Faculty Sch of Business Admin Fax=625-9604

Name	Rank	Phone	E-mail	Fields	Degree	Yr	Institution	Year
Gray, James W.	Dean	625-9319			MBA	69	Arkansas	1969
Eberhardt, Duane O.	Prof	625-9536			PHD	70	S Calif	1986
Jaswal, Jasbir S.	Prof	625-9551			PHD	76	Missouri	1977
La Near, Richard E.	Prof	625-9530		ADGN	PHD	79	Miss	1987
Dr. J. R. Kuhn Chair in Finance								
Miller, Robert J.	Prof	625-9345			MA		Cen Mo St	1968
Larson, Marvin L.	Asst	625-9723			MA		Mo-StLou	1990
Rawlins, Richard B.	Asst	625-9716			PHD	98	Arkansas	1988

Missouri Western St College Saint Joseph, MO 64507-2294 (816) 271-4338 griffon.mwsc.edu
Dept of Business & Economics Div of Professional Std Fax=271-4508 Stephanie Taylor

Name	Rank	Phone	E-mail	Fields	Degree	Yr	Institution	Year
Daffron, Joanne	Dean	271-4207	daffron	Nurs	PHD			
Klimek, Janice L.	C-As	271-4351	klimek	Atg	PHD	96	Nebraska	1995
Hamzaee, Reza G.	Prof	271-4262	hamzaee	E	PHD	85	Ariz St	1984
McMurry, Patrick H.	Prof	271-4276	mcmurray	J	PHD	81	Arkansas	1978
Vargha, Nader	Assoc	271-4339	vargha	B	MA		Oklahoma	1980
Lawson, Catherine L.	Asst	271-4338	lawsonc	EB	PHD	88	Colorado	1995

Molloy College — Rockville Cn, NY 11570-5002 (516) Ext 6342
Economics Faculty — Business Management Dp Fax=256-2288
phone 678-5000

Name	Rank	Phone	Email	Fields	Degree	Yr	School	Since
O'Donoghuo, Joseph	C-Pr	Ext 6342			PHD	75	Catholic	1997
Butler, Sister Agnes	Asst	Ext 6275			ABD		Indiana	

Monmouth University — W Lg Branch NJ 07764 (732) 571-3430 — monmouth.edu
Dept of Economics & Finance — Sch of Business Admin Fax=571-3656 — Beth Boyington

Name	Rank	Phone	Email	Fields	Degree	Yr	School	Since
Dempsey, William A.	Dean	571-3423	dempsey	Mktg	DBA	73	Maryland	1-89
Christofi, Andreas	C-Pr	263-5540	achristo	CFG	PHD	84	Penn St	9-97
Holland, John J. Jr.	Prof	571-3435	jholland	EN	PHD	72	NYU	9-97
Pressman, Steven	Prof	571-3658	pressman		PHD	83	New Sch	1981
Aslanbeigui, Nahid	Assoc	571-3642	naslanbe	E	PHD	84	Michigan	1988
Feist, William R.	Assoc	571-3430	wfeist	G	PHD	87	Temple	
Mahajan, Y. Lal	Assoc	571-3647	ymahajan	CDEG	PHD	95	N Illinois	1979
Moliver, Donald M.	Assoc	571-3660	dmoliver	DE	PHD	78	Va Tech	9-68
Nag, Raja	Asst	263-5344	rnag	G	PHD	98	Michigan	1998

University of Montana — Missoula, MT 59812-1012 (406) 243-2925 — selway.umt.edu
Department of Economics — Col of Arts & Sciences Fax= — Becky Hofstad

Name	Rank	Phone	Email	Fields	Degree	Yr	School	Since
Flightner, James A.	Dean	243-2632		Lang	PHD	72	SUNY-Buf	
Power, Thomas M.	C-Pr	243-2925	tmpower	HQR	PHD	71	Princeton	
Barrett, Richard	Prof	243-4497	rbarrett	EOJQ	PHD	72	Wisconsin	
O'Donnell, Dennis J.	Prof	243-2926	dennisl	OJR	PHD	74	Penn St	
Photiades, John G.	Prof	243-5612	johnp	BOH	PHD	72	Illinois	
Unger, Kay C.	Prof	243-4655	kunger	IDEC	PHD	74	J Hopkins	
Wicks, John H.	Prof	243-4122	jwicks	DH	PHD	62	Illinois	
Dalenberg, Douglas R.	Assoc	243-4406	ecdrd	CRL	PHD	87	Oregon	1990
Kupilik, Michael H.	Assoc	243-4575	radmatt	PHBN	PHD	76	Colorado	1976

Montana State University — Bozeman, MT 59717-2920 (406) 994-3701 — msu.oscs.montana.edu
Department of Economics — Col of Letters & Sci Fax=994-4838 — Rebecca Gwin, Adm Asst

Name	Rank	Phone	Email	Fields	Degree	Yr	School	Since
Watts, Myles	H	994-3701						
Anderson, Terry L.	Prof	994-3701			PHD	72	U Wash	1972
Antle, John M.	Prof	994-3701			PHD	80	Chicago	1987
Johnson, Ronald N.	Prof	994-3701			PHD	77	U Wash	1981
Stroup, Richard L.	Prof	994-3701			PHD	70	U Wash	1969
Young, Douglas J.	Prof	994-3701			PHD	78	Wisconsin	1977
Atwood, Joseph A.	Assoc	994-3701			PHD	87	Nebraska	1987
Brester, Gary	Assoc	994-3701			PHD	90	N Car St	1997
Capalbo, Susan M.	Assoc	994-3710			PHD	82	Ca-Davis	1991
Lueck, Dean L.	Assoc	994-3701			PHD	87	U Wash	1997
Rucker, Randal R.	Assoc	994-3701			PHD	84	U Wash	1991
Smith, Vincent H.	Assoc	994-3701			PHD	87	N Car St	1988
Buschena, David E.	Asst	994-3701			PHD	93	Berkeley	1992
Fleck, Robert K.	Asst	994-3701			PHD	94	Stanford	1995
Hanssen, F. Andrew	Asst	994-3701			PHD	95	Chicago	1995
Stratmann, Thomas	Asst	994-3701			PHD	90	Maryland	1990

Montana State Univ-Billings — Billings, MT 59101-0298 (406) 657-2295 — msubillings.edu
Dept of Bus Academic Prog — College of Business Fax=657-2237

Name	Rank	Phone	Email	Fields	Degree	Yr	School	Since
Nemacek, Barbara H.	Dean	657-1630	bnemecek	Mktg	PHD	87	Minnesota	1997
Lynch, Dan	C-Ac	657-2035	mm_lynch	Mktg	PHD	98	Arkansas	1989
Farsio, Farzad	Prof	657-2033	econ_farsio		PHD	89	Claremont	1987
Harris, R. Scott	Assoc	657-1653	econ_harris		PHD	85	UCLA	1988

Montclair State College — U Montclair, NJ 07043 (973) 655-5255 — saturn.montclair.edu
Dept of Economics & Finance — Sch of Business Admin Fax=655-7629 — Ms. Ida S. Fazio

Name	Rank	Phone	Email	Fields	Degree	Yr	School	Since
Leveen, Serpil Sisik	C-Pr	655-7402	leveen	ADEG	PHD	73	NYU	1974
Desai, Suresh	Prof	655-4370			PHD	68	UCLA	1973
Flint, Harold	Prof	655-7403		AEGP	PHD	72	S Illinois	1971
LeBel, Phillip	Prof	655-7778	lebel	DOQH	PHD	77	Boston U	1981
Baytas, Ahmet	Assoc	655-7633			PHD	86	Illinois	1988
Chakraborty, Chandana	Assoc	655-4125	chankrabortyc	ACDO	PHD	87	Rensselaer	9-89
Honig, Solomon	Assoc	655-5257		ADKR	PHD	76	Columbia	1981
Rawlins, Glenville W.	Assoc	655-4339		AGOQ	PHD	83	NYU	1984
Rezvani, Farahmand	Assoc	655-7568		ACGH	PHD	83	CUNY	1984
Pirouz, Kamrouz	Asst	655-5124		ADGN	PHD	73	Hawaii	1980
Zamanian, Zaman	Asst	655-7399		ACEF	PHD	83	Indiana	1984

University of Montevallo — Montevallo, AL 35115-6000 (205) 665-6540 — um.montevallo.edu
Economics Faculty — Michael E. Stephens COB Fax=665-6560 — Penny Allen
Homepage: www.cob.montevallo.edu

Name	Rank	Phone	Email	Fields	Degree	Yr	School	Since
Bell, Nancy S.	Dean	665-6540	belln	Insr	PHD	85	Georgia	1999
Shinn, Earl W. III	C-Ac	655-6536	shinn		PHD	92	S Carol	1988
Blevins, Dallas	Prof	665-6542	blevins		DBA	76	Fla St	1983
MacPherson, Roderick S.	Assoc	665-6535	macpherson		DBA	77	Miss St	1977

Moorhead State University Moorhead, MN 56563 (218) 236-2842 mhd1.moorhead.msus.edu
Economics Department Business & Industry Fax=236-2168 Brenda Shoemaker

Name	Rank	Phone	Email	Field	Degree	Yr	School	Year
Dobis, Vernon J.	C-Pr	236-4029	dobis		PHD	94	Manitoba	1981
Greenley, Douglas A.	Prof	236-4031	greenley		PHD	79	Colo St	1978
Knighton, Daniel R.	Prof	236-4027	knighton		PHD	73	N Carol	1970
Cooper, John M.	Asst	236-4030			MA	75	Oregon	1972

Moravian College Bethlehem, PA 18018-6650 (610) 861-1381 moravian.edu
Economic Faculty Economics & Bus Dept Fax=861-3980 Mrs. Mayann Weaver
Did Not Respond--1997-98 Listing

Name	Rank	Phone	Email	Field	Degree	Yr	School	Year
West, James P.	C-Pr	861-1381	mejpwo	FM	PHD	87	Lehigh	1989
Ravelle, James J.	Prof	861-1378	mejjrol	KB	DA		Lehigh	1978
Brower, George D.	Assoc	861-1379	megdbol	COM	PHD	85	SUNY-Buf	1989
Ravelle, Linda J.	Assoc	861-1453	meljrol	AG	PHD	90	Lehigh	1989
Von Allmen, Peter	Assoc	861-1413	mepvaol	CDL	PHD	90	Temple	1990
Collins, May N.	Asst	861-1446	memacol	AFO	PHD	92	S Calif	1993

Morehead State University Morehead, KY 40351-1689 (606) 783-2152 morehead-st.edu
Dept of Atg, Econ & Finance Sch of Business & Econ Fax=783-5025 Mary Howard

Name	Rank	Phone	Email	Field	Degree	Yr	School	Year
Miller, Green	C-Pr	783-2721	g.miller		PHD	85	Kentucky	1979
Buck, Roland	Prof	783-2722	r.buck		PHD	79	Tx A&M	1983
Ahmadi, Ali	Asst	783-2797	a.ahmadi		EDD	87	Houston	1995
Creahan, Thomas	Asst	783-2740	t.creahan		PHD	95	Cincinnati	1996
Yasin, Mesghena	Asst	783-2758	m.yasin		PHD	86	Cincinnati	1986

Morehouse College Atlanta, GA 30314-3773 (404) 215-2618 morehouse.edu
Economics Faculty Dept Economics & Bus Ad Fax=215-2719 Mrs. Patricia Allen/Jackson

Name	Rank	Phone	Email	Field	Degree	Yr	School	Year
Williams, John E.	C-Pr	681-2618		Fnce	PHD	86	Geo St	1976
Mills Bee Lane Professor of Finance								
Handy, John	Prof				PHD	85	Geo St	1978
Sheftall, Willis B.	Prof	681-2800			PHD	81	Geo St	1986
Charles E. Merrill Professor of Economics								
Eagan, J. Vincent	Assoc				PHD	86	Geo St	1993
Gissy, William G.	Asst				PHD	87	Geo St	1988
Morman, Martin R.	Asst				PHD	88	Geo St	1990

Morgan State University Baltimore, MD 21239 (443) 319-3438 morgan.edu
Department of Economics Col of Arts & Sciences Fax=319-3358 Jo Ann McCready
Did Not Respond Again--1995-96 Listing

Name	Rank	Phone	Email	Field	Degree	Yr	School	Year
Hollis, Burney	Dean	319-3090						
Fessiehatzen, Tekie	C-Pr	319-3438			PHD		Pittsburgh	
Favor, Homer	Prof	319-3558			PHD	60	Pittsburgh	
Whittaker, Victor A.	Prof	319-3440			PHD	71	Illinois	1974
Amegbe, Annan	Assoc	319-3531			PHD	77	Catholic	1978
Evans, Bernice	Asst	319-3446			MBA		Baruch	
Karangu, Mwangi	Asst	319-3440		CDEG	PHD	81	Walden	9-71
Bagheri, Rashid	Inst	319-3099			MA		Howard	
Kimani, Joseph	Inst	319-3099			MBA		Atlanta	

Morningside College Sioux City, IA 51106-1751 (712) 274-5131 alpha.morningside.edu
Economics Faculty Dept of Economics Fax=274-5101 Deb Protexter

Name	Rank	Phone	Email	Field	Degree	Yr	School	Year
Gilsdorf, Keith F.	C-Ac	274-5289	kgooo1	LJ	PHD	90	Nebraska	1994
Ghoshroy, Atrayee	Asst	274-5318	agoooz	HF	PHD	97	Nebraska	1999

Morris Brown College Atlanta, GA 30314-4140 (404) 220-0233 morrisbrown.edu
Economics Faculty Dept of Econ & Bus Adm Fax=220-3683 Marilyn Judge
Did Not Respond--1997-98 Listing; phone 222-0270

Name	Rank	Phone	Email	Field	Degree	Yr	School	Year
Coleman, Cyiata D.	Dir	Ext 0157	c41c@a	FGOR	PHD	86	S Illinois	8-89

Mount Holyoke College South Hadley, MA 01075-1481 (413) 538-2432 mtholyoke.edu
Economics Faculty Department of Economics Fax=538-2512 Dawn Larder

Name	Rank	Phone	Email	Field	Degree	Yr	School	Year
Robinson, Michael D.	C-Ac	538-2215	mirobins		PHD	87	Tx-Austin	1988
Moseley, Fred B.	Prof	538-2517	fmoseley		PHD	82	Mass	1989
Rapoport, John	Prof	538-2818	rapoport		PHD	70	Penn	1970
Christiansen, Jens	Assoc	538-2750	jchristi		PHD	82	Stanford	1986
Paus, Eva	Assoc	538-2518	epaus		PHD	83	Pittsburgh	1987
Gabriel, Satyananda Jordan	Asst	538-2043	sgabriel		PHD	89	Mass	1989
Hartley, James E.	Asst	538-2566	jhartley		PHD	94	Ca-Davis	1994
Wilson, Lucas	Asst	538-2751	lbwilson		PHD	95	Mass	1995

Mount Saint Mary's College Los Angeles, CA 90049 (310) 954-4155 msmc.la.edu
Economics Faculty Dept Business & Econ Fax=954-4159 Trudi Britt
Chalon Campus

Name	Rank	Phone	Email	Field	Degree	Yr	School	Year
Leese, David	C-Pr	954-4150	dleese	Law	LLD		Nrthwstrn	1977
Whitman, Katherine	Asst	954-4152	kwhitman	ANF	MA		UCLA	1980

Muhlenberg College	Allentown, PA	18104-5586	(610) 821-3280					muhlenberg.edu
Economics Faculty	Department of Economics		Fax=821-3536					Justine Frantz
Heitmann, George Jr.	C-Pr	821-3278	heitmann		PHD	63	Princeton	1-94
Marshall, James N.	Prof	821-3284			PHD	82	Lehigh	1975
Sinha, Rohini P.	Prof	821-3282			PHD	65	New Sch	1965
Kish-Goodling, Donna M.	Asst	821-3479			PHD	92	Lehigh	1990
Raymond, Arthur J.	Asst	821-3278			PHD	90	Tufts	1991
Walsh, Vivian	Lect	821-3290			PHD	53	Trinity	1989
Zumas, Susan	Lect				PHD	94	Lehigh	1992

Murray State University	Murray, KY	42071-0009	(502) 762-4188					murraystate.edu
Dept of Economics & Finance	Col Bus & Public Affair		Fax=762-5478					Marion Elkins
Harrison, Dannie	Dean	762-4181	dannie.harrison	EPO	PHD	74	S Illinois	1969
McCoy, James	C-Pr	762-4274	jim.mccoy	DFOP	PHD	86	N Carol	1985
Mathis, Gilbert L.	Prof	762-4283	gilbert.mathis	DFKQ	PHD	66	Ohio St	1966
Milkman, Martin	Prof	762-4282	martin.milkman	CJH	PHD	89	Oregon	1988
Brasfield, David	Assoc	762-4324	david.brasfield	EGC	PHD	89	N Carol	1986
Hassan, Seid	Assoc	762-4284	seid.hassan	CEFR	PHD	93	Tx A&M	1992
Eaton, David	Asst	762-4290	david.eaton	HCL	PHD	95	Michigan	1996
Brown, Barry	Lect	762-4277	barry.brown	EO	MS	77	Murray St	1991
Reed, Mary Tripp	Lect	762-3932	mary-tripp.reed	ADFJ	MA	95	American	1995

Naval Postgraduate School	Monterey, CA	93943-5000	(408) 656-2161					nps.navy.mil
Economics Faculty	Dept of Systems Mgt		Fax=656-3068					
Boger, Dan C.	Prof	656-2607	dboger	C	PHD	79	Berkeley	1979
Frederiksen, Peter C.	Prof	656-2661	pcfreder	AOR	PHD	74	Wash St	7-74
Jones, Carl R.	Prof	656-2995	crjones	D	PHD	65	Claremont	1965
LaCivita, Charles J.	Prof	656-2445	clacivita	DM	PHD	81	Ca-SnBarb	1985
Looney, Robert	Prof	656-3484	relooney	OF	PHD	69	Berkeley	1977
Mehay, Stephen L.	Prof	656-2643	smehay	IJ	PHD	73	UCLA	1985
Parker, Patrick J.	Prof	656-2097	p.parker@stl.	AH	MBA	55	Chicago	9-74
Thomas, George	Prof	656-2741	gwthomas	J	PHD	71	Purdue	1978
Gates, William R.	Assoc	656-2754	brgates	D	PHD	74	Yale	1988
Henderson, David R.	Assoc	656-2524	drhender	D	PHD	76	UCLA	1984
Hildebrandt, Gregory G.	Assoc	656-2767	ghildebrandt	D	PHD	76	Princeton	1992
Melese, Francois	Assoc	656-2009	fmelese	C	PHD	82	Belgium	1987
Cook, Michael D.	Asst	656-3508	mdcook	J	PHD	96	Maryland	1996
Webb, Natalie J.	Asst	656-2013	njwebb	H	PHD	92	Duke	1992

Nazareth Coll of Rochester	Rochester, NY	14618-3790	(716) Ext 558					naz.edu
Economics Faculty	Dept Bus, Econ, & Mgt		Fax=586-2452					Joan Van du Zer
Did Not Respond Again--1995-96 Listing; phone 586-2525								
Zappia, Gerard	C-Ac	Ext 561			MSED		Nazareth	
Aerni, April Laskey	Assoc	Ext 549			PHD	87	Cincinnati	
DaBoll-Lavoie, Joseph T.	Assoc	Ext 592	jtdaboll	BHJ	PHD	89	SUNY-Bin	9-88
Maley, Leonard A.	Assoc	Ext 550			MBA	62	Cincinnati	
Schroeder, Edward A.	Assoc				PHD	80	UCLA	1988

University of Nebraska	Lincoln, NE	68588-0489	(402) 472-2319					unlnotes.unl.edu
Department of Economics	College of Business Adm		Fax=472-9700					Carol Nelson
Milligan, Sally	Dean	472-9500			JD	67	Geo Wash	1988
Schmidt, James R.	C-Pr	472-2315	jschmidt2		PHD	78	Rice	1977
Anderson, John E.	Prof	472-1190	janderson	H	PHD	77	Claremont	1991
Director of Graduate Program								
Hayden, F. Gregory	Prof	472-2332	ghayden	HQI	PHD	68	Tx-Austin	1967
Lamphear, F. Charles	Prof	472-7928		O	PHD	67	Kansas St	1966
Director, Bureau of Business Research								
MacPhee, Craig R.	Prof	472-2319	cmacphee	F	PHD	70	Mich St	1969
Paul C. Burnmeister College Professor								
Petr, Jerry L.	Prof	472-3003	jpetr	P	PHD	67	Indiana	1966
C. Wheaton Battey Professor of Economics								
Riefler, Roger F.	Prof	472-2327	rriefler	R	PHD	66	U Wash	1973
Rosenbaum, David I.	Prof	472-2318	dir		PHD	85	Wisconsin	1985
Walstad, William B.	Prof	472-2333	wwalstad	I	PHD	78	Minnesota	1982
State Farm Professorship								
Cushing, Matthew J.	Assoc	472-2323	mcushing	EJ	PHD	85	Virginia	1992
Fuess, Scott M.	Assoc	472-6281	sfuess	J	PHD	86	Purdue	1986
Kim, Benjamin J. C.	Assoc	472-3083	kimjc	F	PHD	83	UCLA	1983
May, Ann Mari	Assoc	472-3369	amay	BE	PHD	87	Colo St	1987
McGarvey, Mary G.	Assoc	472-9415	mcgarvey	E	PHD	83	Virginia	1992
Van den Berg, Hendrik F.	Assoc	472-3004	hvan-den-berg	F	PHD	89	Wisconsin	1989
Allgood, Sam	Asst	472-3367	sallgood	DJG	PHD	93	Georgia	
Klaus, Bettina	Asst	472-2129	bklaus	D	PHD	98	Maastricht	1998

Univ of Nebraska at Kearney Kearney, NE 68849-4570 (308) 865-8530 platte.unk.edu
Department of Economics Col of Business & Tech Fax=865-8669 Connie J. Fie

Name	Rank	Phone	Email	Field	Degree	Yr	School	Year
Hadley, Galen D.	Dean	865-8342		Atg	PHD	75	Nebraska	8-91
Kotcherlokota, V. V.	C-Pr	865-8785			PHD	77	India	1986
Blake, Gordon	Prof	865-8459			PHD	70	Nebraska	1963
Eshleman, Tom	Assoc	865-8458			PHD	94	Okla St	1993
Jenkins, Allan	Assoc	865-8461			PHD	87	Nebraska	1987
Marxsen, Craig S.	Assoc	865-8043			PHD	76	Geo St	1987
Bridges, Deborah	Asst	865-8044			PHD	94	Wash St	1997

Univ of Nebraska at Omaha Omaha, NE 68182-0048 (402) 554-2570 unomaha.edu
Department of Economics College of Business Adm Fax=554-3747 Scott Hays

Name	Rank	Phone	Email	Field	Degree	Yr	School	Year
Hille, Stanley J.	Dean	554-2599	shille	Mgt	PHD	66	Minnesota	1996
Sosin, Kim	C-Pr	554-2570	sosin	ECO	PHD	70	Nebraska	1981
Diamond, Arthur M.	Prof	554-3657	adiamond	BJ	PHD	78	Chicago	1986
Nielsen, Donald A.	Prof	554-2453	dnielsen	AR	PHD	70	Syracuse	1972
Sindt, Roger	Prof	554-2802	rsindt	AR	PHD	72	Tx-Austin	1979
Turner, Keith K.	Prof	554-2803	kturner	EM	PHD	68	Nebraska	1969
Wohar, Mark	Prof	554-4342	mwohar	ECGF	PHD	85	Illinois	1988
Zahn, Frank	Prof	554-2257	fzahn	E	PHD	69	Ca-SnBarb	1979
Baum, Donald N.	Assoc		dbaum	HD	PHD	79	Claremont	1987
Corcoran, William J.	Assoc	554-2915	wcorcora	LQD	PHD	75	Rutgers	1980
Lin, Shuanglin	Assoc	554-2815	slin	CDEO	PHD	89	Purdue	1989
Connell, Donald R.	Asst	554-2805	dconnell	AF	MS	58	Ft Hays	1965
West, Janet Mason	Asst	554-2806	jwest	AJ	MA	64	Mich St	1967

Nebraska Wesleyan Univ Lincoln, NE 68504-2796 (402) 465-2213 nebrwesleyan.edu
Div Economics-Social Science Dept Bus Admin & Econ Fax=465-2179 Arleine Kobza

Name	Rank	Phone	Email	Field	Degree	Yr	School	Year
Gleason, Joyce G.	C-Ac	465-2444	jgg		PHD	86	Nebraska	1990
Fairchild, Loretta	Prof	465-2204	llf		PHD	72	Cornell	1975
Hudson, Thomas K.	Assoc	465-2205	tkh	BAdm	PHD	91	Nebraska	1988

Univ of Nevada, Las Vegas Las Vegas, NV 89154-6005 (702) 895-3776 ccmail.nevada.edu
Department of Economics College of Business Fax=895-1354 Debbie Gallant

Name	Rank	Phone	Email	Field	Degree	Yr	School	Year
Malamud, Bernard	C-Pr	895-3294	malamud	E	PHD	71	New Sch	1968
Carroll, Thomas M.	Prof	895-3652	carroll	D	PHD	73	Syracuse	1986
Daneshvary, Nasser Associate Dean	Prof	895-3362	daneshvary	R	PHD	84	Tennessee	1990
Hoppe, Hans Hermann	Prof	895-3227	hoppe	B	PHD		Goethe	1986
Ray, Clarence G.	Prof	895-0817	ray	K	PHD	72	S Carol	1971
Schwer, Keith	Prof	895-3191	schwer	R	PHD	73	Maryland	1986
Karstensson, Lewis	Assoc	895-3653	karstensson	B	PHD	74	Ohio U	1979
Ridgway, Terry R.	Assoc	895-3016	ridgway	D	PHD	74	Arizona	1968
Waddoups, C. Jeffrey	Assoc	895-3497	waddoups	J	PHD	89	Utah	1989
Assane, Djeto	Asst	895-3284	assane	O	PHD	88	Colorado	1988
Bold, Frederick	Asst	895-3376		D	PHD		U Wash	1995
Chen, Lein-Lein	Asst	895-3950	chen	F	PHD	92	U Miami	1993
Cronovich, Ron	Asst	895-3015	cronovich	E	PHD	95	Michigan	1994
Robinson, William J.	Asst	895-3769	robinson	A	PHD	83	Colorado	1980
Wimmer, Bradley	Asst	895-3018	wimmer	L	PHD	92	Kentucky	1998

University of Nevada, Reno Reno, NV 89557-0016 (702) 784-6850 scs.unr.edu
Department of Economics Col of Business Admin Fax=784-4728 Theresa E. Moser
email @1=equinox.unr.edu

Name	Rank	Phone	Email	Field	Degree	Yr	School	Year
Reed, Howard M.	Dean	784-4912	cioreed@1		PHD	75	Utah	1972
Chu, Shih-Fan	C-Pr	784-6850	chu		PHD	68	Illinois	1967
Atkinson, Glendel W.	Prof	784-6678	atkinson		PHD	68	Oklahoma	1967
Cargill, Thomas F.	Prof	784-6812	cargill		PHD	68	Ca-Davis	1973
Eadington, William R.	Prof	784-6887	eading@1		PHD	73	Claremont	1969
Raffiee, Kambiz	Prof	784-6864	raffiee		PHD	83	Oregon	1983
Wendel, Jeanne L.	Prof	784-6695	wendel		PHD	77	So Meth	1985
Dobra, John L.	Assoc	784-6859			PHD	80	Va Tech	1980
Metts, Robert Lyle	Assoc	784-1115			PHD	85	Berkeley	1984
Mitchell, Mike	Assoc	784-1112	mikem		PHD	88	Oregon	1988
Pingle, Mark	Assoc	784-6634	pingle@1		PHD	88	S Calif	1990
Nichols, Mark W.	Asst	784-6936	mnichols	LKJ	PHD	94	Fla St	1996
Parker, Elliott	Asst	784-6408	elliott		PHD	92	U Wash	1992
Song, Shunfeng	Asst	784-6860	song		PHD	92	Ca-Irvine	1992

University of New Hampshire Durham, NH 03824-3593 (603) 862-3457 christa.unh.edu
Department of Economics Whittemore Sch Bus & Ec Fax=862-3383 Sinthy Kounlasa

Name	Rank	Phone	Email	Field	Degree	Yr	School	Year
Merenda, Michael J.	Dean	862-1983	mmerenda	Mgt	PHD	78	Mass	1977
Schmidt, Torsten	C-Ac	862-3349	ts	DL	PHD	90	Florida	1988
England, Richard W.	Prof	662-3335	rwe	OQ	PHD	74	Michigan	1976
Simos, Evangelos O.	Prof	862-3363	eos	EF	PHD	77	N Illinois	1977

Name	Rank	Phone	Email	Fields	Degree	Yr	School	Since
Wible, James R.	Prof	862-3324	jrwible	BE	PHD	80	Penn St	1984
Conway, Karen Smith	Assoc	862-3386	ksconway	HJ	PHD	87	N Carol	1990
Elmslie, Bruce T.	Assoc	862-3347	bte	BF	PHD	88	Utah	1989
Graduate Program Coordinator								
Goldberg, Michael	Assoc	862-3385	michaelg	EF	PHD	91	NYU	1991
Herold, Marc W.	Assoc	862-3375		O	PHD	77	Berkeley	1975
Mills, Richard L.	Assoc	862-3350	rmills	CD	PHD	67	Indiana	1967
Niman, Neil B.	Assoc	862-3336		BL	PHD	85	Tx-Austin	1987
Thompson, Allen R.	Assoc	862-2771	art	GM	PHD	73	Tx-Austin	1974
Huang, Ju-Chin	Asst	862-3279	jehuang	CQ	PHD	94	N Car St	1998
Rork, Jonathan	Asst						Stanford	1999

New Hampshire College — Manchester, NH 03104-1394 (603) 645-9691 — nhc.edu
Economic & Finance Dept — School of Business Fax=645-9603 — Polly Popek

Name	Rank	Phone	Email	Fields	Degree	Yr	School	Since
Doucette, Francis G.	Dean	668-2211			EDD	78	Vanderbilt	8-94
Hall, Yvonne C.	C-Pr	668-2211			PHD	81	Colo St	
Johnson, R. Larry	Prof				DBA	82	Geo Wash	
Hassan, Mahboubul	Assoc				MAPE	82	Boston U	
White, Charles V. A.	Assoc				PHD	73	Ohio St	
Widener, Steven	Assoc	668-2211			PHD	88	NewHamp	

University of New Haven — West Haven, CT 06516-1999 (203) 932-7355 — charger.newhaven.edu
Department of Economics — School of Business Fax=931-6076 — Patricia Skinner

Name	Rank	Phone	Email	Fields	Degree	Yr	School	Since
Martin, Linda R.	Dean	932-7115	lmartin		PHD	81	S Carol	8-95
Parker, Joseph A.	C-Pr	932-7349		JR	PHD	68	Oklahoma	9-69
Kaplan, Phillip	Prof	932-7419		NL	PHD	64	J Hopkins	
Phelan, John	Assoc	932-7355		HI	PHD		Geo Wash	9-95
Shapiro, Steven J.	Assoc	932-7496		GKLM	PHD	88	Geotown	9-87
Suster, Zeljan	Assoc	932-7115	zsuster	FNOP	PHD	88	Belgrade	9-90
Associate Dean								
Woodruff, Mary Martha	Assoc	932-7361			EDD	72	Bridgepr	9-85
Grubacic, Sanja	VAsst	932-6005		EF	PHD	96	Conn	9-98

The College of New Jersey — Ewing, NJ 08628-0718 (609) 771-3496 — tcnj.edu
Economics Program — School of Business Fax=637-5129

Name	Rank	Phone	Email	Fields	Degree	Yr	School	Since
Breslin, Thomas	Dean	771-3050	breslint		PHD	76	W Virginia	
Samanta, Subarna K.	C-Ac	771-3496			PHD	85	So Meth	1987
Liu, Chao-Nan	Prof	771-2240			PHD	76	Tx A&M	
Naples, Michele I.	Assoc	771-2896			PHD	82	Mass	
Datta, Anusua	Asst	771-2657			PHD	99	Wi-Milwa	1999
Leven, Bozen	Asst	771-3140			PHD	91	Cornell	
Vandegrift, Donald	Asst	771-2294			PHD	93	Conn	
Cerf, G.		771-3220			MA	65	Syracuse	

New Jersey City University — Jersey City, NJ 07305-1597 (201) 200-3272 — njcu.edu
Economics Department — Sch of Arts & Science Fax=200-2072 — Ms. Rita Lange

Name	Rank	Phone	Email	Fields	Degree	Yr	School	Since
Hordon, Harris	C-Pr	200-3272	hhordon	AG	PHD	68	NYU	
Ghebrat, Ezra	Assoc	200-3390	eghebrat	ADEF	PHD	82	New Sch	
Anderson, Richard T.	Asst	200-2285	randerson	AI	PHD	91	CUNY	
Steinberg, Ivan	Asst	200-3462	isteinberg	LA	ABD	71	New Sch	
Vohra, Rubina A.	Asst	200-3074	rvohra	AJO	PHD	93	Northeas	9-94

New Jersey Inst Technology — Newark, NJ 07102-1982 (973) 596-3248 — njit.edu
Economics Faculty — Sch of Industrial Mgt Fax=596-3074 — Essie Richardson

Name	Rank	Phone	Email	Fields	Degree	Yr	School	Since
Chakrabarti, Alok K.	Dean	596-3256		Mgt	PHD	72	Nrthwstrn	1989
Distinguished Professor of Management; Sponsored Chair in Management of Tech								
Hasan, Iftekhar	Prof	596-8238			PHD	87	Houston	1994
Anyanwu, Lenard C.	Asst	596-6426			PHD	90	Tx-Dallas	1990
Bonitsis, Theologos H.	Asst	596-3263			PHD	84	CUNY	1990
Sau, Ranjit	Visit	596-4281			PHD	64	Wayne St	1995

University of New Mexico — Albuquerque, NM 87131-1101 (505) 277-5304 — unm.edu
Department of Economics — Col of Arts & Sciences Fax=277-9445 — Dixie Lee Prowell

Name	Rank	Phone	Email	Fields	Degree	Yr	School	Since
Fischer, Michael R.	Dean	277-3046	mfischer		PHD	75	Nrthwstrn	1975
Brookshire, David S.	C-Pr	277-1964	brookshi	Q	PHD	76	New Mex	1989
Bohara, Alok	Prof	277-5903	bohara	CQ	PHD	86	Colorado	1987
Burness, H. Stuart	Prof	277-1952	burness	CDQ	PHD	70	Kansas	1978
Gisser, Micha	Prof	277-2420	gisser	DLQ	PHD	62	Chicago	1973
McKee, Michael	Prof	277-1960	mckee	HKQL	PHD	85	Carleton	1991
Ganderton, Philip	Assoc	277-1962	gandini	DH	PHD	89	Ca-SnBarb	1989
Gawande, Kishore	Assoc	277-1965	gawande	CEFP	PHD	91	UCLA	1991
Santos, Richard	Assoc	277-2107	santos	IJ	PHD	77	Mich St	1989
Sauer, Christine	Assoc	277-1963	sauer	EF	PHD	87	Brown	1985
Anderson, Deborah	Asst	277-5560	andersod	CHJ	PHD	98	Cornell	1998
Berrens, Robert	Asst	277-9004	rberrens	DQ	PHD	93	Oregon St	1994
Binder, Melissa	Asst	277-3548	mbinder	FJO	PHD	95	Columbia	1995
Chermak, Janie	Asst	277-4906	jchermak	DQ	PHD	91	Co Mines	1995
Krause, Kate	Asst	277-3429	kkrause	HK	PHD	96	Wisconsin	1996

New Mexico Highlands Univ	Las Vegas, NM		87701-4211	(505) 454-3579			merlin.nmhu.edu	
Economics Faculty	School of Business		Fax=					
Maestas, Ronald W.	D-Pr	454-3522	ronmaestas	Mis	EDD	79	Ariz St	1972
Ferran, Manuel A.	Assoc	454-3575	m_ferran	ADEG	PHD	69	Oklahoma	1993

New Mexico State Univ	Las Cruces, NM		88003-8001	(505) 646-2113			nmsu.edu	
Dept of Econ & Internl Bus	Col Business Adm & Econ		Fax=646-1915				Stella Barrio	
Arnold, Daniel R.	Dean	646-4083	darnold		DBA	76	La Tech	7-94
Nowotny, Kenneth	H-Pr	646-2113	knowotny	HN	PHD	77	Tx-Austin	1976
Ellis, Michael	Prof	646-4101	mellis	I	PHD	75	Ca-Rivers	1973
Nordyke, James W.	Emer	646-5688		FE	PHD	59	Princeton	1964
Orton, Eliot S.	Emer	646-3800	eorton	N	PHD	71	Cornell	1970
Peach, James T.	Prof	646-3113	jpeach	T	PHD	78	Tx-Austin	1980
Smith, David B	Prof	646-5879	dbsmith	H	PHD	71	Nebraska	1970
Willman, Elliott	Prof	646-1005	ewiillman	EF	PHD	77	Indiana	1979
Brook, Kathleen	Assoc	646-4905	kbrook	E	PHD	76	Tx-Austin	1980
Associate Dean								
Cabe, Richard	Assoc	646-5909	rcabe	K	PHD	83	Wyoming	1988
Enomoto, Carl E.	Assoc	646-1992	cenomote	FE	PHD	82	Tx A&M	1983
Gegax, Douglas A.	Assoc	646-1903	dgegax	HD	PHD	84	Wyoming	1984
Ghosh, Soumendra	Assoc	646-2340	sghosh	O	PHD	87	Utah St	1988
Matta, Benjamin N.	Assoc	646-4085		IJ	PHD	79	Tx-Austin	1972
McGuckin, J. T.	Assoc	646-6302		Q	PHD	90	Wisconsin	1989
Popp, Anthony V.	Assoc	646-5198	apopp	H	PHD	80	N Illinois	1981
Tanski, Janet M.	Assoc	646-1905	jtanski	OI	PHD	91	SUNY-Buf	1989
Adrisson, Rick	Asst	646-4088	radkisso	FH	PHD	94	Nebraska	8-94
Erickson, Christopher A.	Asst	646-5715	chericks	EF	PHD	89	Ariz St	1987
Mora, Marie T.	Asst	646-1595	mmora	JI	PHD	95	Tx A&M	8-95

University of New Orleans	New Orleans, LA		70148-1555	(504) 280-6485			uno.edu	
Dept of Economics & Finance	College of Business Adm		Fax=280-6397				Russel Holliday 280-6487	
Ryan, Timothy P.	Dean	280-6241			PHD	78	Ohio St	1978
Hibernia Professor of Economics								
Mukherjee, Tarun K.	C-Pr	280-7146		Fnce	DBA	77	Tx Tech	
Altazan, John E.	Prof	280-6434			PHD	54	Illinois	1958
Davis, J. Ronnie	Prof	280-7148			PHD	67	Virginia	1989
Hartley, Michael J.	Prof	280-6904			PHD	70	Penn	
Jeffress, Philip W.	Prof	280-6899			PHD	69	Kentucky	1995
Larson, David A.	Prof	280-6902			PHD	68	Maryland	
Miller, Edward M.	Prof	280-6913			PHD	70	MIT	1984
Speyrer, Janet F.	Prof	280-6981			PHD	82	J Hopkins	1987
Director, Division of Business & Economic Research								
Turunen-Red, Arja H.	Prof	280-6912			PHD	85	Brit Colum	1995
Whitney, Gerald A.	Prof	280-6903			PHD	77	Tulane	
Abdel-Rahman, Hesham M.	Assoc	280-7043			PHD	87	Penn	1987
Brite, Robert L.	Assoc	280-6897			PHD	69	Rutgers	1970
Lane, Walter J.	Assoc	280-7145			PHD	78	Ca-SnDgo	1986
McLain, James J.	Assoc	280-6907			PHD	72	Pittsburgh	1972
Naka, Atsuyuki	Assoc	280-6896			PHD	89	Arizona	1989
Tufte, David R.	Assoc	280-7094			PHD	92	SUNY-Buf	1992
Wolfson, Melville Z.	Assoc	280-6917			PHD	71	Illinois	
Maroney, Neal C.	Asst	280-6908			PHD	96	Claremont	1997

College of New Rochelle	New Rochelle, NY		10805	(914) 654-5502				
Div of Social Science-Econ	Sch of Arts & Sciences		Fax=					
Did Not Respond Again--1995-96 Listing								
Bailey, Joan	Dean			Phil	PHD	71	Yale	
Ong, Bruce Nelson	C-Ac			PolS	PHD		Virginia	
Malloy, Mary	Asst			AHJO	PHD	94	Brown	

New York University	New York, NY		10012-1126	(212) 998-0860			stern.nyu.edu	
Economics	Faculty Arts & Sciences		Fax=995-4218				Ms. Laura Tropp	
Homepage: http://www.stern.nyu.economics/								
Daly, George G.	Dean	998-0909	gdale	D	PHD	67	Nrthwstrn	1993
Greene, William H.	C-Pr	998-0876	wgreene	CDE	PHD	76	Wisconsin	1982
Backus, David	Prof	998-0873	dbackus	EFG	PHD	81	Yale	1990
Diamond, Daniel E.	Prof	998-4010	ddiamond	DEN	PHD	58	NYU	1958
Economides, Nicholas S.	Prof	998-0864	neconomi	DKL	PHD	81	Berkeley	1990
Guilfoil, John D.	Prof	998-0045	jguilfoi	DKN	PHD	64	NYU	1964
Katz, Barbara G.	Prof	998-0865	bkatz	CDP	PHD	73	Penn	1974
Kavesh, Robert A.	Prof	998-0863	rkavesh	B	PHD	54	Harvard	1958
Marcus Nadler Professor of Finance & Economics								
Pugel, Thomas A.	Prof	998-0907	tpugel	DEF	PHD	78	Harvard	1978
Ramachandran, Rama	Prof	998-0759	rramacha	DEH	PHD	75	Brown	1987
Sato, Ryuzo	Prof	998-0757	rsato	CO	PHD	62	J Hopkins	1985
C. V. Starr Professor of Economics								

Name	Rank	Phone	Email	Fields	Degree	Yr	School	Since
Smith, George	Prof	998-0860	gsmith	N	PHD	76	Harvard	1988
Sylla, Richard	Prof	998-0869	rsylla	DN	PHD	69	Harvard	1990
Henry Kaufman Professor of the History of Financial Institutions & Markets								
Wachtel, Paul A	Prof	998-0874	pwachtel	EG	PHD	71	Rochester	1972
Research Professor								
Walter, Ingo	Prof	998-0707	iwalter	FG	PHD	66	NYU	1970
Charles Simon Professor of Applied Financial Economics								
White, Lawrence	Prof	998-0880	lwhite	DGKL	PHD	69	Harvard	1976
Arthur E. Imperitore Professor of Economics								
Campa, Jose	Assoc	998-0429	jcampa	DF	PHD	91	Harvard	1991
Roubini, Nouriel	Assoc	998-0886	nroubini	EF	PHD	88	Harvard	1995
Lopomo, Giuseppe	Asst	998-0859	glopomo	CD	PHD	94	Stanford	1994

New York University — New York, NY 10012 (212) 998-8900 — nyu.edu
Department of Economics — Faculty Arts & Sciences Fax=995-4186 — Emily Rizzo

Name	Rank	Phone	Email	Fields	Degree	Yr	School	Since
Schotter, Andrew	C-Pr	998-8909	schotter	D	PHD	73	NYU	1975
Baumol, William J.	Prof	998-8943	baumolw	D	PHD	49	London	1971
Benabou, Roland Jean-Marc	Prof	998-8939	benabou	D	PHD	86	MIT	1994
Benhabib, Jess	Prof	998-8971	benhabib	EO	PHD	76	Columbia	1980
Caplin, Andrew	Prof	99808950	caplina	D	PHD	83	Yale	1995
Fernandez, Raquel	Prof	998-8908	fernande	F	PHD	87	Columbia	1995
Flinn, Christopher	Prof	998-8909	flinnc	J	PHD	84	Chicago	1987
Frydman, Roman	Prof	998-8967	frydman	E	PHD	78	Columbia	1978
Gale, Douglas	Prof	998-8944	galed	D	PHD	75	Cambridge	1996
Gately, Dermot	Prof	998-8955	gatelyd	Q	PHD	73	Princeton	1973
Gertler, Mark	Prof	998-8931	gertlerm	D	PHD	78	Stanford	1990
Jovanovic, Boyan	Prof	998-8953	jovanovi	L	PHD	78	Chicago	1983
Keane, Michael P.	Prof	998-8992	keanem	D	PHD	90	Brown	1998
Kirzner, Israel M.	Prof	998-8914		B	PHD	57	NYU	1957
Nadiri, M. Ishaq	Prof	998-8968	nadirii	O	PHD	65	Berkeley	1971
Nyarko, Yaw	Prof	998-8928	nyarkoy	D	PHD	86	Cornell	1992
Ordover, Janusz A.	Prof	998-8956	ordoverj	G	PHD	73	Columbia	1982
Ramsey, James B.	Prof	998-8947	ramseyj	C	PHD	68	Wisconsin	1976
Ray, Debraj	Prof	998-8900		D	PHD	83	Cornell	1999
Wilson, Charles A.	Prof	998-8954	wilsonc	D	PHD	76	Rochester	1983
Wolff, Edward N.	Prof	998-8917	wolffe	J	PHD	74	Yale	1974
Benoit, Jean-Pierre	Assoc	998-8934	benoitj	D	PHD	83	Stanford	1989
Gali, Jordi	Assoc	998-8926	galij	E	PHD	89	MIT	1994
Prager, Jonas	Assoc	998-8911	pragerj	G	PHD	64	Columbia	1962
Rizzo, Mario J.	Assoc	998-8932	rizzom	K	PHD	77	Chicago	1979
Velasco, Andres	Assoc	998-8958	velasco	F	PHD	88	Columbia	1989
Bisin, Alberto	Asst	998-8916	bisina	D	PHD	93	Chicago	1997
Cummins, Jason	Asst	998-8938	cummins	H	PHD	95	Columbia	1995
Miravete, Eugenio	Asst	998-8904	miravete	L	PHD	96	Nrthwstrn	1998
Ok, Efe	Asst	998-8920	okefe	H	PHD	95	Cornell	1995
Topa, Giorgio	Asst	998-8957	topag	C	PHD	96	Chicago	1996

New York Institute of Tech — New York, NY 11568-8000 (516) 686-7754 — student.nyit.edu
Department of Economics — School of Management Fax=484-8328 — Trudy Waser
261- exchange have 212 area code

Name	Rank	Phone	Email	Fields	Degree	Yr	School	Since
Spender, J. C.	Dean	686-7423		Mgt	PHD	80	Manchest	1996
Chandrasekar, Krishnamurti	Prof	261-1602			PHD	69	New Sch	1969
Lawrence, William	Prof	261-1706			PHD	75	NYU	1971
Schwartz, Carol H.	Prof	686-7739			PHD	63	Columbia	1987
Kutasovic, Paul R.	Assoc	686-7709			PHD	83	Rutgers	1988
Afxentiou, Diamando	Asst	348-3065	afxentiou:jl		PHD	90	W Virginia	1990

Niagara University — Niagara Univ, NY 14109 (716) 286-8160 — eagle.niagara.edu
Dept of Commerce-Economics — Col of Business Admin Fax=286-8206

Name	Rank	Phone	Email	Fields	Degree	Yr	School	Since
Miller, Keith T.	Dean	286-8050	ktm	Mgt	PHD	83	Arizona	1994
Scherer, Philip M.	C-Pr	286-8165	pscherer		PHD	72	Missouri	1980
Lee, Tenpao	Prof	286-8177	jhn		PHD	84	Iowa St	1987
Neimanis, George J.	Prof	286-8169	genne		MA	65	NYU	1970
Warren, Stanton A.	Prof	286-8173	warren		PHD	73	SUNY-Buf	1981
Peek, William A.	Assoc	286-8171	wap		PHD	85	Syracuse	1980
Praetzel, Gary D.	Assoc	286-8182	gdp		PHD	80	SUNY-Buf	1981

Nicholls State University — Thibodaux, LA 70310 (504) 448-4232 — nich-nsunet.nich.edu
Dept of Economics & Finance — Col of Business Admin Fax=448-4922 — Bobbie Taylor

Name	Rank	Phone	Email	Fields	Degree	Yr	School	Since
Gros, Ridley J. Jr.	Dean	448-4170	ba-rjg		PHD	71	LSU	1971
McManis, Bruce L.	H-Pr	448-4188	ecfi-blm	G	PHD	81	LSU	1978
Boyet, Wayne E.	Prof	448-4231	ecfi-web	G	PHD	65	N Car St	1985
Chotigeat, Tosporn	Prof	448-4189	ecfi-tc	FO	PHD	78	S Illinois	1988
Coats, R. Morris	Prof	448-4237	ecfi-rmc	HIRQ	PHD	83	Va Tech	1985
Field, William P. Jr.	Prof	448-4193	ecfi-wpf	E	PHD	71	N Carol	1973
Kooros, Syrous	Prof	448-4407	ecfi-skk	EFOC	PHD	80	Rensselaer	1991
Stanley, Thomas	Prof	448-4194	ecfi-tos	FG	PHD	82	Nebraska	1988
Lejaunie, John	Assoc	448-4210	ecfi-jpl	FG	PHD	92	N Orleans	1991

Nichols College	Dudley, MA	01571-5000	(508) 213-2256					nichols.edu
Department of Economics	College of Business Adm	Fax=213-2225						
Reinhardt, Alan J.	Dean	213-2201			PHD	83	IUP	9-98
Corkum, Keith H.	C-Pr	213-2256			PHD	76	Lehigh	1972
Nordstrom, Louise J.	Prof	213-2259		ADFH	PHD	71	Clark	9-74

Norfolk State University	Norfolk, VA	23504-2954	(757) 683-8955					vger.nsu.edu
Entrepreneurial Studies	Sch of Bus & Entpre	Fax=683-9413						Chelsea Hall
Jones, Dorothy	Dean	683-8870	djones		PHD	93	Ohio St	1993
Achampong, Francis	H	683-8051	f_achampong	Mgt	PHD	85	Geotown	1985
Bowen, Freddie R. Jr.	C-As	623-8790	f.bowen	CHA	MA	70	Wash U	1970
Shiau, Liang-rong	Prof	683-9581	lshiau	CAR'	PHD	72	S Miss	1972

University of North Alabama	Florence, AL	35632-0001	(256)					unanov.edu
Dept of Economics & Finance	School of Business	Fax=765-4811						Debbie Westmoreland
Did Not Respond--1997-98 Listing								
Butler, Michael W.	Dean	765-4261			PHD	74	Arkansas	1973
Morris, Barry K.	C-Pr	760-4411			PHD	74	Arkansas	1974
Copeland, Joe B.	Prof	760-4270			PHD	74	Arkansas	1983
Free, Veronica	Prof	760-4675			PHD	70	Miss St	1984
Rychtanek, Leonard E.	Prof	760-4301			PHD	79	Fla St	1983
Gordon, Bruce	Assoc	760-4415			PHD	93	North Tx	1986
Couch, Jim	Asst	760-4412			MAS	85	Al-Huntsv	1991
VanRensselaer	Asst	760-4417			ABD		Miss St	1991
Thomas, Regina	Inst	760-4371			MA	92	Alabama	1992

North Carolina at Asheville	Asheville, NC	28804-3299	(828) 251-6550					unca.edu
Economics Faculty	Department of Economics	Fax=251-6614						Ms. Kim Moore
email @1=bulldog.unca.edu								
Larson, Bruce D.	C-Pr	251-6562	blarson	ABCD	PHD	83	N Carol	1983
Browning, Shirley C.	Prof	251-6549	sbrowning	AEPQ	PHD	71	Conn	1970
Nickless, Pamela J.	Prof	251-6563	nickless	AJN	PHD	76	Purdue	1983
Sulock, Joseph M.	Prof	251-6568	jsulock	AGH	PHD	76	Virginia	1975
Bell, Christopher Ross	Assoc	251-6552	bell	AGHL	PHD	87	Penn	1989
Konz, Jeffery M.	Asst	251-6570	jkonz	BEFO	PHD	94	N Carol	1996
Mathews, Leah Greden	Asst	251-6561	lmathews@1	HDQO	PHD	97	Minnesota	1997
Bumgarner, Sarah J.	Lect	251-6569	sbumgarner	A	MBA	82	Appalach	1990

University of North Carolina	Chapel Hill, NC	27599-3305	(919) 966-2383					unc.edu
Div Soc Sci-Dept Economics	Col of Arts & Sciences	Fax=966-4986						Mrs. Pago LoRe'
email @1=mail.unc.edu								
Guilkey, David K.	C-Pr	843-9452	david_guilkey	C	PHD	73	N Carol	1983
Akin, John S.	Prof	966-5334	john_akin	IGH	PHD	71	Michigan	1973
Benavie, Arthur	Prof	966-5326		AE	PHD	63	Michigan	1967
Biglaiser, Gary	Prof	966-4884	gbiglais@1	EL	PHD	88	Berkeley	1988
Black, Stanley W.	Prof	966-5926	sblack@1	F	PHD	65	Yale	1983
Lurcy Professor								
Blau, David M.	Prof	966-3962	david_blau	J	PHD	80	Wisconsin	1992
Norman L. Johnson Professor								
Conway, Patrick	Prof	966-5376	patrick_conway	F	PHD	84	Princeton	1983
Darity, William A. Jr.	Prof	966-5392	sandy_darity	E	PHD	78	MIT	1983
Boshamer Professor								
Field, Alfred J. Jr.	Prof	843-9451	afield@1	F	PHD	67	Iowa St	1967
Associate Chairperson; Director, Undergraduate Studies								
Friedman, James W.	Prof	966-3669	friedman@1	DL	PHD	63	Yale	1985
Kenan Professor								
Froyen, Richard T.	Prof	966-5375	froyen@1	E	PHD	72	Maryland	1971
Gallant, A. Ronald	Prof	966-5338	ron_gallant	C	PHD	71	Iowa St	1993
Latane' Professor								
Ingram, James C.	Emer		jcingram@1		PHD	52	Cornell	1952
McFarland, David	Prof	966-5342		BDL	PHD	63	Vanderbilt	1964
Mezzetti, Claudio	Prof	966-5377	mezzetti@1	D	PHD	88	Oxford	1990
Mroz, Thomas A.	Prof	966-5395	tom_mroz	J	PHD	84	Stanford	1989
Murphy, James L.	Prof	966-5346	jlmurphy@1	C	PHD	64	Purdue	1964
Dean, UNC Summer School								
Pfouts, William	Emer				PHD	52	N Carol	1947
Rosefielde, Steven	Prof	966-5371	stevern@1	P	PHD	72	Harvard	1970
Salemi, Michael K.	Prof	966-5391	michael_salemi	E	PHD	76	Minnesota	1976
Zachary Smith Professor								
Stewart, John F.	Prof	966-5345	jstewar@1	L	PHD	76	Wisconsin	1975
Tarascio, Vincent J.	Prof	966-5374	vtarasci@1	N	PHD	66	Rice	1964
Tauchen, Helen	Prof	966-5394	tauchen@1	D	PHD	77	Minnesota	1977
Orsagh, Thomas	Emer				PHD	64	Penn	1965
Parke, William	Assoc	843-9453	parke@1	C	PHD	80	Yale	1988
Director of Graduate Studies								
Rhode, Paul	Assoc	843-9842	prhode@1	N	PHD	90	Stanford	1990

Turchi, Boone A.	Assoc	966-5348	turchi@1	AT	PHD	73	Michigan	1971
Vanderklaauw, H. Wilbert	Assoc	966-2383	vanderkl	J	PHD	92	Brown	1999
Wilde, James A.	Assoc	966-5328	jwilde@1	GH	PHD	68	Princeton	1965
Anderson, Evan	Asst	966-4886	ewanders@1	E	PHD	98	Chicago	1998
Gilleskie, Donna	Asst	966-5372	donna_gilleskie	IJ	PHD	94	Minnesota	1994
Kovalenkov, Alexander	Asst	966-5327	akovalen@1	D	PHD	98	Automoma	1998
Strumpf, Koleman	Asst	966-4485	cigar	GH	PHD	95	MIT	1995
Wu, Xiaodong	Asst	966-2383			PHD	99	Princeton	1999
Willis, Rachel A.	Adj	966-3710	rawillis@1	J	PHD	90	Nrthwstrn	1982

North Carolina at Charlotte Charlotte, NC 28223-0001 (704) 547-2185 uncc.edu
Department of Economics Col of Business Admin Fax=510-6442 Jackie Harper, Sabra Reece

Lilly, Claude C. III	Dean	547-2165		Insu	PHD	73	Geo St	8-97
Schwarz, Peter M.	C-Pr	547-4126			PHD	80	Ohio St	1978
Amato, Louis	Prof	547-4130			PHD	80	S Carol	1980
Connaughton, John E.	Prof	547-4134			PHD	81	Northeas	1978
Director, UNC-Charlotte Economic "Forecast"								
Davis, W. Young Jr.	Prof	547-2187			PHD	70	Georgia	1970
Gandar, John Maxim	Prof	547-4133			PHD	82	Missouri	1982
Madsen, Ron	Prof	547-4127						
Neel, Richard E.	Prof	547-4122			PHD	60	Ohio St	1969
Zuber, Richard A.	Prof	547-4129			PHD	78	Kentucky	1978
Lin, Hwan-Chyang	Assoc	547-3796			PHD	90	Illinois	1993
Liner, Gaines Howard	Assoc	547-4128			PHD	71	Clemson	1971
McGregor, Rob R.	Assoc	547-4121			PHD	91	S Carol	1991
Russo, Benjamin	Assoc	547-4137			PHD	85	Iowa	1984
Tseng, Hui-Kuan	Assoc	547-4123			PHD	88	Illinois	1988
Tucker, Irvin B. III	Assoc	547-4136			PHD	82	S Carol	1981
Dole, Carol	Asst	547-4171			PHD	92	Florida	1993
Miller, Ellen M.	Asst	547-4132			PHD	83	Florida	1982
Troyer, Jennifer	Asst	547-2185			PHD	99	Florida	1999

North Carolina at Greensboro Greensboro, NC 27402-6165 (336) 334-5463 uncg.edu
Department of Economics Bryan Sch of Bus & Econ Fax=334-4089 Ms. Judy Tuttle

Weeks, James K.	Dean	334-5338	jim_weeks	Mgt	PHD	74	S Carol	1976
Allen, Stuart D.	H-Pr	334-3166	stuart_allen	E	PHD	77	Virginia	1976
Caldwell, Bruce J.	Prof	334-4865	bruce_caldwell	B	PHD	79	N Carol	1978
Link, Albert N.	Prof	334-5146	al_link	O	PHD	76	Tulane	1982
Neufeld, John L.	Prof	334-4869	john_neufeld	ND	PHD	75	Michigan	1974
Ruhm, Christopher J.	Prof	334-5148	c_ruhm	JI	PHD	84	Berkeley	1991
Seaks, Terry G.	Emer	228-9048	tgseaks	C	PHD	72	Duke	1972
Layson, Steve	Assoc	334-4868	layson	D	PHD	83	Chicago	1978
Leyden, Dennis P.	Assoc	334-3904	leyden	H	PHD	87	Car Mellon	1984
McCrickard, Donald L.	Assoc	334-5338	don_mccrickard	EF	PHD	76	N Carol	1975
Snowden, Kenneth A.	Assoc	334-4870	snowden	NG	PHD	83	Wisconsin	1983
Bearse, Peter	Asst		pmbearse	CH	PHD	95	Virginia	1998
Freeman, James	VAsst		jafreem2	J	PHD	98	Fla St	1998
Rosenbaum, Dan	Asst		dtrosenb	JI	PHD	98	Nrthwstrn	1998
Brod, Andrew C.	Inst	334-4867	andrew_brod	Q	PHD	92	Minnesota	1989

North Carolina at Wilmington Wilmington, NC 28403-3297 (910) 395-3510 ecn.uncwil.edu
Dept of Economics & Finance Cameron Sch of Bus Adm Fax=395-3815

Rockness, Howard O.	Dean	395-3501	csba@notech	Atg	PHD	73	U Wash	8-93
Lawson, Luther Drew	C-Pr		lawsonl	AJL	PHD	81	Tennessee	
Farrell, Claude H. III	Prof	395-3510	farrell	EGR	PHD	74	N Car St	
Hall, William Woodward Jr.	Prof		hallw	QR	PHD	72	Clemson	
Director, Center for Business & Economics Services								
Hill, Roger Post	Prof	395-3510	hillr	G	PHD	68	Mich St	
Howell, Kristen K.	Assoc		howellk	F	PHD	89	Kentucky	
Robinson, Ned Stephen	Assoc		robinsonn	A	PHD	73	Oklahoma	
Wadman, William Morgan	Assoc		wadmanw	CDH	PHD	76	Claremont	
Burrus, Robert T.	Asst		busserr	D	PHD	97	Virginia	
Dumas, Christopher	Asst		dumusc	Q	PHD	97	Berkeley	
Schuhmann, Peter	Asst		schuhp	Q	PHD	96	N Car St	

U North Carolina at Pembroke Pembroke, NC 28372-1510 (910) 521-6214 sassette.uncp.edu
Economics Faculty School of Business Fax=521-6162 Rena Hill

Clow, Kenneth E.	C-Pr	521-6214		Mktg	PHD	92	Arkansas	1998
Frederick, James R.	Asst	521-6592			PHD	83	Wayne St	1988

North Carolina A&T State Un Greensboro, NC 27411 (336) 334-7746 ncat.edu
Department of Economics Sch of Business & Econ Fax=334-7093 Ms. Cathy Dalton
phone 334-7744

Craig, Quiester	Dean	334-7632		Atg	PHD	72	Missouri	8-72
Simmons, Michael	C-As	Ext 2000	simmonsm		PHD	79	Wash St	

Name	Rank	Phone	Email	Field	Degree	Yr	School	Hired
Benjamin, Julian	Prof	Ext 2020			PHD	77	SUNY-Buf	
Coley, Basil G.	Prof	334-7744			PHD	71	Illinois	1966
Khan, Anwar S.	Prof	Ext 2007			PHD	72	Wisconsin	
Obeng, Kofi	Prof	Ext 2018			PHD	81	Penn	1982
UPS Chair								
Addus, Abdussalam A.	Assoc	Ext 2009			PHD	82	Penn St	1980
Chen, David Y.	Assoc	Ext 2014			PHD	71	Wisconsin	
Jeong, Dong K.	Assoc	Ext 2013			PHD	74	Wayne St	
King, Vereda J.	Assoc	Ext 2008			PHD	84	Duke	
Morse, Lawrence B.	Assoc	Ext 2003			PHD	68	Minnesota	1976
Agesa, Jackie	Asst	Ext 2016			PHD	96	Wi-Milwa	1996
Agesa, Richard	Asst	Ext 6003			PHD	96	Wi-Milwa	1996
Granger, Maury	Asst	Ext 2015			PHD	95	Kentucky	1993
Price, Gregory N.	Asst	Ext 2011	price		PHD	93	Wi-Milwa	
Sakano, Ryoichi	Asst	Ext 2015			PHD	90	Alabama	1992
Simkins, Scott P.	Asst	Ext 2001	simkinss		PHD	88	Iowa	

North Carolina Central Univ — Durham, NC 27707 (919) 560-6127 — nccu1.acc.nccu.edu
Department of Economic — School of Business Fax=560-6163

Name	Rank	Phone	Email	Field	Degree	Yr	School	Hired
Williams, H. James	Dean	560-6175		Atg	PHD	82	Georgia	1999
Balfour, B. Burton	C-Ac	560-6127	bbb		PHD	74	N Car St	1973
Amoateng, Kofi	Assoc	530-7384			PHD	86	Tx-Austin	1990
Dutton, Marilyn	Asst	530-7390			PHD	89	Duke	1991
Gokcekus, Omer	Asst	530-7393			PHD	95	Duke	1996
Hakeem, Salih	Asst	560-6131			PHD	87	N Car St	1988
Maafo, E. Victor	Asst	530-7388			MA	73	Duke	1966

North Carolina State Univ — Raleigh, NC 27695-8110 (919) 515-3274 — ncsu.edu
Department of Economics — College of Management Fax=515-7873 — Carolyn Smith

Name	Rank	Phone	Email	Field	Degree	Yr	School	Hired
Margolis, Stephen E.	H-Pr	515-3274	steve_margolis	LKD	PHD	78	UCLA	1982
Allen, Steven G.	Prof	515-6941	steve_allen	JD	PHD	78	Harvard	1978
Clark, Robert	Prof	515-4568	robert_clark	JD	PHD	74	Duke	1975
Erickson, Edward W.	Prof	515-3201	ed_erickson	LQD	PHD	86	Vanderbilt	1965
Fearn, Robert M.	Emer	515-4616	fearn	JDP	PHD	68	Chicago	1965
Fisher, Douglas	Prof	515-2887	doug_fisher	EN	PHD	65	Chicago	1977
Flath, David	Prof	515-2472	david_flath	LDP	PHD	76	UCLA	1976
Grennes, Thomas	Prof	515-3274	tom_grennes	FD	MA	65	Wisconsin	1968
Hall, Alastair R.	Prof	515-2887	alastair_hall	C	PHD	85	Warwick	1985
Holthausen, Duncan M. Jr.	Prof	515-7680	duncan_holtha+	DC	PHD	76	Nrthwstrn	1974
Hyman, David Neil	Prof	515-2472	hyman_david	HA	PHD	69	Princeton	1969
Knoeber, Charles R.	Prof	515-7680	charles_knoeber	LKDG	PHD	76	UCLA	1976
Palmquist, Raymond B.	Prof	515-3274	palmquist	QDR	PHD	78	U Wash	1979
Pearce, Douglas K.	Prof	515-2472	doug_pearce	EG	PHD	74	Wisconsin	1985
Seater, John J.	Prof	515-2472	john_seater	EH	PHD	75	Brown	1981
Thurman, Walter N.	Prof	515-4545	wally_thurman	QCD	PHD	84	Chicago	1984
Wessels, Walter J.	Prof	515-2472	walt_wessels	JD	PHD	76	Chicago	1975
Ball, David Stafford	Assoc	515-3274	david_bell	FND	PHD	67	N Carol	1966
Craig, Lee A.	Assoc	515-2887	lee_craig	NJD	PHD	89	Indiana	1989
Headen, Alvin E.	Assoc	515-2887	al_headen	IJD	PHD	81	MIT	1986
Lapp, John S.	Assoc	515-7680	john_lapp	EGF	PHD	74	Princeton	1974
McElroy, Michael B.	Assoc	515-7680	mike_mcelroy	E	PHD	70	Nrthwstrn	1970
Newmark, Craig M.	Assoc	515-7680	craig_newmark	LD	PHD	84	UCLA	1984
Levy, Armando	Asst	515-3274	armando	C	PHD	96	Berkeley	1996
Tsoulouhas, Theofanis	Asst	515-7680	fanis_tsoulouhas	CD	PHD	93	Illinois	1993

North Central College — Naperville, IL 60566-7063 (630) 637-5240 — noctrt.edu
Economic Department — Div Economic & Bus Adm Fax=637-5121
Homepage: http://172.16.50.2/intrhome.htm

Name	Rank	Phone	Email	Field	Degree	Yr	School	Hired
Love, Thomas M.	C-Pr	637-5245	tml	F	PHD	67	Wisconsin	1972
Barger, Peter S.	Assoc	637-5246	psb	G	PHD	89	Illinois	1989
Bogart, Marti S.	Assoc	637-5243	msb	J	PHD	86	Purdue	1982
Whitaker, Andrew L.	Assoc	637-5241	alw	G	PHD	88	Illinois	1988
Anstine, Diane	Asst	637-5242	dianstin	D	PHD	97	Kentucky	1997
Hotopp, Susan	Asst	637-5244	sukotopp	A	PHD	89	Illinois	1991

University of North Dakota — Grand Forks, ND 58202-8369 (701) 777-2637 — badlands.nodak.edu
Div of Econ & Public Affairs — Col of Bus & Pub Admin Fax=777-5099 — Ruth Holweger
email @1=prairie.nodak.edu @2=plains.nodak.edu @3=mail.und.nodak.edu

Name	Rank	Phone	Email	Field	Degree	Yr	School	Hired
Elbert, Dennis J.	Dean	777-2135	dennis_elbert@3	Mktg	PHD	76	Missouri	8-80
Ramsett, David E.	C-Pr	777-3349	dramsett	AHQ	PHD	68	Oklahoma	1968
Bagheri, Fatholla	Prof	777-3350	bagheri@1	AJ	PHD	78	Penn	1990
Blackwell, J. Lloyd III	Prof	777-3357	jblackwe@1	C	PHD	73	Geo St	1980
Korbach, Robert J.	Prof	777-3356	korbach	AGH	PHD	73	Maryland	1970
O'Neill, Patrick B.	Assoc	777-3358	poneill@1	ADL	PHD	87	Boston C	1987
Stradley, Scot A.	Assoc	777-3353	stradley@1	ABP	PHD	77	Utah	1970
Biederman, Daniel K.	Asst	777-3347	biederma@2	CGI	PHD	87	Kansas	1987
Clifford, Maryanne	Asst	777-3351		F	MA	96	Kentucky	1998

North Dakota State Univ	Fargo, ND	58105-5075	(701) 231-8567				badlands.nodak.edu	
Department of Economics	Col Humanities & Soc Sc	Fax=231-1047					Jill Blazek, Adm Asst	
Riley, Thomas	Dean	231-7857		Anth	PHD		Hawaii	1996
Lindgren, Jon G.	C-Ac	231-8809	jlindgre	ADH	PHD	68	Missouri	1968
Dobitz, Clifford P.	Prof	231-8653	dobitz	ABDL	PHD	71	Colo St	1970
Gerdes, William D.	Prof	231-8813	gerdes	CEG	PHD	78	Nebraska	1978
Herren, R. Stanley	Prof	231-7698	herren	ABEJ	PHD	75	Duke	1985
O'Relly, Z. Edward	Prof	231-8819	orelley	AFOP	PHD	72	Tennessee	1969

University of North Florida	Jacksonville, FL	32224-2645	(904) 646-2640				unf.edu	
Department of Economics	Col of Business Admin	Fax=646-2594						
Traynham, Earle C. Jr.	Dean	646-2590	traynham		PHD	73	S Carol	1973
Perry, Joseph M.	C-Pr	646-2640	jperry	NOR	PHD	66	Nrthwstrn	1971
Borg, Mary O.	Prof	646-2640	mborg	HT	PHD	85	N Carol	1984
Director of University Scholar Programs								
Mason, Paul M.	Prof	646-2641	pmason	HE	PHD	84	Tx-Austin	1985
Woods, Louis A.	Prof	646-2641		OQR	PHD	72	N Carol	1972
Shapiro, Stephen L.	Assoc	646-2641	sshapiro	AH	PHD	72	S Carol	1972
Director, Center for Economic Education								
Steagall, Jeffrey W.	Assoc	646-260j	steagal	FAC	PHD	90	Wisconsin	1990
Stranahan, Harriett	Assoc	646-2641	hstranah	JGD	PHD	95	Wash	1994
Cobb, Sharon	Asst	620-2640	scobb	AC	PHD	98	Florida	1998
Lynch, Allen	Asst	620-2640	alynch	FAC	PHD	99	Fla St	1999

North Georgia Col & St Univ	Dahlonega, GA	30597	(706) 864-1610				nugget.ngc.peachnet.edu	
Economic Faculty	Dept of Business Admin	Fax=864-1668					Jan Morris	
DeBerry, Thomas W.	H-Ac$	864-1610	tdeberry	A	PHD	94	Tx Tech	1995
Grant, Clayton	Prof	864-1610	cgrant	K	PHD	71	Clemson	1986
Dillard Munford Professor of Business								
Campbell, Noel	Asst	864-1610	ndcampbell	H	PHD	97	GeoMason	1998

University of North Texas	Denton, TX	76203-5457	(940) 565-2573				econ.unt.edu	
Department of Economics	Col of Arts & Sciences	Fax=565-4426					Nancy L. Boyd, Adm Asst	
Homepage: http://www.econ.unt.edu								
Burggrew, Warren	Dean							
Cobb, Steven Lee	C-Ac	565-2184	cobb	AFOP	PHD	87	N Carol	1987
Abernathy, Lewis M.	Prof	565-4322	lewis	J	PHD	67	Oklahoma	1963
Director, Labor & Industrial Relations Institute								
Koelln, Kenneth	Assoc	565-4542	koelln	LI	PHD	91	Florida	1991
Molina, David Jude	Assoc	565-4543	judas	BCN	PHD	83	Tx A&M	1985
Nieswiadomy, Michael L.	Assoc	565-2244	mike	HRIQ	PHD	83	Tx A&M	1985
Jewell, R. Todd	Asst	565-3337	tjewell	HJ	PHD	92	Ca-SnBarb	1996
McPherson, Michael	Asst	565-2270	michael	FO	PHD	92	Mich St	1992
Redfearn, Michael	Asst	565-2220	redfearn	EG	PHD	92	Mich St	1992
Rous, Jeffrey	Asst	565-4545	jrous	HI	PHD	96	N Carol	1996
Tieslau, Margie	Asst	565-3442	tieslau	EC	PHD	92	Mich St	1992
Werger, Jennie	Asst	565-4544	jennie	HJ	PHD	96	N Carol	1996
Battaglia, Kari L.	Lect	565-4541	battagli	A	MA		North Tx	1987
Ellis, Harry Jr.	Lect	565-2246	ellis	A	MA		Mich St	1990
Lynch, Karla	Lect	565-3186	karla	A	MS		North Tx	1993

Northeast Louisiana Univ	Monroe, LA	71209-0130	(318) 342-1150				alpha.nlu.edu	
Dept of Economics & Finance	College of Business Adm	Fax=342-1209					Juanita Hyatt	
Short, Larry E.	Dean	342-1100	dbashort	Mgt	DBA	71	Colorado	1994
Nelson, Paul S.	H-Ac	342-1150	ecnelson	DL	PHD	85	Tx A&M	1989
Moser, Ernest R.	Prof	342-1100	ecmoser	BM	PHD	73	Tx A&M	1972
Associate Dean								
Eisenstadt, Robert C.	Assoc	342-1162	eceisenstadt	JI	PHD	91	Geo St	
Kogut, Carl A.	Assoc	342-1154	eckogut	DLJ	PHD	84	Tx A&M	1992
Scott, John L.	Assoc	342-1160	ecscott	DC	PHD	90	S Carol	1989
Futayyeh, Mohamed-Amin	Asst	342-1163	ecfutayyeh		PHD	70	Oklahoma	
Rapp, Tommy A.	Asst	342-1159	ecrapp	EF	PHD	97	S Illinois	1997
Lee, Tommy R.	Inst	342-1169	eclee		MBA		NE La	

Northeastern University	Boston, MA	02115	(617) 373-2882				neu.edu	
Department of Economics	Col of Arts & Sciences	Fax=373-3640						
email @1=lynx.neu.edu @2=nuhub.neu.edu								
Morrison, Steven A.	C-Pr$	373-3646	sam1		PHD	79	Berkeley	1982
Alam, M. Shahid	Prof	373-2849	salam@1		PHD	79	W Ontario	1988
Fraumeni, Barbara M.	Prof	373-2252			PHD	80	Boston C	1982
Hellman, Daryl A.	Prof	373-7517	dhellman@2		PHD	70	Rutgers	1972
Graduate Coordinator								
Kim, Sungwoo	Prof	373-2893	kim		PHD	57	Berkeley	1972
Schachter, Gustav	Prof	373-2886	gschacte@1		PHD	62	NYU	1965
Sum, Andrew M.	Prof	373-2242			MA	71	MIT	1971

Name	Rank	Phone	E-mail	Area	Degree	Yr	School	Year
Alper, Neil O.	Assoc	373-2839	alper		PHD	77	Pittsburgh	1979
Brookins, Oscar T.	Assoc	373-2251	otbrookins@2		PHD	76	SUNY-Buf	1983
Dadkhah, Kamran N.	Assoc	373-2297	kdadkhah@1		PHD	75	Indiana	1981
Dyer, Alan W.	Assoc	373-2610	dyer		PHD	82	Maryland	1983
Undergraduate Coordinator								
Wassall, Gregory H.	Assoc	373-2196	wassall		PHD	78	Rutgers	1979

Northeastern Illinois Univ Chicago, IL 60625-4699 (773) 794-2638 neiu.edu
Department of Economics Col of Arts & Sciences Fax=794-2708 Martha Kastigar
phone 583-4050

Name	Rank	Phone	E-mail	Area	Degree	Yr	School	Year
Unumb, David F.	Dean$	583-4050			PHD		Loyola	
Easton, Robert F.	C-As	794-2621			MA		Nrthwstrn	
Freiberg, Lewis	Prof	794-2581			PHD	72	Kentucky	1982
Stuart, Edward F.	Prof	794-2574			PHD	78	Oklahoma	1986
Bergan, Daniel J.	Assoc	794-2577			PHD	85	Tx Tech	
Brewton, Audie R.	Assoc	794-2552			PHD	80	Utah	1984
Stehman, Diane	Assoc	794-2579			PHD	78	Il-Chicago	1978
Collum, Thomas E.	Asst	794-2573			MA	75	Nrthwstrn	1977
Rothstein, Sheldon H.	Asst	794-2578			MA		Chicago	

Northeastern State Univ Tahlequah, OK 74464-2399 (918) 458-2091 cherokee.nsuok.edu
Dept of Economics & Mgt Col of Business & Indus Fax=458-2337 Toni Wofford

Name	Rank	Phone	E-mail	Area	Degree	Yr	School	Year
Williams, Earl R.	Dean	458-2091	williame	DMN	PHD	68	Tennessee	1968
Hileman, A. Eugene	C-Pr	456-5511	hileman	AGM	PHD	71	Tennessee	1988
Greubel, Robert T.	Prof		greubel	AEF	PHD	72	Arkansas	1965
Wier, Thomas	Asst	456-5511	weir	RCB	PHD	89	Tennessee	1998

Northern Arizona University Flagstaff, AZ 86011-5066 (520) 523-3657 nau.edu
Dept of Business Admin-Econ Col of Business Admin Fax=523-7331 Sandra Hutchinson

Name	Rank	Phone	E-mail	Area	Degree	Yr	School	Year
Meyers, Patricia	Dean	523-3657		Mktg	PHD	83	Syracuse	8-97
Brown, Douglas	C-Pr	523-7394	douglas.brown	OP	PHD	85	Colo St	1985
Gunderson, Ronald J.	Prof	523-7358	ronald.gunderson	DR	PHD	77	Nebraska	1977
Hildred, William M.	Prof	523-7365	bill.hildred	HA	PHD	64	Colo St	1988
Jerrell, Max E.	Prof	523-7405	max.jerrell	EC	PHD	84	Ariz St	1981
Pinto, James V.	Prof	523-7356	jim.pinto	DC	PHD	75	Oklahoma	1981
Walka, Joseph J.	Prof	523-7345	joseph.walka	HI	PHD	69	Harvard	1986
Campione, Wendy A.	Assoc	523-7360	wendy.campione	HJ	PHD	84	Illinois	1981
Duncan, Wallace H.	Assoc	523-7366	wallace.duncan	EG	PHD	76	Wyoming	1978
Smith, Dean G.	Assoc	523-7396	dean.smith	RC	PHD	85	Tx A&M	1989
Eastwood, John D.	Lect	523-7353	john.eastwood	CD	MS	80	Wyoming	1990

Univ of Northern Colorado Greeley, CO 80639 (970) 351-2709 bentley.univnorthco.edu
Department of Economics Col of Arts & Sciences Fax=351-1571 Linda Jack

Name	Rank	Phone	E-mail	Area	Degree	Yr	School	Year
Flake, Sandra	Dean	351-2707		Eng	PHD	74	Wisconsin	1997
McDaniel, Bruce A.	C-Ac	351-1163		OGMQ	PHD	79	Colo St	1992
Green, John W.	Prof	351-1558		CTQR	PHD	76	Penn	1985
Livingston, Marie L.	Prof	351-2739	mllivin	FHOQ	PHD	84	Colo St	1985
Kallon, Kelfala M.	Assoc	351-2134	kmkallo	EFHO	PHD	83	Virginia	1993
Aske, David	Asst	351-1564		AITR	PHD	92	Nebraska	1992
Graham, Patricia E.	Asst	351-1559		IJOQ	PHD	88	Colo St	1988

Northern Illinois Univ Dekalb, IL 60115-2854 (815) 753-1031 niu.edu
Department of Economics Col Liberal Arts & Sci Fax=752-1019 Ms. Connie Rumer

Name	Rank	Phone	E-mail	Area	Degree	Yr	School	Year
Kitterle, Frederick	Dean	753-1061						7-95
Scaperlanda, Anthony E.	C-Pr	753-6970	tonyscap	F	PHD	64	Tx-Austin	1964
Dalal, Ardeshir J.	Prof	753-6971	adalal	D	PHD	77	Iowa	1977
Gherity, James A.	Emer	753-6964	jgherity	B	PHD	58	Illinois	1964
Kim, Young Chin	Prof	753-6972	ykim	O	PHD	68	Columbia	1970
Kwon, Jene K.	Prof	753-6977	jkwon	E	PHD	68	Iowa	1968
La Tourette, John E.	Prof	753-9500		E	PHD	62	Rutgers	1979
President								
Levy, Lester S.	Emer	753-6982		N	PHD	56	Cornell	1964
Mallela, Parthasaradhi	Emer	753-6974		C	PHD	70	Rochester	1976
Mohabbat, Khan A.	Prof	753-6973	mohabbat	E	PHD	64	SUNY-Buf	1968
Nord, Steven	Prof	753-6976	sen	R	PHD	76	Illinois	1979
Assistant Chairperson								
Skeels, Jack W.	Emer	753-6981	jskeels	J	PHD	57	Wisconsin	1963
Williams, Martin	Prof	753-6960	mwilliams	R	PHD	76	SUNY-Bin	1976
Bechdolt, Burley V.	Emer	753-6959		C	PHD	70	S Calif	1970
Karlson, Stephen	Assoc	753-6980	skarlson1	D	PHD	80	Wisconsin	1986
Porter-Hudak, Susan	Assoc	753-6983	sphudak	C	PHD	82	Wisconsin	1982
Temple, Judy A.	Assoc	753-6962	jtemple	H	PHD	90	Mich St	1989
Wilcox-Gok, Virginia L.	Assoc	753-6957	vlw	J	PHD	84	Wash U	1994
Slotsve, George A.	Asst	753-6966	gslotsve	JD	PHD	89	Wisconsin	1996

University of Northern Iowa Cedar Falls, IA 50614-0129 (319) 273-2412 uni.edu
Department of Economics Col of Business Admin Fax=273-7509 Beverly Barber

Greer, Willis R. Jr.	Dean	273-6240	greer		PHD	71	Michigan	8-96
Abraham, Fred J	H-Pr	273-2412	abrahamf	AEHK	PHD	73	Oregon	1973
Anderson, B. Wylie	Prof	273-2951	andersonbw	AEGJ	PHD	73	Iowa	1966
Hakes, David R.	Prof	273-3597	hakes	BEFG	PHD	85	Iowa St	1992
Krieg, Randall G.	Prof	273-2126	krieg	JRL	PHD	87	Colorado	1987
McCormick, Kenneth J.	Prof	273-6051	mccormick	BEA	PHD	82	Iowa St	1982
Rives, Janet M.	Prof	273-6368	rives	ADJM	PHD	71	Duke	1984
Yousefi, Mahmood	Prof	273-6722	yousefi	GHP	PHD	74	Ca-SnBarb	1981
Strein, Charles T.	Assoc	273-2592	strein	DLMR	PHD	77	Illinois	1970
Uyar, Bulent	Assoc	273-6343	uyar	ACH	PHD	77	Pittsburgh	1991
Alam, M. Imam	Asst	273-7339	alam	CFO	PHD	95	Illinois	1996
Brown, Ken	Asst	273-2956	brownk	CR	PHD	94	Illinois	1994
Thorpe, Steven G.	Asst	273-2103	thorpe	HQ	PHD	95	Colorado	1996
Mardis, Barbara K.	Inst	273-3062	mardis	C	MBA	81	N Iowa	1981

Northern Kentucky Univ Highland Hght KY 41099-0503 (606) 572-6581 nku.edu
Economics & Fnce & Info Sys College of Business Fax=572-6177 Edith Hill
Did Not Respond--1997-98 Listing

Carrell, Michael R.	Dean	572-5165	carrellm	Mgt	DBA	76	Kentucky	7-98
Ramjee, Anju	C-Pr	572-6581		Fnce	PHD	87	Cincinnati	1988
Clayton, Gary E.	Prof	572-6542			PHD	74	Utah	1980
Giesbrecht, Martin G.	Prof	572-5153			PHD	58	Munich	1987
Cate, Thomas H.	Assoc	572-5799			PHD	79	Fla St	1975
Lang, Nancy A.	Assoc	572-5155			EDD	83	Georgia	1983
Director Center for Economic Education								
Noyd, Louis E.	Assoc	572-5160			PHD	73	Oregon	1972
Snyder, Richard S.	Asst	572-5651			PHD	76	Indiana	1978

Northern Michigan Univ Marquette, MI 49855 (906) 227-2220 nmu.edu
Department of Economics Liberal Studies Program Fax=227-2229 Alice McKinney
Did Not Respond Again--1995-96 Listing

Swaine, Howard R.	H-Pr	227-1214		AKDH	PHD	65	UCLA	1966
Aho, Arnold A.	Prof	227-1217		AJ	MA		Lehigh	1969
Carlson, David L.	Prof	227-1218		AEN	BA		N Mich	1961
Holmstrom, Thomas K.	Prof	227-1216		AEF	PHD	73	Okla St	1966
Zaki, Mokhlis Y.	Prof	227-1215		ACDO	PHD	69	Berkeley	1969

Northern State University Aberdeen, SD 57401-7198 (605) 626-2400 wolf.northern.edu
Dept of Business & Economics Sch of Business & Tech Fax=626-3022

Arnold, Clyde L.	Dean	626-2400	PHD	82	Oklahoma	1988
Trierweiler, John	C-Pr	626-2576	PHD	70	Nebraska	1985
Neumann, Hillar Jr.	Assoc	626-7719	PHD	86	Rutgers	1983
Chaudhrey, Mukesh	Asst	626-3001	PHD	94	Clev St	1995
Peterson, John	Asst	626-2434	PHD	97	Kansas	1992
Savitski, David	Asst	626-3002	PHD	97	UCLA	1997

Northwest Missouri St Univ Maryville, MO 64468-6001 (660) 562-1835 mail.nwmissouri.edu
Dept of Atg, Econ & Finance Col Prof & Applied Sci Fax=562-1750 Alisa Meyer

DeYoung, Ronald C.	Dean	562-1277	deyoung	BEd	EDD	71	N Illinois	1984
McLaughlin, Patrick	C-Ac	562-1291	jpat	K	JD	78	Mo-Ks Cty	1978
Jelavich, Mark S.	Prof	562-1763	mjelav	FR	PHD	80	J Hopkins	1981
Kharadia, Virabhai C.	Prof	562-1284	vkharad	AED	PHD	73	Illinois	1973
Collier, Ben	Assoc	562-1762	collier	ADFK	PHD	84	Purdue	1981
Shanklin, James T.	Asst	562-1764	jshakl	AD	MS	66	S Illinois	1966

Northwestern University Evanston, IL 60208-2600 (847) 491-5140 nwu.edu
Department of Economics Weinberg Col Arts & Sci Fax=491-7001 Ethel McKay King

Sunquist, Eric	Dean	491-5697		PHD			1997
Mokyr, Joel	C-Pr	491-5693	j-mokyr	PHD	74	Yale	1974
Robert H. Strotz Professor of Arts & Sciences							
Alexis, Marcus	Prof	467-1318	m-alexis	PHD	59	Minnesota	1985
Daniel F. and Ada L. Rice Professor of Economics							
Altonji, Joseph G.	Prof	491-8218	altonji	PHD	81	Princeton	1990
Braeutigam, Ronald R.	Prof	491-8243	braeutigam	PHD	76	Stanford	1975
Harvey Kapnick Professor of Business Institutions & Transportation Center							
Christiano, Lawrence	Prof	491-8231	l-christiano	PHD	82	Columbia	
Coen, Robert M.	Prof	491-8207	rcoen	PHD	67	Nrthwstrn	1971
Dekel, Eddie	Prof	491-4414	dekel	PHD	86	Harvard	
Eichenbaum, Martin	Prof	491-8232	eich	PHD	81	Minnesota	1988
Gordon, Robert J.	Prof	491-5697	rjg	PHD	67	MIT	1973
Stanley G. Harris Professor of the Social Sciences							
Kamien, Morton I.	Prof	491-5167	m-kamien	PHD	64	Purdue	1970

Name	Rank	Phone	E-mail	Fields	Degree	Yr	Institution	Since
Manski, Charles F.	Prof	491-8223	cfmanski		PHD	73	MIT	1997
Board of Trustees Professor								
Matsuyama, Kiminori	Prof	491-8490	kmatsu		PHD	87	Harvard	
Matzkin, Rosa L.	Prof	491-8220	matzkin		PHD	86	Minnesota	
Meyer, Bruce	Prof	491-8226	bmeyer		PHD	87	MIT	1987
Household International Inc. Professorship								
Mortensen, Dale T.	Prof	491-8230	d-mortensen		PHD	67	Car Mellon	1965
Ida C. Cook Professor of Consumer Economics								
Moses, Leon N.	Prof	491-8209	leon1		PHD	52	Harvard	1959
Myerson, Roger B.	Prof	491-3729	jpanzar		PHD	76	Harvard	1976
Panzar, John C.	Prof	491-8242	jpanzar		PHD	75	Stanford	1983
Louis W. Menk Professor								
Porter, Robert H.	Prof	491-3491	r-porter		PHD	81	Princeton	1987
William R. Kenan Jr. Professor								
Reiter, Stanley	Prof	491-3527	s-reiter		PHD	55	Chicago	
Charles E. and Emma H. Morrison Professor of Economics								
Rogerson, William P.	Prof	491-8484	wrogerson		PHD	81	Cal Tech	
Saari, Donald G.	Prof	491-5580	dsaari		PHD	67	Purdue	
Satterthwaite, Mark A.	Prof	491-5482	m-satterthwaite		PHD	73	Wisconsin	1973
Weisbrod, Burton A.	Prof	491-8704	b-weisbrod		PHD	58	Nrthwstrn	
John Evans Professor of Economic, Director,Ctr for Urban Affairs & Policy Rec								
Whinston, Michael D.	Prof	491-8260	mwhinston	DL	PHD	84	MIT	1996
Robert & Emily King Professor of Business Institutions								
Wolinsky, Asher	Prof	491-4415	wolinsky		PHD	80	Stanford	
Barlevy, Gadi	Asst	491-5395	barley		PHD	97	Harvard	1997
Bassetto, Marco	Asst	491-8233	m-bassetto		PHD	98	Chicago	1998
Conley, Timothy	Asst	491-8266	tconley		PHD	95	Chicago	1995
Ely, Jeffrey	Asst	491-8219	ely		PHD	96	Berkeley	1996
Ferrie, Joseph	Asst	491-8210	j-ferrie		PHD	92	Chicago	
Ramada, Paula	Asst	491-8224	pcramada		PHD	97	MIT	1997
Taber, Christopher	Asst	491-8229	ctaber		PHD	95	Chicago	1995
Valimaki, Juuso	Asst	491-8227	valimaki		PHD	95	Penn	1995
Savage, Ian P.	SLect	491-5140	ipsavage		PHD	84	Leeds	
Assistant Chairperson								

Northwestern State U of LA — Natchitoches, LA 71497 (318) 357-5161 — alpha.nsula.edu
Economics Faculty — Division of Business Fax=357-5990 — Diane Mitchell

Name	Rank	Phone	E-mail	Fields	Degree	Yr	Institution	Since
Aby, Carroll Darden Jr.	Dean				PHD	64	S Miss	
Bacdayan, Andrew W.	Prof	357-5698	bacdayan		PHD	73	Utah St	
Smiley, Barry A	Prof	357-5163	smiley		DBA	75	La Tech	
Elliott, Stephen	Assoc	357-5700	elliott	GM	PHD	83	La Tech	
Jones, Robert C. III	Asst	357-4581	jonesrc		PHD	91	UCLA	

Northwood University — Midland, MI 48640-2398 (517) — northwood.edu
Economics Faculty — Business Fax=

Name	Rank	Phone	E-mail	Fields	Degree	Yr	Institution	Since
Chen, Catherine W.	Dean	837-4371		Lit	PHD	75	Minnesota	1974
Amin, R. John	H-Pr	837-4431		BDFM	PHD	78	Cincinnati	9-86
Haywood, Dale M.	Prof	837-4291			PHD	80	North Tx	
Luptowski, Thomas S.	Prof	837-4263			BS			
Matcheck, Dale C.	Asst	837-4256	matchek_d	Q	PHD	93	Cornell	1995

Norwich University — Northfield, VT 05663 (802) 485-2210 — norwich.edu
Dept of Economics & Finance — Div of Business & Mgt Fax=485-2087 — Sandra Kingsley
Did Not Respond--1997-98 Listing

Name	Rank	Phone	E-mail	Fields	Degree	Yr	Institution	Since
Rotondi, Robert T.	C-Pr	485-2221	rrotondi	Atg	MBA	71	Fordham	9-77
Murtaugh, Frank M. Jr.	H-Ac	485-2216			PHD	81	Emory	1982
Hurd, John II	Prof	485-2217			PHD	69	Penn	1978
Mohaghegh, Mehdi	Assoc	485-2224			PHD	86	Clark	1986

University of Notre Dame — Notre Dame, IN 46556-0783 (219) 631-6335 — nd.edu
Department of Economics — Col of Arts & Sciences Fax=631-8809 — Ms. Juli Tate

Name	Rank	Phone	E-mail	Fields	Degree	Yr	Institution	Since
Dutt, Amitava K.	C-Pr	631-6335	amitava.k.dutt	EFOC	PHD	83	MIT	1988
Bartell, Ernest J.	Prof	631-6580	ernest.j.bartell	O	PHD	66	Princeton	1977
Craypo, Charles	Prof	631-7585	charles.craypo	J	PHD	66	Mich St	1978
Goulet, Denis A.	Prof	631-5250	denis.a.goulet	O	PHD	63	SaoPaulo	1979
Kim, Kwan S.	Prof	631-5179	kwan.s.kim	OF	PHD	67	Minnesota	1975
Leahy, William H.	Prof	631-7238	william.h.leahy	JR	PHD	66	Notre Dm	1963
Mirowski, Philip E.	Prof	631-7580	philip.e.mirowsk	B	PHD	79	Michigan	1990
Ros, Jaime	Prof	631-7009	jaime.ros	OE	PHD	78	Cambridge	1990
Skurski, Roger B.	Prof	631-7010	roger.b.skurski	P	PHD	70	Wisconsin	1974
Swartz, Thomas R.	Prof	631-7737	thomas.r.swartz	HA	PHD	65	Indiana	1965
Wilber, Charles K.	Prof	631-6335	charles.k.wilber	BOP	PHD	66	Maryland	1975
Betson, David M.	Assoc	631-5068	david.m.betson	HI	PHD	80	Wisconsin	1979
Bonello, Frank J.	Assoc	631-7229	frank.j.bonello	EA	PHD	68	Mich St	1968
Ghilarducci, Teresa	Assoc	631-7581	teresa.ghilarduc	J	PHD	84	Berkeley	1983
Lee, Byung	Assoc	631-6837	byungjoo.lee	CD	PHD	88	Wisconsin	1996

Name	Rank	Phone	Email	Fields	Degree	Yr	School	Since
Marsh, Lawrence C.	Assoc	631-6210	lawrence.c.marsh	CD	PHD	76	Mich St	1975
Rakowski, James J.	Assoc	631-6644	james.j.rakowski	DF	PHD	68	Minnesota	1967
Rath, Kali P.	Assoc	631-6954	kali.p.rath	CD	PHD	92	J Hopkins	1990
Ruccio, David F.	Assoc	631-6434	david.f.ruccio	BO	PHD	84	Mass	1982
Warlick, Jennifer L.	Assoc	631-7531	jennifer.l.warli	HI	PHD	79	Wisconsin	1981
Wolfson, Martin H.	Assoc	631-8093	martin.h.wolfson	EG	PHD	84	American	1990
Che, Jiahua	Asst	631-7570	jiahua.che	CDP	PHD	96	Stanford	1996
Sent, Esther-Mirjam	Asst	631-6979	esther-mirjamsen	BE	PHD	94	Stanford	1994

Oakland University Rochester, MI 48309-4401 (248) 370-3523 oakland.edu
Department of Economics School of Business Adm Fax=370-4275 Brenda Payton 370-3283

Name	Rank	Phone	Email	Fields	Degree	Yr	School	Since
Gardner, John C.	Dean			Atg	PHD	83	Mich St	8-96
Fosu, Augustin K.	C-Pr	370-3523	fosu	JOC	PHD	79	Nrthwstrn	1979
Botsas, Eleftherios N.	Prof	370-3289	botsas	FA	PHD	65	Wayne St	1976
Izraeli, Oded	Prof	370-3524	izraeli	RHA	PHD	73	Chicago	1978
Murphy, Kevin J.	Prof	370-3294	murphy	JC	PHD	81	Mich St	1985
Stano, Miron	Prof	370-3291	stano	IL	PHD	71	Cornell	1977
Coppin, Addington M.	Assoc	370-3541	coppin	FO	PHD	87	Illinois	1989
Folland, Sherman T.	Assoc	370-4086	folland	IB	PHD	74	Iowa	1986
Sahu, Anandi P.	Assoc	370-3537	sahu	EG	PHD	85	Wash U	1985
Tracy, Ronald L.	Assoc	370-3514	tracy	CE	PHD	75	Mich St	1983
Mobley, Lee	Asst	370-3277	mobley	LI	PHD	89	Ca-SnBarb	1991
Mukherji, Nivedita	Asst	370-4087	mukherji	EF	PHD	92	Va Tech	1992

Oberlin College Oberlin, OH 44074-1095 (216) 775-8483 oberlin.edu
Department of Economics Col of Arts & Sciences Fax=775-6978 Janice M. Sanborn

Name	Rank	Phone	Email	Fields	Degree	Yr	School	Since
Cleeton, David L.	C-Pr	775-8449	david.cleeton	DGIM	PHD	80	Wash U	1980
Fernandez, Luis	Prof	775-8486	luis.fernandez	CDGL	PHD	83	Berkeley	1980
Hess, Gregory	Prof	775-8592	gregory.hess	E	PHD	89	J Hopkins	1993
Kasper, Hirshel	Prof	775-8489	hirshel.kasper	DJ	PHD	63	Minnesota	1963
Piron, Robert	Prof	775-8485	robert.piron	BD	PHD	66	Nrthwstrn	1961
Sheppard, Stephen C.	Prof	775-8657	stephen.sheppard	CR	PHD	84	Wash U	1990
Zinser, James E.	Prof	775-8484	james.zinser	KLO	PHD	67	Oregon	1967
Craig, Barbara	Assoc	775-8766	barbara.craig	CFQ	PHD	88	Minnesota	1989

Occidental College Los Angeles, CA 90041-3314 (323) 259-2775
Economics Faculty Department of Economics Fax=341-4990 Betty Tracy

Name	Rank	Phone	Email	Fields	Degree	Yr	School	Since
Hirschfeld, Mary L.	C-Ac	259-2932		N	PHD	89	Harvard	1988
Halstead, James F.	Prof	259-2778		A	PHD	72	Stanford	1977
Moore, Robert L.	Prof	259-2779		J	PHD	77	Harvard	1978
Studenmund, A. H.	Prof	259-2776		C	PHD	70	Cornell	1970
Richard W. Millar Professor of Economics & Director of Institutional Planning								
Whitney, James D.	Prof	259-2750		F	PHD	83	Wisconsin	1982
Hamilton, Jean	Asst	259-2971		J	PHD	92	Berkeley	1994
Sicondi, Giorgio	Asst	259-2582		O	PHD	96	Michigan	1998

Oglethorpe University Atlanta, GA 30319 (404) facstaff.ogelthorpe.edu
Department of Economics Div Economics & Bus Adm Fax=364-8500

Name	Rank	Phone	Email	Fields	Degree	Yr	School	Since
Tucker, Dean	C-Pr	261-1441		HMQ	PHD	79	Mich St	1-88
Rikard Chaired Professor								
Hetherington, Bruce W.	Prof	261-1441		NE	PHD	82	Va Tech	1980
Shropshire, William O.	Prof	262-1441		EO	PHD	63	Duke	1979
Callaway Professor of Economics								
Hunger, David	Asst	364-3464	dhunger	LDC	PHD	98	Oregon	1993

Ohio University Athens, OH 45701-2979 (740) 593-2040 ohiou.edu
Department of Economics Col of Arts & Sciences Fax=593-0181

Name	Rank	Phone	Email	Fields	Degree	Yr	School	Since
Palmer, Jan S.	C-Ac	593-2032		A	PHD	74	Mich St	1979
Adie, Douglas K.	Prof	260-2033		BGM	PHD	68	Chicago	1968
Boyd, Roy G.	Prof	593-2050		QH	PHD	81	Duke	1984
Doroodian, Khosrow	Prof	593-2046		QAF	PHD	81	Oregon	1982
Gallaway, Lowell	Prof	593-2036			PHD	59	Ohio St	1967
Distinguished Professor								
Ghazalah, Ismail A.	Prof	593-2034		DFHI	PHD	69	Berkeley	1969
Klingaman, David C.	Prof	593-2047		DE	PHD	67	Virginia	1967
Koshal, Rajindar K.	Prof	593-2038		TACQ	PHD	68	Rochester	1970
Vedder, Richard K.	Prof	593-2037			PHD	65	Illinois	1965
Distinguished Professor								
Caporale, Tony	Assoc	593-2051			PHD	92	GeoMason	1992
Jung, Chulho	Assoc	593-2041		CDFQ	PHD	89	Michigan	1989
Rossiter, Rosemary D.	Assoc	593-2043			PHD	80	Wi-Milwa	1983
Winter, Harold	Assoc	593-2048		KL	PHD	90	Rochester	1992
Caporale, Barbara	Asst	593-2049		EGN	PHD	94	GeoMason	1994
Schwabe, Kurt	Asst	593-2042			PHD	96	N Car St	1996

Ohio Northern University Ada, OH 45810 (419) 772-2082 onu.edu
Department of Economics Col of Business Admin Fax=772-1932 Diane Thede 772-2082

Maris, Terry L.	Dean	772-2070	t-maris	Mgt	PHD	79	Nebraska	1990
Goldberg, Roger H.	Prof	772-2076	r-goldberg		PHD	81	Indiana	1969
Associate Vice President Academic Affairs								
Meininger, Richard P.	Prof	772-2083	r-meininger		PHD	87	Ohio U	1973
Associate Dean								
Meenakshi, Rishi	Assoc	772-2072	m-rishi		PHD	93	Mass	1993
Kloft, Leonard	Asst	772-2080	l-kloft		PHD	95	Iowa	1995

Ohio State University Columbus, OH 43210-1172 (614) 292-6701 osu.edu
Department of Economics Col of Social & Beh Sci Fax=

Hashimoto, Masanori	C-Pr	292-4196	hashimoto.1	J	PHD	71	Columbia	1987
Cecchetti, Stephen G.	Prof	292-9339	cecchetti.1	E	PHD	82	Berkeley	1991
Cosslett, Stephen R.	Prof	292-4106	cosslett.1		PHD	79	Berkeley	1987
Dunn, Lucia	Prof	292-8071	dunn.4	J	PHD	74	Berkeley	1987
Evans, Paul D.	Prof	292-0072	evans.21	E	PHD	76	Chicago	1987
Fleisher, Belton M.	Prof	292-6429	fleisher.1	J	PHD	61	Stanford	1965
Gonzalez-Vega, Claudio	Prof	292-0387	gonzalez.4	O	PHD	76	Stanford	
Haurin, Donald R.	Prof	292-8448	haurin.2	R	PHD	78	Chicago	1975
Associate Dean								
Howitt, Peter	Prof	292-5508	howitt.2	E	PHD	73	Nrthwstrn	1996
University Chaired Professor								
Ichiishi, Tatsuro	Prof	292-0762	ichiishi.1	C	PHD	74	Berkeley	1987
Kagel, John H.	Prof			L	PHD	70	Purdue	1999
University Chaired Professor								
Levin, Dan	Prof	688-4239	levin.36	MI	PHD	82	MIT	1995
Maddala, G. S.	Prof	292-4812	maddala.1		PHD	63	Chicago	1975
Eminent Scholar								
Mark, Nelson C.	Prof	192-0413	mark.1	FG	PHD	83	Chicago	1983
Marvel, Howard P.	Prof	422-1020	marvel.2	L	PHD	75	Chicago	1973
Honors Director								
McCafferty, Stephen A.	Prof	292-7122	mccafferty.1	EF	PHD	77	Brown	1982
McCulloch, J. Huston	Prof	292-0382	mcculloch.2	E	PHD	73	Chicago	1979
Miyazaki, Hajime	Prof	292-7939	miyazaki.1	LJ	PHD	77	Berkeley	1984
Director of Graduate Studies								
Olsen, Randall J.	Prof	292-5654	olsen.6	J	PHD	77	Chicago	1982
Director Center for Human Resource Research								
Ray, Edward J.	Prof	292-5881	ray.1	F	PHD	71	Stanford	1970
Senior Vice Provost								
Schmeidler, David	Prof	292-1148	schmeidler.1		PHD	69	Hebrew	1987
Steckel, Richard H.	Prof	422-5008	steckel.1	N	PHD	77	Chicago	1977
Aly, Hassan	Assoc	292-9133	aly.1		PHD	86	S Illinois	1989
Baack, Bennett D.	Assoc	292-2489	baack.1	N	PHD	72	U Wash	1988
Fisher, Eric O.	Assoc	292-2009	fisher.244	F	PHD	85	Berkeley	1993
Lam, Pok-sang	Assoc	292-6567	lam.1	E	PHD	86	Harvard	1985
Mumy, Gene E.	Assoc	292-0376	mumy.1	D	PHD	74	J Hopkins	1978
Director of Undergraduate Studies								
Ogaki, Masao	Assoc	292-5842	ogaki.1	E	PHD	88	Chicago	1994
Peck, James D.	Assoc	292-0182	peck.33	D	PHD	85	Penn	1992
Reagan, Patricia B.	Assoc	292-0192	reagan.3	LJ	PHD	80	MIT	1989
Sharma, V. V.	Assoc	292-9108	sharma.3		PHD	68	Illinois	1970
Carrasco, Marine	Asst	292-6883	carrasco.4		PHD	95	Toulouse	1996
Glass, Amy J.	Asst	292-1149	glass.29	F	PHD	93	Penn	1993
Light, Audrey	Asst	292-0493	light.20	J	PHD	87	UCLA	1995
Weinberg, Bruce	Asst	292-5642	weinberg.27	J	PHD	96	Chicago	1996
Zhang, Qiang	Asst	292-4094	zhang.100	EF	PHD	98	Ohio St	1998
Zhao, Jingang	Asst	292-6523	zhao.18	CD	PHD	92	Yale	1992
Chen, Jian	Lect	292-2670	chen.65					
Fang, Jiguang	Lect	292-2670	fang.3					
Gill, Leroy	Lect							
Marshall, Kathryn G.	Lect	292-4192	marshall.220	HQ	PHD	90	Berkeley	
McCulloch, Laurence	Lect	292-5528	mcculloch.1					
Osman, Alan	Lect	292-6518	osman.1					
Parsons, Deborah	Lect	292-8863	parsons.5					

Ohio Wesleyan University Delaware, OH 43015-2370 (740) 368-3535 cc.owu.edu
Economics Faculty Department of Economics Fax=368-3551 Pat Masters

Gitter, Robert J.	C-Pr	368-3536	rjgitter	PHD	78	Wisconsin	1976
Gharrity, Norman J.	Prof	368-3538	njgharri	PHD	66	J Hopkins	1962
Simon, Alice E.	Prof	368-3540	aesimon	PHD	84	Ohio St	1985
Yazar, Julide	Asst			MA	98	Ohio St	1999

University of Oklahoma — Norman, OK 73019-2103 (405) 325-2861 — ou.edu
Department of Economics — Col of Arts & Sciences Fax=325-5842 — Tami Kinsey

Name	Rank	Phone	Email	Field	Degree	Yr	School	Since
Dunne, Timothy	C-As	325-2861		DLJ	PHD	87	Penn St	1992
Dauffenbach, Robert C.	Prof	744-5125		J	PHD	73	Illinois	
Kondonassis, Alexander J.	Prof	325-5234		NO	PHD	61	Indiana	1979
David Ross Boyd Professor of Economics								
Clark, William M.	Assoc			O	PHD	81	Virginia	1977
Hartigan, James C.	Assoc	325-2358		FL	PHD	79	Duke	1988
Holmes, Alexander B.	Assoc			RD	PHD	74	SUNY-Bin	
Reed, Robert	Assoc	325-2861		JD	PHD	85	Nrthwstrn	1992
Ju, Jiandong	Asst	325-2861		D	PHD	95	Penn St	1995
Kosmopoulou, Georgia	Asst	325-2861		D	PHD	96	Illinois	1997
Rogers, Cynthia	Asst	325-2861		JR	PHD	94	Pittsburgh	1997

Oklahoma Baptist University — Shawnee, OK 74804-2590 (405) 878-3254 — mail.okbu.edu
Economics Faculty — Dickinson Sch Business Fax=878-3253
phone 878-3254

Name	Rank	Phone	Email	Field	Degree	Yr	School	Since
Babb, Robert M.	Dean	Ext 3254			EDD	89	Kentucky	8-89
Lloyd Minter Professor of Business								
Brattin, Max Alan	Assoc	Ext 3285	max_brattin		MBA	62	LSU	1966

Oklahoma Christian Univ — Oklahoma Cy OK 73136-1100 (405) 425-5560 — oc.edu
Economics Faculty — College of Business Fax=425-5574 — Wanda Neel

Name	Rank	Phone	Email	Field	Degree	Yr	School	Since
Lewis, Phillip V.	Dean	425-5561		Mgt	EDD	70	Houston	7-99
Miller, Ken	C	425-5569		Fnce				

Oklahoma City University — Oklahoma City OK 73106-1493 (405) 521-5357 — frodo.okcu.edu
Economics Faculty — Meinders Sch Business Fax=521-5098 — Ms. Jean Kobs
Did Not Respond--1997-98 Listing

Name	Rank	Phone	Email	Field	Degree	Yr	School	Since
Carmichael, David B.	Dean	521-5276	dcarmich	Hum	PHD	94	Oklahoma	8-94
Moini, Mostafa	C-Ac	521-5357	mmoini		PHD	70	Oklahoma	1985
Alli, Ali M.	Prof	521-5132	aalli	CIP	PHD	68	Okla St	1985
Craig, George	Prof	521-5095	gcraig		PHD	68	Illinois	1982
Shandiz, Mohmood	Assoc	521-5130	mshandiz		PHD	81	Okla St	1985
Associate Dean								
Carter, Thomas J.	Asst	521-5418	tcarter		PHD	87	Wisconsin	1994
Maxcy, Joel	Asst		jmaxcy		PHD	96	Wash St	1997
May, David	Asst	521-5817	dlmay		PHD	96	Fla St	1996
Willner, Jonathan	Asst	521-5133	jwillner	FO	PHD	94	Purdue	1995

Oklahoma State University — Stillwater, OK 74078-4011 (405) 744-5195 — okstate.edu
Dept of Econ & Legal Studies — Col of Business Admin Fax=744-5180 — Ruby Diamond

Name	Rank	Phone	Email	Field	Degree	Yr	School	Since
Trennepohl, Gary L.	Dean	744-5064		Fnce	PHD	76	Tx Tech	1995
Jadlow, Joseph M. Jr.	H-Pr	744-5195	jad1942	L	PHD	70	Virginia	1968
Adkins, Lee C.	Prof	744-8637	ladkins	C	PHD	88	LSU	1988
Amos, Orley M. Jr.	Prof	744-8657	amos	R	PHD	79	Iowa St	1979
Applegate, Michael J.	Prof	744-8656	mja1701	O	PHD	73	Iowa St	1974
Edgmand, Michael R.	Prof	744-5109	edge	E	PHD	68	Mich St	1983
Lage, Gerald M.	Prof	744-5064	glage	FD	PHD	67	Minnesota	1966
Regents Service Professor; Associate Dean for Graduate Studies & Research								
Moomaw, Ronald L.	Prof	744-7359	rmoomaw	R	PHD	76	Princeton	1972
Regents Professor and CBA Associates Chair								
Olson, Kent W.	Prof	744-8655	kolson	HI	PHD	69	Oregon	1974
Rickman, Dan S.	Prof	744-8662	rdan	RC	PHD	87	Wyoming	1996
OG&E Chair in Regional Economic Analysis								
Steindl, Frank G.	Prof	744-5091	steindl	E	PHD	63	Iowa	1962
Regents' Professor and Ardmore Chair								
Willett, Keith D.	Prof	744-5195	kwillet	Q	PHD	82	New Mex	1981
Currier, Kevin M.	Assoc	744-8658	kmcur	C	PHD	85	SUNY-Alb	1984
Fain, James R.	Assoc	744-8651	jrfain	J	PHD	86	Purdue	1986
Gade, Mary N.	Assoc	744-8652	mgade	H	PHD	86	Mich St	1986
Price, Edward O. III	Assoc	744-7669	edprice	B	PHD	80	Tx A&M	1979
Savvides, Andreas	Assoc	744-5110	asavvid	FO	PHD	83	Florida	1985

Old Dominion University — Norfolk, VA 23529-0221 (757) 683-3567 — oduvm.odu.edu
Department of Economics — Col of Bus & Pub Admin Fax=683-5639 — Vicky Curtis

Name	Rank	Phone	Email	Field	Degree	Yr	School	Since
Sims, J. Taylor	Dean	683-3521		Mktg	PHD	70	Illinois	7-94
Yochum, Gilbert R.	C-Pr	683-3535			PHD	74	W Virginia	1975
Agarwal, Vinod	Prof	683-3526			PHD	86	Ca-SnBarb	
Graduate Program Director								
Koch, James V.	Prof	683-3159			PHD	68	Nrthwstrn	1990
President								
Strangways, Raymond S.	Prof	683-4986			PHD	66	Tulane	1962
Talley, Wayne K.	Prof	683-3534			PHD	72	Kentucky	1972
Eminent Professor								

Anderson, Eric E.	Assoc	683-3512			PHD	84	U Wash	1984
Colburn, Christopher B.	Assoc	683-4341		R	PHD	88	Tx A&M	1987
Schwarz-Miller, Ann V.	Assoc	683-3572		DJKM	PHD	74	Nrthwstrn	1978
Turner, Charlie G.	Assoc	683-3576			PHD	81	Harvard	1984
Bezmen, Trisha	Asst	683-3571		F	PHD	98	Georgia	1999
Filer, Larry	Asst				PHD	99	Kentucky	1999
Selover, David D.	Asst	683-3541		F	PHD	91	Ca-SnDgo	1999
Hofler, Martha	Inst	683-3543		F	MA		Old Dom	
Director, CEE								

Olivet College	Olivet, MI	49076	(616) 749-7650				olivetnet.edu	
Economics Faculty	Dept of Bus Adm & Econ		Fax=749-7178					
Hubbel, Michael R.	C-As	749-7626	mhubbel		MBA	94	Insurance	1985
Homer, John S.	Prof	749-7662	jhomer		PHD	91	Hawaii	1979

Olivet Nazarene University	Kankakee, IL	60901-0592	(815) 939-5133				olivet.edu	
Economics Faculty	Business Department		Fax=928-5454				Kay Zoltani	
Rewerts, Glen	C-Ac	939-5277	grewerts	K	JD	87	Illinois	1993
Koch, Paul R.	Prof	939-5100	pkoch	ABHP	EDD	94	Illin St	1992

University of Oregon	Eugene, OR	97403-1285	(541) 346-6027				oregon.uoregon.edu	
Department of Economics	Col of Arts & Sciences		Fax=346 1243				Linda M. Steller 346-1263	
Thoma, Mark A.	C-Ac	346-1266	mthoma	E	PHD	85	Wash St	1987
Ellis, Christopher J.	Prof	346-4657	cjellis	E	PHD	83	Warwick	1983
Evans, George	Prof	346-6027	gevans	E	PHD	80	Berkeley	1994
John B. Hamacher Professor of Economics								
Gray, Jo Anna	Prof	346-4667	jgray	E	PHD	76	Chicago	1989
Associate Dean, College of Arts & Sciences								
Haynes, Stephen E.	Prof	346-4665	shaynes	FE	PHD	76	Ca-SnBarb	1978
Kolpin, Van W.	Prof	346-3011	vkolpin	C	PHD	86	Iowa	1986
Stone, Joe A.	Prof	346-4663	jstone	JFE	PHD	77	Mich St	1970
W. E. Miner Professor of Economics								
Jaeger, William K.	Assoc	346-6027	bjaeger	OQ	PHD	85	Stanford	1998
R.F. Mikesell Visiting Professor of Economics								
Singell, Larry D. Jr.	Assoc	346-4672	lsingell	J	PHD	88	Ca-SnBarb	1988
Wilson, Wesley W.	Assoc	346-4690	wwilson	CD	PHD	86	Wash St	1989
Blonigen, Bruce A.	Asst	346-4680	bruceb	FL	PHD	95	Ca-Davis	1995
Chakraborty, Shakha	Asst	346-6027		EO	PHD	99	UCLA	1999
Davies, Ronald B.	Asst	346-6027		FL	PHD	99	Penn St	1999
Harbaugh, William T.	Asst	346-1244	harbaugh	HQ	PHD	95	Wisconsin	1995
Van den Nouweland, Anne	Asst	346-1267	annev	CL	PHD	93	Tilburg	1996
Ziliak, James P.	Asst	346-4681	jziliak	J	PHD	93	Indiana	1993

Oregon State University	Corvallis, OR	97331-3612	(541) 737-2321				ccmail.orst.edu	
Department of Economics	College of Liberal Arts		Fax=737-5917				Kenn Zappulla	
email @1=ucs.orst.edu								
Schaffer, Kay	Dean	737-4589			PHD	72	Ohio St	9-94
Tremblay, Victor J.	C-Pr	737-2321	v.tremblay	DLC	PHD	83	Wash St	9-90
Fare, Rolf	Prof	737-8184	rolf.fare	CD	DOC	76	Lund	9-98
Farrell, John P.	Prof	737-1479	john.p.farrell	BO	PHD	73	Wisconsin	9-72
Grosskopf, Shawna	Prof	737-8185	shawna.grosskopf	CHJ	PHD	77	Syracuse	9-98
McMullen, B. Starr	Prof	737-1480	s.mcmullen	LE	PHD	79	Berkeley	9-80
O'Sullivan, Arthur M.	Prof	737-2508	arthur.osullivan	DR	PHD	81	Princeton	9-92
Chao, Chi-Chur	Assoc	737-2331	chaoc@1	EF	PHD	87	S Illinois	9-90
Fraundorf, Martha	Assoc	737-1477	martha.n.frau+	J	PHD	76	Cornell	9-76
Kerkvliet, Joe R.	Assoc	737-1482	kerkvlij@1	L	PHD	86	Wyoming	9-88
Martins, Carlos	Assoc	737-1476	carlos.martins	DCL	PHD	92	Tennessee	9-92
Tremblay, Carol	Assoc	737-1468	carol.h.tremblay	CJ	PHD	84	Wash St	9-92
Connolly, Laura	Asst	737-3025	laura.connolly	HL	ABD		Nrthwstrn	9-94

Otterbein College	Westerville, OH	43081	(614) 823-1130				otterbein.edu	
Economics Faculty	Dept Bus, Atg & Econ		Fax=898-1014					
Abdallah, Kamel	C-Ac	823-1892	kabdallah	Mgt	PHD	91	Ohio St	1990
Lewis, J. Patrick	Prof	823-1460	jplewis	FO	PHD	74	Ohio St	1974
Aristotelous, Kyriacos	Assoc	823-1611	karistotelous	EFO	PHD	93	Ohio St	1993
Prindle, Allen M.	Assoc	823-1481	amprindle	DQ	PHD	77	Penn St	1988

Pace University	New York, NY	10038-1502	(212) 346-1469				pace.edu	
Dept of Social Sciences	Dyson Col of Arts & Sci		Fax=346-1467				Mariel Diaz	
Masiello, Charles	Dean	346-1710		Math	PHD	68	CUNY	
Lott, Elizabeth J.	C-Ac	346-1469		ACNR	PHD		Columbia	1990
Bynoe, Ann	Assoc	346-1466			PHD	79	NYU	1997
Keenes, John	Asst	346-1465			PHD			1999
Sadler, Thomas	Asst	346-1465			PHD			1997

University of the Pacific Stockton, CA 95211 (209) 946-2258 uop.edu
Department of Economics College of the Pacific Fax=946-2577 Suzanne B. Westphal
email @1=cs.uop.edu

Name	Rank	Phone	Email	Fields	Degree	Yr	School	Hired
Benedetti, Robert R.	Dean	946-2141	rbenedet	PolS	PHD	75		
Herrin, William E.	C-Ac	946-2259	bherrin	RC	PHD	85	SUNY-Bin	1985
Fulbright to Uganda 1999-2000								
Flynn, Dennis O.	Prof	946-2913	doflynn	DNO	PHD	77	Utah	1979
on leave Fall 1999								
Keefe, David E.	Assoc	946-2258	dkeefe	FT	PHD	80	Berkeley	1978
Meyer, Peter J.	Assoc	946-2258	pmeyer	BJL	PHD	79	Berkeley	1985
Opiela, Timothy P.	Assoc	946-2293	topiela	E	PHD	87	Tx A&M	1986
on leave Visiting Researcher DePaul Univ - Chicago								
Ordovensky, J. Farley	Assoc	946-2910	jfarley	HJ	PHD	92	Duke	1993
Warner, Lori	Assoc	946-2907	lwarner	EN	PHD	86	Utah	1987
on leave spring 2000								
Dennis, Benjamin	Asst	946-2817	bdennis@1	ED	PHD	96	Harvard	1996

Pacific Lutheran University Tacoma, WA 98447-0003 (253) 535-7598 plu.edu
Department of Economics Div of Social Sciences Fax=535-8305 Ms. Peggy Jobe

Name	Rank	Phone	Email	Fields	Degree	Yr	School	Hired
Kelleher, Ann	Dean			PolS	PHD			
Reiman, Mark A.	C Ac	535-8875	reimanma	FPQ	PHD	88	U Wash	1988
Brue, Stanley L.	Prof	535-7634		ABJ	PHD	71	Nebraska	1971
Peterson, Norris A.	Prof	535-7645	petersna	J	PHD	81	Minnesota	1981
Vinje, David L.	Prof	535-7144	vinjedl	O	PHD	64	Wisconsin	1970
Wentworth, Donald R.	Prof	535-7644	wentwodr	A	PHD	65	Minnesota	1972
Jensen, Robert J.	Assoc	535-7594	jensenrj		MA	67	Nebraska	1968
Nugent, Rachel A.	Asst	535-7684	nugentra	DFQH	PHD	94	Geo Wash	1991
Travis, Karen M.	Asst	535-7684	traviskm	I	PHD	95	U Wash	1999

Pacific Union College Angwin, CA 94508-9797 (707) 965-6238 puc.edu
Economics Faculty Dept of Bus Adm & Econ Fax=965-6237

Name	Rank	Phone	Email	Fields	Degree	Yr	School	Hired
Kopitzke, Henry	C-Pr	965-6526		Law	JD	80	Idaho	1973
Neergaard, Keith	Assoc	965-6523	kneergaa		PHD	94	Ca-Irvine	1988
Taylor, Lary			ltaylor					

University of Pennsylvania Philadelphia, PA 19104-6297 (215) 898-7701 econ.sas.upenn.edu
Department of Economics Sch of Arts & Sciences Fax=573-2057
Did Not Respond--1997-98 Listing; email: @1=penndrls.upenn.edu

Name	Rank	Phone	Email	Fields	Degree	Yr	School	Hired
Stevens, Rosemary	Dean	898-2327						
Rosenzweig, Mark R.	C-Pr	898-7408		OJL	PHD	73	Columbia	1990
email markr@markr2.pop.upenn.edu								
Adams, F. Gerard	Prof	898-4477	adams		PHD	56	Michigan	1961
Director, Economic Research Unit								
Ando, Albert K.	Prof	898-7712	aando		PHD	59	Car Mellon	1963
Behrman, Jere R.	Prof	898-7712	jbehrman	OJL	PHD	66	MIT	1965
William R. Kenan Jr. Professor of Economics								
Bloomfield, Arthur I.	Emer				PHD	42	Chicago	1958
Cass, David	Prof	898-5735	dcass	DCG	PHD	65	Stanford	1974
Paul F. & E. Warren Shafer Miller Professor of Economics								
Diebold, Francis X.	Prof	898-1507	diebold		PHD	86	Penn	1989
Undergraduate Chair								
Ethier, Wilfred J.	Prof	898-5105	ethier	F	PHD	70	Rochester	1969
Hess, Arleigh P. Jr.	Emer	898-8473	ahess		PHD	49	Penn	1949
Associate Undergraduate Chair for Advising								
Heston, Alan W.	Prof	898-8485	aheston		PHD	62	Yale	
Inman, Robert P.	Prof	898-8299	inman@wharton		PHD	72	Harvard	
Kehoe, Patrick J.	Prof	898-7409	pkehoe	POF	PHD	86	Harvard	1992
Ronald S. Lauder Term Associate Professor of Economics								
Kihlstrom, Richard	Prof	898-4378	kihlstro@wharton		PHD	64	Minnesota	
Miller-Friedman Professor of Finance & Professor of Economics								
Klein, Lawrence R.	Emer	898-7713	lrk		PHD	44	MIT	1958
Benjamin Franklin Professor of Economics & Finance								
Levine, Herbert S.	Prof	898-7706	hlevine	P	PHD	61	Harvard	1960
Mailath, George J.	Prof	898-7908	gmailath	CDH	PHD	85	Princeton	1985
Graduate Chair								
Mansfield, Edwin	Prof	898-7788			PHD	55	Duke	1963
Mariano, Roberto S.	Prof	898-6771	mariano		PHD	70	Stanford	1971
Matthews, Steven A.	Prof	898-7701			PHD	78	Cal Tech	1997
Phillips, Almarin	Emer	896-5017	phillipa		PHD	53	Harvard	1953
Postlewaite, Andrew W.	Prof	898-7350	apostlew	DH	PHD	74	Nrthwstrn	9-80
Pacific Term Professor in the Social Studies								
Rob, Rafael	Prof	898-6775	rrob		PHD	81	UCLA	1984
Rogerson, Richard D.	Prof	898-7701			PHD	84	Minnesota	1997
Summers, Robert	Emer	898-7717			PHD	56	Stanford	1959
Wolpin, Kenneth I.	Prof	898-7708	wolpink		PHD	74	CUNY	1995
Wright, Randall	Prof	898-7194	rwright	JE	PHD	86	Minnesota	1987
Atkeson, Andrew G.	Asst	898-6691	atkeson	PF	PHD	88	Stanford	1993

Chang, Yongsung	Asst	898-7701			PHD	97	Rochester	1997
Corradi, Valentina	Asst	898-1505	corradi		PHD	94	Ca-SnDgo	1994
Cres, Herve	Asst	898-6260	hres		PHD	94	Geneva	1994
Hahn, Jinyong	Asst	898-5652	hahn		PHD	93	Harvard	1993
Kajii, Atsushi	Asst	898-1875	akajii	G	PHD	91	Harvard	1991
Matsui, Akihiko	Asst	898-7749	amatsui	CDE	PHD	90	Nrthwstrn	1990
William P. Carey Term Assistant Professor of Economics								
Perli, Roberto	Asst	898-1504	perlir	E	PHD	95	NYU	1995
Persico, Nicola	Asst	898-7701			PHD	96	Nrthwstrn	1997
Rios-Rull, Jose-Victor	Asst	898-7767		O	PHD	90	Minnesota	1990
Simon Kuznets Term Assistant Profess of Econ; email vr0j@anaga.sas.upenn.edu								
Todd, Petra	Asst	898-4084	ptodd		PHD	96	Chicago	1996
Zhou, Ruilin	Asst	898-6774	ruilin	FDE	PHD	93	Pittsburgh	1993

Penn State University	Univ Park, PA		16802-3306 (814) 865-1456					psu.edu
Department of Economics	College of Liberal Arts		Fax=863-4775		Linda Spangler/Anna McMullin			
Marshall, Robert C.	H-Pr	865-1456	rcm10		PHD	83	Ca-SnDgo	1995
Bierens, Herman	Prof	865-4921	hbierens		PHD	80	Amsterdm	1996
Bond, Eric W.	Prof	863-0315	ewb1	F	PHD	79	Rochester	1981
Chatterjee, Kalyan	Prof	865-6050	kchatterjee	D	PHD	79	Harvard	1998
Feller, Irwin	Prof	865-9561	iqf	O	PHD	66	Minnesota	1963
Fox, Thomas G.	Prof	863-2650	tgf	A	PHD	66	Syracuse	1966
Ghysels, Eric	Prof	865-7924	eghysels		PHD	84	Nrthwstrn	1996
Jordan, James S.	Prof	865-2201	jxj13	E	PHD	75	Nrthwstrn	1998
Klein, Philip A.	Prof	865-5781	pak11	E	PHD	58	Berkeley	1955
Krishna, Kala	Prof	865-1106	kmk4	F	PHD	84	Princeton	1993
Krishna, Vijay	Prof	863-8543	vxk5	D	PHD	83	Princeton	1993
Lombra, Raymond E.	Prof	865-5452	rl3	E	PHD	71	Penn St	1969
Nelson, Jon P.	Prof	865-8871	jpn	QD	PHD	70	Wisconsin	1969
Roberts, Mark J.	Prof	863-1535	m7r	D	PHD	80	Wisconsin	1980
Rodgers, James D.	Prof	863-2876	jdr	HK	PHD	70	Virginia	1969
Wallace, Neil	Prof			E	PHD	64	Chicago	1997
Coulson, N. Edward	Assoc	863-0625	fyj	R	PHD	83	Ca-SnDgo	1984
Gresik, Thomas A.	Assoc	863-8007	txg8	D	PHD	87	Nrthwstrn	1991
Ickes, Barry W.	Assoc	863-2652	bwickes	P	PHD	84	Berkeley	1983
Laing, Derek	Assoc	863-2656	dxl8	E	PHD	89	Essex	1989
Roberts, Bee-Yan	Assoc	863-1996	byr	O	PHD	80	Wisconsin	1981
Shapiro, David	Assoc	863-1533	dshapiro	J	PHD	72	Princeton	1980
Sjostrom, J. Tomas	Assoc	863-1295	jts10	E	PHD	91	Rochester	1998
Terza, Joseph V.	Assoc	863-3743	jvt	C	PHD	81	Pittsburgh	1986
Li, Jenny	Asst	865-5452	li@math	C	PHD	93	Cornell	1997
Li, Victor	Asst	863-8544	vxl3	E	PHD	92	Nrthwstrn	1992
Imai, Susumu	Lect				PHD			1997
Molico, Miguel	Lect				PHD			1997

Penn State - Erie	Erie, PA		16563-1400 (814) 898-6107					psu.edu
School of Business	Behrend College		Fax=898-6223					
Magenau, John M. III	D-Ac	898-6173	owc	JM	PHD	88	SUNY-Buf	1985
Weller, Barry R.	H-Ac	898-6326	brw	ACE	PHD	71	Penn St	1971
Fizel, John L.	Prof	898-6266	fzk	ALC	PHD	81	Mich St	1985
Kurre, James A.	Assoc	898-6266	k12	RA	PHD	82	Penn St	1977
Louie, Kenneth K. T.	Assoc	898-6265	obr	AFJ	PHD	87	Penn St	1984

Penn State Univ-Harrisburg	Middleton, PA		17057-4808 (717) 948-6141					psu.edu
Finance/Economics Program	School of Business		Fax=948-6456					Becky Dolan
Homepage: www.hbg.psu.edu								
Kulkarni, Mukund	D-Ac$	948-6141	msk5	Fnce	PHD	82	Kentucky	1985
DeRooy, Jacob	C-Ac	948-6155	jxd5		PHD	69	Rutgers	1975
Murti, Vedula N.	Asst	948-6164	vm3		PHD	66	Penn	1969
Sinisi, John	Asst	385-3634			PHD	76	Mass	1982

Pepperdine Univ-Malibu	Malibu, CA		90263-4372 (310) 456-4372					pepperdine.edu
Social Science Division	Seaver College		Fax=317-7271		Ms. Melissa Houghten			
Baird, David	Dean	456-4280	dbarid	Hist	PHD		Oklahoma	1988
Monsma, Stephen	C-Pr	456-4200			PHD	65	Mich St	1987
Batchelder, Ronald W.	Prof	456-4544	rbatch	DEFK	PHD	75	UCLA	1984
Sexton, Robert L.	Prof	456-4345	rsexton	ADNQ	PHD	80	Colorado	1979
Galles, Gary M.	Assoc	456-4250	ggalles	AHLR	PHD	88	UCLA	1982
Carter, Tanja	Asst		tcarter		PHD	99	Ca-SnBarb	1999

Pfeiffer University	Misenheimer, NC		28109-0960 (704)					pfieffer.edu
Economics Program	College of Arts & Sci		Fax=463-1363					
Did Not Respond--1997-98 Listing								
Starr, Bettie C.	Dean	463-1360	bstarr		PHD	76	Duke	1974
Poplin, Toby L.	C-Ac				MA	68	Appalach	1976
Jozsa, Frank	Assoc				PHD	77	Geo St	1991

Piedmont College — Demorest, GA 30535-0010 (706) Ext 250 — piedmont.edu
Economics Faculty — School of Business Fax=776-2811 — Ms. Valerie Williams
phone: 778-8500

Name	Rank	Phone	Email	Field	Degree	Yr	School	Since
Gardner, Mark L.	C-Pr	Ext 250	mgardner		PHD	85	Geo St	1979

Pittsburg State University — Pittsburg, KS 66762-7500 (316) 235-4547 — mail.pittstate.edu
Dept Econ, Finance & Banking — Kelch Sch of Bus & Econ Fax=232-4572 — Mrs. Kathy Bernard

Name	Rank	Phone	Email	Field	Degree	Yr	School	Since
Clement, Ron W.	Dean	235-4590		Mgt	PHD	78	Mich St	
Fischer, Charles C.	C-Pr	235-4547		BJ	PHD	75	Wash St	1974
Smith, Kenneth L.	Prof	235-4547		G	PHD	81	Ca-Rivers	
Cortes, Bienvenido S.	Assoc	235-4547		F	PHD	87	Okla St	
Crough, B. Jane	Lect	235-4547		A	MBA		Pittsburgh	
Lal, Anil K.	Lect	235-4547		A	PHD		Wash St	

University of Pittsburgh — Pittsburgh, PA 15260 (412) 648-1760 — pitt.edu
Department of Economics — Col of Arts & Sciences Fax=648-1793 — Irene Petrovich/Della Sinclair

Name	Rank	Phone	Email	Field	Degree	Yr	School	Since
Cooper, N. John	Dean	624-6090	cooper@fas.		DPHL	76	Oxford	1998
Ochs, Jack N.	C-Pr	624-5711	jochs	H	PHD	66	Indiana	1968
Cassing, James H.	Prof	648-8746	jcassing	F	PHD	75	Iowa	1985
Giarratani, Frank	Prof	648-7378	frankg	R	PHD	75	W Virginia	1979
Gruver, Gene W.	Prof	648-1731	gruver	O	PHD	72	Iowa St	1970
Ham, John	Prof	648-1762	johnham	J	PHD	80	Princeton	1991
Husted, Steven L.	Prof	648-1757	husted1	F	PHD	80	Mich St	1980
Rawski, Thomas G.	Prof	648-7062	tgrawski	O	PHD	72	Harvard	1985
Reny, Philip	Prof	648-5717	reny	D	PHD	88	Princeton	9-94
Richard, Jean Francois	Prof	648-1750	fantin	C	PHD	73	Louvain	1991
Wells, Jerome C.	Prof	648-1749	wells01	O	PHD	64	Michigan	1964
Beeson, Patricia E.	Assoc	648-1754	beeson	R	PHD	83	Oregon	1983
Chesler, Herbert	Assoc	648-1706	chesler	J	PHD	64	MIT	1963
Corbae, P. Dean	Assoc	648-5416	corbae	E	PHD	90	Yale	1998
DeJong, David	Assoc	648-2242	dejong	E	PHD	89	Iowa	1989
Kenkel, James L.	Assoc	648-1767	kenkel	C	PHD	69	Purdue	1969
Sontheimer, Kevin C.	Assoc	648-7071	sontheim	D	PHD	69	Minnesota	1979
Wichers, C. Robert	Assoc	648-1794	wichers	C	PHD	68	Amsterdm	1976
Aoyagi, Masaki	Asst	648-1737	maoyagi	D	PHD	92	Princeton	1992
Berkowitz, Daniel	Asst	648-7072	dmberk	GH	PHD	88	Columbia	1992
Duffy, John	Asst	648-1733	jduffy	E	PHD	92	UCLA	1992
Ichimura, Hidehiko	Asst	648-1732	thide	C	PHD	88	MIT	1996
Kim, Minseong	Asst	648-2823	mkim	E	PHD	96	Brown	1996
Sheppard, Lara Shore	Asst	648-1744	ldshore	J	PHD	96	Princeton	1996
Boerio, Eileen	Lect	648-1760	boerio	D	MA	77	Pittsburgh	1977
Cassing, Shirley	Lect	648-1729	cassing	R	PHD	76	Iowa	1985

U of Pittsburgh at Johnstown — Johnstown, PA 15904 (814) 269-2990 — pitt.edu
Div of Social Sci-Economics — Col of Arts & Sciences Fax=269-7255

Name	Rank	Phone	Email	Field	Degree	Yr	School	Since
Berger, George	C-Ac	269-2982	berger	EJK	PHD	87	Ca-Davis	1989
Yates, Michael Daniel	Prof	269-2986	mikey	JP	PHD	76	Pittsburgh	1969
Long, Stanley G.	Emer		sglong	D-95	PHD	69	Iowa	1973
McGahagan, Thomas A.	Assoc	269-2985	mgahagan	FN	PHD	76	Penn	1982
Strausser, Clark W.	Assoc	269-2980	cstrauss	CG	PHD	70	Minnesota	1973
Lavine, Jeffrey A.	Asst	269-7000	jlavine		MA	68	Pittsburgh	1970

Director of Administration and Budget

Plymouth State College — Plymouth, NH 03264-1600 (603) 535-2610 — plymouth.edu
Economics Faculty — Department of Business Fax=535-2611

Name	Rank	Phone	Email	Field	Degree	Yr	School	Since
Boggess, Trent E.	Prof	535-2414			PHD	80	Kansas	1983
Jang, Soo M.	Prof	535-2413		E	PHD	78	Cincinnati	1983
Couvillion, L. Michael	Assoc	536-2205		I	PHD	82	La Tech	1980
Brickley, Colleen	Inst	535-2278		D	ABD	78	NewHamp	1993

Point Loma Nazarene Univ — San Diego, CA 92106-2899 (619) 849-2305 — ptloma.edu
Economics Faculty — Dept of Acc, Bus & Econ Fax=849-2691 — Lauren Johnson

Name	Rank	Phone	Email	Field	Degree	Yr	School	Since
McEliece, James H.	C-Ac	849-2307	jamesmceliece		PHD	86	Co Mines	1994
Havens, Rebecca A.	Prof	849-2293	beckyhavens		PHD	87	Ca-SnDgo	1990

University of Portland — Portland, OR 97203-5798 (503) 943-7224 — uofport.edu
Economics Faculty — School of Business Adm Fax=978-8041 — Elise Petersen

Name	Rank	Phone	Email	Field	Degree	Yr	School	Since
Hill, Ronald P.	Dean	283-7224	hill	Mktg	PHD	82	Maryland	1996
Adrangi, Bahram	Prof	283-7220	adrangi	CDFR	PHD	82	Oregon	1982
Higgins, Neal O.	Prof	283-7226	higgins	RH	PHD	74	Nebraska	1976
Allender, Mary E.	Assoc	283-7154	allender	LC	PHD	90	Oregon	1985
Easton, Todd E.	Assoc	283-7209	easton	J	PHD	84	Berkeley	1981
Seal, James W.	Assoc	283-7272	seal	HRE	PHD	77	Illinois	1977

Portland State University — Portland, OR 97207-0751 (503) 725-3915 — ch2.ch.pdx.edu
Department of Economics — Col Liberal Arts & Sci Fax=725-3945 — Rita Spears
Homepage: econ.pdx.edu

Name	Rank	Phone	Email	Field	Degree	Yr	School	Year
Kaiser, Marvin	Dean	725-3514			PHD			1993
Potiowsky, Thomas P.	C-Pr$	725-3929	thomasp		PHD	81	Colorado	1982
Brinkman, Richard L.	Prof	725-3938	richard		PHD	65	Rutgers	1961
Hall, John B.	Prof	725-3939	hallj		PHD	84	New Sch	1985
Lin, Kuan-Pin	Prof	725-3931	link		PHD	77	SUNY-SBr	1979
Qayum, Abdul	Prof	725-3936	abdul		DSC	59	Netherld	1970
Walker, John F.	Prof	725-3934	walkerj		PHD	72	Utah	1966
King, Mary C.	Assoc	725-3940	kingm		PHD	91	Berkeley	1992
Koss, Patricia	Asst	725-3942	kossp		PHD	93	Simon Fr	1997
Schmidt, Martin	Asst	725-3940	schmidtm		PHD	94	Colo St	1997
Sharma, Rajiv	Asst	725-3933			PHD	98	Florida	1998

Prairie View A&M University — Prairie View, TX 77446-0638 (409) 857-2122 — pvamu.edu
Dept of Mgt & Marketing — College of Business Fax=857-2797 — Yolanda Kesee

Name	Rank	Phone	Email	Field	Degree	Yr	School	Year
Kruegel, David L.	Dean$	857-4310	kruegel	Mktg	PHD	68	Kentucky	1995
Khan, Mohiuddin M. (Moosa)	H-Ac$	857-2122	mkhan	FEM	PHD	86	Simon Fr	1989
Soliman, Mostafa A.	Assoc		mostafa-soliman	DHQ	PHD	67	Iowa St	1971
Thiagarajan, K. R.	Asst		kthtag	DE	MA	55	Annamali	1967

Presbyterian College — Clinton, SC 29325 (803) 833-8370 — cs1.presby.edu
Economics Faculty — Dept of Econ & Bus Adm Fax=833-8481 — Vernell Smith

Name	Rank	Phone	Email	Field	Degree	Yr	School	Year
Slice, Jerry Kibler	C-Pr	833-8274	jkslice	QFD	PHD	86	Miss St	1989
Lipford, Jody W.	Assoc	833-8353	jlipford	HEFI	PHD	90	Clemson	1991

Princeton University — Princeton, NJ 08544-1021 (609) 258-4000 — princeton.edu
Economics Faculty — Department of Economics Fax=258-6419 — Uta Runyan, Dept Adm
email @1=phoenix.princeton.edu

Name	Rank	Phone	Email	Field	Degree	Yr	School	Year
Bernanke, Ben S.	C-Pr	258-4000	bernanke@wws.		PHD	79	MIT	1985
Ashenfelter, Orley C.	Prof	452-4040	c6789@alfa.		PHD	70	Princeton	1968
Blinder, Alan S.	Prof	258-3358	blinder@pucc.		PHD	71	MIT	1971
Bogan, Elizabeth C.	Prof	258-4035	ebogan		PHD	71	Columbia	
Bradford, David F.	Prof	258-1856	bradford@wws.		PHD	66	Stanford	1966
Branson, William H.	Prof	258-4828	wbranson@wws.		PHD	67	MIT	1967
Chow, Gregory C.	Prof	258-4030	gcnow	CDEP	PHD	55	Chicago	7-70
Deaton, Angus S.	Prof	258-5967	deaton@wws.		PHD	74	Cambridge	1983
Dixit, Avinash K.	Prof	258-4013	dixitak		PHD	68	MIT	1981
Farber, Henry S.	Prof	258-4044	farber@trumph.		PHD	77	Princeton	
Grossman, Gene M.	Prof	258-4823	grossman@wws.		PHD	80	MIT	1980
Gul, Faruk	Prof	258-4009	fgul@phoenix.		PHD	86	Princeton	1995
Kenen, Peter B.	Prof	258-4051	pbkenen@pucc.		PHD	58	Harvard	1971
Walker Professor Economics & International Finance								
Krueger, Alan B.	Prof	258-4046	akrueger@wws.	JH	PHD	87	Harvard	6-87
Malkiel, Burton G.	Prof	258-6445	bmalkiel@pucc.		PHD	64	Princeton	1966
Quandt, Richard E.	Prof	258-4005	quandt@pucc.		PHD	57	Harvard	1959
Reinhardt, Uwe E.	Prof	258-4781	reinhard@wws.		PHD	70	Yale	1967
Rogoff, Kenneth S.	Prof	258-4847	krogoff@wws.		PHD	80	MIT	
Rosen, Harvey S.	Prof	258-4022	hsr@pucc.		PHD	74	Harvard	1974
Rubinstein, Ariel	Prof	258-4000	ariel		PHD	79	Hebrew	
on leave								
Shapiro, Harold T.	Prof	258-6100	hts		PHD	64	Princeton	1988
Trussell, T. James	Prof	258-4801	trussell@opr.	CIT	PHD	75	Princeton	O-74
Watson, Mark W.	Prof	258-4811	mwatson@wws.		PHD	80	Ca-SnDgo	
Willig, Robert D.	Prof	258-4843	willig@wws.		PHD	73	Stanford	1978
Woodford, Michael	Prof	258-4003	woodford@1		PHD	83	MIT	
Paxson, Christina H.	Assoc	258-6474	cpaxson@wws.		PHD	86	Columbia	1986
Case, Anne C.	Asst	258-2177	accase@wws.		PHD	88	Princeton	1991
Lizzeri, Alessandro	Asst	258-4012	lizzeri@1		PHD	95	Nrthwstrn	1995
Hendel, Igal		258-4039	igal					
Honore, Bo Erno		258-4014	honore		PHD	87	Chicago	
Maggi, Giovanni		258-4016	maggi					
Morgan, John		258-4842	rjmorgan					
Rouse, Cecilia		258-6478	rouse					
Shimer, Robert		258-4031	shimer					

Providence College — Providence, RI 02918-0001 (401) 865-2194 — providence.edu
Department of Economics — Economics Fax=865-1264 — Susan Paquin

Name	Rank	Phone	Email	Field	Degree	Yr	School	Year
Lenon, Mary Jane	C-As	865-2566		REI	PHD	89	Conn	1986
Kessler, Alan L.	Assoc	865-2248		DH	PHD	84	Boston C	1985
Latif-Zaman, Nazma	Assoc	865-2572		OFC	PHD		Northeas	
O'Brien, Francis T.	Assoc	865-2156		JK	MA	57	Boston C	1958
Simeone, William J.	Assoc	865-2567		JEI	PHD	85	Boston C	1959
Sawdy, George F.	Asst	865-2570		QEH	PHD	83	Brown	
Kaparakis, Emmanuel	Inst	865-2568		EGF	ABD		Conn	1990
Palumbo, Edwin P.	Inst	865-2189		RJ	MA		Boston C	

University of Puget Sound Tacoma, WA 98416-0140 (253) 756-3136 ups.edu
Economics Faculty Department of Economics Fax=756-3500 Reggie Tison

Name	Rank	Phone	E-mail	Fields	Degree	Yr	School	Hired
Stirling, Kathleen J.	C-Pr	756-3590	stirling	AEIT	PHD	87	Notre Dm	
Goodman, Douglas	Prof	756-3596	goodman	AE	PHD	78	Illinois	1977
Hands, Wade	Prof	756-3592	hands	ABC	PHD	65	U Wash	
Mann, Bruce D.	Prof	756-3593	mann	ADJK	PHD	76	Indiana	1975
Singleton, Ross	Prof	756-3591	singleton	ADKO	PHD	77	Oregon	
Veseth, Michael	Prof	756-3720	veseth	AFH	PHD	76	Purdue	1975
Sable, Karin	Asst	756-3136	sable	AHQ	PHD	97	Colo St	1997
Warning, Matt	Asst	756-3136	warning	ACO	PHD	97	Berkeley	1997

Purdue University W Lafayette, IN 47907-1310 (765) 494-4449 mgt.purdue.edu
Economics Program Krannert Grad Sch Mgt Fax=494-9658 Darsha Lowery

Name	Rank	Phone	E-mail	Fields	Degree	Yr	School	Hired
Weidenaar, Dennis J.	Dean	494-4366	weidend	Mgt	PHD	69	Purdue	1966
Kovenock, Dan J.	C-Pr	494-4468	kovenock		PHD	83	Wisconsin	1983
Aliprantis, C. D. Roko	Prof	494-4404	aliprantis		PHD	73	Cal Tech	1998
Barron, John M.	Prof	494-4451	barron		PHD	76	Brown	1976
Carlson, John A.	Prof	494-4450	carlson		PHD	61	J Hopkins	1962
Loeb Professor of Economics								
Horwich, George	Prof	494-4443	ghorwich		PHD	54	Chicago	1956
Kadiyala, K. Rao	Prof	494-4476	kadiyala		PHD	66	Wisconsin	1970
McCarthy, Patrick S.	Prof	494-4460	mccarthy		PHD	76	Claremont	1978
Moore, James C.	Prof	494-4430	duke		PHD	68	Minnesota	1969
Papke, James A.	Prof	494-4442	papke		PHD	59	Cornell	1962
Thursby, Jerry G.	Prof	494-4462	jgt		PHD	75	N Carol	1988
Thursby, Marie C.	Prof	494-4463	mct		PHD	74	N Carol	1988
Burton D. Morgan Chair of Intl Mgt Policy; Dir Cntr of Intl Busines Education								
Umbeck, John R.	Prof	494-4447	umbeck		PHD	76	U Wash	1975
Watts, Michael W.	Prof	494-8543	bfp		PHD	78	LSU	1981
Director, Purdue Center for Economic Education								
Cason, Timothy	Assoc	494-1737	cason		PHD	91	Berkeley	1998
Hueckel, Glenn R.	Assoc	494-4402	hueckel		PHD	72	Wisconsin	1972
Lynch, Gerald J.	Assoc	494-4388	lynch		PHD	75	Kentucky	1983
Noussair, Charles N.	Assoc	494-4416	noussair		PHD	93	Cal Tech	1994
Novshek, William	Assoc	494-4418	novshek		PHD	79	Nrthwstrn	1986
Pomery, John D.	Assoc	494-4515	pomery		PHD	77	Rochester	1982
Camera, Gabriele	Asst	494-4456	gcamera		PHD	97	Iowa	1997
Netz, Janet S.	Asst	494-4452	netz		PHD	92	Michigan	1994

Purdue University-Calumet Hammond, IN 46323-2904 (219) 989-2388 calumet.purdue.edu
Department of Management Sch of Professional Std Fax=989-2750
Did Not Respond Again--1995-96 Listing

Name	Rank	Phone	E-mail	Fields	Degree	Yr	School	Hired
Sil, Shomir	Dean				DBA	83	Tx Tech	1983
Das, Bhaskar	Assoc	988-2313			PHD	91	Miss	1991
Furdek, Jonathan M.	Assoc	989-2426			PHD	74	Purdue	1974
Jennings, E. James	Assoc	989-2381			PHD	79	So Meth	1978
McGrath, Paul T.	Assoc	989-2425			PHD	88	N Illinois	1986

Quinnipiac College Hamden, CT 06518-1908 (203) Ext 8367 quinnipiac.edu
Department of Economics School of Business Fax=281-8664 Patricia Beale
phone 288-5251

Name	Rank	Phone	E-mail	Fields	Degree	Yr	School	Hired
Frese, Philip B.	Dean	280-8720		Atg	PHD	93	Drexel	1993
DeAndrea, Vincent F.	C-Pr	Ext 8367		CDEN	PHD	72	Mass	1968
Driscoll, Vincent R.	Prof	281-8788		AEG	PHD	75	New Sch	1967
Gius, Mark P.	Assoc			ACDJ	PHD	91	Penn St	1994
Johnson, Donn M.	Assoc			AHQR	PHD	89	Colo St	1996
Kelly, Trish	Assoc	Ext 8318		EFO	PHD	94	Mass	1995
Everett, Michael	Asst	Ext 8256		ADBP	PHD	96	Conn	1996

Radford University Radford, VA 24142 (540) 831-5100 runet.edu
Dept of Economics Col of Business & Econ Fax=831-6209 Ms. Teresa Grubb

Name	Rank	Phone	E-mail	Fields	Degree	Yr	School	Hired
Blaylock, Bruce K.	Dean	831-5300	bblayloc	Mgt	PHD	80	Geo St	1994
Kasturi, Prahlad	C-Pr	831-5884	pkasturi	DOQ	PHD	83	Hawaii	1985
Birecree, Adrienne M.	Prof	831-5887	abirecre	JD	PHD	83	Notre Dm	1988
Hashemzadeh, Nozar	Prof	831-5888	nhashemz	CJG	PHD	74	Va Tech	1983
Santopietro, George D.	Prof	831-5891	gsantopi	QDK	PHD	86	Va Tech	1987
Wooley, Douglas C.	Prof	831-5885	dwoolley	HP	PHD	76	Conn	1975
Ansari, Mohammed	Assoc	831-5889	8mansari	EFGM	PHD	89	Simon Fr	1997
Roufagalas, John	Assoc	831-5892	jroufaga	DGE	PHD	83	Florida	1985
Wilson, Loretta S.	Asst	831-6225	lwilson	FN	PHD	86	Mass	1987
Wade, Ernie	Inst	831-5890	ewwade	AQ	MS	86	Va Tech	1997

Ramapo Coll of New Jersey Mahwah, NJ 07430-1680 (201) ramapo.edu
Economics Faculty School Adm & Business Fax=529-7508
Did Not Respond--Information Taken from College Catalog

Name	Rank	Phone	E-mail	Fields	Degree	Yr	School	Hired
Champlin, Frederick	Dean	529-7377	fchampli	Mgt	PHD	82	Minnesota	1990
McLewin, Phillip J.	Assoc	529-7630			PHD	70	Cornell	1974

Randolph-Macon College — Ashland, VA 23005-5005 (804) 752-7356 — rmc.edu
Economics Faculty — Dept of Economics & Bus Fax=752-7231

Name	Rank	Phone	Email	Fields	Degree	Yr	School	Year
Lang, Steven D.	C-Ac	752-7356	slang	ECR	PHD	90	Pittsburgh	1987
Lowry, George S.	Prof	752-7306	glowry	G	PHD	92	Va Comm	1984
Pfitzner, C. Barry	Prof	752-7307	bpfitzner	DFC	PHD	83	Catholic	1982
Edward W. Seese Professor of Economics and Business								
Schmidt, Edward J.	Assoc	752-7333	eschmidt	E	MA	67	Maryland	1967
Brat, David	Asst	752-7353	dbrat	DBO	PHD	95	American	1996

University of Redlands — Redlands, CA 92373-0999 (909) 335-4068 — uor.edu
Economics Faculty — Dept of Mgt & Business Fax=335-5125
Did Not Respond--1997-98 Listing

Name	Rank	Phone	Email	Fields	Degree	Yr	School	Year
Pick, James	C-Pr	335-4068	pick	RT	PHD	74	Ca-Irvine	1991
Halvorsen, Marcia L.	Prof	793-2121			PHD	78	Geo St	1975
Segur, W. Hubbard	Prof	335-4068		Busi	PHD	80	Ca-Davis	1989
Bandzak, Ruth Anne	Asst				MA		Notre Dm	1988
Fazeli, Rafat R.	Asst	793-2121			PHD	92	New Sch	1989

Reed College — Portland, OR 97202-8199 (503) 771-1112 — reed.edu
Department of Economics — Div History & Soc Sci Fax=777-7776 — Lois Hobbs

Name	Rank	Phone	Email	Fields	Degree	Yr	School	Year
Parker, Jeffrey A.	C-Pr	771-1112	parker	AECF	PHD	81	Stanford	1988
George Hay Professor of Economics								
Hare, Denise	Assoc	771-1112	dhare	AJOD	PHD	92	Stanford	1992
Netusil, Noelwah R.	Assoc	771-1112	netusil	AQDH	PHD	92	Illinois	1990
Clausing, Kimberly	Asst	771-1112	kclausing	ADFH	PHD	97	Harvard	1997

Regent University — Virginia Bch, VA 23464-9850 (757) 579-4302 — regent.edu
Economics Faculty — Robertson Sch of Govt Fax=226-4369 — Mrs. Sherry Hansen
Did Not Respond--1997-98 Listing

Name	Rank	Phone	Email	Fields	Degree	Yr	School	Year
James, Kay C.	Dean	579-4530	kjames	I	BA			1996
Bom, Philip C.	Prof	579-4303	philbom	FOP	PHD		Free	1983

Regis College - MA — Weston, MA 02193-1571 (617) 768-7418
Economics — Div of Social Sciences Fax=768-8339

Name	Rank	Phone	Email	Fields	Degree	Yr	School	Year
Hewins, Dana C.	C-Ac	768-7418			PHD	75	Illinois	
Oates, Mary J.	Prof	768-7420		N	PHD	69	Yale	1970
Coiner, H. Michael	Assoc	768-7419			PHD	79	Yale	

Regis College of Regis Univ — Denver, CO 80221-1099 (303) 458-4170
Economics Program — Div of Business Fax=964-5485 — Sharon Hershfeldt

Name	Rank	Phone	Email	Fields	Degree	Yr	School	Year
Muth, John	D-Ac	458-3584		AGNM	PHD	78	Colorado	9-83
Richard, James S.	Assoc	458-4185			PHD	80	Tx-Austin	1979
Shannon, Lee R.	Assoc	458-4175			PHD	70	N Colo	1978

Rensselaer Poly Institute — Troy, NY 12180-3590 (518) 276-6387 — rpi.edu
Department of Economics — Sch of Human & Soc Sci Fax=276-2235 — Betty Jean Kaufmann

Name	Rank	Phone	Email	Fields	Degree	Yr	School	Year
Duchin, Faye	Dean	276-6575	duchif					1996
Diwan, Romesh K.	Prof	276-6386	diwanr		PHD	65	Birminghm	1967
Gowdy, John M.	Prof	276-8093	gowdyj		PHD	80	W Virginia	1983
Hughes, Greg	Prof	276-	hughesg		PHD	72	Princeton	1997
Vitaliano, Donald F.	Prof	276-8093	vitald		PHD	60	CUNY	1969
Erickson, Tom	Asst	276-2023	erick		PHD	97	Cornell	1997
Heim, John	Asst	276-8092	heinj		PHD	72	SUNY-Alb	1997
O'Hara, Sabine	Asst	276-8095	oharas	BEQR	PHD	84	Goettingen	1-95
Oneiwu, Stephen	Asst	276-4773	onyeis		PHD	97	Conn	1998

University of Rhode Island — Kingston, RI 02881-0808 (401) 874-2212 — uriacc.uri.edu
Department of Economics — Col of Arts & Sciences Fax=874-2588 — Linda Gray
Did Not Respond--1997-98 Listing

Name	Rank	Phone	Email	Fields	Degree	Yr	School	Year
Barnett, Harold C.	C-Pr	874-2070	hbarnett	EKQ	PHD	73	MIT	1970
Burkett, John P.	Prof	874-4122	burkett	CDFI	PHD	81	Berkeley	1981
Lardard, Leonard P.	Prof	874-4128			PHD	79	Indiana	1981
Mead, Arthur C.	Prof	874-4123	acmead		PHD	78	Boston C	1976
Ramsay, Glenworth A.	Prof	874-4129	ramsay		PHD	74	Boston C	1973
Ramstad, Yngve	Prof	874-4113	ramstad	BA	PHD	81	Berkeley	1982
Starkey, James L.	Prof	874-4117	starkey		PHD	71	Boston C	1967
McIntyre, Richard	Assoc	874-4126	macking		PHD	89	Mass	1989
Miller, Carole F.	Assoc	874-4111	cqe101	ACDJ	PHD	88	Syracuse	1986
Charif, Mohammed	Assoc	874-4119	evu101		PHD	83	Boston U	1984
Suzawa, Gilbert S.	Assoc	874-4125	gilsuzawa@a		PHD	73	Brown	1971
Latos, Charles	Asst	277-5169			PHD	77	Brown	1969

Rhode Island College — Providence RI 02908-1991 (401) 456-8036 — ric.edu
Dept of Econ & Management — Center for Mgt & Tech Fax=456-8379 — Ms. Alice Porcelli

Name	Rank	Phone	Email	Field	Degree	Yr	School	Hired
Marks, Peter A.	C-Ac	456-9529			PHD	78	N Carol	
Moore, Peter R.	Prof	456-8037			PHD	75	Illinois	
Blais, Jeffrey	Assoc	456-8037			PHD	75	Pittsburgh	1986
Harman, Peter	Assoc	456-9518			PHD	76	N Carol	
Kazemi, Abbas A.	Assoc	456-9557			PHD	88	SUNY-SBr	
Karim, Alema	Asst	456-9538			PHD	86	Boston U	

Rhodes College — Memphis, TN 38112-1690 (901) 843-3863 — rhodes.edu
Dept of Economics & Business — Div Social Sciences Fax=843-3798 — Amy Radford

Name	Rank	Phone	Email	Field	Degree	Yr	School	Hired
Orvis, Charles C.	H-Ac	843-3922	orvis		PHD	75	Minnesota	1973
Bolch, Ben W.	Prof	843-3995	bolch		PHD	66	N Carol	1987
Iskander, Wasfy B.	Prof	843-3983	iskander		PHD	73	Indiana	
McMahon, Marshall E.	Prof	843-3863	mcmahon		PHD	72	Vanderbilt	1972
Rollosson, Michael	Inst	843-3566	rollesoon		ABD			1993

Rice University — Houston, TX 77005-1892 (713) 527-4875 — rice.edu
Economics Faculty — Dept of Economics MS-22 Fax=285-5278 — Elizabeth Powell
phone 527-8750

Name	Rank	Phone	Email	Field	Degree	Yr	School	Hired
Stein, Robert	Dean	527-8101		PolS				
Zodrow, George R.	C-Pr	527-4875	econ		PHD	80	Princeton	1979
Brito, Dagobert L.	Prof	527-4875	brito		PHD	70	Rice	1984
George A. Peterkin Professor of Political Economy								
Brown, Bryan W.	Prof	527-4875	bwbwn		PHD	77	Penn	1983
Hargrove Professor of Economics								
Brown, James	Prof	527-4875	jbrown		PHD	80	Chicago	1992
Bryant, John B.	Prof	527-4875	jbb		PHD	75	Car Mellon	1981
Henry S. Fox, Sr. Professor of Economics								
Gillis, Malcolm	Prof	527-8101			PHD	68	Illinois	1993
President								
Hartley, Peter R.	Prof	527-4875	hartley		PHD	80	Chicago	1986
Mieszkowski, Peter	Prof	527-4875	mieszko		PHD	63	J Hopkins	1981
Cline Professor of Economics & Finance								
Moulin, Herve	Prof	527-4875		CD	PHD	75	Paris	7-99
Peterkin Professor of Economics								
Sickles, Robin C.	Prof	527-4875	rsickles		PHD	76	N Carol	1985
Smith, Gordon W.	Prof	527-4875	gsmith		PHD	66	Harvard	1968
Soligo, Ronald	Prof	527-4875	soligo		PHD	64	Yale	1967
Chae, Suchan	Assoc	527-4875	chae		PHD	85	Penn	1985
Dudey, Marc Peter	Assoc	527-4875	dudey		PHD	84	Princeton	1990
Barut, Yasar	Asst	527-4875	ybarut		PHD	98	Purdue	7-98
Chang, Yoosoon	Asst	527-4875	yoosoon		PHD	95	Yale	1995
Hasker, Kevin	Asst	527-4875	hasker		PHD	98	Nrthwstrn	7-98
Merz, Monika	Asst	527-4875	mmerz		PHD	94	Nrthwstrn	1994
Ohno, Yuka	Asst	527-4875	yuka	FL	PHD	93	U Wash	9-94

University of Richmond — Richmond, VA 23173 (804) 289-8587 — urvax.urich.edu
Department of Economics — E.C. Robins Sch of Bus Fax=289-8878 — Sue Hopfensberger

Name	Rank	Phone	Email	Field	Degree	Yr	School	Hired
New, J. Randolph	Dean	289-8550		Mgt	PHD	78	Ariz St	1994
Raines, J. Patrick	C-Pr	289-8566	praines		PHD	83	Alabama	1982
Edwards, N. Faye	Prof	289-8590			PHD	68	Kentucky	1968
Cook, Robert W. Jr.	Assoc	289-8561			PHD	81	Va Tech	1980
Dolan, Robert C.	Assoc	289-8562			PHD	82	Rutgers	1980
Nicholson, Robert H.	Assoc	298-8565			PHD	72	N Carol	1972
Schmidt, Robert M.	Assoc	289-8569			PHD	81	Duke	1981
Whitaker, David A.	Assoc	289-8560			PHD	71	Florida	1969
Wight, Jonathan B.	Assoc	289-8570			PHD	82	Vanderbilt	1982
Craft, Erik D.	Asst	287-6573			PHD	95	Chicago	1994
Dean, David H.	Asst	289-8559			PHD	88	Rutgers	1987
McGoldrick, Kim Marie	Asst	289-8575			PHD	93	SUNY-Bin	1992

Rider University — Lawrenceville NJ 08648-3099 (609) 895-5562 — rider.edu
Department of Economics — College of Business Adm Fax=896-5304 — Diana Cook

Name	Rank	Phone	Email	Field	Degree	Yr	School	Hired
Sandberg, Mark E.	Dean$	896-5152		Mgt	PHD	71	Cornell	1970
McCall, Charles W.	C-Ac	895-5562		AL	PHD	82	Temple	1979
Corman, Hope	Prof	895-5559		IJKT	PHD	78	CUNY	1988
Gishlick, Herbert E.	Prof	895-5564		ER	PHD	73	Penn	1964
Bentley, Jerome T.	Assoc	895-5563		D	PHD	74	Pittsburgh	1974
Taga, Leonore S.	Assoc	895-5531		P	PHD	79	Berkeley	1986

University of Rio Grande — Rio Grande, OH 45674 (740) 245-7267 — urgrgcc.edu
Department of Economics — E.E. Evans Col Bus Mgt Fax=245-7123 — Shari Wootan

Name	Rank	Phone	Email	Field	Degree	Yr	School	Hired
Ickinger, William	C-Pr	245-7291		Mgt	PHD	82	Yale	9-92
Kool, Krishna L.	Prof	245-7268	kkool		PHD	76	Tennessee	1970
Koirah, Govinda	Asst	245-7284			PHD	95	NYU	1996

Roanoke College — Salem, VA 24153-3794 (540) 375-2426 — roanoke.edu
Economics Faculty — Dept of Bus Adm & Econ Fax=375-2577 — Nan Watson

Name	Rank	Phone	Email	Field	Degree	Yr	School	Since
Garren, Kenneth	Dean	375-2203	garren	Math	PHD	68	Va Tech	1967
Lynch, Larry A.	C-Pr	375-2413	llynch	Mgt	PHD	87	Va Tech	1978
Fleming, Garry A.	Assoc	375-2509	fleming		PHD	79	Kentucky	1987
Lowry, Darryl W.	Assoc	375-2428	dlowry		PHD	72	Berkeley	1981
Stauffer, Robert F.	Assoc	375-2427			PHD	74	Va Tech	1978

Robert Morris College — Coraopolis, PA 15108-1189 (412) 227-6859 — robert-morris.edu
Dept of Social Science — Sch of Appl Sci & Educ Fax=391-3329
Did Not Respond--1997-98 Listing

Name	Rank	Phone	Email	Field	Degree	Yr	School	Since
Shank, Jon	Dean	262-8279			EDD		Pittsburgh	
Norberg, Robert W.	C-As	227-6859			MA		Ind-Penn	1968
Litzinger, Patrick J.	Prof	262-8438			PHD	75	Pittsburgh	1977
Eschenfelder, Mark J.	Assoc	262-8491			PHD	93	W Illinois	
HOlstein, Adora	Assoc				PHD	87	Penn St	
Lynch, James W.	Assoc	262-8439			MA	72	Pittsburgh	1974
Reiland, Ralph R.	Assoc	227-4055			MBA		Duquesne	
Zeman, Allan H.	Assoc	227-6844			PHD	78	Pittsburgh	1964

University of Rochester — Rochester, NY 14627-0156 (716) 275-7221 — troi.cc.rochester.edu
Department of Economics — Col of Arts & Science Fax=256-2309 — Lynn Enright

Name	Rank	Phone	Email	Field	Degree	Yr	School	Since
LeBlanc, Thomas	Dean							
Stockman, Alan C.	C-Pr	275-7221	stoc		PHD	78	Chicago	1979
Wilson Professor of Economics								
Engerman, Stanley L.	Prof	275-3165	enge		PHD	62	J Hopkins	1963
John Munro Professor of Economics								
Epstein, Larry G.	Prof	275-4320	lepn		PHD	77	Brit Colum	1998
Greenwood, Jeremy	Prof	275-1871	gree	D	PHD	83	Rochester	1992
Hanushek, Eric A.	Prof	275-5059	hanu		PHD	68	MIT	1978
Director, W.A. Wallis Institute of Political Economy								
Jones, Ronald W.	Prof	275-2688	jonr		PHD	56	MIT	1958
Xerox Professor of Economics								
McKenzie, Lionel W.	Emer	275-3096	mcke		PHD	42	Princeton	1957
Oi, Walter Y.	Prof	275-4991	oiwa		PHD	61	Chicago	1967
Elmer B. Milliman Professor of Economics								
Phelps, Charles E.	Prof	275-5149			PHD	73	Chicago	1984
Provost								
Ploberger, Werner	Prof	275-4196	wplo		HAB	93	Vienna T	1997
Plosser, Charles I.	Prof	275-3754			PHD	76	Chicago	1978
John M. Olin Distinguished Professor of Economics								
Thomson, William L.	Prof	275-2236	wth2	CDH	PHD	76	Stanford	9-83
Bils, Mark J.	Assoc	275-0488	bils	D	PHD	85	MIT	1985
Hopenhayn, Hugo	Assoc	275-4081	huho		PHD	80	Minnesota	1994
Krusell, Per	Assoc	275-4903	pekr	O	PHD	92	Minnesota	1994
Director, Center for the Study of Economic Growth and Cycles								
Landsburg, Steven E.	VAsoc	275-4971	landsbur		PHD	79	Chicago	
Alonso, Irasema	VAsst	275-4980	iral		PHD	93	Minnesota	1994
Caucutt, Elizabeth	Asst	275-0093	ecau		PHD	97	Minnesota	1997
Dahl, Gordon B.	Asst	275-6279	dahl		PHD	98	Princeton	1998
Hodgson, Doug	Asst	275-5782	dshn		PHD	95	Yale	1995
Khan, Shakeeb	Asst	275-2180	skhan		PHD	97	Princeton	1998
Lochner, Lance	Asst	275-4239	lance		PHD	98	Chicago	1998
Wolkoff, Michael	Lect	275-5279	wolk		PHD	81	Michigan	1980
Deputy Chairperson, Department of Economics								

Rochester Inst of Technology — Rochester, NY 14623-5604 (716) — ritvax.isc.rit.edu
Div Soc Sci-Dept of Econ — Col of Liberal Arts Fax=475-7120

Name	Rank	Phone	Email	Field	Degree	Yr	School	Since
Vernarelli, Michael J.	C-Pr	475-2455			PHD	78	SUNY-Bin	1976
Hopkins, Thomas D.	Prof	475-6648	tdhgsm	DHK	PHD	71	Yale	1988
Arthur J. Gosnell Professor of Economics								
Humphries, John	Prof	475-6464			PHD	67	Syracuse	1962
Lee, Hoyoung	Prof	475-2406		ABDE	PHD	70	Maryland	1970
Dumangane, Constantino Sr.	Assoc	475-2807	econ.dwelop	GLDM	PHD	88	SUNY-Buf	1986
Mitchell, Jeannette C.	Asst	475-6077	jcmgsm	FOB	PHD	95	Utah	1985

Rockhurst College — Kansas City, MO 64110-2561 (816) 501-4200 — vax1.rockhurst.edu
Department of Economics — School of Management Fax=501-4650
Did Not Respond--1997-98 Listing

Name	Rank	Phone	Email	Field	Degree	Yr	School	Since
Walker, Earl	Dean	501-4201	e_walker		PHD	80	MIT	1998
Tansey, Michael M.	Prof	273-3061			PHD	78	Wisconsin	1982
Arthur, E. Eugene	Assoc	501-4085	arthur	KM	DBA	75	Indiana	1968
Miller, Gerald	Assoc	501-4016			PHD	75	Notre Dm	1982
Stellern, Michael J.	Asst	501-4153			PHD	83	Arizona	1979
Rabbitt, Michael T.	Lect				MA	75	Wash U	1988

Rollins College — Winter Park, FL 32789-4499 (407) 646-2569 — rollins.edu
Economics Faculty — Department of Economics Fax=646-2485 — Sharon Miller

Name	Rank	Phone	Email	Field	Degree	Yr	School	Hired
Taylor, Kenna C.	C-Pr	646-2312	ktaylor		PHD	79	Florida	1974
Rock, Charles Patrick	Prof	646-2152	crock		PHD	86	Cornell	1984
Kypralos, Harry N.	Assoc	646-2510	hkypralos		PHD	87	Virginia	1983
Schutz, Eric A.	Assoc	646-2509	eschutz		PHD	82	N Carol	1987
Skelley, A. Chris	Assoc	646-2489	cskelley		PHD	85	Brown	1987
Steen, Robert C.	Assoc	646-2614	rsteen	RHN	PHD	82	Princeton	1987

Roosevelt University — Chicago, IL 60605-1394 (312) 341-3695 — roosevelt.edu
Dept Econ/Sch Policy Studies — Col of Arts & Sciences Fax=341-3680

Name	Rank	Phone	Email	Field	Degree	Yr	School	Hired
Tallman, Ronald	Dean	341-3670	rtallman					
Langer, Gary F.	D-Ac	341-3767	glander		PHD	80	Ca-Rivers	1983
Balkin, Steven M.	Prof	341-3696			PHD	76	Wayne St	1984
email=eco@interaccess.com								
Rosenberg, Sam	Prof	341-3697	srosenbe		PHD	75	Berkeley	1982
Stein, Howard	Prof	341-3692	hstein		PHD	83	Ca-Rivers	1983
Lapidus, June	Assoc	341-3765	jlapidus		PHD	88	Mass	1990
Baiman, Ron	Asst	341-3879	rbaiman		PHD	89	New Sch	1994

Rowan University — Glassboro, NJ 08028-1748 (856) 256-4060 — rowan.edu
Department of Economics — School of Liberal Arts Fax=256-4921 — Patricia Jenkins
phone 256-4500

Name	Rank	Phone	Email	Field	Degree	Yr	School	Hired
Bartelt, Pearl	Dean	256-4850		Soc	PHD	72	Ohio St	1972
Jam, Habib O. E.	C-Ac	Ext 4061	jam		PHD	75	S Illinois	1979
Hamer, Thomas P.	Prof	256-4062	hamer		PHD	75	Claremont	1974
Kressler, Peter	Assoc	Ext 3321	kressler		PHD	68	Penn	1972
Mukhoti, Bela	Assoc	Ext 3322	mukhoti		PHD	64	London	1974
Reaves, Natalie	Asst	Ext 3320	reaves		PHD	95	Wayne St	1998

The Sage Colleges — Troy, NY 12180-4115 (518) 270-2235 — sage.edu
Social & Global Studies — Russell Sage College Fax=271-4545 — Pam McKee

Name	Rank	Phone	Email	Field	Degree	Yr	School	Hired
Melero, Francisco	D-Ac	270-2241	melerf	DCF	PHD	83	Rensselaer	1982
DiMambro, Carol	Assoc	462-8629	dimamc	AKP	MA	89	SUNY-Alb	1989
Tribble, John A.	Assoc	270-2296	tribbj		PHD	75	Utah St	1976
Lawrence Professor of Economics								
Sabi, Manijeh	Adj	270-2397	sabim	EGO	MA	86	Northeas	1988

Rutgers University-Camden — Camden, NJ 08102 (609) 225-6136 — zodiac.rutgers.edu
Department of Economics — Col of Arts & Sciences Fax=225-6495 — Pennie Prete

Name	Rank	Phone	Email	Field	Degree	Yr	School	Hired
Marsh, Margaret	Dean				PHD	74	Rutgers	
Yamada, Tetsuji	C-Ac	225-6025			PHD	87	CUNY	1987
Seplaki, Les	Prof	225-6319			PHD	70	Ca-Rivers	
Worrall, John D.	Prof	225-6290			PHD	75	Rutgers	1983
Chen, Baolin	Asst	225-6025			PHD	94	Indiana	
Ma, Jinpeng	Asst	225-6025			PHD	93	SUNY-SBr	

Rutgers University-Newark — Newark, NJ 07102 (973) 353-5259 — andromeda.rutgers.edu
Department of Economics — Faculty of Arts & Sci Fax=353-5819 — Marilyn Johnson

Name	Rank	Phone	Email	Field	Degree	Yr	School	Hired
Diner, Steven	Dean							
Loeb, Peter D.	C-Pr	353-5259	ploeb		PHD	73	Rutgers	1973
Coate, Douglas C.	Prof	353-5164	dcoate		PHD	74	CUNY	1971
Graham, John W. III	Prof	353-5354	jwgraham		PHD	78	Nrthwstrn	1986
Troy, Leo	Prof	353-5529	leotroy		PHD	58	Columbia	
VanderHoff, James H.	Prof	353-5256	jhv		PHD	79	N Carol	1980
Rodriguez, Alvaro	Assoc	353-5809	alvaror		PHD	82	Columbia	1994
Seiglie, Carlos C.	Assoc	353-5914	seiglie		PHD	91	Chicago	1986
Goldbaum, David	Asst	353-5164	goldbaum		PHD	96	Wisconsin	1998
Tournas, Ioannis	Asst	353-1320	itournas		PHD	95	Nrthwstrn	1996

Rutgers Univ-New Brunswick — New BrunswickNJ 08903 (732) 932-7363 — fas-econ.rutgers.edu
Department of Economics — Faculty of Arts & Sci Fax=942-7416 — Laura Ford
Did Not Respond--1997-98 Listing

Name	Rank	Phone	Email	Field	Degree	Yr	School	Hired
Foley, Richard F.	Dean	932-7896						
White, Eugene N.	C-Pr	932-7486	white	N	PHD	80	Illinois	1980
Blair, Douglas H.	Prof	932-7858	blair	D	PHD	76	Yale	1981
Bordo, Michael D.	Prof	932-7069	bordo	N	PHD	72	Chicago	1989
Dutta, Manoranjan	Prof	932-7054	dutta	E	PHD	62	Penn	1989
Gigliotti, Gary A.	Prof	932-7466	gag@rci	D	PHD	78	Columbia	1978
Killingworth, Mark R.	Prof	932-7794	illings	J	DPHI	77	Oxford	1978
Klein, Roger W.	Prof	932-7543	klein	C	PHD	70	Yale	1994
Marcus, Matityahu	Prof	932-7344		G	PHD	63	Brown	1962
McLean, Richard P.	Prof	932-7709	mclean	D	PHD	79	SUNY-SBr	1986
Perry, Martin K.	Prof	932-7572	perry	L	PHD	76	Stanford	1989

Name	Rank	Phone	E-mail	Fields	Degree	Yr	School	Since
Rockoff, Hugh T. Undergraduate Director	Prof	932-7857	rockoff	N	PHD	72	Chicago	1971
Rubin, Jeffrey I.	Prof	932-7452	rubin	H	PHD	75	Duke	1973
Russell, Louise B.	Prof	932-6507	lrussell@rci.	I	PHD	71	Harvard	1987
Sato, Kazuo	Prof	932-7077		E	PHD	60	Yale	1984
Seneca, Joseph J.	Prof	932-7821		H	PHD	68	Penn	1976
Stuart, Robert C.	Prof	932-8841	stuart	P	PHD	69	Wisconsin	1968
Tangri, Shanti S.	Prof	932-7460	tangri	O	PHD	61	Berkeley	1970
Taussig, Michael K.	Prof	932-7382	taussig	H	PHD	66	MIT	1967
Tsurumi, Hiroki	Prof	932-7932	tsurumi	C	PHD	67	Penn	1974
Gang, Ira N.	Assoc	932-7405	gang	O	PHD	83	Cornell	1986
Hartline, Jessie C.	Assoc	932-7951		G	PHD	68	Rutgers	1968
Hughes, Joseph P.	Assoc	932-7517		D	PHD	74	N Carol	1975
Mizrach, Bruce	Assoc	932-8261	mizrach	E	PHD	87	Penn	1995
Prusa, Thomas	Assoc	932-7670	prusa	F	PHD	88	Stanford	1994
Sheflin, Neil	Assoc	932-7834	sheflin	C	PHD	79	Rutgers	1975
Sopher, Barry Graduate Director	Assoc	932-7197	sopher	D	PHD	88	Iowa	1987
Altshuler, Rosanne	Asst	932-7783	altshule	H	PHD	88	Penn	1992
Chan, Sewin	Asst	932-8259	chan	H	PHD	95	Columbia	1995
Evenett, Simon	Asst		evenett	F	PHD	95	Yale	1997
Friedman, Eric J.	Asst	932-7797	friedman	D	PHD	93	Berkeley	1996
Moore, Bartholomew J.	Asst	932-8271	moore	E	PHD	90	Columbia	1990
Pietra, Tito	Asst	932-8108		D	PHD	89	Penn	1988
Romeo, Charles J.	Asst	932-8260	romeo	C	PHD	89	Duke	1990
Simard, Dominique	Asst	932-7491	simard	E	PHD	92	Queen's	1991
Vella, Francis G. M.	Asst			C	PHD	90	Rochester	1997

Sacred Heart University — Fairfield, CT 06432-1000 (203) 371-7953 — sacredheart.edu
Economics Program — Fac Fin Stds,Govt & Law Fax=396-6543

Name	Rank	Phone	E-mail	Fields	Degree	Yr	School	Since
Orlowski, Lucjan T.	Prof		orlowskil	EFGP	PHD	79	Poland	1983
Corrigan, Tom D.	Assoc		corrigant	AFG	PHD	69	Maryland	1986
Frangul, Ramzi N.	Assoc		frangulr	G	PHD	73	NYU	1977
Lim, Ralph	Assoc		limr	GLM	MBA		Penn	1981
Mangiero, Susan M.	Asst		mangieros	ACDG	ABD		Conn	1990

Saginaw Valley State Univ — Univ Center, MI 48710 (517) 790-4084 — svsu.edu
Department of Economics — Col of Business & Mgt Fax=249-4699

Name	Rank	Phone	E-mail	Fields	Degree	Yr	School	Since
Uselding, Paul J.	Dean	790-4064		N	PHD	70	Nrthwstrn	1999
Park, Hong Youl	C-Pr	790-4084	hyp	KMEL	PHD	75	Utah St	1975
Kanthi, Mahendra S.	Prof	790-4379	msk	FO	PHD	80	Kentucky	1984
Novey, Donald F.	Prof	790-4352	dfn	DE	MS		S Dak St	1969
Sarkar, Shyamalendu S.	Prof	790-4367	ssarkar		PHD	69	Mich St	1969
Welch, William P.	Assoc	790-5605	welch	CJL	PHD	86	U Wash	1988

St. Ambrose University — Davenport, IA 52803 (319) 333-6382 — saunix.sau.edu
Dept of Econ & Bus Admin — College of Business Fax=333-6268 — Caryl S. Altemus

Name	Rank	Phone	E-mail	Fields	Degree	Yr	School	Since
Collis, John W.	Dean	333-6272	jcollis		PHD	84	Iowa	1984
Harris, Ralph	C-Pr	333-6184	rharris	Stat	PHD	73	Iowa	1993
Begin, Floyd C.	Prof	333-6387	fbegin		PHD	74	Iowa	1985
Chohan, Ray V.	Prof	333-6111	rchohan		PHD	75	Port St	1978
Kabis, Zeinhom M.	Prof	333-6112	zkabis		PHD	68	Illinois	1973
Oberle, Wayne H.	Prof	333-6120	woberle		PHD	69	Missouri	1977
Woodruff, Theodore S.	Prof	333-6420	twoodruf	DEHL	PHD	76	Columbia	8-95
Bereskin, C. Gregory	Assoc	333-6140	gbereskn		PHD	83	Missouri	1991
Brown, Linda K.	Assoc	333-6393	lbrown		DBA	95	Nova SE	1989
Hall, Phillip	Assoc	333-6448	phall		PHD	88	Nebraska	1995
Lee, Christopher	Assoc	333-6120	clee		PHD	90	GeoMason	1995
Lynn, Billy	Assoc	333-6383	blynn		PHD	94	Illinois	1994
Richards, Randy	Assoc	333-6172	rrichard		PHD	96	Iowa	1989
Byrne, John	Asst	333-6406	jbyrne		PHD	96	Iowa	1993
Forret, Monica	Asst	333-6398	mforret		PHD	95	Missouri	1997
Hammermeister, John	Asst	333-6183	jhammerr		MBA		Oregon	
O'Connell, David	Asst	333-6092	doconnel		PHD	97	Boston U	1998
Shoemaker, Craig	Asst	333-6198	cshoemkr		PHD	98	Iowa	1992
Shovlain, Raymond J.	Asst	333-6233	rshovlan		MBA	80	St Ambro	1982
Sztajer, George	Asst	333-6426	gsztajer		MBA	86	E Illinois	1992
Woods, William	Inst	333-6119	wwoods		MBA	96	St Ambro	1995

Saint Anselm College — Manchester, NH 03102-1310 (603)
Economics Faculty — Dept of Economics & Bus Fax=641-7116
Did Not Respond Again--1995-96 Listing

Name	Rank	Phone	E-mail	Fields	Degree	Yr	School	Since
Romps, John F.	C-Ac	641-7140		ABEH	MA	68	Fordham	1968
Kenison, Arthur M.	Prof	641-7138		ACG	PHD	80	Boston U	1980
Kenison, Jeanne H.	Assoc	669-1030		C	EDD	86	Vanderbilt	1988
Minor, Frank J.	Assoc	641-7125			PHD	58	Ohio St	
Moses, Anthony T.	Assoc	641-7139			PHD			
Becker, Gilbert B.	Asst	641-7134		AD	PHD	83	Boston C	1987

College of Saint Benedict St Joseph, MN 56374 (612) 363-3516 csbsju.edu
Economics Faculty Department of Economics Fax=
share faculty with Saint John's Univ, Collegeville MN

Name	Rank	Phone	Email	Field	Degree	Yr	School	Year
Olson, John F.	C-Ac	363-5406	jolson		PHD	84	Rochester	1985
Diedrich, Ernest R.	Prof	363-3518	ediedrich		PHD	83	Colo St	1980
Finn, Daniel Rush	Prof	363-3048	dfinn		PHD	77	Chicago	1977
Clemens Chair in Economics and the Liberal Arts-Dean, School of Theology								
Friedrich, Joseph	Prof	363-3518	jfriedrich		MA	70	Wisconsin	1967
Lewis, Margaret	Assoc	363-5977	mlewis		PHD	89	Maryland	1989
Litterst, Laurence J.	Assoc	363-5917	llitterst		PHD	81	N Illinois	1979
Rambeck, Charles	Assoc	363-3524	crambeck		PHD	79	Minnesota	1975
Johnston, Lewis	Asst	363-2574	ljohnston		PHD	90	Berkeley	

Saint Bonaventure Univ S Bonaventure NY 14778 (716) 375-2202 sbu.edu
Economics Faculty Sch of Business Admin Fax=375-2191

Name	Rank	Phone	Email	Field	Degree	Yr	School	Year
Fischer, Michael J.	Dean	375-2200	mfischer	Atg	PHD	93	Penn St	1985
Kirk, Eugene F.	Asst	375-2069		G	PHD	74	Boston C	1972

College of St. Catherine St Paul, MN 55105 (612) 690-8717 stkate.edu
Economics Faculty Department of Economics Fax=690-6024

Name	Rank	Phone	Email	Field	Degree	Yr	School	Year
Jewell, Nasrin	Prof	690-6830		OA	PHD	81	Wisconsin	1981
Ashley, James R.	Assoc	690-6852	jrashley	AL	PHD	84	Wisconsin	1984
Shikha, Deep	Assoc	690-6577	dshikha	FA	PHD	85	LSU	1985

St. Cloud State University Saint Cloud, MN 56301-4498 (320) 255-2227 stcloudstate.edu
Department of Economics Col of Social Sciences Fax=255-2228 Judi Schindele

Name	Rank	Phone	Email	Field	Degree	Yr	School	Year
Luksetich, William A.	C-Pr	255-4291	a00001		PHD	73	N Illinois	1972
Banaian, King	Prof	255-4797	kbanaian		PHD	86	Claremont	1984
Bodvarsson, Orn B.	Prof	255-2968	i00002		PHD	86	Simon Fr	1988
Edwards, Mary E.	Prof	255-3742	edwards		PHD	88	Tx A&M	1985
Gallagher, Daniel J.	Prof	255-3051	dgallagher		PHD	76	Maryland	1982
Gleisner, Richard F.	Prof	255-3052	b00001		PHD	72	Geotown	1968
Larkin, L. Andrew	Prof	255-2298	larkin		PHD	82	Nebraska	1982
Lofgreen, Harold A.	Prof	255-4250	lofgreen		PHD	72	Iowa	1972
Director, Social Science Research Institute								
Moghaddam, Masoud	Prof	255-4209	masoud		PHD	82	Iowa St	1983
White, Michael D.	Prof	255-3163	mdwhite		PHD	78	Tx Tech	1978
Hampton, Nathan E.	Assoc	255-3825	h00003		PHD	89	Ca-SnBarb	1987
Hughes, Patricia A. Nold	Assoc	255-2076	nold		PHD	91	Ca-SnBarb	1988
Kang, Eungmin B.	Assoc	654-5223	kang		PHD	90	Geo St	1990
Patridge, Mark	Assoc	255-2072	mpartridge		PHD	91	Illinois	1995
Grossman, Philip J.	Asst	255-4232			PHD	84	Virginia	9-99
MacDonald, Richard A.	Asst	255-4781	macdonald		PHD	92	SUNY-Bin	1989
Director, Center for Economic Education								

St. Edward's University Austin, TX 78704-6489 (512) 448-8696 admin.stedwards.edu
Department of Economics School of Business Fax=416-5819
Did Not Respond--1997-98 Listing

Name	Rank	Phone	Email	Field	Degree	Yr	School	Year
Kelliher, Marsha	Dean	448-8658	marshak		LLM	94	San Diego	1993
Tombe, Wani Luan	C-As	448-8599			PHD	85	Tx-Austin	1990
Pluta, Joseph E.	Prof	448-8645			PHD	72	Tx-Austin	1984
Koch, James C.	Assoc	448-8453			MSIR	59	Loyl-Chgo	1960

St. Francis College-NY Brooklyn Hght NY 11201-4398 (718) Ext 266 stfranciscollege.edu
Economics Faculty Department of Economics Fax=522-1274
phone: 522-2300

Name	Rank	Phone	Email	Field	Degree	Yr	School	Year
Quick, Paddy	C-Pr	Ext 266	pquick	ABN	PHD	75	Harvard	9-85
Tabrizi, Behrouz	Asst	Ext 445b	tabrizi		PHD	84	Jawahar	9-97

St. John Fisher College Rochester, NY 14618 (716) sjfc.edu
Economics Faculty Department of Economics Fax=
Did Not Respond--1997-98 Listing

Name	Rank	Phone	Email	Field	Degree	Yr	School	Year
Pate, David S.	C-Ac	385-8120	pate	J	PHD	85	Iowa St	1987
Maley, Jean E.	Prof	385-8097	maley		PHD	72	Rochester	1968
Linsley, Colin A.	Assoc	385-8099	linsley	N	PHD	86	Essex	1987
Maggs, Gary E.	Assoc	385-8432	maggs	E	PHD	86	W Virginia	1986
Roche, John T.	Assoc	385-8119	roche		PHD	81	Mass	1981
Cherry, Monica	VInst	385-8101	cherry		ABD		SUNY-Bin	1996

St. John's University — Jamaica, NY 11439 (718) 990-6419 — stjohns.edu
Dept of Economics & Finance — Col of Business Admin Fax=990-1868

Name	Rank	Phone	Email	Field	Degree	Yr	School	Since
Tobin, Peter	Dean	990-6477						1998
Angelini, Anthony L. P.	C-Ac	990-6420			MA	51	Temple	
Chen, Thomas P.	Prof	990-7347			PHD	76	CUNY	
Clark, Charles	Prof	990-6161			PHD	90	New Sch	1985
Gokturk, S. Sadik	Prof				PHD	72	Columbia	
Gordon, Sara L.	Prof	969-6161			PHD	71	Stanford	1978
Jain, Chaman Lal	Prof				PHD	65	American	
Lawson, Stanley J.	Prof	990-6161			PHD	73	NYU	1978
Lees, Francis A.	Prof	990-6161			PHD	61	NYU	1961
Marshall, John F.	Prof				PHD	82	SUNY-SBr	
Mauer, Laurence J.	Prof	990-6161			PHD	67	Tennessee	1983
Rider, Christine	Prof	969-6161			PHD	79	New Sch	1976
Shapiro, Aharon H.	Prof	969-6161			PHD	66	New Sch	1967
Bansal, Vipul K.	Assoc				PHD	88	Miss	
Buechner, M. Northup	Assoc	990-6161			PHD	71	Virginia	1970
Choi, Young Back	Assoc	876-6161			PHD	86	Michigan	
Ellis, Mary Elizabeth	Assoc				PHD	83	S Carol	
Englander, Valerie	Assoc	390-4545			PHD	75	Rutgers	1982
Flowers, Edward B.	Assoc				PHD	75	Geo St	
Furfero, Arlene J.	Assoc				PHD	80	Rutgers	
Giacalone, Joseph A.	Assoc	990-6161			PHD	71	Columbia	1962
Liaw, K. Thomas	Assoc	990-6161	liawt		PHD	88	Nrthwstrn	9-88
Maran, Michael J.	Assoc				PHD	94	Penn	
Mongiovi, Gary	Assoc	990-7380			PHD	88	New Sch	1985
Moy, Ronald L.	Assoc				PHD	90	Rutgers	
Pappas, Anthony	Assoc				PHD	71	Yale	
Terregrossa, Ralph A.	Assoc				PHD	91	SUNY-Bin	
Tomic, Igor M.	Assoc				PHD	85	CUNY	
Wong, Kwok-Fai Matthew	Assoc	Ext 7313	wongk@sjuvm.	GM	PHD	91	Miss	1990
Eng, Maximo	Adj	990-6161			PHD	66	NYU	1985
Pizzigno, Gregory D.	Adj				MBA		St Johns	
Assistant Dean & Director of Graduate Program								

Saint Joseph's University — Philadelphia, PA 19131-1395 (610) 660-1593 — sju.edu
Department of Economics — Col of Arts & Sciences Fax=660-3300 — Mrs. Dori Pappas

Name	Rank	Phone	Email	Field	Degree	Yr	School	Since
Chapman, Judith G.	Dean	660-1282	jchapman	Psy	PHD	87	Syracuse	1988
Prendergast, George A.	C-Pr	660-1592	gprender	EN	PHD	72	Penn	1956
Bookman, Milica Z.	Assoc	660-1590	mbookman	OP	PHD	83	Temple	1983
Dragonette, Joseph E.	Assoc	660-1594	jdragone	CE	PHD	74	Penn	1967
Fox, Nancy R.	Assoc	660-1596	nfox	DJL	PHD	89	Penn	1986
Sullivan, Edward J.	VInst	660-1591	wmc1998@aol.com	EF	ABD	81	Fordham	1998

St. Lawrence University — Canton, NY 13617-1475 (315) 229-5430 — musci.stlawu.edu
Economics Faculty — Department of Economics Fax=229-5819 — Judith Van Kennen

Name	Rank	Phone	Email	Field	Degree	Yr	School	Since
Richardson, David H.	C-Pr	229-5431	dric	CJEF	PHD	63	Purdue	1979
Charles A. Dana Professor of Economics								
Blewett, Robert Allan	Prof	229-5429	rble	OR	PHD	80	Va Tech	1983
Young, Jeffrey T.	Prof	229-5427	jyou	BQ	PHD	75	Colorado	1980
FitzRandolph, Peter Winfield	Assoc	229-5425	pfit	FN	PHD	79	Tufts	1973
Horwitz, Steven G.	Assoc	229-5731	shor	EPB	PHD	90	GeoMason	1989
Chezum, Brian	Asst	229-5426	bche	JL	PHD	92	Kentucky	1995
Delrossi, Alison	Asst	229-5449	adel	HK	PHD	93	Penn	1999

Saint Louis University — St. Louis, MO 63108 (314) 977-3848 — slu.edu
Department of Economics — Sch of Business Admin Fax=977-3897 — Nancy Young

Name	Rank	Phone	Email	Field	Degree	Yr	School	Since
Seitz, Neil E.	Dean	977-3833		Fnce	PHD	73	Ohio St	1975
Grossman, Leroy J.	C-Pr	977-3830			PHD	63	Vanderbilt	1964
Welch, Patrick J.	Prof	977-3814			PHD	73	Pittsburgh	1983
Islam, Muhammad Q.	Assoc	977-3822			PHD	89	Indiana	1988
Strauss, Jack K.	Assoc	977-3813			PHD	89	Duke	
Chaney, Rick L.	Asst				PHD	84	Illinois	1986
Dean St Louis-Madrid								
Funk, Mark	Asst	977-3844			PHD	98	Ca-Davis	1998
Qian, Hailong	Asst	977-3848			PHD	95	Mich St	1999
Varghese, Adel	Asst	977-3629			PHD	96	Penn	1995

Saint Martin's College — Lacey, WA 98503-1297 (360) 438-4512 — crcstmartin.edu
Economics Faculty — Div Business & Econ Fax=438-4522 — Linda Newman

Name	Rank	Phone	Email	Field	Degree	Yr	School	Since
Knutson, Jerry L.	Dean	438-4512	jknutson		MBA	83	Puget Sd	1987
Wallace, Don	Assoc	438-4329	dwallace		PHD	63	U Wash	

Saint Mary's College-CA	Moraga, CA		94575-4230 (925) 631-4607				stmarys-ca.edu	
Economics Faculty	Sch of Econ & Bus Adm		Fax=376-5625					
Epstein, Edwin M.	Dean	631-4604	eepstein	BLaw	LLB	61	Yale	1994
Hannon, Joan U.	C-Pr	631-4588	jhannon		PHD	78	Wisconsin	1987
Bodily, Jerry J.	Prof	631-4607	jbodily		PHD	74	Purdue	1978
Chase, Kristine L.	Prof	631-4590	kchase		PHD	87	Maryland	1985
Vice President, Finance								
Lee, William C.	Prof	631-4589	wlee		PHD	77	Ca-SnBarb	1982
Allen, Roy E.	Assoc	631-4595	rallen		PHD	83	Berkeley	1985
Moseldjord, Asbjorn	Assoc	631-4596	amoseidj		PHD		Ca-SnBarb	1991
Katz, Elizabeth	Asst			O	PHD	92	Wisconsin	1999

Saint Marys College-IN	Notre Dame, IN		46556-5001 (219) 284-4501				saintmarys.edu	
Economics Faculty	Dept Bus Admin & Econ		Fax=284-4716				Vivian Vargo	
McElroy, Jerome L.	C-Pr	284-4488	jmcelroy	AEFO	PHD	71	Colorado	8-82
Measell, Richard F.	Asst	284-4525	rmeasell	ADHJ	PHD	85	Maryland	8-83

St. Mary's University-TX	San Antonio, TX		78284 (210) 436-3112				stmarytx.edu	
Department of Economics	Sch of Human & Soc Sci		Fax=431-4211					
Did Not Respond--1997-98 Listing								
Miller, Charles H.	Dean	436-3737		Theo	STD	73	Rome	
Robbins, Roy E.	C-As	436-3112	rrobins		MA	75	St MryTX	
Velez, Alejandro	Prof	436-3142	econal		PHD	77	Florida	
Scott, Gary J.	Asst	436-3111	gscott		PHD	93	Notre Dm	1994

Saint Michael's College	Colchester, VT		05439-0125 (802) 654-2298				smcvax.smvt.educ	
Economics Faculty	Department of Economics		Fax=655-3680					
Did Not Respond--1997-98 Listing								
Carvellas, John N.	C-Pr	654-2365	carvellas	ACER	PHD	81	Syracuse	1974
Kessel, Herbert	Prof	654-2460	kessel	AJDC	PHD	81	Boston U	1977
Versteeg, Jennie G.	Prof	654-2298	versteeg	ANFO	PHD	74	Clark	1980
Ramazani, M. Reza	Asst	654-2360	ramazani	AFEC	PHD	90	Colorado	1986

St. Norbert College	DePere, WI		54115-2099 (920) 403-3224				mail.snc.edu	
Department of Economics	Div of Social Sciences		Fax=403-4098					
Elfner, Eliot S.	C-Pr	403-3233	elfnes	BAdm	PHD	77	Wisconsin	1971
Odorzynski, Sandra J.	C-Pr	403-3224	odorsj		PHD	76	Purdue	1978
Paul, Sanjay	Asst	403-3889	paulsa		PHD	92	SUNY-Buf	1992
Quinn, Kevin G.	Asst	403-3447	quinkg		PHD	95	Il-Chicago	1994
vonderRuhr, Marc	Asst		vondma		PHD	99	Indiana	1999

St. Olaf College	Northfield, MN		55057-1098 (507) 646-3149				stolaf.edu	
Economics Faculty	Department of Economics		Fax=646-3523				Lauretta Anderson	
Soderlind, Steven D.	C-Ac	646-3153	soderlin	RA	PHD	80	Mass	1982
Carlson, William L.	Prof	646-3152	carlson	C	PHD	70	Michigan	1973
Dalgaard, Bruce R.	Prof	646-3567	dalgaard	EPA	PHD	76	Illinois	1992
Husby-Johnson Professor in Business & Ecnonmics								
Emery, E. David	Prof	646-3139	emeryd	DIA	PHD	69	Minnesota	1969
Schodt, David W.	Prof	646-3156	schodt	OAH	PHD	80	Wisconsin	1977
Becker, Anthony D.	Assoc	437-2882	becker	DLC	PHD	86	Duke	1987
Chadwick, Kathy	Assoc	646-3154	chadwick	M	PHD	83	Nrthwstrn	1985
Emery, Mary Ann	Assoc	646-3139	emerym	M	MA	65	Minnesota	1969
Judge, Rebecca P.	Assoc	646-3151	judge	ADQ	PHD	76	Duke	1987
Pernecky, Mark L.	Assoc	646-3432	pernecky	EJA	PHD	90	Notre Dm	1990
Wojick, Paul P.	Assoc	646-3152	wojick	AE	PHD	89	Colorado	1988
Geodde, Richard	Asst	646-3126	goedde	M	MBA		Wisconsin	1988
Pomponio, Xun	Asst	646-3151	pomponio	FP	PHD	91	Penn St	1991

Saint Peter's College	Jersey City, NJ		07306 (201) 915-9250				spcvxa.spc.edu	
Economics Faculty	Department of Economics		Fax=				Nancy Carbone	
D'Amico, Thomas F.	C-Pr	915-9250	damico_t	EJT	PHD	83	NYU	1982
Shapiro, Nina	Assoc			DEL	PHD		New Sch	1999
Biolsi, Robert	Asst	915-9251		FG	PHD		CUNY	6-97
Gorcau, Suleyman	Asst			FG	PHD		CUNY	1998

The College of Saint Rose	Albany, NY		12203 (518) 458-5272				mail.strose.edu	
Economics Faculty	School of Business		Fax=458-5449				Maria Freund	
Carlson, Severin C.	Dean	454-2122	scarlson	Fnce	DBA	79	Indiana	1999
Mehtabdin, Khalid R.	Assoc	458-5467	mehtabd	AEFM	PHD	79	Pittsburgh	1986
Sung, Simona	Assoc	458-5869	sungs	CDEL	PHD	90	Rensselaer	8-90

College of St. Scholastica Duluth, MN 55811-4199 (218) 723-6415 css.edu
Economic Faculty Dept of Management Fax=723-6290 Patricia Jones

Goodwin, Larry	Dean	723-6036	lgoodwin		PHD		Chicago	
Smith, George	C-As	723-6415	gsmith		ABD		Nova SE	9-86
Barrett, Anthony	Assoc	723-6471	tbarrett		PHD	84	Geo Wash	
Hoffman, Robert	Asst	723-6715	rhoffman	E	PHD	92	Boston C	

St. Thomas University-FL Miami, FL 33054 (305) 628-6627 stu.edu
Department of Business Adm School of Business Adm Fax=628-6504

Mitchell, Lloyd	C-As	628-6622	lmitchel		MBA	81	U Miami	1984
Carrillo, Raul J.	Assoc				DA		U Miami	1972
Flax, Stanley	Asst				MBA		NYU	1986

University of St. Thomas-MN St. Paul, MN 55105-1096 (651) 962-5675 stthomas.edu
Economics Faculty Div of Social Sciences Fax=962-6360 Christine Igielski
phone 962-5000

Connery, Thomas	Dean	962-6000						
Kreitzer, Joseph L.	C-Pr	962-5683	jlkreitzer	C	PHD	83	Iowa	1981
Blumenthal, Marsha A.	Prof	962-5678	mablumenthal	JH	PHD	85	Minnesota	1984
Garhart, Robert E. Jr.	Prof	962-5679	regarhart	R	PHD	82	Pittsburgh	1981
Gray, Charles M.	Prof	962-4301	cmgray	K	PHD	78	Wash U	1976
Jones, David D.	Prof	962-5675	ddjones	E	PHD	75	Indiana	1972
Alexander, Susan L.	Assoc	962-5677	slalexander	F	PHD	77	So Meth	1981
Fairchild, Daniel R.	Assoc	962-5676	drfairchild	F	PHD	78	St Louis	1976
Langan, Terence G.	Assoc	962-5684	t9langan	L	PHD	88	Minnesota	
Marcott, Craig S.	Assoc	962-5685	csmarcott	C	PHD	83	Purdue	1982
Papagapitos, Agapipos	Assoc	962-5686	a9papagapitos	OP	PHD	92	Ohio St	
Riley, Robert	Assoc	962-5687	rjriley	F	PHD	91	Wisconsin	
Selim, Mohamed Ali	Assoc	962-5180	maselim	A	PHD	81	Minnesota	1959
Vincent, James W.	Assoc	962-5689	jwvincent	Q	PHD	82	Wisconsin	1988
Walsh, William J.	Assoc	962-5690	wjwalsh	E	PHD	70	Notre Dm	1970
Supel, Mary R.	Asst	962-5688	m9supel	L	BA		Denison	1976

University of St. Thomas-TX Houston, TX 77006-4696 (713) 525-2100 basil.stthom.edu
Department of Economics Cameron Sch of Business Fax=525-2110

Ho, Yhi-Min	Dean	522-7911		OQ	PHD	65	Vanderbilt	8-70
Hugh Roy and Lillie Cullen Professor of Economics								
Wilbratte, Barry J.	C-Pr	522-7911		FG	PHD	71	Tulane	1971
Canac, Pierre	Assoc	522-7911		F	PHD	87	Houston	1990
Morefield, Roger D.	Assoc	522-7911		I	PHD	77	Duke	1980
Shirvani, Hassan M.	Assoc	522-7911		FG	PHD	79	Harvard	1986
Yazdi, Khalil	Assoc	522-7911		M	PHD	07	Houston	1990
Ueng, C. Joe	Asst	522-7911		GM	PHD	95	St Louis	1996

Saint Vincent College Latrobe, PA 15650-2690 (724) 537-4597 acad1.stvincent.edu
Economics Faculty Department of Economics Fax=537-4599

Quinlivan, Gary M.	C-Pr	537-4597	gq	CDF	PHD	83	SUNY-Alb	1981
Herr, Andy	Asst		herr	HEQ	PHD	96	Indiana	1991

Salem State College Salem, MA 01970-4589 (978) mecn.mass.edu
Department of Economics Sch of Business & Econ Fax=741-6027
Did Not Respond Again--1995-96 Listing

Burton, Wayne M.	Dean	741-6640			EDD	91	Vanderbilt	
Wesolowski, Karl A.	C-Ac	741-6636			MA		Boston C	
Calabro, Eugene A.	Prof	741-6653			MA		Boston C	
Lucas, Henry A. Jr.	Assoc	741-6683			JD		Suffolk	
Crofts, Robert D.	Asst	741-6615			MA		Northeas	
Pawlak, Andrew T.	Asst	741-6682			MA		Tufts	
Siden, Dorothy R.	Asst	741-6681			PHD	90	Northeas	

Salisbury State University Salisbury, MD 21801-6860 (410) 543-6315 ssu.edu
Department of Economics Perdue Sch of Business Fax=548-2908 Ellen Fykes

Bebee, Richard F.	Dean	543-6316	rfbebee	Atg	PHD	71	Colorado	7-91
Manakyan, Herman	C-Pr	543-6315	hxmanakyan		PHD	89	Alabama	8-99
Khazeh, Kashi	Prof	543-6315	kxkhazeh		PHD	85	Tennessee	O-85
Greene, Benjamin B. Jr.	Assoc	543-6315	bbgreene		PHD	74	Boston C	8-78
Caviglia, Jill	Asst	543-6315	jlcaviglia		PHD	97	Tennessee	8-98
Cheng, Ping	Asst	543-6315	pxcheng		PHD	97	Georgia	8-98
Ervin, Danny	Asst	543-6315	dservin		PHD	96	Kentucky	1-99
Wu, Ying	Asst	543-6315	yxwu		PHD	92	Oregon	8-98
Kincard, Joel	Lect	543-6315	jkincard		PHD	99	N Car St	8-97

Salve Regina University — Newport, RI 02840-4192 (401) Ext 3130 — salve.edu
Economics Faculty — Department of Economics Fax=
phone 847-6650

Name	Rank	Phone	Email	Field	Degree	Yr	School	Since
Tonn, Victor Lux	C-Pr	847-6650	tonnv	AGOP	PHD	94	Utah St	1984
Lawber, Harold E. Jr.	Assoc	847-6650		ABEN	PHD	89	Conn	1988
Coughlan, Carmel	Asst	847-6650		M	MBA	90	Salve Rg	1990

Sam Houston State Univ — Huntsville, TX 77341-2118 (409) 294-1265 — shsu.edu
Dept Economics & Intl Bus — College of Business Adm Fax=294-3612 — Ms. Sally Kundig

Name	Rank	Phone	Email	Field	Degree	Yr	School	Since
Lewis, R. Dean	Dean	294-1254	bed_rdl	Mktg	PHD	72	Arkansas	1980
Green, William B.	C-Pr	294-1265	eco_wbg		PHD	74	LSU	1974
Samuels, George E.	Prof	294-1269	eco_ges		PHD	72	Oregon	1975
Townsend, David C.	Prof	294-1264	eco_dct		PHD	53	LSU	1982
Bumpass, Donald L.	Assoc	294-1268	eco_dlb		PHD	76	Okla St	1992
Greenwade, George D.	Assoc	294-1266	eco_gdg		PHD	88	Tx Tech	1986
Bert, Milo Douglas	Asst	294-1860	eco_mdb		PHD	95	Tx A&M	1995
Blackburne, Edward	Asst	294-3934	exo_efb		PHD	98	Tx A&M	1997
Freeman, Donald	Asst	294-1264	eco_dgf		PHD	88	So Meth	1998
Muehsam, Mitchell J.	Asst	294-1243	eco_mjm		PHD	89	Tx A&M	1989
Muehsam, Valerie P.	Asst	294-3712	eco_vpm		PHD	98	Tx A&M	1993
Miller, John	Lect	294-1293	eco_jmm		MS	65	Rice	1998

Samford University — Birmingham, AL 35229-2306 (205) 726-2364 — mailbox.samford.edu
Economics Faculty — School of Business Fax=726-2464 — M. J. Niesen

Name	Rank	Phone	Email	Field	Degree	Yr	School	Since
Bellas, Carl J.	Dean	726-2308		Mgt	PHD	69	Oregon	1996
Hendon, Fred N.	Prof	726-2549		FN	PHD	68	Alabama	1968
Marshall, Jennings B.	Prof	726-2539		CD	PHD	77	Kentucky	1986
Balaban, Rita	Asst	726-2682		AI	ABD		Pittsburgh	1997

University of San Diego — San Diego, CA 92110-2492 (619) — acusd.edu
Department of Economics — Sch of Business Admin Fax=260-4891

Name	Rank	Phone	Email	Field	Degree	Yr	School	Since
Cook, Curtis	Dean	260-4886		Mgt	DBA	74	S Calif	1997
Anderson, Joan B.	Prof	260-4857	joana		PHD	71	Ca-SnDgo	1981
O'Neil, Robert F.	Prof	260-4855	roneil		PHD	75	Fordham	
Yandell, Dirk	Prof	260-4835	yandell		PHD	81	Purdue	1981
Allen, Andrew T.	Assoc	260-4832	andrewt		PHD	83	Illinois	1984
Dimon, Denise	Assoc	260-4836	dimon		PHD	86	Illinois	1983
Gin, Alan	Assoc	260-4883	agin		PHD	87	Ca-SnBarb	1988
Holt, Charles F.	Assoc	291-6480	cholt		PHD	70	Purdue	1973
Narwold, Andrew	Assoc	260-4875	drew		PHD	91	Ca-SnBarb	1991
Sandy, Jonathan G.	Assoc	260-4880	sandy		PHD	86	Ca-SnBarb	1986

San Diego State University — San Diego, CA 92182-4485 (619) 594-1675 — mail.sdsu.edu
Department of Economics — Col of Arts & Letters Fax=594-5062 — Marie Butler 594-5530

Name	Rank	Phone	Email	Field	Degree	Yr	School	Since
Strand, Paul J.	Dean			PolS	PHD	75	Ohio St	1977
Thayer, Mark A.	C-Pr	594-5510	mthayer		PHD	79	New Mex	1981
Adler, Renatte K.	Prof	594-1662	radler	Q	PHD	79	New Mex	1982
Boddy, Raford D.	Prof	594-6239	rboddy		PHD	68	Michigan	1980
Clement, Norris C.	Prof	594-5860	nclement		PHD	68	Colorado	1968
Frantz, Roger S.	Prof	594-3718	rfrantz		PHD	78	Wash St	1978
Gerber, James B.	Prof	594-5532	jgerber		PHD	86	Ca-Davis	1985
Green, Louis C.	Prof	594-5680	lgreen		PHD	75	Berkeley	1976
Grossbard-Shechtman, Shoshan	Prof	594-5468	shosh		PHD	78	Chicago	1981
Kartman, Arthur E.	Prof	594-5539	akartman		PHD	69	U Wash	1968
Madhavan, Murugappa C.	Prof	594-5492	madhavan		PHD	69	Wisconsin	1968
Nam, Woo Hyun	Prof	594-5478	wnam		PHD	68	U Wash	1968
Stewart, Douglas B.	Prof	594-5502	dstewart		PHD	70	Oregon	1971
Venieris, Yiannis P.	Prof	594-5503	venieris		PHD	69	Oregon	1967
Hambleton, John W.	Assoc	594-5458	jhamble		PHD	71	Wisconsin	1969
Amuedo-Dorantes, Catalina	Asst	594-1663			PHD	98	W Mich	1999
Brunner, Eric	Asst	594-5601	brunner		PHD	95	Ca-SnBarb	1998
Kazimi, Camilla	Asst	594-1675	kazimi		PHD	95	Ca-Irvine	1995

University of San Francisco — San Francisco CA 94117-1080 (415) 422-6784 — usfca.edu
Department of Economics — Col of Arts & Sciences Fax=422-2272 — Cheryl Czekala

Name	Rank	Phone	Email	Field	Degree	Yr	School	Since
Nel, Stanley D.	Dean	422-6172	nel	Fnce	PHD	80	Capetown	1983
Veitch, John	C-Ac	422-6271	veitchj	EG	PHD	85	Nrthwstrn	1985
Fischer, Hartmut	Prof	422-6453	fischer	FA	PHD	73	Berkeley	1970
Kofi, Tetteh A.	Prof	422-6670	kofi	OA	PHD	70	Berkeley	1981
Lehmann, Michael B.	Prof	422-6631	lehmannm	NB	PHD	69	Cornell	1966
Lau, Man-Lui	Assoc	422-6730	laum	CD	PHD	86	Cornell	1992
N'Chu-Oguie, Charles	Assoc	422-6189	nchooguie	CO	PHD	84	Stanford	1984
Garcia, Marilyn	Asst	422-2257	garciam	EO	PHD	97	Berkeley	1997
Wydick, W. Bruce	Asst	422-5863	wydickb	DO	PHD	96	Berkeley	1996

San Francisco State Univ — San Francisco CA 94132 (415) 338-1839 — sfsu.edu
Department of Economics — Col of Behav & Soc Sci Fax=338-1057 — Alex Katz

Name	Rank	Phone	E-mail	Field	Degree	Yr	School	Year
Kasiola, Joel	Dean	338-1846		PolS	PHD	74	Princeton	1995
Potepan, Michael J.	C-Ac	338-2648			PHD	85	Ca-Davis	1991
Anspach, Ralph	Prof	338-7513			PHD	63	Berkeley	1963
Spring Semester only								
Blecha, Betty J.	Prof	338-1447			PHD	76	Iowa	1983
Gemello, John M.	Prof	338-1839			PHD	74	Stanford	1975
Associate Vice President for Academic Resources								
Mason, William J.	Prof	338-7513			PHD	58	Iowa	1958
Moss, Joanna	Prof	338-3026			PHD	78	New Sch	1981
Osman, Jack W.	Prof	338-1116			PHD	66	Rutgers	1967
Schweitzer, Robert N.	Prof	338-1839			PHD	63	Berkeley	1962
Shen, Ruth R.	Prof	338-1009			PHD	61	J Hopkins	1964
Sisk, David E.	Prof	338-1715			PHD	76	UCLA	1978
Vencill, C. Daniel	Prof	338-7514			PHD	71	Stanford	1974
King, Philip G.	Assoc	338-2108			PHD	87	Cornell	1987
Mar, Donald W.	Assoc	338-2499			PHD	85	Berkeley	1987
Hasse, Charles	Asst	338-1839			PHD	96	Ca-Davis	1997
Xu, Peng	Asst	338-7512			PHD	94	Iowa	1994

San Jose State University — San Jose, CA 95192-0114 (408) 924-5400 — sjsu.edu
Department of Economics — Sch of Social Sciences Fax=924-5406 — Janiece Fister

Name	Rank	Phone	E-mail	Field	Degree	Yr	School	Year
Noble, Lela G.	Dean	924-5300		Poly	PHD	70	Fletcher	1965
Gonzalez, Rodolfo	C-Pr	924-5400			PHD	90	Ca-Davis	1990
Cheng, Doris	Prof	924-5423			PHD	76	Notre Dm	1988
Chu, Betty Y.	Prof	924-5419			PHD	73	Notre Dm	1974
Folsom, Roger Nils	Prof	924-5418			PHD	73	Claremont	1976
Garnel, Donald	Prof	924-5407			PHD	66	Berkeley	1958
Greer, Douglas F.	Prof	924-5409			PHD	68	Cornell	1975
Leigh, J. Paul	Prof	924-1368			PHD	79	Wisconsin	1981
Nunn, Geoffrey E.	Prof	924-5410			PHD	73	Virginia	1974
Pogodzinski, Joseph Michael	Prof	924-5421			PHD	80	SUNY-SBr	1987
Saurman, David	Prof	924-1371			PHD	79	Tx A&M	1991
Shieh, Yeung-Nan	Prof	924-5413			PHD	80	Tx A&M	1989
Snowbarger, Marvin R.	Prof	924-5422			PHD	66	Michigan	1966
Watkins, Thayer H.	Prof	924-5420			PHD	65	Colorado	1957
Means, Tom S.	Assoc	924-5414			PHD	83	UCLA	1986
Ortega, Lydia	Assoc	924-1369			PHD	87	GeoMason	1989

Santa Clara University — Santa Clara, CA 95050-0385 (408) 554-4341 — scu.edu
Department of Economics — Leavey Sch of Bus & Adm Fax=554-2331 — Sharon Squyres

Name	Rank	Phone	E-mail	Field	Degree	Yr	School	Year
Posner, Barry Z.	Dean	554-4523	bposner	Mgt	PHD	76	Mass	1978
Sundstrom, William A.	C-Ac	554-6892	wsundstrom		PHD	86	Stanford	1987
Belotti, Mario L.	Prof	554-4086	mbelotti		PHD	69	Tx-Austin	1959
W. M. Keck Foundation Professor-Director, Institute of Agribusiness								
Donnelly, William F.	Prof	554-4948			PHD	69	NYU	1969
Field, Alexander J.	Prof	554-4348	afield		PHD	74	Berkeley	1982
Heineke, John M.	Prof	554-4346	jheineke		PHD	68	Iowa	1968
Iannaccone, Laurence R.	Prof	554-4345	liannaccone		PHD	84	Chicago	1982
Whalen, Thaddeus J. Jr.	Prof	554-4791			PHD	64	Berkeley	1962
Demmert, Henry G.	Assoc	554-4344	hdemmert		PHD	72	Stanford	1968
Associate Dean for Undergraduate Programs								
Kamas, Linda	Assoc	554-6950	lkamas		PHD	82	Berkeley	1988
Klein, Daniel B.	Assoc	554-6051	dklein		PHD	90	NYU	1996
Popper, Helen A.	Assoc	554-6952	hpopper		PHD	90	Berkeley	1991
Russell, Thomas R.	Assoc	554-6953	trussell		PHD	73	Cambridge	1978
Kevane, Michael	Asst	554-4574	mkevane		PHD	94	Berkeley	1995
Roth, David	Asst	554-4340	droth		PHD	92	Yale	1997

University of Scranton — Scranton, PA 18510-4602 (570) 941-4048 — scranton
Dept of Economics & Finance — School of Management Fax=941-4201 — Ms. Susan Trolio 941-4208

Name	Rank	Phone	E-mail	Field	Degree	Yr	School	Year
Did Not Respond Again--1995-96 Listing								
Johnson, Ronald	Dean	941-4208	johnsonr2		DBA	70	Indiana	1997
Ghosh, Satyajit P.	C-Ac	941-6197			PHD	86	SUNY-Buf	1986
Bose, Mrigen	Assoc	941-7727			PHD	72	Utah	1968
Corcione, Frank P.	Assoc	941-7760			PHD	75	Lehigh	1978
Grambo, Ralph W. Jr.	Assoc	941-7417			PHD	81	Penn	1973
Hussain, Riaz	Assoc	941-7497			PHD	73	J Hopkins	1967
Murli, Rajan	Assoc	941-6240			PHD		Temple	1980
Nguyen, Hong V.	Assoc	941-7475			PHD	81	SUNY-Bin	1979
Scahill, Edward M.	Assoc	941-4187			PHD	83	SUNY-Bin	1989
Trussler, Susan	Assoc	941-6122			PHD	89	Penn St	1985
Kallianiotis, John	Asst	941-7577			PHD	85	CUNY	1990

Seattle University
Dept of Economics & Finance
Seattle, WA 98122-4340 (206) 296-2540 seattleu.edu
Albers Sch Bus & Econ Fax=296-2486 Ms. Peggy Allende

Name	Rank	Phone	E-mail	Fields	Degree	Yr	School	Hired
Duggar, Jan W.	Dean	296-5700	jwd		PHD	67	Fla St	1989
Yates, Barbara M.	C-Pr	296-2540	bmyates	AEGH	PHD	69	Michigan	1970
Rivers, Mary J.	Assoc	296-5717	rivers	CDM	PHD	82	Pittsburgh	1978
Sorenson, Timothy L.	Assoc	296-5738	tsore	MDF	PHD	91	Harvard	1991
Hiedemann, Bridget	Asst	296-2803	bgh	DJT	PHD	92	Duke	1994
Peterson, Dean J.	Asst	296-2538	dean	B	PHD	94	Illinois	1991
Weber, Christian E.	Asst	296-5725	cweber	EO	PHD	92	Duke	1993

Seattle Pacific University
Department of Economics
Seattle, WA 98119-1997 (206) 281-2700 spu.edu
Sch of Business & Econ Fax=281-2733 Ruth Myers

Name	Rank	Phone	E-mail	Fields	Degree	Yr	School	Hired
Hill, Alec	Dean	281-2992	adhill	Ethi	JD	80	U Wash	1985
Downing, Douglas A.	C-Ac	281-2890	ddowning	ACH	PHD	87	Yale	1983
Deming, Jonathan C.	Assoc	281-2181	jdeming	BR	PHD	79	Oregon	1977
Surdyk, Lisa	Assoc	281-2709	lsurdyk	G	PHD	91	U Wash	1991

Seton Hall University
Department of Economics
South Orange, NJ 07079-2692 (973) 761-7723 lanmail.shu.edu
Stillman School of Bus Fax=761-9217 Ms. Alliya Cunningham

Name	Rank	Phone	E-mail	Fields	Degree	Yr	School	Hired
Martin, Dolores	Dean	761-9013			PHD	76	Va Tech	
Dall, John J. Jr.	C-Pr	761-9356	dalljohn		PHD	68	Penn	
Jordan, W. John	Prof	761-9236	jordanja		PHD	77	SUNY-Alb	1977
Ketkar, Kusum	Prof	761-9102	ketkarku		PHD	80	Vanderbilt	1983
Tinari, Frank D.	Prof	761-9125	tinarifr		PHD	76	Fordham	
Tzannetakis, George	Prof	761-9211	tzannege		PHD	64	NYU	
Ikpoh, Andrew	Assoc	761-9799	ikpohand		PHD	88	Columbia	
Kant, Chander	Assoc	761-9281	kantchan		PHD	80	So Meth	1987
Loviscek, Anthony	Asst	761-9127	lovisclo		PHD	80	W Virginia	1992

Shenandoah University
Economics Faculty
Winchester, VA 22601-5195 (540) 665-4572 su.edu
Byrd School of Business Fax=665-5437

Name	Rank	Phone	E-mail	Fields	Degree	Yr	School	Hired
Harrison, Stanley E.	Dean	665-4572	sharriso		PHD	89	OSU	1999
Pavsek, Daniel A.	Prof	665-4526	dpavsek		PHD	81	Case Wes	1992
Thies, Clifford F.	Prof	665-5450	cthies		PHD	82	Boston C	1992
Spencer, Theresa	Assoc	665-4572	tspencer		PHD	89	N Car St	1997

Shepherd College
Department of Economics
Shepherdstwn WV 25443-1569 (304) 876-5241 shepherd.wvnet.edu
Business & Soc Sciences Fax=876-5193 Ms. Brenda Baker

Name	Rank	Phone	E-mail	Fields	Degree	Yr	School	Hired
Johnson, E. William	C-Pr	876-5432	bjohnson		PHD	74	Virginia	1971
Reid, Kathleen A.	C-Pr	876-5306	kreid		PHD	86	Penn St	1983
Phillips, Edward S.	Prof	876-5353	sphillips		PHD	70	Colorado	1974
Kinney, Kinney	Assoc	876-5434	lkinney		PHD	85	Maryland	1994
Schultz, John A.	Assoc	876-5352	jschultz		PHD	85	S Carol	1988

Shippensburg University
Department of Economics
Shippensburg, PA 17257-2299 (717) 532-1437 ark.ship.edu
College of Business Fax=530-4003 Vicki Shaak

Name	Rank	Phone	E-mail	Fields	Degree	Yr	School	Hired
Finucane, Brendan P.	C-Pr	532-1437			PHD	82	Pittsburgh	1982
Bastin, Hamid	Prof	532-1679			PHD	89	Geo St	1989
Eggleston, Robert C.	Prof	531-1675			PHD	84	Pittsburgh	1965
Lee, Daniel Y.	Prof	532-1556			PHD	86	Pittsburgh	1986
Mathis, Stephen A.	Prof	532-1696			PHD	79	Iowa St	1979
Posatko, Robert C.	Prof	532-1138			PHD	75	Penn St	1981
Reinwald, Thomas P.	Prof	532-1437			PHD	73	Illinois	1974
Koscianski, Janet	Assoc	532-1174			PHD	90	S Illinois	1990

Siena College
Department of Economics
Loundonville, NY 12211-1462 (518) 783-2398 siena.edu
Business Division Fax=783-4293

Name	Rank	Phone	E-mail	Fields	Degree	Yr	School	Hired
Nolan, James R.	Dean	783-2321	jnolan	Stat	PHD	86	SUNY-Alb	
Trees, W. Scott	C-As		trees		PHD	94	Notre Dm	9-85
Howe, Edward T.	Prof		howe		PHD	73	SUNY-Alb	
Reinhart, Blaise F.	Prof				PHD	62	Catholic	
Shirey, Richard L.	Assoc	783-2398	shirey		PHD	94	SUNY-Alb	9-79

Simmons College
Economics Faculty
Boston, MA 02115-5898 (617) 521-2594 vmsvax.simmons.edu
Col Arts & Sci & Prof S Fax=521-3199 Jaye Smith

Name	Rank	Phone	E-mail	Fields	Degree	Yr	School	Hired
Kenyon, Daphne A.	C-Pr	521-2587	dkenyon	HI	PHD	80	Michigan	1989
Basch, Donald L.	Prof	521-2584	dbasch	D	PHD	77	Yale	1980
Sawtelle, Barbara A.	Prof	521-2582	bsawtelle	E	PHD	76	MIT	1970
Biewener, Carole	Assoc	521-2583	cbiewener	FB	PHD	89	Mass	1987
Aoki, Masato	VAsst	521-2580	maoki	A	PHD	95	Mass	1994

Simpson College — Indianola, IA 50125 (515) 961-1513 — storm.simpson.edu
Dept Mgt, Atg & Economics — Div of Policy Studies Fax=961-1652 — Cindy Hamilton

Name	Rank	Phone	E-mail	Fields	Degree	Yr	School	Since
Mueller, Marilyn	C	961-1574	mueller		JD	81	Drake	1986
Colella, Francis J.	Prof	961-1513	colella	BEFN	PHD	73	Fordham	1977
Palmieri, James	Asst	961-1801	palmieri	DHIJ	PHD	95	Indiana	1997

Skidmore College — Saratoga Sprg NY 12866-1632 (518) Ext 5090 — skidmore.edu
Economics Faculty — Department of Economics Fax=580-5099 — Amelia Clarke

Name	Rank	Phone	E-mail	Fields	Degree	Yr	School	Since
Odekon, Mehmet A.	C-Ac	580-5097	modekon		PHD	77	SUNY-Alb	1983
Baum, Sandra R.	Prof	580-5092	sbaum		PHD	81	Columbia	1987
Rotheim, Roy J.	Prof	580-5115	rrotheim		PHD	77	Rutgers	1980
Jones, Robert J.	Assoc	580-5094	rjones		PHD	78	Columbia	1973
Koechlin, Tim	Assoc	580-5095	tkoechli		PHD	89	Mass	1988
Chiteji, Ngina	Asst	580-5090	nchiteji		PHD	99	N Carol	1999
Shiell, Leslie	Asst	580-5096	lshiell		PHD	98	Toronto	1998
Varsha, Linda	Asst	580-5098	lvarsha		PHD	99	Wisconsin	1999

Slippery Rock University — Slippery Rock PA 16057-1326 (724) 738-2039 — sru.edu
Dept of Economics & Finance — Col Info Sci & Bus Adm Fax=738-2959 — Leigh McGuirk 738-2772

Name	Rank	Phone	E-mail	Fields	Degree	Yr	School	Since
Mastrianna, Frank V.	Dean	738-2008	un3600		PHD	68	Cincinnati	3-87
Culp, David B.	C-Ac	738-2971	david.culp	AEN	PHD	96	S Illinois	1978
Baroutsis, A. Paul	Prof	738-2575	paul.baroutsis	ADP	PHD	72	Purdue	1972
Mamoozadeh, G. Abbas	Assoc	738-2578	abbas.mamooz+	AG	PHD	80	Kent St	
Noorbakhsh, Abbas	Assoc	738-2576	abbas.noorbak+	AG	PHD	89	Kansas St	1990
Tannery, Frederick J.	Assoc	738-2579	frederick.tan+	ACDJ	PHD	80	Pittsburgh	1981
Valencia, Jesus M.	Asst	738-2577	jesus.valencia	ACFJ	PHD	88	Pittsburgh	1983

Smith College — Northampton, MA 01063 (413) 585-3600 — sophia.smith.edu
Economics Faculty — Department of Economics Fax=585-3389 — Judy Fountain

Name	Rank	Phone	E-mail	Fields	Degree	Yr	School	Since
Reinhardt, Nola	C-Ac	585-3617	nreinhar	OPQ	PHD	81	Berkeley	1981
Aldrich, Mark	Prof	585-3603	maldrich	JLN	PHD	69	Tx-Austin	1968
Averitt, Robert T.	Prof	585-3604	raveritt	ABE	PHD	61	Tx-Austin	1961
Bartlett, Randall	Prof	585-3605	rbartlett	AHR	PHD	71	Stanford	1979
Buchele, Robert	Prof	585-3607	rbuchele	CAJP	PHD	76	Harvard	1977
Haas-Wilson, Deborah	Prof	585-3636	dhwilson	DIL	PHD	83	Berkeley	1984
Kaufman, Roger T.	Prof	585-3612	rtkaufman	CEJP	PHD	78	MIT	1983
Leonard, Frederick H.	Prof	585-3614	fleonard	AEG	PHD	66	Michigan	1966
Pfeifer, Karen	Prof	585-3623	kpfeifer	BNOP	PHD	81	American	1979
Savoca, Elizabeth A.	Prof	585-3615	esavoca	CEIT	PHD	82	Berkeley	1982
Zimbalist, Andrew	Prof	585-3622	zimbalis	CJLP	PHD	74	Harvard	1974
Mahdavi, Mahnaz	Assoc	585-3629	mmahdavi	FGM	PHD	86	Michigan	1985
Riddell, Thomas A.	Assoc	585-4910	triddell	AHNO	PHD	75	American	1980
Staelin, Charles P.	Assoc	585-3621	cstaelin	ACDF	PHD	71	Michigan	1981
Miller, James	Asst	585-3613	jdmiller		PHD	97	Chicago	1996
Morey, Matthew	Asst				PHD	93	UCLA	1999

Sonoma State University — Rohnert Park, CA 94928-3609 (707) 664-2377 — sonoma.edu
Department of Economics — Sch of Business & Econ Fax=664-4009 — Sheila Mackintosh

Name	Rank	Phone	E-mail	Fields	Degree	Yr	School	Since
Clark, Lawrence S.	Dean	664-2220		Law	LLM	80	DePaul	1994
Benito, Carlos	C-Pr	664-2366			PHD	73	Ca-Davis	1990
Ben-Zion, Barry	Prof	664-2919			PHD	73	Oregon	1969
Garlin, Victor A.	Prof	664-2702			PHD	65	Berkeley	1970
Hayes, Sue E.	Prof	664-0070			PHD	75	Berkeley	1974
Lewis, Stephen D.	Prof	664-2549			PHD	69	Ca-SnBarb	1982

University of the South — Sewanee, TN 37383-1000 (931) 598-1000 — sewanee.edu
Department of Economics — Col of Arts & Sciences Fax=598-1145

Name	Rank	Phone	E-mail	Fields	Degree	Yr	School	Since
Keele, Robert	Dean	598-1248	bkeele	PolS	PHD	60		
Mohiuddin, Yasmeen	C-Pr	598-1462	ymohiudd	FOE	PHD	83	Vanderbilt	
Gottfried, Robert Richard	Prof	598-1243	rgottri	OQR	PHD	81	N Carol	
Ingles, Jerry Lee	Prof	598-1235	jingles	BL	PHD	75	Cornell	
Schaefer, Arthur McCluny	Prof	598-1146	aschaefer	CD	PHD	67	Penn	
Hendrickson, Jill K.	Asst	598-1805	jhendric	EGC	PHD		Notre Dm	1995

University of South Alabama — Mobile, AL 36688-0002 (334) 460-7171 — usouthal.edu
Dept of Econ & Finance — College of Business Fax=460-6408 — Ms. Lissa Williams

Name	Rank	Phone	E-mail	Fields	Degree	Yr	School	Since
Moore, Carl C.	Dean	460-6902		Mgt	PHD	70	Alabama	1971
Moak, Donald L.	C-Pr	460-7171		Fnce	PHD	74	Miss	9-93
Bobo, James R.	Emer				PHD	61	LSU	1978
Chang, Semoon	Prof	460-6156		M	PHD	71	Fla St	1972
Swofford, James L.	Prof	460-6705	jswoffor@jaguar1	E	PHD	81	Florida	1984
Forbus, Philip R.	Assoc	460-6708		AD	PHD	78	Arkansas	1978
Stutsman, A. Douglas	Emer	460-6706		AB	PHD	70	Miss	1968
Quinn, Robert	Asst	460-6711		ADJI	PHD	95	U Miami	1997

Univ So Carolina at Aiken	Aiken, SC		29801	(803) 641-3340				aiken.sc.edu
Economics Faculty	School Bus Adm & Econ			Fax=641-3445				Gina Buckley
phone 648-6851								
Vyas, Niren M.	H	648-6851	nirenv	Mktg	PHD	81	S Carol	1981
Shelburn, Marsha	Prof	648-6851	marshas		PHD	80	N Carol	1980
Folsom, Davis	Assoc	648-6851	davisf		PHD	79	Conn	1979

Univ of South Carolina	Columbia, SC		29208	(803) 777-7400				darla.badm.sc.edu
Department of Economics	Col of Business Admin			Fax=777-6876				Georgene Dance
Shrock, David L.	Dean	777-3176		Tran	DBA	74	Indiana	1994
Wilder, Ronald P.	C-Pr	777-7400			PHD	69	Vanderbilt	1987
Addison, John T.	Prof	777-4608			PHD	71	London	
Blackburn, McKinley L.	Prof	777-4931			PHD	87	Harvard	1987
Breger, Gerald E.	Emer	777-4780			PHD	64	Arkansas	
Carlsson, Robert J.	Prof	777-6044			PHD	64	Rutgers	
Clower, Robert W.	Prof	777-5919			DLIT	78	Oxford	1986
Hugh C. Lane Professor of Economics								
Cohn, Elchanan	Prof	777-2714			PHD	68	Iowa St	
Harrison, Glenn W.	Prof	777-4943			PHD	82	UCLA	
Dewey H. Johnson Professor of Economics								
Kiker, B. F.	Prof	777-4904			PHD	65	Tulane	1971
Jeff B. Bates Professor of Public Administration & Finance								
Liles, W. Pierce	Prof	777-2306			PHD	72	S Carol	
Martin, Randolph C.	Prof	777-3176			PHD	71	Wash U	1970
Associate Dean								
Putnam, William F.	Emer	777-7602			MS	57	S Carol	
Boucher-Breuer, Janice L.	Assoc	777-7419			PHD	87	N Carol	1987
Chappell, Henry W.	Assoc	777-4940			PHD	79	Yale	1980
McDermott, John H.	Assoc	777-4939			PHD	79	Brown	1983
Phillips, William H.	Assoc	777-4930			PHD	80	MIT	1979
Director Undergraduate Studies								
Rawson, William S.	Emer	777-3865			PHD	67	Duke	1967
Rutstrom, Lisa	Assoc	777-4932	lisar	DFQ	PHD	90	Stockholm	8-91
Johnson, Eric	Asst	777-2583			PHD	97	Ca-SnDgo	8-98
Laury, Susan	Asst				PHD	96	Indiana	8-95
McInnes, Melayne	Asst				PHD	97	Yale	8-97
Woodward, Doug P.	Asst	777-2510			PHD	86	Tx-Austin	
Director, Division of Research								
Balch, Donald C.	Lect	777-6828	sxabalch	AD	MA	88	S Carol	8-84
Bradley, James Jr.	DLect	777-2786	jbradley	AHM	CHPL	70	N Carol	9-74

U South Carolina at Spartanb	Spartanburg, SC		29303	(864) 503-5581				gw.uscs.edu
Department of Economics	Sch of Bus Admin & Econ			Fax=503-5598				Elda Rattie
Word, William R.	Dean	503-5549	bword	ADEJ	PHD	70	Tennessee	1998
Tanyel, Faruk I.	C-Pr	503-5587	ftanyel	Mktg	PHD	83	Tennessee	1981
Bailey, Duncan	Prof	503-5301	dbailey	AEOR	PHD	70	Va Tech	1984
Jilling, Michael	Prof	503-5586	mjilling	ACMF	PHD	76	S Carol	1975
Reese, James W.	Assoc	503-5585	jreese	AFPH	PHD	73	Tennessee	1982
Rook, Sarah P.	Assoc	503-5584	srook	ADEQ	PHD	80	N Car St	1980
Jolly, Eric S.	Asst	503-5288		A	MA		Ohio U	1968
Connelly, Robert A. Jr.	Inst	503-5230		A	MA		Appalach	1972

South Carolina St University	Orangeburg, SC		29117	(803) 536-8070				scsi.edu
Dept Agribusiness & Econ	School of Business			Fax=536-3639				Ms. Patricia McDonald
Reuben, Lucy J.	Dean	536-8086	lreuben	BusA	PHD	81	Michigan	1995
Modeste, Nelson C.	C-Ac	536-8076	nmodeste		PHD	76	Florida	1994
Londhe, Suresh R.	Prof	536-8449	londhe		PHD	65	LSU	1969
Onunkwo, Emmanuel N.	Prof	536-8843	emonunkwo		PHD	73	Geotown	1978
Karemera, David	Assoc	536-7136	kdaremera		PHD	89	Nebraska	1997
Kyereme, Stephen	Assoc	536-8448	skyereme		PHD	84	Cornell	1984
Mustafa, Muhammad	Assoc	536-8459	mmustafa		PHD	88	Wayne St	1989
Selassie, Haile G.	Assoc	536-8456	selassie		PHD	83	Okla St	1984
Sureshwaran, S.	Asst	536-8456	ssuresh		PHD	89	Clemson	1990

University of South Dakota	Vermillion, SD		57069-2390	(605) 677-5455				usd.edu
Dept of Econ, Dec Sci & MIS	School of Business			Fax=677-5427				Ann Ward
Johnson, Jerry W.	Dean	677-5455	jerryj		PHD	71	Iowa St	1967
Powell, John	C	677-5455		Mis				
Brown, Ralph J.	Prof	677-5620	rbrown		PHD	70	Colorado	1977
Johnson, Dennis A.	Prof	677-5552	dajohnson		PHD	72	Iowa	1964
Reinke, Robert W.	Prof	677-5540	rreinke		PHD	82	Minnesota	1987
Ring, Raymond J. Jr.	Prof	677-6861	rring		PHD	73	Kansas	1978
Wymar, Benno	Prof	677-5550	bwymar		PHD	73	Nebraska	1968
Waldron, Randall	Asst	677-6643	rwaldron		PHD	94	Vanderbilt	1994

South Dakota State Univ Brookings, SD 57007-0895 (605) 688-4141 sdstate.edu
Economics Department Col of Agri & Biol Sci Fax=688-6386 June Larkin

Choliac, Fred	Dean	668-4148		PHD	77	Colo St	1998
Shane, Richard C.	C-Pr	688-4141	Q	PHD	78	Wash St	1977
Beutler, Martin K.	Prof	394-2236	Q	PHD	86	Purdue	1986
Dobbs, Thomas L.	Prof	688-4874	Q	PHD	69	Maryland	1978
Gilbert, Howard A.	Prof	688-4844	A	PHD	67	Oregon St	1966
Janssen, Larry L.	Prof	688-4871	Q	PHD	78	Nebraska	1978
Kim, Han J.	Prof	688-4848	C	PHD	69	Oregon St	1967
Lamberton, Charles E.	Prof	688-4865	G	PHD	75	Iowa St	1974
Lyons, Patrick A.	Prof	688-4842	M	JD	74	S Dakota	1975
O'Brien, Jamie L.	Prof	688-4144	K	MPA	84	S Dakota	1984
Peterson, Donald L.	Prof	688-4859	Q	PHD	73	Nebraska	1974
Pflueger, Burton W.	Prof	688-4141	Q	PHD	85	Illinois	1985
Adamson, Dwight W.	Assoc	688-4105	E	PHD	88	Wash St	1989
Fausti, Scott W.	Assoc	688-4868	F	PHD	91	Illinois	1991
Franklin, Douglas R.	Assoc	688-4861	Q	PHD	82	Utah	1988
Sondey, John A.	Assoc	688-4873	H	PHD	89	Wash St	1990
Cumber, Carol J.	Asst	688-4849	M	PHD	94	S Dak St	1990
Dierson, Matthew	Asst	688-4141	Q	PHD	99	Illinois	1999
Klein, Nicole L.	Asst	688-4847	Q	PHD	96	Kansas St	1997
Qasmi, Bashir A.	Asst	688-4870	Q	PHD	86	Iowa St	1987
Sartos, Joseph	Asst	668-4846	E	PHD	96	Rutgers	1997
VanderSluius, Evert	Asst	688-4872	FO	PHD	93	Minnesota	1997
Zimmerman, Jason	Asst	688-4141	MA	PHD	98	Purdue	1999
Ellingson, Wayne D.	Inst	688-4869	C	BS	70	Iowa St	1980
Fredrickson, Trygve G.	Inst	688-4866	M	MBA	89	S Dakota	1990
Gustafson, Curtis O.	Inst	688-4850	M	MPA	86	S Dakota	1989
Rasmussen, Chris H.	Inst	688-4145	M	BA	75	SW State	1978

University of South Florida Tampa, FL 33620-5500 (813) 974-4252 coba.usf.edu
Department of Economics Col of Business Admin Fax=974-6510 Mary L. Bennett

Anderson, Robert L.	Dean	974-3229	randerso		PHD	70	North Tx	1971
DeSalvo, Joseph S.	C-Pr	974-6388	jdesalvo	R	PHD	68	Nrthwstrn	1983
Bellante, Donald M.	Prof	974-6386	dbellant	J	PHD	71	Fla St	1985
Gyimah-Brempong, Kwabena	Prof	974-6520	kgyimah	O	PHD	81	Wayne St	1994
Herander, Mark G.	Prof	974-6540	mherande	F	PHD	80	N Carol	1979
Porter, Philip K.	Prof	974-6539	pporer	H	PHD	78	Tx A&M	1985
Rowe, John W.	Prof	974-6543	jrowe	D	PHD	66	Illinois	1979
Ford, Edward J. Jr.	Assoc	974-6559	eford	R	PHD	71	Boston C	1971
Green-Weishaupt, Carole A.	Assoc	974-6521	cgreen	J	PHD	82	Illinois	1982
Kamp, Bradley P.	Assoc	974-6549	bkamp	L	PHD	93	Ca-SnDgo	1992
Picone, Gabriel A.	Assoc	974-6537	gpicone	C	PHD	93	Vanderbilt	1993
Racine, Jeffrey S.	Assoc	974-6555	jracine	C	PHD	91	W Ontario	1993
Spence, James G. email=jspence2@stpt.usf.edu	Assoc	432-5524		A	PHD	79	Oklahoma	1975
Thomas, Christopher R.	Assoc	974-6546	cthomas	L	PHD	80	Tx A&M	1982
Wilson, R. Mark	Assoc	974-6514	mwilson	I	PHD	77	Nrthwstrn	1978
Saavedra, Luz A.	Asst	974-6554	lsaavedr	F	PHD	98	Illinois	1998
Swinton, John R.	Asst	974-4363	jswinton	Q	PHD	96	Wisconsin	1995
Bartlett, Sue A.	Lect	974-6547	sbartlet	A	MA	93	S Fla	1994
Crummett, Maria A.	Lect	974-3694	mcrummet	F	PHD	85	New Sch	1996

Southeast Missouri St Univ C Girardeau, MO 63701-4799 (573) 651-2181 semovm.semo.edu
Department of Economics Harrison Coll Business Fax=651-2200 Ms. Debbie McKee
Homepage: economics.semo.edu/economics/index.html

McDougall, Gerald S.	Dean	651-2112	c476bux	HL	PHD	74	Claremont	1993
Summary, Rebecca M.	C-Pr	651-2945	c694sse	FA	PHD	83	Illinois	1983
Domazlicky, Bruce R.	Prof	651-2013	c819sse	AK	PHD	76	Wyoming	1986
Fox, Pauline H.	Prof	651-2181	c858sse	AKH	PHD	75	Okla St	1978
Kerr, Peter M.	Prof	651-2012	c446ssb	AEBF	PHD	79	Kansas	1980
Park, Kang Hoon	Prof	651-2942	c382bue	CF	PHD	81	S Illinois	1979
Sutton, Terry	Prof	651-2944	c721bue	B	PHD	70	Kansas St	1972
Weber, William L.	Prof	651-2946	c645sse	GHI	PHD	86	S Illinois	1986
Primont, Diane F.	Assoc	651-2819	c794sse	JDE	PHD	87	N Carol	1990
Redmond, Willie	Asst	651-2181		AFL	PHD	99	S Carol	1999

Southeastern Louisiana Univ Hammond, LA 70402 (504) 549-2086 selu.edu
Dept of General Business College of Business Fax=549-2881 Lou Salisbury

Budden, Michael C.	Dean	549-2258	mbudden	Mktg	PHD	82	Arkansas	1999
Hsing, Yu	H-Pr	549-2086	yhsing	EJOR	PHD	83	Tennessee	1987
Lange, Ralph W.	Prof	549-2081	rlange	AF	PHD	74	LSU	
Gibson, Jo Anne	Assoc	549-3098	jgibson	EF	PHD	72	Miss	
Lewis, Danielle	Asst	549-3084	dlewis2	EL	PHD	96	Kansas St	1996
Pedersen, William E. Director, Business Research Center	Asst	549-5929	pedersen	AGH	PHD	95	N Orleans	1994
Thomasson, Henry E.	Asst	549-3068	htomasson	AJ	MS		LSU	
Wadsworth, Daniel	Inst	549-3091	dwadsworth		MBA	96	LSU	

Southeastern Oklahoma State — Durant, OK 74701-0609 (580) Ext 2713 — sosu.edu
Dept of Economics & Finance — School of Business Fax=920-7479
phone 924-0121

Name	Rank	Phone	Email	Field	Degree	Yr	School	Year
Masters, Robert J.	Dean	Ext 2706		Mgt	PHD	75	Purdue	1995
Chinn, Kenneth	C-Ac	924-0121	kchinn	EC	PHD	91	Colo St	1982
Collier, George A. Jr.	Emer	Ext 2821		ARM	PHD	78	Okla St	1972
Tangesdal, Mark O.	Asst	Ext 2707	mtangesdal		PHD	95	Ca-Rivers	1997

Southern Adventist Univ — Collegedale, TN 37315-0370 (423) 238-2751 — southern.edu
Economics Faculty — Dept of Business & Mgt Fax=238-3151 — Linda Wilhelm

Name	Rank	Phone	Email	Field	Degree	Yr	School	Year
VanOrnam, Don	Dean	238-2750			PHD	95	Claremont	1997
Erickson, Richard	Assoc	238-2755		A	MBA	81	Aust Pea	1984

Southern University — Baton Rouge, LA 70813-9723 (225) 771-2992 — subrvm.subr.edu
Department of Economics — College of Business Fax=771-5262 — Marilyn Doherty

Name	Rank	Phone	Email	Field	Degree	Yr	School	Year
Andrews, Donald R.	Dean$	771-5641		QR	PHD	80	Tx A&M	1995
Jindia, Jaswant R.	C-Pr	771-2992	jaswant	AO	PHD	70	Illinois	1970
Cheng, Benjamin S.	Prof	771-5642		AE	PHD	71	Oklahoma	1971
Yigletu, Ashagre	Assoc	771-2992		AE	PHD	72	Belgrade	1972
Agnihotri, Krisna	Asst	771-2992		A	MA	57	Punjab	1969
Lokhande, Vineeta	Asst	771-2992		G	PHD	94	N Orleans	1994
Osagie, Emmanuel I.	Asst				PHD	85	LSU	1985
Smyser, Michael	Asst	771-2992		G	PHD	91	Fla Intl	1991

Southern Arkansas Univ — Magnolia, AR 71753-5000 (870) 235-4304 — saumag.edu
Dept of Economics & Finance — Sch of Business Admin Fax=235-4800 — Mrs. Gaye Calhoun

Name	Rank	Phone	Email	Field	Degree	Yr	School	Year
Rankin, David F.	Dean	235-4300	dfrankin	Fnce	PHD	70	Miss	1968
Ashby, David J.	C-Ac	235-4304	jdasby	Fnce	DBA		La Tech	1992
Bellamy, D. Scott	Assoc	235-5162	scbellamy	I	PHD		Kentucky	1993

Univ of Southern California — Los Angeles, CA 90089-0253 (213) 740-8335 — usc.edu
Department of Economics — Col of Ltrs, Arts & Sci Fax=740-8543 — Sheila Williams
email @1=almaak.usc.edu

Name	Rank	Phone	Email	Field	Degree	Yr	School	Year
Schapiro, Morton Owen	Dean	740-8218	schapiro@rcf.		PHD	79	Penn	1991
Vuong, Quang	C-Pr	740-3528	qvuong@mizar		PHD	82	Nrthwstrn	1987
Day, Richard H.	Prof	740-2432	rday@rcf.		PHD	61	Harvard	1976
Easterlin, Richard A.	Prof	743-6993	easterl@rcf.		PHD	53	Penn	1982
Elliott, John E.	Prof	740-3510	jeelliot@rcf.		PHD	56	Harvard	1966
Gordon, Peter	Prof	743-2770	pgordon@1		PHD	71	Penn	1971
Hsiao, Cheng	Prof	740-2103	chsiao@1		PHD	72	Stanford	1985
Kalaba, Robert E.	Prof	740-2109	kalaba@rcf.		PHD	58	NYU	1969
Kuran, Timur	Prof	740-7432	kuran@rcf.		PHD	82	Stanford	1982
MacLeod, Bentley	Prof	740-3517	wmacleon@1		PHD	84	Brit Colum	1997
Magill, Michael J. P.	Prof	740-2104	magill@1		PHD	70	Brown	1979
Nugent, Jeffrey B.	Prof	740-2107	nugent@1		PHD	65	New Sch	1973
Richardson, Harry W.	Prof	740-3954	hrichard@rfc.		MA	61	Manchester	1975
Yett, Donald E.	Prof	740-3514	yett@rcf.		PHD	68	Berkeley	1966
Cheng, Harrison C.	Assoc	740-2105	hacheng@mizar.		PHD	77	Berkeley	1978
DePrano, Michael E.	Assoc	740-3525	deprano@rcf.		PHD	63	Illinois	1963
Betts, Caroline	Asst	740-2430	cbetts@rcf.		PHD	94	Brit Colum	1994
Dekle, Robert	Asst	740-2134	dekle@1		PHD	88	Yale	1998
Mui, Vai-Lam	Asst	740-2108	vailam@1		PHD	92	Berkeley	1992
Pendleton, Linwood	Asst	740-3513	linwoodp@1		PHD	96	Yale	1996
Perrigne, Isabelle	Asst	740-3528	perrigne@rcf		PHD	91	Toulouse	1997
Robinson, James A.	Asst	740-3526	jarobins@rcf.		PHD	93	Yale	1995
Rosendorff, Peter	Asst	740-3529	bpeter@1		PHD	93	Columbia	1992
Kamrany, Nake M.	SLect	740-6997	kamrany@rcf.		PHD	62	S Calif	1976

Univ of Southern Colorado — Pueblo, CO 81001-4901 (719) 549-2142 — uscolo.edu
Business Adm Department — Hasan Sch of Business Fax=549-2909

Name	Rank	Phone	Email	Field	Degree	Yr	School	Year
Ward, Bart H.	Dean	549-2142	bward	Atg	PHD	73	Nrthwstrn	1994
Watkins, Donna M.	C-Ac	529-2317	watkins	Mgt	PHD	82	N Mex St	1988
Duncan, Kevin C.	Assoc	549-2228	duncan	JR	PHD	87	Utah	1994
Goodman, David Jay	Asst	549-2155	goodman	FQ	PHD	95	Colorado	1998

Southern Connecticut St Un — New Haven, CT 06515 (203) 392-5629 — scsud.ctstate.edu
Dept of Economics & Finance — School of Business Fax=392-5863 — Gloria Nichols

Name	Rank	Phone	Email	Field	Degree	Yr	School	Year
Smith, Phillip	Dean$	392-5631	smithjp		PHD		Columbia	
Andoh, Samuel Kojo	C-Pr	392-5616	andoh	EO	PHD	86	NYU	
Crakes, Gary M.	Prof	392-5619	crakes	AI	PHD	84	Conn	1980
Hsu, Yu-Chu	Prof	392-5622	hsu	HO	PHD	65	Cornell	
Morgan, Alfred D.	Prof	392-5624		G	PHD	51	Harvard	
Mostaghimi, Mehdi	Prof	392-5625	mostaghimi	CEM	PHD	87	Virginia	8-84
Bodo, Peter	Assoc	392-5617	bodo	CL	PHD	91	Conn	

Eldridge, Robert M.	Assoc	392-5628	eldridge_r	G	DBA	87	Geo Wash	
Gebremariam, Yilma	Assoc	392-5620	gebremariam	FO	PHD	89	S Calif	1990
Gilmore, Clair	Assoc	392-5618		G	PHD		Drexel	
Mills, Judith W.	Assoc	392-5623	mills	CNT	PHD	94	SUNY-SBr	1991
Thorson, James A.	Assoc	392-5626	thorson	R	PHD	91	Il-Chicago	1992
Savage, Deborah A.	Asst	392-5627	savage	I	PHD	93	Conn	

Southern Illinois Univ Carbondale, IL 62901-4515 (618) 536-7746 siu.edu
Department of Economics College of Liberal Arts Fax=453-2717 Mrs. Nancy Mallett
email @1=siucvmb.siu.edu

Jensen, Robert	Dean$	453-2466			PHD	76	N Illinois	1981
Primont, Daniel A.	C-Pr	453-5082	primo	DC	PHD	70	Ca-SnBarb	1978
Edelman, Milton	Emer	453-5063			PHD	51	Illinois	1950
Grabowski, Richard L.	Prof	453-5067	ricardo	OF	PHD	77	Utah	1979
Laumas, G. S.	Prof	453-5740	ga3956@1	EC	PHD	66	Wayne St	1990
Layer, Robert	Emer				PHD	52	Harvard	1955
Myers, John G.	Emer	453-5073			PHD	61	Columbia	1977
Sharma, Subhash	Prof	453-5070	sharma	C	PHD	83	Kentucky	1983
Trescott, Paul B.	Emer	453-5095		EB	PHD	54	Princeton	1976
Ellis, Robert J. Jr.	Emer	453-5063			PHD	66	Virginia	1965
Foran, Terry G.	Emer	453-5066		J	PHD	71	Penn St	1970
Mitchell, Thomas M.	Assoc	453-5072	tmitch	DC	PHD	84	Brown	1983
Chau, Nancy	Asst	453-6250	chauhy	FO	PHD	95	J Hopkins	1995
Dibooglu, Selhattin	Asst	453-5346	sdibo	F	PHD	93	Iowa St	1993
Dworak, Jonathan	Asst			DL	ABD		MIT	1999
Gilbert, Scott	Asst			C	PHD	96	Ca-SnDgo	1999
Sylwester, Kevin	Asst	453-5347	kwylwest	EO	PHD	97	Wisconsin	1998
Zemcik, Petr	Asst	453-5062	petrz	EG	PHD	97	Pittsburgh	1998

So Illinois, Edwardsville Edwardsville, IL 62026-1102 (618) 650-2542 siue.edu
Department of Economics School of Business Fax=650-3047 Sally Moonier

Elliott, Donald S. Jr.	C-Pr	650-2599	delliot	AHMR	PHD	76	Minnesota	1976
Ault, David E.	Prof	650-2578	dault	AFJK	PHD	69	Illinois	1969
Hafer, Rik W.	Prof	650-2747	rhafer	EG	PHD	79	Va Tech	
Levin, Stanford L.	Prof	650-2592	slevin	DL	PHD	74	Michigan	1972
Lin, An-Yhi (Steven)	Prof	650-2580	slin	CDFO	PHD	67	Iowa St	1968
Meisel, John B.	Prof	650-2581	jmeisel	ADL	PHD	78	Boston C	1977
Edmonds, Radcliff G. Jr.	Assoc	650-2598	redmondr	ACF	PHD	79	Michigan	1977
Kutan, Ali M.	Assoc	650-3473	akutan	EFG	PHD	90	Ariz St	1991
Navin, John	Asst	650-3423	jnavin	HIJ	PHD	92	Mich St	
Sullivan, Timothy	Asst	650-3469	tsulliv	IJT	PHD	95	Maryland	1995
Pettit, Mary Ann	Inst	650-2583	mpettit	A	MA	77	Tennessee	1980
Wolff, Laura	Inst	650-2875	lwolff	AO	MS	88	Missouri	1990

Univ of Southern Indiana Evansvillle, IN 47712-3597 (812) 464-1979 usi.edu
Dept of Economics & Finance School of Business Fax=465-1044

Fisher, Philip C.	Dean	464-1718	pfisher	Mgt	PHD	79	Stanford	1991
Cox, Steven R.	Prof	464-1983	scox		PHD	71	Michigan	1989
Quddus, Munir	Prof	464-1745	mquddus		PHD	85	Vanderbilt	1984
Cashel-Cordo, Peter	Assoc	465-7033	cashel		PHD	88	Houston	1994
Khayum, Mohammed	Assoc	464-7034	mkhayum		PHD	90	Temple	1991
Schibik, Timothy J.	Assoc	464-1880	tschibik		PHD	89	W Virginia	1988
Mahoney, Timothy B.	Inst	464-1947	tmahoney		MS	05	Illinois	1987

Univ of Southern Maine Portland, ME 04104-9300 (207) 780-4020 usm.maine.edu
Department of Economics College of Arts & Sci Fax=780-5507

Hillard, Michael	C-Ac	780-4416	mhillard	EJ	PHD	88	Mass	1987
Bay, John W.	Prof	780-4445	jbay	E	PHD	66	Boston C	1965
Executive Director Off Campus Instruction								
Feiner, Susan F.	Assoc	780-4966	sffein	BN	PHD	81	Mass	1995
Goldstein, Nance	Assoc	780-4602	nance	IJ	PHD	88	ThamesPoly	1987
Medley, Joseph E.	Assoc	780-4293	medley	BO	PHD	81	Mass	1983
Phillips, William A.	Assoc	780-4313	phillips	ACDF	PHD	79	Fla St	1980
Roberts, Bruce B.	Assoc	780-5503	broberts	BE	PHD	81	Mass	1995
Mamgain, Vaishali	Asst	780-5807		CO	PHD	79	N Carol	1997

Southern Methodist Univ Dallas, TX 75275-0496 (214) 768-4335 mail.smu.edu
Department of Economics Dedman College Fax=768-1821 Pontip Vattakavanich

Neel, Jasper	Dean	768-3212	jneel		PHD	75	Tennessee	1997
Dean and Vice Provost, Dedman College								
Weber, Shlomo	C-Pr	768-3577	sweber	DHL	PHD	79	Hebrew	1993
Robert H. & Nancy Dedman Trustee Professor								
Batra, Raveendra N.	Prof	768-2707	rbaatra	F	PHD	69	S Illinois	1973
Hayes, Kathy J.	Prof	768-4485	khayes	HIL	PHD	80	Syracuse	1989
Associate Dean for Academic Affairs, Dedman College								

Name	Rank	Phone	Email	Fields	Degree	Yr	School	Since
Maasoumi, Esfandiar	Prof	768-4298	maasoumi	C	PHD	77	LondonSE	1976
Robert H. & Nancy Dedman Professor								
Russell, William R.	Prof	768-2715	wrussell	D	PHD	64	U Wash	1971
Slottje, Daniel J.	Prof	768-2715	dslottje	DJK	PHD	83	Tx A&M	1989
Balke, Nathan S.	Assoc	768-2693	nblake	EG	PHD	86	Nrthwstrn	1986
Deb, Rajat	Assoc	768-3556	rdeb	D	PHD	75	LondonSE	1976
Fomby, Thomas	Assoc	768-2559	tfomby	CD	PHD	75	Missouri	1975
Huffman, Gregory	Assoc	768-3344	ghuffman	EG	PHD	83	Minnesota	1992
Seo, Tae Kun	Assoc	768-3547	tseo	D	PHD	73	Tx A&M	1973
Dolmas, James	Asst	768-3806	jdolmas	CEO	PHD	93	Rochester	1993
Fredriksson, Per	Asst			DF	PHD	94	Penn	1999
Millimet, Danie	Asst			CJO	PHD	99	Brown	1999
Osang, Thomas	Asst	768-4398	tosang	FO	PHD	94	Ca-SnDgo	1994
Saggi, Kamal	Asst	768-3274	ksaggi	FLO	PHD	95	Penn	1995
Sandfort, Mihre	Asst	768-3856	sandfort	DL	PHD	94	Wisconsin	1997

U of Southern Mississippi — Hattiesburg, MS 39406-5072 (601) 266-4648 — cba.usm.edu
Dept Economics & Intl Bus — Col of Business Adm Fax=266-4920 — Ms. Janet McKee

Name	Rank	Phone	Email	Fields	Degree	Yr	School	Since
Gunther, William D.	Dean	266-4659		R	PHD	69	Kentucky	1998
Niroomand, Farhang	C-Pr	266-5028		F	PHD	83	Mich St	1984
Black, Tyrone	Prof	266-6580		E	PHD	70	Tulane	1969
Carter, George H. III	Prof	266-4651		R	PHD	77	Tx A&M	1979
Klinedinst, Mark A.	Prof	266-4649		P	PHD	87	Cornell	1986
Lewis, Eddie Miley Jr.	Prof	266-4652		F	DBA	74	Miss St	1970
Nissan, Edward	Prof	266-4656		R	PHD	69	Tx A&M	1969
Sawyer, W. Charles	Prof	266-4489		F	PHD	83	Arkansas	1983
Dickie, Mark T.	Assoc	266-4648		Q	PHD	89	Wyoming	1994
Goffe, William L.	Assoc	266-4484		C	PHD	90	N Carol	1993
Green, Trellis Garnett	Assoc	266-4662		Q	PHD	84	Fla St	1983
Mixon, Frank	Assoc	266-4648		J	PHD	92	Auburn	1994
Whitesell, Frank Cook	Assoc	266-4366		A	PHD	71	Tulane	1968
Caveny, Regina	Asst	266-5672			PHD	92	Alabama	1979
McQuiston, James M. Jr.	Asst	266-4234			BS	56	S Miss	1960
Trevino, Len	Asst	266-6094		F	PHD	91	Indiana	1999

Southern Nazarene Univ — Bethany, OK 73008 (405) 491-6359 — snu.edu
Economics Faculty — School of Business Fax=491-6384

Name	Rank	Phone	Email	Fields	Degree	Yr	School	Since
Mills, Larry W.	C-Pr	491-6392	lmills	Mgt	PHD	78	Oklahoma	1969
Seyfert, Jeff	Asst	491-6671	jseyfert		MBA	89	Tulsa	1990

Southern Oregon University — Ashland, OR 97520-5082 (541) 552-6251 — sou.edu
Department of Economics — Social Science Area Fax=552-6439

Name	Rank	Phone	Email	Fields	Degree	Yr	School	Since
Burkholder, Sue A.	Dean	562-6255	burkholder		MA	72	Missouri	1985
Young, Linda Wilcox	C-Ac	552-6787	lwyoung	JOF	PHD	87	Berkeley	1994
Pirasteh, Hassan	Prof	552-6434	pirasteh	CEG	PHD	85	Oregon	1982
Rubenson, Daniel L.	Prof	552-6437	drube	CEG	PHD	85	Car Mellon	1986
Holt, Richard P. F.	Assoc	552-6784	rholt	ABDM	PHD	87	Utah	1996
Sigetich, Kip	Assoc	552-6557	sigetich	GHM	PHD	79	Stanford	1989

Southern Utah University — Cedar City, UT 84720 (801) 865-8167 — suu.edu
Dept of Businss-Economics — Sch of Bus, Tech & Comm Fax=586-5493

Name	Rank	Phone	Email	Fields	Degree	Yr	School	Since
Groesbeck, John D.	C-Ac	586-7784			PHD	93	Utah St	1993
Bowman, Rhead S.	Assoc	586-5412			PHD	75	Utah	1978
Chen, Heiwei	Asst	586-5405			PHD	97	Emory	1998
Craft, Kim	Asst	586-5414			PHD	96	Ca-Davis	1996

Southwest Baptist Univ — Bolivar, MO 65613-2496 (417) 326-1951 — sbuniv.edu
Business Administration — College of Business Fax=326-1887 — Ms. Rhonda Agee
Did Not Respond--1997-98 Listing

Name	Rank	Phone	Email	Fields	Degree	Yr	School	Since
Middleton, Kenneth A.	Dean	326-1752		Mgt	PHD	80	Ariz St	1991
DeBauche, Susan	C-As	326-1951		Bus	EDD		Arkansas	1985
Jones, James G.	Asst	326-1757		ECO	MBA		Arkansas	1988
Ritenour, Shawn	Asst	326-1754			PHD		Auburn	1997
Credille, Ronda	Inst	326-1750			MBA		Drury	1990

Southwest Missouri St Univ — Springfield, MO 65804-0094 (417) 836-5516 — mail.smsu.edu
Department of Economics — Col Humanity & Pub Aff Fax=836-4236 — Ms. Sandra K. Wilkins

Name	Rank	Phone	Email	Fields	Degree	Yr	School	Since
Pilant, Denny	Dean$	836-5529		PSci				
Hoftyzer, John	H-Pr	836-5347	joh689f		PHD	74	Indiana	1987
Bell, Joe A.	Prof	836-5140	jab856f		PHD	80	Okla St	1971
Hoppes, Robert B.	Prof	836-5352	rbh018f		PHD	75	Nebraska	1980
Stone, Allan D.	Prof	836-5350	ads98lf		PHD	73	Oklahoma	1972
Wasson, E. Dale	Prof	836-5349	edw389f		PHD	80	Okla St	1969

Wyrick, Thomas L. Prof 836-5060 tlw918f PHD 79 Va Tech 1978
email=twyrick@earthlink.net
Olsen, Reed N. Assoc 836-5379 rno174f PHD 89 Illinois 1990
Sheets, Doris Files Assoc 836-5351 def230f PHD 81 Missouri 1974
Barari, Mahua Asst 836-5171 mab953f PHD 92 Iowa St 1993
Cox, Larry G. Asst 836-5551 MA 70 Kansas St 1970
email=econ99@earthlink.net
Topping, Elizabeth E. Asst 836-5615 eet326f PHD 85 Missouri 1979
Geile, Gerald L. Inst 836-5740 glg138f MA 91 St Louis 1991

Southwest State University Marshall, MN 56258 (507) southwest.msus.edu
Economics Faculty Dept of Business Adm Fax=537-6577
Did Not Respond--1997-98 Listing
Ramos, Melba Dean 537-6218 Anth PHD 82 Mass 1993
Mitchell, George C-Pr 537-6223 Mgt ABD
Blitstein, Allen Prof DFN PHD 72 Minnesota 1976
Cameron, John S. Assoc 537-6560 EFJ PHD 79 Nebraska 1986

Southwest Texas State Univ San Marcos, TX 78666-4616 (512) 245-2547 academia.swt.edu
Dept Finance & Economics School of Business Fax=245-3089 Patty Aranda
Holland, A. Steven C-Pr 245-2547 sh20 E PHD 83 Mich St 1998
Blankmeyer, Eric Prof 245-3253 eb01 F PHD 71 Princeton 1982
Gowens, Paul R. Prof 245-2311 pg01 M PHD 73 Miss 1980
Mogab, John William Prof 245-3244 jm12 O PHD 81 Tennessee 1981
Charles, Joni S. Assoc 245-3243 jc18 D PHD 87 Purdue 1984
Kishan, Ruby Pandey Assoc 245-3248 rk02 E PHD 86 Tx A&M 1986
Campbell, Rebecca Asst 245-3251 rc17 H PHD 98 LSU 1998
Carbacho-Bugos, Andres Asst O ABD Mass 1999
McClung, Bruce Alan Asst 245-3220 bm03 J PHD 88 Tx A&M 1988
Showalter, Dean Asst 245-3194 ds29 L PHD 94 Kentucky 1995

Southwestern University Georgetown, TX 78627-0770 (512) 863-1574 southwestern.edu
Economic & Business Dept Brown Col of Arts & Sci Fax=863-5788 Kathy Buchhorn
Jones, William B. Dean$ 863-1567 jonesw Hist PHD 65 Vanderbilt 1965
Sellers, Fred E. C-Ac 863-1574 sellerf Atg PHD 84 Kansas 1987
Roberts, Kenneth D. Prof 863-1993 robertsk GEOT PHD 80 Wisconsin 1981
Northrop, Emily M. Assoc 863-1591 northroe ENQR PHD 88 Tx-Austin 1994
Young, Mary E. Assoc 863-1994 youngm CDJQ PHD 89 Tx-Austin 1990
Early, Dirk W. Asst 863-1592 earlyd DEHR PHD 95 Virginia 1994

U of Southwestern Louisiana Lafayette, LA 70504-4570 (318) 482-6662 usl.edu
Dept of Economics & Finance Col of Business Admin Fax=482-6195 Sheila Beasley
Underwood, James III Dean$ 482-6491 Mktg DBA 73 Indiana 1989
Heath, W. Cary H-Ac 482-5728 PHD 82 LSU
Greco, Anthony J. Prof 482-6669 ADL PHD 78 Tennessee 8-84
Gale, Louis Asst 482-6663 PHD 94 Ariz St 1995
La Point, James Asst 482-6671
Ressler, Rand W. Asst 482-6666 rwr5011 DJ PHD 93 Auburn 8-93
Waters, Melissa S. Asst 482-6082 msw9633 CJT PHD 89 LSU 8-90
Watson, J. Keith Asst 482-5727 PHD 83 Tx A&M
Rumore, Nancy C. Inst 482-6667 MS 80 LSU

Southwestern Oklahoma St U Weatherford, OK 73096-3098 (580) 774-3066 swosu.edu
Dept Economics & Bus Adm School of Business Fax=774-7067 Nancy Grammer
Did Not Respond--1997-98 Listing
Kaufman, Jerry M. Dean 774-3282 Atg PHD 74 Okla St 1992
Rhee, Anthony C-Pr 774-3049 PHD 79 Kent St 1994
Nowka, Harry E. Prof 774-3754 EDD Okla St 1963
Russell, R. K. Prof 774-3081 PHD 82 Okla St 1973
Hankins, Marvin Asst 774-3750 EDD Okla St 1979
Xiansheng, Duan Asst 774-3706 PHD 97 Illinois 1997

Stanford University Stanford, CA 94305-6072 (650) 725-3266 leland.edu
Department of Economics Sch of Humanities & Sci Fax=725-5702 Nicole Reed 723-3713
Pencavel, John H. C-Pr 723-3981 pencavel PHD 69 Princeton 1979
Amemiya, Takeshi Prof 723-3986 amemiya PHD 64 J Hopkins 1968
Edward Ames Edmonds Professor of Economics
Aoki, Masahiko Prof 723-3975 aoki PHD 67 Minnesota 1984
Henri and Tomoye Takahashi Professor of Japanese Studies
Bernheim, B. Douglas Prof 725-8732 bernheim PHD 82 MIT 1994
Lewis and Virginia Eaton Professor in Economics
Boskin, Michael J. Prof 723-3864 boskin PHD 71 Berkeley 1970
Tully Friedman Professor in Economics
Bresnahan, Timothy F. Prof 723-9471 tbres PHD 80 Princeton 1979

Name	Rank	Phone	E-mail	Degree	Yr	School	Since
David, Paul A.	Prof	723-3710		PHD	73	Harvard	1969
Fuchs, Victor R.	Emer	326-7639		PHD	55	Columbia	1974
Greif, Avner	Prof	725-8936	avner	PHD	89	Nrthwstrn	1993
Hall, Robert E.	Prof	723-2215	hall@hoover	PHD	67	MIT	1978
Hammond, Peter J.	Prof	723-3987	hammond	PHD	74	Cambridge	1979
Harris, Donald J.	Emer	723-3028		PHD	66	Berkeley	1972
Hickman, Bert G.	Emer	723-3417		PHD	51	Berkeley	1966
Krueger, Anne O.	Prof	723-0188	akrueger	PHD	58	Wisconsin	
Herald L. and Caroline L. Reitch Professor in Humanities and Sciences							
Kurz, Mordecai	Prof	723-2220	mordecai	PHD	61	Yale	1966
Joan Kenney Professor of Economics							
Lau, Lawrence J.	Prof	723-3708	ljlau	PHD	69	Berkeley	1966
Kwoh-Ting Li Professor of Economic Development							
MaCurdy, Thomas E.	Prof	723-3983	tmac	PHD	78	Chicago	1983
McKinnon, Ronald I.	Prof	723-3721	mckinnon	PHD	61	Minnesota	1961
William D. Eberle Professor of Economics							
Milgrom, Paul R.	Prof	723-3397	milgrom	PHD	79	Stanford	1987
Shirley R. and Leonard W. Ely, Jr. Professor in Humanities and Sciences							
Noll, Roger G.	Prof	723-2297	rnoll	PHD	67	Harvard	1984
Morris M. Doyle Centennial Professor							
Rosenberg, Nathan	Prof	723-1902	ib.nat@forsythe	PHD	55	Wisconsin	
Fairleigh S. Dickinson, Jr., Professor of Public Policy							
Sargent, Thomas	Prof	725-8161		PHD	68	Harvard	
Shoven, John B.	Prof	326-5377		PHD	73	Yale	1978
Charles R. Schwab Professor of Economics							
Starrett, David A.	Emer	723-3712	dstar@forythe.	PHD	68	Stanford	1973
Stiglitz, Joseph E.	Prof	723-9309		PHD	86	MIT	
on leave							
Taylor, John B.	Prof	723-9677	johntayl	PHD	73	Stanford	
Mary and Robert Raymond Professor of Economics							
Wolak, Frank A.	Prof	723-3944	wolak@zia	PHD	85	Harvard	1986
Wright, Gavin	Prof	723-3837	write	PHD	69	Yale	1982
William Robertson Coe Professor of American Economic History							
Bajari, Patrick	Asst	725-8856	bajari	PHD	97	Minnesota	
Horvath, Michael	Asst	723-4116	mhovath	PHD	94	Nrthwstrn	1994
Jones, Chad	Asst	723-9276	chadj	PHD	93	MIT	1993
Kochar, Anjini	Asst	723-9766	anjini	PHD	91	Chicago	1990
Kumhof, Michael	Asst	725-6120	kumhof				
McClellan, Mark	Asst	723-3982	markm@texas	PHD	93	Harvard	9-95
Nechyba, Thomas	Asst	723-5962	tnechyba	PHD	94	Rochester	1994
Rangel, Antonio	Asst	723-0533	rangel				
Tadelis, Steven	Asst	723-3544	725-8169	PHD		Harvard	

SUNY at Fredonia — Fredonia, NY 14063-1198 (716) 673-3509 fredonia.edu
Economics Faculty — Department of Economics Fax=673-3332 Amy Dorler

Name	Rank	Phone	E-mail	Field	Degree	Yr	School	Since
Sarkar, Amin U.	C-Ac	673-3509	sarkar	OQ	PHD	88	Berkeley	1989
El Nasser, Marwan M.	Prof	673-3827	elnasser	EG	PHD	70	Ohio St	1970
Foeller, William H.	Prof	673-3403	foeller	AJ	PHD	72	Iowa St	1984
Hansen, John A.	Prof	673-3828	hansen	LD	PHD	80	Yale	1984
Hefner, Dennis L.	Prof	673-3456	hefner	IL	PHD	71	Wash St	1996
Parai, Amar K.	Prof	673-3289	parai	AF	PHD	79	So Meth	1988
Choudhary, Munir A. S.	Assoc	673-3830	choudhary	CE	PHD	85	Fla St	1987
Peterson, Janice L.	Assoc	673-3522	peterson	BA	PHD	87	Nebraska	1990

SUNY Col at Cortland — Cortland, NY 13045-0900 (607) 753-4109 syncorva.cortland.edu
Department of Economics — College of Arts & Sci Fax= Denise Riley

Name	Rank	Phone	E-mail	Field	Degree	Yr	School	Since
Prus, Mark J.	C-Ac	753-5758	prus	JN	PHD	85	Utah	
Botwinick, Howard I.	Assoc	753-2435			PHD	88	New Sch	
Doane, Donna L.	Assoc	753-2439		O	PHD	84	Yale	
Krall, Mary Elyse	Assoc	753-2438	krallm	AIJQ	PHD	89	Utah	8-90
Phillips, Timothy P.	Assoc	753-2437		M	MBA	83	Clarkson	1983
Burke, Kathleen	Asst			CD	PHD		SUNY-SBr	1999
Maxey, Joel	Asst			KJ	PHD		Wash St	1998
Polley, Susanne M.	Asst	753-2469	pollys	EHM	PHD	94	Penn St	8-94
Torras, Mariano	Asst			FOP	PHD		Mass	1999
Graham, Katherine	Lect	753-4110			MS		Cornell	
Shirley, John	Lect	753-2190						
VonDonsel, Richard	Lect	753-2469						

State Un College at Geneseo — Geneseo, NY 14454-1401 (716) 245-5367 uno.geneseo.edu
Department of Economics — Jones Sch of Business Fax=245-5467

Name	Rank	Phone	E-mail	Field	Degree	Yr	School	Since
Martin, David A.	Prof	245-5372	martin	BA	PHD	64	Syracuse	1966
Strang, Daniel R.	Prof	245-5365	strang	CQ	PHD	75	Cornell	1992
Asgary, Nader	Asst	245-5366	nader	FJ	PHD	91	Houston	1996
Stone, Leonie L.	Asst	245-4365	stone	OD	PHD	93	Ohio St	1993

SUNY at Old Westbury Old Westbury, NY 11568 (516) snyoldva
Economics Faculty Dept of Bus Econ & Fnce Fax=876-3360
Did Not Respond--1997-98 Listing

Name	Rank	Phone	Email	Field	Degree	Yr	School	Since
O'Sullivan, Patrick	C-Pr				PHD	82	Fordham	
Forti, Annette	Prof				PHD	75	Fordham	
Geyikdogi, Yasar	Prof				PHD		Bath	
Leon, Hyginus	Assoc				PHD	86	S Hamptn	
Mickens, Alvin D.	Assoc	876-3331			PHD	72	NYU	1978
Tabriztchi, Sirousse	Assoc				PHD	70	Columbia	

SUNY College at Oneonta Oneonta, NY 13820-4015 (607) 436-3458 oneonta.edu
Dept of Economics & Business Behavioral & Applied Sc Fax=436-2543 Ms. Dawn Tompkins
Homepage: http://www.oneonta.edu

Name	Rank	Phone	Email	Field	Degree	Yr	School	Since
Lubell, Alfred M.	Dean$	436-3458		ADF	PHD	74	NYU	1974
Thomas, Wade L.	C-Ac	436-3458	thomaswl	DEJ	PHD	82	Nebraska	1989
Clow, John	Prof	436-3275	clowje		EDD		N Illinois	
Ring, David W.	Assoc	436-2127	ringdw	DEPR	PHD	82	SUNY-SBr	1981
Beck, Edward J.	Asst	436-3695	beckei	DE	MBA	82	Syracuse	1977
O'Dea, William P.	Asst	436-2127	odeawp	DEP	PHD	88	SUNY-Alb	1979
Puritz, Frederick A.	Asst	436-3509	poritzfa	ME	MBA		Harvard	

SUNY College at Oswego Oswego, NY 13126 (315) 341-2175 oswego.edu
Economics Faculty Col of Arts & Sciences Fax=341-5444 Betty Bennett

Name	Rank	Phone	Email	Field	Degree	Yr	School	Since
Kane, John C.	C-Ac	341-2581	kane	ACJ	PHD	86	SUNY-SBr	1983
Atri, Said	Prof	341-3954	atri	AFI	PHD	82	SUNY-Alb	1981
Jhun, U-Jin	Prof	341-3455	jhun	EH	PHD	73	SUNY-Alb	1972
Spizman, Lawrence	Prof	341-3479	spizman	AJK	PHD	77	SUNY-Alb	1977
Graham, Glenn	Assoc	341-3482	graham	AIL	PHD	95	SUNY-Bin	1992
Cooper, Brian	Asst	341-3485	bcooper1	ABJ	PHD	97	Harvard	1998
Davis, Lewis	Asst	341-3484	ldavis	AFO	PHD	99	N Carol	1998
Dighe, Ranjit S.	Asst	341-3480	dighe	AEN	ABD		Yale	1997
Dunne, Elizabeth A.	Asst	341-3488	edunne	AEG	ABD		Iowa	1990
Reid, Karen	Asst	341-3472	kreid	AQ	ABD		Tennessee	1998

SUNY at Stony Brook Stony Brook, NY 11794-4384 (516) 632-7550 datalab2.sbs.sunysb.ed
Department of Economics College of Arts & Sci Fax=632-7516

Name	Rank	Phone	Email	Field	Degree	Yr	School	Since
Sanderson, Warren	C-Pr	632-7530	wsanderson		PHD	74	Stanford	1989
Dubey, Pradeep	Prof	632-7549	pdubey		PHD	75	Cornell	1989
Hause, John C.	Prof	632-7530	jhause		PHD	62	Chicago	1978
Hool, Bryce	Prof	632-7012	bhool		PHD	74	Berkeley	1979
Hurd, Michael	Prof	632-7551	mhurd		PHD	71	Berkeley	1978
Muench, Thomas Director of Graduate Studies	Prof	632-7560	tmuench		PHD	65	Purdue	1975
Neuberger, Egon	Prof	632-7545	eneuberger		PHD	58	Harvard	1967
Neyman, Abraham	Prof	632-7546	aneyman		PHD	77	Hebrew	1989
Tauman, Yair	Prof	632-7557	ytauman		PHD	79	Hebrew	1989
Zschock, Dieter	Prof	632-7553	ozschock		PHD	67	Tufts	1966
Zweig, Michael	Prof	632-7536	mzweig		PHD	67	Michigan	1967
Montgomery, Mark	Assoc	632-7523	mmontgomery		PHD	82	Michigan	1988
Armantier, Olivier	Asst	632-1333	4oarmantier		PHD	98	Pittsburgh	1998
Dwyer, Debra	Asst	632-7532			PHD	96	Cornell	1998
Kamihigashi, Takashi	Asst	632-7548	tkamihigashi		PHD	94	Wisconsin	1994
Park, Sangin	Asst	632-7559	spark		PHD	96	Yale	1996
Swann, Christopher	Asst		sswann		PHD	97	Virginia	1999
Dawes, William Director of Undergraduate Studies	Lect	632-7534	wdawes		PHD	72	Purdue	1969

Univ at Albany, SUNY Albany, NY 12222 (518) 442-4735 cnsvax.albany.edu
Department of Economics Col of Arts & Sciences Fax=442-4736 Sue Phillips
email @1=cnsunix.albany.edu @2=csc.albany.edu @3=cnsibm.albany.edu

Name	Rank	Phone	Email	Field	Degree	Yr	School	Since
Hoffmann, Richard	Dean	442-4654	rjh@2					
Kinal, Terrence	C-Pr	442-4744	twk58	CD	PHD	76	Minnesota	1980
Daniel, Betty C.	Prof	442-4747	bd892	EF	PHD	76	N Carol	1983
Jerison, Michael	Prof	442-4287	mi770	DC	PHD	77	Wisconsin	1977
Lahiri, Kajal	Prof	442-4758	kl758	E	PHD	75	Rochester	1977
Reeb, Donald J.	Prof	442-4738	dreeb	RG	PHD	63	Syracuse	1965
Sattinger, Michael	Prof	442-4761	ms339@3	J	PHD	73	Car Mellon	1981
Uppal, Jogindar S.	Prof	442-4748	jsull	OH	PHD	65	Minnesota	1971
Yun, Kwan Koo	Prof	442-4741	ky948	CD	PHD	74	Stanford	1974
Dieffenbach, Bruce C.	Assoc	442-4750	bd455	E	PHD	72	Harvard	1978
Lankford, R. Hamilton	Assoc	442-4743	rh104	HD	PHD	81	N Carol	1981
Mirer, Thad W.	Assoc	442-4755	mirer@3	H	PHD	71	Yale	1973
Joh, Sung-Wook	Asst	442-4737	joh	DL	PHD	94	Harvard	1994
Jones, John	Asst	442-4926	jbjones@2	E	PHD	98	Wisconsin	1998
Kim, Jae Young	Asst	442-4926	jykim@1	CE	PHD	95	Minnesota	1994
Kranich, Laurence J.	Asst	442-4741	l.kranich	DH	PHD	89	Rochester	1998
Marschke, Gerald	Asst	447-3755	marschke@2	DJL	PHD	98	Chicago	1998

SUNY at Binghamton Binghamton, NY 13902-6000 (607) 777-2572 binghamton.edu
Div Soc Sci - Dept Economics Harpur Col Arts & Sci Fax=777-2681 Joanne F. Ardune

Name	Rank	Phone	Email	Field	Degree	Yr	School	Year
Polachek, Solomon W.	Dean	777-2144	bg2776	J	PHD	73	Columbia	1983
Kokkelenberg, Edward C.	C-Pr	777-2550	kokkele	EO	PHD	81	Nrthwstrn	1980
Basmann, Robert L.	Prof	777-2660		C	PHD	66	Iowa St	1988
Bischoff, Charles W.	Prof	777-4351	cbischo	EC	PHD	68	MIT	1977
Britto, Ronald	Prof	777-2660	rbritto	FE	PHD	66	Brown	1974
Clark, Clifford D.	Prof	777-6415	cclark	OF	PHD	53	Chicago	1973
Cowing, Thomas G.	Prof	777-4480	tcowing	LD	PHD	70	Berkeley	1969
Director of Graduate Studies								
Greene, Kenneth V.	Prof	777-2944	kgreene	HK	PHD	68	Virginia	1968
Liu, Jung-Chao	Prof	777-2689	jungliu	FO	PHD	60	Michigan	1970
Masters, Stanley H.	Prof	777-2660		J	PHD	65	Princeton	1981
Kern, Clifford R.	Assoc	777-2228	ckern	R	PHD	74	Harvard	1971
Director of Undergraduate Studies								
Leighton, Richard I.	Assoc	777-2339	rleight	F	PHD	61	Duke	1964
Ofek, Haim	Assoc	777-4351	hofek	J	PHD	71	Columbia	1981
Yoon, Bong J.	Assoc	777-2987	yoon	JC	PHD	78	Illinois	1983
Jones, Barry	Asst			EC	PHD	99	Wash U	1999
Kang, Inbong	Asst	777-2339	inbkang	EO	PHD	95	Rochester	1995
Khanna, Neha	Asst	777-2689	nkhanna	QD	PHD	97	Cornell	1998
Plassmann, Florenz	Asst			HRF	PHD	97	Va Tech	1999
Wong, Linda	Asst	777-4351	lwong	JD	PHD	98	Iowa	1999
Zheng, Mingmei	VAsst			HD	PHD	99	Wash U	1999

SUNY at Buffalo Buffalo, NY 14260-1520 (716) 645-2121 acsu.buffalo.edu
Department of Economics College of Arts & Sci Fax=645-2127 Betty C. Baker

Name	Rank	Phone	Email	Field	Degree	Yr	School	Year
Grant, Kerry	Dean	645-2711		Musi	PHD	77	Berkeley	1991
Ehrlich, Isaac	C-Pr	645-2121	mgtehrl	OLK	PHD	70	Columbia	1977
Anas, Alex	Prof	645-2121	alexanas	DR	PHD	75	Penn	1991
Chang, Winston W.	Prof	645-2121	ecowwc	DF	PHD	68	Rochester	1967
Gort, Michael	Prof	645-2121	gort	O	PHD	54	Columbia	1964
Holmes, James M.	Prof	645-2121	ecoholme	EF	PHD	67	Chicago	1967
Revankar, Nagesh S.	Prof	645-2121	ecorevan	DC	PHD	67	Wisconsin	1967
Zarembka, Paul	Prof	645-2121	zarembka	BO	PHD	67	Wisconsin	1976
Harwitz, Mitchell	Assoc	645-2121	harwitz	COTR	PHD	59	MIT	1958
Morgan, Peter B.	Assoc	645-2121	pbmorgan	D	PHD	78	Canterbu	1989
Romans, Thomas J.	Assoc	645-2121	romans	HR	PHD	63	Brown	1967
Kim, Jinyoung	Asst	645-2121	jinkim	OJ	PHD	94	Chicago	
Li, Hao	Asst	645-2121		DC	PHD	95	Chicago	1999
Mendoza, Juan	Asst	645-2121		ED	PHD	99	Brown	1999
Park, Jungsoo	Asst	645-2121	jungsoo	OF	PHD	99	Stanford	1998
Yin, Yong	Asst	645-2121	yyin	CDE	PHD	95	Ohio St	1995

SUNY Empire State College Saratoga Spr, NY 12866-4391 (518) 587-2100 sescva.esc.edu
Economics Faculty Business Mgt & Econ Fax=587-2660 Jean Carpenter
area codes 598=(212) 587=(518) 358&948=(914) 360&997=(516) 394&886&244=(716)

Name	Rank	Phone	Email	Field	Degree	Yr	School	Year
RyanMann, Duncan	Assoc	587-2100	dryanman	I	PHD	84	Penn	
Cobb, Anne	Asst	244-3884	acobb	I	PHD	69	N Carol	
Angiello, Joseph		358-3990	jangiello	A	PHD	77	Tx-Austin	1983
DuBois, David		244-3884	ddubois	M	PHD	90	Union In	1976
Fortunato, Michael		587-2100	mfortuna	OMF	PHD	84	Harvard	1990
Giordano, Justin		598-0640	jgiordan	M	MBA		St Johns	1992
Herdendorf, Phyllis		886-8020	pherdend	F	PHD	81	SUNY	1987
Jarvis, Leslie		997-4700	ljarvis	A	PHD	82	New Sch	1986
Jones, Otolorin		587-2100	ojones	A	PHD	83	Ohio U	1985
Lill, Lloyd		394-1110	llill	BO	PHD	77	Walden	1973
Musoke, Moses		948-6206	mmusoke	NM	PHD	78	Wisconsin	1985
Pauszek, Ruffin		587-2100	rpauszek	A	MBA		SUNY-Buf	1992
Sussman, Jeffrey		997-4700	jsussman	G	PHD	75	CUNY	1975
Todd, Edward		360-1215		A	PHD	69	Chicago	1985
Weiss, Jeffrey		948-6206	jweiss	A	PHD	67	Harvard	1986

SUNY at New Paltz New Paltz, NY 12561-2499 (914) 257-2969 npvm.newpaltz.edu
Department of Economics Economics Fax=257-3693 Jannette Carcich

Name	Rank	Phone	Email	Field	Degree	Yr	School	Year
Seshu, Chigurupati R.	Assoc	257-3559		AEO	PHD	60	New Sch	1967
Azari-Rad, Hamid	Asst				PHD	96	Utah	1999
Mozayeni, Simin B.	Asst	257-2919	mozayens	ALH	PHD	53	Columbia	1990

SUNY, Col at Plattsburgh Plattsburgh, NY 12901-2697 (518) 564-3184 plattsburgh.edu
Department of Economics Sch of Business & Econ Fax=564-3183 Beverly Cross
Homepage: www.plattsburgh.edu/academics
www.plattsburgh.edu

Name	Rank	Phone	Email	Field	Degree	Yr	School	Year
Gandhi, Prem P.	Dean	564-3184	gandhipp	FO	PHD	73	New Sch	9-66
Dixon, Warren R.	C-Pr	564-4196	dixonwr	BP	PHD	71	Colorado	1968
Jang, Young S.	Prof	564-4193	jangys	CD	PHD	69	SUNY-Alb	1968

Name	Rank	Phone	Email	Field	Degree	Yr	School	Year
Page, Walter	Prof	564-3182	pagewp	DE	PHD	68	Kansas	1983
Withington, Robert P.	Assoc	564-2226	withinpr	NJ	PHD	76	Penn	1972
Christopherson, Robert L.	Asst	564-4218	christrl	GH	PHD	90	Wayne St	1990
Duffy, Neal E.	Asst	564-4194	duffyne	CR	PHD	82	W Virginia	1982
Fitzpatrick, Ellen	Asst	564-3184	fitzpae	FOQ	PHD	97	Mich St	1994

SUNY Col at Potsdam — Potsdam, NY 13676-2294 (315) 267-2206 — sunypotsdam.edu
Department of Economics — Sch of Arts & Sciences Fax=267-2797 — Colleen Wheaton

Name	Rank	Phone	Email	Field	Degree	Yr	School	Year
Pletcher, Galen K.	Dean	267-2231	pletchgk	Phil	PHD	71	Michigan	
Baktari, Paul	C-Ac	267-2204	baktarp		PHD		W Virginia	
Chugh, Ram L.	Prof	267-2206	chughrl		PHD	70	Wayne St	1970
Cliff, Lee	Assoc	267-2295	clliffih		MBA		Clarkson	
Nuwer, Michael J.	Assoc	267-2077	nuwermj		PHD	85	Utah	1986
Shu, Florence P.	Assoc	267-2221	shufp		PHD	86	Mich St	1986
Campbell, Martha	Asst				PHD	91	New Sch	1999
Mosier, Donna	Asst	267-2238	mosierdj		PHD	95	Clarkson	1997
Portugal, Edwin	Asst	267-2212	portugej		PHD	93	SUNY-Alb	

SUNY College at Purchase — Purchase, NY 10577-1400 (914) 251-6601
Division of Social Science — Coll Arts & Letters Fax=251-6603 — Valencia Wallace

Name	Rank	Phone	Email	Field	Degree	Yr	School	Year
Bell, Peter F,	C-Ac	251-6633			PHD	68	Wisconsin	1971
O'Cleiracain, Seamus	Prof	251-6600			PHD	71	Michigan	1974
Christensen, Kimberly	Assoc	251-6622			PHD	86	Mass	1985
Ikeda, Sanford	Assoc	251-6614			PHD	88	NYU	1990

Stephen F. Austin St Univ — Nacogdoches, TX 75962-3009 (409) 468-4301 — sfasu.edu
Dept of Economics & Finance — College of Business Fax=468-1447 — Barbara Roos

Name	Rank	Phone	Email	Field	Degree	Yr	School	Year
Young, Marlin C.	Dean	468-3101	myoung	BEd	EDD	74	Ariz St	1967
Jones, Clifton T.	C-Pr	468-4301	ctjones	CD	PHD	85	Tx A&M	1995
Howard, James E.	Assoc	468-1752	jhoward	AC	PHD	77	Georgia	1976
Ballinger, T. Parker	Asst	468-1442	pballinger	CE	PHD	99	Houston	1999
Ishwaran, Jayvanth	Asst	468-1457	chaos	EF	PHD	97	Purdue	1997
Rummery, Sarah	Asst	468-1783	srummery	J	PHD	94	Austr Natl	1998
Stroup, Michael	Asst	468-1557	mstroup	DH	PHD	93	Fla St	1999
Dumas, Rocky N.	Lect	468-1881	rdumas	A	MBA		SF Austin	1985

Stetson University — Deland, FL 32720-3756 (904) 822-7570 — stetson.edu
Department of Economics — Col of Arts & Sciences Fax=822-7569 — Divina Bungard
Homepage: http://www.stetson.edu/~econ

Name	Rank	Phone	Email	Field	Degree	Yr	School	Year
Ballenger, Grady	Dean	822-7515	gballeng	Eng	PHD	83	N Carol	1998
Long, Neal B.	C-Pr	822-7571	nlong	ACP	PHD	64	Indiana	1974
Wood, Richard H. Jr.	Prof	822-7572	rwood	AFO	PHD	72	Wisconsin	1970
Aldrich, Carole	Visit	822-7542	dickmac660@a	ACD	PHD	72	Car Mellon	1998
Thaver, Ranjini L.	Assoc	822-7573	rthaver	AHP	PHD	95	Notre Dm	1992

Richard Stockton College — Pomona, NJ 08240-0195 (609) 652-1776 — stockton.edu
Department of Economics — Social & Behavioral Sci Fax=748-5559

Name	Rank	Phone	Email	Field	Degree	Yr	School	Year
Carr, David	Dean	652-1776		PolS	PHD	75	SUNY-Bin	1978
Ghorashi, Gholam-Reza	C-Ac	652-1776			PHD	86	Fordham	1981
Elmore, Elizabeth A.	Prof	652-1776			PHD	76	Notre Dm	1972
Figort, Debb	Assoc	652-1776			PHD	95	American	1989
Harrison, Kenneth	Assoc	652-1776	laprod2556		PHD	76	SUNY-Alb	1976
Lakew, Melaku	Assoc	652-1776			PHD	81	Ca-Rivers	1982
Alpan, Erkan	Asst	652-1776			PHD	84	Ca-Rivers	1980

Stonehill College — North Easton, MA 02357-1135 (508) 565-1276 — stonehill.edu
Economics Faculty — Dept of Economics Fax=565-1444
Did Not Respond--1997-98 Listing

Name	Rank	Phone	Email	Field	Degree	Yr	School	Year
Kazemi, Hossein S.	C-Ac	565-1276	kazemi	GE	PHD	83	Clark	1982
Pepin, Raymond A.	Prof	565-1042		AD	PHD	71	Clark	1969
Rosenthal, Robert A.	Prof	565-1230		AI	PHD	78	Boston U	1975
Wiles, James L.	Emer	565-1327		KN	PHD	76	Harvard	1955
Kienzle, Edward C.	Assoc	565-1382		HC	PHD	76	Boston C	1980
Motomura, Akira	Assoc	565-1241		KN	PHD	85	Nrthwstrn	1995
Hammerle, Nancy E.	Asst	565-1257		A	MA		Temple	1980

Suffolk University — Boston, MA 02108-2770 (617) 573-8259 — acad.suffolk.edu
Department of Economics — College of Arts & Sci Fax=720-4272 — Mary K. Anooshian

Name	Rank	Phone	Email	Field	Degree	Yr	School	Year
Ronayne, Michael R.	Dean			Chem	PHD	63	Notre Dm	
Tuerck, David G.	C-Pr	573-8259			PHD	66	Virginia	1982
email=dtuerck@beaconhill.org								
Jaggia, Sanjiv	Assoc	573-8023	sjaggia		PHD	90	Indiana	
Kelly, Alison	Assoc	573-8069	akelly		PHD	93	Boston C	
Mohtadi, Shahruz	Assoc	573-8670	smohtadi		PHD	84	LSU	1983
Shannon, John C.	Assoc	573-8671	jshannon		MA		Boston C	
Baek, In-Mee	Asst	573-8376	ibaek		PHD	90	Indiana	
Haughton, Jonathan H.	Asst		jhaughton		PHD	83	Harvard	1997

Susquehanna University — Selinsgrove, PA 17870-1001 (570) 372-4186 — susqu.edu
Department of Economics — Sigmund Weis Sch Bus Fax=372-4491

Name	Rank	Phone	E-mail	Field	Degree	Yr	School	Year
Brock, James L.	Dean	372-4455	brock	Mktg	PHD	80	Mich St	9-96
Zadeh, Ali Haji-Mohamad	C-Ac	372-4189	azadeh	CEGO	PHD	82	Mich St	1987
Fisher, Warren L.	Prof	372-4186	fisherw	ABQ	PHD	73	Conn	1988
Onafowora, Olugbenga A.	Assoc	372-4187	onafowor	CDOQ	PHD	89	W Virginia	1989
Rusek, Antonin	Assoc	372-4182	rusek	EFP	PHD	84	SUNY-SBr	1986

Swarthmore College — Swarthmore, PA 19081-1397 (610) 328-8125 — swarthmore.edu
Department of Economics — Div of Social Sciences Fax=328-7352 — Mary Anne Stewart

Name	Rank	Phone	E-mail	Field	Degree	Yr	School	Year
Kuperberg, Mark J.	C-Pr	328-8123	mkuperb1	EK	PHD	81	MIT	1977
Caskey, John P.	Prof	328-8128	jcaskey1	EG	PHD	84	Stanford	1988
Golub, Stephen S.	Prof	328-8103	sgolub1	AE	PHD	83	Yale	1981
Hollister, Robinson G. Jr.	Prof	328-8105	rhollis1	IJ	PHD	65	Stanford	1971
Joseph Wharton Professor of Economics								
O'Connell, Stephen A.	Prof	328-8107	soconne1	EO	PHD	86	MIT	1990
Pryor, Frederic	Emer	328-8130	fpryor1	OP	PHD	57	Yale	1972
Saffran, Bernard	Prof	328-8124	bsaffra1	AH	PHD	63	Minnesota	1973
Franklin and Betty Barr Professor of Economics								
Westphal, Larry E.	Prof	328-8096	lwestph1	DO	PHD	69	Harvard	1985
J. Archer & Helen C. Turner Professor of Economics								
Bayer, Amanda	Assoc	328-7821	abayer1	DJ	PHD	95	Yale	1992
Jefferson, Philip N.	Assoc	690-6856	pjeffer1	CE	PHD	87	Virginia	1999
Magenheim, Ellen B.	Assoc	328-8140	emagen1	DI	PHD	86	Maryland	1986
Dee, Thomas S.	Asst	690-5767	tdee1	CI	PHD	97	Maryland	1999

Syracuse University — Syracuse, NY 13244-1090 (315) 443-3843 — maxwell.syr.edu
Department of Economics — Maxwell S Citznship &PA Fax=443-3717 — Kitty Nasto 443-3612

Name	Rank	Phone	E-mail	Field	Degree	Yr	School	Year
Palmer, John L.	Dean	443-2252		I	PHD	70	Stanford	1988
Holtz-Eakin, Douglas	C-Pr	443-9050	djheakin	H	PHD	85	Princeton	
Black, Dan A.	Prof	443-3114	dablac01	DJI	PHD	83	Purdue	
Kelly, Jerry S.	Prof	443-2345	jskelly	D	PHD	69	Harvard	
Ondrich, Jan Ivar	Prof	443-9052	jondrich	C	PHD	83	Wisconsin	
Richardson, J. David	Prof	443-4339	jdrichardson	F	PHD	70	Michigan	
Rosenthal, Stuart S.	Prof	443-3114		RHG	PHD	86	Wisconsin	
Smeeding, Timothy M.	Prof	443-9045	tmsmeeding	I	PHD	75	Wisconsin	
Tussing, A. Dale	Prof	443-2642	adtussing	I	PHD	64	Syracuse	1966
Wasylenko, Michael J.	Prof	443-3612	mjwasyle	H	PHD	75	Syracuse	1989
Yinger, John M.	Prof	443-9062	jyinger	RI	PHD	74	Princeton	1986
Dutkowsky, Donald H.	Assoc	443-1918	dutkow	E	PHD	82	SUNY-Buf	1985
Engelhardt, Gary	Assoc	443-3114			PHD	93	MIT	
Evensky, Jerry	Assoc	443-5863	jevensky	B	PHD	84	Syracuse	1985
Gensemer, Susan H.	Assoc	443-2294	gensemer	D	PHD	84	Purdue	
Hong, Lu	Assoc	443-1746	luhong	D	PHD	91	Minnesota	
Kao, C. H.	Assoc	443-3233	ckao	C	PHD	83	SUNY-SBr	
Lovely, Mary E.	Assoc	443-9048	mlovely	F	PHD	89	Michigan	1988
Dickert-Conlin, Stacy	Asst	443-3232	sdickert	GHJ	PHD	95	Wisconsin	1999
Dunn, Thomas	Asst	443-5053	tadunn	J	PHD	92	Nrthwstrn	
Greaney, Theresa M.	Asst	443-3802	tgreaney	F	PHD	94	Michigan	
Kubik, Jeff	Asst	443-9063	jdkubik		PHD	97	MIT	
Moran, John	Asst	443-3114			PHD	97	Penn St	

University of Tampa — Tampa, FL 33606-1490 (813) Ext 3336 — alpha.utampa.edu
Dept of Finance & Economics — College of Business Fax=258-7408
phone: 253-6221

Name	Rank	Phone	E-mail	Field	Degree	Yr	School	Year
Page, Alfred N.	Dean	253-6221		ADE	PHD	62	Chicago	1997
Truscott, Michael Hugh	C-Pr	253-6221	mhtruscott@a	AEF	PHD	71	LSU	1971
Fesmire, James M.	Prof	253-6221		DKL	PHD	73	Florida	1973
Dana Professor of Economics								
Hoke, Leon R. Jr.	Prof	253-6221		ADJ	PHD	79	Pittsburgh	1981
Brust, Peter J.	Assoc	253-6221		EF	PHD	80	Indiana	1981
LeClair, Daniel R.	Assoc	253-6221		ADL	PHD	88	Florida	1989

Tarleton State University — Stephenville, TX 76402 (254) 968-9047 — tarleton.edu
Dept of Business Systems — College of Business Adm Fax=968-9345 — Mrs. Sharon Iley

Name	Rank	Phone	E-mail	Field	Degree	Yr	School	Year
Collins, Dan	Dean	968-9350		Cis	PHD	83	North Tx	1975
Steed, Steve A.	H-Pr	968-9047		Atg	PHD	85	North Tx	1971
Brocato, Joe M.	Prof	968-9047		CEG	PHD	81	Tennessee	1989
Jafri, Syed Hussain Ali	Assoc	968-9633		AFG	PHD	86	Wisconsin	1989
Zelman, Patricia G.	Assoc	968-9629		N	PHD	80	Ohio St	1982
Beaty, William L.	Asst	968-9622		ADR	MS	73	Utah St	1985

Taylor University — Upland, IN 46989-1001 (765) 998-5135 — tayloru.edu
Dept of Business, Atg & Econ — Division of Business Fax=998-4930 — Nancy Gillespie

Name	Rank	Phone	E-mail	Field	Degree	Yr	School	Year
Bennett, Christopher P.	C-Ac	998-5137	chbennett		MBA	74	UCLA	1988
Associate Dean								
Erickson, Lee E.	Prof	998-5138	leerickso		PHD	75	Michigan	1979
Mitchell, Hadley T.	Assoc	998-4948	hdmitchel		PHD	85	Tennessee	1993

Teikyo Post University	Waterbury, CT 06723-2540 (203) 596-4652					teikyopost.edu
Economic Faculty	School of Business Adm Fax=575-9691					Lisa A. DeLorenzo
Philippides, Andreas	Assoc 596-4661		PHD	94	Conn	1988

Temple University	Philadelphia, PA 19122 (215) 204-8880						templevm
Department of Economics	Sch of Business & Mgt Fax=204-8173						Ms. Karen Robinson
Porat, Moshe	Dean	204-1836	Risk	PHD	81	Temple	1981
Stull, William J.	C-Pr	204-5022	IR	PHD	72	MIT	1976
Bandera, Vladimir N.	Prof	204-5039	FP	PHD	60	Berkeley	1972
Blackstone, Erwin A.	Prof	204-5027	L	PHD	68	Michigan	1976
Buck, Andrew J.	Prof	204-1985	C	PHD	77	Illinois	1977
Dunkelberg, William C.	Prof	204-6686	M	PHD	69	Michigan	1987
Hakim, Simon	Prof	204-5037	R	PHD	76	Penn	1976
Kushnirsky, Fyodor I.	Prof	204-5021	P	PHD	68	Moscow	1980
Raphaelson, Arnold H.	Prof	204-8165	H	PHD	60	Clark	1970
Rima, Ingrid H.	Prof	204-8190	B	PHD	51	Penn	1946
Bernstein, Richard E.	Assoc	204-8182	MG	PHD	73	Brown	1972
Bowman, Gary W.	Assoc	204-5026	D	PHD	71	Car Mellon	1973
Diamantaras, Dimitrios	Assoc	204-8169	CD	PHD	88	Rochester	1988
Fardmanesh, Mohsen	Assoc	204-5043	OF	PHD	85	Yale	1985
Goetz, Michael	Assoc	204-1762	MH	PHD	77	Minnesota	1978
Holmes, William L.	Assoc	204-8175	CD	PHD	66	Illinois	1966
Klotz, Benjamin P.	Assoc	204-8452	E	PHD	69	Minnesota	1975
Lady, George	Assoc	204-8174	CD	PHD	67	J Hopkins	1981
Leeds, Michael A.	Assoc	204-8030	J	PHD	82	Princeton	1982
Phelps, Charlotte D.	Assoc	204-1677	TI	PHD	61	Yale	1967
Rappoport, Paul N.	Assoc	204-5025	C	PHD	74	Ohio St	1977
Seidenstat, Paul	Assoc	204-8893	H	PHD	64	Nrthwstrn	1967
Sorrentino, John A. Jr.	Assoc	204-8164	Q	PHD	73	Purdue	1979
Weintraub, Andrew R.	Assoc	204-1919	A	PHD	66	Rutgers	1973
Weiss, Merle	Assoc	204-5029	IJ	PHD	67	Columbia	1972
Bognanno, Michael	Asst	204-1680	J	PHD	90	Cornell	1990
Ryan, Daniel	Asst	204-8167	PL	PHD	90	Berkeley	1990
Swanson, Charles	Asst	204-8168	E	PHD	91	Minnesota	1993

University of Tennessee	Knoxville, TN 37996-0550 (423) 974-3303							utk.edu
Department of Economics	Col of Business Admin Fax=974-4601							Donna Kemper 974-1697
email @1=utkux.utcc.utk.edu								
Neel, C. Warren	Dean	974-5061	cneel	Mgt	PHD	69	Alabama	9-69
Murray, Matthew N.	C-Ac	974-5441	mmurray@1		PHD	86	Syracuse	1986
Bohm, Robert A.	Prof	974-1687	rbohm		PHD	71	Wash U	1968
Bowlby, Roger L.	Emer	974-1694			PHD	58	Tx-Austin	1965
Carroll, Sidney L.	Prof	974-1708	scarroll3@1		PHD	71	Harvard	1972
Chang, Hui-Shyong	Prof	974-1692	hchang		PHD	73	Vanderbilt	1971
Clark, Don P.	Prof	974-1706	dclark3		PHD	70	Mich St	1970
Cole, William E.	Emer	974-1690			PHD	65	Tx-Austin	1965
Davidson, Paul	Prof	974-4221	pdavidso@1		PHD	59	Penn	1987
J. Fred Holly Professor of Political Economy								
Fox, William F.	Prof	974-1697	billfox		PHD	75	Ohio St	1979
Garrison, Charles B.	Prof	974-1691	cgarris@1		PHD	68	Kentucky	1967
Herzog, Henry W. Jr.	Prof	974-1701	pb55978@utkvm1.		PHD	74	Maryland	1974
Jensen, Hans E.	Emer	974-1688	hjensen1	1993	PHD	61	Tx-Austin	1963
Lee, Feng-Yao	Prof	974-1696	fylee@1		PHD	65	Mich St	1965
Mayhew, Anne	Prof	974-1689	amayhew		PHD	66	Tx-Austin	1968
Neale, Walter C.	Emer	974-1711			PHD		London Ec	1960
Russell, Milton	Prof	974-5672	mrussel4		PHD	63	Oklahoma	1987
Schlottmann, Alan M.	Prof	974-1700	pc46868@utkvm1.		PHD	75	Wash U	1975
Spiva, George A. Jr.	Emer	974-1709			PHD	58	Tx-Austin	1958
Gauger, Jean A.	Assoc	974-1702	jgaugher		PHD	84	Iowa St	1985
Glustoff, Errol	Assoc	974-1705	eglustof@1		PHD	69	Stanford	1970
Kahn, James R.	Assoc	974-1699	jkahn		PHD	81	Maryland	1991
Bruce, Donald	Asst	974-3303					Syracuse	1999
Santore, Rudy	Asst	974-3303			PHD	98	Ohio St	1999
Stango, Victor	Asst	974-1695	stango@1		PHD	96	Ca-Davis	1996
Stanley, Denise	Asst	974-1708	dstanle1@1		PHD	96	Wisconsin	1996

Tennessee at Chattanooga	Chattanooga, TN 37403-2598 (423) 755-4360							utc.edu
Department of Economics	Col of Arts & Sciences Fax=785-2385							Ms. Sissy Markum
Summerlin, Tim	Dean	755-4635	tim-summerlin	Engl	PHD	73	Yale	1994
Clark, J. R.	Prof	755-4118	j-clark	M	PHD	70	Va Tech	1993
Probasco Chair in Free Enterprise								
Garrett, John R.	Prof	755-4080	john-garrett	EFG	PHD	85	Mass	1984
UC Foundation Associate Professor								
Giffin, Phillip E.	Prof	755-4129	phillip-giffin	DBLN	PHD	72	Tennessee	1977
Hutchinson, E. Bruce	Prof	755-4180	bruce-hutchinson	DFLR	PHD	79	Virginia	1982
Keilany, Ziad	Prof	755-4116	ziad-keilany	EO	PHD	68	Indiana	1968
Guerry Professor								

Pratt, Leila J.	Prof	755-4138	leila-pratt	DC	PHD	75	Va Tech	1974
Hart Professor								
Rabin, Alan	Prof	755-4154	alan-rabin	E	PHD	77	Virginia	1977
UC Foundation Professor								
Efaw, Fritz W.	Assoc	755-4688	fritz-efaw	CJ	PHD	87	Rutgers	1988

Univ of Tennessee at Martin Martin, TN 38238-5015 (901) 587-7226 utm.edu
Department of Econ & Finance Sch of Business Admin Fax=587-7241 Tammy McWherter
Did Not Respond--1997-98 Listing

Young, Gary F.	Dean	587-7225			PHD	77	La Tech	
Figgins, Bob G.	C-Pr	587-7232			PHD	73	Arkansas	1973
Bethune, John J.	Prof	587-7228			PHD	87	Fla St	
Cashdollar, Parker D.	Prof	587-7242			PHD	71	Tennessee	
Davis, William L.	Assoc	587-7239			PHD	90	Okla St	

Tennessee State University Nashville, TN 37203-3401 (615) 963-7145 picard.tnstate.edu
Economics Faculty School of Business Fax=963-7139 Ms. C. Brown

Curry, Tilden J.	Dean	963-7124		Plan	PHD	78	Fla St	1976
Hartmann, G. Bruce	H-Pr	963-7146	bhartman		PHD	74	SUNY-Alb	1974
MBA Coordinator								
Hasty, John M. Jr.	Prof	963-7145			PHD	73	Geo St	
Masten, John T.	Prof	963-7145			PHD	67	S Illinois	
Vowels, Robert C.	Prof	963-7145			PHD	64	American	
Wahid, Abu	Prof	963-7145			PHD	89	Manitoba	
Weis, Charles E.	Prof	963-7145			DBA	74	Ariz St	

Tennessee Technological Un Cookeville, TN 38505 (931) 372-3745 tntech.edu
Dept of Econ, Fnce & Mktg Col of Business Admin Fax=372-6112 Hilda McDowell

Bell, Robert R.	Dean	372-3372		Mgt	PHD	70	Florida	1976
Williams, Norman C.	C-Ac	372-3745			PHD	72	Arkansas	1972
Cho, Whewon	Prof	528-3160			PHD	71	Vanderbilt	1983
Throckmorton, H. Bruce	Prof				PHD	72	Arkansas	1971
Isbell, Steven	Assoc				PHD	85	Miss	1985
Rappi, Magdalena	Assoc				PHD	85	S Carol	1985
Stephens, Mark A.	Assoc	528-3368			PHD	85	Tennessee	1980
Jonokin, Jon	Asst	372-3767			PHD	94	Tennessee	1989

U of Texas at Arlington Arlington, TX 76019-0479 (817) 272-3061 uta.edu
Department of Economics College of Business Adm Fax=272-3145 Barbara Sellers, Adm Asst

Schkade, Lawrence L.	Dean$	272-2881	schkade	Insu	PHD	61	LSU	1998
Himarios, Daniel	C-Pr	272-3278	himarios	FE	PHD	84	Va Tech	1983
Amacher, Ryan C.	Prof	272-3888	amacher	FH	PHD	71	Virginia	1992
Hayashi, Paul M.	Prof	272-3257	hayashi	D	PHD	69	So Meth	1965
Meiners, Roger E.	Prof	272-3116	meiners	KJ	PHD	76	Va Tech	1993
Mullendore, Walter	Prof	272-3397		R	PHD	68	Iowa St	1969
Crowder, William J.	Assoc	272-3147	crowder	EF	PHD	93	Arizona	1992
Duwaji, Ghazi	Assoc	272-3148		F	PHD	66	Duke	1966
Depken, Craig	Asst	272-3290	depken	DL	PHD	96	Geo St	1996
Sonora, Robert	Asst	272-3062	sonora	F	PHD	98	Ohio St	1998
Wilson, Richard C.	Asst	272-3383	rwilson	AH	MA	66	Georgia	1966
Himarios, Jane	SLect	272-3293	jhimarios	J	PHD	87	Va Tech	1986
Mitra, Aparna	SLect	272-3284	mitra	DE	PHD	95	Tx-Dallas	1996
Kelly, Kathy	Lect	272-3330	kkelly	DE	MA	89	So Meth	1996
Liggett, Ron	Lect	272-2635	liggett	R	MBA	89	Tx-Arlin	1989
McCraw, Jessica	Lect	272-3286	mccraw	DE	MA	78	DePaul	1990
Wehr, Roger	Lect	272-3287	wehr	DE	MA	96	Tx-Arlin	1993
Wilson, Linda	Lect	272-3282	lindw		MS	92	North Tx	1993

Univ of Texas at Austin Austin, TX 78712-1173 (512) 471-3211 mundo.eco.utexas.edu
Department of Economics College of Liberal Arts Fax=471-3510 Kathy Slade, Exec Asst

Langlois, Judith H.	Dean$	471-4141		Psy	PHD	73	LSU	9-73
Dusansky, Richard	C-Pr$	471-3211		DH	PHD	69	Brown	9-89
Richard J. Gonzales Regents Chair in Economic Progress								
Dacy, Douglas C.	Prof	471-3211		EO	PHD	64	Harvard	1-65
Fullerton, Don	Prof	471-3211		HQ	PHD	78	Berkeley	9-94
Addison Baker Duncan Centennial Professor in Economics								
Geraci, Vincent J.	Prof	471-3211		CI	PHD	74	Wisconsin	9-73
Sue Killam Professorship in the Foundations of Economics								
Glade, William P. Jr.	Prof	471-3211		OR	PHD	55	Tx-Austin	9-70
Hamermesh, Daniel S.	Prof	471-3211		J	PHD	69	Yale	9-73
Eedward Everett Hale Centennial Professor in Economics								
Hansen, Niles M.	Prof	471-3211		RP	PHD	63	Indiana	1-63
Leroy G. Denmann, Jr. Regents Professor in Economics								
Kendrick, David A.	Prof	471-3211		CE	PHD	66	MIT	7-70
Ralph W. Yarborough Centennial Professor of Liberal Arts								

Name	Rank	Phone	Fields	Degree	Yr	School	Since
McAfee, R. Preston	Prof	471-3211	D	PHD	80	Purdue	9-90
Murray S. Johnson Chair in Economics							
Morgan, Daniel C. Jr.	Prof	471-3211	H	PHD	62	Wisconsin	7-76
Norman, Alfred L.	Prof	471-3211	C	PHD	71	Minnesota	7-72
Sibley, David S.	Prof	471-3211	D	PHD	73	Yale	1-91
John Michael Stuart Centennial Professor of Economics							
Slesnick, Daniel T.	Prof	471-3211	CH	PHD	82	Harvard	9-82
Rex G. Baker, Jr., Professorship in Political Economy							
Smith, Bruce D.	Prof	471-3211	E	PHD	81	MIT	9-96
Fred Hofheinz Professor in Economics							
Stahl, Dale O. III	Prof	471-3211	DC	PHD	81	Berkeley	7-88
Malcolm Forsman Centennial Professorship							
Bronars, Stephen G.	Assoc	471-3211	JD	PHD	83	Chicago	9-92
Cleaver, Harry	Assoc	471-3211	P	PHD	75	Stanford	9-76
Freeman, Scott	Assoc	471-3211	E	PHD	83	Minnesota	9-91
Kumbhakar, Subal C.	Assoc	471-3211	CD	PHD	86	S Calif	9-86
Stinchcombe, Maxwell B.	Assoc	471-3211	DC	PHD	86	Berkeley	1-94
Trejo, Stephen J.	Assoc	471-3211	J	PHD	88	Chicago	9-99
Wilson, Paul W.	Assoc	471-3211	RC	PHD	86	Brown	9-90
Debaere, Peter	Asst	471-3211	F	PHD	98	Michigan	9-98
Gan, Li	Asst	471-3211	C	PHD	98	Berkeley	9-98
Keller, Wolfgang	Asst	471-3211	FO	PHD	95	Yale	9-98
Minicozzi, Alexandra	Asst	471-3211	E	PHD	97	Wisconsin	9-97
Oettinger, Gerald	Asst	471-3211	JC	PHD	93	MIT	9-92
Sleet, Christopher	Asst	471-3211	E	PHD	98	Stanford	9-98
Wilcoxen, Peter J.	Asst	471-3211	QD	PHD	89	Harvard	9-91
Williams, Roberton III	Asst	471-3211	H	PHD	99	Stanford	9-99
Zheng, Xu John	Asst	471-3211	CO	PHD	92	Princeton	9-92
Shiue, Carol	Inst	471-3211	ON	PHD	99	Yale	9-98

Univ Texas at Brownsville — Brownsville, TX 78520 (956) 548-8707 — utb.edu
Business Adm Department — School of Business Fax=982-0159 — Magie Aariaga

Name	Rank	Phone	Email	Fields	Degree	Yr	School	Since
Boze, Betsy V.	Dean	982-0231	bboze	Mktg	PHD	84	Arkansas	1994
Lackey, Charles	C-Ac	548-8707	clackey	AFL	PHD	84	S Carol	1995
Banerjee, Guarango	Asst	544-8992	gbanerjee	AE	PHD	97	Al-Birm	1997

Univ of Texas at Dallas — Richardson, TX 75083-0688 (972) 883-2920 — utdallas.edu
Dept of Economics & Finance — Sch of Social Sciences Fax=883-2735 — Sheila Rollerson

Name	Rank	Phone	Email	Degree	Yr	School	Since
Kelly, Rita Mae	Dean	883-2935	rmkelly	PHD		Indiana	1996
Beron, Kurt J.	H-Ac	883-2929	kberon	PHD	85	N Carol	1985
Berry, Brian J. L.	Prof	883-2041	berry	PHD	58	U Wash	
L. V. Berkner Professor							
Dumas, Lloyd J.	Prof	883-2010	ljdumas	PHD	72	Columbia	1979
Hicks, Donald A.	Prof	883-2733	dahicks	PHD	76	N Carol	
Hoch, Irving J.	Prof	883-2928	hoch	PHD	57	Chicago	1985
Kain, John F.	Prof	883-6227	kain	PHD	61	Berkeley	1996
Murdoch, James	Prof	883-2280	murdoch	PHD	82	Wyoming	
Vijverberg, Wim P. M.	Prof	883-2042	vijver	PHD	81	Pittsburgh	1986
Jargowky, Paul	Assoc	883-2992	jargo	PHD	91	Harvard	
Seldon, Barry	Assoc	883-2043	seldon	PHD	85	Duke	
Pineres, Sheila	Asst	883-2920	pineres	PHD	92	Duke	1996

Univ of Texas at El Paso — El Paso, TX 79968-0543 (915) 747-5245 — mail.utep.edu
Dept of Economics & Finance — Col of Business Admin Fax=747-6282 — Gloria Armistead
Did Not Respond--1997-98 Listing

Name	Rank	Phone	Fields	Degree	Yr	School	Since
Hoy, Frank	Dean	747-5241	Mgt	PHD	79	Tx A&M	9-91
Roth, Timothy P.	C-Pr	747-5245	AD	PHD	70	Tx A&M	1970
A.B. Templeton Professor							
Herendeen, James B.	Prof	747-5245	AQ	PHD	63	Penn St	1992
James, Dilmus Delano	Prof	747-5245	AFO	PHD	70	Mich St	1958
Frank & Mary Hanley Professor							
Brannon, Jeffery T.	Assoc	747-5245	JNO	PHD	80	Alabama	1982
Holcomb, James H. Jr.	Assoc	747-5245	CDL	PHD	85	Tx A&M	1985
Associate Dean							
Schauer, David A.	Assoc	747-5245	P	PHD	75	Notre Dm	1975
Smith, William Doyle	Assoc	747-5245	AEC	PHD	81	Tx Tech	1981
Sprinkle, Richard L.	Assoc	747-5245	ABCF	PHD	82	Arkansas	1982
Tollen, Robert D.	Assoc	747-5245	D	PHD	72	Tx-Austin	1972
Fullerton, Thomas	Asst	747-5245	RC	PHD	96	Florida	1996

Univ of Texas-Pan American — Edinburg, TX 78539-2999 (956) 381-3354 — panan1.panan.edu
Dept of Economics & Finance — College of Business Adm Fax=384-5020 — P. Roxanne Cerelli

Name	Rank	Phone	Email	Degree	Yr	School	Since
Avellano, George	Dean$						
Davila, Alberto	C-Pr	326-7136	adavila	PHD	82	Iowa St	1996
Cardenas, Gilbert	Prof	381-3369	gcardenas	PHD	77	Illinois	1975
Ellard, Charles J.	Prof	381-3391	cjeb12b	PHD	74	Houston	1976
Taube, Paul M.	Assoc	381-2579	pmtb00a	PHD	86	SUNY-Alb	1988
Pagan, Jose	Asst	381-3383	jpagan	PHD	95	New Mex	1995
Tijerina, Alfredo	Asst			PHD	92	Cincinnati	1999

U of Texas of Permian Basin Odessa, TX 79762-8301 (915) 552-2171 utpb.edu
Dept of Economics Div of Business Adm Fax=552-2374

Name	Rank	Phone	Email	Field	Degree	Yr	School	Since
Watts, William	Dean$	552-2194	watts_w		PHD	66	Iowa	
Hodges, Paul E.	Prof	552-2193	hodges_p		PHD	74	Stanford	

Un of Texas at San Antonio San Antonio, TX 78249-0633 (210) 458-4315 utsa.edu
Div of Economics & Finance College of Business Fax=458-5837

Name	Rank	Phone	Email	Field	Degree	Yr	School	Since
Gaertner, James F.	Dean	458-4313		Atg	PHD	77	Tx A&M	1983
Flory-Truett, Lila J.	D-Pr	691-4315	ltruett	DFMO	PHD	72	Iowa	1975
de la Vina, Lynda	Prof	458-4317			PHD	82	Rice	1979
on leave; Associate Dean								
Hollas, Daniel R.	Prof	458-4313			PHD	77	Illinois	1988
Associate Vice President for Academic Affairs								
Truett, Dale B.	Prof	458-5313	dtruett@2	DFMO	PHD	67	Tx-Austin	1973
Asbel Smith Professor								
Ayers, Ronald M.	Assoc	458-5302	rayers	GJM	PHD	78	Tulane	1979
Collinge, Robert A.	Assoc	458-5312	rcollinge	FHKQ	PHD	83	Maryland	1987
Firoozi, Fathall K.	Assoc	458-5395	ffiroozi	CF	PHD	87	Oklahoma	1988
Mahdavi, Saeid	Assoc	458-5301	smahdavi	EFO	PHD	85	Ca-SnBarb	1984
Merrifield, John D.	Assoc	458-5310	jmerrifi	HQR	PHD	84	Wyoming	1987
Weiher, Kenneth E.	Assoc	458-5315	kweither	BEN	PHD	75	Indiana	1975
De La Cruz, Justino	Asst	458-5303	jdcruz	CEFH	PHD	94	Iowa St	1996
Zhou, Su	Asst	458-5398	szhou	CEFP	PHD	91	Ariz St	1991

Univ of Texas at Tyler Tyler, TX 75799 (903) 566-7371 mail.uttyl.edu
Social Sciences Department School of Liberal Arts Fax=566-7377 Charlotte Chambers

Name	Rank	Phone	Email	Field	Degree	Yr	School	Since
Lefevre, Stephen	Dean	566-7368		PolS	PHD	75	Ca-Rivers	1975
Hart, Barbara	C-Pr	566-7426		CRIJ	PHD		Sam Hous	
Kane, Tim D.	Prof	566-7430	tkane		PHD	72	Tx-Austin	1981

Texas A&M University Coll Station, TX 77843-4228 (409) 845-7351 tamu.edu
Department of Economics College of Liberal Arts Fax=847-8757 Carolyn Teeter
email @1=econ.tamu.edu @2=acs.tamu.edu @3=econ4.tamu.edu

Name	Rank	Phone	Email	Field	Degree	Yr	School	Since
Jones, Woodrow	Dean$	845-5141	woodyj	PolS	PHD	74	Oregon	1988
Jansen, Dennis W.	H-Pr	845-7358	d-jansen	EG	PHD	83	N Carol	1983
Allen, John William	Prof	845-7397	jwa@1	D	PHD	67	Illinois	1967
Anderson, Richard K.	Prof	845-4547	rka3591@2	CF	PHD	76	Purdue	1975
Auernheimer, Leonardo J. A.	Prof	845-7302	leonardo@3	EF	PHD	73	Chicago	1973
Baltagi, Badi H.	Prof	845-7380	badi@1	C	PHD	79	Penn	1988
George Summey Jr. Professor in Liberal Arts								
Battalio, Ray	Prof	845-7309	rcb@1	C	PHD	69	Purdue	1969
Mary Tucker Currie Professorship in Liberal Arts								
Browning, Edgar K.	Prof	845-7355	jacqueline@1	H	PHD	71	Princeton	1984
Alfred F. Chalk Professor of Economics								
Greenhut, Melvin L.	Emer	845-7351			PHD	51	Wash U	1966
Distinguished Professor of Economics								
Griffin, James M.	Prof	845-9950	jmgrif@2	C	PHD	70	Penn	1982
Hugh Roy Cullen Professor in Liberal Arts								
Gronberg, Timothy J.	Prof	845-8849	tjg@1	H	PHD	78	Nrthwstrn	1977
Hanson, John R. II	Prof	845-4593	hanson@1	N	PHD	72	Penn	1974
Hwang, Hae-Shin	Prof	845-7301	hwang@1	C	PHD	76	Minnesota	1977
Moroney, John R.	Prof	845-1363	jacqueline@1	C	PHD	64	Duke	1981
Pejovich, Svetozar	Prof	845-7347	s-pejovich	P	PHD	63	Geotown	1975
Reynolds, Morgan O.	Prof	845-7307		J	PHD	71	Wisconsin	1974
Saving, Thomas R.	Prof	845-7559	t-saving	DE	PHD	60	Chicago	1968
Distinguished Professor, Jeff Montgomery Prof; Dir Private Enterprise Rsch								
Tian, Guoqlang	Prof	845-7393	gtian	C	PHD	87	Minnesota	1987
Van Huyck, John B.	Prof	845-7392	john.vanhuyck	CD	PHD	86	Brown	1985
Private Enterprise Research Center Rex B. Grey Professor								
Welch, Finis R.	Prof	847-8648	bbc@1	J	PHD	66	Chicago	1991
Distinguished Professor and George T. & Gladys H. Abell Prof of Liberal Arts								
Wiggins, Steven N.	Prof	845-7383	snw@3	L	PHD	79	MIT	1979
Deere, Donald R.	Assoc	845-2059	deere	J	PHD	83	MIT	1983
Gilbert, Roy F.	Assoc	845-7357		C	PHD	69	Mich St	1970
Li, Qi	Assoc	862-8859	qi@1	C	PHD	91	Tx A&M	1999
Neilson, William S.	Assoc	845-9954	wsn@3	CD	PHD	88	Ca-SnDgo	1988
Swanson, Norman	Assoc	845-9345	nswanson		PHD	94	Ca-Sn Dgo	1999
Taylor, Curtis	Assoc	845-9954	crtaylor	L	PHD	92	Yale	1992
Private Enterprise Research Center Mary Julia & George R. Jordan Jr. Prof								
Ureta, Manuelita	Assoc	847-9449	manuelita-ureta	J	PHD	87	UCLA	1991
Ghosh, Parikshit	Asst	845-8506	pghosh@1	LO	PHD	98	Boston U	1997
Jeitschko, Thomas	Asst	845-6929	thosd@2	L	PHD	95	Virginia	1995
Kwark, Noh-sun	Asst	845-7384	kwark	E	PHD	95	Rochester	1995
Sarin, Rajiv	Asst	845-7382	r-sarin	CD	PHD	94	Ca-SnDgo	9-94
Scandizzo, Stefania	Asst	845-8507	scandizzo@1	F	PHD	97	Penn	1997
Strayer, Wayne	Asst	845-8508	strayer@1	J	PHD	97	Ohio St	1997

Texas A&M Univ-Commerce	Commerce, TX	75429-3011 (903) 886-5681					tamu-commerce.edu	
Dept of Economics & Finance	College of Business	Fax=886-5601					Wanda Patterson	
Schmidt, L. Lee	Dean	886-5189	lee_schmidt	Atg	PHD	71	Arkansas	1996
Avard, Stephen L.	H-Ac	886-5681	steve_avard	GFDE	PHD	83	North Tx	1983
Funderburk, Dale R.	Prof	886-5675	dale_funderburk	IEKJ	PHD	71	Okla St	1968
Shwiff, Steven S.	Assoc	886-5679	steve_shwiff	CROD	PHD	77	Tx A&M	1987
Washer, Kenneth	Asst	886-5678	ken_washer	CEG	DBA	98	La Tech	1996

Texas A&M Un- Corpus Christi	Corpus Chr, TX	78412 (361) 825-2665					tamucc.edu	
Finance, Economics & Dec Sci	College of Business	Fax=825-2725						
Abdelsamad, Moustafa H.	Dean	825-6045	moustafa	Fnce	DBA	70	Geo Wash	7-91
McMinn, Robert D.	C-Pr	825-2665	mcminn	A	PHD	73	Oklahoma	9-74
Benavides, Adolfo	Assoc	825-2769		AO	PHD	82	Wash St	9-96
Lee, Jim	Assoc	825-2655			PHD	91	Penn St	7-99

Texas A&M Univ-Kingsville	Kingsville, TX	78363 (361) 593-4174					tamuk.edu	
Economics Faculty	Cl Business Adm Box 187	Fax=593-3912						
Bigbee, Dalton L.	C-Pr$	593-4174	dbigbee	Fnce	DBA	81	Tx Tech	1985
Nash, Robert T.	Prof	595-2355	s-nash		PHD	71	Tx A&M	1971
Rossman, Joseph E.	Assoc	595-2506	j-rossman		PHD	75	Iowa St	1976
Nemec, Richard W.	Asst	595-2507	r-nemec		PHD	97	Kentucky	1981

Texas A&M International Univ	Laredo, TX	78041-1900 (956) 326-2490					tamiu.edu	
Dept of Economics & Finance	College of Business Adm	Fax=326-2494					Norma Ortiz	
Did Not Respond--1997-98 Listing								
Fatemi, Khosrow	Dean	326-2480	fatemi	Mgt	PHD	72	S Calif	8-82
Patrick, J. Michael	C-Pr	326-2515	jmpatrick		PHD	77	Mich St	9-93
Islam, Muhammad	Assoc	326-2511	islam		PHD	87	Vanderbilt	9-90
Carr, Alan Barry	Asst	326-2510	carr		PHD	71	Okla St	9-94
Houser, Cindy	Asst	326-2531	houser		PHD	95	Florida	9-95

Texas Christian University	Fort Worth, TX	76129-8510 (817) 257-7230					tcu.edu	
Dept of Economics Box 298510	AddRan Col/Arts & Sci	Fax=					Ms. Suzanne B. Powell	
McCracken, Michael D.	Dean	257-7160		Biol	PHD	69	Indiana	1971
McNertney, Edward M.	C-Ac	257-7230			PHD	77	Mass	1977
Becker, Charles McVey	Assoc	257-7230			PHD	66	Arizona	1967
Butler, Michael R.	Assoc	257-7230			PHD	86	N Carol	1986
Harvey, John T.	Assoc	257-7230			PHD	87	Tennessee	1987
Elliott, Dawn Richards	Asst	257-7230			PHD	94	New Sch	1995
Klopfenstein, Kristin	Asst	257-7230			PHD	99	Colorado	1999
Quinn, Stephen F.	Asst	257-7230			PHD	94	Illinois	1995

Texas Lutheran University	Seguin, TX	78155-5999 (830) 372-6073					txlutheran.edu	
Economics Faculty	Dept of Econ & Pol Sci	Fax=372-8188					Layne Hoppe	
Citzler, Annette	Prof	372-6072	acitzler	A	PHD	85	Tx A&M	1977
Giesber, Frank W.	Prof	379-6071	fgiesber	A	PHD	78	Tx-Austin	1966
Vaughan, Ben F.	Assoc	372-6567			PHD	97	Berkeley	1998

Texas Southern University	Houston, TX	77004 (713) 313-7210					tsu.edu	
Dept Hst, Geography & Econ	College of Arts & Sci	Fax=						
Did Not Respond Again--1995-96 Listing								
Sapp, John	Dean							
Akalou, Woldie-Michael	H	313-7429			PHD		UCLA	
Horwitz, Sigmund	Prof	313-7735			PHD		Houston	
Keleta, Ethiopia	Assoc	313-7702			PHD	84	Rice	
Norman, Emlyn A.	Asst	313-7892			AM		Harvard	
Norris, Hodge	Asst	313-7814			MS		Tx A&I	
Batie, Clarence	Inst	313-7815			MA		Prairie	

Texas Tech University	Lubbock, TX	79409-1014 (806) 742-2201					ttu.edu	
Dept of Economics & Geog	Col of Arts & Sciences	Fax=742-1137					Karen Davis	
Hill, Lewis E.	Prof	742-2201			PHD	57	Tx-Austin	1967
Steinmeier, Thomas L.	Prof	742-2201			PHD	75	Yale	1982
Becker, Klaus G.	Assoc	742-2201			PHD	87	Kansas	1989
Gilbert, Ronald D.	Assoc	742-2201			PHD	70	Okla St	1977
Kruse, Jamie I.	Assoc	742-2201			PHD	88	Arizona	1990
McComb, Robert P.	Assoc	742-2201			PHD	89	Illinois	1991
Rahnama, Masha	Assoc	742-2201			PHD	88	Iowa St	1996
Al-Hmound, Rasheed	VAsst	742-2201			PHD	94	Tx Tech	1995
Chuderewicz, Russell	Asst	742-2201			PHD	97	Penn St	1997
Von Ende, Eleanor Theresa	Asst	742-2201			PHD	90	Kansas	1990

Texas Wesleyan University — Fort Worth, TX 76105-1536 (817) 531-4840 — txwes.edu
Economics Faculty — School of Business Fax=531-4268 — JoAnn Moore

Name	Rank	Phone	Email	Field	Degree	Yr	School	Since
McLain, Louis P.	Dean$	531-4840	lmclain		MBA	74	So Meth	1976
Klaasen, Thomas Albert	Prof		klaasent		PHD	69	Mich St	1989
Ellis, Charles Michael	Assoc		ellism		PHD	73	Alabama	1983

Texas Woman's University — Denton, TX 76204-5738 (940) 898-2111 — twu.edu
Dept of Business & Economics — Col of Arts & Sciences Fax=898-2120 — Betty Hodge

Name	Rank	Phone	Email	Field	Degree	Yr	School	Since
Griffin, Adelaide	C-Pr	898-2111	f_griffin	Mgt	PHD	79	North Tx	1979
Hersh-Cochran, Mona S.	Prof				PHD	66	So Meth	
Conaro Professor of Business and Economics								

University of Toledo — Toledo, OH 43606-3390 (419) 530-2572 — econ.utoledo.edu
Department of Economics — Col of Arts & Sciences Fax=530-7844 — Jeannie Stambaugh
email: @1=uoft02.utoledo.edu

Name	Rank	Phone	Email	Field	Degree	Yr	School	Since
Bischoff, William	Dean	530-2164		Bio	PHD			
Magura, Michael	C-Pr	530-4631	mm@mm.	RL	PHD	72	Boston C	1969
Lesage, James P.	Prof	530-4754	jpl@jpl.	RC	PHD	83	Boston C	1988
Roy, Raj	Prof	530-4430		F	PHD	68	Wayne St	1963
Weiss, Steven J.	Prof	530-4124	sweiss@1	HI	PHD	71	Colorado	1968
Black, David C.	Assoc	530-4153	dcb@dcb.	E	PHD	92	SUNY-Buf	1990
Chang, Hsin	Assoc	530-4677		OP	PHD	89	Michigan	1989
Dowd, Michael R.	Assoc	530-4603	mrd@mrd.	E	PHD	90	SUNY-Buf	1989
Tank, Frederick E.	Assoc	530-2562	fet@fet.	KQ	PHD	72	Wayne St	1970
Keith, Kristen	Asst	530-4132	kkeith@1	J	PHD	89	Ohio St	1994
Murray, John E.	Asst	530-4148	jmurray@1	B	PHD	92	Ohio St	1994

Towson University — Towson, MD 21252-7097 (410) 830-2959 — towson.edu
Department of Economics — Col of Business & Econ Fax=830-3424 — C. F. Eifert

Name	Rank	Phone	Email	Field	Degree	Yr	School	Since
Leberknight, Alan	Dean	830-3342	leberknight		MBA		Loyola	1995
Georgiou, George C.	C-Pr	830-2146	georgiou		PHD	79	Geo Wash	1980
Dorn, James A.	Prof	830-2956	dorn		PHD	76	Virginia	1973
Fenstermaker, J. Van	Prof	830-2145	fenstermaker		PHD	63	Illinois	1988
Kong, Chang Min	Prof	830-2191	kong		PHD	77	Wi-Milwa	1978
Paul, Harvey	Prof	830-2954	paul		PHD	72	SUNY-Buf	1966
Shin, Bong Ju	Prof	830-2951	shin		PHD	69	Ohio St	1966
Woroby, Tamara	Prof	830-3575	woroby		PHD	81	Queens	1978
Egger, John B.	Assoc	830-3576	egger		PHD	85	NYU	1987
Laurence, Louise	Assoc	830-3275	laurence		PHD	87	Maryland	1987
Lee, Kangoh	Assoc	830-3551	lee		PHD	87	Illinois	1990
Sullivan, Timothy	Assoc	830-2338	sullivan		PHD	87	Illinois	1989
Weintraub, Irvin	Assoc	830-2952	weintraub		MS	51	Columbia	1966
Li, Ling	Asst	830-2675	li		PHD	94	Pittsburgh	1994
Michael, Jeffery	Asst	830-2959	michael		PHD	99	N Carol	1999
Rhoads, Thomas	Asst	830-2959	rhoads		PHD	99	Wyoming	1999

Transylvania University — Lexington, KY 40508-1797 (606) 233-8104 — transy.edu
Economics Faculty — Div of Bus Adm & Econ Fax=233-8749 — Faye Pepperl

Name	Rank	Phone	Email	Field	Degree	Yr	School	Since
Pepper, Michael R.	C-Pr	233-8249			MS	69	NewHamp	1989
Erfani, G. Rod	Prof	233-8196			PHD	84	Fla St	1986
Lynch, Lawrence K.	Emer	233-8157			PHD	66	Kentucky	1979
Shearer, Charles L.	Prof	233-8100			PHD	81	Mich St	
President Transylvania University								
Bartley, Alan	Asst				PHD	99	Vanderbilt	1999

Tri-State University — Angola, IN 46703-0307 (219) 665-4243 — tristate.edu
Dept of Social Sciences — Sch of Arts & Sciences Fax=665-4292
Did Not Respond--1997-98 Listing

Name	Rank	Phone	Email	Field	Degree	Yr	School	Since
Tichenor, Delores	Dean	665-4242						
Morin, John E.	C-Pr	665-4206		SocS	MS		Ind St	1966
Moore, Derald L.	Assoc	665-4207			MA		Mich St	1968
Scheffer, Ronald E.	Assoc	665-4202			MA		Ohio	1967
Dobbert, Duane	Asst	665-4862			MA		Mich St	1995

Trinity College — Hartford, CT 06106-3100 (860) 297-2485
Economics Faculty — Department of Economics Fax=297-2257

Name	Rank	Phone	Email	Field	Degree	Yr	School	Since
Butos, William N.	C-Pr	297-2485			PHD	83	Penn St	1981
Curran, Ward S.	Prof				PHD	61	Columbia	1960
Ramirez, Miguel	Prof				PHD	84	Illinois	1985
Zannoni, Diane C.	Prof				PHD	76	SUNY-SBr	1975
Clark, Carol	Assoc				PHD	91	Cornell	1990
Egan, Francis J.	Assoc				PHD	73	Fordham	1967
Gold, Andrew J.	Assoc				PHD	67	Nrthwstrn	1971
Grossberg, Adam J.	Assoc				PHD	86	Illinois	1986

Setterfield, Mark	Assoc	PHD	92	Dalhousie	1992
Wen, G. James	Assoc	PHD	89	Chicago	1994
Zavareei, Manijeh	VAsoc	PHD	82	SUNY-Buf	1991
Fongemie, Claude A.	Lect	PHD	79	Conn	1977
Jacobs, Cindy	VLect	PHD	89	Illinois	1991
O'Connor, F. William	Lect	JD	78	Conn	1984

Trinity University San Antonio, TX 78212-7200 (210) 999-7221 trinity.edu
Department of Economics Div of Behav & Adm Stds Fax=999-7255 Susie DuBose

Stefl, Mary	Dean	999-7521	mstefl	Hlth				
Gonzalez, Jorge G.	C-Ac	999-7224	jorge.gonzalez	F	PHD	89	Mich St	1989
Breit, William L.	Prof	999-8492	wbreit	B	PHD	61	Mich St	1982
Vernon F. Taylor Distinguished Professor of Economics								
Butler, Richard V.	Prof	999-7256	rbutler	H	PHD	77	MIT	1982
Davis, Joe C.	Prof	999-7226	jdavis	J	PHD	71	Tx-Austin	1969
Salvucci, Richard	Prof	999-8494	rsalvucc	N	PHD	82	Princeton	
Spencer, Roger W.	Prof	999-7222	rspencer	E	PHD	69	Virginia	1980
Huston, John H.	Assoc	999-8471	jhuston	D	PHD	83	Wisconsin	1983
Kamdar, Nipoli	Asst	999-7441	nkamdar	H	PHD	93	Syracuse	1993
Patterson, Debra Moore	Asst	999-7223	dpatters	F	PHD	94	Virginia	1994

Troy State University Troy, AL 36082 (334) 670-3459 asntsu.asn.net
Dept Mktg, Mgt & Economics Sorrell Col of Business Fax=670-3599

Ratcliffe, Thomas A.	Dean	670-3137	tratclif	Atg	PHD	78	Alabama	1986
Eminent Scholar in Accounting and Finance								
Merkel, Edward T.	Prof	670-3194			PHD	74	N Illinois	1978
Kirkland, Jack	Assoc	670-3579			PHD	82	Wash St	1995
Thompson, Charles L.	Asst	670-3195	tsuclt01		MS	82	Auburn	1984
Uze, Barry A.		670-3153			MA	85	Miss	1989
Director, Center for Economic Education								

Truman State University Kirksville, MO 63501-4221 (660) 785-4636 truman.edu
Department of Economics Div of Social Science Fax=785-4181 Kay Anderson, Emily Dittmeier

Lyons, James J.	H-Pr	785-4636		Psyc	PHD	73	Ohio St	1972
Patterson, Seymour	Prof	785-4360	spatters		PHD	80	Oklahoma	1980
Sawani, Mustafa A.	Prof	785-4659	msawani		PHD	85	Missouri	1985
Sublette, Werner Johann	Prof	785-4651	wsublett		PHD	74	Arizona	1974
Gillette, David H.	Assoc	785-4334	dgillette		PHD	90	Wash St	1990
Nnadozie, Emmanuel U.	Assoc	785-4099	ennadozi		PHD	87	Sorbonne	1989
Olson, Terry L.	Assoc	785-4503	tolson		PHD	86	Illinois	1990
Sung, Jane C.	Assoc	785-4658	jsung		PHD	85	Wayne St	1987
Coggins, Bruce	Asst	785-4656	bcoggins		PHD	96	Ca Rivers	1998

Tufts University Medford, MA 02155 (617) 627-3560 tufts.edu
Department of Economics Col of Liberal Arts Fax=627-3917

Ernst, Susan	Dean	627-3864	sernst	Bio	PHD			
Garman, David M.	C-Ac	627-2683	dgarman	C	PHD	84	Michigan	1983
Ioannides, Yannis M.	Prof	627-3294	yioannid	E	PHD	74	Stanford	1995
Neubauer Chair Holder								
Norman, George	Prof	627-3663	gnorman	L	PHD	77	Cambridge	1995
Cummings Chair Holder								
Bianconi, Marcello	Assoc	627-2677	mbiancon	E	PHD	88	Illinois	1989
Brown, Drusilla K.	Assoc	627 3006	dbrown04	F	PHD	84	Michigan	1983
Dapice, David O.	Assoc	627-5947		O	PHD	73	Harvard	1973
Loury, Linda D.	Assoc	627-3348	lloruy	J	PHD	78	MIT	1984
Metcalf, Gilbert	Assoc	627-3685	gmetcalf		PHD	88	Harvard	1994
Pepall, Lynne	Assoc	627-5477	lpepal01	L	PHD	83	Cambridge	1987
Richards, Daniel J.	Assoc	627-2679	dricha03	E	PHD	81	Yale	1985
Rothenberg, Winnie	Assoc	627-5221	wrothenb	N	PHD	85	Brandeis	1986
Zabel, Jeffrey	Assoc	627-2318	jzabel	C	PHD	87	Ca-SnDgo	1989
Downes, Thomas A.	Asst	627-2687	tdownes	H	PHD	88	Stanford	1994
Eggleston, Karen	Asst				PHD	99	Harvard	1999
Kutsoati, Edward	Asst	627-2688	ekutso01	G	PHD	98	Queens	1998
McMillan, Margaret	Asst	627-3560	mmcmilla	O	PHD	97	Columbia	1997
Milyo, Jeffrey	Asst	627-3662	jmilyo	H	PHD	94	Stanford	1992
Mukand, Sharun	Asst	627-3560	smukand	F	PHD	97	Boston U	1997
Yu, David	Asst	627-3138	dyu01	G	PHD	97	Princeton	1998

Tulane University New Orleans, LA 70118-5698 (504) 865-5321 tulane.edu
Department of Economics Col of Arts & Sciences Fax=865-5869

Avery-Peck, Alan J.	Dean	865-5720	PHD		Brown	
McMillen, Daniel P.	C-Pr	862-8344	PHD	87	Nrthwstrn	1994
Freudenberger, Herman	Prof	865-5321	PHD	57	Columbia	
Horiba, Yutaka	Prof	862-8346	PHD	69	Purdue	1971
Oakland, William H.	Prof	862-8343	PHD	65	MIT	1979

Edwards, John H.	Assoc	862-8357			PHD	85	Maryland	1985
Malueg, David A.	Assoc	862-8356			PHD	83	Nrthwstrn	1991
Nelson, Douglas R.	Assoc	865-5317			PHD	81	N Carol	1993
Pritchett, Jonathan B.	Assoc	862-8359			PHD	86	Chicago	1985
Brasington, David	Asst	862-8348			PHD	99	Ohio St	1998
Lei, Fitzray	Asst	862-8347			PHD	97	Geo St	1998
Quispe-Agnoli, Myriam	Asst	862-8354			PHD	96	N Carol	1996
Semenick Alam, Ila	Asst	862-8354			PHD	94	Rice	1994
Smith, Stefani	Asst	862-8358			PHD	97	Illinois	1997
Yates, Andrew J.	Asst	862-8345			PHD	92	Stanford	1998

University of Tulsa Tulsa, OK 74104-3189 (918) 631-2219 utulsa.edu
Department of Economics Kendall Col Arts & Sci Fax=
Did Not Respond--1997-98 Listing

Horne, Thomas	Dean							
Ray, Cadwell L.	C-Ac	631-2221			PHD	67	Tx-Austin	
Dugger, William M.	Prof	631-2951			PHD	74	Tx-Austin	
Steib, Steve B.	Prof	631-2219			PHD	72	Iowa St	1972
Horn, Bobbie L.	Assoc	631-2219			PHD	86	Iowa St	
Karikari, John A.	Assoc	631-3157		AFMO	PHD	85	Queen's	
Soltow, Allen R.	Assoc	631-2335			PHD	69	Iowa St	1973

Tuskegee University Tuskegee, AL 36088 (334) 727-8116 acd.tusk.edu
Dept of Economics Col of Bus, Org & Mgt Fax=727-8604 Susie Stenson

Newhouse, Benjamin	Dean	727-8116	bnewhouse	Atg	PHD	82	Michigan	1-84
Sara, Tejinder S. Associate Dean	H-Ac	727-8705	tsara		PHD	75	Mass	1973
Cheng, William	Assoc	727-6307	chengw		PHD	90	SUNY-Bin	1990
Duncan, Jerome	Assoc	727-2673	jduncan		PHD	80	Florida	1991
Lieu, George	Assoc	727-2673	glieu		PHD	86	Okla St	1988
Upchurch, Leo	Assoc	727-8732	upchurch		PHD	82	Michigan	1990
Olowolayemo, Suryudeen	Asst	727-8712	osuraj		PHD	93	Auburn	1994
Sahai, Sirman	Asst	727-8733	skahai		PHD	95	Auburn	1995
Shalishali, Kasazi	Asst	727-8285	kshalis		PHD	93	Auburn	1993

Union College-NY Schenectady, NY 12308-3163 (518) 388-6200 union.edu
Department of Economics Div of Social Sciences Fax=388-6988 Diana Mirabile

Yaisawarng, Suthathip	C-Ac	388-6606	yaisawas	CD	PHD	89	S Illinois	1989
Fried, Harold O.	Prof	388-6368	friedh	CIL	PHD	78	N Carol	1983
Kenney, James M.	Prof	388-6018	kennyj	QDMG	PHD	72	Stanford	1972
Klein, J. Douglass	Prof	388-6056	kleind	LQD	PHD	75	Wisconsin	1979
Reynolds, Bruce L.	Prof	388-6217	reynoldb	ODP	PHD	75	Michigan	1974
Schmidt, Shelton S.	Prof	388-6218	schmidts	LCA	PHD	77	Virginia	1974
Lewis, Bradley G. Associate Dean for Undergraduate Studies	Assoc	388-6232	lewisb	GMN	PHD	83	Chicago	1979
McCarty, Therese A.	Assoc	388-6045	mccartyt	GI	PHD	87	Michigan	1987
Motahar, Eshragh	Assoc	388-6065	motahare	EFG	PHD	89	J Hopkins	1984
Rafferty, Matt	VAsst	388-6505	raffertm	ENC	PHD	98	Ca-Davis	1998
Schmidt, Stephen J.	Asst	388-6200	schmidsj	LCD	PHD	95	Stanford	1994
Sener, Mehmet F.	Asst			FOEJ	PHD	99	Florida	1999
Tomljanovich, Marc	VAsst	388-6493	tomljanm	ECF	PHD	98	Cornell	1998

Union University Jackson, TN 38305-3697 (901) 661-5360 uu.edu
Department of Economics Sch of Business Admin Fax=661-5366 Judy Leforgee

Lester, Don	Dean	661-5367	dlester		PHD	94	Memphis	1996
Pray, Bwalee	C-As	661-5109	bpray		PHD	92	Memphis	1991
Newell, Howard	Prof	661-5471	hewell		PHD	74	Indiana	1982
Padelford, Walton M.	Prof	661-5362		ABFO	PHD	75	LSU	1980
Holt, Kenneth	Assoc	661-5365	kholt		ABD		Memphis	1987

U.S. Air Force Academy Colorado Spr, CO 80840-6238 (719) 333-3080 usafa.af.mil
Department of Economics Social Science Division Fax=333-7137 Ms. Victoria Armstrong

Franck, Raymond E. Jr	H-Pr	333-3080	franckre.dfeg		PHD	83	Harvard	
Linster, Bruce G.	Prof	333-3080	linsterbg.dfeg		PHD	90	Michigan	1990
Shambert, Vladimir M.	Prof	333-3080	shambergvm.dfeg		PHD	52	Moscow	1992
Slate, Stephen T.	Assoc	333-3080	slatest.dfeg		PHD	94	Colorado	
Waller, Robert L.	Assoc	333-3080	wallerrl.dfeg	AF	PHD	86	Boston U	1998
Carson, Katherine S.	Asst	333-3080	carsonks.dfeg	ACO	PHD	97	Colorado	1977
Lucchesi, Michael S.	Asst	333-3080	lucchesims.dfeg		MA	86	U Wash	1993
Mullin, R. David	Asst	333-3080	mullinrd.dfeg	AD	PHD	93	Virginia	1998
Prosseda, Phil D.	Asst	333-3080	prossedapd.dfeg		ABD	97	Colorado	
Rappaport, Neal J.	Asst	333-3080	rappaportnj.dfeg	DC	PHD	94	MIT	1998
Sikorra, Raymond C.	Asst	333-3080	sikorrarc.dfeg	P	PHD	96	Indiana	1998
Sohan, Gerald	Asst	333-3080	sohange.dfeg		ABD		Tx A&M	
West, James E.	Asst	333-3080	westje.dfeg	AD	PHD	94	Michigan	1997
Barrows, Stephen P.	Inst	333-3080	barrowssp.dfeg		MA	93	Penn St	
Drape, James H.	Inst	333-3080	drapejh		MPP	92	Harvard	
Johanson, Curtis E.	Inst	333-3080	johansonce.dfeg		MA	97	Tx-Austin	
Kovach, David L.	Inst	333-3080	kovachdl.dfeg		MBA	89	Valdosta	
Santoni, Matthew V.	Inst	333-3080	santonimv.dfeg		MS	90	Penn St	

U.S. Military Academy	West Point, NY		10996-1798	(914) 938-3795				usma.edu
Economics Faculty	Dept of Social Sciences		Fax=938-4563					
Messe, Michael J.	D	938-4002	jm6695	HE	PHD	77	Princeton	1990
Gujarati, Damodar N.	Prof	938-3236		CE	PHD	65	Chicago	1990
Smallwood, Dennis	Prof	938-2879		DHL	PHD	66	Yale	1996
Dudley, Dean	Asst	938-3144		DHL	PHD	93	Indiana	1993
Lofgren, Stephanie	Asst	938-2899	js4617	DHF	PHD	96	Nrthwstrn	1995
Onuk, Cengiz	Asst	938-3346		DM	PHD	93	SUNY	1998

U.S. Naval Academy	Annapolis, MD		21402-5042	(410) 293-6880				nadn.navy.mil
Economics Department	Div Humanities & Soc Sc		Fax=293-6899				Ms. Lou Ellen Hazel	
Bowman, William R.	C-Pr	293-6881	bowman		PHD	79	Maryland	1980
Fredland, John E.	Prof	293-6897	fredland		PHD	70	Michigan	1974
Goodman, Rae Jean B.	Prof	293-6891	goodman		PHD	76	Wash U	1973
Little, Roger D.	Prof	293-6889	little		PHD	70	Houston	1970
Morris, Clair E. Jr.	Prof	293-6893	morris		PHD	72	Wisconsin	1966
Gibb, Arthur Jr.	Assoc	293-6886	gibb		PHD	74	Michigan	1974
Thierfelder, Karen	Assoc	293-6887	thier		PHD	92	Wisconsin	1992
Zak, Thomas A.	Assoc	293-6895	zakt		PHD	80	Vanderbilt	1981
Getter, Darryl	Asst	293-6888	getter		PHD	94	Wash U	1994
Krieg, John M.	Asst				PHD	99	Oregon	1999
McCoskey, Suzanne K.	Asst	298-6892	mccoskey		PHD	97	Syracuse	1997

University of Utah	Salt Lake CY, UT		84112	(801) 581-7481				econ.sbs.utah.edu
Department of Economics	Col of Soc & Behav Sci		Fax=585-5649			Ginger Head Adm Officer		
Gelfand, Donna M.	Dean	581-8620		Psyc	PHD	61	Stanford	1964
Hunt, E. K.	C-Pr	581-7656	hunt		PHD	68	Utah	1978
Gander, James P.	Prof	581-5670	gander		PHD	66	Berkeley	1965
Girton, Lance	Prof	581-7622	girton		PHD	76	Chicago	1978
Glick, Mark	Prof	581-7464	glick		PHD	85	New Sch	1985
Jameson, Kenneth P.	Prof	581-8620	jameson		PHD	70	Wisconsin	1989
Mangum, Garth L.	Prof	581-6127	mangum		PHD	60	Harvard	1969
Phillips, Peter W.	Prof	585-6465	phillips		PHD	80	Stanford	1978
Rock, James M.	Prof	581-7481	rock		PHD	66	Nrthwstrn	1967
Sievers, Allen M.	Prof	581-7456	sievers		PHD	48	Columbia	1968
Carlisle, William T.	Assoc	581-8511	carlisle		PHD	75	Cornell	1971
Fowles, Richard G.	Assoc	581-4577	fowles		PHD	85	Utah	1990
Kiefer, David M.	Assoc	581-4308	kiefer		PHD	74	Michigan	1981
Reynolds, Stephen E.	Assoc	581-7603	reynolds		PHD	69	Wisconsin	1969
Waltzman, Norman J.	Assoc	581-7600	waltzman		PHD	88	American	1988
Berik, Gunseli	Asst	581-7435	berik		PHD	86	Mass	1994
Cagatay, Nilufer	Asst	581-7667	cagatay		PHD	86	Stanford	1991
Ehrbar, Hans G.	Asst	581-7797	ehrbar		PHD	85	Michigan	1986
Erturk, Korkut	Asst	581-4576	korkut		PHD	92	New Sch	1992
Lozada, Gabriel A.	Asst	581-7650	lozada		PHD	87	Stanford	1993
Maloney, Tom	Asst	581-7704	maloney		PHD	93	Michigan	1992
Dalendina, Patrick V	Visit	581-4576	dolenc		PHD	93	Utah	
Linebarger, Laura	Visit	581-7697	linebarg		PHD	97	Utah	

Utah State University	Logan, UT		84322-3530	(435) 797-2310				b202.usu.edu
Department of Economics	College of Business		Fax=797-2701			Suzette Alder, Adm Asst		
Stephens, David B.	Dean	797-2272	dstephens	Mgt	PHD	75	Tx-Austin	6-87
Criddle, Keith R.	H-Pr	797-2300	kcriddle	CQ	PHD	89	Ca-Davis	1990
Bailey, DeeVon	Prof	797-2316	dbailey	Q	PHD	83	Tx A&M	1983
Biswas, Basudeb	Prof	797-2304	biswas	CFO	PHD	76	Chicago	1976
Fullerton, Herbert H.	Prof	797-2324	hfullerton	OQR	PHD	71	Iowa St	1969
Glover, Terrence F.	Prof	797-2297	tglover	DCQ	PHD	71	Purdue	1974
Godfrey, E. Bruce	Prof	797-2294	bruceg	Q	PHD	71	Oregon St	1977
Israelsen, L. Dwight	Prof	797-2298	disraelsen	ABDE	PHD	73	MIT	1980
Keith, John E.	Prof	797-2303	jkeith	DEQR	PHD	73	Utah St	1972
Lewis, W. Cris	Prof	797-2327	clewis	MCR	PHD	69	Iowa St	1972
Lyon, Kenneth S.	Prof	797-2292	klyon	CDEQ	PHD	70	Chicago	1966
Petersen, Harold Craig	Prof	797-1170		GM	PHD	73	Stanford	1973
Associate Provost; craigp@champ.usu.edu								
Snyder, Donald L.	Prof	797-2383	dsnyder	CQ	PHD	79	Utah St	1981
Whitaker, Morris D.	Prof	797-1840		FO	PHD	70	Purdue	1970
Director of International Program; morrisw@cscfsl.usu.edu								
Batabyal, Amitrajeet	Assoc	797-2314	batabyal	FOQ	PHD	94	Berkeley	1995
Fawson, Christopher	Assoc	797-2296	cfawson	CGMO	PHD	86	Tx A&M	1990
Aadland, David	Asst	797-2322	aadland	CF	PHD	97	Oregon	1997
Huang, Kevin	Asst	797-2320	khuang	EFG	PHD	98	Minnesota	1998
Hunnicutt, Lynn	Asst	797-2317	hunnicut	DLM	PHD	97	Tx-Austin	1998
Weninger, Quinn	Asst	797-0775	weninger	CQ	PHD	95	Maryland	1995
Bowles, Tyler	Lect	797-2378	tbowles	AF	PHD	91	N Carol	1994
Mohapatra, Sarita	Lect	797-2309	smohapatra	ADF	PHD	95	Utah St	1995
Bentley, Marion	ExtSp	797-2284		H	MPA	70	NYU	1975

Utica College Utica, NY 13502-4892 (315) 792-3055 utica.ucsu.edu
Economics Department Div of Social Sci & Mgt Fax=792-3173 Susan Cox

Name	Rank	Phone	Email	Fields	Degree	Yr	School	Since
Blanchfield, William C.	D-Pr	792-3109		Educ	PHD	70	SUNY-Alb	1966
Neun, Stephen P.	Prof	792-3055	sneu	IJ	PHD	88	Conn	1982
Associate Dean								
Fenner, Richard G.	Assoc	792-3112	rfenner	AIR	PHD	92	Syracuse	1989

Valdosta State University Valdosta, GA 31698-0075 (912) 245-2234 grits.valdosta.peachnet.e
Dept of Mktg & Economics College of Business Adm Fax=245-2248 Bonnie Ely

Name	Rank	Phone	Email	Fields	Degree	Yr	School	Since
Stanley, Kenneth L.	Dean	333-5991	kstanley		PHD	78	Purdue	1984
Allen, Ralph C.	H-Pr	245-2243	rcallen	FDK	PHD	81	Geo St	1982
Love, Jim L.	Prof	245-3824	jllove	R	PHD	83	Okla St	1983
Plumly, L. Wayne Jr.	Prof	245-3815	lwplumly	JA	PHD	83	Geo St	1980
Kushner, Joseph W.	Assoc	245-2249	jkushner	A	PHD	69	Tennessee	1969
Tori, Cynthia R.	Asst	245-2246	crtori	EF	PHD	92	Kentucky	1998

Valparaiso University Valparaiso, IN 46383-6493 (219) 464-5696 valpo.edu
Department of Economics Col of Arts & Sciences Fax=464-5381 Suzanna L. Tudor

Name	Rank	Phone	Email	Fields	Degree	Yr	School	Since
Trost, Albert R.	Dean	464-5314	albert.trost	PolS	PHD	71	Wash U	1963
Shingleton, Virginia	C-Ac	464-5405	virginia.shin+	CJIA	PHD	94	Notre Dm	1992
Henderson, James P.	Prof	464-5404	james.henderson	NBA	PHD	77	N Illinois	1975
Bernard, James A. Jr.	Assoc	464-5045	james.bernard	AOP	PHD	72	Notre Dm	1968
Raman, Jaishankar	Asst	464-6814	jaishankar.raman	OFA	PHD	97	Notre Dm	1996

Vanderbilt University Nashville, TN 37235 (615) 322-2871 ctrvax.vanderbilt.edu
Department of Economics Col of Arts & Science Fax=343-8495 Edda Leithner

Name	Rank	Phone	Email	Fields	Degree	Yr	School	Since
Atack, Jeremy	C-Pr	343-2467	atackj	N	PHD	76	Indiana	1993
Butler, John Scott	Prof	322-3237	butlerjs	GC	PHD	82	Cornell	1982
Senior Fellow, Institute for Public Policy Studies								
Damon, William W.	Prof	322-2871	damonww	DGM	PHD	70	Cornell	1976
Daughety, Andrew F.	Prof	322-2871	andrew.daughety	LK	PHD	72	Case Wes	1995
Driskill, Robert A.	Prof	343-1516	driskira	EFM	PHD	78	J Hopkins	1992
Finegan, T. Aldrich	Prof	322-3445	t.aldrich.fin+	J	PHD	60	Chicago	1970
Foster, James E.	Prof	322-2192	fosterje	DG	PHD	82	Cornell	1990
Huang, Cliff J.	Prof	322-3796	huangxcj	C	PHD	68	N Carol	1969
Margo, Robert A.	Prof	322-2189	margora	NJ	PHD	82	Harvard	1989
Reinganum, Jennifer F.	Prof	322-2871	jennifer.rein+	LK	PHD	79	Nrthwstrn	1995
Russell, Clifford S.	Prof	322-8506	cliff.russell	HQ	PHD	68	Harvard	1986
Director, Institute for Public Policy Studies								
Siegfried, John J.	Prof	322-2429	siegfrjj	LJ	PHD	72	Wisconsin	1972
Weymark, John A.	Prof	322-2871		D	PHD	77	Penn	1999
Wildasin, David E.	Prof	343-2468	wildasin	G	PHD	76	Iowa	1993
Anderson, Kathryn H.	Assoc	322-0263	anderskh	JO	PHD	78	N Car St	1980
Senior Fellow, Inst for Public Policy Studies								
Crucini, Mario J.	Assoc	322-2871		E	PHD	91	Rochester	1999
Getz, Malcolm	Assoc	322-3425	getz	HR	PHD	73	Yale	1973
Hinshaw, C. Elton	Assoc	322-3453	c.elton.hinshaw	N	PHD	66	Vanderbilt	1966
Maneschi, Andrea	Assoc	322-2993	manesca	FO	PHD	64	J Hopkins	1969
Sweeney, George H.	Assoc	322-2845	george.sweeney	DL	PHD	77	Nrthwstrn	1976
Associate Dean								
Mani, Anandi	Asst	322-3582	anandi.mani		PHD	97	Boston	1997
Reilly, Siobhan	Asst	322-2920	siobhan.reilly		PHD	97	Berkeley	1997
Rousseau, Peter L.	Asst	322-2871	peter.l.rouss+	EM	PHD	95	NYU	1995
Schwartz, Jesse	Asst	322-2871		DLQ	PHD	99	Maryland	1999
Watts, Alison	Asst	322-3425	wattsa	DHG	PHD	93	Duke	1993
Weymark, Diana N.	Asst	322-2871		EG	PHD	90	Brit Colum	1999

Vassar College Poughkeepsie, NY 12604 (914) 437-7395 vassar.edu
Economics Faculty Department of Economics Fax=437-7576 Susan M. Conger

Name	Rank	Phone	Email	Fields	Degree	Yr	School	Since
Kennett, David A.	C-Pr	437-7000	kennett	F	PHD	76	Columbia	1976
Jehle, Geoffrey A.	Prof	437-5210	jehle	D	PHD	83	Princeton	1981
Thompson, Alexander M.	Prof	437-5257	thompson	BH	PHD	79	Stanford	1977
Herbst, Lawrence A.	Assoc	437-7398		N	PHD	74	Penn	1970
Johnson, Paul A.	Assoc	437-5213	pajohnson	E	PHD	84	Stanford	1995
Johnson-Lars, Shirley B.	Assoc	437-5214	sjlans	I	PHD	66	Columbia	1967
Lunt, William E.	Assoc	437-7396	lunt	C	PHD	77	Stanford	1974
Bellemore, Fred A.	Asst	437-7393	frbellemore	H	PHD	92	MIT	1992
Jones, Patricia	Asst	437-5209		JO	PHD	98	Oxford	1999
Kilby, Christopher P.	Asst	437-5212	chkilby	O	PHD	94	Stanford	1993
Smith, John Z.	Asst	437-7669	jzsmith	J	PHD	93	MIT	1993

University of Vermont Burlington, VT 05405-4160 (802) uvm.edu
Department of Economics Col of Arts & Sciences Fax=

Smith, Joan	Dean	656-3166	joan.smith					
Rizvi, Saiyid A.	C-Pr	656-3064	saiyid.rizvi	BDF	PHD	90	New Sch	1987
Alnasrawi, Abbas	Prof	656-3064	abbas.alnasrawi	AFOQ	PHD	65	Harvard	1963
Gibson, William A.	Prof	656-3064	william.gibson	CFOQ	PHD	77	Berkeley	1986
Gedeon, Shirley J.	Assoc	656-0188	shirley.gedeon	EP	PHD	82	Mass	1981
Knodell, Jane E.	Assoc	656-3064	jane.knodell	EN	PHD	84	Stanford	1986
McCrate, Elaine D.	Assoc	656-3064	elaine.mccrate	JIT	PHD	85	Mass	1985
Thomson, Ross	Assoc	656-3064	ross.thomson	NDB	PHD	76	Yale	1991
Woolf, Arthur G.	Assoc	656-3064	arthur.woolf	HNR	PHD	80	Wisconsin	1980
Brooks, Nancy	Asst	656-0183	nancy.brooks	DHQR	PHD	94	Penn	1994
Seguino, Stephanie	Asst		stephanie.seg+	EFOP	PHD	94	American	1995

Villanova University Villanova, PA 19085-1678 (610) 519-4370 email.vill.edu
Department of Economics Col of Commerce & Fnce Fax=519-6054 Caroly Mitchell 519-4360

Monahan, Thomas F.	Dean$	519-4354	tmonahan	Atg	PHD	81	Temple	1981
Mathis, Edward J.	C-Pr	519-4387	emathis		PHD	71	SUNY-Buf	1966
DeFina, Robert H.	Prof	519-4482	rdefina		PHD	79	Wash U	1989
Thanawala, Kishor H.	Prof	519-4385	kthanawa		PHD	61	Bombay	1967
Zech, Charles E.	Prof	519-4371	czech		PHD	73	Notre Dm	1974
Clain, Suzanne H.	Assoc	519-6556	sclain		PHD	84	Princeton	1987
Donziger, Alan J.	Assoc	519-4315	adonzige		PHD	72	Bryn Mawr	1967
Giordano, James N.	Assoc	519-4167	jgiordan		PHD	82	Indiana	1983
Kroch, Eugene A.	Assoc	519-6428	ekroch		PHD	78	Harvard	1991
Wolnicki, Miron J.	Assoc	519-4384	mwolnick		PHD	80	Lodz	1984
Zaleski, Peter A.	Assoc	519-4378	pzaleski		PHD	88	Maryland	1987
Alexandrin, Glen	Asst	519-6101	galexand		PHD	67	Clark	1970
Asher, Cheryl	Asst	519-4159	casher		PHD	81	Penn	1984
Casario, Michelle	Asst	519-4362	mcasario		PHD	91	Northeas	1991
Farrell, Rev. John	Asst	519-4324	jfarrell		PHD	72	Catholic	1993
Mao, Wen	Asst	519-4370	wmao		PHD	94	Va Tech	1995
Taylor, Kenneth B.	Asst	519-6430	ktaylor		PHD	80	SUNY-SBr	1985
Walsh, C. Gerald	Asst	519-4165	cwalsh		MA	60	Detroit	1960

University of Virginia Charlottesvil VA 22903-3288 (804) 924-3177 virginia.edu
J. Wilson Dept of Economics Grad Sch of Arts & Sci Fax=982-2904 Bunny Stinnett
Homepage: http://www.virginia.edu/econ/home.html
Did Not Respond--1997-98 Listing

Plog, Stephen E.	Dean	924-3437	sep6n		PHD	77	Michigan	1978
Holt, Charles A.	C-Pr	924-7894	cah2k	CDL	PHD	77	Car Mellon	1989
Merrill Bankard Professor of Economics								
Baxter, Marianne	Prof	924-3997	mb6s	FE	PHD	84	Chicago	1993
Elzinga, Kenneth G.	Prof	924-6752	kge8z	L	PHD	67	Mich St	1967
Epps, Thomas W.	Prof	924-7947	twe	GC	PHD	69	Duke	1972
Undergraduate Director								
James, John A.	Prof	924-3525	jaj8y	NO	PHD	74	MIT	1978
Johnson, William R.	Prof	924-3251	wrj8y	DJ	PHD	75	MIT	1974
King, Robert G.	Prof	924-3994	rgk4m	EG	PHD	80	Brown	1993
A. Willis Robertson Professor of Economics								
Mills, David E.	Prof	924-3061	dem9j	LD	PHD	75	Stanford	1975
Mirman, Leonard J.	Prof	924-6756	lm8h	ACDQ	PHD	70	Rochester	1986
Paul Goodloe McIntire Professor of Economics								
Olsen, Edgar O.	Prof	924-3443	eoo	HI	PHD	68	Rice	1983
Sherman, Roger	Prof	924-6740	rs5w	LD	PHD	66	Car Mellon	1971
Brown-Forman Professor of Economics								
Stern, Steven N.	Prof	924-6754	sns5r	JCI	PHD	85	Yale	1985
Whitaker, John K.	Prof	924-3459	jw9s	BC	PHD	62	Cambridge	1969
Georgia S. Bankard Porfessor of Economics								
Anderson, Simon P.	Assoc	924-3861	sa9w	LDR	PHD	85	Queen's	1987
Engers, Maxim P.	Assoc	924-3130	mpe2m	ACD	PHD	84	UCLA	1982
Graduate Director								
Levine, Ross	Assoc	924-7654	rl9j	FO	PHD	87	UCLA	1997
Michener, Ronald W.	Assoc	924-6753	rwm3n	EN	PHD	81	Chicago	1979
Brien, Michael	Asst	924-6750	brien	JT	PHD	91	Chicago	1993
Goeree, Jacob	Asst	924-7649	jg2n	CDL	PHD	97	Amsterdm	1996
Ihrig, Jane	Asst	924-6751	ihrig	F	PHD	95	Minnesota	1995
John, A. Andrew	Asst	924-6747	aaj9w	AE	PHD	88	Yale	1993
Khan, Aubhik	Asst	924-7581	ak2g	EO	PHD	93	Penn	1993
Khan, Shakeeb	Asst	924-3177		C	PHD	97	Princeton	1997
Kreider, Brent	Asst	924-7845	bk5x	HI	PHD	94	Wisconsin	1994
Pepper, John	Asst	924-3402	jvp3m	HD	PHD	96	Wisconsin	1996
Wright, Jonathan	Asst	924-3177		CE	PHD	97	Harvard	1997

Virginia Commonwealth Univ Richmond, VA 23284-4000 (804) 828-1717 vcu.edu
Department of Economics School of Business Fax=828-1719 Linda Cosby

Name	Rank	Phone	Email	Degree	Yr	School	Since
Miller, E. G.	Dean$	827-0072	egmiller	PHD		Alabama	
Millner, Edward L.	C-Pr	828-1717	elmillne	PHD	82	N Carol	1983
Bowman, John H.	Prof	828-1717	jhbowman	PHD	73	Ohio St	1981
Davis, Douglas D.	Prof	828-7110	dddavis	PHD	84	Indiana	1987
Hoffer, George E.	Prof	828-7089	gehoffer	PHD	72	Virginia	1970
Pratt, Michael D.	Prof	828-1835	mdpratt	PHD	77	Kansas	1979
Reilly, Robert J.	Prof	828-3184	rjreilly	PHD	78	Tennessee	1978
Beall, Larry G.	Assoc	828-7140	lgbeall	PHD	73	Duke	1970
Gallagher, Charles J.	Assoc	828-1745	cjgallag	PHD	70	W Virginia	1971
Associate Dean External Affairs							
Harless, David W.	Assoc	828-7190	dwharles	PHD	88	Indiana	8-93
Mitchell, Shannon K.	Assoc	828-7142	skmitche	PHD	89	Virginia	1990
on leave at University of Virginia							
O'Toole, Dennis M.	Assoc	828-3185	dmotoole	PHD	71	Ohio U	1967
Peterson, Steven P.	Assoc	828-3186	sppeters	PHD	89	Indiana	1989
Wetzel, James N.	Assoc	828-7145	jnwetzel	PHD	74	N Carol	1974
Lehr, Carol A.	Asst	828-7148	cslehr	PHD	91	Penn St	1997
Stratton, Leslie A.	Asst	828-7141	lsstratt	PHD	89	MIT	1997

Virginia Military Institute Lexington, VA 24450-0304 (540) 464-7234 vax.vmi.edu
Dept of Economics & Business Liberal Arts Division Fax=464-7005 Beverley Clements

Name	Rank	Phone	Degree	Yr	School	Since
Reclam, Michael	H-Ac	464-7234	PHD	84	Ca-Rivers	1986
Bush, H. Francis	Prof	464-7234	PHD	89	Florida	1994
Claiborn, Edward L.	Prof	464-7234	PHD	64	Princeton	1981
Daley, Edward V.	Prof	464-7234	PHD	74	Missouri	1981
Duncan, Floyd H.	Prof	464-7234	PHD	72	S Carol	1978
Sexton, Edwin A.	Prof	464-7234	PHD	87	Illinois	1992
Basu, Atin	Asst	464-7234	PHD	98	Miss	1999
Gutermuth, Karen	Asst	464-7234	PHD	96	LSU	1997
West, Clifford T.	Asst	464-7234	PHD	92	Indiana	1996
O'Connor, Roy J.	Inst	464-7234	MBA	69	Hartford	1992

Virginia Poly Inst & St Un Blacksburg, VA 24061-0316 (540) 231-5688 vt.edu
Department of Economics Col of Arts & Sciences Fax=231-5097 Ms. Sherry Williams

Name	Rank	Phone	Email	Fields	Degree	Yr	School	Since
Bates, Robert C.	Dean	231-5421	bates					
Salehi-Isfahani, Djavad	H-Ac	231-7697	salehi	OT	PHD	77	Harvard	1984
Eckel, Catherine C.	Prof	231-7707	eckelc	P	PHD	83	Virginia	1983
Feltenstein, Andrew	Prof	231-7958	afeltens	DHO	PHD	76	Yale	1993
Haller, Hans H.	Prof	231-7591	haller	D	PHD	78	Erlangen	1985
Kats, Amoz	Prof	231-6289	amoz	CDL	PHD	72	Minnesota	1974
Meiselman, David I.	Emer			D	PHD	61	Chicago	1971
Spanos, Aris	Prof	231-7981	aris	CB	PHD	82	London	1988
Tideman, T. Nicolaus	Prof	231-7592	ntideman	H	PHD	69	Chicago	1975
Ashley, Richard A.	Assoc	231-6220	ashleyr	CE	PHD	82	Ca-SnDgo	1981
Ball, Sheryl B.	Assoc	231-4349	sball	DMH	PHD	91	Nrthwstrn	1992
Cothren, Richard D.	Assoc	231-6980	rcothren	E	PHD	81	N Carol	1985
Gilles, Robert P.	Assoc	231-4069	rgilles	DH	PHD	90	Tilburg	1991
Lutz, Nancy A.	Assoc	231-7353	nlutz	DLM	PHD	87	Stanford	1992
Murphy, Russell D. Jr.	Asst	231-4537	rdmurphy	D	PHD	97	Boston U	1997
Snyder, Susan	Asst	231-4431	sksnyder	HDC	PHD	96	Stanford	8-95
Stegeman, Mark W	Asst	231-4923	stegeman	DL	PHD	87	MIT	1994
Verbrugge, Randal J.	Asst	231-7474	rvergrug	EF	PHD	95	Stanford	1995
McLeod, Mark A.	Inst	231-5942	markmc					1998
Cremer, Jacques	Adj				PHD	78	MIT	1983

Virginia State University Petersburg, VA 23806-9398 (804) 524-5335 vsu.edu
Dept of Economics & Finance School of Business Fax=524-6512 Mrs. Shirley Lewis

Name	Rank	Phone	Email	Degree	Yr	School	Since
Gregory, Sadie R.	Dean	524-5166	sgregory	PHD	87	Howard	1-79
Badu, Yaw Agyeman	C-Ac	524-5363	abadu	PHD	80	S Carol	1984
Khan, Agha Nisar	Prof	524-5872	akhan	PHD	70	Va Tech	1972
Meeks, Thomas J.	Prof	524-5364	tmeeks	PHD	71	Duke	1969
Bawuah, Kwado	Assoc	524-5881	kbawuah	PHD	83	Va Tech	1987
Eseonu, Maxwell O.	Assoc	524-5882	meseonu	PHD	83	Howard	1982
Ohn, Jonathan	Asst	524-5324	john	PHD	98	Lehigh	1999
Trainor, William J.	Asst	524-5365	wtrainor	PHD	94	Va Tech	1996

Wake Forest University Winston-SalemNC 27109 (336) 758-5334 wfu.edu
Department of Economics 7505 Reynolda Station Fax=758-4809 Cheryl Denmark

Name	Rank	Phone	Email	Degree	Yr	School	Since
Cottrell, Allin F.	C-Pr	758-5762	cottrell	PHD	81	Edinburgh	1989
Brown, David G.	Prof	758-4878		PHD	61	Princeton	1990
email david_brown@mail.mba.wfu.edu							
Frey, Donald E.	Prof	758-5618	frey	PHD	72	Princeton	1972
Hammond, Claire Holton	Prof	758-5292	hammonc	PHD	82	Virginia	1978
Hammond, J. Daniel	Prof	758-5335	hammond	PHD	79	Virginia	1978

Lawlor, Michael S.	Prof	758-5174	lawlor		PHD	86	Iowa St	1986
Moorhouse, John C.	Prof	758-5130	moorhous		PHD	69	Nrthwstrn	1969
Archie Carroll Professor of Ethical Leadership								
Patterson, Perry L.	Prof	758-5528	patterso		PHD	86	Nrthwstrn	1986
Wood, John H.	Prof	758-5250	jw		PHD	64	Purdue	1985
Reynolds Professor of Economics								
Boko, Sylvain	Asst	758-4461	bokosh		PHD	96	Iowa St	1997
Heckelman, Jac C.	Asst	758-5293	heckeljc		PHD		Maryland	1996
Whaples, Robert M.	Asst	758-4916	whaples		PHD	90	Penn	1991

Walla Walla College	College Place,WA	99324-3000	(509) 527-2951					wwc.edu
Economics Faculty	Department of Business	Fax=527-2962					Ms. Cheri Windemuth	
Anderson, Norman	C-Pr	527-2951	andeno		JD		So Meth	1987
Thompson, Dana	Prof	527-2645	thomda		EDD	89	LLU	1998

Wartburg College	Waverly, IA	50677-0903	(319) 352-8415					wartburg.edu
Economics Faculty	Dept of Bus Adm & Econ	Fax=352-8581					Ann Killion	
Magnall, Paul	C-Ac	352-8428	magnall	Atg	MBA	82	N Iowa	1983
Craft, Rolf	Prof	352-8452	craft		PHD	68	Iowa St	1996
Shipman, William A.	Prof	352-8315	shipman		PHD	77	Pittsburgh	1972
Campbell, Gloria L.	Assoc	352-8229	campbell		MBA	84	N Iowa	1979
Folkers, Kim	Assoc	352-8424	folkers		MIM	89	St Thomas	1989
Legler, James	Assoc	352-8416	legler		PHD	96	Maryhurst	1997
Yee, Janice G.	Assoc	352-8485	yee		PHD	90	Clark	1991

Washburn Univ of Topeka	Topeka, KS	66621	(785) Ext 1308					acc.wuacc.edu
Department of Economics	School of Business	Fax=231-1063					Phyllis Sanderson	
Did Not Respond--1997-98 Listing; phone: 231-1010 Ext 1309								
Mazachek, JuliAnn	Dean	Ext 1309	zzmaza	Atg	PHD	93	Kansas	8-92
Gustavson, Robert L.	Prof	231-1010	zzgust		PHD	76	Colorado	1976
Olson, Richard	Prof	231-1010	zzolso		PHD	65	Nebraska	1980
Kerchner, Robert B.	Assoc	231-1010	zzkerc		PHD	73	Missouri	1976
Smith, Russell E.	Assoc	231-1010	zzsmith		PHD	84	Illinois	1984
Woolf, Linda L.	Assoc	231-1010	zzwool		PHD	70	Kansas St	1969
Dickes, Allen L.	Inst				MA	70	Toledo	1978
Director, Institutional Research								

University of Washington	Seattle, WA	98195	(206) 543-4773					u.washington.edu
Dept of Finance & Bus Econ	Sch of Business Adm	Fax=685-9392					Debra Nastaj, Adm Asst	
Bradford, William D.	Dean	543-4752			PHD	72	Ohio St	1994
Schall, Lawrence D.	C-Pr	543-7689	lschall		PHD	69	Chicago	1967
Alberts, William W.	Emor	543-6579			PHD	61	Chicago	1987
Ferson, Wayne	Prof	543-1843			PHD	82	Stanford	1992
Frost, Peter S.	Prof	543-0992	pfrost		PHD	66	UCLA	1969
Haley, Charles	Prof	543-7697	chiph		PHD	68	Stanford	1966
Hess, Alan C.	Prof	543-4579	hess		PHD	69	Car Mellon	1967
Higgins, Robert C.	Prof	543-4379	rhiggins		PHD	69	Stanford	1967
Kamara, Avraham	Prof	543-0652	kamara		PHD	86	Columbia	1984
Karpoff, Jonathan M.	Prof	685-4954	karpoff		PHD	82	UCLA	1983
Malatesta, Paul H.	Prof	685-1987	phmalat		PHD	81	Rochester	1980
Roley, V. Vance	Prof	543-7476	vroley		PHD	77	Harvard	1983
Siegel, Andrew F.	Prof	543-4476	asiegel		PHD	83	MIT	1990
Dewenter, Kathryn L.	Assoc	685-7893	dowe		PHD	93	Chicago	1992
Koski, Jennifer L.	Assoc	543-7975	jkoski		PHD	91	Stanford	1991
Pontiff, Jeffrey	Assoc	543-3021	pontiff		PHD	94	Rochester	1992
Rice, Edward M.	Assoc	543-4480	erice		PHD	78	UCLA	1979
Novaes, Walter	Asst	543-4435	novaes		PHD	93	MIT	1993
Glassman, Debra	SLect	543-8738	dg2854		PHD	80	Wisconsin	1992
Hadjimichalakis, Karma	SLect	685-8044	karmah		PHD	74	Rochester	1970
Tarhouni, Ali	SLect	543-4577	tarhouni		PHD	84	Mich St	1985

University of Washington	Seattle, WA	98195	(206) 543-5955					u.washington.edu
Dept of Economics Box 353330	Col of Arts & Sciences	Fax=685-7477					Karen Russell	
Startz, Richard	C-Pr	543-5955	startz		PHD	78	MIT	1984
Barzel, Yoram	Prof	543-2510	yoramb		PHD	61	Chicago	1961
Brown, Gardner	Prof	543-5744	gbrown	QDH	PHD	64	Berkeley	1965
Bruce, Neil	Prof	543-5874	brucen		PHD	75	Chicago	1990
Deolalikar, Anil B.	Prof	543-6145	anil		PHD	81	Stanford	1989
Engel, Charles M.	Prof	543-6107	cmengel		PHD	83	Berkeley	1991
Halvorsen, Robert F.	Prof	543-5546	halvor		PHD	73	Harvard	1972
Hartman, Richard C.	Prof	685-1630	rhartman		PHD	71	Berkeley	1971
Lundberg, Shelly J.	Prof	543-6149	lundberg		PHD	81	Nrthwstrn	1984
Nelson, Charles R.	Prof	685-1382	cnelson	EGC	PHD	69	Wisconsin	1975
Parks, Richard	Prof	543-4493	rwparks		PHD	66	Berkeley	1970
Siberberg, Eugene	Prof	543-8664	silber		PHD	64	Purdue	1967

Thornton, Judith Ann	Prof	543-5784	thornj		PHD	60	Harvard	1961
Turnovsky, Stephen J.	Prof	685-8028	sturn		PHD	68	Harvard	1987
Wong, Kar-yiu	Prof	543-1859	karyiu		PHD	83	Columbia	1983
Brock, Philip L.	Assoc	543-5796	plbrock		PHD	82	Stanford	1991
Hadjimichalakis, Michael	Assoc	543-5835	mhadjimi		PHD	69	Rochester	1969
Khalil, Fahad A.	Assoc	543-5836	khalil		PHD	91	Va Tech	1991
Kochin, Levis A.	Assoc	543-5845	lakochin		PHD	75	Chicago	1972
Lawarree, Jacques P.	Assoc	543-5632	lawarree		PHD	90	Berkeley	1990
Leffler, Keith B.	Assoc	543-5795			PHD	77	UCLA	1978
Thomas, Robert P.	Assoc	543-5842	rthomas		PHD	64	Nrthwstrn	1968
Eicher, Theo S.	Asst	685-8082	te		PHD	94	Columbia	1994
Ellis, Gregory M.	Asst	543-4582	ellis		PHD	92	Berkeley	1988
Rose, Elaina	Asst	543-5237	erose		PHD	93	Penn	1993
Zivot, Eric W.	Asst	543-6715	ezivot		PHD	92	Yale	1993
Heyne, Paul T.	SLect	543-0281	pheyne		PHD	63	Chicago	1976
Salehi-Esfahani, Haideh	SLect	543-7463	haideh		PHD	85	Penn	1990
Turnovsky, Michelle H. L.	SLect	543-1967	mturn		PHD	78	Austr Natl	1987

Washington University St. Louis, MO 63130-4899 (314) 935-5670 wuecon.wustl.edu
Department of Economics Col of Arts & Sciences Fax=935-4156 Karen Rensing

Macias, Edward	Dean	935-6820	macias@hilltop		PHD	70	MIT	1970
Fazzari, Steven M.	C-Pr	935-5693	fazz	E	PHD	82	Stanford	1982
Barnett, William A.	Prof	935-4236	barnett	E	PHD	74	Car Mellon	1990
Benham, Lee K.	Prof	935-4535	benham	LP	PHD	70	Stanford	1974
Berliant, Marcus C.	Prof	935-8486	berliant	DHR	PHD	82	Berkeley	1994
Felix, David	Emer	935-5639	felix	O	PHD	55	Berkeley	1964
Greenberg, Edward	Prof	935-5641	edg	DE	PHD	61	Wisconsin	1963
Leven, Charles L.	Emer	935-5836	leven	IR	PHD	58	Nrthwstrn	1964
Meyer, Laurence H.	Prof	935-5648		E	PHD	70	MIT	1969
on leave 1999-2000								
Neuefeind, Wilhelm	Prof	935-5632	wilhelmneuefeind	D	PHD	72	Bonn	1978
on leave 1999-2000								
North, Douglass C.	Prof	935-5809	north	NO	PHD	52	Berkeley	1983
Spencer T. Olin Professor of Arts & Sciences/1993 Nobel Prize in Economics								
Petersen, Bruce C.	Prof	935-5643	petersen	L	PHD	81	Harvard	1991
Pollak, Robert A.	Prof	935-4918	pollak	DJT	PHD	64	MIT	1995
Hernreich Distinguished Professor of Economics								
Schofield, Norman J.	Prof	935-4774	schofld	DH	PHD	76	Essex	1986
William Taussig Professor of Political Economy								
Weidenbaum, Murray L.	Prof	935-5662	moseley@csab	HM	PHD	58	Princeton	1961
Edward Mallinckrodt Distinguished University Professor								
Winter, Eyal	Prof		winter	CD	PHD	88	Hebrew	1995
on leave 1999-2000								
Nachbar, John	Assoc	935-5612	nachbar	CD	PHD	88	Harvard	1990
Nye, John V. C.	Assoc	935-6736	nye	N	PHD	85	Nrthwstrn	1985
Parks, Robert P.	Assoc	935-5665	bparks	H	PHD	71	Purdue	1971
Raines, Fredric Q.	Assoc	935-5636	raines	J	PHD	67	Wisconsin	1964
Rothstein, Paul	Assoc	935-4352	rstein	H	PHD	88	Berkeley	1988
Antinolfi, Gaetano	Asst	935-7335	gaetano	E	PHD	97	Cornell	1997
Ginther, Donna	Asst	935-6607	dginther	J	PHD	95	Wisconsin	1997
on leave 1999-2000								
Kim, Sukkoo	Asst	935-4961	soks	NR	PHD	93	UCLA	1993
Morley, James	Asst		mmorley	E	PHD	99	U Wash	1999

Washington & Jefferson Col Washington, PA 15301-4801 (412) washjeff.edu
Economics Faculty Dept of Economics & Bus Fax=223-5271

Gregor, John J.	C-Pr	223-6150	jgregor	PHD	76	Penn St	1989
Robison, K. Wayne	Prof	223-6253	wrobison	MBA	79	Ohio St	1979
West, James S.	Prof	223-6154	jwest	PHD	97	Nebraska	1997
Moschetta, Judith K.	Assoc	223-6152	jmoschetta	MS	78	W Virginia	1978
Stifflemire, Paul F. Jr.	Assoc	229-5125	pstifflemire	MBA	86	Suffolk	1986
Swint, Kenneth J.	Assoc	223-6156	kswint	PHD	89	Pittsburgh	1988
Lyon, William R.	Asst	223-6516	wlyon	MBA	89	Morehead	1988
Stark, Eric	Asst	229-5127	estark				1998
Tidas, Sam	Asst	223-6157	stidas				1998

Washington and Lee Univ Lexington, VA 24450-0303 (540) 463-8604 fs.commerce.wlu.edu
Department of Economics Sch Comm, Econ & Pol Fax=463-8639 Carol Ruley

Peppers, Larry C.	Dean	463-8602	peppers.l.c		PHD	70	Vanderbilt	1986
Goldsmith, Arthur H.	C-Pr	463-8970	goldsmith.a.h	E	PHD	79	Illinois	1990
Jackson T. Stephens Professor of Economics								
Cline, Philip L.	Prof	463-8622	cline.p.l	C	PHD	75	Okla St	1975
Lewis Whitabker Adams Professor of Economics								
Gunn, John McKenzie	Emer	463-8616	gunn.j.m	E	MA	54	Princeton	1957
Lewis Whitaker Adams Professor of Economics Emeritus								
Herrick, Bruce H.	Prof	463-8615	herrick.b.h	OP	PHD	64	MIT	1980
John F. Hendon Professor of Economics								

Name	Rank	Phone	Email	Fields	Degree	Yr	School	Since
Kaiser, Carl P.	Prof	463-8617	kaiser.c.p	JC	PHD	80	Wash U	1979
Lowry, Stanley T.	Emer	463-8614	lowry.s.t	BK	PHD	58	LSU	1959
Phillips, Charles F. Jr.	Prof	463-8618	phillips.c.f	L	PHD	60	Harvard	1959
Robert C. Brown Professor of Economics								
Winfrey, John C.	Prof	463-8606	winfrey.j.c	DH	PHD	65	Duke	1965
Anderson, Michael A.	Assoc	463-8971	anderson.m.a	F	PHD	90	Wisconsin	1990
Smitka, Michael J.	Assoc	463-8625	smitka.m.j.	FL	PHD	89	Yale	1986
Capra, C. Monica	Asst	463-8604	capra.c.m	D	PHD	98	Virginia	1999
Holliday, A. J.	Asst	463-8628	holliday.a.j.	K	PHD	95	Virginia	1993
Hooks, Linda M.	Asst	463-8621	hooks.l.m	E	PHD	91	UCLA	1993

Washington State University Pullman, WA 99164-4741 (509) 335-6651 wsu.edu
Department of Economics Col of Business & Econ Fax=335-4362 Ms. Frankie Harvey
email @1=mail.wsu.edu @2=wsuvm1.csc.wsu.edu @3=vancouver.wsu.edu

Name	Rank	Phone	Email	Fields	Degree	Yr	School	Since
Johnson, Glenn L.	Dean	335-3596	glennl	Atg	PHD	65	Berkeley	1979
Leigh, Duane E.	C-Pr	335-4441	leighd		PHD	69	Mich St	1968
Berney, Robert E.	Prof	335-5141	bermey@1		PHD	63	Wisconsin	1966
Joerdling, Wayne H.	Prof	335-6468	joerd@1		PHD	79	Nrthwstrn	1979
Krautkraemer, Jeffrey A.	Prof	335-3420	krautkra@2		PHD	82	Stanford	1981
Lowinger, Thomas C.	Prof	335-4913			PHD	70	Mich St	1978
Schaefer, Donald F.	Prof	335-6737	dschaefe		PHD	67	N Carol	1982
Stromsdorfer, Ernst W.	Prof	335-4471	stroms		PHD	62	Wash U	1983
Associate Dean								
Batina, Raymond	Assoc	335-8057	juliab@1		PHD	85	Minnesota	1985
Clark, Carolyn	Assoc	335-6651	clrk		PHD	70	Berkeley	1973
Fort, Rodney D.	Assoc	335-6468	fort@1		PHD	85	Cal Tech	1984
Hallagan, William S.	Assoc	335-6651	hallagan		PHD	77	Ca-Davis	1984
Inaba, Frederick S.	Assoc	335-6651	inaba		PHD	74	Berkeley	1977
Nziramasanga, Mudziviri T.	Assoc	335-6651	nziramasangam		PHD	74	Stanford	1973
Roseman, Robert E.	Assoc	335-1193	yakama@1		PHD	82	Minnesota	1983
Chaudhuri, Ananish	Asst	372-7238			PHD	97	Rutgers	1998
Li, Tong	Asst	335-5314	tli@1		PHD	93	Ca-SnDgo	1997
Michelsen, Ari	Asst	576-9735	michelse@3		PHD	88	Colo St	1994
Perez, Stephen J.	Asst	335-1740	sjperez@1		PHD	94	Ca-Davis	1997

Wayne State College Wayne, NE 68787 (402) 375-7292 wscgate.wsc.edu
Department of Economics Div of Social Sciences Fax=375-7458 L. Teach

Name	Rank	Phone	Email	Fields	Degree	Yr	School	Since
Karlen, Jean	H-Pr	375-7292	jkarlen	Soci	PHD	81	Nebraska	1976
Dalal, Meenakshi N.	Prof	375-7509	dhalal	OE	PHD	84	Northeas	1985
Parker, Charles	Assoc	375-7036	cparker	AEK	PHD	94	Ohio St	8-95

Wayne State University Detroit, MI 48202 (313) 577-3345 econ.wayne.edu
Department of Economics Col of Liberal Arts Fax=577-0149 Cheri Miller/Delores Tennillo

Name	Rank	Phone	Email	Fields	Degree	Yr	School	Since
Rossana, Robert J.	C-Pr	577-3760	rossana		PHD	80	J Hopkins	1991
Braid, Ralph M.	Prof	577-2540	rbraid		PHD	79	MIT	1988
Goodman, Allen C.	Prof	577-3344	agoodman		PHD	76	Yale	1986
Lee, Li Way	Prof	577-2256			PHD	76	Columbia	1981
Levin, Jay H.	Prof	577-3345	jlevin		PHD	68	Michigan	1976
Jensen, Gail A.	Assoc	577-3345			PHD	86	Minnesota	1989
Spurr, Stephen J.	Assoc	577-3345	sspurr	JK	PHD	86	Chicago	1987
Bekdache, Basma	Asst	577-3231	bbekdac		PHD	94	Boston C	1994
Cotter, Kevin D.	Asst	577-3233	kcotter		PHD	84	Minnesota	1989
Hunsaker, Julie	Asst	577-0603	jhunsake		PHD	93	Purdue	1993
Mavros, Panagiotis	Asst	577-3355	pmavros		PHD	93	Cornell	1992

Weber State University Ogden, UT 84408-3807 (801) 626-6066 cobe.weber.edu
Department of Economics Col of Business & Econ Fax=626-7423 Elaine Thompson

Name	Rank	Phone	Email	Fields	Degree	Yr	School	Since
Vaughan, Michael B.	Dean	626-6084		AMK	PHD	80	Nebraska	1981
Nowell, Clifford	C-Pr	626-6488	cnowell	ADQ	PHD	88	Wyoming	1988
Alston, Richard M.	Prof	626-6061	ralston	ABNQ	PHD	70	Cornell	1969
Chi, Wan Fu	Prof	626-6792	wchi	AC	PHD	69	S Illinois	1969
Fuller, Dan A.	Prof	626-6794	dfuller	ADH	PHD	82	N Carol	1981
Mbaku, John M.	Prof	626-7442	jmbaku	AHOP	PHD	85	Georgia	1991
Caplan, Arthur	Asst		acaplan	AQ	PHD	96	Oregon	1996
Geide-Stevenson, Doris	Asst	626-7634	dgsteven	AF	PHD	95	SUNY-Buf	1996

Webster University St. Louis, MO 63119-3194 (314) 968-7021 webster2.websteruni.edu
Business Department Sch of Business & Mgt Fax=968-7077 Kris Andraseck

Name	Rank	Phone	Email	Fields	Degree	Yr	School	Since
Harpool, David	Dean	968-5950		K	PHD	95	St Louis	1991
Berry, Lucille	C-Pr	968-7022		Atg	PHD	87	St Louis	1984
Westerfield, Donald	Prof	968-7025		DIMC	PHD	84	St Louis	1985
Hinson, Steve Y.	Asst	968-7025		AFDH	PHD	93	Kentucky	1993

Wellesley College	Wellesley, MA	02481-8260 (781) 283-2154					wellesley.edu	
Economics Faculty	Department of Economics Fax=283-2177						Helen Graham	
Andrews, Marcellus	C-Ac	283-2179			PHD	86	Yale	1986
Case, Karl E.	Prof	283-2178			PHD	77	Harvard	1987
Goldman, Marshall I.	Prof	283-2161			PHD	61	Harvard	1958
Joyce, Joseph P.	Prof	283-2160			PHD	84	Boston U	1982
Lindauer, David	Prof	283-2159			PHD	79	Harvard	1981
Matthaei, Julie Ann	Prof	283-2181			PHD	78	Yale	1978
Morrison, Rodney J.	Prof	283-2182			PHD	65	Wisconsin	
Witte, Ann D.	Prof	283-2163		DHK	PHD	71	N Car St	1985
Kauffman, Kyle	Assoc	283-2153			PHD	93	Illinois	1993
Levine, Philip	Assoc	283-2493			PHD	91	Princeton	1990
Skeath, Susan E.	Assoc	283-2180			PHD	89	Princeton	1989
Velenchik, Ann D.	Assoc	283-2183			PHD	89	Stanford	1989
Blomberg, Brock	Asst	283-2382			PHD	94	J Hopkins	1995
Johnson, Dan	Asst	283-2236			PHD	98	Yale	1997
Taylor, Corri	Asst	283-2152			PHD	98	Wisconsin	1998

Wesleyan University	Middletown, CT	06459-0007 (860) 685-2340					eagle.wesleyan.edu	
Economics Faculty	Department of Economics Fax=685-2781						Gloria Cone	
Adelstein, Richard P.	C-Pr	685-2366	radelstein	K	PHD	75	Penn	1975
Barber, William J.	Emer	685-2362	wbarber	B	DPHI	57	Oxford	1957
Andrews Professor of Economics								
Bonin, John P.	Prof	685-2353	jbonin	P	PHD	73	Rochester	1970
Kilby, Peter	Prof	685-2365	pkilby	O	DPHI	67	Oxford	1965
Lebergott, Stanley	Emer	685-2364	slebergott	N	MA	39	Michigan	1962
University Professor								
Lovell, Michael C.	Prof	685-2355	mlovell	E	PHD	59	Harvard	1969
Chester D. Hubbard Professor of Economics & Social Science								
Miller, Richard A.	Prof	685-2354	ramiller	L	PHD	62	Yale	1960
Andrews Professor of Economics								
Moore, Basil J.	Prof	685-2363	bmoore	E	PHD	58	J Hopkins	1958
Whitin, Thomson M.	Emer	685-2347	twhitin	C	PHD	52	Princeton	1963
Hubbard Professor								
Yohe, Gary W.	Prof	685-3658	gyohe	D	PHD	75	Yale	1977
Grossman, Richard	Assoc	685-2356	rgrossman	N	PHD	88	Harvard	1990
Jacobsen, Joyce P.	Assoc	685-2357	jjacobson	J	PHD	91	Stanford	1993
Rayack, Wendy	Assoc	685-2358	wrayack	J	PHD	84	Wisconsin	1983
Skillman, Gilbert L.	Assoc	685-2359	gskillman	D	PHD	85	Michigan	1993
Hanson, Michael S.	Asst	685-2348	mhanson	E	PHD	99	Michigan	1999
Rosenblat, Tanya S.	Asst	685-2348	trosenblat	E	PHD	99	MIT	1999

University of West Alabama	Livingston, AL	35470 (205) 652-3471					uwamail.westal.edu	
Dept of Adm & Management	College of Business Fax=652-3576						Sieglinde Fleming	
Peper, Merle J.	Dean	652-3471	mjp		PHD	86	LSU	9-95
Carr, Linda A.	C-Pr	652-3476			EDD	68	Alabama	1965
Sheffield, Howell	Inst	652-3473			MBA		Alabama	1998

West Chester Univ of PA	West Chester, PA	19383-2214 (610) 436-3460					wcupa.edu	
Dept of Economics & Finance	Sch of Bus & Public Aff Fax=436-3170						Pat Mareci	
Fiorentino, Christopher M.	Dean	436-2930	cfiorentino	DQ	PHD	89	Temple	9-85
Benzing, Cynthia D.	C-Pr	436-2217	cbenzing	AEG	PHD	87	Drexel	1988
Naggar, Tahany	Prof	436-2834	tnaggar	ADTN	PHD	76	Oklahoma	1977
Sylvester, Patrick J.	Prof	436-2964	psylvester	AE	PHD	73	Bryn Mawr	1968
Bove, Roger E.	Assoc	436-2134	rbove	FP	PHD	73	Harvard	1984
DeMoss, Philip M.	Assoc	436-2964	pdemoss	AGM	PHD	69	Kansas St	1973
Mohan, Daniel	Assoc	436-3468	dmohan	GM	PHD	75	Rutgers	1980
Andrews, Thomas	Asst	436-1082	tandrews	DHQL	PHD	96	Temple	1997
Dunleavy, Kevin C.	Asst	436-3422	kdunleavy	ACE	PHD	79	Duke	1979
Tolin, Thomas	Asst	436-1082	ttolin	JD	PHD	92	Houston	1992

University of West Florida	Pensacola, FL	32514-5752 (850) 474-2652					uwf.edu	
Dept of Mktg & Economics	College of Business Fax=474-3069						Marianne Baker	
Carper, William B.	Dean	474-2349			PHD	79	Va Tech	1995
Sjolander, Richard J.	C-Pr	474-2663		Mktg	PHD	84	Mich St	1985
Ashraf, Javed	Prof	474-2664		AJ	PHD	86	N Illinois	1990
Huth, William L.	Prof	474-2652		AMG	PHD	80	Arkansas	1989
Arguea, Nestor M.	Assoc	474-3071		ACD	PHD	90	S Calif	1990
Harper, Richard K.	Assoc	474-3072		AFM	PHD	89	Duke	1989
Conroy, Stephen	Asst	474-3072		ACJ	PHD	98	S Calif	1999
Hawkins, Richard R.	Asst	474-2656		ACR	PHD	96	Geo St	1996

State Univ of West Georgia Carrollton, GA 30118-3020 (770) 836-6477 sbf.bus.westga.edu
Department of Economics College of Business Fax=836-6774 Ms. Elizabeth Key

Name	Rank	Phone	Email	Field	Degree	Yr	School	Since
Hovey, David H.	Dean	836-6467	dhovey	Mgt	PHD	78	LSU	8-84
Fryman, Richard F.	C-Pr	836-6477	rfryman	AH	PHD	67	Illinois	1986
Gustafson, Leland Verne	Prof	836-6477	lgustafs	AC	PHD	74	Fla St	
Guynn, Richard Dickson	Prof	836-6477	rguynn	JA	PHD	71	Alabama	
Scott, Carole Elizabeth	Prof	836-6477	cscott	NO	PHD	69	Geo St	
Boldt, David John	Assoc	836-6477	dboldt	AR	PHD	87	New Mex	1988
Dutt, Swarna D.	Assoc	836-6477	sdutt	F	PHD	93	Wayne St	1994
Schaniel, William C.	Assoc	836-6477	wschanie	BP	PHD	85	Tennessee	
Raper, Michael Dennis	Asst	836-6477	mraper	AR	PHD	88	Geo St	

West Liberty State College West Liberty, WV 26074-0295 (304) 336-8053
Dept of Financial Systems School of Business Adm Fax= Sharon Rinderer

Name	Rank	Phone	Email	Field	Degree	Yr	School	Since
McCollough, John P.	Dean	336-8155		Mgt	PHD	71	N Dakota	1971
Reuther, Carol J.	C-Ac	336-8156		CDGH	MS	73	Fla St	1991
Hatzopoulos, Sydma	Assoc	336-8153		CDEI	MA	80	Va Tech	1990
Mullin, Marian V.	Assoc	336-8054		DE	MS	85	Rbt Morr	1975

West Texas A&M University Canyon, TX 79016-0001 (806) 651-2525 mail.wtamu.edu
Dept of Atg, Econ & Finance Pickens Col of Business Fax=651-2514 Betsey Bavousett

Name	Rank	Phone	Email	Field	Degree	Yr	School	Since
Duman, Barry L.	H-Pr	651-2519	bduman	BDP	PHD	71	S Calif	1969
Miller, Jerry D.	Prof	651-2510	jmiller	Fnce	PHD	70	LSU	1993
Kelso, Patrick R.	Assoc	651-2522	pkelso	EHN	PHD	68	Tx-Austin	1967
Rosa, Duane J.	Assoc	651-2276	drosa	EOQ	PHD	89	Tx Tech	1984

West Virginia University Morgantown, WV 26506-6025 (304) 293-7859 wvube1.be.wvu.edu
Department of Economics Col of Business & Econ Fax=293-7061 Barbara Michniak
email: @1=wvu.edu

Name	Rank	Phone	Email	Field	Degree	Yr	School	Since
Dahringer, Lee D.	Dean	293-7800	ldahring	Mktg	DBA	78	Colorado	1999
Trumbull, William N.	C-Ac	293-7860	trumbull	HKD	PHD	85	N Carol	1983
Adams, Donald R. Jr.	Prof	293-7861	adams	N	PHD	67	Penn	1981
Hawley, Clifford B.	Prof	293-7865	hawley	JD	PHD	77	Duke	1978
Hwang, Ming-jeng	Prof	293-7866	hwang	DRC	PHD	73	Tx A&M	1974
Kymn, Kern O.	Prof	293-7867	kymn	EC	PHD	64	Chicago	1976
Labys, Walter C.	Prof	293-6253	wlabys@1	Q	PHD	68	Nottinghm	1975
Mann, Patrick C.	Prof	293-7872	mann	DH	PHD	67	Indiana	1967
Mitchell, Douglas W.	Prof	293-7868	mitchell	E	PHD	78	Princeton	1984
Reece, William S.	Prof	293-4092	reece	CH	PHD	75	Wash U	1990
Witt, Tom S.	Prof	293-7835	witt	CR	PHD	74	Wash U	1970
Balvers, Ronald J.	Assoc	293-7880	balvers	EG	PHD	84	Pittsburgh	1991
Cushing, Brian J.	Assoc	293-7881	cushing	RCH	PHD	81	Maryland	1981
Douglas, Stratford M.	Assoc	293-7863	douglas	CHD	PHD	87	N Carol	990
Fletcher, Jerald J.	Assoc	293-6253	jfletch@1	Q	PHD	82	Berkeley	1989
Phipps, Tim	Assoc	293-6353	tphipps@1	Q	PHD	82	Berkeley	1989
Bandyopadhyay, Subhayu	Asst	293-7879	bandysub	F	PHD	94	Maryland	1993
Bandyopadhyay, Sudeshna	Asst	293-7869	bandy	J	PHD	92	Maryland	1992
Chow, C. Victor	Asst	293-7888	chow	G	PHD	89	Alabama	1989
Sobel, Russell S.	Asst	293-7864	sobel	H	PHD	94	Fla St	1994
Vilasuso, Jon R.	Asst	293-7871		EFG	PHD	94	Conn	1999
Watts, Royce J.	Asst	293-5695		C	MS	61	W Virginia	1955

West Virginia State College Institute, WV 25112-1000 (304) 766-3065 ernie.wvsc.edu
Department of Economics Div of Bus Admin & Econ Fax=766-4127 Norma Bukovac

Name	Rank	Phone	Email	Field	Degree	Yr	School	Since
Islam, Mahmood	C-Ac	766-3057			PHD	85	Wayne St	1987
Carroll, Michael	Asst	766-3065			PHD	97	Colo St	1996
Ghosh, Sudip	Asst	766-3065			PHD	99	W Virginia	1997
Swanke, Thomas A.	Asst	766-3062		AEJO	PHD	93	Colorado	1993

Western Carolina University Cullowhee, NC 28723-9033 (828) 227-7074 wcuvax1.wcu.edu
Dept of Economics & Finance School of Business Fax=227-7414 Kathy Brashear

Name	Rank	Phone	Email	Field	Degree	Yr	School	Since
Shiffler, Ronald E.	Dean	227-7074	rshiffler	Mgt	PHD	80	Florida	7-96
Wade, John	C-Ac	227-7074	jwade		PHD	82	Purdue	1977
Jarrell, Stephen B.	Prof	227-7074	jarrell		PHD	78	Purdue	1988
Jones, Royal Maurice	Prof	227-7074			PHD	67	Maryland	1971
Spencer, Austin Harvey	Prof	227-7074	aspence		PHD	72	Indiana	1980
Allen, Grace	Assoc	227-7074	alleng		PHD	91	S Carol	1992
Hays, Patrick Allen	Assoc	227-7074	hays		PHD	77	N Carol	1985
Kask, Susan B.	Assoc	227-7074	kask		PHD	88	Wyoming	1993
Schreiber, Max M.	Assoc	227-7074	schreibr		PHD	78	S Carol	1977
Mulligan, Richard	Asst	227-7074	mulligan		PHD	93	SUNY-Bin	1997
Murphy, James H.	Asst	227-7074	jmurphy		MA	96	Geo St	1998

Western Conn State Univ Danbury, CT 06810 (203) 837-8484 wcsub.ctstateu.edu
Economics Faculty Sch of Arts & Sciences Fax=837-8525 A. Strucky
email address: wcsu.edu

Name	Rank	Phone	Email	Fields	Degree	Yr	School	Hired
Hawkes, Carol A.	Dean		hawkes	Lang	PHD	53	Columbia	
Bannister, Jerry	C-Pr	837-8454	bannisterj	Soci	MA		Syracuse	
Owoye, Oluwole	Prof	837-8456	owoye	EFHJ	PHD	89	N Illinois	
Skinner, Steven P.	Prof	837-8457	skinner	BJQR	PHD	80	Conn	
Pan, Zuohong	Asst		panz	CJLO	PHD	95	Mich St	

Western Illinois University Macomb, IL 61455-1390 (309) 298-1153 wiu.edu
Department of Economics Col of Business & Tech Fax=298-1020 Mary Sherwood, Esther Grimes

Name	Rank	Phone	Email	Fields	Degree	Yr	School	Hired
Walzer, Norman C.	D-Pr	298-1031	n-walzer	AHR	PHD	70	Illinois	1970
Director, Illinois Institute for Rural Affairs								
Jones, Warren	C-Ac	298-1477	w-jones	AEHN	PHD	82	Iowa	1983
Andrianacos, Dimitri	Prof	298-2331	d-andrianacos	ACE	PHD	89	Chicago	1990
Hattwick, Richard E.	Prof	298-1594	r-hattwick	AM	PHD	65	Vanderbilt	1969
Director Center for Business & Economic Research								
Pledge, Michael T.	Prof	298-1637	m-pledge	AEG	PHD	68	Houston	1968
Rao, Vaman	Prof	298-1321	v-rao	ACEO	PHD	73	Missouri	1979
Rock, Steven M.	Prof	298-1343	s-rock	AJ	PHD	75	Nrthwstrn	1990
Straub, LaVonne	Prof	298-1413	l-straub	AIJR	PHD	83	Utah	1982
Yunker, James A.	Prof	298-1639	j-yunker	ACDP	PHD	71	Nrthwstrn	1968
Fosu, Joseph	Assoc	298-2265	j-fosu	AEO	PHD	87	Iowa St	1987
Kleiner, William C.	Asst	298-1032	w-kleiner	AEF	PHD	74	Mich St	1971
Nussman, Tara D.	Asst	298-1313	tpnussman	ADH	PHD	98	S Carol	1998

Western Kentucky University Bowling Green KY 42101-3576 (502) 745-2249 wku.edu
Dept of Economics & Mktg College of Business Adm Fax=745-3190 Karen Braun

Name	Rank	Phone	Email	Fields	Degree	Yr	School	Hired
Jefferson, Robert M.	Dean	745-6311	robert.jeff+	Mktg	PHD	69	Iowa	1996
Wassom, John C.	H-Pr	745-2249		G	PHD	70	Indiana	1971
Borland, Melvin V.	Prof	745-3112		BDA	PHD	72	Wash U	1978
Goff, Brian L.	Prof	745-3855		GHK	PHD	86	GeoMason	1986
Kim, Hak Youn	Prof	745-3187		CDO	PHD	82	Cincinnati	1983
Lile, Stephen E.	Prof	745-3115		H	PHD	72	Kentucky	1973
Pulsinelli, Robert W.	Prof	745-3118		DK	PHD	74	Rutgers	1967
Wisley, Thomas O.	Prof	745-3127		GHK	PHD	79	Purdue	1985
Brown, J. Michael	Assoc	745-3893		G	PHD	71	Kentucky	1988
Cantrell, Richard P.	Assoc	745-3146		C	MA	63	S Illinois	1967
Davis, William W.	Assoc	745-3123		F	PHD	65	Kentucky	1970
Howsen, Roy M.	Assoc	745-3172		D	PHD	80	Arkansas	1981
Myers, Daniel A.	Assoc	745-3684		R	PHD	86	Vanderbilt	1986
Noser, Thomas C.	Assoc	745-3642		CA	PHD	86	Alabama	1984
Roberts, Charles A.	Assoc	745-3105		BN	PHD	79	Georgia	1969
Carey, Cathrine	Asst	745-6401		F	PHD	92	Kentucky	1992

Western Maryland College Westminster, MD 21157-4390 (410) 857-2450 wmdc.edu
Economics Faculty Dept of Econ & Bus Adm Fax=857-2729 Pat Holford

Name	Rank	Phone	Email	Fields	Degree	Yr	School	Hired
Law, Alton D.	C-Pr	848-7000	ns1		PHD	68	Rutgers	1966
Claycombe, Richard J.	Prof	848-7000	rclaycom		PHD	80	Geo Wash	1981
Milstein, Susan Matz	Prof	848-7000	smilstei		MBA		MtStMary	1983
Olsh, John Lindsay	Prof	848-7000			PHD	74	Ca-Davis	1980
Seidel, Ethan A.	Prof	848-7000	eseidel		PHD	77	J Hopkins	1969
Singer, Diana Sue	Prof	848-7000	ssinger		MBA		Loyola	1983

Western Michigan University Kalamazoo, MI 49008-5023 (616) 387-5535 wmich.edu
Department of Economics Col of Arts & Sciences Fax=387-3999 Mrs. Becky Ryder

Name	Rank	Phone	Email	Fields	Degree	Yr	School	Hired
Sichel, Werner	C-Pr	387-5539	werner.sichel	D	PHD	64	Nrthwstrn	1960
Asefa, Sisay	Prof	387-5540	sisay.asefa	O	PHD	80	Iowa St	1980
Hoffman, Emily P.	Prof	387-5546	emily.hoffman	J	PHD	75	Mass	1981
Huang, Wei-Chiao	Prof	387-5547	wei-chiao.huang	J	PHD	84	Ca-SnBarb	1985
Pozo, Susan	Prof	387-5553	susan.pozo	F	PHD	80	Mich St	1982
Thistle, Paul D.	Prof	387-5528	paul.thistle	D	PHD	83	Tx A&M	1992
Alexander, Donald L.	Assoc	387-5526	donald.alexander	D	PHD	83	Penn St	9900
Alvi, Eskander	Assoc	387-5547	eskander.alvi	E	PHD	85	J Hopkins	1994
Caruso, Phillip P.	Assoc	387-5541	phillip.caruso	E	PHD	77	Mich St	1967
Harik, Bassam	Assoc	387-5554	bassam.harik	E	PHD	78	Wayne St	1979
Harik, Salim	Assoc	387-5544	salim.harik	F	PHD	75	Wayne St	1976
Higgins, Matthew L.	Assoc	387-5543	matthew.higgins	C	PHD	89	Illinois	1995
Kern, William	Assoc	387-5549	william.kern	B	PHD	82	Colo St	1987
Meyer, Donald J.	Assoc	387-5531	donald.meyer	D	PHD	83	Tx A&M	1991
Neill, Jon R.	Assoc	387-5551	jon.neill	H	PHD	83	Pittsburgh	1980
Wheeler, Mark V.	Assoc	387-5563	mark.wheeler	E	PHD	85	Kentucky	1990
Zhou, Huizhong	Assoc	387-5550	huizhong.zhou	C	PHD	86	Nrthwstrn	1990
Brown, Annette N.	Asst	387-5557	a.n.brown	P	PHD	96	Michigan	1996
Masin, Shohreh	Asst	387-5542	shohreh.masin	E	PHD	94	Wi-Milwa	1998

Western New England Coll	Springfield, MA	01119-2684 (413) 782-1252						wnec.edu
Department of Economics	Sch of Arts & Sciences	Fax=782-1746				Donna Utter 782-1480		
Meeropol, Michael A.	C-Pr	782-1252			PHD	73	Wisconsin	1970
Porter, Burton F.	Dean	782-1218		Phil	PHD		StAndrews	
Andrulis, John A.	Prof	782-1601			PHD	75	Purdue	1981
Skillman, Richard K.	Assoc	782-1602			MALD		Tufts	1970
Casimir, Schiller	Asst	782-1741	scasimir		PHD	97	SUNY-Bin	1997
Eskot, Herbert J.	Asst	782-1743	heskot		PHD	84	Tufts	1984
Robinson, Judith	Inst	782-1776	jrobinson		MA	86	Mass	1998

Western Oregon University	Monmouth, OR	97361 (503) 838-8421						wou.edu
Division of Business & Econ	Sch Liberal Arts & Sci	Fax=838-8723					Dianna Hewell	
Bahari-Kashani, Hamid	C-Pr	838-8354	baharih		PHD	83	Wash St	1988
Minahan, John P.	Dean				PHD	69	Geotown	1986
Leadley, John C.	Assoc	838-8719	leadlej		PHD	85	Wisconsin	1991
Zygmont, Zenon X.	Asst	838-8244	zygmouz	APLF	PHD	94	GeoMason	1998

Western State College of CO	Gunnison, CO	81231 (970) 943-7011						western.edu
Economics Faculty	Dept of Business & Atg	Fax=943-3380						
Axelson, David J.	C-Ac	943-3081			EDD	76	Colorado	1982
Plante, David	Asst	943-2207			ABD		Utah	1997

Western Washington Univ	Bellingham, WA	98225-9074 (360) 650-3910						wwu.edu
Department of Economics	Col of Business & Econ	Fax=650-4844					Theresa Gresley	
Homepage: http://www.wwu.edu/~econ/econ.html								
Murphy, Dennis R.	Dean	650-3896	dmurphy@cms.	FM	PHD	74	Indiana	1979
Nelson, David M.	C-Pr	650-4804	david.nelson	EGI	PHD	75	Oregon	1977
Ghali, Moheb A.	Prof	650-2284	ghali@cc.	CDEF	PHD	67	U Wash	1993
Dean of Graduate School								
Globerman, Steven	Prof	650-7708	steven.globerman	DFIL	PHD	71	NYU	1994
Harder, K. Peter	Prof	650-3920	peter.harder	BNP	PHD	68	Nebraska	1970
Merrifield, David E.	Prof	650-3909	david.merrified	M	PHD	82	Claremont	1983
Hagen, Daniel A.	Assoc	650-3964	dan.hagen	JEFQ	PHD	83	Berkeley	1988
Hansen, Julia L.	Assoc	650-3204	julie.hansen	DR	PHD	84	Berkeley	1988
Henson, Steven E.	Assoc	650-4843	steve.henson	QD	PHD	82	Oregon	1985
Sleeman, Allan G.	Assoc	650-3910	allan.sleeman	CD	PHD	83	Simon Fr	1977
Roelofs, Matthew	Asst	650-3910	matthew.roelofs	DL	PHD	96	Purdue	1997
Storer, Paul	Asst	650-6531	paul.storer	EJ	PHD	92	W Ontario	1996
Hendryson, Mary Ann	Lect	650-4799	mary.ann.hend+	DOF	ABD		Wash St	1989
Whalley, Pamela	Lect	650-4823	pam.whally	DG	ABD		Indiana	1989

Westfield State College	Westfield, MA	01086 (413) 572-5590						foma.wsc.mass.edu
Economics Faculty	Dept of Econ & Bus Mgt	Fax=562-3613				Danielle S. Bramucci		
Knipes, Bradford	C-As	572-5574		Mgt	PHD	88	Mass	1988
Bellico, Russell P.	Prof	572-5312			EDD		Mass	1970
Darrow, John J.	Prof	572-5715			PHD	72	Conn	1971
Gural, Michael L.	Assoc	572-5591			MA		Rutgers	1982
Wagner, John R.	Assoc	572-5697			PHD	77	Temple	1986

Westminster College-PA	NewWilmingtonPA	16172-0001 (412) 946-7160						westminster.edu
Economics Faculty	Dept of Business & Econ	Fax=946-7171				Mrs Kathleen A. Proctor		
Miller, Gail L.	C-Pr	946-7160		Bus	DBA		Kentucky	1983
Fischman, Daniel E.	Prof	946-7162			PHD	75	S Illinois	1975
Groothuis, Peter A.	Assoc	946-7163			PHD	89	Kentucky	1989

Westminster Cl of Salt Lk Ct	Salt Lk City, UT	84105-3697 (801) 488-4220						wcslc.edu
Economics Program	Gore School of Business	Fax=466-6916						
Seidelman, James E.	Dean	488-4222	c.seidel		PHD	86	Utah	1980
Watkins, John P.	C-Pr	488-4221	j-watkin	BNQ	PHD	85	Utah	1984
Chapman, Richard	Prof	488-4228	d-chapma	JNB	PHD	92	Utah	1985
Hansen, Ann	Prof	488-4146	a-hansen	CHL	PHD	81	Utah	1990
Wrotniak, Maria	Assoc	488-4155	m-wrotni	BCO	PHD	80	Lodz	1989

Wheaton College-IL	Wheaton, IL	60187-5593 (630) 752-5035						wheaton.edu
Economics Faculty	Dept of Business & Econ	Fax=752-7037					Mrs. Pat Unander	
Howard, Bruce	C-Ac	752-5313	bruce.howard	ABM	PHD	89	N Illinois	1980
Halteman, James	Prof	752-5312	james.haltman	AB	PHD	74	Penn St	1979
Hendrickson Chair								
Hill, Peter J.	Prof	752-5033	p.j.hill	ANPQ	PHD	70	Chicago	1986
George F. Bennett Professor of Economics								
Norton, Seth	Prof	752-5310	seth.norton	GJLM	PHD	82	Chicago	1995
Aldeen Chair								
Ewert, Norman J.	Assoc	752-5311	norman.j.ewert	AF	PHD	76	S Illinois	1973
Tomal, Annette	Asst	752-7058	annette.tomal	AIM	PHD	95	Illinois	1995

Wheaton College-MA Norton, MA 02766 (508) 285-8200 wheatonma.edu
Economics Faculty Department of Economics Fax=
phone 285-8200

Name	Rank	Phone	Email	Fields	Degree	Yr	School	Year
Miller, John A.	C-Pr	Ext 3667	jmiller		PHD	82	Pittsburgh	1979
Gildea, John A.	Prof	Ext 3663	jgildea	EG	PHD	85	Duke	1985
Walgreen, John A.	Prof	Ext 3668	jwalgree		PHD	65	Boston C	1967
Weil, Gordon	Prof	Ext 3666	gweil	FOP	PHD	81	Tufts	1981
Wyss, Brenda	Asst	Ext 3665	bwyss	JTO	PHD	95	Mass	1992

Whitman College Walla Walla, WA 99362 (509) 527-5125 whitman.edu
Economics Faculty Social Sciences Div Fax=527-5026

Name	Rank	Phone	Email	Fields	Degree	Yr	School	Year
Hazlett, Denise J.	C-Ac	527-5155	hazlett	EG	PHD	92	Minnesota	1992
Shepherd, James F.	Prof	527-5149	shepherd	HN	PHD	66	U Wash	1971
Crouter, Jan P.	Assoc	527-5174	crouter	KLQ	PHD	85	Illinois	1985
Parcells, R. J. "Pete"	Assoc	527-5267	parcells	CR	PHD	83	SUNY-Bin	1982
Belay, Halefom	Asst	522-6431	belayh	CEO	PHD	96	SUNY-Bin	1996
Tsournos, Pete	Asst	527-5889		LQ	PHD	99	Wyoming	1998

Whitworth College Spokane, WA 99251 (509) 466-3283 whitworth.edu
Economics Faculty Dept of Economics & Bus Fax=466-3720 Patricia Parker

Name	Rank	Phone	Email	Fields	Degree	Yr	School	Year
Schatz, Richard E.	C-Pr	466-3283	rschatz	DEFO	PHD	74	Hawaii	1989
Hergenrather, Richard A.	Asst	466-3283	rhergenrather	DE	PHD	93	P Drucker	1994

Wichita State University Wichita, KS 67260-0078 (316) 978-3220 twsuvm.uc.twsu.edu
Department of Economics Barton Sch of Business Fax=978-3845 Mrs. Julia Carter

Name	Rank	Phone	Email	Fields	Degree	Yr	School	Year
Graham, Gerald H.	Dean	978-3200		Mgt	PHD	68	LSU	1967
Cheng, Jen-Chi	C-Ac	978-3220	cheng		PHD	89	Vanderbilt	1989
Cho, Dong Woo	Prof	978-3220	dwcho		PHD	73	Illinois	1972
Haydon, Randall B.	Prof	978-3220			PHD	62	Illinois	1970
Hersch, Philip L.	Prof	978-3220	plhersch		PHD	82	Ohio St	1983
Perline, Martin M.	Prof	978-3220			PHD	65	Ohio St	1965
Webb, Samuel C.	Prof	978-3220			PHD	68	Kansas	1966
Clark, James E.	Assoc	978-3220	jeclark		PHD	77	Nrthwstrn	1976
Director Center for Economic Education								
Duell, Dennis	Assoc	978-3220	duell		PHD	69	Illinois	1967
Pfannestiel, Maurice	Assoc	978-3220	pfannest		PHD	67	Okla St	1966
Terrell, William T.	Assoc	978-3220			PHD	70	Vanderbilt	1967
Im, Kyung So	Asst	978-7094			PHD	95	Mich St	1998
Li, Qing	Asst	978-3220			PHD	95	Houston	1995
Miles, William	Asst	978-3220			PHD	98	Illinois	1999
Dimmen, Janet L.	Inst	978-3220			ABD	78	Ohio St	1981

Widener University Chester, PA 19013-5792 (610) 499-4306 widener.edu
Department of Economics School of Business Adm Fax=499-4614 Mrs. Marilyn Lehman

Name	Rank	Phone	Email	Fields	Degree	Yr	School	Year
DiAngelo, Joseph A. Jr.	Dean	499-4301		Mgt	EDD	87	Temple	1980
Saltzman, Cynthia J.	H-Ac	499-4326	cynthia.saltz+	EFGO	PHD	86	Maryland	1980
Duggal, Vijaya G.	Prof	499-1176		CEDQ	PHD	67	Harvard	1983
Fuhr, Joseph P.	Prof	499-1172		DIKQ	PHD	81	Temple	1979
Waldauer, Charles	Prof	499-4329		DEHR	PHD	69	Syracuse	1968
Williams, Mary L.	Prof	499-4324		BOMQ	PHD	84	Temple	1982
Zangeneh, Hamid	Prof	499-1140		EFGP	PHD	84	Missouri	1985
Leppel, Karen	Assoc	499-1170		JCT	PHD	80	Princeton	1985

Wilkes University Wilkes-Barre, PA 18766 (570) 408-4725 wilkes1.wilkes.edu
Dept of Business & Economics Sch Bus,Society &PubPol Fax=408-7874 Ms. Sandra L. Rybak
Did Not Respond--1997-98 Listing

Name	Rank	Phone	Email	Fields	Degree	Yr	School	Year
Bedford, Bonnie C.	Dean	408-4600	bedford	Engl	PHD		SUNY-Bin	8-90
Alves, Jeffrey	C-Ac	408-4725	alves	Fnce	PHD	87	Mass	9-97
Taylor, Wagiha A.	Prof	831-4712		EFO	PHD	66	Clark	1969
Seeley, Robert D.	Assoc	831-4717	rseeley	AIJH	PHD	86	Maryland	9-89
Latzko, David	Asst	831-4718	dlatzko	BEFQ	PHD	92	Maryland	9-93

Willamette University Salem, OR 97301-3922 (503) 370-6060 willamette.edu
Department of Economics College of Liberal Arts Fax=375-5398 Karen Bond

Name	Rank	Phone	Email	Fields	Degree	Yr	School	Year
Cress, Lawrence	Dean	370-6285		Hst	PHD	76	Virginia	
Whiting, Cathleen L.	C-Ac	370-6075			PHD	86	U Wash	1986
Beaton, C. Russell	Prof	370-6306			PHD	68	Claremont	1971
Hanson, James S.	Prof	370-6316			PHD	71	Stanford	1976
Hibbard, Thomas H.	Prof	370-6317			PHD	67	Claremont	1973
Frew, James R.	Assoc	370-6232			PHD	79	Purdue	1984
Gray, Jerry	Assoc	370-6307			PHD	89	Utah	1990
Negri, Donald H.	Assoc	370-6326			PHD	86	Michigan	1990

College of William & Mary Williamsburg, VA 23187-8795 (757) 221-4311 wm.edu
Department of Economics Faculty Arts & Sciences Fax=221-2390 Taylor Cousins

Name	Rank	Phone	Email	Field	Degree	Yr	School	Year
Moody, Carlisle E.	C-Pr	221-2373	cemood		PHD	70	Conn	1970
Archibald, Robert B.	Prof	221-2366	rbarch		PHD	74	Purdue	1976
Baker, Samuel H. III	Prof	221-2371	shbake		PHD	70	Virginia	1969
Campbell, Donald E.	Prof	221-2383	decamp		PHD	72	Princeton	1989
CSX Professor of Economics Public Policy								
Finifter, David H.	Prof	221-2370	dhfini		PHD	74	Pittsburgh	1973
Garrett, Martin A.	Prof	221-2375	mcgarr		PHD	66	Vanderbilt	1963
Haulman, Clyde A.	Prof	221-1276	ahaul		PHD	69	Fla St	1969
Hausman, William J.	Prof	221-2381	wjhaus		PHD	76	Illinois	1981
Pereira, Alfredo M.	Prof				PHD	88	Stanford	1995
Abegaz, Berhanu	Assoc	221-2379	bxabeg		PHD	82	Penn	1982
Feldman, David H.	Assoc	221-2372	dhfeld		PHD	82	Duke	1988
Jensen, Eric R.	Assoc	221-2365	erjens		PHD	82	Michigan	1982
Anderson, Lisa	Asst				PHD	94	Virginia	1997
Basu, Arnab	Asst	221-1318	akbasu		PHD	97	J Hopkins	1998
Mellor, Jennifer	Asst	221-2852	jkmell		PHD	96	Maryland	1998
Rodgers, William	Asst	221-2398	wmrodg		PHD	93	Harvard	1993
Rodgers, Yana	Asst	221-1276	yvrodg		PHD	93	Harvard	1993
Stafford, Sarah	Asst	221-1317			PHD	98	J Hopkins	1998
Weise, Charles	Asst	221-2432	clweis		PHD	93	Wisconsin	1993

William Jewell College Liberty, MO 64068-1896 (816) 781-7700 william.jewell.edu
Economics Faculty Dept of Bus Adm & Econ Fax=415-5027
phone 781-7700

Name	Rank	Phone	Email	Field	Degree	Yr	School	Year
Cook, Michael T.	C-Pr	Ext 5699		EF	PHD	83	Vanderbilt	1978
John W. Boatwright Professor of Economics								

Wm Patterson Univ of NJ Wayne, NJ 07470-2103 (973) 720-2434 frontier.wilpaterson.edu
Dept of Economics & Finance School of Business Fax=720-2809 Mrs. Angela Mazza

Name	Rank	Phone	Email	Field	Degree	Yr	School	Year
Grippo, Frank	Dean	720-2964			MBA		Fairl Dick	
Leung, Cho Kin	C-Pr	595-2434	720-2650		PHD	68	NYU	1974
Dorai, Gopal C.	Prof	720-2430			PHD	67	Wayne St	1974
Ghosh, Arabinda	Prof	720-2221			PHD	72	CUNY	1984
Haroian, Berch	Prof	720-2411			PHD	72	NYU	1978
Cai, Francis	Assoc	720-2178	caif	GCF	PHD	90	CUNY	1993
Ramin, Taghi	Assoc	720-2781			PHD	86	NYU	1984
Swanson, Paul	Assoc	720-2784			PHD	84	Columbia	1982

Williams College Williamstown, MA 01267 (413) 597-2476 williams.edu
Economics Faculty Department of Economics Fax=597-4045 Kathy Butterfield

Name	Rank	Phone	Email	Field	Degree	Yr	School	Year
Hill, Catharine Bond	C-Ac	597-3143			PHD	85	Yale	1985
Winston, Gordon C.	C-Pr	597-2254			PHD	64	Stanford	1963
Orrin Sage Professor of Political Economy								
Bolton, Roger E.	Prof	597-2393			PHD	64	Harvard	1966
William Brough Professor of Economics								
Bradburd, Ralph M.	Prof	597-2300			PHD	76	Columbia	1976
David A. Wells Professor of Political Economy								
Bruton, Henry J.	Emer	597-2357			PHD	52	Harvard	1962
Montiel, Peter J.	Prof	597-2103		EF	PHD	78	MIT	1995
Chair, Center for Development Economics								
Sabot, Richard	Prof	597-3082			DPHI	73	Oxford	
John J. Gibson Emeritus Professor of Economics								
Husbands, Kaye G.	Assoc	597-2469			PHD	90	Harvard	
Macunovich, Diane J.	Assoc	597-2471			PHD	89	S Calif	1989
Brainerd, Elizabeth	Asst	597-2300			PHD	96	Harvard	1996
Conning, Jonathan	Asst	597-2101			PHD	96	Yale	1996
Constantine, Jill M.	Asst	597-2995			PHD	94	Penn	
Frankl, Jennifer	Asst				PHD	96	Berkeley	1997
Gollin, Doug	Asst	597-2449			PHD	96	Minnesota	1996
Samson, Mike	Asst	597-2325			PHD	94	Stanford	
Schulz, Eric	Asst	597-2270			PHD	93	Nrthwstrn	
Siegler, Mark	Asst				PHD	96	Ca-Davis	1997
Zimmerman, David J.	Asst	597-3184			PHD	92	Princeton	1991

Wingate University Wingate, NC 28174-0157 (704) 233-8148 wingate.edu
Economics Program School Business & Econ Fax=233-8146 Ms. Kathryn Rowe

Name	Rank	Phone	Email	Field	Degree	Yr	School	Year
Palmer, Charles F.	Dean	233-8147	palmer	AH	PHD	76	Va Tech	1993
Schwartz, Lisa	Asst	233-8142	schwartz	EG	PHD	96	Tx-Arlin	1998

Winona State University — Winona, MN 55987-0838 (507) 457-5014 — vax2.winona.msus.edu
Dept of Economics & Finance — College of Business Fax=457-5697 — Jan Tollefson

Name	Rank	Phone	Email	Field	Degree	Yr	School	Year
Gorman, Kenneth L.	Dean	457-5014		BusE	EDD		N Illinois	1980
Manrique, Gabriel G.	C-Pr	457-5193	manrique		PHD	82	Notre Dm	1989
Gallegos, Alejandro	Prof	457-5469	agallegos		PHD	86	Wi-Milwa	1988
Gieske, Michael	Prof	457-5171	wngieske		BS		Iowa St	1972
Hyle, Matthew R.	Prof	457-5496	mhyle		PHD	85	Maryland	1988
Kauffman, Daniel E.	Prof	457-5195	kdauffman		PHD	80	Nebraska	1983
Rieder, Mary	Prof				PHD	72		
Salyards, Donald M.	Prof	457-5622	wenonak		PHD	75	Kansas St	1975
Pevas, Mary Ann	Assoc	457-5014	mapevas		PHD	90	Notre Dm	1990

Winston-Salem State Univ — Winston-SalemNC 27110 (336) 750-2342 — wssu.edu
Economics Faculty — Div of Business & Econ Fax=750-2335 — Sandra L. McCracken

Name	Rank	Phone	Email	Field	Degree	Yr	School	Year
King, Arthur T.	D-Pr	750-2330		D	PHD	77	Colorado	8-95
Okonkwo, Valentine	C-Ac	750-2334			PHD		Fla St	4-85
Elassar, Sammy E.	Prof	750-2339			PHD	68	Maryland	1968

Winthrop University — Rock Hill, SC 29733 (803) 323-2186 — mail.winthrop.edu
Dept of Atg, Fin & Econ — College of Business Adm Fax=323-3960

Name	Rank	Phone	Email	Field	Degree	Yr	School	Year
Weikle, Roger D.	Dean	323-2185	weikler	Mgt	PHD	85	S Carol	1974
Bond, James G.	C-Pr	323-2186	bondj	Atg	PHD	77	S Carol	9-79
Parker, Darrell F.	Prof		parkerd	EHRT	PHD	84	Purdue	9-85
Stone, Gary L.	Prof		stoneg	ACD	PHD	80	N Carol	9-75
Vo, Han X.	Assoc		voh	EF	PHD	79	Tennessee	9-79
Pantuosco, Louis J.	Asst		pantuoscol	EHIJ	PHD	92	Northeas	9-97

U of Wisconsin-Eau Claire — Eau Claire, WI 54702-4004 (715) 836-5743 — uwec.edu
Department of Economics — Sch of Arts & Sciences Fax=836-5071 — Mrs. Janna Johnson

Name	Rank	Phone	Email	Field	Degree	Yr	School	Year
Young, Edward G.	C-Pr	836-5743	youngeg	J	PHD	77	Wash St	1977
Carroll, Wayne D.	Prof	836-3388	carrolwd	QE	PHD	84	Minnesota	1986
Egan, James P.	Prof	836-3242	eganjp	E	PHD	82	Syracuse	1970
Hansen, Jan M.	Prof	836-2150	hansenjm	J	PHD	74	Missouri	1985
Kolb, Fredric	Prof	836-3518	kolbfr	ACG	PHD	71	Utah	1971
Leitner, Keith R.	Prof	836-3254	leitnerkr	AMQ	PHD	74	Kansas St	1974
Oyen, Duane B.	Prof	836-3507	oyend	E	PHD	73	Iowa	1976
Avin, Rose Marie	Assoc	836-4513	avinr	FO	PHD	86	Maryland	1987
DaCosta, Maria N.	Assoc	836-4511	dacostmn	RO	PHD	87	Northeas	1989
Monaco, Kristen	Asst	836-3254	monacoka	LJ	PHD	98	Wi-Milwa	1998
Schaffer, David	Asst	836-3513	schaffdl	JEH	PHD	90	MIT	1998
Benesh, Diann	Lect	836-3527	beneshdg	A	ABD		Va Tech	1976
Postlewaite, Richard	Lect	836-3994	postlera	E	MM	89	AGSIM	1997

Univ of Wisconsin-Green Bay — Green Bay, WI 54311-7001 (920) 465-2355 — uwgb.edu
Economics Faculty — Department of Economics Fax=465-2791

Name	Rank	Phone	Email	Field	Degree	Yr	School	Year
Pollis, Carol	Dean	465-2476			PHD		Okla St	
Shariff, Ismail	C-Pr	465-2355			PHD	65	Wisconsin	
Kangayappan, Kumaraswamy	Prof	465-2308			PHD	69	Wisconsin	
Murray, James M.	Prof	465-2426			PHD	62	Oregon	1969
Stoll, John R.	Prof	465-2358			PHD	80	Kentucky	
Smith, Larry J.	Assoc	465-2161			PHD	73	Chicago	
Troyer, Michael D.	Assoc	465-2434			PHD	75	Duke	
Nesslein, Thomas S.	Asst	465-2099	nessleit		PHD	92	U Wash	1996

U of Wisconsin-La Crosse — La Crosse, WI 54601 (608) 785-8099 — mail.uwlax.edu
Department of Economics — College of Business Fax=785-6700 — Jean M.E. Bonde, Prog Asst

Name	Rank	Phone	Email	Field	Degree	Yr	School	Year
Fuller, Rex D.	Dean	785-8090	fuller	JM	PHD	82	Utah	1981
Haupert, Michael J.	C-Pr	785-6863	haupert	AEN	PHD	89	Wash U	1989
Clark, Barry S.	Prof	785-6860	clark_bs	BHOP	PHD	80	Mass	1978
Daellenbach, Lawrence A.	Prof	785-8108	daell¬la	ADR	PHD	69	Iowa St	1969
Hampton, Mary B.	Prof	785-6867	hampton	GHIJ	PHD	91	Wi-Milwa	1991
Khandker, A. Wahhab	Prof	785-6862	khandker	ACF	PHD	80	So Meth	1983
Nyatepe-Coo, Akorlie A.	Prof	785-6865	nyatepec	FHO	PHD	89	N Illinois	1989
Sherony, Deith R.	Prof	785-8101	sherony	ACE	PHD	82	Wi-Milwa	1983
Anderson, Donna M.	Assoc	785-6864	ander_dm	DIJ	PHD	93	Mich St	1994
Knowles, Glenn J.	Assoc	785-6861	knowles	CQR	PHD	80	Minnesota	1985
Brooks, T. J.	Asst			CF	PHD	99	Wi-Milwa	1999

Univ of Wisconsin-Madison — Madison, WI 53706-1393 (608) 263-2989 — wisc.edu
Department of Economics — Col of Letters & Sci Fax=262-2033 — Mary Anne Clarke
email: @1=facstaff.wisc.edu @2=lafollette.wisc.edu

Name	Rank	Phone	Email	Field	Degree	Yr	School	Year
Certain, Phillip	Dean	262-2644		Chem				
Walker, James R.	C-Pr	263-3863	walker@ssc.		PHD	86	Chicago	1987
Andreoni, James R.	Prof	263-3864	andrdeoni@1		PHD	86	Michigan	1986

Name	Rank	Phone	Email	Field	Degree	Yr	School	Since
Brock, William Allen	Prof	263-6665	brock		PHD	69	Berkeley	1981
F. P. Ramsey Professor of Economics								
David, Martin H.	Prof	262-3281	david@ssc.		PHD	60	Michigan	1962
Deneckere, Raymond	Prof	263-6724	rdenecke@1		PHD	83	Wisconsin	1993
Durlauf, Steven N.	Prof	263-3859	durlauf@1		PHD	86	Yale	1993
Goldberger, Arthur S.	Prof	262-4578	asgoldbe@1		PHD	58	Michigan	1960
Harold M. Groves & Vilas Professor of Economics								
Hansen, Bruce	Prof	263-3880	bhansen@ssc.	CE	PHD	89	Yale	1998
Haveman, Robert H.	Prof	263-7398	haveman@2		PHD	63	Vanderbilt	1970
John Bascom Professor of Economics								
Hester, Donald D.	Prof	263-3879	ddhester@1		PHD	61	Yale	1968
Kennan, John F.	Prof	262-5393	jkennan@macc.		PHD	73	Nrthwstrn	1992
Lipman, Barton L.	Prof	262-5373	blipman@ssc.		PHD	85	Michigan	1998
Lyall, Katharine C.	Prof	262-4048			PHD	69	Cornell	1982
President								
Manuelli, Rodolfo	Prof	263-3877	manuelli@1		PHD	86	Minnesota	1993
Nichols, Donald A.	Prof	263-2327	nichols@2		PHD	68	Yale	1983
Samuelson, Larry W.	Prof	263-7791	larrysam@ssc.		PHD	78	Illinois	
Staiger, Robert W.	Prof	262-2265	rstaiger@2		PHD	85	Michigan	1993
West, Kenneth D.	Prof	262-0033	kdwest@2		PHD	83	MIT	1988
Wolfe, Barbara L.	Prof	262-6358	bwolfe@ssc.		PHD	73	Penn	1976
Che, Yeon-Koo	Assoc	262-2819	yche@1		PHD	91	Stanford	1991
Kitamura, Yuichi	Assoc	262-8910	ykitamur@ssc.		PHD	93	Yale	1998
Neal, Derek A.	Assoc	263-3854	dneal@ssc.		PHD	92	Virginia	1998
Scholz, J. Karl	Assoc	262-5380	jkscholz@2		PHD	88	Stanford	1988
Haile, Philip	Asst	263-3867	phaile@1		PHD	96	Nrthwstrn	1996
Levinson, Arik	Asst	262-9890	amlevins@2		PHD	93	Columbia	1993
Sandholm, William	Asst	263-3858	whs@ssc.		PHD	98	Nrthwstrn	1998
Severinov, Sergei	Asst	262-9891	sseverin@ssc.		PHD	98	Stanford	1998

Univ of Wisconsin-Milwaukee Milwaukee, WI 53201 (414) 229-4811 csd.uwm.edu
Department of Economics Col of Letters & Sci Fax=229-3860

Name	Rank	Phone	Degree	Yr	School	Since
Goodman, Marshall	Dean	229-4654	PHD	82	Ohio St	1995
Kandil, Magda	C-Pr	229-6493	PHD	88	Wash St	1992
Bahmani-Oskooee, Mohsen	Prof	229-4334	PHD	81	Mich St	1981
Heywood, John S.	Prof	229-4437	PHD	86	Michigan	1986
Holahan, William L.	Prof	963-5759	PHD	74	Brown	1972
Lee, Tong Hun	Emer	229-4429	PHD	61	Wisconsin	1967
Mamalakis, Markos J.	Prof	229-4449	PHD	62	Berkeley	1967
Niho, Yoshio	Prof	229-4811	PHD	73	Brown	1970
Perlman, Richard W.	Emer	229-4212	PHD	53	Columbia	1964
Pesek, Boris P.	Emer	963-4680	PHD	56	Chicago	1967
Schenker, Eric	Emer	229-4235	PHD	57	Florida	1959
Schur, Leon M.	Emer	963-4670	PHD	55	Wisconsin	1964
Arora, Swarnjit S.	Assoc	229-6617	PHD	71	SUNY-Buf	1978
Belman, Dale	Assoc	229-4374	PHD	86	Wisconsin	1985
Kim, Sunwoong	Assoc	229-6924	PHD	85	MIT	1989
Meadows, G. Richard	Assoc	229-5883	PHD	72	Wash U	1971
Mohtadi, Hamid	Assoc	229-5334	PHD	82	Michigan	1983
Peoples, James A.	Assoc	229-4482	PHD	84	Berkeley	1990
Bender, Keith	Asst	229-4811	PHD	94	Duke	1999
Buchanan, Neil H.	Asst	229-4678	PHD	96	Harvard	1998
Chakrabarti, Avik	Asst	229-4860	PHD	98	Michigan	1998
Tahmiscioglu, Kamil	Asst	229-4429	PHD	96	USC	1997

Univ of Wisconsin-Oshkosh Oshkosh, WI 54901-8634 (920) 424-1441 uwosh.edu
Department of Economics Col Letters & Sciences Fax=424-1734

Name	Rank	Phone	Email	Field	Degree	Yr	School	Since
Zimmerman, Michael	Dean	424-1210	mz	Biol	PHD			1992
Gunderson, Ralph O.	C-Pr	424-1473	gundrson	OR	PHD	78	Arkansas	1987
Grunloh, James J.	Prof	424-2441	grunloh	A	PHD	79	Wash U	1969
Lee, Hy Sang	Prof	424-7150	leehs	O	PHD	65	Wisconsin	1962
Burnett, Nancy J.	Assoc	424-1471	burnett	E	PHD	88	UCLA	1994
Hussain, Syed Bashir	Assoc	424-7149	hussain	F	PHD	83	Ca-Rivers	1982
McGee, M. Kevin	Assoc	424-7155	mcgee	H	PHD	83	Ohio St	1982
Vanscyoc, Lee	Assoc	424-7153	vanscyoc	AL	PHD	87	Nebraska	1987
Brannon, J. Isaac	Asst	424-7154	brannon	J	PHD	93	Indiana	1994
Mitchell, Milt	Asst	424-1473	mitchell	Q	MA	65	Wisconsin	1967
Robson, Denise A.	Asst	424-7152	robson	AF	PHD	93	Nebraska	1994

Univ of Wisconsin-Parkside Kenosha, WI 53141-2000 (414) 595-2316 uwp.edu
Department of Economics College of Arts & Sci Fax=595-2206 Luella Vines

Name	Rank	Phone	Email	Field	Degree	Yr	School	Since
Keehn, Richard	C-Pr	595-2259	richard.keehn	EGN	PHD	72	Wisconsin	1969
Cloutier, Norman R.	Prof	595-2572	norman.cloutier	DJR	PHD	81	W Virginia	1981
Duetsch, Larry L.	Prof	595-2483	larry.duetsch	DKL	PHD	70	Wisconsin	1969
Kaufman, Dennis A.	Assoc	595-2192	dennis.kaufman	CH	PHD	87	Kansas	1987
Khan, Farida C.	Assoc	595-2662	farida.kahn	FO	PHD	90	Maryland	1990
Rosenberg, Richard E.	Assoc	595-2268	richard.rosen+	FOP	PHD	70	Wisconsin	1969

U of Wisconsin-Platteville	Platteville, WI		53818-3099 (608) 342-1550				uwplatt.edu	
Department of Economics	C of Liberal Arts & Edu		Fax=342-1036				Carol Gill	
Ifediora, John O.	C-Ac	342-1051	ifediora		PHD	88	Il-Chicago	1988
Al Yasiri, Kahtan A.	Prof	342-1822	alyasiri		PHD	65	Iowa St	1965
Liska, Terrence L.	Prof	342-1550	liska		PHD	82	Wisconsin	1980
Simonson, John C.	Prof	342-1560	simonson		PHD	72	Wisconsin	1966
Soofi, Abdollah S.	Assoc	342-1570	soofi		PHD	81	Ca-Rivers	1980
Dehghan, Farhad	Asst	342-1755	dehghan		PHD	84	Illinois	1985
Peckham, Brian W.	Asst	342-1752	peckham		PHD	79	Wisconsin	1987

U of Wisconsin-River Falls	River Falls, WI		54022-5001 (715) 425-3991				uwrf.edu	
Department of Economics	School of Bus & Econ		Fax=425-3536				Ms. Eunice Filkins	
Prochnow, Neal H.	Dean	425-3366	neal.h.prochnow	Phys	PHD	71	Duke	9-64
Potts, Glenn T.	C-Pr	425-3125	glenn.t.potts	E	PHD	76	Iowa St	1976
Brux, Jacqueline M.	Prof	425-3991	jacqueline.m.b+	O	PHD	83	Michigan	1986
Cowen, Janna L.	Prof	425-3519	janna.l.cowen	JL	PHD	79	Nebraska	1979
Eftekhari, Hossein	Prof	425-3158	hossein.eftakari	DC	PHD	85	Nebraska	1985
Schultz, Brian L.	Prof	425-3125	brian.l.schultz	C	PHD	80	Notre Dm	1979
Ngoboka, Pascal	Assoc	425-3158	pascal.t.ngoboka	HP	PHD	87	Wi-Milwa	1990
Tabesh, Hamid	Assoc	425-3158	hamid.tabesh	EF	PHD	87	Iowa St	1988
Walker, John	Assoc	425-3519	john.r.walker	JB	PHD	89	Utah	1990

U of Wisconsin-Stevens Point	Stevens Point WI		54481-3897 (715) 346-2728				uwsp.edu	
Div of Business & Economics	Col Letters & Sciences		Fax=346-4215				J. Cayo	
Paul, Justus F.	Dean	346-4224		Hist	PHD	66	Nebraska	1966
Cray, Randy F.	C-Pr	346-2537			PHD	86	Kansas St	8-86
Palmini, Dennis J.	Prof	346-3875			PHD	75	Illinois	1980
Weiser, Lawrence A.	Prof	346-3310			PHD	67	Wisconsin	1972
Christie, Darrell A.	Assoc	346-2018			MS		Illinois	1964
Hofer, Tracy	Asst	346-2728			PHD	97	Texas	1999
Jacobsen, Clifford C.	Asst	346-4576			MA		Ca-Rivers	1969

Univ of Wisconsin-Superior	Superior, WI		54880-4500 (715) 394-8206				uwsuper.edu	
Dept of Bus & Economics	Cl Professional Studies		Fax=394-8180				Sharon McCusker	
Trudeau, Gregory P.	C-Pr	394-8209		Atg	MBA		StThomas	1988
Beam, Robert D.	Prof	394-8302			PHD	80	Cincinnati	1980

U of Wisconsin-Whitewater	Whitewater, WI		53190-1790 (414) 472-1361				uwwvax.uww.edu	
Department of Economics	Col of Business & Econ		Fax=472-4863				Christie Kornhoff	
Domitrz, Joseph S.	Dean	472-1343			PHD	71	S Illinois	1976
Kim, Kirk Y.	C-Pr	472-5576			PHD	70	Utah	1969
Bhargava, Ashok	Prof	472-4704			PHD	75	Wisconsin	1970
Dominguez, John R.	Prof	472-5586			PHD	71	MIT	1988
Laurent, Jerome K.	Prof	472-4715			PHD	73	Indiana	1965
Marks, Denton	Prof	472-5576			PHD	81	Princeton	1990
Parks, Susan	Prof	472-1747			PHD	82	Purdue	1980
Director, Center for Economic Education								
Snow, Sandra L.	Prof	472-1361			PHD	76	Missouri	1981
Zarinnia, Abdullah	Prof	472-5585			PHD	66	Nebraska	1967
Glosser, Stuart M.	Assoc	472-5580			PHD	85	Tx-Austin	1985
Schweigert, Thomas E.	Assoc	472-5582			PHD	90	Wisconsin	1984
Anstine, Jeffrey	Asst	472-5583			PHD	96	Kentucky	1999
Blankenau, William	Asst	472-5583			PHD	96	Iowa	1997
Skidmore, Mark	Asst	472-1354		H	PHD	94	Colorado	1998
Chen, Yvonne	Lect	472-5447			PHD	98	Wi-Milwa	1999
Walker, Rosemary	Lect	472-1776			ABD		Illinois	1998

Wittenberg University	Springfield, OH		45501-0720 (937) 327-7928				wittenberg.edu	
Economics Faculty	Department of Economics		Fax=327-6340				Norma Kettler	
Wishart, David M.	C-Ac	327-7303	dwishart	ABN	PHD	85	Illinois	1983
Ankrom, Jeff A.	Prof	327-7930	jankrom	AEG	PHD	82	Notre Dm	1982
Goulet, Janet C.	Prof	327-7929		AJM	PHD	75	Notre Dm	1975
Gwinn, Lawrence	Assoc	327-7934	lgwinn	ACEF	PHD	83	Kansas	1988
Tiffany, Frederick G.	Asst	327-7933	ftiffany	ACDL	PHD	88	Penn	1987

Wofford College	Spartanburg, SC		29303-3663 (864) 597-4570				wofford.edu	
Economics Faculty	Department of Economics		Fax=597-4019					
Stephenson, Matthew A.	C-Pr	597-4570		DLN	PHD	65	Tulane	1970
T. B. Stackhouse Professor of Economics								
Wallace, Richard M.	Prof	597-4572	wallacerm	ABK	PHD	81	S Carol	1982
Machovec, Frank M.	Assoc	597-4586		EFP	PHD	86	NYU	1988
McArthur, John R.	Assoc	597-4571	mcarthurjr	EHKQ	PHD	91	Claremont	1990

Woodbury University	Burbank, CA	91510-7846	(818) 767-0888				vaxb.woodbury.edu	
Economics Faculty	Sch of Business & Mgt		Fax=504-9320				Vera Hernandez	
King, Richard	Dean	767-0888	king		MA	55	Occidental	9-97
Dhiman, Satinder	C-Pr	767-0888	sdihman	Mgt	EDD	95	Pepperdi	9-92
Gendel, Eugene B.	Prof	767-0888	gendel	AJDE	PHD	79	Boston U	7-94
Afshar, Tahmoures A.	Asst	767-0888	afshar	FGM	PHD	94	Indiana	1-95

The College of Wooster	Wooster, OH	44691-2263	(330) 263-2302				acs.wooster.edu	
Economics Faculty	Department of Economics		Fax=263-2614					
Sell, John W.	C-Pr	263-2383	jwsell		PHD	81	UCLA	1981
Burnell, Barbara S.	Prof	263-2417			PHD	77	Illinois	1977
Burnell, James D.	Prof	263-2308			PHD	77	Illinois	1977
Greenfield, Gail	Asst				PHD	97	Claremont	1997
Vamosi, Alexander	Asst	263-2309			PHD	95	N Carol	1995
Wellington, Alison J.	Asst			J	PHD	90	Michigan	1997

Worcester State College	Worcester, MA	01602-2597	(508) 793-8091				worcester.edu	
Economics Faculty	Dept of Bus Adm & Econ		Fax=793-8048				Esther Golub 793-8091	
Stefanini, Maureen C.	C-Pr	793-8091	mstefanini		EDD		Boston U	7-93
Lee, Wei Pang	Assoc	793-8101			PHD	87	Georgia	
Trimby, F. Stephen	Assoc	793-8093	strimby		ABD			1970
O'Brien, William F. Jr.	Asst	793-8093	wobrien		PHD	89	Northeas	1997

Wright State University	Dayton, OH	45435-0001	(937) 775-3070				wright.edu	
Department of Economics	Col of Business & Admin		Fax=775-2441		Penny Stacy, Fern Freeman			
Kumar, Rishi	Dean	775-4859	rishi.kumar		PHD	72	Wayne St	1974
Traynor, Thomas L.	C-Ac	775-3070	thomas.traynor		PHD	88	Purdue	1988
Blair, John	Prof	775-3484	john.blair		PHD	74	W Virginia	
Fichtenbaum, Rudy H.	Prof	775-3085	rudy.fichten+		PHD	80	Missouri	1980
Premus, Robert	Prof	775-3069	robert.premus		PHD	75	Lehigh	1975
Renas, Stephen M.	Prof	775-3030	stephen.renas		PHD	71	Geo St	
Sav, Thomas G.	Prof	775-3306	tom.sav		PHD	81	Geo Wash	1985
Swaney, James A.	Prof	775-2769	james.swaney		PHD	79	Colo St	
Dung, Tran H.	Assoc	775-2295	tran.dung		PHD	78	Syracuse	1982
Olson, Paulette I.	Assoc	775-2409	paulette.olson		PHD	89	Utah	1988
Hopkins, Barbara	Asst	775-2080	barbara.hopkins		PHD	92	Maryland	1995
Osborne, Evan	Asst	775-4599	evan.osborne		PHD	93	UCLA	1995
Endres, Carole R.	Inst	775-2823	carole.endres		MS	87	Wright St	
Sylvester, Roger A.	Inst	775-2115	roger.sylvester		MS	87	Wright St	
Director, MS Program In Social & Applied Economics								

University of Wyoming	Laramie, WY	82071-3985	(307) 766-2178				uwyo.edu	
Dept of Economics & Finance	College of Business		Fax=766-5090				Jane H. Smith	
Forster, Bruce A.	Dean	766-4194	bforster	FQ	PHD	74	Austrlia	1987
Gerking, Shelby D.	C-Pr	766-4931	sgerking	RC	PHD	75	Indiana	1978
Birch, John W.	Emer	766-4215	birch	1995	PHD	62	J Hopkins	1964
Cramer, Curtis A.	Prof	766-3384	ccramer	BK	PHD	66	Maryland	1966
Crocker, Thomas D.	Prof	766-6423	tcrocker	Q	PHD	67	Missouri	1975
D'Arge, Ralph C.	Emer	766-6425		1996	PHD	69	Cornell	1975
Hersch, Joni	Prof	766-2358	jhersch	CJ	PHD	81	Nrthwstrn	1989
Mason, Charles F.	Prof	766-5336	bambuzlr	DK	PHD	83	Berkeley	1982
Morgan, William E.	Prof	766-6315	wemorgan	H	PHD	64	Colorado	1968
Phillips, Owen R.	Prof	766-2195	exper	DK	PHD	80	Stanford	1985
Shaffer, Sherrill L.	Prof	766-2173	shaffer		PHD	01	Stanford	1997
Shogren, Jason F.	Prof	766-5430	jramses	Q	PHD	86	Wyoming	1995
Tschirhart, John T.	Prof	766-2356	jtsch	DK	PHD	75	Purdue	1985
Sterbenz, Frederic P.	Assoc	766-2201	sterbenz	EG	PHD	81	Penn	1981
Sunderman, Mark	Assoc	766-4199	sundermn		PHD	86	Illinois	1986
Del Rossi, Alison	Asst	766-6424	delrossi	HK	PHD	92	Penn	1992
Godby, Robert	Asst	766-3843	rgodby		PHD	97	McMaster	1997
Hoover, Scott	Asst	766-3848	shoover		PHD	99	Indiana	1997
Hultberg, Patrik	Asst	766-3143	hultberg		PHD	98	Rice	1998
Stamland, Tommy	Asst	766-5438	stamland		PHD	94	Berkeley	1996

Xavier University	Cincinnati, OH	45207-3212	(513) 745-3075				xavier.xu.edu	
Dpt Econ & Human Resources	Col of Business Admin		Fax=745-3692				Ms. Izola White	
Webb, Michael A.	Dean	745-3528		FO	PHD	80	Illinois	1997
Zimmerman, Robert O.	C-Pr	745-3075		ADEF	PHD	69	SUNY-Buf	1970
Bertaux, Nancy E.	Prof	745-2930		ABJN	PHD	87	Michigan	1985
Donnelly, Lawrence I.	Prof	745-3054		AJM	PHD	64	Cincinnati	1956
Marmo, Michael	Prof	745-3056		J	PHD	71	Illinois	1970
Blackwell, Melanie A.	Assoc	745-2037		ACQ	PHD	88	Kentucky	1987
Cobb, Steven A.	Assoc	745-3053		AEHR	PHD	74	Brown	1984
Rankin, Carol A.	Assoc	745-2932		ADJ	PHD	80	Houston	1984
Rashed, Jamal A.	Assoc	745-2938		ACFO	PHD	88	So Meth	1989
Weinberg, David R.	Assoc	745-3052		ARP	PHD	73	Berkeley	1980
Quencau, Herre'	Asst	745-3062			PHD	96	ParisDaup	1996
Wilson, Beth	Asst	745-2931			PHD			

Yale University New Haven, CT 06520-8268 (203) 432-3576 yale.edu
Economics Faculty Department of Economics Fax=432-5779 Pam Warner
email: @1=econ.yale.edu

Name	Rank	Phone	Email	Field	Degree	Yr	School	Year
Srinivasan, T. N.	C-Pr	436-3630	t.srinivasan	FO	PHD	62	Yale	1980
Andrews, Donald W. K.	Prof	432-3698	dandrews@1	C	PHD	82	Berkeley	1982
Berry, Steven T.	Prof	432-3556	steveb@1		PHD	89	Wisconsin	1988
Bewley, Truman F.	Prof	432-3719	truman.bewley	D	PHD	70	Berkeley	1983
Director of Graduate Studies								
Brainard, William C.	Prof	432-3571	william.brainard	DE	PHD	63	Yale	1981
Broude, Henry W.	Prof	432-0556		N	PHD	54	Harvard	1978
Brown, Donald J.	Prof	432-6934	donald.brown					
Director of Undergraduate Studies								
Evenson, Robert E.	Prof	432-3626	robert.everson	DO	PHD	68	Chicago	1977
Fair, Ray C.	Prof	432-3715	fair@1	E	PHD	68	MIT	1974
Geanakoplos, John	Prof	432-3397	john.geanakoplos	CD	PHD	80	Harvard	
Hamada, Koichi	Prof	432-3610	koichi.hamada	F	PHD	65	Yale	1986
Jaynes, Gerald D.	Prof	432-3586	gerald.jaynes	N	PHD	76	Illinois	
Klevorick, Alvin K.	Prof	432-3705	alvin.klevorick	K	PHD	67	Princeton	1975
Levin, Richard C.	Prof	432-2550	richard.levin	O	PHD	74	Yale	1974
President Yale University								
Linton, Oliver	Prof	432-3699	linton@1	C	PHD	91	Berkeley	
Mendelsohn, Robert	Prof	432-5128	robert.mendels+		PHD	78	Yale	1984
Montias, J. Michael	Emer	432-3247		N	PHD	58	Columbia	1963
Morris, Stephen	Prof	432-6903	stephen.morris	D	PHD	91	Yale	1998
Nalebuff, Barry J.	Prof	432-5968	barry.nalebuff	D	DPH	82	Oxford	1989
Nordhaus, William D.	Prof	432-3587	nordhaus@1	E	PHD	67	MIT	1967
Pakes, Ariel	Prof	432-3560	ariel@1	CL	PHD	79	Harvard	
Pearce, David G.	Prof	432-3583	pearce@1	D	PHD	83	Princeton	
Peck, Merton J.	Prof	432-3558	mjpeck@1	LO	PHD	54	Harvard	1978
Phillips, Peter C. B.	Prof	432-3695	peter.phillips	C	PHD	74	London	
Ranis, Gustav	Prof	432-3632	gustav.ranis	O	PHD	56	Yale	1960
Rust, John P.	Prof	432-3569	john.rust		PHD	83	MIT	
Scarf, Herbert E.	Prof	432-3693	herbert.scarf	C	PHD	54	Princeton	1963
Schultz, T. Paul	Prof	432-3620	paul.schultz	J	PHD	66	MIT	1975
Shiller, Robert J.	Prof	432-3708	shiller@1	D	PHD	72	MIT	1982
Shubik, Martin	Prof	432-3704	martin.shubik	G	PHD	53	Princeton	
Sims, Christopher A.	Prof	432-3560	sims@1	D	PHD	68	Harvard	
Udry, Christopher R.	Prof	432-3637	udry	O	PHD	91	Yale	1998
Guinnane, Timothy J.	Assoc	432-3616	timothy.guinn+	N	PHD	87	Stanford	
Hunt, Jennifer A.	Assoc	432-3714	jennifer.hunt	J	PHD	92	Harvard	1992
Lanjouw, Jean Olson	Assoc	432-3568	lanjouw@1	CO	PHD	92	LondonEC	
Polak, Benjamin	Assoc	432-3590	polak@1	N	PHD	92	Harvard	
Bergemann, Dirk	Asst	432-3592	dirk@1		PHD	94	Penn	
Boozer, Michael A.	Asst	432-3623	maboozer@1	DJ	PHD	94	Princeton	1993
Corsetti, Giancurlo	Asst	432-3562	corsetti@1	F	PHD	92	Yale	1998
Hall, George	Asst	432-3566	george.hall	E	PHD	96	Chicago	1996
Krieger, Stefan	Asst		stefan.krieger	E	PHD	99	Chicago	1997
Levy, Philip I.	Asst	432-3638	levy@1	DF	PHD	94	Stanford	
Moscarini, Giuseppe	Asst	432-3596	giuseppe.mosc+	E	PHD	96	MIT	1996
Pesendorfer, Martin	Asst	432-3549	martionp@1	L	PHD	95	Nrthwstrn	9-95
Stevens, Ann Huff	Asst	432-3628	ann.stevens	J	PHD	95	Michigan	1995
Timmins, Christopher	Asst	432-9901	christopher.ti+	LH	PHD	97	Stanford	1997

Yeshiva University New York, NY 10033-3299 (212) 960-5214 yu1.yu.edu
Department of Economics Yeshiva College Fax=960-5245 Ceceil Levinson
Did Not Respond--1997-98 Listing

Name	Rank	Phone	Email	Field	Degree	Yr	School	Year
Adler, Norman	Dean	960-5214		Psyc	PHD	58	Wisconsin	
Levine, Aaron	C-Pr	960-5214			PHD	81	NYU	
Samson and Halina Bitensky Professor of Economics								
Kanovsky, Eliyahu	Prof	960-5214			PHD	61	Columbia	
Ludwig Jesselson Chair in Economics; spring only								
Horowitz, Avery M.	Assoc	960-5214			PHD	84	CUNY	1986
Assistant Dean								
Arluck, Gregory M.	Asst	960-5214			PHD	87	CUNY	
Gutman, Nancy	Adjln	960-5214			BA	82	Barnard	

York College of Pennsylvania York, PA 17405-7199 (717) 846-1423 ycp.edu
Economic Faculty Dept of Business Adm Fax=849-1619 Julie Sterner

Name	Rank	Phone	Email	Field	Degree	Yr	School	Year
Meisenhelter, Mary C.	C-As			Mgt	PHD		Geo Wash	1996
Landis, Brook	Assoc	815-1416	blandis		PHD	74	Cornell	
Scalet, Kenneth G.	Assoc	815-1415	kscalet		MBA		St Johns	1970
Slaysman, Kenneth	Assoc	815-1708	kslaysma		PHD		Penn St	

Youngstown State University Youngstown, OH 44555-0001 (330) cc.ysu.edu
Department of Economics Col of Arts & Sciences Fax= Dena Kay Crissman

Name	Rank	Phone	Email	Fields	Degree	Yr	School	Since
Brothers, Barbara	Dean			Engl	PHD	73	Kent St	
Porter, Tod S.	C-Pr	742-3431	tsporter		PHD	84	Syracuse	1984
Bee, Richard H.	Prof	742-1677	rhbee		DBA	76	Kent St	1966
Liu, Yih-Wu	Prof	742-1674	ywliu		PHD	68	S Illinois	1968
Mehra, Jadish C.	Prof	742-1681			PHD	68	SUNY-Buf	1965
Milley, Donald J.	Prof	742-1676			PHD	74	SUNY-Buf	1969
Petruska, Dennis A.	Prof	742-1679			PHD	84	Ohio St	1984
Morris, Clyde D.	Assoc	742-3434			PHD	87	Case Wes	1970
Riley, Teresa M.	Assoc	742-1675	triley		PHD	84	Syracuse	1984
Usip, Ebenge E.	Assoc	742-1682	eeusip		PHD	84	Conn	1985
Ruffer, Rochelle L.	Asst	742-1673	rlruffer	DH	PHD	94	Wisconsin	1995

Other Schools

McMaster University Hamilton Canada ON L8S 4M4 (905) Ext24630 mcmaster.ca
Finance & Bus Econ Area DeGroote Sch of Bus Fax=521-8995 Ms. Kathy Matthews
Did Not Respond--1997-98 Listing; phone: 525-9140 Ext 24630

Name	Rank	Phone	Email	Fields	Degree	Yr	School	Since
Mountain, Dean C.	C-Pr	Ext23988	mountain	CD	PHD	79	W Ontario	1987
Chamberlain, Trevor W.	Prof	Ext23980	chambert	G	PHD	86	Toronto	1985
Chan, M. W. Luke	Prof	Ext29648	chanmwl	DE	PHD	78	McMaster	1981
Cheung, C. Sherman	Prof	Ext23968	scheung	G	PHD	91	Illinois	1981
Krinsky, Itzhak	Prof	Ext23984	krinsky	G	PHD	83	McMaster	1982
Kwan, Clarence C. Y.	Prof	Ext23797	kwanc	CG	PHD	79	Toronto	1979
Deaves, Richard W.	Assoc	Ext23976	deaves	EG	PHD	87	Toronto	1987
Lee, Jason	Assoc	Ext23987	jasonlee	G	PHD	91	Alberta	1990
Thomas, Hugh A.	Assoc	Ext23983	thomas	G	PHD	91	NYU	1991

Bogazici University Bebek, Instanbul Turkey 90212 287-2453 boun.edu.tr
Economics Faculty Department of Economics Fax=287-2453
Did Not Respond--1997-98 Listing; phone 90 212 263 1540

Name	Rank	Phone	Email	Fields	Degree	Yr	School	Since
Ozmucur, Suleyman	C-Pr	Ext 1505	ozmucur	CEL	PHD	76	Istanbul	1976
Aleskerov, Fuad	Prof	Ext 1803	aleskero	C	PHD	81	Moscow	1995
Balcim, Metin	Prof	Ext 1807	balcim	EH	PHD	73	NYU	1973
Behar, Cem	Prof	Ext 1809	behar	BJT	PHD	72	Paris	1977
Bubik, Osman	Prof	Ext 1508	bubik	QR	PHD	73	Ca-Rivers	1974
Bugray, Ayse	Prof	Ext 1803	bugray	BO	PHD	80	McGill	1985
Cizakca, Murat	Prof	Ext 1807	cizak	N	PHD	79	Penn	1975
Karatas, Cevat	Prof	Ext 1518	karatas	ACDH	PHD	70	Glasgow	1985
Kayalir, Resad	Prof	Ext 1803	kayalir	BE	PHD	76	Istanbul	1972
Kaytaz, Mehmet	Prof	Ext 1808	kaytaz	CE	PHD	78	Nottinghm	1978
Koymen, Oya	Prof	Ext 1524	koymen	NQ	PHD	67	Strathcl	1976
Onis, Ziya	Prof	Ext 1804	onis	AEO	PHD	83	Manchester	1984
Sertel, Murat	Prof	Ext 1522	sertel	AC	PHD	71	MIT	1979
Adaman, Fikret	Assoc	Ext 1809	adaman	BDPQ	PHD	93	Manchester	1993
Erzan, Refik	Assoc	Ext 1809	erzan	F	PHD	83	Stockholm	1992
Evcimen, Gunar	Assoc	Ext 1808	evcimen	FO	PHD	79	Istanbul	1980
Akcay, Cevdet	Asst	Ext 1802	akcay	CE	PHD	92	CUNY	1992
Alper, Emre	Asst	Ext 1526	alper	CEFG	PHD	95	Geotown	1995
Bayazitoglu, Berna	Asst	Ext 1505	bernab	CDO	PHD	96	Cornell	1996
Ercan, Hakan	Asst	Ext 1591	ercanh	CHJ	PHD	94	Iowa	1994
Karasulu, Meral	Asst	Ext 1800	karasulu	CEF	PHD	95	Boston C	1995
Ozar, Semsa	Asst	Ext 1510	ozar	J	PHD	90	Wirtschaf	1990
Sari, Osman	Asst	Ext 1804	sario	FG	PHD	93	CUNY	1993
Zenginobuz, Unal	Asst	Ext 1505	zengin	AHLP	PHD	96	Penn	1996

INSEAD Fontainebleau France 33-1 60724212 insead.fr
Economic & Political Area Business 77305 Fax=60724242

Name	Rank	Phone	Email	Fields	Degree	Yr	School	Since
Borges, Antonio	Dean	60724221	borges		PHD	80	Stanford	9-93
Fatas, Antonio	C-Ac	60724419	antonio		PHD	93	Harvard	1-94
Ayres, Robert	Prof	60724011	ayres		PHD	58	London	9-92
Chairman Sandoz Chair on Environment								
Gabel, Landis	Prof	60724033	gabel	D	PHD	77	Penn	9-82
MBA Dean								
Michaud, Claude	Prof	64224805	michaud		D		Bordeaux	8-70
Roller, Lars-Hendrik	Prof	60724251			PHD	87	Penn	9-87
Story, Jonathan	Prof	60724435	story		PHD	73	J Hopkins	7-74
Walter, Ingo	Prof	60724393		FG	PHD	66	NYU	1999
Cadot, Olivier	Assoc	60724452	cadot		PHD	89	Princeton	9-89
Webber, Douglas	Assoc	60724251	webber		PHD	85	Essex	1-91
Mihov, Ilian	Asst	60724434	mihov		PHD	96	Princeton	9-96
Perrotti, Liesa	Asst	60724478						9-97
Traca, Daniel	Asst	60724184	traca		PHD	96	Columbia	9-96
Van Zandt, Timothy	Asst	60724212		CD	PHD	89	Penn	9-98

University of Lancaster	LancasterLA1 4YX England 01524 594230				lancaster.ac.uk
Economics	The Management School Fax=594244				
Watson, S. R.	Dean		PHD		Cambridge 9-94
Kirby, Maurice W.	H-Pr		PHD		Sheffield
Balasubramanyam, V. N.	Prof		PHD	70	Illinois
Sapsford, David	Prof		PHD		Leeds
Taylor, James	Prof		PHD		Lancaster
Rothschild, Robert	Read		MA		Capetown
Bradley, Steven	SLect		PHD		Lancaster
Johnes, Geraint	SLect		PHD	87	Lancaster
Rose, Mary B.	SLect		PHD		Manchest
Snowden, Peter N.	SLect		PHD		Leeds
Westall, Oliver M.	SLect		BSC		London
Whittenlas, John	SLect		PHD		Capetown
Ingham, Hilary C.	SLect	JCD	PHD		Glasgow
Read, Robert A.	Lect		PHD		Reading
Steele, Gerald R.	Lect		MA		Sheffield
Elliott, Caroline	Lect		PHD		Manchester

Manchester Inst Sci & Tech	Manchester, UK M60 1QD 44-61 200-3438						umist.ac.uk	
Economics Department	Manchester Sch of Mgt Fax=200-3505						Mrs. June Hall	
Did Not Respond--1997-98 Listing								
Little, Dale	H	200-3465	dale.little	Mktg				
Bosworth, Derek L.	Prof	200-3438	bosworth	JOD	PHD		Warwick	1992
Bowe, Michael A.	Lect	200-3407	bowe	EFG	PHD	89	Carleton	1993
Duffy, Martyn H.	Lect	200-3483	duffy	EC	PHD	95	Manchest	1972
Eliot, Stuart J.	Lect	200-3480	eliot	DMA	MA		Manchest	1974
Harrald, Paul D.	Lect	200-3488	harrard	BCDL	PHD		Simon Fr	1994
Jones, Trefor T.	Lect	200-3484	jones	HLR	PHD		Dundee	1976
Simpson, Paul	Lect	200-3485	simpson	LC	MA		Newcastle	1984

ALPHABETICAL BY INDIVIDUAL

Name	Rank	Location	Area	Degree			Start
A'Hearn, Brian	Asst	Frank & Mars		PHD	94	Berkeley	1999
Aadland, David	Asst	Utah State	CE	PHD	97	Oregon	1997
Aarstol, Michael P.	Asst	Georgia	EO	PHD	96	Stanford	1996
Abdel-Rahman, Hesham M.	Assoc	New Orleans		PHD	87	Penn	1987
Abdulahad, Faraj	Assoc	Manhattan	F	PHD	68	Boston C	1970
Abdullah, Dewan A.	Assoc	E Michigan		PHD	84	Kentucky	1988
Abegaz, Berhanu	Assoc	Wm & Mary		PHD	82	Penn	1982
Abel, David R.	Asst	Mankato St	AE	ABD		Minnesota	1969
Abernathy, Lewis M.	Prof	North Texas	J	PHD	67	Oklahoma	1963
Abou-Zeid, Bassem	Assoc	Bethel-MN	FG	PHD	90	Oklahoma	1990
Abraham, Elizabeth	Asst	Gustavus Ado		ABD		Arizona	1997
Abraham, Fred J.	H-Pr	No Iowa	AEHK	PHD	73	Oregon	1973
Abrahamsson, Bernhard J.	Retir	Wis-Superior		PHD	66	Wisconsin	1989
Abrams, Burton A.	Prof	Delaware	EH	PHD	74	Ohio St	1974
Abrams, Eric	Asst	Hawaii Pacif		PHD	97	Iowa	1997
Aburachis, Abdelrahman E.	Prof	Gannon	G	PHD	72	Pittsburgh	
Aby, Carroll Darden Jr.	Dean	NW St of LA		PHD	64	S Miss	
Acemoglu, Daron	Assoc	MIT	J	PHD	92	LondonEc	1993
Acker, Mary H.	Assoc	Iona	FG	PHD	82	Fordham	1982
Ackert, Lucy F.		Fed Reserve		PHD	90	Emory	1996
Acs, Zoltan J.	Prof	Baltimore		PHD	80	New Sch	1989
Adaman, Fikret	Assoc	Bogazici	BDPQ	PHD	93	Manchester	1993
Adamovich, Ljubisa S.	Prof	Florida St	E	PHD	61	Belgrade	1967
Adams, Donald R. Jr.	Prof	W Virginia	N	PHD	67	Penn	1981
Adams, Earl W. Jr.	C-Pr	Allegheny	AEGH	PHD	71	MIT	1972
Andrew Wells Robertson Professor of Economics							
Adams, F. Gerard	Prof	Pennsylvania		PHD	56	Michigan	1961
Adams, Jack E.	Retir	Ark-Ltl Rock		PHD	75	Okla St	1980
Adams, James D.	Prof	Florida	OJ	PHD	76	Chicago	1979
Adams, Jean W.	Prof	Iowa State	L	PHD	73	Illinois	1972
Adams, John	Retir	Northeastern		PHD	68	Tx-Austin	1990
Adams, John P.	Retir	Cal Poly-SLO		PHD	72	Claremont	1970
Adams, Robert J.	Assoc	Edinboro		PHD	71	Penn St	1977
Adams, Ronald G.	Prof	CS-Chico	ACKR	PHD	75	Kansas St	1971
Adams, Roy Dean	Prof	Iowa State	HE	PHD	72	Illinois	1972
Adams, Walter	Retir	Michigan St		PHD	47	Yale	1947
Distinguished Professor; President Emeritus							
Adams, William James	Prof	Michigan		PHD	73	Harvard	1973
Adamson, Dwight W.	Assoc	So Dakota St	E	PHD	88	Wash St	1989
Addison, John T.	Prof	So Carolina		PHD	71	London	
Addus, Abdussalam A.	Assoc	N Carol A&T		PHD	82	Penn St	1980
Adelman, Irma	Prof	Cal-Berkeley		PHD	55	Berkeley	1979
Adelstein, Richard P.	C-Pr	Wesleyan-CT	K	PHD	75	Penn	1975
Adibi, Esmael	Prof	Chapman	AEFC	PHD	80	Claremont	1978
Director, A. Gary Anderson Center for Economic Research; Anderson Chair							
Adie, Douglas K.	Prof	Ohio Univ	BGM	PHD	68	Chicago	1968
Adkins, Lee C.	Prof	Oklahoma St	C	PHD	88	LSU	1988
Adkins, Roger L.	C-Pr	Marshall		PHD	81	Kansas St	1981
Adler, Michael	Prof	Columbia		DBA	68	Harvard	1968
Adler, Renatte K.	Prof	San Diego St	Q	PHD	79	New Mex	1982
Adrangi, Bahram	Prof	Portland	CDFR	PHD	82	Oregon	1982
Adrisson, Rick	Asst	New Mex St	FH	PHD	94	Nebraska	0-94
Aduddell, Robert M.	Retir	Loyola-Chicg		PHD	71	Nrthwstrn	1965
Adusei, Edward O.	Assoc	Longwood		PHD	88	Va Tech	1992
Aerni, April Laskey	Assoc	Nazareth		PHD	87	Cincinnati	
Afiat, Medhi	Prof	Chadron St	MER	PHD	85	Kansas St	1985
Afifi, Ashraf S.	Prof	Ferris State	ADH	PHD	83	Kansas	1980
Afrasiabi, Ahmad	Assoc	Allegheny	BCQR	PHD	85	W Virginia	1985
Afshar, Tahmoures A.	Asst	Woodbury	FGM	PHD	94	Indiana	1-95
Afxentiou, Diamando	Asst	NY Inst Tech		PHD	90	W Virginia	1990
Agahro, Steve B.	Deces	Jackson St		PHD	91	Denver	1988
Agarwal, Rajshree	Asst	Cen Florida	L	PHD	94	SUNY-Buf	1995
Agarwal, Vinod	Prof	Old Dominion		PHD	86	Ca-SnBarb	
Agbetsiafa, Douglas K.	Prof	Ind-So Bend	AGO	PHD	80	Notre Dm	1980
Agbeyegbe, Terence	Prof	CUNY-Hunter		PHD	83	Essex	1994
Agesa, Jackie	Asst	N Carol A&T		PHD	96	Wi-Milwa	1996
Agesa, Richard	Asst	N Carol A&T		PHD	96	Wi-Milwa	1996
Agnello, Richard J.	Assoc	Delaware	C	PHD	70	J Hopkins	1968
Agnihotri, Krisna	Asst	Southern	A	MA	57	Punjab	1969
Aguirre, Sophia	Asst	Catholic	FG	PHD	92	Notre Dm	1993
Ahene, Rexford A.	Assoc	Lafayette	OR	PHD	83	Wisconsin	1982
Ahking, Francis W.	Assoc	Connecticut	EF	PHD	81	Va Tech	1980
Ahlseen, Mark J.	Assoc	Carson-Newmn	DHJL	PHD	86	Tx A&M	1999
Ahmadi, Ali	Asst	Morehead St		EDD	87	Houston	1995
Ahmed, Ehsan	D-Pr	Jms Madison	EC	PHD	83	Mich St	1984
Ahn, Seung C.	Assoc	Arizona St		PHD	90	Mich St	1990

Name	Rank	School	Fields	Degree	Yr	Degree School	Year
Aho, Arnold A.	Prof	No Michigan	AJ	MA		Lehigh	1969
Ai, Chunrong	Asst	Florida	CT	PHD	90	MIT	1994
Aitken, Hugh G. J.	Retir	Amherst		PHD	51	Harvard	1965
Aiyegoro, Ademois	Asst	Howard		PHD	90	GeoMason	
Aizenman, Joshua	Prof	Dartmouth		PHD	81	Chicago	1990
Champion Internation Professor							
Akacemn, Mohammed	Prof	Metro St-CO		PHD	84	Colorado	1991
Akalou, Woldie-Michael	H	Txs Southern		PHD		UCLA	
Akarca, Ali	Lect	Ill-Chicago	E	MS	72	Nrthwstrn	1985
Akbari, Ali	Prof	Calif Luther		PHD	85	S Calif	1984
Akcay, Cevdet	Asst	Bogazici	CE	PHD	92	CUNY	1992
Akerlof, George A.	Prof	Cal-Berkeley		PHD	66	MIT	1966
Akhavi-Pour, Hossein	Assoc	Hamline	FO	PHD	79	Kansas	1988
Akin, John S.	Prof	No Carolina	IGH	PHD	71	Michigan	1973
Akkihal, Ramchandra G.	Prof	Marshall		PHD	69	Tennessee	1970
Akkina, Krishna Rao	Assoc	Kansas State	ECO	PHD	72	Minnesota	1972
Al Yasiri, Kahtan A.	Prof	Wis-Plattev		PHD	65	Iowa St	1965
Al-Hmound, Rasheed	VAsst	Texas Tech		PHD	94	Tx Tech	1995
Al-Sabea, Taha H.	Prof	CS-Pomona		PHD	68	S Calif	1968
Alam, M. Imam	Asst	No Iowa	CFO	PHD	95	Illinois	1996
Alam, M. Shahid	Prof	Northeastern		PHD	79	W Ontario	1988
Alavi, Jafar	Assoc	East Tenn St		PHD	86	Tennessee	1985
Albelda, Randy P.	Prof	Mass-Boston	JI	PHD	83	Mass	1988
Alberini, Anna	Asst	Colorado		PHD	92	Ca-SnDgo	1995
Alberts, William W.	Emer	U Washington		PHD	61	Chicago	1987
Albrecht, James W.	Prof	Georgetown		PHD	76	Berkeley	1992
Albrecht, William P.	Prof	Iowa		PHD	65	Yale	1965
Aldrich, Carole	Visit	Stetson	ACD	PHD	72	Car Mellon	1998
Aldrich, Mark	Prof	Smith	JLN	PHD	69	Tx-Austin	1968
Alesina, Alberto F.	Prof	Harvard		PHD	86	Harvard	1988
Paul Sack Associate Professor of Political Economy							
Aleskerov, Fuad	Prof	Bogazici	C	PHD	81	Moscow	1995
Alexander, Donald L.	Assoc	W Michigan	D	PHD	83	Penn St	9900
Alexander, James	Prof	Alabama A&M	EAOH	PHD	89	Tx-Austin	1983
Alexander, McKinley	Retir	Jackson St		PHD	86	Illinois	1975
Alexander, Peter	Assoc	Hartwick	ACDL	PHD	90	Mass	1997
Alexander, Susan L.	Assoc	St Thomas-MN	F	PHD	77	So Meth	1981
Alexanderson, Peter	Asst	CUNY-Lehman		JD			
Alexandrin, Glen	Asst	Villanova		PHD	67	Clark	1970
Alexeev, Michael	Prof	Indiana		PHD	84	Duke	1992
Alexis, Marcus	Prof	Northwestern		PHD	59	Minnesota	1985
Daniel F. and Ada L. Rice Professor of Economics							
Alger, I.	Asst	Boston Coll	DL	PHD	97	Toulouse	1999
Ali, Mukhtar M.	Prof	Kentucky	C	PHD	69	Wisconsin	1969
Aliprantis, C. D. Roko	Prof	Purdue		PHD	73	Cal Tech	1998
Allen, Andrew T.	Assoc	San Diego		PHD	83	Illinois	1984
Allen, Beth Elaine	Prof	Minnesota		PHD	78	Berkeley	1992
Allen, Bruce T.	Prof	Michigan St		PHD	65	Cornell	1965
Allen, Charles L.	Prof	Lamar	RC	PHD	78	Arkansas	1979
Allen, Grace	Assoc	W Carolina		PHD	91	S Carol	1992
Allen, Joel L.	Asst	Lamar	B	MS	60	Baylor	1960
Allen, John William	Prof	Texas A&M	D	PHD	67	Illinois	1967
Allen, Polly R.	Prof	Connecticut	FE	PHD	70	Brown	1976
Allen, Ralph C.	H-Pr	Valdosta St	FDK	PHD	81	Geo St	1982
Allen, Robert F.	Prof	Creighton	DKL	PHD	69	Mich St	1986
Allen, Roy E.	Assoc	St Marys-Cal		PHD	83	Berkeley	1985
Allen, Steven G.	Prof	N Carol St	JD	PHD	78	Harvard	1978
Allen, Stuart D.	H-Pr	N Car-Greens	E	PHD	77	Virginia	1976
Allen, W. David	Asst	Alabama-Hunt	J	PHD	94	Arkansas	1994
Allender, Mary E.	Assoc	Portland	LC	PHD	90	Oregon	1985
Allgood, Sam	Asst	Nebraska	DJG	PHD	93	Georgia	
Alli, Ali M.	Prof	Okla City	CIP	PHD	68	Okla St	1985
Allison, Michael	Lect	Mo-St Louis	CE	ABD		Virginia	1993
Allison, Robert J.	Prof	CS-Fresno	B	PHD	66	Colorado	1967
Almon, Clopper Jr.	Prof	Maryland		PHD	62	Harvard	1966
Alnasrawi, Abbas	Prof	Vermont	AFOQ	PHD	65	Harvard	1963
Alonso, Irasema	VAsst	Rochester		PHD	93	Minnesota	1994
Alonso, Irma T. de	Prof	Fla Internat	OCFI	PHD	69	York-Eng	1981
Alpan, Erkan	Asst	R Stockton		PHD	84	Ca-Rivers	1980
Alper, Emre	Asst	Bogazici	CEFG	PHD	95	Geotown	1995
Alper, Neil O.	Assoc	Northeastern		PHD	77	Pittsburgh	1979
Alpert, William T.	Assoc	Connecticut	J	PHD	79	Columbia	1983
Alse, Jahardhanan	Asst	Indiana SE	FE	PHD	93	Wisconsin	1992
Alshallah, Mohamed	Assoc	Fairmont St	AF	MBA		Bridgepr	1988
Alshawa, Alaa	Inst	Concordia C	EG	MA	94	Ohio	1997
Alston, Lee	Prof	Illinois	NQ	PHD	78	U Wash	1988
Alston, Richard M.	Prof	Weber State	ABNQ	PHD	70	Cornell	1969
Altazan, John E.	Prof	New Orleans		PHD	54	Illinois	1958
Altieri, Paul L.	Prof	Central Conn	E	PHD	76	Boston C	1975
Altmann, James L.	Prof	Indiana SE	DM	PHD	78	Wisconsin	1978

Altonji, Joseph G.	Prof	Northwestern		PHD	81	Princeton	1990
Altshuler, Rosanne	Asst	Rutgers-N Br	H	PHD	88	Penn	1992
Alvarez, Fernando	Asst	Chicago		PHD	94	Minnesota	1996
Alvi, Eskander	Assoc	W Michigan	E	PHD	85	J Hopkins	1994
Aly, Hassan	Assoc	Ohio State		PHD	86	S Illinois	1989
Amacher, Ryan C.	Prof	Tx-Arlington	FH	PHD	71	Virginia	1992
Amadi, Confidence	Asst	Kentucky St	G	DBA	94	La Tech	1998
Amarante, Massimiliano	Asst	Columbia	DC	PHD	99	MIT	1999
Amariglio, Jack	Prof	Merrimack		PHD	84	Mass	
Amato, Louis	Prof	N Car-Charl		PHD	80	S Carol	1980
Amegbe, Annan	Assoc	Morgan State		PHD	77	Catholic	1978
Amemiya, Takeshi	Prof	Stanford		PHD	64	J Hopkins	1968
Edward Ames Edmonds Professor of Economics							
Amin, R. John	H-Pr	Northwood	BDFM	PHD	78	Cincinnati	9-86
Ammann, Alan	Assoc	Meredith		DBA	78	Miss St	1990
Amoateng, Kofi	Assoc	N Carol Cen		PHD	86	Tx-Austin	1990
Amos, Orley M. Jr.	Prof	Oklahoma St	R	PHD	79	Iowa St	1979
Amott, Teresa Louise	Assoc	Bucknell	JNAB	PHD	80	Boston C	1989
Amrhein, Joseph	Retir	St Michael's		PHD	58	NYU	
Amsler, Christine E.	Assoc	Michigan St		PHD	80	Penn	1980
Amuedo-Dorantes, Catalina	Asst	San Diego St		PHD	98	W Mich	1999
An, Mark	Asst	Duke		PHD	93	Cornell	1993
Anas, Alex	Prof	SUNY-Buffalo	DR	PHD	75	Penn	1991
Anastasopoulos, Petros	Assoc	F Dick-Teane	ADE	PHD	84	New Sch	1986
Anbarci, Nejat M.	Assoc	Fla Internat	DC	PHD	88	Iowa	1995
Anders, Steven L.	Prof	Graceland	ARD	PHD	88	Kansas St	1978
Anderson, B. Wylie	Prof	No Iowa	AEGJ	PHD	73	Iowa	1966
Anderson, Charles E.	Dean	Kean		PHD	75	Stanford	7-88
Anderson, Curtis L.	Prof	Minn-Duluth	QA	PHD	81	Wyoming	1980
Anderson, David A.	Assoc	Centre	ACHK	PHD	92	Duke	1992
Anderson, Deborah	Asst	New Mexico	CHJ	PHD	98	Cornell	1998
Anderson, Donna M.	Assoc	Wis-La Cross	DIJ	PHD	93	Mich St	1994
Anderson, Eric E.	Assoc	Old Dominion		PHD	84	U Wash	1984
Anderson, Evan	Asst	No Carolina	E	PHD	98	Chicago	1998
Anderson, Gary M.	Prof	CS-Northrdge	GLTR	PHD	87	GeoMason	1987
Anderson, James E.	Prof	Boston Coll	DF	PHD	69	Wisconsin	1969
Anderson, Joan B.	Prof	San Diego		PHD	71	Ca-SnDgo	1981
Anderson, John E.	Prof	Nebraska	H	PHD	77	Claremont	1991
Anderson, John Whiting	Retir	Bucknell		PHD	67	Penn	1961
Anderson, Kathryn H.	Assoc	Vanderbilt	JO	PHD	78	N Car St	1980
Anderson, Lee G.	Prof	Delaware	Q	PHD	70	U Wash	1974
Anderson, Lisa	Asst	Wm & Mary		PHD	94	Virginia	1997
Anderson, Michael A.	Assoc	Wash & Lee	F	PHD	90	Wisconsin	1990
Anderson, Patricia Mary	Asst	Dartmouth		PHD	91	Princeton	1991
Anderson, Richard K.	Prof	Texas A&M	CF	PHD	76	Purdue	1975
Anderson, Richard T.	Asst	NewJerseyCty	AI	PHD	91	CUNY	
Anderson, Robert M.	Prof	Cal-Berkeley		PHD	77	Yale	
Anderson, Roy C.	Prof	CS-Long Bch		PHD	65	Tulane	1965
Anderson, Simon P.	Assoc	Virginia	LDR	PHD	85	Queen's	1987
Anderson, Terry L.	Prof	Montana St		PHD	72	U Wash	1972
Anderson, Thomas	Asst	Framingham		PHD	87	Iowa	
Anderson, Thomas C.	Assoc	Kennesaw St	ADM	PHD	72	Berkeley	1985
Anderton, Charles H.	Assoc	Holy Cross	ACDF	PHD	86	Cornell	1986
Ando, Albert K.	Prof	Pennsylvania		PHD	59	Car Mellon	1963
Andoh, Samuel Kojo	C-Pr	So Conn St	EO	PHD	86	NYU	
Andreoni, James R.	Prof	Wisconsin		PHD	86	Michigan	1986
Andrews, Charles Haynes	Prof	Mercer-Macon		PHD	67	Vanderbilt	1973
Stetson Professor of Economics							
Andrews, Donald W. K.	Prof	Yale	C	PHD	82	Berkeley	1982
Andrews, Kim	Assoc	Cen Missouri		PHD	94	Okla St	1990
Andrews, Marcellus	C-Ac	Wellesley		PHD	86	Yale	1986
Andrews, Thomas	Asst	West Chester	DHQL	PHD	96	Temple	1997
Andrianacos, Dimitri	Prof	W Illinois	ACE	PHD	89	Chicago	1990
Andrulis, John A.	Prof	W New Eng		PHD	75	Purdue	1981
Angelini, Anthony L. P.	C-Ac	St John's		MA	51	Temple	
Angiello, Joseph		SUNY-Empire	A	PHD	77	Tx-Austin	1983
Angkatavanich, Virote	C-Pr	F Dick-Teane	AEFG	PHD	67	New Sch	1963
Angrist, Joshua D.	Prof	MIT	J	PHD	89	Princeton	1996
Ankrom, Jeff A.	Prof	Wittenberg	AEG	PHD	82	Notre Dm	1982
Ansari, Mohammed	Assoc	Radford	EFGM	PHD	89	Simon Fr	1997
Anspach, Ralph	Prof	San Fran St		PHD	63	Berkeley	1963
Anstine, Diane	Asst	No Central	D	PHD	97	Kentucky	1997
Anstine, Jeffrey	Asst	Wis-Whitewat		PHD	96	Kentucky	1999
Antecol, Heather	Asst	Illinois St	JIG	PHD	98	McMaster	8-99
Antel, John J.	C-Pr	Houston	J	PHD	82	UCLA	1981
Antinolfi, Gaetano	Asst	Wash Univ	E	PHD	97	Cornell	1997
Antle, John M.	Prof	Montana St		PHD	80	Chicago	1987
Anyamele, Dennis	Asst	Jackson St		PHD	92	Howard	
Anyanwu, Lenard C.	Asst	NJ Inst Tech		PHD	90	Tx-Dallas	1990

Name	Rank	School	Fields	Degree	Yr	Institution	Year
Aoki, Masahiko	Prof	Stanford		PHD	67	Minnesota	1984
Henri and Tomoye Takahashi Professor of Japanese Studies							
Aoki, Masanao	Emer	UCLA		PHD	65	Tokyo In	1983
Aoki, Masato	VAsst	Simmons	A	PHD	95	Mass	1994
Aoyagi, Masaki	Asst	Pittsburgh	D	PHD	92	Princeton	1992
Applegate, Michael J.	Prof	Oklahoma St	O	PHD	73	Iowa St	1974
Appleyard, Dennis R.	Prof	Davidson	F	PHD	66	Michigan	1990
James B. Duke Professor of International Studies							
Aquirregabiria, Victor	Asst	Chicago		PHD	95	Compluten	1999
Arabian, Ghodratollah	Asst	Lincoln-MO		PHD	85	Indiana	1984
Aranson, Peter H.	Prof	Emory	HKL	PHD	72	Rochester	1981
Arbatskaya, Maria	Asst	Emory	DL	ABD		Indiana	9-99
Arce, Daniel G.	Asst	Alabama		PHD	91	Illinois	1991
Archer, Stephen H.	Retir	Willamette		PHD	58	Minnesota	1973
Archibald, Robert B.	Prof	Wm & Mary		PHD	74	Purdue	1976
Arenberg, Yuri	Assoc	CUNY-Brookly	D	PHD	86	NYU	1985
Arguea, Nestor M.	Assoc	West Florida	ACD	PHD	90	S Calif	1990
Argys, Laura M.	Asst	Colo-Denver	IOCD	PHD	93	Colorado	1990
Aristotelous, Kyriacos	Assoc	Otterbein	EFO	PHD	93	Ohio St	1993
Arjomand, H. Lari	Prof	Clayton St		PHD	80	Oklahoma	1980
Arluck, Gregory M.	Asst	Yeshiva		PHD	87	CUNY	
Armantier, Olivier	Asst	SUNY-Stony B		PHD	98	Pittsburgh	1998
Armentano, Dominick T.	Retir	Hartford		PHD	66	Conn	1966
Armstrong, Ken D.	Dean	Anderson U		PHD	85	Nrthwstrn	1990
Arndt, Sven W.	Prof	Claremont		PHD	64	Berkeley	1990
Charles M. Stone Professor of Money, Credit & Trade							
Arnold, Michael	Asst	Delaware	LD	PHD	92	UCLA	1992
Arnold, Roger A.	Prof	CS-S Marcos		PHD	79	Va Tech	
Arnold, Thomas R.	Prof	King's Col		PHD	70	Syracuse	6-60
Herve A. LeBlanc Distinguished Service Professor in Liberal Arts							
Arnott, Richard J.	Prof	Boston Coll	DHR	PHD	75	Yale	1988
Arnould, Richard J.	H-Pr	Illinois	DIKL	PHD	68	Iowa St	1967
Aronson, J. Richard	Prof	Lehigh	HG	PHD	64	Clark	1965
William L. Clayton Professor of Business and Economics							
Arora, Harjit K.	Prof	LeMoyne	EFH	PHD	84	Wi-Milwa	1987
Arora, Swarnjit S.	Assoc	Wis-Milwauke		PHD	71	SUNY-Buf	1978
Arthur, E. Eugene	Assoc	Rockhurst	KM	DBA	75	Indiana	1968
Arvan, Lanny D.	Assoc	Illinois	CD	PHD	81	Nrthwstrn	1980
Arzac, Enrique R.	Prof	Columbia		PHD	68	Columbia	1971
Asadoorian, Malcolm	Lect	Assumption	ACM	ABD		Clark	1997
Asamoah, Yaw	Prof	Indiana U-PA	FO	PHD	85	Wash U	1984
Aschauer, David Alan	Prof	Bates	E	PHD	84	Rochester	1990
Elmer W. Campbell Professor of Economics							
Aschheim, Joseph	Prof	George Wash	E	PHD	54	Harvard	1964
Asdrubali, Pierfederuo	Asst	Michigan St		PHD	96	Brown	1997
Asea, Patrick	Asst	UCLA		PHD	93	J Hopkins	
Asefa, Sally Ann	C-Pr	Brescia		PHD	78	Iowa St	8-80
Asefa, Sisay	Prof	W Michigan	O	PHD	80	Iowa St	1980
Asgary, Nader	Asst	SUNY-Geneseo	FJ	PHD	91	Houston	1996
Asheghian, Par	Prof	CS-San Bern	F	PHD	80	Geo St	1991
Ashenfelter, Orley C.	Prof	Princeton		PHD	70	Princeton	1968
Asher, Cheryl	Asst	Villanova		PHD	81	Penn	1984
Ashley, James R.	Assoc	St Catherine	AL	PHD	84	Wisconsin	1984
Ashley, Richard A.	Assoc	Virg Tech	CE	PHD	82	Ca-SnDgo	1981
Ashman, H. Lowell	C-Pr	Lenoir-Rhyne		PHD	73	Utah	1975
Ashraf, Javed	Prof	West Florida	AJ	PHD	86	N Illinois	1990
Asiedu, Elizabeth	Asst	Kansas	F	PHD	98	Illinois	1998
Askalani, Mohamed H.	Prof	Mankato St	AC	PHD	70	Iowa St	1969
Askari, Ammar	Lect	Ind-Purdue/I		PHD	95	Indiana	1989
Aske, David	Asst	No Colorado	AITR	PHD	92	Nebraska	1992
Aslanbeigui, Nahid	Assoc	Monmouth	E	PHD	84	Michigan	1988
Assad, Jean-Claud	Asst	Jackson St		PHD	87	Howard	1991
Assane, Djeto	Asst	Nev-L Vegas	O	PHD	88	Colorado	1988
Assibey-Mensah, Albert	Asst	Kentucky St	AG	PHD	94	Cincinnati	1994
Atack, Jeremy	C-Pr	Vanderbilt	N	PHD	76	Indiana	1993
Atencio, Leonard D.	Prof	Fort Lewis		PHD	69	Kansas St	1968
Atesoglu, H. Sonmez	Prof	Clarkson	EFO	PHD	72	Pittsburgh	1977
Athey, Susan	Assoc	MIT	L	PHD	95	Stanford	1995
Castle Krob Career Development Associate Professor of Economics							
Atkeson, Andrew G.	Asst	Pennsylvania	PF	PHD	88	Stanford	1993
Atkinson, Glendel W.	Prof	Nevada-Reno		PHD	68	Oklahoma	1967
Atkinson, Scott E.	Prof	Georgia	CQK	PHD	72	Colorado	1985
Atri, Said	Prof	SUNY Oswego	AFI	PHD	82	SUNY-Alb	1981
Attiyeh, Richard E.	Prof	Ca-San Diego	EI	PHD	66	Yale	1982
Atwood, Edward Charles Jr.	Retir	Wash & Lee		PHD	59	Princeton	1969
Atwood, Joseph A.	Assoc	Montana St		PHD	87	Nebraska	1987
Auerbach, Alan J.	Prof	Cal-Berkeley	GEH	PHD	78	Harvard	1994
Auernheimer, Leonardo J. A.	Prof	Texas A&M	EF	PHD	73	Chicago	1973
Ault, David E.	Prof	S Ill-Edward	AFJK	PHD	69	Illinois	1969
Ault, Richard W.	Assoc	Auburn		PHD	83	Virginia	1983

Austen, Andrew	Asst	Bowdoin	HC	PHD	91	Penn	1998
Austin, Adrian	Asst	U Miami	CG	PHD	98	Duke	1998
Austin, Ellis T.	Deces			PHD	55	Mich St	
Austin, John A.	Prof	La St-Shreve		PHD	72	Ariz St	1983
Ausubel, Lawrence M.	Prof	Maryland		PHD	84	Stanford	1992
Autor, David	Asst	MIT	J	PHD	99	Harvard	1999
Auzenne, George R.	Lect	Florida A&M	LM	MS	63	Boston	1976
Avard, Stephen L.	H-Ac	Tx A&M-Comm	GFDE	PHD	83	North Tx	1983
Averett, Susan	Assoc	Lafayette	CJI	PHD	91	Colorado	1991
Averitt, Robert T.	Prof	Smith	ABE	PHD	61	Tx-Austin	1961
Avin, Rose Marie	Assoc	Wis-Eau Clar	FO	PHD	86	Maryland	1987
Awh, Robert Y.	Retir	Miss State		PHD	60	Florida	1968
Axarloglou, Kostas	Asst	Babson	F	PHD	93	Michigan	1994
Axelson, David J.	C-Ac	Western St		EDD	76	Colorado	1982
Ayal, Eliezer B.	Emer	Ill-Chicago	O	PHD	61	Cornell	1970
Ayanian, Robert L.	Retir	CS-Fullerton		PHD	74	UCLA	1977
Ayers, Michael	Assoc	Il-Springfld	HR	PHD	73	Oklahoma	1971
Ayers, Ronald M.	Assoc	Tx-S Antonio	GJM	PHD	78	Tulane	1979
Ayittey, George B. N.	VAsoc	American U		PHD	81	Manitoba	1994
Ayres, Robert	Prof	INSEAD		PHD	58	London	9-92
Chairman Sandoz Chair on Environment							
Azari-Rad, Hamid	Asst	SUNY-N Paltz		PHD	96	Utah	1999
Azariadis, Constantine C.	Prof	UCLA		PHD	75	Car Mellon	
Aziz, Fahima	C-As	Hamline	DJ	PHD	95	Minnesota	1994
Baack, Bennett D.	Assoc	Ohio State	N	PHD	72	U Wash	1988
Babcock, Michael W.	Prof	Kansas State	RQ	PHD	73	Illinois	1972
Babilot, George	Retir	San Diego St		PHD	58	Oregon	1956
Bacdayan, Andrew W.	Prof	NW St of LA		PHD	73	Utah St	
Backus, David	Prof	New York U	EFG	PHD	81	Yale	1990
Badgett, Lee	Asst	Massachusett		PHD	90	Berkeley	1997
Badu, Yaw Agyeman	C-Ac	Virginia St		PHD	80	S Carol	1984
Baek, In-Mee	Asst	Suffolk		PHD	90	Indiana	
Baer, Werner	Prof	Illinois	EFO	PHD	58	Harvard	1974
Bagheri, Fatholla	Prof	North Dakota	AJ	PHD	78	Penn	1990
Bagheri, Rashid	Inst	Morgan State		MA		Howard	
Bagi, Sukhwinder	Asst	Bloomsburg		PHD	87	Vanderbilt	
Bagwell, Kyle W.	Prof	Columbia	LF	PHD	86	Stanford	1996
Bahatiuk, Nicholas G.	Retir	LeMoyne		PHD		Ukranian	1962
Bahl, Roy W. Jr.	Dean	Georgia St	HR	PHD	65	Kentucky	1988
Bahmani-Oskooee, Mohsen	Prof	Wis-Milwauke		PHD	81	Mich St	1981
Bai, Jushan J.	Prof	Boston Coll	CE	PHD	92	Berkeley	1998
Baicker, Katherine	Asst	Dartmouth		PHD	98	Harvard	1998
Bailey BVM, Mary P. F.	Retir	Loyola-Chicg		MA	69	Notre Dm	1991
Bailey, DeeVon	Prof	Utah State	Q	PHD	83	Tx A&M	1983
Bailey, Duncan	Prof	SC-Spartanbu	AEOR	PHD	70	Va Tech	1984
Bailey, Martin J.	Deces	Emory	E	PHD	56	J Hopkins	1989
Bailey, Mary Ann	Adj	George Wash	I	PHD	74	MIT	1983
Baillie, Richard	Prof	Michigan St	CFG	PHD	78	LondonEc	8-86
Pasant Chair of Economics & Finance							
Bails, Dale G.	Assoc	Christian Br		PHD	78	S Dakota	1995
Baiman, Ron	Asst	Roosevelt		PHD	89	New Sch	1994
Baird, Charles W.	Prof	CS-Hayward	BHJ	PHD	68	Berkeley	1972
Baird, Robert N.	Assoc	Case Western	A	PHD	65	Kentucky	1965
Bajari, Patrick	Asst	Stanford		PHD	97	Minnesota	
Baker, Ben	Assoc	Davidson	G	MA	80	S Carol	1997
Baker, Michael	Assoc	Cal-Davis	H	PHD	90	Michigan	1-99
Baker, Samuel H. III	Prof	Wm & Mary		PHD	70	Virginia	1969
Baker, Stephen A.	Prof	Capital		PHD	82	York UK	1987
Bakir, Saad T.	Assoc	Alabama St	CM	PHD	77	Va Tech	1-93
Baktari, Paul	C-Ac	SUNY-Potsdam		PHD		W Virginia	
Balaban, Rita	Asst	Samford	AI	ABD		Pittsburgh	1997
Balabkins, Nicholas W.	Retir	Lehigh		PHD	56	Rutgers	1966
Balasubramanyam, V. N.	Prof	U Lancaster		PHD	70	Illinois	
Balch, Billy W.	Retir	Mid Tenn St		PHD	68	Alabama	1964
Balch, Donald C.	Lect	So Carolina	AD	MA	88	S Carol	8-84
Balch, Michael S.	Assoc	Iowa		PHD	65	NYU	1971
Balcim, Metin	Prof	Bogazici	EH	PHD	73	NYU	1973
Baldani, Jeffrey P.	Assoc	Colgate	CD	PHD	83	Cornell	1982
Baldwin, Marjorie L.	Assoc	East Carol	DIJ	PHD	88	Syracuse	1989
Baldwin, Robert E.	Retir	Wisconsin		PHD	50	Harvard	1964
Baldwin, William Lee	Retir	Dartmouth		PHD	58	Princeton	1956
Balfour, B. Burton	C-Ac	N Carol Cen		PHD	74	N Car St	1973
Bali, Turan	Asst	CUNY-Queens	GE	PHD	98	CUNY	1998
Balkan, Erol M.	C-Ac	Hamilton	OF	PHD	88	SUNY-Bin	1987
Balke, Nathan S.	Assoc	So Methodist	EG	PHD	86	Nrthwstrn	1986
Balkin, Steven M.	Prof	Roosevelt		PHD	76	Wayne St	1984
Ball, David Stafford	Assoc	N Carol St	FND	PHD	67	N Carol	1966
Ball, Laurence M.	Prof	J Hopkins		PHD	86	MIT	1994
Ball, Sheryl B.	Assoc	Virg Tech	DMH	PHD	91	Nrthwstrn	1992

Name	Rank	School	Fields	Degree	Yr	Degree School	Year
Ballantyne, A. Paul	Prof	Colorado Spr	ABEO	PHD	65	Stanford	1967
Ballard, Charles L.	Prof	Michigan St		PHD	83	Stanford	1983
Ballinger, T. Parker	Asst	S F Austin	CE	PHD	99	Houston	1999
Ballman, Richard J. Jr.	C-Pr	Augustana IL	ABDE	PHD	77	Iowa	1972
Ballou, Dale	Assoc	Massachusett		PHD	89	Yale	
Balough, Robert S.	C-Pr	Clarion		PHD	81	N Illinois	1981
Baltagi, Badi H.	Prof	Texas A&M	C	PHD	79	Penn	1988
George Summey Jr. Professor in Liberal Arts							
Balvers, Ronald J.	Assoc	W Virginia	EG	PHD	84	Pittsburgh	1991
Banaian, King	Prof	St Cloud St		PHD	86	Claremont	1984
Bandera, Vladimir N.	Prof	Temple	FP	PHD	60	Berkeley	1972
Bandyopadhayay, Taradas	Prof	Cal-Riversid	AD	PHD	80	So Meth	1987
Bandyopadhyay, Subhayu	Asst	W Virginia	F	PHD	94	Maryland	1993
Bandyopadhyay, Sudeshna	Asst	W Virginia	J	PHD	92	Maryland	1992
Bandzak, Ruth Anne	Asst	Redlands		MA		Notre Dm	1988
Banerjee, Abhijit V.	Prof	MIT	G	PHD	88	Harvard	1993
Banerjee, Guarango	Asst	Tx-Brownsvil	AE	PHD	97	Al-Birm	1997
Banks, Nina	Lect	Hood	AJ	ABD		Mass	1993
Bansal, Vipul K.	Assoc	St John's		PHD	88	Miss	
Baqir, Ghalib M.	Retir	Alabama St	1995	PHD	67	St Louis	1973
Barakeh, A. K.	Retir	So Alabama	F	PHD	68	Indiana	1968
Barari, Mahua	Asst	SW Missouri		PHD	92	Iowa St	1993
Barber, G. Russell Jr.	Assoc	Mercer-Macon		PHD	90	Miss	1973
Barber, William J.	Emer	Wesleyan-CT	B	DPHI	57	Oxford	1957
Andrews Professor of Economics							
Barbezat, Daniel P.	Assoc	Amherst	ANO	PHD	88	Illinois	1988
Barbezat, Debra A.	Assoc	Colby	JIA	PHD	85	Michigan	1992
Barbour, G. Jeffrey	Asst	Cen Michigan		PHD	73	Fla St	1971
Barbour, James L.	Assoc	Elon	AB	PHD	87	Kentucky	1990
Bardhan, Pranab K.	Prof	Cal-Berkeley		PHD		Cambridge	
Barger, Peter S.	Assoc	No Central	G	PHD	89	Illinois	1989
Barkoulas, John	Asst	Louisiana Te	EGF	PHD		Boston C	1997
Barlevy, Gadi	Asst	Northwestern		PHD	97	Harvard	1997
Barlow, Tammy	VAsst	Middlebury	HQ	PHD	99	Mass	1999
Barnes, Clarence H.	Dean	Gonzaga		PHD	73	Tennessee	9-73
Barnes, Robert R.	Retir	Millersville		MA	67	Penn	1963
Barnett, Andy H.	Prof	Auburn		PHD	78	Virginia	1982
Barnett, Harold C.	C-Pr	Rhode Island	EKQ	PHD	73	MIT	1970
Barnett, William	Assoc	Loyola-N Orl	DEFK	PHD	74	Mich St	1974
Barnett, William A.	Prof	Wash Univ	E	PHD	74	Car Mellon	1990
Barnhart, Cora M.	Asst	Lander	AMO	PHD	95	Clemson	1996
Barone, Charles A.	Assoc	Dickinson Cl	AO	PHD	78	American	1975
Baroutsis, A. Paul	Prof	Slippery Roc	ADP	PHD	72	Purdue	1972
Barr, Joseph E.	Prof	Framingham		PHD	76	Boston C	
Barrett, Anthony	Assoc	St Scholasti		PHD	84	Geo Wash	
Barrett, Richard	Prof	Montana	EOJQ	PHD	72	Wisconsin	
Barrington, Linda	Asst	Barnard	NCI	PHD	91	Illinois	1991
Barro, Robert J.	Prof	Harvard		PHD	70	Harvard	1987
Barron, John M.	Prof	Purdue		PHD	76	Brown	1976
Barrows, Stephen P.	Inst	USAF Academy		MA	93	Penn St	
Barsky, Robert	Assoc	Michigan		PHD	86	MIT	
Bartel, Ann	Prof	Columbia		PHD	74	Columbia	1976
Bartell, Ernest J.	Prof	Notre Dame	O	PHD	66	Princeton	1977
Bartell, H. Robert	Prof	East Tenn St		PHD	63	Columbia	1989
Barth, Peter S.	Prof	Connecticut	J	PHD	65	Michigan	1973
Bartholomew, A. Wayne	Prof	Ind-So Bend	AET	PHD	72	Cornell	1972
Bartlett, Randall	Prof	Smith	AHR	PHD	71	Stanford	1979
Bartlett, Robin L.	Prof	Denison	AJ	PHD	74	Mich St	1973
Laura C. Harris Chair							
Bartlett, Sue A.	Lect	South Fla	A	MA	93	S Fla	1994
Bartley, Alan	Asst	Transylvania		PHD	99	Vanderbilt	1999
Barton, William E.	Retir	Colorado Col		PHD	70	Missouri	1958
Barut, Yasar	Asst	Rice		PHD	98	Purdue	7-98
Baryla, Edward	Asst	East Tenn St		PHD	95	Alabama	1995
Barzel, Yoram	Prof	U Washington		PHD	61	Chicago	1961
Basch, Donald L.	Prof	Simmons	D	PHD	77	Yale	1980
Bashir, Abdel H.	H-As	Grambling St		PHD	90	Wisconsin	1990
Baskan, Asuman	Assoc	Allegheny	CDFE	PHD	88	Lehigh	1987
Basmann, Robert L.	Prof	SUNY-Bingham	C	PHD	66	Iowa St	1988
Bassett, Gilbert W.	Prof	Ill-Chicago	C	PHD	73	Michigan	1973
Bassetto, Marco	Asst	Northwestern		PHD	98	Chicago	1998
Bastin, Hamid	Prof	Shippensburg		PHD	89	Geo St	1989
Basu, Arnab	Asst	Wm & Mary		PHD	97	J Hopkins	1998
Basu, Atin	Asst	Va Military		PHD	98	Miss	1999
Basu, Bharati	Prof	Cen Michigan	FODJ	PHD	82	Rochester	1990
Basu, Kaushik	Prof	Cornell	DHLO	PHD	76	LondonEc	
Basu, Parantap	Assoc	Fordham		PHD	85	Ca-SnBarb	1988
Basu, Susanto	Assoc	Michigan		PHD	92	Harvard	1992
Batabyal, Amitrajeet	Assoc	Utah State	FOQ	PHD	94	Berkeley	1995
Batavia, Bala	Prof	DePaul	CD	PHD	74	N Car St	1976

Name	Rank	School	Fields	Degree	Yr	Institution	Year
Batchelder, Ronald W.	Prof	Pepper-Malib	DEFK	PHD	75	UCLA	1984
Bateman, Bradley W.	Prof	Grinnell	B	PHD	84	Kentucky	1987
Bateman, Fred	Prof	Georgia	N	PHD	65	Tulane	1991
Nicholas A. Beadles Professor							
Bates, Laurie	Assoc	Bryant	HD	PHD	89	Conn	
Bates, Lawrence W.	Assoc	E Illinois		PHD	75	Tx-Austin	1970
Batie, Clarence	Inst	Txs Southern		MA		Prairie	
Batina, Raymond	Assoc	Wash State		PHD	85	Minnesota	1985
Batra, Raveendra N.	Prof	So Methodist	F	PHD	69	S Illinois	1973
Battacharya, Radha S.	Asst	CS-Fullerton	E	PHD	90	Penn St	1990
Battaglia, Kari L.	Lect	North Texas	A	MA		North Tx	1987
Battalio, Ray	Prof	Texas A&M	C	PHD	69	Purdue	1969
Mary Tucker Currie Professorship in Liberal Arts							
Battigalli, Pierpaolo	Prof	European U Inst		DE	92	Italian Min	1999
Baum, Christopher F.	Assoc	Boston Coll	CE	PHD	77	Michigan	1977
Baum, Donald N.	Assoc	Neb-Omaha	HD	PHD	79	Claremont	1987
Baum, Sandra R.	Prof	Skidmore		PHD	81	Columbia	1987
Baumol, William J.	Prof	New York U	D	PHD	49	London	1971
Bausor, Randall S.	Prof	Massachusett		PHD	78	Duke	1979
Bawuah, Kwado	Assoc	Virginia St		PHD	83	Va Tech	1987
Bawumia, Muhumudu	Asst	Baylor	F	PHD	95	Simon Fr	1996
Baxter, Marianne	Prof	Virginia	FE	PHD	84	Chicago	1993
Bay, John W.	Prof	So Maine	E	PHD	66	Boston C	1965
Bayazitoglu, Berna	Asst	Bogazici	CDO	PHD	96	Cornell	1996
Baye, Michael R.	Prof	Indiana	DIO	PHD	83	Purdue	1997
Bayer, Amanda	Assoc	Swarthmore	DJ	PHD	95	Yale	1992
Bayer, Arthur A.	Prof	Babson	AH	PHD	68	Mich St	1978
Bays, Carson W.	C-Pr	East Carol	IKL	PHD	74	Michigan	1982
Baytas, Ahmet	Assoc	Montclair St		PHD	86	Illinois	1988
Beall, Larry G.	Assoc	Virg Comm		PHD	73	Duke	1970
Beals, Ralph E.	Prof	Amherst	ACO	PHD	70	MIT	1966
Clarence Francis Professor of Economics							
Beam, Robert D.	Prof	Wis-Superior		PHD	80	Cincinnati	1980
Bean, Richard N.	Assoc	Houston	N	PHD	71	U Wash	1970
Bear, Donald V. T.	Emer	Ca-San Diego	AE	PHD	63	Stanford	1965
Beard, Thomas R.	Emer	Louisiana St	E	PHD	63	Duke	1961
LSU Alumni Professor Emeritus							
Beard, Thomas Randolph	Assoc	Auburn		PHD	88	Vanderbilt	1988
Beardsley, George L.	Prof	Cal Poly-SLO		PHD	74	Penn	1975
Bearse, Peter	Asst	N Car-Greens	CH	PHD	95	Virginia	1998
Beasley, Christine Daughtry	Retir	Campbell		MA		E Carol	1969
Beaton, C. Russell	Prof	Willamette		PHD	68	Claremont	1971
Beaty, William L.	Asst	Tarleton St	ADR	MS	73	Utah St	1985
Beauchemin, Kenneth	Asst	Colorado		PHD	95	Iowa	1995
Beaumont, Marion S.	Prof	CS-Long Bch		PHD	67	Claremont	1967
Beaumont, Paul M.	Assoc	Florida St	C	PHD	84	Penn	1988
Bechdolt, Burley V.	Emer	No Illinois	C	PHD	70	S Calif	1970
Beck, Edward J.	Asst	SUNY-Oneonta	DE	MBA	82	Syracuse	1977
Beck, John H.	D-Ac	Gonzaga	BH	PHD	76	Mich St	1988
Beck, Paul	Assoc	Graceland	AFJE	PHD	94	Missouri	1992
Beck, Stacie E.	Assoc	Delaware	GEF	PHD	87	Penn	1986
Beck, William C. II	Retir	USAF Academy		MA		Michigan	
Becker, Anthony D.	Assoc	St Olaf	DLC	PHD	86	Duke	1987
Becker, Charles McVey	Assoc	Tx Christian		PHD	66	Arizona	1967
Becker, Gary S.	Prof	Chicago		PHD	55	Chicago	1970
Becker, Gilbert D.	Asst	St Anselm	AD	PHD	83	Boston C	1987
Becker, Klaus G.	Assoc	Texas Tech		PHD	87	Kansas	1989
Becker, Robert	C-Pr	Indiana		PHD	78	Rochester	1978
Becker, William	Prof	Indiana		PHD	73	Pittsburgh	1979
Becker, William S.	Prof	Colorado Col		PHD	70	LSU	1970
Beckman, Mary P.	Assoc	Lafayette	OP	PHD	86	Notre Dm	1985
Beckman, Steven R.	Assoc	Colo-Denver	F	PHD	82	Ca-Davis	1988
Bedard, Kelly	Asst	Claremont		PHD	96	Queen's	1998
Bedient, John B.	Assoc	Albion		MBA	79	Indiana	1984
Bee, Richard H.	Prof	Youngstown		DBA	76	Kent St	1966
Beelders, Owen	Asst	Emory	CG	PHD	98	Rochester	1997
Beeson, Bennie E. Jr.	Retir	Radford		PHD	71	Tennessee	
Beeson, Patricia E.	Assoc	Pittsburgh	R	PHD	83	Oregon	1983
Begin, Floyd C.	Prof	St Ambrose		PHD	74	Iowa	1985
Behar, Cem	Prof	Bogazici	BJT	PHD	72	Paris	1977
Behdad, Sohrab	Prof	Denison	BF	PHD	73	Mich St	1985
Behr, Todd	Asst	E Stroudsbur	EH	MBA	78	Lehigh	1989
Behrman, Jere R.	Prof	Pennsylvania	OJL	PHD	66	MIT	1965
William R. Kenan Jr. Professor of Economics							
Beil, Richard O.	Assoc	Auburn		PHD	88	Tx A&M	1988
Bej, Emil	Retir	Shippensburg		DR	70	Ukranian	1969
Bekar, Clifford T.	Asst	Lewis & Clrk	HPIL	ABD		Simon Fr	
Bekdache, Basma	Asst	Wayne State		PHD	94	Boston C	1994
Beladi, Hamid	Prof	Dayton	F	PHD	83	Utah St	1988
Belay, Halefom	Asst	Whitman	CEO	PHD	96	SUNY-Bin	1996

Name	Rank	School	Fields	Degree	Yr	Degree School	Year
Bell, Christine A.	C-As	Albright		MBA	77	Temple	1989
Bell, Christopher Ross	Assoc	N Car-Ashvil	AGHL	PHD	87	Penn	1989
Bell, Duran	Prof	Calif-Irvine		PHD	65	Berkeley	1965
Bell, Edward B.	Assoc	Cleveland St	DHJ	PHD	73	Ohio St	1971
Bell, Frederick W.	Retir	Florida St	7-97	PHD	64	Wayne St	1962
Bell, Joe A.	Prof	SW Missouri		PHD	80	Okla St	1971
Bell, Peter F,	C-Ac	SUNY-Purchas		PHD	68	Wisconsin	1971
Bell, Robert	Prof	CUNY-Brookly	M	PHD	72	Brunel	1986
Bellamy, D. Scott	Assoc	Southern Ark	I	PHD		Kentucky	1993
Bellante, Donald M.	Prof	South Fla	J	PHD	71	Fla St	1985
Bellemore, Fred A.	Asst	Vassar	H	PHD	92	MIT	1992
Bellico, Russell P.	Prof	Westfield St		EDD		Mass	1970
Bellinger, William K.	Asst	Dickinson Cl	JE	PHD	85	Nrthwstrn	1981
Belman, Dale	Assoc	Wis-Milwauke		PHD	86	Wisconsin	1985
Belongia, Michael T.	Prof	Mississippi	E	PHD	82	N Car St	1993
Belotti, Mario L.	Prof	Santa Clara		PHD	69	Tx-Austin	1959
W. M. Keck Foundation Professor-Director, Institute of Agribusiness							
Belsley, David A.	Prof	Boston Coll	CD	PHD	65	MIT	1966
Belton, Willie J. Jr.	Assoc	Georgia Tech	E	PHD	86	Penn St	1987
Ben-Gad, Michael	Asst	Houston	E	PHD	95	Chicago	1995
Ben-Zion, Barry	Prof	Sonoma State		PHD	73	Oregon	1969
Benabou, Roland Jean-Marc	Prof	New York U	D	PHD	86	MIT	1994
Benavides, Adolfo	Assoc	Tx A&M-C Chr	AO	PHD	82	Wash St	9-96
Benavie, Arthur	Prof	No Carolina	AE	PHD	63	Michigan	1967
Benchekroun, Hassan	Asst	Fla Atlantic	DL	PHD	98	Laval	1999
Bender, Keith	Asst	Wis-Milwauke		PHD	94	Duke	1999
Benedict, Mary Ellen	Assoc	Bowling Gr		PHD	91	Car Mellon	1991
Benefield, Michael E.	Asst	Ark Tech		PHD	89	Purdue	1995
Benesh, Diann	Lect	Wis-Eau Clar	A	ABD		Va Tech	1976
Benhabib, Jess	Prof	New York U	EO	PHD	76	Columbia	1980
Benham, Lee K.	Prof	Wash Univ	LP	PHD	70	Stanford	1974
Benito, Carlos	C-Pr	Sonoma State		PHD	73	Ca-Davis	1990
Benjamin, Daniel K.	Prof	Clemson	DEGJ	PHD	75	UCLA	1985
Benjamin, Julian	Prof	N Carol A&T		PHD	77	SUNY-Buf	
Bennett, Charles A.	Asst	Gannon	A	MA	68	Fordham	1968
Bennett, Doris S.	Assoc	Jacksonvl St		PHD	79	Alabama	1986
Bennett, James T.	Prof	George Mason		PHD	70	Case Wes	1975
William P. Snavely Professor of Economics							
Bennett, R. J.	Retir	Aquinas		PHD		St Louis	1969
Bennett, Randall W.	Prof	Gonzaga	HL	PHD	84	Mich St	1988
Bennett, Richard E.	Retir	Kent State	C	PHD	70	Ohio St	1968
Bennett, Robert L.	Retir	Maryland		PHD	63	Tx-Austin	1966
Benoit, Jean-Pierre	Assoc	New York U	D	PHD	83	Stanford	1989
Benson, Bruce L.	Prof	Florida St	K	PHD	78	Tx A&M	1987
VeDoe Moore Distinguished Research Professor							
Benson, C. Scott	Assoc	Idaho State	ABEF	PHD	88	Ca-Davis	1990
Benston, George J.	Prof	Emory	GKLM	PHD	63	Chicago	9-87
John H. Harland Professor of Finance, Economics, and Accounting							
Bentley, Jerome T.	Assoc	Rider	D	PHD	74	Pittsburgh	1974
Bentley, Marion	ExtSp	Utah State	H	MPA	70	NYU	1975
Benz, George A.	Retir	St Marys-Txs		PHD	69	Oklahoma	1985
Benzing, Cynthia D.	C-Pr	West Chester	AEG	PHD	87	Drexel	1988
Bera, Anil K.	Prof	Illinois	C	PHD	83	Austr Natl	1983
Berdell, John	Assoc	DePaul	NE	PHD	91	Cambridge	1991
Bereskin, C. Gregory	Assoc	St Ambrose		PHD	83	Missouri	1991
Berg, Sanford V.	Prof	Florida	T	PHD	70	Yale	1971
Exec Dir Public Utility Research Ctr;Public Utilities & Distinguished Serv Pr							
Bergan, Daniel J.	Assoc	NE Illinois		PHD	85	Tx Tech	
Bergemann, Dirk	Asst	Yale		PHD	94	Penn	
Berger, David E.	Prof	Mass-Dartmou	IJOR	PHD	72	Wash U	1972
Berger, George	C-Ac	Pitts-Johnst	EJK	PHD	87	Ca-Davis	1989
Berger, Mark C.	Prof	Kentucky	J	PHD	81	Ohio St	1981
Bergeron, Suzanne	VAsst	Mich-Dearbor	BENO	PHD	98	Notre Dm	1998
Bergin, Paul	Asst	Cal-Davis	EF	PHD	96	Yale	1996
Bergman, Lila	Lect	CUNY-Hunter		MBA	79	Fordham	9-85
Bergmann, Barbara R.	Retir	American U		PHD	59	Harvard	1988
Bergsten, Gordon S.	Assoc	Dickinson Cl	BNDE	PHD	77	Berkeley	1984
Bergstrom, Theodore C.	Retir	Michigan		PHD	67	Stanford	1975
Berik, Gunseli	Asst	Utah		PHD	86	Mass	1994
Berkowitz, Daniel	Asst	Pittsburgh	GH	PHD	88	Columbia	1992
Berliant, Marcus C.	Prof	Wash Univ	DHR	PHD	82	Berkeley	1994
Berman, Eli	Asst	Boston Univ	CJ	PHD	93	Harvard	1993
Bernanke, Ben S.	C-Pr	Princeton		PHD	79	MIT	1985
Bernard, James A. Jr.	Assoc	Valparaiso	AOP	PHD	72	Notre Dm	1968
Bernasek, Alexandra	Assoc	Colorado St	DA	PHD	92	Michigan	1992
Berney, Robert E.	Prof	Wash State		PHD	63	Wisconsin	1966
Bernhardt, Dan	Asst	Illinois	DGJL	PHD	86	Car Mellon	1998
Bernheim, B. Douglas	Prof	Stanford		PHD	82	MIT	1994
Lewis and Virginia Eaton Professor in Economics							
Bernhofen, Daniel	Asst	Clark		PHD	94	Syracuse	1989

Name	Rank	School	Fields	Degree	Yr	Institution	Year
Bernstein, Richard E.	Assoc	Temple	MG	PHD	73	Brown	1972
Beron, Kurt J.	H-Ac	Texas-Dallas		PHD	85	N Carol	1985
Berrens, Robert	Asst	New Mexico	DQ	PHD	93	Oregon St	1994
Berri, David	Asst	Coe		PHD	97	Colo St	1998
Berry, Brian J. L.	Prof	Texas-Dallas		PHD	58	U Wash	
L. V. Berkner Professor							
Berry, Charles A.	Prof	Cincinnati	O	PHD	68	Cincinnati	1961
Berry, Dale A.	Prof	Drake		PHD	66	Indiana	1962
Berry, Stanley Keith	Assoc	Hendrix		PHD	79	Vanderbilt	1989
Berry, Steven T.	Prof	Yale		PHD	89	Wisconsin	1988
Bert, Milo Douglas	Asst	Sam Houston		PHD	95	Tx A&M	1995
Bertaux, Nancy E.	Prof	Xavier	ABJN	PHD	87	Michigan	1985
Best, Michael	Asst	Berea		PHD	94	Kentucky	1996
Betancourt, Roger R.	Prof	Maryland		PHD	69	Wisconsin	1980
Bethune, John J.	Prof	Tenn-Martin		PHD	87	Fla St	
Betsey, Charles L.	Prof	Howard	J	PHD	76	Michigan	1990
Betson, David M.	Assoc	Notre Dame	HI	PHD	80	Wisconsin	1979
Betts, Caroline	Asst	So Calif		PHD	94	Brit Colum	1994
Betts, Julian R.	Assoc	Ca-San Diego	CJ	PHD	90	Queen's	1990
Beutler, Martin K.	Prof	So Dakota St	Q	PHD	86	Purdue	1986
Beuttenmuller, Doris Henle	Retir	Webster	AIJN	PHD	52	St Louis	1974
Beversluis, Eric H.	C-Ac	Aquinas		PHD	70	Nrthwstrn	1988
Bewley, Truman F.	Prof	Yale	D	PHD	70	Berkeley	1983
Bezmen, Trisha	Asst	Old Dominion	F	PHD	98	Georgia	1999
Bezuneh, Mesfin	C-Ac	Clark Atlant		PHD	85	Va Tech	
Bhagwati, Jagdish	Prof	Columbia	F	PHD	67	MIT	1980
Bhargava, Alok	Prof	Houston	C	PHD	82	London	1989
Bhargava, Ashok	Prof	Wis-Whitewat		PHD	75	Wisconsin	1970
Bhat, Mahadev G.	Asst	Fla Internat	Q	PHD	91	Tennessee	1994
Bhatia, Shyam L.	Assoc	Indiana NW	FDEL	PHD	76	Indiana	1976
Bhattacharya, Gautam	Assoc	Kansas	LDO	PHD	80	Rochester	1980
Bhuiyan, Mohammad	H	Ft Valley St		PHD	93	Florida	9-96
Bianconi, Marcello	Assoc	Tufts	E	PHD	88	Illinois	1989
Bice, Douglas	Asst	E New Mexico		PHD	96	Kentucky	1997
Bidarkota, Prasad V.	Asst	Kansas State	CEG	PHD	96	Ohio St	1999
Biddle, Jeff E.	Prof	Michigan St		PHD	85	Duke	1985
Biederman, Daniel K.	Asst	North Dakota	CGI	PHD	87	Kansas	1987
Biederman, Kenneth R.	Dean$	Delaware	G	PHD	71	Purdue	1991
Biegeleisen, J. Alan	Assoc	Mercer-Atlan		PHD	83	Geo St	1982
Bieker, Richard F.	Prof	Delaware St		PHD	70	Kentucky	
Bierens, Herman	Prof	Penn State		PHD	80	Amsterdm	1996
Bierhanzal, Elwood	Asst	Florida A&M					
Bierman, H. Scott	Prof	Carleton	DHL	PHD	85	Virginia	1982
Biewener, Carole	Assoc	Simmons	FB	PHD	89	Mass	1987
Biglaiser, Gary	Prof	No Carolina	EL	PHD	88	Berkeley	1988
Bilias, Yannis G.	Asst	Iowa State	C	PHD	95	Illinois	1995
Billes, Frank V.	C-Pr	CS-Dominguez	AENP	PHD	74	UCLA	1972
Billings, C. David	Dean	Alabama-Hunt	H	PHD	69	Missouri	1981
Billings, R. Bruce	Lect	Arizona		PHD	69	Claremont	1965
Bilodeau, Marc	Assoc	Ind-Purdue/I	HL	PHD	90	W Ontario	1996
Bils, Mark J.	Assoc	Rochester	D	PHD	85	MIT	1985
Binder, Melissa	Asst	New Mexico	FJO	PHD	95	Columbia	1995
Binder, Michael	Asst	Maryland		PHD	95	Penn	1995
Biolsi, Robert	Asst	St Peters	FG	PHD		CUNY	6-97
Birch, John W.	Emer	Wyoming	1995	PHD	62	J Hopkins	1961
Birckmayer, H. Peter	Retir	SUNY-Empire	O	MBA	56	Cornell	1983
Bird, Michael C	Prof	Colorado Col		PHD	68	Colorado	1968
Birecree, Adrienne M.	Prof	Radford	JD	PHD	83	Notre Dm	1988
Bisakha, Sen	Asst	Cen Florida		PHD			
Bischoff, Charles W.	Prof	SUNY-Bingham	EC	PHD	68	MIT	1977
Bishop, John A.	Prof	East Carol	DHI	PHD	87	Alabama	1988
Biswas, Basudeb	Prof	Utah State	CFO	PHD	76	Chicago	1976
Biven, W. Carl	Prof	Georgia Tech	EB	PHD	56	St Louis	1958
Bivin, David	Assoc	Ind-Purdue/I	E	PHD	80	Purdue	1985
Bjork, Gordon C.	Prof	Claremont		PHD	63	U Wash	1975
Jonathan B. Lovelace Professor							
Black, Dan A.	Prof	Syracuse	DJI	PHD	83	Purdue	
Black, David C.	Assoc	Toledo	E	PHD	92	SUNY-Buf	1990
Black, David E.	Assoc	Delaware	HO	PHD	69	MIT	1975
Black, Duncan	Asst	Calif-Irvine		PHD	99	Brown	1999
Black, Fischer		Goldman Sach		PHD	64	Harvard	1984
Goldman Sachs; 85 Broad 29th Fl; New York NY 10004; 212-902-8859							
Black, Geoffrey	Asst	Marist	QHN	PHD	95	U Wash	1995
Black, Stanley W.	Prof	No Carolina	F	PHD	65	Yale	1983
Lurcy Professor							
Black, Tyrone	Prof	So Miss	E	PHD	70	Tulane	1969
Blackburn, McKinley L.	Prof	So Carolina		PHD	87	Harvard	1987
Blackburne, Edward	Asst	Sam Houston		PHD	98	Tx A&M	1997
Blackley, Dixie M.	Prof	LeMoyne	DRC	PHD	84	Syracuse	1982
Blackley, Paul R.	Prof	LeMoyne	HR	PHD	82	Syracuse	1982

Name	Rank	School	Fields	Degree	Yr	Degree From	Since
Blackstone, Erwin A.	Prof	Temple	L	PHD	68	Michigan	1976
Blackwell, J. Lloyd III	Prof	North Dakota	C	PHD	73	Geo St	1980
Blackwell, Melanie A.	Assoc	Xavier	ACQ	PHD	88	Kentucky	1987
Blair, Douglas H.	Prof	Rutgers-N Br	D	PHD	76	Yale	1981
Blair, John	Prof	Wright State		PHD	74	W Virginia	
Blair, Roger Duncan	Prof	Florida	KT	PHD	68	Mich St	1970
Huber Hurst Professor of Business and Legal Studies							
Blais, Jeffrey	Assoc	Rhode Isl Cl		PHD	75	Pittsburgh	1986
Blake, Daniel R.	Prof	CS-Northrdge		PHD	71	Oregon	1971
Blake, Gordon	Prof	Neb-Kearney		PHD	70	Nebraska	1963
Blakemore, Arthur E.	C-Pr	Arizona St		PHD	77	S Illinois	1979
Blalock, M. Gale	C-Ac	Evansville		PHD	80	Okla St	1977
Blanchard, Olivier J.	H-Pr	MIT	G	PHD	77	MIT	1985
Class of 1941 Professor of Economics							
Blanchflower, David Graham	C-Pr	Dartmouth		PHD	85	London	1989
Blank, Emily	Assoc	Howard	J	PHD	85	Boston C	1985
Blankenau, William	Asst	Wis-Whitewat		PHD	96	Iowa	1997
Blankmeyer, Eric	Prof	SW Texas St	F	PHD	71	Princeton	1982
Blattenberger, Gail R.	Retir	Utah		PHD	77	Michigan	1981
Blau, David M.	Prof	No Carolina	J	PHD	80	Wisconsin	1992
Norman L. Johnson Professor							
Blecha, Betty J.	Prof	San Fran St		PHD	76	Iowa	1983
Blecker, Robert A.	Prof	American U		PHD	87	Stanford	1985
Blevins, Dallas	Prof	Montevallo		DBA	76	Fla St	1983
Blewett, Robert Allan	Prof	St Lawrence	OR	PHD	80	Va Tech	1983
Blinder, Alan S.	Prof	Princeton		PHD	71	MIT	1971
Blitstein, Allen	Prof	SW State	DFN	PHD	72	Minnesota	1976
Bloch, Howard Ruben	Prof	George Mason		PHD	64	Princeton	
Block, Michael K.	Prof	Arizona		PHD	72	Stanford	1981
Block, Walter	C-Pr	Cen Arkansas		PHD	72	Columbia	9-97
Blomberg, Brock	Asst	Wellesley		PHD	94	J Hopkins	1995
Blomquist, Glenn C.	C-Pr	Kentucky	IHQ	PHD	77	Chicago	1980
Blonigen, Bruce A.	Asst	Oregon	FL	PHD	95	Ca-Davis	1995
Bloom, Jay D.	Retir	SUNY-N Paltz	ADJ	MA	58	Chicago	1965
Bloomfield, Arthur I.	Emer	Pennsylvania		PHD	42	Chicago	1958
Bloss, Richard J.	Retir	Chicago St		PHD		Penn	1968
Blume, Andreas	Assoc	Iowa		PHD	89	Ca-SnDgo	1989
Blume, Lawrence E.	Prof	Cornell		PHD	77	Berkeley	
Blumenthal, Marsha A.	Prof	St Thomas-MN	JH	PHD	85	Minnesota	1984
Blumner, Sidney M.	Prof	CS-Pomona		PHD	68	Arizona	1967
Blush, Lawrence D.	Retir	West Liberty		MA	59	Ohio St	1963
Boal, William M.	C-Ac	Drake		PHD	85	Stanford	1995
Bober, Stanley	Prof	Duquesne		PHD	62	NYU	1964
Bobo, James R.	Emer	So Alabama		PHD	61	LSU	1978
Boddy, Raford D.	Prof	San Diego St		PHD	68	Michigan	1980
Bodenhorn, Howard	Assoc	Lafayette	AN	PHD	90	Rutgers	1993
Bodily, Jerry J.	Prof	St Marys-Cal		PHD	74	Purdue	1978
Bodo, Peter	Assoc	So Conn St	CL	PHD	91	Conn	
Bodvarsson, Orn B.	Prof	St Cloud St		PHD	86	Simon Fr	1988
Boeh, Jeanne	C-Ac	Augsburg	I	PHD	89	Il-Chicago	1990
Boerio, Eileen	Lect	Pittsburgh	D	MA	77	Pittsburgh	1977
Bogan, Elizabeth C.	Prof	Princeton		PHD	71	Columbia	
Bogart, Marti S.	Assoc	No Central	J	PHD	86	Purdue	1982
Bogart, William T.	Assoc	Case Western	HRDA	PHD	90	Princeton	1990
Boger, Dan C.	Prof	Naval Postgr	C	PHD	79	Berkeley	1979
Boggess, Trent E.	Prof	Plymouth St		PHD	80	Kansas	1983
Bognanno, Michael	Asst	Temple	J	PHD	90	Cornell	1990
Bohanon, Cecil E.	Prof	Ball State	H	PHD	81	Va Tech	1980
Bohara, Alok	Prof	New Mexico	CQ	PHD	86	Colorado	1987
Bohling, Peter H.	Prof	Bloomsburg		PHD	77	Mass	1978
Bohm, Robert A.	Prof	Tennessee		PHD	71	Wash U	1968
Bohmer, Peter G.		Evergreen St		PHD	85	Mass	1987
Bohn, Henning	Prof	Cal-Santa Br	EF	PHD	86	Stanford	1992
Boileau, Martin	Asst	Colorado		PHD	94	Queen's	1998
Boivin, Jean	Asst	Columbia		PHD	99	Princeton	1999
Boko, Sylvain	Asst	Wake Forest		PHD	96	Iowa St	1997
Boland, Dennis	Assoc	Univ of D C	BA	PHD	70	Illinois	1976
Bolch, Ben W.	Prof	Rhodes		PHD	66	N Carol	1987
Bold, Frederick	Asst	Nev-L Vegas	D	PHD		U Wash	1995
Boldt, David John	Assoc	West Georgia	AR	PHD	87	New Mex	1988
Bolino, August C.	Retir	Catholic		PHD	57	St Louis	
Bollerslev, Tim	Prof	Duke	CG	PHD	86	Ca-SnDgo	1999
Bollinger, Christopher R.	Asst	Kentucky	CDJ	PHD	93	Wisconsin	1998
Bolton, Roger E.	Prof	Williams		PHD	64	Harvard	1966
William Brough Professor of Economics							
Bom, Philip C.	Prof	Regent	FOP	PHD		Free	1983
Bombelles, Joseph T.	Retir	John Carroll	ABOP	PHD	65	Case Wes	1963
Bomberger, William A.	Assoc	Florida		PHD	73	Brown	1977
Bonanno, Giacomo F.	Prof	Cal-Davis	CD	PHD	75	LondonEc	1987
Bond, Eric W.	Prof	Penn State	F	PHD	79	Rochester	1981

Name	Rank	School	Areas	Degree	Yr	Institution	Since
Bond, Larry Keith	Retir	Utah State	Q	PHD	72	Utah St	1972
Bond, Richard E.	Assoc	Duquesne		PHD	69	Maryland	1969
Bonello, Frank J.	Assoc	Notre Dame	EA	PHD	68	Mich St	1968
Bonham, Carl S.	Assoc	Hawaii-Manoa		PHD	89	Tx-Austin	1989
Bonhan, John M.	Retir	Tulsa		PHD	65	Okla St	
Bonin, John P.	Prof	Wesleyan-CT	P	PHD	73	Rochester	1970
Bonitsis, Theologos H.	Asst	NJ Inst Tech		PHD	84	CUNY	1990
Bonsor, Thomas W.	Prof	East Wash		MA	55	Tufts	1958
Bonutti, Karl	Retir	Cleveland St		PHD		Fribourg	1965
Booker, H. Marshall	Prof	Chris Newpor	AFMO	PHD	65	Virginia	1971
Booker, James F.	Asst	Alfred		PHD	90	Colo St	1993
Bookman, Milica Z.	Assoc	St Joseph	OP	PHD	83	Temple	1983
Boor, Randy	Assoc	Mary		MS		N Dak St	
Booth, Donald R.	Prof	Chapman	AD	PHD	70	UCLA	1959
Booth, Douglas E.	Assoc	Marquette	DQ	PHD	72	U Wash	
Booth, John M.	Retir	Stetson		PHD		Penn	1973
Boozer, Michael A.	Asst	Yale	DJ	PHD	94	Princeton	1993
Border, Kim Christian	Assoc	Cal Tech	C	PHD	79	Minnesota	1979
Bordo, Michael D.	Prof	Rutgers-N Br	N	PHD	72	Chicago	1989
Borg, Mary O.	Prof	North Fla	HT	PHD	85	N Carol	1984
Borges, Antonio	Dean	INSEAD		PHD	80	Stanford	9-93
Borland, Melvin V.	Prof	W Kentucky	BDA	PHD	72	Wash U	1978
Borts, George H.	Prof	Brown		PHD	53	Chicago	1964
George S. and Nancy B. Parker Professor of Economics							
Bos, Theodore	Assoc	Alabama-Birm	CG	PHD	82	Illinois	1982
Bose, Mrigen	Assoc	Scranton		PHD	72	Utah	1968
Bose, Pinaki	Asst	Memphis	LD	PHD	90	NYU	9-95
Bose, Subir	Asst	Iowa State	D	PHD	96	Yale	1996
Boskin, Michael J.	Prof	Stanford		PHD	71	Berkeley	1970
Tully Friedman Professor in Economics							
Bossaerts, Peter	Assoc	Cal Tech	G	PHD	86	UCLA	1990
Bosshardt, William D.	Assoc	Fla Atlantic	F	PHD	91	Purdue	1995
Bostaph, Samuel H.	C-Ac	Dallas	BNP	PHD	76	S Illinois	1981
Boston, Thomas D.	Prof	Georgia Tech	JN	PHD	76	Cornell	1985
Bosworth, Derek L.	Prof	Manches Inst	JOD	PHD		Warwick	1992
Botana, Joseph D.	Asst	Lakeland	AFND	MBA		Roosevelt	1990
Botsas, Eleftherios N.	Prof	Oakland	FA	PHD	65	Wayne St	1976
Botticini, Maristella	Asst	Boston Univ	N	ABD		Nrthwstrn	1997
Bottoms, I. Glenn	Prof	Gardner-Webb		PHD	81	Geo St	1983
Botwinick, Howard I.	Assoc	SUNY-Cortlan		PHD	88	New Sch	
Boucher-Breuer, Janice L.	Assoc	So Carolina		PHD	87	N Carol	1987
Boulier, Bryan L.	Prof	George Wash	JT	PHD	74	Princeton	1981
Bound, John	Prof	Michigan		PHD	87	Harvard	
Bourque, Philip J.	Retir	U Washington		PHD	56	Penn	1957
Bove, Roger E.	Assoc	West Chester	FP	PHD	73	Harvard	1984
Bowe, Michael A.	Lect	Manches Inst	EFG	PHD	89	Carleton	1993
Bowen, Freddie R. Jr.	C-As	Norfolk St	CHA	MA	70	Wash U	1970
Bowerman, Priscilla V.		Evergreen St		MPHI	71	Yale	1973
Bowers, Patricia F.	C-Pr	CUNY-Brookly	G	PHD	65	NYU	1964
Bowlby, Roger L.	Emer	Tennessee		PHD	58	Tx-Austin	1965
Bowles, Samuel S.	Prof	Massachusett		PHD	65	Harvard	1973
Bowles, Tyler	Lect	Utah State	AF	PHD	91	N Carol	1994
Bowles, W. Donald	Retir	American U	1994	PHD	58	Columbia	1957
Bowling, James	Retir	Jackson St		PHD	85	Miss	1975
Bowman, Gary W.	Assoc	Temple	D	PHD	71	Car Mellon	1973
Bowman, John H.	Prof	Virg Comm		PHD	73	Ohio St	1981
Bowman, Judy C.	Lect	Baylor		MS	74	Baylor	1974
Bowman, Mary Jean	Emer	Chicago		PHD	38	Harvard	1958
Bowman, Rhead S.	Assoc	So Utah		PHD	75	Utah	1978
Bowman, William R.	C-Pr	USN Academy		PHD	79	Maryland	1980
Boyce, James K.	C-Pr	Massachusett		PHD	85	Oxford	1985
Boyd, David W.	Assoc	Denison	KLD	PHD	91	Ohio St	1991
Boyd, John H. III	Assoc	Fla Internat	DC	PHD	86	Indiana	1998
Boyd, Laura A.	Assoc	Denison	JI	PHD	91	Ohio St	1991
Boyd, Roy G.	Prof	Ohio Univ	QH	PHD	81	Duke	1984
Boyer, Kenneth D.	Prof	Michigan St		PHD	75	Michigan	1984
Boyes, William J.	Prof	Arizona St		PHD	74	Claremont	1969
Boyet, Wayne E.	Prof	Nicholls St	G	PHD	65	N Car St	1985
Brada, Josef C.	Prof	Arizona St		PHD	71	Minnesota	1978
Bradburd, Ralph M.	Prof	Williams		PHD	76	Columbia	1976
David A. Wells Professor of Political Economy							
Bradfield, James	Prof	Hamilton	GD	PHD	73	Rochester	1976
Bradford, Colin	Prof	American U		PHD	70	Columbia	1998
Bradford, David F.	Prof	Princeton		PHD	66	Stanford	1966
Bradford, Scott	Asst	Brigham Yg		PHD	98	Harvard	1998
Bradley, James Jr.	DLect	So Carolina	AHM	CHPL	70	N Carol	9-74
Bradley, Michael D.	Prof	George Wash	E	PHD	82	N Carol	1987
Bradley, Michael E.	Prof	MD-Baltim Co		PHD	67	Cornell	
Bradley, Steven	SLect	U Lancaster		PHD		Lancaster	

Name	Rank	School	Areas	Degree	Yr	Degree School	Since
Brady, James J.	Prof	Jacksonvil U		PHD	69	Notre Dm	
Jessie Ball duPont Professor of Economics							
Braeutigam, Ronald R.	Prof	Northwestern		PHD	76	Stanford	1975
Harvey Kapnick Professor of Business Institutions & Transportation Center							
Braid, Ralph M.	Prof	Wayne State		PHD	79	MIT	1988
Brainard, William C.	Prof	Yale	DE	PHD	63	Yale	1981
Brainerd, Elizabeth	Asst	Williams		PHD	96	Harvard	1996
Brajer, Victor	Assoc	CS-Fullerton	DQ	PHD	83	New Mex	1987
Bramhall, David F.	Emer	Colo-Denver		PHD	61	Penn	
Brandly, Mark	Asst	Ball State	HL	PHD	98	Auburn	1998
Brannon, J. Isaac	Asst	Wis-Oshkosh	J	PHD	93	Indiana	1994
Brannon, Jeffery T.	Assoc	Txs-El Paso	JNO	PHD	80	Alabama	1982
Branson, William H.	Prof	Princeton		PHD	67	MIT	1967
Branstetter, Lee	Asst	Cal-Davis	FL	PH	96	Harvard	1996
Brasfield, David	Assoc	Murray State	EGC	PHD	89	N Carol	1986
Brasington, David	Asst	Tulane		PHD	99	Ohio St	1998
Brastow, Raymond T.	Assoc	Longwood	J	PHD	87	U Wash	1987
Brat, David	Asst	Randolph-Mac	DBO	PHD	95	American	1996
Bratsberg, Bernt	Assoc	Kansas State	JD	PHD	91	Ca-SnBarb	1991
Brattin, Max Alan	Assoc	Okla Baptist		MBA	62	LSU	1966
Brauer, Jurgen	Assoc	Augusta	AFIT	PHD	89	Notre Dm	1991
Braun, Bradley M.	Assoc	Cen Florida	D	PHD	86	Tulane	1986
Bray, Robert T.	Prof	CS-Pomona		PHD	72	UCLA	1965
Brazelton, W. Robert	Prof	Mo-Kansas Ct	EP	PHD	61	Oklahoma	1963
Brechling, Frank P.	Retir	Maryland		PHD	55	Trinity	1979
Breece, James H.	Assoc	Maine	AEF	PHD	82	Boston C	1983
Breeden, Charles H.	Assoc	Marquette	DHK	PHD	77	Va Tech	1979
Breger, Gerald E.	Emer	So Carolina		PHD	64	Arkansas	
Breit, William L.	Prof	Trinity	B	PHD	61	Mich St	1982
Vernon F. Taylor Distinguished Professor of Economics							
Brendler, Michael D.	Prof	La St-Shreve		PHD	77	Tx A&M	1977
Brennan, Michael J.	Retir	Wesleyan-CT	J	PHD	56	Chicago	1974
Brent, Robert J.	Assoc	Fordham		PHD	76	Manchest	1980
Breslin, Thomas	Dean	C New Jersey		PHD	76	W Virginia	
Bresnahan, Timothy F.	Prof	Stanford		PHD	80	Princeton	1979
Bresnock, Anne E.	Prof	CS-Pomona		PHD	81	Colorado	1990
Brester, Gary	Assoc	Montana St		PHD	90	N Car St	1997
Brewer, Stephanie M.	Asst	Indiana U-PA	DHF	PHD	99	Indiana	1999
Brewton, Audie R.	Assoc	NE Illinois		PHD	80	Utah	1984
Brickley, Colleen	Inst	Plymouth St	D	ABD	78	NewHamp	1993
Bridges, Deborah	Asst	Neb-Kearney		PHD	94	Wash St	1997
Briefs, Henry W.	Retir	Georgetown		PHD	54	Geotown	1973
Brien, Michael	Asst	Virginia	JT	PHD	91	Chicago	1993
Briggs, Charles	Inst	Alabama A&M	A	MS	90	Alab A&M	1990
Briley, James	Asst	Cumberland		PHD	98	Tx Tech	1985
Brimmer, Andrew F.	VProf	Massachusett		PHD	57	Harvard	
Brinkman, Richard L.	Prof	Portland St		PHD	65	Rutgers	1961
Brister, Jozell	Assoc	Abilene Chr		MS	73	North Tx	1980
Brite, Robert L.	Assoc	New Orleans		PHD	69	Rutgers	1970
Brito, Dagobert L.	Prof	Rice		PHD	70	Rice	1984
George A. Peterkin Professor of Political Economy							
Britt, Robert D.	Retir	W Virginia	BN	PHD	66	Colorado	1968
Brittingham, Robert L.	C-Pr	Christian Br	AD	PHD	73	St Louis	1989
Britto, Ronald	Prof	SUNY-Bingham	FE	PHD	66	Brown	1974
Britton, Charles R.	Prof	Arkansas	E	PHD	71	Iowa	1978
Brocato, Joe M.	Prof	Tarleton St	CEG	PHD	81	Tennessee	1989
Brock, Baird A.	Prof	Cen Missouri		PHD	77	Arkansas	1969
Brock, Gerald W.	Prof	George Wash	L	PHD	73	Harvard	1990
Brock, Greg J.	Asst	Geo Southern	PO	PHD	89	Ohio St	1999
Brock, James W.	Prof	Miami U-Ohio	AK	PHD	81	Mich St	1979
Bill R. Moeckel Professor of Business							
Brock, John R. Jr.	VAsoc	Colorado Spr	DHKL	PHD	88	Cornell	1998
Brock, Philip L.	Assoc	U Washington		PHD	82	Stanford	1991
Brock, William Allen	Prof	Wisconsin		PHD	69	Berkeley	1981
F. P. Ramsey Professor of Economics							
Brod, Andrew C.	Inst	N Car-Greens	Q	PHD	92	Minnesota	1989
Broder, Ivy E.	Prof	American U		PHD	74	SUNY-SBr	1975
Brodsky, Noel	Assoc	E Illinois		PHD	88	Illinois	1988
Bronars, Stephen G.	Assoc	Texas	JD	PHD	83	Chicago	9-92
Brook, Kathleen	Assoc	New Mex St	E	PHD	76	Tx-Austin	1980
Brooker, Robert F.	Assoc	Gannon	C	PHD	85	N Car St	1982
Brooking, Carl G.	Prof	Millsaps	CDK	PHD	74	Penn	1981
The McRae Chair of Business Administration							
Brookins, Oscar T.	Assoc	Northeastern		PHD	76	SUNY-Buf	1983
Brooks, Nancy	Asst	Vermont	DHQR	PHD	94	Penn	1994
Brooks, Rickey A.	Asst	Freed Hardem	DEF	MBA	91	Miss	8-92
Brooks, Samuel W. III	Deces	Valdosta St		MBA		Georgia	1965
Brooks, T. J.	Asst	Wis-La Cross	CF	PHD	99	Wi-Milwa	1999
Brookshire, David S.	C-Pr	New Mexico	Q	PHD	76	New Mex	1989
Brorby, Bruce M.	Asst	Detroit Merc		MA	67	Detroit	1971

Name	Rank	School	Fields	Degree	Yr	University	Year
Broseta, Bruno	Asst	Arizona		PHD	94	Ca-SnDgo	1995
Brotman, Billie Ann	Prof	Kennesaw St	AGIM	PHD	78	Notre Dm	1989
Broude, Henry W.	Prof	Yale	N	PHD	54	Harvard	1978
Brower, George D.	Assoc	Moravian	COM	PHD	85	SUNY-Buf	1989
Brown, Annette N.	Asst	W Michigan	P	PHD	96	Michigan	1996
Brown, Barry	Lect	Murray State	EO	MS	77	Murray St	1991
Brown, Bryan W.	Prof	Rice		PHD	77	Penn	1983
Hargrove Professor of Economics							
Brown, Byron B.	Retir	So Oregon St	FNOP	PHD	64	Houston	1968
Brown, Byron W.	Prof	Michigan St		PHD	66	J Hopkins	1978
Brown, Carl C.	Prof	Fla Southern	EFHL	PHD	79	Okla St	1980
William F. Chatlos Professorship in Business & Economics							
Brown, Charles C.	Prof	Michigan		PHD	74	Harvard	1985
Brown, Christopher R.	C-Ac	Arkansas St	AEKM	PHD	89	Tennessee	1990
Brown, David G.	Prof	Wake Forest		PHD	61	Princeton	1990
Brown, Donald J.	Prof	Yale					
Brown, Douglas	C-Pr	No Arizona	OP	PHD	85	Colo St	1985
Brown, Douglas M.	Assoc	Georgetown		PHD	69	W Virginia	1972
Brown, Drusilla K.	Assoc	Tufts	F	PHD	84	Michigan	1983
Brown, Gardner	Prof	U Washington	QDH	PHD	64	Berkeley	1965
Brown, J. Michael	Assoc	W Kentucky	G	PHD	71	Kentucky	1988
Brown, James	Prof	Rice		PHD	80	Chicago	1992
Brown, James D.	Retir	So Conn St		PHD		Wisconsin	
Brown, John C.	Assoc	Clark		PHD	86	Michigan	1986
Brown, John H.	Asst	Geo Southern		PHD	89	Mich St	1994
Brown, Ken	Asst	No Iowa	CR	PHD	94	Illinois	1994
Brown, Linda K.	Assoc	St Ambrose		DBA	95	Nova SE	1989
Brown, Lisa Jo	Assoc	East Wash		PHD	86	Colorado	1981
Brown, Mollie B.	Dean	Albany State		PHD	76	Geo St	
Brown, Murray	Retir	SUNY-Buffalo	CD	PHD	56	New Sch	1967
Brown, R. Clair	Prof	Cal-Berkeley	J	PHD	73	Maryland	9-73
Brown, Ralph J.	Prof	South Dakota		PHD	70	Colorado	1977
Brown, Robert E.	Deces	NW Missouri	1994	MA	56	Tx A&I	1971
Brown, Robert W.	Asst	CS-S Marcos	GIKH	PHD	91	Ca-SnBarb	1997
Brown, William	Asst	Claremont		PHD	93	Clemson	1994
Brown, William S.	Prof	Alaska SE		PHD	77	Colorado	1991
Brown, William W.	Prof	CS-Northrdge		MA	66	UCLA	1975
Browne, M. Neil	Prof	Bowling Gr		PHD	69	Tx-Austin	1968
Distinguished Teaching Professor							
Browning, Edgar K.	Prof	Texas A&M	H	PHD	71	Princeton	1984
Alfred F. Chalk Professor of Economics							
Browning, Shirley C.	Prof	N Car-Ashvil	AEPQ	PHD	71	Conn	1970
Brownlee, Robert J.	Prof	Centre	AER	PHD	73	Syracuse	1978
Brownstein, Barry	Assoc	Baltimore		PHD	77	Rutgers	
Brownstone, David	Prof	Calif Irvine		PHD	80	Berkeley	1984
Bruce, Donald	Asst	Tennessee				Syracuse	1999
Bruce, Neil	Prof	U Washington		PHD	75	Chicago	1990
Brue, Stanley L.	Prof	Pacific Luth	ABJ	PHD	71	Nebraska	1971
Brueckner, Jan K.	Prof	Illinois	DHR	PHD	76	Stanford	1976
Bruehler, James	Assoc	E Illinois		PHD	93	Illinois	1993
Bruggink, Thomas H.	Assoc	Lafayette	CQ	PHD	79	Illinois	1978
Bruner, Bill		Evergreen St		BA	67	W Wash	1981
Brunner, Eric	Asst	San Diego St		PHD	95	Ca-SnBarb	1998
Brunner, Lawrence P.	Assoc	Cen Michigan		PHD	81	J Hopkins	1982
Brunsen, William	C-Pr	E New Mexico	GHMA	PHD	76	Virginia	1987
Brunton, Bruce G.	Asst	Jms Madison	FNO	PHD	69	Utah	1984
Bruschko, Heinrich H.	Retir	St Louis		MA	63	Minnesota	1973
Brush, Brian C.	C-Pr	Marquette	DL	PHD	73	N Carol	1968
Brust, Peter J.	Assoc	Tampa	EF	PHD	80	Indiana	1981
Bruton, Henry J.	Emer	Williams		PHD	52	Harvard	1962
Brux, Jacqueline M.	Prof	Wis-Rvr Fall	O	PHD	83	Michigan	1986
Bryant, Harold L.	Retir	Xavier	AF	PHD	67	Cincinnati	1967
Bryant, John B.	Prof	Rice		PHD	75	Car Mellon	1981
Henry S. Fox, Sr. Professor of Economics							
Bryant, Richard R.	Assoc	Mo-Rolla		PHD	84	Ca-Davis	1977
Brzeski, Andrzej	Emer	Cal-Davis	AP	PHD	64	Berkeley	1963
Bubik, Osman	Prof	Bogazici	QR	PHD	73	Ca-Rivers	1974
Bucci, Gabriella A.	Assoc	DePaul	DH	PHD	88	J Hopkins	1989
Buccino, Joan G.	Prof	Fla Southern	A	PHD	90	S Fla	1980
Dorotha Tanner Chair in Ethics in Business & Economics							
Buchanan, James M.	Prof	George Mason		PHD	48	Chicago	1983
University Professor of Economics							
Buchanan, Neil H.	Asst	Wis-Milwauke		PHD	96	Harvard	1998
Buchele, Robert	Prof	Smith	CAJP	PHD	76	Harvard	1977
Buchinsky, Moshe	Prof	Brown	CJ	PHD	91	Harvard	
Buck, Andrew J.	Prof	Temple	C	PHD	77	Illinois	1977
Buck, Donald T.	Retir	So Conn St	G	MA	61	NewHamp	1965
Buck, John	Asst	Jacksonvil U		PHD	89	Wisconsin	1994
Buck, Roland	Prof	Morehead St		PHD	79	Tx A&M	1983
Buechner, M. Northup	Assoc	St John's		PHD	71	Virginia	1970

Buehler, John E.	Retir	Arizona		PHD	67	SUNY-Buf	1968
Buettgen, Elise	Retir	Tx-Brownsvil	AFG	PHD	53	Kiel	1979
Buffie, Edward F.	Prof	Indiana		PHD	82	Yale	1992
Bugray, Ayse	Prof	Bogazici	BO	PHD	80	McGill	1985
Bui, Linda T.	Asst	Boston Univ	HLQ	PHD	93	MIT	1993
Bumgarner, Mary	Prof	Kennesaw St	AERH	PHD	84	Geo St	1985
Bumgarner, Sarah J.	Lect	N Car-Ashvil	A	MBA	82	Appalach	1990
Bumpass, Donald L.	Assoc	Sam Houston		PHD	76	Okla St	1992
Bungum, John L.	Assoc	Gustavus Ado		PHD	77	Nebraska	1979
Bunjun, Seewoonundun	Prof	E Stroudsbur	D	PHD	79	Penn St	1979
Bunn, Julie A.	Asst	Macalester	AFQ	PHD	93	Stanford	1992
Bunting, David C.	Prof	East Wash		PHD	72	Oregon	1971
Burczak, Ted A.	Asst	Dickinson Cl	ELF	PHD	94	Mass	
Burdekin, Richard C. K.	Prof	Claremont		PHD	85	Houston	1989
Burford, William E.	Assoc	Denver	AJM	PHD	70	Ohio St	1969
Burger, John	Asst	Loyola-Maryl	FE	PHD	99	N Carol	1999
Burgess, Paul L.	Prof	Arizona St		PHD	69	Colorado	1969
Burggraf, Shirley	Prof	Florida A&M	CE	PHD	68	Case Wes	1968
Burgstaller, Andre C.	Prof	Barnard	EOB	PHD	79	Columbia	1977
Burke, John F. Jr.	Retir	Cleveland St		PHD		Notre Dm	1967
Burke, John T.	Retir	W Michigan	Atg	PHD	58	Mich St	1962
Burke, Jonathan L.	Asst	Ind-Purdue/I	C	PHD	85	MIT	1998
Burke, Kathleen	Asst	SUNY-Cortlan	CD	PHD		SUNY-SBr	1999
Burke, Mary A.	Asst	Florida St	D	PHD	98	J Hopkins	1997
Burke, Melvin	Prof	Maine	O	PHD	67	Pittsburgh	1966
Burke, Ronald L.	Prof	Chadron St	MQE	PHD	70	Minnesota	1987
Burkett, Evelyn	Asst	Ark-Pine Blf		MA		Houston	
Burkett, John P.	Prof	Rhode Island	CDFI	PHD	81	Berkeley	1981
Burkett, Paul G.	Prof	Indiana St	EO	PHD	84	Syracuse	1991
Burkholder, Sue A.	Dean	So Oregon St		MA	72	Missouri	1985
Burmeister, Edwin	Resr	Duke	GC	PHD	65	MIT	
Burnell, Barbara S.	Prof	Wooster		PHD	77	Illinois	1977
Burness, H. Stuart	Prof	New Mexico	CDQ	PHD	70	Kansas	1978
Burnett, Nancy J.	Assoc	Wis-Oshkosh	E	PHD	88	UCLA	1994
Burnside, A. Craig	Retir	Pittsburgh	4-95	PHD	91	Nrthwstrn	1992
Burrus, Robert T.	Asst	N Car-Wilmin	D	PHD	97	Virginia	
Burton, Mark L.	Asst	Marshall		PHD	91	Tennessee	1999
Burton, Maureen	C-Pr	CS-Pomona		PHD	86	Ca-Rivers	1988
Burton, Robert C.	Deces	Frostburg St		PHD	62	Virginia	
Buschena, David E.	Asst	Montana St		PHD	93	Berkeley	1992
Bush, H. Francis	Prof	Va Military		PHD	89	Florida	1994
Bush, Paul D.	Prof	CS-Fresno	AL	PHD	64	Claremont	1961
Buss, James A.	Assoc	Fairfield	EOP	PHD	72	Conn	1975
Butcher, Kristin F.	Asst	Boston Coll	DJ	PHD	93	Princeton	1995
Butkiewicz, James L.	C-Pr	Delaware	E	PHD	77	Virginia	1976
Butler, Alison	Asst	Kent State	FEO	PHD	89	Oregon	1999
Butler, Donald T.	Retir	Central Iowa		PHD	60	Wisconsin	1953
Butler, James F.	Retir	Ark-Ltl Rock		PHD	68	LSU	1963
Butler, John Scott	Prof	Vanderbilt	GC	PHD	82	Cornell	1982
Butler, Michael R.	Assoc	Tx Christian		PHD	86	N Carol	1986
Butler, Michael W.	Dean	No Alabama		PHD	74	Arkansas	1973
Butler, Richard V.	Prof	Trinity	H	PHD	77	MIT	1982
Butler, Sister Agnes	Asst	Molloy		ABD		Indiana	
Butos, William N.	C-Pr	Trinity-CT		PHD	83	Penn St	1981
Byniyan, Mohammad	Assoc	Hampton		PHD		Geo St	
Bynoe, Ann	Assoc	Pace		PHD	79	NYU	1997
Byrne, Dennis	C-Pr	Akron	AJL	PHD	75	Notre Dm	1975
Byrne, Donald R.	Prof	Detroit Merc		PHD	71	Notre Dm	1966
Byrne, John	Asst	St Ambrose		PHD	96	Iowa	1993
Caassuto, Alexander E.	Prof	CS-Hayward	CEGM	PHD	73	UCLA	1971
Caballero, Ricardo	Prof	MIT	E	PHD	88	MIT	1992
Cabe, Richard	Assoc	New Mex St	K	PHD	83	Wyoming	1988
Cadet, Marc	Assoc	Grambling St		PHD	91	Kansas St	9-68
Cadot, Olivier	Assoc	INSEAD		PHD	89	Princeton	9-89
Cagatay, Nilufer	Asst	Utah		PHD	86	Stanford	1991
Cagliesi, Gabriella	Asst	Rutgers-Newk		PHD	93	Penn	
Cahill, Miles B.	Asst	Holy Cross	AEJ	PHD	95	Purdue	1995
Cahill, Neil S.J.	Asst	Creighton	AN	MA	47	St Louis	1962
Cai, Francis	Assoc	Wm Patterson	GCF	PHD	90	CUNY	1993
Cain, Louis P.	C-Pr	Loyola-Chicg	ADNR	PHD	69	Nrthwstrn	1968
Caines, W. Royce	Assoc	Lander	ALPQ	PHD	88	Clemson	1988
Cairo, Joseph P.	Asst	LaSalle	BE	MA		Penn	1963
Calabro, Eugene A.	Prof	Salem State		MA		Boston C	
Calandri, Kevin	Prof	CS-Sacrament		PHD	85	Ca-Davis	1986
Calcagno, Peter	Asst	Jacksonvl St		PHD	97	Auburn	1997
Caldwell, Bruce J.	Prof	N Car-Greens	B	PHD	79	N Carol	1978
Caldwell, Jean	Prof	Central Okla	AN	EDD	82	N Illinois	1981
Calgaard, Ronald K.	Retir	Trinity		PHD	63	Iowa	1979
Calkins, Lindsay Noble	Assoc	John Carroll	ADH	PHD	86	Michigan	1986
Call, Stephen T.	Prof	Metro St-CO		PHD	77	Indiana	1979

Name	Rank	School	Fields	Degree	Yr	Degree School	Year
Callan, Scott J.	Prof	Bentley	CDQ	PHD	85	Tx A&M	1987
Callari, Antonino	Prof	Frank & Mars		PHD	81	Mass	1979
Calvo, Guillermo	Prof	Maryland		PHD	74	Yale	1994
Camacho, Antonio	Prof	Ill-Chicago	D	PHD	65	Minnesota	1973
Cambronero, Alfredo	C-As	Fisk	DOE	PHD	92	Vanderbilt	1992
Camera, Gabriele	Asst	Purdue		PHD	97	Iowa	1997
Camerer, Colin	Prof	Cal Tech		PHD	81	Chicago	1994
Rea A. & Lela G. Axline Professor of Business Economics							
Cameron, Colin	Asst	Cal-Davis	CIJ	PHD	88	Stanford	1989
Cameron, John S.	Assoc	SW State	EFJ	PHD	79	Nebraska	1986
Cameron, Ottamise C. W.	Retir	So Miss	F	DBA	69	Indiana	1962
Cameron, Rondo	Retir	Emory		PHD	52	Chicago	
Cameron, Stephen	Asst	Columbia	JC	PHD	93	Chicago	1994
Cameron, Trudy Ann	Prof	UCLA		PHD	82	Princeton	1984
Cammarosano, Joseph R.	Prof	Fordham		PHD	56	Fordham	1955
Campa, Jose	Assoc	New York U	DF	PHD	91	Harvard	1991
Campagna, Anthony S.	Retir	Vermont	EH	PHD	66	Rutgers	1965
Campbell, Burnham O.	Retir	Hawaii-Manoa		PHD	61	Stanford	1967
Campbell, Charles A.	Assoc	Miss State		PHD	85	Tennessee	1985
Campbell, Charles W. III	Prof	Centre	AEHF	PHD	66	Virginia	1968
Blazer Professor of Economics							
Campbell, Donald E.	Prof	Wm & Mary		PHD	72	Princeton	1989
CSX Professor of Economics Public Policy							
Campbell, Everett	Retir	Pt Loma Naz	1997	PHD	76	Temple	1989
Campbell, Gary A.	Prof	Mich Tech	Q	PHD	82	Penn St	1982
Campbell, Gloria L.	Assoc	Wartburg		MBA	84	N Iowa	1979
Campbell, Jeffrey	Asst	Chicago		PHD	95	Nrthwstrn	1999
Campbell, John	Prof	Harvard	GE	PHD	84	Yale	7-94
Otto Eckstein Professor of Applied Economics							
Campbell, Martha	Asst	SUNY-Potsdam		PHD	91	New Sch	1999
Campbell, Noel	Asst	No Georgia	H	PHD	97	GeoMason	1998
Campbell, Rebecca	Asst	SW Texas St	H	PHD	98	LSU	1998
Campbell, Thomas C.	Retir	Virg Comm		PHD	47	Pittsburgh	1980
Campbell, William F.	Retir	Louisiana St	N	PHD	66	Virginia	
Campen, James T.	Assoc	Mass-Boston	EG	PHD	76	Harvard	1976
Campione, Wendy A.	Assoc	No Arizona	HJ	PHD	84	Illinois	1981
Canac, Pierre	Assoc	St Thomas-TX	F	PHD	87	Houston	1990
Canals-Cerda, Jose	Asst	Colorado		PHD	98	Virginia	
Canarella, Giorgio	Prof	CS-L Angeles		PHD	73	Virginia	1973
Caniglia, Alan S.	Prof	Frank & Mars		PHD	83	Virginia	1982
Canterbery, E. Ray	Prof	Florida St	F	PHD	66	Wash U	1970
Cantrell, Pat	Assoc	Cen Arkansas		PHD	83	So Meth	8-84
Cantrell, Richard P.	Assoc	W Kentucky	C	MA	63	S Illinois	1967
Canzoneri, Matthew B.	Prof	Georgetown		PHD	75	Minnesota	1985
Capalbo, Susan M.	Assoc	Montana St		PHD	82	Ca-Davis	1991
Caplan, Arthur	Asst	Weber State	AQ	PHD	96	Oregon	1996
Caplan, Bryan	Asst	George Mason		PHD	97	Princeton	1997
Caplin, Andrew	Prof	New York U	D	PHD	83	Yale	1995
Caporale, Barbara	Asst	Ohio Univ	EGN	PHD	94	GeoMason	1994
Caporale, Tony	Assoc	Ohio Univ		PHD	92	GeoMason	1992
Capps, Cory	Asst	Illinois	IL	ABD		Nrthwstrn	1998
Capra, C. Monica	Asst	Wash & Lee	D	PHD	98	Virginia	1999
Carbacho-Bugos, Andres	Asst	SW Texas St	O	ABD		Mass	1999
Carbaugh, Robert John	Prof	Central Wash	AFEK	PHD	74	Colo St	1985
Card, David E.	Prof	Cal-Berkeley		PHD	83	Princeton	
Cardenas, Gilbert	Prof	Tx-Pan Amer		PHD	77	Illinois	1975
Cardon, James H.	Asst	Brigham Yg		PHD	96	Princeton	1996
Carey, Cathrine	Asst	W Kentucky	F	PHD	92	Kentucky	1992
Carey, Kevin	Asst	American U	E	PHD	95	Princeton	1997
Cargill, Thomas F.	Prof	Nevada-Reno		PHD	68	Ca-Davis	1973
Carlin, Paul S.	Assoc	Ind-Purdue/I	J	PHD	85	Pittsburgh	1985
Carlisle, William T.	Assoc	Utah		PHD	75	Cornell	1971
Carlos, Ann M.	C-Pr	Colorado		PHD	80	W Ontario	1990
Carlson, David L.	Prof	No Michigan	AEN	BA		N Mich	1961
Carlson, J. Lon	Asst	Illinois St	PQ	PHD	84	Illinois	1986
Carlson, John A.	Prof	Purdue		PHD	61	J Hopkins	1962
Loeb Professor of Economics							
Carlson, Leonard	Assoc	Emory	DJN	PHD	77	Stanford	1975
Carlson, William L.	Prof	St Olaf	C	PHD	70	Michigan	1973
Carlsson, Bo A.	Prof	Case Western	DFMO	PHD	72	Stanford	1984
William E. Umstattd Professor of Industrial Economics; Assoc Dean							
Carlsson, Robert J.	Prof	So Carolina		PHD	64	Rutgers	
Carney, Kim	Retir	Tx Arlington	I	PHD	68	So Meth	1967
Carpenter, Bruce E.	Assoc	Mansfield		PHD	90	Conn	1987
Carpenter, Jeffrey	Asst	Middlebury	DL	PHD	99	Mass	1999
Carpenter, Robert	Asst	Emory	EL	PHD	92	Wash U	1992
Carr, Alan Barry	Asst	Tx A&M Intl		PHD	71	Okla St	9-94
Carr, Linda A.	C-Pr	West Alabama		EDD	68	Alabama	1965
Carrasco, Marine	Asst	Ohio State		PHD	95	Toulouse	1996
Carreno, Eufronio	Assoc	Kean	DEFO	PHD	80	Rutgers	9-88

Name	Rank	School	Field	Degree	Yr	Degree School	Year
Carrier, Ronald E.	Prof	Jms Madison	A	PHD	60	Illinois	1971
Carrillo, Raul J.	Assoc	St Thomas-FL		DA		U Miami	1972
Carrington, Samantha	Assoc	CS-L Angeles		PHD	85	Ca-SnBarb	1986
Carroll, Christopher D.	Assoc	J Hopkins		PHD	90	MIT	1995
Carroll, Kathleen A.	Asst	MD-Baltim Co		PHD	76	J Hopkins	1980
Carroll, Michael	Asst	W Virg St		PHD	97	Colo St	1996
Carroll, Richard R.	Prof	Lock Haven		PHD	73	Kentucky	1977
Carroll, Sidney L.	Prof	Tennessee		PHD	71	Harvard	1972
Carroll, Thomas M.	Prof	Nev-L Vegas	D	PHD	73	Syracuse	1986
Carroll, Wayne D.	Prof	Wis-Eau Clar	QE	PHD	84	Minnesota	1986
Carson, Katherine S.	Asst	USAF Academy	ACO	PHD	97	Colorado	1977
Carson, Leslie O.	Retir	Augustana SD	ABM	MS	63	Colorado	1958
Carson, Richard T.	Prof	Ca-San Diego	CQ	PHD	85	Berkeley	1985
Carstens, Pamela J.	C-Ac	Coe		PHD	93	Iowa	1985
Carstensen, Fred V.	Prof	Connecticut	N	PHD	76	Yale	1982
Carter, Anne P.	Prof	Brandeis		PHD	49	Harvard	1971
Fred C. Hecht Professor of Economics							
Carter, Charlie	Assoc	Clark Atlant		PHD	75	Illinois	
Carter, George H. III	Prof	So Miss	R	PHD	77	Tx A&M	1979
Carter, Jane	Assoc	Cumberland		MBA	85	Kentucky	1985
Carter, John R.	Prof	Holy Cross	CDL	PHD	76	Cornell	1976
Carter, Michael J.	Assoc	Mass-Lowell	CEQ	PHD	81	Stanford	
Carter, Shawn	Asst	Jacksonvl St		PHD	97	Tx A&M	1998
Carter, Susan B.	Prof	Cal-Riversid	AJNT	PHD	81	Stanford	1990
Carter, Tanja	Asst	Pepper-Malib		PHD	99	Ca-SnBarb	1999
Carter, Thomas J.	Asst	Okla City		PHD	87	Wisconsin	1994
Caruso, Phillip P.	Assoc	W Michigan	E	PHD	77	Mich St	1967
Carvajal, Manuel J.	Prof	Fla Internat	JITQ	PHD	74	Florida	1981
Carvellas, John N.	C-Pr	St Michael's	ACER	PHD	81	Syracuse	1974
Carvounis, Christos C.	Deces	St John's	D-95	PHD	79	New Sch	
Casario, Michelle	Asst	Villanova		PHD	91	Northeas	1991
Case, Anne C.	Asst	Princeton		PHD	88	Princeton	1991
Case, Karl E.	Prof	Wellesley		PHD	77	Harvard	1987
Casella, Alessandra	Prof	Columbia	EF	PHD	88	MIT	1993
Casey, William L. Jr.	Prof	Babson	F	PHD	63	Boston C	1964
Cashdollar, Parker D.	Prof	Tenn-Martin		PHD	71	Tennessee	
Cashel-Cordo, Peter	Assoc	So Indiana		PHD	88	Houston	1994
Casimir, Schiller	Asst	W New Eng		PHD	97	SUNY-Bin	1997
Caskey, John P.	Prof	Swarthmore	EG	PHD	84	Stanford	1988
Casler, Stephen D.	Prof	Allegheny	ACEQ	PHD	83	Illinois	1988
Cason, Timothy	Assoc	Purdue		PHD	91	Berkeley	1998
Casper, Cheryl A.	Prof	Kent State	D	PHD	75	Case Wes	1973
Casperson, Luvonia J.	Retir	La St-Shreve		PHD	74	Oklahoma	1975
Cass, David	Prof	Pennsylvania	DCG	PHD	65	Stanford	1974
Paul F. & E. Warren Shafer Miller Professor of Economics							
Cassimatis, Peter J.	Retir	F Dick-Teane	ACDL	PHD	67	New Sch	1964
Cassing, James H.	Prof	Pittsburgh	F	PHD	75	Iowa	1985
Cassing, Shirley	Lect	Pittsburgh	R	PHD	76	Iowa	1985
Cassou, Steven P.	Assoc	Kansas State	EC	PHD	89	Minnesota	1996
Catanese, Anthony V.	Prof	DePauw		PHD	72	S Illinois	1979
Cate, Thomas H.	Assoc	No Kentucky		PHD	79	Fla St	1975
Cati, Regina C.	Asst	Boston Univ	C	PHD	95	Sao Paulo	1997
Catlett, Robert B.	Asst	Emporia St		MA	75	Nebraska	1976
Caucutt, Elizabeth	Asst	Rochester		PHD	97	Minnesota	1997
Caudill, Steven B.	Prof	Auburn		PHD	82	Florida	1981
Cauley, Jon	Prof	Hawaii-Hilo		PHD	71	Colorado	
Caveny, Regina	Asst	So Miss		PHD	92	Alabama	1979
Caves, Richard E.	Prof	Harvard		PHD	58	Harvard	1962
Nathaniel Ropes Professor of Political Economy							
Caviglia, Jill	Asst	Salisbury St		PHD	97	Tennessee	8-98
Cebula, Richard J.	Prof	Georgia Tech	EDR	PHD	71	Geo St	1992
Cecchetti, Stephen G.	Prof	Ohio State	E	PHD	82	Berkeley	1991
Cecen, A. Aydin	Prof	Cen Michigan		PHD	86	Indiana	1987
Cederlund, Albert M.	Prof	Mass-Lowell	HL	PHD	75	Clark	
Ceglowski, Janet E.	Assoc	Bryn Mawr		PHD	86	Berkeley	1990
Cerf, G.		C New Jersey		MA	65	Syracuse	
Ceyhun, Fikret	Retir	North Dakota	AO	PHD	72	Wayne St	1970
Chade, Hector	Asst	Arizona St		PHD	96	Illinois	1997
Chadwick, Kathy	Assoc	St Olaf	M	PHD	83	Nrthwstrn	1985
Chae, Suchan	Assoc	Rice		PHD	85	Penn	1985
Chaffee, Donald M. Jr.	Prof	Aquinas		PHD	70	Ca-Davis	1992
Chaikind, Stephen B.	C-Pr	Gallaudet		PHD	78	CUNY	1989
Chaing, Alpha C.	Retir	Connecticut		PHD			
Chakrabarti, Avik	Asst	Wis-Milwauke		PHD	98	Michigan	1998
Chakrabarti, Subir	Assoc	Ind-Purdue/I	C	PHD	85	Iowa	1985
Chakraborty, Atreyea	Asst	Brandeis		PHD	93	Boston C	
Chakraborty, Chandana	Assoc	Montclair St	ACDO	PHD	87	Rensselaer	9-89
Chakraborty, Debasish	Prof	Cen Michigan		PHD	87	Pittsburgh	1988
Chakraborty, Shakha	Asst	Oregon	EO	PHD	99	UCLA	1999
Chakravorty, Ujjayant	Assoc	Emory	QRH	PHD	89	Hawaii	1999

Chaloupka, Frank J. IV	Prof	Ill-Chicago	I	PHD	88	CUNY	1988
Chamberlain, Gary	Prof	Harvard		PHD	75	Harvard	1987
Chamberlain, Trevor W.	Prof	McMaster U	G	PHD	86	Toronto	1985
Chambers, Catherine M.	Assoc	Cen Missouri		PHD	90	Kentucky	1990
Chambers, Donald	Prof	Lafayette	MG	PHD	81	N Carol	1992
Walter E. Hanson/KPMG Professor of Business & Finance							
Chambers, Paul	Assoc	Cen Missouri		PHD	89	Kentucky	1990
Chambers, Scott	Assoc	Linfield		PHD	88	Ca-Davis	1990
Chamley, Christophe	Prof	Boston Univ	HEO	PHD	77	Harvard	
Champ, Bruce	Asst	Fordham		PHD	90	Minnesota	1994
Champlin, Dell	Assoc	E Illinois		PHD	90	Utah	1995
Chan, Jimmy	Asst	J Hopkins		PHD	98	Berkeley	1998
Chan, M. W. Luke	Prof	McMaster U	DE	PHD	78	McMaster	1981
Chan, Sewin	Asst	Rutgers-N Br	H	PHD	95	Columbia	1995
Chandler, Clevelend	Prof	Howard	R	PHD	69	Maryland	1976
Chandrasekar, Krishnamurti	Prof	NY Inst Tech		PHD	69	New Sch	1969
Chaney, Rick L.	Asst	St Louis		PHD	84	Illinois	1986
Chang, Cyril F.	Prof	Memphis	IM	PHD	79	Virginia	1981
Chang, Fwu-Ranq	Assoc	Indiana		PHD	85	Chicago	1983
Chang, Hsin	Assoc	Toledo	OP	PHD	89	Michigan	1989
Chang, Hui-Shyong	Prof	Tennessee		PHD	73	Vanderbilt	1971
Chang, Myong-Hun	Assoc	Cleveland St	LDMN	PHD	89	J Hopkins	1988
Chang, Semoon	Prof	So Alabama	M	PHD	71	Fla St	1972
Chang, Winston W.	Prof	SUNY-Buffalo	DF	PHD	68	Rochester	1967
Chang, Yang-Ming	Assoc	Kansas State	DCF	PHD	84	SUNY-Buf	1984
Chang, Yongsung	Asst	Pennsylvania		PHD	97	Rochester	1997
Chang, Yoosoon	Asst	Rice		PHD	95	Yale	1995
Chao, Chi-Chur	Assoc	Oregon State	EF	PHD	87	S Illinois	9-90
Chao, Ching Y.	Retir	Jackson St		PHD	64	Iowa St	1972
Chao, John	Asst	Maryland		PHD	95	Yale	1995
Chao, Kang	Retir	Wisconsin		PHD	62	Michigan	1967
Chapman, Janet G.	Retir	Pittsburgh		PHD	63	Columbia	1964
Chapman, Kenneth S.	Assoc	CS-Northrdge	IG	PHD	86	Minnesota	1991
Chapman, Margaret L.	Prof	Ill Wesleyan	L	PHD	77	Illinois	1977
Chapman, Richard	Prof	Westminst-UT	JNB	PHD	92	Utah	1985
Chappell, Glenn	Assoc	Meredith		PHD		Tennessee	1991
Chappell, Henry W.	Assoc	So Carolina		PHD	79	Yale	1980
Chappell, William	Assoc	Mississippi		PHD	83	S Carol	1987
Chari, V. V.	C-Pr	Minnesota		PHD	81	Car Mellon	1994
Charkins, Ralph James	Prof	CS-San Bern	A	PHD	70	N Carol	1976
Charle, Edwin G.	Retir	Ohio Univ		PHD	58	Indiana	
Charlebois, Cecile M.	Lect	Assumption	AHJ	ABD		Clark	1980
Charles, Joni S.	Assoc	SW Texas St	D	PHD	87	Purdue	1984
Charles, Kerwin	Asst	Michigan		PHD	95	Cornell	1995
Charos, Evangelos N.	Prof	Merrimack		PHD	84	NewHamp	1983
Chase, Kristine L.	Prof	St Marys-Cal		PHD	87	Maryland	1985
Chase, Richard X.	Retir	Vermont	BE	PHD	66	Maryland	1966
Chaston, Kelly	Asst	Davidson	DL	PHD	97	Boston C	1997
Chatha, Jaspal	Asst	CUNY-Lehman		PHD	85	New Sch	
Chatterjee, Kalyan	Prof	Penn State	D	PHD	79	Harvard	1998
Chatterton, R. Edward	Prof	Lock Haven		PHD	80	Wash St	1982
Chau, Nancy	Asst	So Illinois	FO	PHD	95	J Hopkins	1995
Chaudhrey, Mukesh	Asst	Northern St		PHD	94	Clev St	1995
Chaudhuri, Ananish	Asst	Wash State		PHD	97	Rutgers	1998
Chaudhuri, Shubham	Asst	Columbia	HOD	PHD	93	Princeton	1994
Chauvet, Marcelle	Asst	Cal-Riversid	AE	PHD	95	Penn	1995
Chawdhry, M. Arshad	Prof	Calif U-Penn		PHD	74	Illinois	1976
Che, Jiahua	Asst	Notre Dame	CDP	PHD	96	Stanford	1996
Che, Yeon-Koo	Assoc	Wisconsin		PHD	91	Stanford	1991
Cheema, Balwir Singh	Retir	Wittenberg		PHD		American	1966
Chen, Aimin	Assoc	Indiana St	PD	PHD	90	Penn St	1991
Chen, Baolin	Asst	Rutgers-Camd		PHD	94	Indiana	
Chen, David Y.	Assoc	N Carol A&T		PHD	71	Wisconsin	
Chen, Heiwei	Asst	So Utah		PHD	97	Emory	1998
Chen, Jian	Lect	Ohio State					
Chen, Lein-Lein	Asst	Nev-L Vegas	F	PHD	92	U Miami	1993
Chen, Li Hseuh	Asst	CS-L Angeles		PHD	98	Michigan	1998
Chen, Thomas P.	Prof	St John's		PHD	76	CUNY	
Chen, Yan	Asst	Michigan		PHD	94	Cal Tech	1994
Chen, Yongmin	Asst	Colorado		PHD	92	Boston U	1996
Chen, Yvonne	Lect	Wis-Whitewat		PHD	98	Wi-Milwa	1999
Cheng, Benjamin S.	Prof	Southern	AE	PHD	71	Oklahoma	1971
Cheng, Chu-Yuan	Prof	Ball State	OP	PHD	64	Geotown	1971
Cheng, David C.	Retir	Alabama		PHD	73	Yale	1974
Cheng, Doris	Prof	San Jose St		PHD	76	Notre Dm	1988
Cheng, Harrison C.	Assoc	So Calif		PHD	77	Berkeley	1978
Cheng, Jen-Chi	C-Ac	Wichita St		PHD	89	Vanderbilt	1989
Cheng, Juei Ming	Prof	Georgia St	CO	PHD	68	Purdue	1968
Cheng, Ping	Asst	Salisbury St		PHD	97	Georgia	8-98
Cheng, William	Assoc	Tuskegee		PHD	90	SUNY-Bin	1990

Cheng, Xu	Asst	Cal-Riversid	CFO	PHD	99	Columbia	1998
Cheong, Kwang-Soo	Asst	Hawaii-Manoa		PHD	94	Stanford	1994
Chermak, Janie	Asst	New Mexico	DQ	PHD	91	Co Mines	1995
Chernick, Howard	Prof	CUNY-Hunter		PHD	76	Penn	1982
Cherry, Monica	VInst	St John Fshr		ABD		SUNY-Bin	1996
Cherry, Robert D.	Prof	CUNY-Brookly	AJ	PHD	69	Kansas	1977
Chesler, Herbert	Assoc	Pittsburgh	J	PHD	64	MIT	1963
Cheung, C. Sherman	Prof	McMaster U	G	PHD	91	Illinois	1981
Cheung, Kowk Hung (Francis)			DJR	PHD	89	Mich St	
Cheung, Yin-Wong	Assoc	Ca-Santa Crz	C	PHD	90	Penn	1990
Chezum, Brian	Asst	St Lawrence	JL	PHD	92	Kentucky	1995
Chhikara, Rajkumar	Retir	Iowa State		PHD	86	Illinois	1986
Chi, Wan Fu	Prof	Weber State	AC	PHD	69	S Illinois	1969
Chiappori, Pierre Andre	Prof	Chicago		PHD	81	Paris	1997
Chichilnisky, Graciela	Prof	Columbia	FCQ	PHD	74	Berkeley	1979
Chilcote, Ronald H.	Prof	Cal-Riversid	P	PHD	65	Stanford	1963
Chiles, Ted W.	Assoc	Auburn-Montg	ADJM	PHD	90	Penn St	1990
Chin, Wiliam	VAsst	Butler	H	ABD		Iowa St	1999
Chinn, Kenneth	C-Ac	SE Okla St	EC	PHD	91	Colo St	1982
Chinn, Menzie	Asst	Ca-Santa Crz	FCE	PHD	91	Berkeley	1991
Chiong, Winston R.	Prof	Mass-Boston	E	PHD	74	Boston C	1982
Chipman, John S.	Prof	Minnesota		PHD	51	J Hopkins	1955
Regents' Professor							
Chiremba, Daniel S.	Lect	CUNY-Queens	O	MA	69	New Sch	1969
Chirinko, Robert	C-Ac$	Emory	EGH	PHD	82	Nrthwstrn	1994
Chisholm, Darlene C.	Asst	Lehigh	LD	PHD	91	U Wash	1991
Chisholm, Roger	Prof	Ark-Ltl Rock		PHD	67	Chicago	1985
Chisik, Richard	Asst	Connecticut	FL	PHD	97	Nrthwstrn	1997
Chiswick, Barry R.	H-Pr	Ill-Chicago	J	PHD	67	Columbia	1978
Chiswick, Carmel U.	Prof	Ill-Chicago	T	PHD	72	Columbia	1978
Chiteji, Ngina	Asst	Skidmore		PHD	99	N Carol	1999
Chittle, Charles R.	Emer	Bowling Gr		PHD	69	Purdue	1965
Chizmar, John F.	Prof	Illinois St	CM	PHD	71	Boston C	1971
Cho, Dong Woo	Prof	Wichita St		PHD	73	Illinois	1972
Cho, In-Koo	Prof	Illinois	CDE	PHD	86	Princeton	1998
Cho, Whewon	Prof	Tenn Tech		PHD	71	Vanderbilt	1983
Choate, G. Marc	Retir	Willamette		PHD	70	U Wash	1974
Chohan, Ray V.	Prof	St Ambrose		PHD	75	Port St	1978
Choi, Eun Kwan	Prof	Iowa State		PHD	78	Iowa	1985
on leave to Chinese Univ of Hong Kong							
Choi, In	Retir	Ohio State		PHD	90	Yale	1989
Choi, Jai-Young	Prof	Lamar	DF	PHD	82	Oklahoma	1982
Choi, Jin	Assoc	DePaul	GMC	PHD	82	Iowa St	8-88
Choi, Kee	Retir	Worcester St		PHD		Harvard	1970
Choi, Young Back	Assoc	St John's		PHD	86	Michigan	
Choksy, George Dorian	Assoc	Alma	DNRC	PHD	86	Tennessee	1989
Chopin, Marc	Assoc	Louisiana Te	DL	PHD	92	Tx A&M	1992
Chotigeat, Tosporn	Prof	Nicholls St	FO	PHD	78	S Illinois	1988
Chou, Nan-Ting	Assoc	Louisville	E	PHD	86	Ohio St	1991
Choudhary, Munir A. S.	Assoc	SUNY-Fredoni	CE	PHD	85	Fla St	1987
Chow, C. Victor	Asst	W Virginia	G	PHD	89	Alabama	1989
Chow, Gregory C.	Prof	Princeton	CDEP	PHD	55	Chicago	7-70
Chowdhury, A. A. Farhad	C-Pr$	Miss Vall St		PHD	93	Miss St	1993
Chowdhury, Abdur R.	Assoc	Marquette	EFO	PHD	83	Kentucky	1989
Chowdhury, Ashok K.	Prof	Mankato St	AC	PHD	80	Iowa St	1980
Chowdhury, Ma Monayem	Asst	Cheyney		PHD	78	Temple	
Christensen, Kimberly	Assoc	SUNY-Purchas		PHD	86	Mass	1985
Christensen, Paul P.	Assoc	Hofstra	B	PHD	76	Wisconsin	
Christiano, Lawrence	Prof	Northwestern		PHD	82	Columbia	
Christiansen, Daniel S.	Prof	Albion	CD	PHD	75	Stanford	1981
Christiansen, Gregory B.	Prof	CS-Hayward	BEHO	PHD	81	Wisconsin	1983
Christiansen, Jens	Assoc	Mt Holyoke		PHD	82	Stanford	1986
Christie, Darrell A.	Assoc	Wis-Stev Pt		MS		Illinois	1964
Christofi, Andreas	C-Pr	Monmouth	CFG	PHD	84	Penn St	9-97
Christofides, Constantinos A	Prof	E Stroudsbur	CRT	PHD	77	Lehigh	1971
Christopher, Jan E.	Asst	Delaware St	CDMR	PHD	93	Howard	1994
Christopherson, Robert L.	Asst	SUNY-Plattsb	GH	PHD	90	Wayne St	1990
Chu, Betty Y.	Prof	San Jose St		PHD	73	Notre Dm	1974
Chu, Kong	Prof	Georgia Tech	OC	PHD	64	Tulane	1968
Chu, Kwang-Wen	Prof	CS-Fullerton	D	PHD	72	UCLA	1970
Chu, Shih-Fan	C-Pr	Nevada-Reno		PHD	68	Illinois	1967
Chu, Tianshu	VAsst	Ind-Purdue/I	O			Minnesota	1999
Chuak, Sam	Prof	Andrews	CD	PHD	92	Wash St	1998
Chuderewicz, Russell	Asst	Texas Tech		PHD	97	Penn St	1997
Chudzinski, James	Assoc	Heidelberg	AJH	PHD	88	Tx Tech	1988
Chugh, Ram L.	Prof	SUNY-Potsdam		PHD	70	Wayne St	1970
Chung, Hyung C.	Retir	Bridgeport		PHD	70	Columbia	1970
Chung, Jae Wan	Retir	George Mason		PHD	72	NYU	
Chung, Kuk-Soo	Lect	CUNY-Lehman		MA		Yale	
Chung, Nae Hoon	Deces			PHD	63	Mich St	

Name	Rank	School	Codes	Degree	Yr	Institution	Year
Chung, Young-Iob	Prof	E Michigan		PHD	65	Columbia	1966
Ciecka, James E.	Prof	DePaul	CD	PHD	70	Purdue	1970
Cima, Lawrence R.	Assoc	John Carroll	ADEF	PHD	82	W Virginia	1971
Cinar, E. Mine	Prof	Loyola-Chicg	ACDO	PHD	76	Tx A&M	1983
Cirace, John	Prof	CUNY-Lehman		PHD	75	Columbia	
Ciscel, David H.	Prof	Memphis	LM	PHD	71	Houston	1973
Citanna, Alessandro	Asst	Carnegie Mel		PHD	95	Penn	1996
Citzler, Annette	Prof	Tx Lutheran	A	PHD	85	Tx A&M	1977
Cizakca, Murat	Prof	Bogazici	N	PHD	79	Penn	1975
Clague, Christopher K.	Retir	Maryland		PHD	66	Harvard	1979
Claiborn, Edward L.	Prof	Va Military		PHD	64	Princeton	1981
Clain, Suzanne H.	Assoc	Villanova		PHD	84	Princeton	1987
Clarida, Richard	C-Pr	Columbia	FE	PHD	83	Harvard	1988
Clark, Barry S.	Prof	Wis-La Cross	BHOP	PHD	80	Mass	1978
Clark, Carol	Assoc	Trinity-CT		PHD	91	Cornell	1990
Clark, Carol M.	Retir	Guilford	5-99	PHD	79	Michigan	1981
Clark, Carolyn	Assoc	Wash State		PHD	70	Berkeley	1973
Clark, Charles	Prof	St John's		PHD	90	New Sch	1985
Clark, Clifford D.	Prof	SUNY-Bingham	OF	PHD	53	Chicago	1973
Clark, David E.	Assoc	Marquette	DR	PHD	86	SUNY-Bin	1985
Clark, David H.	Retir	Maine	JOA	PHD	62	Wisconsin	1963
Clark, Don P.	Prof	Tennessee		PHD	78	Mich St	1978
Clark, Gregory	Prof	Cal-Davis	NO	PHD	85	Harvard	1990
Clark, J. R.	Prof	Tenn-Chattan	M	PHD	70	Va Tech	1993
Probasco Chair in Free Enterprise							
Clark, James E.	Assoc	Wichita St		PHD	77	Nrthwstrn	1976
Clark, Joy	Assoc	Auburn-Montg	APQB	PHD	88	Tx A&M	1988
Clark, Robert	Prof	N Carol St	JD	PHD	74	Duke	1975
Clark, Wayne Walter	Retir	Brigham Yg		PHD	60	Tx A&M	1962
Clark, William M.	Assoc	Oklahoma	O	PHD	81	Virginia	1977
Clarke, Jere W.	Retir	So Conn St		PHD		Virginia	
Clarke, William A.	C-Pr	Bentley	AD	PHD	73	Rutgers	1972
Clary, Betsy Jane	Prof	Charleston		PHD	81	Miss	1984
Claudon, Michael Paul	Prof	Middlebury	FLMP	PHD	71	J Hopkins	1970
Clausing, Kimberly	Asst	Reed	ADFH	PHD	97	Harvard	1997
Clay, James P.	Prof	Fort Lewis		PHD	74	Kansas St	1982
Claycombe, Richard J.	Prof	W Maryland		PHD	80	Geo Wash	1981
Clayton, Gary E.	Prof	No Kentucky		PHD	74	Utah	1980
Cleaver, Harry	Assoc	Texas	P	PHD	75	Stanford	9-76
Cleeton, David L.	C-Pr	Oberlin	DGIM	PHD	80	Wash U	1980
Clement, Meredith Owen	Retir	Dartmouth		PHD	58	Berkeley	1956
Clement, Norris C.	Prof	San Diego St		PHD	68	Colorado	1968
Clemmer, Richard B.	Assoc	Cen Michigan		PHD	81	Chicago	1982
Cleveland, Paul	Assoc	Birminghm So		PHD	85	Tx A&M	1995
Cliff, Lee	Assoc	SUNY-Potsdam		MBA		Clarkson	
Clifford, Maryanne	Asst	North Dakota	F	MA	96	Kentucky	1998
Cline, Philip L.	Prof	Wash & Lee	C	PHD	75	Okla St	1975
Lewis Whitabker Adams Professor of Economics							
Cloninger, Dale O.	Prof	Houston-Cl L		DBA	73	Fla St	9-74
Cloutier, Norman R.	Prof	Wis-Parkside	DJR	PHD	81	W Virginia	1981
Clow, John	Prof	SUNY-Oneonta		EDD		N Illinois	
Clower, Robert W.	Prof	So Carolina		DLIT	78	Oxford	1986
Hugh C. Lane Professor of Economics							
Co, Catherine	Asst	Cen Florida		PHD	95	Rutgers	1996
Coate, Douglas C.	Prof	Rutgers-Newk		PHD	74	CUNY	1971
Coate, Stephen	Prof	Cornell		PHD	88	Nrthwstrn	
Coats, R. Morris	Prof	Nicholls St	HIRQ	PHD	83	Va Tech	1985
Cobb, Anne	Asst	SUNY-Empire	I	PHD	69	N Carol	
Cobb, Sharon	Asst	North Fla	AC	PHD	98	Florida	1998
Cobb, Steven A.	Assoc	Xavier	AEHR	PHD	74	Brown	1984
Cobb, Steven Lee	C-Ac	North Texas	AFOP	PHD	87	N Carol	1987
Cobbe, James H.	C-Pr	Florida St	O	PHD	77	Yale	1976
Cocheba, Donald John	Prof	Central Wash	QR	PHD	71	Wash St	1970
Distinguished Professor, Research (1992)							
Cochi Ficano, Carlena	Asst	Hartwick	ACDJ	PHD	97	Cornell	1997
Cochran, Howard H. Jr.	Assoc	Belmont	AFM	DA	94	Mid Tenn	1989
Cochran, John	C-Pr	Metro St-CO		PHD	85	Colorado	1984
Cochrane, Harold	Prof	Colorado St	EA	PHD	75	Colorado	1975
Coehlo, Philip R. P.	Prof	Ball State	NT	PHD	69	U Wash	1986
Coen, Edward	Emer	Minnesota		PHD	53	London	
Coen, Robert M.	Prof	Northwestern		PHD	67	Nrthwstrn	1971
Coffin, Donald A.	Dean	Indiana NW	JNR	PHD	79	W Virginia	1987
Coffman, Richard B.	Assoc	Idaho	DL	PHD	72	U Wash	1978
Coggins, Bruce	Asst	Truman State		PHD	95	Ca-Rivers	1998
Cogley, Timothy	Assoc	Arizona St		PHD	88	Berkeley	1999
Cohen, Alvin	Retir	Lehigh	FO	PHD	62	Florida	1970
Cohen, Linda	C-Pr	Calif-Irvine		PHD	79	Cal Tech	1988
Cohen, Richard H.	Asst	Lyon College	EG	PHD	92	Indiana	1998
Cohn, Cheryl L.	Asst	Millikin		DA	85	Illin St	1984
Cohn, Elchanan	Prof	So Carolina		PHD	68	Iowa St	

Name	Rank	School	Fields	Degree	Yr	Degree School	Hired
Cohn, Raymond L.	Prof	Illinois St	DN	PHD	77	Oregon	1983
Coiner, H. Michael	Assoc	Regis-MA		PHD	79	Yale	
Colander, David C.	Prof	Middlebury	ABE	PHD	76	Columbia	1982
Christian A. Johnson Distinguished Professor of Economics							
Colburn, Christopher B.	Assoc	Old Dominion	R	PHD	88	Tx A&M	1987
Cole, Charles L.	Prof	CS-Long Bch		PHD	63	S Calif	1967
Cole, Donald P.	Prof	Drew	AH	PHD	68	Ohio St	1966
Cole, Ismail	Prof	Calif U-Penn		PHD	86	Pittsburgh	1984
Cole, Raymond E.	Prof	Ark Tech		PHD	76	Arkansas	1970
Cole, William E.	Emer	Tennessee		PHD	65	Tx-Austin	1965
Colella, Francis J.	Prof	Simpson	BEFN	PHD	73	Fordham	1977
Coleman, Cyiata D.	Dir	Morris Brown	FGOR	PHD	86	S Illinois	8-89
Coley, Basil G.	Prof	N Carol A&T		PHD	71	Illinois	1966
Collier, Ben	Assoc	NW Missouri	ADFK	PHD	84	Purdue	1981
Collier, George A. Jr.	Emer	SE Okla St	ARM	PHD	78	Okla St	1972
Collinge, Robert A.	Assoc	Tx-S Antonio	FHKQ	PHD	83	Maryland	1987
Collins, May N.	Asst	Moravian	AFO	PHD	92	S Calif	1993
Collins, Susan M.	Assoc	Georgetown		PHD	84	MIT	1992
Collum, Thomas E.	Asst	NE Illinois		MA	75	Nrthwstrn	1977
Colonna, Carl M.	Assoc	Chris Newpor	AEIR	MA		Old Dom	1970
Colton, Nora Ann	Asst	Drew	FPT	DPHL	92	Oxford	1994
Comanor, William S.	Prof	Cal-Santa Br	LD	PHD	64	Harvard	1975
Combs, Ernest F.	Retir	Puget Sound	AOQ	PHD	71	U Wash	1967
Combs, J. Paul	Prof	Appalach St	MR	PHD	73	N Car St	1971
Combs, Kathryn L.	Assoc	CS-L Angeles		PHD	88	Minnesota	1986
Comolli, Paul M.	Assoc	Kansas	QF	PHD	75	Purdue	1975
Conant, John L.	C-Pr	Indiana St	DJB	PHD	84	Tennessee	1981
Condon, Carol M.	Asst	Kean		PHD	78	Columbia	9-85
Condon, Clarence M. III	Dean	Charleston		PHD	78	S Carol	1980
Congleton, Roger D.	Prof	George Mason		PHD	78	Va Tech	1988
Conhaim, Louis E.	Retir	St John's		PHD	60	Columbia	1979
Conley, John	Assoc	Illinois	DGH	PHD	90	Rochester	1989
Conley, Timothy	Asst	Northwestern		PHD	95	Chicago	1995
Conlin, Michael	Asst	Cornell	LJ	PHD	95	Wisconsin	8-95
Conlisk, John	Prof	Ca-San Diego	ET	PHD	65	Stanford	1968
Conlon, John	Assoc	Mississippi		PHD	78	Chicago	1987
Connaughton, John E.	Prof	N Car-Charl		PHD	81	Northeas	1978
Connell, Donald R.	Asst	Neb-Omaha	AF	MS	58	Ft Hays	1965
Connell, James A.	Asst	Mercer-Atlan		DBA	92	La Tech	1996
Connelly, Rachel E.	Assoc	Bowdoin	JT	PHD	85	Michigan	1985
Connelly, Robert A. Jr.	Inst	SC-Spartanbu	A	MA		Appalach	1972
Connery, Thomas	Dean	St Thomas-MN					
Conning, Jonathan	Asst	Williams		PHD	96	Yale	1996
Connolly, Laura	Asst	Oregon State	HL	ABD		Nrthwstrn	9-94
Connolly, Michael B.	Prof	U Miami	F	PHD	69	Chicago	1987
Connolly, Michelle	Asst	Duke		PHD	96	Yale	1997
Conover, Roger	Asst	Azusa Pacif		MA	82	Ca-SnDgo	9-90
Conrad, James M.	Assoc	Indianapolis		PHD	70	Kentucky	1979
Conroy, Stephen	Asst	West Florida	ACJ	PHD	98	S Calif	1999
Constantine, Jill M.	Asst	Williams		PHD	94	Penn	
Conway, Karen Smith	Assoc	New Hampshir	HJ	PHD	87	N Carol	1990
Conway, Patrick	Prof	No Carolina	F	PHD	84	Princeton	1983
Conway, William B.	Retir	Augustana IL	AIJK	PHD	69	Minnesota	1970
Cook, John	Asst	Heidelberg	AG	PHD	94	Kentucky	1995
Cook, Michael D.	Asst	Naval Postgr	J	PHD	96	Maryland	1996
Cook, Michael T.	C-Pr	Wm Jewell	EF	PHD	83	Vanderbilt	1978
John W. Boatwright Professor of Economics							
Cook, Robert W. Jr.	Assoc	Richmond		PHD	81	Va Tech	1980
Cooke, John P.	Retir	South Fla	H	PHD	67	Colorado	1968
Cooke, Priscilla	Asst	Kenyon	OQCD	PHD	95	U Wash	7-97
Cookingham, Mary E.	Assoc	Michigan St		PHD	80	Berkeley	1979
Coolidge, Cathleen J.	Assoc	CS-Chico	AHKL	PHD	83	Va Tech	1984
Coomes, Paul A.	D-Ac	Louisville	R	PHD	85	Tx-Austin	1985
Cooper, Brian	Asst	SUNY Oswego	ABJ	PHD	97	Harvard	1998
Cooper, David J.	Asst	Case Western	CD	PHD	92	Princeton	1999
Cooper, John M.	Asst	Moorhead St		MA	75	Oregon	1972
Cooper, Richard N.	Prof	Harvard		PHD	62	Harvard	1981
Maurits C. Boas Professor ofInternational Economics							
Cooper, Russell W.	Prof	Boston Univ	CDE	PHD	79	Penn	
Cooper, Thomas E.	C-Ac	Lyon College	DGHL	PHD	84	Princeton	1987
Anne J. Stewart Professor of Economics							
Copeland, Joe B.	Prof	No Alabama		PHD	74	Arkansas	1983
Coppejans, Mark	Asst	Duke		PHD	96	Nrthwstrn	1996
Coppin, Addington M.	Assoc	Oakland	FO	PHD	87	Illinois	1989
Coppock, Lee	Asst	Hillsdale		PHD	94	GeoMason	1994
Corbae, P. Dean	Assoc	Pittsburgh	E	PHD	90	Yale	1998
Corcione, Frank P.	Assoc	Scranton		PHD	75	Lehigh	1978
Corcoran, William J.	Assoc	Neb-Omaha	LQD	PHD	75	Rutgers	1980
Cordato,	Prof	Campbell		PHD		GeoMason	1993
Cordes, Joseph J.	Prof	George Wash	H	PHD	77	Wisconsin	1975

Name	Rank	Institution	Fields	Degree	Yr	Degree Institution	Year
Corkum, Keith H.	C-Pr	Nichols Col		PHD	76	Lehigh	1972
Corley, Edward M.	Prof	E Illinois		PHD	64	Okla St	1967
Corman, Hope	Prof	Rider	IJKT	PHD	78	CUNY	1988
Cornwall, Richard R.	Retir	Middlebury		PHD	68	Berkeley	1977
Cornwell, Christopher M.	Assoc	Georgia	CHJ	PHD	85	Mich St	1988
Corradi, Valentina	Asst	Pennsylvania		PHD	94	Ca-SnDgo	1994
Corrigan, Tom D.	Assoc	Sacred Heart	AFG	PHD	69	Maryland	1986
Corsetti, Giancurlo	Asst	Yale	F	PHD	92	Yale	1998
Cortes, Bienvenido S.	Assoc	Pittsburg St	F	PHD	87	Okla St	
Cosgel, Metin M.	Assoc	Connecticut	N	PHD	89	Iowa	1989
Cosslett, Stephen R.	Prof	Ohio State		PHD	79	Berkeley	1987
Costa, Dora L.	Assoc	MIT	N	PHD	93	Chicago	1993
on leave; Ford Career Development Associate Professor of Economics							
Coston, Robert D.	Prof	Geo Southern		PHD	73	Arkansas	1970
Costrell, Robert M.	Prof	Massachusett		PHD	78	Harvard	1978
Cothren, Richard D.	Assoc	Virg Tech	E	PHD	81	N Carol	1985
Cotter, Kevin D.	Asst	Wayne State		PHD	84	Minnesota	1989
Cotton, Jeremiah	Assoc	Mass-Boston	IJ	PHD	83	Michigan	1985
Cottrell, Allin F.	C-Pr	Wake Forest		PHD	81	Edinburgh	1989
Couch, Jim	Asst	No Alabama		MAS	85	Al-Huntsv	1991
Couch, Kenneth A.	Asst	Connecticut	J	PHD	92	Wisconsin	1995
Coughlan, Carmel	Asst	Salve Regina	M	MBA	90	Salve Rg	1990
Coughlin, Peter J.	Assoc	Maryland		PHD	76	SUNY-Alb	1982
Coulson, N. Edward	Assoc	Penn State	R	PHD	83	Ca-SnDgo	1984
Coultrap-McQuin, Susan	Dean	Mankato St		PHD		Iowa	1995
Coupe, John D.	Retir	Maine	ACD	PHD	60	Clark	1962
Courant, Paul N.	Prof	Michigan		PHD	74	Princeton	1973
Courbois, Jean-Pierre	Prof	Appalach St	F	PHD	68	American	1968
Courington, John M.	Prof	Cameron		PHD	87	Okla St	1979
Couvillion, L. Michael	Assoc	Plymouth St	I	PHD	82	La Tech	1980
Cover, James P.	Assoc	Alabama		PHD	82	Virginia	1982
Cowen, Janna L.	Prof	Wis-Rvr Fall	JL	PHD	79	Nebraska	1979
Cowen, Tyler	Prof	George Mason		PHD	87	Harvard	
Cowing, Thomas G.	Prof	SUNY-Bingham	LD	PHD	70	Berkeley	1969
Cox, Donald C.	Prof	Boston Coll	DJ	PHD	80	Brown	1987
Cox, James C.	Prof	Arizona		PHD	71	Harvard	1977
Cox, Larry G.	Asst	SW Missouri		MA	70	Kansas St	1970
Cox, Steven R.	Prof	So Indiana		PHD	71	Michigan	1989
Coyle, Sister Ann	Assoc	Immaculata		MA		Temple	1978
Cozzi, Guido	Asst	Cornell		PHD	98	NYU	
Cracraft, Scott	Retir	Albion	1997	MS	60	Miss	1977
Craft, Erik D.	Asst	Richmond		PHD	95	Chicago	1994
Craft, Kim	Asst	So Utah		PHD	96	Ca-Davis	1996
Craft, Rolf	Prof	Wartburg		PHD	68	Iowa St	1996
Craig, Barbara	Assoc	Oberlin	CFQ	PHD	80	Minnesota	1989
Craig, Eleanor D.	Assoc	Delaware	H	MA	61	Penn	1962
Craig, George	Prof	Okla City		PHD	68	Illinois	1982
Craig, Lee A.	Assoc	N Carol St	NJD	PHD	89	Indiana	1989
Craig, Steven C.	Prof	Houston	HR	PHD	81	Penn	1989
Crain, W. Mark	Prof	George Mason		PHD	76	Tx A&M	
Craine, Roger	Prof	Cal-Berkeley		PHD	72	Maryland	1977
Crakes, Gary M.	Prof	So Conn St	AI	PHD	84	Conn	1980
Cramer, Curtis A.	Prof	Wyoming	BK	PHD	66	Maryland	1966
Cramton, Peter C.	Prof	Maryland		PHD	84	Stanford	1993
Crane, Steven E.	Assoc	Marquette	DHLR	PHD	81	Colorado	1980
Crary, David B.	Asst	E Michigan		PHD	82	Maryland	1980
Crawford, Gregory	Asst	Duke		PHD	96	Stanford	1996
Crawford, Jerry L.	Prof	Arkansas St	ADTM	PHD	69	Arkansas	1966
Crawford, Vincent	Prof	Ca-San Diego	D	PHD	76	MIT	1976
Cray, Randy F.	C-Pr	Wis-Stev Pt		PHD	86	Kansas St	8-86
Craycraft, Joseph L.	Retir	Cincinnati	L	PHD	64	Cincinnati	1962
Craypo, Charles	Prof	Notre Dame	J	PHD	66	Mich St	1978
Creahan, Thomas	Asst	Morehead St		PHD	95	Cincinnati	1996
Creane, Anthony J.	Assoc	Michigan St		PHD	91	Virginia	1990
Credille, Ronda	Inst	SW Baptist		MBA		Drury	1990
Cremer, Jacques	Adj	Virg Tech		PHD	78	MIT	1983
Cres, Herve	Asst	Pennsylvania		PHD	94	Geneva	1994
Cribari-Neto, Francisco		Brazil	E	PHD	94	Illinois	
Universidade Federal de Pernambuco; Brazil							
Crick, Nelson B.	Retir	Portland St		PHD	67	Colorado	1967
Criddle, Keith R.	H-Pr	Utah State	CQ	PHD	89	Ca-Davis	1998
Crist, William D.	Prof	CS-Stanislau		PHD	72	Nebraska	1969
Crocker, Thomas D.	Prof	Wyoming	Q	PHD	67	Missouri	1975
Crofts, Robert D.	Asst	Salem State		MA		Northeas	
Cron, William R.	Prof	Cen Mich	Atg	PHD	73	Mich St	1982
Cronovich, Ron	Asst	Nev-L Vegas	E	PHD	95	Michigan	1994
Cropper, Maureen L.	Prof	Maryland		PHD	73	Cornell	1980
Cross, John D.	Prof	Michigan		PHD	65	Princeton	1965
Cross, John W.	Assoc	Indiana U-PA	EG	MA	68	Mass	1969
Crotty, James R.	Prof	Massachusett		PHD	73	Car Mellon	1974

Name	Rank	School	Fields	Degree	Yr	Institution	Year
Crouch, Robert L.	Prof	Cal-Santa Br	A	PHD	67	Essex	1973
Crough, B. Jane	Lect	Pittsburg St	A	MBA		Pittsburgh	
Crouter, Jan P.	Assoc	Whitman	KLQ	PHD	85	Illinois	1985
Crowder, William J.	Assoc	Tx-Arlington	EF	PHD	93	Arizona	1992
Crowell, Elizabeth	Assoc	Mich-Dearbor	DHIJ	PHD	71	Indiana	1978
Crowley, Patrick	Asst	Middlebury	BEF	PHD	95	McGill	1998
Crowther, Simeon J.	Prof	CS-Long Bch		PHD	70	Penn	1968
Crucini, Mario J.	Assoc	Vanderbilt	E	PHD	91	Rochester	1999
Crummett, Maria A.	Lect	South Fla	F	PHD	85	New Sch	1996
Cruz, Robert D.	Assoc	Barry		PHD	85	Penn	1993
Cruz-Saco, Maria A.	C-Ac	Conn Coll	O	PHD	83	Pittsburgh	1990
Cuddington, John T.	C-Pr	Georgetown		PHD	78	Wisconsin	1986
Culbertson, W. Patton Jr.	Prof	Louisiana St	F	PHD	72	Tx-Austin	
Cullenberg, Stephen E.	C-Ac	Cal-Riversid	ABCP	PHD	87	Mass	1988
Cullie, Julie	Asst	Michigan					
Cullity, John P.	Retir	Rutgers-Newk		PHD	63	Columbia	1977
Culp, David B.	C-Ac	Slippery Roc	AEN	PHD	96	S Illinois	1978
Culver, Sarah E.	Asst	Alabama-Birm	CEFG	PHD	93	Houston	1993
Cumber, Carol J.	Asst	So Dakota St	M	PHD	94	S Dak St	1990
Cummings, Donald G.	Retir	No Iowa	AEH	PHD	75	Tulane	1963
Cummings, Ronald G.	Prof	Georgia St	Q	PHD	68	Kansas	1993
Noah Langdale Jr. Eminent Scholar Chair of Environmental Policy							
Cummins, Jason	Asst	New York U	H	PHD	95	Columbia	1995
Cunningham, Steven R.	Assoc	Connecticut	EB	PHD	89	Fla St	1989
Cupper, Robert Dean	Prof	Allegheny	ACD	PHD	74	Pittsburgh	1977
Curington, William P.	Prof	Arkansas	J	PHD	79	Syracuse	1989
Curley, Michael D.	Prof	Kennesaw St	ADMG	PHD	74	Kentucky	1984
Curme, Michael A.	Assoc	Miami U-Ohio	JD	PHD	89	Illinois	1988
Curran, Christopher	Assoc	Emory	CDK	PHD	72	Purdue	1970
Curran, Ward S.	Prof	Trinity-CT		PHD	61	Columbia	1960
Currie, Janet	Prof	UCLA		PHD	88	Princeton	1988
Currier, Kevin M.	Assoc	Oklahoma St	C	PHD	85	SUNY-Alb	1984
Curtis, Fred	Prof	Drew	BJO	PHD	83	Mass	1978
Curtis, Thomas D.	Retir	South Fla	B	PHD	65	Indiana	1974
Cushing, Brian J.	Assoc	W Virginia	RCH	PHD	81	Maryland	1981
Cushing, Matthew J.	Assoc	Nebraska	EJ	PHD	85	Virginia	1992
Cutler, David M.	Prof	Harvard		PHD	91	MIT	
Cutler, Harvey	Assoc	Colorado St	EC	PHD	85	U Wash	1980
Cwik,	Asst	Campbell		ABD		Auburn	1998
Cyert, Richard M.	Deces	Carnegie Mel		PHD	51	Columbia	1948
Cypher, James M.	C-Pr	CS-Fresno	OP	PHD	73	Ca-Rivers	1967
D'Ambrosio, Charles A.	Retir	U Washington		PHD	82	Illinois	1980
D'Amico, Thomas F.	C-Pr	St Peters	EJT	PHD	83	NYU	1982
D'Arge, Ralph C.	Emer	Wyoming	1996	PHD	69	Cornell	1975
DaBoll-Lavoie, Joseph T.	Assoc	Nazareth	BHJ	PHD	89	SUNY-Bin	9-88
DaCosta, Maria N.	Assoc	Wis-Eau Clar	RO	PHD	87	Northeas	1989
Dacy, Douglas C.	Prof	Texas	EO	PHD	64	Harvard	1-65
Dadgie, Frank	Lect	Clark Atlant		MA			
Dadkhah, Kamran N.	Assoc	Northeastern		PHD	75	Indiana	1981
Daellenbach, Lawrence A.	Prof	Wis-La Cross	ADR	PHD	69	Iowa St	1969
Daghestani, Eddie	Assoc	Barry		PHD	71	Colo St	1988
Dahl, Gordon B.	Asst	Rochester		PHD	98	Princeton	1998
Dahms, Joseph E.	C-Ac	Hood	NOP	PHD	83	American	1978
Daigle, Ronald R.	Prof	Central Conn	EG	PHD	75	Clark	1976
Dalal, Ardeshir J.	Prof	No Illinois	D	PHD	77	Iowa	1977
Dalal, Meenakshi N.	Prof	Wayne St Col	OE	PHD	84	Northeas	1985
Dale, Lawrence Raymond	Prof	Arkansas St	ABPQ	PHD	79	Ohio U	1986
Dalenberg, Douglas R.	Assoc	Montana	CRL	PHD	87	Oregon	1990
Dalendina, Patrick V	Visit	Utah		PHD	93	Utah	
Daley, Edward V.	Prof	Va Military		PHD	74	Missouri	1981
Dalgaard, Bruce R.	Prof	St Olaf	EPA	PHD	76	Illinois	1992
Husby-Johnson Professor in Business & Ecnonmics							
Dall, John J. Jr.	C-Pr	Seton Hall		PHD	68	Penn	
Dalmia, Sonia	Asst	Grand Valley		PHD	99	Iowa	1999
Dalton, George	Deces	Northwestern		PHD		Oregon	
Dalton, Margaret M.	Prof	Frostburg St		PHD	86	W Virginia	1981
Dalton, W. Robert	Adj	Carnegie Mel		PHD	72	Missouri	1985
Daly, George G.	Dean	New York U	D	PHD	67	Nrthwstrn	1993
Damon, William W.	Prof	Vanderbilt	DGM	PHD	70	Cornell	1976
Damooei, Jamshid	Assoc	Calif Luther		PHD		Surrey	1987
Dane, Andrew J.	Prof	Angelo State		PHD	75	Oklahoma	1973
Daneshvary, Nasser	Prof	Nev-L Vegas	R	PHD	84	Tennessee	1990
Daneshyar, Arifeen M.	Prof	Kutztown	AE	PHD	76	S Illinois	1984
Daniel, Betty C.	Prof	SUNY-Albany	EF	PHD	76	N Carol	1983
Daniel, Coldwell III	Prof	Memphis	IL	PHD	68	Virginia	1970
Daniels, Joseph P.	Assoc	Marquette	EFG	PHD	92	Indiana	1989
Daniels, Michael J.	Prof	Columbus	JKR	PHD	79	Geo St	1980
Daniels, Rudolph	Prof	Florida A&M	DJQ	PHD	80	Fla St	1977
Danielsen, Albert L.	Prof	Georgia	MH	PHD	66	Duke	1963
Dao, Minh Quang	Prof	E Illinois		PHD	87	Illinois	1987

Name	Rank	School	Fields	Degree	Yr	Institution	Year
Dapice, David O.	Assoc	Tufts	O	PHD	73	Harvard	1973
Dardis, Rachel	Retir	Maryland		PHD	65	Minnesota	1992
Darity, William A. Jr.	Prof	No Carolina	E	PHD	78	MIT	1983
Boshamer Professor							
Darrat, Ali F.	Prof	Louisiana Te	EG	PHD	81	Indiana	1987
Darrow, John J.	Prof	Westfield St		PHD	72	Conn	1971
Das, Bhaskar	Assoc	Purdue-Calmu		PHD	91	Miss	1991
Das, Jayoti	Asst	Elon	FL	PHD	93	Cincinnati	1996
Das, Mitali	Asst	Columbia	IDC	PHD	98	MIT	1998
Dasgupta, Manabendra	Assoc	Alabama-Birm	CDHL	PHD	89	So Meth	1992
Datta, Anusua	Asst	C New Jersey		PHD	99	Wi-Milwa	1999
Datta, Manjira	Asst	Arizona St		PHD	92	Cornell	1995
Dauffenbach, Robert C.	Prof	Oklahoma	J	PHD	73	Illinois	
Daughety, Andrew F.	Prof	Vanderbilt	LK	PHD	72	Case Wes	1995
Dauterive, Jerry W.	Assoc	Loyola-N Orl	ADH	PHD	76	Tx Tech	1979
David, Martin H.	Prof	Wisconsin		PHD	60	Michigan	1962
David, Paul A.	Prof	Stanford		PHD	73	Harvard	1969
Davidson, Audrey	Asst	Louisville	L	PHD	93	Auburn	1993
Davidson, Carl	Prof	Michigan St		PHD	87	Wisconsin	1982
Davidson, Larry	Prof	Indiana		PHD	77	N Carol	1990
Davidson, Paul	Prof	Tennessee		PHD	59	Penn	1987
J. Fred Holly Professor of Political Economy							
Davies, Anthony	Asst	Duquesne		PHD	94	SUNY-Alb	1999
Davies, Ronald B.	Asst	Oregon	FL	PHD	99	Penn St	1999
Davila, Alberto	C-Pr	Tx-Pan Amer		PHD	82	Iowa St	1996
Davis, Ann E.	Asst	Marist	RT	PHD	83	Boston C	1981
Davis, Donald R.	Assoc	Harvard		PHD	92	Columbia	1992
Davis, Douglas D.	Prof	Virg Comm		PHD	84	Indiana	1987
Davis, Elynor G.	Prof	Geo Southern		PHD	78	Tx A&M	1979
Davis, George K.	Prof	Miami U-Ohio	EO	PHD	84	So Meth	1985
Davis, J. Ronnie	Prof	New Orleans		PHD	67	Virginia	1989
Davis, Joe C.	Prof	Trinity	J	PHD	71	Tx-Austin	1969
Davis, John B.	Prof	Marquette	BI	PHD	85	Mich St	
Davis, Lance E.	Prof	Cal Tech	N	PHD	56	J Hopkins	1968
Mary Stillman Harkness Professor of Social Science							
Davis, Lewis	Asst	SUNY Oswego	AFO	PHD	99	N Carol	1998
Davis, Mary	Lect	MD-Baltim Co		MBA	78	Maryland	
Davis, Tom E.	Prof	Cornell		PHD	56	J Hopkins	
Davis, Victor	Inst	Graceland	ACHD	ABD		Wisconsin	1998
Davis, W. Young Jr.	Prof	N Car-Charl		PHD	70	Georgia	1970
Davis, William L.	Assoc	Tenn-Martin		PHD	90	Okla St	
Davis, William W.	Assoc	W Kentucky	F	PHD	65	Kentucky	1970
Dawes, William	Lect	SUNY-Stony B		PHD	72	Purdue	1969
Dawson, John	Asst	Bellarmine		PHD		N Car St	
Dawson, John C.	Retir	Grinnell	1994	PHD	57	Cornell	1971
Day, A. Edward	Assoc	Cen Florida	D	PHD	76	Purdue	1983
Day, Richard H.	Prof	So Calif		PHD	61	Harvard	1976
De La Cruz, Justino	Asst	Tx-S Antonio	CEFH	PHD	94	Iowa St	1996
de la Vina, Lynda	Prof	Tx-S Antonio		PHD	82	Rice	1979
de Lima, Pedro F.	Assoc	J Hopkins		PHD	92	Wisconsin	1993
De los Santos, Tomas	Assoc	Central Okla	AEFO	PHD	88	Clark	1991
Deacon, Robert T.	C-Pr	Cal-Santa Br	QH	PHD	72	U Wash	1972
Deak, Edward J.	C-Pr	Fairfield	LRK	PHD	74	Conn	1970
Dean, David H.	Asst	Richmond		PHD	88	Rutgers	1987
DeAndrea, Vincent F.	C-Pr	Quinnipiac	CDEN	PHD	72	Mass	1968
Dearden, James A.	Assoc	Lehigh	DH	PHD	87	Penn St	1989
Deardorff, Alan V.	Prof	Michigan		PHD	71	Cornell	1970
Deaton, Angus S.	Prof	Princeton		PHD	74	Cambridge	1983
Deaves, Richard W.	Assoc	McMaster U	EG	PHD	87	Toronto	1987
Deb, Partha	Asst	Ind-Purdue/I	C	PHD	91	Rutgers	1991
Deb, Rajat	Assoc	So Methodist	D	PHD	75	LondonSE	1976
Debaere, Peter	Asst	Texas	F	PHD	98	Michigan	9-98
deBartolome, Charles	Assoc	Colorado		PHD	85	Penn	1993
DeBerry, Thomas W.	H-Ac$	No Georgia	A	PHD	94	Tx Tech	1995
DeBoer, Dale	Asst	Colorado Spr	DFO	PHD	93	Ca-Davis	1993
Debrecht, Dennis M.	Asst	Carroll		PHD	81	Iowa	1984
Debreu, Gerard	Prof	Cal-Berkeley		DSC	56	Paris	1962
DeBrock, Lawrence	Prof	Illinois	DIL	PHD	80	Cornell	1979
DeCanio, Stephen J.	Prof	Cal-Santa Br	NCD	PHD	72	MIT	1978
Dechert, W. Davis	Prof	Houston	C	PHD	77	Cornell	
DeCosmo, Michael C.	Assoc	E Stroudsbur		MBA	84	Lehigh	1984
DeCoster, Gregory Paul	C-Ac	Bowdoin	ER	PHD	85	Tx-Austin	1985
Dee, Thomas S.	Asst	Swarthmore	CI	PHD	97	Maryland	1999
Deere, Carmon D.	Prof	Massachusett		PHD	78	Berkeley	1977
Deere, Donald R.	Assoc	Texas A&M	J	PHD	83	MIT	1983
DeFina, Robert H.	Prof	Villanova		PHD	79	Wash U	1989
DeFreitas, Gregory E.	Assoc	Hofstra	J	PHD	79	Columbia	
DeGraff, Deborah S.	Asst	Bowdoin	OT	PHD	89	Michigan	1991
DeGregori, Thomas R.	Prof	Houston	O	PHD	65	Tx-Austin	1967
Dehghan, Farhad	Asst	Wis-Plattev		PHD	84	Illinois	1985

Dehijia, Rajeev	Asst	Columbia	DJC	PHD	97	Harvard	1998
Deily, Mary E.	Assoc	Lehigh	LQ	PHD	85	Harvard	1991
Deitsch, Clarence R.	Prof	Ball State	J	PHD	74	NewHamp	1974
DeJong, David	Assoc	Pittsburgh	E	PHD	89	Iowa	1989
deJong, Robert	Asst	Michigan St		PHD	93	Free	1997
Dekel, Eddie	Prof	Northwestern		PHD	86	Harvard	
Dekle, Robert	Asst	So Calif		PHD	88	Yale	1998
Del Rossi, Alison	Asst	Wyoming	HK	PHD	92	Penn	1992
Delemeester, Gregory	Assoc	Marietta	DJK	PHD	89	Tx A&M	1986
Milton Friedman Chair in Economics							
DeLoach, Stephen B.	Asst	Elon	EF	PHD	93	Mich St	1996
DeLong, J. Bradford	Assoc	Cal-Berkeley		PHD	87	Harvard	1995
DeLorme, Charles D. Jr.	H-Pr	Georgia	EH	PHD	66	LSU	1968
Delrossi, Alison	Asst	St Lawrence	HK	PHD	93	Penn	1999
Deltas, George M.	Asst	Illinois	CDKL	PHD	96	Yale	1995
DeMarchi, Neil B.	Prof	Duke		PHD	70	Austr Natl	1983
Deme, Mamit	Asst	Mid Tenn St	FE	PHD	90	Tx-Austin	1990
Deming, Jonathan C.	Assoc	Seattle Pac	BR	PHD	79	Oregon	1977
Demmert, Henry G.	Assoc	Santa Clara		PHD	72	Stanford	1968
DeMoss, Philip M.	Assoc	West Chester	AGM	PHD	69	Kansas St	1973
Demsetz, Harold	Emer	UCLA		PHD	59	Nrthwstrn	1971
Deneckere, Raymond	Prof	Wisconsin		PHD	83	Wisconsin	1993
denHaan, Wouter	Assoc	Ca-San Diego	AE	PHD	91	Car Mellon	1991
Dennis, Benjamin	Asst	Pacific	ED	PHD	96	Harvard	1996
Denslow, David A. Jr.	Prof	Florida	EH	PHD	74	Yale	1970
Distinguished Service Professor							
Denson, Chad	Asst	Delta State		PHD	87	La Tech	8-97
Denzer, Thomas F.	Retir	Rockhurst	1994	STB	62		1957
Deolalikar, Anil B.	Prof	U Washington		PHD	81	Stanford	1989
Depken, Craig	Asst	Tx-Arlington	DL	PHD	96	Geo St	1996
Depperschmidt, Thomas O.	Prof	Memphis	KH	PHD	65	Tx-Austin	1966
DePrano, Michael E.	Assoc	So Calif		PHD	63	Illinois	1963
DePrince, Albert E. Jr.	Prof	Mid Tenn St	GM	PHD	78	NYU	1991
Deravi, M. Keivan	Prof	Auburn-Montg	DFGJ	PHD	85	Okla St	1985
Dernburg, Thomas F.	Retir	American U		PHD	57	Yale	1975
DeRooy, Jacob	C-Ac	Penn St-Harr		PHD	69	Rutgers	1975
Derrick, Frederick W.	Prof	Loyola-Maryl	CI	PHD	76	N Car St	1982
Dery, George C.	Assoc	Mass-Lowell	CD	MA		Boston C	
Desai, Padma	Prof	Columbia	O	PHD	60	Harvard	1980
Desai, Suresh	Prof	Montclair St		PHD	68	UCLA	1973
DeSalvo, Joseph S.	C-Pr	South Fla	R	PHD	68	Nrthwstrn	1983
DeSerpa, Allan C.	Prof	Arizona St		PHD	70	Ca-SnBarb	1975
DeSimone, Jeffrey	Asst	East Carol	DIJ	PHD	98	Yale	1999
DeVany, Arthur S.	Prof	Calif-Irvine		PHD	70	UCLA	1984
DeVault, James M.	Assoc	Lafayette	EFQ	PHD	90	Wisconsin	1989
Devereux, John J.	Assoc	CUNY-Queens	DFO	PHD	89	Chicago	1998
Devine, James N.	Prof	Loyola Marym	AEJN	PHD	81	Berkeley	1985
Devine, Robert	Asst	Framingham		MA		Northeas	
Devino, William S.	Retir	Maine		PHD	59	Mich St	1960
DeVries, Jan	Prof	Cal-Berkeley		PHD	70	Yale	
DeVries, Rick	Asst	Calvin		ABD	95	Notre Dm	1995
Dewenter, Kathryn L.	Assoc	U Washington		PHD	93	Chicago	1992
Dezhbakhsh, Hashem	Assoc	Emory	CG	PHD	89	Ohio St	1992
Dhrymes, Phoebus	Prof	Columbia	B	PHD	61	MIT	1973
Diamantaras, Dimitrios	Assoc	Temple	CD	PHD	88	Rochester	1988
Diamond, Arthur M.	Prof	Neb-Omaha	BJ	PHD	78	Chicago	1986
Diamond, Daniel E.	Prof	New York U	DEN	PHD	58	NYU	1958
Diamond, James J.	Emer	DePaul	EC	PHD	62	Nrthwstrn	9-55
Diamond, Peter A.	Prof	MIT	E	PHD	63	MIT	1966
Institute Professor							
Diba, Behzad T.	Assoc	Georgetown		PHD	84	Brown	1988
Dibooglu, Selhattin	Asst	So Illinois	F	PHD	93	Iowa St	1993
Dickens, Edwin T.	Asst	Drew	EG	PHD	90	New Sch	1996
Dickert-Conlin, Stacy	Asst	Syracuse	GHJ	PHD	95	Wisconsin	1999
Dickes, Allen L.	Inst	Washburn		MA	70	Toledo	1978
Dickey, Steven W.	Assoc	E Kentucky		PHD	85	S Illinois	1983
Dickhaus, Elizabeth	Retir	Missouri	IN	PHD	74	Missouri	1974
Dickie, Mark T.	Assoc	So Miss	Q	PHD	89	Wyoming	1994
Didia, Dal	Asst	Jackson St		PHD	93	LSU	1997
Diduch, Amy	Asst	Mary Baldwin	J	PHD	95	Harvard	1995
Diebold, Francis X.	Prof	Pennsylvania		PHD	86	Penn	1989
Diedrich, Ernest R.	Prof	St Benedict		PHD	83	Colo St	1980
Dieffenbach, Bruce C.	Assoc	SUNY-Albany	E	PHD	72	Harvard	1978
Dierson, Matthew	Asst	So Dakota St	Q	PHD	99	Illinois	1999
Dietz, James L.	Prof	CS-Fullerton	O	PHD	74	Ca-Rivers	1973
Diffine, Donald P.	Prof	Harding		PHD	75	Miss	1971
Dighe, Ranjit S.	Asst	SUNY Oswego	AEN	ABD		Yale	1997
DiLiberto, Maryann	Asst	CUNY-Lehman		PHD	84	Columbia	
Dill, Floyd R.	Asst	DePaul	N	PHD	73	Cornell	1975
DiLorenzo, Thomas J.	Prof	Loyola-Maryl	KLH	PHD	80	Va Tech	1992

Name	Rank	School	Fields	Degree	Yr	Degree Univ	Year
DiMambro, Carol	Assoc	Russell Sage	AKP	MA	89	SUNY-Alb	1989
Dimmen, Janet L.	Inst	Wichita St		ABD	78	Ohio St	1981
Dimon, Denise	Assoc	San Diego		PHD	86	Illinois	1983
DiNardo, John	Assoc	Calif-Irvine		PHD	90	Princeton	1991
Ding, John	Asst	Framingham		PHD	91	Mass	
Dinopoulos, Elias	Prof	Florida	FO	PHD	85	Columbia	1988
DiNoto, Michael J.	Prof	Idaho	JR	PHD	73	SUNY-Buf	1970
DiPrimio, Anthony	H	Holy Family		PHD			7-98
Diskin, Jonathan	C-Ac	Earlham		PHD	89	Mass	1988
Diulio, Eugene A.	Assoc	Fordham		PHD	66	Columbia	1963
Diwan, Romesh K.	Prof	Rensselaer		PHD	65	Birminghm	1967
Dixit, Avinash K.	Prof	Princeton		PHD	68	MIT	1981
Dixon, Bruce	Prof	Arkansas	TQ	PHD	76	Ca-Davis	1986
Dixon, Warren R.	C-Pr	SUNY-Plattsb	BP	PHD	71	Colorado	1968
Djimopoulos, Evangelos	Prof	F Dick-Teane	ADEF	PHD	69	Columbia	
Doak, Paul D.	Retir	Iowa State	1994	PHD	65	Iowa St	1961
Doane, Donna L.	Assoc	SUNY-Cortlan	O	PHD	84	Yale	
Dobbert, Duane	Asst	Tri-State		MA		Mich St	1995
Dobbs, Thomas L.	Prof	So Dakota St	Q	PHD	69	Maryland	1978
Dobis, Vernon J.	C-Pr	Moorhead St		PHD	94	Manitoba	1981
Dobitz, Clifford P.	Prof	N Dakota St	ABDL	PHD	71	Colo St	1970
Dobkins, Linda H.	Asst	Emory Henry	ROF	PHD	95	Va Tech	1996
Dobra, John L.	Assoc	Nevada-Reno		PHD	80	Va Tech	1980
Doeringer, Peter B.	Prof	Boston Univ	JL	PHD	66	Harvard	1974
Dohan, Michael R.	Assoc	CUNY-Queens	PQ	PHD	69	MIT	1971
Dolan, Robert C.	Assoc	Richmond		PHD	82	Rutgers	1980
Dolbear, F. Treanery Jr.	C-Pr	Brandeis		PHD	63	Yale	1968
Clinton S. Darling Professor of Economics							
Dole, Carol	Asst	N Car-Charl		PHD	92	Florida	1993
Dolmas, James	Asst	So Methodist	CEO	PHD	93	Rochester	1993
Domazlicky, Bruce R.	Prof	SE Missouri	AK	PHD	76	Wyoming	1986
Dominguez, John R.	Prof	Wis-Whitewat		PHD	71	MIT	1988
Domitrz, Joseph S.	Dean	Wis-Whitewat		PHD	71	S Illinois	1976
Dompere, Kofi	Assoc	Howard	HEC	PHD	80	Temple	1977
Donald, Stephen	Assoc	Boston Univ	CE	PHD	90	Brit Colum	1993
Donaldson, John B.	Prof	Columbia		PHD	76	Car Mellon	1977
Donihue, Michael R.	Assoc	Colby	CEA	PHD	89	Michigan	1989
Donley, Thomas D.	Assoc	DePaul	C	PHD	93	Wisconsin	8-90
Donnelley, Lawrence P.	Assoc	Delaware	O	PHD	70	Brown	1968
Donnelly, Lawrence I.	Prof	Xavier	AJM	PHD	64	Cincinnati	1956
Donnelly, William F.	Prof	Santa Clara		PHD	69	NYU	1969
Donovan, Elaine M.	Assoc	Merrimack		PHD	81	Houston	
Donziger, Alan J.	Assoc	Villanova		PHD	72	Bryn Mawr	1967
Dooley, Michael	Prof	Ca-Santa Crz	F	PHD	71	Penn	1992
Dor, Avi	Assoc	Case Western	I	PHD	86	CUNY	1995
John R. Mannix Blue Cross & Blue Shield Professor of Health Care Economics							
Dorai, Gopal C.	Prof	Wm Patterson		PHD	67	Wayne St	1974
Dorfman, Mark	Retir	Ark-Ltl Rock		PHD	70	Illinois	1987
Dorn, James A.	Prof	Towson		PHD	76	Virginia	1973
Dornbusch, Rudiger	Prof	MIT	F	PHD	71	Chicago	1975
on leave; Ford International Professor of Economics							
Doroodian, Khosrow	Prof	Ohio Univ	QAF	PHD	81	Oregon	1982
Dorsainvil, Kathleen	Asst	Howard	CEO	PHD	97	Penn St	1995
Dorsey, John W.	Prof	Maryland		PHD	65	Harvard	1989
Dorsey, Robert	Assoc	Mississippi	ED	PHD	89	Arizona	1989
Doss, Veda	Retir	Wingate	BDJF	PHD	69	Syracuse	1984
Doti, James L.	Prof	Chapman	AEC	PHD	76	Chicago	1974
Dotterweich, Douglas P.	Assoc	East Tenn St		PHD	78	Delaware	1984
Dougan, William R.	C-Pr	Clemson	HDEL	PHD	81	Chicago	1988
Douglas, Richard W. Jr.	Assoc	Bowling Gr		PHD	75	Iowa	1976
Douglas, Stratford M.	Assoc	W Virginia	CHD	PHD	87	N Carol	990
Dowd, Michael R.	Assoc	Toledo	E	PHD	90	SUNY-Buf	1989
Dowling, Edward T.	Prof	Fordham		PHD	73	Cornell	1973
Downes, Thomas A.	Asst	Tufts	H	PHD	88	Stanford	1994
Downing, Douglas A.	C-Ac	Seattle Pac	ACH	PHD	87	Yale	1983
Downing, Paul B.	Prof	Florida St		PHD	67	Wisconsin	1980
Doyle, George A.	Prof	Assumption	FBOP	PHD	51	Fordham	1961
Doyle, Joanne M.	Asst	Jms Madison	DC	PHD	93	Boston C	1993
Doyle, William	Asst	Dallas	GN	PHD	91	Tennessee	1991
Doyle-Burke, Christine	Assoc	Framingham		MA		Boston C	
Draayer, Gerald F.	Assoc	Boise State	HNA	PHD	70	Ohio U	1976
Drabicki, John Z.	Assoc	Arizona		PHD	73	Purdue	1970
Drabkin, Eric	C-As	Hawaii Pacif	MCEF	PHD	93	UCLA	1994
Dragonette, Joseph E.	Assoc	St Joseph	CE	PHD	74	Penn	1967
Drape, James H.	Inst	USAF Academy		MPP	92	Harvard	
Drazen, Allen	Prof	Maryland		PHD	76	MIT	1990
Driscoll, John	Asst	Brown		PHD	95	Harvard	1995
Driscoll, Vincent R.	Prof	Quinnipiac	AEG	PHD	75	New Sch	1967
Driskill, Robert A.	Prof	Vanderbilt	EFM	PHD	78	J Hopkins	1992
Dropsy, Vincent	Asst	CS-Fullerton	FE	PHD	90	S Calif	1989

Du Boff, Richard B.	Retir	Bryn Mawr		PHD	64	Penn	1964
Dube, Smile W.	Assoc	CS-Sacrament		PHD	89	Tx-Austin	1989
Dubey, Pradeep	Prof	SUNY-Stony B		PHD	75	Cornell	1989
Dubin, Jeffrey A.	Assoc	Cal Tech		PHD	82	MIT	1982
Dubin, Robin A.	Assoc	Case Western	RCD	PHD	82	J Hopkins	1988
DuBois, David		SUNY-Empire	M	PHD	90	Union In	1976
Duchesneau, Thomas D.	Prof	Maine	AO	PHD	69	Boston C	1967
Dudey, Marc Peter	Assoc	Rice		PHD	84	Princeton	1990
Dudley, Dean	Asst	USM Academy	DHL	PHD	93	Indiana	1993
Duell, Dennis	Assoc	Wichita St		PHD	69	Illinois	1967
Duetsch, Larry L.	Prof	Wis-Parkside	DKL	PHD	70	Wisconsin	1969
Duffy, John	Asst	Pittsburgh	E	PHD	92	UCLA	1992
Duffy, John A.	Retir	LaSalle		PHD	71	Boston C	1964
Duffy, Martyn H.	Lect	Manches Inst	EC	PHD	95	Manchest	1972
Duffy, Neal E.	Asst	SUNY-Plattsb	CR	PHD	82	W Virginia	1982
Duffy, Niev	Asst	Hofstra	ITJ	PHD	96	NYU	
Duflo, Ester	Asst	MIT	O	PHD	99	MIT	1999
Duggal, Vijaya G.	Prof	Widener	CEDQ	PHD	67	Harvard	1983
Duggar, Jan W.	Dean	Seattle		PHD	67	Fla St	1989
Dugger, William M.	Prof	Tulsa		PHD	74	Tx-Austin	
Dulaney, Ronald A.	Retir	Montana	DJ	PHD	73	Columbia	
Duman, Barry L.	H-Pr	West Tx A&M	BDP	PHD	71	S Calif	1969
Dumangane, Constantino Sr.	Assoc	Rochest Tech	GLDM	PHD	88	SUNY-Buf	1986
Dumas, Christopher	Asst	N Car-Wilmin	Q	PHD	97	Berkeley	
Dumas, Lloyd J.	Prof	Texas-Dallas		PHD	72	Columbia	1979
Dumas, Rocky N.	Lect	S F Austin	A	MBA		SF Austin	1985
Dumont, David A.	Prof	Lander	ADJR	PHD	77	SUNY-Alb	1972
Duncan, Brian	Asst	Colo-Denver	HC	PHD	98	Ca-SnBarb	1998
Duncan, Floyd H.	Prof	Va Military		PHD	72	S Carol	1978
Duncan, Jerome	Assoc	Tuskegee		PHD	80	Florida	1991
Duncan, Kevin C.	Assoc	So Colorado	JR	PHD	87	Utah	1994
Duncan, Wallace H.	Assoc	No Arizona	EG	PHD	76	Wyoming	1978
Dung, Tran H.	Assoc	Wright State		PHD	78	Syracuse	1982
Dunham, Heather	Prof	Centenary	ADEM	EDD	99	St Johns	8-82
Dunkelberg, William C.	Prof	Temple	M	PHD	69	Michigan	1987
Dunleavy, Kevin C.	Asst	West Chester	ACE	PHD	79	Duke	1979
Dunlevy, James A.	Prof	Miami U-Ohio	JF	PHD	74	Nrthwstrn	1980
Dunn, James R.	Prof	Edinboro		PHD	81	SUNY-Bin	1974
Dunn, Leroy	Retir	Trinity-CT	1990	PHD	56	LondonEc	1957
Dunn, Lucia	Prof	Ohio State	J	PHD	74	Berkeley	1987
Dunn, Robert M. Jr.	Prof	George Wash	F	PHD	67	Stanford	1978
Dunn, Thomas	Asst	Syracuse	J	PHD	92	Nrthwstrn	
Dunne, Elizabeth A.	Asst	SUNY Oswego	AEG	ABD		Iowa	1990
Dunne, Maureen E.	Prof	Framingham		MBA		Detroit	
Dunne, Timothy	C-As	Oklahoma	DLJ	PHD	87	Penn St	1992
Dupree, Jill L.	Asst	Holy Cross	FNT	PHD	96	Colorado	1996
Durden, Gary C.	Prof	Appalach St	EH	PHD	71	Fla St	1982
Durell, Alan	Asst	Dartmouth		PHD	99	Harvard	1999
Durgin, Frank A. Jr.	Retir	So Maine	NPQ	DRD	56	France	1964
Durham, Yvonne	Asst	Arkansas	LD	PHD	94	Arizona	1994
Durlauf, Steven N.	Prof	Wisconsin		PHD	86	Yale	1993
Durtschi, Reed R.	Retir	Utah State	AE	PHD	67	U Wash	1958
Dusansky, Richard	C-Pr$	Texas	DH	PHD	69	Brown	9-89
Richard J. Gonzales Regents Chair in Economic Progress							
Duston, Thomas E.	Assoc	Keene State		PHD	72	Brown	1984
Dutkowsky, Donald H.	Assoc	Syracuse	E	PHD	82	SUNY-Buf	1985
Dutt, Amitava K.	C-Pr	Notre Dame	EFOC	PHD	83	MIT	1988
Dutt, Swarna D.	Assoc	West Georgia	F	PHD	93	Wayne St	1994
Dutta, Manoranjan	Prof	Rutgers-N Br	E	PHD	62	Penn	1989
Dutta, Prajit	Prof	Columbia	DLG	PHD	87	Cornell	1992
Dutton, Marilyn	Asst	N Carol Cen		PHD	89	Duke	1991
Duwaji, Ghazi	Assoc	Tx-Arlington	F	PHD	66	Duke	1966
Dvorak, Eldon J.	Retir	CS-Long Bch	1994	PHD	62	U Wash	1961
Dworak, Jonathan	Asst	So Illinois	DL	ABD		MIT	1999
Dwyer, Debra	Asst	SUNY-Stony B		PHD	96	Cornell	1998
Dyal, James A.	Prof	Indiana U-PA	JR	PHD	75	Illinois	1977
Dye, Alan	Asst	Barnard	N	PHD	91	Illinois	1995
Dye, Howard S.	Retir	0retirFla		PHD	49	Cornell	1973
Dyer, Alan W.	Assoc	Northeastern		PHD	82	Maryland	1983
Dykema, Eugene R.	Prof	George Fox		PHD	83	Notre Dm	
Dymski, Gary A.	Assoc	Cal-Riversid	AEHP	PHD	87	Mass	1991
Eadington, William R.	Prof	Nevada-Reno		PHD	73	Claremont	1969
Eagan, J. Vincent	Assoc	Morehouse		PHD	86	Geo St	1993
Eapen, A. Thomas	Retir	SUNY-Bingham		PHD	61	Michigan	1966
Earley, Joseph E.	Assoc	Loyola Marym	AC	PHD	74	Fordham	1974
Early, Dirk W.	Asst	Southwestern	DEHR	PHD	95	Virginia	1994
Earnhart, Dietrich	Asst	Kansas	QK	PHD	95	Wisconsin	8-97
Easley, David A.	Prof	Cornell	DGC	PHD	79	Nrthwstrn	9-79
Henry Scarborough Professor of Social Sciences							
Easterlin, Richard A.	Prof	So Calif		PHD	53	Penn	1982

Eastham, George M.	Retir	Cal Poly-SLO		PHD	78	Claremont	1966
Easton, Robert F.	C-As	NE Illinois		MA		Nrthwstrn	
Easton, Todd E.	Assoc	Portland	J	PHD	84	Berkeley	1981
Eastwood, John D.	Lect	No Arizona	CD	MS	80	Wyoming	1990
Eaton, David	Asst	Murray State	HCL	PHD	95	Michigan	1996
Eaton, Jonathan	C-Pr	Boston Univ	FG	PHD	76	Yale	
Eaton, Peter J.	Assoc	Mo-Kansas Ct	CI	PHD	76	Florida	1979
Ebeling, Richard M.	C-Ac	Hillsdale		MA	80	Rutgers	1988
Ludwig von Mises Chair							
Eberhardt, Duane O.	Prof	Missouri So		PHD	70	S Calif	1986
Ebert, Robert R.	Prof	Baldwin-Wal	DFP	PHD	74	Case Wes	1967
Eckalbar, John C.	Prof	CS-Chico	CE	PHD	75	Colorado	1978
Eckaus, Richard S.	Retir	MIT	O	PHD	54	MIT	1965
Eckel, Catherine C.	Prof	Virg Tech	P	PHD	83	Virginia	1983
Economides, Nicholas S.	Prof	New York U	DKL	PHD	81	Berkeley	1990
Edelman, Milton	Emer	So Illinois		PHD	51	Illinois	1950
Edelstein, Michael	Prof	CUNY-Queens	NOF	PHD	70	Penn	1974
Ederington, William	Asst	U Miami	F	PHD	98	Wisconsin	1998
Edgmand, Michael R.	Prof	Oklahoma St	E	PHD	68	Mich St	1983
Edgren, John A.	Prof	E Michigan		PHD	79	Michigan	1979
Edlin, Aaron	Assoc	Cal-Berkeley		PHD	93	Stanford	1995
Edlund, Lena	Asst	Columbia	J	PHD	96	SSE	1999
Edmiston, Kelly D.	Asst	Georgia St	EGHR	PHD	98	Tennessee	1998
Edmonds, Eric V.	Asst	Dartmouth		PHD	99	Princeton	1999
Edmonds, Radcliff G. Jr.	Assoc	S Ill-Edward	ACF	PHD	79	Michigan	1977
Edmondson, Rob	Asst	Barton		MBA		Wake For	8-91
Edwards, Alejandra C.	Prof	CS-Long Bch		PHD	84	Chicago	1966
Edwards, Bruce E.	Retir	Bowling Gr		PHD		Michigan	1966
Edwards, Franklin R.	C-Pr	Columbia		PHD	64	Harvard	1980
Arthur F. Burns Professor of Free and Competitive Enterprise							
Edwards, John H.	Assoc	Tulane		PHD	85	Maryland	1985
Edwards, Linda N.	Prof	CUNY-Queens	JC	PHD	71	Columbia	1971
Edwards, Mary E.	Prof	St Cloud St		PHD	88	Tx A&M	1985
Edwards, N. Faye	Prof	Richmond		PHD	68	Kentucky	1968
Edwards, Sebastian	Prof	UCLA		PHD	81	Chicago	1985
Efaw, Fritz W.	Assoc	Tenn-Chattan	CJ	PHD	87	Rutgers	1988
Eff, E. Anthon	Assoc	Mid Tenn St	RB	PHD	89	Tx-Austin	1990
Eftekhari, Hossein	Prof	Wis-Rvr Fall	DC	PHD	85	Nebraska	1985
Egan, Francis J.	Assoc	Trinity-CT		PHD	73	Fordham	1967
Egan, James P.	Prof	Wis-Eau Clar	E	PHD	82	Syracuse	1970
Egge, Karl A.	Prof	Macalester	AGM	PHD	73	Ohio St	1970
F. R. Bigelow Professor of Economics							
Egger, John B.	Assoc	Towson		PHD	85	NYU	1987
Eggleston, Brian D.	C-Ac	Augustana SD	ABQ	PHD	91	Wash St	1988
Eggleston, Karen	Asst	Tufts		PHD	99	Harvard	1999
Eggleston, Robert C.	Prof	Shippensburg		PHD	84	Pittsburgh	1965
Ehrbar, Hans G.	Asst	Utah		PHD	85	Michigan	1986
Ehrenberg, Ronald G.	Prof	Cornell		PHD	70	Nrthwstrn	1985
Irving M. Ives Professor of Industrial & Labor Relations and Economics							
Ehrlich, Isaac	C-Pr	SUNY-Buffalo	OLK	PHD	70	Columbia	1977
Eichenbaum, Martin	Prof	Northwestern		PHD	81	Minnesota	1988
Eichengreen, Barry	Prof	Cal-Berkeley		PHD	79	Yale	1987
Eicher, Theo S.	Asst	U Washington		PHD	94	Columbia	1994
Eide, Eric	Asst	Brigham Yg		PHD	93	Ca-SnBarb	1993
Eisenhauer, Joseph G.	Asst	Canisius		PHD	91	SUNY-Buf	1986
Eisenstadt, Robert C.	Assoc	NE Louisiana	JI	PHD	91	Geo St	
Eisner, Robert	Retir	Northwestern		PHD	51	J Hopkins	1952
Eissa, Nada	Asst	Cal-Berkeley		PHD	95	Harvard	1995
Ekanem, Frank	Asst	Howard	EGHR	PHD	74	Geo Wash	1987
Ekelund, Robert B. Jr.	Prof	Auburn		PHD	67	LSU	1979
Lowder Eminent Scholar							
El Nasser, Marwan M.	Prof	SUNY-Fredoni	EG	PHD	70	Ohio St	1970
El-Hodiri, Mohamed A.	Prof	Kansas		PHD	66	Minnesota	1966
Elassar, Sammy E.	Prof	Winston-Sal		PHD	68	Maryland	1968
Elbaum, Bernard	Assoc	Ca-Santa Crz	N	PHD	82	Harvard	1986
Elder, Erick	Asst	Ark-Ltl Rock		PHD	97	Pittsburgh	8-96
Elder, Harold W.	Assoc	Alabama		PHD	82	Va Tech	1981
Elder, John	Asst	Middlebury	CEG	PHD	95	Virginia	1998
Eldridge, Robert M.	Assoc	So Conn St	G	DBA	87	Geo Wash	
Elike, Uchenna I.	Asst	Alabama A&M	AOF	PHD	85	Alabama	1985
Eliot, Stuart J.	Lect	Manches Inst	DMA	MA		Manchest	1974
Elkes, Lynne C.	Asst	Baltimore					
Elkins, Ron	Inst	Central Wash					1996
Ellard, Charles J.	Prof	Tx-Pan Amer		PHD	74	Houston	1976
Elledge, Barry	Prof	Appalach St	IM	PHD	70	N Car St	1969
Eller, Eric	Asst	Bellarmine		PHD		Virginia	
Ellickson, Bryan C.	C-Pr	UCLA		PHD	70	MIT	1973
Ellickson, Donald L.	Retir	Wis-Eau Clar		PHD	66	Wisconsin	1958
Ellingson, Wayne D.	Inst	So Dakota St	C	BS	70	Iowa St	1980
Elliott, Caroline	Lect	U Lancaster		PHD		Manchester	

Elliott, Dawn Richards	Asst	Tx Christian		PHD	94	New Sch	1995
Elliott, Donald S. Jr.	C-Pr	S Ill-Edward	AHMR	PHD	76	Minnesota	1976
Elliott, Graham	Asst	Ca-San Diego	CEF	PHD	94	Harvard	1994
Elliott, John E.	Prof	So Calif		PHD	56	Harvard	1966
Elliott, Stephen	Assoc	NW St of LA	GM	PHD	83	La Tech	
Ellis, Charles M.	Prof	Dallas Bapt		PHD	73	Alabama	
Ellis, Charles Michael	Assoc	Txs Wesleyan		PHD	73	Alabama	1983
Ellis, Christopher J.	Prof	Oregon	E	PHD	83	Warwick	1983
Ellis, Gregory M.	Asst	U Washington		PHD	92	Berkeley	1988
Ellis, Harry Jr.	Lect	North Texas	A	MA		Mich St	1990
Ellis, Larry V.	Assoc	Appalach St	E	PHD	78	Missouri	1978
Ellis, Mary Elizabeth	Assoc	St John's		PHD	83	S Carol	
Ellis, Michael	Prof	New Mex St	I	PHD	75	Ca-Rivers	1973
Ellis, Michael A.	Asst	Kent State	EF	PHD	91	Tx A&M	1990
Ellis, Randall P.	Prof	Boston Univ	CILQ	PHD	81	MIT	1981
Ellis, Robert J. Jr.	Emer	So Illinois		PHD	66	Virginia	1965
Ellis, Steffany G.	Asst	Mich-Dearbor	CEFG	PHD	93	NC-Charl	1992
Ellis, Theodore	Prof	Adams State		PHD	72	Colo St	1967
Ellison, Glenn D.	Prof	MIT	L	PHD	92	MIT	1994
Ellison, Sara	Lect	MIT	L	PHD	93	MIT	1997
Elmore, Elizabeth A.	Prof	R Stockton		PHD	76	Notre Dm	1972
Elmslie, Bruce T.	Assoc	New Hampshir	BF	PHD	88	Utah	1989
Elston, Julie Ann	Asst	Cen Florida		PHD			
Elul, Ronel	Asst	Brown		PHD	95	Yale	
Elwood, S. Kirk	Asst	Jms Madison	EFC	PHD	93	Ca-Davis	1992
Ely, Jeffrey	Asst	Northwestern		PHD	96	Berkeley	1996
Elzinga, Kenneth G.	Prof	Virginia	L	PHD	67	Mich St	1967
Emery, E. David	Prof	St Olaf	DIA	PHD	69	Minnesota	1969
Emery, Mary Ann	Assoc	St Olaf	M	MA	65	Minnesota	1969
Enders, Walter	Prof	Iowa State	EF	PHD	75	Columbia	1974
Endres, Carole R.	Inst	Wright State		MS	87	Wright St	
Eng, Maximo	Adj	St John's		PHD	66	NYU	1985
Engel, Charles M.	Prof	U Washington		PHD	83	Berkeley	1991
Engelhardt, Gary	Assoc	Syracuse		PHD	93	MIT	
Engelmann, Paul H.	C-Pr	Cen Missouri		PHD	76	Okla St	1972
Engerman, Stanley L.	Prof	Rochester		PHD	62	J Hopkins	1963
John Munro Professor of Economics							
Engers, Maxim P.	Assoc	Virginia	ACD	PHD	84	UCLA	1982
England, Richard W.	Prof	New Hampshir	OQ	PHD	74	Michigan	1976
Englander, Frederick	Prof	F Dick-Madis	DE	PHD	75	Rutgers	
Englander, Valerie	Assoc	St John's		PHD	75	Rutgers	1982
Engle, Fred A. Jr.	Retir	E Kentucky		EDD	66	Kentucky	1959
Engle, Robert F.	Prof	Ca-San Diego	CGR	PHD	66	Cornell	1975
Chancellor's Associates Chair in Econometrics							
English, Mary P.	Assoc	DePauw		PHD	89	So Meth	1988
Enomoto, Carl E.	Assoc	New Mex St	FE	PHD	82	Tx A&M	1983
Epple, Dennis N.	Prof	Carnegie Mel		PHD	74	Princeton	1974
Epps, Thomas W.	Prof	Virginia	GC	PHD	69	Duke	1972
Epstein, Gerald A.	Prof	Massachusett		PHD	81	Princeton	1987
Epstein, Jose D.	Deces	American U		PHD	85	San Andres	
Epstein, Larry G.	Prof	Rochester		PHD	77	Brit Colum	1998
Epstein, Seth	Asst	DePaul	D	PHD	88	Arizona	1992
Ercan, Hakan	Asst	Bogazici	CHJ	PHD	94	Iowa	1994
Erdilek, Asim	Prof	Case Western	F	PHD	72	Harvard	1971
Erekson, O. Homer	Prof	Miami U-Ohio	HR	PHD	80	N Carol	1978
Erenburg, Sharon J.	Assoc	E Michigan		PHD	86	Illinois	1987
Erfani, G. Rod	Prof	Transylvania		PHD	84	Fla St	1986
Erickson, Christopher A.	Asst	New Mex St	EF	PHD	89	Ariz St	1987
Erickson, Edward C.	C-Pr	CS-Stanislau		PHD	70	S Calif	1970
Erickson, Edward W.	Prof	N Carol St	LQD	PHD	86	Vanderbilt	1965
Erickson, Elizabeth L.	Assoc	Akron	AOQ	PHD	72	Illinois	1969
Erickson, Erick Lee	Prof	Metro St-CO		PHD		New Mex	1984
Erickson, Lee E.	Prof	Taylor		PHD	75	Michigan	1979
Erickson, Richard	Assoc	So Adventist	A	MBA	81	Aust Pea	1984
Erickson, Tom	Asst	Rensselaer		PHD	97	Cornell	1997
Ericson, Richard	Prof	Columbia	O	PHD	79	Berkeley	1985
Erikkila, John	Prof	Lk Superior	ADEF	PHD	87	W Ontario	9-90
Erturk, Korkut	Asst	Utah		PHD	92	New Sch	1992
Ervin, Danny	Asst	Salisbury St		PHD	96	Kentucky	1-99
Erzan, Refik	Assoc	Bogazici	F	PHD	83	Stockholm	1992
Eschenfelder, Mark J.	Assoc	Robt Morris		PHD	93	W Illinois	
Eschker, Erik	Asst	CS-Humboldt		PHD	97	Ca-Davis	1998
Escoe, Gisela Meyer	Assoc	Cincinnati	O	PHD	91	Ohio St	1991
Esensoy, Yilmaz	Retir	Alabama A&M	AOD	PHD	69	Ohio St	
Eseonu, Maxwell O.	Assoc	Virginia St		PHD	83	Howard	1982
Esfahani, Hadi S.	Assoc	Illinois	EFLO	PHD	84	Berkeley	1984
Eshleman, Tom	Assoc	Neb-Kearney		PHD	94	Okla St	1993
Eskot, Herbert J.	Asst	W New Eng		PHD	84	Tufts	1984
Espiritu, Antonina	Asst	Hawaii Pacif		PHD	98	Nebraska	1998
Esposito, Frances F.	Prof	Mass-Dartmou		PHD	67	Boston C	1967

Name	Rank	School	Fields	Degree	Yr	Institution	Year
Esposito, Louis	Retir	Mass-Boston	L	PHD	68	Boston C	1968
Esposto, Alfredo G.	Assoc	E Michigan		PHD	83	Temple	1990
Essenburg, Timothy J.	C-Pr	Bethel-MN	AI	PHD	91	Tennessee	1989
Estenson, Paul	Asst	Gustavus Ado		PHD	86	Nebraska	1986
Ethier, Wilfred J.	Prof	Pennsylvania	F	PHD	70	Rochester	1969
Eubank, Wayne F.	Retir	SE Missouri		PHD		Kentucky	1964
Eubanks, Larry S.	C-Ac	Colorado Spr	DHQ	PHD	80	Wyoming	1986
Eusufzai, Zaki	Asst	Loyola Marym	ACFD	PHD	94	UCLA	1989
Euzent, Patricia	Inst	Cen Florida		MA		Clemson	1991
Evans, Bernice	Asst	Morgan State		MBA		Baruch	
Evans, Boyd	Assoc	Mid Tenn St	A	MA	64	Auburn	1965
Evans, George	Prof	Oregon	E	PHD	80	Berkeley	1994
John B. Hamacher Professor of Economics							
Evans, Hugh G. Jr.	C-Ac	Elizabethtwn		MA	66	Penn St	1968
Evans, John S.	Retir	Alabama		PHD	71	Wisconsin	1968
Evans, Keith D.	Assoc	CS-Northrdge		PHD	71	U Wash	1971
Evans, Mark O.	Prof	CS-Bakersf	AIQR	PHD	77	New Mex	1978
Evans, Martin D. D.	Prof	Georgetown	EFG	PHD	87	Princeton	1996
Evans, Paul D.	Prof	Ohio State	E	PHD	76	Chicago	1987
Evans, Richard D.	Prof	Memphis	CM	PHD	70	Harvard	1978
Evans, Robert Jr.	Retir	Brandeis		PHD	59	Chicago	1967
Evans, William N.	Prof	Maryland		PHD	87	Duke	1987
Evcimen, Gunar	Assoc	Bogazici	FO	PHD	79	Istanbul	1980
Even, William E.	Prof	Miami U-Ohio	JC	PHD	84	Iowa	1983
Evenett, Simon	Asst	Rutgers-N Br	F	PHD	95	Yale	1997
Evensky, Jerry	Assoc	Syracuse	B	PHD	84	Syracuse	1985
Evenson, Robert E.	Prof	Yale	DO	PHD	68	Chicago	1977
Everett, Michael	Asst	Quinnipiac	ADBP	PHD	96	Conn	1996
Everett, Michael David	Assoc	East Tenn St		PHD	67	Wash U	1977
Ewert, Norman J.	Assoc	Wheaton-IL	AF	PHD	76	S Illinois	1973
Ezeani, Eboh	Prof	Univ of D C	O	PHD	76	American	1976
Fabritius, Michael	Prof	Mary Hrdn-By	ABDE	PHD	87	Tx-Austin	1987
Claude McBryde Professor of Finance-Economics							
Fackler, James S.	Prof	Kentucky	E	PHD	77	Indiana	1982
Fagal, Frederick F. Jr.	Assoc	Marywood		PHD	81	Syracuse	1987
Fahy, Colleen A.	Asst	Assumption	HLCD	PHD	89	SUNY-Bin	1994
Fahy, Paul R.	Assoc	E Illinois		PHD	76	Conn	1976
Fain, James R.	Assoc	Oklahoma St	J	PHD	86	Purdue	1986
Fair, Ray C.	Prof	Yale	E	PHD	68	MIT	1974
Fairchild, Daniel R.	Assoc	St Thomas-MN	F	PHD	78	St Louis	1976
Fairchild, Loretta	Prof	Nebraska Wes		PHD	72	Cornell	1975
Fairlie, Robert	Asst	Ca-Santa Crz	J	PHD	94	Nrthwstrn	1994
Fairris, David H.	Assoc	Cal-Riversid	AJP	PHD	84	Duke	1989
Faith, Roger L.	Prof	Arizona St		PHD	73	UCLA	1981
Falaris, Evangelos M.	Assoc	Delaware	O	PHD	70	Minnesota	1986
Falero, Frank Jr.	Prof	CS-Bakersf	ADEG	PHD	67	Fla St	1972
Falk, Barry L.	Assoc	Iowa State	E	PHD	82	Minnesota	1980
Falls, Gregory A.	Prof	Cen Michigan		PHD	82	Purdue	1981
Fan, Chuen-mei	Prof	Colorado St	HD	PHD	72	Minnesota	1978
Fan, Liang-Shing	Prof	Colorado St	AOF	PHD	65	Minnesota	1968
Fanchon, Phillip F.	Assoc	Cal Poly-SLO		PHD	82	Ca-SnBarb	
Fang, Jiguang	Lect	Ohio State					
Farber, Henry S.	Prof	Princeton		PHD	77	Princeton	
Fardmanesh, Mohsen	Assoc	Temple	OF	PHD	85	Yale	1985
Fare, Rolf	Prof	Oregon State	CD	DOC	76	Lund	9-98
Farina, Louis	Asst	Framingham		MBA		Babson	
Farley, Noel J. J.	Prof	Bryn Mawr		PHD	65	Yale	1971
Farmer, Amy F.	Assoc	Arkansas	DK	PHD	91	Duke	1999
Farmer, Berkwood M.	Dean	Longwood	Q	PHD	70	N Car St	1991
Farmer, Roger E. A.	Prof	UCLA		PHD	82	W Ontario	1988
Farnham, Paul G.	Assoc	Georgia St	DHI	PHD	78	Berkeley	1977
Farr, William Kendrick	Assoc	Georgia Col	ADQ	PHD	85	Georgia	1985
Farrell, Claude H. III	Prof	N Car-Wilmin	EGR	PHD	74	N Car St	
Farrell, John P.	Prof	Oregon State	BO	PHD	73	Wisconsin	9-72
Farrell, Joseph V.	Prof	Cal-Berkeley		PHD	81	Oxford	
Farrell, Michael J.	Prof	CS-Long Bch		PHD	69	Stanford	1969
Farrell, Rev. John	Asst	Villanova		PHD	72	Catholic	1993
Farsio, Farzad	Prof	Mont St-Bill		PHD	89	Claremont	1987
Fatas, Antonio	C-Ac	INSEAD		PHD	93	Harvard	1-94
Faulk, Dagney	Asst	Indiana SE	R	PHD	99	Geo St	1999
Faurot, David J.	Assoc	Kansas	J	PHD	75	Nrthwstrn	1975
Fausti, Scott W.	Assoc	So Dakota St	F	PHD	91	Illinois	1991
Favor, Homer	Prof	Morgan State		PHD	60	Pittsburgh	
Fawson, Christopher	Assoc	Utah State	CGMO	PHD	86	Tx A&M	1990
Fayazmanesh, Sasan	Asst	CS-Fresno	BCE	PHD	84	Ca-Rivers	1990
Fayissa, Bichaka	Prof	Mid Tenn St	D	PHD	82	Tennessee	1980
Fazeli, Rafat R.	Asst	Redlands		PHD	92	New Sch	1989
Fazzari, Steven M.	C-Pr	Wash Univ	E	PHD	82	Stanford	1982
Fearn, Robert M.	Emer	N Carol St	JDP	PHD	68	Chicago	1965
Feeney, JoAnne	Asst	Colorado		MA	91	Rochester	1990

Feenstra, Robert	Prof	Cal-Davis	F	PHD	81	MIT	1986
Feiedberg, Leora	VAsst	MIT		PHD			1999
Feige, Edgar L.	Retir	Wisconsin		PHD	63	Chicago	1963
Feigenbaum, Susan K.	Prof	Mo-St Louis	DHKP	PHD	80	Wisconsin	1988
Feinberg, Robert M.	C-Pr	American U		PHD	76	Virginia	1989
Feiner, Susan F.	Assoc	So Maine	BN	PHD	81	Mass	1995
Feist, William R.	Assoc	Monmouth	G	PHD	87	Temple	
Felder, Joseph	Assoc	Bradley		PHD	79	UCLA	1981
Feldman, Allan M.	Assoc	Brown		PHD	72	J Hopkins	1977
Feldman, David H.	Assoc	Wm & Mary		PHD	82	Duke	1988
Feldman, Roger D.	Prof	Minnesota		PHD	76	Rochester	1985
Feldstein, Martin S.	Prof	Harvard		DPHL	67	Oxford	1969
George F. Baker Professor of Economics							
Feliciano, Zadia M.	Asst	CUNY-Queens	JFN	PHD	95	Harvard	1994
Felix, David	Emer	Wash Univ	O	PHD	55	Berkeley	1964
Feller, Irwin	Prof	Penn State	O	PHD	66	Minnesota	1963
Feltenstein, Andrew	Prof	Virg Tech	DHO	PHD	76	Yale	1993
Feltner, Richard L.	Retir	Bellarmine		PHD	65	N Car St	6-86
Fender, Ann Harper	Prof	Gettysburg	ADNL	PHD	76	J Hopkins	1978
Fenner, Richard G.	Assoc	Utica	AIR	PHD	92	Syracuse	1989
Fenstermaker, J. Van	Prof	Towson		PHD	63	Illinois	1988
Fenton, Sister Helen M.	Retir	Regis-MA		PHD	73	Boston C	
Ferber, Marianne A.	Retir	Illinois		PHD	54	Chicago	1956
Ferderer, J. Peter	Assoc	Macalester	EFN	PHD	89	Wash U	1996
Ferdowsi, Abdollah	Prof	Ferris State		PHD	82	Mich St	1984
Ferguson, J. David	C-Pr	Miami U-Ohio	EF	PHD	74	Brown	1970
Ferguson, William D.	Assoc	Grinnell	JE	PHD	89	Mass	1989
Ferleger, Louis	Prof	Mass-Boston	NOQ	PHD	78	Temple	1978
Fernandez, Luis	Prof	Oberlin	CDGL	PHD	83	Berkeley	1980
Fernandez, Raquel	Prof	New York U	F	PHD	87	Columbia	1995
Ferran, Manuel A.	Assoc	New Mex High	ADEG	PHD	69	Oklahoma	1993
Ferrie, Joseph	Asst	Northwestern		PHD	92	Chicago	
Ferrier, Gary D.	Assoc	Arkansas	DC	PHD	88	N Carol	1993
Ferson, Wayne	Prof	U Washington		PHD	82	Stanford	1992
Fesmire, James M.	Prof	Tampa	DKL	PHD	73	Florida	1973
Dana Professor of Economics							
Fessiehatzen, Tekie	C-Pr	Morgan State		PHD		Pittsburgh	
Fethke, Carol	Prof	Iowa		PHD	71	Iowa	1975
Fichtenbaum, Rudy H.	Prof	Wright State		PHD	80	Missouri	1980
Field, Alexander J.	Prof	Santa Clara		PHD	74	Berkeley	1982
Field, Alfred J. Jr.	Prof	No Carolina	F	PHD	67	Iowa St	1967
Field, William Joseph	Prof	DePauw		PHD	80	Michigan	1979
Field, William P. Jr.	Prof	Nicholls St	E	PHD	71	N Carol	1973
Field-Hendrey, Elizabeth	Assoc	CUNY-Queens	NJC	PHD	85	Duke	1989
Fielding, Gordon J.	Emer	Calif-Irvine		PHD	62	UCLA	1965
Fielding, William T.	Dean	Jacksonvl St		PHD	76	S Carol	1968
Fields, Judith M.	Asst	CUNY-Lehman		PHD	84	NYU	1984
Fields, T. Windsor	Prof	Jms Madison	EC	PHD	78	Virginia	1990
Figgins, Bob G.	C-Pr	Tenn-Martin		PHD	73	Arkansas	1973
Figort, Debb	Assoc	R Stockton		PHD	95	American	1989
Filer, Larry	Asst	Old Dominion		PHD	99	Kentucky	1999
Filer, Randall K.	Assoc	CUNY-Hunter		PHD	79	Princeton	1986
Finch, Eugene B.	Retir	Kean		PHD		Syracuse	9-69
Fincher, Phillip E.	Retir	Louisiana Te		PHD	78	Miss	1964
Findlay, David W.	C-Ac	Colby	EGA	PHD	86	Purdue	1985
Dana Professor							
Findlay, Ronald	Prof	Columbia	FB	PHD	60	MIT	1970
Finegan, T. Aldrich	Prof	Vanderbilt	J	PHD	60	Chicago	1970
Finifter, David H.	Prof	Wm & Mary		PHD	74	Pittsburgh	1973
Finley, Henry E.	Retir	Florida A&M		PHD		Indiana	1959
Finn, Daniel Rush	Prof	St Benedict		PHD	77	Chicago	1977
Clemens Chair in Economics and the Liberal Arts-Dean, School of Theology							
Finn, Thomas J. Jr.	Retir	Wayne State		PHD	59	Harvard	1963
Finney, Miles	Assoc	CS-L Angeles		PHD	92	Houston	1991
Finster, Ronald D.	Retir	W Oregon St		PHD	70	Arizona	1971
Finucane, Brendan P.	C-Pr	Shippensburg		PHD	82	Pittsburgh	1982
Fiorentino, Christopher M.	Dean	West Chester	DQ	PHD	89	Temple	9-85
Firoozi, Fathall K.	Assoc	Tx-S Antonio	CF	PHD	87	Oklahoma	1988
First, Ramona K.	Retir	San Fran St		PHD	49	Wisconsin	1956
Fischbaum, Marvin N.	Prof	Indiana St	DP	PHD	65	Columbia	1965
Fischel, William Alan	Prof	Dartmouth		PHD	73	Princeton	1973
Fischer, Charles C.	C-Pr	Pittsburg St	BJ	PHD	75	Wash St	1974
Fischer, Hartmut	Prof	San Francisc	FA	PHD	73	Berkeley	1970
Fischer, Stanley	Retir	MIT	G	PHD	69	MIT	1977
Fischmar, Daniel E.	Prof	Westminst-PA		PHD	75	S Illinois	1975
Fish, Mary	Prof	Alabama		PHD	63	Oklahoma	1965
Fishback, Price V.	Prof	Arizona		PHD	83	U Wash	1990
Fishbaugh, Charles P.	Retir	New Orleans	1995	PHD	66	Indiana	1967
Fishe, Raymond P. H.	Prof	U Miami	CD	PHD	79	Florida	1981
Fisher, Douglas	Prof	N Carol St	EN	PHD	65	Chicago	1977

Fisher, Eric O.	Assoc	Ohio State	F	PHD	85	Berkeley	1993
Fisher, Franklin M.	Prof	MIT	P	PHD	60	Harvard	1960
Fisher, Robert B.	Prof	CS-Chico	H	PHD		Oregon	1968
Fisher, Ronald C.	Prof	Michigan St		PHD	77	Brown	1976
Fisher, Warren L.	Prof	Susquehanna	ABQ	PHD	73	Conn	1988
Fisman, Raymond	Asst	Columbia		PHD	98	Harvard	1999
Fitzgerald, John M.	Prof	Bowdoin	HC	PHD	83	Wisconsin	1983
Fitzpatrick, Ellen	Asst	SUNY-Plattsb	FOQ	PHD	97	Mich St	1994
FitzRandolph, Peter Winfield	Assoc	St Lawrence	FN	PHD	79	Tufts	1973
Fitzsimmons, Edward L.	Assoc	Creighton	AD	PHD	84	Nebraska	1984
Fizel, John L.	Prof	Penn St-Erie	ALC	PHD	81	Mich St	1985
Flaherty, Diane P.	Prof	Massachusett		PHD	78	NYU	
Flaherty, E. E.	VAsst	Charleston		PHD	96	Fla St	1999
Flaherty, Sean	Prof	Frank & Mars	J	PHD	81	Berkeley	1980
Flammang, Robert A.	Retir	SW Texas St		PHD	62	Iowa	1991
Flanagan, Edward J.	Retir	Bradley		PHD	69	Mich St	1963
Flath, David	Prof	N Carol St	LDP	PHD	76	UCLA	1976
Flavin, Marjorie A.	Assoc	Ca-San Diego	E	PHD	81	MIT	1992
Flax, Stanley	Asst	St Thomas-FL		MBA		NYU	1986
Fleck, Robert K.	Asst	Montana St		PHD	94	Stanford	1995
Fleisher, Belton M.	Prof	Ohio State	J	PHD	61	Stanford	1965
Fleming, Garry A.	Assoc	Roanoke		PHD	79	Kentucky	1987
Flessig, Adrian	Assoc	CS-Fullerton	EF	PHD	93	N Car St	1999
Fletcher, Daniel O.	Retir	Denison		PHD	60	Michigan	1966
Fletcher, Jean W.	Assoc	Gettysburg	AJD	PHD	83	Wash U	1986
Fletcher, Jerald J.	Assoc	W Virginia	Q	PHD	82	Berkeley	1989
Fletcher, Lehman B.	Prof	Iowa State	O	PHD	69	Berkeley	1960
Flinn, Christopher	Prof	New York U	J	PHD	84	Chicago	1987
Flint, Harold	Prof	Montclair St	AEGP	PHD	72	S Illinois	1971
Flores, Nicholas E.	Asst	Colorado		PHD	95	Ca-SnDgo	1995
Floro, Maria Sagrario	Assoc	American U	OGDQ	PHD	87	Stanford	1988
Flory-Truett, Lila J.	D-Pr	Tx-S Antonio	DFMO	PHD	72	Iowa	1975
Flowers, Edward B.	Assoc	St John's		PHD	75	Geo St	
Flowers, Marilyn	C-Pr	Ball State	H	PHD	74	Va Tech	1990
Flueckiger, Gerald E.	Deces	Miami U-Ohio	CD	PHD	70	Purdue	1968
Flynn, Dennis O.	Prof	Pacific	DNO	PHD	77	Utah	1979
Foeller, William H.	Prof	SUNY-Fredoni	AJ	PHD	72	Iowa St	1984
Fogarty, Michael S.	Prof	Case Western	RO	PHD	75	Pittsburgh	1986
Fogel, Robert W.	Prof	Chicago		PHD	63	J Hopkins	1981
Charles R. Walgreen Professor/Director, Center for Population Economics							
Fohlin, Caroline	Asst	Cal Tech	NFL	PHD	94	Berkeley	1994
Folbre, Nancy	Prof	Massachusett		PHD	79	Mass	1985
Foley, James W.	Assoc	U Miami	O	PHD	69	Mich St	1968
Folkers, Kim	Assoc	Wartburg		MIM	89	St Thomas	1989
Folland, Sherman T.	Assoc	Oakland	IB	PHD	74	Iowa	1986
Folsom, Davis	Assoc	So Car-Aiken		PHD	79	Conn	1979
Folsom, Roger Nils	Prof	San Jose St		PHD	73	Claremont	1976
Fomby, Thomas	Assoc	So Methodist	CD	PHD	75	Missouri	1975
Fon, Vincy	Asst	George Wash	CD	PHD	81	Kansas	1979
Fong, Tat P.	Asst	Geneva	F	PHD	91	Pittsburgh	1996
Fongemie, Claude A.	Lect	Trinity-CT		PHD	79	Conn	1977
Foote, Chris	Asst	Harvard		PHD	96	Michigan	
Foran, Terry G.	Emer	So Illinois	J	PHD	71	Penn St	1970
Forbes, Kevin F.	Assoc	Catholic	DHLQ	PHD	82	Maryland	1983
Forbus, Philip R.	Assoc	So Alabama	AD	PHD	78	Arkansas	1978
Ford, Edward J. Jr.	Assoc	South Fla	R	PHD	71	Boston C	1971
Ford, Richard	Prof	Ark-Lil Rock		PHD	79	Arkansas	1981
Ford, William F.	Prof	Mid Tenn St	GHM	PHD	66	Michigan	1991
Weatherford Chair							
Formby, John P.	Prof	Alabama		PHD	65	Colorado	1982
Hayes Professor of Economics							
Forret, Monica	Asst	St Ambrose		PHD	95	Missouri	1997
Forstater, Mathew B.	Asst	Mo-Kansas Ct	ABF	PHD	96	New Sch	1999
Forster, Bruce A.	Dean	Wyoming	EQ	PHD	74	Austrlia	1987
Forsythe, Robert	Prof	Iowa		PHD	75	Car Mellon	1981
Fort, Rodney D.	Assoc	Wash State		PHD	85	Cal Tech	1984
Forti, Annette	Prof	SUNY Old Wes		PHD	75	Fordham	
Fortunato, Michael		SUNY-Empire	OMF	PHD	84	Harvard	1990
Foshee, Andrew W.	Prof	McNeese St		PHD	80	LSU	1978
Foster, Edward M.	Prof	Minnesota		PHD	61	MIT	1983
Foster, James E.	Prof	Vanderbilt	DG	PHD	82	Cornell	1990
Fosu, Augustin K.	C-Pr	Oakland	JOC	PHD	79	Nrthwstrn	1979
Fosu, Joseph	Assoc	W Illinois	AEQ	PHD	87	Iowa St	1987
Fournier, Gary M	Prof	Florida St	L	PHD	81	Virginia	1980
Fowles, Richard G.	Assoc	Utah		PHD	85	Utah	1990
Fox, Eugene H.	Retir	NE Louisiana		PHD	62	Alabama	1965
Fox, Jerrald Mark	Assoc	CUNY-Brookly	J	PHD	92	Union	1988
Fox, Nancy R.	Assoc	St Joseph	DJL	PHD	89	Penn	1986
Fox, Pauline H.	Prof	SE Missouri	AKH	PHD	75	Okla St	1978
Fox, Thomas G.	Prof	Penn State	A	PHD	66	Syracuse	1966

Name	Rank	School	Fields	Degree	Yr	Institution	Year
Fox, William F.	Prof	Tennessee		PHD	75	Ohio St	1979
France, Robert R.	Retir	Rochester		PHD	52	Princeton	
Francis, Gary E.	Prof	CS-Chico	ABGH	PHD	72	Colorado	1967
Franck, Raymond E. Jr	H-Pr	USAF Academy		PHD	83	Harvard	
Frangul, Ramzi N.	Assoc	Sacred Heart	G	PHD	73	NYU	1977
Frank, Robert H.	Prof	Cornell		PHD	72	Berkeley	1972
Goldwin Smith Professor of Economics, Ethics, and Public Policy							
Frankl, Jennifer	Asst	Williams		PHD	96	Berkeley	1997
Franklin, Douglas R.	Assoc	So Dakota St	Q	PHD	82	Utah	1988
Franklin, Raymond S.	Prof	CUNY-Queens	JBP	PHD	66	Berkeley	1966
Franko, Patrice	Assoc	Colby	FAO	PHD	86	Notre Dm	1986
Frantz, Roger S.	Prof	San Diego St		PHD	78	Wash St	1978
Franz, Wolfgang W.	Retir	Central Wash	HJK	PHD	70	Wash St	1969
Frasca, Ralph R.	Prof	Dayton	A	PHD	75	Indiana	1972
Frascatore, Mark	Asst	Clarkson	DHL	PHD	94	Va Tech	1994
Fratianni, Michele	C-Pr	Indiana		PHD	71	Ohio St	1971
Fraumeni, Barbara M.	Prof	Northeastern		PHD	80	Boston C	1982
Fraundorf, Martha	Assoc	Oregon State	J	PHD	76	Cornell	9-76
Frech, H. E. III	Prof	Cal-Santa Br	LAI	PHD	74	UCLA	1973
Frederick, James R.	Asst	NC-Pembroke		PHD	83	Wayne St	1988
Frederiksen, Peter C.	Prof	Naval Postgr	AOR	PHD	74	Wash St	7-74
Fredland, John E.	Prof	USN Academy		PHD	70	Michigan	1974
Fredrickson, Trygve G.	Inst	So Dakota St	M	MBA	89	S Dakota	1990
Fredriksson, Per	Asst	So Methodist	DF	PHD	94	Penn	1999
Free, Rhona C.	Assoc	Eastern Conn		PHD	83	Notre Dm	1983
Free, Veronica	Prof	No Alabama		PHD	70	Miss St	1984
Freed, Rodney Alan	Prof	CS-Dominguez	ACR	PHD	77	Virginia	1979
Freeman, Albert Myrick III	Prof	Bowdoin	QD	PHD	65	U Wash	1965
William Shipman Professor of Economics							
Freeman, Donald	Asst	Sam Houston		PHD	88	So Meth	1998
Freeman, James	VAsst	N Car-Greens	J	PHD	98	Fla St	1998
Freeman, James	Retir	Columbia		MBA	70	Penn	1991
Freeman, Katherine	Assoc	Denver	AD	PHD	78	Fla St	1983
Freeman, Patricia A.	Assoc	Jackson St		PHD	88	LSU	1998
Freeman, Scott	Assoc	Texas	E	PHD	83	Minnesota	9-91
Freiberg, Lewis	Prof	NE Illinois		PHD	72	Kentucky	1982
Freudenberger, Herman	Prof	Tulane		PHD	57	Columbia	
Frevert, Peter	Assoc	Kansas	DF	PHD	64	Purdue	1964
Frew, James R.	Assoc	Willamette		PHD	79	Purdue	1984
Frey, Donald E.	Prof	Wake Forest		PHD	72	Princeton	1972
Frieberg, Leora	Asst	Ca-San Diego	HDJE	PHD	96	MIT	1996
Fried, Harold O.	Prof	Union	CIL	PHD	78	N Carol	1983
Friedberg, Rachel	Asst	Brown		PHD	93	MIT	
Friedman, Benjamin M.	Prof	Harvard		PHD	71	Harvard	1972
William Joseph Maier Professor of Political Economy							
Friedman, Daniel	C-Pr	Ca-Santa Crz	FG	PHD	77	Ca-SanCrz	1979
Friedman, Eric J.	Asst	Rutgers-N Br	D	PHD	93	Berkeley	1996
Friedman, Gerald	Assoc	Massachusett		PHD	86	Harvard	1984
Friedman, Hershey	Prof	CUNY-Brookly	M	PHD	77	CUNY	1986
Friedman, James W.	Prof	No Carolina	DL	PHD	63	Yale	1985
Kenan Professor							
Friedman, Milton	Emer	Chicago		PHD	46	Columbia	1946
Paul Snowden Russell Distinguished Service Professor Emeritus							
Friedman, Richard	Retir	CS-Northrdge		ABD		CUNY	1961
Friedrich, Joseph	Prof	St Benedict		MA	70	Wisconsin	1967
Frost, Peter S.	Prof	U Washington		PHD	66	UCLA	1969
Froyen, Richard T.	Prof	No Carolina	E	PHD	72	Maryland	1971
Frydman, Roman	Prof	New York U	E	PHD	78	Columbia	1978
Fryman, Richard F.	C-Pr	West Georgia	AH	PHD	67	Illinois	1986
Fuchs, Victor R.	Emer	Stanford		PHD	55	Columbia	1974
Fudenberg, Drew D.	Prof	Harvard		PHD	81	MIT	1987
Fuentes, Gabriel	Asst	Loyola Marym	DLO	PHD	94	Berkeley	1994
Fuerst, Timothy S.	Assoc	Bowling Gr		PHD	90	Chicago	1993
Fuess, Scott M.	Assoc	Nebraska	J	PHD	86	Purdue	1986
Fugar, Christian	Asst	Dillard		PHD	89	Howard	
Fuhr, Joseph P.	Prof	Widener	DIKQ	PHD	81	Temple	1979
Fujii, Edwin T.	Deces	Hawaii-Manoa		PHD	73	Stanford	
Fukasawa, Yoshikazu	Dean	Midwest St	EF	PHD	79	Kansas St	1978
Fuller, Dan A.	Prof	Weber State	ADH	PHD	82	N Carol	1981
Fuller, John W.	Prof	Iowa		PHD	68	Wash St	1979
Fuller, Rex D.	Dean	Wis-La Cross	JM	PHD	82	Utah	1981
Fullerton, Don	Prof	Texas	HQ	PHD	78	Berkeley	9-94
Addison Baker Duncan Centennial Professor in Economics							
Fullerton, Herbert H.	Prof	Utah State	OQR	PHD	71	Iowa St	1969
Fullerton, Thomas	Asst	Txs-El Paso	RC	PHD	96	Florida	1996
Fulton, Betty	Retir	SE Missouri	P	PHD	75	Missouri	1968
Funderburk, Dale R.	Prof	Tx A&M-Comm	IEKJ	PHD	71	Okla St	1968
Fung, Kwok-Chiu	Assoc	Ca-Santa Crz	F	PHD	70	Wisconsin	1989
Fung, Kwok-Kwan	Prof	Memphis	OP	PHD	70	Harvard	1975
Funk, Herbert J.	Emer	Creighton	AC	PHD	64	Iowa St	1967

Name	Rank	School	Fields	Degree	Yr	Degree School	Year
Funk, Mark	Asst	St Louis		PHD	98	Ca-Davis	1998
Funkhouser, Ed	Asst	Cal-Santa Br	OJ	PHD	90	Harvard	1992
Furdek, Jonathan M.	Assoc	Purdue-Calmu		PHD	74	Purdue	1974
Furfero, Arlene J.	Assoc	St John's		PHD	80	Rutgers	
Furubotn, Eirik G.	Retir	Tx-Arlington	DNB	PHD	59	Columbia	1982
Furuya, K.	Asst	Calif-Irvine		PHD	96	Berkeley	1996
Futayyeh, Mohamed-Amin	Asst	NE Louisiana		PHD	70	Oklahoma	
Futrell, Gene Allen	Deces	Iowa State	1994	PHD	64	Ohio St	1964
Gabaix, Xavier	Asst	MIT	G	PHD	99	Harvard	1999
Gabel, David J.	Assoc	CUNY-Queens	DNC	PHD	87	Wisconsin	1987
Gabel, Landis	Prof	INSEAD	D	PHD	77	Penn	9-82
Gabriel, Albert H.	Retir	SW Okla St		PHD	65	Mich St	1956
Gabriel, Paul E.	Assoc	Loyola-Chicg	ADJ	PHD	87	Kentucky	1990
Gabriel, Satyananda Jordan	Asst	Mt Holyoke		PHD	89	Mass	1989
Gade, Mary N.	Assoc	Oklahoma St	H	PHD	86	Mich St	1986
Gaertner, Robert C.	Assoc	Lk Superior	DM	MBA	65	Notre Dm	1-70
Gafar, John S.	C-Pr	Lg Isl-Post		PHD	79	W Indies	1980
Gaffney, M. Mason	Prof	Cal-Riversid	AHR	PHD	56	Berkeley	1976
Gahvari, Firouz	Prof	Illinois	DH	PHD	81	UCLA	1994
Galbreath, George T.	Retir	CS-Pomona		MA	49	Stanford	1953
Galchus, Kenneth	Prof	Ark-Ltl Rock		PHD	70	Wash U	1976
Gale, Douglas	Prof	New York U	D	PHD	75	Cambridge	1996
Gale, Ian L.	Assoc	Georgetown		PHD	86	Princeton	1995
Gale, James R.	Prof	Mich Tech	E	PHD	72	Iowa	1971
Gale, Louis	Asst	SW Louisiana		PHD	94	Ariz St	1995
Galenson, David W.	Prof	Chicago		PHD	79	Harvard	1978
Gali, Jordi	Assoc	New York U	E	PHD	89	MIT	1994
Gallagher, Charles J.	Assoc	Virg Comm		PHD	70	W Virginia	1971
Gallagher, Daniel J.	Prof	St Cloud St		PHD	76	Maryland	1982
Gallant, A. Ronald	Prof	No Carolina	C	PHD	71	Iowa St	1993
Latane' Professor							
Gallaway, Lowell	Prof	Ohio Univ		PHD	59	Ohio St	1967
Distinguished Professor							
Gallegos, Alejandro	Prof	Winona State		PHD	86	Wi-Milwa	1988
Galles, Gary M.	Assoc	Pepper-Malib	AHLR	PHD	88	UCLA	1982
Gallet, Craig	Asst	Cen Florida	CDL	PHD	94	Iowa St	1996
Gallman, Robert E.	Deces	No Carolina		PHD	56	Penn	1962
Gallo, David E.	Prof	CS-Chico	AEHQ	PHD	74	Oregon	1970
Gallo, Joseph C.	H-Pr	Cincinnati	L	PHD	69	Missouri	1967
Gallup, Lanny W.	Retir	Okla City		MS	63	Okla St	1964
Galor, Oded	Prof	Brown		PHD	84	Columbia	1986
Gamba, Maria V.	Asst	Findlay	AD	MS		Wright St	1988
Gamber, Edward N.	Assoc	Lafayette	EC	PHD	86	Va Tech	1992
Gamble, Ralph C. Jr.	C-Pr	Fort Hays St	AEG	PHD	89	Okla St	1984
Gambles, Glenn C.	Prof	CS-Sacrament		PHD	70	Maryland	1969
Gan, Li	Asst	Texas	C	PHD	98	Berkeley	9-98
Gandar, John Maxim	Prof	N Car-Charl		PHD	82	Missouri	1982
Gander, James P.	Prof	Utah		PHD	66	Berkeley	1965
Ganderton, Philip	Assoc	New Mexico	DH	PHD	89	Ca-SnBarb	1989
Gandhi, Prem P.	Dean	SUNY-Plattsb	FO	PHD	73	New Sch	9-66
Gang, Ira N.	Assoc	Rutgers-N Br	O	PHD	83	Cornell	1986
Gangnes, Byron S.	Assoc	Hawaii-Manoa		PHD	90	Penn	1990
Gao, Ting	Asst	Missouri	FJ	PHD	98	Michigan	1998
Gapinski, James H.	Prof	Florida St	O	PHD	71	SUNY-Buf	1979
Garber, Peter M.	Prof	Brown		PHD	77	Chicago	1985
Garcia, Javier	Assoc	Ashland		JD		Akron	1980
Garcia, Marilyn	Asst	San Francisc	EO	PHD	97	Berkeley	1997
Gardner, B. Delworth	Retir	Brigham Yg		PHD	60	Chicago	1986
Gardner, H. Stephen	Prof	Baylor	FP	PHD	78	Berkeley	1978
Herman Brown Professor of Economics							
Gardner, Mark L.	C-Pr	Piedmont		PHD	85	Geo St	1979
Gardner, Roy J.	Prof	Indiana		PHD	75	Cornell	1983
Gardner, Wayland D.	Retir	W Michigan	H	PHD	58	Wisconsin	1964
Garen, John E.	Prof	Kentucky	J	PHD	82	Ohio St	1982
Garfinkel, Michelle	Assoc	Calif-Irvine		PHD	88	Brown	1991
Garhart, Robert E. Jr.	Prof	St Thomas-MN	R	PHD	82	Pittsburgh	1981
Garlick, Peter C.	Retir	SUNY-N Paltz	BEHN	PHD	72	London	1967
Garlin, Victor A.	Prof	Sonoma State		PHD	65	Berkeley	1970
Garman, David M.	C-Ac	Tufts	C	PHD	84	Michigan	1983
Garnel, Donald	Prof	San Jose St		PHD	66	Berkeley	1958
Garofalo, Gasper A.	Prof	Akron	ADR	PHD	74	Pittsburgh	1979
Garratt, Rodney J.	Asst	Cal-Santa Br	AEH	PHD	91	Cornell	1991
Garrett, John R.	Prof	Tenn-Chattan	EFG	PHD	85	Mass	1984
UC Foundation Associate Professor							
Garrett, Martin A.	Prof	Wm & Mary		PHD	66	Vanderbilt	1963
Garrison, Charles B.	Prof	Tennessee		PHD	68	Kentucky	1967
Garrison, Roger W.	Prof	Auburn		PHD	81	Virginia	1983
Garston, Neil H.	Prof	CS-L Angeles		PHD	73	Brown	1975
Garvin, Alexander	Retir	Indiana U-PA	CE	PHD	73	Tennessee	1969
Gashugi, Leonard K.	C-Pr	Andrews	CF	PHD	92	Boston U	1979

Name	Rank	School	Fields	Degree	Yr	Institution	Since
Gately, Dermot	Prof	New York U	Q	PHD	73	Princeton	1973
Gates, William R.	Assoc	Naval Postgr	D	PHD	74	Yale	1988
Gau, Carolina	Prof	Alcorn State		PHD		Missouri	
Gau, Paul K.	Prof	Alcorn State		PHD	71	Illinois	1972
Gauger, Jean A.	Assoc	Tennessee		PHD	84	Iowa St	1985
Gawande, Kishore	Assoc	New Mexico	CEFP	PHD	91	UCLA	1991
Gay, David E.	Prof	Arkansas	H	PHD	73	Tx A&M	1983
Gaynor, Patricia E.	Prof	Appalach St	C	PHD	73	U Miami	1976
Ge, Wei	Asst	Bucknell	DFOR	PHD	93	Penn	9-95
Geanakoplos, John	Prof	Yale	CD	PHD	80	Harvard	
Gebremariam, Yilma	Assoc	So Conn St	FO	PHD	89	S Calif	1990
Gebremikael, Fesseha	Inst	Alabama A&M	A	MS	97	Alab A&M	1996
Geddes, Raymond R.	Asst	Fordham		PHD	91	Chicago	1991
Gedeon, Shirley J.	Assoc	Vermont	EP	PHD	82	Mass	1981
Gegax, Douglas A.	Assoc	New Mex St	HD	PHD	84	Wyoming	1984
Geide-Stevenson, Doris	Asst	Weber State	AF	PHD	95	SUNY-Buf	1996
Geile, Gerald L.	Inst	SW Missouri		MA	91	St Louis	1991
Geiss, Charles G.	Assoc	Missouri	C	PHD	74	N Carol	1972
Geisst, Charles R.	Prof	Manhattan	N	PHD	72	LondonEC	1985
Gelbach, Jonah	Asst	Maryland		PHD	98	MIT	1998
Gelles, Gregory	C-Ac	Mo-Rolla		PHD	89	W Virginia	1989
Gemello, John M.	Prof	San Fran St		PHD	74	Stanford	1975
Gemery, Henry A.	Prof	Colby	NAB	PHD	67	Penn	1961
Pugh Family Professor of Economics							
Gemmill, Robert M.	Retir	Gettysburg	AEG	ABD		Nrthwstrn	1958
Gendel, Eugene B.	Prof	Woodbury	AJDE	PHD	79	Boston U	7-94
Genicot, Garance	Asst	Calif-Irvine		PHD	99	Cornell	1999
Gensemer, Bruce L.	C-Pr	Kenyon	HPDI	PHD	66	Michigan	1966
Gensemer, Susan H.	Assoc	Syracuse	D	PHD	84	Purdue	
Gentenaar, Robert	Assoc	Hope	EC	PHD	77	Mich St	1977
Geodde, Richard	Asst	St Olaf	M	MBA		Wisconsin	1988
Geoghegan, Jacqueline	Asst	Clark		PHD	95	Berkeley	1996
George, David L.	Assoc	LaSalle	ABN	PHD	84	Temple	1979
George, Nashwa E.	Asst	CUNY-Hunter		PHD	88	Baruch	9-85
Georges, Christophre	Assoc	Hamilton	EJB	PHD	89	Michigan	1989
Georgianna, Daniel L.	Prof	Mass-Dartmou		PHD	77	Mass	1977
Georgiou, George C.	C-Pr	Towson		PHD	79	Geo Wash	1980
Geraci, Vincent J.	Prof	Texas	CI	PHD	74	Wisconsin	9-73
Sue Killam Professorship in the Foundations of Economics							
Gerber, James B.	Prof	San Diego St		PHD	86	Ca-Davis	1985
Gerdes, William D.	Prof	N Dakota St	CEG	PHD	78	Nebraska	1978
Gerlowski, Daniel A.	H-Ac	Baltimore	ALM	PHD	87	Pittsburgh	8-87
Gerking, Shelby D.	C-Pr	Wyoming	RC	PHD	75	Indiana	1978
Gernant, Paul L.	Retir	Ferris State		PHD		Michigan	1979
Gershenberg, Irving	Prof	Mass-Boston	FOL	PHD	67	Berkeley	1982
Gerson, Janet	Lect	Michigan	AD	PHD	81	Michigan	
Gersovitz, Mark	Prof	J Hopkins		PHD	75	Yale	1994
Gertler, Mark	Prof	New York U	D	PHD	78	Stanford	1990
Geruson, Richard T.	Retir	LaSalle	TR	PHD	73	Penn	1958
Gery, Frank W.	Retir	St Olaf		PHD	57	Boston U	1962
Getter, Darryl	Asst	USN Academy		PHD	94	Wash U	1994
Getz, Malcolm	Assoc	Vanderbilt	HR	PHD	73	Yale	1973
Geweke, John F.	Prof	Minnesota		PHD	75	Minnesota	1990
Geyikdogi, Yasar	Prof	SUNY Old Wes		PHD		Bath	
Ghali, Moheb A.	Prof	Western Wash	CDEF	PHD	67	U Wash	1993
Gharrity, Norman J.	Prof	Ohio Wesley		PHD	66	J Hopkins	1962
Ghatak, Maintreesh	Asst	Chicago		PHD	96	Harvard	1996
Ghazalah, Ismail A.	Prof	Ohio Univ	DFHI	PHD	69	Berkeley	1969
Ghazanfar, Shaikh M.	H-Pr	Idaho	HOB	PHD	69	Wash St	1968
Ghebrat, Ezra	Assoc	NewJerseyCty	ADEF	PHD	82	New Sch	
Ghebreyesus, Ghirmay	Asst	Grambling St	EFJO	PHD	88	Strathcl	1990
Ghebreyohannes, Keleta	Assoc	Grambling St		PHD		Colo St	9-81
Ghent, Linda	VAsst	East Carol	DJ	PHD	92	N Car St	1993
Gherity, James A.	Emer	No Illinois	B	PHD	58	Illinois	1964
Ghiara, Ranjetta	Asst	CS-S Marcos		PHD	94	Ca-Rivers	1994
Ghilarducci, Teresa	Assoc	Notre Dame	J	PHD	84	Berkeley	1983
Ghirardato, Paolo	Asst	Cal Tech	D	PHD	95	Berkeley	1995
Ghorashi, Gholam-Reza	C-Ac	R Stockton		PHD	86	Fordham	1981
Ghosal, Vivek	Assoc	Miami U-Ohio	DE	PHD	88	Florida	1990
Ghosh, Arabinda	Prof	Wm Patterson		PHD	72	CUNY	1984
Ghosh, Dipak	VProf	Emporia St		PHD	94	Tulane	1997
Ghosh, Koushik	Asst	Central Wash		PHD		Wash St	
Ghosh, Parikshit	Asst	Texas A&M	LO	PHD	98	Boston U	1997
Ghosh, Satyajit P.	C-Ac	Scranton		PHD	86	SUNY-Buf	1986
Ghosh, Soumendra	Assoc	New Mex St	O	PHD	87	Utah St	1988
Ghosh, Sucharita	Asst	Akron	AEF	PHD	93	Kansas	1993
Ghosh, Sudip	Asst	W Virg St		PHD	99	W Virginia	1997
Ghoshal, Animesh	Prof	DePaul	DE	PHD	74	Michigan	1981
Ghoshroy, Atrayee	Asst	Morningside	HF	PHD	97	Nebraska	1999
Ghysels, Eric	Prof	Penn State		PHD	84	Nrthwstrn	1996

Giacalone, Joseph A.	Assoc	St John's		PHD	71	Columbia	1962
Giannakouros, George	Prof	Loras		PHD	74	Iowa	1966
Giannoros, Demetrios	Prof	Hartford	AEMP	PHD	81	Boston U	
Giarratani, Frank	Prof	Pittsburgh	R	PHD	75	W Virginia	1979
Giavazzi, Francesco	VProf	MIT		PHD			1999
Gibb, Arthur Jr.	Assoc	USN Academy		PHD	74	Michigan	1974
Gibbens, John M.	Retir	Wis-Whitewat		PHD	64	Iowa St	1961
Gibbons, Donna M.	Asst	Carleton	DOR	PHD	95	Brown	1993
Gibbs, W. Ernest	Assoc	Cen Florida	D	PHD	87	Rutgers	1987
Gibson, Eleanor	Asst	Bloomfield		MA		Columbia	1965
Gibson, Jo Anne	Assoc	SE Louisiana	EF	PHD	72	Miss	
Gibson, William A.	Prof	Vermont	CFOQ	PHD	77	Berkeley	1986
Gidwani, Sushila J.	Retir	Manhattan		PHD	64	Minnesota	1965
Giertz, J. Fred	Prof	Illinois	HO	PHD	70	Nrthwstrn	1980
Giesber, Frank W.	Prof	Tx Lutheran	A	PHD	78	Tx-Austin	1966
Giesbrecht, Martin G.	Prof	No Kentucky		PHD	58	Munich	1987
Giesecke, Leonard F.	Deces	Southwestern		PHD	75	Tx-Austin	1968
Gieske, Michael	Prof	Winona State		BS		Iowa St	1972
Giffin, Phillip E.	Prof	Tenn-Chattan	DBLN	PHD	72	Tennessee	1977
Gifford, Adam Jr.	C-Pr	CS-Northrdge		PHD	72	Ca-SnDgo	1975
Gift, Richard E.	Prof	Kentucky	FB	PHD	65	Duke	1965
Gigliotti, Gary A.	Prof	Rutgers-N Br	D	PHD	78	Columbia	1978
Gilbert, Howard A.	Prof	So Dakota St	A	PHD	67	Oregon St	1966
Gilbert, Richard J.	Prof	Cal-Berkeley		PHD	76	Stanford	1976
Gilbert, Ronald D.	Assoc	Texas Tech		PHD	70	Okla St	1977
Gilbert, Roy F.	Assoc	Texas A&M	C	PHD	69	Mich St	1970
Gilbert, Scott	Asst	So Illinois	C	PHD	96	Ca-SnDgo	1999
Gilbreath, L. Kent	Prof	Baylor	GN	PHD	71	Florida	1973
Stevens Professor of Private Enterprise							
Gilchrist, Simon	Asst	Boston Univ	C	PHD	90	Wisconsin	1995
Gildea, John A.	Prof	Wheaton-MA	EG	PHD	85	Duke	1985
Giles, John	Asst	Michigan St		PHD	99	Berkeley	1999
Gill, Andrew M.	Prof	CS-Fullerton	J	PHD	85	Wash St	1984
Gill, Leroy	Lect	Ohio State					
Gilles, Robert P.	Assoc	Virg Tech	DH	PHD	90	Tilburg	1991
Gilles, William	Retir	Nebraska		EDE	73	Nebraska	1963
Gilleskie, Donna	Asst	No Carolina	IJ	PHD	94	Minnesota	1994
Gillespie, Robert W.	Retir	Illinois		PHD	61	MIT	1960
Gillette, David H.	Assoc	Truman State		PHD	90	Wash St	1990
Gillette, Lynn G.	Dean	Houston Bapt		PHD	81	Tx A&M	1998
Gillette, Robert	Assoc	Kentucky	A	PHD	86	Tx A&M	1994
Gilley, Otis W.	Prof	Louisiana Te	D	PHD	79	Purdue	1988
Gilliam, Kenneth P.	Prof	Kennesaw St	ACD	PHD	76	Lehigh	1984
Gilliam, Lynde O.	Assoc	Metro St-CO		PHD	80	Colo St	1986
Gillis, Malcolm	Prof	Rice		PHD	68	Illinois	1993
Gilmore, Clair	Assoc	So Conn St	G	PHD		Drexel	
Gilsdorf, Keith F.	C-Ao	Morningside	LJ	PHD	90	Nebraska	1994
Gilson, Preston	Asst	Fort Hays St	F	PHD	93	St Louis	1988
Gin, Alan	Assoc	San Diego		PHD	87	Ca-SnBarb	1988
Gindling, Thomas H.	Assoc	MD-Baltim Co	O	PHD	87	Cornell	
Ginsburg, Helen	Retir	CUNY-Brookly	J	PHD	67	New Sch	1977
Ginther, Donna	Asst	Wash Univ	J	PHD	95	Wisconsin	1997
Gintis, Herbert M.	Prof	Massachusett		PHD	69	Harvard	1975
Giordano, James N.	Assoc	Villanova		PHD	82	Indiana	1983
Giordano, Justin		SUNY-Empire	M	MBA		St Johns	1992
Giraud, Kelly	Asst	Alaska-Fairb		PHD	99	Colo St	
Girton, Lance	Prof	Utah		PHD	76	Chicago	1978
Gishlick, Herbert E.	Prof	Rider	ER	PHD	73	Penn	1964
Gisser, Micha	Prof	New Mexico	DLQ	PHD	62	Chicago	1973
Gissy, William G.	Asst	Morehouse		PHD	87	Geo St	1988
Gitter, Robert J.	C-Pr	Ohio Wesley		PHD	78	Wisconsin	1976
Giunta, A. John	Retir	Scranton		PHD		Syracuse	1960
Gius, Mark P.	Assoc	Quinnipiac	ACDJ	PHD	91	Penn St	1994
Gjerde, Kathy A. Paulson	Asst	Butler	LJ	PHD	93	Purdue	1997
Glade, William P. Jr.	Prof	Texas	OR	PHD	55	Tx-Austin	9-70
Glaeser, Edward L.	Assoc	Harvard		PHD	92	Chicago	
Glahe, Fred R.	Prof	Colorado		PHD	64	Purdue	1965
Glass, Amy J.	Asst	Ohio State	F	PHD	93	Penn	1993
Glassman, Debra	SLect	U Washington		PHD	80	Wisconsin	1992
Glazer, Amihai	Prof	Calif-Irvine		PHD	78	Yale	1978
Gleason, Joyce G.	C-Ac	Nebraska Wes		PHD	86	Nebraska	1990
Gleicher, David	C-Ac	Adelphi	BJ	PHD	84	Columbia	1981
Gleisner, Richard F.	Prof	St Cloud St		PHD	72	Geotown	1968
Glendening, Richard N.	Prof	Central Iowa	EFHO	PHD	93	Iowa St	1966
Glezakos, Constantine	Prof	CS-Long Bch		PHD	70	S Calif	1968
Glick, Lee	Retir	Duquesne		PHD		Pittsburgh	
Glick, Mark	Prof	Utah		PHD	85	New Sch	1985
Globerman, Steven	Prof	Western Wash	DFIL	PHD	71	NYU	1994
Glomm, Gerhard	Assoc	Michigan St		PHD	88	Minnesota	1995
Glosser, Stuart M.	Assoc	Wis-Whitewat		PHD	85	Tx-Austin	1985

Name	Rank	School	Fields	Degree	Yr	Institution	Year
Glover, Terrence F.	Prof	Utah State	DCQ	PHD	71	Purdue	1974
Glustoff, Errol	Assoc	Tennessee		PHD	69	Stanford	1970
Gnuschke, John E.	Prof	Memphis	MR	PHD	75	Missouri	1976
Gobin, Roy T.	Assoc	Loyola-Chicg	AEHO	PHD	78	Illinois	1978
Godby, Robert	Asst	Wyoming		PHD	97	McMaster	1997
Goddard, Frederick O.	Assoc	Florida		PHD	67	Duke	1966
Goddard, Haynes C.	Assoc	Cincinnati	H	PHD	70	Indiana	
Goddeeris, John H.	C-Pr	Michigan St		PHD	80	Wisconsin	1980
Godfrey, E. Bruce	Prof	Utah State	Q	PHD	71	Oregon St	1977
Goel, Rajeev Kumar	Assoc	Illinois St	CO	PHD	87	Houston	1989
Goeree, Jacob	Asst	Virginia	CDL	PHD	97	Amsterdm	1996
Goering, Gregory	Assoc	Alaska-Fairb		PHD	90	Purdue	1990
Goetz, Michael	Assoc	Temple	MH	PHD	77	Minnesota	1978
Goff, Brian L.	Prof	W Kentucky	GHK	PHD	86	GeoMason	1986
Goffe, William L.	Assoc	So Miss	C	PHD	90	N Carol	1993
Gohmann, Stephan F.	Prof	Louisville	J	PHD	84	N Car St	1988
Gokcekus, Omer	Asst	N Carol Cen		PHD	95	Duke	1996
Gokturk, S. Sadik	Prof	St John's		PHD	72	Columbia	
Golan, Amos	VAsoc	American U		PHD	88	Berkeley	1996
Golbe, Devra L.	Assoc	CUNY-Hunter		PHD	79	NYU	1987
Gold, Andrew J.	Assoc	Trinity-CT		PHD	67	Nrthwstrn	1971
Goldbaum, David	Asst	Rutgers-Newk		PHD	96	Wisconsin	1998
Goldberg, Kalman	Prof	Bradley		PHD	54	Cornell	1952
Goldberg, Michael	Assoc	New Hampshir	EF	PHD	91	NYU	1991
Goldberg, Paul A.	Assoc	CUNY-Brookly	HP	PHD	84	Columbia	1978
Goldberg, Pinelopi	Prof	Columbia	FLC	PHD	92	Stanford	1999
Goldberg, Roger H.	Prof	Ohio Northrn		PHD	81	Indiana	1969
Goldberger, Arthur S.	Prof	Wisconsin		PHD	58	Michigan	1960
Harold M. Groves & Vilas Professor of Economics							
Goldfarb, Marsha G.	Prof	MD-Baltim Co		PHD	68	Nrthwstrn	1973
Goldfarb, Robert S.	Prof	George Wash	BJ	PHD	68	Yale	1980
Goldfeld, Stephen M.	Deces	Princeton		PHD	63	MIT	1969
Goldin, Claudia D.	Prof	Harvard		PHD	72	Chicago	1990
Goldman, Marshall I.	Prof	Wellesley		PHD	61	Harvard	1958
Goldman, Steven M.	Prof	Cal-Berkeley		PHD	66	Stanford	1979
Goldsmith, Arthur H.	C-Pr	Wash & Lee	E	PHD	79	Illinois	1990
Jackson T. Stephens Professor of Economics							
Goldsmith, O. Scott	Prof	Alaska-Ancho	CH	PHD	76	Wisconsin	1975
Goldstein, Donald	Assoc	Allegheny	ABG	PHD	91	Mass	1989
Goldstein, Harold M.	Retir	Northeastern		PHD	61	Clark	1961
Goldstein, Henry	Retir	Oregon	1997	PHD	67	J Hopkins	1967
Goldstein, Jonathan Paul	Prof	Bowdoin	EC	PHD	82	Mass	1979
Goldstein, Nance	Assoc	So Maine	IJ	PHD	88	ThamesPoly	1987
Gollin, Doug	Asst	Williams		PHD	96	Minnesota	1996
Gollop, Frank M.	Prof	Boston Coll	DO	PHD	74	Harvard	1979
Golub, Stephen S.	Prof	Swarthmore	AE	PHD	83	Yale	1981
Gomersall, C. Nicholas	Asst	Luther		PHD	91	Cornell	1991
Gonce, Richard A.	Prof	Grand Valley	ABDK	PHD	66	Wisconsin	1972
Gondwe, Derrick K.	C-Pr	Gettysburg	ABEO	PHD	78	Manitoba	1977
Gonzalez, Jorge G.	C-Ac	Trinity	F	PHD	89	Mich St	1989
Gonzalez, Rodolfo	C-Pr	San Jose St		PHD	90	Ca-Davis	1990
Gonzalez-Rivera, Gloria	Assoc	Cal-Riversid	CG	PHD	91	Ca-SnDgo	1991
Gonzalez-Vega, Claudio	Prof	Ohio State	O	PHD	76	Stanford	
Good, Delmar	C-Pr	Goshen	AH	PHD	70	Illinois	2-67
Gooding, Elmer R.	Prof	Arizona St		PHD	69	Kansas	1988
Goodman, Allen C.	Prof	Wayne State		PHD	76	Yale	1986
Goodman, David Jay	Asst	So Colorado	FQ	PHD	95	Colorado	1998
Goodman, Douglas	Prof	Puget Sound	AE	PHD	78	Illinois	1977
Goodman, Rae Jean B.	Prof	USN Academy		PHD	76	Wash U	1973
Goodstein, Eban	Assoc	Lewis & Clrk	QDGL	PHD	89	Michigan	1995
Goodwin, Craufurd	Prof	Duke	ABFN	PHD	58	Duke	9-62
James D. Duke Professor							
Goodwin, Randall B.	Assoc	Kennesaw St	ADM	PHD	82	Georgia	1982
Goodwin, Susan A.	Assoc	Mass-Lowell	G	PHD	75	Tufts	
Gootzeit, Michael J.	Prof	Memphis	BE	PHD	66	Purdue	1975
Gorcau, Suleyman	Asst	St Peters	FG	PHD		CUNY	1998
Gordon, Bruce	Assoc	No Alabama		PHD	93	North Tx	1986
Gordon, Brunhild	Retir	South Fla		PHD	57	S Calif	1960
Gordon, David B.	Assoc	Clemson	DE	PHD	95	Chicago	1992
Gordon, Peter	Prof	So Calif		PHD	71	Penn	1971
Gordon, Robert J.	Prof	Northwestern		PHD	67	MIT	1973
Stanley G. Harris Professor of the Social Sciences							
Gordon, Sara L.	Prof	St John's		PHD	71	Stanford	1978
Gormely, Patrick J.	Assoc	Kansas State	OF	PHD	67	Duke	1967
Gort, Michael	Prof	SUNY-Buffalo	O	PHD	54	Columbia	1964
Goss, Ernest P.	Prof	Creighton	RC	PHD	83	Tennessee	1992
MacAllister Chair in Regional Economics							
Gottfried, Robert Richard	Prof	Univ South	OQR	PHD	81	N Carol	
Gottheil, Fred	Prof	Illinois	AB	PHD	59	Duke	1959
Gottschalk, Peter	Prof	Boston Coll	CDIJ	PHD	73	Penn	1987

Gottschang, Thomas R.	C-Ac	Holy Cross	AOP	PHD	82	Michigan	1979
Gouke, Cecil G.	Retir	Ohio State	M	PHD	67	NYU	1973
Goulet, Denis A.	Prof	Notre Dame	O	PHD	63	SaoPaulo	1979
Goulet, Janet C.	Prof	Wittenberg	AJM	PHD	75	Notre Dm	1975
Gowdy, John M.	Prof	Rensselaer		PHD	80	W Virginia	1983
Gowens, Paul R.	Prof	SW Texas St	M	PHD	73	Miss	1980
Gownsaukaran, Gautam	Asst	Minnesota		PHD	95	Yale	1995
Grabowski, Henry G.	Prof	Duke		PHD	67	Princeton	1972
Grabowski, Richard L.	Prof	So Illinois	OF	PHD	77	Utah	1979
Graddy, Duane B.	Prof	Mid Tenn St	GHA	PHD	74	Lehigh	1972
Grady, John	Assoc	LaSalle	BE	MA		Temple	1960
Graeser, Paul	Deces	No Illinois	L	PHD	67	Columbia	1967
Graham, D. A.	Prof	Duke		PHD	69	Duke	1969
Graham, Fred C.	Assoc	American U		PHD	85	Virginia	1988
Graham, Glenn	Assoc	SUNY Oswego	AIL	PHD	95	SUNY-Bin	1992
Graham, John W. III	Prof	Rutgers-Newk		PHD	78	Nrthwstrn	1986
Graham, Katherine	Lect	SUNY-Cortlan		MS		Cornell	
Graham, Patricia E.	Asst	No Colorado	IJOQ	PHD	88	Colo St	1988
Graham, William R.	Retir	CS-L Angeles		PHD	69	Arizona	1969
Gram, Harvey H.	Prof	CUNY-Queens	FCE	PHD	73	Wisconsin	1974
Grambo, Ralph W. Jr.	Assoc	Scranton		PHD	81	Penn	1973
Gramlich, Edward M.	Prof	Michigan		PHD	65	Yale	1976
Grammy, Abbas P.	C-Pr	CS-Bakersf	ACOR	PHD	82	Colorado	1989
Granderson, Gerald	Assoc	Miami U-Ohio	DG	PHD	93	N Carol	1993
Granger, Clive W. J.	Prof	Ca-San Diego	C	PHD	74	Nottinghm	1974
Chancellor's Associates Chair in Economics							
Granger, George L.	Retir	East Tenn St		PHD	71	Penn	1961
Granger, Maury	Asst	N Carol A&T		PHD	95	Kentucky	1993
Grant, Alan	Asst	E Illinois		PHD	96	Kansas St	1997
Grant, Clayton	Prof	No Georgia	K	PHD	71	Clemson	1986
Dillard Munford Professor of Business							
Grant, Darren P.	Asst	Geo Southern		PHD	95	Fla St	1996
Grant, James H.	Asst	Lewis & Clrk	CDJA	PHD	79	Mich St	1987
Grant, Randy R.	Assoc	Linfield		PHD	96	Nebraska	1993
Grant, Stephen K.	Retir	Mass Lib Art		PHD	74	Clark	
Grapard, Ulla A.	Assoc	Colgate	AB	PHD	90	Cornell	1985
Grass, R. Gail	Assoc	Jackson St		PHD	89	Harvard	1989
Gray, Charles M.	Prof	St Thomas-MN	K	PHD	78	Wash U	1976
Gray, Jerry	Assoc	Willamette		PHD	89	Utah	1990
Gray, Jo Anna	Prof	Oregon	E	PHD	76	Chicago	1989
Gray, Wayne B.	C-Ac	Clark		PHD	83	Harvard	1984
Greaney, Theresa M.	Asst	Syracuse	F	PHD	94	Michigan	
Greckel, Fay E.	Retir	Indiana SE	OJR	PHD	69	Indiana	1967
Greco, Anthony J.	Prof	SW Louisiana	ADL	PHD	78	Tennessee	8-84
Green, Gregory G.	Asst	Idaho State	ACEF	PHD	97	Temple	1997
Green, Jeffery	Assoc	Ball State	C	PHD	72	Cornell	1972
Green, Jeffery	Prof	Indiana		PHD	67	Illinois	1985
Green, Jerry R.	Prof	Harvard		PHD	70	Rochester	1973
David A. Wells Professor of Political Economy							
Green, John W.	Prof	No Colorado	CTQR	PHD	76	Penn	1985
Green, Louis C.	Prof	San Diego St		PHD	75	Berkeley	1976
Green, Rodney D.	Prof	Howard	R	PHD	80	American	1977
Green, Steven L.	Prof	Baylor		PHD	84	Brown	1986
Green, Trellis Garnett	Assoc	So Miss	Q	PHD	84	Fla St	1983
Green, William B.	C-Pr	Sam Houston		PHD	74	LSU	1974
Green-Weishaupt, Carole A.	Assoc	South Fla	J	PHD	82	Illinois	1982
Greenbaum, Harry	Retir	So Dakota St	E	PHD	61	Ohio St	1961
Greenberg, Edward	Prof	Wash Univ	DE	PHD	61	Wisconsin	1963
Greene, Benjamin B. Jr.	Assoc	Salisbury St		PHD	74	Boston C	8-78
Greene, Clinton	Asst	Mo-St Louis	CE	PHD	92	Ca-Davis	1994
Greene, Kenneth V.	Prof	SUNY-Bingham	HK	PHD	68	Virginia	1968
Greene, William H.	C-Pr	New York U	CDE	PHD	76	Wisconsin	1982
Greenfield, Gail	Asst	Wooster		PHD	97	Claremont	1997
Greenfield, Robert L.	Prof	F Dick-Madis	GP	PHD	79	Rutgers	8-79
Greenhut, Melvin L.	Emer	Texas A&M		PHD	51	Wash U	1966
Distinguished Professor of Economics							
Greenlaw, Steven A.	C-Ac	Mary Wash	EFA	PHD	87	SUNY-Bin	1982
Greenley, Douglas A.	Prof	Moorhead St		PHD	79	Colo St	1978
Greenwade, George D.	Assoc	Sam Houston		PHD	88	Tx Tech	1986
Greenwald, Bruce C. N.	Prof	Columbia		PHD	78	MIT	1991
Robert Heilbrunn Professo of Finance and Asset Management							
Greenwood, Daphne T.	Assoc	Colorado Spr	HJT	PHD	80	Oklahoma	1980
Greenwood, Jeremy	Prof	Rochester	D	PHD	83	Rochester	1992
Greenwood, Michael J.	Prof	Colorado		PHD	67	Nrthwstrn	1980
Greer, Douglas F.	Prof	San Jose St		PHD	68	Cornell	1975
Greer, Mark	Asst	Dowling		PHD	90	Michigan	1994
Gregor, John J.	C-Pr	Wash & Jeff		PHD	76	Penn St	1989
Gregorowicz, Phillip	H-Pr	Auburn-Montg	EFGJ	PHD	82	N Illinois	1980
Gregory, Paul R.	Prof	Houston	P	PHD	69	Harvard	1972
Gregory, Sadie R.	Dean	Virginia St		PHD	87	Howard	1-79

Name	Rank	School	Fields	Degree	Yr	Institution	Year
Greif, Avner	Prof	Stanford		PHD	89	Nrthwstrn	1993
Grennes, Thomas	Prof	N Carol St	FD	MA	65	Wisconsin	1968
Gresik, Thomas A.	Assoc	Penn State	D	PHD	87	Nrthwstrn	1991
Grether, David M.	Prof	Cal Tech		PHD	69	Stanford	1970
Greubel, Robert T.	Prof	NE St-Okla	AEF	PHD	72	Arkansas	1965
Greytak, David	Retir	Syracuse	D	PHD	68	Wash U	
Grieson, Ronald E.	Prof	Ca-Santa Crz	RHD	PHD	72	Rochester	1980
Griffin, James M.	Prof	Texas A&M	C	PHD	70	Penn	1982
Hugh Roy Cullen Professor in Liberal Arts							
Griffin, Keith B.	Prof	Cal-Riversid	AOP	DPHI	65	Oxford	1988
Griffith, Jacqueline	Asst	Kean		MBA			
Griffith, Winston Harold	Prof	Bucknell	FOD	PHD	81	Howard	1987
Griffiths, L. Christopher	Prof	Colorado Col		PHD	70	Colorado	1967
Grigg, Vernon H.	Retir	South Fla		PHD	54	MIT	1981
Griliches, Zvi	Prof	Harvard		PHD	57	Chicago	1969
Paul M. Warburg Professor of Economics							
Grimes, Paul W.	Prof	Miss State		PHD	84	Okla St	1987
Grinols, Earl L.	Prof	Illinois	DFO	PHD	77	MIT	1984
Grobar, Lisa M.	Prof	CS-Long Bch		PHD	89	Michigan	1989
Grobey, John H.	Prof	CS-Humboldt		PHD	75	U Wash	1967
Groesbeck, John D.	C-Ac	So Utah		PHD	93	Utah St	1993
Gronberg, Timothy J.	Prof	Texas A&M	H	PHD	78	Nrthwstrn	1977
Groothuis, Peter A.	Assoc	Westminst-PA		PHD	89	Kentucky	1989
Gropper, Daniel M.	Assoc	Auburn		PHD	89	Fla St	1988
Grossbard-Shechtman, Shoshan	Prof	San Diego St		PHD	78	Chicago	1981
Grossberg, Adam J.	Assoc	Trinity-CT		PHD	86	Illinois	1986
Grosskopf, Shawna	Prof	Oregon State	CHJ	PHD	77	Syracuse	9-98
Grossman, Gene M.	Prof	Princeton		PHD	80	MIT	1980
Grossman, Gregory	Prof	Cal-Berkeley		PHD	53	Harvard	1953
Grossman, Herschel I.	Prof	Brown		PHD	65	J Hopkins	1973
Merton P. Stolz Professor in the Social Sciences							
Grossman, Leroy J.	C-Pr	St Louis		PHD	63	Vanderbilt	1964
Grossman, Peter Z.	Assoc	Butler	NL	PHD	92	Wash U	1994
Efroymson Chair in Economics							
Grossman, Philip J.	Asst	St Cloud St		PHD	84	Virginia	9-99
Grossman, Richard	Assoc	Wesleyan-CT	N	PHD	88	Harvard	1990
Groves, Theodore	Prof	Ca-San Diego	DHM	PHD	70	Berkeley	1978
Grubacic, Sanja	VAsst	New Haven	EF	PHD	96	Conn	9-98
Grubaugh, Stephen G.	Prof	Bentley	CF	PHD	82	Chicago	1981
Grubb, Farley	Prof	Delaware	N	PHD	84	Chicago	1983
Gruber, Jonathan H.	Prof	MIT	G	PHD	92	Harvard	1992
Grunloh, James J.	Prof	Wis-Oshkosh	A	PHD	79	Wash U	1969
Gruver, Gene W.	Prof	Pittsburgh	O	PHD	72	Iowa St	1970
Guell, Robert	Assoc	Indiana St	HC	PHD	91	Syracuse	1991
Guffey, Loren	Retir	Cen Arkansas		PHD	66	Arkansas	9-65
Guiler, Charles J.	Retir	Grove City		MED	66	Ind-Penn	1967
Guilfoil, John D.	Prof	New York U	DKN	PHD	64	NYU	1964
Guilkey, David K.	C-Pr	No Carolina	C	PHD	73	N Carol	1983
Guinnane, Timothy J.	Assoc	Yale	N	PHD	87	Stanford	
Gujarati, Damodar N.	Prof	USM Academy	CE	PHD	65	Chicago	1990
Gul, Faruk	Prof	Princeton		PHD	86	Princeton	1995
Gullason, Edward T.	Assoc	Dowling		PHD	86	Penn	
Gulley, O. David	Assoc	Bentley	EG	MA	89	Kentucky	1990
Gummerson, A.	Lect	Fla Internat	AEF	PHD	71	Wisconsin	1989
Gumpper, Michael R.	Asst	Millersville		PHD	97	Kentucky	1995
Gunden, Randal G.	Assoc	Goshen	EIO	ABD		Notre Dm	1984
Gunderson, Elizabeth W.	Assoc	Hamline	C	PHD	91	Union In	1980
Gunderson, Ralph O.	C-Pr	Wis-Oshkosh	OR	PHD	78	Arkansas	1987
Gunderson, Ronald J.	Prof	No Arizona	DR	PHD	77	Nebraska	1977
Gunn, John McKenzie	Emer	Wash & Lee	E	MA	54	Princeton	1957
Lewis Whitaker Adams Professor of Economics Emeritus							
Gunter, Frank R.	Assoc	Lehigh	FK	PHD	85	J Hopkins	1984
Gunther, William D.	Dean	So Miss	R	PHD	69	Kentucky	1998
Guo, Jang-Ting	Asst	Cal-Riversid	AC	PHD	93	UCLA	1993
Gupta, Barnali	Assoc	Miami U-Ohio	DR	PHD	90	Florida	1993
Gupta, Harish C.	Retir	Nebraska	FO	PHD	69	Tennessee	1969
Gupta, Satya P.	Prof	Augsburg		PHD	75	S Illinois	1976
Gupta, Shiv K.	Prof	Findlay	AJ	DBA	83	London	1983
Gupta, Srabana	Asst	Fla Atlantic	DL	PHD	95	Florida	1995
Gural, Michael L.	Assoc	Westfield St		MA		Rutgers	1982
Gurmu, Shiferaw	Assoc	Georgia St	CI	PHD	92	Indiana	1998
Gurtunca, Esen Z.	Prof	Indianapolis		PHD	73	Purdue	1974
Donald W. Tanselle Professor of Economics							
Gustafson, Curtis O.	Inst	So Dakota St	M	MPA	86	S Dakota	1989
Gustafson, Elizabeth F.	C-Ac	Dayton	C	PHD	74	N Carol	1983
Gustafson, Leland Verne	Prof	West Georgia	AC	PHD	74	Fla St	
Gustafson, W. Eric	Emer	Cal-Davis	AO	PHD	59	Harvard	1978
Gustavson, Robert L.	Prof	Washburn		PHD	76	Colorado	1976
Gustman, Alan Leslie	Prof	Dartmouth		PHD	69	Michigan	1969
Loren M. Berry Professor							

Gutermuth, Karen	Asst	Va Military		PHD	96	LSU	1997
Gutman, Nancy	Adjln	Yeshiva		BA	82	Barnard	
Gutmann, Peter M.	Prof	CUNY-Baruch	EF	PHD	57	Harvard	1963
Gutowsky, Albert R.	Prof	CS-Sacrament		PHD	65	Oregon	1967
Guttmann, Robert P.	Prof	Hofstra	F	PHD	79	London	
Guynn, Richard Dickson	Prof	West Georgia	JA	PHD	71	Alabama	
Gwartney, James D.	Prof	Florida St	A	PHD	69	U Wash	1968
Gwin, Carl	Asst	Babson	DLM	PHD	97	Indiana	1997
Gwinn, Lawrence	Assoc	Wittenberg	ACEF	PHD	83	Kansas	1988
Gyimah-Brempong, Kwabena	Prof	South Fla	O	PHD	81	Wayne St	1994
Gylys, Julius A.	Retir	Toledo		PHD	69	Wayne St	1967
Haab, Timothy C.	Asst	East Carol	CDQ	PHD	95	Maryland	1995
Haas, Paul F.	Prof	Bowling Gr		PHD	70	Boston C	1967
Haas-Wilson, Deborah	Prof	Smith	DIL	PHD	83	Berkeley	1984
Haberland, Chris		Clayton St		MBA	76	Geo St	1987
Habib, Ahsan M.	Assoc	Adrian		PHD	80	McMaster	1981
Hackett, Steven C.	Assoc	CS-Humboldt		PHD	89	Tx A&M	1994
Hadjimichalakis, Karma	SLect	U Washington		PHD	74	Rochester	1970
Hadjimichalakis, Michael	Assoc	U Washington		PHD	69	Rochester	1969
Hadley, Lawrence H.	Assoc	Dayton	J	PHD	75	Conn	1977
Hafer, Gail	Assoc	Lindenwood		PHD	87	S Illinois	9-93
Hafer, Rik W.	Prof	S Ill-Edward	EG	PHD	79	Va Tech	
Hagan, Oliver	Dean	Lindenwood		DMGT		Webster	9-90
Hagen, Daniel A.	Assoc	Western Wash	JEFQ	PHD	83	Berkeley	1988
Haggerty, Mark E.	Assoc	Clarion		PHD	88	Wash St	1989
Hagstrom, Paul Alan	Assoc	Hamilton	JHI	PHD	91	Wisconsin	1991
Hahn, Jinyong	Asst	Pennsylvania		PHD	93	Harvard	1993
Hahn, Youngki	Prof	Hawaii-Hilo		PHD	71	Ca-Rivers	
Hahnel, Robin E.	Prof	American U		PHD	79	American	1976
Hai, Wen	Asst	Fort Lewis		PHD	91	Ca-Davis	1992
Haight, Alan D.	Assoc	Bowling Gr		PHD	90	Wisconsin	1991
Haile, Philip	Asst	Wisconsin		PHD	96	Nrthwstrn	1996
Hailstones, Thomas J.	Deces	South Fla		PHD	51	St Louis	1988
Haines, Michael R.	Prof	Colgate	TN	PHD	71	Penn	1990
Banfi Vintners Professor of Economics							
Hajizadeh, Avaz	Assoc	Mass Lib Art		PHD	85	Rensselaer	
Hakeem, Salih	Asst	N Carol Cen		PHD	87	N Car St	1988
Hakes, David R.	Prof	No Iowa	BEFG	PHD	85	Iowa St	1992
Hakes, John K.	Asst	Clemson	HQC	PHD	96	Duke	1999
Hakim, Simon	Prof	Temple	R	PHD	76	Penn	1976
Halcoussis, Dennis	Asst	CS-Northrdge	C	PHD	92	Penn	1991
Haley, Charles	Prof	U Washington		PHD	68	Stanford	1966
Halil, Kiymaz	Asst	Houston-Cl L					1-97
Hall, Alastair R.	Prof	N Carol St	C	PHD	85	Warwick	1985
Hall, Bernard	Retir	Kent State	BNH	PHD	55	Berkeley	1955
Hall, Brian J.	Assoc	Harvard		PHD	83	Harvard	1993
Hall, Bronwyn H.	Assoc	Cal-Berkeley		PHD	88	Stanford	1987
Hall, Darwin C.	Prof	CS-Long Bch		PHD	77	Berkeley	1986
Hall, George	Asst	Yale	E	PHD	96	Chicago	1996
Hall, Jane V.	Prof	CS-Fullerton	Q	PHD	77	Berkeley	1981
Hall, John	Asst	Ark-Ltl Rock		PHD	92	Indiana	
Hall, John B.	Prof	Portland St		PHD	84	New Sch	1985
Hall, Phillip	Assoc	St Ambrose		PHD	88	Nebraska	1995
Hall, Robert E.	Prof	Stanford		PHD	67	MIT	1978
Hall, Thomas E.	Prof	Miami U-Ohio	EC	PHD	82	Ca-SnBarb	1982
Hall, W. Clayton	Assoc	Illinois Tch		PHD	04	Illinois	
Hall, William Woodward Jr.	Prof	N Car-Wilmin	QR	PHD	72	Clemson	
Hall, Yvonne C.	C-Pr	New Hamp Col		PHD	81	Colo St	
Hallagan, William S.	Assoc	Wash State		PHD	77	Ca-Davis	1984
Hallam, Arne	Assoc	Iowa State	D	PHD	83	Berkeley	1983
Haller, Hans H.	Prof	Virg Tech	D	PHD	78	Erlangen	1985
Hallock, Kevin F.	Asst	Illinois	HJ	PHD	95	Princeton	1995
Hallwood, C. Paul	Prof	Connecticut	F	PHD	88	Aberdeen	1986
Halstead, James F.	Prof	Occidental	A	PHD	72	Stanford	1977
Halteman, James	Prof	Wheaton-IL	AB	PHD	74	Penn St	1979
Hendrickson Chair							
Haltiwanger, John C.	Prof	Maryland		PHD	81	J Hopkins	1987
Halvorsen, Marcia L.	Prof	Redlands		PHD	78	Geo St	1975
Halvorsen, Robert F.	Prof	U Washington		PHD	73	Harvard	1972
Ham, C. L.	Retir	CS-Northrdge	8-94	PHD	72	S Calif	1963
Ham, John	Prof	Pittsburgh	J	PHD	80	Princeton	1991
Hamada, Koichi	Prof	Yale	F	PHD	65	Yale	1986
Hambleton, John W.	Assoc	San Diego St		PHD	71	Wisconsin	1969
Hamer, Thomas P.	Prof	Rowan Col-NJ		PHD	75	Claremont	1974
Hamermesh, Daniel S.	Prof	Texas	J	PHD	69	Yale	9-73
Eedward Everett Hale Centennial Professor in Economics							
Hamid, M. Khalil	Prof	Millersville		PHD	66	Iowa	1968
Hamilton, Bruce W.	Prof	J Hopkins		PHD	72	Princeton	1973
Hamilton, James D.	C-Pr	Ca-San Diego	D	PHD	83	Berkeley	1992
Hamilton, Jean	Asst	Occidental	J	PHD	92	Berkeley	1994

Name	Rank	School	Fields	Degree	Yr	Degree School	Year
Hamilton, Johnathan H.	Assoc	Florida	HRD	PHD	82	MIT	1984
Hammack, Judd	Retir	CS-L Angeles		PHD	69	U Wash	1970
Hammerle, Nancy E.	Asst	Stonehill	A	MA		Temple	1980
Hammermeister, John	Asst	St Ambrose		MBA		Oregon	
Hammes, David L.	C-Pr	Hawaii-Hilo		PHD	85	Simon Fr	1988
Hammond, Claire Holton	Prof	Wake Forest		PHD	82	Virginia	1978
Hammond, J. Daniel	Prof	Wake Forest		PHD	79	Virginia	1978
Hammond, Peter J.	Prof	Stanford		PHD	74	Cambridge	1979
Hammoudeh, Shawka M.	Assoc	Drexel		PHD	80	Kansas	1990
Hampton, Mary B.	Prof	Wis-La Cross	GHIJ	PHD	91	Wi-Milwa	1991
Hampton, Nathan E.	Assoc	St Cloud St		PHD	89	Ca-SnBarb	1987
Hamzaee, Reza G.	Prof	Missouri Wes	E	PHD	85	Ariz St	1984
Han, Hsiang-Ling	Asst	Babson	CE	PHD	92	Rochester	1997
Hanchate, Amresh	Asst	Case Western	OQDC	PHD	92	Wisconsin	1992
Hands, Wade	Prof	Puget Sound	ABC	PHD	65	U Wash	
Handy, John	Prof	Morehouse		PHD	85	Geo St	1978
Hankins, Marvin	Asst	SW Okla St		EDD		Okla St	1979
Hanna, Raouf S.	H-Pr	E Michigan		PHD	73	Indiana	1977
Hannah, Richard	Prof	Mid Tenn St	J	PHD	81	Utah	1992
Hannan, Michael J.	C-Pr	Edinboro		PHD	88	W Virginia	1988
Hannes, Lance E.	Assoc	Edinboro		MBA	87	SUNY-Buf	1978
Hanni, Eila A.	Retir	South Fla		PHD	70	Yale	1970
Hannon, Joan U.	C-Pr	St Marys-Cal		PHD	78	Wisconsin	1987
Hansen, Ann	Prof	Westminst-UT	CHL	PHD	81	Utah	1990
Hansen, Bradley	Asst	Mary Wash	N	PHD	95	Wash U	1995
Hansen, Bruce	Prof	Wisconsin	CE	PHD	89	Yale	1998
Hansen, David	Prof	Linfield		MS		Portland	1969
Hansen, Dwight W.	Assoc	Coe		MA	76	Nebraska	1978
Hansen, Gary B.	Retir	Utah State	J	PHD	71	Cornell	1967
Hansen, Gary D.	Prof	UCLA		PHD	86	Minnesota	1987
Hansen, Jan M.	Prof	Wis-Eau Clar	J	PHD	74	Missouri	1985
Hansen, John A.	Prof	SUNY-Fredoni	LD	PHD	80	Yale	1984
Hansen, Julia L.	Assoc	Western Wash	DR	PHD	84	Berkeley	1988
Hansen, Lars Peter	Prof	Chicago		PHD	78	Minnesota	1982
Homer J. Livingston Professor							
Hansen, Niles M.	Prof	Texas	RP	PHD	63	Indiana	1-63
Leroy G. Denmann, Jr. Regents Professor in Economics							
Hansen, W. Lee	Retir	Wisconsin		PHD	58	J Hopkins	1965
Hanson, Gordon H.	Assoc	Michigan	FO	PHD	92	MIT	
Hanson, James S.	Prof	Willamette		PHD	71	Stanford	1976
Hanson, John R. II	Prof	Texas A&M	N	PHD	72	Penn	1974
Hanson, Michael S.	Asst	Wesleyan-CT	E	PHD	99	Michigan	1999
Hanson, Robin	Asst	George Mason		PHD	99	Cal Tech	1999
Hanssen, F. Andrew	Asst	Montana St		PHD	95	Chicago	1995
Hanushek, Eric A.	Prof	Rochester		PHD	68	MIT	1978
Happel, Stephen K.	Prof	Arizona St		PHD	76	Duke	1975
Harbaugh, Richard	Asst	Claremont		PHD	97	Pittsburgh	1999
Harbaugh, William T.	Asst	Oregon	HQ	PHD	95	Wisconsin	1995
Harberger, Arnold C.	Emer	Chicago		PHD	50	Chicago	1953
Gustavus F. and Ann M. Swift Distinguished Service Professor							
Harder, K. Peter	Prof	Western Wash	BNP	PHD	68	Nebraska	1970
Hare, Denise	Assoc	Reed	AJOD	PHD	92	Stanford	1992
Harford, Jon D.	C-Ac	Cleveland St	DHKQ	PHD	74	Stanford	1982
Harger, Bruce T.	Prof	Lk Superior	A	PHD	91	Mich St	9-67
Harik, Bassam	Assoc	W Michigan	E	PHD	78	Wayne St	1979
Harik, Salim	Assoc	W Michigan	F	PHD	75	Wayne St	1976
Haririan, Mehdi	Prof	Bloomsburg		PHD	87	New Sch	1982
Harju, Melvin W.	Dean	La St-Shreve		PHD	72	Florida	8-77
Harl, Neil E.	Prof	Iowa State	QK	PHD	65	Iowa St	1964
Harless, David W.	Assoc	Virg Comm		PHD	88	Indiana	8-93
Harman, Peter	Assoc	Rhode Isl Cl		PHD	76	N Carol	
Harmel, Robert	Assoc	Midwest St	DL	PHD	74	Iowa St	1989
Harmon, Oskar R.	Assoc	Connecticut	H	PHD	80	Rutgers	1982
Haroian, Berch	Prof	Wm Patterson		PHD	72	NYU	1978
Harper, Richard K.	Assoc	West Florida	AFM	PHD	89	Duke	1989
Harpool, David	Dean	Webster	K	PHD	95	St Louis	1991
Harraf, Abe	C-Pr	Embry-Riddle		PHD	84	Utah St	
Harrald, Paul D.	Lect	Manches Inst	BCDL	PHD		Simon Fr	1994
Harrington, David E.	Assoc	Kenyon	QRHC	PHD	84	Wisconsin	1986
Himmelright Associate Professor in Economics							
Harrington, Joseph E.	Prof	J Hopkins		PHD	84	Duke	1983
Harris, Donald J.	Emer	Stanford		PHD	66	Berkeley	1972
Harris, James G.	Prof	CS-Dominguez	AEDH	PHD	70	Oregon	1969
Harris, Jeffrey E.	Prof	MIT	I	PHD	75	Penn	1976
Harris, John R.	Prof	Boston Univ	ER	PHD	67	Nrthwstrn	1975
Harris, R. Scott	Assoc	Mont St-Bill		PHD	85	UCLA	1988
Harris, Robert	Assoc	Ind-Purdue/I	A	PHD	79	Ohio St	1981
Harris, William G.	Retir	Georgetown		PHD	67	Oregon	
Harrison, Ann E.	Assoc	Columbia		PHD	91	Princeton	1994
Harrison, Dannie	Dean	Murray State	EPO	PHD	74	S Illinois	1969

Name	Rank	Institution	Fields	Degree	Yr	Degree School	Year
Harrison, Glenn W.	Prof	So Carolina		PHD	82	UCLA	
Dewey H. Johnson Professor of Economics							
Harrison, Kenneth	Assoc	R Stockton		PHD	76	SUNY-Alb	1976
Harrison, Sharon	Asst	Barnard	E	PHD	97	Nrthwstrn	1997
Harrison, William B. III	Retir	Virg Comm		PHD	72	Maryland	1972
Hart, Barbara	C-Pr	Texas-Tyler	CRIJ	PHD		Sam Hous	
Hart, Oliver D'Arcy	Prof	Harvard		PHD	74	Princeton	1993
Hart, William R.	Prof	Miami U-Ohio	EA	PHD	76	Wash U	1974
Hart-Landsberg, Martin	Prof	Lewis & Clrk	POFA	PHD	74	Wisconsin	1978
Harter, John F. R.	Asst	E Kentucky		PHD	92	Purdue	1999
Hartigan, James C.	Assoc	Oklahoma	FL	PHD	79	Duke	1988
Hartley, James E.	Asst	Mt Holyoke		PHD	94	Ca-Davis	1994
Hartley, Michael J.	Prof	New Orleans		PHD	70	Penn	
Hartley, Peter R.	Prof	Rice		PHD	80	Chicago	1986
Hartline, Jessie C.	Assoc	Rutgers-N Br	G	PHD	68	Rutgers	1968
Hartman, Harrison G.	C-Pr	E Stroudsbur	J	PHD	76	NYU	1964
Hartman, Richard C.	Prof	U Washington		PHD	71	Berkeley	1971
Hartmann, G. Bruce	H-Pr	Tenn State		PHD	74	SUNY-Alb	1974
Harvey, Curtis E.	Prof	Kentucky	P	PHD	63	S Calif	1963
Harvey, John T.	Assoc	Tx Christian		PHD	87	Tennessee	1987
Harwitz, Mitchell	Assoc	SUNY-Buffalo	COTR	PHD	59	MIT	1958
Hasan, Iftekhar	Prof	NJ Inst Tech		PHD	87	Houston	1994
Hasan, Nazmul	Asst	Illinois St	G	PHD	93	Illinois	1993
Hashemzadeh, Nozar	Prof	Radford	CJG	PHD	74	Va Tech	1983
Hashimoto, Masanori	C-Pr	Ohio State	J	PHD	71	Columbia	1987
Hasker, Kevin	Asst	Rice		PHD	98	Nrthwstrn	7-98
Hassan, Mahboubul	Assoc	New Hamp Col		MAPE	82	Boston U	
Hassan, Seid	Assoc	Murray State	CEFR	PHD	93	Tx A&M	1992
Hassanein, Saad A.	Prof	Marymount		PHD	88	Catholic	1988
Hasse, Charles	Asst	San Fran St		PHD	96	Ca-Davis	1997
Hasty, John M. Jr.	Prof	Tenn State		PHD	73	Geo St	
Hattwick, Richard E.	Prof	W Illinois	AM	PHD	65	Vanderbilt	1969
Hatzopoulos, Sydma	Assoc	West Liberty	CDEI	MA	80	Va Tech	1990
Hau, Jong-Chol	Retir	Millersville		PHD	67	St Louis	1969
Haughton, Jonathan H.	Asst	Suffolk		PHD	83	Harvard	1997
Haulman, Clyde A.	Prof	Wm & Mary		PHD	69	Fla St	1969
Haupert, Michael J.	C-Pr	Wis-La Cross	AEN	PHD	89	Wash U	1989
Haurin, Donald R.	Prof	Ohio State	R	PHD	78	Chicago	1975
Hause, John C.	Prof	SUNY-Stony B		PHD	62	Chicago	1978
Hausman, Jerry A.	Prof	MIT	C	DPHI	73	Oxford	1973
John and Jennie S. MacDonald Professor of Economics							
Hausman, William J.	Prof	Wm & Mary		PHD	76	Illinois	1981
Haveman, Robert H.	Prof	Wisconsin		PHD	63	Vanderbilt	1970
John Bascom Professor of Economics							
Havens, Rebecca A.	Prof	Pt Loma Naz		PHD	87	Ca-SnDgo	1990
Havrilesky, Thomas	Deces	Duke		PHD	66	Illinois	1969
Hawkins, Charles F.	C-Pr	Lamar	RK	PHD	80	LSU	1966
Regents' Professor of Economics							
Hawkins, Richard R.	Asst	West Florida	ACR	PHD	96	Geo St	1996
Hawley, Clifford B.	Prof	W Virginia	JD	PHD	77	Duke	1978
Haworth, Barry	Asst	Louisville	L	PHD	94	Ca-Davis	1995
Hay, George A.	Prof	Cornell		PHD	69	Nrthwstrn	1979
Edward Cornell Professor Law and Professor of Economics							
Hayashi, Paul M.	Prof	Tx-Arlington	D	PHD	69	So Meth	1965
Hayden, F. Gregory	Prof	Nebraska	HQI	PHD	68	Tx-Austin	1967
Haydon, Randall B.	Prof	Wichita St		PHD	62	Illinois	1970
Hayes, Kathy J.	Prof	So Methodist	HIL	PHD	80	Syracuse	1989
Hayes, Sue E.	Prof	Sonoma State		PHD	75	Berkeley	1974
Hayford, Marc D.	Assoc	Loyola-Chicg	AE	PHD	87	Brown	1986
Haynes, C. Beth	Prof	Brighm Yg-Hl	DG	PHD	81	Purdue	1994
Haynes, James F.	Dean	Athens State		PHD	80	Vanderbilt	1980
Haynes, Michael C.	Retir	So Oregon St	ADK	MS	64	Brighm Yg	1964
Haynes, Stephen E.	Prof	Oregon	FE	PHD	76	Ca-SnBarb	1978
Hays, Patrick Allen	Assoc	W Carolina		PHD	77	N Carol	1985
Haywood, Dale M.	Prof	Northwood		PHD	80	North Tx	
Hayworth, Steve	Assoc	E Michigan		PHD	87	MIT	1977
Hazilla, Michael	Assoc	American U		PHD	78	SUNY-Bin	1988
Hazlett, Denise J.	C-Ac	Whitman	EG	PHD	92	Minnesota	1992
Head, Tom	C-Ac	George Fox		MA	80	Berkeley	
Headen, Alvin E.	Assoc	N Carol St	IJD	PHD	81	MIT	1986
Heal, Geoffrey M.	Prof	Columbia		PHD	68	Cambridge	1983
Paul Garett Professor of Public Policy and Business Responsibility							
Heath, Julia A.	Prof	Memphis	JI	PHD	86	S Carol	1986
Heath, W. Cary	H-Ac	SW Louisiana		PHD	82	LSU	
Heavey, Jerome F.	C-Ac	Lafayette	DHP	PHD	76	Penn St	1973
Heberling, Gregory Dean	Assoc	Anderson U		MBA		Ball St	1978
Hebert, Robert F.	Prof	Auburn		PHD	70	LSU	1974
Russell Professor							
Heckelman, Jac C.	Asst	Wake Forest		PHD		Maryland	1996
Heckerman, Donald G.	Assoc	Arizona		PHD	67	MIT	1971

Name	Rank	School	Fields	Degree	Yr	Degree Institution	Year
Heckman, James J.	Prof	Chicago		PHD	71	Princeton	1973
Henry Schultz Professor of Economics & Soc Sciences							
Hecox, Walter E.	Prof	Colorado Col		PHD	69	Syracuse	1970
Hedrick, David W.	Assoc	Central Wash	AIO	PHD	84	Oregon	1987
Heffley, Dennis R.	Prof	Connecticut	RI	PHD	75	Ca-SnBarb	193
Hefner, Dennis L.	Prof	SUNY-Fredoni	IL	PHD	71	Wash St	1996
Hefner, Frank L.	Asst	Charleston		PHD	88	Kansas	1995
Hegji, Charles E.	Prof	Auburn-Montg	DFMJ	PHD	80	Wash U	1985
Heilbrun, James	Retir	Fordham		PHD	64	Columbia	1970
Heim, Carol E.	Assoc	Massachusett	NRE	PHD	82	Yale	1-81
Heim, John	Asst	Rensselaer		PHD	72	SUNY-Alb	1997
Heineke, John M.	Prof	Santa Clara		PHD	68	Iowa	1968
Heiner, Ronald A.	Prof	George Mason		PHD	75	UCLA	1989
Heiney, Joseph N.	D-Pr	Elmhurst		PHD	83	Chicago	1977
Coleman Foundation Distinguished Chair in Business							
Heinicke, Craig W.	Assoc	Baldwin-Wal	NOE	PHD	91	Toronto	1991
Heins, A. James	Retir	Illinois		PHD	61	Wisconsin	1960
Heisler, James B.	C-Pr	Hope	PD	PHD	75	Nebraska	1981
Heitmann, George Jr.	C-Pr	Muhlenberg		PHD	63	Princeton	1-94
Hekmat, Ali	C-Pr	Estrn Utah	E	PHD	93	Wi-Milwa	1994
Helburn, Suzanne W.	Emer	Colo-Denver	BI	PHD	61	Indiana	1970
Helfand, Steven	Asst	Cal-Riversid	AOQ	PHD	94	Berkeley	1995
Helland, Eric	Asst	Claremont		PHD	95	U Wash	1998
Heller, Dana	Asst	Chicago		PHD	98	Stanford	1998
Heller, Walter P.	Prof	Ca-San Diego	DE	PHD	70	Stanford	1974
Hellerstein, Judith	Asst	Maryland		PHD	94	Harvard	1996
Hellman, Daryl A.	Prof	Northeastern		PHD	70	Rutgers	1972
Helms, L. Jay	Assoc	Cal-Davis	DHI	PHD	79	MIT	1985
Helper, Susan	Assoc	Case Western	ONM	PHD	87	Harvard	1990
Helpman, Elhanen	Prof	Harvard		PHD		Harvard	1974
Hemesath, Michael	C-Ac	Carleton	AFP	PHD	88	Harvard	1989
Hendel, Igal		Princeton					
Henderson, David R.	Assoc	Naval Postgr	D	PHD	76	UCLA	1984
Henderson, J. Vernon	Prof	Brown		PHD	72	Chicago	1974
Eastman Professor of Political Economy							
Henderson, James M.	Deces	Duke		PHD	55	Harvard	1986
Henderson, James P.	Prof	Valparaiso	NBA	PHD	77	N Illinois	1975
Henderson, James W.	Prof	Baylor	IJ	PHD	81	So Meth	1981
Ben H. Williams Professor of Economics							
Henderson, Sandra R.	Retir	W Virg St	AFR	MA	60	Pittsburgh	1968
Henderson, Upton B.	Retir	Central Okla		PHD	65	Missouri	1971
Hendon, Fred N.	Prof	Samford	FN	PHD	68	Alabama	1968
Hendricks, Lutz	Asst	Arizona St		PHD	96	Penn	1996
Hendricks, Wallace E.	Prof	Illinois	J	PHD	73	Berkeley	1973
Hendrickson, Jill K.	Asst	Univ South	EGC	PHD		Notre Dm	1995
Hendryson, Mary Ann	Lect	Western Wash	DOF	ABD		Wash St	1989
Henry, Jacqueline	Asst	Immaculata		MA		Cen Mich	1998
Henry, John F.	Prof	CS-Sacrament		PHD	74	McGill	1970
Henry, Marc	Asst	Columbia	CG	PHD	98	LondonSE	1998
Henson, Steven E.	Assoc	Western Wash	QD	PHD	82	Oregon	1985
Hentzel, David	Prof	Mo-Rolla		PHD	67	S Illinois	1969
Herander, Mark G.	Prof	South Fla	F	PHD	80	N Carol	1979
Herbener, Jeffrey M.	Prof	Grove City		PHD	82	Okla St	1997
Herber, Bernard P.	Retir	Arizona		PHD	69	U Wash	1957
Herbst, Lawrence A.	Assoc	Vassar	N	PHD	74	Penn	1970
Herdendorf, Phyllis		SUNY-Empire	F	PHD	81	SUNY	1987
Herendeen, James B.	Prof	Txs-El Paso	AQ	PHD	63	Penn St	1992
Hergenrather, Richard A.	Asst	Whitworth	DE	PHD	93	P Drucker	1994
Hermalin, Benjamin E.	Assoc	Cal-Berkeley		PHD	88	MIT	1988
Herman, E. Edward	Prof	Cincinnati	J	PHD	65	McGill	1966
Herman, Walter J.	Retir	South Fla	E	PHD	65	Florida	1980
Hermann, Mark	Assoc	Alaska-Fairb		PHD	90	Wash St	1990
Herold, Marc W.	Assoc	New Hampshir	O	PHD	77	Berkeley	1975
Herr, Andy	Asst	St Vincent	HEQ	PHD	96	Indiana	1991
Herren, R. Stanley	Prof	N Dakota St	ABEJ	PHD	75	Duke	1985
Herrick, Bruce H.	Prof	Wash & Lee	OP	PHD	64	MIT	1980
John F. Hendon Professor of Economics							
Herrin, William E.	C-Ac	Pacific	RC	PHD	85	SUNY-Bin	1985
Herrnstadt, Irwin L.	Retir	Northeastern		PHD	64	MIT	1960
Hersch, Joni	Prof	Wyoming	CJ	PHD	81	Nrthwstrn	1989
Hersch, Philip L.	Prof	Wichita St		PHD	82	Ohio St	1983
Herschede, Alfred J.	Prof	Ind-So Bend	ADP	PHD	76	Illinois	1976
Hersh-Cochran, Mona S.	Prof	Txs Woman's		PHD	66	So Meth	
Conaro Professor of Business and Economics							
Hervitz, Hugo M.	Prof	Barry		PHD	83	Indiana	1982
Herzog, Henry W. Jr.	Prof	Tennessee		PHD	74	Maryland	1974
Hess, Alan C.	Prof	U Washington		PHD	69	Car Mellon	1967
Hess, Arleigh P. Jr.	Emer	Pennsylvania		PHD	49	Penn	1949
Associate Undergraduate Chair for Advising							
Hess, Gregory	Prof	Oberlin	E	PHD	89	J Hopkins	1993

Hess, Peter N.	C-Pr	Davidson	OT	PHD	82	N Carol	1980
Gail M. and Ernst G. Doe Professor of Economics							
Hester, Donald D.	Prof	Wisconsin		PHD	61	Yale	1968
Heston, Alan W.	Prof	Pennsylvania		PHD	62	Yale	
Hetherington, Bruce W.	Prof	Ogelthorpe	NE	PHD	82	Va Tech	1980
Hettich, Walter	Prof	CS-Fullerton	H	PHD	67	Yale	1983
Hettler, Paul	Asst	Duquesne		PHD	98	Pittsburgh	1999
Heung, C. James	Asst	Alabama		PHD	97	Wisconsin	1997
Hewett, Roger S.	Assoc	Drake		PHD	84	Illinois	1981
Hewins, Dana C.	C-Ac	Regis-MA		PHD	75	Illinois	
Heyne, Paul T.	SLect	U Washington		PHD	63	Chicago	1976
Heywood, John S.	Prof	Wis-Milwauke		PHD	86	Michigan	1986
Hibbard, Thomas H.	Prof	Willamette		PHD	67	Claremont	1973
Hickerson, Steven	Prof	Mankato St	ABK	PHD	80	Nebraska	1980
Hickey, Kevin L.	Assoc	Assumption		MLA	76	Harvard	1972
Hickman, Bert G.	Emer	Stanford		PHD	51	Berkeley	1966
Hicks, Donald A.	Prof	Texas-Dallas		PHD	76	N Carol	
Hicks, W. Whitney	Prof	Missouri	O	PHD	65	Stanford	1965
Hiebert, L. Dean	Prof	Illinois St	ADE	PHD	72	Wisconsin	1973
Hiedemann, Bridget	Asst	Seattle	DJT	PHD	92	Duke	1994
Hiestand, Thomas W.	Assoc	Concordia C	CD	PHD	74	Kansas St	1972
Higgins, Matthew L.	Assoc	W Michigan	C	PHD	89	Illinois	1995
Higgins, Neal O.	Prof	Portland	RH	PHD	74	Nebraska	1976
Higgins, Robert C.	Prof	U Washington		PHD	69	Stanford	1967
Highfill, Jannett K.	Prof	Bradley		PHD	85	Kansas	1985
Hildebrandt, Gregory G.	Assoc	Naval Postgr	D	PHD	76	Princeton	1992
Hildred, William M.	Prof	No Arizona	HA	PHD	64	Colo St	1988
Hileman, A. Eugene	C-Pr	NE St-Okla	AGM	PHD	71	Tennessee	1988
Hill, Catharine Bond	C-Ac	Williams		PHD	85	Yale	1985
Hill, Cynthia D.	Asst	Idaho State	AIJQ	PHD	97	Wash St	1998
Hill, James Richard	Assoc	Cen Michigan		PHD	80	Kentucky	1981
Hill, John A.	Asst	Hardin-Simm		PHD	95	Tennessee	1998
Hill, Lawrence G.	C-Pr	Lewis		PHD	76	N Illinois	1968
Hill, Lewis E.	Prof	Texas Tech		PHD	57	Tx-Austin	1967
Hill, M. Anne	C-Pr	CUNY-Queens	JC	PHD	80	Duke	1989
Hill, Pershing J.	Assoc	Alaska-Ancho	EFH	PHD	76	Wash St	1975
Hill, Peter J.	Prof	Wheaton-IL	ANPQ	PHD	70	Chicago	1986
George F. Bennett Professor of Economics							
Hill, R. Carter	Prof	Louisiana St	C	PHD	75	Missouri	
Marjory B. Ourso Excellence in Teaching Professor							
Hill, Roger Post	Prof	N Car-Wilmin	G	PHD	68	Mich St	
Hillard, Michael	C-Ac	So Maine	EJ	PHD	88	Mass	1987
Hilmer, Michael	Asst	Louisville	H	PHD	96	Ca-SnBarb	8-97
Hilton S.J., F. G.	Asst	Loyola-Maryl	QF	PHD	96	Wisconsin	1996
Himarios, Daniel	C-Pr	Tx-Arlington	FE	PHD	84	Va Tech	1983
Himarios, Jane	SLect	Tx-Arlington	J	PHD	87	Va Tech	1986
Himmelberg, Charles P.	Assoc	Columbia	DEL	PHD	90	Nrthwstrn	1995
Hinderliter, Roger H.	Assoc	Ithaca	BE	PHD	70	Wash U	1970
Hinshaw, C. Elton	Assoc	Vanderbilt	N	PHD	66	Vanderbilt	1966
Hinson, Steve Y.	Asst	Webster	AFDH	PHD	93	Kentucky	1993
Hinton, William Valentine	Prof	Delta State		PHD	82	Arkansas	8-87
Hippie, F. Steb	Prof	East Tenn St		PHD	72	So Meth	1982
Hirsch, Barry T.	Prof	Florida St	J	PHD	77	Virginia	1990
Hirschfeld, Mary L.	C-Ac	Occidental	N	PHD	89	Harvard	1988
Hitchner, Benjamin	Retir	Rowan Col-NJ		MS		Penn	1964
Ho, Franklin Y. H.	Prof	CS-Pomona		PHD	57	S Calif	1961
Ho, Peter S. W.	Assoc	Denver	FO	PHD	89	Stanford	1987
Ho, Yhi-Min	Dean	St Thomas-TX	OQ	PHD	65	Vanderbilt	8-70
Hugh Roy and Lillie Cullen Professor of Economics							
Hoag, John H.	C-Pr	Bowling Gr		PHD	72	Kansas	1972
Hoch, Irving J.	Prof	Texas-Dallas		PHD	57	Chicago	1985
Hochman, Harold M.	Prof	Lafayette	HIK	PHD	65	Yale	1992
Wm. E. Simon Professor of Political Economics							
Hodges, Paul E.	Prof	Txs-Perm Bas		PHD	74	Stanford	
Hodgin, Gary L.	Assoc	Belmont		PHD	85	Tennessee	1983
Hodgin, Robert F.	Assoc	Houston-Cl L		DA	80	Illin St	9-81
Hodgson, Doug	Asst	Rochester		PHD	95	Yale	1995
Hofer, Tracy	Asst	Wis-Stev Pt		PHD	97	Texas	1999
Hoffer, George E.	Prof	Virg Comm		PHD	72	Virginia	1970
Hoffman, Dennis L.	Prof	Arizona St		PHD	78	Mich St	1979
Hoffman, Elizabeth	Prof	Ill-Chicago	N	PHD	79	Cal Tech	1997
Hoffman, Emily P.	Prof	W Michigan	J	PHD	75	Mass	1981
Hoffman, Naphtali	C-Ac	Elmira		PHD	80	Case Wes	1976
Hoffman, Robert	Asst	St Scholasti	E	PHD	92	Boston C	
Hoffman, Saul D.	Prof	Delaware	TJ	PHD	77	Michigan	1977
Hofler, Martha	Inst	Old Dominion	F	MA		Old Dom	
Hofler, Richard A.	C-Pr	Cen Florida	CIJ	PHD	82	N Carol	1989
Hofman, Cornelius A.	Retir	Idaho State	5-97	PHD	64	Utah	1960
Hoftyzer, John	H-Pr	SW Missouri		PHD	74	Indiana	1987
Hogan, Timothy D.	Prof	Arizona St		PHD	71	Va Tech	1970

Name	Rank	School	Fields	Degree	Yr	Degree School	Year
Hogan, William V.	C-Pr	Mass-Dartmou		PHD	76	Cornell	1976
Hogendorn, Jan S.	Prof	Colby	FOA	PHD	66	London	1966
Grossman Professor of Economics							
Hohenberg, Paul M.	Retir	Rensselaer		PHD	63	MIT	1977
Hoke, Leon R. Jr.	Prof	Tampa	ADJ	PHD	79	Pittsburgh	1981
Hoksbergen, Roland G.	C-Pr	Calvin		PHD	86	Notre Dm	1983
Holahan, William L.	Prof	Wis-Milwauke		PHD	74	Brown	1972
Holbrook, Robert S.	Prof	Michigan		PHD	65	Berkeley	1965
Holcomb, James H. Jr.	Assoc	Txs-El Paso	CDL	PHD	85	Tx A&M	1985
Holcombe, Randall G.	Prof	Florida St	H	PHD	76	Va Tech	1988
DeVoe Moore Professor							
Holland, A. Steven	C-Pr	SW Texas St	E	PHD	83	Mich St	1998
Holland, John J. Jr.	Prof	Monmouth	EN	PHD	72	NYU	9-97
Holland, Larry C.	Asst	Ark-Ltl Rock		PHD	96	Okla St	1995
Holland, Thomas E.	Retir	Tx-Arlington	D	PHD	63	Duke	1970
Hollas, Daniel R.	Prof	Tx-S Antonio		PHD	77	Illinois	1988
Holliday, A. J.	Asst	Wash & Lee	K	PHD	95	Virginia	1993
Hollister, Robinson G. Jr.	Prof	Swarthmore	IJ	PHD	65	Stanford	1971
Joseph Wharton Professor of Economics							
Holman, Jill Ann	Asst	Georgia	EF	PHD	97	Colorado	1997
Holman, Mary A.	Prof	George Wash	L	PHD	63	Geo Wash	1963
Holmes, Alexander B.	Assoc	Oklahoma	RD	PHD	74	SUNY-Bin	
Holmes, George M.	Asst	East Carol	CIJ	PHD	99	N Carol	1999
Holmes, James M.	Prof	SUNY-Buffalo	EF	PHD	67	Chicago	1967
Holmes, Thomas J.	Assoc	Minnesota		PHD	85	Nrthwstrn	1995
Holmes, William L.	Assoc	Temple	CD	PHD	66	Illinois	1966
Holmstrom, Bengt	Prof	MIT	L	PHD	78	Stanford	1995
Paul A. Samuelson Professor of Economics							
Holmstrom, Thomas K.	Prof	No Michigan	AEF	PHD	73	Okla St	1966
HOlstein, Adora	Assoc	Robt Morris		PHD	87	Penn St	
Holt, Charles A.	C-Pr	Virginia	CDL	PHD	77	Car Mellon	1989
Merrill Bankard Professor of Economics							
Holt, Charles F.	Assoc	San Diego		PHD	70	Purdue	1973
Holt, Harry G.	Retir	Indiana U-PA	IP	MS	61	Bucknell	1968
Holt, Kenneth	Assoc	Union-TN		ABD		Memphis	1987
Holt, Richard P. F.	Assoc	So Oregon St	ABDM	PHD	87	Utah	1996
Holthausen, Duncan M. Jr.	Prof	N Carol St	DC	PHD	76	Nrthwstrn	1974
Holtmann, Alphonse G.	Prof	U Miami	DI	PHD	63	Wash U	1981
Holtz-Eakin, Douglas	C-Pr	Syracuse	H	PHD	85	Princeton	
Holzer, Harry J.	Prof	Michigan St		PHD	83	Harvard	1983
Holzman, Franklyn Dunn	Retir	Tufts		PHD	52	Harvard	1961
Homer, John S.	Prof	Olivet		PHD	91	Hawaii	1979
Hong, Lu	Assoc	Syracuse	D	PHD	91	Minnesota	
Hong, Youngmaio	Assoc	Cornell		PHD	93	Ca-SnDgo	7-93
Honig, Marjorie	C-Pr	CUNY-Hunter		PHD	71	Columbia	
Honig, Solomon	Assoc	Montclair St	ADKR	PHD	76	Columbia	1981
Honig, Susan	Asst	CUNY-Lehman		MS		Pace	
Honkalehto, Oswald	Retir	Colgate	C	PHD	69	MIT	1962
Honore, Bo Erno		Princeton		PHD	87	Chicago	
Hood, Frank	Prof	Miss College		PHD	72	Miss	1972
Hooks, Donald L.	Assoc	Alabama		PHD	71	Tx A&M	1971
Hooks, Jon A.	Asst	Albion	G	PHD	89	Mich St	1989
Hooks, Linda M.	Asst	Wash & Lee	E	PHD	91	UCLA	1993
Hool, Bryce	Prof	SUNY-Stony B		PHD	74	Berkeley	1979
Hoover, Gary A.	Asst	Alabama		PHD	98	U Wash	1998
Hoover, Kevin D.	Prof	Cal-Davis	BE	DPHI	85	Oxford	1985
Hoover, Scott	Asst	Wyoming		PHD	99	Indiana	1997
Hope, Barney F.	C-Pr	CS-Chico	RFO	PHD	79	Ca-Rivers	1977
Hopenhayn, Hugo	Assoc	Rochester		PHD	89	Minnesota	1994
Hopkins, Barbara	Asst	Wright State		PHD	92	Maryland	1995
Hopkins, Thomas D.	Prof	Rochest Tech	DHK	PHD	71	Yale	1988
Arthur J. Gosnell Professor of Economics							
Hoppe, Hans Hermann	Prof	Nev-L Vegas	B	PHD		Goethe	1986
Hoppes, Robert B.	Prof	SW Missouri		PHD	75	Nebraska	1980
Hoppie, Maurice R.	Assoc	Elizabethtwn		PHD	85	Tennessee	1980
Hordon, Harris	C-Pr	NewJerseyCty	AG	PHD	68	NYU	
Horiba, Yutaka	Prof	Tulane		PHD	69	Purdue	1971
Horn, Bobbie L.	Assoc	Tulsa		PHD	86	Iowa St	
Horn, Robert N.	Prof	Jms Madison	JD	PHD	78	NewHamp	1978
Horner, James	Prof	Cameron		PHD	85	Tx-Dallas	1976
Horney, Mary Jean	Prof	Furman		PHD	77	Duke	1979
Frederick W. Symmes Professor of Economics							
Hornsten, James	Asst	Bowdoin	L	ABD		Nrthwstrn	1999
Horowitz, Andrew W.	Assoc	Arkansas	OFD	PHD	89	Wisconsin	1998
Horowitz, Ann R.	Assoc	Florida		PHD	66	Indiana	1972
Horowitz, Avery M.	Assoc	Yeshiva		PHD	84	CUNY	1986
Horowitz, John B.	Assoc	Ball State	HJ	PHD	88	Tx A&M	1989
Horowtiz, Joel	Prof	Iowa		PHD	67	Cornell	1982
Horrace, William	Asst	Arizona		PHD	96	Mich St	1996
Horton, Joseph J.	Dean	Cen Arkansas		PHD	68	So Meth	7-96

Horvath, Janos	Retir	Butler	FE	PHD	67	Columbia	
Horvath, Michael	Asst	Stanford		PHD	94	Nrthwstrn	1994
Horwich, George	Prof	Purdue		PHD	54	Chicago	1956
Horwitz, Sigmund	Prof	Txs Southern		PHD		Houston	
Horwitz, Steven G.	Assoc	St Lawrence	EPB	PHD	90	GeoMason	1989
Hoselitz, Bert F.	Retir	Chicago		JD	36	Vienna	1945
Hosni, Djehane	Assoc	Cen Florida	O	PHD	78	Arkansas	1977
Hosseini, Hamid S.	C-Ac	King's Col		PHD	77	Oregon	9-86
Hosseinzadeh, Esmail	Assoc	Drake		PHD	87	New Sch	1988
Hotchkiss, Julie L.	Assoc	Georgia St	CJ	PHD	89	Cornell	1989
Hotelling, Harold	C-Ac	Lawrence Tec	KL	PHD	82	Duke	9-89
Hotopp, Susan	Asst	No Central	A	PHD	89	Illinois	1991
Hott, David D.	C-Ac	Fla Inst Tec		PHD	77	Lehigh	1995
Hou, Chi-Ming	Deces	Colgate	1994	PHD	54	Columbia	1956
Hou, Jack W.	Prof	CS-Long Bch		PHD	89	Yale	1989
Houlihan, Colleen	Asst	Grand Canyon	L	PHD	98	Illinois	1998
Houser, Cindy	Asst	Tx A&M Intl		PHD	95	Florida	9-95
Houser, Daniel	Asst	Arizona		PHD	97	Minnesota	1997
Houser, Scott	Asst	CS-Fresno	HRI	PHD	96	Wisconsin	1996
Houston, A. Craig	Retir	Dickinson Cl		PHD	62	Penn St	1956
Houston, Robert G.	Asst	E Kentucky		ABD	99	Kentucky	1998
Houthakker, Hendrick S.	Emer	Harvard		ECD	49	Amsterdm	
Henry Lee Professor of Economics							
Howard, Bruce	C-Ac	Wheaton-IL	ABM	PHD	89	N Illinois	1980
Howard, James E.	Assoc	S F Austin	AC	PHD	77	Georgia	1976
Howe, Charles W.	Prof	Colorado		PHD	59	Stanford	1970
Howe, Edward T.	Prof	Siena		PHD	73	SUNY-Alb	
Howell, Kristen K.	Assoc	N Car-Wilmin	F	PHD	89	Kentucky	
Howitt, Peter	Prof	Ohio State	E	PHD	73	Nrthwstrn	1996
University Chaired Professor							
Howrey, E. Philip	Prof	Michigan	CE	PHD	64	N Carol	9-73
Howsen, Roy M.	Assoc	W Kentucky	D	PHD	80	Arkansas	1981
Hoxby, Caroline Minter	Assoc	Harvard	JH	PHD	94	MIT	7-94
Hoynes, Hilary	Asst	Cal-Berkeley		PHD	95	Stanford	1995
Hoyt, Gail Mitchell	Asst	Kentucky	A	PHD	92	Kentucky	1994
Hoyt, William H.	Assoc	Kentucky	RHG	PHD	86	Iowa	1969
Hsia, Ke Ting	Retir	CS-L Angeles		PHD	66	Wisconsin	1963
Hsiao, Cheng	Prof	So Calif		PHD	72	Stanford	1985
Hsiao, Frank S. T.	Prof	Colorado		PHD	67	Rochester	1975
Hsiao, James C.	Retir	So Conn St		PHD		Conn	
Hsiao, Mei-chu W.	Assoc	Colo-Denver	OC	PHD	67	Rochester	1981
Hsiao, Yu-Mong	Prof	Campbell		PHD	85	N Car St	1984
Hsieh, Edward T.	Assoc	CS-L Angeles		PHD	88	Houston	1989
Hsieh, Eric	Assoc	La St-Shreve		PHD		LSU	1989
Hsing, Yu	H-Pr	SE Louisiana	EJOR	PHD	83	Tennessee	1987
Hsu, Robert C.	Prof	Clark		PHD	70	Berkeley	1971
Hsu, Yu-Chu	Prof	So Conn St	HO	PHD	65	Cornell	
Hu, Sheng C.	Retir	Purdue		PHD	70	Rochester	1968
Hu, Wei-Yin	Asst	UCLA		PHD	94	Stanford	
Huang, Cliff J.	Prof	Vanderbilt	C	PHD	68	N Carol	1969
Huang, Ju-Chin	Asst	New Hampshir	CQ	PHD	94	N Car St	1998
Huang, Kevin	Asst	Utah State	EFG	PHD	98	Minnesota	1998
Huang, Lien-fu	Prof	Howard	I	PHD	71	Rochester	
Huang, Wei-Chiao	Prof	W Michigan	J	PHD	84	Ca-SnBarb	1985
Hubbard, R. Glenn	Prof	Columbia		PHD	83	Harvard	1988
Russell L. Carson Professor of Finance and Economics							
Hubbard, Thomas	Asst	UCLA		PHD	96	Stanford	
Hubbell, L. Kenneth	Prof	Mo-Kansas Ct	GHM	PHD	70	Nebraska	1968
Huckins, Larry E.	Asst	CUNY-Baruch		PHD	83	Chicago	1980
Huddle, Donald L.	Retir	Rice		PHD	64	Vanderbilt	1964
Huddleston, Kenneth M.	Asst	Georgia SW		MBA		Geo St	
Hueckel, Glenn R.	Assoc	Purdue		PHD	72	Wisconsin	1972
Huenneke, Steve	Assoc	Minot State	AR	PHD	92	Kansas St	1991
Huetter, David A.	Retir	Oklahoma	L	PHD	72	Case Wes	1974
Huffman, Gregory	Assoc	So Methodist	EG	PHD	83	Minnesota	1992
Huffman, Wallace E.	Prof	Iowa State	J	PHD	72	Chicago	1974
Hughes, Greg	Prof	Rensselaer		PHD	72	Princeton	1997
Hughes, James W.	C-As	Bates	J	PHD	87	Michigan	1987
Hughes, Johnathan R. T.	Deces	Northwestern		PHIL		Oxford	
Hughes, Joseph P.	Assoc	Rutgers-N Br	D	PHD	74	N Carol	1975
Hughes, Patricia A. Nold	Assoc	St Cloud St		PHD	91	Ca-SnBarb	1988
Hughes, Woodrow W. Jr.	C-As	Converse		PHD	89	S Carol	1986
Hull, Brooks B.	C-Pr	Mich-Dearbor	LQ	PHD	82	U Wash	1981
Hull, Everson W.	Asst	Howard		PHD	77	Howard	
Hultberg, Patrik	Asst	Wyoming		PHD	98	Rice	1998
Hulten, Charles R.	Prof	Maryland		PHD	73	Berkeley	1985
Hultman, Charles W.	Retir	Kentucky	F	PHD	60	Iowa	1969
Humphreys, Brad	Inst	MD-Baltim Co		MA	91	J Hopkins	
Humphries, John	Prof	Rochest Tech		PHD	67	Syracuse	1962
Hung, Chao-shun	Prof	Fla Atlantic	D	PHD	82	Tx A&M	1982

Hung, Gregory	Prof	Howard	O	PHD	65	Virginia	
Hunger, David	Asst	Ogelthorpe	LDC	PHD	98	Oregon	1993
Hunnicutt, Lynn	Asst	Utah State	DLM	PHD	97	Tx-Austin	1998
Hunsaker, Julie	Asst	Wayne State		PHD	93	Purdue	1993
Hunt, E. K.	C-Pr	Utah		PHD	68	Utah	1978
Hunt, Gary	Prof	Maine	AR	PHD	84	Colorado	1993
Hunt, Jennifer A.	Assoc	Yale	J	PHD	92	Harvard	1992
Hunt, Joseph W.	Retir	Shippensburg		PHD	66	Indiana	1980
Hunte, C. Kenrick	Asst	Howard	OF	PHD		Ohio St	
Hunter, Thomas Kenneth	Retir	S F Austin		PHD	68	Tennessee	1968
Hunter, William J.	Assoc	Marquette	DH	PHD	79	Va Tech	1982
Hurd, John II	Prof	Norwich		PHD	69	Penn	1978
Hurd, Michael	Prof	SUNY-Stony B		PHD	71	Berkeley	1978
Hurley, John F.	C-Ac	Jackson St		PHD	71	Illinois	1972
Hurwicz, Leo	Prof	Minnesota		LLM	38	Warsaw	1951
Husbands, Kaye G.	Assoc	Williams		PHD	90	Harvard	
Husby, Ralph D.	Assoc	Illinois	EJ	PHD	69	Cornell	1967
Huskey, Lee	C-Pr	Alaska-Ancho	AJR	PHD	77	Wash U	1977
Hussain, Riaz	Assoc	Scranton		PHD	73	J Hopkins	1967
Hussain, Syed Bashir	Assoc	Wis-Oshkosh	F	PHD	83	Ca-Rivers	1982
Hussen, Ahmed M.	C-Pr	Kalamazoo	DQ	PHD	78	Oregon St	1985
Husted, Steven L.	Prof	Pittsburgh	F	PHD	80	Mich St	1980
Husted, Thomas A.	Assoc	American U		PHD	86	N Carol	1986
Huston, John H.	Assoc	Trinity	D	PHD	83	Wisconsin	1983
Hutcheson, Aaron A.	Retir	Austin Peay	AQ	PHD	68	Clemson	1967
Hutchinson, E. Bruce	Prof	Tenn-Chattan	DFLR	PHD	79	Virginia	1982
Hutchinson, Gladstone	Asst	Lafayette	AO	PHD	90	Clark	1992
Hutchinson, William K.	Prof	Miami U-Ohio	EF	PHD	75	Iowa	1972
Hutchison, Michael M.	Prof	Ca-Santa Crz	EFG	PHD	83	Oregon	1985
Huth, William L.	Prof	West Florida	AMG	PHD	80	Arkansas	1989
Huttman, John P.	Retir	San Fran St		PHD	69	London	1970
Hutton, Patricia A.	Prof	Canisius		PHD	80	Wisconsin	1981
Hvidding, James M.	C-Pr	Kutztown	EB	PHD	76	Maryland	1986
Hwang, Hae-Shin	Prof	Texas A&M	C	PHD	76	Minnesota	1977
Hwang, Ming-jeng	Prof	W Virginia	DRC	PHD	73	Tx A&M	1974
Hyclak, Thomas J.	C-Pr	Lehigh	JR	PHD	76	Notre Dm	1979
Hyle, Matthew R.	Prof	Winona State		PHD	85	Maryland	1988
Hyman, David Neil	Prof	N Carol St	HA	PHD	69	Princeton	1969
Hymans, Saul H.	Prof	Michigan		PHD	64	Berkeley	1964
Hyslop, Dean	Asst	UCLA		PHD	95	Princeton	
Iannaccone, Laurence R.	Prof	Santa Clara		PHD	84	Chicago	1982
Ibister, John W.	Prof	Ca-Santa Crz	O	PHD	69	Princeton	1968
Ichiishi, Tatsuro	Prof	Ohio State	C	PHD	74	Berkeley	1987
Ichimura, Hidehiko	Asst	Pittsburgh	C	PHD	88	MIT	1996
Ickes, Barry W.	Assoc	Penn State	P	PHD	84	Berkeley	1983
Idson, Todd	Assoc	Columbia	JC	PHD	86	Columbia	1990
Ierulli, Kathryn	Asst	Ill-Chicago	D	PHD	94	Chicago	1993
Ifediora, John O.	C-Ac	Wis-Plattev		PHD	88	Il-Chicago	1988
Ignatin, George	Assoc	Alabama-Birm	AJK	PHD	69	Tx-Austin	1969
Ihlanfeldt, Keith R.	Prof	Georgia St	HR	PHD	78	Wash U	1981
Ihrig, Jane	Asst	Virginia	F	PHD	95	Minnesota	1995
Ikeda, Sanford	Assoc	SUNY-Purchas		PHD	88	NYU	1990
Ikpoh, Andrew	Assoc	Seton Hall		PHD	88	Columbia	
Ilacqua, Joseph A.	Prof	Bryant	AJ	EDD	93	Boston U	1968
Im, Eric I.	Prof	Hawaii-Hilo		PHD	82	Hi-Manoa	
Im, Kyung So	Asst	Wichita St		PHD	95	Mich St	1998
Imai, Susumu	Lect	Penn State		PHD			1997
Inaba, Frederick S.	Assoc	Wash State		PHD	74	Berkeley	1977
Ingham, Hilary C.	SLect	U Lancaster	JCD	PHD		Glasgow	
Ingles, Jerry Lee	Prof	Univ South	BL	PHD	75	Cornell	
Ingram, David	Asst	Coe		PHD	97	Kansas St	1999
Ingram, James C.	Emer	No Carolina		PHD	52	Cornell	1952
Ingram, Marlynne B. F.	Assoc	Iowa		PHD	86	Iowa	1988
Inman, Robert P.	Prof	Pennsylvania		PHD	72	Harvard	
Innes, Jon T.	Prof	Lehigh	EB	PHD	67	Oregon	1987
Intriligator, Michael D.	Emer	UCLA		PHD	63	MIT	1972
Ioannatos, Petros	Asst	Kettering		PHD	89	Wayne St	
Ioannides, Yannis M.	Prof	Tufts	E	PHD	74	Stanford	1995
Neubauer Chair Holder							
Ireland, Peter N.	Assoc	Boston Coll	E	PHD	91	Chicago	1998
Ireland, Thomas R.	Prof	Mo-St Louis		PHD	68	Virginia	1972
Irvine, F. Owen	Assoc	Michigan St		PHD	76	MIT	1982
Irwin, Douglas	VAsst	MIT		PHD		Columbia	1999
Irwin, Douglas A.	Prof	Dartmouth		PHD	88	Columbia	1997
Irwin, James R.	Asst	Cen Michigan		PHD	86	Rochester	1989
Isaac, Alan G.	Assoc	American U		PHD	86	Ca-Davis	1987
Isaac, R. Mark	Prof	Arizona		PHD	80	Cal Tech	1980
Isaacs, Patricia	Assoc	Berea		DBA	94	Kentucky	1989
Isbell, Steven	Assoc	Tenn Tech		PHD	85	Miss	1985
Isely, Paul N.	Asst	Grand Valley		PHD	95	Purdue	1997

Name	Rank	School	Fields	Degree	Yr	Institution	Year
Isenberg, Dorene L.	Assoc	Drew	E	PHD	86	Ca-Rivers	
Isham, Jonathan T. Jr.	Asst	Middlebury	OQ	PHD	94	Ca-Rivers	1997
Ishimine, Tomotaka	Prof	CS-Long Bch		PHD	71	Wisconsin	1967
Ishwaran, Jayvanth	Asst	S F Austin	EF	PHD	97	Purdue	1997
Iskander, Wasfy B.	Prof	Rhodes		PHD	73	Indiana	
Islam, Anisul	Assoc	Houston-Down		PHD	84	Alberta	1990
Islam, Muhammad	Assoc	Tx A&M Intl		PHD	87	Vanderbilt	9-90
Islam, Muhammad Q.	Assoc	St Louis		PHD	89	Indiana	1988
Islam, Nazrul	Asst	Emory	ECO	PHD	93	Harvard	1997
Ispahani, Ahmed S.	Prof	LaVerne		PHD	66	S Calif	1964
Israelsen, L. Dwight	Prof	Utah State	ABDE	PHD	73	MIT	1980
Ito, Harumi	Asst	Brown		PHD	97	Stanford	
Iwand, Thomas	Retir	Nebraska	D	PHD	59	Oregon	1967
Iwata, Shigeru	Assoc	Kansas	EJ	PHD	88	UCLA	1988
Iwomi, Peter O.	Assoc	Cen St-Ohio		EDD		Cincinnati	1981
Izraeli, Oded	Prof	Oakland	RHA	PHD	73	Chicago	1978
Izyumov, Alexei	Asst	Louisville	F	PHD	85	USSR	8-97
Jackson, Don C.	Assoc	Abilene Chr		DBA	65	Geo Wash	1987
Jackson, John D.	Prof	Auburn		PHD	77	Claremont	1984
Jackson, Marvin R. Jr.	Retir	Arizona St		PHD	67	Berkeley	1962
Jackson, Matthew O.	Prof	Cal Tech		PHD	88	Stanford	1997
Jackson, Peter	Assoc	Kean		PHD		Harvard	
Jackstadt, Stephen L.	Prof	Alaska-Ancho	AEH	EDD	81	Indiana	1985
Jacobs, Cindy	VLect	Trinity-CT		PHD	89	Illinois	1991
Jacobsen, Clifford C.	Asst	Wis-Stev Pt		MA		Ca-Rivers	1969
Jacobsen, Joyce P.	Assoc	Wesleyan-CT	J	PHD	91	Stanford	1993
Jacques, Kevin T.	Asst	John Carroll	EG	PHD	90	Mich St	1999
Jadlow, Joseph M. Jr.	H-Pr	Oklahoma St	L	PHD	70	Virginia	1968
Jaeger, David	Asst	CUNY-Hunter		PHD	95	Michigan	9-97
Jaeger, William K.	Assoc	Oregon	OQ	PHD	85	Stanford	1998
R.F. Mikesell Visiting Professor of Economics							
Jaffe, Adam B.	Assoc	Brandeis		PHD	85	Harvard	
Jaffee, Bruce	Prof	Indiana		PHD	71	J Hopkins	1971
Jafri, Syed Hussain Ali	Assoc	Tarleton St	AFG	PHD	86	Wisconsin	1989
Jaggi, Anand P.	Prof	Barton		PHD		Jabalpur	1971
Jaggia, Sanjiv	Assoc	Suffolk		PHD	90	Indiana	
Jain, Chaman Lal	Prof	St John's		PHD	65	American	
Jain, Sanjay	Asst	George Wash	ODL	PHD	95	Princeton	1994
Jalili, Reza	Assoc	Mercer-Atlan		PHD	94	NewHamp	1993
Jam, Habib O. E.	C-Ac	Rowan Col-NJ		PHD	75	S Illinois	1979
James, Dilmus Delano	Prof	Txs-El Paso	AFO	PHD	70	Mich St	1958
Frank & Mary Hanley Professor							
James, Duncan	Asst	Fordham		PHD	98	Arizona	1999
James, Harvey Jr.	Asst	Hartford	ADKL	PHD	95	Wash U	1995
James, John A.	Prof	Virginia	NO	PHD	74	MIT	1978
James, John B.	Retir	Mid Tenn St		PHD	70	Tx A&M	1969
James, Kay C.	Dean	Regent	I	BA			1996
James, Robert G.	Prof	CS-Chico	EFG	PHD	78	Oregon	1981
Jameson, Kenneth P.	Prof	Utah		PHD	70	Wisconsin	1989
Janeba, Eckhard	Asst	Colorado		PHD	94	Bonn	
Jang, Soo M.	Prof	Plymouth St	E	PHD	78	Cincinnati	1983
Jang, Young S.	Prof	SUNY-Plattsb	CD	PHD	69	SUNY-Alb	1968
Jannuzi, F. Tomasson	Retir	Texas	OR	PHD	58	LondonEc	9-68
Jansen, Dennis W.	H-Pr	Texas A&M	EG	PHD	83	N Carol	1983
Janssen, Arthur J.	Asst	Emporia St		MA		Missouri	1976
Janssen, Larry L.	Prof	So Dakota St	Q	PHD	78	Nebraska	1978
Jantzen, Robert H	Assoc	Iona	CIJ	PHD	82	Northeas	1982
Jaques, David G.	Prof	CS-Pomona		PHD	73	Claremont	1965
Jargowky, Paul	Assoc	Texas-Dallas		PHD	91	Harvard	
Jarrell, Stephen B.	Prof	W Carolina		PHD	78	Purdue	1988
Jarvis, Leslie		SUNY-Empire	A	PHD	82	New Sch	1986
Jasek-Rysdahl, Kelvin	Asst	CS-Stanislau		PHD	96	Colo St	1996
Jaswal, Jasbir S.	Prof	Missouri So		PHD	76	Missouri	1977
Jaynes, Gerald D.	Prof	Yale	N	PHD	76	Illinois	
Jeannero, Marshall J.	Retir	Bentley	AGP	PHD	69	Fletcher	1966
Jefferson, Gary H.	Assoc	Brandeis		PHD	86	Yale	1984
Jefferson, Philip N.	Assoc	Swarthmore	CE	PHD	87	Virginia	1999
Jeffress, Philip W.	Prof	New Orleans		PHD	69	Kentucky	1995
Jeffries, Christopher N.	Asst	Jackson St		PHD	88	Fla St	1992
Jehle, Geoffrey A.	Prof	Vassar	D	PHD	83	Princeton	1981
Jeitschko, Thomas	Asst	Texas A&M	L	PHD	95	Virginia	1995
Jelavich, Mark S.	Prof	NW Missouri	FR	PHD	80	J Hopkins	1981
Jenkins, Allan	Assoc	Neb-Kearney		PHD	87	Nebraska	1987
Jenkins, Glenn P.	Lect	Harvard		PHD	72	Chicago	1972
Jenkins, Sidney L.	Retir	SE Okla St	AQ	MS	59	Okla St	1968
Jennings, Donna	Asst	East Tenn St		PHD	95	Vanderbilt	1994
Jennings, E. James	Assoc	Purdue-Calmu		PHD	79	So Meth	1978
Jensen, Elizabeth J.	Prof	Hamilton	LN	PHD	84	MIT	1983
Jensen, Eric R.	Assoc	Wm & Mary		PHD	82	Michigan	1982
Jensen, Farrell	C-Pr	Brigham Yg		PHD	72	Kansas St	1982

Name	Rank	School	Field	Degree	Yr	Institution	Year
Jensen, Gail A.	Assoc	Wayne State		PHD	86	Minnesota	1989
Jensen, George	Retir	CS-L Angeles		PHD	68	U Wash	1962
Jensen, Hans E.	Emer	Tennessee	1993	PHD	61	Tx-Austin	1963
Jensen, Mark	Asst	Missouri	EC	PHD	94	Wash U	1997
Jensen, Paul	Asst	Drexel		PHD	97	Penn St	1997
Jensen, Richard A.	Prof	Kentucky	D	PHD	80	Nrthwstrn	1980
Jensen, Robert J.	Assoc	Pacific Luth		MA	67	Nebraska	1968
Jensen, Rolf W.	Assoc	Conn Coll	O	PHD	81	Mass	
Jeon, Bang Nam	Assoc	Drexel		PHD	87	Indiana	1988
Jeong, Dong K.	Assoc	N Carol A&T		PHD	74	Wayne St	
Jepsen, Lisa	Lect	Mo-Kansas Ct		PHD	98	Vanderbilt	1998
Jerison, Michael	Prof	SUNY-Albany	DC	PHD	77	Wisconsin	1977
Jerome, Robert T. Jr.	Assoc	Jms Madison	DF	PHD	82	Virginia	1981
Jerrell, Max E.	Prof	No Arizona	EC	PHD	84	Ariz St	1981
Jessup, Paul F.	Prof	Hamline	G	PHD	66	Nrthwstrn	1988
William Kahlert Professor							
Jesswein, Wayne A.	H-Pr	Minn-Duluth	FA	PHD	69	Illinois	1968
Jewell, Nasrin	Prof	St Catherine	OA	PHD	81	Wisconsin	1981
Jewell, R. Todd	Asst	North Texas	HJ	PHD	92	Ca-SnBarb	1996
Jezefowicz, James J.	Asst	Indiana U-PA	CEL	PHD	99	SUNY-Alb	1999
Jhun, U-Jin	Prof	SUNY Oswego	EH	PHD	73	SUNY-Alb	1972
Jianakoplos, Nancy A.	Assoc	Colorado St	CE	PHD	83	Ohio St	1990
Jilling, Michael	Prof	SC-Spartanbu	ACMF	PHD	76	S Carol	1975
Jindia, Jaswant R.	C-Pr	Southern	AO	PHD	70	Illinois	1970
Joerdling, Wayne H.	Prof	Wash State		PHD	79	Nrthwstrn	1979
Joh, Sung-Wook	Asst	SUNY-Albany	DL	PHD	94	Harvard	1994
Johansen, Thomas C.	Asst	Fort Hays St	GE	PHD	90	Okla St	1989
Johanson, Curtis E.	Inst	USAF Academy		MA	97	Tx-Austin	
John, A. Andrew	Asst	Virginia	AE	PHD	88	Yale	1993
Johnes, Geraint	SLect	U Lancaster		PHD	87	Lancaster	
Johnson, Bruce H.	C-Ac	Gustavus Ado		PHD	79	Houston	1986
Johnson, Bruce K.	C-Ac	Centre	ADL	PHD	85	Virginia	1987
James Graham Brown Associate Professor of Economics							
Johnson, Byron L.	Emer	Colo-Denver		PHD	47	Wisconsin	1947
Johnson, Colleen	Assoc	E Oregon St	AEJM	PHD	88	Wash St	9-86
Johnson, D. Gale	Emer	Chicago		PHD	45	Iowa St	1944
Eliakim Hastings Moore Distinguished Service Professor							
Johnson, Dan	Asst	Wellesley		PHD	98	Yale	1997
Johnson, David B.	Prof	Louisiana St	H	PHD	68	Virginia	
Johnson, Denise H.	Asst	Alma	CFJP	PHD	93	Mass	1994
Johnson, Dennis A.	Prof	South Dakota		PHD	72	Iowa	1964
Johnson, Donn M.	Assoc	Quinnipiac	AHQR	PHD	89	Colo St	1996
Johnson, Dudley W.	Retir	U Washington		PHD	57	Nrthwstrn	1960
Johnson, E. William	C-Pr	Shepherd		PHD	74	Virginia	1971
Johnson, Eric	Asst	So Carolina		PHD	97	Ca-SnDgo	8-98
Johnson, George	Prof	Michigan		PHD	66	Berkeley	
Johnson, Ivan C.	Prof	CS-Northrdge		PHD	71	W Ontario	1973
Johnson, James A.	Retir	Colorado Col		MA	59	Stanford	1956
Johnson, Jeffery	C	E Oregon St		PHD	78	Ca-Rivers	9-82
Johnson, Joseph T.	Asst	Central Okla	AMR	PHD	80	Chicago	1992
Johnson, Karen R.	Lect	Baylor		MIM		Baylor	1979
Johnson, Lowell E.	Prof	Bemidji St		PHD	75	Cornell	1976
Johnson, M. Bruce	Retir	Cal-Santa Br		PHD	62	Nrthwstrn	1968
Johnson, Mark	Assoc	Chicago St		PHD	85	Stanford	1995
Johnson, Paul A.	Assoc	Vassar	E	PHD	84	Stanford	1995
Johnson, R. Larry	Prof	New Hamp Col		DBA	82	Geo Wash	
Johnson, Robert S.	Dean	Columbus		PHD	64	Virginia	1993
Bill Heard Chair of Business Administration							
Johnson, Ronald N.	Prof	Montana St		PHD	77	U Wash	1981
Johnson, W. Clint	Prof	Cen Arkansas		PHD	75	Tx Tech	1975
Johnson, Walter L.	Assoc	Missouri	AEGH	PHD	63	Duke	1965
Johnson, William R.	Prof	Virginia	DJ	PHD	75	MIT	1974
Johnson-Lars, Shirley B.	Assoc	Vassar	I	PHD	66	Columbia	1967
Johnston, Charles W.	Asst	Mich-Flint		PHD	88	Tx-Austin	1988
Johnston, John	Emer	Calif-Irvine		PHD	57	Wales	1978
Johnston, Lewis	Asst	St Benedict		PHD	90	Berkeley	
Johnstone, Robert L.	Retir	Berea		PHD	61	Illinois	1964
Jolly, Eric S.	Asst	SC-Spartanbu	A	MA		Ohio U	1968
Jones, Barbara A. P.	Dean	Alabama A&M	AP	PHD	73	Geo St	1997
Jones, Barry	Asst	SUNY-Bingham	EC	PHD	99	Wash U	1999
Jones, Bryce J.	Retir	Rockhurst	1994	PHD	55	St Louis	1964
Jones, Carl R.	Prof	Naval Postgr	D	PHD	65	Claremont	1965
Jones, Chad	Asst	Stanford		PHD	93	MIT	1993
Jones, Charlotte	Prof	La St-Shreve		DBA	85	La Tech	1984
Jones, Clifton T.	C-Pr	S F Austin	CD	PHD	85	Tx A&M	1995
Jones, David D.	Prof	St Thomas-MN	E	PHD	75	Indiana	1972
Jones, Derek C.	Prof	Hamilton	PJ	PHD	74	Cornell	1972
Jones, Ellis J.	Retir	Gustavus Ado		EDD	65	N Dakota	1958
Jones, Ethel B.	Retir	Auburn		PHD	61	Chicago	1975
Jones, James G.	Asst	SW Baptist	ECO	MBA		Arkansas	1988

Jones, John	Asst	SUNY-Albany	E	PHD	98	Wisconsin	1998
Jones, Kenneth D.	Prof	Georgia Col		PHD	77	La Tech	1987
Jones, Kent A.	C-Pr	Babson	F	PHD	81	Geneva	1982
Jones, Lamar B.	Prof	Louisiana St	J	PHD	65	Tx-Austin	1967
Jones, Leroy P.	Prof	Boston Univ	HLO	PHD	74	Harvard	1976
Jones, Marcia Noreen	Prof	Geo Southern		PHD	86	Illinois	1986
Jones, Michael	Assoc	Bowdoin	F	PHD	79	Yale	1987
Jones, Otolorin		SUNY-Empire	A	PHD	83	Ohio U	1985
Jones, Patricia	Asst	Vassar	JO	PHD	98	Oxford	1999
Jones, Robert C. III	Asst	NW St of LA		PHD	91	UCLA	
Jones, Robert J.	Assoc	Skidmore		PHD	78	Columbia	1973
Jones, Ronald W.	Prof	Rochester		PHD	56	MIT	1958
Xerox Professor of Economics							
Jones, Royal Maurice	Prof	W Carolina		PHD	67	Maryland	1971
Jones, Trefor T.	Lect	Manches Inst	HLR	PHD		Dundee	1976
Jones, Warren	C-Ac	W Illinois	AEHN	PHD	82	Iowa	1983
Jonnard, Claude	Prof	F Dick-Madis	A	PHD			
Jonokin, Jon	Asst	Tenn Tech		PHD	94	Tennessee	1989
Jonsson, Petur	Assoc	Fayetteville		PHD	86	Penn St	
Joray, Paul A.	Prof	Ind-So Bend	ADJ	PHD	71	Illinois	1971
Jorda, Oscar	Asst	Cal-Davis	E	PHD	97	Ca-SnDgo	1997
Jordan, James S.	Prof	Penn State	E	PHD	75	Nrthwstrn	1998
Jordan, W. John	Prof	Seton Hall		PHD	77	SUNY-Alb	1977
Jorge, Antonio	Prof	Fla Internat	BPO	PHD		Villanova	
Jorgenson, Dale W.	Prof	Harvard		PHD	59	Harvard	1969
Frederick E. Abbe Professor of Economics							
Joseph, Hyman	Prof	Iowa		PHD	69	Nrthwstrn	1966
Joshi, Sumit	Assoc	George Wash	CD	PHD	91	Indiana	1992
Joskow, Paul L.	Prof	MIT	O	PHD	72	Yale	1972
on leave; Mitsui Professor of Economics and Management							
Joutz, Frederick L.	Assoc	George Wash	EC	PHD	87	U Wash	1988
Jovanovic, Boyan	Prof	New York U	L	PHD	78	Chicago	1983
Joyce, B. Patrick	Prof	Mich Tech	D	PHD	74	Missouri	1972
Joyce, Joseph P.	Prof	Wellesley		PHD	84	Boston U	1982
Joyce, Theodore	Prof	CUNY-Baruch		PHD	85	CUNY	1986
Jozsa, Frank	Assoc	Pfeiffer		PHD	77	Geo St	1991
Ju, Jiandong	Asst	Oklahoma	D	PHD	95	Penn St	1995
Judge, Rebecca P.	Assoc	St Olaf	ADQ	PHD	76	Duke	1987
Juhn, Chinhui	Assoc	Houston	J	PHD	91	Chicago	1992
Jung, Chulho	Assoc	Ohio Univ	CDFQ	PHD	89	Michigan	1989
Junk, Paul E.	Retir	Minn-Duluth	E	PHD	62	Nrthwstrn	1979
Jursa, Paul E.	Assoc	Charleston		PHD	72	Tx-Austin	1976
Juster, F. Thomas	Prof	Michigan		PHD	56	Columbia	1973
Kabir, MD Mahbabul	Asst	Concordia C	FO	PHD	98	Nebraska	1997
Kabis, Zeinhom M	Prof	St Ambrose		PHD	68	Illinois	1973
Kabot, Alvin	Retir	CUNY-Hunter	1-99	LLM	63	NYU	9-67
Kacapyr, Ella W.	Assoc	Ithaca	AG	PHD	85	Geo St	1985
Kader, Ahmad A.	Prof	Carroll		PHD	74	W Virginia	1974
Kadiyala, K. Rao	Prof	Purdue		PHD	66	Wisconsin	1970
Kaempfer, William H.	Prof	Colorado		PHD	79	Duke	1981
Kafoglis, Milton Z.	Retir	Emory	LI	PHD	58	Ohio St	1979
Kaganovich, M.	Assoc	Indiana		PHD	85	USSR	1991
Kagel, John H.	Prof	Ohio State	L	PHD	70	Purdue	1999
University Chaired Professor							
Kahane, Leo H.	Assoc	CS-Hayward	CFL	PHD	91	Columbia	1991
Kahn, Abraham	Assoc	Mass Lib Art		MA	79	SUNY-Alb	
Kahn, Daniel S.	Asst	Georgetown		PHD	95	Columbia	1994
Kahn, James R.	Assoc	Tennessee		PHD	81	Maryland	1991
Kahn, Matthew	Assoc	Columbia	JQR	PHD	93	Chicago	1993
Kahwar, Mariam	Asst	Elmira		PHD	97	J Hopkins	1997
Kain, John F.	Prof	Texas-Dallas		PHD	61	Berkeley	1996
Kaiser, Carl P.	Prof	Wash & Lee	JC	PHD	80	Wash U	1979
Kajii, Atsushi	Asst	Pennsylvania	G	PHD	91	Harvard	1991
Kakoli, Philip	Asst	Dallas Bapt	F	MBA	88	DallasBpt	1988
Kalaba, Robert E.	Prof	So Calif		PHD	58	NYU	1969
Kali, Raja	Asst	Arkansas	LOFD	PHD	96	Maryland	1999
Kalish, Richard J.	Retir	SUNY-Albany	N	PHD	63	Colorado	1969
Kallianiotis, John	Asst	Scranton		PHD	85	CUNY	1990
Kallon, Kelfala M.	Assoc	No Colorado	EFHO	PHD	83	Virginia	1993
Kamara, Avraham	Prof	U Washington		PHD	86	Columbia	1984
Kamas, Linda	Assoc	Santa Clara		PHD	82	Berkeley	1988
Kamath, Shyam J.	Prof	CS-Hayward	BFMO	PHD	87	Simon Fr	1986
Kamdar, Nipoli	Asst	Trinity	H	PHD	93	Syracuse	1993
Kamen, Michele	Asst	CUNY-Lehman		MBA		St Johns	
Kamerschen, David R.	Prof	Georgia	DK	PHD	64	Mich St	1974
Jasper N. Dorsey Professor							
Kamery, Rob H.	Assoc	Christian Br	ABJ	MS	81	Arkansas	1987
Kamien, Morton I.	Prof	Northwestern		PHD	64	Purdue	1970
Kamihigashi, Takashi	Asst	SUNY-Stony B		PHD	94	Wisconsin	1994
Kaminarides, John S.	Prof	Arkansas St	AFTO	PHD	68	Houston	1968

Kaminsky, Graciela	Prof	George Wash	F	PHD	83	MIT	1998
Kamm, Judy	Asst	Lindenwood		MS		Mo-StLou	8-96
Kamp, Bradley P.	Assoc	South Fla	L	PHD	93	Ca-SnDgo	1992
Kamps, William E.	Retir	So Dakota St	E	PHD	74	Wash St	1972
Kamrany, Nake M.	SLect	So Calif		PHD	62	S Calif	1976
Kanazawa, Mark T.	Assoc	Carleton	DKNQ	PHD	87	Stanford	1985
Kanbur, Sanjiv	Prof	Cornell		PHD	81	Oxford	
Lee Teng-hui Professor of World Arts							
Kandil, Magda	C-Pr	Wis-Milwauke		PHD	88	Wash St	1992
Kane, John C.	C-Ac	SUNY Oswego	ACJ	PHD	86	SUNY-SBr	1983
Kane, Joseph A.	Retir	LaSalle		PHD	72	Temple	1961
Kane, Mamadou	Assoc	E Stroudsbur	EFN	MA	72	NYU	1973
Kane, Tim D.	Prof	Texas-Tyler		PHD	72	Tx-Austin	1981
Kaneda, Hiromitsu	Emer	Cal-Davis	AFOQ	PHD	64	Stanford	1973
Kang, Eungmin B.	Assoc	St Cloud St		PHD	90	Geo St	1990
Kang, Inbong	Asst	SUNY-Bingham	EO	PHD	95	Rochester	1995
Kang, Keejoon	Prof	Indiana		PHD	80	U Wash	1980
Kangayappan, Kumaraswamy	Prof	WI-Green Bay		PHD	69	Wisconsin	
Kannappan, Subbiah	Retir	Michigan St		PHD	56	Tufts	1961
Kanovsky, Eliyahu	Prof	Yeshiva		PHD	61	Columbia	
Ludwig Jesselson Chair in Economics; spring only							
Kant, Chander	Assoc	Seton Hall		PHD	80	So Meth	1987
Kantarelis, Demetrius	Assoc	Assumption	DCKL	PHD	83	Clark	1983
Kanthi, Mahendra S.	Prof	Saginaw Vall	FO	PHD	80	Kentucky	1984
Kantor, Shawn E.	Assoc	Arizona		PHD	90	Cal Tech	1990
Kao, C. H.	Assoc	Syracuse	C	PHD	83	SUNY-SBr	
Kaparakis, Emmanuel	Inst	Providence	EGF	ABD		Conn	1990
Kaplan, Phillip	Prof	New Haven	NL	PHD	64	J Hopkins	
Kapler, Janis	Asst	Mass-Boston	FL	PHD	93	American	1993
Kapuria-Foreman, Vibha	Assoc	Colorado Col		PHD	87	Pittsburgh	1989
Karangu, Mwangi	Asst	Morgan State	CDEG	PHD	81	Walden	9-71
Karasulu, Meral	Asst	Bogazici	CEF	PHD	95	Boston C	1995
Karatas, Cevat	Prof	Bogazici	ACDH	PHD	70	Glasgow	1985
Karatjas, Nicholas	C-Pr	Indiana U-PA	ADI	PHD	76	SUNY-SBr	1978
Karayaicin, Ali Cem	Assoc	Fla Internat	EF	PHD	89	Columbia	1989
Karbassioon, Ebrahim	C-Pr	E Illinois		PHD	81	Nebraska	1980
Kareken, John H.	Retir	Minnesota		PHD	56	MIT	1958
Karemera, David	Assoc	So Carol St		PHD	89	Nebraska	1997
Karier, Thomas M.	Prof	East Wash		PHD	85	Berkeley	1981
Karikari, John A.	Assoc	Tulsa	AFMO	PHD	85	Queen's	
Karim, Alema	Asst	Rhode Isl Cl		PHD	86	Boston U	
Karlson, Stephen	Assoc	No Illinois	D	PHD	80	Wisconsin	1986
Karni, Edi	Prof	J Hopkins		PHD	71	Chicago	1981
Karns, James M.	Retir	E Kentucky		PHD	75	Oklahoma	1975
Karpoff, Jonathan M.	Prof	U Washington		PHD	82	UCLA	1983
Karras, Georgios	Assoc	Ill-Chicago	E	PHD	90	Ohio St	1990
Karscig, Mark P.	Prof	Cen Missouri		PHD	87	Pittsburgh	1981
Karsten, Siegfried G.	Retir	West Georgia	8-94	PHD	70	Utah	1978
Karstensson, Lewis	Assoc	Nev-L Vegas	B	PHD	74	Ohio U	1979
Kartman, Arthur E.	Prof	San Diego St		PHD	69	U Wash	1968
Kaschins, Edward A.	H-Pr	Luther		PHD	73	Iowa	1961
Kaserman, David L.	Prof	Auburn		PHD	76	Florida	1986
Torchmark Professor							
Kask, Susan B.	Assoc	W Carolina		PHD	88	Wyoming	1993
Kasper, Hirshel	Prof	Oberlin	DJ	PHD	63	Minnesota	1963
Kassouf, Sheen T.	Emer	Calif-Irvine		PHD	65	Columbia	1965
Kasturi, Prahlad	C-Pr	Radford	DOQ	PHD	83	Hawaii	1985
Kasun, Jacqueline R.	Retir	CS-Humboldt		PHD	56	Columbia	1969
Kato, Takao	C-Ac	Colgate	J	PHD	86	Queen's	1986
Kats, Amoz	Prof	Virg Tech	CDL	PHD	72	Minnesota	1974
Katz, Arnold M.	Retir	Pittsburgh	J	PHD	61	Yale	
Katz, Barbara G.	Prof	New York U	CDP	PHD	73	Penn	1974
Katz, Elizabeth	Asst	St Marys-Cal	O	PHD	92	Wisconsin	1999
Katz, Lawrence F.	Prof	Harvard		PHD	85	MIT	1986
Katz, Michael	Prof	Cal-Berkeley		PHD		Oxford	
Katzman, Brett E.	Asst	U Miami	DL	PHD	96	Duke	1996
Katzner, Donald W.	Prof	Massachusett		PHD	65	Minnesota	1975
Kauffman, Daniel E.	Prof	Winona State		PHD	80	Nebraska	1983
Kauffman, Kyle	Assoc	Wellesley		PHD	93	Illinois	1993
Kaufman, Bruce E.	Prof	Georgia St	JN	PHD	78	Wisconsin	1977
Kaufman, Dennis A.	Assoc	Wis-Parkside	CH	PHD	87	Kansas	1987
Kaufman, Roger T.	Prof	Smith	CEJP	PHD	78	MIT	1983
Kaufmann, Hugo M.	Prof	CUNY-Queens	FE	PHD	68	Columbia	1967
Kaun, David E.	Prof	Ca-Santa Crz	J	PHD	64	Stanford	1966
Kavesh, Robert A.	Prof	New York U	B	PHD	54	Harvard	1958
Marcus Nadler Professor of Finance & Economics							
Kaviani, Mohammad	Asst	Ind-Purdue/I		MA	85	Indiana	1986
Kawahito, Kiyoshi	Prof	Mid Tenn St	FE	PHD	71	Maryland	1971
Kayaalp, Orhan	Assoc	CUNY-Lehman		PHD	84	CUNY	1979
Kayalir, Resad	Prof	Bogazici	BE	PHD	76	Istanbul	1972

Kayser, Hilke A.	Asst	Hamilton	HIQ	PHD	94	Wisconsin	1993
Kaytaz, Mehmet	Prof	Bogazici	CE	PHD	78	Nottinghm	1978
Kazemi, Abbas A.	Assoc	Rhode Isl Cl		PHD	88	SUNY-SBr	
Kazemi, Hossein S.	C-Ac	Stonehill	GE	PHD	83	Clark	1982
Kazimi, Camilla	Asst	San Diego St		PHD	95	Ca-Irvine	1995
Kazmer, Daniel R.	Lect	Georgetown		PHD	73	MIT	
Kazura, Martie	C-As	Berea		MBA	90	Montana	1991
Keane, Michael P.	Prof	New York U	D	PHD	90	Brown	1998
Kearl, James R.	Prof	Brigham Yg		PHD	75	MIT	1975
Kearney, Adrienne	Asst	Maine	AF	PHD	92	Penn St	1997
Kearns, Robert	Retir	Carroll	1995				
Keating, John W.	Asst	Kansas	E	PHD	89	Nrthwstrn	8-97
Keefe, David E.	Assoc	Pacific	FT	PHD	80	Berkeley	1978
Keehn, Richard	C-Pr	Wis-Parkside	EGN	PHD	72	Wisconsin	1969
Keeler, James	Assoc	Kenyon	CEB	PHD	81	Indiana	1984
Keeler, Theodore E.	Prof	Cal-Berkeley		PHD	71	MIT	1977
Keenan, Donald C.	Prof	Georgia	CHR	DSC	78	Wash U	1978
Keener, Gary	Asst	Heidelberg	AHKR	PHD	93	Kentucky	1991
Keenes, John	Asst	Pace		PHD			1999
Kehoe, Patrick J.	Prof	Pennsylvania	POF	PHD	86	Harvard	1992
Ronald S. Lauder Term Associate Professor of Economics							
Kehoe, Timothy J.	Prof	Minnesota		PHD	79	Yale	1987
Keil, Manfred W.	Assoc	Claremont	ECJA	PHD	85	LondonEc	7-95
Keil, Stanley R.	Assoc	Ball State	QR	PHD	73	Oregon	1973
Keilany, Ziad	Prof	Tenn-Chattan	EO	PHD	68	Indiana	1968
Guerry Professor							
Keith, John E.	Prof	Utah State	DEQR	PHD	73	Utah St	1972
Keith, Kristen	Asst	Toledo	J	PHD	89	Ohio St	1994
Kelejian, Harry	Prof	Maryland		PHD	68	Wisconsin	1968
Keleta, Ethiopia	Assoc	Txs Southern		PHD	84	Rice	
Keller, Anita	Inst	Ark-Ltl Rock		MBA	76	Ark St	1991
Keller, Robert R.	Prof	Colorado St	EN	PHD	71	Wisconsin	1974
Keller, Wolfgang	Asst	Texas	FO	PHD	95	Yale	9-98
Kelley, Allen C.	Prof	Duke		PHD	64	Stanford	1972
James D. Duke Professor							
Kelley, George T.	Retir	Worcester St		PHD	71	Clark	1969
Kelly, Alison	Assoc	Suffolk		PHD	93	Boston C	
Kelly, David	Asst	U Miami	E	PHD	95	Car Mellon	1998
Kelly, Eamon M.	Retir	Tulane		PHD	65	Columbia	1981
Kelly, Jerry S.	Prof	Syracuse	D	PHD	69	Harvard	
Kelly, Kathy	Lect	Tx-Arlington	DE	MA	89	So Meth	1996
Kelly, Robert A.	Asst	Fairfield	HKC	PHD	71	Geotown	1978
Kelly, Thomas	Asst	Middlebury	OQ	PHD	97	Ca-Rivers	1997
Kelly, Thomas M.	Prof	Baylor	R	PHD	70	Okla St	1969
Kelly, Trish	Assoc	Quinnipiac	EFO	PHD	94	Mass	1995
Kelso, Patrick R.	Assoc	West Tx A&M	EHN	PHD	68	Tx-Austin	1967
Kelsy, Michael	Lect	Mo-Kansas Ct	CQ	PHD	91	Tennessee	1996
Kelton, Christina	Assoc	Cincinnati		PHD	79	Wisconsin	1996
Kemme, David M.	Prof	Memphis	FCP	PHD	80	Ohio St	1994
Morris Chair of Excellence in International Econ							
Kempey, William M.	C-Pr	Kean		PHD	70	NYU	9-78
Kendrick, David A.	Prof	Texas	CE	PHD	66	MIT	7-70
Ralph W. Yarborough Centennial Professor of Liberal Arts							
Kenen, Peter B.	Prof	Princeton		PHD	58	Harvard	1971
Walker Professor Economics & International Finance							
Kenison, Arthur M.	Prof	St Anselm	ACG	PHD	00	Boston U	1980
Kenison, Jeanne H.	Assoc	St Anselm	C	EDD	86	Vanderbilt	1988
Kenkel, James L.	Assoc	Pittsburgh	C	PHD	69	Purdue	1969
Kennett, David A.	C-Pr	Vassar	F	PHD	76	Columbia	1976
Kenney, James M.	Prof	Union	QDMG	PHD	72	Stanford	1972
Kenny, Lawrence W.	C-Pr	Florida	DHJ	PHD	77	Chicago	1975
Kent, Calvin A.	Dean	Marshall		PHD	67	Missouri	1993
Kent, Richard J.	C-Ac	Kent State	E	PHD	76	Berkeley	1983
Kenyon, Daphne A.	C-Pr	Simmons	HI	PHD	80	Michigan	1989
Kerby, William C.	Prof	CS-Sacrament		PHD	71	Oregon	1967
Kerchner, Robert B.	Assoc	Washburn		PHD	73	Missouri	1976
Kercsmar, John	Assoc	E Stroudsbur	M	PHD	85	Houston	
Kerkvliet, Joe R.	Assoc	Oregon State	L	PHD	86	Wyoming	9-88
Kermani, Taghi T.	Retir	Youngstown		PHD	59	Nebraska	1959
Kern, Clifford R.	Assoc	SUNY-Bingham	R	PHD	74	Harvard	1971
Kern, William	Assoc	W Michigan	B	PHD	82	Colo St	1987
Kerr, Peter M.	Prof	SE Missouri	AEBF	PHD	79	Kansas	1980
Kersten, Timothy W.	Prof	Cal Poly-SLO		PHD	73	Oregon	1971
Kessel, Herbert	Prof	St Michael's	AJDC	PHD	81	Boston U	1977
Kesselring, Randall G.	Prof	Arkansas St	ACJF	PHD	80	Oklahoma	1984
Kessler, Adam	Assoc	F Dick-Teane	ACDE	PHD	78	NYU	
Kessler, Alan L.	Assoc	Providence	DH	PHD	84	Boston C	1985
Ketkar, Kusum	Prof	Seton Hall		PHD	80	Vanderbilt	1983
Kevane, Michael	Asst	Santa Clara		PHD	94	Berkeley	1995
Key, Euell Dwyane	Retir	S F Austin	A	PHD	70	S Illinois	1970

Name	Rank	School	Fields	Degree	Yr	Degree School	Since
Khactu, Dominique	Retir	North Dakota	FG	PHD	65	Minnesota	1966
Khalil, Fahad A.	Assoc	U Washington		PHD	91	Va Tech	1991
Khalil, Mohamad	C-Pr	Fairmont St	C	PHD	88	W Virginia	1988
Khan, Agha Nisar	Prof	Virginia St		PHD	70	Va Tech	1972
Khan, Anwar S.	Prof	N Carol A&T		PHD	72	Wisconsin	
Khan, Aubhik	Asst	Virginia	EO	PHD	93	Penn	1993
Khan, Azizur Rahman	Prof	Cal-Riversid	FOPR	PHD	66	Cambridge	1988
Khan, B. Zorina	Asst	Bowdoin	GN	PHD	91	UCLA	1996
Khan, Farida C.	Assoc	Wis-Parkside	FO	PHD	90	Maryland	1990
Khan, M. Ali	Prof	J Hopkins		PHD	73	Yale	1988
Khan, Mohiuddin M. (Moosa)	H-Ac$	Prairie View	FEM	PHD	86	Simon Fr	1989
Khan, Saleem M.	C-Pr	Bloomsburg	AEOP	PHD	67	J Gutenb	1-78
Khan, Shakeeb	Asst	Rochester		PHD	97	Princeton	1998
Khan, Shakeeb	Asst	Virginia	C	PHD	97	Princeton	1997
Khandke, Kailash	Asst	Furman		PHD	93	Ca-Davis	1995
Khandker, A. Wahhab	Prof	Wis-La Cross	ACF	PHD	80	So Meth	1983
Khang, Chulsoon	Retir	Oregon	1997	PHD	65	Minnesota	1966
Khanna, Jyoti	Assoc	Colgate	H	PHD	90	Iowa	1992
Khanna, Neha	Asst	SUNY-Bingham	QD	PHD	97	Cornell	1998
Kharadia, Virabhai C.	Prof	NW Missouri	AED	PHD	73	Illinois	1973
Khayum, Mohammed	Assoc	So Indiana		PHD	90	Temple	1991
Khazeh, Kashi	Prof	Salisbury St		PHD	85	Tennessee	O-85
Khorassani, Jacqueline	Asst	Marietta	AEFH	PHD	97	W Virginia	1994
Kidane, Abraham Z.	Prof	CS-Dominguez	AFOI	PHD	71	UCLA	1971
Kidman, Peter N.	Prof	E Stroudsbur	K	PHD	71	W Virginia	1977
Kiefer, David M.	Assoc	Utah		PHD	74	Michigan	1981
Kiefer, Nicholas M.	Prof	Cornell		PHD	76	Princeton	1980
Ta-Chung Liu Professor of Economics							
Kiel, Katherine A.	Asst	Holy Cross	CDQR	PHD	89	Ca-SnDgo	1998
Kienzle, Edward C.	Assoc	Stonehill	HC	PHD	76	Boston C	1980
Kiernan, Joseph J.	Asst	F Dick-Teane	AEG	PHD	80	Fordham	
Kiesling, Herbert J.	Retir	Indiana		PHD	65	Harvard	1965
Kihlstrom, Richard	Prof	Pennsylvania		PHD	64	Minnesota	
Miller-Friedman Professor of Finance & Professor of Economics							
Kiker, B. F.	Prof	So Carolina		PHD	65	Tulane	1971
Jeff B. Bates Professor of Public Administration & Finance							
Kilby, Christopher P.	Asst	Vassar	O	PHD	94	Stanford	1993
Kilby, Peter	Prof	Wesleyan-CT	O	DPHI	67	Oxford	1965
Kilian, Lutz	Asst	Michigan					
Killingworth, Mark R.	Prof	Rutgers-N Br	J	DPHI	77	Oxford	1978
Kim, Benjamin J. C.	Assoc	Nebraska	F	PHD	83	UCLA	1983
Kim, Gew-Rae	Asst	Bridgeport		PHD	92	CUNY	
Kim, Hak Youn	Prof	W Kentucky	CDO	PHD	82	Cincinnati	1983
Kim, Han J.	Prof	So Dakota St	C	PHD	69	Oregon St	1967
Kim, Jae-Young	Asst	SUNY-Albany	CE	PHD	95	Minnesota	1994
Kim, Jinyoung	Asst	SUNY-Buffalo	OJ	PHD	94	Chicago	
Kim, Jong Sung	Asst	Bryant	AJ	PHD	98	J Hopkins	1998
Kim, Juho	Prof	Miss Vall St		PHD	73	Oklahoma	1973
Kim, Ki Hoon	Prof	Central Conn	FO	PHD	68	Conn	1967
Kim, Kil-Joong	Prof	Austin Peay	FO	PHD	80	Cincinnati	1980
Kim, Kirk Y.	C-Pr	Wis-Whitewat		PHD	70	Utah	1969
Kim, Kwan S.	Prof	Notre Dame	OF	PHD	67	Minnesota	1975
Kim, Kyoo H.	Prof	Bowling Gr		PHD	78	Wisconsin	1978
Kim, Minseong	Asst	Pittsburgh	E	PHD	96	Brown	1996
Kim, Soyoung	Asst	Illinois	EF	PHD	96	Yale	1997
Kim, Sukkoo	Asst	Wash Univ	NR	PHD	93	UCLA	1993
Kim, Sun K.	Prof	CS-L Angeles		PHD	66	S Calif	1964
Kim, Sungwoo	Prof	Northeastern		PHD	57	Berkeley	1972
Kim, Sunwoong	Assoc	Wis-Milwauke		PHD	85	MIT	1989
Kim, Yang H.	Retir	Alabama A&M	AOE	PHD	67	Utah	1965
Kim, Yoonbai	Assoc	Kentucky	EFG	PHD	87	Stanford	1991
Kim, Youn Suk	Prof	Kean		PHD	73	New Sch	9-74
Kim, Young Chin	Prof	No Illinois	O	PHD	68	Columbia	1970
Kimani, Joseph	Inst	Morgan State		MBA		Atlanta	
Kimball, Miles S.	Assoc	Michigan		PHD	87	Harvard	1987
Kimbrough, Kent P.	Assoc	Duke		PHD	80	Chicago	1980
Kimenyi, Samson M.	Assoc	Connecticut	HI	PHD	86	GeoMason	1991
Kimzey, Bruce W.	Prof	Brighm Yg-HI		PHD	70	Wash St	1989
Kinal, Terrence	C-Pr	SUNY-Albany	CD	PHD	76	Minnesota	1980
Kincard, Joel	Lect	Salisbury St		PHD	99	N Car St	8-97
Kindahl, James K.	Retir	Massachusett		PHD	58	Chicago	1967
King, Arthur E.	Prof	Lehigh	FP	PHD	76	Ohio St	1976
King, Arthur T.	D-Pr	Winston-Sal	D	PHD	77	Colorado	8-95
King, Clay B.	Retir	Minot State	A	PHD	72	Wash St	1975
King, Mary C.	Assoc	Portland St		PHD	91	Berkeley	1992
King, Paul G.	Prof	Denison	OAQ	PHD	71	Illinois	1967
John Harris Chair							
King, Philip G.	Assoc	San Fran St		PHD	87	Cornell	1987
King, Randall H.	Assoc	Akron	ADJ	PHD	78	Ohio St	1978

Name	Rank	School	Field	Degree	Yr	Institution	Hired
King, Robert G.	Prof	Virginia	EG	PHD	80	Brown	1993
A. Willis Robertson Professor of Economics							
King, Vereda J.	Assoc	N Carol A&T		PHD	84	Duke	
Kingston, Jerry L.	Prof	Arizona St		PHD	69	Penn St	1969
Kinnaman, Thomas	Asst	Bucknell	HQ	PHD	94	Virginia	9-94
Kinney, Kinney	Assoc	Shepherd		PHD	85	Maryland	1994
Kirby, Maurice W.	H-Pr	U Lancaster		PHD		Sheffield	
Kiriazis, David M.	Lect	Frostburg St		PHD	97	Wayne St	
Kirk, Eugene F.	Asst	St Bonaventu	G	PHD	74	Boston C	1972
Kirk, Robert	Prof	Ind-Purdue/I	HR	PHD	69	Iowa St	1972
Kirkland, Jack	Assoc	Troy State		PHD	82	Wash St	1995
Kirklin, Wayne	Assoc	Heidelberg	G	MBA		NYU	1978
Kirkpatrick, Rickey C.	Assoc	Appalach St	FM	PHD	78	Tulane	1980
Kirzner, Israel M.	Prof	New York U	B	PHD	57	NYU	1957
Kiser, Larry L.	Prof	East Wash		PHD	73	Rutgers	1971
Kish-Goodling, Donna M.	Asst	Muhlenberg		PHD	92	Lehigh	1990
Kishan, Ruby Pandey	Assoc	SW Texas St	E	PHD	86	Tx A&M	1986
Kitamura, Yuichi	Assoc	Wisconsin		PHD	93	Yale	1998
Kjetsaa, Richard W.	Assoc	F Dick-Teane	AEG	PHD	85	Fordham	
Klaasen, Thomas Albert	Prof	Txs Wesleyan		PHD	69	Mich St	1989
Klaus, Bettina	Asst	Nebraska	D	PHD	98	Maastricht	1998
Klauser, Jack E.	Prof	Chaminade		PHD	77	NYU	1970
Klay, Robin	Assoc	Hope	BO	PHD	73	Princeton	1979
Klein, Benjamin	Prof	UCLA		PHD	70	Chicago	1978
Klein, Daniel B.	Assoc	Santa Clara		PHD	90	NYU	1996
Klein, J. Douglass	Prof	Union	LQD	PHD	75	Wisconsin	1979
Klein, Judy L.	C-Ac	Mary Baldwin	BC	PHD	86	London	1982
Klein, Lawrence R.	Emer	Pennsylvania		PHD	44	MIT	1958
Benjamin Franklin Professor of Economics & Finance							
Klein, Nicole L.	Asst	So Dakota St	Q	PHD	96	Kansas St	1997
Klein, Peter G.	Asst	Georgia	GKL	PHD	95	Berkeley	1995
Klein, Philip A.	Prof	Penn State	E	PHD	58	Berkeley	1955
Klein, Roger W.	Prof	Rutgers-N Br	C	PHD	70	Yale	1994
Klein, Yehuda L.	Assoc	CUNY-Brookly	CDQ	PHD	85	Berkeley	1985
Kleinberg, Norman L.	Assoc	CUNY-Baruch		PHD	77	MIT	
Kleiner, William C.	Asst	W Illinois	AEF	PHD	74	Mich St	1971
Klepper, Steven I.	Prof	Carnegie Mel		PHD	75	Cornell	1980
Kletzer, Kenneth M.	Prof	Ca-Santa Crz	FDOH	PHD	82	Berkeley	1992
Kletzer, Lori Gladstein	Asst	Ca-Santa Crz	J	PHD	86	Berkeley	1993
Klevorick, Alvin K.	Prof	Yale	K	PHD	67	Princeton	1975
Klinedinst, Mark A.	Prof	So Miss	P	PHD	87	Cornell	1986
Kling, Robert W.	C-Ac	Colorado St	DQ	PHD	85	Kansas	1984
Klingaman, David C.	Prof	Ohio Univ	DE	PHD	67	Virginia	1967
Kloft, Leonard	Asst	Ohio Northrn		PHD	95	Iowa	1995
Klopfenstein, Kristin	Asst	Tx Christian		PHD	99	Colorado	1999
Klose, Gilbert	Prof	Earlham		MA		Nrthwstrn	1960
Klotz, Benjamin P.	Assoc	Temple	E	PHD	69	Minnesota	1975
Knapp, Gunnar P.	Prof	Alaska-Ancho	QR	PHD	81	Yale	1981
Knapp, Kimberly A.	Asst	MD-Baltim Co		PHD	88	Brown	
Kniesner, Thomas J.	Prof	Indiana		PHD	76	Ohio St	1988
Knight, Robert E. L.	Retir	Maryland		PHD	58	Berkeley	1960
Knighton, Daniel R.	Prof	Moorhead St		PHD	73	N Carol	1970
Knodell, Jane E.	Assoc	Vermont	EN	PHD	84	Stanford	1986
Knoeber, Charles R.	Prof	N Carol St	LKDG	PHD	76	UCLA	1976
Knoedler, Janet T.	Assoc	Bucknell	LNO	PHD	91	Tennessee	9-92
Knowles, Glenn J.	Assoc	Wis-La Cross	CQR	PHD	80	Minnesota	1985
Knox, Robert L.	Retir	Arizona St		PHD	63	N Carol	1963
Knudsen, James J.	Asst	Creighton	CHJ	PHD	89	Iowa St	1989
Knudsen, John W.	Retir	Idaho	EP	PHD	70	Minnesota	1972
Knusel, Jack L.	Retir	Wis-Whitewat		PHD		Colorado	1965
Koch, James C.	Assoc	St Edwards		MSIR	59	Loyl-Chgo	1960
Koch, James V.	Prof	Old Dominion		PHD	68	Nrthwstrn	1990
Koch, Paul D.	Prof	Kansas	Fnce	PHD	80	Mich St	1988
Koch, Paul R.	Prof	Olivet Nazar	ABHP	EDD	94	Illin St	1992
Koch, S.	Asst	Geo Southern		PHD	97	Penn St	1998
Kochanowski, Paul S.	Prof	Ind-So Bend	CDR	DBA	72	Indiana	1972
Kochar, Anjini	Asst	Stanford		PHD	91	Chicago	1990
Kochin, Levis A.	Assoc	U Washington		PHD	75	Chicago	1972
Kockesen, Levent	Asst	Columbia	DL	PHD	99	NYU	1999
Koechlin, Tim	Assoc	Skidmore		PHD	89	Mass	1988
Koelln, Kenneth	Assoc	North Texas	LI	PHD	91	Florida	1991
Koenker, Roger	Prof	Illinois	CL	PHD	74	Michigan	1983
Kofi, Tetteh A.	Prof	San Francisc	OA	PHD	70	Berkeley	1981
Koford, Kenneth	Prof	Delaware	H	PHD	77	UCLA	1979
Kogut, Carl A.	Assoc	NE Louisiana	DLJ	PHD	84	Tx A&M	1992
Kohen, Andrew I.	Prof	Jms Madison	JD	PHD	73	Ohio St	1976
Kohler, Heinz	Emer	Amherst	APCD	PHD	61	Michigan	1961
Willard Long Thorp Professor of Economics							
Kohlhase, Janet E.	Assoc	Houston	RHD	PHD	80	Penn	1983
Kohn, Meir G.	Prof	Dartmouth		PHD	73	MIT	1978

Koirah, Govinda	Asst	Rio Grande		PHD	95	NYU	1996
Koizumi, Tetsunori	Retir	Ohio State	E	PHD	70	Brown	1970
Kokkelenberg, Edward C.	C-Pr	SUNY-Bingham	EO	PHD	81	Nrthwstrn	1980
Kolb, Fredric	Prof	Wis-Eau Clar	ACG	PHD	71	Utah	1971
Kolberg, William	Assoc	Ithaca	AQ	PHD	84	Rhode Isl	1984
Kolluri, Bharat R.	C-Pr	Hartford	CEGH	PHD	77	SUNY-Buf	1976
Kolmer, Lee Roy	Retir	Iowa State	1994	PHD	54	Iowa St	1973
Kolpin, Van W.	Prof	Oregon	C	PHD	86	Iowa	1986
Kolstad, Charles	Prof	Cal-Santa Br	QLD	PHD	82	Stanford	1992
Konan, Denise	Asst	Hawaii-Manoa		PHD	93	Colorado	1993
Kondeas, Alexander G.	Asst	Greensboro	EG	PHD	98	Auburn	1999
Kondonassis, Alexander J.	Prof	Oklahoma	NO	PHD	61	Indiana	1979
David Ross Boyd Professor of Economics							
Kong, Chang Min	Prof	Towson		PHD	77	Wi-Milwa	1978
Konishi, Hideo	Assoc	Boston Coll	DHL	PHD	94	Rochester	1999
Konow, James D.	Assoc	Loyola Marym	ACD	PHD	93	UCLA	1989
Kontos, Nicholas C.	Assoc	Marshall		MA	58	Indiana	1961
Konyar, Kazim	Assoc	CS-San Bern	CQ	PHD	85	Ca-Rivers	1991
Konz, Jeffery M.	Asst	N Car-Ashvil	BEFO	PHD	94	N Carol	1996
Konzelmann, Suzanne	Assoc	Ind-So Bend	ADJ	PHD	91	Notre Dm	1989
Koo, Anthony Y.	VProf	Florida St	F	PHD	46	Harvard	
Kool, Krishna L.	Prof	Rio Grande		PHD	76	Tennessee	1970
Koont, Sinan	C-As	Dickinson Cl	CFE	PHD	87	Mass	1986
Kooros, Syrous	Prof	Nicholls St	EFOC	PHD	80	Rensselaer	1991
Kopecky, Helen Pauline	Retir	Oklahoma St		PHD	72	Houston	1973
Koppl, Roger	Assoc	F Dick-Madis	BEG	PHD	88	Auburn	1988
Koray, Faik A.	Prof	Louisiana St	EF	PHD	84	Duke	1984
Korbach, Robert J.	Prof	North Dakota	AGH	PHD	73	Maryland	1970
Kordsmeier, William F.	Assoc	Cen Arkansas		PHD	86	Tx A&M	
Kornai, Janos	Prof	Harvard		DSC	66	Hungaria	1986
Kornecki, Lucyna	Asst	Embry-Riddle		PHD	80	Krakow	
Kortum, Sam	Asst	Boston Univ	ELO	PHD	92	Yale	1991
Koscianski, Janet	Assoc	Shippensburg		PHD	90	S Illinois	1990
Koshal, Rajindar K.	Prof	Ohio Univ	TACQ	PHD	68	Rochester	1970
Kosicki, George	Assoc	Holy Cross	ADJL	PHD	85	Cornell	9-85
Koski, Jennifer L.	Assoc	U Washington		PHD	91	Stanford	1991
Kosmopoulou, Georgia	Asst	Oklahoma	D	PHD	96	Illinois	1997
Kosobud, Richard F.	Prof	Ill-Chicago	D	PHD	63	Penn	1966
Koss, Joseph J.	Retir	Youngstown		EDD	87	Akron	1967
Koss, Patricia	Asst	Portland St		PHD	93	Simon Fr	1997
Kossoudji, Sherrie A.	Asst	Michigan		PHD	84	Michigan	1987
Kotcherlokota, V. V.	C-Pr	Neb-Kearney		PHD	77	India	1986
Kotlikoff, Laurence J.	Prof	Boston Univ	EH	PHD	77	Harvard	
Kotz, David M.	Prof	Massachusett		PHD	75	Berkeley	
Kovach, David L.	Inst	USAF Academy		MBA	89	Valdosta	
Kovalenkov, Alexander	Asst	No Carolina	D	PHD	98	Automoma	1998
Kovenock, Dan J.	C-Pr	Purdue		PHD	83	Wisconsin	1983
Kowal, Lubomyr M.	Prof	Mich-Flint		PHD	65	Illinois	1966
Koymen, Oya	Prof	Bogazici	NQ	PHD	67	Strathcl	1976
Koziara, Edward C.	Prof	Drexel		PHD	65	Wisconsin	1966
Kozlov, Nicholas N.	Assoc	Hofstra	P	PHD	88	NewHamp	
Kozmetsky, George	Retir	Texas	O	PHD	57	Harvard	9-66
Kraft, John L.	Dean	Florida		PHD	71	Pittsburgh	1990
Krall, Mary Elyse	Assoc	SUNY-Cortlan	AIJQ	PHD	89	Utah	8-90
Kramer, Melvin L.	Retir	Wartburg		PHD	66	Iowa	1956
Kranich, Laurence J.	Asst	SUNY-Albany	DH	PHD	89	Rochester	1998
Kranton, Rachel E.	Asst	Maryland		PHD	93	Berkeley	1993
Krasa, Stefan	Assoc	Illinois	DG	PHD	87	Vienna	1990
Kraus, James A.	Asst	CUNY-Lehman		JD		Columbia	
Kraus, Marvin C.	Prof	Boston Coll	DR	PHD	73	Minnesota	1972
Krause, Kate	Asst	New Mexico	HK	PHD	96	Wisconsin	1996
Krautkraemer, Jeffrey A.	Prof	Wash State		PHD	82	Stanford	1981
Krautmann, Anthony C.	Prof	DePaul	DL	PHD	85	Iowa	1985
Krebs, Tom	Asst	Brown		PHD	95	Columbia	1999
Kreider, Brent	Asst	Virginia	HI	PHD	94	Wisconsin	1994
Kreinin, Mordechai E.	Prof	Michigan St		PHD	54	Michigan	1959
University Distinguished Professor							
Kreitzer, Joseph L.	C-Pr	St Thomas-MN	C	PHD	83	Iowa	1981
Kresl, Peter K.	Prof	Bucknell	FO	PHD	70	Tx-Austin	1969
Kressler, Peter	Assoc	Rowan Col-NJ		PHD	68	Penn	1972
Kreutzer, David W.	Assoc	Jms Madison	FH	PHD	84	GeoMason	1984
Kridel, Donald	Asst	Mo-St Louis	CD	PHD	87	Arizona	1993
Krieg, John M.	Asst	USN Academy		PHD	99	Oregon	1999
Krieg, Randall G.	Prof	No Iowa	JRL	PHD	87	Colorado	1987
Krieger, Stefan	Asst	Yale	E	PHD	99	Chicago	1997
Krienke, Albert B.	Prof	Midwest St	DP	PHD	67	Tx A&M	1965
Krier, Donald F.	Prof	Framingham		PHD	69	Boston C	1973
Krinsky, Itzhak	Prof	McMaster U	G	PHD	83	McMaster	1982
Krishna, Kala	Prof	Penn State	F	PHD	84	Princeton	1993
Krishna, Pravin	Asst	Brown		PHD	95	Columbia	1995

Name	Rank	School	Fields	Degree	Yr	Degree School	Year
Krishna, Vijay	Prof	Penn State	D	PHD	83	Princeton	1993
Krishnan, V. N.	Retir	Bowling Gr		PHD	68	Mich St	1965
Krislov, Joseph	Prof	Kentucky	JN	PHD	54	Wisconsin	1954
Kroch, Eugene A.	Assoc	Villanova		PHD	78	Harvard	1991
Krohn, Gregory A.	Assoc	Bucknell	EGA	PHD	85	Wisconsin	1983
Krol, Robert	Prof	CS-Northrdge	FGT	PHD	82	S Illinois	1983
Krouse, Clement G.	Prof	Cal-Santa Br	D	PHD	69	UCLA	1979
Krueger, Alan B.	Prof	Princeton	JH	PHD	87	Harvard	6-87
Krueger, Anne O.	Prof	Stanford		PHD	58	Wisconsin	
Herald L. and Caroline L. Reitch Professor in Humanities and Sciences							
Krueger, Gary J.	Assoc	Macalester	ACP	PHD	89	Wisconsin	1989
Krugman, Paul R.	Prof	MIT	F	PHD	77	MIT	1979
on leave; Ford International Professor of Economics							
Kruse, Jamie I.	Assoc	Texas Tech		PHD	88	Arizona	1996
Krusell, Per	Assoc	Rochester	O	PHD	92	Minnesota	1994
Kuan, Chen I.	Retir	SUNY-Albany	OF	PHD		Berkeley	
Kubik, Jeff	Asst	Syracuse		PHD	97	MIT	
Kudek, James F.	Assoc	Lakeland	ABCD	MBA		Wi-Milwa	1982
Kuenne, Robert E.	Retir	Princeton	6-97	PHD	53	Harvard	1969
Kuersteiner, Guido	Asst	MIT	E	PHD	92	Princeton	1997
Kugler, Penny L.	Inst	Cen Missouri		MA	88	Cen Mo St	1988
Kuhn, Kai-uwe	Assoc	Michigan					
Kulkarni, Kishore G.	Prof	Metro St-CO		PHD	82	Pittsburgh	1989
Kumar, Rishi	Dean	Wright State		PHD	72	Wayne St	1974
Kumar, Vikram	Assoc	Davidson	E	PHD	87	Vanderbilt	1986
Kumbhakar, Subal C.	Assoc	Texas	CD	PHD	86	S Calif	9-86
Kumhof, Michael	Asst	Stanford					
Kuntz, Dale F.	Prof	Bentley	AEO	PHD	79	Conn	1975
Kuperberg, Mark J.	C-Pr	Swarthmore	EK	PHD	81	MIT	1977
Kupilik, Michael H.	Assoc	Montana	PHBN	PHD	76	Colorado	1976
Kuran, Timur	Prof	So Calif		PHD	82	Stanford	1982
Kurre, James A.	Assoc	Penn St-Erie	RA	PHD	82	Penn St	1977
Kurth, Michael M.	Prof	McNeese St		PHD	82	Va Tech	1984
Kurz, Mordecai	Prof	Stanford		PHD	61	Yale	1966
Joan Kenney Professor of Economics							
Kushner, Joseph W.	Assoc	Valdosta St	A	PHD	69	Tennessee	1969
Kushnirsky, Fyodor I.	Prof	Temple	P	PHD	68	Moscow	1980
Kutan, Ali M.	Assoc	S Ill-Edward	EFG	PHD	90	Ariz St	1991
Kutasovic, Paul R.	Assoc	NY Inst Tech		PHD	83	Rutgers	1988
Kutsoati, Edward	Asst	Tufts	G	PHD	98	Queens	1998
Kuznets, Paul W.	Retir	Indiana		PHD	64	Yale	1964
Kwack, Sung Y.	Prof	Howard	E	PHD	68	Berkeley	
Kwak, Young-sik	Assoc	Delaware St		PHD	94	Miss	1993
Kwan, Clarence C. Y.	Prof	McMaster U	CG	PHD	79	Toronto	1979
Kwark, Noh-sun	Asst	Texas A&M	E	PHD	95	Rochester	1995
Kwoka, John E. Jr.	Prof	George Wash	L	PHD	72	Penn	1981
Kwon, Jene K.	Prof	No Illinois	E	PHD	68	Iowa	1968
Kydland, Finn	Prof	Carnegie Mel		PHD	73	Car Mellon	1977
Kyer, Ben L.	Prof	Fran Marion		PHD	84	W Virginia	
Kyereme, Stephen	Assoc	So Carol St		PHD	84	Cornell	1984
Kyle, James T.	Assoc	Indiana St	J	ABD	63	Indiana	1963
Kyle, Reuben	Prof	Mid Tenn St	L	PHD	72	Tennessee	1972
Kymn, Kern O.	Prof	W Virginia	EC	PHD	64	Chicago	1976
Kyn, Oldrich	Prof	Boston Univ	CEP	PHD		Charles	1971
Kynski, Kathy	Assoc	Kenyon	CDIJ	PHD	86	Wisconsin	7-86
Himmelright Associate Professor of Economics							
Kypralos, Harry N.	Assoc	Rollins		PHD	87	Virginia	1983
Kyriazidou, Ekaterina	Asst	Chicago		PHD	95	Nrthwstrn	1995
La Croix, Sumner J.	Prof	Hawaii-Manoa		PHD	81	U Wash	1981
La Near, Richard E.	Prof	Missouri So	ADGN	PHD	79	Miss	1987
Dr. J. R. Kuhn Chair in Finance							
La Point, James	Asst	SW Louisiana					
La Tourette, John E.	Prof	No Illinois	E	PHD	62	Rutgers	1979
Labadie, Pamela A.	Prof	George Wash	E	PHD	84	Chicago	1996
Laband, David N.	H-Pr	Auburn		PHD	81	Va Tech	1994
Labys, Walter C.	Prof	W Virginia	Q	PHD	68	Nottinghm	1975
LaCivita, Charles J.	Prof	Naval Postgr	DM	PHD	81	Ca-SnBarb	1985
Lackey, Charles	C-Ac	Tx-Brownsvil	AFL	PHD	84	S Carol	1995
Lacy, Allen W.	Emer	Auburn-Montg	ETIH	PHD	71	Iowa St	1976
Ladd, George W.	Retir	Iowa State	1994	PHD	55	Illinois	1955
Lady, George	Assoc	Temple	CD	PHD	67	J Hopkins	1981
Lage, Gerald M.	Prof	Oklahoma St	FD	PHD	67	Minnesota	1966
Regents Service Professor; Associate Dean for Graduate Studies & Research							
Lage, Maureen J.	Assoc	Miami U Ohio	AE	PHD	91	Penn St	1990
Lages, John David	Deces	SW Missouri		PHD	67	Iowa St	1963
Lagunoff, Roger D.	Asst	Georgetown		PHD	89	Minnesota	1996
Lahiri, Amartya	Asst	UCLA		PHD	95	Maryland	
Lahiri, Kajal	Prof	SUNY-Albany	E	PHD	75	Rochester	1977
Lahiri, Supriya	Assoc	Mass-Lowell	CQ	PHD	75	Delhi	
Lai, Kon Sun	C-Pr	CS-L Angeles		PHD	87	Penn	1987

Lai, T. H.	Assoc	Liberty	AEFG	PHD	84	Ohio St	9-85
Laibman, David	Prof	CUNY-Brookly	AP	PHD	73	New Sch	1967
Laibson, David	Asst	Harvard	DE	PHD	94	MIT	7-94
Laing, Derek	Assoc	Penn State	E	PHD	89	Essex	1989
Laird, William E.	Retir	Florida St	6-97	PHD	62	Virginia	1960
Laitner, John	Prof	Michigan		PHD	76	Harvard	1975
Lakew, Melaku	Assoc	R Stockton		PHD	81	Ca-Rivers	1982
Lal, Anil K.	Lect	Pittsburg St	A	PHD		Wash St	
Lal, Deepak	Prof	UCLA		PHD	65	Oxford	
Lam, David A.	Prof	Michigan		PHD	83	Berkeley	1983
Lam, Pok-sang	Assoc	Ohio State	E	PHD	86	Harvard	1985
Lambertini, Luisa	Asst	UCLA		PHD	95	Berkeley	
Lamberton, Charles E.	Prof	So Dakota St	G	PHD	75	Iowa St	1974
Lambson, Val E.	Prof	Brigham Yg		PHD	83	Rochester	1989
Lamdin, Douglas J.	Asst	MD-Baltim Co		PHD	91	Maryland	1989
Lamoreaux, Naomi	Prof	UCLA		PHD	79	J Hopkins	
Lamphear, F. Charles	Prof	Nebraska	O	PHD	67	Kansas St	1966
Lamson, George H.	Prof	Carleton	EF	PHD	71	Nrthwstrn	1969
Wadsworth W. Williams Professor of Economics							
Lancaster, Anthony	C-Pr	Brown		PHD	64	St Cathe	
Lancaster, Kelvin	Prof	Columbia	B	PHD	58	London	1966
Landau, Daniel L.	Assoc	Connecticut	O	PHD	74	Chicago	1981
Landis, Brook	Assoc	York Penn		PHD	74	Cornell	
Landsburg, Steven E.	VAsoc	Rochester		PHD	79	Chicago	
Lane, Julia I.	Prof	American U		PHD	82	Missouri	1990
Lane, Philip J.	Assoc	Fairfield	EGR	PHD	83	Tufts	1981
Lane, Walter J.	Assoc	New Orleans		PHD	78	Ca-SnDgo	1986
Lang, Kevin	Prof	Boston Univ	JC	PHD	82	MIT	1987
Lang, Nancy A.	Assoc	No Kentucky		EDD	83	Georgia	1983
Lang, Steven D.	C-Ac	Randolph-Mac	ECR	PHD	90	Pittsburgh	1987
Langan, Terence G.	Assoc	St Thomas-MN	L	PHD	88	Minnesota	
Lange, Ralph W.	Prof	SE Louisiana	AF	PHD	74	LSU	
Langer, Gary F.	D-Ac	Roosevelt		PHD	80	Ca-Rivers	1983
Langlois, Richard N.	Prof	Connecticut	B	PHD	81	Stanford	1983
Langston, Vicky	Assoc	Austin Peay	RM	PHD	83	Tx-Austin	1997
Lanjouw, Jean Olson	Assoc	Yale	CO	PHD	92	LondonEC	
Lankford, R. Hamilton	Assoc	SUNY-Albany	HD	PHD	81	N Carol	1981
Lanzillotti, Robert F.	Prof	Florida	T	PHD	53	Berkeley	1969
Dir Public Pol Resr Center; American Econ Int Free Enterprise Eminent Scholar							
Laopodis, Nikiforos T.	Asst	Villa Julie	CFOG	PHD	91	Catholic	1994
Lapan, Harvey E.	Prof	Iowa State	DF	PHD	71	MIT	1972
Lapidus, June	Assoc	Roosevelt		PHD	88	Mass	1990
LaPorta, Rafael	Asst	Harvard		PHD	94	Harvard	
Lapp, John S.	Assoc	N Carol St	EGF	PHD	74	Princeton	1974
Laramie, Anthony J.	C-Pr	Merrimack		PHD	86	Clark	
Lardard, Leonard P.	Prof	Rhode Island		PHD	79	Indiana	1981
Larew, Barbara	Assoc	Coe		PHD	96	Iowa	1981
Larkin, L. Andrew	Prof	St Cloud St		PHD	82	Nebraska	1982
LaRoe, Ross M.	C-Ac	Denison	AHQ	PHD	82	American	1985
Larriviere, James	Asst	Adams State		PHD	95	Auburn	1997
Larson, Bruce D.	C-Pr	N Car-Ashvil	ABCD	PHD	83	N Carol	1983
Larson, David A.	Prof	New Orleans		PHD	68	Maryland	
Larson, John C.	C-Pr	Loyola-Maryl	E	PHD	77	Minnesota	1974
Larson, Marvin L.	Asst	Missouri So		MA		Mo-StLou	1990
Larson, Tom Edward	Prof	CS-L Angeles		PHD	86	Berkeley	1987
Larudee, Mehrene	Asst	Kansas	F	ABD		Mass	1984
Lastrapes, William D.	Assoc	Georgia	CEF	PHD	86	N Carol	1990
Latanich, Gary A.	Assoc	Arkansas St	AREM	PHD	78	Nebraska	1981
Latham, William R. III	Assoc	Delaware	RC	PHD	73	Illinois	1971
Latif-Zaman, Nazma	Assoc	Providence	OFC	PHD		Northeas	
Latos, Charles	Asst	Rhode Island		PHD	77	Brown	1969
Latzko, David	Asst	Wilkes	BEFQ	PHD	92	Maryland	9-93
Lau, Lawrence J.	Prof	Stanford		PHD	69	Berkeley	1966
Kwoh-Ting Li Professor of Economic Development							
Laughlin, William	Assoc	Fairmont St	AE	MA		Cincinnati	1966
Laumas, G. S.	Prof	So Illinois	EC	PHD	66	Wayne St	1990
Laumas, Prem S.	Retir	No Illinois	1995	PHD	65	Wayne St	1971
Laurence, Louise	Assoc	Towson		PHD	87	Maryland	1987
Laurent, Jerome K.	Prof	Wis-Whitewat		PHD	73	Indiana	1965
Laury, Susan	Asst	So Carolina		PHD	96	Indiana	8-95
Lave, Charles	Emer	Calif-Irvine		PHD	68	Stanford	1964
Lave, Lester B.	Prof	Carnegie Mel		PHD	63	Harvard	1963
James H. Higgins Professor of Economics							
Lavine, Jeffrey A.	Asst	Pitts-Johnst		MA	68	Pittsburgh	1970
Lavry, Susan K.	Asst	Georgia St	HC	PHD	96	Indiana	1999
Law, Alton D.	C-Pr	W Maryland		PHD	68	Rutgers	1966
Lawarree, Jacques P.	Assoc	U Washington		PHD	90	Berkeley	1990
Lawber, Harold E. Jr.	Assoc	Salve Regina	ABEN	PHD	89	Conn	1988
Lawlor, Michael S.	Prof	Wake Forest		PHD	86	Iowa St	1986
Lawrence, William	Prof	NY Inst Tech		PHD	75	NYU	1971

Lawson, Catherine L.	Asst	Missouri Wes	EB	PHD	88	Colorado	1995
Lawson, Luther Drew	C-Pr	N Car-Wilmin	AJL	PHD	81	Tennessee	
Lawson, Robert	Asst	Capital		PHD		Fla St	1996
Lawson, Robert L.	Retir	Ball State		PHD	67	Iowa	1963
Lawson, Stanley J.	Prof	St John's		PHD	73	NYU	1978
Layer, Robert	Emer	So Illinois		PHD	52	Harvard	1955
Layson, Steve	Assoc	N Car-Greens	D	PHD	83	Chicago	1978
Lazarcik, Gregor	Prof	CUNY-Brookly	O	PHD	60	Columbia	1985
Lazonick, William H.	Retir	Barnard		PHD		Harvard	1985
Leach, Elroy M.	Prof	Chicago St		PHD	85	Il-Chicago	1985
Leadley, John C.	Assoc	W Oregon St		PHD	85	Wisconsin	1991
Leahy, John V.	Assoc	Boston Univ	E	PHD	90	Princeton	1997
Leahy, William H.	Prof	Notre Dame	JR	PHD	66	Notre Dm	1963
Leake, Richard S.	Assoc	Luther		MBA		Wisconsin	1975
Leamer, Edward E.	Prof	UCLA		PHD	70	Michigan	1975
Leathers, Charles G.	Prof	Alabama		PHD	68	Oklahoma	1968
LeBel, Phillip	Prof	Montclair St	DOQH	PHD	77	Boston U	1981
Lebergott, Stanley University Professor	Emer	Wesleyan-CT	N	MA	39	Michigan	1962
Lebrenz, Eugene R.	Prof	Fla Southern	J	EDD		N Illinois	1987
LeClair, Daniel R.	Assoc	Tampa	ADL	PHD	88	Florida	1989
LeClair, Mark S.	Assoc	Fairfield	FGC	PHD	87	Rutgers	1988
Ledyard, John O.	C-Pr	Cal Tech		PHD	67	Purdue	1985
Lee, Albert Yin-Po	Emer	CS-Stanislau		PHD	70	S Illinois	1970
Lee, Byung	Assoc	Howard	CDH	PHD	73	Catholic	8-73
Lee, Byung	Assoc	Notre Dame	CD	PHD	88	Wisconsin	1996
Lee, Christopher	Assoc	St Ambrose		PHD	90	GeoMason	1995
Lee, Chung H.	Prof	Hawaii-Manoa		PHD	66	Berkeley	1980
Lee, Dae Sung	Dean	Kentucky St	ADEC	PHD	69	Mass	1969
Lee, Daniel Y.	Prof	Shippensburg		PHD	86	Pittsburgh	1986
Lee, Dwight R. Bernard B. & Eugenia A. Ramsey Professor	Prof	Georgia	DHM	PHD	72	Ca-SnDgo	1985
Lee, Eric Y.	Prof	F Dick-Madis	F	PHD	73	Columbia	
Lee, Feng-Yao	Prof	Tennessee		PHD	65	Mich St	1965
Lee, Gerald R.	Prof	Miss College		PHD	73	Miss	1970
Lee, Hoyoung	Prof	Rochest Tech	ABDE	PHD	70	Maryland	1970
Lee, Hy Sang	Prof	Wis-Oshkosh	O	PHD	65	Wisconsin	1962
Lee, Jae Won	Assoc	CUNY-Baruch		PHD	69	CUNY	1972
Lee, Jaewoo	Asst	Calif-Irvine		PHD	92	MIT	1992
Lee, Jason	Assoc	McMaster U	G	PHD	91	Alberta	1990
Lee, Jim	Assoc	Tx A&M-C Chr		PHD	91	Penn St	7-99
Lee, Jimmy	Assoc	Fort Hays St	EKL	PHD	91	Penn St	1989
Lee, Joe W.	Retir	Howard		DBA		Indiana	
Lee, John T.	C-Pr	Mid Tenn St		PHD	77	Georgia	1984
Lee, Joseph S.	Retir	Mankato St	JK	PHD	70	Mass	1970
Lee, Junsoo	Asst	Cen Florida	E	PHD	91	Mich St	
Lee, Kangoh	Assoc	Towson		PHD	87	Illinois	1990
Lee, Kie Bok	Retir	Skidmore		PHD	67	Virginia	1963
Lee, Li Way	Prof	Wayne State		PHD	76	Columbia	1981
Lee, Maw Lin	Retir	Missouri	C	PHD	61	Wisconsin	1968
Lee, Ronald D.	Prof	Cal-Berkeley		PHD	71	Harvard	1979
Lee, Seung-Dong	C-Ac	Alabama-Birm	CDFQ	PHD	79	So Meth	1979
Lee, Soyon	Prof	Benedictn-IL	GO	PHD	77	N Illinois	1974
Lee, Tae-Hwy	Asst	Cal-Riversid	ACG	PHD	90	Ca-SnDgo	1995
Lee, Tenpao	Prof	Niagara		PHD	84	Iowa St	1987
Lee, Tommy R.	Inst	NE Louisiana		MBA		NE La	
Lee, Tong Hun	Emer	Wis-Milwauke		PHD	61	Wisconsin	1967
Lee, Wei Pang	Assoc	Worcester St		PHD	87	Georgia	
Lee, William C.	Prof	St Marys-Cal		PHD	77	Ca-SnBarb	1982
Lee, Woo Bong	Prof	Bloomsburg		PHD	72	Rutgers	1977
Leeds, Michael A.	Assoc	Temple	J	PHD	82	Princeton	1982
Leekley, Robert M.	C-Ac	Ill Wesleyan	H	PHD	74	Mich St	1974
Leeper, Eric M.	Assoc	Indiana		PHD	89	Minnesota	1995
Lees, Francis A.	Prof	St John's		PHD	61	NYU	1961
Leet, Don R.	Prof	CS-Fresno	TNA	PHD	72	Penn	1969
Leete, Laura	Asst	Case Western	IJ	PHD	92	Harvard	1991
Leeth, John D.	Prof	Bentley	GCJ	PHD	83	N Carol	1987
Leffler, Keith B.	Assoc	U Washington		PHD	77	UCLA	1978
Leftwich, Howard M.	Prof	Cincinnati	J	PHD	65	Illinois	1964
Legler, James	Assoc	Wartburg		PHD	96	Maryhurst	1997
Lehman, Dale E.	Assoc	Fort Lewis		PHD	81	Rochester	1983
Lehmann, Michael B.	Prof	San Francisc	NB	PHD	69	Cornell	1966
Lehr, Carol A.	Asst	Virg Comm		PHD	91	Penn St	1997
Lehrer, Evelyn L.	Prof	Ill-Chicago	T	PHD	78	Nrthwstrn	1980
Lei, Fitzray	Asst	Tulane		PHD	97	Geo St	1998
Leigh, Duane E.	C-Pr	Wash State		PHD	69	Mich St	1968
Leigh, J. Paul	Prof	San Jose St		PHD	79	Wisconsin	1981
Leightner, Jonathan E.	Assoc	Augusta	DTOP	PHD	89	N Carol	1989
Leighton, Linda S.	Assoc	Fordham		PHD	78	Columbia	1979
Leighton, Richard I.	Assoc	SUNY-Bingham	F	PHD	61	Duke	1964

Name	Rank	School	Fields	Degree	Yr	Institution	Year
Leijonhufvud, Axel S. B.	Emer	UCLA		PHD	87	Nrthwstrn	
Leitner, Keith R.	Prof	Wis-Eau Clar	AMQ	PHD	74	Kansas St	1974
Lejaunie, John	Assoc	Nicholls St	FG	PHD	92	N Orleans	1991
Lemke, Robert J.	Asst	Fla Internat	DJ	PHD	97	Wisconsin	1997
Lenihan, Patrick M.	Prof	E Illinois		PHD	68	Wisconsin	1967
Lenon, Mary Jane	C-As	Providence	REI	PHD	89	Conn	1986
Leon, Hyginus	Assoc	SUNY Old Wes		PHD	86	S Hamptn	
Leonard, Frederick H.	Prof	Smith	AEG	PHD	66	Michigan	1966
Leonard, John	VAsst	Cen Arkansas		PHD	81	Ca-SnBarb	9-98
Leonard, William J.	Retir	St Joseph		MA	69	Notre Dm	1957
Leontief, Wassily W.	Retir	New York U		PHD	28	Berlin	
LePage, James	Assoc	Lincoln-MO		PHD		Kansas	1984
Leppel, Karen	Assoc	Widener	JCT	PHD	80	Princeton	1985
Lerman, Robert I.	Prof	American U		PHD	70	MIT	1989
LeRoy, Stephen F.	Prof	Cal-Santa Br	GE	PHD	71	Penn	1997
Lesage, James P.	Prof	Toledo	RC	PHD	83	Boston C	1988
Lester, Bijou	Assoc	Drexel		PHD	81	Penn	1988
Lester, Don	Dean	Union-TN		PHD	94	Memphis	1996
Leube, Kurt R.	Prof	CS-Hayward	DBHK	DLE	71	Salzburg	1985
Leung, Cho Kin	C-Pr	Wm Patterson		PHD	68	NYU	1974
Leuthold, Jane H.	Prof	Illinois	HO	PHD	68	Wisconsin	1967
Leveen, Serpil Sisik	C-Pr	Montclair St	ADEG	PHD	73	NYU	1974
Leven, Bozen	Asst	C New Jersey		PHD	91	Cornell	
Leven, Charles L.	Emer	Wash Univ	IR	PHD	58	Nrthwstrn	1964
Levenson, Albert M.	Prof	CUNY-Queens	DFC	PHD	59	Columbia	1961
Lever, Jacqueline	Assoc	Albright		PHD	82	Pittsburgh	1990
Levernier, William B.	Assoc	Geo Southern		PHD	88	W Virginia	1989
Levin, Dan	Prof	Ohio State	MI	PHD	82	MIT	1995
Levin, Jay H.	Prof	Wayne State		PHD	68	Michigan	1976
Levin, Richard C.	Prof	Yale	O	PHD	74	Yale	1974
Levin, Sharon G.	Prof	Mo-St Louis	DJ	PHD	73	Michigan	1974
Levin, Stanford L.	Prof	S Ill-Edward	DL	PHD	74	Michigan	1972
Levine, Aaron	C-Pr	Yeshiva		PHD	81	NYU	
Samson and Halina Bitensky Professor of Economics							
Levine, David K.	Prof	UCLA		PHD	81	MIT	1981
Levine, Herbert S.	Prof	Pennsylvania	P	PHD	61	Harvard	1960
Levine, Philip	Assoc	Wellesley		PHD	91	Princeton	1990
Levine, Ross	Assoc	Virginia	FO	PHD	87	UCLA	1997
Levinsohn, James A.	Assoc	Michigan		PHD	88	Princeton	1987
Levinson, Arik	Asst	Wisconsin		PHD	93	Columbia	1993
Levinson, Marshall M.	Retir	Duquesne		MA	50	Columbia	1966
Levitt, Steven D.	Asst	Chicago		PHD	94	MIT	1997
Levy, Armando	Asst	N Carol St	C	PHD	96	Berkeley	1996
Levy, Daniel	Assoc	Emory	EC	PHD	90	Ca-Irvine	1992
Levy, David M.	Assoc	George Mason		PHD	79	Chicago	1983
Levy, David T.	Prof	Baltimore		PHD		N Carol	
Levy, Lester S.	Emer	No Illinois	N	PHD	56	Cornell	1964
Levy, Philip I.	Asst	Yale	DF	PHD	94	Stanford	
Lewbel, Arthur	Prof	Boston Coll	CD	PHD	84	MIT	1998
Lewis, Bradley G.	Assoc	Union	GMN	PHD	83	Chicago	1979
Lewis, Carl	Retir	Neb-Kearney		PHD		Nebraska	1969
Lewis, Danielle	Asst	SE Louisiana	EL	PHD	96	Kansas St	1996
Lewis, David P.	Retir	Alabama-Birm	CER	PHD	68	Tennessee	1969
Lewis, Eddie Miley Jr.	Prof	So Miss	F	DBA	74	Miss St	1970
Lewis, J. Patrick	Prof	Otterbein	FO	PHD	74	Ohio St	1974
Lewis, Kenneth A.	Prof	Delaware	CE	PHD	69	Princeton	1973
Lewis, Margaret	Assoc	St Benedict		PHD	89	Maryland	1989
Lewis, Stephen D.	Prof	Sonoma State		PHD	69	Ca-SnBarb	1982
Lewis, Stephen R. Jr.	Prof	Carleton	FO	PHD	63	Stanford	1987
Lewis, Tracy R.	Prof	Florida	TDQ	PHD	75	Ca-SnDgo	1991
James Walter Eminent Scholar in Economics							
Lewis, W. Cris	Prof	Utah State	MCR	PHD	69	Iowa St	1972
Ley, Robert D.	C-Pr	Bemidji St		PHD	77	Wash St	1977
Leyden, Dennis P.	Assoc	N Car-Greens	H	PHD	87	Car Mellon	1984
Li, David	Asst	Michigan		PHD	92	Harvard	1992
Li, Haizheng C.	Asst	Georgia Tech	C	PHD	97	Colorado	1997
Li, Hao	Asst	SUNY-Buffalo	DC	PHD	95	Chicago	1999
Li, Jenny	Asst	Penn State	C	PHD	93	Cornell	1997
Li, Ling	Asst	Towson		PHD	94	Pittsburgh	1994
Li, Qi	Assoc	Texas A&M	C	PHD	91	Tx A&M	1999
Li, Qing	Asst	Wichita St		PHD	95	Houston	1995
Li, Tien En	Retir	Delaware St		PHD		Tx A&M	
Li, Tong	Asst	Wash State		PHD	93	Ca-SnDgo	1997
Li, Victor	Asst	Penn State	E	PHD	92	Nrthwstrn	1992
Liaw, K. Thomas	Assoc	St John's		PHD	88	Nrthwstrn	9-88
Libecap, Gary D.	Prof	Arizona		PHD	76	Penn	1984
Liberatore, Anthony F.	Assoc	Millikin		PHD	78	Conn	1984
Lichtenberg, Frank R.	Prof	Columbia		PHD	82	Penn	1983
Courtney C. Brown Professor of Business							
Lichtenstein, Larry	Assoc	Canisius		PHD	81	SUNY-Bin	1981

Lichtenstein, Peter M.	Prof	Boise State	PEF	PHD	74	Colorado	1975
Lichty, Richard W.	Prof	Minn-Duluth	R	PHD	71	Kansas St	1971
Lidman, Russell M.		Evergreen St		PHD	72	Wisconsin	1974
Lieberman, Sima	Retir	Utah		PHD	67	Berkeley	1967
Liechty, Elden E.	Retir	Weber State		PHD	72	Utah	1972
Liedholm, Carl E.	Prof	Michigan St		PHD	65	Michigan	1967
Lien, Da-Hsiang D.	Prof	Kansas	O	PHD	86	Cal Tech	1986
Lieu, George	Assoc	Tuskegee		PHD	86	Okla St	1988
Liew, Chong K.	Deces	Oklahoma		PHD	68	Berkeley	1969
Liggett, Ron	Lect	Tx-Arlington	R	MBA	89	Tx-Arlin	1989
Light, Audrey	Asst	Ohio State	J	PHD	87	UCLA	1995
Lile, Stephen E.	Prof	W Kentucky	H	PHD	72	Kentucky	1973
Liles, W. Pierce	Prof	So Carolina		PHD	72	S Carol	
Lilien, David M.	Prof	Calif-Irvine		PHD	77	MIT	1984
Lill, Lloyd		SUNY-Empire	BO	PHD	77	Walden	1973
Lillard, Lee	Prof	Michigan		PHD	72	N Car St	
Lilly, Gregory A.	C-As	Elon	CDA	PHD	88	Duke	1990
Lillydahl, Jane H.	Prof	Colorado		PHD	76	Duke	1976
Lim, Ralph	Assoc	Sacred Heart	GLM	MBA		Penn	1981
Lima, Anthony K.	Prof	CS-Hayward	CEGM	PHD	80	Stanford	1979
Lin, An-Yhi (Steven)	Prof	S Ill-Edward	CDFO	PHD	67	Iowa St	1968
Lin, Emily	Asst	Connecticut	HJ	PHD	98	Michigan	1998
Lin, Hwan-Chyang	Assoc	N Car-Charl		PHD	90	Illinois	1993
Lin, Kuan-Pin	Prof	Portland St		PHD	77	SUNY-SBr	1979
Lin, Lung-Ho	Assoc	Akron	AE	PHD	74	Notre Dm	1978
Lin, Shuanglin	Assoc	Neb-Omaha	CDEO	PHD	89	Purdue	1989
Lindauer, David	Prof	Wellesley		PHD	79	Harvard	1981
Lindeman, Bruce	Prof	Ark-Ltl Rock		PHD	68	Duke	1975
Lindert, Peter H.	Prof	Cal-Davis	FN	PHD	67	Cornell	1978
Lindgren, Jon G.	C-Ac	N Dakota St	ADH	PHD	68	Missouri	1968
Lindsay, Cotton M.	Prof	Clemson	DHJK	PHD	68	Virginia	1984
J. Wilson Newman Professor							
Lindsey, Debra A.	Assoc	Howard		PHD	83	Howard	
Linebarger, Laura	Visit	Utah		PHD	97	Utah	
Liner, Gaines Howard	Assoc	N Car-Charl		PHD	71	Clemson	1971
Link, Albert N.	Prof	N Car-Greens	O	PHD	76	Tulane	1982
Link, Charles R.	Prof	Delaware	J	PHD	71	Wisconsin	1701
Linsley, Colin A.	Assoc	St John Fshr	N	PHD	86	Essex	1987
Linster, Bruce G.	Prof	USAF Academy		PHD	90	Michigan	1990
Linton, Oliver	Prof	Yale	C	PHD	91	Berkeley	
Linz, Susan	Prof	Michigan St		PHD	80	Illinois	1988
Liossatos, Panagis S.	C-Pr	Fla Internat	CODR	PHD	68	Penn	1981
Lipford, Jody W.	Assoc	Presbyterian	HEFI	PHD	90	Clemson	1991
Lipman, Barton L.	Prof	Wisconsin		PHD	85	Michigan	1998
Lipner, Kenneth	Assoc	Fla Internat	RJA	PHD	77	Rutgers	1981
Lippit, Victor D.	Prof	Cal-Riversid	AOP	PHD	71	Yale	1971
Lipsey, Robert E.	Emer	CUNY-Queens	FC	PHD	61	Columbia	1967
Liska, Terrence L.	Prof	Wis-Plattev		PHD	82	Wisconsin	1980
List, John	Asst	Cen Florida		PHD	96	Wyoming	1996
Litterst, Laurence J.	Assoc	St Benedict		PHD	81	N Illinois	1979
Little, Charles H.	Retir	St John's		PHD	65	Berkeley	
Little, Roger D.	Prof	USN Academy		PHD	70	Houston	1970
Litzinger, Patrick J.	Prof	Robt Morris		PHD	75	Pittsburgh	1977
Liu, Chao-Nan	Prof	C New Jersey		PHD	76	Tx A&M	
Liu, Jung-Chao	Prof	SUNY-Bingham	FO	PHD	60	Michigan	1970
Liu, Tsung-Hua	Prof	East Wash		PHD	69	Toronto	1970
Liu, Tung	Assoc	Ball State	C	PHD	90	Ca-SnDgo	1990
Liu, Yih-Wu	Prof	Youngstown		PHD	68	S Illinois	1968
Liu, Zheng	Asst	Clark		PHD	97	Minnesota	1997
Liveson, Avi	Asst	CUNY-Hunter		LLM	75	NYU	9-86
Livingston, Marie L.	Prof	No Colorado	FHOQ	PHD	84	Colo St	1985
Lizzeri, Alessandro	Asst	Princeton		PHD	95	Nrthwstrn	1995
Locay, Luis	Assoc	U Miami	DJOT	PHD	83	Chicago	1989
Lochner, Lance	Asst	Rochester		PHD	98	Chicago	1998
Loeb, Peter D.	C-Pr	Rutgers-Newk		PHD	73	Rutgers	1973
Loeb, Susanna	Asst	Cal-Davis	JH	PHD	98	Michigan	7-98
Lofgreen, Harold A.	Prof	St Cloud St		PHD	72	Iowa	1972
Lofgren, Stephanie	Asst	USM Academy	DHF	PHD	96	Nrthwstrn	1995
Logan, Robert	Assoc	Alaska-Fairb		PHD	86	Iowa	1986
Lokhande, Vineeta	Asst	Southern	G	PHD	94	N Orleans	1994
Lombard, John	Prof	Eastern Conn		PHD	78	Conn	
Lombardi, Waldo J.	Prof	Lg Isl-Brook	ACD	PHD	70	Columbia	
Lombra, Raymond E.	Prof	Penn State	E	PHD	71	Penn St	1969
Londhe, Suresh R.	Prof	So Carol St		PHD	65	LSU	1969
Lonergan, Janis	Prof	Augustana IL	AFIC	PHD	79	S Illinois	1999
Long, C. Richard	Emer	Georgia St	BE	PHD	68	Vanderbilt	1968
Long, James E.	Prof	Auburn		PHD	74	Fla St	1974
Torchmark Professor							
Long, Neal B.	C-Pr	Stetson	ACP	PHD	64	Indiana	1974
Long, Stanley G.	Emer	Pitts-Johnst	D-95	PHD	69	Iowa	1973

Name	Rank	School	Fields	Degree	Yr	Degree School	Year
Long, Stewart L.	Prof	CS-Fullerton	N	PHD	74	Illinois	1973
Long, Teresa M.	C-Pr	Marymount		PHD	80	Iowa St	1981
Looney, Lawrence J.	Assoc	Merrimack		MA		Boston C	
Looney, Robert	Prof	Naval Postgr	OF	PHD	69	Berkeley	1977
Lopomo, Giuseppe	Asst	New York U	CD	PHD	94	Stanford	1994
Lopus, Jane S.	Assoc	CS-Hayward	AEH	PHD	90	Ca-Davis	1979
Lord, William A.	Assoc	MD-Baltim Co		PHD	84	Indiana	1987
Loschky, David J.	Retir	Missouri	TN	PHD	62	Harvard	1967
Lotspeich, Richard	Assoc	Indiana St	PQ	PHD	86	New Mex	1990
Lott, Elizabeth J.	C-Ac	Pace	ACNR	PHD		Columbia	1990
Lott, William F.	Assoc	Connecticut	C	PHD	69	N Car St	1969
Loucks, Christine	Prof	Boise State	ELH	PHD	83	Wash St	1989
Loughlin, James C.	Prof	Central Conn	DH	PHD	65	Clark	1968
Louie, Kenneth K. T.	Assoc	Penn St-Erie	AFJ	PHD	87	Penn St	1984
Loury, Glenn C.	Prof	Boston Univ	DJ	PHD	76	MIT	1991
Loury, Linda D.	Assoc	Tufts	J	PHD	78	MIT	1984
Love, Barry A.	C-Ac	Emory Henry		PHD	78	Virginia	1984
Holbert L. Harris Professorship in Free Enterprise							
Love, Jim L.	Prof	Valdosta St	R	PHD	83	Okla St	1983
Love, Thomas M.	C-Pr	No Central	F	PHD	67	Wisconsin	1972
Lovejoy, Robert M.	Retir	SUNY-Bingham	E	PHD	63	Michigan	1965
Lovell, Hugh G.	Retir	Portland St		PHD	51	MIT	1964
Lovell, Knox	Prof	Georgia	D	PHD	66	Duke	1994
Herman & Mary Virginia Terry Professor							
Lovell, Michael C.	Prof	Wesleyan-CT	E	PHD	59	Harvard	1969
Chester D. Hubbard Professor of Economics & Social Science							
Lovely, Mary E.	Assoc	Syracuse	F	PHD	89	Michigan	1988
Loviscek, Anthony	Asst	Seton Hall		PHD	80	W Virginia	1992
Low, Stuart A.	Prof	Arizona St		PHD	79	Illinois	1979
Lowenberg, Tony	Prof	CS-Northrdge	GH	PHD	84	Simon Fr	1984
Lowinger, Thomas C.	Prof	Wash State		PHD	70	Mich St	1978
Lowry, Darryl W.	Assoc	Roanoke		PHD	72	Berkeley	1981
Lowry, George S.	Prof	Randolph-Mac	G	PHD	92	Va Comm	1984
Lowry, Stanley T.	Emer	Wash & Lee	BK	PHD	58	LSU	1959
Lozada, Gabriel A.	Asst	Utah		PHD	87	Stanford	1993
Lu, Laura	Asst	Lg Isl-Post		PHD	89	SUNY-SBr	
Lu, Xiaohua	Asst	Kansas State	LDC	PHD	95	Tx-Austin	1997
Lubell, Alfred M.	Dean$	SUNY-Oneonta	ADF	PHD	74	NYU	1974
Lucas, Eruesto	Asst	Hawaii Pacif		PHD	69	Hi-Manoa	1993
Lucas, Henry A. Jr.	Assoc	Salem State		JD		Suffolk	
Lucas, Robert E. B.	Prof	Boston Univ	CFJO	PHD	72	MIT	1976
Lucas, Robert E. Jr.	D-Pr	Chicago		PHD	64	Chicago	1974
John Dewey Distinguished Service Professor; 1995 Nobel Prize							
Lucchesi, Michael S.	Asst	USAF Academy		MA	86	U Wash	1993
Luce, Ducan	Emer	Calif-Irvine		PHD	50	MIT	1988
Lucier, Richard L.	Prof	Denison	ADF	PHD	72	Claremont	1971
Luckett, Dudley G.	Retir	Iowa State	EN	PHD	58	Tx-Austin	1957
Ludolf, Gordon W.	Retir	East Tenn St		PHD	64	Ohio St	1961
Lueck, Dean L.	Assoc	Montana St		PHD	87	U Wash	1997
Luizer, James C.	Assoc	Kutztown	JC	PHD	84	Lehigh	1984
Luksetich, William A.	C-Pr	St Cloud St		PHD	73	N Illinois	1972
Lumsdaine, Robin	Prof	Brown		PHD	91	Harvard	
Lund, Mark	Prof	Luther		PHD	75	Iowa St	1978
Lund, Peter B.	C-Pr	CS-Sacrament		PHD	67	Berkeley	1970
Lundberg, Shelly J.	Prof	U Washington		PHD	81	Nrthwstrn	1984
Lunn, John E.	Prof	Hope	LD	PHD	80	UCLA	1992
Lunt, William E.	Assoc	Vassar	C	PHD	77	Stanford	1974
Luptowski, Thomas S.	Prof	Northwood		BS			
Lusardi, Annamaria	Asst	Dartmouth		PHD	92	Princeton	1993
Lustgarten, Steven	Prof	CUNY-Baruch		PHD	71	UCLA	
Lutz, Mark A.	Prof	Maine	AB	PHD	72	Berkeley	1970
Lutz, Nancy A.	Assoc	Virg Tech	DLM	PHD	87	Stanford	1992
Lutzker, Adam	Inst	Hamilton	EB	ABD		Michigan	1995
Lwamugira, Pirudas L.	Assoc	Fitchburg St		PHD	90	Temple	1991
Lyall, Katharine C.	Prof	Wisconsin		PHD	69	Cornell	1982
Lyman, R. Ashley	Assoc	Idaho	DC	PHD	72	Nrthwstrn	1976
Lynch, Allen	Asst	North Fla	FAC	PHD	99	Fla St	1999
Lynch, Gary	Prof	Indiana NW	RTE	PHD	70	Wash St	1981
Lynch, Gerald J.	Assoc	Purdue		PHD	75	Kentucky	1983
Lynch, James G.	Lect	CS-Bakersf	AFJ	PHD	98	Colorado	1999
Lynch, James W.	Assoc	Robt Morris		MA	72	Pittsburgh	1974
Lynch, Karla	Lect	North Texas	A	MS		North Tx	1993
Lynch, Lawrence K.	Emer	Transylvania		PHD	66	Kentucky	1979
Lynch, Vernon E. Jr.	Prof	Fort Lewis		PHD	76	Arizona	1972
Lynde, Catherine	Assoc	Mass-Boston	EF	PHD	85	Ca-Davis	1983
Lynn, Billy	Assoc	St Ambrose		PHD	94	Illinois	1994
Lynn, Stuart R.	C-Ac	Assumption	DBFO	PHD	71	N Carol	1987
Lyon, Andrew B.	Assoc	Maryland		PHD	86	Princeton	1987
Lyon, Kenneth S.	Prof	Utah State	CDEQ	PHD	70	Chicago	1966
Lyon, Tom	Assoc	Indiana		PHD	89	Stanford	1989

Lyon, William R.	Asst	Wash & Jeff		MBA	89	Morehead	1988
Lyons, John S.	Asst	Miami U-Ohio	NO	PHD	77	Berkeley	1985
Lyons, Patrick A.	Prof	So Dakota St	M	JD	74	S Dakota	1975
Lyons, Thomas P.	Assoc	Cornell		PHD	83	Cornell	1988
Ma, Barry K.	Asst	CUNY-Baruch		PHD	86	Stanford	1989
Ma, Ching-to Albert	Assoc	Boston Univ	DIL	PHD	88	LondonEc	1987
Ma, Jinpeng	Asst	Rutgers-Camd		PHD	93	SUNY-SBr	
Maafo, E. Victor	Asst	N Carol Cen		MA	73	Duke	1966
Maasoumi, Esfandiar	Prof	So Methodist	C	PHD	77	LondonSE	1976
Robert H. & Nancy Dedman Professor							
MacBeth, Thomas G.	Prof	Mass-Lowell	AC	PHD	62	S Calif	
Maccini, Louis J.	C-Pr	J Hopkins		PHD	70	Nrthwstrn	1969
MacDonald, John	Asst	Clarkson	GM	PHD	87	Va Tech	1995
MacDonald, Richard A.	Asst	St Cloud St		PHD	92	SUNY-Bin	1989
Macesich, George	Prof	Florida St	E	PHD	58	Chicago	1959
MacEwan, Arthur	Prof	Mass-Boston	FOI	PHD	69	Harvard	1975
Machina, Mark J.	Prof	Ca-San Diego	D	PHD	79	MIT	1979
Machlis, David	Assoc	Adelphi	E	PHD	71	Rutgers	1968
Machovec, Frank M.	Assoc	Wofford	EFP	PHD	86	NYU	1988
Mack, Richard Stanley	Prof	Central Wash	RQP	PHD	72	Colo St	1972
Distinguished Professor, Research (1988)							
Mackara, W. Frederick	Assoc	East Tenn St		PHD	76	Tx A&M	1975
Mackey, M. Cecil	Prof	Michigan St		PHD	55	Illinois	1980
Mackie-Mason, Jeffrey K.	Assoc	Michigan		PHD	86	MIT	1986
Maclachlan, Fiona C.	Asst	Manhattan		PHD	91	NYU	1992
MacLeod, Bentley	Prof	So Calif		PHD	84	Brit Colum	1997
MacPhee, Craig R.	Prof	Nebraska	F	PHD	70	Mich St	1969
Paul C. Burnmeister College Professor							
Macpherson, David A.	Prof	Florida St	J	PHD	87	Penn St	1992
MacPherson, Roderick S.	Assoc	Montevallo		DBA	77	Miss St	1977
MacRitchie, Donald R.	Assoc	Framingham		MA	85	Boston C	1987
Macunovich, Diane J.	Assoc	Williams		PHD	89	S Calif	1989
MaCurdy, Thomas E.	Prof	Stanford		PHD	78	Chicago	1983
Madajewicz, Margaret	Asst	Columbia	DLO	PHD	98	Harvard	1999
Madan, Vibhas	C-Ac	Drexel		PHD	89	Mich St	1989
Maddala, G. S.	Prof	Ohio State		PHD	63	Chicago	1975
Eminent Scholar							
Madden, John L.	Retir	Kentucky	N	PHD	68	Kansas St	1968
Madden, Kirsten K.	Asst	Millersville		PHD	95	N Carol	1996
Maddox, D. Pat	Assoc	Angelo State		PHD	82	Tx Tech	1982
Madhavan, Murugappa C.	Prof	San Diego St		PHD	69	Wisconsin	1968
Madresehee, Mehrdad	C-Ac	Lycoming	FKLR	PHD	85	Wash St	1986
Madsen, Ron	Prof	N Car-Charl					
Maeshiro, Asatoshi	Retir	Pittsburgh	C	PHD	65	Michigan	1979
Magaddino, Joseph P.	C-Pr	CS-Long Bch		PHD	72	Va Tech	1973
Magenau, John M. III	D-Ac	Penn St-Erie	JM	PHD	88	SUNY-Buf	1985
Magenheim, Ellen B.	Assoc	Swarthmore	DI	PHD	86	Maryland	1986
Maggi, Giovanni		Princeton					
Maggs, Gary E.	Assoc	St John Fshr	E	PHD	86	W Virginia	1986
Magill, Michael J. P.	Prof	So Calif		PHD	70	Brown	1979
Magura, Michael	C-Pr	Toledo	RL	PHD	72	Boston C	1969
Mahajan, Y. Lal	Assoc	Monmouth	CDEG	PHD	95	N Illinois	1979
Mahan, Gary P.	Assoc	Gannon		PHD	78	N Car St	1977
Mahdavi, Mahnaz	Assoc	Smith	FGM	PHD	86	Michigan	1985
Mahdavi, Saeid	Assoc	Tx-S Antonio	EFO	PHD	85	Ca-SnBarb	1984
Mahdi, Syed I.	Prof	Benedict Col		PHD	76	Mass	1975
Maher, William F. X.	Retir	St Peters		PHD	71	Boston C	1965
Mahoney, Timothy B.	Inst	So Indiana		MS	65	Illinois	1987
Mailath, George J.	Prof	Pennsylvania	CDH	PHD	85	Princeton	1985
Main, Robert S.	C-Ac	Butler	HQ	PHD	73	UCLA	1981
Majumdar, Mukul K.	Prof	Cornell		PHD	70	Berkeley	
H.T. & R.I. Warshow Professor of Economics							
Mak, James	Prof	Hawaii-Manoa		PHD	70	Purdue	1970
Makowski, Louis	Prof	Cal-Davis	DE	PHD	75	UCLA	1985
Malamud, Bernard	C-Pr	Nev-L Vegas	E	PHD	71	New Sch	1968
Malatesta, Paul H.	Prof	U Washington		PHD	81	Rochester	1980
Malenbaum, Wilfred	Retir	Pennsylvania		PHD	41	Harvard	1959
Maley, Jean E.	Prof	St John Fshr		PHD	72	Rochester	1968
Maley, Leonard A.	Assoc	Nazareth		MBA	62	Cincinnati	
Malhotra, Devinder	Prof	Akron	ADR	PHD	79	Kansas St	1979
Malik, Arun	Assoc	George Wash	Q	PHD	84	J Hopkins	1992
Malixi, Margaret M.	Prof	CS-Bakersf	ACFP	PHD	88	Wisconsin	1988
Malkiel, Burton G.	Prof	Princeton		PHD	64	Princeton	1966
Mallela, Parthasaradhi	Emer	No Illinois	C	PHD	70	Rochester	1976
Malliaris, Tassos	Prof	Loyola-Chicg	ACG	PHD	72	Oklahoma	1972
Mallick, Naresh	Asst	Alabama A&M	CE	PHD	95	Illinois	2-99
Malloy, Mary	Asst	New Rochelle	AHJO	PHD	94	Brown	
Malone, Laurence J.	C-Ac	Hartwick	ABFN	PHD	91	New Sch	1986
Maloney, Michael T.	Prof	Clemson	DGKL	PHD	78	LSU	
Maloney, Tom	Asst	Utah		PHD	93	Michigan	1992

Maltsev, Yuri N.	Assoc	Carthage	DFJP	PHD	80	Inst Labor	1991
Malueg, David A.	Assoc	Tulane		PHD	83	Nrthwstrn	1991
Mamalakis, Markos J.	Prof	Wis-Milwauke		PHD	62	Berkeley	1967
Mamgain, Vaishali	Asst	So Maine	CO	PHD	79	N Carol	1997
Mammen, Thampy	Retir	St Norbert		PHD	67	Penn	1968
Mamoozadeh, G. Abbas	Assoc	Slippery Roc	AG	PHD	89	Kent St	
Manage, Neela D.	Assoc	Fla Atlantic	FE	PHD	81	Geo Wash	1981
Mandle, Jay R.	Prof	Colgate	ON	PHD	69	Penn	
W. Bradford Wiley Professor of Economics							
Mandler, Michael A.	Assoc	Harvard		PHD	87	Yale	
Mandy, David M.	Assoc	Missouri	CD	PHD	87	Illinois	1994
Manelli, Alejandro	Assoc	Arizona St		PHD	88	Berkeley	1997
Maneschi, Andrea	Assoc	Vanderbilt	FO	PHD	64	J Hopkins	1969
Mangiero, Susan M.	Asst	Sacred Heart	ACDG	ABD		Conn	1990
Mangum, Garth L.	Prof	Utah		PHD	60	Harvard	1969
Mangum, James M.	Retir	Louisiana Te		PHD	72	Okla St	1970
Mani, Anandi	Asst	Vanderbilt		PHD	97	Boston	1997
Manion, Thomas A.	Retir	St Norbert		PHD	74	Clark	1983
Mankiw, N. Gregory	Prof	Harvard		PHD	84	MIT	1985
Mann, Bruce D.	Prof	Puget Sound	ADJK	PHD	76	Indiana	1975
Mann, Patrick C.	Prof	W Virginia	DH	PHD	67	Indiana	1967
Mann, Prem S.	Assoc	Eastern Conn		PHD	88	UCLA	1986
Manning, Linda M.	Assoc	Mo-Rolla		PHD	90	Il-Chicago	1989
Manove, Michael	Prof	Boston Univ	D	PHD	70	MIT	1975
Manrique, Gabriel G.	C-Pr	Winona State		PHD	82	Notre Dm	1989
Mansfield, Edwin	Prof	Pennsylvania		PHD	55	Duke	1963
Mansfield, Jon	VAsst	Georgia St	AM	PHD	92	Geo St	1996
Manski, Charles F.	Prof	Northwestern		PHD	73	MIT	1997
Board of Trustees Professor							
Mansori, Kashif	Asst	Colby	EF	PHD	97	Princeton	1997
Manuelli, Rodolfo	Prof	Wisconsin		PHD	86	Minnesota	1993
Mao, Wen	Asst	Villanova		PHD	94	Va Tech	1995
Mapalad, Claret	Asst	Alfred		PHD	94	Ca-Rivers	7-99
Mar, Donald W.	Assoc	San Fran St		PHD	85	Berkeley	1987
Maran, Michael J.	Assoc	St John's		PHD	94	Penn	
Marburger, Daniel R.	Assoc	Arkansas St	AJMD	PHD	89	Ariz St	1989
Marcal, Leah	Asst	CS-Northrdge		PHD	96	Wisconsin	1996
Marcis, John G.	Assoc	Fran Marion		PHD		Missouri	
Marcott, Craig S.	Assoc	St Thomas-MN	C	PHD	83	Purdue	1982
Marcouiller, Douglas	Asst	Boston Coll	FO	PHD	94	Tx-Austin	1994
Marcus, Matityahu	Prof	Rutgers-N Br	G	PHD	63	Brown	1962
Marcus, Morton	Lect	Indiana		MA	63	Wash U	1973
Mardfin, Ward	Assoc	Hawaii Pacif		PHD	79	Hi-Manoa	1992
Mardis, Barbara K.	Inst	No Iowa	C	MBA	81	N Iowa	1981
Marett, Pamela	Asst	Embry-Riddle		PHD	82	Tennessee	
Marglin, Stephen A.	Prof	Harvard		PHD	65	Harvard	
Walter S. Barker Professor of Economics							
Margo, Robert A.	Prof	Vanderbilt	NJ	PHD	82	Harvard	1989
Margolis, H. Albert	Prof	Kutztown	NC	PHD	69	Purdue	1976
Margolis, Julius	Emer	Calif-Irvine		PHD	49	Harvard	1976
Margolis, Marvin S.	Prof	Millersville		PHD	69	Purdue	1981
Margolis, Stephen E.	H-Pr	N Carol St	LKD	PHD	78	UCLA	1982
Mariano, Roberto S.	Prof	Pennsylvania		PHD	70	Stanford	1971
Marion, Nancy P.	Prof	Dartmouth		PHD	77	Princeton	1976
Mark, Adolph E.	Emer	DePaul	A	PHD	63	Illinois	9-61
Mark, Nelson C.	Prof	Ohio State	FG	PHD	83	Chicago	1983
Marker, William	Inst	Lewis		MA	85	N Illinois	1988
Market, Donald R.	Retir	Arkansas	E	PHD	67	LSU	1975
Marks, Denton	Prof	Wis-Whitewat		PHD	81	Princeton	1990
Marks, Melanie B.	Assoc	Longwood		PHD	93	Tx A&M	1993
Marks, Peter A.	C-Ac	Rhode Isl Cl		PHD	78	N Carol	
Markusen, James R.	Prof	Colorado		PHD	73	Boston C	1990
Marlin, Matthew R.	Assoc	Duquesne		PHD	81	Fla St	1987
Marlow, Michael L.	Prof	Cal Poly-SLO		PHD	78	Va Tech	1988
Marme, Christopher B.	Asst	Augustana IL	ACEO	PHD	94	Illinois	1988
Marmo, Michael	Prof	Xavier	J	PHD	71	Illinois	1970
Maroney, Neal C.	Asst	New Orleans		PHD	96	Claremont	1997
Marquis, Milton H.	Prof	Florida St	E	PHD	85	Indiana	1986
Marschke, Gerald	Asst	SUNY-Albany	DJL	PHD	98	Chicago	1998
Marsh, Lawrence C.	Assoc	Notre Dame	CD	PHD	76	Mich St	1975
Marshall, James N.	Prof	Muhlenberg		PHD	82	Lehigh	1975
Marshall, Jennings B.	Prof	Samford	CD	PHD	77	Kentucky	1986
Marshall, John F.	Prof	St John's		PHD	82	SUNY-SBr	
Marshall, John M.	Prof	Cal-Santa Br	A	PHD	69	MIT	1972
Marshall, Kathryn G.	Lect	Ohio State	HQ	PHD	90	Berkeley	
Marshall, Louise	Prof	Marymount		PHD	89	Maryland	1976
Marshall, Robert C.	H-Pr	Penn State		PHD	83	Ca-SnDgo	1995
Marshall, Robert H.	Emer	Arizona		PHD	57	Ohio St	1957
Martel, Arthur H.	Prof	Indiana U-PA	JK	PHD	74	Mass	1970
Martellaro, Joseph A.	Retir	No Illinois		PHD	62	Notre Dm	

Name	Rank	School	Fields	Degree	Yr	Degree School	Year
Marthinsen, John E.	C-Pr	Babson	FD	PHD	74	Conn	1974
Martin, David A.	Prof	Albright		DA	80	Lehigh	1983
Martin, David A.	Prof	SUNY-Geneseo	BA	PHD	64	Syracuse	1966
Martin, David W.	Prof	Davidson	GQ	PHD	84	Illinois	1984
Martin, Dolores	Dean	Seton Hall		PHD	76	Va Tech	
Martin, Lawrence W.	Prof	Michigan St		PHD	81	Maryland	1982
Martin, Linda R.	Dean	New Haven		PHD	81	S Carol	8-95
Martin, Randolph C.	Prof	So Carolina		PHD	71	Wash U	1970
Martin, Richard S.	Retir	Hartford		PHD		Cornell	1968
Martin, Robert E.	Prof	Centre	CD	PHD	79	So Meth	1996
Ewing T. Boles Professor of Economics							
Martin, Thomas L.	Assoc	Cen Florida	B	PHD	81	Rice	1983
Martinez, John	Prof	Midwest St	ABCO	PHD	84	Oklahoma	1997
Martinez, Jorge L.	Prof	Georgia St	DF	PHD	78	Wash U	1977
Martins, Carlos	Assoc	Oregon State	DCL	PHD	92	Tennessee	9-92
Marty, Alvin L.	Prof	CUNY-Baruch		PHD	55	Berkeley	1960
Marvasti, Akbar B.	Assoc	Houston-Down		PHD	85	LSU	1990
Marvel, Howard P.	Prof	Ohio State	L	PHD	75	Chicago	1973
Marx, Karl B.	Retir	W Illinois	ADH	PHD	61	Illinois	1961
Marxsen, Craig S.	Assoc	Neb-Kearney		PHD	76	Geo St	1987
Masih, Nolin	Retir	St Cloud St		PHD	88	Kansas	1964
Masin, Shohreh	Asst	W Michigan	E	PHD	94	Wi-Milwa	1998
Maskin, Eric S.	Prof	Harvard		PHD	76	Harvard	
Maskus, Keith E.	Prof	Colorado		PHD	81	Michigan	1981
Mason, Andrew	C-Pr	Hawaii-Manoa		PHD	75	Michigan	1975
Mason, Charles F.	Prof	Wyoming	DK	PHD	83	Berkeley	1982
Mason, Patrick L.	Assoc	Florida St	J	PHD	91	New Sch	1999
Mason, Paul M.	Prof	North Fla	HE	PHD	84	Tx-Austin	1985
Mason, Timothy I.	Assoc	E Illinois		PHD	87	Indiana	1989
Mason, W. Joe Jr.	Assoc	East Tenn St		PHD	87	S Carol	1984
Mason, William J.	Prof	San Fran St		PHD	58	Iowa	1958
Masson, Robert T.	Prof	Cornell		PHD	69	Berkeley	1976
Masten, John T.	Prof	Tenn State		PHD	67	S Illinois	
Masters, Stanley H.	Prof	SUNY-Bingham	J	PHD	65	Princeton	1981
Mastrianna, Frank V.	Dean	Slippery Roc		PHD	68	Cincinnati	3-87
Matcheck, Dale C.	Asst	Northwood	Q	PHD	93	Cornell	1995
Mateer, G. Dirk	Assoc	Grove City		PHD	91	Fla St	1993
Mateer, Robert N.	C-Pr	Liberty		MBA	64	Tulane	1984
Mathews, Leah Greden	Asst	N Car-Ashvil	HDQO	PHD	97	Minnesota	1997
Mathis, Edward J.	C-Pr	Villanova		PHD	71	SUNY-Buf	1966
Mathis, Gilbert L.	Prof	Murray State	DFKQ	PHD	66	Ohio St	1966
Mathis, Stephen A.	Prof	Shippensburg		PHD	79	Iowa St	1979
Mathur, Vijay K.	Prof	Cleveland St	DR	PHD	69	Wayne St	1968
Matsui, Akihiko	Asst	Pennsylvania	CDE	PHD	90	Nrthwstrn	1990
William P. Carey Term Assistant Professor of Economics							
Matsumoto, Keishiro	Retir	So Conn St		PHD		Minnesota	
Matsuyama, Kiminori	Prof	Northwestern		PHD	87	Harvard	
Matta, Benjamin N.	Assoc	New Mex St	IJ	PHD	79	Tx-Austin	1972
Matthaei, Julie Ann	Prof	Wellesley		PHD	78	Yale	1978
Matthews, Peter H.	Asst	Middlebury	BCEJ	PHD	95	Yale	1995
Matthews, Steven A.	Prof	Pennsylvania		PHD	78	Cal Tech	1997
Matthews, Warren T.	Assoc	Houston Bapt		PHD	72	Tx A&M	1995
Mattila, John Peter	Prof	Iowa State	J	PHD	69	Wisconsin	1973
Mattox, Bruce W. Sr.	Retir	NC-Pembroke		PHD	71	Oregon St	1988
Matusz, Steven J.	Prof	Michigan St		PHD	83	Penn	1983
Matzkin, Rosa L.	Prof	Northwestern		PHD	86	Minnesota	
Mauer, Laurence J.	Prof	St John's		PHD	67	Tennessee	1983
Mauney, William M.	Prof	Lenoir-Rhyne	AE	MA	76	Appalach	1967
Centennial Professor of Economics - Director Broyhill Institute							
Maurer-Fazio, Margaret	Asst	Bates	O	PHD	94	Pittsburgh	1985
Maurice, S. Charles	Deces	Texas A&M		PHD	67	Georgia	1967
Mavros, Panagiotis	Asst	Wayne State		PHD	93	Cornell	1992
Maxcy, Joel	Asst	Okla City		PHD	96	Wash St	1997
Maxey, Joel	Asst	SUNY-Cortlan	KJ	PHD		Wash St	1998
Maxwell, Don P.	Prof	Central Okla	ADEH	PHD	82	Okla St	1981
Maxwell, John	Asst	Indiana		PHD	93	Queen's	1992
Maxwell, Nan L.	Prof	CS-Hayward	ADJT	PHD	83	Fla St	1985
May, Ann Mari	Assoc	Nebraska	BE	PHD	87	Colo St	1987
May, David	Asst	Okla City		PHD	96	Fla St	1996
Mayer, Thomas	Emer	Cal-Davis	BE	PHD	53	Columbia	1962
Mayer, Walt	Assoc	Mississippi	E	PHD	86	Florida	1987
Mayer, Wolfgang	Prof	Cincinnati	FD	PHD	71	SUNY-Buf	1970
David Sinton Professor							
Mayhew, Anne	Prof	Tennessee		PHD	66	Tx-Austin	1968
Mayor, Thomas H.	Prof	Houston	AK	PHD	65	Maryland	1969
Mazumdar, Joy	Asst	Emory	FEO	PHD	96	Michigan	1996
Mazzarella, James	Asst	Holy Family		PHD	87	Columbia	
Mazzucato, Mariana	Asst	Denver	CL	PHD	98	New Sch	1997
Mbaku, John M.	Prof	Weber State	AHOP	PHD	85	Georgia	1991

Name	Rank	School	Fields	Degree	Yr	Institution	Year
McAfee, R. Preston	Prof	Texas	D	PHD	80	Purdue	9-90
Murray S. Johnson Chair in Economics							
McArthur, John R.	Assoc	Wofford	EHKQ	PHD	91	Claremont	1990
McAuliffe, Robert E. Jr.	Assoc	Babson	EL	PHD	82	Virginia	1982
McBearty, James C.	Assoc	Arizona		PHD	68	Illinois	1968
McBride, Howard	Retir	Cincinnati		PHD	59	Illinois	
McBride, Mark E.	Prof	Miami U-Ohio		PHD	79	Wash U	1983
McBride, Timothy	Assoc	Mo-St Louis	IH	PHD	87	Wisconsin	1991
McCabe, Kevin A.	Assoc	Arizona		PHD	85	Penn	1996
McCabe, Mark J.	Asst	Georgia Tech	L	PHD	91	MIT	1998
McCafferty, Stephen A.	Prof	Ohio State	EF	PHD	77	Brown	1982
McCain, Roger A. III	Prof	Drexel		PHD	71	LSU	1988
McCaleb, Thomas S.	Assoc	Florida St		PHD	75	N Carol	1980
McCall, Charles W.	C-Ac	Rider	AL	PHD	82	Temple	1979
McCall, John B.	Retir	Tx-Arlington	OQ	PHD	68	Okla St	1964
McCall, John J.	Emer	UCLA		PHD	59	Chicago	
McCallie, John	Lect	Maine	EA	PHD	90	Auburn	1992
McCallum, Bennett T.	Prof	Carnegie Mel		PHD	69	Rice	1981
H. J. Heinz Professor of Economics							
McCallum, George E.	Retir	St Norbert		PHD		Calif	1967
McCarl, Henry N.	Prof	Alabama-Birm	AR	PHD	69	Penn St	1969
McCarley, James F.	C-Pr	Albion	J	PHD	70	Mich St	1965
McCarthy, Patrick S.	Prof	Purdue		PHD	76	Claremont	1978
McCarty, Cynthia S.	Asst	Jacksonvl St		PHD	94	N Carol	1990
McCarty, Marilu H.	Assoc	Georgia Tech	EH	PHD	72	Geo St	1972
McCarty, Therese A.	Assoc	Union	GI	PHD	87	Michigan	1987
McClellan, Mark	Asst	Stanford		PHD	93	Harvard	9-95
McClelland, Peter D.	Prof	Cornell		PHD	67	Harvard	1968
McClintock, Brent	Assoc	Carthage	EFG	PHD	90	Colo St	1991
McCloskey, Deirdre N.	Prof	Iowa		PHD	70	Harvard	1980
McClung, Bruce Alan	Asst	SW Texas St	J	PHD	88	Tx A&M	1988
McClure, James Edward	Assoc	Ball State	J	PHD	83	Purdue	1982
McCollum, James B.	Retir	Columbus		PHD	68	Tulane	1976
McComb, Robert P.	Assoc	Texas Tech		PHD	89	Illinois	1991
McConnell, Virginia D.	Assoc	MD-Baltim Co		PHD	78	Maryland	
McCorkle, Sarapage	Asst	Mo-St Louis	A	EDD	87	Mo-StLou	1970
McCormack, Edward	Asst	Berea		MBA	80	Estrn Ky	1985
McCormick, Kenneth J.	Prof	No Iowa	BEA	PHD	82	Iowa St	1982
McCormick, Robert E.	Prof	Clemson	DGKH	PHD	78	Tx A&M	
McCoskey, Suzanne K.	Asst	USN Academy		PHD	97	Syracuse	1997
McCown, James	Asst	Fla Atlantic	FE	PHD	97	Ohio St	1997
McCoy, James	C-Pr	Murray State	DFOP	PHD	86	N Carol	1985
McCracken, Michael	Asst	Louisiana St	C	PHD	98	Wisconsin	8-98
McCrate, Elaine D.	Assoc	Vermont	JIT	PHD	85	Mass	1985
McCraw, Jessica	Lect	Tx-Arlington	DE	MA	78	DePaul	1990
McCrickard, Donald L.	Assoc	N Car-Greens	EF	PHD	76	N Carol	1975
McCrickard, Myra J.	D-As	Bellarmine	CE	PHD	89	N Car St	1989
McCulloch, J. Huston	Prof	Ohio State	E	PHD	73	Chicago	1979
McCulloch, Laurence	Lect	Ohio State					
McCulloch, Rachel	Prof	Brandeis		PHD	73	Chicago	1987
McDaniel, Bruce A.	C-Ac	No Colorado	OGMQ	PHD	79	Colo St	1992
McDermott, John H.	Assoc	So Carolina		PHD	79	Brown	1983
McDevitt, Catherine L.	Asst	Cen Michigan		PHD	86	Rochester	1989
McDonald, James B.	Prof	Brigham Yg		PHD	70	Purdue	1972
McDonald, John F.	Prof	Ill-Chicago	R	PHD	71	Yale	1971
McDonald, Judith Ann	Assoc	Lehigh	FE	PHD	86	Princeton	1990
McDonald, Michael	Assoc	Coe		MA	81	Iowa	1981
McDonald, Stephen L.	Retir	Texas	HQ	PHD	51	Tx-Austin	9-61
McDonald, Vincent R.	Prof	Howard		PHD	68	Maryland	
McDonough, Carol C.	Prof	Mass-Lowell	DN	PHD	69	Boston C	1970
McDougall, Gerald S.	Dean	SE Missouri	HL	PHD	74	Claremont	1993
McDowell, John M.	Prof	Arizona St		PHD	79	UCLA	1978
McEachern, William A.	Prof	Connecticut	H	PHD	75	Virginia	1978
McEliece, James H.	C-Ac	Pt Loma Naz		PHD	86	Co Mines	1994
McElroy, F. William	Retir	Georgetown		PHD	67	Geotown	1968
McElroy, Jerome L.	C-Pr	St Marys-Ind	AEFO	PHD	71	Colorado	8-82
McElroy, Marjorie B.	C-Pr	Duke		PHD	69	Nrthwstrn	1976
McElroy, Michael B.	Assoc	N Carol St	E	PHD	70	Nrthwstrn	1970
McFadden, Daniel L.	Prof	Cal-Berkeley		PHD	62	Minnesota	1963
McFarland, David	Prof	No Carolina	BDL	PHD	63	Vanderbilt	1964
McFarland, Earl L. Jr.	Retir	Williams		PHD	73	Columbia	1968
McFerrin, Randy	Asst	E New Mexico		PHD	95	Tx A&M	1995
McGahagan, Thomas A.	Assoc	Pitts-Johnst	FN	PHD	76	Penn	1982
McGarrity, Joseph	Asst	Cen Arkansas		PHD	94	GeoMason	8-95
McGarry, Kathleen	Asst	UCLA		PHD	92	SUNY-SBr	
McGarvey, Mary G.	Assoc	Nebraska	E	PHD	83	Virginia	1992
McGee, L. Randolph	Retir	Kentucky	MG	PHD	63	Tulane	1963
McGee, M. Kevin	Assoc	Wis-Oshkosh	H	PHD	83	Ohio St	1982
McGibany, James M.	Assoc	Marquette	CER	PHD	83	Mich St	1983
McGill-Tillman, Patricia	Inst	Jackson St		MA	65	Atlanta	1968

Name	Rank	School	Fields	Degree	Yr	Institution	Hired
McGoldrick, Kim Marie	Asst	Richmond		PHD	93	SUNY-Bin	1992
McGowan, Susan	Prof	CS-Sacrament		PHD	77	Ca-Davis	1974
McGrath, Paul T.	Assoc	Purdue-Calmu		PHD	88	N Illinois	1986
McGrath, Richard	Asst	Armstrong At	DHG	PHD	97	Virginia	1997
McGregor, Rob R.	Assoc	N Car-Charl		PHD	91	S Carol	1991
McGuckin, J. T.	Assoc	New Mex St	Q	PHD	90	Wisconsin	1989
McGuire, Martin C.	Prof	Calif-Irvine		PHD	64	Harvard	1992
McGuire, Robert A.	Prof	Akron	AKN	PHD	78	U Wash	1990
McGuire, Thomas G.	Prof	Boston Univ	HIL	PHD	76	Yale	1976
McHale, John	Asst	Harvard		PHD	96	Harvard	
McHone, W. Warren	Prof	Cen Florida	R	PHD	80	Penn	1982
McInnes, Melayne	Asst	So Carolina		PHD	97	Yale	8-97
McIntyre, Richard	Assoc	Rhode Island		PHD	89	Mass	1989
McKee, David L.	Prof	Kent State	OR	PHD	66	Notre Dm	1967
McKee, Michael	Prof	New Mexico	HKQL	PHD	85	Carleton	1991
McKenna, Edward J.	Assoc	Conn Coll	E	PHD	81	SUNY-SBr	
McKenzie, Lionel W.	Emer	Rochester		PHD	42	Princeton	1957
McKinney, Charles W.	Retir	Whitworth	DE	PHD	73	Wash St	1985
McKinney, Hannah J.	Asst	Kalamazoo	HJR	PHD	84	Penn	1988
McKinney, Joseph A.	Prof	Baylor	F	PHD	70	Mich St	1976
McKinney, Marie M.	Prof	Framingham		PHD	83	SUNY-Bin	1985
McKinnon, Ronald I.	Prof	Stanford		PHD	61	Minnesota	1961
William D. Eberle Professor of Economics							
McKinnon, Thomas	Prof	Arkansas	NA	PHD	72	Miss	1981
McLain, James J.	Assoc	New Orleans		PHD	72	Pittsburgh	1972
McLain, Louis P.	Dean$	Txs Wesleyan		MBA	74	So Meth	1976
McLaren, John	Prof	Columbia	OD	PHD	92	Princeton	1992
McLaughlin, Francis M.	Assoc	Boston Coll	JN	PHD	64	MIT	1961
McLaughlin, Kenneth J.	Assoc	CUNY-Hunter		PHD	87	Chicago	9-94
McLaughlin, Patrick	C-Ac	NW Missouri	K	JD	78	Mo-Ks Cty	1978
McLean, Richard P.	Prof	Rutgers-N Br	D	PHD	79	SUNY-SBr	1986
McLean, Roy	Asst	Cen Arkansas		PHD	95	S Carol	9-97
McLean, Thomas A.	Retir	Portland St		PHD	66	Utah	1962
McLellan, Jacquelynne W.	Assoc	Frostburg St		PHD	93	Wayne St	1994
McLennan, Andrew M.	Assoc	Minnesota		PHD	82	Princeton	1987
McLeod, Darryl L.	Asst	Fordham		PHD	82	Berkeley	1984
McLewin, Phillip J.	Assoc	Ramapo		PHD	70	Cornell	1974
McMahon, Marshall E.	Prof	Rhodes		PHD	72	Vanderbilt	1972
McMahon, Robert C.	Retir	So Maine	R	PHD	70	Lehigh	1969
McMahon, Walter W.	Retir	Illinois		PHD	57	Iowa	1957
McManis, Bruce L.	H-Pr	Nicholls St	G	PHD	81	LSU	1978
McMillan, Margaret	Asst	Tufts	O	PHD	97	Columbia	1997
McMillen, Daniel P.	C-Pr	Tulane		PHD	87	Nrthwstrn	1994
McMillin, W. Douglas	Prof	Louisiana St	E	PHD	79	LSU	1985
South Central Bell Business Partnership Professor							
McMinn, Jim Thomas	Retir	Austin Peay	GM	DBA	75	Miss St	1977
McMinn, Robert D.	C-Pr	Tx A&M-C Chr	A	PHD	70	Oklahoma	9-74
McMullen, B. Starr	Prof	Oregon State	LE	PHD	79	Berkeley	9-80
McMurry, Patrick H.	Prof	Missouri Wes	J	PHD	81	Arkansas	1978
McNamara, John R.	Prof	Lehigh	MO	PHD	71	Rensselaer	1973
Lee Iacocca Professor of Business & Economics							
McNelis, Paul D.	Prof	Georgetown		PHD	74	J Hopkins	1977
McNertney, Edward M.	C-Ac	Tx Christian		PHD	77	Mass	1977
McNiel, Douglas W.	Prof	McNeese St		PHD	77	Okla St	1984
McNown, Robert F.	Prof	Colorado		PHD	71	Ca-SnDgo	1971
McPherson, Michael	Asst	North Texas	FO	PHD	92	Mich St	1992
McPherson, S.	Asst	Geo Southern		PHD	97	Indiana	1997
McPheters, Lee R.	Prof	Arizona St		PHD	72	Va Tech	1976
McQuiston, James M. Jr.	Asst	So Miss		BS	56	S Miss	1960
McRae, Larry T.	Assoc	Appalach St	CDE	PHD	78	N Carol	1977
McRostie, Clair	Retir	Gustavus Ado		PHD	64	Wisconsin	1957
Mead, Arthur C.	Prof	Rhode Island		PHD	78	Boston C	1976
Meadows, G. Richard	Assoc	Wis-Milwauke		PHD	72	Wash U	1971
Meadows, Tommy C.	C-Pr	Austin Peay	HJ	PHD	78	Clemson	1977
Meaney, Martha M.	Assoc	Framingham		MA		Boston C	
Means, Tom S.	Assoc	San Jose St		PHD	83	UCLA	1986
Measell, Richard F.	Asst	St Marys-Ind	ADHJ	PHD	85	Maryland	8-83
Medema, Steven G.	C-Pr	Colo-Denver	BHDK	PHD	89	Mich St	1989
Medley, Joseph E.	Assoc	So Maine	BO	PHD	81	Mass	1983
Medoff, James L.	Prof	Harvard		PHD	75	Harvard	
Meyer Kestnbaum Professor of Labor & Industry							
Medoff, Marshall H.	Prof	CS-Long Bch		PHD	73	Berkeley	1979
Meehan, James P.	Retir	Edinboro		MA	61	Notre Dm	1966
Meehan, James W.	Prof	Colby	DM	PHD	67	Boston C	1973
Herbert E. Wadsworth Professor of Economics							
Meeks, Thomas J.	Prof	Virginia St		PHD	71	Duke	1969
Meenakshi, Rishi	Assoc	Ohio Northrn		PHD	93	Mass	1993
Meepagaia, Gaminie	Asst	Howard	C	PHD	86	SUNY-Alb	1988
Meeropol, Michael A.	C-Pr	W New Eng		PHD	73	Wisconsin	1970
Mehay, Stephen L.	Prof	Naval Postgr	IJ	PHD	73	UCLA	1985

Name	Rank	School	Fields	Degree	Yr	Institution	Year
Mehdizadeh, Mostafa	Assoc	Miami U-Ohio	A	PHD	80	Oklahoma	1982
Mehra, Jadish C.	Prof	Youngstown		PHD	68	SUNY-Buf	1965
Mehra, Rajnish	Prof	Cal-Santa Br	GF	PHD	78	Car Mellon	1988
Mehrez, Gil	Asst	Georgetown		PHD	95	Berkeley	1995
Mehrling, Perry G.	C-Ac	Barnard	EGB	PHD	88	Harvard	1987
Mehtabdin, Khalid R.	Assoc	St Rose	AEFM	PHD	79	Pittsburgh	1986
Meiners, Roger E.	Prof	Tx-Arlington	KJ	PHD	76	Va Tech	1993
Meininger, Richard P.	Prof	Ohio Northrn		PHD	87	Ohio U	1973
Meisel, John B.	Prof	S Ill-Edward	ADL	PHD	78	Boston C	1977
Meiselman, David I.	Emer	Virg Tech	D	PHD	61	Chicago	1971
Meister, J. Patrick	VAsst	Butler	L	PHD	92	Michigan	1996
Melancon, Melissa	Asst	Grambling St		ABD		La Tech	
Melero, Francisco	D-Ac	Russell Sage	DCF	PHD	83	Rensselaer	1982
Melese, Francois	Assoc	Naval Postgr	C	PHD	82	Belgium	1987
Melick, William R.	Assoc	Kenyon	EGCF	PHD	87	Ohio St	7-98
Mellor, Jennifer	Asst	Wm & Mary		PHD	96	Maryland	1998
Meltzer, Allan H.	Prof	Carnegie Mel		PHD	58	UCLA	1957
John M. Olin University Professor of Political Economy and Public Policy							
Meltzer, Yale L.	Asst	CUNY-Stn Isl	EG	MBA	66	NYU	1983
Melvin, Michael T.	Prof	Arizona St		PHD	80	UCLA	1980
Menchik, Paul L.	Prof	Michigan St		PHD	76	Penn	1979
Mendelsohn, Robert	Prof	Yale		PHD	78	Yale	1984
Mendez, Jose A.	Prof	Arizona St		PHD	80	So Meth	1980
Mendoza, Enrique	Assoc	Duke		PHD	89	W Ontario	1997
Mendoza, Juan	Asst	SUNY-Buffalo	ED	PHD	99	Brown	1999
Menes, Rebecca	Asst	George Mason		PHD	97	Harvard	1999
Menezes, Carmen F.	Prof	Missouri	DF	PHD	66	Nrthwstrn	1965
Menge, John A.	Prof	Dartmouth		PHD	59	MIT	1956
Mengistu, Tadessa	Assoc	Dillard		PHD	86	Indiana	
Menz, Fredric C.	Dean	Clarkson	HQD	PHD	70	Virginia	1974
Mercer, Lloyd J.	Prof	Cal-Santa Br	ND	PHD	67	U Wash	1966
Mercuro, Nicholas	Retir	New Orleans		PHD	77	Mich St	1977
Merkel, Edward T.	Prof	Troy State		PHD	74	N Illinois	1978
Merkle, Paul E.	Retir	La St-Shreve		PHD	77	La Tech	1976
Merrifield, David E.	Prof	Western Wash	M	PHD	82	Claremont	1983
Merrifield, John D.	Assoc	Tx-S Antonio	HQR	PHD	84	Wyoming	1987
Merrill, William C.	Prof	Iowa State	O	PHD	64	Berkeley	1964
Merriman, David F.	Assoc	Loyola-Chicg	ADHO	PHD	83	Wisconsin	1987
Merz, Monika	Asst	Rice		PHD	94	Nrthwstrn	1994
Merz, Thomas E.	Assoc	Mich Tech		PHD	80	Pittsburgh	1980
Mesa-Lago, Carmelo	Retir	Pittsburgh	P	PHD	68	Cornell	1968
Mescon, Timothy S.	Dean	Kennesaw St		PHD	79	Georgia	1990
Messe, Michael J.	D	USM Academy	HE	PHD	77	Princeton	1990
Messerschmidt, Daniel C.	C-Pr	Lynchburg		PHD	84	Iowa St	1985
Metcalf, Gilbert	Assoc	Tufts		PHD	88	Harvard	1994
Metrick, Andrew P.	Asst	Harvard		PHD	94	Harvard	
Metts, Robert Lyle	Assoc	Nevada-Reno		PHD	85	Berkeley	1984
Metzger, Michael R.	C-Pr	Central Okla	DIL	PHD	78	Stanford	1991
Meurs, Mieke E.	Assoc	American U		PHD	88	Mass	1989
Meyer, Bruce	Prof	Northwestern		PHD	87	MIT	1987
Household International Inc. Professorship							
Meyer, Carrie A.	Assoc	George Mason		PHD	88	Illinois	1988
Meyer, Charles W.	Retir	Iowa State	G	PHD	61	J Hopkins	1961
Meyer, Christine	Asst	Bentley	EFH	PHD	95	MIT	1995
Meyer, Donald J.	Assoc	W Michigan	D	PHD	83	Tx A&M	1991
Meyer, Jack	Prof	Michigan St		PHD	74	Stanford	1983
Meyer, Laurence H.	Prof	Wash Univ	E	PHD	70	MIT	1969
Meyer, Peter	Retir	Louisville		PHD	70	Wisconsin	
Meyer, Peter J.	Assoc	Pacific	BJL	PHD	79	Berkeley	1985
Mezzetti, Claudio	Prof	No Carolina	D	PHD	88	Oxford	1990
Miceli, Thomas J.	Prof	Connecticut	KR	PHD	88	Brown	1987
Michael, Jeffery	Asst	Towson		PHD	99	N Carol	1999
Michaels, Robert J.	Prof	CS-Fullerton	L	PHD	72	UCLA	1968
Michailidis, Lazaros	Assoc	Bloomfield		PHD	80	SUNY-Buf	1978
Michalik, Benjamin A.	Retir	St Peters	1987	PHD	57	Fordham	1947
Michaud, Claude	Prof	INSEAD		D		Bordeaux	8-70
Michelsen, Ari	Asst	Wash State		PHD	88	Colo St	1994
Michener, Ronald W.	Assoc	Virginia	EN	PHD	81	Chicago	1979
Michl, Thomas R.	Assoc	Colgate	EJ	PHD	84	New Sch	1983
Mickens, Alvin D.	Assoc	SUNY Old Wes		PHD	72	NYU	1978
Mieczkowski, Bogdan	Prof	Ithaca	AF	PHD	54	Illinois	1954
Mieszkowski, Peter	Prof	Rice		PHD	63	J Hopkins	1981
Cline Professor of Economics & Finance							
Mihov, Ilian	Asst	INSEAD		PHD	96	Princeton	9-96
Miklius, Walter	Retir	Hawaii-Manoa		PHD	64	UCLA	
Milener, Eugene D. III	Retir	Hartwick		PHD		NYU	1960
Miles, William	Asst	Wichita St		PHD	98	Illinois	1999
Milgrom, Paul R.	Prof	Stanford		PHD	79	Stanford	1987
Shirley R. and Leonard W. Ely, Jr. Professor in Humanities and Sciences							
Milkman, Martin	Prof	Murray State	CJH	PHD	89	Oregon	1988

Name	Rank	School	Fields	Degree	Yr	Institution	Year
Millar, James R.	Prof	George Wash	P	PHD	65	Cornell	1989
Millea, Meghan	Asst	Miss State		PHD	98	Nebraska	1998
Miller, Carole F.	Assoc	Rhode Island	ACDJ	PHD	88	Syracuse	1986
Miller, Dennis D.	Assoc	Baldwin-Wal	OQ	PHD	85	Colorado	1987
Miller, Edward M.	Prof	New Orleans		PHD	70	MIT	1984
Miller, Ellen M.	Asst	N Car-Charl		PHD	83	Florida	1982
Miller, Gerald	Assoc	Rockhurst		PHD	75	Notre Dm	1982
Miller, Gerald M.	SInst	Miami U-Ohio	DC	MA	73	Brown	1971
Miller, Green	C-Pr	Morehead St		PHD	85	Kentucky	1979
Miller, James	Asst	Smith		PHD	97	Chicago	1996
Miller, Jeffrey B.	Prof	Delaware	EP	PHD	76	Penn	1976
Miller, John	Lect	Sam Houston		MS	65	Rice	1998
Miller, John A.	C-Pr	Wheaton-MA		PHD	82	Pittsburgh	1979
Miller, Jon R.	Prof	Idaho	BQ	PHD	74	Wash U	1989
Miller, Michael S.	Assoc	DePaul	E	PHD	80	Pittsburgh	1980
Miller, Norman C.	Prof	Miami U-Ohio	EF	PHD	66	Pittsburgh	1985
Julian G. Lange Professor of Economics & American Enterprise							
Miller, Oscar	Prof	Ill-Chicago	A	MA	46	Chicago	1948
Miller, Otis E.	Retir	Wm Jewell		PHD	62	Missouri	1978
Miller, Richard A.	Prof	Wesleyan-CT	L	PHD	62	Yale	1960
Andrews Professor of Economics							
Miller, Robert A.	Assoc	Carnegie Mel		PHD	82	Chicago	1982
Miller, Robert J.	Prof	Missouri So		MA		Cen Mo St	1968
Miller, Ronald	Asst	Columbia	EO	PHD	94	Princeton	1994
Miller, Stephen M.	H-Pr	Connecticut	EF	PHD	72	SUNY-Buf	1970
Miller, Timothy I.	Prof	Denison	CE	PHD	79	S Illinois	1978
Miller, Tracy C.	Assoc	Grove City		PHD	86	Chicago	1995
Milley, Donald J.	Prof	Youngstown		PHD	74	SUNY-Buf	1969
Milliman, Scott R.	Assoc	Jms Madison	DQ	PHD	85	Wisconsin	1986
Millimet, Danie	Asst	So Methodist	CJO	PHD	99	Brown	1999
Millner, Edward L.	C-Pr	Virg Comm		PHD	82	N Carol	1983
Mills, David E.	Prof	Virginia	LD	PHD	75	Stanford	1975
Mills, Jeffrey A.	Assoc	Cincinnati	C	PHD	89	Wash U	1992
Mills, Judith W.	Assoc	So Conn St	CNT	PHD	94	SUNY-SBr	1991
Mills, Richard L.	Assoc	New Hampshir	CD	PHD	67	Indiana	1967
Millsaps, Steven	Prof	Appalach St	CDQ	PHD	73	N Car St	1973
Milstein, Susan Matz	Prof	W Maryland		MBA		MtStMary	1983
Milyo, Jeffrey	Asst	Tufts	H	PHD	94	Stanford	1992
Minehart, Deborah	Asst	Boston Univ	CDL	PHD	94	Berkeley	1994
Miner, Jerry	Retir	Syracuse		PHD	58	Michigan	
Miners, Cathy	VAsst	Fairfield	EG	PHD	81	N Carol	1998
Miners, Laurence A.	Assoc	Fairfield	CIJA	PHD	79	N Carol	1981
Minet, Lawrence J.	Retir	Canisius		PHD	53	Columbia	1958
Ming, Xing	Asst	Indiana		PHD	95	Rice	1995
Mini, Peter S.	Assoc	Bryant	BN	PHD	65	Tulane	
Minick, Robert A.	Retir	CS-Fresno		PHD	67	Tx-Austin	1962
Minicozzi, Alexandra	Asst	Texas	E	PHD	97	Wisconsin	9-97
Minier, Jenny	Asst	U Miami	EO	PHD	98	Wisconsin	1998
Minisian, Jora	Retir	CS-Northrdge		PHD	60	Chicago	1972
Minkler, Alanson P.	Assoc	Connecticut	DK	PHD	88	Ca-Davis	1989
Minniti, Maria	Asst	Babson	E	PHD	97	NYU	1997
Minor, Frank J.	Assoc	St Anselm		PHD	58	Ohio St	
Minsky, Hyman P.	Retir	Wash Univ		PHD	54	Harvard	1965
Miranne, Martha	Retir	Pace		MA		Pace	1977
Miranowski, John A.	C-Pr	Iowa State	Q	PHD	75	Harvard	1995
Miravete, Eugenio	Asst	New York U	L	PHD	96	Nrthwstrn	1998
Mirer, Thad W.	Assoc	SUNY-Albany	H	PHD	71	Yale	1973
Mirman, Leonard J.	Prof	Virginia	ACDQ	PHD	70	Rochester	1986
Paul Goodloe McIntire Professor of Economics							
Mirmirani, Sam	C-Pr	Bryant	IMO	PHD	85	Clark	1982
Miron, Jeffrey A.	Prof	Boston Univ	EKN	PHD	84	MIT	1990
Mirowski, Philip E.	Prof	Notre Dame	B	PHD	79	Michigan	1990
Mirza, David B.	Assoc	Loyola-Chicg	AF	PHD	73	Nrthwstrn	1969
Misdzar, Sujetlana	Asst	Gustavus Ado		PHD	96	Minnesota	1994
Mishkin, Frederic S.	Prof	Columbia		PHD	76	MIT	1983
A. Barton Hepburn Professor of Economics							
Misiolek, Walter S.	Prof	Alabama		PHD	76	Cornell	1975
Mitch, David F.	Assoc	MD-Baltim Co		PHD	82	Chicago	1983
Mitchell, Douglas W.	Prof	W Virginia	E	PHD	78	Princeton	1984
Mitchell, Hadley T.	Assoc	Taylor		PHD	85	Tennessee	1993
Mitchell, Jeannette C.	Asst	Rochest Tech	FOB	PHD	95	Utah	1985
Mitchell, Lloyd	C-As	St Thomas-FL		MBA	81	U Miami	1984
Mitchell, Mike	Assoc	Nevada-Reno		PHD	88	Oregon	1988
Mitchell, Milt	Asst	Wis-Oshkosh	Q	MA	65	Wisconsin	1967
Mitchell, Shannon K.	Assoc	Virg Comm		PHD	89	Virginia	1990
Mitchell, Thomas M.	Assoc	So Illinois	DC	PHD	84	Brown	1983
Mitchell, William E.	Retir	Mo-St Louis	EG	PHD	67	Duke	1965
Mitra, Aparna	SLect	Tx-Arlington	DE	PHD	95	Tx-Dallas	1996
Mitra, Devashish	Asst	Fla Internat	FLO	PHD	96	Columbia	1996
Mitra, Tapan	C-Pr	Cornell		PHD	75	Rochester	

Mixon, Frank	Assoc	So Miss	J	PHD	92	Auburn	1994
Mixon, J. Wilson	Prof	Berry		PHD	74	U Wash	1986
Miyagawa, Eiichi	Asst	Columbia	DH	PHD	98	Rochester	1998
Miyagiwa, Kaz	Assoc	Louisiana St	FO	PHD	85	Tx-Austin	8-95
Miyazaki, Hajime	Prof	Ohio State	LJ	PHD	77	Berkeley	1984
Mizak, Daniel A.	Prof	Frostburg St		PHD	84	Pittsburgh	1977
Mizrach, Bruce	Assoc	Rutgers-N Br	E	PHD	87	Penn	1995
Moberly, H. Dean	Retir	Auburn-Montg	ADIQ	PHD	68	Tx A&M	1970
Mobley, Lee	Asst	Oakland	LI	PHD	89	Ca-SnBarb	1991
Mocan, Naci H.	Prof	Colo-Denver	CJI	PHD	89	CUNY	1990
Modeste, Nelson C.	C-Ac	So Carol St		PHD	76	Florida	1994
Modigliani, Franco	Retir	MIT		PHD	44	New Sch	1960
Moe, Karine S.	Asst	Macalester	AJ	PHD	95	Minnesota	1995
Moen, Jon R.	Assoc	Mississippi		PHD	87	Chicago	1990
Moewes, David S.	Prof	Concordia C	EH	PHD	82	Utah	1968
Moffett, Russell E.	Retir	Ferris State		PHD	61	Ca-Davis	1965
Moffit, Tim	Asst	Kalamazoo	M	MBA	84	Dartmouth	1994
Moffitt, Robert A.	Prof	J Hopkins		PHD	75	Brown	1995
Mogab, John William	Prof	SW Texas St	O	PHD	81	Tennessee	1981
Moghadam, Fatemeh	C-Pr	Hofstra	NOQ	PHD	79	Oxford	
Moghaddam, Masoud	Prof	St Cloud St		PHD	82	Iowa St	1983
Mohabbat, Khan A.	Prof	No Illinois	E	PHD	64	SUNY-Buf	1968
Mohaghegh, Mehdi	Assoc	Norwich		PHD	86	Clark	1986
Mohammadi, Hassan	Assoc	Illinois St	E	PHD	88	Wash St	1988
Mohan, Daniel	Assoc	West Chester	GM	PHD	75	Rutgers	1980
Mohanty, Madhu	Assoc	CS-L Angeles		PHD	90	Wi-Milwa	1990
Mohapatra, Sarita	Lect	Utah State	ADF	PHD	95	Utah St	1995
Mohindru, Rajesh K.	Prof	Bloomsburg		PHD	69	Penn	
Mohiuddin, Yasmeen	C-Pr	Univ South	FOE	PHD	83	Vanderbilt	
Mohring, Herbert D.	Emer	Minnesota		PHD	59	MIT	1961
Mohtadi, Hamid	Assoc	Wis-Milwauke		PHD	82	Michigan	1983
Mohtadi, Shahruz	Assoc	Suffolk		PHD	84	LSU	1983
Moini, Mostafa	C-Ac	Okla City		PHD	70	Oklahoma	1985
Moite, Leonard M.	Assoc	CS-Dominguez	AEDJ	PHD	84	UCLA	1980
Mokyr, Joel	C-Pr	Northwestern		PHD	74	Yale	1974
Robert H. Strotz Professor of Arts & Sciences							
Molico, Miguel	Lect	Penn State		PHD			1997
Molina, David Jude	Assoc	North Texas	BCN	PHD	83	Tx A&M	1985
Moliver, Donald M.	Assoc	Monmouth	DE	PHD	78	Va Tech	9-68
Monacelli, T.	Asst	Boston Coll		PHD	99	NYU	1999
Monaco, Kristen	Asst	Wis-Eau Clar	LJ	PHD	98	Wi-Milwa	1998
Moncur, James E. T.	Prof	Hawaii-Manoa		PHD	71	Wash St	1969
Mondschean, Thomas H.	Assoc	DePaul	EG	PHD	89	Wisconsin	1987
Mongell, Susan	Assoc	Calif U-Penn		PHD		Pittsburgh	1990
Mongiovi, Gary	Assoc	St John's		PHD	88	New Sch	1985
Monhollon, Jimmie R.	Dean	Hardin-Simm		PHD	61	Vanderbilt	1995
Distinguished Professor							
Monsma, George N. Jr.	Prof	Calvin		PHD	69	Princeton	1969
Monson, Terry D.	Prof	Mich Tech	F	PHD	72	Minnesota	1977
Montano, Carl B.	Prof	Lamar	OQ	PHD	82	Mich St	1981
Monteith, Chalmers A.	Retir	Kent State	N	PHD	58	Ohio St	1958
Montgomery, Edward B.	Prof	Maryland		PHD	82	Harvard	1990
Montgomery, Mark	Assoc	Grinnell	JQH	PHD	82	Wisconsin	1989
Montgomery, Mark	Assoc	SUNY-Stony B		PHD	82	Michigan	1988
Montgomery, Michael	Assoc	Maine	AE	PHD	88	Florida	1991
Montias, J. Michael	Emer	Yale	N	PHD	58	Columbia	1963
Montiel, Peter J.	Prof	Williams	EF	PHD	78	MIT	1995
Moody, Carlisle E.	C-Pr	Wm & Mary		PHD	70	Conn	1970
Moohr, Michael	Assoc	Bucknell	FNO	PHD	71	Cambridge	1975
Mookherjee, Dilip M.	Prof	Boston Univ	HLO	PHD	82	LondonEc	1995
Moomaw, Ronald L.	Prof	Oklahoma St	R	PHD	76	Princeton	1972
Regents Professor and CBA Associates Chair							
Moon, Hyunsik Roger	Asst	Cal-Santa Br	C	PHD	98	Yale	1998
Moore, B. C.	C-Pr	Delta State	AG	PHD	95	Miss	8-86
Moore, Barbara	Inst	Cen Florida		MAAE			
Moore, Bartholomew J.	Asst	Rutgers-N Br	E	PHD	90	Columbia	1990
Moore, Basil J.	Prof	Wesleyan-CT	E	PHD	58	J Hopkins	1958
Moore, Derald L.	Assoc	Tri-State		MA		Mich St	1968
Moore, Gary A.	Dean$	Lamar	J	PHD	74	Nebraska	1998
Moore, James C.	Prof	Purdue		PHD	68	Minnesota	1969
Moore, Joseph L.	Prof	Ark Tech		PHD	75	Arkansas	1988
Moore, M.	Asst	Calif-Irvine		PHD	97	MIT	1997
Moore, Mack A.	Retir	Georgia Tech	J	PHD	63	Wisconsin	1963
Moore, Margaret D.	Retir	Franklin		PHD	86	Ohio St	
Moore, Michael Owen	Assoc	George Wash	F	PHD	88	Wisconsin	1988
Moore, Peter R.	Prof	Rhode Isl Cl		PHD	75	Illinois	
Moore, Robert E.	Assoc	Georgia St	FO	PHD	88	Cornell	1989
Moore, Robert L.	Prof	Occidental	J	PHD	77	Harvard	1978
Moore, William J.	Prof	Louisiana St	IJ	PHD	70	Tx-Austin	
Gulf Coast Coca Cola Business Partnership Professor							

Name	Rank	School	Fields	Degree	Yr	Institution	Since
Moorhouse, John C.	Prof	Wake Forest		PHD	69	Nrthwstrn	1969
Archie Carroll Professor of Ethical Leadership							
Mora, Marie T.	Asst	New Mex St	JI	PHD	95	Tx A&M	8-95
Moran, John	Asst	Syracuse		PHD	97	Penn St	
Morand, Oliver	Asst	Connecticut	DO	PHD	97	Ariz St	1997
Morefield, Roger D.	Assoc	St Thomas-TX	I	PHD	77	Duke	1980
Morehouse, Thomas	Retir	Alaska-Ancho		PHD	68	Minnesota	
Moreland, Kemper W.	Prof	E Michigan		PHD	80	Wisconsin	1980
Morelli, Massimo	Asst	Iowa State	D	PHD	96	Harvard	1996
Morey, Edward R.	Prof	Colorado		PHD	78	Brit Colum	1980
Morey, Matthew	Asst	Smith		PHD	93	UCLA	1999
Morgan, Alfred D.	Prof	So Conn St	G	PHD	51	Harvard	
Morgan, Celia A.	Retir	SW Texas St		PHD	71	Houston	1971
Morgan, Daniel C. Jr.	Prof	Texas	H	PHD	62	Wisconsin	7-76
Morgan, J. Michael	C-Pr	Charleston		PHD	77	S Carol	1967
Morgan, John		Princeton					
Morgan, Peter B.	Assoc	SUNY-Buffalo	D	PHD	78	Canterbu	1989
Morgan, W. Douglas	Prof	Cal-Santa Br	HDE	PHD	69	Berkeley	1973
Morgan, William E.	Prof	Wyoming	H	PHD	64	Colorado	1968
Morley, James	Asst	Wash Univ	E	PHD	99	U Wash	1999
Morley, John	Asst	Marist	N	PHD	87	Yale	1995
Morlock, Mark J.	Prof	CS-Chico	J	PHD	78	Wash St	1980
Morman, Martin R.	Asst	Morehouse		PHD	88	Geo St	1990
Moroney, John R.	Prof	Texas A&M	C	PHD	64	Duke	1981
Morra, Wayne A.	Assoc	Beaver	ALR	PHD	84	Temple	8-81
Morrell, Stephen O.	Prof	Barry		PHD	77	Va Tech	1990
Morris, Barry K.	C-Pr	No Alabama		PHD	74	Arkansas	1974
Morris, Clair E. Jr.	Prof	USN Academy		PHD	72	Wisconsin	1966
Morris, Clyde D.	Assoc	Youngstown		PHD	87	Case Wes	1970
Morris, Cynthia T.	Retir	Smith	BNOP	PHD	59	Yale	1983
Morris, John R. Jr.	Emer	Colo-Denver	BI	PHD	66	Purdue	1970
Morris, Stephen	Prof	Yale	D	PHD	91	Yale	1998
Morrison, Clarence C.	Retir	Indiana		PHD	64	N Carol	1970
Morrison, Rodney J.	Prof	Wellesley		PHD	65	Wisconsin	
Morrison, Steven A.	C-Pr$	Northeastern		PHD	79	Berkeley	1982
Morrow, William R.	Retir	E Kentucky		PHD	68	Tennessee	1968
Morse, Lawrence B.	Assoc	N Carol A&T		PHD	68	Minnesota	1976
Mortensen, Dale T.	Prof	Northwestern		PHD	67	Car Mellon	1965
Ida C. Cook Professor of Consumer Economics							
Mosby, James B.	Asst	Detroit Merc		MA	70	Detroit	1972
Moscarini, Giuseppe	Asst	Yale	E	PHD	96	MIT	1996
Moschetta, Judith K.	Assoc	Wash & Jeff		MS	78	W Virginia	1978
Moseldjord, Asbjorn	Assoc	St Marys-Cal		PHD		Ca-SnBarb	1991
Moseley, Fred B.	Prof	Mt Holyoke		PHD	82	Mass	1989
Moser, Ernest R.	Prof	NE Louisiana	BM	PHD	73	Tx A&M	1972
Moses, Anthony T.	Assoc	St Anselm		PHD			
Moses, Leon N.	Prof	Northwestern		PHD	52	Harvard	1959
Moses, Ronald P.	Asst	Ill-Chicago	F	PHD	69	Chicago	1964
Moshtagh, Ali R.	Assoc	E Illinois		PHD	88	Arkansas	1987
Mosier, Donna	Asst	SUNY-Potsdam		PHD	95	Clarkson	1997
Moskwa, Antoni	Assoc	Allegheny	AFCP	PHD	75	Warsaw	1982
Moss, Joanna	Prof	San Fran St		PHD	78	New Sch	1981
Moss, Laurence S.	Prof	Babson	K	PHD	71	Columbia	1977
Moss, Richard L.	Prof	CS-San Bern	A	PHD	73	New Mex	1973
Mostaghimi, Mehdi	Prof	So Conn St	CEM	PHD	87	Virginia	8-84
Mostashari, Shahriar	C-Pr	Campbell		PHD	78	N Car St	1982
Motahar, Eshragh	Assoc	Union	EFG	PHD	89	J Hopkins	1984
Motomura, Akira	Assoc	Stonehill	KN	PHD	85	Nrthwstrn	1995
Mott, Tracy L.	C-Ac	Denver	BE	PHD	82	Stanford	1991
Mouhammed, Adil	Assoc	Il-Springfld	FP	PHD	85	Nebraska	1988
Moulin, Herve	Prof	Rice	CD	PHD	75	Paris	7-99
Peterkin Professor of Economics							
Mount, Randall I.	Prof	Kent State	CD	PHD	69	Purdue	1966
Mountain, Dean C.	C-Pr	McMaster U	CD	PHD	79	W Ontario	1987
Mounts, William S. Jr.	Prof	Mercer-Macon		PHD	77	Georgia	1978
Mourdoukoutas, Panos	Prof	Lg Isl-Post		PHD	83	SUNY-SBr	1984
Moy, Ronald L.	Assoc	St John's		PHD	90	Rutgers	
Moyer, James T.	Prof	Albright		PHD	76	Lehigh	9-68
Mozayeni, Simin B.	Asst	SUNY-N Paltz	ALH	PHD	53	Columbia	1990
Mroz, Thomas A.	Prof	No Carolina	J	PHD	84	Stanford	1989
Mrozek, Janusz R.	Asst	Georgia Tech	QD	PHD	95	Stanford	1993
Mshomba, Richard	Asst	LaSalle	FO	PHD	92	Illinois	1991
Mudambi, Ram	Assoc	Case Western	CLM	PHD	85	Cornell	1998
Muehsam, Mitchell J.	Asst	Sam Houston		PHD	89	Tx A&M	1989
Muehsam, Valerie P.	Asst	Sam Houston		PHD	98	Tx A&M	1993
Mueller, Hans G.	Retir	Mid Tenn St		PHD	68	Vanderbilt	1961
Mueller, James V.	C-Ac	Alma	ABEH	ABD		Ca-Irvine	1976
Mueller, Marilyn	C	Simpson		JD	81	Drake	1986
Mueller, Richard	Asst	Maine	JA	PHD	97	Tx-Austin	1996
Muench, Thomas	Prof	SUNY-Stony B		PHD	65	Purdue	1975

Name	Rank	School	Fields	Degree	Yr	Degree Institution	Year
Mueser, Peter R.	Assoc	Missouri	DJT	PHD	83	Chicago	1985
Mui, Vai-Lam	Asst	So Calif		PHD	92	Berkeley	1992
Mukand, Sharun	Asst	Tufts	F	PHD	97	Boston U	1997
Mukerjee, Swati	Assoc	Bentley	DFI	PHD	86	Boston U	1989
Mukherjee, Kankana	Asst	Clarkson	EFG	PHD	97	Conn	1997
Mukherji, Nivedita	Asst	Oakland	EF	PHD	92	Va Tech	1992
Mukhoti, Bela	Assoc	Rowan Col-NJ		PHD	64	London	1974
Mullainathan, Sendhlil	Asst	MIT		PHD	98	Harvard	1998
Mullen, John K.	Prof	Clarkson	GHR	PHD	78	SUNY-Bin	1977
Mullendore, Walter	Prof	Tx-Arlington	R	PHD	68	Iowa St	1969
Muller, Herman J.	Retir	Detroit Merc		PHD		Loyola	1956
Muller, Ronald E.	Prof	American U		PHD		American	1970
Mulligan, Casey	Asst	Chicago		PHD	93	Chicago	1993
Mulligan, James G.	Prof	Delaware	L	PHD	80	Minnesota	1980
Mulligan, Richard	Asst	W Carolina		PHD	93	SUNY-Bin	1997
Mulligan, Robert M.	Retir	Providence	EK	MA	61	Boston C	1965
Mullin, Marian V.	Assoc	West Liberty	DE	MS	85	Rbt Morr	1975
Mullin, R. David	Asst	USAF Academy	AD	PHD	93	Virginia	1998
Mullin, Wallace P.	Asst	Michigan St		PHD	92	MIT	1992
Mullings, Llewellyn M.	Retir	Bridgeport		PHD	64	Clark	
Mullins, Steven	Assoc	Drury		PHD	83	Okla St	1982
Mumy, Gene E.	Assoc	Ohio State	D	PHD	74	J Hopkins	1978
Munasinghe, Lalith	Asst	Barnard	JC	PHD	95	Columbia	1997
Mundell, Cyril Lee	Assoc	Loyola-N Orl	AC	PHD	76	N Carol	1981
Mundell, Robert	Prof	Columbia	EF	PHD	56	MIT	1974
Munkirs, John R.	Dean	Il-Springfld	BN	PHD	73	Oklahoma	1972
Munley, Vincent G.	Prof	Lehigh	HI	PHD	79	SUNY-Bin	1980
Munyon, Paul G.	Assoc	Grinnell	L	PHD	75	Harvard	1982
Murans, Frank	Retir			PHD	57	Mich St	
Muraoka, Dennis D.	Prof	CS-Long Bch		PHD	81	Ca-SnBarb	1982
Murdoch, James	Prof	Texas-Dallas		PHD	82	Wyoming	
Murdock, E. Wayne	Retir	S F Austin	AR	PHD	71	Oklahoma	1972
Murli, Rajan	Assoc	Scranton		PHD		Temple	1989
Murphy, Caroline	Retir	Fitchburg St		PHD	71	Clark	1971
Murphy, Dennis R.	Dean	Western Wash	FM	PHD	74	Indiana	1979
Murphy, George G. S.	Emer	UCLA		PHD	57	U Wash	
Murphy, James H.	Asst	W Carolina		MA	96	Geo St	1998
Murphy, James L.	Prof	No Carolina	C	PHD	64	Purdue	1964
Murphy, John J.	Retir	Catholic		PHD	61	Yale	1967
Murphy, Kevin J.	Prof	Oakland	JC	PHD	81	Mich St	1985
Murphy, Robert G.	Assoc	Boston Coll	EF	PHD	84	MIT	1984
Murphy, Russell D. Jr.	Asst	Virg Tech	D	PHD	97	Boston U	1997
Murra, Gene E.	Retir	So Dakota St	Q	PHD	63	Ohio St	1959
Murray, Chris	Asst	Houston	E	PHD	98	U Wash	1998
Murray, Jack W.	Retir	Tarleton St	1995	PHD	66	Tx-Arlin	1968
Murray, James M.	Prof	WI-Green Bay		PHD	62	Oregon	1969
Murray, John E.	Asst	Toledo	B	PHD	92	Ohio St	1994
Murray, Matthew N.	C-Ac	Tennessee		PHD	86	Syracuse	1986
Murray, Michael P.	Prof	Bates	RH	PHD	74	Iowa St	1986
Phillips Professor of Economics							
Murray, Sheila	Asst	Kentucky	I	PHD	95	Maryland	1995
Murray, Tracy W.	Prof	Arkansas	F	PHD	69	Mich St	1978
Distinguished Professor & Chairholder, Phillips Petroleum Company Chair/IEB							
Murrell, Peter	Prof	Maryland		PHD	77	Penn	1977
Murry, Donald A.	Retir	Oklahoma	L	PHD	66	Missouri	
Murtaugh, Frank M. Jr.	H-Ac	Norwich		PHD	81	Emory	1982
Murthy, N. R. Vasudeva	Prof	Creighton	CDH	PHD	75	SUNY-Bin	1979
Murti, Vedula N.	Asst	Penn St-Harr		PHD	66	Penn	1969
Musgrave, Frank W.	C-Pr$	Ithaca	IJ	PHD	68	Rutgers	1968
Mushinski, David	Asst	Colorado St	CHO	PHD	96	Wisconsin	1997
Musoke, Moses		SUNY-Empire	NM	PHD	78	Wisconsin	1985
Mustafa, Muhammad	Assoc	So Carol St		PHD	88	Wayne St	1989
Mustard, David B.	Asst	Georgia	DJK	PHD	97	Chicago	1997
Muth, John	D-Ac	Regis-CO	AGNM	PHD	78	Colorado	9-83
Muth, Richard F.	Prof	Emory	N	PHD	58	Chicago	1983
Fuller E. Callaway Professor of Economics							
Mutti, John	Prof	Grinnell	FHQ	PHD	74	Wisconsin	1987
Sydney Meyer Professor of International Economics							
Myers, Daniel A.	Assoc	W Kentucky	R	PHD	86	Vanderbilt	1986
Myers, George G.	Retir	East Tenn St		EDD	65	Tennessee	1957
Myers, John G.	Emer	So Illinois		PHD	61	Columbia	1977
Myers, Steven	Assoc	Akron	ACJ	PHD	80	Ohio St	1979
Myerson, Roger B.	Prof	Northwestern		PHD	76	Harvard	1976
N'Chu-Oguie, Charles	Assoc	San Francisc	CO	PHD	84	Stanford	1984
Nachbar, John	Assoc	Wash Univ	CD	PHD	88	Harvard	1990
Nadenichek, Jon	Asst	CS-Northrdge		PHD	96	Rochester	1996
Nadiri, M. Ishaq	Prof	New York U	O	PHD	65	Berkeley	1971
Nadler, Mark A.	C-Ac	Ashland		PHD	83	Iowa St	1989
A. L. Garber Family Chair of Economics							
Nafziger, E. Wayne	Prof	Kansas State	OPF	PHD	67	Illinois	1966

Nag, Raja	Asst	Monmouth	G	PHD	98	Michigan	1998
Naggar, Tahany	Prof	West Chester	ADTN	PHD	76	Oklahoma	1977
Nahata, Babu L.	Prof	Louisville	D	PHD	77	N Illinois	8-78
Nair, Usha C.	Asst	Georgia Tech	F	PHD	95	Purdue	1996
Naish, Howard F.	Prof	CS-Fullerton	E	PHD	83	S Calif	1988
Naito, Hisahiro	Asst	Calif-Irvine		PHD	98	Michigan	1999
Naka, Atsuyuki	Assoc	New Orleans		PHD	89	Arizona	1989
Nakajami, Tomoyuki	Asst	Brown		PHD	99	Chicago	1999
Nalebuff, Barry J.	Prof	Yale	D	DPH	82	Oxford	1989
Nam, Woo Hyun	Prof	San Diego St		PHD	68	U Wash	1968
Nantz, Kathryn A.	Assoc	Fairfield	JDPA	PHD	87	Purdue	1986
Naples, Michele I.	Assoc	C New Jersey		PHD	82	Mass	
Narwold, Andrew	Assoc	San Diego		PHD	91	Ca-SnBarb	1991
Nas, Tevfik F.	Prof	Mich-Flint		PHD	77	Fla St	1982
Nash, Robert T.	Prof	Tx A&M-Kings		PHD	71	Tx A&M	1971
Nasser, Alan		Evergreen St		PHD	71	Indiana	1975
Natke, Paul A.	Prof	Cen Michigan		PHD	82	Notre Dm	1981
Navin, John	Asst	S Ill-Edward	HIJ	PHD	92	Mich St	
Navin, Leo J.	Retir	Bowling Gr		PHD	68	Mich St	
Navratil, Frank J.	Dean	John Carroll	G	PHD	74	Notre Dm	1973
Naya, Seiji	Prof	Hawaii-Manoa		PHD	66	Wisconsin	1961
Nazemzadah, Asghar	C-Pr	Houston-Down		PHD	83	Fla St	1989
Ndikumana, Leonce	Asst	Massachusett		PHD	96	Wash U	1996
Neal, Derek A.	Assoc	Wisconsin		PHD	92	Virginia	1998
Neal, Larry	Prof	Illinois	EGN	PHD	68	Berkeley	1967
Neale, Walter C.	Emer	Tennessee		PHD		London Ec	1968
Nechyba, Thomas	Asst	Stanford		PHD	94	Rochester	1994
Neel, Richard E.	Prof	N Car-Charl		PHD	60	Ohio St	1969
Neelakantan, P.	Asst	E Stroudsbur	D	PHD	92	SUNY-Buf	1992
Neeman, Zvika	Asst	Boston Univ	CD	PHD	95	Nrthwstrn	1995
Neenan, William B.	Retir	Boston Coll	HR	PHD	66	Michigan	1980
Neergaard, Keith	Assoc	Pacific Unio		PHD	94	Ca-Irvine	1988
Negbenebor, Anthony I.	Prof	Gardner-Webb		PHD	88	Miss St	1989
Negri, Donald H.	Assoc	Willamette		PHD	86	Michigan	1990
Nehman, Gerlad	Retir	Tx-Arlington	Q	PHD	73	Ohio St	1993
Nehring, Klaus D.	Assoc	Cal-Davis	DG	PHD	91	Harvard	1992
Neill, Jon R.	Assoc	W Michigan	H	PHD	83	Pittsburgh	1980
Neils, Allan E.	Retir	East Wash		JD		Gonzaga	1969
Neilson, William S.	Assoc	Texas A&M	CD	PHD	88	Ca-SnDgo	1988
Neimanis, George J.	Prof	Niagara		MA	65	NYU	1970
Nelson, Charles R.	Prof	U Washington	EGC	PHD	69	Wisconsin	1975
Nelson, David M.	C-Pr	Western Wash	EGI	PHD	75	Oregon	1977
Nelson, Dennis L.	Retir	Minn-Duluth	A	PHD	70	Minnesota	1964
Nelson, Douglas R.	Assoc	Tulane		PHD	81	N Carol	1993
Nelson, Forrest D.	Prof	Iowa		PHD	75	Rochester	1980
Nelson, John P.	Prof	Louisville	H	PHD	68	Kentucky	
Nelson, Jon P.	Prof	Penn State	QD	PHD	70	Wisconsin	1969
Nelson, Michael A.	Prof	Illinois St	G	PHD	80	Purdue	1981
Nelson, Paul A.	Assoc	Mich Tech	M	PHD	74	Wisconsin	1972
Nelson, Paul S.	H-Ac	NE Louisiana	DL	PHD	85	Tx A&M	1989
Nelson, Phillip J.	Retir	SUNY-Bingham	L	PHD	67	Columbia	1969
Nelson, Ralph L.	Retir	CUNY-Queens	MG	PHD	55	Columbia	1964
Nelson, Randy A.	Prof	Colby	GM	PHD	79	Illinois	1987
Douglas Professor of Economics							
Nelson, Richard R.	Retir	Columbia		PHD	56	Yale	1986
Nemec, Richard W.	Asst	Tx A&M-Kings		PHD	97	Kentucky	1981
Neral, John A.	Assoc	Frostburg St		PHD	89	Pittsburgh	1986
Nesiba, Reynold	Asst	Augustana SD	EG	PHD	95	Notre Dm	1995
Nesslein, Thomas S.	Asst	WI-Green Bay		PHD	92	U Wash	1996
Netusil, Noelwah R.	Assoc	Reed	AQDH	PHD	92	Illinois	1990
Netz, Janet S.	Asst	Purdue		PHD	92	Michigan	1994
Neuberger, Egon	Prof	SUNY-Stony B		PHD	58	Harvard	1967
Neuefeind, Wilhelm	Prof	Wash Univ	D	PHD	72	Bonn	1978
Neufeld, John L.	Prof	N Car-Greens	ND	PHD	75	Michigan	1974
Neumann, George R.	Prof	Iowa		PHD	74	Nrthwstrn	1984
Neumann, Hillar Jr.	Assoc	Northern St		PHD	86	Rutgers	1983
Neumark, David B.	Prof	Michigan St		PHD	87	Harvard	1995
Neun, Stephen P.	Prof	Utica	IJ	PHD	88	Conn	1982
Neville, Howard R.	Deces			PHD	56	Mich St	
Newburger, Harriet B.	Assoc	Bryn Mawr		PHD	84	Wisconsin	1987
Newell, Barbara W.	Retir	Florida St	1996	PHD	58	Wisconsin	1987
Newell, Howard	Prof	Union-TN		PHD	74	Indiana	1982
Newey, Whitney K.	Prof	MIT	CDH	PHD	83	MIT	6-90
Newkirk, Wayne	Retir	Drake		PHD	65	LSU	1967
Newman, Andrew F.	Assoc	Columbia	DLO	PHD	89	Harvard	1993
Newman, Robert J.	Prof	Louisiana St	IJ	PHD	80	UCLA	1983
South Central Bell Business Partnership Professor							
Newmark, Craig M.	Assoc	N Carol St	LD	PHD	84	UCLA	1984
Newsome, Heather	Lect	Baylor		MS	96	Baylor	1996
Newsome, Mike	Asst	Marshall		PHD	97	Kentucky	1999

Newton, Dahlia	Asst	Athens State	A	MBA	80	W Carol	1987
Newton, James E.	C-Pr	Franklin		PHD	97	Ohio St	
Neyman, Abraham	Prof	SUNY-Stony B		PHD	77	Hebrew	1989
Ng, Kenneth	Assoc	CS-Northrdge	N	PHD	88	Rochester	1986
Ng, Serena	Assoc	Boston Coll	CE	PHD	93	Princeton	1996
Ngoboka, Pascal	Assoc	Wis-Rvr Fall	HP	PHD	87	Wi-Milwa	1990
Nguyen, Hong V.	Assoc	Scranton		PHD	81	SUNY-Bin	1979
Nguyen, Nghiep H.	Assoc	Mid Tenn St	L	PHD	81	Tennessee	1981
Ni, Xiagoguang	Asst	Missouri	EH	PHD	91	Minnesota	1990
Nichols, Archie J.	Retir	Butler	B	PHD	61	Penn	1957
Nichols, Donald A.	Prof	Wisconsin		PHD	68	Yale	1983
Nichols, Mark W.	Asst	Nevada-Reno	LKJ	PHD	94	Fla St	1996
Nicholson, Robert H.	Assoc	Richmond		PHD	72	N Carol	1972
Nicholson, Walter E.	Prof	Amherst	ACDK	PHD	70	MIT	1968
Ward H. Patton, Jr. Professor of Economics							
Nickerson, David	Assoc	American U		PHD	82	Nrthwstrn	1992
Nickless, Pamela J.	Prof	N Car-Ashvil	AJN	PHD	76	Purdue	1983
Nielsen, Darwin B.	Retir	Utah State	Q	PHD	64	Oregon St	1965
Nielsen, Donald A.	Prof	Neb-Omaha	AR	PHD	70	Syracuse	1972
Nieswiadomy, Michael L.	Assoc	North Texas	HRIQ	PHD	83	Tx A&M	1985
Niho, Yoshio	Prof	Wis-Milwauke		PHD	73	Brown	1970
Nijhawan, Inder P.	C-Pr	Fayetteville		PHD	71	N Carol	
Nilsson, Eric A.	Assoc	CS-San Bern	FJ	PHD	89	Mass	1989
Niman, Neil B.	Assoc	New Hampshir	BL	PHD	85	Tx-Austin	1987
Niroomand, Farhang	C-Pr	So Miss	F	PHD	83	Mich St	1984
Nirro, Katsuyuki	Assoc	Gettysburg	AC	PHD	75	Pittsburgh	1972
Nisbet, Charles T.		Evergreen St		PHD	67	Oregon	1971
Nisbet, Mary J.	SLect	Cal-Santa Br	G	PHD	91	Glasgow	1991
Niss, James F.	Retir	W Illinois	1994	PHD		Illinois	1968
Nissan, Edward	Prof	So Miss	R	PHD	69	Tx A&M	1969
Nitsch, Thomas O.	Emer	Creighton	ENP	PHD	63	Ohio St	1969
Nix, Joan	Assoc	CUNY-Queens	DG	PHD	89	NYU	1988
Njoku, Anthanasius O.	Prof	Benedict Col		PHD	71	Illinois	1971
Nnadozie, Emmanuel U.	Assoc	Truman State		PHD	87	Sorbonne	1989
Noam, Eli	Prof	Columbia		PHD	75	Harvard	1976
Noble, Nicholas R.	Prof	Miami U-Ohio	EC	PHD	78	Cincinnati	1976
Noll, Roger G.	Prof	Stanford		PHD	67	Harvard	1984
Morris M. Doyle Centennial Professor							
Nonnenmacher, Tomas	Asst	Allegheny	DKLN	PHD	96	Illinois	1996
Noorbakhsh, Abbas	Assoc	Slippery Roc	AG	PHD	89	Kansas St	1990
Norberg, Robert W.	C-As	Robt Morris		MA		Ind-Penn	1968
Nord, Steven	Prof	No Illinois	R	PHD	76	Illinois	1979
Nordhaus, William D.	Prof	Yale	E	PHD	67	MIT	1967
Nordin, Harold D.	Prof	E Illinois		PHD	76	Illinois	1967
Nordquist, Gerald L.	Emer	Iowa		PHD	60	Iowa	1968
Nordstrom, Louise J.	Prof	Nichols Col	ADFH	PHD	71	Clark	9-74
Nordyke, James W.	Emer	New Mex St	FE	PHD	59	Princeton	1964
Norman, Alfred L.	Prof	Texas	C	PHD	71	Minnesota	7-72
Norman, Emlyn A.	Asst	Txs Southern		AM		Harvard	
Norman, George	Prof	Tufts	L	PHD	77	Cambridge	1995
Cummings Chair Holder							
Norman, Lee	Prof	Idaho State	ALN	PHD	80	Utah	1981
Norman-Zietz, Emily	Assoc	Mid Tenn St	M	PHD	94	Fla St	1993
Norrbin, Stefan C.	Prof	Florida St	F	PHD	86	Ariz St	1990
Norris, Hodge	Asst	Txs Southern		MS		Tx A&I	
North, Charles	Asst	Baylor	K	PHD	99	Tx-Austin	1998
North, Douglass C.	Prof	Wash Univ	NO	PHD	52	Berkeley	1983
Spencer T. Olin Professor of Arts & Sciences/1993 Nobel Prize in Economics							
Northrop, Emily M.	Assoc	Southwestern	ENQR	PHD	88	Tx-Austin	1994
Norton, R. D.	Prof	Bryant	FR	PHD	77	Princeton	1985
Sarkesian Professor of Business Economics							
Norton, Seth	Prof	Wheaton-IL	GJLM	PHD	82	Chicago	1995
Aldeen Chair							
Norton, Virgil	Retir	W Virginia	QI	PHD	64	Oregon St	1986
Norwood, Dwight Lamar	Assoc	Campbell		PHD	74	Arkansas	1973
Noser, Thomas C.	Assoc	W Kentucky	CA	PHD	86	Alabama	1984
Nourzad, Farrokh	Assoc	Marquette	CEO	PHD	82	Kansas	1981
Noussair, Charles N.	Assoc	Purdue		PHD	93	Cal Tech	1994
Novaes, Walter	Asst	U Washington		PHD	93	MIT	1993
Novey, Donald F.	Prof	Saginaw Vall	DE	MS		S Dak St	1969
Novshek, William	Assoc	Purdue		PHD	79	Nrthwstrn	1986
Nowell, Clifford	C-Pr	Weber State	ADQ	PHD	88	Wyoming	1988
Nowka, Harry E.	Prof	SW Okla St		EDD		Okla St	1963
Nowotny, Kenneth	H-Pr	New Mex St	HN	PHD	77	Tx-Austin	1976
Noyd, Louis E.	Assoc	No Kentucky		PHD	73	Oregon	1972
Nugent, Jeffrey B.	Prof	So Calif		PHD	65	New Sch	1973
Nugent, Rachel A.	Asst	Pacific Luth	DFQH	PHD	94	Geo Wash	1991
Nunn, Geoffrey E.	Prof	San Jose St		PHD	73	Virginia	1974
Nussman, Tara D.	Asst	W Illinois	ADH	PHD	98	S Carol	1998
Nuwer, Michael J.	Assoc	SUNY-Potsdam		PHD	85	Utah	1986

Nwefor, Ferdinand C.	Asst	Bethune-Cook		PHD	97	Howard	1997
Nyamwange, Richard	Assoc	E Stroudsbur	D	MBA	82	Long Isl	1987
Nyarko, Yaw	Prof	New York U	D	PHD	86	Cornell	1992
Nyatepe-Coo, Akorlie A.	Prof	Wis-La Cross	FHO	PHD	89	N Illinois	1989
Nye, John V. C.	Assoc	Wash Univ	N	PHD	85	Nrthwstrn	1985
Nyomba, Ajamu	Asst	Clark Atlant		PHD	91	Tx-Austin	
Nziramasanga, Mudziviri T.	Assoc	Wash State		PHD	74	Stanford	1973
O'Boyle, Edward John	Assoc	Louisiana Te		PHD	72	St Louis	1977
O'Brien, A. Maureen	Assoc	Minn-Duluth	J	PHD	83	W Virginia	1982
O'Brien, Anthony P.	Assoc	Lehigh	NE	PHD	86	Berkeley	1987
O'Brien, Francis T.	Assoc	Providence	JK	MA	57	Boston C	1958
O'Brien, J. Patrick	Dean	Loyola-N Orl	AEHR	PHD	77	Okla St	1995
O'Brien, Jamie L.	Prof	So Dakota St	K	MPA	84	S Dakota	1984
O'Brien, Kevin M.	Assoc	Bradley		PHD	88	Illinois	1992
O'Brien, M. Barry	Assoc	Fran Marion		PHD	86	S Carol	
O'Brien, Peter A. Jr.	Retir	Pace		MBA	57	Rutgers	1964
O'Brien, William F. Jr.	Asst	Worcester St		PHD	89	Northeas	1997
O'Cleiracain, Seamus	Prof	SUNY-Purchas		PHD	71	Michigan	1974
O'Connell, David	Asst	St Ambrose		PHD	97	Boston U	1998
O'Connell, John F.	Prof	Holy Cross	CDIJ	PHD	70	Wisconsin	1974
O'Connell, Stephen A.	Prof	Swarthmore	EO	PHD	86	MIT	1990
O'Connor, Catherine	Asst	Bucknell	DJC	PHD	96	Virginia	9-96
O'Connor, Dennis A.	Prof	Loras		PHD	84	Notre Dm	1983
O'Connor, F. William	Lect	Trinity-CT		JD	78	Conn	1984
O'Connor, J. Francis	Prof	E Kentucky		PHD	74	Minnesota	1989
O'Connor, Roy J.	Inst	Va Military		MBA	69	Hartford	1992
O'Dea, William P.	Asst	SUNY-Oneonta	DEP	PHD	88	SUNY-Alb	1979
O'Donnell, Dennis J.	Prof	Montana	OJR	PHD	74	Penn St	
O'Donnell, Margaret G.	Deces	SW Louisiana		PHD	76	Tx A&M	
O'Donoghue, Joseph	C-Pr	Molloy		PHD	75	Catholic	1997
O'Donoghue, Ted	Asst	Cornell		PHD	96	Berkeley	
O'Flaherty, Brendan	Assoc	Columbia	RA	PHD	80	Harvard	1987
O'Hara, Sabine	Asst	Rensselaer	BEQR	PHD	84	Goettingen	1-95
O'Neil, Robert F.	Prof	San Diego		PHD	75	Fordham	
O'Neill, James B.	Prof	Delaware	A	PHD	71	Purdue	1971
O'Neill, June E.	Prof	CUNY-Baruch		PHD	70	Columbia	1987
O'Neill, Patrick B.	Assoc	North Dakota	ADL	PHD	87	Boston C	1987
O'Relly, Z. Edward	Prof	N Dakota St	AFOP	PHD	72	Tennessee	1969
O'Sullivan, Arthur M.	Prof	Oregon State	DR	PHD	81	Princeton	9-92
O'Sullivan, Patrick	C-Pr	SUNY Old Wes		PHD	82	Fordham	
O'Toole, Dennis M.	Assoc	Virg Comm		PHD	71	Ohio U	1967
O'Toole, James K.	Prof	CS-Chico	ADR	PHD	83	Va Tech	1984
Oakland, William H.	Prof	Tulane		PHD	65	MIT	1979
Oates, Mary J.	Prof	Regis-MA	N	PHD	69	Yale	1970
Oates, Wallace	Prof	Maryland		PHD	65	Stanford	1979
Oaxaca, Ronald L.	Prof	Arizona		PHD	71	Princeton	1976
Obar, Ruth I.	Asst	Hood	CEF	PHD	96	Alabama	1994
Obeng, Kofi	Prof	N Carol A&T		PHD	81	Penn	1982
UPS Chair							
Oberle, Wayne H.	Prof	St Ambrose		PHD	69	Missouri	1977
Obst, Norman P.	Prof	Michigan St		PHD	70	Purdue	1973
Obstfeld, Maurice	Prof	Cal-Berkeley		PHD	79	MIT	
Obutelewicz, Robert S.	Assoc	Bloomsburg		PHD	71	Mass	
Ochs, Jack N.	C-Pr	Pittsburgh	H	PHD	66	Indiana	1968
Odegaard, Thomas A.	Lect	Baylor		MA	70	Rice	1985
Odekon, Mehmet A.	C-Ac	Skidmore		PHD	77	SUNY-Alb	1983
Odorzynski, Sandra J.	C-Pr	St Norbert		PHD	76	Purdue	1978
Oerther, Frederick J.	Asst	Greensboro		PHD	89	GeoMason	1990
Oettinger, Gerald	Asst	Texas	JC	PHD	93	MIT	9-92
Ofek, Haim	Assoc	SUNY-Bingham	J	PHD	71	Columbia	1981
Officer, Lawrence H.	Prof	Ill-Chicago	F	PHD	65	Harvard	1987
Ogaki, Masao	Assoc	Ohio State	E	PHD	88	Chicago	1994
Oguledo, Victor I.	Assoc	Florida A&M	FL	PHD	89	Nebraska	1990
Ogum, George	Assoc	LaSierra		DBA	90	Memphis	1997
Ohly, John H.	Assoc	Mass-Dartmou	A	PHD	76	Boston U	1977
Ohn, Jonathan	Asst	Virginia St		PHD	98	Lehigh	1999
Ohno, Yuka	Asst	Rice	FL	PHD	93	U Wash	9-94
Oi, Walter Y.	Prof	Rochester		PHD	61	Chicago	1967
Elmer B. Milliman Professor of Economics							
Ojemakindel, Abiodun	Assoc	Albany State		PHD	89	LSU	1989
Ok, Efe	Asst	New York U	H	PHD	95	Cornell	1995
Okonkwo, Valentine	C-Ac	Winston-Sal		PHD		Fla St	4-85
Okpala, Amon O.	Assoc	Fayetteville		PHD	84	LSU	1984
Okten, Cagla	Asst	Louisiana St	L	PHD	99	Nrthwstrn	8-99
Okun, Bernard	Retir	CUNY-Brookly	CO	PHD	57	J Hopkins	1966
Okunade, Albert A.	Prof	Memphis	JI	PHD	86	Arkansas	1987
Oldfather, Michael	Assoc	Kansas State	EJ	PHD	80	Ohio	1983
Olili, Una O.	Asst	Ind-Purdue/I	O	PHD	97	Nrthwstrn	1999
Olley, G. Steven	Asst	Georgetown	L	PHD	92	Wisconsin	1997
Olmstead, Alan L.	Prof	Cal-Davis	HN	PHD	70	Wisconsin	1969

Name	Rank	School	Fields	Degree	Yr	Institution	Year
Olmstead, Jennifer C.	Asst	Mich-Flint		PHD	94	Ca-Davis	1993
Olmsted, George M.	Assoc	Indiana NW	HI	PHD	84	Nrthwstrn	1987
Olowolayemo, Suryudeen	Asst	Tuskegee		PHD	93	Auburn	1994
Olsen, Edgar O.	Prof	Virginia	HI	PHD	68	Rice	1983
Olsen, Randall J.	Prof	Ohio State	J	PHD	77	Chicago	1982
Olsen, Reed N.	Assoc	SW Missouri		PHD	89	Illinois	1990
Olsh, John Lindsay	Prof	W Maryland		PHD	74	Ca-Davis	1980
Olson, Dennis D.	Asst	Ferris State		ABD		Minnesota	1972
Olson, Edwin G.	Retir	Kansas State	HBM	PHD	71	U Wash	1968
Olson, Gerald W.	Prof	Mo-Kansas Ct	CGH	PHD	73	Rutgers	1971
Olson, John F.	C-Ac	St Benedict		PHD	84	Rochester	1985
Olson, Kent W.	Prof	Oklahoma St	HI	PHD	69	Oregon	1974
Olson, Mancur	Deces	Maryland		PHD	60	Harvard	1969
Olson, Paulette I.	Assoc	Wright State		PHD	89	Utah	1988
Olson, Richard	Prof	Washburn		PHD	65	Nebraska	1980
Olson, Terry L.	Assoc	Truman State		PHD	86	Illinois	1990
Omar, Hanai	Assoc	Univ of D C	AH	MS		Maryland	1976
Omarzai, Mahmood	Prof	Calif U-Penn		PHD	76	Indiana	1979
Onafowora, Olugbenga A.	Assoc	Susquehanna	CDOQ	PHD	89	W Virginia	1989
Ondrich, Jan Ivar	Prof	Syracuse	C	PHD	83	Wisconsin	
Oneiwu, Stephen	Asst	Rensselaer		PHD	97	Conn	1998
Onis, Ziya	Prof	Bogazici	AEO	PHD	83	Manchester	1984
Onuk, Cengiz	Asst	USM Academy	DM	PHD	93	SUNY	1998
Onunkwo, Emmanuel N.	Prof	So Carol St		PHD	73	Geotown	1978
Opara-Nadi, Gregory	Inst	Jackson St		MBA	77	Rust	
Opdahl, Roger W.	Retir	Lycoming	AENR	DED	70	Penn St	1962
Opiela, Timothy P.	Assoc	Pacific	E	PHD	87	Tx A&M	1986
Oppenheimer, Margaret M.	C-Pr	DePaul	JDK	PHD	74	Nrthwstrn	9-76
Orazem, Peter F.	Prof	Iowa State	J	PHD	83	Yale	1982
Orcutt, Bonnie	C-As	American Int	ADJH	PHD	94	Clark	1992
Ordovensky, J. Farley	Assoc	Pacific	HJ	PHD	92	Duke	1993
Ordover, Janusz A.	Prof	New York U	G	PHD	73	Columbia	1982
Orlowski, Lucjan T.	Prof	Sacred Heart	EFGP	PHD	79	Poland	1983
Ormiston, Michael B.	Prof	Arizona St		PHD	77	J Hopkins	1984
Orr, Daniel	Retir	Illinois		PHD	60	Princeton	1989
Orr, Lloyd D.	Retir	Indiana		PHD	64	Nrthwstrn	1964
Orsagh, Thomas	Emer	No Carolina		PHD	64	Penn	1965
Ortega, Lydia	Assoc	San Jose St		PHD	87	GeoMason	1989
Ortiz, L.	Asst	Frank & Mars		PHD	98	Berkeley	1996
Orton, Eliot S.	Emer	New Mex St	N	PHD	71	Cornell	1970
Orvis, Charles C.	H-Ac	Rhodes		PHD	75	Minnesota	1973
Osagie, Emmanuel I.	Asst	Southern		PHD	85	LSU	1985
Osakue, John U.	Asst	CUNY-Stn Isl	FO	PHD	80	Nebraska	1991
Osang, Thomas	Asst	So Methodist	FO	PHD	94	Ca-SnDgo	1994
Osborne, Evan	Asst	Wright State		PHD	93	UCLA	1995
Osborne, Theresa	Asst	CUNY-Hunter		PHD	97	Princeton	9-97
Oseghale, Braimoh	Assoc	F Dick-Teane	F	PHD	89	Temple	1994
Osman, Alan	Lect	Ohio State					
Osman, Jack W.	Prof	San Fran St		PHD	66	Rutgers	1967
Ossella, Ilaria	Asst	Ill Wesleyan	O	PHD	99	Cornell	1999
Ostas, James R.	Retir	Bowling Gr		PHD		Indiana	1969
Ostrosky, Anthony L. Jr.	Prof	Illinois St	ADEC	PHD	73	Pittsburgh	1973
Ostroy, Joseph M.	Prof	UCLA		PHD	70	Nrthwstrn	
Oswald, Donald J.	Assoc	CS-Bakersf	ABKN	PHD	74	Wash St	1961
Ott, Attiat F.	Prof	Clark		PHD	62	Michigan	1969
Ovitsky, Nancy L.	Asst	Mass Lib Art		PHD	82	Illinois	
Oweiss, Ibrahim M.	Assoc	Georgetown		PHD	69	Minnesota	1967
Owen, Ann	Asst	Hamilton	EO	PHD	95	Brown	1997
Owen, John D.	Retir	Wayne State		PHD	64	Columbia	1975
Owen, Laura J.	Assoc	DePaul	NJ	PHD	91	Yale	1990
Owoye, Oluwole	Prof	Western Conn	EFHJ	PHD	89	N Illinois	
Oyen, Duane B.	Prof	Wis-Eau Clar	E	PHD	73	Iowa	1976
Ozaki, Robert S.	Prof	CS-Hayward	EFNO	PHD	60	Harvard	1960
Ozar, Semsa	Asst	Bogazici	J	PHD	90	Wirtschaf	1990
Ozawa, Terutomo	Prof	Colorado St	FO	PHD	66	Columbia	1974
Ozden, Caglar	Asst	Emory	FL	PHD	98	Stanford	1998
Ozler, Sule	Assoc	UCLA		PHD	86	Stanford	1985
Ozmucur, Suleyman	C-Pr	Bogazici	CEL	PHD	76	Istanbul	1976
Paarsch, Harry	Assoc	Iowa		PHD	87	Stanford	1996
Paas, Martha W.	Prof	Carleton	BNO	PHD	79	Bryn Mawr	1975
Pachis, Dimitrios S.	Assoc	Eastern Conn		PHD	82	Mass	
Pack, Spencer J.	Prof	Conn Coll	B	PHD	83	NewHamp	1981
Padelford, Walton M.	Prof	Union-TN	ABFO	PHD	75	LSU	1980
Pae, Ki-Tai	C-Pr	Central Conn		PHD	71	Conn	1971
Pagan, Jose	Asst	Tx-Pan Amer		PHD	95	New Mex	1995
Page, Alfred N.	Dean	Tampa	ADE	PHD	62	Chicago	1997
Page, Marianne E.	Asst	Cal-Davis	HJ	PHD	95	Michigan	1996
Page, Scott	Assoc	Iowa	H	PHD	93	Nrthwstrn	1997
Page, Talbot	Prof	Brown		PHD	72	Cornell	
Page, Walter	Prof	SUNY-Plattsb	DE	PHD	68	Kansas	1983

Name	Rank	School	Fields	Degree	Yr	Institution	Joined
Paglin, Morton	Retir	Portland St		PHD	56	Berkeley	1961
Pakes, Ariel	Prof	Yale	CL	PHD	79	Harvard	
Pal, Debashis	Assoc	Cincinnati	L	PHD	90	Florida	1994
Palacios-Huercta, Ignacid	Asst	Brown		PHD	95	Chicago	
Paleisek,	Inst	Campbell		PHD		GeoMason	1993
Palfrey, Thomas R.	Prof	Cal Tech		PHD	81	Cal Tech	1986
Palivos, Theodore	Assoc	Louisiana St	F	PHD	92	Penn St	1992
Mack Hornbeak Business Partnership Professor							
Palm, Thomas	Retir	Portland St		PHD	67	Michigan	1967
Palmer, Charles F.	Dean	Wingate	AH	PHD	76	Va Tech	1993
Palmer, Jan S.	C-Ac	Ohio Univ	A	PHD	74	Mich St	1979
Palmer, Ransford W.	C-Pr	Howard	HO	PHD	66	Clark	1973
Palmini, Dennis J.	Prof	Wis-Stev Pt		PHD	75	Illinois	1980
Palmquist, Raymond B.	Prof	N Carol St	QDR	PHD	78	U Wash	1979
Palomba, Neil A.	Dean	Ball State		PHD	66	Minnesota	8-84
Palumbo, Edwin P.	Inst	Providence	RJ	MA		Boston C	
Palumbo, George M.	C-Pr	Canisius		PHD	77	Syracuse	1978
Palumbo, Michael G.	Asst	Houston	H	PHD	92	Virginia	1992
Pan, Zuohong	Asst	Western Conn	CJLO	PHD	95	Mich St	
Panagariya, Arvind	Prof	Maryland		PHD	78	Princeton	1978
Pande, Rohini	Asst	Columbia	OD	PHD		London	1999
Panik, Michael J.	Prof	Hartford	CDHO	PHD	70	Boston C	1968
Pantuosco, Louis J.	Asst	Winthrop	EHIJ	PHD	92	Northeas	9-97
Panzar, John C.	Prof	Northwestern		PHD	75	Stanford	1983
Louis W. Menk Professor							
Papachristou, Patricia T.	Prof	Christian Br	TI	MBA	79	Memphis	1980
Papagapitos, Agapipos	Assoc	St Thomas-MN	OP	PHD	92	Ohio St	
Papageorgio, Chris	Asst	Louisiana St	E	PHD	96	Pittsburgh	8-97
Papakyriazis, Artemis	H-Pr	Cal Poly-SLO		PHD	82	Ca-Rivers	1982
Papakyriazis, Panagiotis A.	Prof	Cal Poly-SLO		PHD	74	Ca-SnDgo	1971
Papathanasis, Anastasios	Prof	Central Conn	LK	PHD	79	Ca-Davis	1984
Papell, David H.	Prof	Houston	E	PHD	81	Columbia	1984
Papke, James A.	Prof	Purdue		PHD	59	Cornell	1962
Papke, Leslie E.	Assoc	Michigan St		PHD	87	MIT	1990
Pappas, Anthony	Assoc	St John's		PHD	71	Yale	
Parai, Amar K.	Prof	SUNY-Fredoni	AF	PHD	79	So Meth	1988
Parcells, R. J. "Pete"	Assoc	Whitman	CR	PHD	83	SUNY-Bin	1982
Parigi, Sam F.	Prof	Lamar	J	PHD	64	Tx-Austin	1961
Regents' Professor of Economics							
Paringer, Lynn C.	Prof	CS-Hayward	CDI	PHD	78	Wisconsin	1981
Park, David J.	Retir	CS-Pomona		PHD	62	S Calif	1965
Park, Gon Yung	Prof	LaVerne		PHD	93	Brown	1995
Park, Hong Youl	C-Pr	Saginaw Vall	KMEL	PHD	75	Utah St	1975
Park, Jong-Heum	Prof	Kennesaw St	ADFO	PHD	74	Okla St	1988
Park, Jungsoo	Asst	SUNY-Buffalo	OF	PHD	99	Stanford	1998
Park, Kang Hoon	Prof	SE Missouri	CF	PHD	81	S Illinois	1979
Park, Sang O.	C-Pr	Chris Newpor	DFOR	PHD	63	N Carol	1982
Park, Sangin	Asst	SUNY Stony B		PHD	96	Yale	1996
Park, Walter G.	Assoc	American U		PHD	91	Yale	1991
Park, William Laird	Retir	Brigham Yg		PHD	63	Cornell	1977
Park, Young J.	Prof	Calif U-Penn		PHD	74	Temple	1977
Parke, William	Assoc	No Carolina	C	PHD	80	Yale	1988
Parker, Carl D.	Prof	Fort Hays St	DIJM	PHD	71	Okla St	1976
Parker, Charles	Assoc	Wayne St Col	AEK	PHD	94	Ohio St	8-95
Parker, Darrell F.	Prof	Winthrop	EHRT	PHD	84	Purdue	9-85
Parker, Elliott	Asst	Nevada-Reno		PHD	92	U Wash	1992
Parker, Jeffrey A.	C-Pr	Reed	AECF	PHD	81	Stanford	1988
George Hay Professor of Economics							
Parker, Joseph A.	C-Pr	New Haven	JR	PHD	68	Oklahoma	9-69
Parker, Patrick J.	Prof	Naval Postgr	AH	MBA	55	Chicago	9-74
Parker, Randall E.	Assoc	East Carol	EN	PHD	86	Kentucky	1986
Parkison, Kathy	Asst	Ind-Kokomo		PHD	83	Purdue	1993
Parks, Richard	Prof	U Washington		PHD	66	Berkeley	1970
Parks, Robert P.	Assoc	Wash Univ	H	PHD	71	Purdue	1971
Parks, Susan	Prof	Wis-Whitewat		PHD	82	Purdue	1980
Parks, Terrance C.	Prof	Indiana St	OED	PHD	74	Illinois	1966
Parlour, Christine	Asst	Carnegie Mel		PHD	95	Queen's	1995
Parsons, Christina	Asst	Fairfield	HR	PHD	97	Ohio St	1997
Parsons, Deborah	Lect	Ohio State					
Parsons, Donald O.	Prof	Geo Wash	J	PHD	70	Chicago	1997
Parsons, George R.	Asst	Delaware	Q	PHD	85	Wisconsin	1985
Parvin, Manoucher	Retir	Akron	ACP	PHD	79	Columbia	1978
Parzych, Kenneth M.	C-Pr	Eastern Conn		PHD	70	Conn	
Pasternak, Richard E.	Prof	Metro St-CO		PHD	62	Alabama	1968
Pasupathy, Meenakshi	Asst	CUNY Baruch		PHD	96	Wash U	1996
Patch, Elizabeth P.	Assoc	Bloomsburg		PHD	90	Lehigh	
Pate, David S.	C-Ac	St John Fshr	J	PHD	85	Iowa St	1987
Patrick, Hugh T.	Prof	Columbia		PHD	60	Michigan	1984
R. D. Calkins Professor of International Business							
Patrick, J. Michael	C-Pr	Tx A&M Intl		PHD	77	Mich St	9-93

Patridge, Mark	Assoc	St Cloud St		PHD	91	Illinois	1995
Patrono, Michael Frank	Asst	Berry		MS	88	Fla St	1989
Pattanaik, Prasanta	Prof	Cal-Riversid	AO	PHD	68	Delhi	1991
Patterson, Braxton I.	Retir	Wis-Oshkosh		PHD	61	Mich St	1967
Patterson, Debra Moore	Asst	Trinity	F	PHD	94	Virginia	1994
Patterson, Perry L.	Prof	Wake Forest		PHD	86	Nrthwstrn	1986
Patterson, Seymour	Prof	Truman State		PHD	80	Oklahoma	1980
Paul, Chris W.	Emer	Alabama-Hunt	K	PHD	79	Tx A&M	1982
Paul, Harvey	Prof	Towson		PHD	72	SUNY-Buf	1966
Paul, Sanjay	Asst	St Norbert		PHD	92	SUNY-Buf	1992
Paulin, Elizabeth	Assoc	LaSalle	J	PHD	87	Tx-Austin	1988
Paus, Eva	Assoc	Mt Holyoke		PHD	83	Pittsburgh	1987
Pauszek, Ruffin		SUNY-Empire	A	MBA		SUNY-Buf	1992
Pavcnik, Nina	Asst	Dartmouth		PHD	99	Princeton	1999
Pavsek, Daniel A.	Prof	Shenandoah		PHD	81	Case Wes	1992
Pawlak, Andrew T.	Asst	Salem State		MA		Tufts	
Paxson, Christina H.	Assoc	Princeton		PHD	86	Columbia	1986
Paxton, Donald	Retir	Jacksonvl St		PHD	71	Tulane	1977
Payne, Bill	Retir	Murray State	DFMQ	PHD	70	Oregon St	1975
Payne, Bruce C.	Assoc	Barry		PHD	77	LSU	8-98
Payne, James E.	Assoc	E Kentucky		PHD	89	Fla St	1992
Payne, Richard D.	Prof	Boise State	HEA	PHD	70	S Calif	1970
Peach, James T.	Prof	New Mex St	T	PHD	78	Tx-Austin	1980
Peake, Charles F.	Assoc	MD-Baltim Co		PHD	68	Maryland	1967
Pearce, David G.	Prof	Yale	D	PHD	83	Princeton	
Pearce, Douglas K.	Prof	N Carol St	EG	PHD	74	Wisconsin	1985
Pearce, John F.	Retir	No Georgia		PHD	66	Alabama	1970
Pearson, Donald W.	Prof	E Michigan		PHD	70	Tx-Austin	1969
Peart, Sandra Joan	Assoc	Baldwin-Wal	BD	PHD	89	Toronto	1989
Pecchenino, Rowena A.	Prof	Michigan St		PHD	85	Wisconsin	1985
Peck, James D.	Assoc	Ohio State	D	PHD	85	Penn	1992
Peck, Merton J.	Prof	Yale	LO	PHD	54	Harvard	1978
Peck, Richard M.	Assoc	Ill-Chicago	D	PHD	83	Princeton	1981
Peckham, Brian W.	Asst	Wis-Plattev		PHD	79	Wisconsin	1987
Pecorino, Paul	Assoc	Alabama		PHD	90	Duke	1994
Pedersen, William E.	Asst	SE Louisiana	AGH	PHD	95	N Orleans	1994
Pedroni, Peter	Asst	Indiana		PHD	93	Columbia	1993
Peek, Joe	Prof	Boston Coll	E	PHD	79	Nrthwstrn	1978
Peek, William A.	Assoc	Niagara		PHD	85	Syracuse	1980
Peirce, William S.	C-Pr	Case Western	HOQ	PHD	66	Princeton	1966
Pejovich, Svetozar	Prof	Texas A&M	P	PHD	63	Geotown	1975
Pelzman, Joseph	Prof	George Wash	F	PHD	76	Boston C	1980
Pemberton, Donald K.	Prof	Detroit Merc		PHD	70	Kansas	1969
Pencavel, John H.	C-Pr	Stanford		PHD	69	Princeton	1979
Pendleton, Linwood	Asst	So Calif		PHD	96	Yale	1996
Pendse, Dilip C.	Assoc	Ind-Kokomo		PHD	71	Oregon St	
Penn, William M.	Prof	Belhaven	AM	PHD	68	Duke	1981
Pennington, Robert L.	Assoc	Cen Florida	D	PHD	77	Tx A&M	1983
Peoples, James A.	Assoc	Wis-Milwauke		PHD	84	Berkeley	1990
Pepall, Lynne	Assoc	Tufts	L	PHD	83	Cambridge	1987
Peper, Merle J.	Dean	West Alabama		PHD	86	LSU	9-95
Pepin, Raymond A.	Prof	Stonehill	AD	PHD	71	Clark	1969
Peppard, Donald M. Jr.	Prof	Conn Coll	R	PHD	75	Mich St	
Pepper, John	Asst	Virginia	HD	PHD	96	Wisconsin	1996
Peppers, Larry C.	Dean	Wash & Lee		PHD	70	Vanderbilt	1986
Perelman, Michael A.	Prof	CS-Chico	N	PHD	71	Berkeley	1971
Peretto, Pietro	Asst	Duke	EFLM	PHD	94	Yale	9-94
Perez, Stephen J.	Asst	Wash State		PHD	94	Ca-Davis	1997
Perkins, Dwight H.	Prof	Harvard		PHD	64	Harvard	1963
Harold Hitchings Burbank Professor of Political Economy							
Perkins, Garey B.	Assoc	Freed Hardem	DEQ	PHD	71	Tennessee	8-98
Perkins, Mary	Assoc	Howard	D	PHD	82	American	
Perktold, Josef	Asst	Chicago		PHD	95	UCLA	1995
Perli, Roberto	Asst	Pennsylvania	E	PHD	95	NYU	1995
Perline, Martin M.	Prof	Wichita St		PHD	65	Ohio St	1965
Perlman, Mark	Retir	Pittsburgh		PHD	50	Columbia	1963
Perlman, Richard W.	Emer	Wis-Milwauke		PHD	53	Columbia	1964
Pernecky, Mark L.	Assoc	St Olaf	EJA	PHD	90	Notre Dm	1990
Perotti, Roberto	Assoc	Columbia	E	PHD	91	MIT	1991
Perri, Timothy J.	Prof	Appalach St	DJ	PHD	78	Ohio St	1980
Perrigne, Isabelle	Asst	So Calif		PHD	91	Toulouse	1997
Perron, Pierre	Prof	Boston Univ	C	PHD	86	Yale	1997
Perrotti, Liesa	Asst	INSEAD					9-97
Perry, Joseph M.	C-Pr	North Fla	NOR	PHD	66	Nrthwstrn	1971
Perry, Mark J.	Asst	Mich-Flint		PHD	93	GeoMason	1996
Perry, Martin K.	Prof	Rutgers-N Br	L	PHD	76	Stanford	1989
Persico, Nicola	Asst	Pennsylvania		PHD	96	Nrthwstrn	1997
Persky, Joseph J.	Prof	Ill-Chicago	R	PHD	71	Harvard	1974
Pescatrice, Donn R.	C-Pr	Iona	CDE	PHD	75	Purdue	1983
Pesek, Boris P.	Emer	Wis-Milwauke		PHD	56	Chicago	1967

Pesendorfer, Martin	Asst	Yale	L	PHD	95	Nrthwstrn	9-95
Petersen, Bruce C.	Prof	Wash Univ	L	PHD	81	Harvard	1991
Petersen, Harold A.	Assoc	Boston Coll	G	PHD	63	Brown	1960
Petersen, Harold Craig	Prof	Utah State	GM	PHD	73	Stanford	1973
Peterson, Dean J.	Asst	Seattle	B	PHD	94	Illinois	1991
Peterson, Donald L.	Prof	So Dakota St	Q	PHD	73	Nebraska	1974
Peterson, Elaine J.	Asst	CS-Stanislau		PHD	96	Wisconsin	1996
Peterson, Janice L.	Assoc	SUNY-Fredoni	BA	PHD	87	Nebraska	1990
Peterson, Jerrold M.	Prof	Minn-Duluth	HE	PHD	70	Illinois	1969
Peterson, John	Asst	Northern St		PHD	97	Kansas	1992
Peterson, Kenneth D.	Asst	Furman		PHD	91	SUNY-SBr	1990
Peterson, Norris A.	Prof	Pacific Luth	J	PHD	81	Minnesota	1981
Peterson, Rodney	Retir	Colorado St	1994	PHD		Nebraska	
Peterson, Steven P.	Assoc	Virg Comm		PHD	89	Indiana	1989
Peterson, Thomas C.	Retir	Cen Michigan		PHD	70	UCLA	1972
Petr, Jerry L.	Prof	Nebraska	P	PHD	67	Indiana	1966
C. Wheaton Battey Professor of Economics							
Petrakis, John T.	Retir	Lg Isl-Post		PHD		American	
Petratos, Vasilios	C-Ac	CUNY-Stn Isl	BF	PHD	70	NYU	1974
Petree, Daniel L.	C-Ac	Concordia C	JT	PHD	93	Kansas	1995
Petri, Peter A.	Prof	Brandeis		PHD	76	Harvard	1974
Petruska, Dennis A.	Prof	Youngstown		PHD	84	Ohio St	1984
Pettit, Mary Ann	Inst	S Ill-Edward	A	MA	77	Tennessee	1989
Pevas, Mary Ann	Assoc	Winona State		PHD	90	Notre Dm	1990
Pfaff, Alexander	Asst	Columbia	DQ	PHD	95	MIT	1995
Pfannestiel, Maurice	Assoc	Wichita St		PHD	67	Okla St	1966
Pfeifer, Karen	Prof	Smith	BNOP	PHD	81	American	1979
Pfitzner, C. Barry	Prof	Randolph-Mac	DFC	PHD	83	Catholic	1982
Edward W. Seese Professor of Economics and Business							
Pflueger, Burton W.	Prof	So Dakota St	Q	PHD	85	Illinois	1985
Pfouts, William	Emer	No Carolina		PHD	52	N Carol	1947
Pham, Chung	Retir	New Mexico	CEGO	PHD	62	Penn	1963
Pham, Van	Asst	Missouri	FL	PHD	98	Cornell	1998
Phares, Donald	C-Pr	Mo-St Louis	HR	PHD	70	Syracuse	1969
Phares, Kathleen	Lect	Mo-St Louis	A	MA	76	Mo-StLou	1977
Phelan, John	Assoc	New Haven	HI	PHD		Geo Wash	9-95
Phelps, Charles E.	Prof	Rochester		PHD	73	Chicago	1984
Phelps, Charlotte D.	Assoc	Temple	TI	PHD	61	Yale	1967
Phelps, Edmund	Prof	Columbia	EG	PHD	59	Yale	1971
Phelps, Janie	Asst	Miss State		PHD	98	Kansas	1998
Philippides, Andreas	Assoc	Teikyo Post		PHD	94	Conn	1988
Philipps, Eugene A.	Retir	Moorhead St		PHD		Illinois	1966
Philipson, Tomas J.	Assoc	Chicago		PHD	89	Penn	1996
Phillips, Almarin	Emer	Pennsylvania		PHD	53	Harvard	1953
Phillips, Charles F. Jr.	Prof	Wash & Lee	L	PHD	60	Harvard	1959
Robert C. Brown Professor of Economics							
Phillips, Edward S.	Prof	Shepherd		PHD	70	Colorado	1974
Phillips, Joseph M. Jr.	Prof	Creighton	EO	PHD	82	Notre Dm	1988
Phillips, K. E.	Retir	Tennessee		PHD		U Wash	
Phillips, Kerk	Assoc	Brigham Yg		PHD	91	Rochester	1992
Phillips, Llad	Prof	Cal-Santa Br	JC	PHD	69	Harvard	1972
Phillips, Owen R.	Prof	Wyoming	DK	PHD	80	Stanford	1985
Phillips, Peter C. B.	Prof	Yale	C	PHD	74	London	
Phillips, Peter W.	Prof	Utah		PHD	80	Stanford	1978
Phillips, Robert F.	Assoc	George Wash	C	PHD	85	Columbia	1985
Phillips, Ronnie J.	Prof	Colorado St	GB	PHD	80	Tx-Austin	1993
Phillips, Timothy P.	Assoc	SUNY-Cortlan	M	MBA	83	Clarkson	1983
Phillips, William A.	Assoc	So Maine	ACDF	PHD	79	Fla St	1980
Phillips, William H.	Assoc	So Carolina		PHD	80	MIT	1979
Phipps, Tim	Assoc	W Virginia	Q	PHD	82	Berkeley	1989
Photiades, John G.	Prof	Montana	BOH	PHD	72	Illinois	
Pickett, John C.	Prof	Ark-Ltl Rock		PHD	70	Missouri	1986
Picone, Gabriel A.	Assoc	South Fla	C	PHD	93	Vanderbilt	1993
Piedra, Alberto M.	Prof	Catholic	BNO	PHD			
Pieper, Paul J.	Assoc	Ill-Chicago	E	PHD	84	Nrthwstrn	1982
Pierce, James L.	Prof	Cal-Berkeley		PHD	64	Berkeley	1976
Pierce, Thomas J.	Prof	CS-San Bern	E	PHD	76	Notre Dm	1976
Pierson, Lynne M.	Prof	Chapman	NE	PHD	78	Ca-Rivers	1972
Pietra, Tito	Asst	Rutgers-N Br	D	PHD	89	Penn	1988
Pietrykowski, Bruce	Asst	Mich-Dearbor	BJNR	PHD	90	New Sch	1988
Pillsbury, Warren A.	Retir	Lehigh		PHD	63	Virginia	1962
Pillutla, Padmaja	Asst	East Tenn St		ABD		Wash St	1998
Pinchin, Hugh M.	Prof	Colgate	F	PHD	70	Yale	1965
Pineres, Sheila	Asst	Texas-Dallas		PHD	92	Duke	1996
Pingkarawat, Nampeang	Prof	Chicago St		PHD	83	Il-Chicago	1982
Pingle, Mark	Assoc	Nevada-Reno		PHD	88	S Calif	1990
Pinto, James V.	Prof	No Arizona	DC	PHD	75	Oklahoma	1981
Piore, Michael J.	Prof	MIT	J	PHD	66	Harvard	1966
David W. Skinner Professor of Political Economy							
Pippenger, John E.	Retir	Cal-Santa Br		PHD	66	UCLA	1965

Pippenger, Michael	H-As	Alaska-Fairb		PHD	90	Purdue	1991
Pirasteh, Hassan	Prof	So Oregon St	CEG	PHD	85	Oregon	1982
Piron, Robert	Prof	Oberlin	BD	PHD	66	Nrthwstrn	1961
Pirouz, Kamrouz	Asst	Montclair St	ADGN	PHD	73	Hawaii	1980
Pischke, Jorn-Steffen	Assoc	MIT	J	PHD	92	Princeton	1993
Pisciotta, John L.	Assoc	Baylor		PHD	71	Tx-Austin	1980
Pisciottoli, Louis F.	Retir	CS-Fresno		PHD	72	Duke	1967
Pitt, Mark M.	Prof	Brown		PHD	77	Berkeley	
Pitts, M. Melinda	Asst	Georgia St	IJ	PHD	97	N Car St	1998
Pizzi, Robert	Deces	Colorado Col		PHD	82	Wash	1990
Pizzigno, Gregory D.	Adj	St John's		MBA		St Johns	
Placone, Dennis L.	Assoc	Clemson	FPH	PHD	82	Pittsburgh	1976
Plagens, Les	Dean	Howard Payne		PHD	84	Tx A&M	1997
Plante, David	Asst	Western St		ABD		Utah	1997
Plassmann, Florenz	Asst	SUNY-Bingham	HRF	PHD	97	Va Tech	1999
Platt, Glenn	Assoc	Miami U-Ohio	CR	PHD	93	Car Mellon	1993
Platt, Henry M.	Retir	Pace		PHD		Columbia	1966
Pledge, Michael T.	Prof	W Illinois	AEG	PHD	68	Houston	1968
Pliskin, Jeffrey L.	Assoc	Hamilton	CF	PHD	85	Michigan	1982
Ploberger, Werner	Prof	Rochester		HAB	93	Vienna T	1997
Plosser, Charles I.	Prof	Rochester		PHD	76	Chicago	1978
John M. Olin Distinguished Professor of Economics							
Plott, Charles R.	Prof	Cal Tech		PHD	65	Virginia	1971
Edward S. Harkness Professor of Economics and Political Science							
Plumly, L. Wayne Jr.	Prof	Valdosta St	JA	PHD	83	Geo St	1980
Plummer, Michael G.	Assoc	Brandeis		PHD	88	Mich St	1993
Pluta, Joseph E.	Prof	St Edwards		PHD	72	Tx-Austin	1984
Pluta, Joseph E.	Retir	SW Texas St		PHD	72	Tx-Austin	1991
Podgursky, Michael J.	C-Pr	Missouri	IJ	PHD	80	Wisconsin	1995
Pogodzinski, Joseph Michael	Prof	San Jose St		PHD	80	SUNY-SBr	1987
Pogue, Thomas F.	Prof	Iowa		PHD	68	Yale	1965
Poirier, Dale	Prof	Calif-Irvine		PHD	73	Wisconsin	1999
Poirier, J. Eugene	Retir	Georgetown		PHD	66	Yale	
Poitras, Marc	Asst	Dayton	A	PHD	95	GeoMason	1998
Polachek, Solomon W.	Dean	SUNY-Bingham	J	PHD	73	Columbia	1983
Polak, Benjamin	Assoc	Yale	N	PHD	92	Harvard	
Polavarapu, Ramana V.	Asst	Colo-Denver	IOCD	PHD	93	Ca-Davis	1993
Polkinghorn, Bette A.	Prof	CS-Sacrament		PHD	72	Ca-Davis	1971
Pollak, Robert A.	Prof	Wash Univ	DJT	PHD	64	MIT	1995
Hernreich Distinguished Professor of Economics							
Polley, Susanne M.	Asst	SUNY-Cortlan	EHM	PHD	94	Penn St	8-94
Polley, William	Asst	Bradley		PHD	99	Iowa	1999
Pollin, Robert N.	Prof	Massachusett		PHD	82	New Sch	1998
Pollock, Gene Edward	Retir	Wooster		PHD	71	Ohio St	1961
Pollock, Richard L.	Deces	Hawaii-Manoa		PHD	67	Wisconsin	1968
Polutnik, Lidija	Asst	Babson	HJ	PHD	94	Geo St	1991
Pomery, John D.	Assoc	Purdue		PHD	77	Rochester	1982
Pompe, Jeffrey	Assoc	Fran Marion		PHD	90	Fla St	
Pomponio, Xun	Asst	St Olaf	FP	PHD	91	Penn St	1991
Pongracic, Ivan	Asst	Indiana Wesl	AEFP	MA	68	Zagreb	1987
Pontiff, Jeffrey	Assoc	U Washington		PHD	94	Rochester	1992
Poole, Keith T.	Prof	Carnegie Mel		PHD	78	Rochester	1982
Poole, Richard W.	Retir	Oklahoma St		PHD	60	Okla St	1965
Poole, William	Retir	Brown		PHD	66	Chicago	1974
Pope, C. Arden III	Prof	Brigham Yg		PHD	81	Iowa St	1984
Pope, Clayne L.	Dean	Brigham Yg		PHD	72	Chicago	1970
Pope, Rulon D.	Prof	Brigham Yg		PHD	76	Berkeley	1982
Poper, Frank J.	Assoc	Christian Br		PHD		NYU	1995
Poplin, Toby L.	C-Ac	Pfeiffer		MA	68	Appalach	1976
Popp, Anthony V.	Assoc	New Mex St	H	PHD	80	N Illinois	1981
Popp, David	Asst	Kansas	O	PHD	97	Yale	8-97
Popper, Helen A.	Assoc	Santa Clara		PHD	90	Berkeley	1991
Pordeli, Hassan	Prof	Jacksonvil U		PHD	83	Nebraska	1983
Hugh F. Culverhouse Professor of Economics							
Porter, Jack	Asst	Harvard		PHD	96	MIT	
Porter, Philip K.	Prof	South Fla	H	PHD	78	Tx A&M	1985
Porter, Richard C.	Prof	Michigan		PHD	57	Yale	1964
Porter, Robert H.	Prof	Northwestern		PHD	81	Princeton	1987
William R. Kenan Jr. Professor							
Porter, Tod S.	C-Pr	Youngstown		PHD	84	Syracuse	1984
Porter-Hudak, Susan	Assoc	No Illinois	C	PHD	82	Wisconsin	1982
Portugal, Edwin	Asst	SUNY-Potsdam		PHD	93	SUNY-Alb	
Posatko, Robert C.	Prof	Shippensburg		PHD	75	Penn St	1981
Possen, Uri M.	Prof	Cornell		PHD	71	Yale	1971
Postlewaite, Andrew W.	Prof	Pennsylvania	DH	PHD	74	Nrthwstrn	9-80
Pacific Term Professor in the Social Studies							
Postlewaite, Richard	Lect	Wis-Eau Clar	E	MM	89	AGSIM	1997
Potepan, Michael J.	C-Ac	San Fran St		PHD	85	Ca-Davis	1991
Poterba, James M.	Prof	MIT	H	DPHI	83	Oxford	1983
Mitsui Professor of Economics							

Potlowsky, Thomas P.	C-Pr$	Portland St		PHD	81	Colorado	1982
Potter, Gordon Alwyn	Retir	Pace		MDIV		Gen Theo	1969
Potter, Simon M.	Asst	UCLA		PHD	90	Wisconsin	1990
Potter, William	Assoc	Fairmont St	AN	MA		Memphis	1970
Potts, Glenn T.	C-Pr	Wis-Rvr Fall	E	PHD	76	Iowa St	1976
Poulson, Barry W.	Prof	Colorado		PHD	65	Ohio St	1965
Powell, Irene	Assoc	Grinnell	IL	PHD	85	Wisconsin	1989
Powelson, John P.	Retir	Colorado		PHD	51	Harvard	1966
Power, James	Prof	Cal-Berkeley		PHD	82	Stanford	1995
Power, Thomas M.	C-Pr	Montana	HQR	PHD	71	Princeton	
Powers, Elizabeth	Asst	Illinois	IJR	PHD	94	Penn	1996
Powers, John A.	Assoc	Cincinnati	C	PHD	66	Purdue	1965
Pozo, Susan	Prof	W Michigan	F	PHD	80	Mich St	1982
Praetzel, Gary D.	Assoc	Niagara		PHD	80	SUNY-Buf	1981
Prager, Jonas	Assoc	New York U	G	PHD	64	Columbia	1962
Prasad, Kislaya	Assoc	Florida St	D	PHD	88	Syracuse	1988
Pratt, Leila J.	Prof	Tenn-Chattan	DC	PHD	75	Va Tech	1974
Hart Professor							
Pratt, Michael D.	Prof	Virg Comm		PHD	77	Kansas	1979
Pray, Bwalee	C-As	Union-TN		PHD	92	Memphis	1991
Premus, Robert	Prof	Wright State		PHD	75	Lehigh	1975
Prendergast, George A.	C-Pr	St Joseph	EN	PHD	72	Penn	1956
Prescott, Edward C.	Prof	Minnesota		PHD	67	Car Mellon	1980
Regent's Professor							
Prescott, James R.	Retir	Iowa State	R	PHD	64	Harvard	1973
Pressman, Steven	Prof	Monmouth		PHD	83	New Sch	1981
Price, Donald I.	Prof	Lamar	MO	PHD	80	Arkansas	1981
Price, Edward O. III	Assoc	Oklahoma St	B	PHD	80	Tx A&M	1979
Price, Gregory N.	Asst	N Carol A&T		PHD	93	Wi-Milwa	
Price, Hollis F. Jr.	Retir	U Miami	HR	PHD	72	Colorado	1971
Pries, Michael	Asst	Maryland		PHD	99	Stanford	1999
Prime, Penelope B.	Prof	Kennesaw St	ADFO	PHD	87	Michigan	1991
Primont, Daniel A.	C-Pr	So Illinois	DC	PHD	70	Ca-SnBarb	1978
Primont, Diane F.	Assoc	SE Missouri	JDE	PHD	87	N Carol	1990
Prince, Steven	Asst	CS-Humboldt		PHD	93	Utah	1998
Prindle, Allen M.	Assoc	Otterbein	DQ	PHD	77	Penn St	1988
Prinzinger, Joseph M.	Prof	Lynchburg		PHD	74	Geo St	1987
Pritchett, Jonathan B.	Assoc	Tulane		PHD	86	Chicago	1985
Prosper, Peter A. Jr.	Retir	Union	JA	PHD	70	Cornell	1964
Prosseda, Phil D.	Asst	USAF Academy		ABD	97	Colorado	
Proulx, Christopher	Asst	Cal-Santa Br	D	PHD	98	Michigan	1998
Prucha, Ingmar R.	Prof	Maryland		PHD	77	Vienna	1981
Prus, Mark J.	C-Ac	SUNY-Cortlan	JN	PHD	85	Utah	
Prusa, Thomas	Assoc	Rutgers-N Br	F	PHD	88	Stanford	1994
Pryor, Frederic	Emer	Swarthmore	OP	PHD	57	Yale	1972
Puffer, Frank W.	Prof	Clark		PHD	68	Brown	1968
Pugel, Thomas A.	Prof	New York U	DEF	PHD	78	Harvard	1978
Pulchritudoff, Nikolai	Assoc	CS-L Angeles		PHD	71	Ca-Davis	1972
Pulikonda, Naga	Assoc	Ind-Kokomo		PHD	77	Illinois	
Pulsinelli, Robert W.	Prof	W Kentucky	DK	PHD	74	Rutgers	1967
Puri, Anil K.	C-Pr	CS-Fullerton	HR	PHD	77	Minnesota	1977
Puritz, Frederick A.	Asst	SUNY-Oneonta	ME	MBA		Harvard	
Purkayastha, Dipankar	Assoc	CS-Fullerton	O	PHD	90	Wash St	1990
Puth, Robert C.	Retir	New Hampshir	N	PHD	67	Nrthwstrn	1967
Putnam, William F.	Emer	So Carolina		MS	57	S Carol	
Putterman, Louis G.	Prof	Brown		PHD	80	Yale	1980
Pyle, William	Asst	Middlebury	EP	PHD	97	Duke	1999
Qasmi, Bashir A.	Asst	So Dakota St	Q	PHD	86	Iowa St	1987
Qastin, Abdul Masesh	Assoc	Lakeland	DGNP	PHD		Kennedy W	1985
Qayum, Abdul	Prof	Portland St		DSC	59	Netherld	1970
Qi, Min	Asst	Kent State	CDFG	PHD	96	Ohio St	1996
Qian, Hailong	Asst	St Louis		PHD	95	Mich St	1999
Qian, Yingyi	Prof	Maryland		PHD	90	Harvard	1999
Qin, Cheng-Zhong	Assoc	Cal-Santa Br	D	PHD	89	Iowa	1989
Quade, Ane M.	Assoc	CS-Sacrament		PHD	88	Illinois	1989
Quadrini, Vincenzo	Asst	Duke		PHD	96	Penn	1998
Quandt, Richard E.	Prof	Princeton		PHD	57	Harvard	1959
Quddus, Munir	Prof	So Indiana		PHD	85	Vanderbilt	1984
Quencau, Herre'	Asst	Xavier		PHD	96	ParisDaup	1996
Quick, Paddy	C-Pr	St Fran-NY	ABN	PHD	75	Harvard	9-85
Quigley, Herbert G.	C-Pr	Univ of D C		DBA	77	Geo Wash	1969
Quigley, John M.	Prof	Cal-Berkeley		PHD	72	Harvard	1970
Quinlivan, Gary M.	C-Pr	St Vincent	CDF	PHD	83	SUNY-Alb	1981
Quinn, J. Kevin	Assoc	Bowling Gr		PHD	89	American	1990
Quinn, Joseph F.	Prof	Boston Coll	DJ	PHD	75	MIT	1975
Quinn, Kevin G.	Asst	St Norbert		PHD	95	Il-Chicago	1994
Quinn, Robert	Asst	So Alabama	ADJI	PHD	95	U Miami	1997
Quinn, Stephen F.	Asst	Tx Christian		PHD	94	Illinois	1995
Quinzii, Martine	C-Pr	Cal-Davis	CDG	PHD	74	U Paris	1991
Quirmbach, Herman C.	Assoc	Iowa State	L	PHD	83	Princeton	1990

Quispe-Agnoli, Myriam	Asst	Tulane		PHD	96	N Carol	1996
Qunjian, Daniel	Deces	Tufts		PHD		Harvard	1962
Raab, Raymond L.	Prof	Minn-Duluth	L	PHD	71	Colo St	1970
Rabbitt, Michael T.	Lect	Rockhurst		MA	75	Wash U	1988
Rabin, Alan	Prof	Tenn-Chattan	E	PHD	77	Virginia	1977
UC Foundation Professor							
Rabin, Matthew J.	Prof	Cal-Berkeley		PHD	89	MIT	
Racine, Jeffrey S.	Assoc	South Fla	C	PHD	91	W Ontario	1993
Radakovic, George	Assoc	Indiana U-PA	JR	PHD	79	Pittsburgh	1986
Radell, Willard W.	Prof	Indiana U-PA	NP	PHD	80	Illinois	1981
Radsich, Aleksander	Asst	CS-Long Bch		PHD	99	Princeton	1999
Raehsler, Rod D.	Asst	Clarion		PHD	93	Iowa	
Rafeld, Frederick J.	Prof	Ashland		PHD	68	Ohio St	9-70
Raff, Horst	Asst	Indiana		PHD	91	W Ontario	1993
Raffa, Frederick A.	Retir	Cen Florida	E	PHD	69	Fla St	1969
Rafferty, Matt	VAsst	Union	ENC	PHD	98	Ca-Davis	1998
Raffiee, Kambiz	Prof	Nevada-Reno		PHD	83	Oregon	1983
Ragan, James F. Jr.	H-Pr	Kansas State	JA	PHD	75	Wash U	1977
Raha, Arun	Asst	Boise State	EFO	PHD	91	Wash St	1990
Rahim, Niazur	Asst	Chris Newpor		PHD	94	Va Comm	1998
Rahimian, Eric N.	C-Pr	Alabama A&M	ADOF	PHD	75	Indiana	1975
Rahmatian, Morteza	Prof	CS-Fullerton	Q	PHD	82	Wyoming	1988
Rahnama, Masha	Assoc	Texas Tech		PHD	88	Iowa St	1996
Railing, William F.	Prof	Gettysburg	AHP	PHD	58	Cornell	1964
Raines, Fredric Q.	Assoc	Wash Univ	J	PHD	67	Wisconsin	1964
Raines, J. Patrick	C-Pr	Richmond		PHD	83	Alabama	1982
Rajan, Uday	Asst	Carnegie Mel		PHD	95	Stanford	1995
Rajanikauth, N.	Inst	Miss Vall St		MBA		Miss St	1987
Raji, Seyed	Prof	Dowling		PHD	72	NYU	
Rakowski, James J.	Assoc	Notre Dame	DF	PHD	68	Minnesota	1967
Ram, Rati	Prof	Illinois St		PHD	76	Chicago	1982
Distinguished Professor							
Ramachandran, Rama	Prof	New York U	DEH	PHD	75	Brown	1987
Ramada, Paula	Asst	Northwestern		PHD	97	MIT	1997
Ramakomud, Sriprinya	Deces	Howard		PHD		Indiana	
Raman, Jaishankar	Asst	Valparaiso	OFA	PHD	97	Notre Dm	1996
Ramanathan, Ramu	Emer	Ca-San Diego	CFO	PHD	67	Minnesota	1967
Ramaswamy, Sunder	C-As	Middlebury	DFO	PHD	90	Purdue	1990
Ramazani, M. Reza	Asst	St Michael's	AFEC	PHD	90	Colorado	1986
Rambeck, Charles	Assoc	St Benedict		PHD	79	Minnesota	1975
Ramdas, Ganga P.	Asst	Lincoln-PA		PHD	87	Temple	
Ramey, Garey	Assoc	Ca-San Diego	D	PHD	87	Stanford	1987
Ramey, James	Prof	N Carolina	GH	PHD	80	Kentucky	
Ramey, Valerie	Prof	Ca-San Diego	E	PHD	87	Stanford	1987
Ramin, Taghi	Assoc	Wm Patterson		PHD	86	NYU	1984
Ramirez, Carlos D.	Asst	George Mason		PHD	93	Harvard	
Ramirez, Miguel	Prof	Trinity-CT		PHD	84	Illinois	1985
Ramsay, Glenworth A.	Prof	Rhode Island		PHD	74	Boston C	1973
Ramsett, David E.	C-Pr	North Dakota	AHQ	PHD	68	Oklahoma	1968
Ramsey, David D.	C-Ac	Illinois St	DEH	PHD	67	Minnesota	1973
Ramsey, James B.	Prof	New York U	C	PHD	68	Wisconsin	1976
Ramstad, Yngve	Prof	Rhode Island	BA	PHD	81	Berkeley	1982
Randall, Laura	Prof	CUNY-Hunter		PHD	62	Columbia	
Randolph, Susan M.	Assoc	Connecticut	O	PHD	83	Cornell	1984
Rangazas, Peter	Assoc	Ind-Purdue/I	EH	PHD	83	Indiana	1989
Rangel, Antonio	Asst	Stanford					
Ranis, Gustav	Prof	Yale	O	PHD	56	Yale	1960
Ranjan, Priya	Asst	Calif-Irvine		PHD	97	Columbia	1997
Rankin, Carol A.	Assoc	Xavier	ADJ	PHD	80	Houston	1984
Ransom, Michael R.	Prof	Brigham Yg		PHD	83	Princeton	1988
Rao, J. Mohan	Prof	Massachusett		PHD	82	Harvard	1989
Rao, Vaman	Prof	W Illinois	ACEO	PHD	73	Missouri	1979
Raper, Michael Dennis	Asst	West Georgia	AR	PHD	88	Geo St	
Raphael, Steven	Asst	Ca-San Diego	JF	PHD	96	Berkeley	1996
Raphaelson, Arnold H.	Prof	Temple	H	PHD	60	Clark	1970
Rapoport, John	Prof	Mt Holyoke		PHD	70	Penn	1970
Rapp, Tommy A.	Asst	NE Louisiana	EF	PHD	97	S Illinois	1997
Rappaport, Neal J.	Asst	USAF Academy	DC	PHD	94	MIT	1998
Rappi, Magdalena	Assoc	Tenn Tech		PHD	85	S Carol	1985
Rapping, Leonard A.	Deces	Massachusett		PHD	60	Chicago	1972
Rappoport, Paul N.	Assoc	Temple	C	PHD	74	Ohio St	1977
Rasche, Robert H.	Retir	Michigan St		PHD	66	Michigan	1975
Rashed, Jamal A.	Assoc	Xavier	ACFO	PHD	88	So Meth	1989
Rashid, Khadijat	Asst	Gallaudet		MBA	93	Maryland	
Rashid, Salim	Prof	Illinois	BGO	PHD	76	Yale	1981
Rask, Kevin N.	Assoc	Colgate	QI	PHD	91	Duke	1991
Rask, Kolleen J.	Assoc	Holy Cross	EFOP	PHD	89	Yale	1989
Rasmusen, Eric	Prof	Indiana		PHD	84	MIT	1992
Rasmussen, Chris H.	Inst	So Dakota St	M	BA	75	SW State	1978
Rasmussen, David W.	Prof	Florida St	K	PHD	69	Wash U	1968

Name	Rank	School	Areas	Degree	Yr	Institution	Year
Rassekh, Farhad	Assoc	Hartford	ADFO	PHD	83	Houston	1989
Ratajczak, Donald	Prof	Georgia St	MN	PHD	72	MIT	1973
Rath, Kali P.	Assoc	Notre Dame	CD	PHD	92	J Hopkins	1990
Ratkus, Mark J.	C-As	LaSalle	O	PHD	76	Notre Dm	1973
Ratowsky, Henry	Asst	CUNY-Lehman		PHD	76	CUNY	1988
Ratti, Ronald A.	Prof	Missouri	EFG	PHD	75	So Meth	1975
Rauch, James	Asst	Gustavus Ado		PHD	94	Nebraska	1998
Rauch, James E.	Prof	Ca-San Diego	FO	PHD	85	Yale	1986
Ravelle, James J.	Prof	Moravian	KB	DA		Lehigh	1978
Ravelle, Linda J.	Assoc	Moravian	AG	PHD	90	Lehigh	1989
Ravikumar, B.	Assoc	Iowa		PHD	89	Iowa	1996
Rawlins, Glenville W.	Assoc	Montclair St	AGOQ	PHD	83	NYU	1984
Rawlins, Richard B.	Asst	Missouri So		PHD	98	Arkansas	1988
Rawski, Thomas G.	Prof	Pittsburgh	O	PHD	72	Harvard	1985
Rawson, William S.	Emer	So Carolina		PHD	67	Duke	1967
Ray, Cadwell L.	C-Ac	Tulsa		PHD	67	Tx-Austin	
Ray, Clarence G.	Prof	Nev-L Vegas	K	PHD	72	S Carol	1971
Ray, Debraj	Prof	New York U	D	PHD	83	Cornell	1999
Ray, Edward J.	Prof	Ohio State	F	PHD	71	Stanford	1970
Ray, Margaret A.	Assoc	Mary Wash	LQRA	PHD	88	Tennessee	
Ray, Subhash C.	Prof	Connecticut	CD	PHD	81	Ca-SnBarb	1982
Rayack, Wendy	Assoc	Wesleyan-CT	J	PHD	84	Wisconsin	1983
Raymon, Neil A.	Assoc	Missouri	CDEF	PHD	77	Colorado	1983
Raymond, Arthur J.	Asst	Muhlenberg		PHD	90	Tufts	1991
Raymond, Richard D.	Retir	Kent State	DR	PHD	63	Brown	1970
Raynold, Prosper	Assoc	Miami U-Ohio	EG	PHD	89	LSU	1989
Razzolini, Laura	Asst	Mississippi	D	PHD	94	So Meth	1994
Read, Colin	Assoc	Alaska-Fairb		PHD	88	Queen's	1989
Read, Robert A.	Lect	U Lancaster		PHD		Reading	
Reagan, Patricia B.	Assoc	Ohio State	LJ	PHD	80	MIT	1989
Reagle, Derrick	Asst	Fordham		PHD	98	Vanderbilt	1998
Reaves, Natalie	Asst	Rowan Col-NJ		PHD	95	Wayne St	1998
Rebitzer, James B.	Assoc	Case Western	J	PHD	85	Mass	1997
Reclam, Michael	H-Ac	Va Military		PHD	84	Ca-Rivers	1986
Reddy, Nallapu N.	C-Pr	Mich-Flint		PHD	67	Penn St	1974
Redfearn, Michael	Asst	North Texas	EG	PHD	92	Mich St	1992
Redington, Douglas B.	Asst	Elon	Q	PHD	89	Wyoming	1995
Redmon, Patrick	Assoc	Austin Peay	IJ	PHD	93	Mich St	1998
Redmond, Willie	Asst	SE Missouri	AFL	PHD	99	S Carol	1999
Redmount, Esther R.	C-Ac	Colorado Col		PHD	85	Virginia	1987
Reeb, Donald J.	Prof	SUNY-Albany	RG	PHD	63	Syracuse	1965
Reece, William S.	Prof	W Virginia	CH	PHD	75	Wash U	1990
Reed, J. David	Emer	Bowling Gr		PHD	70	Kansas St	1968
Reed, Mary Tripp	Lect	Murray State	ADFJ	MA	95	American	1995
Reed, Morris D.	Retir	East Central		MBA	70	Hawaii	1975
Reed, Robert	Asst	Iowa State	EFJ	PHD	98	Penn St	1998
Reed, Robert	Assoc	Oklahoma	JD	PHD	85	Nrthwstrn	1992
Rees, Daniel I.	Asst	Colo-Denver	J	PHD	92	Cornell	1993
Rees, David M.	Assoc	Mesa State		PHD	73	Oregon	1983
Reese, David A.	Assoc	Gustavus Ado		PHD	80	Va Tech	1979
Reese, James W.	Assoc	SC-Spartanbu	AFPH	PHD	73	Tennessee	1982
Reffett, Kevin	Assoc	Arizona St		PHD	90	Purdue	1995
Register, Charles A.	C-Pr	Fla Atlantic	JL	PHD	84	Okla St	1997
Reich, Michael	Prof	Cal-Berkeley		PHD	74	Harvard	1974
Reid, Clifford E.	Prof	Colby	DCHR	PHD	73	Princeton	1987
Dana Professor							
Reid, John Joseph	C-Ac	Memphis	EF	PHD	62	Virginia	1966
Reid, Joseph D.	Assoc	George Mason		PHD	74	Chicago	1983
Reid, Karen	Asst	SUNY Oswego	AQ	ABD		Tennessee	1998
Reid, Kathleen A.	C-Pr	Shepherd		PHD	86	Penn St	1983
Reifel, John W.	Prof	Grand Valley	AHOR	PHD	72	Mich St	1971
Reiland, Ralph R.	Assoc	Robt Morris		MBA		Duquesne	
Reilly, Robert J.	Prof	Virg Comm		PHD	78	Tennessee	1978
Reilly, Siobhan	Asst	Vanderbilt		PHD	97	Berkeley	1997
Reiman, Mark A.	C-Ac	Pacific Luth	FPQ	PHD	88	U Wash	1988
Reimers, Cordelia W.	Prof	CUNY-Hunter		PHD	77	Columbia	1982
Reinert, Kenneth	Asst	Kalamazoo	FDE	PHD	88	Maryland	1993
Reinganum, Jennifer F.	Prof	Vanderbilt	LK	PHD	79	Nrthwstrn	1995
Reinhardt, Nola	C-Ac	Smith	OPQ	PHD	81	Berkeley	1981
Reinhardt, Uwe E.	Prof	Princeton		PHD	70	Yale	1967
Reinhart, Blaise F.	Prof	Siena		PHD	62	Catholic	
Reinke, Robert W.	Prof	South Dakota		PHD	82	Minnesota	1987
Reinwald, Thomas P.	Prof	Shippensburg		PHD	73	Illinois	1974
Reiter, Stanley	Prof	Northwestern		PHD	55	Chicago	
Charles E. and Emma H. Morrison Professor of Economics							
Renas, Stephen M.	Prof	Wright State		PHD	71	Geo St	
Rencher, Robert	Assoc	Liberty		MBA	81	Fairl Dick	1991
Renner, Donald E.	Prof	Mankato St	ACHR	PHD	78	Cincinnati	1979
Rennie, Henry	Prof	Heidelberg	CFG	PHD	73	Ohio St	1993
Renning, H. Dieter	Emer	CS-Stanislau		DR	61	Freiburg	1970

Name	Rank	School	Fields	Degree	Yr	Institution	Since
Renshaw, Edward F.	Retir	SUNY-Albany	H	PHD	58	Chicago	
Renshaw, Robert H.	Retir	No Illinois	A	PHD	64	Mich St	1965
Reny, Philip	Prof	Pittsburgh	D	PHD	88	Princeton	9-94
Resek, Robert W.	Prof	Illinois	CR	PHD	61	Harvard	1961
Resnick, Stephen A.	Prof	Massachusett		PHD	64	MIT	
Ressler, Rand W.	Asst	SW Louisiana	DJ	PHD	93	Auburn	8-93
Rethwisch, Kurt	Prof	Duquesne		PHD	69	Maryland	1967
Reuther, Carol J.	C-Ac	West Liberty	CDGH	MS	73	Fla St	1991
Revankar, Nagesh S.	Prof	SUNY-Buffalo	DC	PHD	67	Wisconsin	1967
Revier, Charles F.	Assoc	Colorado St	EH	PHD	78	MIT	1974
Rewerts, Glen	C-Ac	Olivet Nazar	K	JD	87	Illinois	1993
Reynolds, Bruce L.	Prof	Union	ODP	PHD	75	Michigan	1974
Reynolds, Douglas	Asst	Alaska-Fairb		PHD			
Reynolds, Morgan O.	Prof	Texas A&M	J	PHD	71	Wisconsin	1974
Reynolds, R. Larry	Prof	Boise State	BID	PHD	77	Wash St	1979
Reynolds, Stanley	H-Pr	Arizona		PHD	83	Nrthwstrn	1982
Reynolds, Stephen E.	Assoc	Utah		PHD	69	Wisconsin	1969
Rezvani, Farahmand	Assoc	Montclair St	ACGH	PHD	83	CUNY	1984
Rhoads, Thomas	Asst	Towson		PHD	99	Wyoming	1999
Rhode, Paul	Assoc	No Carolina	N	PHD	90	Stanford	1990
Rhodes, George F.	Retir	Colorado St	LC	PHD	74	Tx A&M	1978
Rhodus, W. Gregory	Asst	Bentley	ACG	MA	75	Conn	1992
Ricciardi, Joseph M.	Assoc	Babson	EO	PHD	85	Tx-Austin	1985
Rice, Edward M.	Assoc	U Washington		PHD	78	UCLA	1979
Rice, G. Randolph	C-Pr	Louisiana St	C	PHD	70	Kentucky	1969
Thomas J. Singletary Business Partnership Professor							
Rice, Walter E.	Prof	Cal Poly-SLO		PHD	73	Claremont	1964
Rich, Daniel P.	Assoc	Illinois St	DJ	PHD	87	Houston	1987
Rich, Stuart	Retir	Wis-Whitewat		DBA	60	Indiana	1959
Richard, James S.	Assoc	Regis-CO		PHD	80	Tx-Austin	1979
Richard, Jean Francois	Prof	Pittsburgh	C	PHD	73	Louvain	1991
Richards, Alan	Prof	Ca-Santa Crz	ONQ	PHD	75	Wisconsin	1976
Richards, Daniel J.	Assoc	Tufts	E	PHD	81	Yale	1985
Richards, Donald G.	Prof	Indiana St	FO	PHD	83	Conn	1985
Richards, Randy	Assoc	St Ambrose		PHD	96	Iowa	1989
Richardson, David H.	C-Pr	St Lawrence	CJEF	PHD	63	Purdue	1979
Charles A. Dana Professor of Economics							
Richardson, Gary	Asst	Calif-Irvine		PHD	99	Berkeley	1999
Richardson, Harry W.	Prof	So Calif		MA	61	Manchester	1975
Richardson, J. David	Prof	Syracuse	F	PHD	70	Michigan	
Richardson, James A.	Prof	Louisiana St	H	PHD	71	Michigan	1970
Alumni Professor of Economics; Director Public Administration Institute							
Richter, Marcel K.	Prof	Minnesota		PHD	59	MIT	1959
Rickman, Bill D.	Prof	Fort Hays St	DEJ	PHD	82	Okla St	1972
Rickman, Dan S.	Prof	Oklahoma St	RC	PHD	87	Wyoming	1996
OG&E Chair in Regional Economic Analysis							
Riddell, Thomas A.	Assoc	Smith	AHNO	PHD	75	American	1980
Ridder, Geert	Prof	J Hopkins		PHD	87	Amsterdm	1998
Rider, Christine	Prof	St John's		PHD	79	New Sch	1976
Rider, Robert L.	C-Ac	CS-S Marcos	CDHK	PHD	89	S Calif	1992
Ridgway, Terry R.	Assoc	Nev-L Vegas	D	PHD	74	Arizona	1968
Rieber, Michael	Prof	Arizona		PHD	63	MIT	1978
Rieber, William J.	Prof	Butler	F	PHD	79	Pittsburgh	1989
Rieder, Mary	Prof	Winona State		PHD	72		
Riefler, Roger F.	Prof	Nebraska	R	PHD	66	U Wash	1973
Ries, Christine P.	C-Pr	Georgia Tech		PHD	77	Chicago	1997
Riker, David	Asst	Ca-San Diego	FEC	PHD	96	MIT	1996
Riley, John G.	Prof	UCLA		PHD	72	MIT	1973
Riley, Robert	Assoc	St Thomas-MN	F	PHD	91	Wisconsin	
Riley, Teresa M.	Assoc	Youngstown		PHD	84	Syracuse	1984
Rima, Ingrid H.	Prof	Temple	B	PHD	51	Penn	1946
Rinehart, James R.	C-Pr	Fran Marion		PHD	62	Virginia	
Phillip N. Truluck Professor of Economics and Public Policy							
Ring, David W.	Assoc	SUNY-Oneonta	DEPR	PHD	82	SUNY-SBr	1981
Ring, Raymond J. Jr.	Prof	South Dakota		PHD	73	Kansas	1978
Ringel, Jeanne	Asst	Louisiana St	D	PHD	97	Maryland	8-97
Rioja, Felix K.	Asst	Georgia St	EFG	PHD	97	Ariz St	1997
Riordan, Michael H.	Prof	Columbia	LD	PHD	81	Berkeley	1999
Rios, Roberto J.	Asst	CUNY-Lehman		PHD	87	Columbia	1979
Rios-Rull, Jose-Victor	Asst	Pennsylvania	O	PHD	90	Minnesota	1990
Simon Kuznets Term Assistant Profess of Econ; email vr0j@anaga.sas.upenn.edu							
Riskin, Carl A.	Prof	CUNY-Queens	POQ	PHD	69	Berkeley	1974
Ritchey, Barry	Prof	Anderson U	DHR	PHD	88	Syracuse	1991
Ritenour, Shawn	Asst	SW Baptist		PHD		Auburn	1997
Rittenberg, Libby T.	Prof	Colorado Col		PHD	80	Rutgers	1989
Rittenoure, R. Lynn	Deces	Tulsa		PHD	70	Tx-Austin	1977
Rivera-Batiz, Francisco L.	Assoc	Columbia	FOJ	PHD	79	MIT	1991
Rivers, Mary J.	Assoc	Seattle	CDM	PHD	82	Pittsburgh	1978
Rives, Janet M.	Prof	No Iowa	ADJM	PHD	71	Duke	1984
Rivkin, Steven G.	Asst	Amherst	AIJ	PHD	91	UCLA	1993

Rizvi, Saiyid A.	C-Pr	Vermont	BDF	PHD	90	New Sch	1987
Rizzo, Mario J.	Assoc	New York U	K	PHD	77	Chicago	1979
Roayaei, A. Jean	Assoc	Fayetteville		PHD	84	Fla St	
Rob, Rafael	Prof	Pennsylvania		PHD	81	UCLA	1984
Robbani, Mohammad G.	Asst	Alabama A&M	GO	PHD	94	Fla Intl	9-94
Robbins, Edward	Assoc	Manhattan		PHD	86	Stanford	1997
Robbins, Roy E.	C-As	St Marys-Txs		MA	75	St MryTX	
Roberts, Bee-Yan	Assoc	Penn State	O	PHD	80	Wisconsin	1981
Roberts, Charles A.	Assoc	W Kentucky	BN	PHD	79	Georgia	1969
Roberts, Helen	Lect	Ill-Chicago	E	PHD	95	Chicago	1995
Roberts, Kenneth D.	Prof	Southwestern	GEOT	PHD	80	Wisconsin	1981
Roberts, Mark C.	Assoc	Mich Tech		PHD	85	Arizona	1985
Roberts, Mark J.	Prof	Penn State	D	PHD	80	Wisconsin	1980
Roberts, Ray C. Jr.	Retir	Furman		PHD	61	N Carol	1969
Roberts, William W.	Prof	CS-Northrdge		PHD	74	Ca-SnDgo	1973
Robertson, Gary L.	Assoc	Aquinas		MA		Detroit	1969
Robertson, Marvin	Prof	Harding	EDK	JD	73	Arkansas	8-79
Robertson, Raymond	Asst	Macalester	AEF	PHD	97	Texas	1999
Robertson, Robert L. Jr.	Retir	Mt Holyoke		PHD	60	Wisconsin	1962
Robins, Philip K.	C-Pr	U Miami	IJ	PHD	72	Wisconsin	1982
Robinson, James A.	Asst	So Calif		PHD	93	Yale	1995
Robinson, Judith	Inst	W New Eng		MA	86	Mass	1998
Robinson, Michael D.	C-Ac	Mt Holyoke		PHD	87	Tx-Austin	1988
Robinson, Ned Stephen	Assoc	N Car-Wilmin	A	PHD	73	Oklahoma	
Robinson, William J.	Asst	Nev-L Vegas	A	PHD	83	Colorado	1980
Robison, H. David	Assoc	LaSalle	LQC	PHD	83	Maryland	1988
Robison, K. Wayne	Prof	Wash & Jeff		MBA	79	Ohio St	1979
Robles, Jack	Asst	Colorado		PHD	96	Ca-SnDgo	1996
Robson, Denise A.	Asst	Wis-Oshkosh	AF	PHD	93	Nebraska	1994
Roca, Sergio G.	Deces	Adelphi		PHD	75	Rutgers	1971
Roche, John T.	Assoc	St John Fshr		PHD	81	Mass	1981
Rochon, Louis-Phillip	Asst	Kalamazoo		PHD	98	New Sch	1999
Rock, Charles Patrick	Prof	Rollins		PHD	86	Cornell	1984
Rock, James M.	Prof	Utah		PHD	66	Nrthwstrn	1967
Rock, Steven M.	Prof	W Illinois	AJ	PHD	75	Nrthwstrn	1990
Rockoff, Hugh T.	Prof	Rutgers-N Br	N	PHD	72	Chicago	1971
Rockwood, Charles E.	Emer	Florida St	O	PHD	63	Indiana	1960
Rodgers, James D.	Prof	Penn State	HK	PHD	70	Virginia	1969
Rodgers, William	Asst	Wm & Mary		PHD	93	Harvard	1993
Rodgers, Yana	Asst	Wm & Mary		PHD	93	Harvard	1993
Rodriguez, Ada	Lect	CUNY-Lehman		MBA			
Rodriguez, Alvaro	Assoc	Rutgers-Newk		PHD	82	Columbia	1994
Rodriguez, Carolyn	Asst	CS-San Bern	E	PHD	95	Ca-Rivers	1995
Rodriguez, Francisco	Asst	Maryland		PHD	98	Harvard	1998
Rodriguez, Louis J.	Prof	Midwest St	EF	PHD	63	LSU	1081
Roe, R. David	C-Pr	Furman		PHD	78	Duke	1977
Roehl, Richard	Prof	Mich-Dearbor	BJNR	PHD	68	Berkeley	1976
Roelofs, Matthew	Asst	Western Wash	DL	PHD	96	Purdue	1997
Roemer, John E.	Prof	Cal-Davis	DP	PHD	74	Berkeley	1974
Roemer, Michael	Deces	Harvard		PHD	68	MIT	1974
Rogers, Augustus J.	Deces			PHD	69	Mich St	
Rogers, Carol Ann	Assoc	Georgetown		PHD	83	Princeton	1984
Rogers, Cynthia	Asst	Oklahoma	JR	PHD	94	Pittsburgh	1997
Rogers, Kevin	Asst	Miss State		PHD	96	Georgia	1996
Rogers, Mary T.	Assoc	Framingham		PHD	89	Mass	
Rogers, Robert	Assoc	Ashland		PHD	83	Geo Wash	1993
Rogers, Walter B.	Retir	Mid Tenn St		PHD	69	Okla St	1981
Rogerson, Richard D.	Prof	Pennsylvania		PHD	84	Minnesota	1997
Rogerson, William P.	Prof	Northwestern		PHD	81	Cal Tech	
Rogoff, Kenneth S.	Prof	Princeton		PHD	80	MIT	
Rohacek, Jerry K.	Prof	Alaska-Ancho	DEN	MA	69	Ca-SnBarb	1973
Rohlf, William D. Jr.	Prof	Drury		PHD	72	Kansas St	1972
Roistacher, Elizabeth A.	Prof	CUNY-Queens	RH	PHD	72	Penn	1974
Roley, V. Vance	Prof	U Washington		PHD	77	Harvard	1983
Roller, Lars-Hendrik	Prof	INSEAD		PHD	87	Penn	9-87
Rolleston, Barbara Sherman	C-Ac	Baldwin-Wal	HR	PHD	83	Cornell	1983
Rollosson, Michael	Inst	Rhodes		ABD			1993
Roman, Paul D.	Retir	St Louis		PHD	67	St Louis	1966
Romano, Richard E.	Prof	Florida	THOD	PHD	82	Pittsburgh	1982
Romans, Thomas J.	Assoc	SUNY-Buffalo	HR	PHD	63	Brown	1967
Romeo, Charles J.	Asst	Rutgers-N Br	C	PHD	89	Duke	1990
Romer, Christina D.	Prof	Cal-Berkeley		PHD	85	MIT	1988
Romer, David H.	Prof	Cal-Berkeley		PHD	85	MIT	1988
Romig, Rodney	Dean	Hawaii Pacif		PHD	75	Nebraska	8-87
Romps, John F.	C-Ac	St Anselm	ABEH	MA	68	Fordham	1968
Ronaghy, Hassan A.	Retir	Youngstown		PHD	69	Wisconsin	
Rook, Sarah P.	Assoc	SC-Spartanbu	ADEQ	PHD	80	N Car St	1980
Rooney, Patrick	Assoc	Ind-Purdue/I	JH	PHD	87	Notre Dm	1987
Rooney, Robert F.	Prof	CS-Long Bch		PHD	65	Stanford	1970
Roper, Don E.	Prof	Colorado		PHD	70	Chicago	1985

Name	Rank	School	Fields	Degree	Yr	Degree From	Hired
Rork, Jonathan	Asst	New Hampshir				Stanford	1999
Ros, Jaime	Prof	Notre Dame	OE	PHD	78	Cambridge	1990
Rosa, Duane J.	Assoc	West Tx A&M	EOQ	PHD	89	Tx Tech	1984
Rose, David C.	Assoc	Mo-St Louis	CDIJ	PHD	87	Virginia	1985
Rose, Elaina	Asst	U Washington		PHD	93	Penn	1993
Rose, Louis	Prof	Hawaii-Manoa		PHD	70	UCLA	1969
Rose, Margarita M.	Asst	King's Col		PHD	89	Notre Dm	9-90
Rose, Mary B.	SLect	U Lancaster		PHD		Manchest	
Rose, Nancy E.	Prof	CS-San Bern	IN	PHD	85	MIT	1985
Rosefielde, Steven	Prof	No Carolina	P	PHD	72	Harvard	1970
Rosegger, Gerhard	Emer	Case Western	OFND	DIUR	53	Austria	1965
Frank Tracy Carlton Professor Emeritus of Economics							
Roseman, Robert E.	Assoc	Wash State		PHD	82	Minnesota	1983
Rosen, George	Retir	Ill-Chicago		PHD	49	Princeton	
Rosen, Harvey S.	Prof	Princeton		PHD	74	Harvard	1974
Rosen, Harvey S.	Retir	Cleveland St		PHD	69	Case Wes	1967
Rosen, Sherwin	Prof	Chicago		PHD	66	Chicago	1977
Edwin A. and Betty L. Bergman Professor of Economis & Social Sciences							
Rosenbaum, Dan	Asst	N Car-Greens	JI	PHD	98	Nrthwstrn	1998
Rosenbaum, David I.	Prof	Nebraska		PHD	85	Wisconsin	1985
Rosenberg, Nathan	Prof	Stanford		PHD	55	Wisconsin	
Fairleigh S. Dickinson, Jr., Professor of Public Policy							
Rosenberg, Richard	Retir	Penn State	A	PHD	69	Minnesota	1965
Rosenberg, Richard E.	Assoc	Wis-Parkside	FOP	PHD	70	Wisconsin	1969
Rosenberg, Sam	Prof	Roosevelt		PHD	75	Berkeley	1982
Rosenblat, Tanya S.	Asst	Wesleyan-CT	E	PHD	99	MIT	1999
Rosenbloom, Joshua L.	Assoc	Kansas	NJ	PHD	88	Stanford	1988
Rosendorff, Peter	Asst	So Calif		PHD	93	Columbia	1992
Rosenthal, Jean-Laurent	Prof	UCLA		PHD	88	Cal Tech	1988
Rosenthal, Robert A.	Prof	Stonehill	AI	PHD	78	Boston U	1975
Rosenthal, Robert W.	Prof	Boston Univ	CD	PHD	71	Stanford	1987
Rosenthal, Stuart S.	Prof	Syracuse	RHG	PHD	86	Wisconsin	
Rosenzweig, Mark R.	C-Pr	Pennsylvania	OJL	PHD	73	Columbia	1990
Rosovsky, Henry	Emer	Harvard		PHD	59	Harvard	1965
Lewis P. and Linda L. Geyser University Professor, Emeritus							
Ross, Clark G.	Prof	Davidson	P	PHD	76	Boston C	1979
Frontis Johnston Professor of Economics							
Ross, David R.	C-Ac	Bryn Mawr		PHD	84	Nrthwstrn	1992
Ross, Howard N.	Prof	CUNY-Baruch		PHD	64	Columbia	1964
Ross, Larry L.	Prof	Alaska-Ancho	ADE	MS	71	Oregon	1971
Ross, Robert P.	Assoc	Bloomsburg		MA	58	Wash U	1967
Ross, Stephen	Asst	Connecticut	R	PHD	94	Syracuse	1994
Ross, Stephen A.	Prof	MIT	G	PHD	69	Harvard	1998
Franco Modiglani Professor of Finance and Economics							
Ross, Thomas A.	Assoc	Baldwin-Wal	CG	MA		Bowl Gr	
Ross, William N.	Retir	Clarion		PHD	71	Kansas St	1972
Rossana, Robert J.	C-Pr	Wayne State		PHD	80	J Hopkins	1991
Rosser, J. Barkley Jr.	Prof	Jms Madison	R	PHD	76	Wisconsin	1977
Rosser, Marina V.	Assoc	Jms Madison	FP	PHD	79	MoscowSt	1987
Rossi, Armond A.	Asst	Frostburg St		PHD	93	W Virginia	1988
Rossiter, Rosemary D.	Assoc	Ohio Univ		PHD	80	Wi-Milwa	1983
Rossman, Joseph E.	Assoc	Tx A&M-Kings		PHD	75	Iowa St	1976
Rossman, Kathleen	Asst	Birminghm So		PHD	99	Colorado	1999
Rotella, Elyce J.	Assoc	Indiana		PHD	77	Penn	1981
Roth, Alvin E.	Prof	Harvard		PHD	74	Stanford	
Roth, David	Asst	Santa Clara		PHD	92	Yale	1997
Roth, Margarete P.	C-Pr	Benedictn-IL	FA	PHD	67	Cologne	1970
Roth, Timothy P.	C-Pr	Txs-El Paso	AD	PHD	70	Tx A&M	1970
A.B. Templeton Professor							
Rotheim, Roy J.	Prof	Skidmore		PHD	77	Rutgers	1980
Rothenberg, Jerome	Retir	MIT	R	PHD	54	Columbia	1966
Rothenberg, Winnie	Assoc	Tufts	N	PHD	85	Brandeis	1986
Rothenburg, Thomas J.	Prof	Cal-Berkeley		PHD	66	MIT	1966
Rothman, Philip	Assoc	East Carol	CE	PHD	90	NYU	1992
Rothschild, Robert	Read	U Lancaster		MA		Capetown	
Rothstein, Paul	Assoc	Wash Univ	H	PHD	88	Berkeley	1988
Rothstein, Sheldon H.	Asst	NE Illinois		MA		Chicago	
Rottenberg, Simon	Retir	Massachusett		PHD	50	Harvard	1971
Roubini, Nouriel	Assoc	New York U	EF	PHD	88	Harvard	1995
Roufagalas, John	Assoc	Radford	DGE	PHD	83	Florida	1985
Roumasset, James A.	Prof	Hawaii-Manoa		PHD	73	Wisconsin	1976
Rous, Jeffrey	Asst	North Texas	HI	PHD	96	N Carol	1996
Rouse, Cecilia		Princeton					
Rousseau, Peter L.	Asst	Vanderbilt	EM	PHD	95	NYU	1995
Routledge, Bryan	Asst	Carnegie Mel		PHD	95	Brit Colum	1995
Rowe, John W.	Prof	South Fla	D	PHD	66	Illinois	1979
Rowland, Patrick	Asst	Fordham		PHD	98	Ca-SnBarb	1996
Rowley, Charles K.	Prof	George Mason		PHD	64	Nottinghm	1984
Roy, Raj	Prof	Toledo	F	PHD	68	Wayne St	1963
Roy, Santanu	Assoc	Fla Internat	DLQF	PHD	91	Cornell	1998

Name	Rank	School	Fields	Degree	Yr	Institution	Joined
Roy, Suddhasatwa	Asst	CS-Fullerton	LF	PHD	96	Purdue	1998
Roy, Tapan K.	Assoc	Eastern Conn		PHD	80	Temple	1977
Roy, Udayan	Assoc	Lg Isl-Post		PHD	91	SUNY-SBr	
Royalty, Anne B.	Asst	Ind-Purdue/I	J	PHD	93	Yale	1999
Rubenson, Daniel L.	Prof	So Oregon St	CEG	PHD	85	Car Mellon	1986
Rubin, Jeffrey I.	Prof	Rutgers-N Br	H	PHD	75	Duke	1973
Rubin, Paul	Prof	Emory	K	PHD	70	Purdue	1991
Rubin, Rose M.	Prof	Memphis	JI	PHD	68	Kansas St	1994
Rubinfeld, Daniel L.	Prof	Cal-Berkeley		PHD	72	MIT	1983
Rubinstein, Ariel	Prof	Princeton		PHD	79	Hebrew	
Rucci, Anthony	Dean	Ill-Chicago		PHD	78	Bowl Gr	1998
Ruccio, David F.	Assoc	Notre Dame	BO	PHD	84	Mass	1982
Rucker, Randal R.	Assoc	Montana St		PHD	84	U Wash	1991
Ruffer, Rochelle L.	Asst	Youngstown	DH	PHD	94	Wisconsin	1995
Ruffin, Roy J.	Prof	Houston	F	PHD	67	Nrthwstrn	1976
Ruggiero, John	Assoc	Dayton	R	PHD	95	Syracuse	1995
Ruhm, Christopher J.	Prof	N Car-Greens	JI	PHD	84	Berkeley	1991
Ruiz, Nestor M.	Assoc	CS-Pomona		PHD	89	Ca-Davis	1990
Rummery, Sarah	Asst	S F Austin	J	PHD	94	Austr Natl	1998
Rumore, Nancy C.	Inst	SW Louisiana		MS	80	LSU	
Rundle, Steve	Asst	Biola	DEFN	PHD	97	Claremont	1998
Rungeling, Brian S.	Prof	Cen Florida	J	PHD	69	Kentucky	1981
Rupp, Daniel G.	Deces	Fort Hays St	AFH	PHD	81	Kansas St	1968
Ruppel, Fred J.	C-Ac	E Kentucky		PHD	84	Maryland	1997
Ruprecht, Theodore K.	Retir	CS-Humboldt		PHD		Berkeley	1958
Rusek, Antonin	Assoc	Susquehanna	EFP	PHD	84	SUNY-SBr	1986
Rush, Lynda M.	Prof	CS-Pomona		PHD	84	Ca-Davis	1986
Rush, Mark	Prof	Florida	EF	PHD	82	Rochester	1982
Rushing, Francis W.	Prof	Georgia St	ANP	PHD	67	N Carol	1974
Holder of the Eugenia A. and Bernard B. Ramsey Chair of Private Enterprise							
Russell, Clifford S.	Prof	Vanderbilt	HQ	PHD	68	Harvard	1986
Russell, Louise B.	Prof	Rutgers-N Br	I	PHD	71	Harvard	1987
Russell, Malcolm B.	Prof	Andrews	EN	PHD	78	J Hopkins	1979
Russell, Milton	Prof	Tennessee		PHD	63	Oklahoma	1987
Russell, Paul	Prof	Buena Vista		EDD	65	N Colo	9-67
Russell, R. K.	Prof	SW Okla St		PHD	82	Okla St	1973
Russell, R. Robert	Prof	Cal-Riversid	ADH	PHD	65	Harvard	1986
Russell, Steven	Asst	Ind-Purdue/I		PHD	89	Minnesota	1993
Russell, Thomas R.	Assoc	Santa Clara		PHD	73	Cambridge	1978
Russell, William R.	Prof	So Methodist	D	PHD	64	U Wash	1971
Russo, Benjamin	Assoc	N Car-Charl		PHD	85	Iowa	1984
Russo, Daniel M.	Retir	East Tenn St		BA	61	Rutgers	1967
Russo, Gerard G.	Assoc	Hawaii-Manoa		PHD	89	Nrthwstrn	1987
Rust, John P.	Prof	Yale		PHD	83	MIT	
Rutherford, Thomas F.	Assoc	Colorado		PHD	87	Stanford	1995
Rutman, Gilbert L.	Retir	S Ill-Edward	JKD	PHD	65	Duke	1969
Rutstrom, Lisa	Assoc	So Carolina	DFQ	PHD	90	Stockholm	8-91
Ruttan, Vernon W	Emer	Minnesota		PHD	52	Chicago	1976
Regents' Professor							
Ruud, Paul A.	Prof	Cal-Berkeley		PHD	81	MIT	1981
Ryan, Daniel	Asst	Temple	PL	PHD	90	Berkeley	1990
Ryan, Julie	Asst	Immaculata		MA		St MryCA	1999
Ryan, Peter C.	Asst	Framingham		PHD	77	Mass	
Ryan, Timothy P.	Dean	New Orleans		PHD	78	Ohio St	1978
Hibernia Professor of Economics							
RyanMann, Duncan	Assoc	SUNY-Empire	I	PHD	84	Penn	
Rychtanek, Leonard E.	Prof	No Alabama		PHD	79	Fla St	1983
Rycroft, Robert S.	Prof	Mary Wash	CHJG	PHD	78	Maryland	1977
Ryder, Harl E.	Prof	Brown		PHD	67	Stanford	1965
Saadatmand, Yassaman	Assoc	Armstrong At	FO	PHD	88	NewHamp	1989
Saari, Donald G.	Prof	Northwestern		PHD	67	Purdue	
Saavedra, Luz A.	Asst	South Fla	F	PHD	98	Illinois	1998
Saba, Richard P.	Assoc	Auburn		PHD	74	Tx A&M	1974
Sabbarese, Donald M.	Assoc	Kennesaw St	AEM	PHD	84	Geo St	1978
Sabella, Edward M.	Prof	Augsburg		PHD	71	Minnesota	1961
Sabi, Manijeh	Adj	Russell Sage	EGO	MA	86	Northeas	1988
Sable, Karin	Asst	Puget Sound	AHQ	PHD	97	Colo St	1997
Saboori, Farhad	Assoc	Albright		PHD	85	Indiana	1986
Sabot, Richard	Prof	Williams		DPHI	73	Oxford	
John J. Gibson Emeritus Professor of Economics							
Sacerdote, Bruce I.	Asst	Dartmouth		PHD	98	Harvard	1998
Sachs, Jeffrey D.	Prof	Harvard		PHD	80	Harvard	1983
Galen L. Stone Professor of International Trade							
Sackrey, Charles Melvin	C-Ac	Bucknell	A	PHD	65	Tx-Austin	1980
Sacks, Stephen R.	Prof	Connecticut	H	PHD	71	Berkeley	1971
Sadler, Michael A.	Asst	Kansas State	EO	PHD	97	Tx-Austin	1996
Sadler, Thomas	Asst	Pace		PHD			1997
Safarzadeh, Mohammad R.	Prof	CS-Pomona		PHD	84	Claremont	1987
Saffer, Henry	Assoc	Kean		PHD	77	CUNY	9-85

Name	Rank	School	Fields	Degree	Yr	Degree School	Year
Saffran, Bernard	Prof	Swarthmore	AH	PHD	63	Minnesota	1973
Franklin and Betty Barr Professor of Economics							
Saft, Lester F.	Prof	CS-Northrdge		PHD	76	UCLA	1971
Sage, Lewis C.	Assoc	Baldwin-Wal	CIJ	PHD	85	Maryland	1985
Saggi, Kamal	Asst	So Methodist	FLO	PHD	95	Penn	1995
Sahai, Sirman	Asst	Tuskegee		PHD	95	Auburn	1995
Sahu, Anandi P.	Assoc	Oakland	EG	PHD	85	Wash U	1985
Sakai, Marcia	Assoc	Hawaii-Hilo		PHD	85	Hi-Manoa	1991
Sakano, Ryoichi	Asst	N Carol A&T		PHD	90	Alabama	1992
Sakata, Shinichi	Asst	Michigan					
Sakellaris, Plutarchos	Assoc	Maryland		PHD	92	Harvard	1992
Sala-i-Martin, Xavier	Prof	Columbia	OE	PHD	90	Harvard	1996
Salant, Stephen W.	Prof	Michigan		PHD	73	Penn	1981
Salazar-Carrillo, Jorge	Prof	Fla Internat	OFA	PHD	67	Berkeley	
Sale, Tom S. III	Retir	Louisiana Te		PHD	72	LSU	1965
Salehi-Esfahani, Haideh	SLect	U Washington		PHD	85	Penn	1990
Salehi-Isfahani, Djavad	H-Ac	Virg Tech	OT	PHD	77	Harvard	1984
Salemi, Michael K.	Prof	No Carolina	E	PHD	76	Minnesota	1976
Zachary Smith Professor							
Salib, Anis B.	Retir	Alabama A&M	AI	PHD	72	Vanderbilt	1982
Saliba, Michael T.	Assoc	Loyola-N Orl	ADM	PHD	72	Oklahoma	1973
Saltzman, Cynthia J.	H-Ac	Widener	EFGO	PHD	86	Maryland	1980
Saltzman, Gregory M.	Assoc	Albion		PHD	82	Wisconsin	1982
Salvatore, Dominick	C-Pr	Fordham		PHD	71	CUNY	1970
Salvucci, Richard	Prof	Trinity	N	PHD	82	Princeton	
Salyards, Donald M.	Prof	Winona State		PHD	75	Kansas St	1975
Salyer, Kevin D.	Assoc	Cal-Davis	EG	PHD	85	Ca-SnBarb	1990
Samanta, Subarna K.	C-Ac	C New Jersey		PHD	85	So Meth	1987
Samprone, Joseph C. Jr.	Prof	Georgia Col	AD	PHD	75	Ca-SnBarb	1983
Samson, Mike	Asst	Williams		PHD	94	Stanford	
Samuels, George E.	Prof	Sam Houston		PHD	72	Oregon	1975
Samuels, Warren J.	Retir	Michigan St		PHD	57	Wisconsin	1968
Samuelson, Larry W.	Prof	Wisconsin		PHD	78	Illinois	
Samuelson, Paul A.	Retir	MIT	D	PHD	41	Harvard	1940
Samwick, Andrew A.	Asst	Dartmouth		PHD	93	MIT	1994
Sanchez, Nicolas	Assoc	Holy Cross	DENO	PHD	72	S Calif	1977
Sandberg, Lars G.	Retir	Ohio State	NO	PHD	64	Harvard	
Sandberg, Michael L.	Prof	Coe	EJKM	PHD	76	Iowa	1976
Louie J. & Ella Pocho Bradsky Professor of Bus Adm; Assoc Dean of Faculty							
Sander, William III	Prof	DePaul	RD	PHD	78	Cornell	1989
Sanders, Seth	Assoc	Maryland		PHD	93	Chicago	1999
Sanders, William V.	Prof	Clarion		PHD	81	Penn St	1981
Sanderson, Allen	SLect	Chicago		MA	70	Chicago	
Sanderson, Patricia L.	Assoc	Miss State		PHD	77	Oklahoma	1979
Sanderson, Warren	C-Pr	SUNY-Stony B		PHD	74	Stanford	1989
Sandfort, Mihre	Asst	So Methodist	DL	PHD	94	Wisconsin	1997
Sandholm, William	Asst	Wisconsin		PHD	98	Nrthwstrn	1998
Sandler, Todd M.	Prof	Iowa State	HD	PHD	71	SUNY-Bin	1986
Sands, Barbara N.	Assoc	Arizona		PHD	85	U Wash	1985
Sandy, Jonathan G.	Assoc	San Diego		PHD	86	Ca-SnBarb	1986
Sandy, Robert	C-Ac	Ind-Purdue/I	J	PHD	77	Mich St	1974
Santerre, Rexford E.	Prof	Bentley	DHI	PHD	83	Conn	1983
Santoni, Gary J.	Prof	Ball State	E	PHD	72	New Mex	1988
Santoni, Matthew V.	Inst	USAF Academy		MS	90	Penn St	
Santopietro, George D.	Prof	Radford	QDK	PHD	86	Va Tech	1987
Santore, Rudy	Asst	Tennessee		PHD	98	Ohio St	1999
Santos, Manuel	Prof	Arizona St		PHD	84	Chicago	1999
Bank One Professor							
Santos, Richard	Assoc	New Mexico	IJ	PHD	77	Mich St	1989
Sanz, Ernesto	C-Pr	Mass-Lowell	FNP	PHD	75	Boston C	
Saposnik, Rubin	Emer	Georgia St	D	PHD	59	Minnesota	1970
Sappington, David A.	Prof	Florida	TD	PHD	80	Princeton	1989
Lanzillotti-McKethan Eminent Scholar							
Sapra, Sunil	Prof	CS-L Angeles		PHD	83	Columbia	1991
Sapsford, David	Prof	U Lancaster		PHD		Leeds	
Sara, Tejinder S.	H-Ac	Tuskegee		PHD	75	Mass	1973
Sarauiti, Brett	Asst	Hawaii Pacif		PHD	97	Nrthwstrn	1997
Sardy, Hyman	Prof	CUNY-Brookly	C	PHD	63	New Sch	1957
Sargent, Thomas	Prof	Stanford		PHD	68	Harvard	
Sari, Osman	Asst	Bogazici	FG	PHD	93	CUNY	1993
Sarin, Rajiv	Asst	Texas A&M	CD	PHD	94	Ca-SnDgo	9-94
Sarkar, Amin U.	C-Ac	SUNY-Fredoni	OQ	PHD	88	Berkeley	1989
Sarkar, Shyamalendu S.	Prof	Saginaw Vall		PHD	69	Mich St	1969
Sarki, Ayuba J.	Assoc	Hampton		PHD	84	Georgia	1982
Sartos, Joseph	Asst	So Dakota St	E	PHD	96	Rutgers	1997
Sarver, Lee	Assoc	Mid Tenn St	M	PHD	87	Tennessee	1991
Sass, Tim R.	Assoc	Florida St	L	PHD	84	U Wash	1990
Sassone, Peter G.	Deces	Georgia Tech	DH	PHD	73	Purdue	1972
Sato, Kazuo	Prof	Rutgers-N Br	E	PHD	60	Yale	1984

Name	Rank	School	Fields	Degree	Yr	Institution	Year
Sato, Ryuzo	Prof	New York U	CO	PHD	62	J Hopkins	1985
C. V. Starr Professor of Economics							
Satterthwaite, Mark A.	Prof	Northwestern		PHD	73	Wisconsin	1973
Sattinger, Michael	Prof	SUNY-Albany	J	PHD	73	Car Mellon	1981
Sattler, Edward L.	Prof	Bradley		PHD	79	Illinois	1977
Sau, Ranjit	Visit	NJ Inst Tech		PHD	64	Wayne St	1995
Sauer, Christine	Assoc	New Mexico	EF	PHD	87	Brown	1985
Saunders, Kent T.	Asst	LeMoyne	ADG	PHD	95	Clemson	1998
Saunders, Lisa F.	Asst	Massachusett		PHD	87	Berkeley	1987
Saunders, Peter J.	C-Pr	Central Wash	EHQ	PHD	81	Colorado	1988
Saunders, Phillip	Retir	Indiana		PHD	64	MIT	1970
Saurman, David	Prof	San Jose St		PHD	79	Tx A&M	1991
Saussy, Gordon A.	Retir	New Orleans		PHD	72	Yale	1970
Sav, Thomas G.	Prof	Wright State		PHD	81	Geo Wash	1985
Savage, Deborah A.	Asst	So Conn St	I	PHD	93	Conn	
Savage, Ian P.	SLect	Northwestern		PHD	84	Leeds	
Savage, Vernon H.	Retir	SW Texas St		PHD	72	Tx-Austin	1971
Savin, Nathan E.	Prof	Iowa		PHD	69	Berkeley	1986
Saving, Thomas R.	Prof	Texas A&M	DE	PHD	60	Chicago	1968
Distinguished Professor, Jeff Montgomery Prof; Dir Private Enterprise Rsch							
Savitski, David	Asst	Northern St		PHD	97	UCLA	1997
Savoca, Elizabeth A.	Prof	Smith	CEIT	PHD	82	Berkeley	1982
Savvides, Andreas	Assoc	Oklahoma St	FO	PHD	83	Florida	1985
Sawani, Mustafa A.	Prof	Truman State		PHD	85	Missouri	1985
Sawdy, George F.	Asst	Providence	QEH	PHD	83	Brown	
Sawers, Larry B.	Prof	American U		PHD	69	Michigan	1969
Sawhney, Bansi L.	Prof	Baltimore		PHD	75	Geo Wash	1971
Sawtelle, Barbara A.	Prof	Simmons	E	PHD	76	MIT	1970
Sawyer, Juliet	Assoc	Cheyney					
Sawyer, W. Charles	Prof	So Miss	F	PHD	83	Arkansas	1983
Saxonhouse, Gary R.	Prof	Michigan		PHD	71	Yale	1970
Sayre, Edward A.	VAsst	Kenyon	JROA	PHD	99	Texas	7-99
Sazama, Gerald W.	Assoc	Connecticut	H	PHD	67	Wisconsin	1966
Scafidi, Benjamin P.	Asst	Georgia St	HIR	PHD	97	Virginia	1998
Scahill, Edward M.	Assoc	Scranton		PHD	83	SUNY-Bin	1989
Scalet, Kenneth G.	Assoc	York-Penn		MBA		St Johns	1970
Scandizzo, Stefania	Asst	Texas A&M	F	PHD	97	Penn	1997
Scannell, Nancy	Asst	Il-Springfld	AG	PHD	92	Il-Chicago	1996
Scaperlanda, Anthony E.	C-Pr	No Illinois	F	PHD	64	Tx-Austin	1964
Scarf, Herbert E.	Prof	Yale	C	PHD	54	Princeton	1963
Schachter, Gustav	Prof	Northeastern		PHD	62	NYU	1965
Schad, Tom	Asst	Detroit Merc					
Schaefer, Arthur McCluny	Prof	Univ South	CD	PHD	67	Penn	
Schaefer, Donald F.	Prof	Wash State		PHD	67	N Carol	1982
Schaefer, Kurt C.	Assoc	Calvin		PHD	84	Michigan	1987
Schaffer, Beverly K.	Prof	Emory	D	PHD	67	Duke	1965
Schaffer, David	Asst	Wis-Eau Clar	JEH	PHD	90	MIT	1998
Schaffer, William A.	Prof	Georgia Tech	R	PHD	63	Duke	1963
Schall, Lawrence D.	C-Pr	U Washington		PHD	69	Chicago	1967
Schaniel, William C.	Assoc	West Georgia	BP	PHD	85	Tennessee	
Schansberg, D. Eric	Asst	Indiana SE	HJC	PHD	91	Tx A&M	1992
Schap, David J.	Prof	Holy Cross	CDK	PHD	82	Wash U	1981
Schatz, Richard E.	C-Pr	Whitworth	DEFO	PHD	74	Hawaii	1989
Schauer, David A.	Assoc	Txs-El Paso	P	PHD	75	Notre Dm	1975
Scheel, Daniel Curtis	Prof	CS-Sacrament		PHD	70	Oregon	1969
Scheffer, Ronald E.	Assoc	Tri-State		MA		Ohio	1967
Scheinkman, Jose	C-Pr	Chicago		PHD	74	Rochester	1973
Alvin H. Baum Professor							
Schelling, Thomas	Prof	Maryland		PHD	51	Harvard	1991
Schenker, Eric	Emer	Wis-Milwauke		PHD	57	Florida	1959
Scher, Frances	Retir	Montclair St	AHIT	MA		Columbia	1975
Scherer, Philip M.	C-Pr	Niagara		PHD	72	Missouri	1980
Scheuch, Richard	Retir	Trinity-CT	1989	PHD	52	Princeton	1950
Schhwalberg, Barney K.	Retir	Brandeis		PHD	66	Harvard	
Schiantarelli, Fabio	Prof	Boston Coll	CEF	PHD	81	LondonEc	1992
Schibik, Timothy J.	Assoc	So Indiana		PHD	89	W Virginia	1988
Schieren, George A.	C-Ac	Appalach St	CDE	PHD	75	N Carol	1977
Schifrin, Leonard	Retir	Wm & Mary		PHD	64	Michigan	1964
Schilcutt, J. Garland	C-Pr	Lakeland	M	LLD		Marian	1958
Schilling, Donald J.	Retir	Missouri	EF	PHD	67	N Carol	1964
Schiming, Richard C.	Prof	Mankato St	AE	PHD	74	Ohio St	1981
Schlack, Robert F.	C-Pr	Carthage	FPRC	PHD	77	Wayne St	1975
Schlagenhauf, Don E.	Prof	Florida St	E	PHD	77	Illinois	1998
Brim Eminent Scholar Chair							
Schlee, Edward E.	Assoc	Arizona St		PHD	88	Illinois	1990
Schlesinger, Harris	Prof	Alabama		PHD	80	Illinois	1987
Schlottmann, Alan M.	Prof	Tennessee		PHD	75	Wash U	1975
Schmalensee, Richard L.	Dean	MIT	O	PHD	70	MIT	1977
Goldon Y. Billard Professor Economics & Management							
Schmeidler, David	Prof	Ohio State		PHD	69	Hebrew	1987

Schmertmann, Carl P.	Assoc	Florida St	C	PHD	88	Berkeley	1990
Schmidt, David R.	Asst	Indiana		PHD	94	CIT	1993
Schmidt, Edward J.	Assoc	Randolph-Mac	E	MA	67	Maryland	1967
Schmidt, James R.	C-Pr	Nebraska		PHD	78	Rice	1977
Schmidt, Martin	Asst	Portland St		PHD	94	Colo St	1997
Schmidt, Peter J.	Prof	Michigan St		PHD	70	Mich St	1977
University Distinguished Professor							
Schmidt, Robert M.	Assoc	Richmond		PHD	81	Duke	1981
Schmidt, Shelton S.	Prof	Union	LCA	PHD	77	Virginia	1974
Schmidt, Stephen J.	Asst	Union	LCD	PHD	95	Stanford	1994
Schmidt, Torsten	C-Ac	New Hampshir	DL	PHD	90	Florida	1988
Schmitz, Suzanne	Asst	Elmhurst		PHD	89	Kentucky	1990
Schneider, Geoffrey	Asst	Bucknell	NOBA	ABD	97	N Carol	9-96
Schneider, Lynn	Asst	Auburn-Montg		PHD	96	Houston	1998
Schnell, John F.	Prof	Alabama-Hunt	J	PHD	84	Illinois	1990
Schodt, David W.	Prof	St Olaf	OAH	PHD	80	Wisconsin	1977
Schoening, Niles C.	Prof	Alabama-Hunt	R	PHD	83	Tennessee	1983
Schofield, Norman J.	Prof	Wash Univ	DH	PHD	76	Essex	1986
William Taussig Professor of Political Economy							
Scholland, Ken	Assoc	Hawaii Pacif	MLFB	MSFB		Geotown	1991
Scholz, J. Karl	Assoc	Wisconsin		PHD	88	Stanford	1988
Schotter, Andrew	C-Pr	New York U	D	PHD	73	NYU	1975
Schrag, Joel	Asst	Emory	DKL	PHD	93	Berkeley	1993
Schran, Peter	Retir	Illinois		PHD	61	Berkeley	1965
Schreiber, Max M.	Assoc	W Carolina		PHD	78	S Carol	1977
Schroeder, Edward A.	Assoc	Nazareth		PHD	80	UCLA	1988
Schroeter, John R.	Assoc	Iowa State	L	PHD	81	Minnesota	1983
Schuh, G. Edward	Prof	Minnesota		PHD	61	Chicago	1979
Schuhmann, Peter	Asst	N Car-Wilmin	Q	PHD	96	N Car St	
Schulman, Craig	Assoc	Arkansas	F	PHD	89	Tx A&M	1989
Schultz, Brian L.	Prof	Wis-Rvr Fall	C	PHD	80	Notre Dm	1979
Schultz, John A.	Assoc	Shepherd		PHD	85	S Carol	1988
Schultz, T. Paul	Prof	Yale	J	PHD	66	MIT	1975
Schultz, Theodore	Retir	Chicago		PHD	39	Wisconsin	1943
Schulz, Eric	Asst	Williams		PHD	93	Nrthwstrn	
Schumacher, Edward	Asst	East Carol	DIJ	PHD	94	Fla St	1994
Schumacher, Howard	Retir	Kean		MA		Columbia	9-56
Schupack, Mark B.	Emer	Brown		PHD	60	Princeton	1970
Schur, Leon M.	Emer	Wis-Milwauke		PHD	55	Wisconsin	1964
Schutte, David	Prof	Birminghm So		PHD	81	Minnesota	1999
Schuttler, Robert D.	Inst	Marian		MBA	80	Evansville	1985
Schutz, Eric A.	Assoc	Rollins		PHD	82	N Carol	1987
Schwab, Robert M.	Prof	Maryland		PHD	80	J Hopkins	1980
Schwabe, Kurt	Asst	Ohio Univ		PHD	96	N Car St	1996
Schwalbenberg, Henry M.	Asst	Fordham		PHD	88	Columbia	1988
Schwartz, Adina Tzur	Assoc	Lakeland	AEFG	MA		Wi-Milwa	1986
Schwartz, Carol H.	Prof	NY Inst Tech		PHD	63	Columbia	1987
Schwartz, David Lamar	Prof	Albright		MA	64	Mich St	1965
Schwartz, Jesse	Asst	Vanderbilt	DLQ	PHD	99	Maryland	1999
Schwartz, Lisa	Asst	Wingate	EG	PHD	96	Tx-Arlin	1998
Schwartz, Marius	Prof	Georgetown		PHD	82	UCLA	1982
Schwarz, Peter M.	C-Pr	N Car-Charl		PHD	80	Ohio St	1978
Schwarz, Samuel	Prof	CUNY-Stn Isl	KC	PHD	78	Columbia	1986
Schwarz-Miller, Ann V.	Assoc	Old Dominion	DJKM	PHD	74	Nrthwstrn	1978
Schweigert, Thomas E.	Assoc	Wis-Whitewat		PHD	90	Wisconsin	1984
Schweitzer, Robert N.	Prof	San Fran St		PHD	63	Berkeley	1962
Schwer, Keith	Prof	Nev-L Vegas	R	PHD	73	Maryland	1986
Schwinn, Carl R.	Assoc	Bates	IO	PHD	78	Cornell	1975
Schydlowsky, Daniel M.	Prof	American U		PHD	66	Harvard	1990
Scott, Carole Elizabeth	Prof	West Georgia	NO	PHD	69	Geo St	
Scott, Charles E.	Prof	Loyola-Maryl	MJH	PHD	79	Vanderbilt	1985
Scott, Frank A. Jr.	Prof	Kentucky	GH	PHD	79	Virginia	1979
Scott, Gary J.	Asst	St Marys-Txs		PHD	93	Notre Dm	1994
Scott, J. T.	Retir	Iowa State		PHD	57	Iowa St	1955
Scott, John L.	Assoc	NE Louisiana	DC	PHD	90	S Carol	1989
Scott, John T.	Prof	Dartmouth		PHD	76	Harvard	1977
Scott, Loren C.	Emer	Louisiana St	J	PHD	69	Okla St	1969
Scott, Ralph D.	Prof	Hendrix		PHD	83	Tulane	1979
Scott, Robert C.	Prof	Bradley		PHD	75	Iowa	1975
Seaks, Terry G.	Emer	N Car-Greens	C	PHD	72	Duke	1972
Seal, James W.	Assoc	Portland	HRE	PHD	77	Illinois	1977
Seaman, Bruce A.	Assoc	Georgia St	DL	PHD	78	Chicago	1978
Seater, John J.	Prof	N Carol St	EH	PHD	75	Brown	1981
Sebestyen, Zoltan H.	Retir	SUNY-N Paltz	DFA	PHD	68	Columbia	1969
Sechtem, Everett A.	Retir	Neb-Kearney		PHD	86	Nebraska	1970
Seeborg, Michael C.	Prof	Ill Wesleyan	J	PHD	76	Utah	1989
Robert S. Eckley Distinguished Professor of Economics							
Seeley, Robert D.	Assoc	Wilkes	AIJH	PHD	86	Maryland	9-89
Segelhorst, Elbert W.	Retir	CS-Long Bch	1994	PHD	63	Columbia	1964
Segerson, Kathleen	Prof	Connecticut	QD	PHD	84	Cornell	1986

Segerstrom, Paul S.	Prof	Michigan St		PHD	84	Rochester	1984
Seguino, Stephanie	Asst	Vermont	EFOP	PHD	94	American	1995
Seidel, Ethan A.	Prof	W Maryland		PHD	77	J Hopkins	1969
Seidelman, James E.	Dean	Westminst-UT		PHD	86	Utah	1980
Seidenstat, Paul	Assoc	Temple	H	PHD	64	Nrthwstrn	1967
Seidenstricker, Kenneth C.	Retir	Regis-CO		MA		Marquette	
Seidman, Laurence S.	Prof	Delaware	H	PHD	74	Berkeley	1982
Seifried, Edmond J.	Prof	Lafayette	JM	PHD	71	W Virginia	1978
Seiglie, Carlos C.	Assoc	Rutgers-Newk		PHD	91	Chicago	1986
Seiver, Daniel A.	Prof	Miami U-Ohio	TG	PHD	74	Yale	1978
Seiz, Janet A.	C-Ac	Grinnell	BO	PHD	85	Duke	1989
Selassie, Haile G.	Assoc	So Carol St		PHD	83	Okla St	1984
Seldon, Barry	Assoc	Texas-Dallas		PHD	85	Duke	
Selgin, George A.	Assoc	Georgia	EN	PHD	86	NYU	1989
Selim, Mohamed Ali	Assoc	St Thomas-MN	A	PHD	81	Minnesota	1959
Selivanoff, George A.	C-Pr	LaSierra	AF	PHD	64	American	1984
Sell, John W.	C-Pr	Wooster		PHD	81	UCLA	1981
Sellers, Gary	Assoc	Akron	AKL	PHD	77	Cincinnati	1976
Sellgrew, Andrew	Asst	George Mason		PHD	98	Chicago	1999
Selover, David D.	Asst	Old Dominion	F	PHD	91	Ca-SnDgo	1999
Semenick Alam, Ila	Asst	Tulane		PHD	94	Rice	1994
Sen, Amartya K.	Retir	Harvard		PHD	59	Cambridge	1988
Sen, Amit	Asst	Mo-Rolla		PHD	97	N Carol	1997
Sen, Swapan	Assoc	Chris Newpor		PHD	91	Nebraska	1998
Seneca, Joseph J.	Prof	Rutgers-N Br	H	PHD	68	Penn	1976
Seneca, Rosalind S.	Prof	Drew	DL	PHD	71	Penn	1981
Sener, Mehmet F.	Asst	Union	FOEJ	PHD	99	Florida	1999
Sengupta, Jati K.	Prof	Cal-Santa Br	CO	PHD	62	Iowa St	1976
Sent, Esther-Mirjam	Asst	Notre Dame	BE	PHD	94	Stanford	1994
Seo, Tae Kun	Assoc	So Methodist	D	PHD	73	Tx A&M	1973
Seplaki, Les	Prof	Rutgers-Camd		PHD	70	Ca-Rivers	
Seppi, Duane J.	Assoc	Carnegie Mel		PHD	88	Chicago	1986
Serow, William J.	Prof	Florida St	T	PHD	72	Duke	1981
Serrano, Roberto	Prof	Brown		PHD	92	Harvard	
Sertel, Murat	Prof	Bogazici	AC	PHD	71	MIT	1979
Seshu, Chigurupati R.	Assoc	SUNY-N Paltz	AEO	PHD	60	New Sch	1967
Sethi, Rajiv	Asst	Barnard	DQ	PHD	93	New Sch	1995
Setterfield, Mark	Assoc	Trinity-CT		PHD	92	Dalhousie	1992
Settle, Russell F.	Prof	Delaware	H	PHD	74	Wisconsin	1974
Severinov, Sergei	Asst	Wisconsin		PHD	98	Stanford	1998
Sexton, Edwin A.	Prof	Va Military		PHD	87	Illinois	1992
Sexton, Robert L.	Prof	Pepper-Malib	ADNQ	PHD	80	Colorado	1979
Sexton, Terri A.	Prof	CS-Sacrament		PHD	81	Minnesota	1987
Seyfert, Jeff	Asst	S Nazarene		MBA	89	Tulsa	1990
Sfeir, Raymond	Assoc	Chapman	AC	PHD	82	Ca-SnBarb	1985
Sgontz, Larry G.	Emer	Iowa		PHD	64	Illinois	1964
Shaaf, Mohammad	Prof	Central Okla	BDEG	PHD	82	Tx Tech	1980
Shaanan, Joseph	Prof	Bryant	FL	PHD	79	Cornell	
Shabahang, Homa		Chapman	F	PHD	83	Oklahoma	1991
Shaban, Radwan Ali	Assoc	Georgia Tech	DO	PHD	85	Stanford	1991
Shabbir, Tayyeb	Asst	Frank & Mars		PHD	87	Penn	1998
Shachat, Jason	Asst	Ca-San Diego	CD	PHD	96	Arizona	1996
Shackelford, Jean A.	Prof	Bucknell	ABE	PHD	74	Kentucky	1975
Shadbegian, Ronald	Asst	Mass-Dartmou	HKQ	PHD	91	Clark	1993
Shadoan, Donald	Retir	E Kentucky		PHD		Kentucky	1962
Shafer, Wayne	Prof	Illinois	CD	PHD	72	Ca-SnBarb	1990
Shaffer, Linda J.	Prof	CS-Fresno	CJ	PHD	78	Nrthwstrn	1984
Shaffer, Sherrill L.	Prof	Wyoming		PHD	81	Stanford	1997
Shah, Parth	Asst	Mich-Dearbor	EFO	PHD	90	Auburn	1991
Shah, Umanglal	Asst	Albany State		MA	64	Houston	
Shahjahan, Mirza	Assoc	Ark-Pine Blf		PHD		Bonn	
Shalishali, Kasazi	Asst	Tuskegee		PHD	93	Auburn	1993
Shambert, Vladimir M.	Prof	USAF Academy		PHD	52	Moscow	1992
Shandiz, Mohmood	Assoc	Okla City		PHD	81	Okla St	1985
Shane, Richard C.	C-Pr	So Dakota St	Q	PHD	78	Wash St	1977
Shanklin, James T.	Asst	NW Missouri	AD	MS	66	S Illinois	1966
Shannon, John C.	Assoc	Suffolk		MA		Boston C	
Shannon, Lee R.	Assoc	Regis-CO		PHD	70	N Colo	1978
Shapiro, Aharon H.	Prof	St John's		PHD	66	New Sch	1967
Shapiro, David	Assoc	Penn State	J	PHD	72	Princeton	1980
Shapiro, Edward	Retir	Toledo	1994	PHD		Harvard	1967
Shapiro, Harold T.	Prof	Princeton		PHD	64	Princeton	1988
Shapiro, Matthew D.	Prof	Michigan		PHD	84	MIT	1989
Shapiro, Nina	Assoc	St Peters	DEL	PHD		New Sch	1999
Shapiro, Perry	Prof	Cal-Santa Br	DH	PHD	67	Berkeley	1969
Shapiro, Stephen L.	Assoc	North Fla	AH	PHD	72	S Carol	1972
Shapiro, Steven J.	Assoc	New Haven	GKLM	PHD	88	Geotown	9-87
Shapley, Lloyd S.	Prof	UCLA		PHD	53	Princeton	
Sharav, Itzhak	Prof	CUNY-Lehman		PHD	71	CUNY	9-67
Sharif, Mohammed	Assoc	Rhode Island		PHD	83	Boston U	1984

Name	Rank	School	Fields	Degree	Yr	Univ	Since
Shariff, Ismail	C-Pr	WI-Green Bay		PHD	65	Wisconsin	
Sharma, Rajiv	Asst	Portland St		PHD	98	Florida	1998
Sharma, Subhash	Prof	So Illinois	C	PHD	83	Kentucky	1983
Sharma, V. V.	Assoc	Ohio State		PHD	68	Illinois	1970
Sharma, Ved P.	C-Pr	Mankato St	CDT	PHD	77	Wash U	1976
Sharp, Ansel M.	Retir	Univ South		PHD	56	LSU	1985
Sharp, Robert R.	Retir	E Kentucky		PHD	69	Kentucky	1969
Shatten, Richard	Prof	Case Western	HR	MBA	80	Harvard	1997
Shatto, Gloria M.	Prof	Berry		PHD	66	Rice	1979
Shaw, John A. Jr.	Prof	CS-Fresno	DNF	PHD	69	Purdue	1965
Shaw, Kathryn L.	Assoc	Carnegie Mel		PHD	81	Harvard	1981
Shaw, Sue O.	Prof	Longwood		PHD	67	Harvard	1986
Shea, John	Assoc	Maryland		PHD	90	MIT	1996
Sheahan, John B.	Retir	Williams		PHD	54	Harvard	1954
Shearer, Charles L.	Prof	Transylvania		PHD	81	Mich St	
President Transylvania University							
Sheets, Doris Files	Assoc	SW Missouri		PHD	81	Missouri	1974
Sheffield, Howell	Inst	West Alabama		MBA		Alabama	1998
Sheffrin, Steven M.	Dean	Cal-Davis	EH	PHD	76	MIT	1976
Sheflin, Neil	Assoc	Rutgers-N Br	C	PHD	79	Rutgers	1975
Sheftall, Willis B.	Prof	Morehouse		PHD	81	Geo St	1986
Charles E. Merrill Professor of Economics							
Shelburn, Marsha	Prof	So Car-Aiken		PHD	80	N Carol	1980
Shell, Karl	Prof	Cornell		PHD	65	Stanford	1986
Robert Julius Thorne Professor of Economics							
Shelton, David H.	Retir	N Car-Greens		PHD	58	Ohio St	1965
Shen, Raphael	Prof	Detroit Merc		PHD	75	Mich St	1977
Shen, Ruth R.	Prof	San Fran St		PHD	61	J Hopkins	1964
Shen, T. Y.	Emer	Cal-Davis	L	PHD	56	Yale	7-63
Shepard, Delynne	Asst	Andrews	EJ	PHD	95	Purdue	1995
Shepard, Edward M.	C-Ac	LeMoyne	HJL	PHD	87	Boston C	1990
Shepherd, A. Ross	Prof	Mo-Kansas Ct	DF	PHD	63	Syracuse	1967
Shepherd, James F.	Prof	Whitman	HN	PHD	66	U Wash	1971
Shepherd, Robert J.	Lect	Ca-Santa Crz		MSA	70	S Calif	
Shepherd, William G.	Prof	Massachusett		PHD	63	Yale	1986
Sheppard, Lara Shore	Asst	Pittsburgh	J	PHD	96	Princeton	1996
Sheppard, Stephen C.	Prof	Oberlin	CR	PHD	84	Wash U	1990
Sheriff, Mohamed A.	Asst	Dillard		PHD	91	Howard	
Sherman, Howard J.	Retir	Cal-Riversid	EK	PHD	60	S Calif	1966
Sherman, Robert P.	Asst	Cal Tech		PHD	91	Yale	1996
Sherman, Roger	Prof	Virginia	LD	PHD	66	Car Mellon	1971
Brown-Forman Professor of Economics							
Sherony, Deith R.	Prof	Wis-La Cross	ACE	PHD	82	Wi-Milwa	1983
Sherry, Robert L.	Assoc	Keene State		PHD	79	Yale	1984
Shiau, Liang-rong	Prof	Norfolk St	CAR'	PHD	72	S Miss	1972
Shieh, John T.	Prof	CS-Pomona		DBA	81	S Calif	1967
Shieh, Yeung-Nan	Prof	San Jose St		PHD	80	Tx A&M	1989
Shields, Michael P.	C-Pr	Cen Michigan		PHD	75	Utah	1993
Shiell, Leslie	Asst	Skidmore		PHD	98	Toronto	1998
Shiers, Alden F.	Assoc	Cal Poly-SLO		PHD	77	Ca-SnBarb	1975
Shikha, Deep	Assoc	St Catherine	FA	PHD	85	LSU	1985
Shiller, Robert J.	Prof	Yale	D	PHD	72	MIT	1982
Shimer, Robert		Princeton					
Shin, Bong Ju	Prof	Towson		PHD	69	Ohio St	1966
Shin, Kwanho	Asst	Kansas	E	ABD		UCLA	1984
Shingleton, Virginia	C-Ac	Valparaiso	CJIA	PHD	94	Notre Dm	1992
Shinn, Earl W. III	C-Ac	Montevallo		PHD	92	S Carol	1988
Shipman, William A.	Prof	Wartburg		PHD	77	Pittsburgh	1972
Shippen, Benjamin S.	Asst	Mercer-Macon		PHD	95	Fla St	1995
Shirey, Richard L.	Assoc	Siena		PHD	94	SUNY-Alb	9-79
Shirley, John	Lect	SUNY-Cortlan					
Shirvani, Hassan M.	Assoc	St Thomas-TX	FG	PHD	79	Harvard	1986
Shiue, Carol	Inst	Texas	ON	PHD	99	Yale	9-98
Shively, Philip	Asst	Lafayette	CG	PHD	97	Michigan	1997
Shleifer, Andrei	Prof	Harvard		PHD	86	MIT	1991
Shmanske, Steven	Prof	CS-Hayward	CDHL	PHD	82	UCLA	1979
Shockley, Frederica	Prof	CS-Chico	HMOR	PHD	78	Geo St	1978
Shoemaker, Craig	Asst	St Ambrose		PHD	98	Iowa	1992
Shogren, Jason F.	Prof	Wyoming	Q	PHD	86	Wyoming	1995
Shojai, Siamack	Assoc	Manhattan		PHD	84	Fordham	1989
Shoukry, Kamal	Assoc	Loyola Marym	ABCE	PHD	72	S Calif	1980
Shoven, John B.	Prof	Stanford		PHD	73	Yale	1978
Charles R. Schwab Professor of Economics							
Shovlain, Raymond J.	Asst	St Ambrose		MBA	80	St Ambro	1982
Showalter, Dean	Asst	SW Texas St	L	PHD	94	Kentucky	1995
Showalter, Mark	Assoc	Brigham Yg		PHD	91	MIT	1991
Shows, E. Warren	Retir	South Fla	L	PHD	68	Geo St	1964
Shreiber, Chanoch	C-Pr	CUNY-Lehman		PHD	73	Columbia	
Shropshire, William O.	Prof	Ogelthorpe	EO	PHD	63	Duke	1979
Callaway Professor of Economics							

Name	Rank	School	Fields	Degree	Yr	Institution	Date
Shu, Florence P.	Assoc	SUNY-Potsdam		PHD	86	Mich St	1986
Shubik, Martin	Prof	Yale	G	PHD	53	Princeton	
Shughart, William F. II	Prof	Mississippi		PHD	78	Tx A&M	1988
Shukla, Vishwa S.	Retir	Ohio Univ		PHD	72	Wisconsin	1966
Shuklian, Steve	Assoc	Marshall		PHD	88	Utah	1988
Shull, Bernard Jr.	Prof	CUNY-Hunter		PHD	57	Wisconsin	1970
Shull, Ralph	Prof	Ark-Ltl Rock		PHD	72	Arkansas	1971
Shulman, Steven J.	Prof	Colorado St	JKEI	PHD	84	Mass	1984
Shupp, Franklin R.	Retir	Illinois		PHD	59	Princeton	1960
Shute, Laurence	Prof	CS-Pomona		PHD	73	Columbia	1988
Shwiff, Steven S.	Assoc	Tx A&M-Comm	CROD	PHD	77	Tx A&M	1987
Siberberg, Eugene	Prof	U Washington		PHD	64	Purdue	1967
Sibley, David S.	Prof	Texas	D	PHD	73	Yale	1-91
John Michael Stuart Centennial Professor of Economics							
Sichel, Werner	C-Pr	W Michigan	D	PHD	64	Nrthwstrn	1960
Sicherman, Nachum	Prof	Columbia		PHD	87	Columbia	1991
Sicilian, Joseph M.	C-Ac	Kansas	D	PHD	77	Purdue	1977
Sicilian, Paul	Asst	Grand Valley	ACDJ	PHD	91	Illinois	1987
Sickles, Robin C.	Prof	Rice		PHD	76	N Carol	1985
Sicondi, Giorgio	Asst	Occidental	O	PHD	96	Michigan	1998
Siconolfi, Paolo	Prof	Columbia		PHD	87	Penn	1989
Siddiquee, Baker A.	H-Ac	Il-Springfld	EFO	PHD	88	Manitoba	1987
Siden, Dorothy R.	Asst	Salem State		PHD	90	Northeas	
Sidwell, Richard J.	Prof	E Illinois		PHD	72	Utah	1970
Siebert, Calvin D.	Prof	Iowa		PHD	66	Berkeley	1965
Sieg, Holger	Asst	Duke		PHD	96	Car Mellon	1996
Siegel, Abraham J.	Retir	MIT		PHD	61	Berkeley	
Siegel, Andrew F.	Prof	U Washington		PHD	83	MIT	1990
Siegel, Rachel S.	Assoc	Lyndon State	CGQN	MBA	89	Yale	9-90
Siegfried, John J.	Prof	Vanderbilt	LJ	PHD	72	Wisconsin	1972
Siegler, Mark	Asst	Williams		PHD	96	Ca-Davis	1997
Sievers, Allen M.	Prof	Utah		PHD	48	Columbia	1968
Sigetich, Kip	Assoc	So Oregon St	GHM	PHD	79	Stanford	1989
Sigman, Hilary	Asst	UCLA		PHD	93	MIT	
Sihag, Balbir S.	Prof	Mass-Lowell	CI	PHD	78	MIT	1980
Sikes, Ellen	Assoc	Campbell		MS		N Carol	1966
Sikorra, Raymond C.	Asst	USAF Academy	P	PHD	96	Indiana	1998
Silva, Donald H.	Retir	Wis-Whitewat		PHD	64	Missouri	1964
Silver, J. Lew	Assoc	Alabama		PHD	80	Duke	1990
Silver, Stephen J.	Assoc	Citadel		PHD	83	Maryland	8-90
Silvestre, Joaquim	Prof	Cal-Davis	D	PHD	73	Minnesota	1983
Simard, Dominique	Asst	Rutgers-N Br	E	PHD	92	Queen's	1991
Simeone, William J.	Assoc	Providence	JEI	PHD	85	Boston C	1959
Simkins, Scott P.	Asst	N Carol A&T		PHD	88	Iowa	
Simler, Norman J.	Retir	Macalester	AE	PHD	59	Minnesota	1991
Simmons, Michael	C-As	N Carol A&T		PHD	79	Wash St	
Simmons, Walter O.	Asst	John Carroll	JKNO	PHD	94	Wayne St	1995
Simon, Alice E.	Prof	Ohio Wesley		PHD	84	Ohio St	1985
Simon, Carl P.	Prof	Michigan	CDT	PHD	70	Nrthwstrn	7-72
Simon, Curtis J.	Assoc	Clemson	JOR	PHD	85	SUNY-Bin	1985
Simon, Peter J.	C-Ac	Loras		PHD	89	N Illinois	1989
Simons, Gerald P.	Asst	Grand Valley		PHD	95	Kansas	1995
Simonson, John C.	Prof	Wis-Plattev		PHD	72	Wisconsin	1966
Simonson, Robert D.	Prof	Mankato St	AJ	PHD	79	Nebraska	1981
Simos, Evangelos O.	Prof	New Hampshir	EF	PHD	77	N Illinois	1977
Simpson, Murray S.	Asst	Davidson	O	PHD	94	Illinois	1993
Simpson, Paul	Lect	Manches Inst	LO	MA		Newcastle	1984
Sims, Christopher A	Prof	Yale	D	PHD	68	Harvard	
Sindt, Roger	Prof	Neb-Omaha	AR	PHD	72	Tx-Austin	1979
Singamsetti, Nageswara Rao	Assoc	Hartford	CDLM	PHD	73	SUNY-Buf	1974
Singell, Larry D.	Prof	Colorado		PHD	65	Wayne St	1968
Singell, Larry D. Jr.	Assoc	Oregon	J	PHD	88	Ca-SnBarb	1988
Singer, Diana Sue	Prof	W Maryland		MBA		Loyola	1983
Singer, Les	Retir	Indiana NW	RTE	PHD	58	Indiana	1958
Singer, Russell	C-As	King's Col		BS	58	Wilkes	9-67
Singh, Ajmer	Retir	W Oregon St		PHD	64	Oregon St	1965
Singh, Davinder	Prof	CS-Long Bch		PHD	78	S Carol	1983
Singh, Harinder	C-Pr	Grand Valley		PHD	85	Il-Chicago	1995
Singh, Nirvikar	Prof	Ca-Santa Crz	DLO	PHD	82	Berkeley	1982
Singh, Ram Das	Prof	Illinois St	TIO	PHD	70	N Delhi	1981
Singh, Sarjit	Retir	Clarion		PHD		Okla St	1964
Singleton, Robert	C-As	Loyola Marym	AJR	PHD	83	UCLA	1982
Singleton, Ross	Prof	Puget Sound	ADKO	PHD	77	Oregon	
Sinha, Rohini P.	Prof	Muhlenberg		PHD	65	New Sch	1965
Sinisi, John	Asst	Penn St-Harr		PHD	76	Mass	1982
Sisk, David E.	Prof	San Fran St		PHD	76	UCLA	1978
Sjaastad, Larry A.	Prof	Chicago		PHD	61	Chicago	1965
Sjoquist, David L.	Prof	Georgia St	DR	PHD	71	Minnesota	1970
Sjostrom, J. Tomas	Assoc	Penn State	E	PHD	91	Rochester	1998
Skaggs, Jimmy M.	Retir	Wichita St		PHD	70	Tx Tech	1970

Name	Rank	School	Fields	Degree	Yr	Institution	Year
Skaggs, Neil T.	Prof	Illinois St	BDE	PHD	80	Duke	1979
Skaperdas, Stergios	Assoc	Calif-Irvine		PHD	88	J Hopkins	1988
Skeath, Susan E.	Assoc	Wellesley		PHD	89	Princeton	1989
Skeels, Jack W.	Emer	No Illinois	J	PHD	57	Wisconsin	1963
Skelley, A. Chris	Assoc	Rollins		PHD	85	Brown	1987
Skidmore, Mark	Asst	Wis-Whitewat	H	PHD	94	Colorado	1998
Skillman, Gilbert L.	Assoc	Wesleyan-CT	D	PHD	85	Michigan	1993
Skillman, Richard K.	Assoc	W New Eng		MALD		Tufts	1970
Skinner, Gordon S.	Retir	Cincinnati		PHD	53	Wisconsin	
Skinner, Jonathan	Prof	Dartmouth		PHD	83	UCLA	1995
John French Professor							
Skinner, Steven P.	Prof	Western Conn	BJQR	PHD	80	Conn	
Skogstad, Samuel L.	C-Pr	Georgia St	EFO	PHD	65	Wash U	1994
Skoorka, Bruce	Asst	Kean		PHD	92	NYU	
Skoro, Charles L.	C-Pr	Boise State	JBI	PHD	77	Columbia	1982
Skorr, Arlen J.	Prof	Mankato St	AE	PHD	70	Nebraska	1965
Skov, Iva L.	Prof	CS-Long Bch		PHD	76	S Calif	1972
Skrabis, Kristin	Asst	Dickinson Cl	QD				
Skurski, Roger B.	Prof	Notre Dame	P	PHD	70	Wisconsin	1974
Slamim, Robert L.	Asst	Case Western	CD	PHD	95	Duke	1998
Slate, Stephen T.	Assoc	USAF Academy		PHD	94	Colorado	
Slaughter, Matthew J.	Asst	Dartmouth		PHD	94	MIT	1994
Slaysman, Kenneth	Assoc	York-Penn		PHD		Penn St	
Sleeman, Allan G.	Assoc	Western Wash	CD	PHD	83	Simon Fr	1977
Sleet, Christopher	Asst	Texas	E	PHD	98	Stanford	9-98
Slemrod, Joel B.	C-Pr	Michigan		PHD	80	Harvard	1987
Slesnick, Daniel T.	Prof	Texas	CH	PHD	82	Harvard	9-82
Rex G. Baker, Jr., Professorship in Political Economy							
Slesnick, Frank L.	Prof	Bellarmine	AIKJ	PHD	72	Minnesota	1975
Slice, Jerry Kibler	C-Pr	Presbyterian	QFD	PHD	86	Miss St	1989
Sliger, Bernard F.	Prof	Florida St	A	PHD	55	Mich St	1972
Sloan, Frank A.	Prof	Duke		PHD	69	Harvard	1993
Alexander McMahon Professor							
Slotkin, M.	Asst	Fla Inst Tec		PHD	95	N Carol	1996
Slotsve, George A.	Asst	No Illinois	JD	PHD	89	Wisconsin	1996
Slottje, Daniel J.	Prof	So Methodist	DJK	PHD	83	Tx A&M	1989
Slutsky, Steven M.	Prof	Florida	DH	PHD	75	Yale	1984
Smale, Stephen	Prof	Cal-Berkeley		PHD	57	Michigan	
Small, Kenneth A.	Prof	Calif-Irvine		PHD	76	Berkeley	1983
Smallwood, Dennis	Prof	USM Academy	DHL	PHD	66	Yale	1996
Smeeding, Timothy M.	Prof	Syracuse	I	PHD	75	Wisconsin	
Smiles, Ronald	C-Pr	Dallas Bapt	R	PHD	87	Tx-Arlin	1987
Smiley, William G.	Prof	Marquette	DN	PHD	73	Iowa	1973
Smith, Allen W.	Retir	E Illinois		PHD	70	Indiana	1970
Smith, Anthony A.	Asst	Carnegie Mel		PHD	91	Duke	1992
Smith, Barton A.	Prof	Houston	ADR	PHD	74	Chicago	1973
Smith, Bernard	C-Ac	Drew	HOP	PHD	89	Yale	1986
Smith, Bruce D.	Prof	Texas	E	PHD	81	MIT	9-96
Fred Hofheinz Professor in Economics							
Smith, David B	Prof	New Mex St	H	PHD	71	Nebraska	1970
Smith, Dean G.	Assoc	No Arizona	RC	PHD	85	Tx A&M	1989
Smith, Galen	Assoc	Cedarville	ABFH	DMIN	98	Trinity	1981
Smith, George	Prof	New York U	N	PHD	76	Harvard	1988
Smith, George	C-As	St Scholasti		ABD		Nova SE	9-86
Smith, Gerald A.	Prof	Mankato St	AOQ	PHD	79	LSU	1979
Smith, Gordon W.	Prof	Rice		PHD	66	Harvard	1968
Smith, Harlan	Emer	Minnesota		PHD	49	Chicago	
Smith, Harlan II	Assoc	Marshall		PHD	89	Yale	1991
Smith, Janet K.	C-Pr	Claremont		PHD	80	UCLA	1996
Smith, John Z.	Asst	Vassar	J	PHD	93	MIT	1993
Smith, Jon L.	Assoc	East Tenn St		PHD	82	S Carol	1980
Smith, Kenneth L.	Prof	Pittsburg St	G	PHD	81	Ca-Rivers	
Smith, Kenneth R.	Prof	Arizona		PHD	68	Nrthwstrn	1980
Smith, Larry J.	Assoc	WI-Green Bay		PHD	73	Chicago	
Smith, Lawrence C.	Prof	Louisiana Te		PHD	68	Miss	1970
Smith, Lewis	Prof	Mississippi	E	PHD	71	Tennessee	1971
Smith, Lones A.	Assoc	Michigan	D	PHD	91	Chicago	
Smith, Lynn A.	Assoc	Clarion		PHD	85	Pittsburgh	1989
Smith, Mark Griffin	Assoc	Colorado Col		PHD	87	Duke	1988
Smith, Patricia	Assoc	Mich-Dearbor	IJK	PHD	86	Va Tech	1988
Smith, Paula	Assoc	Central Okla	IJ	PHD	84	Okla St	1987
Smith, Richard S.	H-Ac	Ark Tech		PHD	74	Tx-Austin	1991
Smith, Ronald G. E.	Retir	CUNY-Hunter	1-99	DBA	68	LSU	
Smith, Russell E.	Assoc	Washburn		PHD	84	Illinois	1984
Smith, Stanley K.	Prof	Florida	J	PHD	76	Michigan	1976
Smith, Stefani	Asst	Tulane		PHD	97	Illinois	1997
Smith, Stephen C.	Assoc	George Wash	O	PHD	83	Cornell	1983
Smith, V. Kerry	Prof	Duke	QDC	PHD	70	Rutgers	1994
Smith, Vardaman Russell	Assoc	Jms Madison	B	PHD	80	Penn St	1979

Smith, Vernon L.	Prof	Arizona		PHD	55	Harvard	1975
Regents' Professor							
Smith, Vincent H.	Assoc	Montana St		PHD	87	N Car St	1988
Smith, W. James	Dean	Colo-Denver		PHD	76	Colorado	
Smith, William	Assoc	Memphis	EF	PHD	87	Virginia	1993
Smith, William Doyle	Assoc	Txs-El Paso	AEC	PHD	81	Tx Tech	1981
Smitka, Michael J.	Assoc	Wash & Lee	FL	PHD	89	Yale	1986
Smolowitz, Ira E.	Prof	American Int		PHD	84	Rensselaer	1988
Smyser, Michael	Asst	Southern	G	PHD	91	Fla Intl	1991
Smyth, David J.	Retir	Louisiana St	E	PHD	68	Birminghm	1987
Smyth, John W.	Retir	Youngstown		PHD	73	Nebraska	
Snoonian, Paul E.	Assoc	Mass-Lowell	EQ	PHD	71	Mich St	
Snow, Arthur	Assoc	Georgia	DH	PHD	79	Wisconsin	1989
Snow, Karl N.	Asst	Brigham Yg		PHD	91	Chicago	1995
Snow, Marcellus S.	Retir	Hawaii-Manoa		PHD	74	Berkeley	1974
Snow, Sandra L.	Prof	Wis-Whitewat		PHD	76	Missouri	1981
Snowbarger, Marvin R.	Prof	San Jose St		PHD	66	Michigan	1966
Snowden, Kenneth A.	Assoc	N Car-Greens	NG	PHD	83	Wisconsin	1983
Snowden, Peter N.	SLect	U Lancaster		PHD		Leeds	
Snyder, Christopher	Asst	George Wash	L	PHD	94	MIT	1994
Snyder, Donald L.	Prof	Utah State	CQ	PHD	79	Utah St	1981
Snyder, James M. Jr.	Prof	MIT		PHD	85	Cal Tech	
Snyder, Marcia	Inst	Charleston		MA	95	London	1999
Snyder, Richard S.	Asst	No Kentucky		PHD	76	Indiana	1978
Snyder, Susan	Asst	Virg Tech	HDC	PHD	96	Stanford	8-95
Soares, Jorge	Asst	George Wash	E	PHD	96	Rochester	1998
Sobel, Joel	Prof	Ca-San Diego	D	PHD	78	Berkeley	1978
Sobel, Russell S.	Asst	W Virginia	H	PHD	94	Fla St	1994
Sockwell, William D.	Assoc	Berry		PHD	89	Vanderbilt	1988
Soderlind, Steven D.	C-Ac	St Olaf	RA	PHD	80	Mass	1982
Sohan, Gerald	Asst	USAF Academy		ABD		Tx A&M	
Sohng, Soong Nark	Prof	Clarion		PHD	82	Wayne St	1981
Sokoloff, Joel J.	Asst	Kentucky St	ACE	MA	67	Mass	1974
Sokoloff, Kenneth L.	Prof	UCLA		PHD	82	Harvard	1980
Solar, Donald	Prof	Lg Isl-Post		PHD	63	Columbia	1965
Solberg, Eric J.	Prof	CS-Fullerton	J	PHD	74	Claremont	1973
Soligo, Ronald	Prof	Rice		PHD	64	Yale	1967
Soliman, Mostafa A.	Assoc	Prairie View	DHQ	PHD	67	Iowa St	1971
Sollars, David L.	Assoc	Auburn-Montg	KHAE	PHD	91	Fla St	1990
Soller, Elizabeth	Asst	Drexel		PHD	97	Indiana	1997
Solnick, Sara J.	Asst	U Miami	DIJ	PHD	96	Penn	1996
Solomon, Elinor H.	Adj	George Wash	E	PHD	48	Harvard	1982
Solomon, Henry	Retir	George Wash	I	PHD	59	NYU	
Solomon, Lynnette K.	Retir	S F Austin		PHD	70	Arkansas	1979
Solon, Babette S.	Emer	CUNY-Queens	DJ	PHD	58	MIT	1961
Solon, Gary R.	C Pr	Michigan		PHD	83	Princeton	1903
Solow, John L.	Assoc	Iowa		PHD	83	Stanford	1081
Solow, Robert M.	Retir	MIT	E	PHD	51	Harvard	1958
Soltow, Allen R.	Assoc	Tulsa		PHD	69	Iowa St	1973
Sommers, Paul M.	Prof	Middlebury	CDT	PHD	76	Ca-SnDgo	1976
Sonanathan, Rohini	Asst	Michigan					
Sondey, John A.	Assoc	So Dakota St	H	PHD	89	Wash St	1990
Song, Frank M.	Assoc	Cleveland St	EG	PHD	91	Ohio St	1991
Song, Inbum	Retir	Louisville		PHD		Oklahoma	
Song, Shunfeng	Asst	Nevada-Reno		PHD	92	Ca-Irvine	1992
Song, Yoon K.	Prof	Detroit Merc		PHD	69	Illinois	1069
Songha, W. A.	Assoc	Cheyney					
Sonmez, Tayfun O.	Asst	Michigan	CDH	PHD	95	Rochester	1995
Sonnenschein, Hugo F.	Prof	Chicago		PHD	64	Purdue	
Sonny, Jacob	Assoc	Dowling		PHD	71	New Sch	
Sonora, Robert	Asst	Tx-Arlington	F	PHD	98	Ohio St	1998
Sonstegaard, Miles H.	Assoc	Arkansas	H	PHD	58	Oregon	1969
Sonstelie, Jon C.	Prof	Cal-Santa Br	HR	PHD	75	Nrthwstrn	1977
Sontheimer, Kevin C.	Assoc	Pittsburgh	D	PHD	69	Minnesota	1979
Soofi, Abdollah S.	Assoc	Wis-Plattev		PHD	81	Ca-Rivers	1980
Soper, John C.	Prof	John Carroll	ENA	PHD	70	Mass	1982
Sopher, Barry	Assoc	Rutgers-N Br	D	PHD	88	Iowa	1987
Sorensen, Duane L.	Retir	Indiana St	R	MS	61	Iowa St	1968
Sorensen, Phillip E.	Prof	Florida St	Q	PHD	66	Berkeley	1971
Sorensen, Robert L.	Prof	Mo-St Louis	KMAO	PHD	71	Va Tech	1970
Sorenson, David	Asst	Augustana SD	RG	PHD	97	W Virginia	1997
Sorenson, Timothy L.	Assoc	Seattle	MDF	PHD	91	Harvard	1991
Soriano, Beverly	Asst	Framingham		MS		Bentloy	
Sorkin, Alan L.	C-Pr	MD-Baltim Co		PHD	66	J Hopkins	1974
Sorrentino, John A. Jr.	Assoc	Temple	Q	PHD	73	Purdue	1979
Sosin, Kim	C-Pr	Neb-Omaha	ECO	PHD	70	Nebraska	1981
Soskin, Mark D.	Assoc	Cen Florida	C	PHD	79	Penn St	1988
Sowell, Clifford	Prof	Berea		PHD	78	Georgia	1981
Sowell, Fallaw B.	Assoc	Carnegie Mel		PHD	86	Duke	1988
Spagnolo, John A.	Assoc	Iona	R	PHD	82	Fordham	1978

Spanos, Aris	Prof	Virg Tech	CB	PHD	82	London	1988
Sparks, Donald L.	Prof	Citadel		PHD	85	London	8-86
Spatt, Chester S.	Prof	Carnegie Mel		PHD	79	Penn	1979
Spear, Stephen E.	H-Pr	Carnegie Mel		PHD	82	Penn	1982
Spears, Philip V.	Prof	Berea		PHD	71	Kentucky	1968
Spechler, Martin	Prof	Ind-Purdue/I	BFNP	PHD	71	Harvard	1986
Spector, David	Asst	MIT	E	PHD	96	LondonEc	1996
Spector, Lee C.	Assoc	Ball State	E	PHD	85	Iowa	1985
Speir, Edwin G.	Prof	Georgia Col		PHD	65	Denver	1981
Spence, James G.	Assoc	South Fla	A	PHD	79	Oklahoma	1975
Spencer, Austin Harvey	Prof	W Carolina		PHD	72	Indiana	1980
Spencer, David E.	Prof	Brigham Yg		PHD	74	Tx A&M	1986
Spencer, Roger W.	Prof	Trinity	E	PHD	69	Virginia	1980
Spencer, Theresa	Assoc	Shenandoah		PHD	89	N Car St	1997
Speyrer, Janet F.	Prof	New Orleans		PHD	82	J Hopkins	1987
Spiva, George A. Jr.	Emer	Tennessee		PHD	58	Tx-Austin	1958
Spizman, Lawrence	Prof	SUNY Oswego	AJK	PHD	77	SUNY-Alb	1977
Spolaore, Enrico	Asst	Brown		PHD	93	Harvard	
Spraberry, Hubert O.	Prof	Howard Payne		PHD	85	Tx Tech	1986
Sprenkle, Case	Retir	Illinois		PHD	60	Yale	1960
Sprinkle, Richard L.	Assoc	Txs-El Paso	ABCF	PHD	82	Arkansas	1982
Sprunger, Philip W.	Asst	Lycoming	AJQH	PHD	93	Indiana	1993
Spurr, Stephen J.	Assoc	Wayne State	JK	PHD	86	Chicago	1987
Sraiheen, Abdulwahab	Assoc	Kutztown	CM	PHD	86	Penn St	1990
Sridharan, K. P.	Assoc	Delta State	ACFG	PHD	92	Miss	8-92
Srinivasan, T. N.	C-Pr	Yale	FO	PHD	62	Yale	1980
Srivastava, Sanjay	Prof	Carnegie Mel		PHD	82	MIT	1982
St. Clair, David J.	Prof	CS-Hayward	BENP	PHD	79	Utah	1979
Staab, Martin	Lect	Howard	EQ	PHD		Indiana	
Stachetti, Ennio	Prof	Michigan		PHD	83	Wisconsin	1992
Staelin, Charles P.	Assoc	Smith	ACDF	PHD	71	Michigan	1981
Stafford, Frank P.	Prof	Michigan		PHD	68	Chicago	1974
Stafford, Sarah	Asst	Wm & Mary		PHD	98	J Hopkins	1998
Stageberg, Stephen P.	Assoc	Mary Wash	CFN	PHD	84	Geotown	1982
Stahl, Dale O. III	Prof	Texas	DC	PHD	81	Berkeley	7-88
Malcolm Forsman Centennial Professorship							
Staiger, Douglas O.	Assoc	Dartmouth		PHD	90	MIT	1998
Staiger, Robert W.	Prof	Wisconsin		PHD	85	Michigan	1993
Stair, Anthony G.	C-Ac	Frostburg St		PHD	93	W Virginia	1984
Staller, George J.	Prof	Cornell		PHD	59	Cornell	1960
Stallings, Dale G.	Retir	CS-Pomona	1994	PHD	62	Minnesota	1964
Stamland, Tommy	Asst	Wyoming		PHD	94	Berkeley	1996
Stanfield, James Ronald	Prof	Colorado St	BA	PHD	72	Oklahoma	1976
Stanford, Richard A.	Prof	Furman		PHD	71	Georgia	1968
David C Garrett Jr. Professor of Economics							
Stanford, Robert	Prof	Alabama-Birm	C	PHD	71	Berkeley	1982
Stanford, William G.	Assoc	Ill-Chicago	C	PHD	84	Nrthwstrn	1983
Stango, Victor	Asst	Tennessee		PHD	96	Ca-Davis	1996
Stanley, Denise	Asst	Tennessee		PHD	96	Wisconsin	1996
Stanley, Thomas	Prof	Nicholls St	FG	PHD	82	Nebraska	1988
Stanley, Tom D.	Assoc	Hendrix		PHD	82	Purdue	1986
Stano, Miron	Prof	Oakland	IL	PHD	71	Cornell	1977
Stark, Eric	Asst	Wash & Jeff					1998
Starkey, James L.	Prof	Rhode Island		PHD	71	Boston C	1967
Starleaf, Dennis R.	Retir	Iowa State	E	PHD	67	Vanderbilt	1963
Starr, Ross	Prof	Ca-San Diego	DE	PHD	72	Stanford	1980
Starrett, David A.	Emer	Stanford		PHD	68	Stanford	1973
Startz, Richard	C-Pr	U Washington		PHD	78	MIT	1984
Stauffer, Robert F.	Assoc	Roanoke		PHD	74	Va Tech	1978
Steagall, Jeffrey W.	Assoc	North Fla	FAC	PHD	90	Wisconsin	1990
Steckel, Richard H.	Prof	Ohio State	N	PHD	77	Chicago	1977
Steele, Gerald R.	Lect	U Lancaster		MA		Sheffield	
Steele, Henry B.	Prof	Houston	A	PHD	57	MIT	
Steen, Robert C.	Assoc	Rollins	RHN	PHD	82	Princeton	1987
Steen, Todd P.	Assoc	Hope	JT	PHD	93	Harvard	1988
Steenstra, Alex	Asst	E Oregon St	ABDQ	PHD	97	Utah	9-97
Stegeman, Mark W	Asst	Virg Tech	DL	PHD	87	MIT	1994
Steger, Eric K.	Prof	East Central		PHD	80	La Tech	1970
Stegner, Tesa	C-Ac	Idaho State	AHQ	PHD	89	Wash St	1992
Stehman, Diane	Assoc	NE Illinois		PHD	78	Il-Chicago	1978
Steib, Steve B.	Prof	Tulsa		PHD	72	Iowa St	1972
Steigerwald, Douglas G.	Assoc	Cal-Santa Br	C	PHD	89	Berkeley	1988
Stein, Bruno	Retir	New York U		PHD	59	NYU	1959
Stein, Howard	Prof	Roosevelt		PHD	83	Ca-Rivers	1983
Stein, Jerome L.	Emer	Brown		PHD	55	Yale	1956
Eastman Professor of Political Economy - Emeritus							
Stein, Sheldon H.	Assoc	Cleveland St	CER	PHD	78	J Hopkins	1976
Steinberg, Ivan	Asst	NewJerseyCty	LA	ABD	71	New Sch	
Steinberg, Richard	Prof	Ind-Purdue/I	HL	PHD	84	Penn	1991

Name	Rank	School	Fields	Degree	Yr	Institution	Year
Steindl, Frank G.	Prof	Oklahoma St	E	PHD	63	Iowa	1962
Regents' Professor and Ardmore Chair							
Steiner, Peter	Retir	Michigan					
Steinhauer, Larry	Prof	Albion		PHD	74	Chicago	1968
Steinkamp, Stanley W.	Retir	Illinois		PHD	58	Michigan	1958
Steinmeier, Thomas L.	Prof	Texas Tech		PHD	75	Yale	1982
Steinnes, Donald N.	Prof	Minn-Duluth	C	PHD	72	Nrthwstrn	1975
Stellern, Michael J.	Asst	Rockhurst		PHD	83	Arizona	1979
Stephan, Paula E.	Prof	Georgia St	JO	PHD	71	Michigan	1971
Stephens, Mark A.	Assoc	Tenn Tech		PHD	85	Tennessee	1980
Stephenson, E. Frank	Asst	Berry		PHD	97	N Carol	1997
Stephenson, James A.	Retir	Iowa State		PHD	65	Berkeley	1964
Stephenson, Matthew A.	C-Pr	Wofford	DLN	PHD	65	Tulane	1970
T. B. Stackhouse Professor of Economics							
Sterbenz, Frederic P.	Assoc	Wyoming	EG	PHD	81	Penn	1981
Stern, Andrew	Prof	CS-Long Bch		PHD	67	Columbia	1967
Stern, Robert M.	Prof	Michigan		PHD	58	Columbia	1961
Stern, Steven N.	Prof	Virginia	JCI	PHD	85	Yale	1985
Stevens, Ann Huff	Asst	Yale	J	PHD	95	Michigan	1995
Stevens, David W.	Prof	Baltimore		PHD	65	Colorado	
Stevens, Flumo	Prof	Lawrence Tec	G	PHD	74	Nebraska	1987
Stevens, George E.	Dean	Kent State	ADMS	DBA	79	Kent St	1995
Stevenson, Mary H.	Assoc	Mass-Boston	JIR	PHD	74	Michigan	1972
Stevenson, Thomas M. Jr.	Retir	St Louis		PHD	64	Illinois	1965
Stewart, Douglas B.	Prof	San Diego St		PHD	70	Oregon	1971
Stewart, Douglas O.	Assoc	Cleveland St	DH	PHD	74	Michigan	1972
Stewart, John F.	Prof	No Carolina	L	PHD	76	Wisconsin	1975
Stewart, Milton D. Jr.	Retir	S F Austin		PHD	72	Tx-Austin	1966
Stieber, Jack	Retir	Michigan St		PHD	56	Harvard	1956
Stifflemire, Paul F. Jr.	Assoc	Wash & Jeff		MBA	86	Suffolk	1986
Stiglitz, Joseph E.	Prof	Stanford		PHD	86	MIT	
Stillwaggon, Eileen	Asst	Gettysburg	AFQO	PHD	79	American	1995
Stinchcombe, Maxwell B.	Assoc	Texas	DC	PHD	86	Berkeley	1-94
Stine, William F.	Prof	Clarion		PHD	83	Fordham	1981
Stirling, Kathleen J.	C-Pr	Puget Sound	AEIT	PHD	87	Notre Dm	
Stober, William J.	Retir	Kentucky	D	PHD	65	Duke	1965
Stock, Wendy A.	Asst	Kansas State	JCQ	PHD	96	Mich St	1996
Stockhausers, Gerard L. S.J.	Assoc	Creighton	AEFN	PHD	85	Michigan	1985
Stockman, Alan C.	C-Pr	Rochester		PHD	78	Chicago	1979
Wilson Professor of Economics							
Stockman, David	Asst	Delaware	CE	PHD	97	Chicago	1998
Stocks, Anthony H.	Retir	Youngstown		PHD	63	SUNY-Buf	1968
Stokes, Houston H.	Prof	Ill-Chicago	D	PHD	69	Chicago	1967
Stokey, Nancy	Prof	Chicago		PHD	78	Harvard	1990
Frederick Henry Prince Professor							
Stoll, John R.	Prof	WI-Green Bay		PHD	80	Kentucky	
Stollar, Andrew J.	Prof	Bentley	CFP	PHD	73	Boston C	1976
Stolnitz, George J.	Retir	Indiana		PHD	52	Princeton	
Stolte, William F.	Retir	Berea		PHD	71	Syracuse	1970
Stone, Allan D.	Prof	SW Missouri		PHD	73	Oklahoma	1972
Stone, Courtney C.	Prof	Ball State	EM	PHD	73	UCLA	1991
Stone, Gary L.	Prof	Winthrop	ACD	PHD	80	N Carol	9-75
Stone, Gerald W. Jr.	Retir	Metro St-CO		PHD	73	Rice	1975
Stone, Irving	Prof	CUNY-Baruch		PHD	62	Columbia	1962
Stone, Joe A.	Prof	Oregon	JFE	PHD	77	Mich St	1970
W. E. Miner Professor of Economics							
Stone, Leonie L.	Asst	SUNY Geneseo	OD	PHD	93	Ohio St	1993
Stone, Richard G.	Assoc	Elizabethtwn		PHD	80	Temple	1987
Stonebraker, Robert J.	Prof	Indiana U-PA	EK	PHD	73	Princeton	1971
Storer, Paul	Asst	Western Wash	EJ	PHD	92	W Ontario	1996
Story, Jonathan	Prof	INSEAD		PHD	73	J Hopkins	7-74
Stradley, Scot A.	Assoc	North Dakota	ABP	PHD	77	Utah	1970
Straight, Ronald L.	Asst	Howard		DBA	79	Geo Wash	1988
Strait, Roger H.	Retir	F Dick-Teane	BN	STB		Harvard	
Stranahan, Harriett	Assoc	North Fla	JGD	PHD	95	Wash	1994
Strand, Larry D.	Dean	Biola		MBA	69	S Calif	1986
Strand, Stephen H.	Prof	Carleton	DL	PHD	76	Vanderbilt	1981
Raymond Plank Professor of Economics							
Strang, Daniel R.	Prof	SUNY-Geneseo	CQ	PHD	75	Cornell	1992
Strangways, Raymond S.	Prof	Old Dominion		PHD	66	Tulane	1962
Strasma, John D.	Retir	Wisconsin		PHD	60	Harvard	1966
Strassmann, W. Paul	Retir	Michigan St		PHD	56	Maryland	
Straszheim, Mahlon R.	C-Pr	Maryland		PHD	66	Harvard	
Stratmann, Thomas	Asst	Montana St		PHD	90	Maryland	1990
Stratton, Leslie A.	Asst	Virg Comm		PHD	89	MIT	1997
Stratton, Peter J.	Retir	W Illinois	AD	PHD	70	N Illinois	1970
Stratton, Richard	Assoc	Akron	ADJ	PHD	77	Conn	1978
Straub, LaVonne	Prof	W Illinois	AIJR	PHD	83	Utah	1982
Strauss, Jack K.	Assoc	St Louis		PHD	89	Duke	
Strauss, John	Prof	Michigan St		PHD	81	Mich St	1992

Name	Rank	School	Fields	Degree	Yr	Institution	Year
Strausser, Clark W.	Assoc	Pitts-Johnst	CG	PHD	70	Minnesota	1973
Strayer, Wayne	Asst	Texas A&M	J	PHD	97	Ohio St	1997
Strazicich, Mark	VAsst	Cen Florida		PHD			
Street, Barbara P.	Prof	Chaminade	ACEI	PHD	86	Virginia	1981
Street, Donald R.	Retir	Auburn		PHD	65	Penn St	1965
Streeter, Lanny E.	Assoc	U Miami	C	PHD	70	Illinois	1967
Strein, Charles T.	Assoc	No Iowa	DLMR	PHD	77	Illinois	1970
Stromsdorfer, Ernst W.	Prof	Wash State		PHD	62	Wash U	1983
Strong, Jerome C.	Retir	Hartwick		PHD		Columbia	1965
Stronge, William B.	Prof	Fla Atlantic		PHD	71	Iowa St	1971
Stroup, Michael	Asst	S F Austin	DH	PHD	93	Fla St	1999
Stroup, Richard L.	Prof	Montana St		PHD	70	U Wash	1969
Strumpf, Koleman	Asst	No Carolina	GH	PHD	95	MIT	1995
Stuart, Charles	Prof	Cal-Santa Br	HKD	PHD	75	Lunds	1980
Stuart, Edward F.	Prof	NE Illinois		PHD	78	Oklahoma	1986
Stuart, Robert C.	Prof	Rutgers-N Br	P	PHD	69	Wisconsin	1968
Stubblebine, William Craig	Prof	Claremont		PHD	63	Virginia	1966
Studenmund, A. H.	Prof	Occidental	C	PHD	70	Cornell	1970
Richard W. Millar Professor of Economics & Director of Institutional Planning							
Stuligross, John D.	Retir	Hartwick	AEGR	PHD	71	Oklahoma	1980
Stull, Charles	Inst	Kalamazoo		ABD		Wisconsin	
Stull, William J.	C-Pr	Temple	IR	PHD	72	MIT	1976
Stumph, Carolyn F.	Asst	Ill Wesleyan	E	PHD	99	Lehigh	1998
Sturgeon, James I.	Prof	Mo-Kansas Ct	BO	PHD	74	Oklahoma	1977
Sturges, David M.	Asst	Colgate	EG	PHD	94	Yale	1995
Stutsman, A. Douglas	Emer	So Alabama	AB	PHD	70	Miss	1968
Su, Dongwei	Asst	Akron	AC	PHD	97	Ohio St	1997
Su, Vincent	Prof	CUNY-Baruch		PHD	70	Rutgers	1971
Suarez, James M.	Dean	Manhattan		PHD	72	Columbia	1984
Sublette, Werner Johann	Prof	Truman State		PHD	74	Arizona	1974
Subramanian, Shankar	Asst	Cornell	OQ	PHD	88	Berkeley	8-93
Sukar, Abdul Hamid	Assoc	Cameron		PHD	89	Tx Tech	1987
Sukhatme, Vasant A.	C-Pr	Macalester	ADO	PHD	77	Chicago	1978
Edward J. Noble Professor of Economics							
Sula, Laddie J.	Prof	Loras		PHD	76	Geo St	1983
Suliman, Osman	C-Pr	Millersville		PHD	84	Indiana	1993
Sullivan, Dennis H.	Prof	Miami U-Ohio	HI	PHD	75	Princeton	1973
Sullivan, Edward J.	VInst	St Joseph	EF	ABD	81	Fordham	1998
Sullivan, John J.	Retir	Hartford		PHD	67	Conn	
Sullivan, Timothy	Asst	S Ill-Edward	IJT	PHD	95	Maryland	1995
Sullivan, Timothy	Assoc	Towson		PHD	87	Illinois	1989
Sulock, Joseph M.	Prof	N Car-Ashvil	AGH	PHD	76	Virginia	1975
Sulter, Mary	Lect	Mo-St Louis	A	MIEE		Delaware	
Sum, Andrew M.	Prof	Northeastern		MA	71	MIT	1971
Summary, Rebecca M.	C-Pr	SE Missouri	FA	PHD	83	Illinois	1983
Summers, Jeffrey A.	Assoc	Linfield		PHD	87	Purdue	1992
Summers, Robert	Emer	Pennsylvania		PHD	56	Stanford	1959
Sumner, Scott B.	Prof	Bentley	EN	PHD	84	Chicago	1982
Sumpta, Sister Virginia A.	Assoc	Immaculata		MA		Catholic	1968
Sunderman, Mark	Assoc	Wyoming		PHD	86	Illinois	1986
Sundstrom, William A.	C-Ac	Santa Clara		PHD	86	Stanford	1987
Sung, Jane C.	Assoc	Truman State		PHD	85	Wayne St	1987
Sung, Simona	Assoc	St Rose	CDEL	PHD	90	Rensselaer	8-90
Supel, Mary R.	Asst	St Thomas-MN	L	BA		Denison	1976
Suranovic, Steven M.	Assoc	George Wash	F	PHD	87	Cornell	1988
Surdam, David	Asst	Loyola-Chicg	AILN	PHD	94	Chicago	1994
Surdyk, Lisa	Assoc	Seattle Pac	G	PHD	91	U Wash	1991
Sureshwaran, S.	Asst	So Carol St		PHD	89	Clemson	1990
Sussman, Jeffrey		SUNY-Empire	G	PHD	75	CUNY	1975
Suster, Zeljan	Assoc	New Haven	FNOP	PHD	88	Belgrade	9-90
Sutch, Richard C.	Prof	Cal-Riversid	AN	PHD	68	MIT	1998
Sutliffe, James S.	Deces	SUNY-Potsdam		PHD		Fla St	
Sutton, James E.	Prof	CS-Pomona		BS	55	Wisconsin	1964
Sutton, Terry	Prof	SE Missouri	B	PHD	70	Kansas St	1972
Suwanakul, Sontachai	Assoc	Alabama St		PHD	86	Arkansas	1989
Suzawa, Gilbert S.	Assoc	Rhode Island		PHD	73	Brown	1971
Svorny, Shirley V.	Assoc	CS-Northrdge	IG	PHD	79	UCLA	1978
Swaine, Howard R.	H-Pr	No Michigan	AKDH	PHD	65	UCLA	1966
Swan, Craig E.	Prof	Minnesota		PHD	70	Yale	1969
Swaney, James A.	Prof	Wright State		PHD	79	Colo St	
Swanke, Thomas A.	Asst	W Virg St	AEJO	PHD	93	Colorado	1993
Swann, Christopher	Asst	SUNY-Stony B		PHD	97	Virginia	1999
Swanson, Charles	Asst	Temple	E	PHD	91	Minnesota	1993
Swanson, Gerald	Assoc	Arizona		PHD	72	Illinois	1970
Swanson, James A.	Assoc	Cen Missouri		PHD	87	Wash St	1986
Swanson, Norman	Assoc	Texas A&M		PHD	94	Ca-Sn Dgo	1999
Swanson, Paul	Assoc	Wm Patterson		PHD	84	Columbia	1982
Swartz, Thomas R.	Prof	Notre Dame	HA	PHD	65	Indiana	1965
Sweeney, George H.	Assoc	Vanderbilt	DL	PHD	77	Nrthwstrn	1976
Sweeney, Vernon E.	Retir	Sam Houston		PHD	68	Tx-Austin	1971

Sweeney, William B. Jr.	Prof	Bryant	AE	PHD	73	Sarasota	
Swenson, Deborah	Asst	Cal-Davis	FH	PHD	91	MIT	1993
Swint, Kenneth J.	Assoc	Wash & Jeff		PHD	89	Pittsburgh	1988
Swinton, John R.	Asst	South Fla	Q	PHD	96	Wisconsin	1995
Swofford, James L.	Prof	So Alabama	E	PHD	81	Florida	1984
Sylla, Richard	Prof	New York U	DN	PHD	69	Harvard	1990
Henry Kaufman Professor of the History of Financial Institutions & Markets							
Sylvester, Patrick J.	Prof	West Chester	AE	PHD	73	Bryn Mawr	1968
Sylvester, Roger A.	Inst	Wright State		MS	87	Wright St	
Sylwester, Kevin	Asst	So Illinois	EO	PHD	97	Wisconsin	1998
Syropoulos, Constantinos	Assoc	Fla Internat	FLO	PHD	89	Yale	1996
Sztajer, George	Asst	St Ambrose		MBA	86	E Illinois	1992
Tabb, William K.	Prof	CUNY-Queens	RO	PHD	68	Wisconsin	1971
Taber, Christopher	Asst	Northwestern		PHD	95	Chicago	1995
Tabesh, Hamid	Assoc	Wis-Rvr Fall	EF	PHD	87	Iowa St	1988
Tabrizi, Behrouz	Asst	St Fran-NY		PHD	84	Jawahar	9-97
Tabriztchi, Sirousse	Assoc	SUNY Old Wes		PHD	70	Columbia	
Tacker, Thomas L.	Assoc	Embry-Riddle		PHD	87	N Carol	
Tadelis, Steven	Asst	Stanford		PHD		Harvard	
Taga, Leonore S.	Assoc	Rider	P	PHD	79	Berkeley	1986
Tahmiscioglu, Kamil	Asst	Wis-Milwauke		PHD	96	USC	1997
Tailby, Don	Retir	New Mexico	ABNO	PHD	61	Rutgers	1967
Taira, Koji	Retir	Illinois		PHD	61	Stanford	1970
Takacs, Wendy E.	Assoc	MD-Baltim Co		PHD	76	J Hopkins	1981
Takayama, Akira	Deces	So Illinois	FEDC	PHD	62	Rochester	1983
Takeyama, Lisa N.	Asst	Amherst	ADLQ	PHD	92	Stanford	1994
Talarico, Joseph F.	Retir	Rider	F	PHD	58	Rutgers	1967
Talbert, Lonnie E.	Retir	Arkansas St	AQMT	PHD	64	N Car St	1966
Tallarini, Thomas	Asst	Carnegie Mel		PHD	95	Chicago	1995
Talley, Wayne K.	Prof	Old Dominion		PHD	72	Kentucky	1972
Eminent Professor							
Tam, Mo-Yin S.	Prof	Ill-Chicago	P	PHD	74	SUNY-SBr	1974
Tamura, Robert F.	Assoc	Clemson	IJO	PHD	88	Chicago	1996
Tan, Chin	Assoc	Cumberland		MBA	88	Tenn Tech	1988
Tandon, Pankaj	Assoc	Boston Univ	DO	PHD	79	Harvard	1978
Tang, Linghui	Asst	Drexel		PHD	98	Syracuse	1998
Tangesdal, Mark O.	Asst	SE Okla St		PHD	95	Ca-Rivers	1997
Tangri, Shanti S.	Prof	Rutgers-N Br	O	PHD	61	Berkeley	1970
Tank, Frederick E.	Assoc	Toledo	KQ	PHD	72	Wayne St	1970
Tanner, J. Ernest	Retir	Tulane		PHD	68	Brown	1971
Tannery, Frederick J.	Assoc	Slippery Roc	ACDJ	PHD	80	Pittsburgh	1981
Tansey, Francis B.	Lect	CUNY-Baruch		MBA	65	CUNY	1967
Tansey, Michael M.	Prof	Rockhurst		PHD	78	Wisconsin	1982
Tanski, Janet M.	Assoc	New Mex St	OI	PHD	91	SUNY-Buf	1989
Tarascio, Vincent J.	Prof	No Carolina	N	PHD	66	Rice	1964
Tarhouni, Ali	SLect	U Washington		PHD	84	Mich St	1985
Tarpley, Fred A. Jr.	Prof	Georgia Tech	D	PHD	67	Tulane	1962
Tarullo, P. Ronald	Prof	Calif U-Penn		PHD	76	Pittsburgh	1978
Taub, Allan J.	Assoc	Cleveland St	CD	PHD	73	Nrthwstrn	1971
Taub, Bart	Prof	Illinois	E	PHD	81	Chicago	1989
Taube, Paul M.	Assoc	Tx-Pan Amer		PHD	86	SUNY-Alb	1988
Tauber, Linda	Asst	CUNY-Lehman		MBA			
Tauchen, George	Prof	Duke		PHD	78	Minnesota	1977
Tauchen, Helen	Prof	No Carolina	D	PHD	77	Minnesota	1977
Tauman, Yair	Prof	SUNY-Stony B		PHD	79	Hebrew	1989
Taussig, Michael K.	Prof	Rutgers-N Br	H	PHD	00	MIT	1967
Tay, Abigail	Asst	Columbia	LHI	PHD	99	Stanford	1999
Taylor, Addis C.	Assoc	Florida A&M	JM	PHD	83	Fla St	1976
Taylor, Beck	Asst	Baylor	D	PHD	97	Purdue	1997
Taylor, Corri	Asst	Wellesley		PHD	98	Wisconsin	1998
Taylor, Curtis	Assoc	Texas A&M	L	PHD	92	Yale	1992
Private Enterprise Research Center Mary Julia & George R. Jordan Jr. Prof							
Taylor, Donald C.	Retir	So Dakota St	O	PHD	65	Minnesota	1980
Taylor, James	Prof	U Lancaster		PHD		Lancaster	
Taylor, John B.	Prof	Stanford		PHD	73	Stanford	
Mary and Robert Raymond Professor of Economics							
Taylor, Kenna C.	C-Pr	Rollins		PHD	79	Florida	1974
Taylor, Kenneth B.	Asst	Villanova		PHD	80	SUNY-SBr	1985
Taylor, Larry W.	Assoc	Lehigh	CE	PHD	84	N Carol	1984
Taylor, Lary		Pacific Unio					
Taylor, Laura L.	Asst	Georgia St	C	PHD	94	N Car St	1994
Taylor, Lester D.	Prof	Arizona		PHD	63	Harvard	1972
Taylor, Millicent M.	C-Ac	Carson-Newmn	DFCE	PHD	85	Tennessee	8-95
Taylor, Patrick A.	C-Ac	Millsaps	AD	PHD	85	Alabama	1984
Taylor, Susan W.	Assoc	Millsaps	AFH	PHD	89	LSU	1992
The J. A. Brown Chair of Business Administration							
Taylor, Wagiha A.	Prof	Wilkes	EFO	PHD	66	Clark	1969
Tchakerian, Viken	Asst	CS-Northrdge	N	PHD	91	UCLA	1991
Teeples, Ronald K.	Prof	Claremont		PHD	70	UCLA	1969
Boswell Professor of Economics							

Teferra, Daniel	C-Pr	Ferris State		PHD	79	Wisconsin	1980
Tellew, Fuad H.	Retir	Cal Poly-SLO		PHD	59	S Calif	1960
Telmer, Chris I.	Asst	Carnegie Mel		PHD	92	Queen's	1992
Telser, Lester G.	Emer	Chicago	1-98	PHD	56	Chicago	1958
Temimi, Akram	Asst	Alabama		PHD	96	Illinois	1996
Temin, Peter	Prof	MIT	N	PHD	64	MIT	1965
Elish Gray II Professor							
Temple, Frederick C.	Retir	Southern		PHD		Wisconsin	1950
Temple, Judy A.	Assoc	No Illinois	H	PHD	90	Mich St	1989
Tenenbaum, Marcel	Retir	Hofstra		PHD	69	Columbia	1964
Terkla, David G.	C-Pr	Mass-Boston	QRH	PHD	79	Berkeley	1987
Terrebonne, Peter	Asst	Georgia St	A	PHD	92	Emory	1992
Terregrossa, Ralph A.	Assoc	St John's		PHD	91	SUNY-Bin	
Terrell, Dek	Assoc	Louisiana St	C	PHD	91	Duke	8-96
Mack H. Hornbeak Business Professorship Professor							
Terrell, Timothy	Asst	Liberty	ACPQ	PHD	98	Auburn	1998
Terrell, William T.	Assoc	Wichita St		PHD	70	Vanderbilt	1967
Terry, Andy	C-Ac	Ark-Ltl Rock		PHD	89	Michigan	1989
Terry, Rory	Asst	Fort Hays St	GE	PHD	92	Utah	1997
Terza, Joseph V.	Assoc	Penn State	C	PHD	81	Pittsburgh	1986
Tesar, Linda L.	Assoc	Michigan	FGE	PHD	90	Rochester	
Tesfatsion, Leigh S.	Prof	Iowa State	E	PHD	75	Minnesota	1990
Thakur, Rita	Prof	LaVerne		MBA		NW Mo St	1978
Thanawala, Kishor H.	Prof	Villanova		PHD	61	Bombay	1967
Thanh, Pham Chi	Prof	American U		PHD		NS Wales	1976
Thaver, Ranjini L.	Assoc	Stetson	AHP	PHD	95	Notre Dm	1992
Thayer, Mark A.	C-Pr	San Diego St		PHD	79	New Mex	1981
Thewell, Raphael R.	Retir	Howard		PHD		Geo Wash	
Thiagarajan, K. R.	Asst	Prairie View	DE	MA	55	Annamali	1967
Thierfelder, Karen	Assoc	USN Academy		PHD	92	Wisconsin	1992
Thies, Clifford F.	Prof	Shenandoah		PHD	82	Boston C	1992
Thimester, Renate	Assoc	Loyola Marym	ABKM	PHD	67	Alabama	1971
Thistle, Paul D.	Prof	W Michigan	D	PHD	83	Tx A&M	1992
Thoma, George A. Jr.	Prof	Elmhurst		PHD	73	N Illinois	1970
Thoma, Mark A.	C-Ac	Oregon	E	PHD	85	Wash St	1987
Thomakos, Dimitrios	Asst	Fla Internat	CEO	PHD	98	Columbia	1998
Thomas, Christopher R.	Assoc	South Fla	L	PHD	80	Tx A&M	1982
Thomas, Duncan	Prof	UCLA		PHD	86	Princeton	
Thomas, George	Prof	Naval Postgr	J	PHD	71	Purdue	1978
Thomas, Hugh A.	Assoc	McMaster U	G	PHD	91	NYU	1991
Thomas, Janet M.	Prof	Bentley	DHQ	PHD	87	Boston C	1987
Thomas, John R.	Inst	Lehigh		PHD	96	SanDiego	1995
Thomas, Johnny	Asst	LaSierra	C	MBA	88	LomaLinda	1989
Thomas, Julia	Asst	Carnegie Mel					
Thomas, Lloyd B. Jr.	Prof	Kansas State	EA	PHD	70	Nrthwstrn	1968
Thomas, Michael	Asst	Florida A&M					
Thomas, Philip S.	Retir	Kalamazoo	FO	PHD	61	Michigan	1965
Thomas, Regina	Inst	No Alabama		MA	92	Alabama	1992
Thomas, Robert P.	Assoc	U Washington		PHD	64	Nrthwstrn	1968
Thomas, Robert W. Jr.	Deces	Iowa State	1994	PHD	62	Iowa St	1957
Thomas, Wade L.	C-Ac	SUNY-Oneonta	DEJ	PHD	82	Nebraska	1989
Thomas, William J.	Deces			PHD	57	Mich St	
Thomasson, Henry E.	Asst	SE Louisiana	AJ	MS		LSU	
Thompson, Alexander M.	Prof	Vassar	BH	PHD	79	Stanford	1977
Thompson, Allen R.	Assoc	New Hampshir	GM	PHD	73	Tx-Austin	1974
Thompson, Charles L.	Asst	Troy State		MS	82	Auburn	1984
Thompson, Dana	Prof	Walla Walla		EDD	89	LLU	1998
Thompson, Earl A.	Prof	UCLA		PHD	61	Harvard	1965
Thompson, Eric	Asst	Kentucky	R	PHD	92	Wisconsin	1995
Thompson, Frank W.	Lect	Michigan		PHD	73	Harvard	1990
Thompson, G. Richard	Prof	Clemson	HLM	PHD	72	Virginia	
Thompson, Gerald E.	Retir	Nebraska		PHD	53	Iowa	1954
Thompson, Henry L.	Prof	Auburn		PHD	81	Houston	1987
Thompson, Mary M.	Asst	Belmont		MA		Notre Dm	1983
Thompson, Paul J.	Retir	Mankato St	AI	PHD	68	Iowa	1963
Thompson, Paul W.	Retir	Jacksonvl St		PHD	70	Duke	1974
Thompson, Peter	Asst	Houston		PHD	94	Florida	1996
Thompson, Philip B.	Asst	Mo-Rolla		PHD	88	Arizona	1994
Thompson, William F.	Prof	E Illinois		PHD	79	Arkansas	1981
Thomson, Ross	Assoc	Vermont	NDB	PHD	76	Yale	1991
Thomson, William L.	Prof	Rochester	CDH	PHD	76	Stanford	9-83
Thorbecke, Erik	Prof	Cornell		PHD	57	Berkeley	1974
H. Edward Babcock Professor of Economics and Food Economics							
Thorbecke, Willem	Assoc	George Mason		PHD	88	Berkeley	
Thornberg, Christopher	Asst	Clemson	FJL	PHD	97	UCLA	1997
Thorne, Emanuel D.	Asst	CUNY-Brookly	A	PHD	94	Yale	1994
Thornton, James	Assoc	E Michigan		PHD	91	Oregon	1991
Thornton, James R.	Assoc	Delaware	P	PHD	74	Cornell	1973
Thornton, Judith Ann	Prof	U Washington		PHD	60	Harvard	1961
Thornton, Richard M.	Retir	DePaul		PHD	76	N Illinois	1974

Thornton, Robert J.	Prof	Lehigh	JI	PHD	70	Illinois	1970
Charles W. MacFarlane Professor of Economics							
Thorpe, Steven G.	Asst	No Iowa	HQ	PHD	95	Colorado	1996
Thorsnes, Paul E.	Asst	Grand Valley		PHD	94	Oregon	1995
Thorson, Douglas Y.	Retir	Bradley		PHD	62	Wisconsin	1960
Thorson, James A.	Assoc	So Conn St	R	PHD	91	Il-Chicago	1992
Throckmorton, H. Bruce	Prof	Tenn Tech		PHD	72	Arkansas	1971
Thurman, Walter N.	Prof	N Carol St	QCD	PHD	84	Chicago	1984
Thurow, Lester C.	Prof	MIT	F	PHD	64	Harvard	1968
Jerome and Dorothy Lemelson Professor of Economics and Management							
Thursby, Jerry G.	Prof	Purdue		PHD	75	N Carol	1988
Thursby, Marie C.	Prof	Purdue		PHD	74	N Carol	1988
Burton D. Morgan Chair of Intl Mgt Policy; Dir Cntr of Intl Busines Education							
Thurston, Norman	Asst	Brigham Yg	HIJ	PHD	95	Princeton	1995
Thurston, Thom B.	Prof	CUNY-Queens	EC	PHD	70	Berkeley	1971
Thweatt, William O.	Retir	Vanderbilt		BPHI	55	Oxford	1963
Tian, Guoqiang	Prof	Texas A&M	C	PHD	87	Minnesota	1987
Tidas, Sam	Asst	Wash & Jeff					1998
Tideman, T. Nicolaus	Prof	Virg Tech	H	PHD	69	Chicago	1975
Tiefenthaler, Jill M.	Assoc	Colgate	TO	PHD	91	Duke	1991
Tiemann, Thomas K.	Prof	Elon	RC	PHD	75	Vanderbilt	1984
Tiemstra, John P.	Prof	Calvin		PHD	75	MIT	1975
Tieslau, Margie	Asst	North Texas	EC	PHD	92	Mich St	1992
Tietenberg, Thomas H.	Prof	Colby	QK	PHD	71	Wisconsin	1977
Mitchell Family Professor of Economics							
Tiffany, Frederick G.	Asst	Wittenberg	ACDL	PHD	88	Penn	1987
Tijerina, Alfredo	Asst	Tx-Pan Amer		PHD	92	Cincinnati	1999
Timmer, C. Peter	Retir	Harvard		PHD	69	Harvard	1980
Timmermann, Allan	Assoc	Ca-San Diego	CG	PHD	92	Cambridge	1994
Timmins, Christopher	Asst	Yale	LH	PHD	97	Stanford	1997
Tinari, Frank D.	Prof	Seton Hall		PHD	76	Fordham	
Tirole, Jean	VProf	MIT	O	PHD	81	MIT	1984
Titus, Varkey K.	C-Ac	Emporia St		PHD	80	Wash St	8-79
Tiwari, Kashi N.	Assoc	Kennesaw St	CEG	PHD	81	So Meth	1988
Tix, Paul	Asst	Mankato St	AC	MS		N Dak St	1984
Tobias, Justin	Asst	Calif-Irvine		PHD	99	Chicago	1999
Toda, Yasushi	Assoc	Florida	RP	PHD	69	Harvard	1974
Todd, Edward		SUNY-Empire	A	PHD	69	Chicago	1985
Todd, Petra	Asst	Pennsylvania		PHD	96	Chicago	1996
Tohamy, Soumaya	Asst	Berry		PHD	94	Emory	1997
Tokar, Bette L.	Prof	Holy Family	AFED	EDD	93	Temple	9-75
Tokle, Robert J.	Asst	Idaho State	AGL	PHD	86	Iowa St	1986
Tolin, Thomas	Asst	West Chester	JD	PHD	92	Houston	1992
Tollen, Robert D.	Assoc	Txs-El Paso	D	PHD	72	Tx-Austin	1972
Tolley, George S.	Prof	Chicago		PHD	55	Chicago	1966
Tollison, Robert	Retir	George Mason		PHD	69	Virginia	
Tolliver, R. Wayne	Assoc	Berea		DBA	87	Kentucky	1975
Tolpin, Harriet G.	Retir	Simmons	I	PHD	73	Boston C	1974
Toma, Eugenia F.	Prof	Kentucky	H	PHD	77	Va Tech	1977
Toma, Mark	Assoc	Kentucky	E	PHD	51	Va Tech	1989
Toma, Michael	Asst	Armstrong At	RE	PHD	96	GeoMason	1997
Tomal, Annette	Asst	Wheaton-IL	AIM	PHD	95	Illinois	1995
Tomaske, John A.	Retir	CS-L Angeles		PHD	68	U Wash	1965
Tombe, Wani Luan	C-As	St Edwards		PHD	85	Tx-Austin	1990
Tomer, John F.	C-Pr	Manhattan		PHD	73	Rutgers	1983
Tomic, Igor M.	Assoc	St John's		PHD	85	CUNY	
Tomlin, KaSaundra	Asst	Cen Florida		PHD			
Tomljanovich, Marc	VAsst	Union	ECF	PHD	98	Cornell	1998
Toniolo, Gianni	Resr	Duke		LAUR	66	Venice	
Tonn, Victor Lux	C-Pr	Salve Regina	AGOP	PHD	94	Utah St	1984
Tontar, Charles F.	Assoc	Merrimack		MA		New Sch	
Tontz, Jay L.	Dean	CS-Hayward	EGM	PHD	66	N Carol	9-69
Topa, Giorgio	Asst	New York U	C	PHD	96	Chicago	1996
Toporovsky, Rinaldo	Retir	F Dick-Teane	AEG	PHD	72	Columbia	1969
Topping, Elizabeth E.	Asst	SW Missouri		PHD	85	Missouri	1979
Topyan, Kudret	Assoc	Manhattan		PHD	92	CUNY	1991
Tori, Cynthia R.	Asst	Valdosta St	EF	PHD	92	Kentucky	1998
Torras, Mariano	Asst	SUNY-Cortlan	FOP	PHD		Mass	1999
Toruno, Mayo C.	C-Pr	CS-San Bern	B	PHD	83	Ca-Rivers	1983
Tosh, Dennis S.	Assoc	Mississippi		PHD	80	Geo St	1980
Toumanoff, Peter	Assoc	Marquette	DOPC	PHD	77	U Wash	1995
Tourk, Khairy A.	Assoc	Illinois Tch		PHD	71	Berkeley	
Tournas, Ioannis	Asst	Rutgers-Newk		PHD	95	Nrthwstrn	1996
Towor, Edward	Prof	Duke		PHD	71	Harvard	1974
Townsend, David C.	Prof	Sam Houston		PHD	53	LSU	1982
Townsend, Ralph E.	Prof	Maine	CHQA	PHD	83	Wisconsin	1980
Townsend, Robert M.	Prof	Chicago		PHD	75	Minnesota	1985
Charles E. Merriam Professor							
Traca, Daniel	Asst	INSEAD		PHD	96	Columbia	9-96
Tracy, Ronald L.	Assoc	Oakland	CE	PHD	75	Mich St	1983

Name	Rank	School	Fields	Degree	Yr	Institution	Hired
Trainor, William J.	Asst	Virginia St		PHD	94	Va Tech	1996
Tran, Dang	Prof	CS-L Angeles		PHD	77	Syracuse	1987
Trandel, Gregory A.	Assoc	Georgia	GK	PHD	92	Princeton	1989
Trask, Kathleen	Asst	Kentucky	FO	PHD	98	Penn St	1998
Travis, Karen M.	Asst	Pacific Luth	I	PHD	95	U Wash	1999
Trawick, Michelle	Asst	Bellarmine		PHD	96	N Car St	1999
Traynham, Earle C. Jr.	Dean	North Fla		PHD	73	S Carol	1973
Traynor, Thomas L.	C-Ac	Wright State		PHD	88	Purdue	1988
Treacy, John J.	Retir	Wright State		PHD	64	Tulane	1967
Trebing, Harry M.	Retir	Michigan St		PHD	58	Wisconsin	1966
Trees, W. Scott	C-As	Siena		PHD	94	Notre Dm	9-85
Tregarthen, Timothy D.	Retir	Colorado Spr	DEHR	PHD	72	Ca-Davis	1971
Trejo, Stephen J.	Assoc	Texas	J	PHD	88	Chicago	9-99
Tremblay, Carol	Assoc	Oregon State	CJ	PHD	84	Wash St	9-92
Tremblay, Victor J.	C-Pr	Oregon State	DLC	PHD	83	Wash St	9-90
Treml, Vladimir G.	Emer	Duke		PHD	63	N Carol	1967
Trenary, Roger C.	Inst	Kansas State	A	MA	72	Wayne St	1977
Tresch, Richard W.	C-Ac	Boston Coll	H	PHD	73	MIT	1969
Trescott, Paul B.	Emer	So Illinois	EB	PHD	54	Princeton	1976
Trethewey, Richard L.	Assoc	Kenyon	NFKB	PHD	71	U Wash	1969
Trevino, Len	Asst	So Miss	F	PHD	91	Indiana	1999
Treyz, George I.	Retir	Massachusett	1995	PHD	67	Cornell	1969
Tribble, John A.	Assoc	Russell Sage		PHD	75	Utah St	1976
Lawrence Professor of Economics							
Trierweiler, John	C-Pr	Northern St		PHD	70	Nebraska	1985
Trimby, F. Stephen	Assoc	Worcester St		ABD			1970
Trimm, John M.	Deces			PHD	67	Mich St	
Trivedi, Pravin K.	Prof	Indiana		PHD	70	LondonEc	1987
Trogen, Paul	Asst	East Tenn St		PHD	95	Fla St	1995
Troske, Kenneth	Asst	Missouri	J	PHD	92	Chicago	1997
Trost, Alice	Asst	Mass-Boston	RH	PHD	95	SUNY-Bin	1992
Trost, Robert P.	Prof	George Wash	C	PHD	77	Florida	1981
Troy, Leo	Prof	Rutgers-Newk		PHD	58	Columbia	
Troyer, Jennifer	Asst	N Car-Charl		PHD	99	Florida	1999
Troyer, Michael D.	Assoc	WI-Green Bay		PHD	75	Duke	
Truett, Dale B.	Prof	Tx-S Antonio	DFMO	PHD	67	Tx-Austin	1973
Asbel Smith Professor							
Truitt, Terry	Assoc	Anderson U	G	PHD	96	Miss St	1995
Truitt, W. James	C-Pr	Baylor	D	PHD	68	Illinois	1968
Herman W. Lay Prof Private Enterprise, & Director Cntr/Priv Entrp							
Trulove, William T.	C-Pr	East Wash		PHD	73	Oregon	1969
Trumbull, William N.	C-Ac	W Virginia	HKD	PHD	85	N Carol	1983
Truscott, Michael Hugh	C-Pr	Tampa	AEF	PHD	71	LSU	1971
Trussell, T. James	Prof	Princeton	CIT	PHD	75	Princeton	O-74
Trussler, Susan	Assoc	Scranton		PHD	89	Penn St	1985
Tryon, Joseph L.	Retir	Georgetown		PHD	61	Harvard	
Tsai, Mau-Sung	Retir	Evansville		PHD	66	S Illinois	1964
Tschirhart, John T.	Prof	Wyoming	DK	PHD	75	Purdue	1985
Tseng, Hui-Kuan	Assoc	N Car-Charl		PHD	88	Illinois	1988
Tseng, S. C.	Prof	Catawba		PHD	72	Oklahoma	
Tsiang, Grace	SLect	Chicago		PHD	91	Chicago	1990
Tsoulouhas, Theofanis	Asst	N Carol St	CD	PHD	93	Illinois	1993
Tsournos, Pete	Asst	Whitman	LQ	PHD	99	Wyoming	1998
Tsurumi, Hiroki	Prof	Rutgers-N Br	C	PHD	67	Penn	1974
Tu, Yien-I	Retir	Arkansas	C	PHD	61	Iowa St	1981
Tuck, Bradford H.	Prof	Alaska-Ancho	CDL	PHD	73	Boston U	1977
Tucker, Dean	C-Pr	Ogelthorpe	HMQ	PHD	79	Mich St	1-88
Rikard Chaired Professor							
Tucker, Irvin B. III	Assoc	N Car-Charl		PHD	82	S Carol	1981
Tuerck, David G.	C-Pr	Suffolk		PHD	66	Virginia	1982
Tufte, David R.	Assoc	New Orleans		PHD	92	SUNY-Buf	1992
Tullock, Gordon	Prof	Arizona		JD	47	Chicago	1987
Tully, Cathyann	Asst	Kean					
Tuma, Elias H.	Emer	Cal-Davis	ANO	PHD	62	Berkeley	1967
Turchi, Boone A.	Assoc	No Carolina	AT	PHD	73	Michigan	1971
Turek, Joseph H.	Assoc	Lynchburg		PHD	87	SUNY-Alb	1986
Turk, Michael	Assoc	Fitchburg St		PHD	76	Harvard	1982
Turnbull, Geoffrey K.	Prof	Louisiana St	DH	PHD	83	Wi-Milwa	1984
CJ Brown Distinguished Professor of Real Estate; Gulfcoast Bottling Dist Prof							
Turner, Charlie G.	Assoc	Old Dominion		PHD	81	Harvard	1984
Turner, Keith K.	Prof	Neb-Omaha	EM	PHD	68	Nebraska	1969
Turner, Robert W.	Assoc	Colgate	CH	PHD	84	MIT	1983
Turnovsky, Michelle H. L.	SLect	U Washington		PHD	78	Austr Natl	1987
Turnovsky, Stephen J.	Prof	U Washington		PHD	68	Harvard	1987
Turunen-Red, Arja H.	Prof	New Orleans		PHD	85	Brit Colum	1995
Tussing, A. Dale	Prof	Syracuse	I	PHD	64	Syracuse	1966
Tutterow, Roger C.	C-Ac	Kennesaw St	CDGM	PHD	90	Geo St	1991
Twight, Charlotte	Prof	Boise State	HKN	PHD	83	U Wash	1986
Twomey, Michael J.	Prof	Mich-Dearbor	FNO	PHD	73	Cornell	1977
Tyler, Thomas P.	Dean	Ark Tech		PHD	80	Arkansas	1967

Tyson, Laura D.	Prof	Cal-Berkeley		PHD	74	MIT	1977
Tzannetakis, George	Prof	Seton Hall		PHD	64	NYU	
Uctum, Merih	Asst	CUNY-Brookly		PHD	89	Queens	1996
Udis, Bernard	Retir	Colorado		PHD	59	Princeton	1965
Udry, Christopher R.	Prof	Yale	O	PHD	91	Yale	1998
Ueng, C. Joe	Asst	St Thomas-TX	GM	PHD	95	St Louis	1996
Ukpolo, Victor	Prof	Austin Peay	FO	PHD	85	American	1988
Ullah, Aman	Prof	Cal-Riversid	C	PHD	71	Delhi	1989
Ullerich, Stan	Assoc	Buena Vista	AQMA	PHD	95	Purdue	9-94
Ulveling, Edwin F.	Retir	Georgia St	AO	PHD	81	Iowa St	1967
Umbeck, John R.	Prof	Purdue		PHD	76	U Wash	1975
Unger, Kay C.	Prof	Montana	IDEC	PHD	74	J Hopkins	
Upchurch, Leo	Assoc	Tuskegee		PHD	82	Michigan	1990
Uppal, Jogindar S.	Prof	SUNY-Albany	OH	PHD	65	Minnesota	1971
Upton, Charles W.	Prof	Kent State	EQ	PHD	69	Car Mellon	8-89
Ureta, Manuelita	Assoc	Texas A&M	J	PHD	87	UCLA	1991
Urquhart, Robert	Assoc	Denver	BN	PHD	88	New Sch	1988
Uselding, Paul J.	Dean	Saginaw Vall	N	PHD	70	Nrthwstrn	1999
Usip, Ebenge E.	Assoc	Youngstown		PHD	84	Conn	1985
Uyar, Bulent	Assoc	No Iowa	ACH	PHD	77	Pittsburgh	1991
Uze, Barry A.		Troy State		MA	85	Miss	1989
Vachris, Michelle A.	Asst	Chris Newpor	DFHK	PHD	92	GeoMason	1994
Vafaie, Massie S.	C-As	Cen St-Ohio		PHD	79	Cincinnati	1991
Vahaly, John	Assoc	Louisville	R	PHD	75	Vanderbilt	1975
Vaidya, Ashish K.	Assoc	CS-L Angeles		PHD	90	Ca Davis	1991
Vail, David Jeremiah	Prof	Bowdoin	OQ	PHD	71	Yale	1970
Adams-Catlin Professor of Economics							
Vaitheswaran, Ramakrishna	Retir	Coe	AFOP	PHD	77	Iowa St	1973
Valencia, Jesus M.	Asst	Slippery Roc	ACFJ	PHD	88	Pittsburgh	1983
Valentine, John	Dean	McMurry		MBA		Abilene	1980
Valentine, Lloyd M.	Retir	Cincinnati		MA	51	UCLA	1954
Valentino, Salvatore	Retir	Creighton	A	PHD	54	Nebraska	1961
Valev, Neven T.	Asst	Georgia St	EF	PHD	97	Purdue	1998
Valimaki, Juuso	Asst	Northwestern		PHD	95	Penn	1995
Vamosi, Alexander	Asst	Wooster		PHD	95	N Carol	1995
Van Boening, Mark V.	Assoc	Mississippi	BDL	PHD	91	Arizona	1990
Van Cott, T. Norman	Prof	Ball State	FH	PHD	69	U Wash	1977
Van den Berg, Hendrik F.	Assoc	Nebraska	F	PHD	89	Wisconsin	1989
Van den Nouweland, Anne	Asst	Oregon	CL	PHD	93	Tilburg	1996
Van Der Heide, Evert M.	Prof	Calvin		PHD	82	Wayne St	1982
Van Huyck, John B.	Prof	Texas A&M	CD	PHD	86	Brown	1985
Private Enterprise Research Center Rex B. Grey Professor							
Van Zandt, Timothy	Asst	INSEAD	CD	PHD	89	Penn	9-98
Van't Veld, Klaas	Asst	Michigan					
Vandegrift, Donald	Asst	C New Jersey		PHD	93	Conn	
Vander Linde, Scott H.	Asst	Calvin		PHD	89	Notre Dm	
Vander Meulen, Allen Jr.	Retir	No Central		PHD	75	Brown	1978
Vanderhart, Peter G.	Assoc	Bowling Gr		PHD	91	Wisconsin	1991
VanderHoff, James H.	Prof	Rutgers-Newk		PHD	79	N Carol	1980
Vanderklaauw, H. Wilbert	Assoc	No Carolina	J	PHD	92	Brown	1999
Vanderporten, Bruce S.	Assoc	Loyola-Chicg	ACD	PHD	73	Wayne St	1978
VanderSluius, Evert	Asst	So Dakota St	FO	PHD	93	Minnesota	1997
Vandewetering, Hylke	Prof	Iowa State	O	PHD	64	Iowa St	1964
VanEaton, Charles D.	Retir	Hillsdale		PHD	74	Tulane	1978
Vanek, Jaroslav	Retir	Cornell		PHD	58	MIT	
VanHoose, David D.	Prof	Alabama		PHD	84	N Carol	1990
VanMatre, Joe G	Prof	Alabama-Birm	C	PHD	70	Alabama	1971
VanRensselaer	Asst	No Alabama		ABD		Miss St	1991
Vanscyoc, Lee	Assoc	Wis-Oshkosh	AL	PHD	87	Nebraska	1987
Vargha, Nader	Assoc	Missouri Wes	B	MA		Oklahoma	1980
Varghese, Adel	Asst	St Louis		PHD	96	Penn	1995
Varghese, K. Thomas	Prof	Jms Madison	E	PHD	71	Wayne St	1970
Varma, Ranbir	C-Pr	Lg Isl-Brook	AFOP	PHD	57	New Sch	1959
Varma, Umesh C.	Inst	Campbell		MS		Jackson	1988
Varsha, Linda	Asst	Skidmore		PHD	99	Wisconsin	1999
Vasigh, Bijan	Prof	Embry-Riddle		PHD	84	SUNY-Bin	
Vaughan, Ben F.	Assoc	Tx Lutheran		PHD	97	Berkeley	1998
Vaughan, Michael B.	Dean	Weber State	AMK	PHD	80	Nebraska	1981
Vaughn, Karen I.	Prof	George Mason		PHD	71	Duke	1978
Vedder, Richard K.	Prof	Ohio Univ		PHD	65	Illinois	1965
Distinguished Professor							
Veendorp, Emiel C.	Prof	Clark		PHD	63	Rice	1976
Vegh, Carlos	Assoc	UCLA		PHD	87	Chicago	
Veitch, John	C-Ac	San Francisc	EG	PHD	85	Nrthwstrn	1985
Velasco, Andres	Assoc	New York U	F	PHD	88	Columbia	1989
Velenchik, Ann D.	Assoc	Wellesley		PHD	89	Stanford	1989
Velez, Alejandro	Prof	St Marys-Txs		PHD	77	Florida	
Vella, Francis G. M.	Asst	Rutgers-N Br	C	PHD	90	Rochester	1997
Vencill, C. Daniel	Prof	San Fran St		PHD	71	Stanford	1974
Venieris, Yiannis P.	Prof	San Diego St		PHD	69	Oregon	1967

Name	Rank	School	Fields	Degree	Yr	Institution	Since
Venti, Steven F.	Prof	Dartmouth		PHD	82	Harvard	1982
Ventocilla, Antonio A.	Retir	Ferris State		MA		American	1967
Ventura, Jaume	Assoc	MIT	E	PHD	95	Harvard	1995
Verbrugge, Randal J.	Asst	Virg Tech	EF	PHD	95	Stanford	1995
Vercella, Kit J.	Prof	Alaska-Ancho	ADEO	MA	72	Ca-SnDgo	1974
Verdugo, Paul	Asst	Azusa Pacif		MA	76	Ca Poly	9-80
Vernarelli, Michael J.	C-Pr	Rochest Tech		PHD	78	SUNY-Bin	1976
Vernon, Jack R.	Prof	Florida	E	PHD	61	Nrthwstrn	1967
Vernon, John M.	Prof	Duke		PHD	66	MIT	1969
Vernon, Thomas T.	Retir	Clarion		PHD	71	Kansas St	1969
Verrall, George	C-Ac	Miss State		DBA	72	Miss St	1965
Versteeg, Jennie G.	Prof	St Michael's	ANFO	PHD	74	Clark	1980
Veseth, Michael	Prof	Puget Sound	AFH	PHD	76	Purdue	1975
Vesterlund, Lise	Asst	Iowa State	H	PHD	97	Wisconsin	1997
Vickers, Douglas W.	Retir	Massachusett	1995	PHD	56	London	1977
Vijverberg, Wim P. M.	Prof	Texas-Dallas		PHD	81	Pittsburgh	1986
Viksnins, George J.	Prof	Georgetown		PHD	64	Geotown	1968
Vilasuso, Jon R.	Asst	W Virginia	EFG	PHD	94	Conn	1999
Villamil, Anne P.	Assoc	Illinois	EG	PHD	88	Minnesota	1988
Villegas, Daniel J.	Asst	Cal Poly-SLO		PHD	79	Stanford	1987
Vincent, Daniel	Assoc	Maryland		PHD	87	Princeton	1998
Vincent, James W.	Assoc	St Thomas-MN	Q	PHD	82	Wisconsin	1988
Vines, Timothy	C-Ac	La St-Shreve		PHD	92	Tennessee	1989
Vinje, David L.	Prof	Pacific Luth	O	PHD	64	Wisconsin	1970
Vinod, Hrishinesh D.	Prof	Fordham		PHD	65	Harvard	1982
Virts, Nancy L.	Asst	CS-Northrdge	N	PHD	85	UCLA	1985
Visgilio, Gerald R.	Prof	Conn Coll	K	PHD	73	Rhode Isl	
Vishwasrao, Sharmila	Asst	Fla Atlantic	F	PHD	94	Purdue	1995
Vissing-Jorgensen,	Asst	Chicago		PHD		MIT	1998
Vitallano, Donald F.	Prof	Rensselaer		PHD	69	CUNY	1969
Vo, Han X.	Assoc	Winthrop	EF	PHD	79	Tennessee	9-79
Voelker, Keith E.	Retir	Wis-Oshkosh	J	PHD	69	Wisconsin	1970
Vogelsang, Ingo	Prof	Boston Univ	HL	PHD	69	Heidelbe	1981
Vogt, Michael G.	Prof	E Michigan		PHD	76	Wisconsin	1978
Vogt, Walter H.	Retir	San Diego St		PHD		Syracuse	1974
Vohra, Rajiv	Prof	Brown		PHD	83	J Hopkins	
Vohra, Rubina A.	Asst	NewJerseyCty	AJO	PHD	93	Northeas	9-94
Volij, Oscar	Assoc	Brown		PHD	94	Hebrew	
Von Allmen, Peter	Assoc	Moravian	CDL	PHD	90	Temple	1990
Von Ende, Eleanor Theresa	Asst	Texas Tech		PHD	90	Kansas	1990
von Furstenberg, George	Prof	Indiana		PHD	66	Princeton	1970
Rudy Professor of Economics							
vonderRuhr, Marc	Asst	St Norbert		PHD	99	Indiana	1999
VonDonsel, Richard	Lect	SUNY-Cortlan					
VonHagen, Jurgen	Prof	Indiana		PHD	86	Bonn	1987
Vonortas, Nicholas S.	Assoc	George Wash	OL	PHD	89	NYU	
Vorst, Karen S.	Prof	Mo-Kansas Ct	EC	PHD	80	Indiana	1980
Vose, David	Assoc	Minn-Duluth	QA	PHD	66	Wisconsin	1966
Votey, Harold L. Jr.	Retir	Cal-Santa Br		PHD	68	Berkeley	1976
Vowels, Robert C.	Prof	Tenn State		PHD	64	American	
Vredeveld, George	Prof	Cincinnati		PHD	73	Indiana	1977
Vroman, Susan	Prof	Georgetown		PHD	77	J Hopkins	1978
Vrooman, David H. Jr.	Retir	St Lawrence	GE	PHD	76	SUNY-Alb	1965
Vruwink, Carol J.	C-Ac	Central Iowa		MS	82	Drake	1979
Vuong, Quang	C-Pr	So Calif		PHD	82	Nrthwstrn	1987
Wachtel, Howard M.	Prof	American U		PHD	69	Michigan	1969
Wachtel, Paul A.	Prof	New York U	EG	PHD	71	Rochester	1972
Research Professor							
Wachter, Daniel R.	C-Ac	DePauw		PHD	82	Purdue	1979
Waddoups, C. Jeffrey	Assoc	Nev-L Vegas	J	PHD	89	Utah	1989
Wade, Ernie	Inst	Radford	AQ	MS	86	Va Tech	1997
Wade, John	C-Ac	W Carolina		PHD	82	Purdue	1977
Wadhawan, Satish C.	Prof	Howard	FO	PHD		Nehru	
Wadman, William Morgan	Assoc	N Car-Wilmin	CDH	PHD	76	Claremont	
Wadsworth, Daniel	Inst	SE Louisiana		MBA	96	LSU	
Waggle, J. Douglas	Asst	Berry		PHD	94	Alabama	1994
Wagner, F. Eugene	Prof	Mo-Kansas Ct	AJO	PHD	67	Syracuse	1967
Wagner, John R.	Assoc	Westfield St		PHD	77	Temple	1986
Wagner, Richard E.	Prof	George Mason		PHD	66	Virginia	1988
Holbert I. Harris Professor of Economics							
Wagoner, Charles	Asst	Delta State	ACFG	PHD	93	Tulane	8-95
Wahid, Abu	Prof	Tenn State		PHD	89	Manitoba	
Wahl, Jenny Bourne	Asst	Carleton	JKN	PHD	86	Chicago	1998
Wakeman, Douglas	Assoc	Meredith		PHD	86	N Carol	1987
Walbert, Mark S.	Assoc	Illinois St	CDE	PHD	84	New Mex	1984
Waldauer, Charles	Prof	Widener	DEHR	PHD	69	Syracuse	1968
Waldman, Don E.	Prof	Colgate	L	PHD	76	Cornell	1981
Richard M. Kessler Professor of Economic Studies							
Waldman, Donald M.	Prof	Colorado		PHD	79	Wisconsin	1984
Waldo, Douglas G.	Assoc	Florida	EFO	PHD	80	N Carol	1981

Waldron, Randall	Asst	South Dakota		PHD	94	Vanderbilt	1994
Walgreen, John A.	Prof	Wheaton-MA		PHD	65	Boston C	1967
Walgreen, Sonia	VLect	Mass-Dartmou		MA	63	Boston C	1984
Walka, Joseph J.	Prof	No Arizona	HI	PHD	69	Harvard	1986
Walker, Craig	Asst	Delta State	ACFG	PHD	96	So Meth	8-96
Walker, Deborah L.	C-Ac	Loyola-N Orl	ABDJ	PHD	87	GeoMason	1987
Walker, Donald A.	Retir	Indiana U-PA	BD	PHD	61	Harvard	1969
Walker, Franklin V.	Retir	SUNY-Albany	FE	PHD	58	Harvard	1966
Walker, James M.	Prof	Indiana		PHD	78	Tx A&M	1984
Walker, James R.	C-Pr	Wisconsin		PHD	86	Chicago	1987
Walker, John	Assoc	Wis-Rvr Fall	JB	PHD	89	Utah	1990
Walker, John F.	Prof	Portland St		PHD	72	Utah	1966
Walker, Mark A.	Prof	Arizona		PHD	70	Purdue	1990
Walker, Mary Beth	Assoc	Georgia St	DC	PHD	86	Rice	1991
Walker, Roger	Deces	Hamline	J	PHD	59	Cornell	1969
Walker, Rosemary	Lect	Wis-Whitewat		ABD		Illinois	1998
Wallace, Don	Assoc	St Martin		PHD	63	U Wash	
Wallace, Frederick H.	Assoc	Appalach St	E	PHD	87	Rice	1986
Wallace, Myles S.	Prof	Clemson	EFC	PHD	76	Colorado	1980
Wallace, Neil	Prof	Penn State	E	PHD	64	Chicago	1997
Wallace, Richard L.	Prof	Missouri		PHD	65	Vanderbilt	1967
Wallace, Richard M.	Prof	Wofford	ABK	PHD	81	S Carol	1982
Wallace, Robert	C-Pr	Framingham		PHD	72	Nrthwstrn	
Wallace, Sally	Assoc	Georgia St	GH	PHD	88	Syracuse	1991
Wallace, Suzanne	Assoc	Central Iowa	DJE	PHD	91	Georgia	1991
Wallace, T. Dudley	Emer	Duke					
James D. Duke Professor							
Waller, Christopher J.	Assoc	Kentucky	E	PHD	86	Wash St	1998
Waller, Robert L.	Assoc	USAF Academy	AF	PHD	86	Boston U	1998
Wallis, John J.	Prof	Maryland		PHD	81	U Wash	1983
Walsh, C. Gerald	Asst	Villanova		MA	60	Detroit	1960
Walsh, Carl E.	Prof	Ca-Santa Crz	E	PHD	76	Berkeley	1987
Walsh, Vivian	Lect	Muhlenberg		PHD	53	Trinity	1989
Walsh, William J.	Assoc	St Thomas-MN	E	PHD	70	Notre Dm	1970
Walstad, William B.	Prof	Nebraska	I	PHD	78	Minnesota	1982
State Farm Professorship							
Walter, Ingo	Prof	New York U	FG	PHD	66	NYU	1970
Charles Simon Professor of Applied Financial Economics							
Walters, Joan G.	Retir	Fairfield	EF	PHD	52	Harvard	1963
Walters, Stephen J. K.	Prof	Loyola-Maryl	KL	PHD	82	UCLA	1981
Walther, Theodore	Prof	Bates	FG	PHD	64	New Sch	1958
Walton, Gary M.	Prof	Cal-Davis	ADN	PHD	66	U Wash	1981
Waltzman, Norman J.	Assoc	Utah		PHD	88	American	1988
Walzer, Norman C.	D-Pr	W Illinois	AHR	PHD	70	Illinois	1970
Wan, Henry Y. Jr.	Prof	Cornell		PHD	61	MIT	
Wan, Siaw-Peng	Asst	Elmhurst		PHD	94	Illinois	1995
Wang, Cheng	Asst	Carnegie Mel		PHD	94	W Ontario	1994
Wang, Xinghe	Asst	Missouri	CDO	PHD	90	Iowa	1990
Ward, Benjamin N.	Retir	Cal-Berkeley		PHD		Berkeley	
Ward, John O.	C-Pr	Mo-Kansas Ct	KIO	PHD	70	Oklahoma	1969
Ware, Stephen B.	Retir	Indiana U-PA	BE	BA	61	Ohio Wes	1969
Warlick, Jennifer L.	Assoc	Notre Dame	HI	PHD	79	Wisconsin	1981
Warner, Geoffrey	Asst	Ind-Purdue/I	I	PHD	94	CUNY	1998
Warner, John T.	Prof	Clemson	DJE	PHD	76	N Car St	1980
Warner, Larkin B.	Retir	Oklahoma St		PHD	61	Indiana	1960
Warner, Lori	Assoc	Pacific	EN	PHD	86	Utah	1987
Warning, Matt	Asst	Puget Sound	ACO	PHD	97	Berkeley	1997
Warren, J. Harold	Assoc	East Tenn St		PHD	69	Okla St	1969
Warren, Ronald S.	Assoc	Georgia	JC	PHD	76	N Carol	1985
Warren, Stanton A.	Prof	Niagara		PHD	73	SUNY-Buf	1981
Washer, Kenneth	Asst	Tx A&M-Comm	CEG	DBA	98	La Tech	1996
Wasnich, Wendy	Asst	Ashland		MA		Ohio St	1985
Wassall, Gregory H.	Assoc	Northeastern		PHD	78	Rutgers	1979
Wassink, Darwin	Retir	Wis-Eau Clar	FO	PHD	68	Stanford	1976
Wassmer, Robert W.				PHD	89	Mich St	
Wassom, John C.	H-Pr	W Kentucky	G	PHD	70	Indiana	1971
Wasson, E. Dale	Prof	SW Missouri		PHD	80	Okla St	1969
Wasylenko, Michael J.	Prof	Syracuse	H	PHD	75	Syracuse	1989
Waters, Melissa S.	Asst	SW Louisiana	CJT	PHD	89	LSU	8-90
Watkins, John P.	C-Pr	Westminst-UT	BNQ	PHD	85	Utah	1984
Watkins, Thayer H.	Prof	San Jose St		PHD	65	Colorado	1957
Watkins, Thomas G.	Prof	E Kentucky		PHD	79	Iowa St	1984
Watkins, Todd A.	Asst	Lehigh	LO	PHD	95	Harvard	1992
Watson, Harry S.	C-Pr	George Wash	H	PHD	81	Indiana	1980
Watson, J. Keith	Asst	SW Louisiana		PHD	83	Tx A&M	
Watson, James O.	Assoc	Millikin		PHD	76	Purdue	1979
Watson, Joel	Assoc	Ca-San Diego	CF	PHD	92	Stanford	1994
Watson, Mark W.	Prof	Princeton		PHD	80	Ca-SnDgo	
Watters, Francis M.	Retir	CS-Chico		PHD	66	Berkeley	1966
Watts, Alison	Asst	Vanderbilt	DHG	PHD	93	Duke	1993

Name	Rank	School	Fields	Degree	Yr	Granting Inst.	Year
Watts, Harold	Retir	Columbia	P	PHD	57	Yale	1976
Watts, Michael W.	Prof	Purdue		PHD	78	LSU	1981
Watts, Royce J.	Asst	W Virginia	C	MS	61	W Virginia	1955
Waud, Roger N.	Retir	No Carolina		PHD	65	Berkeley	1969
Way, Philip K.	Assoc	Cincinnati	J	PHD	86	Warwick	1985
Weathers, Milledge W.	Retir	Adrian		PHD	61	Munich	1968
Weaver, James H.	Retir	American U		PHD	63	Oklahoma	1963
Weaver, Janice E.	Assoc	Drake		PHD	76	Illinois	1983
Webb, Michael A.	Dean	Xavier	FO	PHD	80	Illinois	1997
Webb, Natalie J.	Asst	Naval Postgr	H	PHD	92	Duke	1992
Webb, Samuel C.	Prof	Wichita St		PHD	68	Kansas	1966
Webber, Douglas	Assoc	INSEAD		PHD	85	Essex	1-91
Weber, Arnold R.	Retir	Northwestern	1994	PHD		MIT	
Weber, Charles T.	Assoc	Mich-Flint		PHD	77	Wayne St	1977
Weber, Christian E.	Asst	Seattle	EO	PHD	92	Duke	1993
Weber, Richard E.	Retir	Monmouth		PHD	74	Rutgers	9-79
Weber, Shlomo	C-Pr	So Methodist	DHL	PHD	79	Hebrew	1993
Robert H. & Nancy Dedman Trustee Professor							
Weber, William L.	Prof	SE Missouri	GHI	PHD	86	S Illinois	1986
Weckstein, Richard S.	Retir	Brandeis		PHD	53	Yale	1962
Weeks, Gregory C.		Evergreen St		PHD	78	Wash St	1981
Wegge, Leon L.	Emer	Cal-Davis	F	PHD	63	MIT	1966
Wehr, Roger	Lect	Tx-Arlington	DE	MA	96	Tx-Arlin	1993
Weida, William J.	Prof	Colorado Col		DBA	75	Colorado	1985
Weidenbaum, Murray L.	Prof	Wash Univ	HM	PHD	58	Princeton	1961
Edward Mallinckrodt Distinguished University Professor							
Weidenmeir, Marc	Asst	Claremont		PHD	99	Illinois	1999
Weiher, Kenneth E.	Assoc	Tx-S Antonio	BEN	PHD	75	Indiana	1975
Weil, David	Prof	Brown		PHD	90	Harvard	
Weil, Gordon	Prof	Wheaton-MA	FOP	PHD	81	Tufts	1981
Weil, Philippe	VProf	MIT		PHD	85	Harvard	1999
Weiler, John E.	Prof	Dayton	H	PHD	73	Cincinnati	1967
Weiler, Stephan	Asst	Colorado St	RO	PHD	94	Berkeley	1996
Weiman, David F.	Assoc	CUNY-Queens	NOE	PHD	84	Stanford	1994
Weinberg, Bruce	Asst	Ohio State	J	PHD	96	Chicago	1996
Weinberg, David R.	Assoc	Xavier	ARP	PHD	73	Berkeley	1980
Weinrobe, Maurice D.	Prof	Clark		PHD	69	Cornell	1976
Weinstein, David E.	Prof	Columbia	FL	PHD	91	Michigan	1999
Weinstein, Paul A.	Deces	Maryland		PHD	61	Nrthwstrn	1965
Weintraub, Andrew R.	Assoc	Temple	A	PHD	66	Rutgers	1973
Weintraub, Irvin	Assoc	Towson		MS	51	Columbia	1966
Welr, David R.	VAsoc	Chicago		PHD	83	Stanford	1995
Weis, Charles E.	Prof	Tenn State		DBA	74	Ariz St	
Weisbrod, Burton A.	Prof	Northwestern		PHD	58	Nrthwstrn	
John Evans Professor of Economic, Director,Ctr for Urban Affairs & Policy Rec							
Weise, Charles	Asst	Wm & Mary		PHD	93	Wisconsin	1993
Weisenborn, David E.	Retir	Geo Southern		PHD	68	Florida	1976
Weiser, Lawrence A.	Prof	Wis-Stev Pt		PHD	67	Wisconsin	1972
Weisman, Dennis	Assoc	Kansas State	LKD	PHD	93	Florida	1993
Weiss, Andrew M.	Prof	Boston Univ	DGJ	PHD	76	Stanford	1987
Weiss, Jeffrey		SUNY-Empire	A	PHD	67	Harvard	1986
Weiss, Jeffrey H.	Assoc	CUNY-Baruch		PHD	81	Wisconsin	1981
Weiss, Merle	Assoc	Temple	IJ	PHD	67	Columbia	1972
Weiss, Steven J.	Prof	Toledo	HI	PHD	71	Colorado	1968
Weiss, Thomas J.	Prof	Kansas	NF	PHD	67	N Carol	1967
Weisskopf, Thomas E.	Prof	Michigan		PHD	66	MIT	1972
Weitzman, Martin L.	Prof	Harvard		PHD	67	MIT	1989
Ernest E. Monrad Professor of Economics							
Welch, Finis R.	Prof	Texas A&M	J	PHD	66	Chicago	1991
Distinguished Professor and George T. & Gladys H. Abell Prof of Liberal Arts							
Welch, Patrick J.	Prof	St Louis		PHD	73	Pittsburgh	1983
Welch, Robert G.	H-Pr	Midwest St	ADP	PHD	62	Oregon St	1966
Welch, William P.	Assoc	Saginaw Vall	CJL	PHD	86	U Wash	1986
Welki, Andrew M.	Asst	John Carroll	HR	PHD	83	Penn St	1982
Welle, Patrick G.	Prof	Bemidji St		PHD	86	Wisconsin	1982
Weller, Barry R.	H-Ac	Penn St-Erie	ACE	PHD	71	Penn St	1971
Wellington, Alison J.	Asst	Wooster	J	PHD	90	Michigan	1997
Wellington, Donald C.	Prof	Cincinnati	D	PHD	66	Chicago	
Wellisz, Stanislaw	Prof	Columbia	O	PHD	54	Harvard	1964
Wells, Arnold R.	Prof	Mankato St	ADM	PHD	66	Minnesota	1966
Wells, Donald A.	Prof	Arizona		PHD	61	Oregon	1969
Wells, Donald R.	Retir	Memphis		PHD	65	S Calif	1967
Wells, Jerome C.	Prof	Pittsburgh	O	PHD	64	Michigan	1964
Wells, John M.	Asst	Auburn		PHD	94	Tx A&M	1994
Wells, Robin	Asst	MIT	L	PHD	89	Berkeley	1996
Welsh, Arthur	Retir	Penn State	A	PHD	63	Illinois	1986
Wen, G. James	Assoc	Trinity-CT		PHD	89	Chicago	1994
Wendel, Jeanne L.	Prof	Nevada-Reno		PHD	77	So Meth	1985
Wenders, John T.	Retir	Idaho	DL	PHD	67	Nrthwstrn	1981
Weninger, Quinn	Asst	Utah State	CQ	PHD	95	Maryland	1995

Name	Rank	School	Fields	Degree	Yr	Institution	Year
Wentworth, Donald R.	Prof	Pacific Luth	A	PHD	65	Minnesota	1972
Werger, Jennie	Asst	North Texas	HJ	PHD	96	N Carol	1996
Werner, Jan	Assoc	Minnesota		PHD		Bonn	1987
Werner, Megan	Asst	Florida	CHQ	PHD	94	Ca-SnDgo	1994
Wesolowski, Karl A.	C-Ac	Salem State		MA		Boston C	
Wessel, Robert H.	Retir	Cincinnati		PHD	53	Cincinnati	1957
Wessels, Walter J.	Prof	N Carol St	JD	PHD	76	Chicago	1975
West, Carol Taylor	Prof	Florida	RQC	PHD	74	Michigan	1989
West, Clifford T.	Asst	Va Military		PHD	92	Indiana	1996
West, James E.	Asst	USAF Academy	AD	PHD	94	Michigan	1997
West, James P.	C-Pr	Moravian	FM	PHD	87	Lehigh	1989
West, James S.	Prof	Wash & Jeff		PHD	97	Nebraska	1997
West, Janet Mason	Asst	Neb-Omaha	AJ	MA	64	Mich St	1967
West, Kenneth D.	Prof	Wisconsin		PHD	83	MIT	1988
Westall, Oliver M.	SLect	U Lancaster		BSC		London	
Westbrook, M. Daniel	Asst	Georgetown		PHD	78	Ohio St	1978
Westerfield, Donald	Prof	Webster	DIMC	PHD	84	St Louis	1985
Westfield, Fred M.	Retir	Vanderbilt	D	PHD	57	MIT	1965
Westhoff, Frank H.	C-Pr	Amherst	ADHC	PHD	74	Yale	1973
Weston, Gerald A.	Deces	Wis-Whitewat	2-99	PHD	65	Wash St	1968
Weston, Rafael R.	Dean	Adams State		PHD	72	Harvard	1988
Weston, Samuel C.	Asst	Dallas	B	PHD	87	Pittsburgh	1987
Westphal, Larry E.	Prof	Swarthmore	DO	PHD	69	Harvard	1985
J. Archer & Helen C. Turner Professor of Economics							
Wetzel, James N.	Assoc	Virg Comm		PHD	74	N Carol	1974
Wexler, Imanuel	Retir	Connecticut		PHD	59	Harvard	1961
Weymark, Diana N.	Asst	Vanderbilt	EG	PHD	90	Brit Colum	1999
Weymark, John A.	Prof	Vanderbilt	D	PHD	77	Penn	1999
Whalen, Thaddeus J. Jr.	Prof	Santa Clara		PHD	64	Berkeley	1962
Whalley, Pamela	Lect	Western Wash	DG	ABD		Indiana	1989
Whaples, Robert M.	Asst	Wake Forest		PHD	90	Penn	1991
Whatley, Warren	Prof	Michigan	NJOR	PHD	82	Stanford	1981
Wheaton, William C.	Prof	MIT	R	PHD	72	Penn	1972
Wheeler, Bert	Assoc	Cedarville	AFOP	PHD	85	Tennessee	1992
Wheeler, Clifford	Retir	NE St-Okla	1995	PHD		Missouri	1971
Wheeler, Mark V.	Assoc	W Michigan	E	PHD	85	Kentucky	1990
Whinston, Michael D.	Prof	Northwestern	DL	PHD	84	MIT	1996
Robert & Emily King Professor of Business Institutions							
Whitaker, Andrew L.	Assoc	No Central	G	PHD	88	Illinois	1988
Whitaker, David A.	Assoc	Richmond		PHD	71	Florida	1969
Whitaker, John K.	Prof	Virginia	BC	PHD	62	Cambridge	1969
Georgia S. Bankard Porfessor of Economics							
Whitaker, Morris D.	Prof	Utah State	FO	PHD	70	Purdue	1970
Whitaker, William M.	C-Pr	Geo Southern		PHD	68	Kentucky	1989
White, Charles	Prof	Framingham	EC	PHD	81	Chicago	9-85
White, Charles V. A	Assoc	New Hamp Col		PHD	73	Ohio St	
White, Eugene N.	C-Pr	Rutgers-N Br	N	PHD	80	Illinois	1980
White, Halbert L.	Prof	Ca-San Diego	C	PHD	76	MIT	1979
White, Harry Ruff	Retir	W Carolina		PHD	66	Kentucky	1968
White, Kenneth R.	Assoc	Cen Florida	C	PHD	71	Oklahoma	1968
White, Lawrence	Prof	New York U	DGKL	PHD	69	Harvard	1976
Arthur E. Imperitore Professor of Economics							
White, Lawrence H.	Assoc	Georgia	ENB	PHD	82	UCLA	1988
White, Leonard A.	Retir	Arkansas	D	PHD	63	St Louis	1971
White, Mark D.	Asst	CUNY-Stn Isl	C	PHD		Cincinnati	1997
White, Michael D.	Prof	St Cloud St		PHD	78	Tx Tech	1978
White, Michelle J.	Prof	Michigan		PHD	73	Princeton	1984
White, Nancy E.	Assoc	Bucknell	RH	PHD	87	Colorado	1986
White, Thomas J.	Asst	Assumption	EGQ	PHD	89	SUNY-Bin	1995
White-Means, Shelley L.	Prof	Memphis	DJI	PHD	83	Nrthwstrn	1988
Whited, Toni	Assoc	Delaware	GE	PHD	90	Princeton	1994
Whitehead, John C.	Assoc	East Carol	DQ	PHD	89	Kentucky	1989
Whiteman, Charles H.	C-Pr	Iowa		PHD	81	Minnesota	1980
Whitesell, Frank Cook	Assoc	So Miss	A	PHD	71	Tulane	1968
Whitesell, William E.	C-Pr	Frank & Mars		PHD	63	Tx-Austin	1965
Henry P. & Mary B. Stager Professor of Economics							
Whitin, Thomson M.	Emer	Wesleyan-CT	C	PHD	52	Princeton	1963
Hubbard Professor							
Whiting, Cathleen L.	C-Ac	Willamette		PHD	86	U Wash	1986
Whitman, Katherine	Asst	Mt St Mary's	ANF	MA		UCLA	1980
Whitman, Raymond D.	Prof	Univ of D C	JHA	PHD	71	Columbia	1985
Whitmore, Harland W. Jr.	Prof	Cincinnati	E	PHD	69	Mich St	1967
Whitney, Chet	Retir	Augustana SD	C	PHD	65	Kansas	1960
Whitney, Gerald A.	Prof	Now Orleans		PHD	77	Tulane	
Whitney, James D.	Prof	Occidental	F	PHD	83	Wisconsin	1982
Whittaker, Victor A.	Prof	Morgan State		PHD	71	Illinois	1974
Whitten, David O.	Prof	Auburn		PHD	70	Tulane	1968
Whittenlas, John	SLect	U Lancaster		PHD		Capetown	
Whyte, Charles D.	Retir	Virginia St		PHD	69	Ohio St	1974
Wible, James R.	Prof	New Hampshir	BE	PHD	80	Penn St	1984

Wichers, C. Robert	Assoc	Pittsburgh	C	PHD	68	Amsterdm	1976
Wicker, Elmus R.	Retir	Indiana		PHD	56	Duke	
Wickman, Kenneth P.	Retir	SUNY-Cortlan		PHD	62	Syracuse	1968
Wicks, John H.	Prof	Montana	DH	PHD	62	Illinois	
Widener, Steven	Assoc	New Hamp Col		PHD	88	NewHamp	
Wiegersma, Nancy A.	Prof	Fitchburg St		PHD	76	Maryland	1979
Wier, Thomas	Asst	NE St-Okla	RCB	PHD	89	Tennessee	1998
Wiest, Philip Ray	Assoc	George Mason		PHD	76	Pittsburgh	
Wiggins, Steven N.	Prof	Texas A&M	L	PHD	79	MIT	1979
Wight, Jonathan B.	Assoc	Richmond		PHD	82	Vanderbilt	1982
Wightman, James W.	Retir	SUNY-Potsdam		PHD	67	Clark	
Wihry, David F.	C-Ac	Maine	HIA	PHD	72	Syracuse	1969
Wilber, Charles K.	Prof	Notre Dame	BOP	PHD	66	Maryland	1975
Wilbratte, Barry J.	C-Pr	St Thomas-TX	FG	PHD	71	Tulane	1971
Wilcox, Nathaniel	Assoc	Houston	D	PHD	92	Chicago	1991
Wilcox-Gok, Virginia L.	Assoc	No Illinois	J	PHD	84	Wash U	1994
Wilcoxen, Peter J.	Asst	Texas	QD	PHD	89	Harvard	9-91
Wildasin, David E.	Prof	Vanderbilt	G	PHD	76	Iowa	1993
Wilde, James A.	Assoc	No Carolina	GH	PHD	68	Princeton	1965
Wilder, Lisa A.	Asst	Bowling Gr		PHD	95	Va Tech	1995
Wilder, Ronald P.	C-Pr	So Carolina		PHD	69	Vanderbilt	1987
Wiles, James L.	Emer	Stonehill	KN	PHD	76	Harvard	1955
Wilford, W. Terry	Deces	New Orleans	4-94	PHD	64	So Meth	1968
Wilhelm, Mark	Assoc	Ind-Purdue/I	CH	PHD	90	NYU	1998
Wilhite, Allen W.	C-Pr	Alabama-Hunt	JK	PHD	81	Illinois	1988
Wilkes, William	Asst	Athens State	AF	DA	98	Mid Tenn	1996
Wilkie, Simon	Asst	Cal Tech	L	PHD	90	Rochester	1995
Wilkins, Allen J.	Assoc	Marshall		PHD	84	Wisconsin	1985
Wilkins, Mira	Prof	Fla Internat	NF	PHD	57	Cambridge	1974
Wilkinson, Maurice	Prof	Columbia		PHD	65	Harvard	1965
Willard, Kristen L.	Asst	Columbia	DFH	PHD	94	Princeton	9-94
Willett, Keith D.	Prof	Oklahoma St	Q	PHD	82	New Mex	1981
Willett, Thomas D.	Prof	Claremont		PHD	67	Virginia	1977
Horton Professor of Economics							
Williams, Anne D.	Prof	Bates	O	PHD	76	Chicago	1981
Williams, Arlington W.	Prof	Indiana		PHD	78	Arizona	1979
Williams, C. Glyn	Retir	So Carolina		PHD	60	Virginia	
Williams, D. C. Jr.	Retir	So Miss		PHD		LSU	
Williams, Darrell L.	Asst	UCLA	GKL	PHD	91	Wash U	F-90
Williams, Donald R.	Prof	Kent State	J	PHD	84	Nrthwstrn	1983
Williams, Earl R.	Dean	NE St-Okla	DMN	PHD	68	Tennessee	1968
Williams, Eugene	Prof	McMurry		PHD	71	Arkansas	1988
Williams, Harold R.	Retir	Kent State	EF	PHD	65	Nebraska	1966
Williams, Martin	Prof	No Illinois	R	PHD	76	SUNY-Bin	1976
Williams, Mary L.	Prof	Widener	BOMQ	PHD	84	Temple	1982
Williams, Mike M.	Retir	Bethune-Cook		PHD	70	Ohio U	1991
Williams, Nancy A.	Assoc	Loyola-Maryl	QH	PHD	84	Berkeley	1987
Williams, Nicolas	Assoc	Cincinnati	J	PHD	89	Nrthwstrn	1990
Williams, Norman C.	C-Ac	Tenn Tech		PHD	72	Arkansas	1972
Williams, Raburn M.	Retir	Hawaii-Manoa		PHD	70	Chicago	1969
Williams, Robert B.	Assoc	Guilford	HQRL	PHD	84	N Carol	1987
Williams, Robert G.	C-Pr	Guilford	POFE	PHD	78	Stanford	1978
Williams, Roberton III	Asst	Texas	H	PHD	99	Stanford	9-99
Williams, Steven R.	Assoc	Illinois	CD	PHD	82	Nrthwstrn	1992
Williams, Walter E.	C-Pr	George Mason		PHD	72	UCLA	1981
John M. Olin Distinguished Professor of Economics							
Williams, William V.	Retir	Hamline	1994	PHD	61	Colorado	1961
Williamson, Daniel P.	H-Pr	Cal Poly-SLO		PHD	73	Ca-SnDgo	1970
Williamson, H. F. Jr.	Assoc	Illinois	AR	PHD	69	Yale	1964
Williamson, Jeffrey G.	C-Pr	Harvard		PHD	61	Stanford	1983
Laird Bell Professor of Economics							
Williamson, Oliver E.	Prof	Cal-Berkeley		PHD	63	Car Mellon	1988
Williamson, Samuel H.	Prof	Miami U-Ohio	NI	PHD	68	Purdue	1983
Willig, Robert D.	Prof	Princeton		PHD	73	Stanford	1978
Willis, James F.	Retir	San Jose St		PHD	66	So Meth	1966
Willis, Rachel A.	Adj	No Carolina	J	PHD	90	Nrthwstrn	1982
Willman, Elliott	Prof	New Mex St	EF	PHD	77	Indiana	1979
Willner, Jonathan	Asst	Okla City	FO	PHD	94	Purdue	1995
Willoughby, John A.	Assoc	American U		PHD	79	Berkeley	1979
Willumsen, Maria Jose	Assoc	Fla Internat	RO	PHD	84	Cornell	1984
Wilson, Beth	Asst	Xavier		PHD			
Wilson, Bradley	Asst	Alabama-Birm	CEF	PHD	97	Kansas	1997
Wilson, Charles A.	Prof	New York U	D	PHD	76	Rochester	1983
Wilson, Dwayne H.	Dean	Freed Hardem	CDEQ	PHD	91	Miss	8-75
Wilson, Erika G.	Prof	CS-L Angeles		PHD	79	S Calif	1968
Wilson, F. Scott	Prof	Canisius		PHD	76	Minnesota	1977
Wilson, George W.	Prof	Cen Missouri		PHD	76	Okla St	1972
Wilson, John D.	Prof	Michigan St		PHD	79	MIT	1998
Wilson, Kathryn S.	Asst	Kent State	DHIJ	PHD	96	Wisconsin	1996
Wilson, Linda	Lect	Tx-Arlington		MS	92	North Tx	1993

Name	Rank	School	Fields	Degree	Yr	Institution	Since
Wilson, Loretta S.	Asst	Radford	FN	PHD	86	Mass	1987
Wilson, Lucas	Asst	Mt Holyoke		PHD	95	Mass	1995
Wilson, Paul W.	Assoc	Texas	RC	PHD	86	Brown	9-90
Wilson, R. Mark	Assoc	South Fla	I	PHD	77	Nrthwstrn	1978
Wilson, Richard C.	Asst	Tx-Arlington	AH	MA	66	Georgia	1966
Wilson, Wesley W.	Assoc	Oregon	CD	PHD	86	Wash St	1989
Wiltgen, Richard J.	Prof	DePaul	B	PHD	74	Illinois	1973
Wimberly, Jack Cook	Retir	So Miss		PHD		LSU	
Wimmer, Bradley	Asst	Nev-L Vegas	L	PHD	92	Kentucky	1998
Wimmer, Larry T.	Prof	Brigham Yg		PHD	68	Chicago	1963
Winczewski, Greg A.	Asst	Fordham		PHD	92	Fordham	1995
Winder, Robert C.	Assoc	Chris Newpor		PHD	81	Rutgers	1991
Winfrey, John C.	Prof	Wash & Lee	DH	PHD	65	Duke	1965
Wing, Martin M.	Asst	Kettering		PHD	89	Wayne St	
Winkelman, Richard D.	Assoc	Arizona St		PHD	66	Illinois	1965
Winkler, Anne E.	Assoc	Mo-St Louis	JT	PHD	89	Illinois	1989
Winrich, J. Steven	Assoc	Centre	APN	PHD	78	Kentucky	1981
Winston, Barbara	Retir	NE Illinois		PHD	74	Nrthwstrn	1974
Winston, Gordon C.	C-Pr	Williams		PHD	64	Stanford	1963
Orrin Sage Professor of Political Economy							
Winter, Eyal	Prof	Wash Univ	CD	PHD	88	Hebrew	1995
Winter, Harold	Assoc	Ohio Univ	KL	PHD	90	Rochester	1992
Wion, Douglas A.	Assoc	Lock Haven		PHD	80	Penn St	1980
Wiseman, A. Clark	Prof	Gonzaga	AFQ	PHD	68	U Wash	1981
Wishart, David M.	C-Ac	Wittenberg	ABN	PHD	85	Illinois	1983
Wisley, Thomas O.	Prof	W Kentucky	GHK	PHD	79	Purdue	1985
Wisman, Jon D.	Prof	American U		PHD	74	American	1971
Withington, Robert P.	Assoc	SUNY-Plattsb	NJ	PHD	76	Penn	1972
Witt, Tom S.	Prof	W Virginia	CR	PHD	74	Wash U	1970
Witte, Ann D.	Prof	Fla Internat	DHK	PHD	71	N Car St	1996
Witte, Ann D.	Prof	Wellesley	DHK	PHD	71	N Car St	1985
Witte, Willard E.	Assoc	Indiana		PHD	75	Wisconsin	1981
Wittman, Donald A.	Prof	Ca-Santa Crz	KD	PHD	70	Berkeley	1969
Woglom, Geoffrey R.	Prof	Amherst	AEG	PHD	74	Yale	1978
Wohar, Mark	Prof	Neb-Omaha	ECGF	PHD	85	Illinois	1988
Wojcikewych, Raymond	C-Ac	Bradley		PHD	80	Penn St	1977
Wojick, Paul P.	Assoc	St Olaf	AE	PHD	89	Colorado	1988
Wolak, Frank A.	Prof	Stanford		PHD	85	Harvard	1986
Wolaver, Amy	Asst	Bucknell	IJH	PHD	98	Wisconsin	9-98
Wolcott, Susan	Assoc	Mississippi		PHD	88	Stanford	1999
Wolcowitz, Jeffrey	SLect	Harvard	HDRJ	PHD	82	Harvard	7-78
Wolf, Avner	C-Pr	CUNY-Baruch		PHD	83	Columbia	
Wolfe, Barbara L.	Prof	Wisconsin		PHD	73	Penn	1976
Wolfe, Janet C.	Lect	Michigan		MPP	80	Michigan	1987
Wolfenbarger, J. Larry	C Pr	Georgia Col	ABPE	PHD	74	Tennessee	1987
Wolff, Edward N.	Prof	New York U	J	PHD	74	Yale	1974
Wolff, Laura	Inst	S Ill-Edward	AO	MS	88	Missouri	1990
Wolff, Richard D.	Prof	Massachusett	ABNP	PHD	69	Yale	9-73
Wolfram, Catherine	Asst	Harvard		PHD	96	MIT	
Wolfram, Gary	Assoc	Hillsdale		PHD	76	Berkeley	1989
Wolfson, Martin H.	Assoc	Notre Dame	EG	PHD	84	American	1990
Wolfson, Melville Z.	Assoc	New Orleans		PHD	71	Illinois	
Wolfson, Murray	Prof	CS-Fullerton	BC	PHD	63	Wisconsin	1986
Wolinsky, Asher	Prof	Northwestern		PHD	80	Stanford	
Wolkoff, Michael	Lect	Rochester		PHD	81	Michigan	1980
Wolnicki, Miron J.	Assoc	Villanova		PHD	80	Lodz	1984
Wolozin, Harold	Prof	Mass-Boston	B	PHD	55	Columbia	1966
Wolpin, Kenneth I.	Prof	Pennsylvania		PHD	74	CUNY	1995
Womeldorf, Thomas		Evergreen St		PHD	89	American	1991
Womer, N. Keith	Prof	Mississippi		PHD	70	Penn St	1986
Wong, David C.	Prof	CS-Fullerton	CO	PHD	84	Ca-SnBarb	1981
Wong, Kar-yiu	Prof	U Washington		PHD	83	Columbia	1983
Wong, Kwok-Fai Matthew	Assoc	St John's	GM	PHD	91	Miss	1990
Wong, Linda	Asst	SUNY-Bingham	JD	PHD	98	Iowa	1999
Wonnacott, Paul	Prof	Middlebury	EF	PHD	59	Princeton	1994
Alan R. Holmes Visiting Professor in Monetary Economics							
Woo, Wing T.	Prof	Cal-Davis	EFOP	PHD	82	Harvard	1985
Wood, Clinton F.	Prof	Delta State		JD	80	Miss	8-84
Wood, Edgar	Retir	Mississippi		PHD	67	LSU	1967
Wood, J. Stuart	Assoc	Loyola-N Orl	GM	PHD	80	NYU	1984
Wood, John H.	Prof	Wake Forest		PHD	64	Purdue	1985
Reynolds Professor of Economics							
Wood, Richard H. Jr.	Prof	Stetson	AFO	PHD	72	Wisconsin	1970
Wood, William C.	Prof	Jms Madison	DA	PHD	80	Virginia	1989
Woodbury, Denise	Assoc	Brighm Yg-HI	AG	PHD	92	Utah	1996
Woodbury, Stephen A.	Prof	Michigan St		PHD	81	Wisconsin	1982
Wooders, John C.	Asst	Arizona		PHD	91	Cornell	1991
Woodford, Michael	Prof	Princeton		PHD	83	MIT	
Woodland, Bill M.	Prof	E Michigan		PHD	81	Purdue	1981
Woodruff, Mary Martha	Assoc	New Haven		EDD	72	Bridgepr	9-85

Name	Rank	School	Fields	Degree	Yr	Degree School	Hired
Woodruff, Theodore S.	Prof	St Ambrose	DEHL	PHD	76	Columbia	8-95
Woodruff, William D.	Retir	Florida	N	PHD	52	Nottinghm	1966
Woods, Louis A.	Prof	North Fla	OQR	PHD	72	N Carol	1972
Woods, William	Inst	St Ambrose		MBA	96	St Ambro	1995
Woodward, Doug P.	Asst	So Carolina		PHD	86	Tx-Austin	
Wooldridge, Jeffrey	Prof	Michigan St	C	PHD	86	Ca-SnDgo	9-91
Wooley, Douglas C.	Prof	Radford	HP	PHD	76	Conn	1975
Woolf, Arthur G.	Assoc	Vermont	HNR	PHD	80	Wisconsin	1980
Woolf, Linda L.	Assoc	Washburn		PHD	70	Kansas St	1969
Woolley, Peter J.	C	F Dick-Madis		PHD	89	Pittsburgh	1987
Woolsey, W. William	Assoc	Citadel		PHD	86	GeoMason	8-86
Word, William R.	Dean	SC-Spartanbu	ADEJ	PHD	70	Tennessee	1998
Worden, Debra	Asst	George Fox		PHD	84	Purdue	
Woroby, Tamara	Prof	Towson		PHD	81	Queens	1978
Worrall, John D.	Prof	Rutgers-Camd		PHD	75	Rutgers	1983
Woudenberg, Henry W. Jr.	Retir	Kent State	E	PHD	68	Mich St	1967
Wray, L. Randall	Assoc	Denver	E	PHD	88	Wash U	1987
Wray, Randall	Prof	Mo-Kansas Ct		PHD	88	U Wash	1999
Wright, Arthur W.	Prof	Connecticut	KD	PHD	69	MIT	1979
Wright, Colin	Prof	Claremont		PHD	66	Chicago	1977
Norwood and Frances Berger Professor of Business & Soc							
Wright, Gavin	Prof	Stanford		PHD	69	Yale	1982
William Robertson Coe Professor of American Economic History							
Wright, Jeffrey J.	Prof	Lenoir-Rhyne	AFK	PHD	87	Conn	1989
Wright, Jonathan	Asst	Virginia	CE	PHD	97	Harvard	1997
Wright, Randall	Prof	Pennsylvania	JE	PHD	86	Minnesota	1987
Wright, Virginia B.	Prof	E Kentucky		PHD	71	Geo Wash	1982
Wrightsman, Dwayne E.	Retir	New Hampshir	Fnce	PHD	64	Mich St	1964
Wrotniak, Maria	Assoc	Westminst-UT	BCO	PHD	80	Lodz	1989
Wu, De-Min	Prof	Kansas		PHD	63	Wisconsin	1964
Wu, Mickey Tai Chuen	Prof	Coe	ACEF	PHD	79	Kentucky	1979
George R. Baker Professor of Economics and Business Administration							
Wu, Roland Y.	Assoc	MD-Baltim Co		PHD	71	Stanford	
Wu, Shih-Yen	Emer	Iowa		PHD	60	Nrthwstrn	1964
Wu, Xiaodong	Asst	No Carolina		PHD	99	Princeton	1999
Wu, Yeen-Kuen	Assoc	Ark-Pine Blf		MA		Atlanta	
Wu, Ying	Asst	Salisbury St		PHD	92	Oregon	8-98
Wuilleumier, Rudolph B.	Asst	E Kentucky		BS	67	Estrn Ky	1971
Wunnava, Phanindra V.	Prof	Middlebury	ACIJ	PHD	86	SUNY-Bin	1985
Wydick, W. Bruce	Asst	San Francisc	DO	PHD	96	Berkeley	1996
Wymar, Benno	Prof	South Dakota		PHD	73	Nebraska	1968
Wyrick, Thomas L.	Prof	SW Missouri		PHD	79	Va Tech	1978
Wyss, Brenda	Asst	Wheaton-MA	JTO	PHD	95	Mass	1992
Xander, James A.	Assoc	Cen Florida	D	PHD	74	Georgia	1969
Xiansheng, Duan	Asst	SW Okla St		PHD	97	Illinois	1997
Xiao, Zhijie	Asst	Illinois	CL	PHD	97	Yale	1997
Xu, Bin	Asst	Florida	FO	PHD	95	Columbia	1995
Xu, Peng	Asst	San Fran St		PHD	94	Iowa	1994
Xu, Yongsheng	Assoc	Georgia St	DHC	PHD	92	Tulane	1999
Yacovissi, William A.	Prof	Mansfield		PHD	89	SUNY-Bin	1976
Yalsawarng, Suthathip	C-Ac	Union	CD	PHD	89	S Illinois	1989
Yamada, Tetsuji	C-Ac	Rutgers-Camd		PHD	87	CUNY	1987
Yamarik, Steven	Asst	Akron	AE	PHD	96	N Carol	1997
Yamazaki, Masato	Asst	Aquinas		PHD	84	Duke	1987
Yamoah, David A.	Assoc	Kean		PHD	90	Rutgers	9-87
Yan, Chiou-shuang	Prof	Drexel		PHD	66	Purdue	1967
Yandell, Dirk	Prof	San Diego		PHD	81	Purdue	1981
Yandle, T. Bruce Jr.	Prof	Clemson	QKH	PHD	70	Geo St	1969
Yang, Bill	Asst	Minot State	LG	PHD	93	Iowa	1997
Yang, Chin-Wei	Prof	Clarion	DFHR	PHD	79	W Virginia	1981
Yang, Dennis	Asst	Duke		PHD	93	Chicago	1992
Yang, Wei-Hsein	Deces	Ark-Pine Blf		PHD		Nebraska	
Yang, Yung Y.	Prof	CS-Sacrament		PHD	74	Oregon	1974
Yannelis, Nicholas C.	Prof	Illinois	D	PHD	83	Rochester	1988
Yarbrough, Beth V.	Prof	Amherst	ADF	PHD	83	U Wash	1982
Yaron, Amir	Asst	Carnegie Mel		PHD	94	Chicago	1994
Yasin, Jehad	Assoc	Ft Valley St	ETAC	PHD	87	Fla St	9-88
Yasin, Mesghena	Asst	Morehead St		PHD	86	Cincinnati	1986
Yates, Andrew J.	Asst	Tulane		PHD	92	Stanford	1998
Yates, Barbara M.	C-Pr	Seattle	AEGH	PHD	69	Michigan	1970
Yates, Michael Daniel	Prof	Pitts-Johnst	JP	PHD	76	Pittsburgh	1969
Yazar, Julide	Asst	Ohio Wesley		MA	98	Ohio St	1999
Yazdi, Khalil	Assoc	St Thomas-TX	M	PHD	87	Houston	1990
Yee, Janice G.	Assoc	Wartburg		PHD	90	Clark	1991
Yeh, Chiou-Nan	C-Pr	Alabama St		PHD	74	Mass	1974
Yeh, Yeong-Her	Prof	Hawaii-Manoa		PHD	66	Minnesota	1965
Yellen, Janet L.	Prof	Cal-Berkeley		PHD	71	Yale	
Yelowitz, Aaron	Asst	UCLA		PHD	94	MIT	
Yerger, David B.	Asst	Lycoming	JFTN	PHD	94	Penn St	1996
Yett, Donald E.	Prof	So Calif		PHD	68	Berkeley	1966

Yezer, Anthony M.	Prof	George Wash	R	PHD	74	MIT	1972
Yigletu, Ashagre	Assoc	Southern	AE	PHD	72	Belgrade	1972
Yiheyis, Zelealm	Asst	Clark Atlant		PHD			
Yin, Yong	Asst	SUNY-Buffalo	CDE	PHD	95	Ohio St	1995
Ying, John S.	Assoc	Delaware	L	PHD	87	Berkeley	1987
Yinger, John M.	Prof	Syracuse	RI	PHD	74	Princeton	1986
Yochum, Gilbert R.	C-Pr	Old Dominion		PHD	74	W Virginia	1975
Yohe, Gary W.	Prof	Wesleyan-CT	D	PHD	75	Yale	1977
Yohe, William P.	Emer	Duke		PHD	59	Michigan	1958
Yoho, Devon L.	Assoc	Ball State	A	PHD	74	Missouri	1978
Yoon, Bong J.	Assoc	SUNY-Bingham	JC	PHD	78	Illinois	1983
Yoon, lee	Retir	Wichita St	5-95	PHD	67	Minnesota	1968
Yoon, Mann	Assoc	CS-L Angeles		PHD	91	Illinois	1991
Yordon, Wesley J.	Retir	Colorado		PHD		Harvard	
York, Anne	Asst	Meredith		PHD		N Car St	1999
Yorukoglu, Mehmet	Asst	Chicago		PHD	96	Rochester	1996
Young, Ben	Lect	Mo-Kansas Ct	A	PHD	73	Oklahoma	1993
Young, Douglas J.	Prof	Montana St		PHD	78	Wisconsin	1977
Young, Edward G.	C-Pr	Wis-Eau Clar	J	PHD	77	Wash St	1977
Young, H. Peyton	Prof	J Hopkins		PHD	70	Michigan	1994
Young, Jeffrey T.	Prof	St Lawrence	BQ	PHD	75	Colorado	1980
Young, Linda Wilcox	C-Ac	So Oregon St	JOF	PHD	87	Berkeley	1994
Young, Madelyn V.	Asst	Converse		PHD	91	Geo St	1991
Young, Mary E.	Assoc	Southwestern	CDJQ	PHD	89	Tx-Austin	1990
Young, Richard D.	Retir	Rice		PHD	65	Car Mellon	1965
Young, Shik C.	Retir	East Wash		PHD	69	Wash St	1966
Youngelson-Neal, Helen L.	Retir	Portland St		PHD	66	Columbia	1967
Yousefi, Mahmood	Prof	No Iowa	GHP	PHD	74	Ca-SnBarb	1981
Yousif, Salah A.	Asst	Alabama A&M	AJ	MA		Howard	1976
Yu, Ben T.	Assoc	CS-Northrdge		PHD	78	U Wash	1984
Yu, David	Asst	Tufts	G	PHD	97	Princeton	1998
Yu, Tie-Liu	Assoc	Mercer-Atlan		PHD	90	Miss St	1990
Yuhn, Ky-hyang	Assoc	Fla Atlantic	ECG	PHD	85	N Illinois	8-93
Yun, Kwan Koo	Prof	SUNY-Albany	CD	PHD	74	Stanford	1974
Yunker, James A.	Prof	W Illinois	ACDP	PHD	71	Nrthwstrn	1968
Zabel, Edward	Retir	Florida	D	PHD	56	Princeton	1981
Zabel, Jeffrey	Assoc	Tufts	C	PHD	87	Ca-SnDgo	1989
Zadeh, Ali Haji-Mohamad	C-Ac	Susquehanna	CEGO	PHD	82	Mich St	1987
Zahka, William J.	Retir	Widener	ABNO	ABD		Bryn Mawr	1959
Zahn, Frank	Prof	Neb-Omaha	E	PHD	69	Ca-SnBarb	1979
Zahrt Geib, Elizabeth	Asst	Lewis & Clrk	GEBJ	PHD	97	Calif	1997
Zajac, Edward E.	Prof	Arizona		PHD	54	Stanford	1983
Zak, Thomas A.	Assoc	USN Academy		PHD	80	Vanderbilt	1981
Zaki, Mokhlis Y.	Prof	No Michigan	ACDO	PHD	69	Berkeley	1969
Zaleski, Peter A.	Assoc	Villanova		PHD	88	Maryland	1987
Zamanian, Zaman	Asst	Montclair St	ACEF	PHD	83	Indiana	1984
Zame, William	Prof	UCLA		PHD	70	Tulane	
Zampelli, Ernest M.	C-Ac	Catholic	DHQ	PHD	82	Maryland	9-85
Zampieron, Alexander Alg	Prof	Bentley	ABF	PHD	72	Fletcher	1965
Zandvakili, Sourushe	Assoc	Cincinnati	J	PHD	87	Indiana	1987
Zangeneh, Hamid	Prof	Widener	EFGP	PHD	84	Missouri	1985
Zannoni, Diane C.	Prof	Trinity-CT		PHD	76	SUNY-SBr	1975
Zapalska, Alina	Assoc	Marshall		PHD	91	Kentucky	1991
Zaporowski, Mark P.	Assoc	Canisius		PHD	85	SUNY-Alb	1983
Zappia, Gerard	C-Ac	Nazareth		MSED		Nazareth	
Zarembka, Paul	Prof	SUNY-Buffalo	BO	PHD	67	Wisconsin	1976
Zarinnia, Abdullah	Prof	Wis-Whitewat		PHD	66	Nebraska	1967
Zavareei, Manijeh	VAsoc	Trinity-CT		PHD	82	SUNY-Buf	1991
Zax, Jeffrey S.	Prof	Colorado		PHD	84	Harvard	1990
Zeager, Lester A.	Assoc	East Carol	DIJ	PHD	87	Pittsburgh	1986
Zech, Charles E.	Prof	Villanova		PHD	73	Notre Dm	1974
Zegeye, Abera	Assoc	Ball State	A	PHD	77	Indiana	1974
Zein-Elabdin, Eiman	Asst	Frank & Mars		PHD	93	Tennessee	1995
Zeineldin, Aly	Assoc	Lg Isl-Post		PHD	79	NYU	
Zekavat, Seid M.	Assoc	Loyola Marym	ACG	PHD	64	S Calif	1964
Zelcer, Moishe	Assoc	CUNY-Brookly	G	PHD	91	Baruch	1992
Zeldes, Stephen P.	Prof	Columbia		PHD	84	Brown	1996
Zelleke, Girma	Assoc	Kutztown	FO	PHD	84	Colorado	1986
Zelman, Patricia G.	Assoc	Tarleton St	N	PHD	80	Ohio St	1982
Zeman, Allan H.	Assoc	Robt Morris		PHD	78	Pittsburgh	1964
Zembrowski-Chanmala, Adriana	VInst	Cen Florida		MAAE			
Zemcik, Petr	Asst	So Illinois	EG	PHD	97	Pittsburgh	1998
Zenginobuz, Unal	Asst	Bogazici	AHLP	PHD	96	Penn	1996
Zestos, George K.	Assoc	Chris Newpor	CFHO	PHD	91	Indiana	1993
Zewail, Amin A.	Assoc	Lg Isl-Brook	AEHR	PHD	75	Fordham	
Zhang, Harold H.	Asst	Carnegie Mel		PHD	94	Duke	1994
Zhang, Jianbo	Assoc	Kansas	D	PHD	90	Penn St	1990
Zhang, Kevin	Asst	Illinois St	F	PHD	96	Colorado	8-97
Zhang, Qiang	Asst	Ohio State	EF	PHD	98	Ohio St	1998
Zhao, Jingang	Asst	Ohio State	CD	PHD	92	Yale	1992

Zheng, Buhong	Assoc	Colo-Denver	O	PHD	93	W Virginia	1995
Zheng, Mingmei	VAsst	SUNY-Bingham	HD	PHD	99	Wash U	1999
Zheng, Xu John	Asst	Texas	CO	PHD	92	Princeton	9-92
Zhou, Huizhong	Assoc	W Michigan	C	PHD	86	Nrthwstrn	1990
Zhou, Lin	Assoc	Duke	CF	PHD	89	Princeton	1996
Zhou, Ruilin	Asst	Pennsylvania	FDE	PHD	93	Pittsburgh	1993
Zhou, Su	Asst	Tx-S Antonio	CEFP	PHD	91	Ariz St	1991
Ziegert, Andrea	Asst	Denison		PHD	85	N Carol	1997
Ziegler, Joseph A.	H-Pr	Arkansas	R	PHD	71	Notre Dm	1980
Ziegler, William	Asst	Bethune-Cook		ABD		Nova SE	1991
Zietz, Joachim	Prof	Mid Tenn St	EC	PHD	81	Gottingen	1989
Ziliak, James P.	Asst	Oregon	J	PHD	93	Indiana	1993
Ziliak, Stephen T.	Asst	Bowling Gr		PHD	96	Iowa	1996
Zimbalist, Andrew	Prof	Smith	CJLP	PHD	74	Harvard	1974
Zimmer, Basil G.	Asst	Cen Michigan		PHD	72	Rutgers	1969
Zimmer, Michael A.	Prof	Evansville		PHD	77	Tennessee	1976
Zimmerman, David J.	Asst	Williams		PHD	92	Princeton	1991
Zimmerman, Jason	Asst	So Dakota St	MA	PHD	98	Purdue	1999
Zimmerman, Robert O.	C-Pr	Xavier	ADEF	PHD	69	SUNY-Buf	1970
Zin, Stanley E.	Assoc	Carnegie Mel		PHD	87	Toronto	1988
Zinam, Oleg	Retir	Cincinnati		PHD	63	Cincinnati	
Zinser, James E.	Prof	Oberlin	KLO	PHD	67	Oregon	1967
Zivot, Eric W.	Asst	U Washington		PHD	92	Yale	1993
Zlatoper, Thomas J.	C-Pr	John Carroll	ACD	PHD	80	Nrthwstrn	1984
Zodrow, George R.	C-Pr	Rice		PHD	80	Princeton	1979
Zomorrodian, Reza	Asst	Mass Lib Art		EDD	90	Mass	
Zottola, Armand J.	Prof	Central Conn	JRT	PHD	70	Catholic	1970
Zschock, Dieter	Prof	SUNY-Stony B		PHD	67	Tufts	1966
Zuber, Richard A.	Prof	N Car-Charl		PHD	78	Kentucky	1978
Zuberi, Habib A.	Prof	Cen Michigan		PHD	71	S Illinois	1971
Zuehlke, Thomas W.	Assoc	Florida St	C	PHD	83	Florida	1983
Zumas, Susan	Lect	Muhlenberg		PHD	94	Lehigh	1992
Zupan, Mark	Dean	Arizona		PHD	87	MIT	1996
Zweig, Michael	Prof	SUNY-Stony B		PHD	67	Michigan	1967
Zygmont, Zenon X.	Asst	W Oregon St	APLF	PHD	94	GeoMason	1998